MANCHESTER
COMMUNITY
COLLEGE

Manchester Community College is pleased to offer a number of options for students who wish to study psychology. Students can enroll in the Liberal Arts & Science Associate of Arts (A.A.) program, the Liberal Arts & Science Associate of Science (A.S.) program, or the CSCU Transfer Pathway in Psychology Studies (A.A.). The Liberal Arts degree programs are good options for students who want to continue their study of psychology at any baccalaureate institution of higher learning. The CSCU Psychology Studies program is specifically designed for students who wish to transfer to one of the four Connecticut State Universities (CSU) for further study in psychology.

Psychology courses that can be completed at MCC include:
- PSY*111: General Psychology I
- PSY*112: General Psychology II
- PSY*201: Life Span Development
- PSY*203: Child Development
- PSY*240: Social Psychology
- PSY*243: Theories of Personality
- PSY*245: Abnormal Psychology

For more information, please contact any of the faculty members in the Department of Psychology:

Dr. Jean Wynn, Chair
860-512-2784
jwynn@manchestercc.edu

Dr. Nancy Bray
860-512-2790
nbray@manchestercc.edu

Dr. Len Dupille
860-512-2779
ldupille@manchestercc.edu

Dr. Stacy Giguere
860-512-2796
sgiguere@manchestercc.edu

Dr. Francine Rosselli-Navarra
860-512-2711
frosselli-navarra@manchestercc.edu

Working with Sources
Using APA, Sixth Edition Style
By Barbara Fister, Gustavus Adolphus College

A A Checklist for Working with Sources

B For APA-Style In-Text Citations

C For an APA-Style Reference List

▶ Author variations, 3 • Articles, 3 • Books, 4 • Online Sources, 4 • Other Sources, 5

[W] = online sources

Sources not only provide information and ideas but can help establish your credibility and strengthen your argument when used as "expert witnesses." You should cite your sources to allow readers to track down those sources and to avoid plagiarizing words and ideas, a serious academic offense. For additional examples and advice, consult the *Publication Manual of the American Psychological Association*, 6th edition (2010).

A — A Checklist for Working with Sources

■ **Did I use the best possible evidence for my assertions?**

☑ **Are all of my claims supported by evidence?** If a section of your paper needs stronger support or if you need to verify a fact, consult with a reference librarian for suggestions.

☑ **Do my sources present balanced perspectives?** If a source you rely on ignores alternative viewpoints, substitute one that is more balanced and less likely to be considered unreliable.

☑ **Will my readers find my sources persuasive?** If your assignment calls for scholarly sources, look for those written by researchers that include documented references to other sources.

☑ **In a literature review, have I highlighted the most significant publications?** A review gives a concise overview of important research. Organize a review so readers can quickly grasp the various approaches and key issues relevant to your topic.

■ **Are my sources integrated into my writing smoothly and correctly?**

☑ **Do my sources back up what I say—or do they speak for me?** Use sources to support your ideas, but write in your own words. Don't quote a source when a paraphrase or summary will do.

☑ **Have I used my sources ethically?** Provide a reference for anything that isn't common knowledge, even if you have used your own words. Facts available in multiple sources—such as dates and well-known historical events—are considered common knowledge and do not need to be cited.

☑ **Have I introduced each source effectively?** Never drop in a quotation without introducing it. Use signal phrases such as "according to . . ." or ". . . Smith (2001) argued."

■ Are my sources cited clearly and completely?

☑ **Did I provide a citation for every idea that came from a source?** Indicate the original source by naming the author and year of publication. If you include a page number, put it in parentheses at the end of the quotation: (p. 112).

☑ **Did I provide complete details for all of my in-text citations and reference list entries?** Make sure every source referred to in the text can be found easily in your reference list. Provide all required publication information in the reference list.

B For APA-Style In-Text Citations

In-text citations allow your readers to locate the full citations for sources in the reference list at the end of your text.

- Refer to the author's name in the text or include it with the year in parentheses: Jones (2009) asserted . . . or (Jones, 2009). When quoting directly from a source, include the page number: (Jones, 2009, p. 33).
- If there is no author, use a shortened version of the title: ("Mind," 2008).
- For multiple works by the same author published in the same year, use the lowercase letter assigned to the year in the reference list: (Peters, 2005b).
- When a work has two authors, cite both names and the year: (Smith & Jones, 2009). For three to five authors, cite all authors in the first reference; for subsequent references, use the first author followed by "et al." For a source with six or more authors, use the first author's name followed by "et al." in the first and subsequent references.
- Include in-text citations for personal communications and interviews by providing the person's name, type of communication, and date: J. Smith (interview by the author, March 3, 2009) or (J. Smith, personal communication, February 12, 2009).

C For an APA-Style Reference List

At the end of your paper, provide all the details readers need to find the sources you used in your text. For some sources, all the details may not be available, but do your best to uncover all the information about your sources.

- Arrange the entries in alphabetical order by authors' last names (or by title if a work has no author).

- Do not list personal communications, unpublished interviews, or other unrecoverable sources in the reference list.

- Some online sources include a DOI (digital object identifier). APA uses the DOI, when available, instead of a URL.

- Use the state abbreviation for all US cities or the country (not abbreviated) for non-US cities; also give the province for Canadian cities.

- For sources with up to seven authors, use all authors' names. For sources with eight or more authors, use the first six names followed by an ellipsis mark and the last author's name.

- Use volume and issue numbers only for journals that begin each issue with page 1; use the volume number alone for journals that number pages continuously throughout the volume.

- Give the retrieval date for a source only if the content of the source is likely to change. (Use "n.d." if a source has no date.)

- To divide a URL or a DOI at the end of a line, break it after a double slash or before any other mark of punctuation. Do not insert a hyphen; do not add a period at the end of the entry.

Author variations

■ ONE AUTHOR

Last name, First initial(s).

Craske, M. G.

■ TWO TO SEVEN AUTHORS

Last name, First initial(s), Last name, First initial(s), & [before last author] Last name, First initial(s).

Brunstein, A., Betts, S., & Anderson, J. R.

Lent, R. W., Cinamon, R. G., Bryan, N. A., Jezzi, M. M., Martin, H. M., & Lim, R.

■ EIGHT OR MORE AUTHORS

Last name, First initial(s), Last name, First initial(s), Last name, First initial(s), Last name, First initial(s), Last name, First initial(s), Last name, First initial(s), . . . Last name, First initial(s).

Fleisher, A. S., Podraza, K. M., Bangen, K. J., Taylor, C., Sherzai, A., Sidhar, K., . . . Buxton, R. B.

Articles

■ ARTICLE IN A JOURNAL PAGINATED BY VOLUME

Last name, First initial(s). (Date). Title of article. *Title of Journal, volume*, pages.

Quane, H. (2005). The rights of indigenous peoples and the development process. *Human Rights Quarterly, 27*, 652-682.

■ ARTICLE IN A JOURNAL PAGINATED BY ISSUE

Last name, First initial(s). (Date). Title of article. *Title of Journal, volume*(issue), pages.

Fuchs, A. (2009). Family tradition. *Film Journal International, 112*(9), 16-19.

■ ARTICLE FROM AN ELECTRONIC DATABASE Ⓦ

Last name, First initial(s). (Date). Title of article. *Title of Journal* [or *Magazine or Newspaper*], publication information. doi:number *or* Retrieved from URL for journal home page

Kravitz, D. A. (2005). Diversity in teams. *Psychological Science in the Public Interest, 6,* i-ii. doi:10.1111/j.1529-1006.2005.00021.x

Oliver, M., Nelson, K., Cade, R., & Cueva, C. (2007). Therapeutic letter writing from school counselors to students, parents, and teachers. *Professional School Counseling, 10,* 510-515. Retrieved from http://schoolcounselor.org/

■ MAGAZINE ARTICLE

Last name, First initial(s). (Year, month and day [if any]). Title of article. *Title of Magazine, volume*(issue), pages.

Anderson, J. L. (2005, December 19). American viceroy. *The New Yorker, 81*(91), 54-65.

■ NEWSPAPER ARTICLE

Last name, First initial(s). (Year, month and day). Title of article. *Title of Newspaper,* p. page(s).

Fairclough, F., & Seo, H. (2005, December 24). Probe finds scientist faked results. *The Wall Street Journal,* p. B3.

Books

■ BASIC FORMAT FOR A BOOK

Last name, First initial(s). (Date). *Title of book.* Place: Publisher.

Martinson, T. (2000). *American dreamscape: The pursuit of happiness in postwar suburbia.* New York, NY: Carroll & Graf.

■ EDITED BOOK

Last name(s) of editor(s), First initial(s). (Ed. *or* Eds.). (Date). *Title of book.* Place: Publisher.

Pieterse, J. N. (Ed.). (2000). *Global futures: Shaping globalization.* London, England: Zed.

■ EDITION OTHER THAN FIRST

Last name, First initial(s). (Date). *Title of book* (number ed.). Place: Publisher.

Gudykunst, W. B. (2004). *Bridging differences: Effective intergroup communication* (4th ed.). Thousand Oaks, CA: Sage.

■ ARTICLE OR CHAPTER IN AN EDITED BOOK

Last name, First initial(s). (Date). Title of article or chapter.
In First initial(s) Last name (Ed.), *Title of book* (pp. pages).
Place: Publisher.

Ehrenfeld, D. (2002). Hard times for diversity. In A. Kimbrell (Ed.), *The fatal harvest reader: The tragedy of industrial agriculture* (pp. 77-86). Washington, DC: Island Press.

Online Sources

■ DOCUMENT FROM A WEB SITE ⒲

Last name, First initial(s). (Date). *Title of document.* Retrieved from URL

Maathai, W. (2004). *Nobel lecture.* Retrieved from http://nobelprize.org/peace /laureates/2004/maathai-lecture.html

■ DOCUMENT FROM A UNIVERSITY PROGRAM WEB SITE ⒲

Last name, First initial(s) *or* Organization Name. (Date). *Title of document.* Retrieved from Name of University Program website: URL

Richelson, J. (Ed.). (2006, March 21). *U.S. intelligence and the French nuclear weapons program.* Retrieved from George Washington University National Security Archives website: http://www.gwu.edu/~nsarchiv/NSAEBB /NSAEBB184/index.htm

■ WEBLOG (BLOG) POST ⒲

Last name, First initial(s). (Date). Title *or* Subject of post [Web log post]. Retrieved from URL

Eggers, A. (2008, February 23). Publication bias in drug trials. [Web log post]. Retrieved from http://www.iq.harvard.edu/blog/sss/archives/2008/02 /publication_bia_1.shtml#more

■ PODCAST ⒲

Last name, First initial(s). (Host, Producer, *or* Writer [if appropriate]). (Date). Title of podcast (No. number, if any) [Audio podcast]. *Series title* [if any]. Retrieved from URL

Olney, W. (Host), & Konecky, D., Scott, G., & Cooper, K. (Producers). (2008, March 13). Energy security and global warming [Audio podcast]. *To the point.* Retrieved from http://www.kcrw.com/news/programs/tp/tp080313energy _security_and_

■ ENTRY IN A WIKI ⒲

Title of entry. (Date of posting). Retrieved date from URL

Intelligent design. (2007, November 10). Retrieved March 17, 2008, from http://dkosopedia.com/wiki/Intelligent_Design

■ GOVERNMENT DOCUMENT

Agency. (Date). *Title of document*. Place: Publisher.

U.S. Census Bureau. (2005). *Statistical abstract of the United States*. Washington, DC: Government Printing Office.

■ CONFERENCE PROCEEDINGS

Last name(s) of editor(s), First initial(s). (Ed. *or* Eds.). (Date). *Title of proceedings*. Place: Publisher.

Dykstra-Erickson, E., & Tscheligi, M. (Eds.). (2004). *Proceedings of the SIGCHI Conference on Human Factors in Computing Systems*. New York, NY: Association for Computing Machinery.

■ FILM OR VIDEO (MOTION PICTURE)

Last name of director *or* producer, First initial(s). (Director *or* Producer). (Date). *Title* [DVD *or* Videocassette *or* Motion picture]. Country: Name of studio.

Niccol, A. (Director). (2005). *Lord of war* [Motion picture]. United States: Lions Gate Films.

■ TELEVISION PROGRAM

Last name of producer, First initial(s). (Producer). (Year, date aired). *Title of program* [Television broadcast]. Place: Network or channel.

Bikel, O. (Producer). (2004, June 17). *The plea* [Television broadcast]. Boston, MA: WGBH.

■ BROCHURE

Last name, First initial(s) [if given]. (Date). *Title of brochure* [Brochure]. Place: Publisher.

Information about hate crimes [Brochure]. (n.d.). San Diego, CA: Office of the District Attorney.

■ DATA FILE OR DATA SET [W]

Sponsoring Organization. (Date). *Title* [Data file *or* Data set]. Retrieved from URL

Data and Program Library Service, University of Wisconsin. (1973). *Records of slave ship movement between Africa and the Americas, 1817-1843* [Data file]. Retrieved from http://dpls.dacc.wisc.edu/slavedata/slaintro1.html

Copyright © 2009, 2007 by Bedford/St. Martin's
ISBN-13: 978-0-312-65356-9
ISBN-10: 0-312-65356-5

To order this quick-reference card for FREE with student copies of Bedford/St. Martin's texts, please contact your local Bedford/St. Martin's sales representative or visit bedfordstmartins.com.

1 2 3 4 f e d c

ISBN-13: 978-0-312-65356-9
ISBN-10: 0-312-65356-5

9 780312 653569

Careers in Psychology: Planning for Success[1]

Jennifer Zwolinski
University of San Diego

THE PSYCHOLOGY MAJOR

What can you do with a degree in psychology?

Lots! As a psychology major, you will graduate college with a scientific mind-set and an awareness of basic principles of human behavior (biological, developmental, mental disorder–related, social). This background will prepare you for success in many areas, including business, helping professions, health services, marketing, law, sales, and teaching. You may even go on to graduate school for specialized training to become a psychology professional. Here, you'll find the answers to important questions about pursuing the study of psychology: Is psychology the right major for you? What are the various levels of psychology education, and what kinds of jobs are available at those levels? What are psychology's specialized subfields? What are some ways you can improve your chances of admission to graduate school?

How do you know if psychology is the right major for you?

To see if you would be well matched with a major in psychology, start by considering the questions below.

Do you:

- enjoy learning about the ways we think and behave, and why?
- appreciate the value of applying the scientific method to answer questions?
- have an interest in a career that requires interpersonal skills?
- want to learn critical thinking and analytical skills?
- want to learn communication and presentation skills?
- want to gain computer skills in data processing, and research methodology skills such as assessment and statistics?
- want to work in human or animal services?
- have a desire to apply psychological principles to understand or solve personal, social, organizational, or environmental problems?

If you answered "yes" to most or all of these questions, then psychology may be the right major for you.

---

[1]Although "Careers in Psychology" draws primarily from available U.S. data, its descriptions of psychology's subfields and suggestions for preparing to enter the profession are applicable to students in many other countries.

How popular is the psychology major?

Psychology is a very popular major. In 2011–2012, psychology was the fourth most popular major as defined by the number of degrees conferred (6 percent). (Business, social science and history, and health professions and related programs occupied the top three spots, with 21 percent, 10 percent, and 9 percent of graduates, respectively [National Center for Education Statistics (NCES), 2013a]). In that year, more than 108,000 psychology majors graduated with a bachelor's degree from U.S. colleges and universities (NCES, 2013a) **(FIGURE 1)**.

Given that this number has been steadily increasing over the last 50 years (NCES, 2013a), it is very likely that psychology will remain a popular major among undergraduate students. The popularity of psychology is observed at the graduate level as well. Over the last decade, the number of graduate degrees in psychology has increased dramatically by 32 percent at the master's level and 54 percent at the doctoral level (APA Center for Workplace Studies, 2015) **(FIGURE 2)**.

Who is studying psychology at the undergraduate and graduate levels?

In 2011–2012, 76 percent of the graduating majors with bachelor's degrees were women. This tendency for most degree recipients in psychology to be women was also observed for master's degrees (79 percent) and doctoral degrees (74 percent) (NCES, 2013b). In 2011–2012, approximately 78 percent of doctorates in psychology were earned by Caucasian students, continuing a 30-year trend (APA Center for Workplace Studies, 2014).

What are the main reasons that undergraduate students choose to study psychology?

One study found that the number one reason psychology majors chose their major was a positive experience in their Introduction to Psychology class (Marrs, Barb, & Ruggiero,

FIGURE 1   **Number of Psychology Degrees Conferred by Level of Degree: 2011–2012** (Data from NCES, 2013b.)

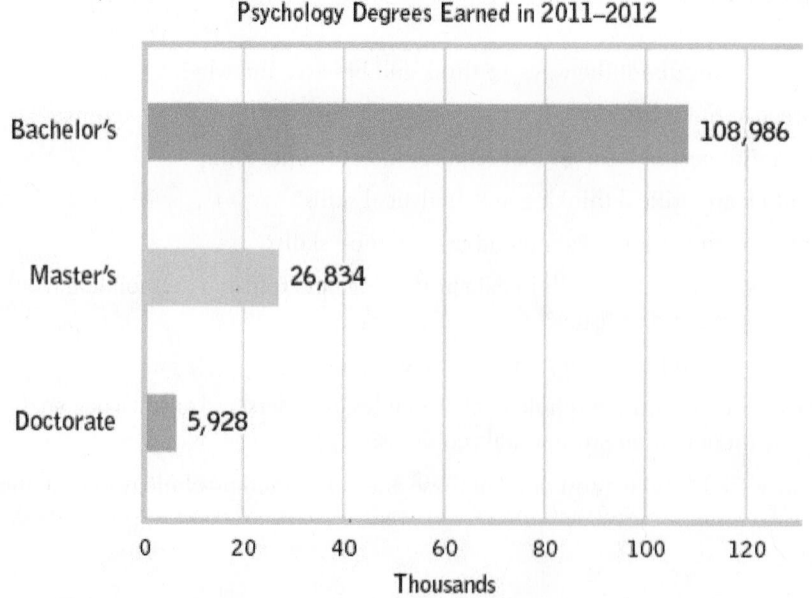

Psychology Degrees Earned in 2011–2012

Bachelor's — 108,986
Master's — 26,834
Doctorate — 5,928

(Thousands: 0, 20, 40, 60, 80, 100, 120)

FIGURE 2   Number of Psychology Master's and Doctoral Degrees Awarded by Year: 2004–2013 (Data from APA Center for Workplace Studies, 2015.)

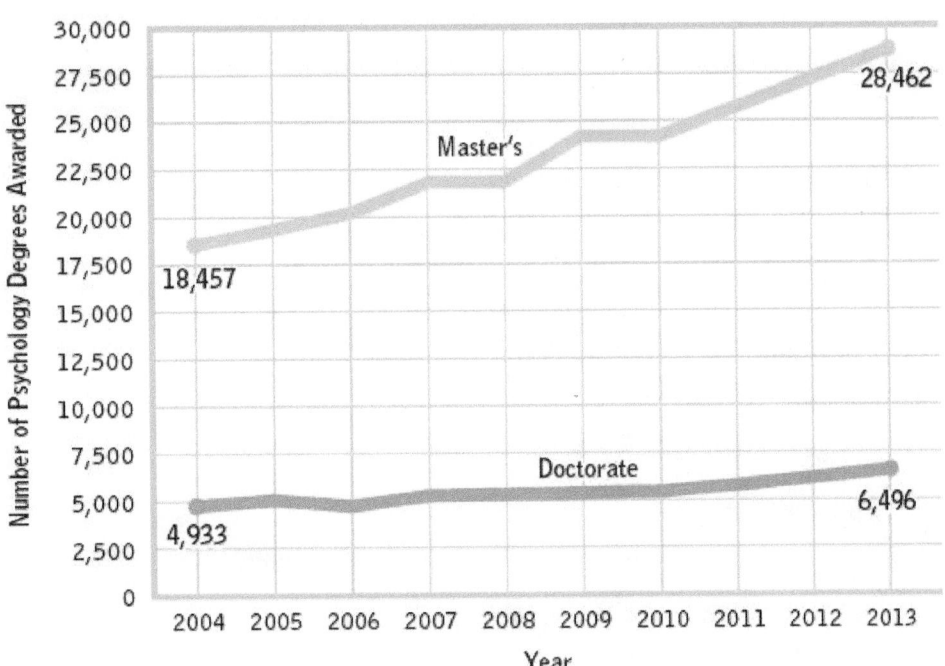

2007). Other research has found that the top five reasons students choose a psychology major are that it provides the ability to help others, incorporates interesting subject matter, produces a better understanding of self and others, includes good career or salary potential, and offers the ability to conduct research (Mulvey & Grus, 2010).

What types of skills will you learn as a psychology major?

The wide range of skills that psychology majors develop makes this major a "premier choice" for versatile career preparation (Halonen, 2014). This skill set is guided by the American Psychological Association (APA)'s learning goals and outcomes for psychology majors **(FIGURE 3)**.

Across all occupations, the skill set that twenty-first-century employers value includes social perceptiveness, reading comprehension, critical thinking, and speaking and active listening skills (Carnevale & Smith, 2014). These skills align with APA's learning goals and outcomes (Figure 3), which means that psychology majors will be well prepared for numerous professional opportunities and a range of graduate training options. In addition to exceptional interpersonal and communication skills, psychology majors develop a number of methodological skills that result from the focus on the scientific study of human and animal behavior. The study of statistics and research methodology contributes to a scientific mind-set that emphasizes exploring and managing uncertainty, critical thinking and analytical skills, and logical thinking abilities. The ability to analyze data using statistics, conduct database searches, and integrate multiple sources of information are helpful in a number of professional settings. Prospective employers appreciate the excellent written and verbal communication skills among students who present their research projects at conferences and master APA style.

FIGURE 3   **APA Guidelines for the Undergraduate Psychology Major: Learning Goals and Outcomes** (APA, 2013. For complete Guidelines, see apa.org/ed/precollege/about/psymajor-guidelines.aspx)

GOAL 1:
KNOWLEDGE BASE

1.1 Describe key concepts, principles, and overarching themes in psychology.

1.2 Develop a working knowledge of psychology's content domains.

1.3 Describe applications of psychology.

GOAL 2:
SCIENTIFIC INQUIRY & CRITICAL THINKING

2.1 Use scientific reasoning to interpret psychological phenomena.

2.2 Demonstrate psychology information literacy.

2.3 Engage in innovative and integrative thinking and problem solving.

2.4 Interpret, design, and conduct basic psychological research.

2.5 Incorporate sociocultural factors in scientific inquiry.

GOAL 3:
ETHICAL & SOCIAL RESPONSIBILITY IN A DIVERSE WORLD

3.1 Apply ethical standards to evaluate psychological science and practice.

3.2 Build and enhance interpersonal relationships.

3.3 Adopt values that build community at local, national, and global levels.

GOAL 4:
COMMUNICATION

4.1 Demonstrate effective writing for different purposes.

4.2 Exhibit effective presentation skills for different purposes.

4.3 Interact effectively with others.

GOAL 5:
PROFESSIONAL DEVELOPMENT

5.1 Apply psychological content and skills to career goals.

5.2 Exhibit self-efficacy and self-regulation.

5.3 Refine project-management skills.

5.4 Enhance teamwork capacity.

5.5 Develop meaningful professional direction for life after graduation.

CAREER OPTIONS WITH A DEGREE IN PSYCHOLOGY

What can you do with a bachelor's degree in psychology?

A psychology major will prepare you for many possible career paths. Approximately 40 percent of students with a bachelor's degree in psychology attend graduate school or receive professional training, so the majority of psychology majors will be in the job market after graduation (Halonen, 2014). With a bachelor's degree, most graduates find work in business administration, sales, or education (U.S. Bureau of Labor Statistics, 2014). Many psychology majors also work in public affairs, service industries, the health field, or biological sciences and computer programming (APA, n.d.); popular occupations include employment counselor, interviewer, personnel analyst, probation officer, or writer (APA, n.d.). If you choose to work more directly in the field of psychology, a bachelor's degree will qualify you to work as an assistant to psychologists, researchers, or other professionals in community mental health centers, vocational rehabilitation offices, and correctional programs (U.S. Bureau of Labor Statistics, 2014).

A second option for psychology majors after graduation is to pursue a graduate master's or doctorate degree in psychology. Snyder and Dillow (2010) estimate that 20–24 percent of psychology baccalaureate recipients continue on to graduate study in psychology (approximately 8–10 percent pursue doctorate degrees).

A third option is to pursue advanced training in other disciplines such as law, business, education, or medicine.

Drew Appleby provides a list of 280 careers that would be of interest to psychology majors (2015)—including those pursuing advanced degrees. The list includes links for more information about professional responsibilities, salaries, and job outlook for each of these positions.

How can you maximize your ability to get a job after graduating with a major in psychology?

Betsy Morgan and Ann Korschgen (2009) offer the following helpful tips for increasing your chances of getting a job after graduation. Many of these tools will benefit students who plan to apply to graduate school as well.

1. **Get to know your instructors.** Talk with them about the field of psychology and get their advice on your career plan. Ask them to support you on an independent study internship or research project. By learning more about your skills and ambitions, faculty members can help you accomplish your goals. This may even result in an enthusiastic reference for future employment.

2. **Familiarize yourself with available resources.** Talk to alumni and senior students. Career Services can help you identify and market your job skills and emphasize your knowledge and abilities in your resume. They can also help you to network with other alumni who are working in your area of interest and who can help you to prepare for the career that you want. Take advantage of Career Services and other online resources.

3. **Volunteer some of your time and talent to campus or community organizations, such as Psi Chi (the national honor society in psychology) or your school's psychology club.** In addition to showing that you are an active citizen in your department, you will gain important skills, such as meeting and event planning, how to work with a group, and improved communication skills, all of which enhance your marketability.

4. **Participate in an internship experience.** Many employers want students to gain relevant experience outside the classroom. Internships are offered during the school year as well as the summer break. Some are paid and others are not, but you may be able to earn course credit while completing your internship. In addition to gaining relevant work experience before you graduate, you will increase your network of mentors who can provide supervision and support for your career goals as well as letters of endorsement when you apply for jobs.

5. **Take courses that support your interests and plans.** Although the psychology major offers a range of skills that will benefit you in the job market, don't assume the psychology curriculum will offer all the skills necessary to get a job in your area of interest. Add courses to increase your knowledge base and skills. This will also show prospective employers that your specific interests are in line with the demands of the job.

What type of salary can you expect with a degree in psychology? Will a graduate degree increase your salary?

The average starting salary for 2013 bachelor's degree recipients was $37,210, up 5.7 percent from the prior year (National Association of Colleges and Employers [NACE], 2013). By comparison, the average starting salary for 2013 master's recipients was $48,700 (NACE, 2013). Across a lifetime, individuals with a psychology bachelor's are expected to earn $2,001,000, whereas individuals with a doctorate in psychology are expected to earn $3,157,000 (U.S. Census Bureau, 2012) **(FIGURE 4)**. Clearly, earnings tend to increase with education, and higher levels of education will almost always yield greater financial rewards (Carnevale, Strohl, & Melton, 2011).

When considering new doctoral recipients in 2009, women reported a median salary that was $8,000 lower than that reported by men ($62,000 versus $70,000, respectively). Median salaries reported by ethnic minorities were similar to those indicated by nonminorities: $65,000. The mean salaries for these two groups were also close, at $65,962 and $66,314, respectively (Michalski et al., 2011).

Among psychologists with new doctoral degrees in 2009, clinical psychologists working in criminal justice earned the highest median starting salary of $80,500. Psychology graduates working in consulting firms ($75,000) and those working in applied psychology positions ($73,332) tended to have the next two highest median salaries (Michalski et al., 2011).

Psychologists rank number seven (shared with medical scientists) among the top-paying occupations for those with doctoral degrees. The lifetime salary in 2009 dollars was $2,515,000 for graduate level psychologists whereas the lifetime average for all doctoral occupations was $3,252,000 (Carnevale, Rose, & Cheah, 2011).

Of course, earnings potential should not be the only reason that individuals choose a major. Job satisfaction is another important consideration.

What kind of job satisfaction can you expect if you are working in a psychology field?

In a study of 27,000 Americans, the most satisfying jobs were those that involve "caring for, teaching and protecting others and creative pursuits" (Smith, 2007, pp. 1–2). Most of the occupations with the highest-ranking happiness levels involved helping others, using technical and scientific expertise, or using creativity (pp. 1–2). A bachelor's degree in psychology can increase the likelihood that you will be working in a job that fosters these skills (Landrum, 2009).

Positive job satisfaction has also been observed among individuals who attend graduate school in psychology. In 2009, approximately 72 percent of new doctoral recipients

FIGURE 4   **U.S. Census: Pathways After a Bachelor's Degree in Psychology** (Data from U.S. Census Bureau, 2012.)

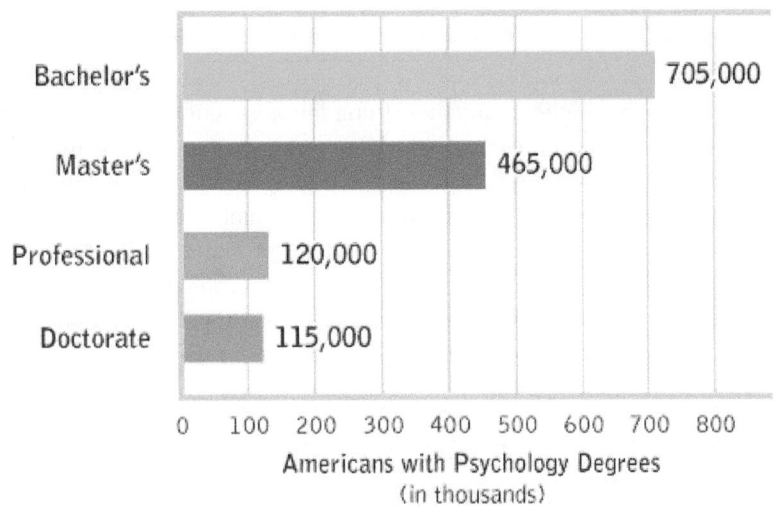

Bachelor's — 705,000
Master's — 465,000
Professional — 120,000
Doctorate — 115,000

Americans with Psychology Degrees
(in thousands)

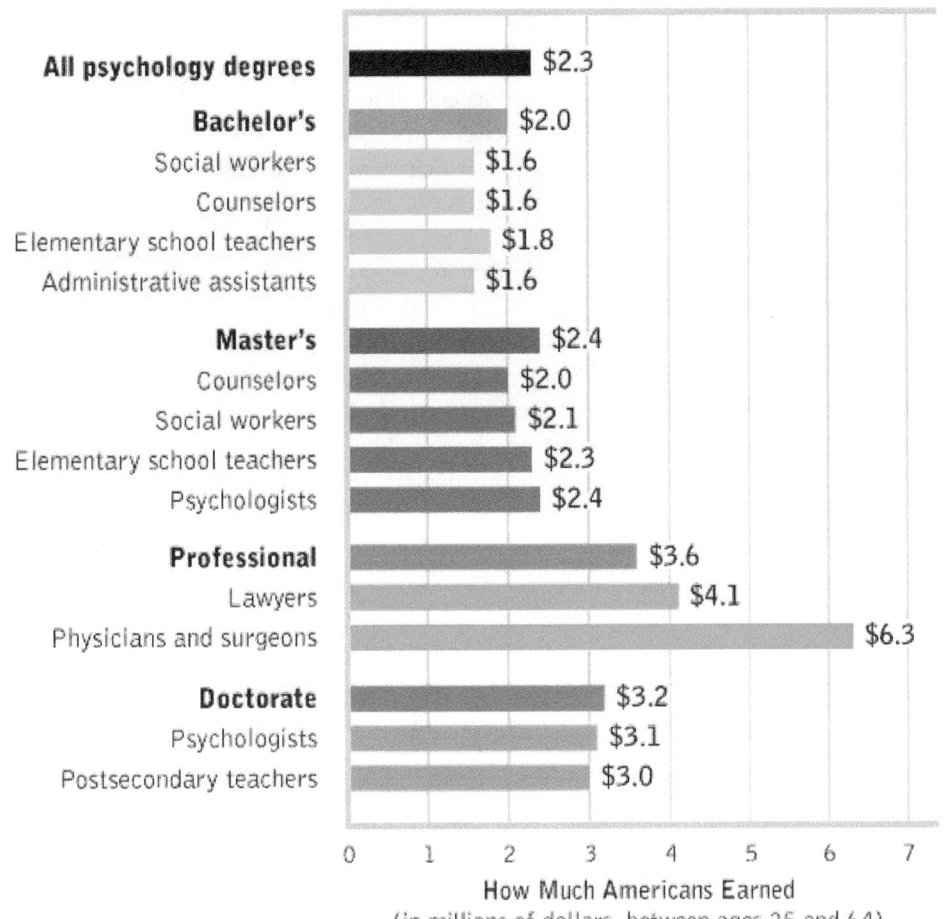

All psychology degrees — $2.3
Bachelor's — $2.0
Social workers — $1.6
Counselors — $1.6
Elementary school teachers — $1.8
Administrative assistants — $1.6
Master's — $2.4
Counselors — $2.0
Social workers — $2.1
Elementary school teachers — $2.3
Psychologists — $2.4
Professional — $3.6
Lawyers — $4.1
Physicians and surgeons — $6.3
Doctorate — $3.2
Psychologists — $3.1
Postsecondary teachers — $3.0

How Much Americans Earned
(in millions of dollars, between ages 25 and 64)

indicated that their primary occupational position was their first choice. Most new graduates with a Ph.D. are fairly satisfied with their current position in terms of salary, benefits, opportunities for personal development, supervisors, colleagues, and working conditions (Michalski et al., 2011).

POSTGRADUATE DEGREES

Why should you consider attending graduate school in psychology?

In addition to a higher salary and strong job satisfaction, a graduate degree in psychology will give you proficiency in an area of psychological specialization and increased opportunities to work in diverse areas of psychology.

Job prospects in the field of psychology are much better for individuals with graduate degrees. According to the U.S. Bureau of Labor Statistics (2014), job prospects will be best for those with a doctoral degree in school psychology or a specialty degree. Individuals with a master's degree will still face keener competition for positions in psychology than those with a doctoral degree—even in fields such as industrial/organization (I/O) psychology, which are experiencing faster than average employment growth.

Employment for psychologists is expected to grow 12 percent from 2012 to 2022, which is in keeping with the average across all occupations. Employment will grow because of increased demand for psychological services in schools, hospitals, social service agencies, and mental health centers (U.S. Bureau of Labor Statistics, 2014).

What's the difference between a master's degree and a doctorate degree in psychology?

Both degrees will prepare you for more specialized training in psychology and increase your job opportunities in the field of psychology beyond the bachelor's degree.

A master's degree in psychology requires at least two years of full-time graduate study in a specific subfield of psychology. In addition to specialized course work in psychology, requirements usually include practical experience in an applied setting or a master's thesis reporting on an original research project. You might acquire a master's degree to do specialized work in psychology. As a graduate with a master's degree, you might handle research and data collection and analysis in a university, government, or private industry setting. You might work under the supervision of a psychologist with a doctorate, providing some clinical service such as therapy or testing. Or you might find a job in the health, government, industry, or education fields. You might also acquire a master's degree as a stepping stone for more advanced study in a doctoral program in psychology, which will expand the number of employment opportunities available to you.

You will probably need five to seven years of graduate study in a specific subfield of psychology to earn your doctoral degree. The degree you choose to pursue will depend on your career goals. You will probably choose to earn a doctor of philosophy (Ph.D.) in psychology if your career goals are geared toward conducting research, or a doctor of psychology (Psy.D.) if you are more interested in pursuing professional practice. Training for the Ph.D. culminates in a dissertation (an extensive research paper you will be required to defend orally) based on original research. Courses in quantitative research methods, which include the use of computer-based analysis, are an important part of graduate study and are necessary to complete the dissertation. Psy.D. training may be based on clinical (therapeutic) work and examinations rather than a dissertation. It is important to note, however, that psychologists with Psy.D. degrees are not the only ones who work in professional practice. Many psychologists who earn a Ph.D. in clinical or counseling psychology conduct research and work in professional settings. If you pursue clinical and counseling psychology programs, you should expect at least a one-year internship in addition to the regular course work, clinical practice, and research.

FIGURE 5 lists by subfield the Ph.D.s earned in the United States in 2012, the most recent year for which these data are available. Among the doctorates awarded in the

FIGURE 5   **Psychology Degrees Awarded by Subfield, 2012** (Data from National Center for Education Statistics, Integrated Postsecondary Education Data System [IPEDS], 2012 Completion Survey.)

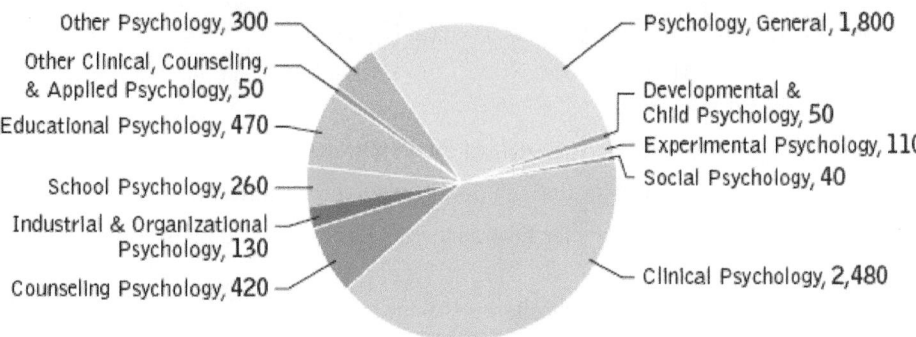

Number of Doctorates Awarded by Psychology Subfield, 2012

Other Psychology, 300

Other Clinical, Counseling, & Applied Psychology, 50

Educational Psychology, 470

School Psychology, 260

Industrial & Organizational Psychology, 130

Counseling Psychology, 420

Psychology, General, 1,800

Developmental & Child Psychology, 50

Experimental Psychology, 110

Social Psychology, 40

Clinical Psychology, 2,480

2011–2012 academic year, the most popular subfield was clinical psychology, followed by general psychology. Of these doctorates, the majority were classified as research/scholarship (74 percent), with fewer designated as professional practice (24 percent) or other types (1 percent) (APA Center for Workplace Studies, 2014).

What are some of the subfields of psychology?

If you are like most psychology students, you may be unaware of the wide variety of specialties and work settings available in psychology (Terre & Stoddart, 2000). To date, the APA has 54 active divisions (FIGURE 6). The following paragraphs (arranged alphabetically) describe some careers in the main specialty areas of psychology, most of which require a graduate degree in psychology.

Clinical psychologists promote psychological health in individuals, groups, and organizations. Some clinical psychologists specialize in specific psychological disorders. Others treat a range of disorders, from adjustment difficulties to severe psychopathology. Clinical psychologists might engage in research, teaching, assessment, and consultation. Some hold workshops and lectures on psychological issues for other professionals or for the public. Clinical psychologists work in a variety of settings, including private practice, mental health service organizations, schools, universities, industries, legal systems, medical systems, counseling centers, government agencies, and military services.

To become a clinical psychologist, you will need to earn a doctorate from a clinical psychology program. The APA sets the standards for clinical psychology graduate programs, offering accreditation (official recognition) to those who meet their standards. In all U.S. states, clinical psychologists working in independent practice must obtain a license to offer services such as therapy and testing.

Cognitive psychologists study thought processes and focus on such topics as perception, language, attention, problem solving, memory, judgment and decision making, forgetting, and intelligence. Recent areas of research interest include designing computer-based models of thought processes and identifying biological correlates of cognition. As a cognitive psychologist, you might work as a professor, industrial consultant, or human factors specialist in an educational or business setting.

Community psychologists move beyond focusing on specific individuals or families and deal with broad problems of mental health in community settings. These psychologists believe that human behavior is powerfully influenced by the interaction between people and their physical, social, political, and economic environments. They seek to

FIGURE 6   **APA Divisions by Number and Name**

APA Divisions by Name and Number

1. Society for General Psychology
2. Society for the Teaching of Psychology
3. Experimental Psychology
4. There is no active Division 4.
5. Division for Quantitative and Qualitative Methods
6. Behavioral Neuroscience and Comparative Psychology
7. Developmental Psychology
8. Society for Personality and Social Psychology
9. Society for the Psychological Study of Social Issues (SPSSI)
10. Society for the Psychology of Aesthetics, Creativity, and the Arts
11. There is no active Division 11.
12. Society of Clinical Psychology
13. Society of Consulting Psychology
14. Society for Industrial and Organizational Psychology
15. Educational Psychology
16. School Psychology
17. Society of Counseling Psychology
18. Psychologists in Public Service
19. Military Psychology
20. Adult Development and Aging
21. Applied Experimental and Engineering Psychology
22. Rehabilitation Psychology
23. Society for Consumer Psychology
24. Theoretical and Philosophical Psychology
25. Behavior Analysis
26. Society for the History of Psychology
27. Society for Community Research and Action: Division of Community Psychology
28. Psychopharmacology and Substance Abuse
29. Society for the Advancement of Psychotherapy
30. Society of Psychological Hypnosis
31. State, Provincial, and Territorial Psychological Association Affairs
32. Society for Humanistic Psychology
33. Intellectual and Developmental Disabilities
34. Society for Environmental, Population, and Conservation Psychology
35. Society for the Psychology of Women
36. Society for the Psychology of Religion and Spirituality
37. Society for Child and Family Policy and Practice
38. Health Psychology
39. Psychoanalysis
40. Society for Clinical Neuropsychology
41. American Psychology-Law Society
42. Psychologists in Independent Practice
43. Society for Family Psychology
44. Society for the Psychological Study of Lesbian, Gay, Bisexual, and Transgender Issues
45. Society for the Psychological Study of Culture, Ethnicity and Race
46. Society for Media Psychology and Technology
47. Exercise and Sport Psychology
48. Society for the Study of Peace, Conflict, and Violence: Peace Psychology Division
49. Society of Group Psychology and Group Psychotherapy
50. Society of Addiction Psychology
51. Society for the Psychological Study of Men and Masculinity
52. International Psychology
53. Society of Clinical Child and Adolescent Psychology
54. Society of Pediatric Psychology
55. American Society for the Advancement of Pharmacotherapy
56. Trauma Psychology

Source: American Psychological Association.

Note: There is no active Division 4 or Division 11. See *A Chronological History of Divisions* for more details.

improve individual functioning by enhancing environmental settings to promote psychological health.

Community psychologists focus on prevention, promotion of positive mental health, and crisis intervention, with special attention to the problems of underserved groups and ethnic minorities. Given the shared emphasis on prevention, some community psychologists collaborate with professionals in other areas, such as public health. As a community psychologist, your work settings could include federal, state, and local departments of mental health, corrections, and welfare systems. You might conduct research or help evaluate research in health service settings, serve as an independent consultant for a private or government agency, or teach and consult as a college or university faculty member.

Counseling psychologists help people adjust to life transitions or make lifestyle changes. This field is very similar to clinical psychology, except that counseling psychologists typically help people with adjustment problems rather than severe psychopathology. Like clinical psychologists, counseling psychologists conduct therapy and provide assessments to individuals and groups. As a counseling psychologist, you would emphasize your clients' strengths, helping clients cope during a transitional time using their own skills, interests, and abilities. You might find yourself working in an academic setting as a faculty member or administrator or in a university counseling center, community mental health center, business, or private practice. As with clinical psychology, if you plan to work in independent practice you will need to obtain a state license to provide counseling services to the public.

Developmental psychologists conduct research in age-related behavioral changes and apply their scientific knowledge to educational, child care, policy, and related settings. As a developmental psychologist, you would investigate change across a broad range of topics, including the biological, social, psychological, and cognitive aspects of development. Developmental psychology informs a number of applied fields, including educational psychology, school psychology, child psychopathology, and gerontology. The field also informs public policy in areas such as education and child-care reform, maternal and child health and attachment, and adoption. You would probably specialize in behavior during infancy, childhood, adolescence, or middle or late adulthood. Your work setting could be an educational institution, day-care center, youth group program, or senior center.

Educational psychologists study the relationship between learning and our physical and social environments. They study the psychological processes involved in learning and develop strategies for enhancing the learning process. As an educational psychologist, you might work in a university—in a psychology department or a school of education. You might conduct basic research on topics related to learning or develop innovative methods of teaching to enhance the learning process. You might design effective tests, including measures of aptitude and achievement. You might be employed by a school or government agency or charged with designing and implementing effective employee-training programs in a business setting.

Experimental psychologists are a diverse group of scientists who investigate a variety of basic behavioral processes in research involving humans and other animals. Prominent areas of study in experimental research include comparative methods of science, motivation, learning, thought, attention, memory, perception, and language. Most experimental psychologists identify with a particular subfield such as cognitive psychology, depending on their area of study. It is also important to note that the experimental method for conducting research studies is not limited to the field of experimental psychology, as many other subfields rely on experimental methodology to conduct studies. As an experimental psychologist, you would most likely work in an academic setting, teaching courses and supervising students' research in addition to conducting your own research using experimental methodology. Or you might be employed by a research institution, zoo, business, industry affiliate, or government agency.

Forensic psychologists apply psychological principles to legal issues. They conduct research on the interface of law and psychology, help to create public policies related to mental health, help law-enforcement agencies in criminal investigations, or assist in forensic consultation involving jury selection and deliberation research. They also provide therapy and assessment to assist the legal community. Some forensic psychologists hold law degrees and provide clients with legal services as well. Although most forensic psychologists are clinical psychologists, they might have expertise in other areas of psychology, such as social or cognitive psychology. As a forensic psychologist, you might work in a university psychology department, law school, research organization, community mental health agency, law-enforcement agency, court, or correctional setting.

Health psychologists are researchers and practitioners concerned with psychology's contribution to promoting health and preventing disease. As applied psychologists or clinicians, they may help individuals lead healthier lives by designing, conducting, and evaluating programs to stop smoking, lose weight, improve sleep, manage pain, treat psychosocial problems associated with chronic and terminal illness, or prevent the spread of sexually transmitted infections. As researchers and clinicians, they identify conditions and practices associated with health and illness to help create effective interventions. In public service, health psychologists study and work to improve government policies and health care systems. As a health psychologist, you could be employed in a hospital, medical school, rehabilitation center, public health agency, college or university, or, if you are also a clinical psychologist, in private practice.

Industrial/organizational (I/O) psychologists study the relationship between people and their working environments. They may develop new ways to increase productivity, improve personnel selection, or promote job satisfaction in a business setting. Their interests include organizational structure and change, consumer behavior, and personnel selection and training. As an I/O psychologist, you might conduct workplace training or provide organizational analysis and development. You may find yourself working in business, industry, the government, or a college or university. Or you may be self-employed as a consultant or work for a management counseling firm.

Neuropsychologists investigate the relationship between neurological processes (structure and function of the brain) and behavior. As a neuropsychologist you might assess, diagnose, or treat disorders related to the central nervous system, such as Alzheimer's disease or stroke. You might also evaluate individuals for evidence of head injuries, learning and developmental disabilities such as autism spectrum disorder, and other psychiatric disorders including ADHD. If you are a clinical neuropsychologist, you might work in the neurology, neurosurgery, or psychiatric unit of a hospital. Neuropsychologists also work in academic settings, where they conduct research and teach.

Psychometric and quantitative psychologists study the methods and techniques used to acquire psychological knowledge. A psychometrician may update existing neurocognitive or personality tests or devise new tests for use in clinical and school settings or in business and industry. These psychologists also administer, score, and interpret such tests. Quantitative psychologists collaborate with researchers to design, analyze, and interpret the results of research programs. As a psychometric or quantitative psychologist, you will need to be well trained in research methods, statistics, and computer technology. You will most likely be employed by a university or college, testing company, private research firm, or government agency.

Rehabilitation psychologists are researchers and practitioners who work with people who have lost optimal functioning after an accident, illness, or other event. As a rehabilitation psychologist, you would probably work in a medical rehabilitation institution or hospital. You might also work in a medical school, university, state or federal vocational rehabilitation agency, or in private practice serving people with physical disabilities.

School psychologists are involved in the assessment of and intervention for children in educational settings. They diagnose and treat cognitive, social, and emotional problems that may negatively influence children's learning or overall functioning at school. As a school psychologist, you would collaborate with teachers, parents, and administrators, making recommendations to improve student learning. You would work in an academic setting, a federal or state government agency, a child guidance center, or a behavioral research laboratory.

Social psychologists are interested in our interactions with others. Social psychologists investigate how our beliefs, feelings, and behaviors are affected by and influence other people. They study topics such as attitudes, aggression, prejudice, interpersonal attraction, group behavior, and leadership. As a social psychologist, you would probably be a faculty member at a college or university. You might also work in organizational consultation, marketing research, or other applied psychology fields, including social neuroscience. Some social psychologists work for hospitals, federal agencies, or businesses performing applied research.

As a **sport psychologist**, you would study the psychological factors that influence, and are influenced by, participation in sports and other physical activities. Professional activities of sport psychologists include coach education and athlete preparation, as well as research and teaching. Sport psychologists who also have a clinical or counseling degree can apply those skills to working with athletes with psychological problems such as anxiety or substance-abuse problems that might interfere with optimal performance. If you were not working in an academic or research setting, you would most likely work as part of a team or organization or in a private capacity.

PREPARING EARLY FOR GRADUATE STUDY IN PSYCHOLOGY

Why do you need to prepare for graduate study in psychology?

Competition for the openings in psychology graduate programs is keen. During the 2009–2010 academic year, just over one in five, or 22 percent of applicants, were accepted into doctoral programs in psychology. The acceptance rate for applicants to clinical psychology programs was approximately 32 percent among Psy.D. programs and 8 percent among Ph.D. programs (Kohout & Wicherski, 2010). The acceptance rate for U.S. master's programs was higher than for doctoral programs, with just under half (48 percent) of all applicants accepted by master's programs during the 2009–2010 school year (Kohout & Wicherski, 2010).

What kind of debt can you expect after earning a doctorate degree in psychology?

Tuition costs vary by type of doctoral degree sought, and education-related debt levels, too, differ by degree type. In 2009, approximately 68 percent of doctorate recipients reported some debt from their graduate training. A total of 89 percent of Psy.D. recipients reported debt, compared to 62 percent of Ph.D. recipients. Among graduates who reported any debt, individuals who received a Psy.D. reported a median debt of $120,000 whereas those receiving a Ph.D. reported a median debt of $50,000 (Michalski et al., 2011). Approximately half (52 percent) of Ph.D. students reported that their primary funding was from university sources of support. By comparison, only 4 percent of Psy.D. recipients reported university sources as their primary source of support; most (65 percent) reported that their primary source of support was nonuniversity or federal loans (Michalski et al., 2011).

What can you do to increase your chances of acceptance into graduate school?

If you choose to go to graduate school, there are a number of things you can do now to maximize your chances of gaining admission to the school of your choice. If possible, begin preparing during your first year on campus to maximize opportunities and obtain the experience needed to gain admission to a competitive program. Kristy Arnold and Kelly Horrigan (2002) offer a number of suggestions to facilitate this process.

1. **Network.** Get to know faculty members and the psychology department by attending activities and meetings. This will be especially helpful when you apply to graduate school or for a professional position, because many applications require two to three letters of reference. Become involved in psychology clubs and in Psi Chi, the national honor society in psychology. These meetings connect students with similar interests and expose them to a broader study of the field.

2. **Become actively involved in research as early as possible.** Start by doing simple tasks such as data entry and data collection, and over time you will be prepared to conduct your own research project under the supervision of a research mentor. Consider applying for summer research positions through your university or from other organizations such as the American Psychological Association Summer Science Fellowship program or the National Science Foundation Research Experiences for Undergraduates (REU) program, which will test your interest in academic careers and build your skills for future study in psychology.

3. **Volunteer or get a job in a psychology-related field.** Getting involved will demonstrate your willingness to apply psychological concepts to real-world settings. Further, it will showcase your ability to juggle a number of tasks successfully, such as those in work and school—an important skill for graduate school success.

4. **Maintain good grades and prepare early for the GRE.** Demonstrate your ability to do well in graduate school by successfully completing challenging courses, especially those related to your interests in graduate school. In your junior year, you should begin studying for the Graduate Record Exam (GRE), the standardized test that applicants to graduate school must complete. Many graduate programs in psychology require both the general GRE and the psychology subject tests. If you start preparing early for the GRE and maintain high grades, you will be ready for success in your graduate school application and study.

So, the next time someone asks you what you will do with your psychology degree, tell them you have a lot of options. You might use your acquired skills and understanding to get a job and succeed in any number of fields, or you might pursue graduate school and then career opportunities in associated professions. In any case, what you have learned about behavior and mental processes will surely enrich your life (Hammer, 2003).

FOR MORE INFORMATION

How can you learn more about the psychology major and the field of psychology?

1. Talk with as many people as possible who have experience in the discipline of psychology. This includes psychology majors, graduate students in psychology, psychology instructors, advisors, and other professionals who train in psychology or work in the field.

2. Go to your college's Career Services office. Learn more about what your college has to offer in terms of career planning for psychology.

3. Attend your school's events in psychology. Attend Psychology Club, <u>Psi Chi</u>, or <u>Psi Beta</u> meetings, and other psychology-related offerings where you can learn more about careers in the field.

4. Read available <u>books</u>.

5. Take advantage of online resources, which can help you to determine whether you would be well matched for a major and a career in psychology.

- <u>Watch online videos showcasing different careers in psychology.</u>
- <u>Play the Career Interest Game.</u>
- Get more information about specific jobs in psychology from the <u>Bureau of Labor Statistics</u>, the <u>Occupational Information Network</u> (O*NET), or the <u>Occupational Outlook Handbook</u> (OOH).
- Visit the <u>American Psychological Association</u> and <u>Association for Psychological Science</u> websites. Become a student affiliate of these organizations.
- Learn more about the national honor societies in psychology, <u>Psi Chi</u> and <u>Psi Beta</u>.

What are some books that can help you to learn more about the major, careers, and graduate school in psychology?

American Psychological Association (2015). *Graduate study in psychology, 2016 edition*. Washington, DC: Author.

Hettich, P., & Landrum, R. E. (2014). *Your undergraduate degree in psychology: From college to career*. Thousand Oaks, CA: Sage.

Kracen, A. C., & Wallace, I. J. (Eds.) (2008). *Applying to graduate school in psychology: Advice from successful students and prominent psychologists*. Washington, DC: American Psychological Association.

Kuther, T., & Morgan, R. D. (2012). *Careers in psychology: Opportunities in a changing world*. Boston, MA: Wadsworth Cengage.

Landrum, E., & Davis, S. (2013). *The psychology major: Career options and strategies for success* (5th ed.). Upper Saddle River, NJ: Pearson/Prentice Hall.

Morgan, B., & Korschgen, A. (2014). *Majoring in psychology? Career options for psychology undergraduates* (5th ed.). Boston, MA: Pearson.

Wegenek, A. R., & Buskist, W. (2010). *The insider's guide to the psychology major. Everything you need to know about the degree and the profession*. Washington, DC: American Psychological Association.

REFERENCES

American Psychological Association. (n.d.). *Your career: Psychology can take you to great places*. Retrieved from apa.org/action/careers/facts.aspx

APA Center for Workplace Studies. (2014). How many psychology doctorates are awarded by U.S. institutions? *Monitor on Psychology, 45*, 13. Retrieved from apa.org/monitor/2014/07-08/datapoint.aspx

APA Center for Workplace Studies. (2015). How much has the number of advanced degrees in psychology increased in the past decade? *Monitor on Psychology, 46,* 13. Retrieved from apa.org/monitor/2015/01/datapoint.aspx

Appleby, D. C. (2015). *An online career-exploration resource for psychology majors.* Retrieved from teachpsych.org/page-1603066

Arnold, K. L., & Horrigan, K. L. (2002). Gaining admission into the graduate program of your choice. *Eye on Psi Chi, 7,* 30–33.

Carnevale, A. P., Rose, S. J., & Cheah, B. (2011). *The college payoff. Education, occupations, lifetime earnings.* Center on Education and the Workforce, Georgetown University. Retrieved from http://cew.georgetown.edu/collegepayoff/

Carnevale, A. P., & Smith, N. (2014). *Workplace basics: The skills employees need and employers want.* Center on Education and the Workforce, Georgetown University. Retrieved from cew.georgetown.edu/wp-content/uploads/2014/11/HRDI.Editorial.pdf

Carnevale, A. P., Strohl, J., & Melton, M. (2011). *What's it worth: The economic value of college majors.* Center on Education and the Workforce, Georgetown University. Retrieved from cew.georgetown.edu/wp-content/uploads/2014/11/whatsitworth-complete.pdf

Hammer, E. Y. (2003). How lucky you are to be a psychology major. *Eye on Psi Chi, 7,* 4–5.

Halonen, J. (2014). Why would you want to major in *that? Psychology Student Network.* Retrieved from apa.org/ed/precollege/psn/2014/01/why-major.aspx

Kohout, J., & Wicherski, M. (2010). *2009–10: Applications, acceptances, enrollments, and degrees awarded to master's- and doctoral-level students in U.S. and Canadian graduate departments of psychology.* APA Center for Workforce Studies. Retrieved from apa.org/workforce/publications/11-grad-study/applications.aspx?tab=1

Landrum, E. (2009). *Finding jobs with a psychology bachelor's degree: Expert advice for launching your career.* Washington, DC: American Psychological Association.

Marrs, H., Barb, M., & Ruggiero, J. (2007). Self-reported influences on psychology major choice and personality. *Individual Differences Research, 5,* 289–299.

Michalski, D., Kohout, J., Wicherski, M., & Hart, B. (2011). 2009 doctorate employment survey. APA Center for Workforce Studies. Retrieved from apa.org/workforce/publications/09-doc-empl/index.aspx

Morgan, B. L., & Korschgen, A. J. (2009). *Majoring in psych?: Career options for psychology undergraduates.* Boston, MA: Pearson Allyn & Bacon.

Mulvey, T. A., & Grus, C. A. (2010). *What do I do with a degree in psychology? APA Center for Workforce Studies.* Accessed May 24, 2010, from apa.org/workforce/presentations/2010-convention.aspx

National Association of Colleges and Employers. (2013). *NACE salary survey: Starting salary for new college graduates. Data reported by employers.* Retrieved from careers.washington.edu/sites/default/files/all/editors/docs/2013-september-salary-survey.pdf

National Center for Education Statistics. (2013a). *Bachelor's degrees conferred by postsecondary institutions, by field of study: Selected years, 1970–71 through 2011–12.* Retrieved from nces.ed.gov/programs/digest/d13/tables/dt13_322.10.asp

National Center for Education Statistics. (2013b). *Degrees in psychology conferred by post-secondary institutions, by level of degree and sex of student: Selected years, 1949–50 through 2011–12*. Retrieved from nces.ed.gov/programs/digest/d13/tables/dt13_325.80.asp

Smith, T. W. (2007). *Job satisfaction in the United States*. Retrieved from www-news.uchicago.edu/releases/07/pdf/070417.jobs.pdf

Snyder, T. D., & Dillow, S. A. (2010). *Digest of Education Statistics 2009 (NCES 2010-013)*. National Center for Education Statistics, Institute of Education Sciences, U.S. Department of Education. Washington, DC.

Terre, L., & Stoddart, R. M. (2000). Cutting-edge specialties for graduate study in psychology. *Eye on Psi Chi, 5*, 23–26.

U.S. Bureau of Labor Statistics. (2014). *Occupational Outlook Handbook, 2014–2015 Edition, Psychologists*. Accessed January 4, 2015, from bls.gov/ooh/life-physical-and-social-science/psychologists.htm

U. S. Census Bureau. (2012). *Pathways after a bachelor's degree in psychology: Educational attainment, common occupations, and synthetic work-life earnings estimates.* Retrieved from census.gov/library/infographics/psyc_majors.html

A Practical Guide to Study Skills

Amy Himsel
El Camino College

Like most of you, I had never been taught the best way to study. I am writing this chapter because I want studying to be less confusing and frustrating for you than it was for me, and I want you to know about study techniques that are effective and efficient. So, if you are ready for a change in your study habits, prepare to open your mind to some of the surprising findings from the science of studying. They reveal successful study strategies that will help you improve specific class and overall school performance. You'll discover that the brain has an incredible capacity to change when given the proper exercise—an ability you can apply to any area of your life.

Learning How to Learn

How do we learn? It's a simple question, but the answer is more complicated than you might expect.

Let Go of What You Think You Know

My study plan as a college freshman was straightforward: to memorize as many words as possible from my textbooks and professors' lectures. I was pretty good at this, furiously taking notes in class or as I read the course materials. I spent countless hours repeating the information in an effort to make it sink into my brain, and I earned a reputation for being one of the most studious (okay, obsessive) students in my dorm. So why wasn't I, master memorizer with a will of steel, earning straight As? Like many students, my assumptions about studying were guided more by "common sense" than by scientific reality. Unfortunately, then as now, "common-sense" notions are frequently incorrect (Stanovich, 2010).

It's easy to get tricked into thinking rote methods work because they *feel* so effective in the moment. During my marathon sessions of rote learning, I certainly *felt* like I was doing the right thing. But the proof is in the pudding, and my grades that first year did not match my feeling of mastery. Has this ever happened to you? If so, you are not alone. We are poor judges of how well we have learned something, and we chronically underestimate how much we know about a topic we have studied. Furthermore, the less we know about a topic, the less we realize we *don't* really know it (Kruger & Dunning, 1999). In the quest to become a better and more efficient learner, you must let go of what you think you know about studying and follow methods backed by science.

No matter what your grades were in the past or what your current habits or attitudes are, you can change for the better. Please don't underestimate the brain's potential for change. It is constantly changing due to experience, and you are capable of creating new experiences while you study. As you'll find out, if you learn how the brain works and give it proper attention and exercise, it can change to your benefit.

How Your Brain Really Works

Studying is about making memories, but memories are not made in a straightforward manner. We do not "place" information in one spot—like placing an item on a closet shelf, returning later to pick it up, dust it off, and then use it to answer a question on a test. Instead, we make memories when our brain's networks of connections are activated in patterns. Basically, here's what science tells us: Mental exercise creates and strengthens networks of connections in your brain similar to the way lifting weights strengthens your muscles (Medina, 2008). The more you "work" the information (for example, by explaining a concept in your own words), the more neural connections are made or strengthened and the stronger your memory becomes. As a result, you remember more when it's time to take a test.

But here's a surprising fact: Memories—including those formed while you study—are deeply personal, customized to fit your brain and nobody else's in exactly the same way. Why? Because learning is not like painting on a blank canvas. Rather, you start with a backdrop of networks that represent your current knowledge, preferences, and habits.

Simply put, you are your connections. You make long-lasting memories by weaving the new information into your unique brain cell connections. No two people will do this in exactly the same way. Likewise, there is no magic formula for studying well. With this in mind, start experimenting with the techniques described in this chapter to find out what works best for your brain. But please don't worry: You don't have to become an expert in neuroscience to learn how best to exercise your brain cell networks. Take a look at Figure 1, and then stay with me to learn the basics of brain change and how to apply that information to your everyday life as a student.

(a)

(a) Tom Barrick, Chris Clark, SGHMS/Photo Researchers

FIGURE 1 The Connectome These images are models created to represent the incredibly complex and unique networks of connections among brain cells. Nobody's connections are exactly the same as yours. Shown in (a) is a model of neuronal connections across different regions of the brain as a whole. The model in (b) shows a close-up of the complex connections that have formed between individual neurons.

(b)

(b) Image courtesy of Dr. Sebastian Seung: Neural "wiring" reconstructed from the retina V. Jain, J. Murray, S. Turaga, and S. Seung (MIT); K. Briggman, M. Helmstaedter, and W. Denk (MPG)

Getting Things into Your Head: Brain-Change Fundamentals

When you study, you start by bringing new information into your brain, a process referred to as encoding. Basically, when you pay attention to information, you encode it. Reading, listening to lectures, taking notes, and reviewing notes are all forms of encoding. But not all forms of encoding are equally helpful. Common study strategies—like rereading the text or notes, or trying to memorize definitions word for word—are rote methods that involve shallow processing, which results in very limited brain change. This kind of encoding produces only the weakest of neural connections, without generating enough raw material from which to later construct an accurate memory.

To study better, move beyond shallow encoding to process information at a deeper level. For example, relate the new information you are trying to learn to something that is already familiar to you. Let's say you need to learn the definition of the term *homeostasis* ("the maintenance of a steady internal state in the body"). That may seem very abstract until you think about your actual experiences with homeostasis—say, a time when you have felt hot and sweaty. That's your body trying to cool itself off, and that's a homeostatic experience. Ever felt dehydrated? That's your body signaling that more liquid is needed. Thinking in this way, you will find that homeostasis now seems far more familiar because you've connected it to knowledge and experiences that are already represented in your networks of brain cells. Even the simple act of putting things into your own words triggers deeper processing because you are converting the material into words that are more familiar to you. (See more about this in Table 1.)

Quality studying also requires practice in getting the learned information out again, a process referred to as *retrieval*. As a student, when I tried to remember the exact words of a definition, I was practicing retrieval—but only in a very shallow form. It is much better exercise for the brain when studying involves deeper methods of retrieval, like restating definitions in your own words (without peeking at your notes first!) or trying to explain the material to someone else.

TABLE 1 **Rote Method Makeover**

Common rote strategy	New and improved strategy
Reading	• Previewing each section before you read, and writing questions • Using questions to think while you read, and to test yourself after reading
Copying definitions	• Writing definitions in your own words
Memorizing definitions	• Stating definitions in your own words, as though you were trying to explain the terms to someone else
Copying notes	• Elaborating on your notes • Noting connections between your notes and your past knowledge or experience • Making connections between terms and concepts within the material
Rereading the text or your notes	• Processing your notes or the text in different ways • Self-testing with questions you wrote or those provided in the text • Testing yourself to see if you can repeat in your own words the material you have just read
Taking notes focused on the professor's words	• Writing down not only what is on the slide, board, or outline, but also supplementing with your own words • Marking spots of confusion and asking the professor for clarification later
Comparing your notes with a classmate to make sure you "got everything down"	• Discussing your notes with a classmate; explaining to each other the material in your notes • Filling in any gaps with your own words

The mental exercise involved in studying takes time to sink in and stabilize into lasting brain change. This is a process called *memory consolidation,* one that is similar to how your muscles need some rest after exercise in order to develop best. Memories settle into the fabric of the brain gradually, aided by time, sleep, and further mental exercise. Imagine what happens when you spend several hours drilling with rote methods and skimping on sleep in an effort to cram it all in: You actually make the task of learning harder on yourself by shortchanging your brain's memory consolidation process.

How do you apply these fundamentals to studying? What follows are some basic study tips to keep in mind.

Keep Things Challenging

Learning should not feel easy. To be more specific, creating strong, reliable memories—memories that are still there for you on the day of the exam—should not feel easy. Sorry, but that is true. Ignoring this fact is like expecting to housetrain your new puppy on day one. It's funny how this same advice is completely non-controversial when it comes to physical exercise. Who expects to develop impressive biceps by doing curls with only 1-pound weights? Challenging study stimulates deeper brain change, resulting in stronger memories that are more easily retrieved on demand. Scientists call this a "desirable difficulty" because the more you struggle to learn now, the stronger your neural networks become—and the less likely you are to forget the information later (Bjork & Bjork, 2011).

It all makes sense when you spell it out, but it's fascinating how quickly we forget and get tricked by our feelings in the moment. I used to parrot back all kinds of information and definitions in the midst of my marathon rote-method study sessions. It didn't feel difficult, especially after three hours of memorizing. I felt like I was really learning something, which made it all the more disappointing when my test scores showed otherwise. Sound familiar? If so, it's time once again to let go of what you think you know. When studying feels easy in the moment, that's exactly when you should doubt your mastery the most. In contrast, when you feel frustrated and unsure while studying, smile and pat yourself on the back—you are engaging in a vigorous mental workout. Those difficulties are desirable and will pay off big time later.

Space Out Your Study Sessions

I used to study for long stretches of time for each class. I figured the longer I kept at it, the better I would learn the material. Wrong. Contrary to common sense, it's much better exercise for your brain if you space out your study sessions for each class. Consider a weight-lifting analogy: If you wanted to tone up, would you expect your muscles to respond better to one five-hour workout a week than to five one-hour sessions a week? Of course not. Similarly, the brain responds best to short, focused study sessions spaced across several days.

Learning experts recommend you spend two to three hours studying for every hour spent at lectures. That's a lot of time, but it's much less overwhelming if you spread it out across several days. You'll see possible study schedules in the calendars in Figure 2.

Mix Things Up

Exercise your brain connections with some cross-training—that is, by varying the way you encode new information (see Figure 3 on page 6). Of course, it's a great idea to engage in traditional tasks like reading. But monitor your encoding: Are you just focused on memorizing words? If so, you are focused only on *visual encoding.* At that level, processing is shallow. So take another step and encode the information further. For example, the definition of a term will be most memorable if you focus on the meaning *(semantic encoding),* which is aided by putting the definition into your own words. Perhaps also try relating what you read to a body movement or gesture (Cook,

Marisol

2011	Sunday, Jul 17	Monday, Jul 18	Tuesday Jul 19	Wednesday Jul 20	Thursday Jul 21	Friday, Jul 22	Saturday, Jul 23
11 AM						11:00 AM Study Psychology	11:00 AM Study English
Noon							
12 PM						12:00 PM Study Biology	12:00 PM Study Biology
1 PM	1:00 PM Study Chemistry			1:00 PM Study English			1:00 PM Study Chemistry
2 PM					2:00 PM Study Biology		
3 PM			3:00 PM Study English		3:00 PM Study English		
4 PM			4:00 PM Study Psychology		4:00 PM Study Psychology	4:00 PM Study Psychology	
5 PM			5:00 PM Study Chemistry	5:00 PM Study Chemistry		5:00 PM Study English	
6 PM		6:00 PM Study Psychology		6:00 PM Study Psychology		6:00 PM Study Chemistry	
7 PM		7:00 PM Study Chemistry		7:00 PM Study Biology			
8 PM		8:00 PM Study Biology	8:00 PM Study Biology				
9 PM		9:00 PM Study English					
10 PM							

Noah

2011	Sunday, Jul 17	Monday, Jul 18	Tuesday Jul 19	Wednesday Jul 20	Thursday, Jul 21	Friday, Jul 22	Saturday, Jul 23
11 AM						11:00 AM Study Psychology	11:00 AM Study English
Noon							
12 PM						12:00 PM Study Biology	12:00 PM Study Biology
1 PM	1:00 PM Study Chemistry					1:00 PM Study English	1:00 PM Study Chemistry
2 PM	2:00 PM Study Psychology					2:00 PM Study Chemistry	2:00 PM Study Psychology
3 PM	3:00 PM Study Biology						
4 PM	4:00 PM Study English						
5 PM							
6 PM							
7 PM		7:00 PM Study Chemistry	7:00 PM Study Chemistry	7:00 PM Study Chemistry	7:00 PM Study Biology		
8 PM		8:00 PM Study Biology	8:00 PM Study English	8:00 PM Study English	8:00 PM Study English		
9 PM		9:00 PM Study Psychology	9:00 PM Study Biology	9:00 PM Study Psychology	9:00 PM Study Psychology		
10 PM							

FIGURE 2 Two Possible Study Calendars With this customized plan, both Marisol and Noah spend 2 to 3 hours studying for each hour of lecture. They space their studying out across the week in 1-hour blocks per subject—this practice allows rest between subjects for the brain connections they have exercised.

FIGURE 3 Levels of Processing
Processing a word deeply—by its meaning (semantic encoding)—produces better recognition of it at a later time than does shallow processing by attending to its appearance or sound. (From Craik & Tulving, 1975.)

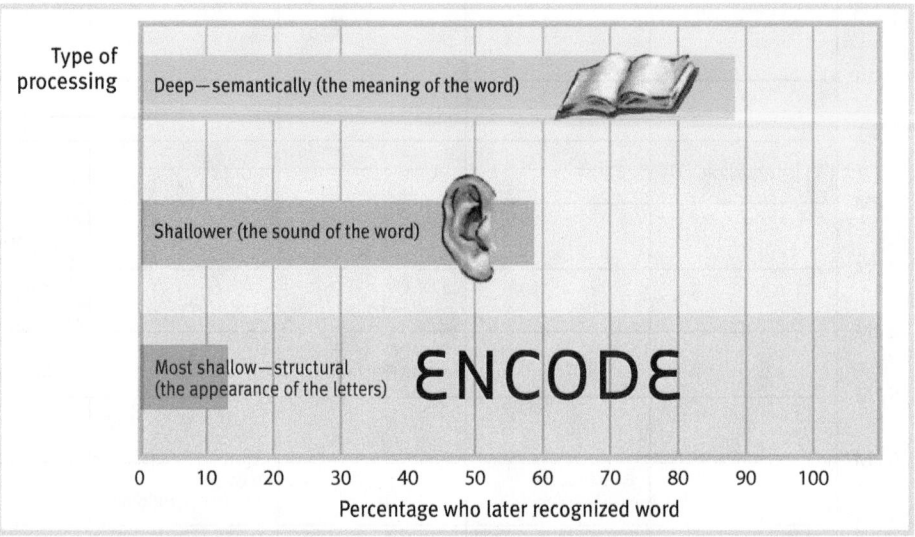

Mitchell, & Goldin-Meadow, 2008). For example, to remember that two variables move in opposite directions in a negative correlation, try moving your arms in different directions as you rehearse the material. You could also try linking the material with a catchy phrase or tune, anything to add an auditory component to the memory. Each encoding experience will present an opportunity to make connections; with more connections formed, more paths will lead to the memory. Remember to never turn down the opportunity to strengthen your memory with more connections!

Test Yourself, Early and Often

If just the mention of the word *test* increases your heart rate, then here's another opportunity to let go of what you think you know: Testing is your friend. Self-testing is one of the best ways to overcome the tendency to overestimate how much you know by providing a reality check of your actual knowledge (Rohrer & Pashler, 2010).

For everyone, self-testing not only reveals current competence but also provides another set of exercises to train the brain. Every time you test yourself, you engage the brain in an attempt to retrieve a memory. This act alone helps strengthen connections among your brain cells. Nevertheless, networks strengthened through study weaken over time. The fact that you once knew something provides no guarantee that you will know it when you are assessed. So test yourself repeatedly to ensure that those memories stay strong.

Combining self-testing with well-spaced study sessions is an even more useful strategy. Spread your self-testing out to create the best opportunity for a strenuous mental workout. When some time has elapsed, even just a day or two, some forgetting will inevitably occur. You would think that's bad, right? It's not. Experts are finding that forgetting helps us learn (Kornell, 2009). Basically, a little forgetting now provides you with a lot of desirable difficulties the next time you study the material. Think of it as one step backward that leads to two steps forward.

SECTION REVIEW

- Rote methods, like rereading the text or memorizing definitions, may *feel* like they work, but they are not very effective for long-term learning.
- The best way to study is to work the to-be-learned information into the unique set of connections that already exist among your brain cells.
- You exercise your brain (and learn best) when you keep study sessions challenging but brief, utilizing a variety of strategies and testing yourself often.

Test Yourself

Hint: Don't look back at the text until you have pulled out of your memory as much information as you can.

- What are rote methods, and why are they less effective than other study methods?
- Why is self-testing such a valuable study skill?

Try It

- Set a timer to go off at regular intervals (perhaps every 15 minutes) while you study. When the buzzer sounds, simply ask yourself: "Does this feel easy?" If so, evaluate your study methods and strive to create more desirable difficulties.
- Give yourself an exam reality check. After you take your next assessment in a class, predict the grade you earned and write it down in your notebook. When the assessment is returned, write your actual grade next to your prediction. Is there a discrepancy? If so, consider why.
- Create your own study calendar for the week ahead. Remember to allow 2 to 3 hours of study for each hour of lecture, and be sure to space out your study sessions for each class.

Crafting Your Mental Workout Plan

Let's get practical and discuss how to translate brain-change knowledge into your everyday life as a student before, during, and after classes.

Exercise Your Brain by Reading Before Class

Reading before class is one of the most overlooked ways to boost your learning in a college course. Think of how a warm-up prepares the body for a workout. Reading the material before class serves a similar function. If you first process this new information and get the neural networks primed, the result will be a much more productive time in class. Why? You will have an easier time figuring out which information is most important. What you hear in class will more easily connect with the networks in your brain because of the mental warm-up. So make the most of your reading by following these tips:

Invite Desirable Difficulties

Get a good workout while you read: If you feel your eyes skimming across the page, or if you reach the bottom and don't remember much (if anything) of what you just read, then you are barely processing the information at all. It happens to the best of us. The important thing is to catch yourself, shake the cobwebs out of your head, and start again with the goal of staying more engaged. Awareness is a step in the right direction. See Table 2 on the next page for specific tips on how to keep your brain active while reading.

Space It Out

If you have a 50-page chapter to read for Monday's class, break it down into smaller chunks (perhaps 15- to 20-page sections), and spread your reading out across a couple of days. Here's another reason to space things out: If you are zipping through a 50-page chapter in one sitting, I doubt that you are engaging desirable difficulties! Pace yourself. Course materials are often organized into sections with headers. Read one or two sections in one sitting, but no more than that. Remember, your brain needs breaks in order for memories to consolidate. Also, this will help you manage your attention better and help reading become more enjoyable.

TABLE 2 Desirable Difficulties While You Read

Here are two specific methods to trigger challenges that help you get the most out of your reading.

SQ3R: The Survey, Question, Read, Rehearse, and Review Strategy
One structured approach to reading for deep processing is SQ3R (Robinson, 1970). Here are the steps:

- Before you read, survey the section to get a general idea of what information you will encounter.
- Next, formulate a question to keep in mind as you read. Your text may already include learning objectives or preview questions that help with this step.
- Now you are ready to read, but you should read with your question in mind, actively considering what the answer might be. Take notes, putting things in your own words as much as you can.
- After you have finished reading a section, take time to rehearse: put the text material in your own words, then ask yourself the question again (but no peeking at the text or your notes until you have answered!).
- The last step is to review what you have learned, paying special attention to the notes in your own words.

3R: The Read-Recite-Review Strategy
The 3R approach (McDaniel, Howard, & Einstein, 2009) is another method to encourage deep processing while reading. You can use this technique repeatedly with your texts or your notes.

- Read a brief section or passage.
- Close your book or cover the text, then recite in your own words anything you can remember about what you have just read.
- Open the book and review the passage to check yourself.

Self-Test While You Read

As you read, think of questions you could ask yourself to test your learning. Write them down somewhere. When you reach the end of the section, use these questions as a self-test quiz. How much did you remember? Take note of the information that you left out, and go back to review that material.

Work the Information in Different Ways

First and foremost, make sure you are focused on the meaning of the words, not memorizing the author's words, which triggers only shallow encoding. How can you do this? Take notes while you read, but don't just copy from a book or screen. Instead, put things into your own words. Consider how this new information fits in with your uniquely wired brain. How does it link to your experiences? Does an image come to mind? If so, draw it. Does a silly thought occur to you? For example, I remember reading about the hippocampus, a brain structure involved with memory, and I immediately thought: "Hippos are similar to elephants, and elephants supposedly have good memories." It stuck. It worked for me, but it might not work for you. Remember, you are your connections, so make what you read stick in a way that makes sense to you!

Go to Class and Train with an Expert

Go to your classes—each and every one of them. These are golden opportunities your brain shouldn't miss. This is a chance to have a mental workout with an expert on the topic. At the very least, a missed class is a lost opportunity to find out what the professor thinks is most important (in other words, what material is most likely to appear on assessments).

Your professor will present the material in at least a slightly different way than it is presented in the readings, so that alone will provide some helpful cross-training to strengthen your neural networks. But it's ultimately up to you to make class worth your time. Just as simply moving your eyes across the page fails to result in much learning, sitting there and simply writing down whatever is on the board or slides only triggers the most shallow processing. So try the following procedures.

Create a Set of Complete and Personally Meaningful Notes

Notice that I said "create" instead of "take." This is an important distinction. When you "take" notes, you write down the exact words from the board or a slide, and that's it. Some students who are obsessive (as I was) attempt to write down as many words spoken by the professor as possible. In both cases, there is a misconception that the professor's words are magical: If you can just transfer them directly into your brain, you will be in good shape. It's simply not true. Research indicates that students who "create" comprehensive and elaborated notes tend to earn better grades (Peverly et al., 2007).

How do you do this? Of course you should write down the outline, terms, or key examples the professor has provided on the board or slides. And it's wise to jot down additional helpful details your professor may state, as long as you are not attempting to transcribe the words verbatim. What's most important is that you churn the information through your brain so it makes sense to you. You have to work with the information, and transform it in some way so it will become embedded within your neural networks. This strategy can range from simply putting things into your own words to jotting down a related example or a personal experience. It will build bridges that connect the professor's words with your brain.

Try some of these strategies to "create" your own notes:

- *Remind yourself to focus on the meaning, not just the words.* As much as possible, put things into your own words. Make your notes personally meaningful. If note taking seems quick and easy, view this as a warning sign. Keep desirable difficulties in mind.

- *Listen for organizational cues from your professor* (Kiewra, 2002). For example, a statement like "So we have just discussed X, and now I'd like to move to Y" is a clear signal that the lecture is shifting to a new topic. If the instructor tells you "There are four components of Z," use that as a signal to start a numbered list in your notes.

- *Develop a set of abbreviations and symbols.* Save time by abbreviating or using symbols whenever possible. Include those an individual professor uses and invent some of your own (see examples in Table 3). Just make sure the abbreviations and symbols help you make sense of the material.

- *Draw a representation of how concepts relate to each other.* Try venturing outside the standard outline structure. Consider using arrows, for example. Create drawings to represent the information.

- *Check yourself by noting spots where you got lost or confused.* I used to do this by writing a big question mark next to the spot where I got lost. After you mark the spot, shake out the mental cobwebs and then move on to keep up with the pace of the class. Stay after class to discuss the confusing part with the professor or a classmate. Do not wait.

- *As soon as possible after class, review your notes and jot down any additional information that comes to mind.* It's important to do this while the information is still fresh. Better yet, do this with a classmate. You may be able to fill in some blanks for each other. Kiewra (2002) calls this "the reconstruction strategy." But beware of shifting into rote mode! Don't just read and copy verbatim; actually discuss the notes, explain what they mean, and focus on which parts of the meaning either of you may have missed or misunderstood.

TABLE 3 Using Abbreviations in Your Notes

Allow your hands to keep up with the pace of class by using abbreviations in your notes. Here are just a few ideas to get you started, but the most important thing is to use symbols that make sense to your brain. What abbreviations could you add for some of the common words or phrases in your classes?

w/o	without
w/n	within
b/c	because
diffs	differences
beh	behavior
♂	male
♀	female
Ψ	psychology
?	ask professor
+	and
→	leads to, causes
≈	is similar to
≠	is not the same as

Train Your Brain for Exams and Other Assessments

Students often ask me how best to prepare for exams. It's a great question, but the problem is that most ask it less than a week before the exam. When should you start preparing for the exam? Today! But that doesn't mean you have to spend hours studying today. A little goes a long way, especially when you revisit the material several times a week. It's like going to the gym a few times a week instead of spending 10 hours there on Saturday to make up for a week of sloth. Here are some suggestions for how to proceed.

Process Your Notes Regularly

Research indicates that you will learn more from processing your notes than you learned while taking them (Kiewra, 2002; Knight & McKelvie, 1986). Rereading is not enough, and neither is copying notes verbatim. Oh, how I wish someone had told me this when I was a student! I wasted loads of time on this particular rote method. Of course, there is nothing wrong with rereading your notes the first time you revisit them. The problem is expecting that you will somehow be able to "write" the contents of your notes directly into your brain (Bjork & Bjork, 2011). This ignores the reality that each of us begins with a brain full of unique connections, where new information sticks best by being woven into the networks that already exist.

Use your notes as a springboard to organize and integrate the course material (see Figure 4). Consider how the different pieces of information connect to one another (*internal connections*), and then think about how the information relates to your prior knowledge and experiences (*external connections*) (Mayer, 1996). This is great exercise for the brain, helping to form and strengthen neural networks that can later consolidate into stronger memories.

- *Make internal links.* There are often numerous ways that the course material could be organized to show internal links, such as terms that can be grouped by some shared characteristic or terms that are notable for how they reveal opposite tendencies. Experiment with different ways to show internal links. You could construct a memory matrix, where you identify categories and appropriately place terms, concepts, or other information. Concept maps are another option; these are diagrams or figures you draw to show relationships among the various aspects of the material (see Figure 5).

- *Make external links.* You can relate the course material to information you currently know by forming mental representations. Depending on the way your mind works, this could come out in many different ways. The links could be visual. For example, I think of neural connections as colorful strands of yarn and of building strong memories as similar to knitting a blanket with that yarn. With further processing (strands/connections), the blanket (memory) becomes more and more resilient.

The links could also be verbal—for instance, analogies. Does a certain concept remind you of something else? If so, write in your notes: "It's like . . ." To understand how brain cells communicate, for example, you could note: "It's like a conversation." You could also imagine methods of linking the material to movements or sounds. Studies indicate that engaging the senses and motor skills when creating a memory yields additional cues that can help embed the new information more deeply into your brain (Glenberg, Brown, & Levin, 2007; Stevanoni & Salmon, 2005). The bottom line: You create stronger memories when you process the new information in a variety of ways.

FIGURE 4 Internal and External Links
While making notes, try to connect the new information with things you already know. This is one specific way to weave the material into your uniquely connected brain, as shown in blue. In addition, pay attention to the connections you see between the bits of new information you encounter, as shown in green. Both methods help you process the material deeply. (Illustration after Kiewra, 2002)

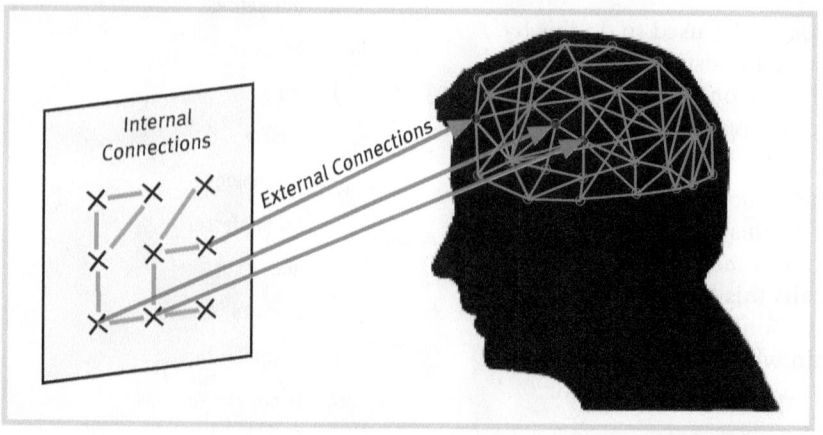

- *Simply ask "why"?* Doing so is a very effective and straightforward way to make external links. This method of triggering self-explanation has been shown to improve learning more than does simple summarizing or rereading of notes (Kiewra, 2002). Why does it work? It forces you to think about the meaning of the material instead of focusing on the memorization of words.

(a)

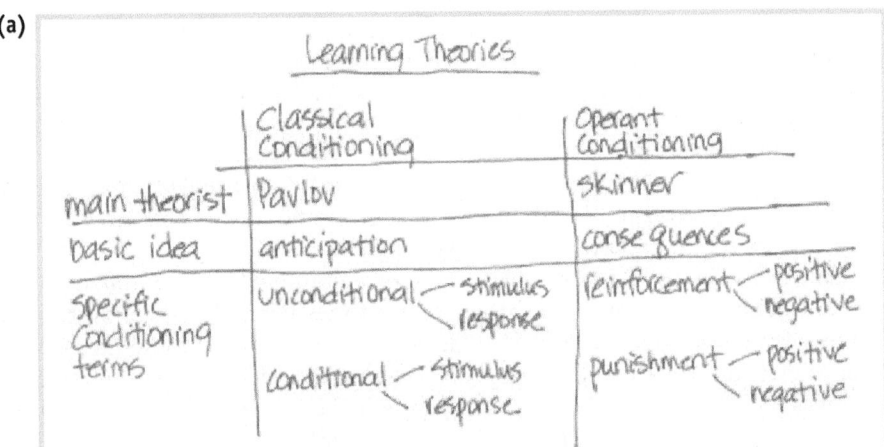

FIGURE 5 **Memory Matrixes (a) and Concept Maps (b)** **(a)** This memory matrix shows the distinctions a student made between two theories about learning. **(b)** This concept map shows how one student has organized her learning about energy and the natural laws governing it.

(b)

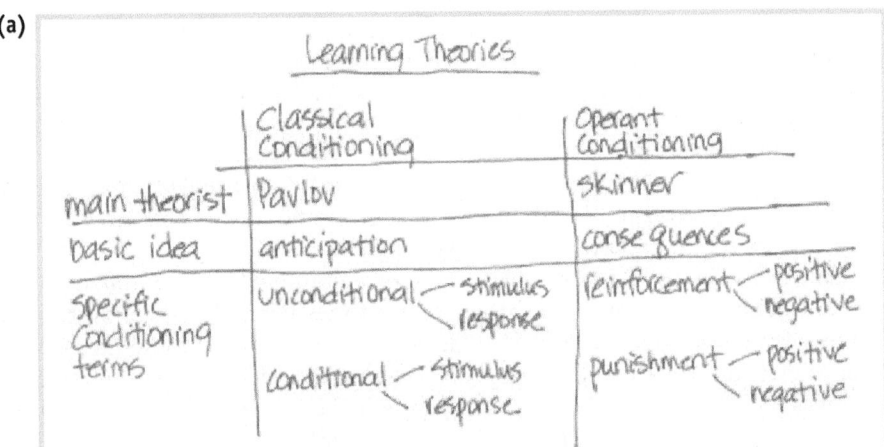

Check Your Learning Through Self-Testing—Repeatedly

How did you know that you could ride a bicycle? I remember the exhilarating feeling I had when the training wheels on my bike were removed and I rode down the driveway all on my own. It was scary at first, but eventually I brought the wobbles under control.

How do you know when you have really learned something? Most students rely on how familiar the material seems as they reread it or on how well they do on multiple-choice quizzes or test questions. Think about why that might be the case. Your notes, readings, and multiple-choice questions all contain the verbal equivalent of training wheels: words and organizational features that act as cues for your performance. The trouble is that, unlike training wheels on a bike, we don't realize how much our performance is assisted by these aids. The wheels come off for the exam—questions are in random order, unfamiliar wording is used, you're required to apply what you've learned—and suddenly your confidence is shaken. You feel wobbly. You discover that you really didn't know the material well.

Let's take the training wheels off for a moment, right now. Without looking back on the chapter, answer this question: How are memories formed in the brain?

Now look back to page 2 to check your answer. How much did you remember?

When you self-test like this, you get a more accurate view of how much you understand. This is especially true when you ask open-ended questions, like the one I used above—to answer, you are required to pull all of the information you can from the depths of your own brain. The real challenge is to put the course material away (for a few hours or a day) and then later see what you can still retrieve from the strands of information that were encoded. This strategy tests recall memory—a good countermeasure against that annoying human tendency to overestimate what you know.

There is another excellent reason to self-test: The act of trying to retrieve information helps us embed the information in the brain more deeply, which leads to stronger and more readily accessible memories. Remember, brain cell connections are strengthened by both encoding and retrieval. Making yourself come up with an answer (especially to an open-ended question) is one of the most effective exercises for your memory networks (Bjork & Bjork, 2011).

In short, self-testing is a great workout that will show you what you really do and don't know. Don't be surprised to find that there are some big gaps in your memory. Be happy you found them and can remedy the problem! Also, remember that if it's difficult while you're studying, it's more likely to be easier while you're being tested later. Self-testing creates desirable difficulties that strengthen your memories for long-term retention.

Here are some self-testing options you can try:

- *Use the tools the professor or text author gave you.* Many professors and texts provide lists of objectives, preview questions, or review questions. Just make sure to move beyond multiple-choice questions because, to begin with, they are easier. Focus on open-ended questions, like fill-in-the-blank or essay questions.

- *Make your own tests.* This is a lot easier than you might think. For example, go back to the questions you wrote in your notes while reading. Create flashcards and, on the back of each, write where in your notes the answer can be found. This will remind you not to try to rote-memorize "answers." You can also use the 3R method (look back at Table 2) as a simple and effective way to check your understanding while you study.

- *Mix up the order of questions.* This is a form of brain cross-training. If you always study everything in the same order, the order itself becomes a context cue that fools you into overestimating what you really know. Besides, many professors arrange their exam items in random order.

- *Try out a variety of study locations.* Even without our conscious awareness, cues from the places where we study help us form associations with the new material we are trying to learn (Smith, 2007; Smith & Vela, 2001). If we study in only one location, we create only one set of context cues to link to the material. Studying in many different locations gives you the chance to form multiple context cues. In other words, trying out different study locations can actually help you form more connections between brain cells relevant to the material. More connections equal stronger memories.

- *Sort items back into their categories.* Shuffle your flashcards and then sort them into piles by chapter or topic. Now you are forced to think about how the items are similar to or different from one another, which is excellent exercise for the mind. Even if this seems too hard, it can trigger deep learning because of the workout it gives your brain (Kornell, in press). Remember, difficulties help you learn!

- *Pretend it is your job to teach someone else this material, someone who really needs the information.* This makes you think about the meaning of the material instead of just focusing on the literal words. Actors often use this method (Noice & Noice, 2006). They are encouraged not to rote-memorize the script but to think of the motivations, goals, and reasons why the person would be saying these things. Even just talking to someone about the material—a classmate, friend, or family member—can serve as a self-test. The concepts that are hard for you to explain are those that need more attention.

- *It is never too early to self-test.* In fact, some research shows that it helps to start testing yourself even *before* you've read the text or attended a lecture on the topic, especially if you follow up by investigating the correct answer afterwards (Richland, Kornell, & Kao, 2009). Aren't you likely to answer incorrectly? Yes, but creating that initial challenge of retrieval for your brain cells prepares you for longer-term retention of the material over time. The answer is less important than the mental exercise the question triggers.

- *Self-test to keep memories strong.* Knowing something now doesn't mean you'll know it at test time. Why? Because your brain has undoubtedly changed, at least a little bit, since you first made that memory. Some students make the mistake of studying only the difficult material, assuming that they already know the easier material. But if brain cell pathways haven't been exercised, even if that material once felt "easy," you may fail to retrieve the information when it matters at a later date (like during an exam!). Remember, the brain responds like a muscle. Imagine that you have finally reached the point where your biceps are perfectly toned. Congratulations! But that doesn't mean you never have to work them again. The same is true of memory.

Remember: Self-test to study; test early and often. Don't wait until it's too late!

SECTION REVIEW
- Warm up your brain by taking a deep-processing approach to reading the assigned material before class.
- View each class as an opportunity to further exercise your brain. Create notes that go beyond the professor's words, and compare your notes with those of classmates afterwards.
- To find out what you have really learned, and to continue the workout of your brain cells, test yourself early and often.

Test Yourself
Hint: Don't look back at the text until you have pulled out of your memory as much information as you can.

- From the perspective of training your brain, what is the purpose of reading the assigned material before class?

- What is the difference between rereading your notes and processing your notes?
- How early and how often should you test yourself while studying?

Try It

- Flip back to a section of this chapter that you found challenging, and use the 3R method (look back at Table 2): Read the section, cover it, then recite anything at all that you remember from the passage. Be patient and give yourself enough time to truly drain the contents of your brain. Finally, uncover the section and review it to check your understanding. Remember, you can use this strategy anytime you read a text or process your notes.
- Ask another student to "reconstruct" lecture notes with you shortly after a class. Discuss the content of your notes to see if either of you missed any information. Resist the urge to simply copy missed information. Instead, explain the material to each other in your own words, focusing on the meaning.
- Examine a set of notes you have recently taken during class. "Re-create" these notes, putting the material in your own words and making internal or external linkages as much as possible. Then devise a plan for how to incorporate more note-creating techniques during the next class.
- Create a "cheat sheet" list of self-testing strategies to keep close at hand as a reminder while you study. During every session of studying on your calendar for the week ahead, strive to incorporate one or two of these strategies at regular intervals.

The Moment of Truth: Exam Day

I am a very anxious test-taker. I dealt with my anxiety by getting to class early on the day of a test and frantically scanning my notes to pack in as many last-minute bits of information as possible. I thought I was improving my chances of success. In reality, I was stressing myself out and making things worse. I was usually sleep-deprived as well, heaping another unnecessary burden on my maxed-out brain (see the feature Help Your Brain Help You: The Importance of Sleep).

The First Thing to Do Is to Manage Your Stress

Of course you are nervous: You feel motivated to do your best yet worried about the uncertainty inherent in testing. (What questions will be on the test? Will I know the answers?) The stress is even greater with past experiences of disappointment related to testing. Stress makes us feel threatened, and the body responds by increasing heart rate, generating sweat, and pumping stress hormones through the bloodstream. Unfortunately, those worries steal valuable brain energy and make it difficult for you to function at top capacity. Instead of worrying about your stress response, take action. Here are some ways to manage test-day stress:

Breathe Deeply to Reduce Your Stress Response

This advice is simple but absolutely true. You may not be able to prevent the stress reaction, but you can have an impact on how long it lasts and how intense it becomes. Your body is simply unable to sustain that intense fight-or-flight reaction forever. And you can hasten its decline by taking charge of the things you can control, like the rate of your breathing.

HELP YOUR BRAIN HELP YOU

The Importance of Sleep

Take care of yourself. This advice is obvious when it comes to physical health; for example, no runner in her right mind would suggest staying up all night before a marathon. Yet, like me, I bet many of you have treated your brain poorly in pursuit of better grades. Pressed for time, we assume we must skimp on sleep to learn the material. Let go of what you think you know, and let sleep improve your memory!

No, I'm not talking about sleeping with your book beneath your pillow. Getting a good night's sleep helps the brain form and keep memories. How? A well-rested brain is better at encoding (Walker, 2008). In other words, if you're chronically sleep deprived, your brain has a harder time processing new information. You make learning harder on yourself.

Sleep also helps us strengthen and maintain the networks of memories we have recently formed. While you sleep, the brain reactivates the memories you worked on during the day, a form of mental exercise that knits those memories more deeply into your network of connections (Rasch & Born, 2008). Even a short period of daytime sleep can trigger the consolidation process that helps stabilize new memories in the brain (Mednick, Cai, Kanady, & Drummond, 2008).

Why not just power through sleepiness with caffeine? That was my "solution." I thought that Diet Coke and coffee made up for the hours of sleep I regularly skipped. Nope. In fact, research suggests that a nap may benefit your brain more than a double-shot latte. One study found that a 60- to 90-minute nap boosted memory significantly more than a 200- to 300-mg dose of caffeine (Mednick et al., 2008). Sure, caffeine makes you feel more alert, but a nap actually helps you *strengthen* the memories you've studied so hard to create.

I'm sure it's obvious why all-nighters before an exam are an absolutely terrible idea: You harm your brain's natural ability to cement memories at the very time it's most critical that your brain be working at top capacity! But even skipping a couple of hours of sleep is enough to decrease your brain's potential. Of all the advice in this chapter, this is the piece I most desperately wish I had known back when I was in college. I could have studied less and slept more? That's right! And I probably would have earned the same, or even better, grades. It's too late for me, but not for you: Get plenty of sleep and help your brain help you learn!

Have a Stress-Reduction Plan for the Moments Before the Test Is Passed Out

Figure out what helps reduce your stress response, and take action. Are you a social person who relaxes by talking to others? If so, engage in conversation with another student. Or do you need to focus inward in order to calm yourself down? Does music help you relax? Recent research suggests that highly test-anxious students relax and perform better when they write out their test-related worries for 10 minutes before the exam (Ramirez & Beilock, 2011). Try some of these suggestions, and find out what works best for you.

Identify Factors That Influence Your Ability to Stay Focused During the Exam, and Ask About Possible Accommodations

For minor requests, ask your professor. For example, if you are easily distracted by noise, ask your professor if you can use earplugs (not earbuds) during the exam. If it is noisy in the hallway, ask if the professor could close the door. If you think you may have a disability that warrants more significant accommodations, make an appointment with the disabilities services department on campus well in advance of any exams. Typically, professors are unable to make significant accommodations without this kind of expertise involved.

Be Strategic in Completing the Exam

Try some of these tips to give your brain the best chance to perform.

Start by Skimming

Skim the exam from start to finish before starting to answer questions. Why? On a practical level, skimming lets you take stock of what is coming. It reminds you of how many items are on the exam. It allows you to check whether the exam is printed on both sides of the page, so you don't accidentally fail to answer any of the questions. But skimming is also an overlooked strategy for warming up your brain. As you quickly read each question, you are exposing yourself to a treasure-trove of cues that will spark activation of your neural networks. This may not happen immediately, and you may not be fully aware of it happening. But, when it helps, you will be happy you gave it a chance!

Write on the Exam (if permitted)

Your brain is very busy while you are taking an exam, so anything you can do to ease the cognitive strain can make a big difference. Circle important words (e.g., *not*, *all*, *except for*). Cross out answers you know are incorrect. Jot down notes, charts, figures—anything that comes to mind that could help you answer the question.

If You Are Uncertain, Mark the Question, Move On, and Return to It Later

As you work on other questions, the cues you encounter may begin to jostle connections and activate a pathway to the answer. When I was taking the statistics portion of my comprehensive exams in graduate school, I kept going back to the same question again and again. I just didn't know the answer. But eventually, after working on other parts of the test, the answer just popped into my head like a gift from the universe. I can't tell you how it happened, but obviously my work on the test shook up my neural networks and spread the activation to enough spots that allowed me to construct the memory. Sometimes you have to give your brain time to activate the proper networks. Remember, each memory may consist of thousands of connections, and any of these could serve as a lifeline to the information you need.

A Special Tip for Multiple-Choice Questions: Cover the Answer Choices, and Read Only the Stem of the Question First

Basically, treat a multiple-choice question like an open-ended question first, and try to recall the answer. Think of it as a strategy to warm up the relevant neural networks. Next, uncover the answer choices and make a decision. Why do this? Sometimes it's easy to overanalyze the answer choices, which can lead to confusion. Answer choices often contain a variety of cues that can lead you down the wrong neural pathways. Focus on the stem first, trigger those associations, and then consider the answer choices.

Don't Assume Your First Hunch Is Always Correct

Many of us have received the well-intentioned but misguided advice to trust our instincts and not change our initial answers. Let go of what you think you know! To the contrary, research indicates that students more often change from an incorrect to a correct answer than vice versa (Lilienfeld, Lynn, Ruscio, & Beyerstein, 2010). If you really don't know the answer, randomly making changes is not going to help improve your score. But if you are struck by compelling reasons that suggest your initial answer is incorrect, trust your reasoning.

A Special Tip for Essay Questions: Brainstorm and Outline First

You probably get more nervous about essay questions than multiple-choice ones, but don't let this fear freeze your brain. In the margins or on the back (if writing on the exam is permissible), sketch out any ideas that come to mind in response to the essay question. Try to organize these thoughts into some structure. This helps activate the relevant brain cell networks, basically warming up the brain. If the answer isn't coming to you, move on to other questions and come back to it later. Sometimes the act of answering other questions will remind you of other bits of relevant information. As that happens, write those ideas alongside the others. When you are ready to answer the essay question, make sure you provide the information that is requested. For example, compare/contrast questions require you not only to define concepts but also to show how they are similar to and different from one another. Application questions require that you not only provide definitions but also show how terms or concepts relate to a given example.

Don't Rush Through the Exam Just to "Get It Over With"

We all look forward to unpleasant experiences coming to an end. My dentist is a terrific person, but dental work is unpleasant, and I want appointments to be over as quickly as possible. It's only natural that you would feel the same way about exams. However, unlike being at the dentist, you decide how quickly to work on a test; within the overall testing-time framework, you decide when the ordeal is over. The anticipation is enticing: You look forward to the feeling of relief.

In my class, I often hear audible sighs as students walk out the door after taking a test. This desire for relief can lead you to work faster than you should, increasing your odds of misreading questions or making other careless mistakes. So take all the time you are given to show all of what you know on an exam.

SECTION REVIEW

- Manage your pre-exam stress so you can devote more of your brain's resources to demonstrating your mastery.
- Be strategic in completing the exam: Skim to get an overview, make notes to aid your memory, and allow the experience of taking the exam to activate the connections you made while studying.
- Do not rush. Take the time you are given to show what you really know!

Test Yourself

Hint: Don't look back at the text until you have pulled out of your memory as much information as you can.

- What impact does stress have on your brain?
- How can skimming the exam influence your memory?
- What should you do if you are having second thoughts about an answer you chose?

Try It

- Reflect on your typical pre-exam experience. What changes could you make to improve your brain's ability to do its best for you? Identify at least one strategy you could incorporate when you take your next exam.
- Evaluate the strategies you typically follow while taking exams, and plan out the changes you could make to improve your performance on the next one.
- The next time you take an exam, introduce a "mindful moment" whenever you feel overwhelmed. Try the S.T.O.P. method (Stahl & Goldstein, 2010): *Stop* (simply take a brief moment to pause). *Take* a deep breath. Without passing judgment, *Observe* what's going on in your mind and body (Is your heart rate elevated? Are anxious thoughts interfering with your reasoning?). Finally, *Proceed* (check the time, note how many more items you have to complete, and decide which test-taking strategies to use next). Remind yourself of this strategy by writing "STOP" at the top of your exam.

Actually Doing It

Consider this question: What are the observable behaviors that successful students engage in consistently? At this point, you should have all kinds of answers. That's the easy part. But consider a trickier question: Once successful, how do you prevent yourself from slipping back into old, ineffective patterns of study behavior, like cramming, depriving yourself of sleep, and rote memorizing? Unfortunately, "saying" is much easier than "doing." But take heart: Any pattern of behavior or thinking you engage in that is detrimental to your learning is still just a habit. Habits reflect well-worn pathways in the neural networks of the brain, like a map of our current default settings. Habits are not eliminated overnight, but they can be changed through awareness, persistence, and motivation (see the feature Help Your Brain Help You: The Trouble with Multitasking to learn about a common habit that makes learning more difficult).

Developing Habits of Self-Regulation and Self-Control

Changing habits requires plenty of self-regulation, something that is challenging for most of us. If you've ever known what you needed to do but had trouble actually doing it, you know what this is like. We need to exercise self-control, putting off something very interesting right now in order to do something else that is less interesting but will pay off big time later. Luckily, we can build self-control over time; it's another mental muscle that responds to training (Muraven, 2010). The benefits extend well beyond studying, too; our strengthened self-control helps us modify any habit or learn any new skill—from quitting smoking to learning a new job.

HELP YOUR BRAIN HELP YOU

The Trouble with Multitasking

Are you easily bored? I am. I get bored while I'm cleaning or doing laundry, so I often listen to a podcast or audiobook. It makes the time pass more quickly. As long as one of the tasks is virtually mindless (like folding laundry), multitasking can work just fine. But when you try to do two cognitively complex tasks at once—like studying while texting or IMing—the brain protests. Why? The brain cannot simultaneously engage in two tasks requiring complex cognition. Instead, it shifts back and forth between tasks. When you study, you exercise one set of networks in the brain. When you read and answer a text message, you switch to a completely different network. All of this switching puts a lot of stress on your brain. It's like requiring one conductor to switch back and forth between two different orchestras performing different pieces. Your brain is designed to do its best work when focused on one task (Rubenstein, Myer, & Evans, 2001). When you try to multitask while studying, you activate a less flexible and more basic area of the brain capable of only the most shallow processing (Foerde, Knowlton, & Poldrack, 2006).

You may feel like multitasking is necessary in order to keep you from feeling so bored. Maybe it seems like you're able to study longer while watching TV, using Facebook, or talking to friends. If this is the case, I need you to let go of what you think you know. Yes, time may seem to pass more quickly, but you are making things much harder on your brain by providing it with a very weak form of exercise. By eliminating distractions, you make your studying more efficient and effective. In short, multitasking wastes time; performing one task at a time saves time.

What if you are a chronic multitasker? Can you train your brain to switch between tasks without any declines in brain performance? The scientific evidence suggests the answer is no: Practice does not make perfect. In fact, those who multitask most often tend to show the steepest declines in their cognitive performance while multitasking (Ophir, Nass, & Wagner, 2009)!

If you are easily bored while studying, evaluate your study habits. Spending several hours memorizing definitions or rereading notes? That's boring. Instead of pulling out your cell phone or turning on the TV, use the strategies discussed in this chapter. Remember, studying that feels challenging now pays off the most later, and it also happens to be much less boring than memorizing flashcards. So try something different. Spend shorter periods of time on each subject, and alternate between subjects. Make a concept map. Create some open-ended questions and test yourself. Pretend you are teaching the material to someone else. Focus on having a high-quality mental workout, and your urge to multitask won't be so strong.

Procrastination is one of the biggest self-control challenges we face. It feels good in the moment because we have avoided an aversive task. In regard to studying, students procrastinate for many reasons. Some are afraid of failure, and some believe they do their best work under the pressure of the last minute. Whatever the reason, procrastination gives us an escape from an unpleasant feeling. But it always catches up with us in the end. One study found that students who procrastinated reported more health problems near the end of the term, perhaps because of the stress of all of that cramming. On top of that, their grades suffered as well (Tice & Baumeister, 1997). Here are some strategies you can use to strengthen your self-control.

Start with a Short Burst

If you are having trouble getting started with a task, make it very easy at first. Work on the dreaded task for only 10 minutes, and then take a 2-minute break to do something more interesting. Go back for another 10-minute work session, and then take another 2-minute break. Repeat as necessary! I do this to kick-start my grading, which at first leaves me feeling overwhelmed. But when I think about only spending 10 minutes on grading, it's no longer a big deal. What usually happens next is that the simple act of getting started breaks the spell of procrastination. I find that after a few 10-minute bursts, I can work longer.

Make Sure You Are Spacing Out Your Studying

Remember, it's better for your brain if your study sessions are short and frequent. This helps with procrastination as well, because a 1-hour study session seems far less dreadful than a 5-hour marathon.

Capitalize on Your Strengths and Interests

Fuse something that provides immediate rewards with something that advances you toward your long-term goal (Steel, 2007). For example, if you are a very social person who loves meeting new people, form a study group early in the semester and start meeting regularly. If you love nature, incorporate a short session of reading into your next hike. In other words, find ways to link studying with some of the things you love.

Make Small Changes in Your Environment to Stay Focused on Your Goals

People striving to meet health-related goals do this by eliminating unhealthy foods from their pantry at home. You can do something similar to advance your academic goals. Reduce distractions by turning off any indicators of new texts or e-mails. Better yet, put your cell phone in a different room. Is the Internet a constant temptation? Temporarily disable your online access. Do you have trouble staying focused in class? Sit where you are not able to see the clock, or put your watch or cell phone away so you can't see the time. Why? The more we check the time, the more slowly time seems to pass (Sackett, Meyvis, Nelson, Converse, & Sackett, 2010). Try sitting in the front row, where the professor is more likely to notice your behavior. That way, you're less likely to feel tempted to give into your urge to text, sleep, or daydream.

Act "As If"

Have you ever felt your attitude needed an adjustment? Try changing your behavior first. Do you think this is the most boring class in the world? Act "as if" you are interested: Get to class early, sit near the front, listen intently with an expression of interest, and create great notes. Quite literally, play the role of "interested student." Do this to boost your studying outside class (if necessary) as well. Obviously, this will feel very strange at first, but research indicates that our attitudes often shift to line up with our behaviors (Festinger, 1957). This may not become your favorite class, but acting "as if" is likely to help improve your attitude and motivation. As a result, you have more energy to apply effective study strategies!

SECTION REVIEW

- Habits are behaviors learned over time. As such, habits can be unlearned through persistence and patience.
- Self-control and self-regulation habits are central to long-term, effective studying.
- You should focus on making small changes first.

Test Yourself

Hint: Don't look back at the text until you have pulled out of your memory as much information as you can.

- How is practicing self-control like engaging a muscle?
- Why can it be beneficial to your studying to act "as if" you are more interested and motivated than you sometimes really feel?

Try It

- Think back to a time when you successfully changed a habit. How did you do it? Adapt elements of that experience to change your least effective study habits.
- If you tend to put things off, choose one procrastination-reduction method to apply in the week ahead.
- Identify the biggest distractions you face while studying, and make changes to your environment to minimize these distractions the next time you study.

If At First You Don't Succeed . . .

Effective habits for studying and self-regulation come from the same place: the well-trained brain. Imagine your brain cells lifting weights, getting stronger and building more connections every day. It will take time to figure out which strategies work best for you, so be prepared to experiment. Remember, your brain is wired uniquely; the strategies that work best for you may be different from those that work best for others. You may also find that different classes require different strategies, so prepare to modify your approach accordingly.

Allow yourself to be human. You will probably lapse back into ineffective strategies or habits occasionally. What matters most is what you do next. Take a lesson from a recent study on procrastination (Wohl, Pychyl, & Bennet, 2010). Students who forgave themselves for procrastinating before Exam 1 were much less likely to procrastinate before Exam 2. Self-forgiveness prevented them from spiraling into apathy, like a dieter who slips up with one cookie and decides he might as well eat the whole box. The self-forgivers acknowledged their slip-up and took the next opportunity to get back on track again. So with these findings in mind, keep persisting!

Whether your future plans include academics or not, I hope the practical advice offered in this chapter will help you make long-lasting changes in the way you approach any type of learning experience.

References

Bjork, E., & Bjork, R. (2011). Making things hard on yourself, but in a good way: Creating desirable difficulties to enhance learning. In M. A. Gernsbacher, R. W. Pew, L. W. Hough, & J. R. Pomerantz (Eds.), *Psychology and the real world: Essays illustrating fundamental contributions to society* (pp. 56–64). New York: Worth Publishers.

Cook, S. W., Mitchell, Z., & Goldin-Meadow, S. (2008). Gesturing makes learning last. *Cognition, 106* (2), 1047–1058. doi:10.1016/j.cognition.2007.04.010

Craik, F.I.M., & Tulving, E. (1975). Depth of processing and the retention of words in episodic memory. *Journal of Experimental Psychology: General, 104,* 268-294.

Festinger, L. (1957). *A theory of cognitive dissonance.* Evanston, IL: Row, Peterson.

Foerde, K., Knowlton, B. J., & Poldrack, R. A. (2006). Modulation of competing memory systems by distraction. *Proceedings of the National Academy of Sciences, 103*(31), 11778–11783. doi:10.1073/pnas.0602659103

Glenberg, A., Brown, M., & Levin, J. (2007). Enhancing comprehension in small reading groups using a manipulation strategy. *Contemporary Educational Psychology, 32*(3), 389–399. doi:10.1016/j.cedpsych.2006.03.001

Karpicke, J. D., & Blunt, J. R. (2011). Retrieval practice produces more learning than elaborative studying with concept mapping. *Science, 331*(6018), 772–775. doi:10.1126/science.1199327

Kiewra, K. A. (2002). How classroom teachers can help students learn and teach them how to learn. *Theory into Practice, 41*(2), 71–80.

Knight, L. J., & McKelvie, S. J. (1986). Effects of attendance, note-taking, and review on memory for a lecture: Encoding vs. external storage functions of notes. *Canadian Journal of Behavioural Science/Revue canadienne des sciences du comportement, 18*(1), 52–61. doi:10.1037/h0079957

Kornell, N. (in press). Discrimination learning: Training methods. In H. Pashler (Ed.), *Encyclopedia of the mind.* Thousand Oaks: Sage Reference.

Kornell, N. (2009). Optimising learning using flashcards: Spacing is more effective than cramming. *Applied Cognitive Psychology, 23*(9), 1297–1317. doi:10.1002/acp.1537

Kruger, J., & Dunning, D. (1999). Unskilled and unaware of it: How difficulties in recognizing one's own incompetence lead to inflated self-assessments. *Journal of Personality and Social Psychology, 77*(6), 1121–1134. doi:10.1037/0022-3514.77.6.1121

Lilienfeld, S. O., Lynn, S. J., Ruscio, J., & Beyerstein, B. L. (2010). *50 great myths of popular psychology: Shattering widespread misconceptions about human behavior.* Malden, MA: Wiley-Blackwell.

Mayer, R. E. (1996). Learning strategies for making sense out of expository text: The SOI model for guiding three cognitive processes in knowledge construction. *Educational Psychology Review, 8*(4), 357–371. doi:10.1007/BF01463939

McDaniel, M. A., Howard, D. C., & Einstein, G. O. (2009). The Read-Recite-Review study strategy: Effective and portable. *Psychological Science, 20*(4), 516–522. doi:10.1111/j.1467-9280.2009.02325.x

Medina, J. (2008). *Brain rules: 12 principles for surviving and thriving at work, home, and school.* Seattle, WA: Pear Press.

Mednick, S., Cai, D., Kanady, J., & Drummond, S. (2008). Comparing the benefits of caffeine, naps and placebo on verbal, motor and perceptual memory. *Behavioural Brain Research, 193*(1), 79–86. doi:10.1016/j.bbr.2008.04.028

Muraven, M. (2010). Practicing self-control lowers the risk of smoking lapse. *Psychology of Addictive Behaviors, 24*(3), 446–452. doi:10.1037/a0018545

Noice, H., & Noice, T. (2006). What studies of actors and acting can tell us about memory and cognitive functioning. *Current Directions in Psychological Science, 15*(1), 14–18.

Ophir, E., Nass, C., & Wagner, A. D. (2009). From the cover: Cognitive control in media multitaskers. *Proceedings of the National Academy of Sciences, 106*(37), 15583–15587. doi:10.1073/pnas.0903620106

Peverly, S. T., Ramaswamy, V., Brown, C., Sumowski, J., Alidoost, M., & Garner, J. (2007). What predicts skill in lecture note taking? *Journal of Educational Psychology, 99*(1), 167–180. doi:10.1037/0022-0663.99.1.167

Ramirez, G., & Beilock, S. L. (2011). Writing about testing worries boosts exam performance in the classroom. *Science, 331*(6014), 211–213. doi:10.1126/science.1199427

Rasch, B., & Born, J. (2008). Reactivation and consolidation of memory during sleep. *Current Directions in Psychological Science, 17*(3), 188–192.

Richland, L. E., Kornell, N., & Kao, L. S. (2009). The pretesting effect: Do unsuccessful retrieval attempts enhance learning? *Journal of Experimental Psychology: Applied, 15*(3), 243–257. doi:10.1037/a0016496

Robinson, F. P. (1970). *Effective study.* New York: HarperCollins.

Rohrer, D., & Pashler, H. (2010). Recent research on human learning challenges conventional instructional strategies. *Educational Researcher, 39*(5), 406–412. doi:10.3102/0013189X10374770

Rubinstein, J. S., Meyer, D. E., & Evans, J. E. (2001). Executive control of cognitive processes in task switching. *Journal of Experimental Psychology: Human Perception and Performance, 27*(4), 763–797. doi:10.1037//0096-1523.27.4.763

Sackett, A. M., Meyvis, T., Nelson, L. D., Converse, B. A., & Sackett, A. L. (2010). You're having fun when time flies: The hedonic consequences of subjective time progression. *Psychological Science, 21*(1), 111–117. doi:10.1177/0956797609354832

Smith, S. M. (2007). Context and human memory. In H. L. Roediger, Y. Dudai, & S. M. Fitzpatrick (Eds.), *Science of memory: Concepts* (pp. 111–114). Oxford: Oxford University Press.

Smith, S. M., & Vela, E. (2001). Environmental context dependent memory: A review and meta analysis. *Psychonomic Bulletin and Review, 8,* 203–220.

Stahl, B., & Goldstein, E. (2010). *A mindfulness-based stress reduction workbook.* Oakland, CA: New Harbinger Publications.

Stanovich, K. (2010). *How to think straight about psychology* (9th ed.). Boston: Allyn & Bacon.

Stanovich, K. E. (2010). *Rationality and the reflective mind.* New York: Oxford University Press.

Steel, P. (2007). The nature of procrastination: A meta-analytic and theoretical review of quintessential self-regulatory failure. *Psychological Bulletin, 133*(1), 65–94. doi:10.1037/0033-2909.133.1.65

Stevanoni, E., & Salmon, K. (2005). Giving memory a hand: Instructing children to gesture enhances their event recall. *Journal of Nonverbal Behavior, 29*(4), 217–233. doi:10.1007/s10919-005-7721-y

Tice, D. M., & Baumeister, R. F. (1997). Longitudinal study of procrastination, performance, stress, and health: The costs and benefits of dawdling. *Psychological Science, 8*(6), 454–458. doi:10.1111/j.1467-9280.1997.tb00460.x

Walker, M. P. (2008). Sleep-dependent memory processing. *Harvard Review of Psychiatry, 16*(5), 287–298. doi:10.1080/10673220802432517

Wohl, M. J., Pychyl, T. A., & Bennett, S. H. (2010). I forgive myself, now I can study: How self-forgiveness for procrastinating can reduce future procrastination. *Personality and Individual Differences, 48*(7), 803–808. doi:10.1016/j.paid.2010.01.029

PSYCHOLOGY

PSYCHOLOGY

FOURTH EDITION

Schacter | Gilbert | Nock | Wegner

RJ MUNA

When we view the striking poses adopted by each of these dancers, it's hard to resist wondering: What thoughts and feelings are they trying to express through their actions? What came before each pose and what comes next? What stories are they trying to tell?

Psychological scientists grapple with such questions when they attempt to unravel the complexities of human thought, emotion, and behavior. These photos by RJ Muna grabbed us because they invite precisely the kinds of questions that we find endlessly fascinating in our own work and that of our colleagues in the field. They also hint at the beauty and complexity of human behavior, which drew us to the field in the first place.

PSYCHOLOGY

FOURTH EDITION

DANIEL L. SCHACTER

HARVARD UNIVERSITY

DANIEL T. GILBERT

HARVARD UNIVERSITY

MATTHEW K. NOCK

HARVARD UNIVERSITY

DANIEL M. WEGNER

HARVARD UNIVERSITY

worth publishers

Macmillan Learning

New York

Vice President, Social Sciences and High School: Charles Linsmeier

Senior Acquisitions Editor: Daniel DeBonis

Senior Development Editor: Valerie Raymond

Assistant Editor: Kimberly Morgan Smith

Senior Marketing Manager: Lindsay Johnson

Marketing Assistant: Morgan Ratner

Executive Media Editor: Noel Hohnstine

Media Editor: Stefani Wallace

Media Producer: Joseph Tomasso

Director, Content Management Enhancement: Tracey Kuehn

Managing Editor, Sciences and Social Sciences: Lisa Kinne

Senior Project Editor: Jane O'Neill

Senior Production Supervisor: Sarah Segal

Director of Design, Content Management: Diana Blume

Senior Design Manager and Cover Designer: Vicki Tomaselli

Interior Designer: Marsha Cohen, Parallelogram Graphics

Senior Photo Editor: Cecilia Varas

Photo Researcher: Elyse Rieder

Art Manager: Matt McAdams

Illustrations: Eli Ensor, Mapping Specialists, Evelyn Pence, Jackie Heda, Matthew McAdams, Matt Holt, Christy Krames, Don Stewart, and Todd Buck

Composition: MPS Ltd.

Printing and Binding: King Printing Co., Inc.

Cover Photographs: RJ Muna

Library of Congress Control Number: 2016958177

ISBN-13: 978-1-4641-5546-8
ISBN-10: 1-4641-5546-1

Printed in the United States of America

First printing

Worth Publishers
One New York Plaza
Suite 4500
New York, NY 10004-1562
www.macmillanlearning.com

We dedicate this edition to the memory of

Dan Wegner

our co-author, colleague, and deeply missed friend.

About the Authors

Daniel Schacter is William R. Kenan, Jr. Professor of Psychology at Harvard University. Dan received his BA degree from the University of North Carolina at Chapel Hill. He subsequently developed a keen interest in amnesic disorders associated with various kinds of brain damage. He continued his research and education at the University of Toronto, where he received his PhD in 1981. He taught on the faculty at Toronto for the next six years before joining the psychology department at the University of Arizona in 1987. In 1991, he joined the faculty at Harvard University. His research explores the relationship between conscious and unconscious forms of memory, the nature of distortions and errors in remembering, and the ways in which we use memory to imagine future events. Many of his studies are summarized in his 1996 book, *Searching for Memory: The Brain, the Mind, and the Past,* and his 2001 book, *The Seven Sins of Memory: How the Mind Forgets and Remembers,* both winners of the American Psychological Association's William James Book Award. He has also received a number of awards for teaching and research, including the Harvard-Radcliffe Phi Beta Kappa Teaching Prize, the Award for Distinguished Scientific Contributions from the American Psychological Association, and the William James Fellow Award from the Association for Psychological Science. In 2013, he was elected to the National Academy of Sciences.

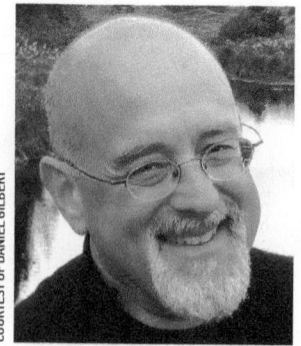

Daniel Gilbert is the Edgar Pierce Professor of Psychology at Harvard University. Dan received his BA from the University of Colorado at Denver and his PhD from Princeton University. From 1985 to 1996 he taught at the University of Texas at Austin, and in 1996 he joined the faculty of Harvard University. He has received the American Psychological Association's Distinguished Scientific Award for an Early Career Contribution to Psychology and the Diener Award for Outstanding Contributions to Social Psychology, and has won teaching awards that include the Phi Beta Kappa Teaching Prize and the Harvard College Professorship. His research focuses on how and how well people think about their emotional reactions to future events. He is the author of the international best seller *Stumbling on Happiness,* which won the Royal Society's General Prize for best popular science book of the year, he is the co-writer and host of the PBS television series *This Emotional Life,* and yes, he's that guy in the Prudential commercials.

Matthew Nock is a Professor of Psychology at Harvard University. Matt received his BA from Boston University (1995) and his PhD from Yale University (2003), and he completed his clinical internship at Bellevue Hospital and the New York University Child Study Center (2003). He joined the faculty of Harvard University in 2003 and has been there ever since. While an undergraduate, he became very interested in the question of why people do things to intentionally harm themselves, and he has been conducting research aimed at answering this question since that time. His research is multidisciplinary in nature and involves a range of methodological approaches (e.g., epidemiologic surveys, laboratory-based experiments, and clinic-based studies) to understand better how these behaviors develop, how to predict them, and how to prevent their occurrence. He has received multiple teaching awards at Harvard and four early career awards recognizing his research, and in 2011 was named a MacArthur Fellow.

Daniel Wegner was the John Lindsley Professor of Psychology in Memory of William James at Harvard University. He received his BS in 1970 and his PhD in 1974, both from Michigan State University. He began his teaching career at Trinity University in San Antonio, Texas, before receiving his appointments at the University of Virginia in 1990 and then at Harvard University in 2000. He was a Fellow of the American Academy of Arts and Sciences and also the recipient of the William James Award from the Association for Psychological Science, the Award for Distinguished Scientific Contributions from the American Psychological Association, and the Distinguished Scientist Award from the Society of Experimental Social Psychology. His research focused on thought suppression and mental control, transactive memory in relationships and groups, and the experience of conscious will. His work on thought suppression and consciousness served as the basis of two popular books, *White Bears and Other Unwanted Thoughts* and the *Illusion of Conscious Will,* both of which were named *Choice* Outstanding Academic Books. He died in 2013.

BRIEF CONTENTS

CONTENTS

YAGI STUDIO/GETTY IMAGES

PHOTOSINDIA/GETTY IMAGES

x

AURORA/GETTY IMAGES

ANDREW GEIGER

4   Sensation and Perception   125

5   Consciousness   171

STONE/GETTY IMAGES

6   Memory   **215**

ICONICA/GETTY IMAGES

7 Learning 261

IMAGE SOURCE/AGE FOTOSTOCK

8 Emotion and Motivation 309

9 Language and Thought   349

OHMEGA1982/AGE FOTOSTOCK

10 Intelligence   395

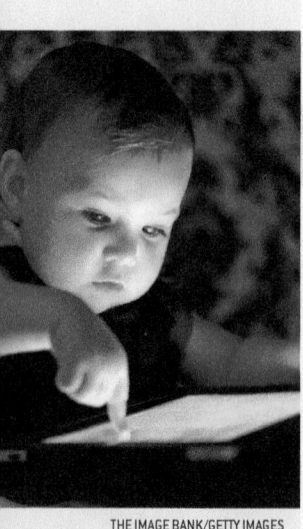

CHRISTOPHER WILSON

11 Development   427

THE IMAGE BANK/GETTY IMAGES

12   Personality   471

PEOPLEIMAGES/GETTY IMAGES

STONE/GETTY IMAGES

FOTOSEARCH/AGE FOTOSTOCK

15   Psychological Disorders   587

EASYFOTOSTOCK/AGE FOTOSTOCK

MOMENT SELECT/GETTY IMAGES

16   Treatment of Psychological Disorders 633

Preface

Why are you reading this? This book doesn't really get going for another 10 pages, so why are you starting here instead of skipping ahead? Are you the kind of person who just can't stand the thought of missing something? Are you trying to justify the cost of the book by consuming every word of it? Or maybe you opened to this page out of habit or obligation? Are you starting to think that maybe you made a big mistake?

For as long as we can remember, we've been asking questions like these about ourselves, about our friends, and about anyone else who didn't run away fast enough. Our curiosity about why people think, feel, and act as they do drew each of us into our first psychology course, and although we remember being swept away by the lectures, we don't remember much about our textbooks. That's probably because those textbooks were little more than colorful encyclopedias of facts and jargon, names and dates. No wonder we sold them back to the bookstore the moment we finished our final exams.

Then we became psychology professors and did all the things psychology professors do: We taught classes, we conducted research, and we wore sweater vests long after they stopped being fashionable. We also wrote some things that people really enjoyed reading—magazine articles and popular books, for instance—and that made us wonder why no one had ever written an introductory psychology textbook that students really enjoyed reading. After all, psychology is the single most interesting subject in the known universe, so why shouldn't a psychology textbook be the single most interesting object in a student's backpack? We couldn't think of a reason, so we sat down and wrote the book that we wished our professors had given us when we were students. The first edition of *Psychology* was published in 2008, and the reaction to it was astounding. We'd never written a textbook before, so we didn't know exactly what to expect, but never in our wildest dreams did we imagine that we would *win the Pulitzer Prize!*

Which was good, because we didn't. But what actually happened was even better: We started getting e-mails from students all over the world who wanted to tell us how much they actually *liked* reading our book. They liked the content, of course, because as we already mentioned, psychology is the single most interesting subject in the known universe. But they also liked the fact that our textbook didn't *sound* like a textbook. It wasn't written in the stodgy voice of the announcer from one of those nature films that we all saw in seventh-grade biology class ("Behold the sea otter, nature's furry little scavenger"). Rather, it was written in *our* voices—the same voices we use when we talk to our students, our spouses, our kids, and our pets (which explains why the original title of Chapter 12 was "Stop Chewing My Shoes!"). We made a conscious effort to tell the *story* of psychology—to integrate topics rather than just listing them, to illustrate ideas rather than just describing them. We realized that because science is a complicated and serious business, some teachers might think that a science textbook should be complicated and serious, too. With all due respect, we just didn't see it that way ourselves. We thought that writing was the art of making complicated things seem simple and of making serious things seem fun. The students who sent us nice letters seemed to agree, even if the Pulitzer Prize committee didn't.

The last edition of our book was a big hit—so why have we replaced it? Two reasons. First, we got tired of being asked about the people dancing in mid-air on the cover.

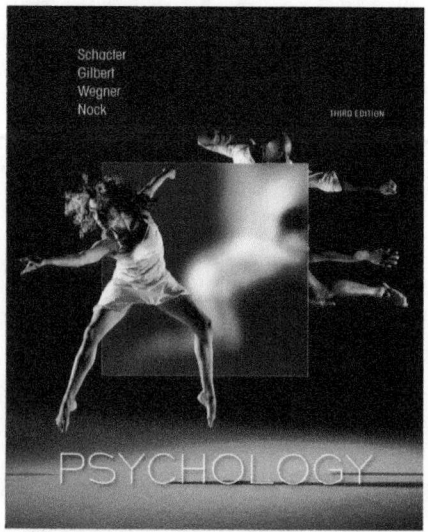

They are gone now, and we're only going to say this one more time: No, we don't know them, and no, we don't know why they are levitating in their pajamas. The second and somewhat more important reason for bringing out a new edition is that things change. Science changes (psychologists know all sorts of things about the mind and the brain that they didn't know just a few years ago), the world changes (when we wrote the last edition, no one had heard of Snapchat or Caitlyn Jenner), and we change (our research and reading gave us new perspectives on psychological issues, and our writing and teaching showed us new ways to help students learn). With all of these changes happening around us and to us, we felt that our book should change as well.

Changes in the Fourth Edition

NEW LEARNING OUTCOMES

In preparing this new edition, we heard from teachers across the country who are increasingly being asked to describe the goals of their course and how they are assessing those goals. To aid them in their efforts, we considered how to articulate the goals of this text in a way that will aid students as well as teachers and allow them to better track their learning progress. The result is a new set of pedagogical features:

▶ **Learning Outcomes,** introduced at the beginning of each major section of each chapter, have been written to align with the goals of the American Psychological Association (APA). These outcomes describe the key points presented in the section and can be used to preview the material. We believe that a first course in psychology is about more than just being able to recite a bunch of facts; rather, it should foster the ability to understand and draw connections among concepts. Consequently, the outcomes set the expectation that students will not only learn about psychology but also will learn *how to think about* psychology.

▶ **Build to the Outcomes** questions conclude each section and provide the scaffolding necessary to reach the outcomes. Students can use them as a study guide, or instructors can use them as writing assignments. Guides for answering the questions can be found in the **Chapter Review** section at the end of each chapter.

▶ **Quiz questions in LearningCurve** offer readers an additional means of interleaved practice in the new outcomes. This builds on what we know about learning (covered in the Learning chapter): that self-testing and mixing study tools improves understanding and retention. LearningCurve also allows instructors to track students' learning at a glance.

▶ The **Test Bank**, also aligned to the outcomes, allows the flexibility to create additional formative and summative assessments. This new program offers a new way of setting and tracking goals consistently throughout the course.

NEW! DATA VISUALIZATION ACTIVITIES

Is SAT performance related to family income and education level? How do concussion rates for high school sports differ? How important is a good night's sleep? The Data Visualization Activities invite readers to consider these questions as scientists by looking at real experimental data. Available in LaunchPad, each activity is based around an interactive graph that displays actual data from a published study. After reading a description of the study, students have to answer questions that test their ability to understand and reason about the data. Integrated lessons in statistical concepts further build students' quantitative-reasoning skills. The Data Visualization Activities engage students in the science of psychology and help to prepare them for later courses in statistics and research methods.

CULTURE AND BEYOND

In the last decade, many psychologists have become interested in culture, and we've become interested in it, too. Previous editions of our book had special sections and boxes on culture. But human beings differ along many important dimensions, and culture is just one of them. Thought, feeling, and behavior are influenced by culture, but also by gender, race, religion, age, sexual orientation, and all the other individual differences that make us so diverse. So in this edition, we've expanded our focus on culture to include many of these other interesting differences as well. You'll notice this especially in two new features:

▶ "A World of Difference" is a new boxed feature that covers exciting research on a wide range of human differences, from culture to gender to social class.

▶ "Paired photos" are visual reminders that people across our planet differ in interesting and consequential ways.

Chapter Number	A World of Difference
1	To Have and Have Not, p. 25
2	Are Heroes and Sheroes Divided by Zeroes? p. 40
4	The Dress, p. 137
5	Dreaming Blind, p. 196
6	Childhood Amnesia in Western and Eastern Cultures, p. 235
7	Implicit Learning in Autism Spectrum Disorder, p. 297
8	Say Cheese, p. 323
9	Exploring the 30-Million-Word Gap, p. 356
10	Equality in Smartland, p. 401
11	That's the Dumbest Thing I Never Heard!, p. 439
12	Why Do Males and Females Have Different Personality Traits? p. 481
13	Do Me a Favor? p. 517
14	Can Discrimination Cause Stress and Illness? p. 554
15	The Impact of Culture on Mental Disorders, p. 593
16	Differences in People's Responses to Treatment, p. 656

NEW RESEARCH

A textbook should give students a complete tour of the classics, of course, but it should also take them on a tour of the cutting edge. Psychology has a history. But in addition to being a collection of past events, it is also a collection of current events. We want students to realize that this young and evolving science is about them—and that it even has a place for them if they want it. So we've packed the fourth edition with information about what's happening in the field right this very minute. (Okay, well, not *this* minute, because we had to write the book in the past so you could read it in the present, but you get the point.) Not only have we included more than

350 new citations but we've also featured some of the hottest new science in a box that we creatively called "Hot Science." You'll find one in every chapter.

Chapter Number	Hot Science
1	Psychology as a Hub Science, pp. 29–30
2	Is Science Gender Biased? p. 57
3	The Power of Thought: Brain–Machine Interfaces, p. 91
3	Epigenetics and the Persisting Effects of Early Experiences, p. 108
4	Music Training: Worth the Time, p. 156
5	The Mind Wanders, p. 178
6	Sleep on It, p. 228
7	Dopamine and Reward Learning in Parkinson's Disease, p. 287
8	The Nutritionist Behind Your Eyes, p. 334
9	Creative Problem Solving: Insiders and Outsiders, p. 384
10	Brains Wide Open, p. 416
11	I Won't Make *That* Mistake Again! p. 462
12	Personality on the Surface, p. 479
13	Through Other Eyes, p. 544
14	Stress, Health, and Money, p. 559
15	Optimal Outcome in Autism Spectrum Disorder, p. 620
16	"Rebooting" Psychological Treatment, p. 648

Proven Strengths

FOCUS ON CRITICAL THINKING

Flip-flopper. Waffler. Wishy-washy. Namby-pamby. Those are just some of the inventive invectives we use to describe people who change their minds. But science is constantly uncovering new evidence that changes the way we think about old evidence, so good scientists change their minds all the time. Some of the facts that students learn in their first psychology course still will be facts a century from now, but others will require qualification or will turn out to have been just plain wrong. That's why students need not only to learn the facts but also how to think about facts—how to examine, question, and weigh the kinds of evidence that scientists produce. We call this *critical thinking,* and although we emphasize it throughout our textbook, we discuss it specifically in a section designed to help students understand the kinds of mistakes that human beings commonly make when they consider evidence (see "Thinking Critically about Evidence" in Chapter 2, Methods in Psychology, pp. 62–66). This section is meant to help students learn how to develop well-founded beliefs—about psychological science and about the stuff of which their lives are made.

The "Changing Minds" questions that are included at the end of every chapter are another way that we try to get students to think critically. These questions ask

> **CHANGING MINDS**
>
> **1.** One of the senators from your state is supporting a bill that would impose heavy fines on aggressive drivers who run red lights. One of your classmates thinks this is a good idea. "The textbook taught us a lot about punishment and reward. It's simple. If we punish aggressive driving, its frequency will decline." Is your classmate right? Might the new law backfire? Might another policy be more effective in promoting safe driving?

students to consider everyday situations in which a common misconception about human behavior might arise, and then to use psychological science to overcome that misconception. These exercises are meant to encourage students to apply what they are learning in their psychology course to their daily lives.

MANY NEW "OTHER VOICES"

Long before psychologists appeared on earth, the human nature business was dominated by poets, playwrights, pundits, philosophers, and several other groups whose names begin with *p*. Those folks are still in that business today, and they continue to have deep and original insights into how and why human beings behave as they do. So we decided to invite some of them to share their thoughts with students via a feature that we call "Other Voices." In every chapter, students will find a short essay by someone who has three important qualifications: (1) They think deeply; (2) they write beautifully; and (3) they know things we don't. For example, students will find essays by leading journalists and writers such as David Brooks, Ted Gup, Tina Rosenberg, David Ewing Duncan, Susan Kruglinski, and Peter Brown; by award-winning educators such as Linda Moore and Julie Lythcott-Haims; by renowned legal scholars such as Gustin Reichbach, Cass Sunstein, Stephen Carter, Karen L. Daniel, and Elyn Saks; and by eminent scientists such as the neurobiologist Robert Sapolsky and the psychologists V. S. Ramachandran, Timothy Wilson, Christopher Chabris, Daniel Simons, Henry Roediger, and Mark McDaniel. Every one of these amazing people has something important to say about human nature, and we are delighted that they've agreed to say it in these pages. Not only do these essays encourage students to think critically about a variety of topical issues, but they also demonstrate psychology's relevance and growing importance in the public forum.

Chapter Number	Other Voices
1	Is Psychology a Science? Timothy D. Wilson, p. 14
2	Can We Afford Science? Cass R. Sunstein, p. 68
3	Neuromyths, Chris Chabris and Daniel Simons, p. 118
4	Hallucinations and the Visual System, V. S. Ramachandran as reported to Susan Kruglinski, p. 150
5	A Judge's Plea for Pot, the Honorable Gustin L. Reichbach, p. 207
6	Memories Inside Out, Karen L. Daniel, p. 249
7	Learning at Jiffy Lube University, Peter Brown, Henry Roediger, and Mark McDaniel, p. 301
8	Should We Pay People to Vote? Stephen L. Carter, p. 339
9	Americans' Future Has to Be Bilingual, Linda Moore, p. 364
10	How Science Can Build a Better You, David Ewing Duncan, p. 423
11	What Time Leaves Behind, Robert Sapolsky, p. 453
12	Does the Study of Personality Lack . . . Personality? David Brooks, p. 501
13	Ninety-one Percent of All Students Read This Box and Love It, Tina Rosenberg, p. 531
14	The Dangers of Overparenting, Julie Lythcott-Haims, p. 582
15	Successful and Schizophrenic, Elyn R. Saks, p. 613
16	Diagnosis: Human, Ted Gup, p. 659

PRACTICAL APPLICATION: "THE REAL WORLD" BOXES

From cells in petri dishes to rats in mazes to participants in experimental cubicles, a psychology textbook can seem like a report about things that happened in places that aren't much like the place students are sitting in right now. That's why in every chapter we have included a box called "The Real World" that shows students how the facts and concepts of psychology have been or can be applied to the stuff of everyday life, from dating to studying to going on a job interview. Additionally, this edition continues to celebrate the rich diversity of human beings throughout the text, as detailed below.

Chapter Number	The Real World
1	Improving Study Skills, pp. 8–9
2	Oddsly Enough, p. 58
3	Brain Plasticity and Sensations in Phantom Limbs, p. 101
4	Multitasking, p. 130
5	Drugs and the Regulation of Consciousness, p. 205
6	Is Google Hurting Our Memories? p. 243
7	Understanding Drug Overdoses, p. 264
8	A Feast for the Eyes, p. 333
9	From Zippers to Political Extremism: An Illusion of Understanding, p. 390
10	Look Smart, p. 407
11	Coming to Terms, p. 457
12	Does Your Personality Change Depending on Who You're With? p. 491
13	Making the Move, p. 519
14	This is Your Brain on Placebos, p. 575
15	How Are Mental Disorders Defined and Diagnosed? p. 595
16	Types of Psychotherapists, p. 636
16	Treating Severe Mental Disorders, p. 652

CULTURE AND MULTICULTURAL EXPERIENCE

Aggression and culture, p. 510
    and geography, p. 511
Aging population, pp. 460–466
Alcohol, binge drinking, p. 200
Attachment style, pp. 443–445
Attractiveness, pp. 519–524
Autism, pp. 297, 438, 619–621
Beauty, standards of (paired photo), p. 522
Body ideal, pp. 522–523
Children and happiness (paired photo), pp. 465–466

Concept of time (paired photo), p. 367
Conformity, pp. 529–530
Culture, discovering, pp. 440–441
Cultural norms, pp. 528–529
Cultural psychology,
    definition, pp. 24–25
Deaf culture, pp. 356, 438
Depression, pp. 605–610
Development
    adolescence, protracted, pp. 451–452
    attachment, pp. 442–445
    cognitive development, pp. 432–441

counting ability, p. 440
    moral development, pp. 445–449
Dreams, meaning of, pp. 194–195
Drugs, psychological effects of, pp. 651–655
Eating disorders, pp. 330–335
Expression, display rules, pp. 322–324
Expression, universality, pp. 319–320
False memories, pp. 352–353
Family therapy, pp. 647–649
First memories (paired photo), p. 235
Homosexuality
    genes, pp. 454–456

THE PSYCHOLOGY OF MEN AND WOMEN

Focus on Learning Outcomes

TEACHING WITH THE APA LEARNING GOALS AND OUTCOMES: MORE SPECIFICS

In every chapter in this book, you will see references to "Learning Outcomes." What in the world are these? you ask. In an effort to develop greater consensus on what undergraduate students should be learning in their psychology courses, the APA formed the Task Force on Undergraduate Psychology Major Competencies to provide a framework for educators. The task force published comprehensive recommendations in *The APA Guidelines for the Undergraduate Psychology Major,* with the revised version 2.0 released in August 2013. These revised guidelines present a rigorous standard for what students should gain from foundational courses and from the psychology major as a whole. They comprise five goals relating to the following:

Goal 1:   Knowledge Base in Psychology

Goal 2:   Scientific Inquiry and Critical Thinking

Goal 3:   Ethical and Social Responsibility in a Diverse World

Goal 4:   Communication

Goal 5:   Professional Development

In order to make sure that you know everything that students of psychology should know, this textbook, and the people who created it—Worth Publishers—offer a wide variety of resources to support you in achieving the APA outcomes. Most important, a document showing how the content of this textbook maps onto the APA goals is available for download from the Resources area of LaunchPad at launchpadworks.com. To assist with assessment, Worth has tagged all of the items included in the Test Bank accompanying this book to the relevant outcomes. In addition, the Instructor's Resources and LaunchPad learning system feature a variety of activities and additional content items that contribute to the APA goals. All of these resources in combination offer instructors (and their students!) a powerful set of tools for achieving their course outcomes.

PREPARING FOR THE MCAT

Are any of your students thinking about going to medical school? If so, all the more reason to make sure they master the material in this revised edition of our textbook, because psychological science now makes up a significant portion of the material in the standardized test that students must take when applying to medical school. More specific, from 1977 to 2014, the Medical College Admission Test (MCAT) focused only on biology, chemistry, and physics, but as of 2015, 25% of its questions now cover "Psychological, Social, and Biological Foundations of Behavior," with most of those questions concerning the psychological science taught in introductory psychology courses. According to the *Preview Guide for the MCAT 2015 Exam* (second edition), the addition of this content "recognizes the importance of socio-cultural and behavioral determinants of health and health outcomes." The psychology material in the new MCAT covers the breadth of topics in this textbook. The table below offers a sample of how the topics in this textbook's Sensation and Perception chapter correspond precisely to the topics laid out in the MCAT *Preview Guide.* A complete correlation of the MCAT psychology topics with this book's contents is available for download from the Resources area of LaunchPad at launchpadworks.com. In addition, since the MCAT sets a global standard for assessing the ability to reason about scientific information, the Test Bank for *Psychology,* Fourth Edition, features a new set of data-based questions for each chapter that are designed to test students' quantitative reasoning. These questions are available for preview in LaunchPad.

Media and Supplements

LAUNCHPAD WITH LEARNINGCURVE QUIZZING

A comprehensive web resource for teaching and learning psychology

LaunchPad combines Worth Publishers' award-winning media with an innovative platform for easy navigation. For students, it is the ultimate online study guide, with rich interactive tutorials and videos, as well as an e-Book and the LearningCurve adaptive quizzing system. For instructors, LaunchPad is a full course space where class documents can be posted, quizzes easily assigned and graded, and students' progress assessed and recorded. The fourth edition integrates the new Data Visualization activities in each chapter for easy access. Whether you are looking for the most effective study tools or a robust platform for an online course, LaunchPad is a powerful way to enhance your class.

> LaunchPad to accompany *Psychology*, Fourth Edition, can be previewed and purchased at launchpadworks.com.
>
> *Psychology*, Fourth Edition, and LaunchPad can be ordered together with ISBN-10: 1-319-11450-4 / ISBN-13: 978-1-319-11450-3.

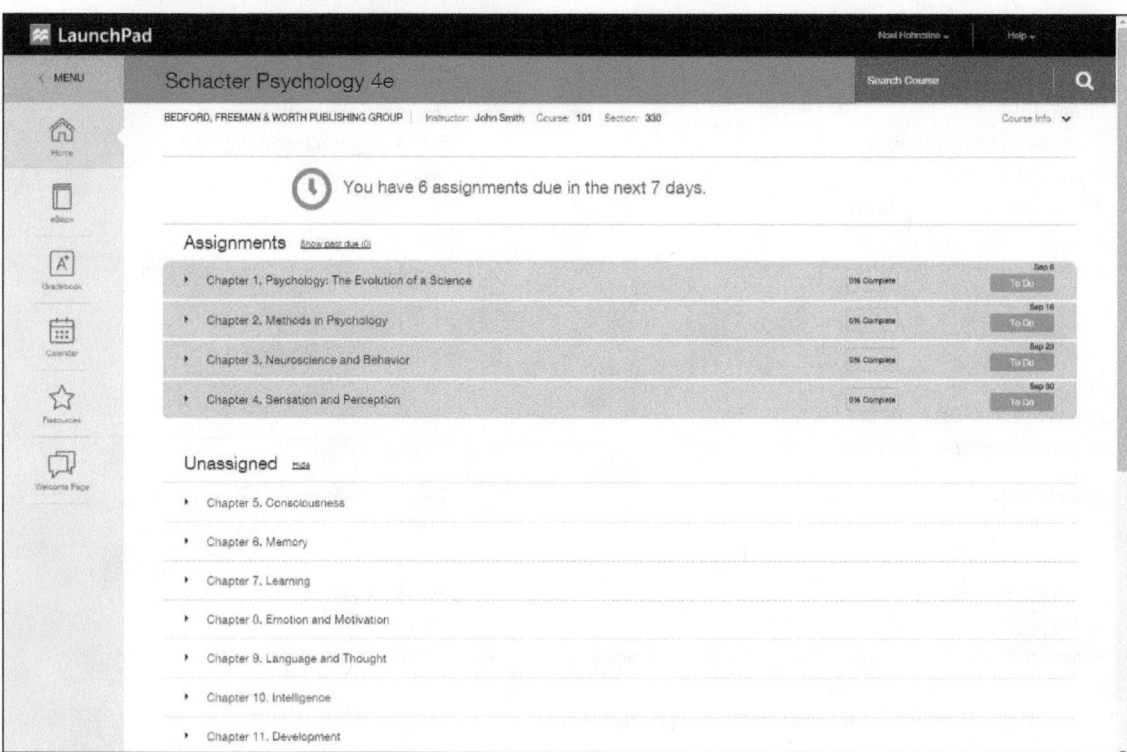

LaunchPad for *Psychology*, Fourth Edition, includes all the following resources:

▶ The design of the **LearningCurve** quizzing system is based on the latest findings from learning and memory research. It combines adaptive question selection, immediate and valuable feedback, and a gamelike interface to engage students in a learning experience that is unique to them. Each LearningCurve quiz is fully integrated with other resources in LaunchPad through the Personalized Study Plan, so students will be able to review using Worth's extensive library of videos

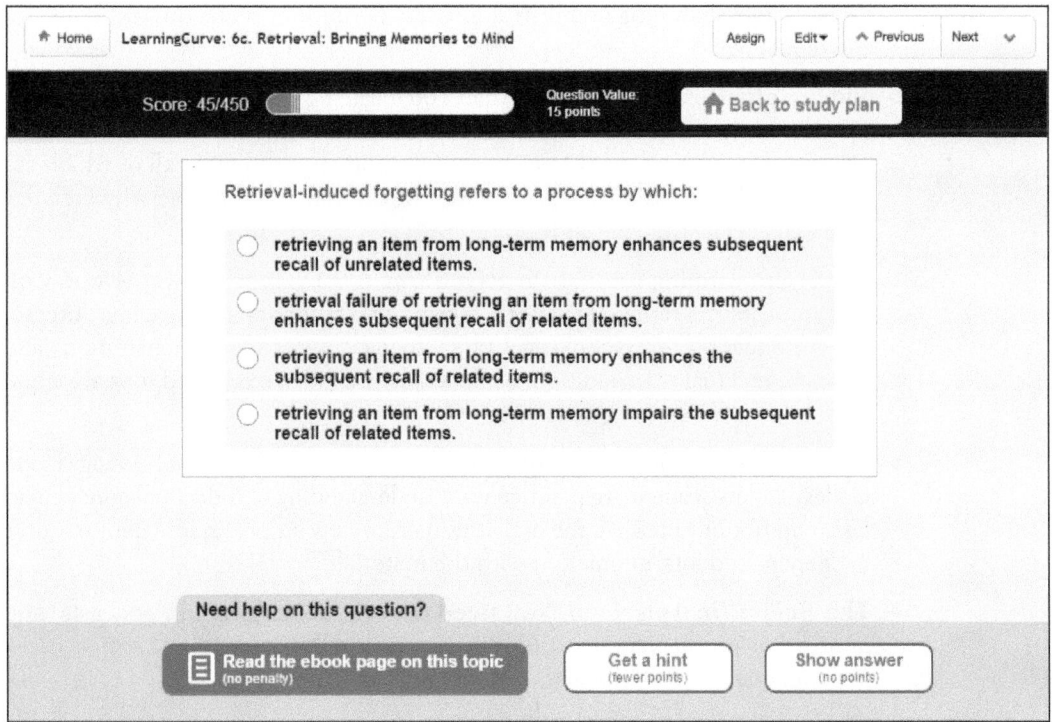

and activities. And state-of-the-art question analysis reports allow instructors to track the progress of individual students as well as their class as a whole.

▶ **New! Immersive Learning Activities: Data Visualization Activities** offer students practice in understanding and reasoning about data. In each activity, students interact with a graph or visual display of data and must think like scientists to answer the accompanying questions. These activities build quantitative reasoning skills and offer a deeper understanding of how science works.

▶ **An interactive e-Book** allows students to highlight, bookmark, and add their own notes on the e-Book page, just as they would in a printed textbook.

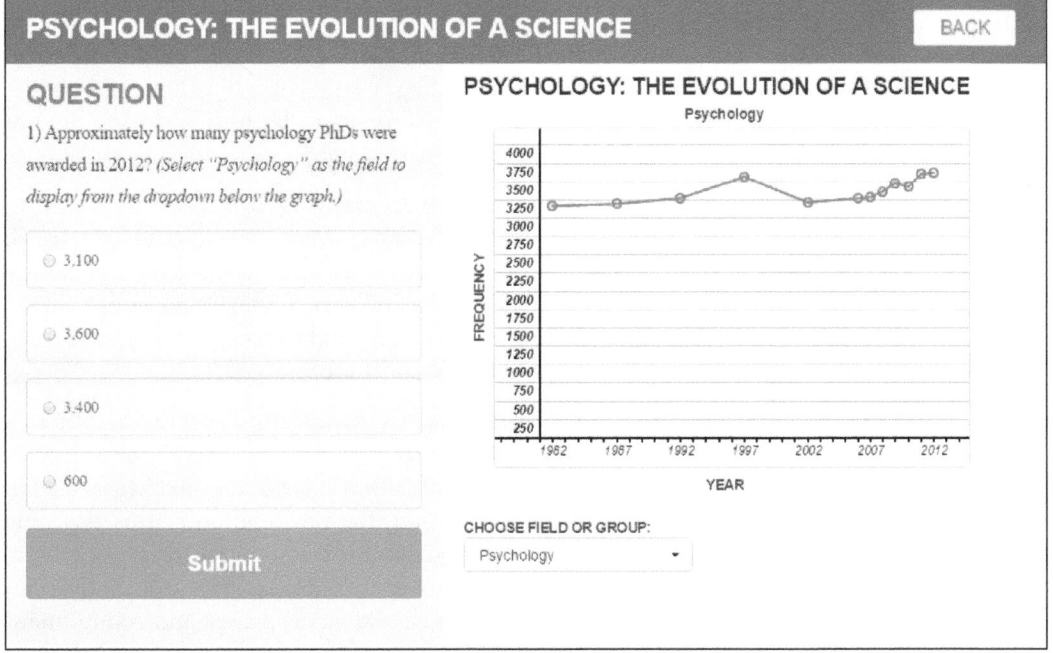

Google-style searching and in-text glossary definitions make the text ready for the digital age.

▶ **Video Activities** comprise more than 100 engaging video modules that instructors can easily assign and customize for student assessment. Videos cover classic experiments, current news footage, and cutting-edge research, all of which are sure to spark discussion and encourage critical thinking. Each activity includes a quiz to check students' understanding.

▶ The award-winning tutorials in **PsychSim 6.0** by Tom Ludwig (Hope College) and John Krantz (Hanover College) give students an engaging, interactive introduction to psychological phenomena, integrating demonstrations and experimental tasks. In addition, each activity includes integrated formative and summative assessment questions.

▶ The newly revised series of **Concept Practice** activities by Tom Ludwig (Hope College) allow students to practice their understanding of individual concepts in less than five minutes. All the activities feature new art and assessment features to deepen students' interaction with the material.

▶ The *Scientific American* **Newsfeed** delivers weekly articles, podcasts, and news briefs on the very latest developments in psychology from the first name in popular-science journalism.

▶ **Deep integration** is available between LaunchPad products and most learning management systems including Blackboard, Brightspace by D2L, Canvas, and Moodle. These deep integrations offer educators single sign-on and grade-book sync, now with auto refresh. These best-in-class integrations offer deep linking to all Macmillan digital content at the chapter and asset levels, giving professors maximum flexibility within their LMS.

Additional Student Supplements

Macmillan offers a wide variety of texts to supplement students' first course in psychology. Find out more about these titles or request an examination copy at www.macmillanlearning.com.

▶ *Pursuing Human Strengths: A Positive Psychology Guide,* **Second Edition,** by Martin Bolt (Calvin College) and Dana S. Dunn (Moravian College), is a perfect way to introduce students to both the amazing field of positive psychology and their own personal strengths.

▶ *The Psychology Major's Companion: Everything You Need to Know to Get Where You Want to Go,* by Dana S. Dunn (Moravian College) and Jane S. Halonen (University of West Florida), helps students to declare the psychology major if it is in their best interests to do so, to learn strategies regarding how to produce optimal gains in the major experience, and to prepare for either graduate school or a psychology-related professional life.

▶ *Psychology and the Real World: Essays Illustrating Fundamental Contributions to Society,* **Second Edition,** is a superb collection of essays by major researchers that describe their landmark studies. Published in association with the not-for-profit FABBS Foundation, the new edition of this engaging reader includes Alan Kazdin's reflections on his research on treating children with severe aggressive behavior, Adam Grant's look at work and motivation, and Steven Hayes's research on mindfulness and acceptance and commitment therapy. A portion of all proceeds is donated to FABBS to support societies of cognitive, psychological, behavioral, and brain sciences.

▶ *The Critical Thinking Companion for Introductory Psychology,* **Third Edition,** by Jane S. Halonen (University of West Florida) and Cynthia Gray (Beloit College), contains a guide to critical thinking strategies as well as exercises in pattern recognition, practical problem solving, creative problem solving, scientific problem solving, psychological reasoning, and perspective taking.

▶ *The Worth Expert Guide to Scientific Literacy: Thinking Like a Psychological Scientist,* by Kenneth D. Keith (University of San Diego) and Bernard Beins (Ithaca College), helps students foster solid habits of scientific thought, learning to apply an empirical attitude and data-driven decision making in their lives. With this increased level of scientific literacy, students will be better able to make sense of complex scientific information and to recognize pseudoscientific claims that are not only invalid but also potentially harmful.

TAKE ADVANTAGE OF OUR MOST POPULAR SUPPLEMENTS!

Worth Publishers is pleased to offer cost-saving packages of *Psychology,* Fourth Edition, with our most popular supplements. Below is a list of some of the most popular combinations available for order through your local bookstore.

Psychology, 4th Ed. & LaunchPad Access Card
ISBN-10: 1-319-11450-4 / ISBN-13: 978-1-319-11450-3

Psychology, 4th Ed. & *Pursuing Human Strengths: A Positive Psychology Guide*
ISBN-10: 1-319-12375-9 / ISBN-13: 978-1-319-12375-8

Psychology, 4th Ed. & *The Psychology Major's Companion*
ISBN-10: 1-319-12097-0 / ISBN-13: 978-1-319-12097-9

Psychology, 4th Ed. & *Psychology and the Real World*
ISBN-10: 1-319-11526-8 / ISBN-13: 978-1-319-11526-5

Psychology, 4th Ed. & *The Critical Thinking Companion for Introductory Psychology*
ISBN-10: 1-319-12096-2 / ISBN-13: 978-1-319-12096-2

Psychology, 4th Ed. & *The Worth Expert Guide to Scientific Literacy*
ISBN-10: 1-319-12098-9 / ISBN-13: 978-1-319-12098-6

ForeWords Custom Publishing Library

The ForeWords Library contains special chapters and other print content to supplement *Psychology,* Fourth Edition, through Macmillan's custom publishing program. ForeWords content is authored by recognized experts and can be added to a custom book at little or no cost. Current offerings include:

▶ **New!** *Psychology and Sustainability* by Susan Clayton of The College of Wooster

▶ *A Practical Guide to Study Skills* by Amy Himsel of El Camino College

▶ *Industrial/Organizational Psychology and Human Factors* by Paul Levy of The University of Akron and Karen Marando of Argosy University

▶ *The Basics of Scientific Writing in APA Style* by Pam Marek of Kennesaw State University

▶ And many others!

For more information, visit our Curriculum Solutions webpage at www.worthpublishers .com/psychologyforewords.

ASSESSMENT

▶ **The Computerized Test Bank,** powered by Diploma, includes a full assortment of test items from author Chad Galuska (College of Charleston). Each chapter features over 200 multiple-choice, true/false, and essay questions to test students at several levels of Bloom's taxonomy. All the questions are tagged to the text's learning outcomes, the book page, the chapter section, and the outcomes recommended in the 2013 APA Guidelines for the Undergraduate Psychology Major, allowing for incredible ease in finding and selecting items for a wide variety of assessments. In the new edition, the Test Bank items are divided into two forms with similar characteristics to make it even easier to create two different tests covering the same material at comparable levels of difficulty.

This title also features a special set of data-based reasoning questions to test advanced critical thinking skills in a manner similar to the MCAT. They pair perfectly with the Data Visualization exercises featured in LaunchPad for an incomparable introduction to scientific literacy. Adopters also have access to a special collection of integrative questions which require students to connect material from multiple chapters—a challenging addition for midterm and final exams. The accompanying grade book software makes it easy to record students' grades throughout a course, to sort student records, to view detailed analyses of test items, to curve tests, to generate reports, and to add weights to grades.

▶ The **iClicker** Classroom Response System is a versatile polling system developed by educators for educators that makes class time more efficient and interactive. iClicker allows you to ask questions and instantly record your students' responses, take attendance, and gauge students' understanding and opinions. iClicker is available at a 10% discount when packaged with *Psychology,* Fourth Edition.

PRESENTATION

▶ **Lecture Slides** are complimentary to adopters of *Psychology,* Fourth Edition, and are perfect for technology novices and experts alike. Fully updated to support the new edition, they include images from the text and in-class discussion prompts. The Presentation Slides are available to download in LaunchPad at launchpadworks.com.

▶ The **Instructor's Resources** by Jeffrey Henriques (University of Wisconsin-Madison) feature a variety of materials that are valuable to new and veteran teachers alike. In addition to background on the chapter reading and suggestions for in-class lectures, the manual is rich with activities to engage students in different modes of learning. The Instructor's Resources are available to download in LaunchPad at launchpadworks.com.

▶ The **Video Collection for Introductory Psychology** includes over 300 unique video clips to bring lectures to life. Provided complimentary to adopters of *Psy-*

chology, Fourth Edition, this rich collection includes clinical footage, interviews, animations, and news segments that vividly illustrate topics across the psychology curriculum. Request a copy from your local Macmillan representative.

▶ **Macmillan Community** is an online forum where teachers can find and share favorite teaching ideas and materials, including videos, animations, images, PowerPoint slides, news stories, articles, web links, and lecture activities. It is also the home of Worth's abundant social media content, including tweets, blog posts, webinars (featuring Daniel Schacter, Daniel Gilbert, Matthew Nock, and others), and more! Browse the site and share your favorite materials for teaching psychology at https://community.macmillan.com

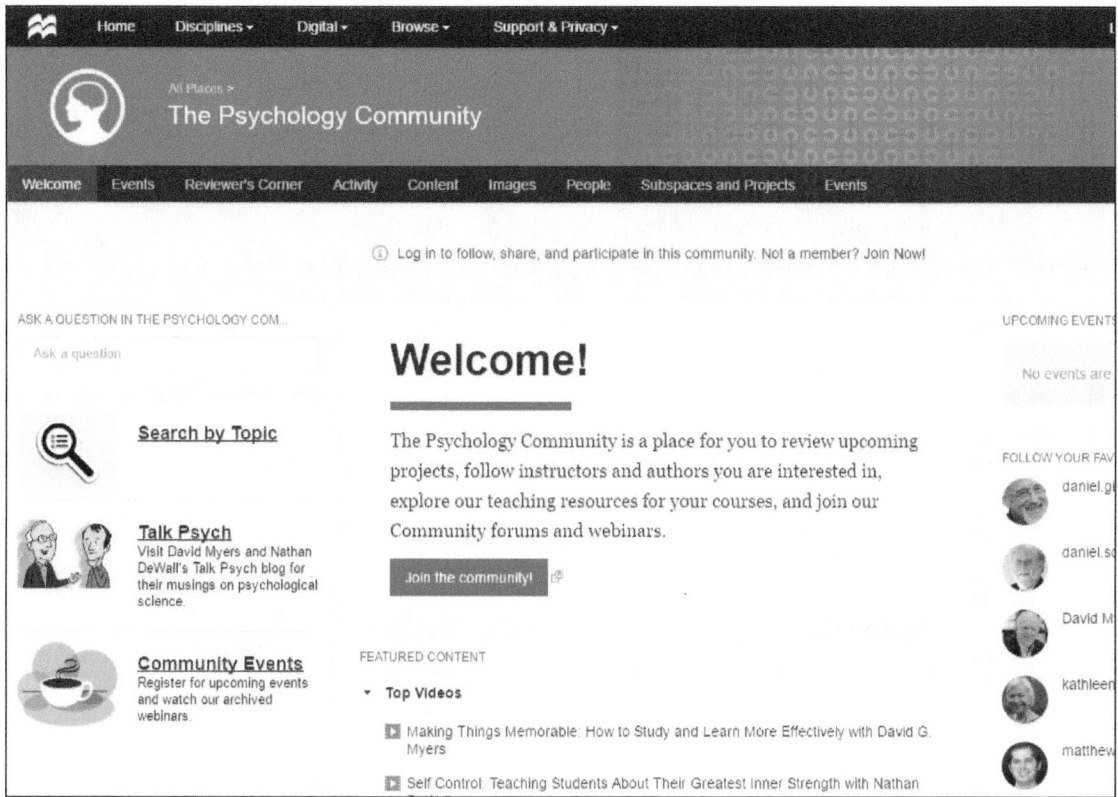

Acknowledgments

Despite what you might guess by looking at our photographs, we all found women who were willing to marry us, though in some cases it required special pleading. We are grateful to our amazing wives—Susan McGlynn, Marilynn Oliphant, and Keesha Nock—who never once complained on all those long nights and weekends when we were busy writing this book instead of hanging out with them. Hey, wait a minute. You did miss us, didn't you?

Although ours are the only names on the cover, writing a textbook is a team sport, and we were lucky to have a terrific group of professionals in our dugout. We greatly appreciate the contributions of our distinguished colleagues, Martin M. Antony, Mark Baldwin, Michelle A. Butler, Patricia Csank, Denise D. Cummins, Ian J. Deary, Howard Eichenbaum, Sam Gosling, Paul Harris, Melanie Maggard, Catherine Myers, Shigehiro Oishi, Arthur S. Reber, Morgan T. Sammons, Dan Simons, Alan Swinkels, Richard M. Wenzlaff, and Steven Yantis.

We thank our core supplements authors, who provided insight into the role our book can play in the classroom and adeptly developed the materials to support it. Chad Galuska, Jeff Henriques, and Russ Frohardt, we appreciate your tireless work in the classroom and the experience you brought to our book's supplements. We also appreciate the editorial, clerical, and research assistance we received from Molly Evans and Franchesca Ramirez. What would we have done without you?

We would also like to thank the faculty members who reviewed our book. These dedicated teachers showed a level of engagement we have come to expect from our best colleagues:

Eileen Achorn
University of Texas, San Antonio

Jim Allen
SUNY Geneseo

Randy Arnau
University of Southern Mississippi

Joanne Bagshaw
Montgomery College

Kathryn Becker-Blease
Oregon State University

Benjamin Bennett-Carpenter
Oakland University

Joan Bihun
University of Colorado, Denver

Kristin Biondolillo
Arkansas State University

Stephen Blessing
University of Tampa

Jeffrey Blum
Los Angeles City College

Richard Bowen
Loyola University of Chicago

Nicole Bragg
Mt. Hood Community College

Jennifer Breneiser
Valdosta State University

Christopher Brill
Old Dominion University

Michele Brumley
Idaho State University

Josh Burk
College of William and Mary

Jennifer Butler
Case Western Reserve University

Richard Cavasina
California University of Pennsylvania

Amber Chenoweth
Kent State University

Stephen Chew
Samford University

Chrisanne Christensen
Southern Arkansas University

Sheryl Civjan
Holyoke Community College

Jennifer Dale
Community College of Aurora

Jennifer Daniels
University of Connecticut

Joshua Dobias
Marywood University

Dale Doty
Monroe Community College

Julie Evey-Johnson
University of Southern Indiana

Valerie Farmer-Dugan
Illinois State University

Diane Feibel
University of Cincinnati,
Raymond Walters College

Jocelyn Folk
Kent State University

Chad Galuska
College of Charleston

Afshin Gharib
Dominican University of California

Jeffrey Gibbons
Christopher Newport University

Adam Goodie
University of Georgia

John Governale
Clark College

Patricia Grace
Kaplan University Online

Stephanie Griffiths
Okanagan College

Sarah Grison
University of Illinois at
Urbana-Champaign

Deletha Hardin
University of Tampa

Jason Hart
Christopher Newport University

Lesley Hathorn
Metropolitan State College of Denver

Mark Hauber
Hunter College

Jacqueline Hembrook
University of New Hampshire

Allen Huffcutt
Bradley University

Mary Hughes-Stone
San Francisco State University

Mark Hurd
College of Charleston

Linda Jackson
Michigan State University

Jennifer Johnson
Rider University

Linda Johnson
Butte College

Lance Jones
Bowling Green State University

Linda Jones
Blinn College

Katherine Judge
Cleveland State University

Don Kates
College of DuPage

Martha Knight-Oakley
Warren Wilson College

Ken Koenigshofer
Chaffey College

Neil Kressel
William Patterson University

Josh Landau
York College of Pennsylvania

Fred Leavitt
California State University, East Bay

Tera Letzring
Idaho State University

Karsten Loepelmann
University of Alberta

Laura Loewen
Okanagan College

Ray Lopez
University of Texas at San Antonio

Jeffrey Love
Penn State University

Greg Loviscky
Penn State University, University Park

Julianne Ludlam
University of Missouri, Columbia

Keith Maddox
Tufts University

Lynda Mae
Arizona State University at Tempe

Caitlin Mahy
University of Oregon

Gregory Manley
University of Texas at San Antonio

Karen Marsh
University of Minnesota at Duluth

Sarah Marsh
Minnesota State University

Robert Mather
University of Central Oklahoma

Wanda McCarthy
University of Cincinnati at Clermont College

Daniel McConnell
University of Central Florida

Robert McNally
Austin Community College

Dawn Melzer
Sacred Heart University

Dennis Miller
University of Missouri

Mignon Montpetit
Miami University

William P. Neace
Lindsey Wilson College

Todd Nelson
California State University at Stanislaus

Margaret Norwood
Community College of Aurora

Aminda O'Hare
University of Kansas

Gina A. O'Neal-Moffitt
Florida State University

Melissa Pace
Kean University

Brady Phelps
South Dakota State University

Raymond Phinney
Wheaton College

Claire St. Peter Pipkin
West Virginia University, Morgantown

Christy Porter
College of William and Mary

Jens Pruessner
McGill University

Douglas Pruitt
West Kentucky Community and
Technical College

Elizabeth Purcell
Greenville Technical College

Gabriel Radvansky
University of Notre Dame

Celia Reaves
Monroe Community College

Diane Reddy
University of Wisconsin,
Milwaukee

Cynthia Shinabarger Reed
Tarrant County College

David Reetz
Hanover College

Ann Renken
University of Southern California

Tanya Renner
Kapi'olani Community College

Anthony Robertson
Vancouver Island University

Nancy Rogers
University of Cincinnati

Wendy Rote
University of Rochester

Larry Rudiger
University of Vermont

Sharleen Sakai
Michigan State University

Matthew Sanders
Marquette University

Phillip Schatz
Saint Joseph's University

Vann Scott
Armstrong Atlantic State University

Colleen Seifert
University of Michigan at Ann Arbor

Keith Shafritz
Hofstra University

Wayne Shebilske
Wright State University

Elisabeth Sherwin
University of Arkansas at Little Rock

Lisa Shin
Tufts University

Kenith Sobel
University of Central Arkansas

Genevieve Stevens
Houston Community College

Mark Stewart
American River College

Holly Straub
University of South Dakota

Mary Strobbe
San Diego Miramar College

William Struthers
Wheaton College

Donald Tellinghuisen
Calvin College

Lisa Thomassen
Indiana University

Ross Thompson
University of California, Davis

Jeremy Tost
Valdosta State University

Susan Troy
Northeast Iowa Community College

Laura Turiano
Sacred Heart University

Jeffrey Wagman
Illinois State University

Alexander Williams
University of Kansas

John Wright
Washington State University

Dean Yoshizumi
Sierra College

Keith Young
University of Kansas

We continue to be grateful to the good folks at Worth Publishers. They include vice president Charles Linsmeier, who provided guidance and encouragement at all stages of the project; our senior acquisitions editor, Dan DeBonis, who managed the project with brio; our brilliant, talented, and preternaturally cheerful senior development editor, Valerie Raymond, who made us sound a lot smarter than we actually are; our director, content management enhancement, Tracey Kuehn; our senior project editor Jane O'Neill, our senior production supervisor Sarah Segal, and our assistant editor Kimberly Morgan, all of whom somehow turned a manuscript into a real book; our senior design manager, Vicki Tomaselli, our art manager, Matt McAdams, our senior photo editor Cecilia Varas, and our photo researcher Elyse Rieder, all of whom worked to make our book an aesthetic delight; our executive media editor Noel Hohnstine, who guided the development and creation of a superb supplements package; and our senior marketing manager Lindsay Johnson who continues to be a tireless public advocate for our vision. Gracias, arigato, danke, merci, xie xie, and Way Big Thanks to all of you.

Finally, allow us to acknowledge the essential contributions of our dear friend, colleague, and coauthor, Dan Wegner. Dan was diagnosed with ALS and passed away before we began work on this edition, but his brilliant ideas and beautiful words remain—in our pages and in our hearts. *Ad perpetuam rei memoriam.*

Daniel L. Schacter

Daniel T. Gilbert

Matthew K. Nock

Cambridge, 2017

PSYCHOLOGY

Psychology: Evolution of a Science

1

A lot was happening in 1860. Abraham Lincoln had just been elected president of the United States, the Pony Express had just begun to deliver mail between Missouri and California, and a woman named Anne Kellogg had just given birth to a child who would one day grow up to invent the cornflake. But none of this mattered very much to William James, a bright, taciturn, 18-year-old who had no idea what to do with his life. He loved to paint and draw but worried that he wasn't talented enough to become a serious artist. He had enjoyed studying biology in school but doubted that a naturalist's salary would ever allow him to get married and have a family of his own. So, like many young people who are faced with difficult decisions about their futures, William abandoned his dreams and chose to do something in which he had little interest but of which his family heartily approved. Alas, within a few months of his arrival at Harvard Medical School, his lack of interest in medicine blossomed into a troubling lack of enthusiasm, and with a bit of encouragement from the faculty, he put his medical studies on hold to join a biological expedition to the Amazon. The adventure failed to focus his wandering mind (although he learned a great deal about leeches), and when he returned to medical school, both his physical and mental health began to deteriorate. It was clear to everyone that William James was not the sort of person who should be put in charge of a scalpel and a bag of drugs.

Had James become an artist, a biologist, or a physician, we would probably remember nothing about him today. Fortunately for us, he was a somewhat confused young man who could speak five languages, and when he became so depressed that he was once again forced to leave medical school, he decided to travel around Europe, where at least he knew how to talk to people. As he talked and

Throughout his youth, William James (1842–1910) was a bit mixed up. He began college as a chemistry major, then switched to anatomy, then set sail on a biological expedition to the Amazon, and then traveled to Europe, where he became interested in the new science of psychology. Luckily for us, he stuck with it for a while.

LETTERS TO WILLIAM JAMES FROM VARIOUS CORRESPONDENTS AND PHOTOGRAPH ALBUM, 1865–1929. MS AM 1092 (1185) #8. HOUGHTON LIBRARY, HARVARD UNIVERSITY

listened, he learned about a new science called *psychology* (from a combination of the Greek *psyche* [soul] and *logos* [to study]). He saw that this developing field was taking a modern, scientific approach to age-old questions about human nature—questions that had become painfully familiar to him during his personal search for meaning but to which only poets and philosophers had ever before offered answers (Bjork, 1983; Simon, 1998). Excited about the new discipline, James returned to America and quickly finished his medical degree. But he never practiced medicine and never intended to do so. Rather, he became a professor at Harvard University and devoted the rest of his life to philosophy and psychology. His landmark book *The Principles of Psychology* is still widely read and remains one of the most influential books ever written on the subject (James, 1890).

A LOT HAS HAPPENED SINCE THEN. Abraham Lincoln has become the face on the penny, the Pony Express has been replaced by Snapchat, and the Kellogg Company made about $15 billion in net sales last year. If William James (1842–1910) were alive today, he would surely be amazed by these things. But he would be even more amazed by the intellectual advances that have taken place in the science that he helped create. James wanted to learn about human nature, but he confronted a very different situation than a similarly curious student would confront today, largely because psychology did not yet exist as an independent field of study. As he famously joked, "The first lecture in psychology that I ever heard was the first I ever gave." Of course, that doesn't mean no one had ever thought about human nature before. For 2,000 years, thinkers with scraggly beards and poor dental hygiene had pondered such questions, and in fact, modern psychology acknowledges its deep roots in philosophy.

W e will begin by examining those roots and then describe some of the early attempts to develop a scientific approach to psychology by relating the mind to the brain. Next, we discuss important developments in the evolution of psychological science, including the emergence of clinical psychology, behaviorism, cognitive psychology, and social and cultural psychology. We conclude by describing how the profession of psychology has changed in important ways, and what it is that professional psychologists actually do today.

Psychology's Roots: The Path to a Science of Mind

Learning Outcomes

▶ Explain what makes psychology a science.

▶ Identify key steps in the early development of the field of psychology.

psychology The scientific study of mind and behavior.

Psychology is *the scientific study of mind and behavior.* The **mind** refers to *the private inner experience of perceptions, thoughts, memories, and feelings,* an ever-flowing stream of consciousness. **Behavior** refers to *observable actions of human beings and nonhuman animals,* the things that we do in the world, by ourselves or with others. As you will see in the chapters to come, psychology is an attempt to use scientific methods to address fundamental questions about mind and behavior such as:

▶ How do we experience the electrical and chemical activity in our brains as things like thoughts, feelings, and behaviors?

▶ How do our minds respond to, and learn from, the world around us so quickly, and in ways that ensure our survival?

▶ What leads the mind to function so ineffectively in some people, such as in those who experience hallucinations, dramatic mood swings, or intense urges to end their own lives?

These questions are merely the tip of the iceberg, and this textbook is a guide to exploring the rest of it. But before we don our parkas and grab our pickaxes, we need to understand how the iceberg got here in the first place. To understand psychology in the 21st century, we need to become familiar with the psychology of the past.

PSYCHOLOGY'S ANCESTORS: THE GREAT PHILOSOPHERS

The desire to understand ourselves is not new. Greek thinkers such as Plato (428–347 BCE) and Aristotle (384–322 BCE) were among the first to struggle with questions about how the mind works (Robinson, 1995). Greek philosophers debated many of the questions that psychologists continue to debate today. For example, are cognitive abilities and knowledge inborn, or are they acquired only through experience? Plato argued in favor of **nativism,** *the philosophical view that certain kinds of knowledge are innate or inborn.* Children in every culture figure out early on that sounds can have meanings that can be arranged into words, which then can be arranged into sentences. Before a child is old enough to poop in the proper place, he or she has already mastered the fundamentals of language without any formal instruction. Is the propensity to learn language "hard-wired" (something that children are born with)? Or does the ability to learn language depend on the child's experience? Aristotle believed that the child's mind was a *tabula rasa* (blank slate) on which experiences were written, and he argued for **philosophical empiricism,** *the view that all knowledge is acquired through experience.*

Although few modern psychologists believe that either nativism or empiricism is entirely correct, the issue of just how much "nature" and "nurture" explain any given behavior is still a matter of controversy. In some ways, it is quite amazing that ancient philosophers were able to articulate so many of the important questions in psychology and offer many excellent insights into their answers without any access to scientific evidence. Their ideas came from personal observations, intuition, and speculation. Although they were quite good at arguing with one another, they usually found it impossible to settle their disputes because their approach provided no means of testing their theories. As you will see in the Methods chapter, the ability to test a theory is the cornerstone of the scientific approach and the basis for reaching conclusions in modern psychology.

LINKING THE MIND TO THE BRAIN: THE FRENCH CONNECTION

We all know that the brain and the body are physical objects that we can see and touch and that the subjective contents of our minds—our perceptions, thoughts, and feelings—are not. Inner experience is perfectly real, but where in the world is it? The French philosopher René Descartes (1596–1650) argued that body and mind are different things—that the body is made of a material substance, whereas the mind (or soul) is made of an immaterial or spiritual substance. But if the mind and the body are different things made of different substances, how do they interact? How does the mind tell the body to put its foot forward, and when the body steps on a rusty nail, why does the mind say "ouch"? This is the problem of *dualism,* or how mental activity can be reconciled and coordinated with physical behavior.

GEO MARTINEZ/FEATURE PICS

How do young children learn about the world? Plato believed that certain kinds of knowledge are innate, whereas Aristotle believed that the mind is a blank slate on which experiences are written.

mind The private inner experience of perceptions, thoughts, memories, and feelings.

behavior Observable actions of human beings and nonhuman animals.

nativism The philosophical view that certain kinds of knowledge are innate or inborn.

philosophical empiricism The view that all knowledge is acquired through experience.

▲ **Figure 1.1**

PHRENOLOGY Franz Joseph Gall (1758–1828) developed a theory called phrenology, which suggested that psychological capacities (such as the capacity for friendship) and traits (such as cautiousness and mirth) were located in particular parts of the brain. The more of these capacities and traits a person had, the larger the corresponding bumps on the skull.

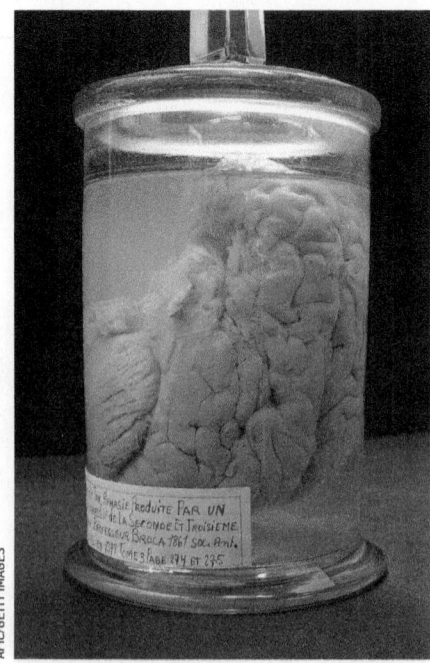

Louis Victor Leborgne was nicknamed "Tan" because it was the only word he could say. When he died in 1861, Paul Broca dissected his brain and found a lesion in the left hemisphere that he believed was responsible for Leborgne's loss of speech. Leborgne's brain now resides in a jar at the Musée Dupuytren in Paris, France.

The British philosopher Thomas Hobbes (1588–1679) argued that the mind and body aren't different things at all; rather, the mind *is* what the brain *does*. From Hobbes's perspective, looking for a place in the brain where the mind meets the body is like looking for the place in a television where the picture meets the flat panel display.

The French physician Franz Joseph Gall (1758–1828) also thought that brains were related to minds. He examined the brains of animals and of people who had died of disease, or as healthy adults, or as children, and observed that mental ability often increases with larger brain size and decreases with damage to the brain. These aspects of Gall's findings were generally accepted (and the part about brain damage still is today). But Gall went far beyond his evidence to develop a psychological theory known as **phrenology,** *a now discredited theory that specific mental abilities and characteristics, ranging from memory to the capacity for happiness, are localized in specific regions of the brain* (see **FIGURE 1.1**). The idea that different parts of the brain are specialized for specific psychological functions turned out to be right; as you'll learn later in this textbook, a part of the brain called the *hippocampus* is intimately involved in memory, just as a structure called the *amygdala* is intimately involved in fear. But phrenology took this idea to an absurd extreme. Gall asserted that the size of bumps or indentations on the skull reflected the size of the brain regions beneath them and that by feeling those bumps, one could tell whether a person was friendly, cautious, assertive, idealistic, and so on. What Gall didn't realize was that bumps on the skull do not necessarily reveal anything about the shape of the brain underneath.

Phrenology made a nice parlor game and gave young people a good excuse for touching each other, but in the end it amounted to a series of strong claims based on weak evidence. Not surprisingly, his critics were galled (so to speak), and they ridiculed many of his proposals. Despite an initially large following, phrenology was quickly discredited (Fancher, 1979).

While Gall was busy playing bumpologist, other French scientists were beginning to link the brain and the mind in a more convincing manner. The biologist Marie Jean Pierre Flourens (1794–1867) was appalled by Gall's far-reaching claims and sloppy methods, so he conducted experiments in which he surgically removed specific parts of the brain from dogs, birds, and other animals and found (no surprise!) that their actions and movements differed from those of animals with intact brains.

The French surgeon Paul Broca (1824–1880) worked with a patient who had suffered damage to a small part of the left side of the brain (now known as *Broca's area*). The patient, Louis Victor Leborgne, was virtually unable to speak and could utter only the single syllable "tan." Yet Leborgne understood everything that was said to him and was able to communicate using gestures. Broca had the crucial insight that damage to a specific part of the brain impaired a specific mental function, clearly demonstrating that the brain and mind are closely linked. This was important in the 19th century because at that time many people still accepted Descartes' idea that the mind is separate from, but interacts with, the brain and the body. Broca and Flourens, then, were the first to demonstrate that the mind is grounded in a material substance, the brain. Their work jump-started the scientific investigation of mental processes.

STRUCTURALISM: A FIRST STEP TOWARD THE SCIENTIFIC METHOD

In the middle of the 19th century, psychology benefited from the work of German scientists who were trained in the field of **physiology,** *the study of biological processes, especially in the human body.* Physiologists had developed methods that allowed them to measure such things as the speed of nerve impulses, and some of them had begun to use these methods to measure mental abilities. William James was drawn to the work of two such physiologists: Hermann von Helmholtz (1821–1894) and Wilhelm Wundt (1832–1920). "It seems to me that perhaps the time has come for psychology to begin to be a science," James wrote in a letter during his visit to Berlin in 1867. "Helmholtz and a man called Wundt at Heidelberg are working at it." What attracted James to the work of these two scientists?

Helmholtz Measures the Speed of Responses

A brilliant experimenter with a background in both physiology and physics, Helmholtz had developed a method for measuring the speed of nerve impulses in a frog's leg that he then adapted to the study of human beings. Helmholtz trained his human partici-pants to respond when he applied a **stimulus**—*sensory input from the environment*—to different parts of the leg. He recorded his participants' **reaction time,** or *the amount of time taken to respond to a specific stimulus,* after applying the stimulus. Helmholtz found that people generally took longer to respond when the toe was stimulated than when the thigh was stimulated, and the difference between these reaction times al-lowed him to estimate how long it took a nerve impulse to travel to the brain. These results were astonishing to 19th-century scientists because, at that time, just about everyone thought that mental processes occurred instantaneously. When you move your hands in front of your eyes, you don't feel your hands move a fraction of a second before you see them. The real world doesn't appear like one of those late-night mov-ies in which the video and the audio are off by just a fraction of a second. Scientists assumed that the neurological processes underlying mental events *must* be instanta-neous for everything to be so nicely synchronized, but Helmholtz showed that this wasn't true. In so doing, he also demonstrated that reaction time could be a useful way to study the mind and the brain.

Wundt Opens the First Psychology Lab

Although Helmholtz's contributions were important, historians generally credit the official emergence of psychology to Helmholtz's research assistant, Wilhelm Wundt (Rieber, 1980). In 1867, at the University of Heidelberg, Wundt taught what was probably the first course in physiological psychology, which led to the publication of his book *Principles of Physiological Psychology,* in 1874. Wundt called the book "an at-tempt to mark out [psychology] as a new domain of science" (Fancher, 1979, p. 126). In 1879, at the University of Leipzig, Wundt opened the first laboratory exclusively devoted to psychological studies, an event that marked the official birth of psychology as an independent field of study. The new lab was full of graduate students carrying out research on topics assigned by Wundt, and it soon attracted young scholars from all over the world who were eager to learn about the new science that Wundt had developed.

Wundt believed that scientific psychology should focus on analyzing **consciousness,** *a person's subjective experience of the world and the mind.* Consciousness encompasses a broad range of subjective experiences. We may be conscious of sights, sounds, tastes, smells, bodily sensations, thoughts, or feelings. As Wundt tried to figure out a way to study consciousness scientifically, he noted that chemists try to understand the structure of matter by breaking down natural substances into basic elements. His students built on this approach, which later came to be known as **structuralism,** *the analysis of the basic elements that consti-tute the mind.* This approach involved breaking down consciousness into elemental sensations and feelings.

Introspection: An Attempt to Measure Consciousness You can do a bit of structuralism right now without leaving your chair. Consider the contents of your own consciousness. At this very moment you may be aware of the meaning of these words, the visual appearance of the letters on the page, the key ring pressing uncomfortably

By measuring a person's reaction times to different stimuli, Hermann von Helmholtz (1821–1894) estimated the length of time it takes a nerve impulse to travel to the brain.

HULTON ARCHIVE/GETTY IMAGES

phrenology A now discredited theory that specific mental abilities and characteristics, ranging from memory to the capacity for happiness, are localized in specific regions of the brain.

physiology The study of biological processes, especially in the human body.

stimulus Sensory input from the environment.

reaction time The amount of time taken to respond to a specific stimulus.

consciousness A person's subjective experience of the world and the mind.

structuralism The analysis of the basic elements that constitute the mind.

Wilhelm Wundt (1832–1920), far right, founded the first laboratory devoted exclusively to psychology at the University of Leipzig in Germany. He sought to understand consciousness by breaking it down into its basic parts, including individual sensations and feelings.

introspection The subjective observation of one's own experience.

Edward Titchener wasn't the first to try to identify the elements of conscious experience. As this drawing shows, the 17th-century physician and artist Robert Fludd tried to do the same thing—and was about equally successful.

against your thigh, your feelings of excitement or boredom (probably excitement), the smell of curried chicken salad, or the nagging question of how Ice Cube got his name. At any given moment, all sorts of things are swimming in your stream of consciousness. Wundt tried to analyze them in a systematic way using the method of **introspection,** *the subjective observation of one's own experience.* In a typical experiment, observers (usually students) were presented with a stimulus (usually a color or a sound) and then asked to report their introspections. The observers described the brightness of a color or the loudness of a tone. They reported on their "raw" sensory experience, rather than on their interpretations of that experience. For example, an observer presented with this page would not report seeing words on the page (which counts as an interpretation of the experience), but instead might describe a series of black marks, some straight and others curved, against a bright white background. Wundt also attempted to describe carefully the feelings associated with elementary perceptions. For example, when Wundt listened to the ticks produced by a metronome, some of the patterns of sounds were more pleasant than others. By analyzing the relation between feelings and perceptual sensations, Wundt and his students hoped to uncover the basic structure of conscious experience.

Wundt tried to provide objective measurements of conscious processes by using reaction-time techniques similar to those first developed by Helmholtz. Wundt used reaction times to examine a distinction between the perception and interpretation of a stimulus. His research participants were instructed to press a button as soon as a tone sounded. Some participants were told to concentrate on perceiving the tone before pressing the button, whereas others were told to concentrate only on pressing the button. Those people who concentrated on the tone responded about one tenth of a second more slowly than those told to concentrate only on pressing the button. Wundt reasoned that both fast and slow participants had to register the tone in consciousness, but only the slower participants also had to interpret the significance of the tone and press the button. The faster research participants, focusing only on the response they were to make, could respond automatically to the tone because they didn't have to engage in the additional step of interpretation (Fancher, 1979). This type of experimentation broke new ground by showing that psychologists could use scientific techniques to disentangle even subtle conscious processes. In fact, as you'll see in later chapters, reaction-time procedures have proven extremely useful in modern research.

Titchener Spreads Structuralism in North America The pioneering efforts of Wundt's laboratory launched psychology as an independent science and profoundly influenced the field for the remainder of the 19th century. Many European and American psychologists journeyed to Leipzig to study with Wundt. Among the most eminent was the British-born Edward Titchener (1867–1927), who studied with Wundt for 2 years in the early 1890s. Titchener then came to the United States and set up a psychology laboratory at Cornell University (where, if you'd ever like to see it, his brain is still on display in the psychology department). Titchener brought some parts of Wundt's approach to America, but he also made some changes (Brock, 1993; Rieber, 1980). For instance, whereas Wundt emphasized the relationship between elements of consciousness, Titchener focused on identifying the basic elements themselves. In his textbook *An Outline of Psychology* (1896), Titchener put forward a list of more than 44,000 elemental qualities of conscious experience, most of them visual (32,820) or auditory (11,600) (Schultz & Schultz, 1987).

Flaws Emerge The influence of the structuralist approach gradually faded, due mostly to the introspective method. Science requires replicable observations; we could never determine the structure of a cell or the life span of a dust mite if every scientist who looked through a microscope saw something different. Alas, even trained observers provided conflicting introspections about their conscious experiences

("I see a cloud that looks like a duck"—"No, I think that cloud looks like a horse"), thus making it difficult for different psychologists to agree on the basic elements of conscious experience. Indeed, some psychologists had doubts about whether it was even possible to identify such elements through introspection alone. One of the most prominent skeptics was someone you've already met: a young man with a bad attitude and a useless medical degree named William James.

FUNCTIONALISM: MENTAL PROCESSES AS ADAPTATIONS

James returned from his European tour inspired by the idea of approaching psychological issues from a scientific perspective. He received a teaching appointment at Harvard (primarily because the president of the university was a neighbor and family friend), and his position at Harvard enabled him to purchase laboratory equipment for classroom experiments. As a result, James taught the first course at an American university to draw on the new experimental psychology developed by Wundt and his German followers (Schultz & Schultz, 1987).

James agreed with Wundt on some points, including the importance of focusing on immediate experience and the usefulness of introspection as a technique (Bjork, 1983), but he disagreed with Wundt's claim that consciousness could be broken down into separate elements. James believed that trying to isolate and analyze a particular moment of consciousness (as the structuralists did) distorted the essential nature of consciousness. Consciousness, he argued, was more like a flowing stream than a bundle of individual components. So James decided to approach psychology from a different perspective entirely and developed an approach known as **functionalism,** the study of how mental processes enable people to adapt to their environments. In contrast to structuralism, which examined the structure of mental processes, functionalism set out to understand the functions those mental processes served. (See the Real World box for some strategies to enhance one of those functions—learning.)

James Draws Inspiration from Darwin

James's thinking was inspired by Charles Darwin's (1809–1882) recently published book on biological evolution, *On the Origin of Species by Means of Natural Selection* (1859). Darwin proposed the principle of **natural selection:** *The features of an organism that help it survive and reproduce are more likely than other features to be passed on to subsequent generations.* From this perspective, James reasoned, mental abilities must have evolved because they were adaptive, that is, because they helped people solve problems and increased their chances of survival. Like other animals, people have always needed to avoid predators, locate food, and attract mates. Applying Darwin's principle of natural selection, James (1890) reasoned that consciousness must serve an important biological function and that the task for psychologists was to understand what those functions are. Wundt and the other structuralists worked in laboratories, and James believed that such work was limited in its ability to tell us how consciousness functioned in the natural environment. Wundt, in turn, believed that James did not focus enough on new findings from the laboratory that he and the structuralists had begun to produce. Commenting on *The Principles of Psychology,* Wundt conceded that James was a topflight writer but disapproved of his approach: "It is literature, it is beautiful, but it is not psychology" (Bjork, 1983, p. 12).

Hall Champions Functionalism

The rest of the world did not agree, and James's functionalist psychology quickly gained followers, especially in North America, where Darwin's ideas were influencing many thinkers. G. Stanley Hall (1844–1924), who studied with both Wundt and

You don't have to look at this photo for more than a half-second to know that Vladimir Putin, the president of Russia, is not feeling very happy. William James suggested that your ability to read emotional expressions in an instant serves an important function that promotes your survival and well-being.

functionalism The study of how mental processes enable people to adapt to their environments.

natural selection Charles Darwin's theory that the features of an organism that help it survive and reproduce are more likely than other features to be passed on to subsequent generations.

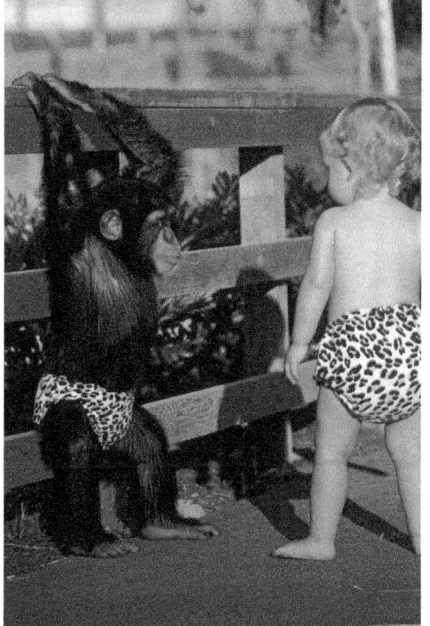

G. Stanley Hall believed that as they develop, children retrace the evolutionary history of our species, starting out as "mental cavemen" and ending up as . . . well, us.

Improving Study Skills

To get the most out of taking this course, you should begin by doing something that might seem a bit strange: Make it hard on yourself. But by making it hard on yourself in the right way, you will end up making the course easier and take away a lot more from it than you would otherwise.

What do we mean by making it hard on yourself? Our minds don't work like video cameras, passively recording everything that happens and then faithfully storing the information. In order to retain new information, you need to take an active role in learning, by doing such things as rehearsing, interpreting, and testing yourself. These activities initially might seem difficult, but in fact they are what psychologists call *desirable difficulties* (Bjork & Bjork, 2011): Making it more difficult by actively engaging during critical phases of learning will increase your retention and ultimately result in improved performance. Here are some specific suggestions:

- **Rehearse.** One useful type of active manipulation is rehearsal: repeating to-be-learned information to yourself. Psychologists have found that *spaced rehearsal* is a particularly effective strategy. In spaced rehearsal, you repeat information to yourself at increasingly longer intervals (Maddox & Balota, 2015). For example, suppose that you want to learn the name of a person you've just met named Eric. Repeat the name to yourself right away, wait a few seconds and think of it again, wait a bit longer (maybe 30 seconds) and bring the name to mind once more, then rehearse the name again after a minute and once more after 2 or 3 minutes. Making rehearsal gradually more difficult will improve retention; studies show that this type of rehearsal improves long-term learning more than rehearsing the name without any spacing between rehearsals (Landauer & Bjork, 1978). You can apply this technique to names, dates, definitions, and many other kinds of information, including concepts presented in this textbook.

- **Interpret.** Simple rehearsal can be beneficial, but one of the most important lessons from psychological research is that we acquire information most effectively when we think about its meaning and reflect on its significance. In fact, we don't even have to try to remember something if we think deeply enough about what we want to remember; the act of reflection itself will virtually guarantee good memory. For example, suppose that you want to learn the basic ideas behind Skinner's approach to behaviorism (see page 15). Ask yourself the following kinds of questions: How did behaviorism differ from previous approaches in psychology? How would a behaviorist such as Skinner think about psychological issues that interest you (for example, whether a mentally disturbed individual should be held responsible for committing a crime, or what factors would contribute to your choice of a major subject or career path)? In attempting to answer such questions, you will need to review what you've learned about behaviorism and then relate it to other things you already know about. This may seem like a demanding activity, but it is much easier to remember new information when you can relate it to something that already is familiar. The Critical Thinking questions that are sprinkled throughout this textbook will help you to reflect on and interpret the material. A happy consequence of that activity is that you will be more likely to remember the information that the questions engage you to think about.

- **Build.** Think about and review the information you have acquired in class on a regular basis. Begin soon after class, and then try to schedule regular "booster" sessions. Don't wait until the last second to cram your review into one sitting; as discussed in the "Rehearse" section, research shows that spacing out review and repetition leads to longer-lasting recall.

- **Test.** Don't just look at your class notes or this textbook; test yourself on the material as often as you can. As you will learn in the Memory and Learning chapters, research also shows that actively testing yourself on information you've acquired helps you to remember that information later more than just looking at it again. Testing yourself can also guard against a common pitfall. You may think that you have learned the material because it seems familiar to you after reviewing it several times, but just because the material seems familiar, that doesn't necessarily mean that you have learned it well enough to answer a test question. Testing yourself will alert you to when you need to study more, even when the information seems familiar. The Build to Outcomes questions that you will encounter at the ends of sections throughout this textbook are designed to test you and thereby increase learning and retention. Be sure to use them. The Learning Curve study aid will also help you to test and learn. (See the Preface for further discussion of Learning Curve.)

- **Hit the main points.** Take some of the load off your memory by developing effective note-taking and outlining skills. Students often scribble down vague and fragmentary notes during lectures, figuring that the notes will be good enough to jog their memory later. But when the time comes to study, they've forgotten so much that their notes are no longer clear. Realize that you can't write down everything an instructor says, and try to focus on making detailed notes about the main ideas, facts, and people mentioned in the lecture.

- **Organize.** The act of organizing an outline in a way that clearly highlights the major concepts will force you to reflect on the information in a way that promotes retention and will also provide you with a helpful study guide to promote self-testing and review. Again, this activity may seem

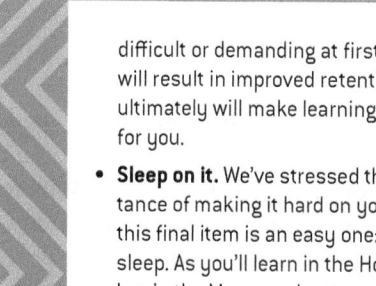

difficult or demanding at first, but it will result in improved retention and ultimately will make learning easier for you.

- **Sleep on it.** We've stressed the importance of making it hard on yourself, but this final item is an easy one: Get some sleep. As you'll learn in the Hot Science box in the Memory chapter, research shows that sleep helps us form lasting

memories. In fact, research shows that sleep does a particularly good job of increasing memory for important, meaningful material. So be sure to enlist sleep as an ally in your studying and test preparation.

▶ Anxious feelings about an upcoming exam may be unpleasant, but as you've probably experienced yourself, they can motivate much-needed study.

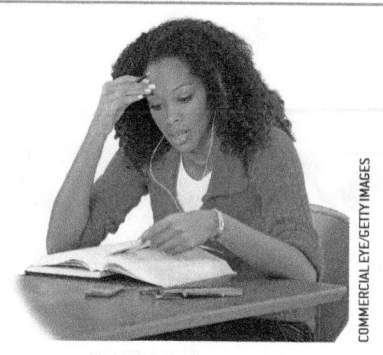

COMMERCIAL EYE/GETTY IMAGES

James, set up the first psychology research laboratory in North America at Johns Hopkins University in 1881. Hall's work focused on development and education and was strongly influenced by evolutionary thinking (Schultz & Schultz, 1987).

Hall believed that as children develop, they pass through stages that repeat the evolutionary history of the human race. Thus, the mental capacities of a young child resemble those of our ancient ancestors, and children grow over a lifetime in the same way that a species evolves over eons. Hall founded the *American Journal of Psychology* in 1887 (the first psychology journal in the United States), and went on to play a key role in founding the American Psychological Association (the first national organization of psychologists in the United States), serving as its first president.

The efforts of James and Hall set the stage for functionalism to develop as a major school of psychological thought in North America. Psychology departments that embraced a functionalist approach started to spring up at many major American universities, and in a struggle for survival that would have made Darwin proud, functionalism became more influential than structuralism had ever been. By the 1920s, functionalism was the dominant approach to psychology in North America.

Build to the Outcomes

1. What specifically do psychologists study?
2. Why were Greek philosophers unable to settle the dispute between nativism and philosophical empiricism?
3. How did Broca's study of a patient with brain damage help demonstrate the mind–brain connection?
4. How did Helmholtz's discovery about stimulus reaction time disprove previous assumptions about mental processes?
5. How did the approach of chemists influence Wundt's work?
6. What aspects of the theory of natural selection inspired James and Hall and the functionalist approach?

The Development of Clinical Psychology

At about the same time that some psychologists were developing structuralism and functionalism, other psychologists working in hospitals and outpatient health care clinics were beginning to study people with psychological disorders (psychologists and other mental health professionals working in outpatient clinics are referred to as *clinicians*). They began to realize that one can often understand how something works by examining how it breaks, and their observations of mental disorders influenced the development of clinical psychology.

Learning Outcomes

- ▶ Explain the insights that early clinicians brought to psychology.
- ▶ Outline Freud's major contributions.
- ▶ Explain how the humanist approach came to overtake Freud's ideas.

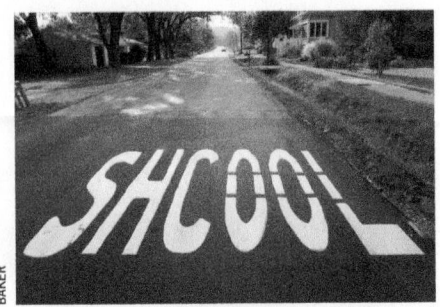

Mistakes can teach us a lot about how people think—or fail to think, as the case may be.

hysteria A temporary loss of cognitive or motor functions, usually as a result of emotionally upsetting experiences.

unconscious The part of the mind that operates outside of conscious awareness but influences conscious thoughts, feelings, and actions.

psychoanalytic theory An approach that emphasizes the importance of unconscious mental processes in shaping feelings, thoughts, and behavior.

psychoanalysis A therapeutic approach that focuses on bringing unconscious material into conscious awareness to better understand psychological disorders.

LESSONS FROM WORK WITH PATIENTS

The French physicians Jean-Martin Charcot (1825–1893) and Pierre Janet (1859–1947) reported striking observations when they interviewed patients who had developed a condition known then as **hysteria,** a *temporary loss of cognitive or motor functions, usually as a result of emotionally upsetting experiences.* Hysteric patients became blind, paralyzed, or lost their memories, even though there was no known physical cause of their problems. However, when the patients were put into a trance-like state through the use of hypnosis (an altered state of consciousness characterized by suggestibility), their symptoms disappeared: Blind patients could see, paralyzed patients could walk, and forgetful patients could remember. After coming out of the hypnotic trance, the patients forgot what had happened under hypnosis and again showed their symptoms. Each patient behaved like two different people in the waking versus hypnotic states.

These peculiar disorders were ignored by Wundt, Titchener, and other laboratory scientists, who did not consider them a proper subject for scientific psychology (Bjork, 1983). But William James believed they had important implications for understanding the nature of the mind (Taylor, 2001). He thought it was important to capitalize on these mental disruptions as a way of understanding the normal operation of the mind. During our ordinary conscious experience we are only aware of a single "me" or "self," but the aberrations described by Charcot, Janet, and others suggested that the brain can create many conscious selves that are not aware of each other's existence (James, 1890, p. 400). These striking observations also fueled the imagination of a young physician from Vienna, Austria, who had studied with Charcot in Paris in 1885. His name was Sigmund Freud (1856–1939).

FREUD DEVELOPS PSYCHOANALYTIC THEORY

After his visit to Charcot's clinic in Paris, Freud returned to Vienna, where he continued his work with hysteric patients. (The word *hysteria,* by the way, comes from the Latin word *hyster* [womb]. It was once believed that only women suffered from hysteria, which was thought to be caused by a "wandering womb.") Working with the physician Joseph Breuer (1842–1925), Freud began to make his own observations of hysteric patients and develop theories to explain their strange behaviors and symptoms. Freud theorized that many of the patients' problems could be traced to the effects of painful childhood experiences that the person could not remember, and he suggested that the powerful influence of these seemingly lost memories revealed the presence of an unconscious mind. According to Freud, the **unconscious** is *the part of the mind that operates outside of conscious awareness but influences conscious thoughts, feelings, and actions.* This idea led Freud to develop **psychoanalytic theory,** *an approach that emphasizes the importance of unconscious mental processes in shaping feelings, thoughts, and behaviors.* From a psychoanalytic perspective, it is important to uncover a person's early experiences and to illuminate a person's unconscious anxieties, conflicts, and desires. Psychoanalytic theory formed the basis for a therapy that Freud called **psychoanalysis,** which focuses on *bringing unconscious material into conscious awareness to better understand psychological disorders.* During psychoanalysis, patients recalled past experiences ("When I was a toddler, I was frightened by a masked man on a black horse") and related their dreams and fantasies ("Sometimes I close my eyes and imagine not having to pay for this session"). Psychoanalysts used Freud's theoretical approach to interpret what their patients said.

In the early 1900s, Freud and a growing number of followers formed a psychoanalytic movement. Carl Gustav Jung (1875–1961) and Alfred Adler (1870–1937) were prominent in the movement, but both were independent thinkers, and Freud apparently had little tolerance for individuals who challenged his ideas. Soon enough,

In this photograph, Sigmund Freud (1856–1939) sits by the couch reserved for his psychoanalytic patients, where they would be encouraged to recall past experiences and bring unconscious thoughts into awareness.

HISTORICAL/CORBIS

This famous psychology conference, held in 1909 at Clark University, was organized by G. Stanley Hall and brought together many notable figures, such as William James and Sigmund Freud. Both men are circled, with James on the left.

Freud broke off his relationships with both men so that he could shape the psychoanalytic movement himself (Sulloway, 1992). Psychoanalytic theory became quite controversial (especially in America) because it suggested that understanding a person's thoughts, feelings, and behavior required a thorough exploration of the person's early sexual experiences and unconscious sexual desires. In those days these topics were considered far too racy for scientific discussion.

Most of Freud's followers, like Freud himself, were trained as physicians and did not conduct psychological experiments in the laboratory (although early in his career, Freud did do some nice laboratory work on the sexual organs of eels). By and large, psychoanalysts did not hold positions in universities and developed their ideas in isolation from the research-based approaches of Wundt, Titchener, James, Hall, and others. One of the few times that Freud met with the leading academic psychologists was at a conference that G. Stanley Hall organized at Clark University in 1909. It was there that William James and Sigmund Freud met for the first time. Although James worked in an academic setting and Freud worked with clinical patients, both men believed that mental aberrations provide important clues into the nature of mind.

Most historians consider Freud to be one of the two or three most influential thinkers of the 20th century, and the psychoanalytic movement influenced everything from literature and history to politics and art. Within psychology, psychoanalysis had its greatest impact on clinical practice, but that influence has been considerably diminished over the past 40 years.

THE RISE OF HUMANISTIC PSYCHOLOGY

Freud's influence diminished partly because his vision of human nature was a dark one, emphasizing limitations and problems rather than possibilities and potentials. He saw people as hostages to their forgotten childhood experiences and primitive sexual

©CBW/ALAMY

Humanistic psychology offered a positive view of human nature that matched the zeitgeist of the 1960s, when open-air music festivals such as Woodstock drew massive crowds seeking peace and love.

humanistic psychology An approach to understanding human nature that emphasizes the positive potential of human beings.

impulses, and the inherent pessimism of his perspective frustrated those psychologists who had a more optimistic view of human nature. In America, the years after World War II were positive, invigorating, and upbeat: Poverty and disease were being conquered by technology, the standard of living of ordinary Americans was rising sharply, and people were landing on the moon. The era was characterized by the accomplishments—not the foibles—of the human mind, and Freud's viewpoint was out of step with the spirit of the times.

Freud's ideas were also difficult to test, and a theory that can't be tested is of limited use in psychology or other sciences. Although Freud's emphasis on unconscious processes has had an enduring impact on psychology, psychologists began to have serious misgivings about many aspects of Freud's theory.

It was in these times that psychologists such as Abraham Maslow (1908–1970) and Carl Rogers (1902–1987) pioneered a new movement called **humanistic psychology,** *an approach to understanding human nature that emphasizes the positive potential of human beings*. Humanistic psychologists focused on the highest aspirations that people have for themselves. Rather than regarding people as prisoners of events in their remote pasts, humanistic psychologists viewed people as free agents who have an inherent need to develop, grow, and attain their full potential. This movement reached its peak in the 1960s, when a generation of "flower children" found it easy to see psychological life as a kind of blossoming of the spirit. Humanistic therapists sought to help people realize their full potential; in fact, they called them *clients* rather than *patients*. In this relationship, the therapist and the client (unlike the psychoanalyst and the patient) were on an equal footing. The development of the humanistic perspective was one more reason that Freud's ideas eventually became less influential.

Build to the Outcomes

1. What did early clinicians learn from hypnotizing patients with hysteria?

2. What are the basic ideas behind psychoanalytic theory?

3. Why are Freud's ideas less influential today?

4. What are the basic ideas behind humanistic psychology?

The Search for Objective Measurement: Behaviorism Takes Center Stage

Learning Outcomes

▶ Compare the behaviorist approach with earlier approaches.

▶ Explain Skinner's principle of reinforcement.

behaviorism An approach that advocates that psychologists restrict themselves to the scientific study of objectively observable behavior.

Our discussion of the development of clinical psychology into the 1960s took us a little ahead of ourselves—we need to turn our attention back a few decades to understand some other important developments.

The schools of psychological thought that had developed by the early 20th century—structuralism, functionalism, and psychoanalysis—differed substantially from each other. But they shared an important similarity: Each tried to understand the inner workings of the mind by examining conscious perceptions, thoughts, memories, and feelings or by trying to elicit previously unconscious material, all of which were reported by participants in experiments or patients in a clinical setting. In each case it proved difficult to establish with much certainty just what was going on in people's minds, due to the unreliable nature of the methodology. As the 20th century unfolded, a new approach developed as psychologists challenged the idea that psychology should focus on mental life at all. This new approach was called **behaviorism,** which *advocated that psychologists* *restrict themselves* to *the scientific study of objectively observable behavior.* (See Other Voices: Is Psychology a Science? for a modern discussion of the science of psychology.) Behaviorism was a dramatic departure from previous schools of thought.

WATSON AND THE EMERGENCE OF BEHAVIORISM

John Broadus Watson (1878–1958) believed that private experience was too idiosyncratic and vague to be an object of scientific inquiry. Science required replicable, objective measurements of phenomena that were accessible to all observers, and the introspective methods used by structuralists and functionalists were far too subjective for that. So instead of describing conscious experiences, Watson proposed that psychologists focus entirely on the study of behavior—what people *do,* rather than what people *experience*—because behavior can be observed by anyone and it can be measured objectively. Watson thought that a focus on behavior would put a stop to the endless philosophical debates among psychologists and that it would foster practical applications in such areas as business, medicine, law, and education. The goal of scientific psychology, according to Watson, should be to predict and to control behavior in ways that benefit society.

Why would someone want to throw the mind out of psychology? This may seem excessive, until you notice that Watson studied the behavior of animals such as rats and birds. In such studies, inferring a mind is a matter of some debate. Shall we say that dogs have minds, for instance, but leave out pigeons? If we include pigeons, what about worms? Animal behavior specialists staked out claims in this area. In 1908, Margaret Floy Washburn (1871–1939) published *The Animal Mind,* in which she reviewed what was then known about perception, learning, and memory in different animal species. She argued that nonhuman animals, much like human ones, have conscious mental experiences (Scarborough & Furumoto, 1987). Watson reacted to this claim with venom. Because we cannot ask pigeons about their private, inner experiences (well, we can ask, but they never will tell us), Watson decided that the only way to understand how animals learn and adapt was to focus solely on their behavior, and he suggested that the study of human beings should proceed on the same basis.

Watson was influenced by the work of the Russian physiologist Ivan Pavlov (1849–1936), who carried out pioneering research on the physiology of digestion. In the course of that work, Pavlov noticed something interesting about the dogs he was studying (Fancher, 1979). Not only did the dogs salivate at the sight of food; they also salivated at the sight of the person who fed them. The feeders were not dressed in Alpo suits, so why should the mere sight of them trigger a basic digestive response in the dogs? To answer this question, Pavlov developed a procedure in which he sounded a tone every time he fed the dogs, and after a while he observed that the dogs would salivate when they heard the tone alone. In Pavlov's experiments, the sound of the tone was a *stimulus* (sensory input from the environment) that influenced the salivation of the dogs, which was a **response:** *an action or physiological change elicited by a stimulus.* Watson and other behaviorists made these two notions the building blocks of their theories, which is why behaviorism is sometimes called *stimulus–response* (S–R) psychology.

Watson applied Pavlov's techniques to human infants. In a famous and controversial study, Watson and his student Rosalie Rayner taught an infant known as "Little Albert" to have a strong fear of a harmless white rat (and other white furry animals and toys) that he had previously not feared. Why would they do such a thing? You'll learn more about this study in the Learning chapter, but the short answer is this: Watson believed that human behavior is powerfully influenced by the environment, and the experiments with Little Albert provided a chance to demonstrate such influence at the earliest stage of life. Neither Watson nor later behaviorists believed that the environment was the *only* influence on behavior (Todd & Morris, 1992), but they did think it was the most important one.

In 1894, Margaret Floy Washburn (1871–1939), a student of Edward Titchener at Cornell, became the first woman to receive a PhD degree in psychology. Washburn went on to a highly distinguished career, spent mainly in teaching and research at Vassar College in Poughkeepsie, New York. Washburn wrote an influential book, *The Animal Mind;* developed a theory of consciousness; and contributed to the development of psychology as a profession.

response An action or physiological change elicited by a stimulus.

Is Psychology a Science?

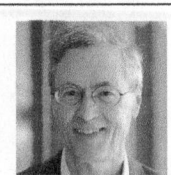

Timothy D. Wilson is a professor of psychology at the University of Virginia and the author of several popular books, including *Redirect: The Surprising New Science of Psychological Change* (2011).

PHOTO BY JEN FARIELLO, COURTESY TIMOTHY D. WILSON

Nobody can dispute that you are taking a course in psychology, but are you taking a science course? Some critics maintain that psychology fails to meet accepted criteria for what constitutes a science. Timothy Wilson, a psychology professor at the University of Virginia, took on the critics by drawing from an appropriate source: the scientific literature (Wilson, 2012).

Once, during a meeting at my university, a biologist mentioned that he was the only faculty member present from a science department. When I corrected him, noting that I was from the Department of Psychology, he waved his hand dismissively, as if I were a Little Leaguer telling a member of the New York Yankees that I too played baseball. There has long been snobbery in the sciences, with the "hard" ones (physics, chemistry, biology) considering themselves to be more legitimate than the "soft" ones (psychology, sociology). It is thus no surprise that many members of the general public feel the same way. But of late, skepticism about the rigors of social science has reached absurd heights.

The U.S. House of Representatives recently voted to eliminate funding for political science research through the National Science Foundation. In the wake of that action, an opinion writer for the *Washington Post* suggested that the House didn't go far enough. The NSF should not fund any research in the social sciences, wrote Charles Lane, because "unlike hypotheses in the hard sciences, hypotheses about society usually can't be proven or disproven by experimentation."

Lane's comments echoed ones by Gary Gutting in the Opinionator blog of the *New York Times*. "While the physical sciences produce many detailed and precise predictions," wrote Gutting, "the social sciences do not. The reason is that such predictions almost always require randomized controlled experiments, which are seldom possible when people are involved."

This is news to me and the many other social scientists who have spent their careers doing carefully controlled experiments on human behavior, inside and outside the laboratory. What makes the criticism so galling is that those who voice it, or members of their families, have undoubtedly benefited from research in the disciplines they dismiss.

Most of us know someone who has suffered from depression and sought psychotherapy. He or she probably benefited from therapies, such as cognitive behavioral therapy, that have been shown to work in randomized clinical trials.

Problems such as child abuse and teenage pregnancy take a huge toll on society. Interventions developed by research psychologists, tested with the experimental method, have been found to lower the incidence of child abuse and reduce the rate of teenage pregnancies.

Ever hear of stereotype threat? It is the double jeopardy that people face when they are at risk of confirming a negative stereotype of their group. When African American students take a difficult test, for example, they are concerned not only about how well they will do but also about the possibility that performing poorly will reflect badly on their entire group. This added worry has been shown time and again, in carefully controlled experiments, to lower academic performance. But fortunately, experiments have also showed promising ways to reduce this threat. One intervention, for example, conducted in a middle school, reduced the achievement gap by 40%.

If you know someone who was unlucky enough to be arrested for a crime he didn't commit, he may have benefited from social psychological experiments that have resulted in fairer lineups and interrogations, making it less likely that innocent people are convicted.

An often-overlooked advantage of the experimental method is that it can demonstrate what doesn't work. Consider three popular programs that research psychologists have debunked: Critical Incident Stress Debriefing, used to prevent post-traumatic stress disorders in first responders and others who have witnessed horrific events; the D.A.R.E. anti-drug program, used in many schools throughout America; and Scared Straight programs designed to prevent at-risk teens from engaging in criminal behavior.

All three of these programs have been shown, with well-designed experimental studies, to be ineffective or, in some cases, to make matters worse. And as a result, the programs have become less popular or have changed their methods. By discovering what doesn't work, social scientists have saved the public billions of dollars.

To be fair to the critics, social scientists have not always taken advantage of the experimental method as much as they could. Too often, for example, educational programs have been implemented widely without being adequately tested. But increasingly, educational researchers are employing better methodologies. For example, in a recent study, researchers randomly assigned teachers to a program called My Teaching Partner, which is designed to improve teaching skills, or to a control group. Students taught by the teachers who participated in the program did significantly better on achievement tests than did students taught by teachers in the control group.

Are the social sciences perfect? Of course not. Human behavior is complex, and it is not possible to conduct experiments to test all aspects of what people do or why. There are entire disciplines devoted to the experimental study of human behavior, however, in tightly controlled, ethically acceptable ways. Many people benefit from the results, including those who, in their ignorance, believe that science is limited to the study of molecules.

Wilson's examples of psychological investigations that have had beneficial effects on society are excellent, but perhaps even more important is his point that much of psychology is based on carefully controlled experimentation using randomization procedures that the critics apparently believe—mistakenly—cannot be applied to the study of human beings. The next chapter in this textbook is devoted to explaining how psychologists apply the scientific method to the study of the mind and behavior. It should come as no surprise to learn that your textbook authors believe that psychology is indeed a science. But what *kind* of science is psychology? (See the Hot Science box for one approach to this question.) Should psychology strive to come up with general laws like those of physics or try to make precise predictions like those made by the so-called hard sciences? Should psychologists focus on laboratory experimentation or spend more effort attempting to study behavior in everyday life? What methods seem most promising to you as tools for psychological investigations? There is room for debate about what kind of science psychology is and should be; we hope that you think about these questions as you read this textbook.

Wilson, T. D. (July 12, 2012). Stop Bullying the 'Soft' Sciences. In *The Los Angeles Times* (Op Ed). Copyright 2012 Timothy D. Wilson and Sherrell J. Aston. Reproduced by permission.

B. F. SKINNER AND THE DEVELOPMENT OF BEHAVIORISM

In 1926, Burrhus Frederick Skinner (1904–1990) graduated from Hamilton College. Like William James, Skinner was a young man who couldn't decide what to do with his life. He aspired to become a writer, and his interest in literature led him indirectly to psychology. Skinner wondered whether a novelist could portray a character without understanding why the character behaved as he or she did, and when he came across Watson's books, he knew he had the answer. Skinner completed his PhD studies in psychology at Harvard (Wiener, 1996) and began to develop a new kind of behaviorism. In Pavlov's experiments, the dogs had been passive participants that stood around, listened to tones, and drooled. Skinner recognized that in everyday life, animals don't just stand there—they do something! Animals *act* on their environments in order to find shelter, food, or mates, and Skinner wondered if he could develop behaviorist principles that would explain how they *learned* to act in those situations.

Skinner built what he called a *conditioning chamber* but what the rest of the world would forever call a *Skinner box*. The box has a lever and a food tray, and a hungry rat could get food delivered to the tray by pressing the lever. Skinner observed that when a rat was put in the box, it would wander around, sniffing and exploring, and would usually press the bar by accident, at which point a food pellet would drop into the tray. After that happened, the rate of bar pressing would increase dramatically and remain high until the rat was no longer hungry. Skinner saw evidence for what he called the principle of **reinforcement,** which states that *the consequences of a behavior determine whether it will be more or less likely to occur again*. The concept of reinforcement became the foundation for Skinner's new approach to behaviorism (see the Learning chapter), which he formulated in a landmark book, *The Behavior of Organisms: An Experimental Analysis* (Skinner, 1938).

Real-World Application

Skinner set out to use his ideas about reinforcement to help improve the quality of everyday life. He was visiting his daughter's fourth-grade class when he realized that he might be able to improve classroom instruction by breaking a complicated task into small bits and then using the principle of reinforcement to teach the children each bit (Bjork, 1993). He developed automatic devices known as *teaching machines* that did exactly that (Skinner, 1958). The teaching machine asked a series of increasingly difficult questions that built on the students' answers to the simpler ones. To solve a complicated math problem, for instance, students would first be asked an easy question about the simplest part of the problem. They would then be told whether the answer was right or wrong, and if they gave a correct response, the machine would move on to a more difficult question. (This important innovation is incorporated in modern approaches to enhancing learning, such as the LearningCurve program discussed in the Preface [p. xxx]). Skinner thought that the satisfaction of knowing they were correct would be reinforcing and help students learn.

Real-World Overreach

If fourth graders and rats could be successfully trained, then why stop there? In the controversial books *Beyond Freedom and Dignity* (1971) and *Walden II* (1948/1986), Skinner laid out his vision of a utopian society in which behavior was controlled by the judicious application of the principle of reinforcement (Skinner, 1971). In those books he put forth the simple but stunning claim that our subjective sense of free will is an illusion and that when we think we are exercising free will, we are actually responding to present and past patterns of reinforcement. We do things in the present that were rewarding in the past, and our sense of "choosing" to do them is nothing more than an illusion. In this, Skinner echoed the sentiments of philosopher Baruch

Inspired by John B. Watson's behaviorism, B. F. Skinner (1904–1990) investigated the way an animal learns by interacting with its environment. Here, he demonstrates the Skinner box, in which rats learn to press a lever to receive food: The lever press is the learned behavior, and the food is the reinforcement that increases the frequency of future lever pressing.

reinforcement The consequences of a behavior determine whether it will be more or less likely to occur again.

B. F. Skinner's well-publicized questioning of such cherished notions as free will led to a rumor that he had raised his own daughter in a Skinner box. This urban legend, though untrue, likely originated from the climate-controlled, glass-encased crib that he invented to protect his daughter from the cold Minnesota winter. Skinner marketed the crib under various names, including the "Air-Crib" and the "Heir Conditioner," but it failed to catch on with parents.

Spinoza (1632–1677), who several centuries earlier had noted that "men are deceived in thinking themselves free, a belief that consists only in this, that they are conscious of their actions and ignorant of the causes by which they are determined. As to their saying that human actions depend on the will, these are mere words without any corresponding idea" (1677/1982, p. 86).

Skinner argued that his insights could be used to increase human well-being and solve social problems. It is not surprising that this claim sparked an outcry from critics who believed that Skinner was giving away one of our most cherished attributes—free will—and calling for a repressive society that manipulated people for its own ends. One magazine even called his ideas "the taming of mankind through a system of dog obedience schools for all" (Bjork, 1993, p. 201). Given the nature of Skinner's ideas, the critics' attacks were understandable—he had seriously underestimated how much people cherish the idea of free will—but in the sober light of hindsight, they were clearly overblown. Skinner did not want to turn society into a "dog obedience school" or strip people of their personal freedoms. Rather, he argued that an understanding of the principles by which behavior is generated could be used to improve the social welfare, which is precisely what happens when a government launches advertisements to encourage citizens to drink milk or quit smoking. The result of all the controversy, however, was that Skinner's fame reached a level rarely attained by psychologists. A popular magazine that listed the 100 most important people who have ever lived ranked Skinner just 39 points below Jesus Christ (Herrnstein, 1977).

Build to the Outcomes

1. What shared idea behind structuralism, functionalism, and psychoanalysis did the behaviorists challenge?

2. What did Watson believe should be the goal of scientific psychology?

3. What technique, borrowed from Pavlov, did Watson famously apply to a human infant?

4. What were the results of the research done with the Skinner box?

5. Which of Skinner's claims provoked an outcry?

Return of the Mind: Psychology Expands

Learning Outcomes

▶ Outline the research into mental processes that filled gaps left by the work of behaviorists.

▶ Explain how new technologies furthered the field of cognitive neuroscience.

▶ Describe the ideas behind evolutionary psychology.

Watson, Skinner, and the behaviorists dominated psychology from the 1930s to the 1950s. The psychologist Ulric Neisser recalled the atmosphere when he was a student at Swarthmore in the early 1950s:

> Behaviorism was the basic framework for almost all of psychology at the time. It was what you had to learn. That was the age when it was supposed that no psychological phenomenon was real unless you could demonstrate it in a rat (quoted in Baars, 1986, p. 275).

Behaviorism wouldn't dominate the field for much longer, however, and Neisser himself would play an important role in developing an alternative perspective. Why was behaviorism replaced? Although behaviorism allowed psychologists to measure, predict, and control behavior, it did this by ignoring some important things. First, it ignored the mental processes that had fascinated psychologists such as Wundt and James and, in so doing, found itself unable to explain some very important phenomena, such as how children learn language. Second, it ignored the evolutionary history of the organisms it studied and was thus unable to explain why, for example, a rat could learn to associate nausea with food much more quickly than it could learn to associate nausea with a tone or a light. As we will see, the approaches that ultimately replaced behaviorism met these kinds of problems head-on.

PIONEERING IDEAS LEAD TO COGNITIVE PSYCHOLOGY

Even at the height of behaviorist domination, there were a few revolutionaries whose research and writings were focused on mental processes. This research, which came to be known as cognitive psychology, focused on the study of mental or cognitive processes such as perception, memory, subjective experience, attention, and language.

Insights Into How the Mind Organizes What We See

The German psychologist Max Wertheimer (1880–1943) focused on the study of **illusions,** *errors of perception, memory, or judgment in which subjective experience differs from objective reality.* In one of Wertheimer's experiments, a person was shown two lights that flashed quickly on a screen, one after the other. One light was flashed through a vertical slit, the other through a diagonal slit. When the time between two flashes was relatively long (one fifth of a second or more), an observer would see that it was just two lights flashing in alternation. But when Wertheimer reduced the time between flashes to around one twentieth of a second, observers saw a single flash of light moving back and forth (Fancher, 1979; Sarris, 1989). Wertheimer reasoned that the perceived motion could not be explained in terms of the separate elements that cause the illusion (the two flashing lights) but instead that the moving flash of light is perceived as a *whole* rather than as the sum of its two parts. This unified whole, which in German is called *Gestalt,* makes up the perceptual experience. Wertheimer's interpretation of the illusion led to the development of **Gestalt psychology,** *a psychological approach that emphasizes that we often perceive the whole rather than the sum of the parts.* In other words, the mind imposes organization on what it perceives, so people don't see what the experimenter actually shows them (two separate lights); instead, they see the elements as a unified whole (one moving light).

Insights into How the Mind Organizes Memory

Another pioneer who focused on the mind was Sir Frederic Bartlett (1886–1969), a British psychologist interested in memory. Bartlett was dissatisfied with existing research, especially the research of the German psychologist Hermann Ebbinghaus (1850–1909), who had performed groundbreaking experiments on memory in 1885 (described in the Memory chapter). Ebbinghaus, serving as his own research subject, tried to discover how quickly and how well he could memorize and recall meaningless information, such as the three-letter nonsense syllables *dap, kir,* and *sul.* Bartlett believed that it was more important to examine memory for the kinds of information people actually encounter in everyday life, so he gave people stories to remember and carefully observed the kinds of errors they made when they tried to recall them at a later time (Bartlett, 1932). Bartlett discovered many interesting things that Ebbinghaus could never have learned with his nonsense syllables. For example, he found that research participants often remembered what *should* have happened or what they *expected* to happen rather than what actually *did* happen. These and other errors led Bartlett to suggest that memory is not a photographic reproduction of past experience and that our attempts to recall the past are powerfully influenced by our knowledge, beliefs, hopes, aspirations, and desires.

Insights into Child Development

Jean Piaget (1896–1980) was a Swiss psychologist who studied children's perceptual and cognitive errors in order to gain insight into the nature and

What do you see when you look at this image? Why do you see more than just random markings?

illusions Errors of perception, memory, or judgment in which subjective experience differs from objective reality.

Gestalt psychology A psychological approach that emphasizes that we often perceive the whole rather than the sum of the parts.

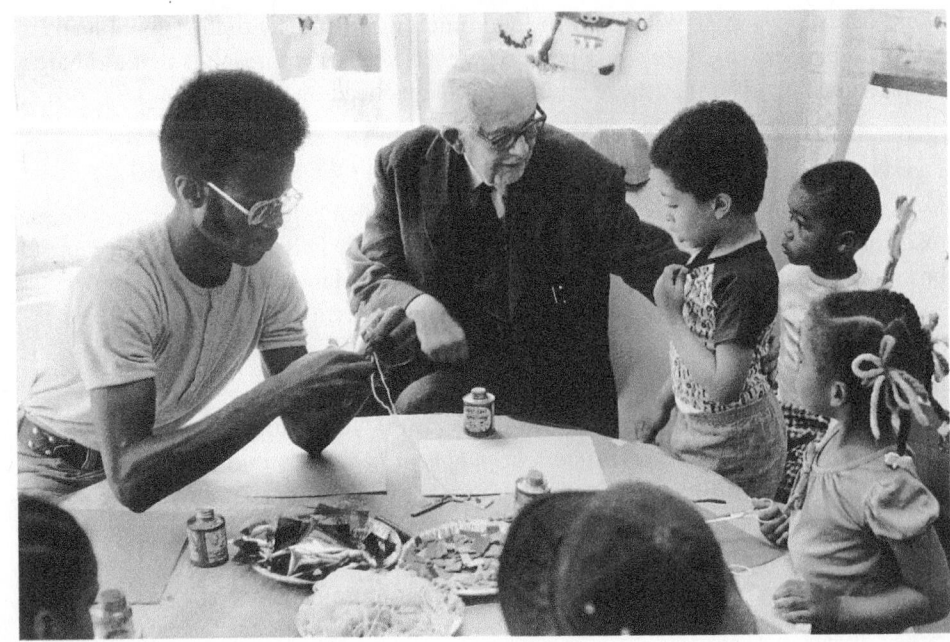

Jean Piaget (1896–1980) studied and theorized about the developing mental lives of children. How were his methods a marked departure from the methods of the behaviorists?

development of the human mind. For example, in one of his tasks, Piaget gave 3-year-olds a large and a small mound of clay and told the child to make the two mounds equal. Then Piaget broke one of the clay mounds into smaller pieces and asked the child which mound now had more clay. Although the amount of clay remained the same, of course, 3-year-olds usually said that the mound that was broken into smaller pieces was bigger, but by the age of 6 or 7, they no longer made this error. As you'll see in the Development chapter, Piaget theorized that younger children lack a particular cognitive ability that allows older children to appreciate the fact that the mass of an object remains constant even when it is divided. For Piaget, errors such as these provided key insights into the mental world of the child (Piaget & Inhelder, 1969).

The Importance of Personal Experience

The German psychologist Kurt Lewin (1890–1947), another pioneer in the study of thought, argued that a person's behavior in the world could be predicted best by understanding the person's subjective experience of the world. A television soap opera is a meaningless series of unrelated physical movements unless one thinks about the characters' experiences (how Karen feels about Bruce; what Van was planning to say to Kathy about Emily; and whether Linda's sister, Nancy, will always hate their mother for meddling in her marriage, etc.). Lewin realized that it was not the stimulus but rather the person's *construal* of the stimulus, that determined the person's subsequent behavior. A pinch on the cheek can be pleasant or unpleasant depending on who administers it, under what circumstances, and to which set of cheeks. Lewin used a special kind of mathematics called *topology* to model the person's subjective experience, and although his topological theories were not particularly influential, his attempts to model mental life and his insistence that psychologists study how people construe their worlds had a lasting impact on psychology.

Computers Enter the Scene

Aside from a handful of pioneers such as these, most psychologists happily ignored mental processes until the 1950s, when something important happened: the computer. The advent of computers had enormous practical impact, of course, but

Kurt Lewin argued that people react to the world as they see it and not to the world as it is.

it also had an enormous conceptual impact on psychology. People and computers differ in important ways, but both seem to register, store, and retrieve information, leading psychologists to wonder whether the computer might be useful as a model for the human mind. Computers are information-processing systems, and the flow of information through their circuits is clearly no fairy tale. If psychologists could think of mental events—such as remembering, attending, thinking, believing, evaluating, feeling, and assessing—as the flow of information through the mind, then they might be able to study the mind scientifically after all. The emergence of the computer led to a reemergence of interest in mental processes all across the discipline of psychology, and spawned a new approach called **cognitive psychology,** *the scientific study of mental processes, including perception, thought, memory, and reasoning.*

Insights into the Limits of Attention

Although the contributions of psychologists such as Wertheimer, Bartlett, Piaget, and Lewin provided early alternatives to behaviorism, they did not depose it. That job required the army. During World War II, the military turned to psychologists to help understand how soldiers could best learn to use new technologies, such as radar. Radar operators had to pay close attention to their screens for long periods while trying to decide whether blips were friendly aircraft, enemy aircraft, or flocks of wild geese in need of a good chasing (Ashcraft, 1998; Lachman, Lachman, & Butterfield, 1979). How could radar operators be trained to make quicker and more accurate decisions? The answer to this question clearly required more than the swift delivery of pellets to the radar operator's food tray. It required that those who designed the equipment think about and talk about cognitive processes, such as perception, attention, identification, memory, and decision making.

The British psychologist Donald Broadbent (1926–1993) was among the first to study what happens when people try to pay attention to several things at once. For instance, Broadbent observed that pilots can't attend to many different instruments at once and must actively move the focus of their attention from one to another (Best, 1992). Broadbent (1958) showed that the limited capacity to handle incoming information is a fundamental feature of human cognition and that this limit could explain many of the errors that pilots (and other people) made. At about the same time, the American psychologist George Miller (1956) pointed out a striking consistency in our capacity limitations across a variety of situations: We can pay attention to, and briefly hold in memory, about seven (give or take two) pieces of information. Cognitive psychologists began conducting experiments and devising theories to better understand the mind's limited capacity, a problem that behaviorists had ignored.

The Gift of Human Language

As you have already read, the invention of the computer in the 1950s had a profound impact on psychologists' thinking. A computer is made of hardware (e.g., chips and disk drives today; magnetic tapes and vacuum tubes a half century ago) and software (stored on optical disks today; on punch cards a half century ago). If the brain was roughly analogous to the computer's hardware, then perhaps the mind was roughly analogous to a software program. This line of thinking led cognitive psychologists to begin writing computer programs to see what kinds of software could be made to mimic human speech and behavior (Newell, Shaw, & Simon, 1958).

It is ironic that the emergence of cognitive psychology was also energized by the appearance of B. F. Skinner's (1957) book *Verbal Behavior,* which offered a behaviorist analysis of language. A linguist at the Massachusetts Institute of Technology (MIT), Noam Chomsky (b. 1928), published a devastating critique of this book, arguing that Skinner's insistence on observable behavior had caused him to miss some of

This 1950s computer was among the first generation of digital computers. How was the computer analogy helpful in the early days of cognitive psychology?

cognitive psychology The scientific study of mental processes, including perception, thought, memory, and reasoning.

Noam Chomsky (b. 1928) pointed out that even young children generate sentences they have never heard before and therefore could not possibly be learning language by reinforcement. This critique of Skinner's theory signaled the end of behaviorism's dominance in psychology and helped spark the development of cognitive psychology.

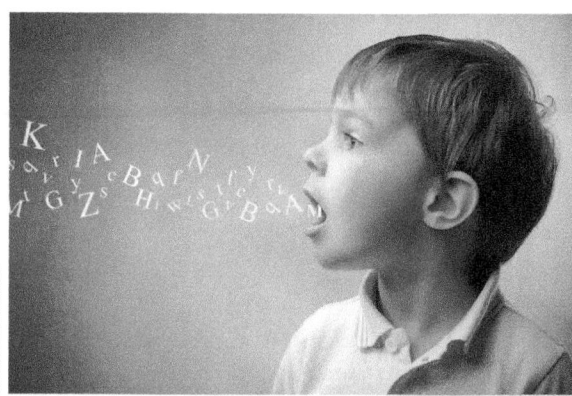

the most important features of language. According to Chomsky, language relies on mental rules that allow people to understand and produce novel words and sentences. The ability of even the youngest child to generate new sentences that he or she has never heard before flew in the face of the behaviorist claim that children learn to use language by reinforcement. Chomsky provided a clever, detailed, and thoroughly cognitive account of language that could explain many of the phenomena that the behaviorist account could not (Chomsky, 1959).

These developments during the 1950s set the stage for an explosion of cognitive studies during the 1960s. Cognitive psychologists did not return to the old introspective procedures of the 19th century but instead developed new and ingenious methods that allowed them to study cognitive processes. The excitement of the new approach was summarized in a landmark book, *Cognitive Psychology*, written by someone you met earlier in this chapter, Ulric Neisser. Neisser's (1967) book provided a foundation for the development of cognitive psychology, which grew and thrived in the years that followed.

THE BRAIN MEETS THE MIND: THE RISE OF COGNITIVE NEUROSCIENCE

Although cognitive psychologists studied the software of the mind, they had little to say about the hardware of the brain. And yet, as any computer scientist knows, the relationship between software and hardware is crucial: Each element needs the other to get the job done. Our mental activities often seem so natural and effortless—noticing the shape of an object, using words in speech or writing, recognizing a face as familiar—that we fail to appreciate the fact that they depend on intricate operations carried out by the brain. This dependence is revealed by dramatic cases in which damage to a particular part of the brain causes a person to lose a specific cognitive ability. Recall that in the 19th century, the French physician Paul Broca described a patient who, after damage to a limited area in the left side of the brain, could not produce words, even though he could understand them perfectly well. As you'll see later in this textbook, damage to other parts of the brain can also result in syndromes that are characterized by the loss of specific mental abilities (e.g., prosopagnosia, in which the person cannot recognize human faces) or by the emergence of bizarre behavior or beliefs (e.g., Capgras syndrome, in which the person believes that a close family member has been replaced by an imposter). These striking—sometimes startling—cases remind us that even the simplest cognitive processes depend on the brain.

Behavioral Neuroscience Emerges

Karl Lashley (1890–1958), a psychologist who studied with John B. Watson, conducted a famous series of studies in which he trained rats to run mazes, surgically removed parts of their brains, and then measured how well they could run the maze again. Lashley hoped to find the precise spot in the brain where *learning* occurred. Alas, no one spot seemed to uniquely and reliably eliminate learning (Lashley, 1960). Rather, Lashley simply found that the more of the rat's brain he removed, the more poorly the rat ran the maze. Lashley was frustrated by his inability to identify a specific site of learning, but his efforts inspired other scientists to take up the challenge. They developed a research area called *physiological psychology*. Today, this area has grown into **behavioral neuroscience,** *an approach to psychology that links psychological processes to activities in the nervous system and to other bodily processes.* To learn about the relationship between brain and behavior, behavioral neuroscientists observe animals' responses as the animals perform specially constructed tasks, such as running through a maze to obtain food rewards. The neuroscientist can record electrical or chemical responses in the brain as the task is being performed or later remove specific parts of the brain to see how performance is affected.

behavioral neuroscience An approach to psychology that links psychological processes to activities in the nervous system and other bodily processes.

Noninvasive Brain Scanning Techniques Unravel Mysteries

Of course, experimental brain surgery cannot ethically be performed on human beings; thus, psychologists who want to study the human brain often have to rely on nature's cruel and inexact experiments. Birth defects, accidents, and illnesses often cause damage to particular brain regions, and if that damage disrupts a particular ability, then psychologists deduce that the region is involved in producing the ability. For example, in the Memory chapter you'll learn about a patient whose memory was virtually eliminated by damage to a specific part of the brain, and you'll see how this tragedy provided scientists with remarkable clues about how memories are stored (Scoville & Milner, 1957). But in the late 1980s, technological breakthroughs led to the development of noninvasive brain scanning techniques that made it possible for psychologists to watch what happens inside a human brain as a person performs a task such as reading, imagining, listening, or remembering. Brain scanning is an invaluable tool because it allows us to observe the brain in action and to see which parts are involved in which operations (see the Neuroscience and Behavior chapter).

For example, researchers used scanning technology to identify the parts of the brain in the left hemisphere that are involved in specific aspects of language, such as understanding or producing words (Peterson et al., 1989). Later scanning studies showed that people who are deaf from birth, but who learn to communicate using American Sign Language (ASL), rely on regions in the right hemisphere (as well as the left) when using ASL. In contrast, people with normal hearing who learned ASL after puberty seemed to rely only on the left hemisphere when using ASL (Newman et al., 2002). These findings suggest that although both spoken and signed language usually rely on the left hemisphere, the right hemisphere also can become involved—but only for a limited period (perhaps until puberty). The findings also provide a nice example of how psychologists can now use scanning techniques to observe people with various kinds of cognitive capacities and use their observations to unravel the mysteries of the mind and the brain (see **FIGURE 1.2**).

▼ Figure 1.2

FUNCTIONAL MAGNETIC RESONANCE IMAGING (fMRI) is one of several brain imaging technologies that psychologists use to observe the living brain. These images come from a study by O'Brien and colleagues (2010) in which 51 elderly adults (average age 74.8 years) were scanned when they first entered the study and then again two years later. The top row shows scans from 21 participants who were judged to be cognitively normal on a Clinical Dementia Rating (CDR 0). The bottom row shows scans from 30 participants who initially showed mild cognitive impairment (CDR 0.5). When the scans were repeated two years later, and compared with the baseline scans (Baseline - 2 Year on the right side of the figure), CDR 0.5 participants showed significantly reduced activity in the hippocampus, a structure that is important for memory, whereas CDR 0 patients showed no change in hippocampal activity.

In 1925, the schoolteacher John Scopes was arrested for teaching students about Darwin's theory of evolution. Today, that theory is the centerpiece of modern biology—and of evolutionary psychology.

cognitive neuroscience The field of study that attempts to understand the links between cognitive processes and brain activity.

evolutionary psychology A psychological approach that explains mind and behavior in terms of the adaptive value of abilities that are preserved over time by natural selection.

Behaviorists explain behavior in terms of organisms learning to make particular responses that are paired with reinforcement (and to avoid responses that are paired with punishment). Evolutionary psychology focuses on how abilities are preserved over time if they contribute to an organism's ability to survive and reproduce. How might a proponent of each approach explain the fact that a rat placed in an unfamiliar environment will tend to stay in dark corners and avoid brightly lit open areas?

In fact, there's a name for this area of research. **Cognitive neuroscience** is the *field of study that attempts to understand the links between cognitive processes and brain activity* (Gazzaniga, 2000).

THE ADAPTIVE MIND: THE EMERGENCE OF EVOLUTIONARY PSYCHOLOGY

Psychology's renewed interest in mental processes and its growing interest in the brain were two developments that led psychologists away from behaviorism. A third development also pointed them in a different direction. In experiments conducted during the 1960s and 1970s, the psychologist John Garcia and his colleagues showed that rats can learn to associate nausea with the smell of food much more quickly than they can learn to associate nausea with a flashing light (Garcia, 1981). Why should this be? Behaviorism did not provide an explanation of these striking findings, so psychologists looked elsewhere for clues: the world outside the laboratory. In the real world of forests, sewers, and garbage cans, nausea is usually caused by spoiled food and not by lightning, and although these particular rats had been born in a laboratory and had never left their cages, millions of years of evolution had prepared their brains to learn the natural association more quickly than the artificial one. In other words, it was not only the rat's learning history but also the rat's *ancestors'* learning histories that determined the rat's ability to learn.

This critical insight became the credo for a new kind of psychology. **Evolutionary psychology** *explains mind and behavior in terms of the adaptive value of abilities that are preserved over time by natural selection.* Evolutionary psychology has its roots in Charles Darwin's theory of natural selection, which, as we saw earlier, holds that the features of an organism that help it survive and reproduce are more likely than other features to be passed on to subsequent generations.

Natural selection inspired the functionalist approaches of William James and G. Stanley Hall because it led them to focus on how mental abilities help people to solve problems and therefore increase their chances of survival. But it is only since the publication in 1975 of *Sociobiology,* by the biologist E. O. Wilson, that evolutionary thinking has had an identifiable presence in psychology. That presence is steadily increasing (Buss, 1999; Pinker, 1997a, 1997b; Tooby & Cosmides, 2000). Evolutionary psychologists think of the mind as a collection of specialized "modules" that solve the human problems our ancestors faced as they attempted to eat, mate, and reproduce over millions of years. According to evolutionary psychology, the brain is not an all-purpose computer that can do or learn one thing just as easily as it can do or learn another; rather, it is a computer that does a few things well and everything else not at all. It is a computer that comes with a small suite of built-in applications that are designed to do the things that previous versions of that computer needed to have done.

Consider, for example, how evolutionary psychology treats the emotion of jealousy. All of us who have been in romantic relationships have experienced jealousy, if only because we noticed our partner noticing someone else. Jealousy can be a powerful, overwhelming emotion that we might wish to avoid, but according to evolutionary psychology, it exists today because it once served an adaptive function. If some of our hominid ancestors experienced jealousy and others did not, then those who experienced it might have been more likely to guard their mates and aggress against their rivals and thus may have been more likely to reproduce and pass on their "jealous genes" to the next generation (Buss, 2000, 2007; Buss & Haselton, 2005).

However, many current traits of people and other animals probably evolved to serve different functions than those they currently serve. For example, biologists believe that the feathers of birds probably evolved initially to perform such functions as regulating body temperature or capturing prey and only later served the entirely different function of flight. Likewise, people are reasonably adept at learning to drive a car, but nobody would argue that such an ability is the result of natural selection; the learning abilities that allow us to become skilled car drivers must have evolved for purposes other than driving cars.

Complications such as these have led critics to wonder how evolutionary hypotheses can ever be tested (Coyne, 2000; Sterelny & Griffiths, 1999). We don't have a record of our ancestors' thoughts, feelings, and actions, and fossils won't provide much information about the evolution of mind and behavior. Testing ideas about the evolutionary origins of psychological phenomena is indeed a challenging task, but not an impossible one (Buss et al., 1998; Pinker, 1997a, 1997b).

Start with the assumption that if an adaptation has been favored by natural selection, it should be possible to find some evidence of this in the numbers of offspring that are produced by the trait's bearers. Consider, for instance, the hypothesis that men tend to have deep voices because women prefer to mate with baritones rather than sopranos. To investigate this hypothesis, researchers studied a group of modern hunter-gatherers, the Hadza people of Tanzania. The researchers found that consistent with the evolutionary hypothesis, the pitch of a man's voice did indeed predict how many children he would have, but the pitch of a woman's voice did not (Apicella, Feinberg, & Marlowe, 2007). This kind of study provides evidence that allows evolutionary psychologists to test their ideas. Not every evolutionary hypothesis can be tested, of course, but evolutionary psychologists are becoming increasingly inventive in their strategies.

Build to the Outcomes

1. What is the fundamental idea behind Gestalt psychology?

2. How is memory *un*like a photograph?

3. What did Piaget discover a 6- or 7-year-old would understand that a 3-year-old usually could not?

4. What is the relationship of subjective experience to behavior?

5. How did the advent of computers change psychology?

6. What did psychologists learn from pilots during World War II?

7. How did Chomsky's work dispute Skinner's theory?

8. How have new technologies furthered the understanding of the relationship between the brain and behavior?

9. What evidence suggests that some traits can be inherited?

Beyond the Individual: Social and Cultural Perspectives

The picture we have painted so far may vaguely suggest a scene from some 1950s science-fiction film in which the protagonist is a living brain that thinks, feels, hopes, and worries while suspended in a vat of pink jelly in a basement laboratory. Although psychologists often do focus on the brain and the mind of the individual, they have not lost sight of the fact that human beings are fundamentally social animals who are part of a vast network of family, friends, teachers, and coworkers. Trying to understand people in the absence of that fact is a bit like trying to understand an ant or a bee without considering the function and influence of the colony or hive. People are the most important and most complex organisms that we ever encounter; thus it is not surprising that our behavior is strongly influenced by their presence—or their absence. The two areas of psychology that most strongly emphasize these facts are social and cultural psychology.

Learning Outcomes

► Explain how historical events are tied to the emergence of social psychology.

► Give examples of the range of cultural psychology.

THE DEVELOPMENT OF SOCIAL PSYCHOLOGY

social psychology The study of the causes and consequences of sociality.

Social psychology is *the study of the causes and consequences of sociality.* As this definition suggests, social psychologists address a remarkable variety of topics. Historians trace the birth of social psychology to an experiment conducted in 1895 by the psychologist and bicycle enthusiast Norman Triplett, who noticed that cyclists seemed to ride faster when they rode with others. Intrigued by this observation, he conducted an experiment that showed that children reeled in a fishing line faster when tested in the presence of other children than when tested alone. Triplett was not trying to improve the fishing abilities of American children, of course, but rather was trying to show that the mere presence of other people can influence performance on even the most mundane kinds of tasks.

Social psychology's development began in earnest in the 1930s and was driven by several historical events. The rise of Nazism led many of Germany's most talented scientists to immigrate to America, and among them were psychologists such as Solomon Asch (1907–1996) and Kurt Lewin. These psychologists had been strongly influenced by Gestalt psychology, which you'll recall held that "the whole is greater than the sum of its parts." Although the Gestaltists had been talking about the visual perception of objects, these psychologists felt that the phrase also captured a basic truth about the relationship between social groups and the individuals who constitute them. Philosophers had speculated about the nature of sociality for thousands of years, and political scientists, economists, anthropologists, and sociologists had been studying social life scientifically for some time. But these German refugees were the first to generate theories of social behavior that resembled the theories generated by natural scientists, and more important, they were the first to conduct experiments to test their social theories. For example, Lewin (1936) adopted the language of midcentury physics to develop a "field theory" that viewed social behavior as the product of "internal forces" (such as personality, goals, and beliefs) and "external forces" (such as social pressure and culture), whereas Asch (1946) performed laboratory experiments to examine the "mental chemistry" that allows people to combine small bits of information about another person into a full impression of that person's personality.

Other historical events also shaped social psychology in its early years. For example, the Holocaust brought the problems of conformity and obedience into sharp focus, leading psychologists such as Asch (1956) and others to examine the conditions under which people can influence each other to think and act in inhuman or irrational ways. The civil rights movement and the rising tensions between African Americans and White Americans led psychologists such as Gordon Allport (1897–1967) to study stereotyping, prejudice, and racism and to shock the world of psychology by suggesting that prejudice was the result of a perceptual error that was every bit as natural and unavoidable as an optical illusion (Allport, 1954). Allport argued that the same perceptual processes that allow us to efficiently categorize elements of our social and physical world allow us to erroneously categorize entire groups of people. Social psychologists today study a wider variety of topics (from social memory to social relationships) and use a wider variety of techniques (from opinion polls to neuroimaging) than did their forebears, but this field of psychology remains dedicated to understanding the brain as a social organ, the mind as a social adaptation, and the individual as a social creature.

Social psychology studies how the thoughts, feelings, and behaviors of individuals can be influenced by the presence of others. Members of the Reverend Sun Myung Moon's Unification Church are often married to each other in ceremonies of 10,000 people or more; in some cases couples don't know each other before the wedding begins. Social movements such as this have the power to sway individuals.

AP IMAGES/AHN YOUNG-JOON

THE EMERGENCE OF CULTURAL PSYCHOLOGY

North Americans and western Europeans are sometimes surprised to realize that most of the people on the planet are members of neither culture. Although we're all more alike than we are different, there is nonetheless considerable diversity within the human species in social practices, customs, and ways of living. *Culture* refers to the values, traditions, and beliefs that are shared by a particular group of people. Although we usually think of culture in terms of nationality and ethnic groups, cultures can also be defined by age (youth culture, elderly culture), gender (female culture,

To Have and Have Not

A WORLD OF DIFFERENCE

When we think about "other cultures," most of us imagine faraway lands filled with people eating exotic foods, wearing unusual clothes, and speaking languages we can't understand. But you don't have to board an airplane to visit a culture much different from your own, because in just about every place on earth there are two distinctly different cultures living side by side: those who have more—more money, more education, more prestige—and those who have less (Kraus, Piff, & Keltner, 2011). In even the most egalitarian societies, people can be divided into higher and lower social classes, and as it turns out, social class is a powerful determinant of human behavior.

Consider an example. Because upper-class people have ample material resources, they don't need to depend much on others. When problems arise, upper-class people rely on their bank accounts, whereas lower-class people rely on family, friends, and neighbors with whom they must maintain good relationships. In a way, upper-class people have the *luxury* of not worrying too much about what others feel or think. Does that influence their behavior?

Indeed it does. In laboratory studies, upper-class people often prove to be less generous, less charitable, less trusting, and less helpful toward others (Piff, Kraus, Côté, Cheng, & Keltner, 2010), as well as more likely to lie and cheat for personal gain (Gino & Pearce, 2009; Piff, Stancato, Côté, Mendoza-Denton, & Keltner, 2012). This "me first" orientation is easy to see outside of the laboratory, too. For example, in one study, researchers stood near the intersection of two busy streets and recorded the make, model, and year of the

DATA FROM PIFF, P. K., STANCATO, D. M., CÔTÉ, S., MENDOZA-DENTON, R., & KELTNER, D. (2012). HIGHER SOCIAL CLASS PREDICTS INCREASED UNETHICAL BEHAVIOR. *PROCEEDINGS OF THE NATIONAL ACADEMY OF SCIENCES OF THE UNITED STATES OF AMERICA, 109*(11), 4086–91. http://doi.org/10.1073/pnas.1118373109

cars that approached, and then watched to see whether they cut off other cars and pedestrians in the intersection. As the two graphs show, the drivers of new, expensive cars were considerably more likely to zip through intersections without regard for others. Is this because being upper-class makes people selfish? Or because being selfish makes people upper-class? Some studies suggest that the first explanation is the right one. For example, when participants in experiments are randomly assigned to *think* of themselves as upper-class—for instance, when they are asked to compare their incomes to those who have less—they

also behave more selfishly (Piff, Stancato, Côté, Mendoza-Denton, & Keltner, 2012).

Social class matters. And so do gender, race, religion, age, and most of the other dimensions on which human beings differ. Psychological science often produces conclusions about "people on average," but it is important to keep in mind that while averages are useful for understanding and predicting behavior, people actually come in nearly infinite varieties, and the things that distinguish them are often as interesting as the things that make them one. We hope to prove that to you throughout the rest of this textbook in the boxes called "A World of Difference."

---

transgender culture), sexual orientation (straight culture, gay culture), religion (Jewish culture, Christian culture), occupation (student culture, academic culture), and other of the many dimensions on which people differ (see "A World of Difference" box). **Cultural psychology** is *the study of how cultures reflect and shape the psychological processes of their members* (Shweder & Sullivan, 1993). Cultural psychologists study a wide range of phenomena, ranging from visual perception to social interaction, as they seek to understand which of these phenomena are universal and which vary from place to place and time to time.

Oddly enough, one of the first psychologists to pay attention to the influence of culture was Wilhelm Wundt, who is recognized today for his pioneering development of experimental psychology. Wundt believed that a complete psychology would have to combine a laboratory approach with a broader cultural perspective (Wundt, 1900–1920).

cultural psychology The study of how cultures reflect and shape the psychological processes of their members.

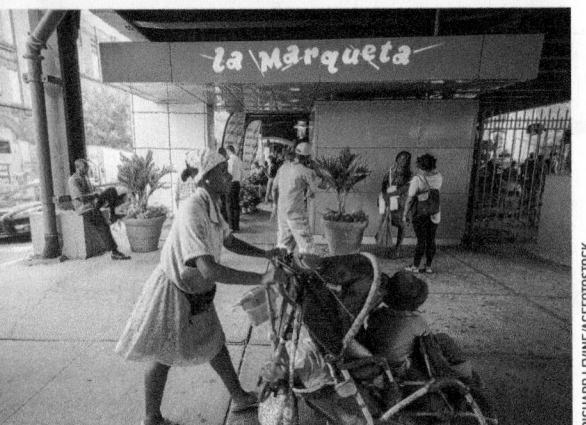

Psychologists don't necessarily have to travel the world to study the effects of culture on psychological phenomena. In big cities like New York, shown in both photos above, different subcultures live in close proximity under the umbrella of the American culture.

But Wundt's ideas failed to spark much interest in other psychologists, who had their hands full trying to make sense of results from laboratory experiments and formulating general laws of human behavior. Outside of psychology, anthropologists such as Margaret Mead (1901–1978) and Gregory Bateson (1904–1980) attempted to understand the workings of culture by traveling to far-flung regions of the world and carefully observing child-rearing patterns, rituals, religious ceremonies, and the like. Such studies revealed practices—some bizarre from a North American perspective—that served important functions in a culture, such as the painful ritual of violent body mutilation and bloodletting in mountain tribes of New Guinea, which initiates young boys into training to become warriors (Mead, 1935/1968; Read, 1965).

Yet, at the time, most anthropologists paid as little attention to psychology as psychologists did to anthropology. Cultural psychology began to emerge as a strong force in psychology only during the 1980s and 1990s, when psychologists and anthropologists began to communicate with each other about their ideas and methods (Stigler, Shweder, & Herdt, 1990). It was then that psychologists rediscovered Wundt as an intellectual ancestor of this area of the field (Jahoda, 1993).

Physicists assume that $E = mc^2$ whether the m is located in Cleveland, Moscow, or the Orion Nebula. Chemists assume that water is made of hydrogen and oxygen and that it was made of hydrogen and oxygen in 1609 as well. The laws of physics and chemistry are assumed to be universal, and for much of psychology's history, the same assumption was made about the principles that govern human behavior (Shweder, 1991). *Absolutism* holds that culture makes little or no difference for most psychological phenomena, that "honesty is honesty and depression is depression, no matter where one observes it" (Segall, Lonner, & Berry, 1998, p. 1103). And yet, as any world traveler knows, cultures differ in exciting, delicious, and frightening ways, and things that are true of people in one culture are not necessarily true of people in another. *Relativism* holds that psychological phenomena are likely to vary considerably across cultures and should be viewed only in the context of a specific culture (Berry et al., 1992). Although depression is observed in nearly every culture, the symptoms associated with it vary dramatically from one place to another. For example, Western cultures place greater emphasis on cognitive symptoms such as worthlessness, whereas Eastern cultures place greater focus on somatic symptoms such as fatigue and body aches (Draguns & Tanaka-Matsumi, 2003).

Today, most cultural psychologists fall somewhere between these two extremes. Most psychological phenomena can be influenced by culture, some are completely determined by it, and others seem to be entirely unaffected. For example, the age of a person's earliest memory differs dramatically across cultures (MacDonald, Uesiliana, & Hayne, 2000), whereas judgments of facial attractiveness do not (Cunningham et al., 1995). As noted when we discussed evolutionary psychology, it seems likely that the most universal phenomena are those that are closely associated with the basic biology that all human beings share. Conversely, the least universal phenomena are those rooted in the varied socialization practices that different cultures develop. Of course, the only way to determine whether a phenomenon is variable or constant across cultures is to design research to investigate these possibilities, and cultural psychologists do just that (Cole, 1996; Segall et al., 1998).

Build to the Outcomes

1. What was important about what Triplett discovered while watching bicycle riders?

2. Why did social psychology arise as a field in response to events such as the rise of Nazism and the civil rights movement?

3. What is the scope of the study of cultural psychology?

The Profession of Psychology: Past and Present

If ever you find yourself on an airplane with an annoying seatmate who refuses to let you read your magazine, there are two things you can do. First, you can turn to the person and say in a calm and friendly voice, "Did you know that I am covered with strange and angry bacteria?" If that seems a bit extreme, you might instead try saying, "Did you know that I am a psychologist, and I'm forming an evaluation of you as you speak?" as this will usually eliminate the problem without getting you arrested. The truth is that most people don't really know what psychology is or what psychologists do, but they do have some vague sense that it isn't wise to talk to one. Now that you've been briefly acquainted with psychology's past, let's consider its present by looking at psychology as a profession. We'll look first at the origins of psychology's professional organizations, next at the contexts in which psychologists tend to work, and finally at the kinds of training required to become a psychologist.

PSYCHOLOGISTS BAND TOGETHER: THE AMERICAN PSYCHOLOGICAL ASSOCIATION

You'll recall that when we last saw William James, he was wandering around the greater Boston area, expounding on the virtues of the new science of psychology. In July 1892, James and five other psychologists traveled to Clark University to attend a meeting called by G. Stanley Hall. Each worked at a large university, teaching psychology courses, performing research, and writing textbooks. Although they were too few to make up a jury or even a respectable hockey team, these seven men decided that it was time to form an organization that represented psychology as a profession, and on that day the American Psychological Association (APA) was born. The seven psychologists could scarcely have imagined that today their little club would have more than 150,000 members—approximately the population of a decent-sized city in the United States. Although all of the original members were employed by universities or colleges, today academic psychologists make up only 20% of the membership, whereas nearly 70% of the members work in clinical and health-related settings. Because the APA is no longer so focused on academic psychology as it once was, the American Psychological Society (APS) was formed in 1988 by 450 academic psychologists who wanted an organization that focused specifically on the needs of psychologists carrying out scientific research. The APS, renamed the Association for Psychological Science in 2006, grew quickly, attracting 5,000 members within 6 months; today it numbers nearly 12,000 psychologists.

The Growing Roles of Women and Minorities

In 1892, the APA had 31 members, all of whom were White and all of whom were male. Today, about half of all APA members are women, and the percentage of non-White members continues to grow. Surveys of recent PhD recipients reveal a picture of increasing diversification in the field. The proportion of women receiving PhDs in psychology increased from only 15% in 1950 to 70% in 2010, and the proportion of racial minorities receiving PhDs in psychology grew from a very small number to 24% during that same period. Clearly, psychology is increasingly reflecting the diversity of American society.

The current involvement of women and minorities in the APA, and in psychology more generally, can be traced to early pioneers who blazed a trail that others followed. In 1905, Mary Whiton Calkins (1863–1930) became the first woman to serve as president of the APA. Calkins became interested in psychology while teaching

Mary Whiton Calkins (1863–1930), the first woman elected APA president, suffered from the sex discrimination that was common during her lifetime. Despite academic setbacks (such as Harvard University's refusal to grant a woman an official PhD), Calkins went on to a distinguished career in research and teaching at Wellesley College.

NEW YORK TIMES CO./GETTY IMAGES

Kenneth B. Clark (1914–2005) studied the developmental effects of prejudice, discrimination, and segregation on children. In one classic study from the 1950s, he found that African American preschoolers preferred White dolls to Black ones. Clark's research was cited by the U.S. Supreme Court in its decision for the landmark *Brown v. Board of Education* case that ended school segregation.

Greek at Wellesley College. She studied with William James at Harvard and later became a professor of psychology at Wellesley College, where she worked until retiring in 1929. In her presidential address to the APA, Calkins described her theory of the role of the "self" in psychological function. Arguing against Wundt's and Titchener's structuralist ideas that the mind can be dissected into components, Calkins claimed that the self is a single unit that cannot be broken down into individual parts. Calkins wrote four books and published over 100 articles during her illustrious career (Calkins, 1930; Scarborough & Furumoto, 1987; Stevens & Gardner, 1982). Today, women play leading roles in all areas of psychology. Some of the men who formed the APA might have been surprised by the prominence of women in the field today, but we suspect that William James, a strong supporter of Mary Calkins, would not be one of them.

Just as there were no women at the first meeting of the APA, there weren't any non-White people either. The first member of a minority group to become president of the APA was Kenneth Clark (1914–2005), who was elected in 1970. Clark worked extensively on the self-image of African American children and argued that segregation of the races causes severe psychological harm. Clark's conclusions had a great influence on public policy, and his research contributed to the Supreme Court's 1954 ruling (*Brown v. Board of Education*) that outlawed segregation in public schools (Guthrie, 2000). Clark's interest in psychology was sparked when he was an undergraduate at Howard University, where he took a course taught by Francis Cecil Sumner (1895–1954), the first African American to receive a PhD in psychology (from Clark University in 1920). Sumner's main interest focused on the education of African American youth (Sawyer, 2000).

WHAT PSYCHOLOGISTS DO: RESEARCH CAREERS

Before we describe what psychologists do, we should note that most people who major in psychology do not go on to become psychologists. Psychology has become a major academic, scientific, and professional discipline with links to many other disciplines and career paths (see the Hot Science box). That being said, what should you do if you *do* want to become a psychologist, and what should you fail to do if you desperately want to avoid it? You can become "a psychologist" by a variety of routes, and the people who call themselves psychologists may hold a variety of different degrees. Typically, students finish college and enter graduate school in order to obtain a PhD (doctor of philosophy) degree in some particular area of psychology (social, cognitive, developmental). During graduate school, students generally gain exposure to the field by taking classes and learn to conduct research by collaborating with their professors. Although William James was able to master every area of psychology because the areas were so small during his lifetime, today a student can spend the better part of a decade mastering just one.

After receiving a PhD, you can go on for more specialized research training by pursuing a postdoctoral fellowship under the supervision of an established researcher in his or her area, or apply for a faculty position at a college or university or a research position in government or industry. Academic careers usually involve a combination of teaching and research, whereas careers in government or industry are typically dedicated to research alone.

The Variety of Career Paths

As you saw earlier, research is not the only career option for a psychologist. Most people who call themselves psychologists neither teach nor do research. Rather, they assess or treat people with psychological problems. Most of these *clinical psychologists* work in private practice, often in partnerships with other psychologists or with psychiatrists (who have earned an MD, or medical degree, and are allowed to prescribe medication). Other clinical psychologists work

DATA VISUALIZATION

Psychology: Understanding How to Read and Use (or Misuse!) Data

Go to launchpadworks.com.

in hospitals or medical schools, some have faculty positions at universities or colleges, and some combine private practice with an academic job. Many clinical psychologists focus on specific problems or disorders, such as depression or anxiety, whereas others focus on specific populations such as children, ethnic

HOT SCIENCE

Psychology as a Hub Science

This chapter describes how psychology emerged as a field of study, and the Other Voices box on page 14 illustrates some of the ways in which psychology is indeed a *scientific* field of study. But where does psychology stand in relation to other areas of science? That is, how big a field is it? What links does it have to other scientific disciplines? What fields (if any) are influenced by psychological science? With recent advances in computing and electronic record keeping, researchers are now able to answer these questions by literally creating maps of science. Information about scientific articles, the journals in which they are published, and the frequency and patterns with which articles in one field are cited by articles in another field, is now fully electronic and available online (in the Science Citation and Social Science Citation Indexes). Researchers can use this information to learn about the interconnectedness of different scientific disciplines.

As an example, in an article called "Mapping the Backbone of Science," Kevin Boyack and his colleagues (2005) used data from more than 1 million articles, with more than 23 million references, published in more than 7,000 journals to create a map showing the interconnectedness of different areas of science based on how frequently journal articles from different disciplines cite each other. The results are fascinating. As shown in the figure on the right, seven major fields, or "hub sciences," that link with and influence smaller subfields emerged in the data: math, physics, chemistry, earth sciences, medicine, *psychology,* and social science. The organization of the hubs is interesting to note. As you can see in the figure, psychology sits between medicine and social sciences, whereas physics sits between math and chemistry. The location of subfields also matches with what you might expect: public health and neurology fall between psychology and medicine, statistics between psychology and math, and economics between social science and math.

Another study used data from more than 6 million citations, found in more than 6,000 journals, to create a map of citation patterns focusing only on citations to articles published in a recent 5-year period (in this case from 2000 to 2004; Rosvall & Bergstrom, 2008). In that analysis, psychology again emerged as a major scientific hub (see the figure on page 30). The largest scientific fields, in order, are molecular and cell biology, medicine, physics, neuroscience, ecology and evolution, economics, geosciences, psychology, and chemistry. Psychological research has strong links (based on the frequency of citations of work in journals in each field) with neuroscience, psychiatry, education, sociology, business and marketing, medicine, and ecology and evolution. More recent and larger studies continue to support the overall structure of these maps of science (Börner et al., 2012) and also have demonstrated the value of research, such as that in psychology, that stretches across disciplinary boundaries. For instance, one recent study examining over 9 million published research papers showed that research that spans across different disciplines tends to have a much higher impact on the field, and the further apart the subdisciplines (according to distances on the maps shown here) the bigger the impact (Larivière, Haustein, & Börner, 2015). The message for you: Think about how work from one course you are taking might inform that in another—such considerations could make the biggest impact on the world!

Studies such as these are useful to university administrators and funding agencies, and also to students to help them understand the relationships among different academic departments and how the scientific work of one field relates to science as a whole. They also show the reach of psychology into other disciplines and support the idea that knowledge about psychology has relevance for many related disciplines and career paths. Good thing you are taking this class!

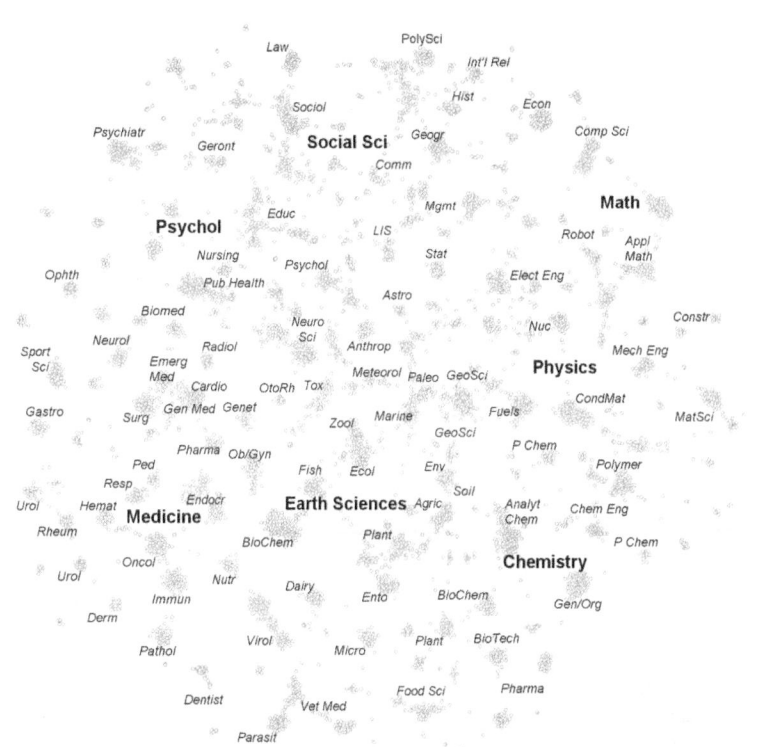

REPUBLISHED WITH PERMISSION OF SPRINGERVERLAG/AKADEMIAI DIADO, "MAPPING THE BACKBONE OF SCIENCE," BY K. W. BOYACK, R. KLAVANS, AND K. BORNER, 2005, *SCIENTOMETRICS, 64,* P. 364; PERMISSION CONVEYED THROUGH COPYRIGHT CLEARANCE CENTER, INC.

(Continued on page 30)

[Continued from Hot Science on page 29]

Fluid Mechanics

Material Engineering

Circuits

Computer Science

Operations Research

Tribology

Geosciences

Astronomy & Astrophysics

Computer Imaging

Mathematics

Power Systems

Telecommunication

Physics

Electromagnetic Engineering

Control Theory

Chemical Engineering

Probability & Statistics

Chemistry

Environmental Chemistry & Microbiology

Business & Marketing

Applied Acoustics

Analytic Chemistry

Economics

Geography

Crop Science

Sociology

Psychology

Pharmacology

Ecology & Evolution

Political Science

Education

Agriculture

Law

Neuroscience

Psychiatry

Environmental Health

Medical Imaging

Anthropology

Molecular & Cell Biology

Orthopedics   Veterinary

Parasitology

Medicine

Dentistry

Otolaryngology

Ophthalmology

Citation flow from B to A	Citation flow within field
A	B
Citation flow from A to B	Citation flow out of field

Urology

Gastroenterology

Dermatology   Rheumatology   Pathology

ROSVALL, MARTIN AND BERGSTROM, CARL T., MAPS OF RANDOM WALKS ON COMPLEX NETWORKS REVEAL COMMUNITY STRUCTURE. *PROCEEDINGS OF THE NATIONAL ACADEMY OF SCIENCES*, JAN. 29, 2008, VOL. 105, NO. 2, P. 1118. © 2008 NATIONAL ACADEMY OF SCIENCES, U.S.A.

minority groups, or older adults (see **FIGURE 1.3**). Just over 10% of APA members are *counseling psychologists,* who assist people in dealing with work or career issues and changes or help people deal with common crises such as divorce, the loss of a job, or the death of a loved one. Counseling psychologists may have a PhD or an MA (master's degree) in counseling psychology or an MSW (master of social work).

Psychologists are also quite active in educational settings. About 5% of APA members are *school psychologists,* who offer guidance to students, parents, and teachers. A similar proportion of APA members, known *as industrial/organizational psychologists,* focus on issues in the workplace. These psychologists typically work in business or industry and may be involved in assessing potential employees, finding ways to improve productivity, or helping staff and management to develop effective planning strategies for coping with

A person earning a PhD in psychology can go on to a wide range of fields, such as these three (*from left to right*): Lynne Madden is a clinical psychologist who works with individuals and groups. Gloria Balague applies her training as a clinical psychologist to her work with athletes. Lynne Owens Mock directs a community mental health center in Chicago.

▶ Figure 1.3

THE MAJOR SUBFIELDS OF PSYCHOLOGY Psychologists are drawn to many different subfields in psychology. Here are the percentages of people receiving PhDs in various subfields. Clinical psychology makes up over half of the doctorates awarded in psychology.

Data from *Graduate Study in Psychology, 2016 Edition*. Prepared by APA Office of Graduate and Postgraduate Education and Training.

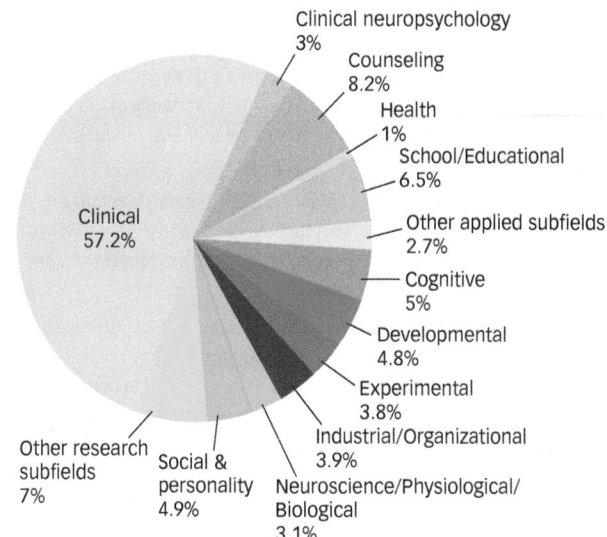

change or anticipated future developments. Of course, this brief list doesn't begin to cover all the different career paths that someone with training in psychology might take. For instance, sports psychologists help athletes improve their performance, forensic psychologists assist attorneys and courts, and consumer psychologists help companies develop and advertise new products. Indeed, we can't think of any major enterprise that *doesn't* employ psychologists.

Even this brief and incomplete survey of the APA membership provides a sense of the wide variety of contexts in which psychologists operate. You can think of psychology as an international community of professionals devoted to advancing scientific knowledge; assisting people with psychological problems and disorders; and trying to enhance the quality of life in work, school, and other everyday settings.

Build to the Outcomes

1. How has the face of psychology changed as the field has evolved?

2. What are a few of the possible career choices for people trained in psychology?

3. Where does psychology stand in relation to other areas of science?

Chapter Review

Psychology's Roots: The Path to a Science of Mind

▶ Psychologists use scientific methods to study mind and behavior.

▶ Early philosophers pondered and debated ideas about human nature, but could not provide empirical evidence to support their claims.

▶ Some of the earliest successful efforts to develop a science linking mind and behavior came from the French scientists Marie Jean Pierre Flourens and Paul Broca, who showed that damage to the brain can result in impairments of behavior and mental functions.

▶ Hermann von Helmholtz developed methods for measuring how long it takes a nerve impulse to travel to the brain, demonstrating that mental processes do not occur instantaneously.

▶ Wilhelm Wundt is credited with the founding of psychology as a scientific discipline. He focused on analyzing the basic elements of consciousness, an approach that became known as structuralism. Wundt's student Edward Titchener brought structuralism to the United States.

▶ William James applied Darwin's theory of natural selection to the study of the mind. His functionalist approach focused on how mental processes enable people to adapt to their environments. The approach influenced G. Stanley Hall in his focus on how children develop.

The Development of Clinical Psychology

▶ After observing that some patients' symptoms disappeared under a hypnotic state, psychologists began to focus on studying mental disruptions as a way of better understanding the human mind and behavior.

▶ Through his work with hysteric patients, Sigmund Freud developed psychoanalysis, which emphasized the importance of unconscious influences and childhood experiences in shaping thoughts, feelings, and behavior.

▶ Freud's influence waned both because his dark view of human nature fell out of step later, more optimistic times and because his ideas were difficult to test.

▶ Humanistic psychologists offered a more positive view of the human condition, suggesting that people are inherently disposed toward growth and can usually reach their full potential with a little help from their friends.

The Search for Objective Measurement: Behaviorism Takes Center Stage

▶ Behaviorists advocated the study of observable actions and responses and held that inner mental processes were private events that could not be studied scientifically.

▶ John B. Watson proposed that psychologists focus on what people do rather than on what they experience.

▶ Working with dogs, Ivan Pavlov studied the association between a stimulus and a response and emphasized the importance of the environment in shaping behavior. Watson believed the same techniques could be applied to human infants.

▶ Influenced by Watson's behaviorism, B. F. Skinner developed the concept of reinforcement, using a Skinner box. He demonstrated that animals and humans repeat behaviors that generate pleasant results and avoid performing those that generate unpleasant results.

▶ Skinner extended Watson's contentions about the importance of the environment in shaping behavior by suggesting that free will is an illusion and that the principle of reinforcement can be used to benefit society.

Return of the Mind: Psychology Expands

▶ Significant research on mental processes undercut behavioralism's dominance.
  – Gestalt psychology revealed that we perceive the whole rather than the sum of the parts.
  – Memory studies revealed that what we recall is heavily influenced by our knowledge and beliefs.
  – Jean Piaget studied the evolution of cognitive development in children.
  – Kurt Lewin emphasized the importance of personal experience.
  – The invention of the computer offered a useful model of the human mind.
  – Psychologists' efforts to improve the performance of the military revealed insight into the limitations of attention.
  – Noam Chomsky's theories about language showed that children have abilities that they have not been taught.

▶ Noninvasive brain scanning techniques made it possible for cognitive neuroscientists to observe the brain in action, furthering attempts to link psychology and physiology.

▶ Evolutionary psychology focuses on the adaptive function that minds and brains serve and seeks to understand the nature and origin of psychological processes in terms of natural selection.

Beyond the Individual: Social and Cultural Perspectives

▶ Triplett observed that the mere presence of others influences behavior. Social psychology recognizes that people exist as part of a network of other people and examines how individuals influence and interact with each other.

▶ Social psychology was pioneered by psychologists who desired to understand how people can influence each other to think and act in inhuman or irrational ways.

▶ Cultural psychology is concerned with the effects of the broader culture on individuals and with similarities and differences among people in different cultures. Within this perspective, absolutists hold that culture has little impact on most psychological phenomena, whereas relativists believe that culture has a powerful effect. Together, social and cultural psychology help expand the discipline's horizons beyond just an examination of individuals. These areas of psychology examine behavior within the broader context of human interaction.

The Profession of Psychology: Past and Present

▶ The American Psychological Association (APA) has grown dramatically since it was formed in 1892 and now includes over 150,000 members working in clinical, academic, and applied settings. Psychologists are also represented by professional organizations such as the Association for Psychological Science (APS), which focuses on scientific psychology.

▶ Through the efforts of pioneers such as Mary Calkins, women have come to play an increasingly important role in the field and are now as well represented as men. Minority involvement in psychology took longer, but the pioneering work of Francis Cecil Sumner, Kenneth B. Clark, and others have led to increased participation of minorities in psychology.

▶ Psychologists prepare for research careers through graduate and postdoctoral training and work in a variety of applied settings, including schools, clinics, and industry.

▶ Research into the interconnectedness of scientific disciplines shows that psychology has a high impact on a variety of other areas.

KEY CONCEPT QUIZ

1. In the 1800s, the French biologist Marie Jean Pierre Flourens and the French surgeon Paul Broca conducted research that demonstrated a connection between
   a. animals and humans.
   b. the mind and the brain.
   c. brain size and mental ability.
   d. skull indentations and psychological attributes.

2. The functional approach to psychology was inspired by
   a. Darwin's *On the Origin of Species by Means of Natural Selection*.
   b. James's *Principles of Psychology*.
   c. Wundt's *Principles of Physiological Psychology*.
   d. Titchener's *Outline of Psychology*.

3. The psychological theory that emphasizes the positive potential of human beings is known as
   a. structuralism.
   b. psychoanalytic theory.
   c. humanistic psychology.
   d. functionalism.

4. Behaviorism involves the study of
   a. observable actions and responses.
   b. the potential for human growth.
   c. unconscious influences and childhood experiences.
   d. human behavior and memory.

5. The experiments of Ivan Pavlov and John B. Watson centered on
   a. perception and behavior.
   b. stimulus and response.
   c. reward and punishment.
   d. conscious and unconscious behavior.

6. The study of mental processes such as perception and memory is called
   a. behavioral determinism.   c. social psychology.
   b. Gestalt psychology.   d. cognitive psychology.

7. The use of scanning techniques to observe the brain in action and to see which parts are involved in which operations helped the development of
   a. evolutionary psychology.
   b. cognitive neuroscience.
   c. cultural psychology.
   d. cognitive accounts of language formation.

8. Central to evolutionary psychology is the ___ function that minds and brains serve.

   a. emotional
   b. adaptive
   c. cultural
   d. physiological

9. Social psychology differs most from other psychological approaches in its emphasis on

   a. human interaction.
   b. behavioral processes.
   c. the individual.
   d. laboratory experimentation.

10. Cultural psychology emphasizes that

    a. all psychological processes are influenced to some extent by culture.
    b. psychological processes are the same across all human beings, regardless of culture.
    c. culture shapes some but not all psychological phenomena.
    d. insights gained from studying individuals from one culture will only rarely generalize to individuals from other cultures, which have different social identities and rituals.

 LearningCurve   Don't stop now! Quizzing yourself is a powerful study tool. Go to LaunchPad to access the LearningCurve adaptive quizzing system and your own personalized learning plan. Visit launchpadworks.com.

KEY TERMS

psychology (p. 2)
mind (p. 2)
behavior (p. 2)
nativism (p. 3)
philosophical empiricism (p. 3)
phrenology (p. 4)
physiology (p. 4)
stimulus (p. 5)

reaction time (p. 5)
consciousness (p. 5)
structuralism (p. 5)
introspection (p. 6)
functionalism (p. 7)
natural selection (p. 7)
hysteria (p. 10)
unconscious (p. 10)

psychoanalytic theory (p. 10)
psychoanalysis (p. 10)
humanistic psychology (p. 12)
behaviorism (p. 12)
response (p. 13)
reinforcement (p. 15)
illusions (p. 17)
Gestalt psychology (p. 17)

cognitive psychology (p. 19)
behavioral neuroscience (p. 20)
cognitive neuroscience (p. 22)
evolutionary psychology (p. 22)
social psychology (p. 24)
cultural psychology (p. 25)

CHANGING MINDS

1. One of your classmates says that she's taking this class only because it's required for her education major. "Psychology is all about understanding mental illness and treatment. I don't know why I have to learn this stuff when I'm going to be a teacher, not a psychologist." Why should your friend reconsider her opinion? What subfields of psychology are especially important for a teacher?

2. One of your friends confesses that he really enjoys his psychology courses, but he's decided not to declare a major in psychology. "You have to get a graduate degree to do anything with a psychology major," he says, "and I don't want to stay in school for the rest of my life. I want to get out there and work in the real world." Knowing what you've read in this chapter about careers in psychology, what might you tell him?

3. On May 6, you spot a news item announcing that it's the birthday of Sigmund Freud, "the father of psychology." How accurate is it to call Freud the "father of psychology?" Having read about psychology's subfields, do you think other people are as important or more important than Freud?

4. One of your classmates has flipped ahead in this textbook and noticed that there is going to be a lot of material—including an entire chapter—on the brain. "I don't see why we have to learn so much biology," he says. "I want to be a school counselor, not a brain surgeon. I don't need to understand the parts of the brain or chemical reactions in order to help people." How are the brain and the mind connected? In what specific ways might knowing about the brain help us to understand the mind?

5. Another classmate is very unsettled after reading about B. F. Skinner's claim that free will is an illusion. "Psychology always tries to treat human beings like lab rats, whose behavior can be manipulated," she says. I have free will, and I decide what I'm going to do next." What would you tell your friend? Does an understanding of the basic principles of psychology allow us to predict every detail of what individual humans will do?

ANSWERS TO KEY CONCEPT QUIZ

1. b; 2. a; 3.c; 4. a; 5. b; 6. d; 7. b; 8. b; 9. a; 10. c.

 LaunchPad   macmillan learning   LaunchPad features the full e-Book of *Psychology*, the LearningCurve adaptive quizzing system, videos, and a variety of activities to boost your learning. Visit LaunchPad at launchpadworks.com.

Methods in Psychology

2

Y OU CAN HEAL YOUR LIFE has sold over 35 million copies. Its author, Louise Hay, suggests that everything that happens to us is a result of the thoughts we choose to think. She claims that she cured herself of cancer simply by changing her thoughts, and she says that others can learn to do the same by buying her books, CDs, and DVDs, and by attending her seminars. In a television interview, Hay explained how she knows that her technique is effective.

Interviewer: How do you know what you're saying is right?

Hay: Oh, my inner ding.

Interviewer: Ding?

Hay: My inner ding. It speaks to me. It feels right or it doesn't feel right. Happiness is choosing thoughts that make you feel good. It's really very simple.

Interviewer: But I hear you saying that even if there were no proof for what you believed, or even if there were scientific evidence against it, it wouldn't change.

Hay: Well, I don't believe in scientific evidence, I really don't. Science is fairly new. It hasn't been around that long. We think it's such a big deal, but it's, you know, it's just a way of looking at life.

Louise Hay says she doesn't "believe" in scientific evidence, but what could that possibly mean? After all, if Hay's techniques really do cure cancer, then even she would have to expect cancer victims who practice her techniques to have a higher rate of remission than cancer victims who don't. That isn't "a way of looking at life." It's just plain, old-fashioned, common sense—exactly the kind of common sense that lies at the heart of science.

Science tells us that the only way to know for sure whether a claim is true is to go out and have a look. But that sounds easier than it is. For example, where would you look to see whether Louise Hay's claims are true? Would you go to one of her seminars and ask people in the audience whether or not they'd been healed? Would you examine the medical records of people who had and hadn't bought her books? Would you invite people to sign up for a class that teaches her techniques and then

Louise Hay says she doesn't believe in scientific evidence and instead trusts her "inner ding."

wait to see how many got cancer? All of these things sound reasonable, but the fact is that none of them would be particularly informative. There are a few good ways to test claims like Louise Hay's and a whole lot of bad ways, and in this chapter you will learn to tell one from the other. Scientists have developed powerful tools for determining when an inner ding is right and when it is wrong, and it is these tools that make science special. As the philosopher Bertrand Russell (1945, p. 527) wrote, "It is not *what* the man of science believes that distinguishes him, but *how* and *why* he believes it." That, it turns out, goes for women of science too.

WE'LL START BY EXAMINING THE GENERAL PRINCIPLES THAT GUIDE scientific research and distinguish it from every other way of knowing. Next, we'll see that the methods of psychology are meant to answer two basic questions: *What* do people do, and *why* do they do it? Psychologists answer the first question by observing and measuring, and they answer the second question by looking for relationships between the things they measure. We'll see that scientific research allows us to draw certain kinds of conclusions and not others, and we'll see that most people have problems thinking critically about scientific evidence. Finally, we'll consider the unique ethical questions that confront scientists who study people and other animals.

Empiricism: How to Know Stuff

When ancient Greeks sprained their ankles, caught the flu, or accidentally set their nose hair on fire, they had to choose between two kinds of doctors: dogmatists (from *dogmatikos,* meaning "belief"), who thought that the best way to understand illness was to speculate about the body's functions, and empiricists (from *empeirikos,* meaning "experience"), who thought that the best way to understand illness was to observe sick people. The rivalry between these two schools of medicine didn't last long because the people who went to see dogmatists tended to die, which was bad for business. Today we use the word *dogmatism* to describe people's tendency to cling to their assumptions, and the word **empiricism** to describe *the belief that accurate knowledge can be acquired through observation.* The fact that we can answer questions about the natural world by examining it may seem painfully obvious to you, but this painfully obvious fact has only recently gained wide acceptance. For most of human history, people trusted authority to answer important questions, and it is only in the last millennium (and especially in the past three centuries) that people have begun to trust their eyes and ears more than their elders.

empiricism The belief that accurate knowledge can be acquired through observation.

The astronomer Galileo Galilei (1564–1642) was excommunicated and sentenced to prison for sticking to his own observations of the solar system rather than accepting the teachings of the Church. In 1597 he wrote to his friend and fellow astronomer Johannes Kepler (1571–1630), "What would you say of the learned here, who, replete with the pertinacity of the asp, have steadfastly refused to cast a glance through the telescope? What shall we make of this? Shall we laugh, or shall we cry?" As it turned out, the answer was *cry*.

BETTMANN/CORBIS

THE SCIENTIFIC METHOD

Empiricism is the essential element of the **scientific method**, which is *a procedure for finding facts by using empirical evidence.* In essence, the scientific method suggests that when we have an idea about the world—about how bats navigate, or where the moon came from, or why people can't forget traumatic events—we should gather empirical evidence relevant to that idea and then modify the idea to fit with the evidence. Scientists usually refer to an idea of this kind as a **theory**, which is *a hypothetical explanation of a natural phenomenon.* We might theorize that bats navigate by making sounds and then listening for the echo, that the moon was formed when a small planet collided with the earth, or that the brain responds to traumatic events by producing chemicals that facilitate memory. Each of these theories is an explanation of how something in the natural world works.

When scientists set out to develop a theory, they generally follow *the rule of parsimony*, which says that the *simplest* theory that explains all the evidence is the best one. Parsimony comes from the Latin word *parcere,* meaning "to spare," and this rule is often credited to the 14th-century logician William Ockham, who wrote "Plurality should not be posited without necessity." Ockham wasn't suggesting that nature is simple or that complex theories are wrong. He was merely suggesting that it makes sense to *start* with the simplest theory and then make the theory more complicated only if one must. Part of what makes $E = mc^2$ such a lovely theory is that it has exactly three letters and one number.

We want our theories to be as simple as possible, but we also want them to be right. How do we decide if a theory is right? Theories make specific predictions about what we should observe in the world. For example, if bats really do navigate by making sounds and then listening for echoes, then we should observe that deaf bats can't navigate. That "should statement" is technically known as a **hypothesis,** which is *a falsifiable prediction made by a theory.* The word *falsifiable* is a critical part of that definition. Some theories, such as "God created the universe," simply do not specify what we should observe if they are true, and thus no observation can ever falsify them. Because these theories do not give rise to hypotheses, they can never be the subject of scientific investigation. That doesn't mean they're wrong—it just means that we can't evaluate them by using the scientific method.

So what happens when we test a hypothesis? Albert Einstein is reputed to have said, "No amount of experimentation can ever prove me right, but a single experiment can prove me wrong." Why should that be? Well, just imagine what

SCIENCE SOURCE/COLORIZATION BY: MARY MARTIN

Classical thinkers such as Euclid and Ptolemy believed that our eyes work by emitting rays that travel to the objects we see. Ibn al-Haytham (965–1039) reasoned that if this were true, then when we open our eyes it should take longer to see something far away than something nearby. And guess what? It doesn't. And with that single observation, a centuries-old theory vanished—in the blink of an eye.

scientific method A procedure for finding truth by using empirical evidence.

theory A hypothetical explanation of a natural phenomenon.

hypothesis A falsifiable prediction made by a theory.

SEFANO BIANCHETTI/CORBIS

INTERFOTO/ALAMY

Scientists once believed that all combustible objects contain an element called *phlogiston* that is released during burning. But in 1779, the chemist Antoine Lavoisier (1734–1794) demonstrated that when metals such as mercury are burned, they don't get lighter, as the phlogiston theory said they must. Lavoisier (*left*) and his theory-killing apparatus (*right*).

you could possibly learn about the navigation-by-sound theory if you observed a few bats. If you saw the deaf bats navigating every bit as well as the hearing bats, then the navigation-by-sound theory would instantly be proved wrong; but if you saw the deaf bats navigating more poorly than the hearing bats, your observation would be *consistent* with the navigation-by-sound theory but would not prove it. After all, even if you didn't see a deaf bat navigating perfectly today, it is still possible that someone else did, or that you will see one tomorrow. We can't observe every bat that has ever been and will ever be, which means that even if the theory wasn't disproved by your observation, some chance always remains that it will be disproved by some other observation. When evidence is consistent with a theory, it increases our confidence in it, but it never makes us completely certain. The next time you see a newspaper headline that says "Scientists prove theory X correct," you are hereby authorized to roll your eyes.

The scientific method suggests that the best way to learn the truth about the world is to develop theories, derive hypotheses from them, test those hypotheses by gathering evidence, and then use that evidence to modify the theories. But what exactly does gathering evidence entail?

THE ART OF LOOKING

For centuries, people rode horses. And for centuries, when they got off their horses, they sat around and argued about whether all four of a horse's feet ever leave the ground at the same time. Some said yes, some said no, and some said they really wished they could talk about something else for a change. In 1877, Eadweard Muybridge invented a technique for taking photographs in rapid succession, and his photos showed that when horses gallop, all four feet do indeed leave the ground. And that was that. Never again did two riders have the pleasure of a flying-horse debate because Muybridge had settled the matter once and for all.

But why did it take so long? After all, people had been watching horses gallop for quite a few years, so why did some say that they clearly saw the horse going airborne while others said that they clearly saw at least one hoof on the ground at all times? Because as wonderful as our eyes may be, there are a lot of things they cannot see and a lot of things they see incorrectly. We can't see germs, but they are very real. The earth looks perfectly flat, but it is imperfectly round. As Muybridge knew, we have to do more than just look if we want to know the truth about the world. Empiricism is the right approach, but to do it properly requires an **empirical method,** which is *a set of rules and techniques for observation.*

In many sciences, the word *method* refers primarily to technologies that enhance the powers of the senses. Biologists use microscopes and astronomers use telescopes because the things they want to observe are invisible to the naked eye. Human behavior, on the other hand, is quite visible, so you might expect psychology's methods to be relatively simple. In fact, the empirical challenges facing psychologists are among the most daunting in all of modern science, which is why psychology's empirical methods are among the most sophisticated in all of modern science. These empirical challenges arise because people have three qualities that make them unusually difficult to study:

▶ *Complexity:* No galaxy, particle, molecule, or machine is as complicated as the human brain. Scientists can describe the birth of a star or the death of a cell in exquisite detail, but they can barely begin to say how the 500 million interconnected neurons that constitute the brain give rise to the thoughts, feelings, and actions that are psychology's core concerns.

▶ *Variability:* In almost all the ways that matter, one *E. coli* bacterium is pretty much like another. But people are as varied as their fingerprints. No two

Frames 2 and 3 of this historic series of photos by Eadweard Muybridge (1830–1904) show that horses can indeed fly, albeit briefly and only in coach.

EADWEARD MUYBRIDGE/CORBIS

empirical method A set of rules and techniques for observation.

individuals ever do, say, think, or feel exactly the same thing under exactly the same circumstances, which means that when you've seen one, you've most definitely not seen them all.

▶ *Reactivity:* An atom of cesium-133 oscillates 9,192,631,770 times per second, regardless of whether anyone is watching. But people often think, feel, and act one way when they are being observed and a different way when they are not. When people know they are being studied, they don't always behave as they otherwise would.

The fact that human beings are complex, variable, and reactive presents a major challenge to the scientific study of their behavior, and psychologists have developed two kinds of methods that are designed to meet these challenges head on: *methods of observation,* which allow them to determine what people do, and *methods of explanation,* which allow them to determine why people do it. We'll examine both of these methods in the sections that follow.

People behave differently when they are and are not being observed. For example, President Obama might have inhibited that neck swivel if he'd realized that a photographer (as well as a rather amused French President Nicolas Sarkozy) were watching him.

Build to the Outcomes

1. How does empiricism differ from dogmatism?

2. What is the difference between a theory and a hypothesis?

3. Why can theories be proven wrong but not right?

4. What makes human beings especially difficult to study?

Observation: What Do People Do?

To *observe* means to use one's senses to learn about the properties of an event (e.g., a storm or a parade) or an object (e.g., an apple or a person). For example, when you observe a round, red apple, your brain is using the pattern of light that is coming into your eyes to draw an inference about the apple's identity, shape, and color. That kind of informal observation is fine for buying fruit but not for doing science. Why? First, casual observations are notoriously unstable. The same apple may appear red in the daylight and crimson at night or spherical to one person and elliptical to another. Second, casual observations can't tell us about all of the properties that might interest us. No matter how long and hard you look, you will never be able to discern an apple's crunchiness or pectin content simply by watching it.

Luckily, scientists have devised techniques that allow them to overcome these problems. In the first section below (Measurement), we'll see how psychologists design instruments and then use them to make measurements. In the second section (Description), we'll see what psychologists do with their measurements once they've made them.

Learning Outcomes

▶ Explain what measurement involves, and what properties a good definition and a good instrument must have.

▶ Identify some of the methods psychologists use to avoid demand characteristics and observer bias.

▶ Explain what a frequency distribution is, and describe the two main types of descriptive statistics.

MEASUREMENT

For most of human history, people had no idea how old they were because there was no simple way to keep track of time—or weight, or volume, or density, or temperature, or anything else for that matter. Today we live in a world of clocks and calendars, odometers and thermometers. Measurement is not just a basic part of science, it is a basic part of modern life. But what exactly does measurement require? Whether we

A WORLD OF DIFFERENCE

Are Heroes and Sheroes Divided by Zeroes?

Galileo, Newton, Mendel, Darwin, Faraday, Einstein, Turing, Tesla—what do all these people have in common? First, they were all brilliant scientists. And second, they were all men. The history of science is pretty much the history of smart men having big ideas and making big discoveries. So where are all the women hiding? There are two answers to this question. The first is that until quite recently, educational and employment opportunities for women were limited. For most of history, women were either subtly discouraged or actively prohibited from studying science—and you really can't win the Nobel Prize in Physics if they won't let you take algebra. Women, it seems, have been hiding right where men put them: in the kitchen.

Of course, another possible reason why most great scientists have been men is that men and women may have different talents, and the talents men have may be precisely the talents people need to become great scientists. Is there any truth to this suggestion? A few years ago, a group of male and female scientists got together, surveyed all the scientific evidence on sex differences in cognitive abilities, and drew a striking conclusion: Yes, they concluded, the evidence does show that men and women differ with regard to certain talents (Halpern et al., 2007). Specifically, men are more *variable* than women on almost every measure of quantitative ability (the ability to use numbers) and visuo-spatial ability (the ability to use images), both of which are important to success in many sciences. Being more variable means that although men and women have the same average amount of talent on these dimensions, there are more men at both the very lowest and very highest ends of the spectrum. If great scientists tend to come from the highest end of the quantitative and visuo-spatial ability spectrums, then men will naturally be overrepresented among great scientists. And indeed, recent data show that men are overrepresented in scientific fields that are "math intensive" such as geoscience, engineering, economics, mathematics, computer science, and the physical sciences, but not in other scientific fields such as biology, psychology, and sociology (Ceci, Ginther, Khan, & Williams, 2014).

So men are more variable than women on certain dimensions. But *why*? Is it because they are encouraged to hone their quantitative and visuo-spatial skills by parents who buy them video games instead of dolls, and by teachers who encourage them to join the math team rather than the debate team? Or is it because there is some innate difference in the structure or function of the male and female brains? Once again, an expert review of the evidence concludes that "sex differences in spatial and mathematical reasoning need not stem from biological bases, that the gap between average female and male math ability is narrowing (suggesting strong environmental influences), and that sex differences in math ability at the right tail (which is the "high" end of the ability spectrum) show variation over time and across nationalities, ethnicities, and other factors, indicating that the ratio of males to females at the right tail can and does change" (Ceci, Ginther, Khan, & Williams, 2014, p. 75). In short, no one really knows why men are more variable, but the smart money seems to be on nurture rather than nature.

We agree with the experts who concluded that "there are no single or simple answers to the complex questions about sex differences in science and mathematics" (Halpern et al., 2007, p. 75). However, we feel confident that one day in the not-too-distant future, a brilliant young psychological scientist will discover the answer to this important and complex question. We just hope she does it soon.

---

want to measure the intensity of an earthquake, the distance between molecules, or the attitude of a registered voter, we must always do two things—*define* the property we wish to measure and then find a way to *detect* it.

Definition and Detection: What to Measure and How to Measure It

The last time you said, "I'll be there in a second," you probably didn't know you were talking about atomic decay. Every unit of time has an **operational definition,** which is *a description of a property in concrete, measurable terms.* For example, the operational definition of a second is *the duration of 9,192,631,770 cycles of microwave light absorbed or emitted by the hyperfine transition of cesium-133 atoms in their ground state undisturbed by external fields* (which takes roughly 6 seconds just to say). To actually count the cycles of light emitted as cesium-133 decays requires an **instrument,** which is *anything that can detect the condition to which an operational definition refers.* An instrument known as a cesium clock can count cycles of light, and when it counts 9,192,631,770 of them, one second has officially passed.

The steps we take to measure a physical property are the same steps we take to measure a psychological property. For example, if we wanted to measure a person's intelligence, or shyness, or happiness, we would have to start by generating an operational definition of that property—that is, by specifying some concrete, measurable event that indicates it. For example, we might define happiness as *the frequency with*

operational definition A description of a property in concrete, measurable terms.

instrument Anything that can detect the condition to which an operational definition refers.

which a person smiles. Once we do, we just need a smile-detecting instrument, such as a computer with a camera attached or a human brain with an eye attached. Having an operational definition that specifies a measurable event and an instrument that measures that event are the keys to scientific measurement.

A Good Definition Is Valid There are many ways to define and detect a property such as happiness, so which ways are best? The most important feature of an operational definition is **validity,** *the extent to which a concrete event defines a property.* For example, the concrete event called *frequency of smiling* is a valid way to define the property called *happiness* because, as we all know, people tend to smile more often when they feel happy. Do they eat more or talk more or spend more money? Well, maybe. But maybe not. And that's why most people probably would regard food consumption or verbal output or financial expenditures as invalid measures of happiness (though perfectly valid measures of something else). Validity is to some extent in the eye of the beholder, but most beholders would agree that the frequency of smiles is a more valid way to operationally define happiness than is the frequency of eating, talking, or spending.

A Good Instrument Is Reliable and Powerful If validity is the most important feature of an operational definition, then what is the most important feature of a measuring instrument? Actually, there are two. First, a good instrument has **reliability,** which is *the tendency for an instrument to produce the same measurement whenever it is used to measure the same thing.* For example, if a person smiles just as much on Tuesday as on Wednesday, then a smile-detecting instrument should produce identical results on those two days. If it produced different results (i.e., if the instrument detected differences that weren't actually there), it would lack reliability. Second, a good instrument has **power,** which is *an instrument's ability to detect small magnitudes of the property.* If a person smiled just *slightly* more often on Tuesday than on Wednesday, then a good smile-detector should produce different results on those two days. If it produced the same result (i.e., if it failed to detect a small difference that was actually there), then it would lack power (see **FIGURE 2.1**).

Demand Characteristics: Doing What Is Expected

Once we have a valid definition and a reliable and powerful instrument, are we *finally* ready to measure behavior? Yes—as long as we want to measure the behavior of an amoeba or a raindrop or anything else that doesn't care if we are watching it. But if we want to measure the behavior of a human being, then we still have some work to do, because while we are trying to discover how people normally behave, normal people will be trying to behave as they think we want or expect them to. **Demand characteristics** are *those aspects of an observational setting that cause people to behave as they think someone else wants or expects.* We call these demand characteristics because they seem to "demand" or require that people say and do certain things. When someone you love asks, "Do these jeans make me look fat?" the right answer is always no, and if you've ever been asked this question, then you have experienced demand. Demand characteristics make it hard to measure behavior as it typically unfolds. Luckily, psychologists have several ways to get around this problem.

Naturalistic Observation One way that psychologists avoid the problem of demand characteristics is by observing people without their knowledge. **Naturalistic observation** is *a technique for gathering scientific information by unobtrusively observing people in their natural environments.* For example, naturalistic observation has shown that the biggest groups leave the smallest tips in restaurants (Freeman et al., 1975), that hungry shoppers buy the most impulse items at the grocery store (Gilbert, Gill, & Wilson, 2002), that golfers are most likely to cheat when they play several opponents at once (Erffmeyer, 1984), that men do not usually approach the most beautiful woman at a singles' bar (Glenwick, Jason, & Elman, 1978), and that Olympic athletes

Define the Property

Generate an operational definition that has validity

↓

Detect the Property

Design an instrument that has reliability and power

▲ Figure 2.1
MEASUREMENT There are two steps in the measurement of a property.

validity The extent to which a concrete event defines a property.

reliability The tendency for an instrument to produce the same measurement whenever it is used to measure the same thing.

power An instrument's ability to detect small magnitudes of the property.

demand characteristics Those aspects of an observational setting that cause people to behave as they think someone else wants or expects.

naturalistic observation A technique for gathering scientific information by unobtrusively observing people in their natural environments.

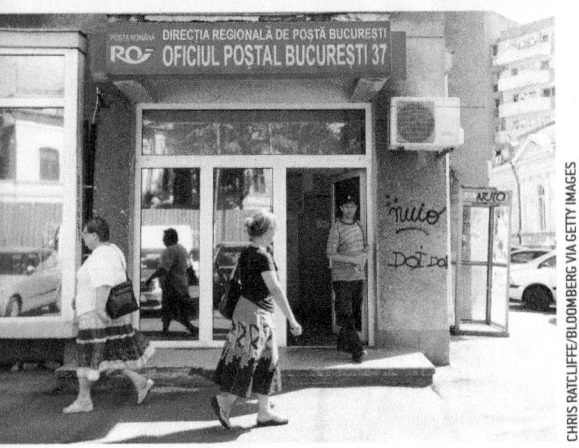

Countries that have a faster pace of life tend to have higher rates of heart disease but also greater happiness. How do researchers measure the "pace of life"? They make naturalistic observations, in this case, by measuring the average walking speed of pedestrians in different cities. By the way, the fastest pedestrians are the Irish (top) and the slowest are the Romanians (bottom) (Levine & Norenzayan, 1999).

smile more when they win the bronze medal than the silver medal (Medvec, Madey, & Gilovich, 1995). Each of these conclusions is the result of measurements made by psychologists who observed people who didn't know they were being observed. It seems unlikely that the psychologists could have made the same observations if the diners, shoppers, golfers, singles, and athletes had realized that they were being scrutinized.

Unfortunately, naturalistic observation isn't always a viable solution to the problem of demand characteristics. First, some of the things psychologists want to observe simply don't occur naturally. If we wanted to know whether people who have undergone sensory deprivation perform poorly on motor tasks, we would have to hang around the shopping mall for a very long time before a few dozen blindfolded people with earplugs just happened to wander by and start typing. Second, some of the things that psychologists want to observe can be gathered only from direct interaction with a person, for example, by administering a survey, giving tests, conducting an interview, or hooking someone up to a machine. If we wanted to know how often people worry about dying, how accurately they can remember their high school graduations, how quickly they can solve a logic puzzle, or how much electrical activity their brains produce when they feel jealous, then simply watching them from the bushes won't do. So what *can* we do?

Privacy and Control When naturalistic observation isn't possible, psychologists use a number of other techniques to avoid demand characteristics. For instance, people are less likely to be influenced by demand characteristics when they cannot be identified as the originators of their actions, and psychologists often take advantage of this fact by allowing people to respond privately (e.g., by having them complete questionnaires when they are alone) or anonymously (e.g., by not collecting personal information, such as people's names or addresses). In addition, psychologists can measure behaviors that cannot easily be demanded. For instance, a person's behavior can't be influenced by demand characteristics if that behavior isn't under the person's voluntary control. You may not want a psychologist to know that you are extremely interested in the celebrity gossip magazine that she's asked you to read, but you can't prevent your pupils from dilating, which is what they do when you are engaged. Behaviors are also unlikely to be influenced by demand characteristics when people don't know that the demand and the behavior are related. For example, you may want the psychologist to believe that you are concentrating hard on the *Wall Street Journal* article that she's asked you to read, but you probably don't realize that your blink rate slows when you are concentrating, and thus you probably won't fake a slow blink.

Unawareness Of course, one of the best ways to avoid demand characteristics is simply to make sure that the people who are being observed are unaware of the true purpose of the observation. When people are unaware of the purpose of an observation, they can't behave the way they think they should behave because they don't *know* how they should behave. For instance, if you didn't know that a psychologist was studying the effects of music on mood, you wouldn't feel obligated to smile when music was played. This is why psychologists typically don't reveal the true purpose of an observation to the people who are being observed until the study is over.

Of course, people are clever and curious, and when psychologists don't tell them the purpose of their observations, people generally try to figure it out for themselves. That's why psychologists sometimes use *cover stories,* or misleading explanations that are meant to keep people from discerning the true purpose of an observation. For example, if a psychologist wanted to know how music influenced your mood, he or she might falsely tell you that the purpose of the study was to determine how quickly people can do logic puzzles while music plays in the background. (We will discuss the ethical implications of deceiving people later in this chapter.) In addition, the psychologist might use *filler items,* pointless measures that are designed to mislead you about the true purpose of the observation. So, for example, the psychologist might ask you a few questions whose answers are of real interest to him or her (How happy are you right now?), as well as a few questions whose answers are not (Do you like cats more or less than dogs?). This makes it difficult for you to guess the true purpose of the observation from the nature of the questions you were asked.

Observer Bias: Seeing What Is Expected

The people being observed aren't the only ones who can make measurement a bit tricky. In one study, students in a psychology class were asked to measure the speed with which a rat learned to run through a maze (Rosenthal & Fode, 1963). Some students were told that their rat had been specially bred to be "maze-dull" (i.e., slow to learn a maze) and others were told that their rat had been specially bred to be "maze-bright" (i.e., quick to learn a maze). Although all the rats were actually the same breed, the students who *thought* they were measuring the speed of a maze-dull rat reported that their rats took longer to learn the maze than did the students who *thought* they were measuring the speed of a maze-bright rat. In other words, the measurements revealed precisely what the students expected them to reveal.

Why did this happen? First, *expectations can influence observations.* It is easy to make errors when measuring the speed of a rat, and our expectations often determine the kinds of errors we make. When the rat puts one paw over the finish line, does that count as learning the maze? If the rat falls asleep, should the stopwatch be left running or should the rat be awakened and given a second chance? If a rat runs a maze in 18.5 seconds, should that number be rounded up or rounded down before it is recorded in the log book? The answers to these questions may depend on whether one thinks the rat is bright or dull. The students who timed the rats probably tried to be honest, vigilant, fair, and objective, but their expectations influenced their observations in subtle ways that they could neither detect nor control.

Second, *expectations can influence reality.* Students who expected their rats to learn quickly may have unknowingly done things to help that learning along, for example, by

(Photo 1)

(Photo 2)

THINKSTOCK

One way to avoid demand characteristics is to measure behaviors that people are unable or unlikely to control. For example, our pupils contract when we are bored (photo 1) and dilate when we are interested (photo 2), which makes pupillary dilation a useful measure of a person's level of engagement in a task.

BETTMANN/CORBIS

THE GRANGER COLLECTION, NYC. ALL RIGHTS RESERVED.

People's expectations can cause the phenomena they expect. In 1929, investors who expected the stock market to collapse sold their stocks and thereby caused the very crisis they feared. In this photo, panicked citizens stand outside the New York Stock Exchange the day after the crash, which the *New York Times* attributed to "mob psychology."

double-blind observation A technique whose true purpose is hidden from both the observer and the person being observed.

frequency distribution A graphical representation of measurements arranged by the number of times each measurement was made.

normal distribution A mathematically defined distribution in which the frequency of measurements is highest in the middle and decreases symmetrically in both directions.

mode The value of the most frequently observed measurement

mean The average value of all the measurements.

median The value that is in the middle, that is, greater than or equal to half the measurements and less than or equal to half the measurements.

muttering, "Oh no!" when the bright rat looked the wrong direction or by petting the dull rat less affectionately. (We'll discuss both of these phenomena more extensively in the Social Psychology chapter.)

Observers' expectations, then, can have a powerful influence on both their observations and on the behavior of those whom they observe. Psychologists use many techniques to avoid these influences, and one of the most common is the **double-blind** observation, which is *an observation whose true purpose is hidden from both the observer and the person being observed.* For example, if the students had not been told which rats were bright and which were dull, then they wouldn't have *had* any expectations about their rats; thus their expectations couldn't have influenced their measurements. That's why it is common practice in psychology to keep the observers as blind as the participants. For example, measurements are often made by research assistants who do not know what is being studied or why, and who therefore don't have any expectations about what the people being observed will or should do. Indeed, studies nowadays are often carried out by the world's blindest experimenter—a computer—which can present information to people and measure their responses while having no expectations at all.

DESCRIPTION

You now know how to generate a valid operational definition, how to design a reliable and powerful instrument, and how to use that instrument while avoiding demand characteristics and observer bias. So where does that leave you? With a big page filled with numbers—and if you are like most people, a big page filled with numbers just doesn't seem very informative. Don't worry—most psychologists feel the same way, and that's why they have two techniques for making sense of big pages full of numbers: graphic representations and descriptive statistics.

Graphic Representations: Picturing the Measurements

A picture may be worth a thousand words, but it is worth a million digits. As you'll learn in the Sensation and Perception chapter, vision is our most sophisticated sense, and human beings typically find it easier to understand things when they are represented visually than numerically or verbally. Psychologists are people too, and they often create graphic representations of the measurements they collect. The most common kind is the **frequency distribution,** which is *a graphic representation of measurements arranged by the number of times each measurement was made.* **FIGURE 2.2** shows a pair of frequency distributions that represent the hypothetical

▲ Figure 2.2

FREQUENCY DISTRIBUTIONS This graph shows how a hypothetical group of men and women scored on a test of fine motor skills. Test scores are listed along the horizontal axis, and the frequency with which each score was obtained is represented along the vertical axis.

performances of a group of men and women who took a test of fine motor skills (i.e., the ability to manipulate things with their hands). Every possible test score is shown on the horizontal axis. The number of times (or the *frequency* with which) each score was observed is shown on the vertical axis. Although a frequency distribution can have any shape, a common shape is the *bell curve,* which is technically known as the *Gaussian distribution* or the **normal distribution,** which is *a mathematically defined distribution in which the frequency of measurements is highest in the middle and decreases symmetrically in both directions.* The mathematical definition of the normal distribution isn't important. (Well, not for you, anyway. For statisticians it is slightly more important than breathing.) What is important for you is what you can easily see for yourself: the normal distribution is symmetrical (i.e., the left half is a mirror image of the right half), has a peak in the middle, and trails off at both ends.

The graph in Figure 2.2 reveals in a single optical gulp what a page full of numbers never can. For instance, the shape of the distributions instantly tells you that most people have moderate motor skills, and that only a few have exceptionally good or exceptionally bad motor skills. You can also see that the distribution of men's scores is displaced a bit to the left of the distribution of women's scores, which instantly tells you that women tend to have somewhat better motor skills than men. And finally, you can see that the two distributions have a great deal of overlap, which tells you that although women tend to have better motor skills than men, there are still plenty of men who have better motor skills than plenty of women.

Descriptive Statistics: Talking About the Measurements

A frequency distribution depicts every measurement and thus provides a full and complete picture of those measurements. But sometimes a full and complete picture is just TMI.[1] When we ask a friend how she's been, we don't want her to show us a frequency distribution of her happiness scores on each day of the previous 6 months. We want a brief summary statement that captures the essential information that such a graph would provide (e.g., "I've been doing pretty well," or, "I've been having some ups and downs"). In psychology, brief summary statements that capture the essential information from a frequency distribution are called *descriptive statistics*. There are two important kinds of descriptive statistics: those that describe the *central tendency* of a frequency distribution and those that describe the *variability* in a frequency distribution.

Central Tendency: Where Is the Middle? Descriptions of *central tendency* are statements about the value of the measurements that *tend* to lie near the *center* or midpoint of the frequency distribution. When a friend says that she's been "doing pretty well," she is describing the central tendency (or approximate location of the midpoint) of the frequency distribution of her happiness over time (see **FIGURE 2.3**). The three most common descriptions of central tendency are: the **mode** (*the value of the most frequently observed measurement*); the **mean** (*the average value of all the measurements*); and the **median** (*the value that is in the middle, i.e., greater than or equal to half the measurements and less than or equal to half the measurements*). **FIGURE 2.4** shows how each of these descriptive statistics is calculated. When you hear a descriptive statistic such as "the average American

On average, men are taller than women, but there are still many women (such as Nicole Kidman) who are taller than many men (such as her husband, Keith Urban).

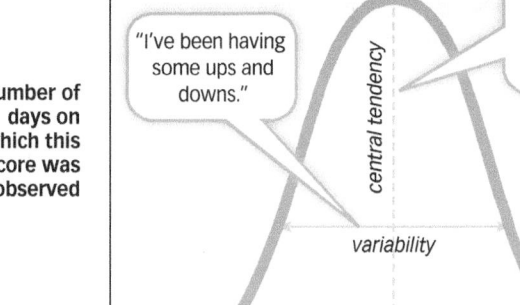

▲ Figure 2.3

TWO KINDS OF DESCRIPTIVE STATISTICS Descriptive statistics are used to describe two important features of a frequency distribution: central tendency (where do most of the scores lie?) and variability (how much do the scores differ from one another?).

---

[1] Our editor thinks you need four professors with a combined age of 190 to tell you that this means "too much information." ROFL.

- Mode = 3 because there are five 3s and only three 2s, two 1s, two 4s, one 5, one 6, and one 7.
- Mean = 3.27 because (1 + 1 + 2 + 2 + 2 + 3 + 3 + 3 + 3 + 3 + 4 + 4 + 5 + 6 + 7)/15 = 3.27
- Median = 3 because 10 scores are ≥ 3 and 10 scores are ≤ 3

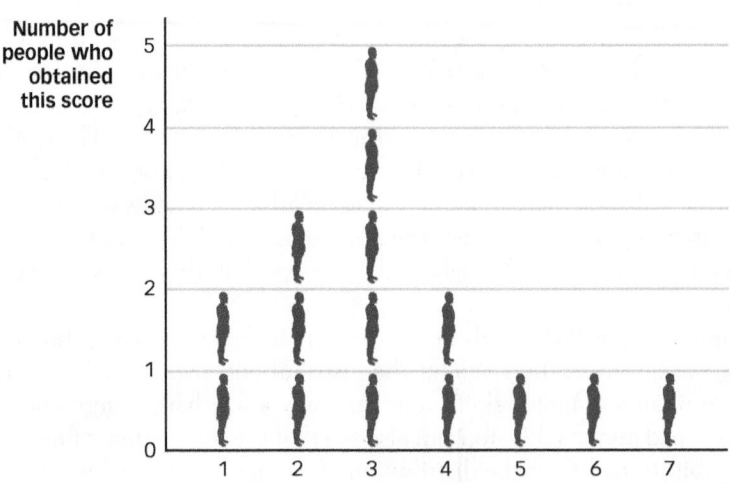

▲ Figure 2.4

SOME DESCRIPTIVE STATISTICS This frequency distribution shows the scores of 15 individuals on a 7-point test. Descriptive statistics include measures of central tendency (such as the mean, median, and mode) and measures of variability (such as the range and the standard deviation).

college student sleeps 8.3 hours per day," you are hearing about the central tendency of a frequency distribution (in this case, the mean).

In a normal distribution, the mean, median, and mode all have the same value, but when the distribution is not normal, these three descriptive statistics can differ. For example, imagine that you measured the net worth of 40 college professors and Mark Zuckerberg. The frequency distribution of your measurements would not be normal, but *positively skewed*. As you can see in **FIGURE 2.5**, the mode and the median of a positively skewed distribution are much lower than the mean because the mean is more strongly influenced by the value of a single extreme measurement (which, in case you've been sleeping for the last few years, would be the net worth of Mark Zuckerberg). When distributions become skewed, the mean gets dragged off toward the tail, the mode stays home at the hump, and the median goes to live between the two. When distributions are skewed, a single measure of central tendency can paint a misleading picture of the measurements. For example, the average net worth of the people you measured is probably about a billion dollars each, but that statement makes the college professors sound a whole lot richer than they are. You could provide a much better description of the net worth of the people you measured if you also mentioned that the median net worth is $300,000 and that the modal net worth is $288,000. Indeed, you should always be suspicious when you hear some new fact about the "average person" but don't hear anything about the shape of the frequency distribution.

Variability: How Far from the Middle? Whereas descriptions of central tendency are statements about the location of the measurements in a frequency distribution, descriptions of variability are statements about the extent to which the measurements differ from each other. When a friend says that she has been "having some ups and downs," she is offering a brief summary statement that describes how measurements of her happiness taken at different times tend to differ from one another. The simplest description of variability is the **range,** which is *the value of the largest measurement in a frequency distribution minus the value of the smallest measurement.* When the range is

When Mark Zuckerberg walks into a room, he dramatically increases the mean income of the people in it, but doesn't much change the median and does nothing at all to the mode. Facebook is trying to fix that.

range The value of the largest measurement in a frequency distribution minus the value of the smallest measurement.

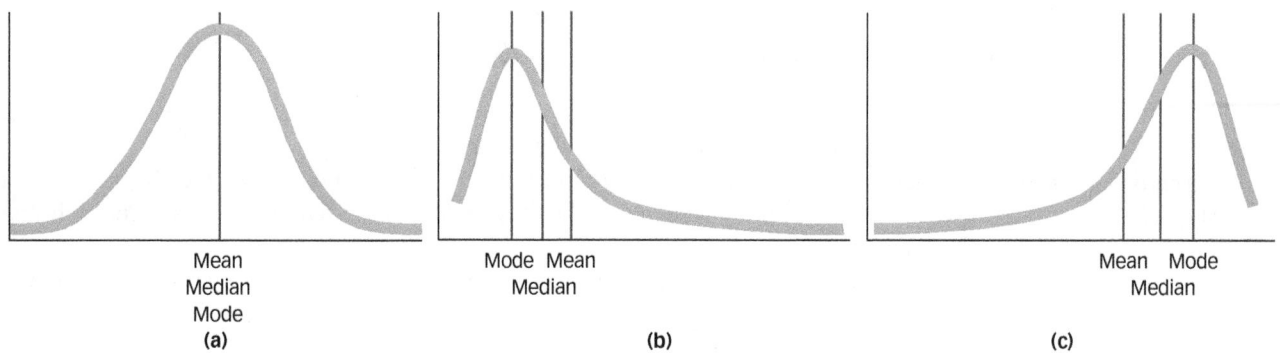

Mean
Median
Mode
(a)

Mode Mean
Median
(b)

Mean   Mode
Median
(c)

small, the measurements don't vary as much as when the range is large. The range is easy to compute, but like the mean it can be dramatically affected by a single measurement. If you said that the net worth of people you had measured ranged from $40,000 to $14 billion, a listener might get the impression that these people were all remarkably different from each other when, in fact, they were all quite similar, save for one very rich guy from California.

Other descriptions of variability aren't quite as susceptible to this problem. For example, the **standard deviation** is *a statistic that describes the average difference between the measurements in a frequency distribution and the mean of that distribution*. In other words, on average, how far are the measurements from the center of the distribution? As **FIGURE 2.6** shows, two frequency distributions can have the same mean, but very different ranges and standard deviations. For example, studies show that men and women have the same mean IQ, but that men have a larger range and standard deviation, which is to say that a man is more likely than a woman to be much more or much less intelligent than the average person of his or her own gender.

▲ **Figure 2.5**
SKEWED DISTRIBUTIONS When a frequency distribution is normal (a), the mean, median, and mode are all the same, but when it is positively skewed (b) or negatively skewed (c), these three measures of central tendency are quite different.

standard deviation A statistic that describes the average difference between the measurements in a frequency distribution and the mean of that distribution.

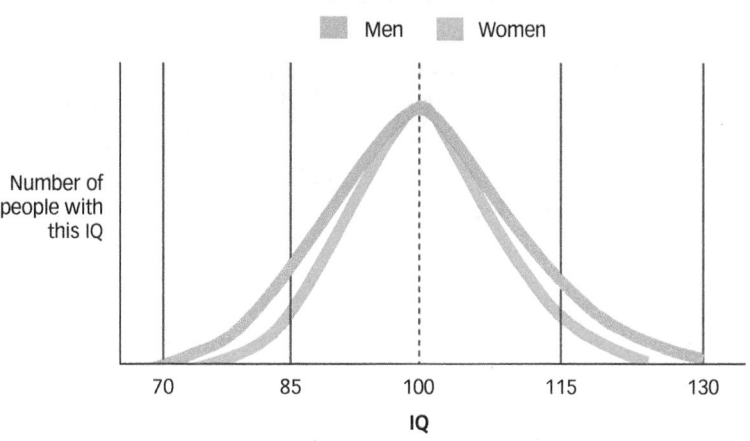

Men   Women

Number of
people with
this IQ

70   85   100   115   130

IQ

▲ **Figure 2.6**
IQS OF MEN AND WOMEN Men and women have the same average IQ, but men are more variable than women.

Build to the Outcomes

1. What property does a good operational definition have?

2. What two properties does a good measuring instrument have?

3. What methods do psychologists use to avoid demand characteristics?

4. What methods do psychologists use to avoid observer bias?

5. What is a frequency distribution, and how is the normal distribution special?

6. What is the difference between measures of central tendency and variability?

Explanation: Why Do People Do What They Do?

It would be interesting to know whether happy people are healthier than unhappy people, but it would be even more interesting to know why. Does happiness make people healthier? Does being healthy make people happier? Does being rich make people healthy and happy? These are the kinds of questions scientists often wish to answer, and scientists have developed some clever ways of using their measurements to do just that. In the first section (Correlation) we'll examine techniques that can tell us whether two things are related. In the second section (Causation), we'll examine techniques that can tell us whether the relationship between two things is one of cause and effect. In the third section (Drawing Conclusions) we'll see what kinds of conclusions these techniques allow us to draw. Finally, in the fourth section, we'll discuss the difficulty that most of us have thinking critically about scientific evidence.

CORRELATION

How much sleep did you get last night? Okay, now, how many U.S. presidents can you name? If you asked a dozen college students those two questions, you'd probably find that the students who got a good night's sleep are better president namers than are students who pulled an all-nighter. A pattern of responses like the one shown in **TABLE 2.1** would probably lead you to conclude that sleep deprivation causes memory problems. But on what basis did you draw that conclusion? How did you manage to use measurement to tell you not only about *how much* sleeping and remembering had occurred among the students you measured, but also about the *relationship* between sleeping and remembering?

variable A property whose value can vary across individuals or over time.

correlation Two variables are said to "be correlated" when variations in the value of one variable are synchronized with variations in the value of the other.

Seeing Relationships: Patterns of Variation

Measurements tell us about the properties of objects and events. We can learn about the relationships between those objects and events by comparing the *patterns of variation in a series of measurements*. When you asked college students questions about sleep and presidents, you actually did three things:

▶ First, you measured a pair of **variables,** which are *properties whose values can vary across individuals or over time.* (When you took your first algebra course you were probably horrified to learn that everything you'd been taught in grade school about the distinction between letters and numbers was a lie, that mathematical equations could contain Xs and Ys as well as 7s and 4s, and that the letters are called *variables* because they can have different values under different circumstances. Same idea here.) You measured one variable (number of hours slept) whose value could vary from 0 to 24, and you measured a second variable (number of presidents named) whose value could vary from 0 to 44.

▶ Second, you did this again. And then again. And then again. That is, you made a *series* of measurements rather than making just one.

▶ Third and last, you tried to discern a pattern in your series of measurements. If you look at the second column of Table 2.1, you will see that it contains values that vary as your eyes move down the column. That column has a particular *pattern of variation.* If you compare the third column with the second, you will notice that the patterns of variation in the two columns are synchronized: in this case, both increase as you move from top to bottom. This synchrony is known as a *pattern of covariation* or a **correlation** (as in "co-relation"). Two variables are said to "covary" or to "be correlated" when *variations in the value of one variable are synchronized with variations in the value of the other.* As the values in the second column vary from small to large, the values in the third column do the same.

TABLE 2.1

Hypothetical Data Showing the Relationship Between Sleep and Memory

Participant	Hours of Sleep	No. of Presidents Named
A	0	11
B	0	17
C	2.7	16
D	3.1	21
E	4.4	17
F	5.5	16
G	7.6	31
H	7.9	41
I	8	40
J	8.1	35
K	8.6	38
L	9	43

By looking for synchronized patterns of variation, we can use measurement to discover the relationships between variables. Indeed, this is the only way anyone has *ever* discovered the relationship between variables, which is why most of the facts you know about the world can be thought of as correlations. For example, you know that people who smoke generally die younger than people who don't, but this is just a shorthand way of saying that as the value of *cigarette consumption* increases, the value of *longevity* decreases. Correlations not only describe the world as it is, they also allow us to predict the world as it will be. For example, given the correlation between smoking and longevity, you can predict with some confidence that a young person who starts smoking today will probably not live as long as a young person who doesn't. In short, when two variables are correlated, knowledge of the value of one variable allows us to make predictions about the value of the other variable.

Measuring the Direction and Strength of a Correlation

If you predict that a well-rested person will have better memory than a sleep-deprived person, you will be right more often than wrong. But you won't be right in every single instance. Statisticians have developed a way to estimate how accurate such predictions are likely to be by measuring the *direction* and *strength* of the correlation on which the predictions are based.

Direction is easy to measure because the direction of a correlation is either positive or negative. A positive correlation exists when two variables have a "more-is-more" or "less-is-less" relationship. So, for example, when we say that *more sleep* is associated with *more memory* or that *less sleep* is associated with *less memory*, we are describing a positive correlation. Conversely, a negative correlation exists when two variables have a "more-is-less" or "less-is-more" relationship. When we say that *more cigarette smoking* is associated with *less longevity* or that *less cigarette smoking* is associated with *more longevity*, we are describing a negative correlation.

The direction of a correlation is easy to measure, but the strength is a little more complicated. The **correlation coefficient** is *a mathematical measure of both the direction and strength of a correlation*, and it is symbolized by the letter *r* (as in "relationship"). Like most measures, the correlation coefficient has a limited range. What does that mean? Well, if you were to measure the number of hours of sunshine per day in your hometown, that number could range from 0 to 24. Numbers such as –7 and 36.8 would be meaningless. Similarly, the value of *r* can range from –1 to 1, and numbers outside that range are meaningless. What, then, do the numbers *inside* that range mean?

▶ If every time the value of one variable increases by a fixed amount the value of the second variable also increases by a fixed amount, then the relationship between the variables is called a *perfect positive correlation*, and *r* = 1 (see **FIGURE 2.7a**). For example, if every 30-minute increase in sleep was associated with a 2-president increase in memory, then sleep and memory would be *perfectly positively correlated*.

> **correlation coefficient** A mathematical measure of both the direction and strength of a correlation, which is symbolized by the letter *r*.

▼ Figure 2.7
GRAPHING CORRELATIONS These figures show what three different kinds of correlations look like when graphed.

r = 1
Perfect Positive Correlation
(a)

r = –1
Perfect Negative Correlation
(b)

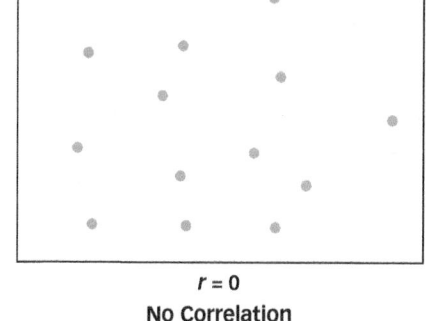

r = 0
No Correlation
(c)

▶ If every time the value of one variable increases by a fixed amount the value of the second variable *decreases* by a fixed amount, then the relationship between the variables is called a *perfect negative correlation*, and $r = -1$ (see Figure 2.7b). For example, if every 30-minute increase in sleep was associated with a 2-president decrease in memory, then sleep and memory would be *perfectly negatively correlated*.

▶ If every time the value of one variable increases by a fixed amount the value of the second variable neither increases nor decreases systematically, then the two variables are said to be *uncorrelated,* and $r = 0$ (see Figure 2.7c). For example, if a 30-minute increase in sleep was sometimes associated with an increase in memory, sometimes associated with a decrease in memory, and sometimes associated with no change in memory at all, then sleep and memory would be uncorrelated.

Perfect correlations are extremely rare. As you'll learn in the Consciousness chapter, sleep really does enhance memory performance, but the relationship is not perfect. It isn't as though every 18 minutes of sleep buys you exactly one third of a remembered president! Sleep and memory are *positively* correlated (i.e., as one increases, the other also increases), but they are *imperfectly* correlated, thus r will lie somewhere between 0 and 1. But where? That depends on how many exceptions there are to the "X more minutes of sleep = Y more presidents remembered" rule. If there are only a few exceptions, then r will be much closer to 1 than to 0. But as the number of exceptions increases, then the value of r will begin to move toward 0.

FIGURE 2.8 shows four cases in which two variables are positively correlated but have different numbers of exceptions, and as you can see, the number of exceptions changes the value of r quite dramatically. Two variables can have a perfect correlation ($r = 1$), a strong correlation (e.g., $r = .90$), a moderate correlation (e.g., $r = .70$), or a weak correlation (e.g., $r = .30$). The correlation coefficient, then, is a measure of both the *direction* and *strength* of the relationship between two variables. The sign of r (plus or minus) tells us the direction of the relationship and the absolute value of r (between 0 and 1) tells us about the number of exceptions and hence about how confident we can be when using the correlation to make predictions.

CAUSATION

We observe correlations all the time: between automobiles and pollution, between bacon and heart attacks, between sex and pregnancy. **Natural correlations** are *the correlations observed in the world around us,* and although such observations can tell us whether two variables have a relationship, they cannot tell us what *kind* of relationship those variables have. For example, many studies have found a positive correlation between the amount of violence to which a child is exposed through media such as television, movies, and video

natural correlation A correlation observed in the world around us.

Cigarettes are the deadliest device ever created by human beings, causing about 1.5 million deaths every year. So why do people smoke them? As early as 1912, scientists noticed a correlation between smoking and lung cancer, but tobacco companies argued that this natural correlation was not evidence of a causal relationship. In 1964, the U. S. Surgeon General finally determined that they were wrong: Smoking cigarettes causes lung cancer. What kinds of tools allow scientists to go from observing correlations to inferring causal relationships?

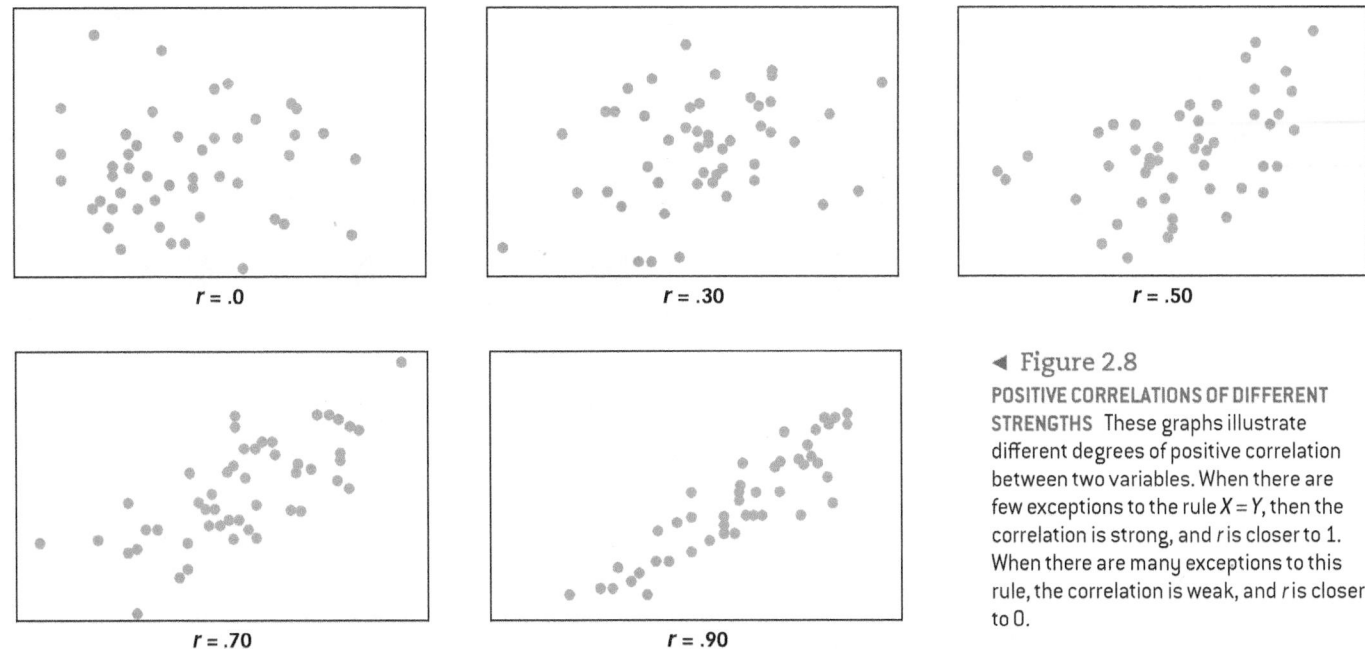

r = .0   r = .30   r = .50

r = .70   r = .90

◀ Figure 2.8
POSITIVE CORRELATIONS OF DIFFERENT STRENGTHS These graphs illustrate different degrees of positive correlation between two variables. When there are few exceptions to the rule $X = Y$, then the correlation is strong, and r is closer to 1. When there are many exceptions to this rule, the correlation is weak, and r is closer to 0.

games (variable X) and the aggressiveness of the child's behavior (variable Y; Anderson & Bushman, 2002; Anderson et al., 2003; Huesmann et al., 2003). The more media violence a child is exposed to, the more aggressive that child is likely to be. These variables clearly have a relationship—they are imperfectly positively correlated—but why?

The Third-Variable Problem: Why We Can't Draw Causal Conclusions From Correlations

One possibility is that exposure to media violence (X) causes aggressiveness (Y). For example, media violence may teach children that aggression is a reasonable way to vent anger and solve problems. A second possibility is that aggressiveness (Y) causes children to be exposed to media violence (X). For example, children who are naturally aggressive may be especially likely to seek opportunities to play violent video games or watch violent movies. A third possibility is that a *third variable* (Z) causes children to be aggressive (Y) and to be exposed to media violence (X), neither of which is causally related to the other. For example, lack of adult supervision (Z) may allow children to get away with bullying others and to get away with watching television shows that adults would normally not allow. If so, then being exposed to media violence (X) and behaving aggressively (Y) may not be causally related to each other at all and may instead be the independent effects of a lack of adult supervision (Z). In other words, the relation between aggressiveness and exposure to media violence may be a case of **third-variable correlation,** which means that *two variables are correlated only because each is causally related to a third variable.* **FIGURE 2.9** shows three possible causes of any correlation.

third-variable correlation Two variables are correlated only because each is causally related to a third variable.

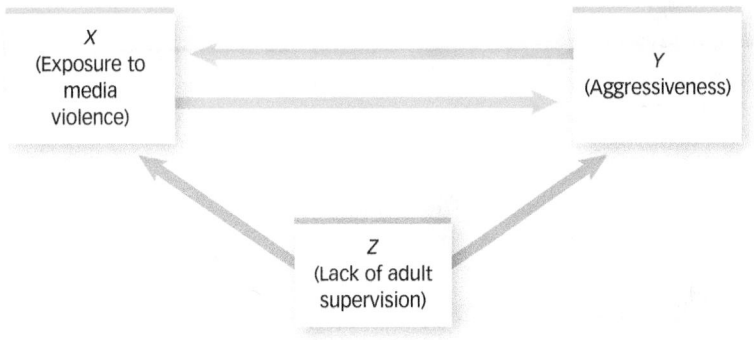

◀ Figure 2.9
CAUSES OF CORRELATION If X and Y are correlated, then there are at least three possible explanations: X causes Y, Y causes X, or Z causes both Y and X, neither of which causes the other.

▶ Figure 2.10

MATCHED SAMPLES AND PAIRS Both the matched samples technique (*left*) and the matched pairs technique (*right*) ensure that children in the exposure and no-exposure groups have the same amount of adult supervision on average. Thus, any differences we observe between the groups can't be due to differences in adult supervision.

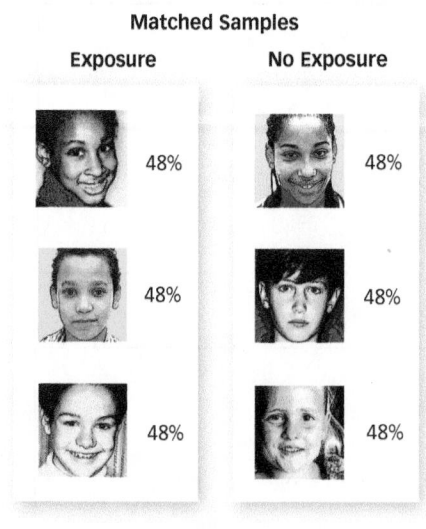

Matched Samples

Exposure	No Exposure
48%	48%
48%	48%
48%	48%

Matched Pairs

Exposure	No Exposure
20%	20%
91%	91%
33%	33%
Mean = 48%	Mean = 48%

matched samples technique A technique whereby the participants in two groups are identical in terms of a third variable.

matched pairs technique A technique whereby each participant is identical to one other participant in terms of a third variable.

In 1949, Dr. Benjamin Sandler noticed a correlation between the incidence of polio and ice cream consumption, and concluded that sugar made children susceptible to the disease. Public health officials issued warnings. As it turned out, a third variable—warm weather—caused both an increase in disease (viruses become more active in the summer) and an increase in ice cream consumption.

How can we determine by simple observation which of these three possibilities best describes the relationship between exposure to media violence and aggressiveness? Take a deep breath. The answer is: *We can't.* When we observe a natural correlation, the possibility of third-variable correlation can never be dismissed. But don't take this claim on faith. Let's try to dismiss the possibility of third-variable correlation and you'll see why such efforts are always doomed to fail.

The most straightforward way to determine whether a third variable, such as lack of adult supervision (Z), causes both exposure to media violence (X) and aggressive behavior (Y) is to eliminate differences in adult supervision (Z) among a group of children and see if the correlation between exposure (X) and aggressiveness (Y) is eliminated too. For example, we could observe children using the **matched samples technique,** which is *a technique whereby the participants in two groups are identical in terms of a third variable* (see **FIGURE 2.10**). For instance, we could measure only children who are supervised by an adult exactly $Q\%$ of the time, thus ensuring that every child who was exposed to media violence had exactly the same amount of adult supervision as every child who was not exposed. Alternatively, we could observe children using the **matched pairs technique,** which is *a technique whereby each participant is identical to one other participant in terms of a third variable*. We could measure children who have different amounts of adult supervision, but we could make sure that for every child we measure who is exposed to media violence and is supervised $Q\%$ of the time, we also observe a child who is not exposed to media violence and is supervised $Q\%$ of the time, thus ensuring that children who are and are not exposed to media violence have the same amount of adult supervision *on average*.

Regardless of which technique we used, we would know that children who were and were not exposed to media violence had equal amounts of adult supervision on average. So if those who were exposed are on average more aggressive than those who were not exposed, we can be sure that lack of adult supervision was not the cause of this difference.

So we've solved the problem, right? Well, not exactly. The matched samples technique and the matched pairs technique can be useful, but neither eliminates the possibility of third-variable correlation entirely. Why? Because even if we used these techniques to dismiss a *particular* third variable (such as lack of adult supervision), we would not be able to dismiss *all* third variables. For example, as soon as we finished making these observations, it might suddenly occur to us that emotional instability could cause children to gravitate toward violent television or video games and to behave aggressively. Emotional instability would be a new third variable (Z) and we would have to design a new test to investigate whether it explains the correlation between exposure (X) and aggression (Y). Unfortunately, we could keep dreaming up new third variables all day long without ever breaking a sweat, and every time we dreamed one up, we would have to rush out and do a new test using matched samples or matched pairs to determine whether *this* third variable was the cause of the correlation between exposure and aggressiveness.

Are you starting to see the problem? There are a humongous number of third variables, so there are a humongous number of reasons that X and Y might be correlated. And because we can't perform a humongous number of studies with matched samples or matched pairs, we cannot be absolutely sure that the correlation we observe between X and Y is evidence of a causal relationship between them. The **third-variable problem** is the fact that *a causal relationship between two variables cannot be inferred from the naturally occurring correlation between them because of the ever-present possibility of third-variable correlation*. In other words, if we care about causality, then naturally occurring correlations just won't tell us what we really want to know. Luckily, another technique will.

Experimentation: A Solution to the Third-Variable Problem

The matched pairs and matched samples techniques eliminate a single difference between two groups: for example, the difference in adult supervision between groups of children who were and were not exposed to media violence. The problem is that they eliminate only one difference, and a humongous number remain. If we could just find a technique that eliminated *all* of the humongous number of differences, then we *could* conclude that exposure and aggression are causally related. If exposed kids were more aggressive than unexposed kids, and if the two groups didn't differ in *any* way except for that exposure, then we could be sure that their level of exposure had caused their level of aggression.

In fact, scientists have a technique that does exactly that. It is called an **experiment,** which is *a technique for establishing the causal relationship between variables*. The best way to understand how experiments eliminate all the differences between groups is by examining their two key features: *manipulation* and *random assignment*.

Manipulation: Making Changes in the Independent Variable

The most important thing to know about experiments is that you already know the most important thing about experiments because you've been doing them all your life. Imagine that you are surfing the Web on a laptop when all of a sudden you lose your wireless connection. You suspect that another device—say, your roommate's new cell phone—has somehow bumped you off the network. What would you do to test your suspicion? Observing a natural correlation wouldn't be much help. You could carefully note when you did and didn't have a connection and when your roommate did and didn't use his cell phone, but even if you observed a correlation between these two variables you still couldn't conclude that the cell phone was *causing* you to lose your network connection. After all, if your roommate was afraid of loud noises and called his mommy for comfort whenever there was an electrical storm, and if that storm zapped your router and crashed your wireless network, then the storm (Z) would be the cause of both your roommate's cell phone usage (X) and your connectivity problem (Y).

third-variable problem The fact that a causal relationship between two variables cannot be inferred from the naturally occurring correlation between them because of the ever-present possibility of third-variable correlation.

experiment A technique for establishing the causal relationship between variables.

(a)   (b)

MACMILLAN LEARNING

Where should you put the "sign up" button on a Web page? Developers often create two versions of their Web pages. Some visitors see one version, some see the other, and the developer measures the number of clicks that each version elicits. Developers call this "A/B Testing," but scientists just call it experimentation.

How do you determine whether eating 62 hot dogs will make you sick? You eat them one day, don't eat them the next day, and then see which day you barf. *That's* manipulation! By the way, in 2015, the world champion Matt Stonie ate 62 hot dogs in 10 minutes by folding them up. *That's* manipulation, too!

So how could you test your suspicion? Well, rather than *observing* the correlation between cell phone usage and connectivity, you could try to *create* a correlation by intentionally making a call on your roommate's cell phone, hanging up, making another call, hanging up again, and observing changes in your laptop's connectivity as you did so. If you observed that "laptop connection off" occurred only in conjunction with "cell phone on," then you could conclude that your roommate's cell phone was the *cause* of your failed connection, and you could sell the phone on eBay and then lie about it when asked. The technique you intuitively used to solve the third-variable problem is called **manipulation,** which involves *changing a variable in order to determine its causal power.* Congratulations! You are now officially a manipulator.

Manipulation is a critical ingredient in experimentation. Until now, we have approached science like polite dinner guests, taking what we were offered and making the best of it. Nature offered us children who differed in how much violence they were exposed to and who differed in how aggressively they behaved, and we dutifully measured the natural patterns of variation in these two variables and computed their correlations. The problem with this approach is that when all was said and done, we still didn't know what we really wanted to know, namely, whether these variables had a causal relationship. No matter how many matched samples or matched pairs we observed, there was always another third variable that we hadn't yet dismissed.

Experiments solve this problem. Rather than *measuring* exposure and *measuring* aggression and then computing the correlation between these two naturally occurring variables, experiments require us to *manipulate* exposure in exactly the same way that you manipulated your roommate's cell phone. In essence, we need to systematically switch exposure on and off in a group of children and then watch to see whether aggression goes on and off too.

There are many ways to do this. For example, we might ask some children to participate in an experiment, then have half of them play violent video games for an hour and make sure the other half does not. Then, at the end of the hour, we could measure the children's aggression and compare the measurements across the two groups. When we compared these measurements, we would essentially be computing the correlation between a variable that we manipulated (exposure) and a variable that we measured (aggression). Because we *manipulated* rather than *measured* exposure, we would never have to ask whether a third variable (such as lack of adult supervision) caused children to experience different levels of exposure. After all, we already *know* what caused that to happen. *We* did!

Experimentation involves three critical steps (and several ridiculously confusing terms):

manipulation   Changing a variable in order to determine its causal power.

independent variable   The variable that is manipulated in an experiment

experimental group   The group of participants who are exposed to a particular manipulation, compared with the control group, in an experiment

control group   The group of participants who are not exposed to the particular manipulation, compared with the experimental group, in an experiment

dependent variable   The variable that is measured in a study.

▶ First, we perform a manipulation. We call *the variable that is manipulated* the **independent variable** because it is under our control, and thus it is "independent" of what the participant says or does. When we manipulate an independent variable (such as exposure to media violence), we create at least two groups of participants: an **experimental group,** which is *the group of participants who are exposed to a particular manipulation,* and a **control group,** which is *the group of participants who are not exposed to that particular manipulation.*

▶ Second, having manipulated one variable (exposure), we now measure another variable (aggression). We call *the variable that is measured* the **dependent variable** because its value "depends" on what the participant says or does.

▶ Third and last, we look to see whether our manipulation of the independent variable produced changes in the dependent variable. **FIGURE 2.11** shows exactly how manipulation works.

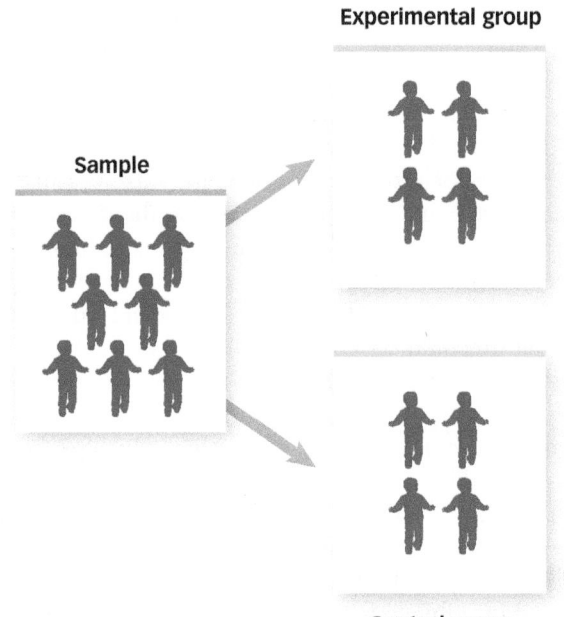

Experimental group

Exposed to media violence?	Aggression
Yes	High
Yes	High
Yes	High
Yes	High

Sample

Exposed to media violence?	Aggression
No	Low
No	Low
No	Low
No	Low

Control group

◀ **Figure 2.11**

MANIPULATION The independent variable is exposure to media violence, and the dependent variable is aggression. Manipulation of the independent variable results in an experimental group and a control group. When we compare the behavior of participants in these two groups, we are actually computing the correlation between the independent variable and the dependent variable.

Random Assignment: Making Sure Conditions Differ in Only One Way

Once we have manipulated an independent variable and measured a dependent variable, we've done one of the two things that experimentation requires. The second thing is a little less intuitive but equally important. Imagine that we began our exposure and aggression experiment by finding a group of children and asking each child whether he or she would like to be in the experimental group or the control group. Imagine that half the children said that they'd like to play violent video games and the other half said they would rather not. Imagine that we let the children do what they wanted to do, measured aggression some time later, and found that the children who had played the violent video games were more aggressive than those who had not. Would this experiment allow us to conclude that playing violent video games causes aggression? Definitely not—but *why* not? After all, we switched exposure on and off like a cell phone, and we watched to see whether aggression went on and off too. So where did we go wrong?

We went wrong when we let the children decide for themselves whether or not they would play violent video games. After all, children who ask to play such games are probably different in many ways from those who ask not to. They may be older, or stronger, or smarter—or younger, weaker, or not so smart—or less often supervised or more often supervised. The list of possible differences goes on and on. The whole point of doing an experiment was to divide children into two groups that differed in *only one way,* namely, in terms of their exposure to media violence. The moment we let the children decide for themselves whether they would be in the experimental group or the control group, we had two groups that differed in countless ways, and any of those countless differences could have been a third variable that was responsible for any differences we may have observed in their measured aggression. **Self-selection** is *a problem that occurs when anything about a participant determines whether he or she will be included in the experimental or control group.* Just as we cannot allow nature to decide which of the children in our study is exposed to media violence, we cannot allow the children to decide either. Okay, then who decides?

The answer to this question is a bit spooky: *No one does.* If we want to be sure that there is one and only one difference between the children in our study who are and are not exposed to media violence, then their inclusion in the experimental or control

self-selection A problem that occurs when anything about a participant determines whether he or she will be included in the experimental or control group.

There is no evidence that Louise Hay's techniques can cure cancer. But even if cancer victims who bought her books did show a higher rate of remission than those who didn't, there would still be no evidence because buyers are self-selected and thus may differ from nonbuyers in countless ways.

INGRAM PUBLISHING/GETTY IMAGES

Do strawberries taste better when dipped in chocolate? If you dip the big juicy ones and don't dip the small dry ones, then you won't know if the chocolate is what made the difference. But if you randomly assign some to be dipped and others not to be dipped, and if the dipped ones taste better on average, then you will have demonstrated scientifically what every 3-year-old already knows.

random assignment A procedure that lets chance assign participants to the experimental or control group.

groups must be *randomly determined*. If you flipped a coin and a friend asked what had *caused* it to land heads up, you would correctly say that *nothing* had. This is what it means for the outcome of a coin flip to be random. Because the outcome of a coin flip is random, we can put coin flips to work for us to solve the problem that self-selection creates. If we want to be sure that a child's inclusion in the experimental or control group was not caused by nature, was not caused by the child, and was not caused by *any* of the countless third variables we could name if only we had the time to name them, then all we have to do is let it be caused by the outcome of a coin flip—which itself has no cause! For example, we could walk up to each child in our experiment, flip a coin, and, if the coin lands heads up, assign the child to play violent video games. If the coin lands heads down, then we could assign the child to play no violent video games. **Random assignment** is a *procedure that lets chance assign participants to the experimental or the control group.*

What would happen if we assigned children to groups with a coin flip? As **FIGURE 2.12** shows, the first thing we would expect is that about half the children would be assigned to play violent video games and about half would not. Second—and *much* more important—we could expect the experimental group and the control group to have roughly equal numbers of supervised kids and unsupervised kids, roughly equal numbers of emotionally stable and unstable kids, roughly equal numbers of big kids and small kids, of active kids, fat kids, tall kids, funny kids, and blue-haired kids named Larry McSweeny. In other words, we could expect the two groups to have roughly equal numbers of kids who are anything-you-can-ever-name-and-everything-you-can't! Because the kids in the two groups will be the same *on average* in terms of height, weight, emotional stability, adult supervision, and every other variable in the known universe *except the one we manipulated*, we can be sure that the variable we manipulated (exposure) was the one and only cause of any differences in the variable we measured (aggression). Because exposure was the *only* difference between the two groups of children when we started the experiment, it *must* be the cause of any differences in aggression we observe at the end of the experiment. And that, it turns out, is how experiments solve the third-variable problem (see Hot Science: Is Science Gender Biased?).

▶ Figure 2.12

RANDOM ASSIGNMENT Children with adult supervision are shown in orange; those without adult supervision are shown in blue. The independent variable is exposure to media violence; the dependent variable is aggression. Random assignment ensures that participants in the experimental and the control groups are on average equal in terms of all possible third variables. In essence, it ensures that there is no correlation between a third variable and the dependent variable.

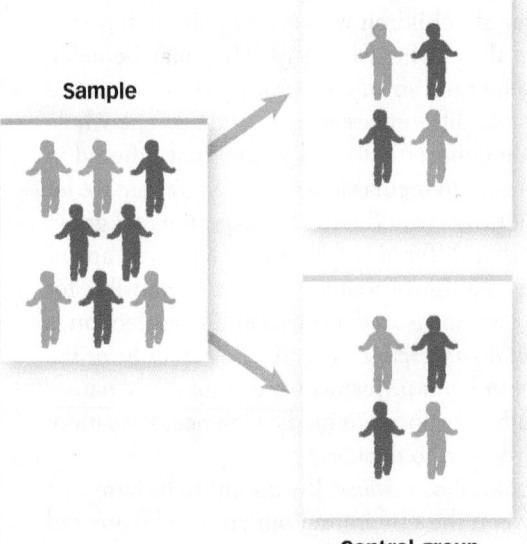

Experimental group

Exposed to media violence?	Adult supervision?	Aggression
Yes	Yes	High
Yes	No	High
Yes	Yes	High
Yes	No	High

Sample

Exposed to media violence?	Adult supervision?	Aggression
No	Yes	Low
No	No	Low
No	Yes	Low
No	No	Low

Control group

HOT SCIENCE

Is Science Gender Biased?

Women are often discouraged from pursuing scientific careers because they notice that many scientific disciplines are dominated by men, and that makes them worry that they may experience discrimination when it comes time to find a job. Is that worry well founded? Traditionally, scientists who have been interested in the problem of sexism in hiring have examined natural correlations, and when they find that a larger percentage of men than women are hired, promoted, or given a raise, they become suspicious. But what they don't become is certain because, as you know from reading this chapter, the third-variable problem means that natural correlations can never provide clear evidence of causation. If the psychology department at a major university hires a smaller percentage of female than male applicants, that could be due to gender discrimination. But it could also be due to the fact that the female applicants got their degrees at less prestigious universities, or published fewer scientific papers, or were just less aggressive in pestering the faculty for an interview. And as you also know, even if we rule out these particular possibilities, another will always arise to take its place. Correlations just can't answer this important question.

But experiments can. Recently, the psychologists Wendy Williams and Stephen Ceci (2015) tried to use experiments to do just that. The participants in their experiments were nearly a thousand professors from biology, engineering, economics, and psychology departments at several hundred universities and colleges from every

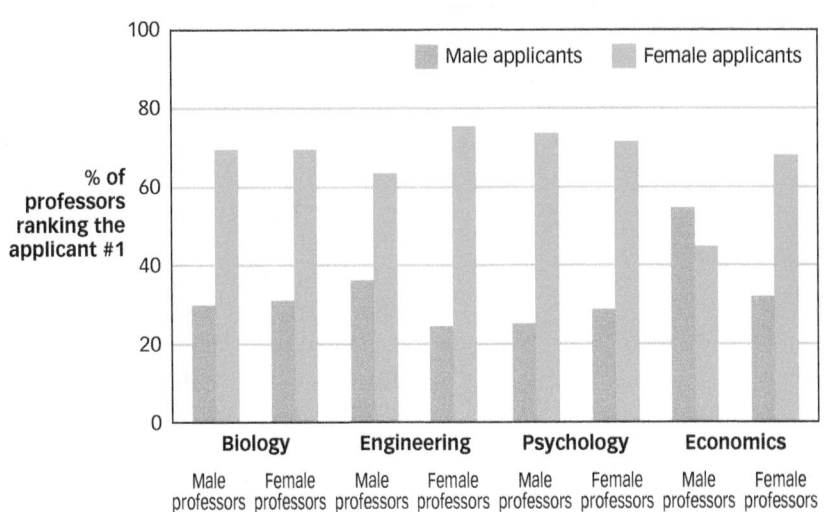

state in the nation. These professors were shown descriptions of several applicants who were applying for a professorship, and were asked to rank the applicants from the most to least hirable. What the professors were not told was that the researchers had manipulated the applicants' genders, so if one professor was randomly assigned to see an applicant referred to as "he," another professor was randomly assigned to see the same applicant referred to as "she." Because the professors were randomly assigned to condition, and because the only thing that differed between those conditions was the gender of otherwise identical applicants (which the experimenters had manipulated), Williams and Ceci were able to determine whether professors were gender biased. And indeed they were—but not in the way you might think. Results showed that both male and

female professors in all fields showed a strong preference for female applicants. The only exception to that rule was male economics professors, who showed no gender bias at all.

Of course, experiments are not miniature versions of the real world, so isn't it possible that in real hiring situations, real professors would show the opposite bias? It is possible, of course, but the data suggest that it probably isn't true. "Research on actual hiring shows female Ph.D.s are disproportionately less likely to apply for tenure-track positions, but if they do apply, they are more likely to be hired, sometimes by a 2:1 ratio" (Williams & Ceci, 2015, p. 5365). Although no research can ever answer a question like this once and for all, it appears that now is a very good time for women to choose a career in science.

Statistical Testing: What Do the Differences Between Conditions Actually Mean?

Random assignment is a powerful tool, but like a lot of tools, it doesn't work every time you use it. If we randomly assigned children to be exposed or not exposed to media violence, we could expect the two groups to have roughly equal numbers of supervised and unsupervised kids, roughly equal numbers of emotionally stable and unstable kids, and so on. The key word in that sentence is *roughly.* When you flip a coin 100 times, you can expect it to land heads up *roughly* 50 times. But every once in a while, 100 coin flips will produce 80 heads, or 90 heads, or even 100 heads, by sheer chance alone (see The Real World: Oddsly Enough). This does not happen often, of course, but it does happen. Because random assignment is achieved by using a randomizing device such as a coin, every once in a long while the coin will assign more unsupervised, emotionally unstable kids to play violent video games and more supervised, emotionally stable kids to play none. When this happens, random assignment has failed—and when random assignment fails, the third-variable problem rises up out of its grave like a guy with a hockey mask and a grudge. When random assignment fails, we cannot conclude that there is a causal relationship between the independent and dependent variables.

How can we tell when random assignment has failed? Unfortunately, we can't tell for sure. But we can calculate the *odds* that random assignment has failed each time we use it. It isn't important for you to know how to do this calculation, but it is important for you to understand how psychologists interpret its results. Psychologists perform this calculation every time they do an experiment, and they do not accept the results of those experiments unless the calculation tells them that if random assignment had failed, then there is less than a 5% chance that they would have seen those particular results.

When there is less than a 5% chance that a result would happen if random assignment had failed, then that result is said to be *statistically significant*. You've already learned about descriptive statistics, such as the mean, median, mode, range, and

Oddsly Enough

A recent Gallup survey found that 53% of college graduates believe in extrasensory perception, or ESP. Very few psychologists share that belief. What makes them such a skeptical lot is their understanding of the laws of probability.

Consider the case of the Truly Amazing Coincidence. One night you dream that a panda is piloting an airplane over the Indian Ocean, and the next day you tell a friend, who says, "Wow, I had exactly the same dream!" One morning you wake up humming an old Radiohead tune (probably "Paranoid Android"), and an hour later you hear it playing in the mall. You and your roommate are sitting around watching television when suddenly you turn to each other and say in perfect unison, "Want pizza?" Coincidences like these might make anyone believe in supernatural mental weirdness.

Well, not anyone. The Nobel laureate Luis Alvarez was reading the newspaper one day, and a particular story got him thinking about an old college friend whom he hadn't seen in years. A few minutes later, he turned the page and was shocked to see the very same friend's obituary. But before concluding that he had an acute case of ESP, Alvarez decided to use probability theory to determine just how amazing this coincidence really was.

First he estimated the number of friends an average person has, and then he estimated how often an average person thinks about each of those friends. With these estimates in hand, he did a few simple calculations and determined the likelihood that someone would think about a friend five minutes before learning about that friend's death. The odds were astonishing. In a country the size of the United States, for example, Alvarez predicted that this amazing coincidence should happen to 10 people every day (Alvarez, 1965). Another Nobel laureate disagreed. He put the number closer to 80 people a day (Charpak & Broch, 2004)!

"In 10 years there are 5 million minutes," says the statistics professor Irving Jack. "That means each person has plenty of opportunity to have some remarkable coincidences in his life" (quoted in Neimark, 2004). For example, 250 million Americans dream for about two hours every night (that's a half billion hours of dreaming!), so it isn't surprising that two people sometimes have the same dream, or that we sometimes dream about something that actually happens the next day. As the mathematics professor John Allen Paulos (quoted in Neimark, 2004) put it, "In reality, the most astonishingly

"Idaho! What a coincidence—I'm from Idaho."

incredible coincidence imaginable would be the complete absence of all coincidence."

If all of this seems surprising to you, then you are not alone. Research shows that people routinely underestimate the likelihood of coincidences happening by chance (Diaconis & Mosteller, 1989; Falk & McGregor, 1983; Hintzman, Asher, & Stern, 1978). If you want to profit from this fact, assemble a group of 24 or more people and bet anyone that at least 2 of the people share a birthday. The odds are in your favor, and the bigger the group, the better the odds. In fact, in a group of 35, the odds are 85%. Happy fleecing!

standard deviation. Another kind of statistics—called *inferential statistics*—tells scientists what kinds of conclusions or inferences they can draw from observed differences between the experimental and control groups. For example, *p* (for "probability") is an inferential statistic that tells psychologists the likelihood that random assignment failed in a particular experiment. When psychologists report that $p < .05$, they are saying that according to the inferential statistics they calculated, the odds that their results would have occurred if random assignment had failed are less than 5%, and given that those results *did* occur, a failure of random assignment is unlikely to have happened. Therefore, differences between the experimental and control groups were unlikely to have been caused by a third variable.

DRAWING CONCLUSIONS: WHAT DO MEASUREMENTS TELL US?

If we applied all the techniques discussed so far, we could design an experiment that had a very good chance of establishing the causal relationship between two variables. That experiment would have **internal validity,** which is *an attribute of an experiment that allows it to establish causal relationships.* When we say that an experiment is internally valid, we mean that everything *inside* the experiment is working exactly as it must in order for us to draw conclusions about causal relationships. But what exactly are those conclusions? If our imaginary experiment revealed a difference between the aggressiveness of children in the exposed and unexposed groups, then we could conclude that media violence *as we defined it* caused aggression *as we defined it* in the people *whom we studied.* Notice those phrases in italics. Each corresponds to an important restriction on the kinds of conclusions we can draw from an experiment, so let's consider each in turn.

Representative Variables

The results of any experiment depend, in part, on how the independent and dependent variables are defined. For instance, we are more likely to find that exposure to media violence causes aggression when we define exposure as "watching two hours of gory axe murders" rather than "watching 10 minutes of football," or when we define aggression as "interrupting another person" rather than "smacking someone silly with a tire iron." The way we define variables can have a profound influence on what we find, so which of these is the *right* way?

One answer is that we should define variables in an experiment as they are defined in the real world. **External validity** is *an attribute of an experiment in which variables have been defined in a normal, typical, or realistic way.* It seems pretty clear that the kind of aggressive behavior that concerns teachers and parents lies somewhere between an interruption and an assault, and that the kind of media violence to which children are typically exposed lies somewhere between sports and torture. If the goal of an experiment is to determine whether the kinds of media violence to which children are typically exposed causes the kinds of aggression with which societies are typically concerned, then external validity is essential. When variables are defined in an experiment as they typically are in the real world, we say that the variables are *representative* of the real world.

External validity sounds like such a good idea that you may be surprised to learn that most psychology experiments are externally *in*valid—and that most psychologists don't mind. The reason for this is that psychologists are rarely trying to learn about the real world by creating tiny replicas of it in their laboratories. Rather, they are usually trying to learn about the real world by using experiments to test hypotheses derived from theories, and externally invalid experiments can often do that quite nicely (Mook, 1983).

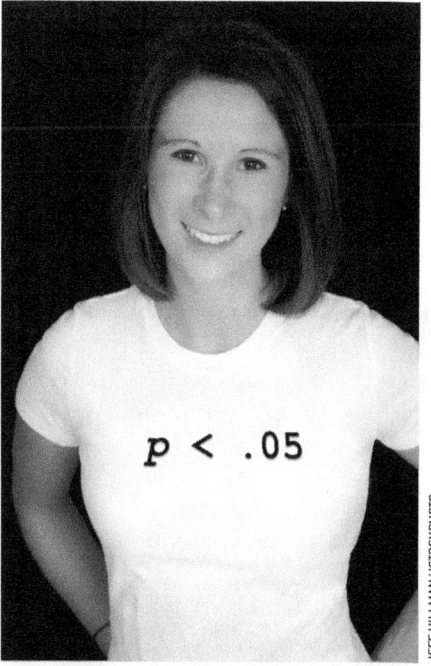

Some scientists wear this T-shirt under their clothing at all times so that if they ever get in a car accident and are rushed unconscious to the emergency room, the doctors will know they are allergic to fashion.

internal validity An attribute of an experiment that allows it to establish causal relationships.

external validity An attribute of an experiment in which variables have been defined in a normal, typical, or realistic way.

Does piercing make a person more or less attractive? The answer, of course, depends entirely on your operational definition of *piercing*.

To see how, consider an example from physics. Physicists have a theory stating that heat is the result of the rapid movement of molecules. This theory gives rise to a hypothesis, namely, that when the molecules that constitute an object are slowed, the object should become cooler. Now imagine that a physicist tested this hypothesis by performing an experiment in which a laser was used to slow the movement of the molecules in a rubber ball, whose temperature was then measured. Would you criticize this experiment by saying, "Sorry, but your experiment teaches us nothing about the real world because in the real world, no one actually uses lasers to slow the movement of the molecules in rubber balls"? Let's hope not. The physicist's theory (molecular motion causes heat) led to a hypothesis about *what would happen in the laboratory* (slowing the molecules in a rubber ball should cool it), and the events that the physicist manipulated and measured in the laboratory tested the hypothesis. Similarly, a well-thought-out theory about the causal relationship between exposure to media violence and aggression should lead to hypotheses about how children in a laboratory will behave after watching a violent movie, and thus their reaction to the movie tests the hypothesis. If children who watch *Warcraft* are more likely to push and shove each other on their way out of the laboratory, then any theory that says that media violence cannot influence aggression has just been proved wrong.

In short, theories allow us to generate hypotheses about what can, must, or will happen under particular circumstances, and experiments are usually meant to create those circumstances, test the hypotheses, and thereby provide evidence for or against the theories that generated them. Experiments are not usually meant to be miniature versions of everyday life, and thus external invalidity is not necessarily a problem.

Representative People

Our imaginary experiment on exposure to media violence and aggression would allow us to conclude that exposure as we defined it caused aggression as we defined it in the people *whom we studied.* That last phrase names another important restriction on the kinds of conclusions we can draw from experiments.

Who are the people whom psychologists study? Psychologists rarely observe an entire **population,** which is *a complete collection of people*, such as the population of human beings (about 7 billion), the population of Californians (about 38 million), or the population of people with Down syndrome (about 1 million). Rather, they observe a **sample,** which is *a partial collection of people drawn from a population*. How big can a sample be? The size of a population is signified by the uppercase letter N, the size of a sample is signified by the lowercase letter n, so $0 < n < N$. If you read this as an emoticon it means . . . oh well, never mind.

In most studies n is closer to 0 than to N, and in some cases $n = 1$. For example, sometimes single individuals are so remarkable that they deserve close study, and when psychologists study them they use the **case method,** which is *a procedure for gathering scientific information by studying a single individual*. We can learn a lot about memory by studying someone such as Rajveer Meena, who memorized the first 70,000 digits of pi; about consciousness by studying someone such as Henry Molaison, whose ability to look backward and forward in time was destroyed by damage to his brain; about intelligence and creativity by studying someone such as Tanishq Abraham, who graduated from college at the age of 11 and began consulting in the aerospace industry. Cases such as these are interesting in their own right, but they also provide important insights into how the rest of us work.

Of course, most of the psychological studies you will read about in this book included samples of ten, a hundred, a thousand, or a few thousand people. So how do psychologists decide which people to include in their samples? One way to select a sample from a population is by **random sampling,** which is *a technique for choosing participants that ensures that every member of a population has an equal chance of being included in the sample*. When we randomly sample participants from a population,

population A complete collection of participants who might possibly be measured.

sample A partial collection of people drawn from a population.

case method A procedure for gathering scientific information by studying a single individual.

random sampling A technique for choosing participants that ensures that every member of a population has an equal chance of being included in the sample.

the sample is said to be *representative* of the population. This allows us to *generalize* from the sample to the population—that is, to conclude that what we observed in our sample would also have been observed if we had measured the entire population. You probably already have solid intuitions about the importance of random sampling. For example, if you stopped at a farm stand to buy a bag of cherries and the farmer offered to let you taste a few that he had handpicked from the bag, you'd be reluctant to generalize from that sample to the population of cherries in the bag. But if the farmer invited you to pull a few cherries from the bag at random, you'd probably be willing to take those cherries as representative of the cherry population.

Random sampling sounds like such a good idea that you might be surprised to learn that most psychological studies involve nonrandom samples—and that most psychologists don't mind. Indeed, virtually every participant in every psychology experiment you will ever read about was a volunteer, and most were college students who were significantly younger, smarter, healthier, wealthier, and Whiter than the average Earthling. About 96% of the people whom psychologists study come from countries that have just 12% of the world's population, and 70% come from the United States alone (Henrich, Heine, & Norenzayan, 2010).

So why do psychologists sample nonrandomly? They have no choice. Even if there were a computerized list of all the world's human inhabitants from which we could randomly choose our research participants, how would we ever *find* the 72-year-old Bedouin woman whose family roams the desert so that we could measure the electrical activity in her brain while she watched cartoons? How would we convince the 3-week-old infant in New Delhi to complete a lengthy questionnaire about his political beliefs? Most psychology experiments are conducted by professors and graduate students at colleges and universities in the Western Hemisphere, and as much as they might *like* to sample the population of the planet randomly, the practical truth is that they are pretty much stuck studying the folks who volunteer for their studies.

So how can we learn *anything* from psychology experiments? Isn't the failure to sample randomly a fatal flaw? No, it's not, and there are three reasons why. First, sometimes the similarity of a sample and a population doesn't matter. If one pig flew over the Statue of Liberty just one time, it would instantly disprove the traditional theory of porcine locomotion. It wouldn't matter if all pigs flew or if any other pigs flew. If one did, then that's enough. An experimental result can be illuminating even when the sample isn't typical of the population.

Second, when the ability to generalize an experimental result *is* important, psychologists perform a **direct replication**, which is *an experiment that uses the same*

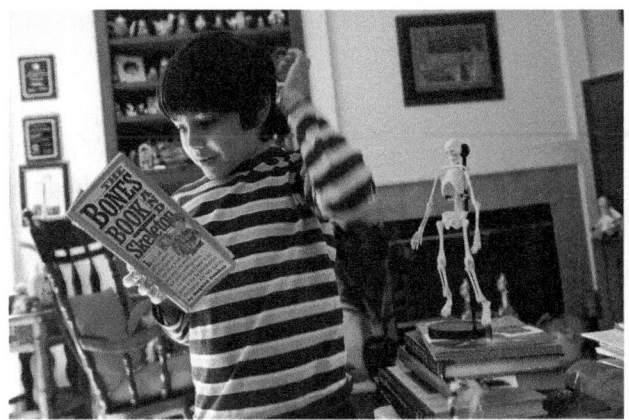

Tanishq Abraham graduated from college in 2015 at the age of 11. He told reporters, "I want to become a doctor, but I also want to become a medical researcher, and also the President of the United States." Is there any reason why he can't do all three?

direct replication An experiment that uses the same procedures as a previous experiment but with a new sample.

Nonrandom sampling can lead to errors. In the presidential election of 1948, the *Chicago Tribune* mistakenly predicted that Thomas Dewey would beat Harry Truman. Why? Because polling was done by telephone, and Dewey Republicans were more likely to have telephones than were Truman Democrats. In the presidential election of 2004, exit polls mistakenly predicted that John Kerry would beat George Bush. Why? Because polling was done by soliciting voters as they left the polls, and Kerry supporters were more willing to stop and talk.

This mouse died after drinking the green stuff. Want to drink the green stuff? Why not? You're not a mouse, are you?

procedures as a previous experiment but with a new sample. For example, after measuring how a nonrandomly selected group of American children behaved after playing violent video games, we might try to replicate our experiment with Japanese children, or with American teenagers, or with deaf adults. In essence, we could treat the attributes of our sample, such as culture and age and ability, as independent variables, and we could do experiments to determine whether these attributes influenced our dependent variable. If the results of our study were replicated in these other samples, then we would be more confident (but never completely confident) that the results describe a basic human tendency. If the results are not replicated, then we would learn something about the influence of culture or age or ability on aggressiveness. Replicating research with new samples drawn from different populations is a win–win strategy: No matter what happens, we learn something interesting.

Third, sometimes the similarity of the sample and the population is simply a reasonable starting assumption. Instead of asking, "Do I have a compelling reason to believe that my sample is representative of the population?" we could instead ask, "Do I have a compelling reason not to?" For example, few of us would be willing to take an experimental medicine if a nonrandom sample of 7 participants took it and died. Indeed, we would probably refuse the medicine even if the 7 participants were mice. Although these nonrandomly sampled participants were different from us in many ways (including tails and whiskers), most of us would be willing to generalize from their experience to ours because we know that even mice share enough of our basic biology to make it a good bet that what harms them can harm us too. By this same reasoning, if a psychology experiment demonstrated that some American children behaved violently after playing violent video games, we might ask whether there is a compelling reason to suspect that Ecuadorian college students or middle-aged Australians would behave any differently. If the answer was yes, then experiments would provide a way for us to investigate that possibility.

Build to the Outcomes

1. What is a natural correlation and how can it be measured?

2. What does it mean for a correlation to be positive or negative, strong or weak?

3. What is the correlation coefficient and what do its values mean?

4. What is the third-variable problem?

5. What are the key ingredients for an experiment?

6. How do manipulation and random assignment solve the third-variable problem?

7. Why is self-selection a problem?

8. What is the difference between a dependent and independent variable?

9. What is the difference between internal validity and external validity?

10. What is the difference between a population and a sample?

Thinking Critically About Evidence

Learning Outcomes

▶ Identify the two psychological tendencies that make critical thinking so difficult.

▶ Describe the two steps people can take to help them think critically.

In 1620, Sir Francis Bacon published a book called *Novum Organum,* in which he described a new method for discovering facts about the natural world. Today, this so-called Baconian method is more simply known as the scientific method, and that method has allowed human beings to learn more about themselves and the world in the last four centuries than in all the previous centuries combined.

As you've seen in this chapter, the scientific method allows us to produce empirical evidence. But empirical evidence is useful only if we know how to think about it—and the fact is that most of us don't. Using evidence requires *critical thinking*, which involves asking ourselves tough questions about whether we have interpreted the evidence in an unbiased way, and about whether the evidence tells not just the truth, but the *whole* truth. Research suggests that most people have trouble doing both of these things, and that educational programs designed to teach or improve critical thinking skills are not particularly effective (Willingham, 2007). Why do people have so much trouble thinking critically?

Consider the armadillo. Some animals freeze when threatened; others duck, run, or growl. Armadillos jump. This natural tendency served armadillos quite well for millennia because for millennia the most common threat to an armadillo's well-being was a rattlesnake. Alas, this natural tendency serves armadillos rather poorly today, because when they wander onto a Texas highway and are threatened by a speeding car, they jump up and hit the bumper. No armadillo makes this mistake twice.

Human beings also have natural tendencies that once served them well but no longer do. Our natural and intuitive ways of thinking about evidence, for example, worked just fine when we were all hunter-gatherers living in small groups on the African savannah. But now most of us live in large-scale, complex societies, and these natural ways of thinking interfere with our ability to reason in the modern world. Sir Francis Bacon understood this well. In the very same book in which he developed the scientific method, he argued that two ancient and all-too-human-tendencies—the tendency to see what we expect or want to see and the tendency to ignore what we can't see—are the hallmarks of natural or intuitive thinking, and therefore the enemies of critical thinking.

WE SEE WHAT WE EXPECT AND WANT

When two people are presented with the same evidence, they often draw different conclusions. Sir Francis Bacon thought he knew why: "The human understanding, once it has adopted opinions . . . draws everything else to support and agree with them." Thus our "first conclusion colors and brings into conformity with itself all that come after." In other words, our preexisting beliefs color our view of new evidence, causing us to see what we expect to see. As such, evidence often seems to confirm what we believed all along.

This tendency has been widely documented in psychological science. For instance, participants in one study (Darley & Gross, 1983) learned about a little girl named Hannah. One group of participants was told that Hannah came from an affluent family, and another group was told that Hannah came from a poor family. All participants were then shown some evidence about Hannah's academic abilities (specifically, they watched a video of Hannah taking a reading test) and were then asked to rate Hannah. Although the video was exactly the same for all participants, those who believed that Hannah was affluent rated her performance more positively than did those who believed that Hannah was poor. What's more, both groups of participants defended their conclusions by citing evidence from the video! Experiments like this one suggest that when we consider evidence, what we see depends on what we *expected* to see.

Our beliefs aren't the only things that color our views of evidence. Those views are also colored by our preferences and prejudices, our ambitions and aversions, our hopes and needs and wants and dreams. As Bacon noted, "The human understanding is not a dry light, but is infused by desire and emotion which give rise to wishful science. For man prefers to believe what he wants to be true."

Research suggests that Bacon was right about this, too. For example, participants in one study (Lord, Ross, & Lepper, 1979) were shown some scientific evidence about the effectiveness of the death penalty. Some of the evidence suggested that the death penalty deterred crime, and some suggested it did not. What did participants make of this mixed bag of evidence? Participants who originally supported the death penalty became even *more* supportive, and participants who originally opposed the death

Sir Francis Bacon (1561–1626) is credited with having devised the scientific method, which he used until he died from pneumonia, which he caught while studying the effects of low temperatures on the preservation of meat.

DATA VISUALIZATION

Does SAT Performance Correlate with Family Income and Education Level? Go to launchpadworks.com.

DAVID J. GREEN/ALAMY STOCK PHOTO

The first rule of critical thinking is to doubt your own conclusions—but that's hard to do when everyone tells you you're right! Recent research shows that Facebook users create "echo chambers" by sharing stories and links only with friends who already share their points of view (Del Vicario et al., 2016).

penalty became even *more* opposed. In other words, when presented with exactly the same evidence, participants saw what they *wanted* to see and ended up feeling even more sure about their initial views. Subsequent research has shown that the same pattern emerges when professional scientists are asked to rate the quality of scientific studies that either confirm or disconfirm what they want to believe (Koehler, 1993).

Exactly how do beliefs and desires shape our view of the evidence? People hold different kinds of evidence to different standards. When evidence confirms what we believe or want to believe, we tend to ask ourselves, *"Can* I believe it?" and our answer is usually yes; but when evidence disconfirms what we believe or want to believe, we tend to ask ourselves, *"Must* I believe it?" and the answer is often no (Gilovich, 1991). *Can* you believe that people with college degrees are happier than people without them? Yes! Plenty of surveys show that just such a relationship exists, and a reasonable person who studied the evidence could easily defend this conclusion. Now, *must* you believe it? Well, no. After all, those surveys didn't measure every single person on earth, did they? And if the survey questions had been asked differently, they might well have produced different answers, right? A reasonable person who studied the evidence could easily conclude that the relationship between education and happiness is not yet clear enough to warrant an opinion.

Our beliefs and desires also influence *which* evidence we consider in the first place. Most people surround themselves with others who believe what they believe and want what they want, which means that our friends and families are much more likely to validate our beliefs and desires than to challenge them. Studies also show that when given the opportunity to search for evidence, people preferentially search for evidence that confirms their beliefs and fulfills their desires (Hart et al., 2009). What's more, when people find evidence that confirms their beliefs and fulfills their desires, they tend to stop looking, but when they find evidence that does the opposite, they keep searching for more evidence (Kunda, 1990).

What all of these studies suggest is that evidence leaves room for interpretation, and that's the room in which our beliefs and desires spend most of their time. Because it is so easy to see what we expect to see or to see what we want to see, the first rule of critical thinking is this: *Doubt your own conclusions.* One of the best ways to reduce your own certainty is to seek out people who doubt you and listen carefully to what they have to say. Scientists go out of their ways to expose themselves to criticism by sending their papers to the colleagues who are most likely to disagree with them or by presenting their findings to audiences full of critics, and they do this in large part so that they can achieve a more balanced view of their own conclusions. If you want to be happy, take your friend to lunch; if you want to be right, take your enemy.

We Consider What We See and Ignore What We Don't

In another part of his remarkable book, Bacon recounted an old story about a man who visited a Roman temple. The priest showed the man a portrait of several sailors who had taken religious vows and then miraculously survived a shipwreck, and suggested that this was clear evidence of the power of the gods. The visitor paused a moment and then asked precisely the right question: "But where are the pictures of those who perished after taking their vows?" According to Bacon, most of us never think to ask this kind of question. We consider the evidence we can see and forget about the evidence we can't. Bacon claimed that "little or no attention is paid to things invisible" and he argued that this natural tendency was "the greatest impediment and aberration of the human understanding."

Bacon was right when he claimed that people rarely consider what they can't see. For example, participants in one study (Newman, Wolff, & Hearst, 1980) played a game in which they were shown a set of trigrams, which are three-letter combinations such as *SXY*, *GTR*, *BCG*, and *EVX*. On each trial, the experimenter pointed to one of the trigrams in the set and told the participants that *this* trigram was the special one. The participants' job was to figure out what made the special trigram so special. How many trials did it take before participants figured it out? It depended on the trigram's special feature. For half the participants, the special trigram was always the one that contained the letter *T*, and participants in this condition needed to see about 34 sets of trigrams before they figured out that the presence of *T* was what made the trigram special. But for the other half of the participants, the special trigram was always the one that *lacked* the letter *T*. How many trials did it take before participants figured it out? They *never* figured it out—never. What this study shows is that we naturally consider the evidence we see and rarely, if ever, consider the evidence we don't.

The tendency to ignore missing evidence can cause us to draw all kinds of erroneous conclusions. Consider a study in which participants were randomly assigned to play one of two roles in a game (Ross, Amabile, & Steinmetz, 1977). The "quizmasters" were asked to make up a series of difficult questions, and the "contestants" were asked to answer them. If you give this a quick try, you will discover that it's very easy to generate questions that you can answer but that most other people cannot. For example, think of the last city you visited. Now give someone the name of the hotel you stayed in and ask them what street it's on. Very few will know.

So participants who were cast in the role of quizmaster asked lots of clever-sounding questions, and participants who were cast in the role of contestant gave lots of wrong answers. Now comes the interesting part. Quizmasters and contestants played this game while another participant—the observer—watched. After the game was over, the observer was asked to make some guesses about what the players were like in their everyday lives. The results were clear: observers consistently concluded that the quizmaster was a more knowledgeable person than the contestant! Observers *saw* the quizmaster asking sharp questions and *saw* the contestant saying, "Um, gosh, I don't know," and observers considered this evidence. What they failed to consider was the evidence they did *not* see. Specifically, they failed to consider what would have happened if the person who had been assigned to play the role of quizmaster had instead been assigned to play the role of contestant, and vice versa. If that had happened, then surely the contestant would have been the one asking clever questions and the quizmaster would have been the one struggling to answer them. Bottom line? If the first rule of critical thinking is to doubt what you do see, then the second rule is to *consider what you don't see*. To practice these and other critical thinking skills, check out the Changing Minds questions in the review section at the conclusion of each chapter.

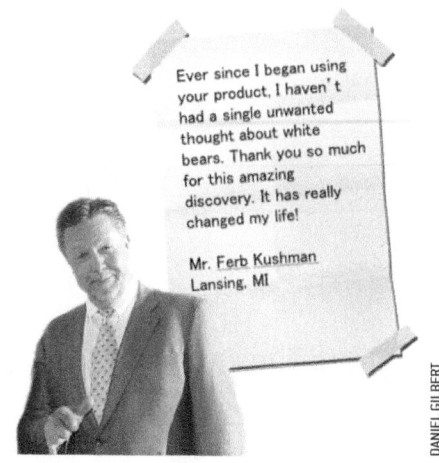

The second rule of critical thinking is to consider what you don't see. Business often provides testimonials from satisfied customers, but where are all the dissatisfied customers, and what might they have to say?

THE SKEPTICAL STANCE

Winston Churchill once said that democracy is the worst form of government, except for all the others. Similarly, science is not an infallible method for learning about the world; it's just a whole lot less fallible than the other methods. Science is a human enterprise, and humans make mistakes. They see what they expect to see, they see what they want to see, and they rarely consider what they can't see at all.

What makes science different from most other human enterprises is that science actively seeks to discover and remedy its own biases and errors. Scientists are constantly striving to make their observations more accurate and their reasoning more rigorous, and they invite anyone and everyone to examine their evidence and challenge their conclusions. Thus, science is the ultimate democracy—one of the only institutions in the world in which the lowliest nobody can triumph over the most celebrated someone. When an unknown Swiss patent clerk named Albert Einstein challenged the greatest physicists of his day, he didn't have a famous name, a fancy degree, powerful friends, or a fat wallet. He just had evidence. And he prevailed for one reason: His evidence was right.

So think of the remaining chapters in this textbook as a report from the field—a description of the work that psychological scientists have done as they stumble toward knowledge. These chapters tell the story of the men and women who have put their faith in Sir Francis Bacon's method and used it to pry loose small pieces of the truth about who we are, how we work, and what we are all doing here together on the third stone from the sun. Read it with interest, but also with skepticism. Some of the things we are about to tell you simply aren't true; we just don't yet know which things they are. We hope you will think critically about what you read here—and everywhere else.

Build to the Outcomes

1. According to Sir Francis Bacon, what are the two enemies of critical thinking?

2. What does it mean to say, *If you want to be happy, take your friend to lunch; if you want to be right, take your enemy*?

3. What makes science different from most other human enterprises?

The Ethics of Science: What's Right?

Learning Outcomes

▶ Identify the things that ethical research must always respect.

▶ Identify the ways in which psychologists ensure that their research respects people.

▶ Identify the ways in which psychologists ensure that their research respects truth.

Somewhere along the way, someone probably told you that it isn't nice to treat people like objects. And yet, it may seem that psychologists do just that by creating situations that cause people to feel fearful or sad, to do things that are embarrassing or immoral, and to learn things about themselves and others that they might not really want to know. Don't be fooled by appearances. The fact is that psychologists go to great lengths to protect the well-being of their research participants, and they are bound by a code of ethics that is as detailed and demanding as the professional codes that bind physicians, lawyers, and accountants. That code requires that psychologists show respect for people, for animals, and for the truth. Let's examine each of these obligations in turn.

RESPECTING PEOPLE

During World War II, Nazi doctors performed truly barbaric experiments on human subjects, such as removing organs or submerging them in ice water just to see how long it would take them to die. After the war ended, the international community developed the Nuremberg Code of 1947 and then the Declaration of Helsinki in 1964, which spelled out rules for the ethical treatment of human subjects. Unfortunately, not everyone obeyed them. For example, from 1932 until 1972, the U.S. Public Health Service conducted the infamous Tuskegee experiment, in which 399 African American men with syphilis were denied treatment so that researchers could observe the progression of the disease. As one journalist noted, the government "used human beings as laboratory animals in a long and inefficient study of how long it takes syphilis to kill someone" (Coontz, 2008).

In 1974, the U.S. Congress created the National Commission for the Protection of Human Subjects of Biomedical and Behavioral Research. In 1979, the U.S. Department of Health, Education and Welfare released what came to be known as the Belmont Report, which described three basic principles that all research involving human subjects should follow. First, research should show *respect for persons* and their right to make decisions for and about themselves without undue influence or coercion. Second, research should be *beneficent*, which means that it should attempt to maximize benefits and reduce risks to the participant. Third, research should be *just*, which means that it should distribute benefits and risks equally to participants without prejudice toward particular individuals or groups.

The specific ethical code that psychologists follow incorporates these basic principles and expands them. (You can find the American Psychological Association's *Ethical Principles of Psychologists and Code of Conduct* [2002] at http://www.apa.org/ethics/code/index.aspx.) Here are a few of the most important rules that govern the conduct of psychological research:

The man at this bar is upset. He just saw another man slip a drug into a woman's drink and he is alerting the bartender. What he doesn't know is that all the people at the bar are actors and that he is being filmed for the television show *What Would You Do?* Was it ethical for ABC to put this man in such a stressful situation without his consent? And how did the men who didn't alert the bartender feel when they turned on their televisions months later and were confronted by their own shameful behavior?

▶ *Informed consent*: Participants may not take part in a psychological study unless they have given **informed consent,** which is *a written agreement to participate in a study made by an adult who has been informed of all the risks that participation may entail.* This doesn't mean that the person must know everything about the study (e.g., the hypothesis), but it does mean that the person must know about anything that might potentially be harmful or painful. If people cannot give informed consent (e.g., because they are minors or are mentally incapable), then informed consent must be obtained from their legal guardians. And even after people give informed consent, they always have the right to withdraw from the study at any time without penalty.

▶ *Freedom from coercion*: Psychologists may not coerce participation. Coercion not only means physical and psychological coercion but monetary coercion as well. It is unethical to offer people large amounts of money to persuade them to do something that they might otherwise decline to do. College students may be invited to participate in studies as part of their training in psychology, but they are ordinarily offered the option of learning the same things by other means.

▶ *Protection from harm*: Psychologists must take every possible precaution to protect their research participants from physical or psychological harm. If there are two equally effective ways to study something, the psychologist must use the safer method. If no safe method is available, the psychologist may not perform the study.

▶ *Risk-benefit analysis*: Although participants may be asked to accept small risks, such as a minor shock or a small embarrassment, they may not even be *asked* to accept large risks, such as severe pain, psychological trauma, or any risk that is greater than the risks they would ordinarily take in their everyday lives. Furthermore, even when participants are asked to take small risks, the psychologist must first demonstrate that these risks are outweighed by the social benefits of the new knowledge that might be gained from the study.

▶ *Deception*: Psychologists may use deception only when it is justified by the study's scientific, educational, or applied value and when alternative procedures are not feasible. They may never deceive participants about any aspect of a study that could cause them physical or psychological harm or pain.

▶ *Debriefing*: If a participant is deceived in any way before or during a study, the psychologist must provide a **debriefing,** which is *a verbal description of the true nature and purpose of a study.* If the participant was changed in any way (e.g., made to feel sad), the psychologist must attempt to undo that change (e.g., ask the person to do a task that will make him or her happy) and restore the participant to the state he or she was in before the study.

▶ *Confidentiality*: Psychologists are obligated to keep private and personal information obtained during a study confidential.

informed consent A written agreement to participate in a study made by an adult who has been informed of all the risks that participation may entail.

debriefing A verbal description of the true nature and purpose of a study.

These are just some of the rules that psychologists must follow. But how are those rules enforced? Almost all psychology studies are done by psychologists who work at

Can We Afford Science?

Cass R. Sunstein is a law professor at Harvard University and was the administrator of the White House Office of Information and Regulatory Affairs under President Barack Obama.

Who pays for all the research described in textbooks like this one? The answer is you. By and large, scientific research is funded by government agencies, such as the National Science Foundation, which give scientists grants (also known as money) to do particular research projects that the scientists have proposed. Of course, this money could be spent on other things, for example, feeding the poor, housing the homeless, caring for the ill and elderly, and so on. Does it make sense to spend taxpayer dollars on psychological science when some of our fellow citizens are cold and hungry?

The legal scholar Cass Sunstein argues that research in the behavioral sciences is not an expenditure—it is an investment that pays for itself, and more. Here's some of what he has to say:

When government programs fail, it is often because public officials are clueless about how human beings think and act. Federal, state and local governments make it far too hard for small businesses, developers, farmers, veterans and poor people to get permits, licenses, training and economic assistance. It's one thing to make financial aid available to students, so they can attend college. It's another thing to design forms that students can actually fill out.

Building on impressive new findings from the White House's Social and Behavioral Sciences Team, Mr. Obama ordered his government to use behavioral insights to simplify forms, cut wait times, eliminate administrative hurdles and reduce regulatory burdens. A new report from the team, which has been up and running for more than a year, shows that small reforms can make a big difference.

For example, the team helped to design a new email campaign to increase savings by service members, which nearly doubled enrollment in federal savings plans. It found that simple text messages to lower-income students, reminding them to complete required pre-matriculation tasks, increased college enrollment among those students by 5.7 percentage points. An outreach letter to farmers, designed to promote awareness of a loan program, produced a 22 percent increase in the proportion of farmers who ultimately obtained loans. A new signature box on an online form, requiring vendors to confirm the accuracy of self-reported sales, produced an additional $1.59 million in fees collected by the government in just one quarter, apparently because the box increased honest reporting.

Notwithstanding the success stories, official use of behavioral science raises two legitimate concerns. The first is practical: How much good can it do? Improvements might be a matter of just a few percentage points—and perhaps a distraction from ambitious fiscal or regulatory reforms that could make a much bigger difference. It's a fair point, but incremental improvements should not be disparaged, especially if they help hundreds of thousands of people. And if the goal is to produce large-scale change, behaviorally informed approaches might accomplish more than we expect. For example, behavioral scientists have found that the default rule, establishing what happens if people do nothing, has surprisingly big effects. If employers automatically enroll new employees in savings programs, they can produce significant increases in participation—in one study, an increase of more than 30 percentage points. And more controversially, if utility companies automatically enrolled people in green energy, there would inevitably be reductions in greenhouse gas emissions, even with the right to opt out.

These examples raise a second concern, about ethics: What about the risk of manipulation? Should the national government really be conducting psychological experiments on the American people? It is true that behavioral science can be misused. A graphic warning, designed to produce fear, might discourage people from purchasing products that create little harm. People might be automatically enrolled in programs that do them no good. The best safeguard against manipulation is accountability. Official uses of behavioral science should never be hidden, and they should always be undertaken within the limits of law and for legitimate ends, such as promoting retirement security, lowering barriers to college, increasing employment and saving taxpayers money. If the law requires people to obtain licenses or permits, to pay taxes, or to apply for benefits or training, the government must select some method of communication. Public officials need to experiment if they want to know the effects of different methods.

Behavioral research shows that efforts at simplification, or slight variations in wording, can make all the difference. Since 2010, Britain has had its own Behavioral Insights Team, which experimented with a brief addition to a letter to late-paying taxpayers: "The great majority of people in your local area pay their tax on time." The change, which is being introduced nationally, produced a 15 percent increase in on-time payments and is projected to bring in millions of dollars worth of revenue. When government programs aren't working, those on the left tend to support more funding, while those on the right want to scrap them altogether. It is better to ask whether the problem is complexity and poor design. We can solve those problems — sometimes without spending a penny.

What do you think? Is Sunstein right? Is psychological science a wise use of public funds? Or is it a luxury that we simply can't afford?

SUNSTEIN, S. (2015, SEPTEMBER 19). MAKING GOVERNMENT LOGICAL. *NEW YORK TIMES.* HTTP://WWW.NYTIMES.COM/2015/09/20/OPINION/SUNDAY/CASS-SUNSTEIN-MAKING-GOVERNMENT-LOGICALHTML.HTML

colleges and universities. These institutions have institutional review boards (IRBs) that are composed of instructors and researchers, university staff, and laypeople from the community (e.g., business leaders or members of the clergy). If the research is federally funded, then the law requires that the IRB include at least one nonscientist and one person who is not affiliated with the institution. (See Other Voices: Can We Afford Science? for more about the federal funding of psychological science). A psychologist may conduct a study only after the IRB has reviewed and approved it.

As you can imagine, the code of ethics and the procedure for approval are so strict that many studies simply cannot be performed anywhere, by anyone, at any time. For example, psychologists would love to know how growing up without exposure to language affects a person's subsequent ability to speak and think, but they cannot ethically manipulate that variable in an experiment. They can only study the natural correlations between language exposure and speaking ability, and so may never be able to firmly establish the causal relationships between these variables. Indeed, there are many questions that psychologists will never be able to answer definitively because doing so would require unethical experiments that violate basic human rights.

RESPECTING ANIMALS

Not all research participants have human rights because not all research participants are human. Some are chimpanzees, rats, pigeons, or other nonhuman animals. The American Psychological Association's code specifically describes the special rights of these nonhuman participants, and some of the more important ones are these:

▶ All procedures involving animals must be supervised by psychologists who are trained in research methods and experienced in the care of laboratory animals and who are responsible for ensuring appropriate consideration of the animals' comfort, health, and humane treatment.

▶ Psychologists must make reasonable efforts to minimize the discomfort, infection, illness, and pain of animals.

▶ Psychologists may use a procedure that subjects an animal to pain, stress, or privation only when an alternative procedure is unavailable and when the procedure is justified by the scientific, educational, or applied value of the study.

▶ Psychologists must perform all surgical procedures under appropriate anesthesia and must minimize an animal's pain during and after surgery.

That's good—but is it good enough? Some people don't think so. For example, philosopher Peter Singer (1975) argued that all creatures capable of feeling pain have the same fundamental rights, and that treating nonhumans differently from humans is a form of speciesism that is every bit as abhorrent as racism or sexism. Singer's philosophy has inspired groups such as People for the Ethical Treatment of Animals

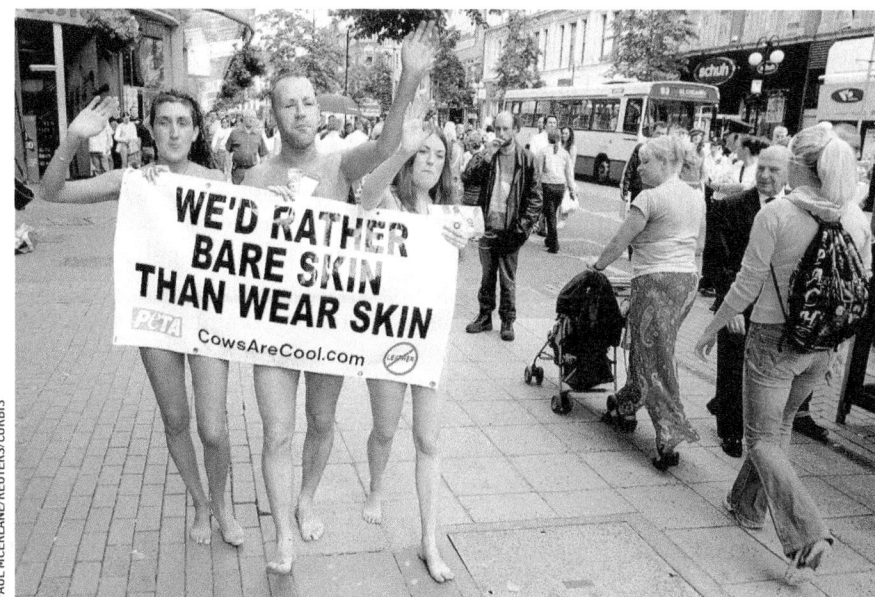

Some people consider it unethical to use animals for clothing or research. Others see an important distinction between these two purposes.

PAUL MCERLANE/REUTERS/CORBIS

to call for an end to all research involving nonhuman animals. Unfortunately, it has also inspired some groups to attack psychologists who legally conduct such research. As two researchers (Ringach & Jentsch, 2009, p. 11417) reported:

> We have seen our cars and homes firebombed or flooded, and we have received letters packed with poisoned razors and death threats via e-mail and voicemail. Our families and neighbors have been terrorized by angry mobs of masked protesters who throw rocks, break windows, and chant that "you should stop or be stopped" and that they "know where you sleep at night." Some of the attacks have been cataloged as attempted murder. Adding insult to injury, misguided animal-rights militants openly incite others to violence on the Internet, brag about the resulting crimes, and go as far as to call plots for our assassination "morally justifiable."

Where do most people stand on this issue? The vast majority of Americans consider it morally acceptable to use nonhuman animals in research and say they would reject a governmental ban on such research (Kiefer, 2004; Moore, 2003). Indeed, most Americans eat meat, wear leather, and support the rights of hunters, which is to say that most Americans see a sharp distinction between animal and human rights. Science is not in the business of resolving moral controversies, and every individual must draw his or her own conclusions about this issue. But whatever position you take, it is important to note that only a small percentage of psychological studies involve animals, and only a small percentage of those studies cause animals pain or harm. Psychologists mainly study people, and when they do study animals, they mainly study their behavior.

RESPECTING TRUTH

Institutional review boards ensure that data are collected ethically. But once the data are collected, who ensures that they are ethically analyzed and reported? No one does. Psychology, like all sciences, works on the honor system. No authority is charged with monitoring what psychologists do with the data they've collected, and no authority is charged with checking to see if the claims they make are true. You may find that a bit odd. After all, we don't use the honor system in stores ("Take the television set home and pay us next time you're in the neighborhood"), banks ("I don't need to look up your account, just tell me how much money you want to withdraw"), or courtrooms ("If you say you're innocent, well then, that's good enough for me"), so why would we expect it to work in science? Are scientists more honest than everyone else?

Definitely! Okay, we just made that up. But the honor system doesn't depend on scientists being especially honest, but on the fact that science is a community enterprise. When scientists claim to have discovered something important, other scientists don't just applaud. They start studying it too. When the physicist Jan Hendrik Schön announced in 2001 that he had produced a molecular-scale transistor, other physicists were deeply impressed—that is, until they tried to replicate his work and discovered that Schön had fabricated his data (Agin, 2007). Schön lost his job, and his doctoral degree was revoked, but the important point is that such frauds can't last long because one scientist's conclusion is the next scientist's research question. This doesn't mean that all frauds are uncovered swiftly: The psychologist Diederik Stapel lied, cheated, and made up his data for decades before people became suspicious enough to investigate (Levelt Committee, Noort Committee, Drenth Committee, 2012). But it does mean that the *important* frauds are uncovered eventually. The psychologist who fraudulently claims to have shown that chimps are smarter than goldfish may never get caught because no one is likely to follow up on such an obvious finding, but the psychologist who fraudulently claims to have shown the opposite will soon have a lot of explaining to do.

What exactly are psychologists on their honor to do? At least three things. First, when they write reports of their studies and publish them in scientific journals,

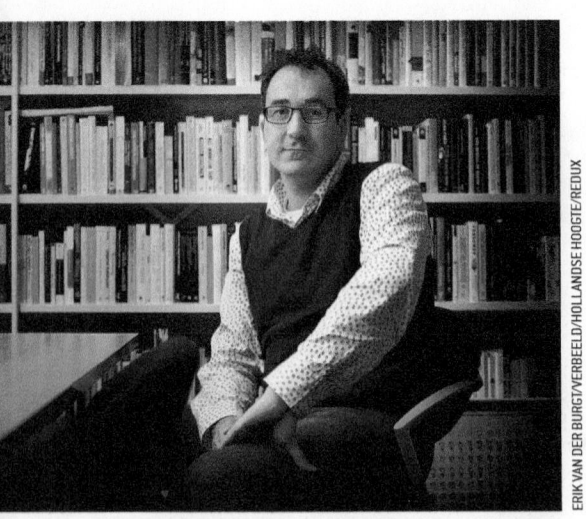

In 2012, the psychologist Diederik Stapel was found to have committed massive fraud over the course of many years. He was fired from his job as a professor and dozens of his published scientific articles were retracted.

psychologists are obligated to report truthfully on what they did and what they found. They can't fabricate results (e.g., by claiming to have performed studies that they never really performed) or fudge results (e.g., by changing records of data that were actually collected), and they can't mislead by omission (e.g., by reporting only the results that confirm their hypothesis and saying nothing about the results that don't). Second, psychologists are obligated to share credit fairly by including as co-authors of their reports the other people who contributed to the work, and by mentioning in their reports the other scientists who have done related work. And third, psychologists are obligated to share their data. The American Psychological Association's code of conduct states that ethical psychologists "do not withhold the data on which their conclusions are based from other competent professionals who seek to verify the substantive claims through reanalysis." The fact that anyone can check up on anyone else is part of why the honor system works as well as it does.

Build to the Outcomes

1. What is an institutional review board (IRB)?

2. What is informed consent?

3. What is debriefing?

4. What steps must psychologists take to protect nonhuman subjects?

5. What three things must psychologists do when they report the results of their research?

6. How does science uncover fraud?

Chapter Review

Empiricism: How to Know Stuff

▶ Empiricism is the belief that the best way to understand the world is to observe it firsthand. It is only in the last few centuries that people have begun systematically collecting and evaluating evidence to test the accuracy of their beliefs about the world.

▶ Observation doesn't just mean "looking." It requires a method. The scientific method involves (a) developing a theory that gives rise to a falsifiable hypothesis; and then (b) making observations that serve to test that hypothesis. Although these tests may prove that a theory is false, they can prove that it is true.

▶ The methods of psychology are special because human beings are more complex, variable, and reactive than almost anything else that scientists study.

Observation: What Do People Do?

▶ Measurement involves (a) defining a property in terms of a concrete, measurable condition, and then (b) using an instrument that can detect that condition. A good definition is valid (the concrete condition it measures is conceptually related to the property of interest), and a good instrument is both reliable (it produces the same measurement whenever it is used to measure the same thing) and powerful (it can detect the concrete conditions when they actually exist).

▶ When people know they are being observed, they may behave as they think they should. Demand characteristics are features of a setting that suggest to people that they should behave in a particular way. Psychologists try to reduce or eliminate demand characteristics by observing participants in their natural habitats or by hiding their expectations from the participant. Observer bias is the tendency for observers to see what they expect to see or cause others to behave as they expect them to behave. Psychologists try to eliminate observer bias by making double-blind observations.

▶ Psychologists often describe the measurements they make with a graphic representation called a frequency distribution, which often has a special shape known as the normal distribution. They also describe their measurements with descriptive statistics; the most common are descriptions of central tendency (such as the mean, median, and mode) and descriptions of variability (such as the range and the standard deviation).

Explanation: Why Do People Do What They Do?

▶ To determine whether two variables are causally related, we must first determine whether they are related at all. This can be done by measuring each variable many times and then comparing the patterns of variation within each series of measurements. If the patterns covary, then the variables are correlated. Correlations allow us to predict the value of one variable from knowledge of the value of the other. The direction and strength of a correlation are measured by the correlation coefficient (r).

▶ Even when we observe a correlation between two variables, we can't conclude that they are causally related because there are an infinite number of third variables that might be causing them both. Experiments solve this third-variable problem by manipulating an independent variable, randomly assigning participants to the experimental and control groups that this manipulation creates, and measuring a dependent variable. These measurements are then compared across groups. If inferential statistics show that random assignment failed, then the results would only happen 5% of the time, then differences in the measurements across groups are assumed to have been caused by the manipulation.

▶ An internally valid experiment establishes a causal relationship between variables as they were operationally defined and among the participants whom they included. When an experiment mimics the real world, it is externally valid. But most psychology experiments are not attempts to mimic the real world, but to test hypotheses derived from theories.

Thinking Critically About Evidence

▶ Thinking critically about evidence is difficult because people have a natural tendency to see what they expect to see, to see what they want to see, and to consider what they see but not what they don't.

▶ Critical thinkers consider evidence that disconfirms their own opinions. They also consider the evidence that is absent, and not just the evidence that is present.

▶ What makes science different from most other human enterprises is that science actively seeks to discover and remedy its own biases and errors.

The Ethics of Science: What's Right?

▶ Institutional review boards ensure that the rights of human beings who participate in scientific research are based on the principles of respect for persons, beneficence, and justice.

▶ Psychologists are obligated to uphold these principles by getting informed consent from participants, not coercing participation, protecting participants from harm, weighing benefits against risks, avoiding deception, and keeping information confidential.

▶ Psychologists are obligated to respect the rights of animals and treat them humanely. Most people are in favor of using animals in scientific research.

▶ Psychologists are obligated to tell the truth about their studies, to share credit appropriately, and to grant others access to their data.

KEY CONCEPT QUIZ

1. The belief that accurate knowledge can be acquired through observation is
   a. parsimony.
   b. dogmatism.
   c. empiricism.
   d. scientific research.

2. Which of the following is the best definition of a hypothesis?
   a. empirical evidence
   b. a scientific investigation
   c. a falsifiable prediction
   d. a theoretical idea

3. If a measure produces the same measurement whenever it is used to measure the same thing, it is said to have
   a. validity.
   b. reliability.
   c. power.
   d. concreteness.

4. Aspects of an observational setting that cause people to behave as they think they should are called
   a. observer biases.
   b. reactive conditions.
   c. natural habitats.
   d. demand characteristics.

5. Which of the following describes the average value of all the measurements in a particular distribution?
   a. mean
   b. median
   c. mode
   d. range

6. What does a correlation coefficient show?
   a. the value of one specific variable
   b. the direction and strength of a correlation
   c. the efficiency of the relevant research method
   d. the degree of natural correlation

7. When two variables are correlated, what keeps us from concluding that one is the cause and the other is the effect?
   a. the possibility of third-variable correlation
   b. random assignment of control groups
   c. the existence of false-positive correlation
   d. correlation strength is impossible to measure accurately

8. A researcher administers a questionnaire concerning attitudes toward global warming to people of both genders and of all ages who live all across the country. The dependent variable in the study is the _____ of the participants.
   a. age
   b. gender
   c. attitudes toward global warming
   d. geographic location

9. An experiment that operationally defines variables in a realistic way is said to be
   a. externally valid.
   b. controlled.
   c. operationally defined.
   d. statistically significant.

10. When people find evidence that confirms their beliefs, they often
    a. tend to stop looking.
    b. seek evidence that disconfirms their conclusions.
    c. seek evidence that presents both sides.
    d. talk to their colleagues.

 LearningCurve   **Don't stop now! Quizzing yourself is a powerful study tool. Go to LaunchPad to access the LearningCurve adaptive quizzing system and your own personalized learning plan. Visit launchpadworks.com.**

KEY TERMS

empiricism (p. 36)

scientific method (p. 37)

theory (p. 37)

hypothesis (p. 37)

empirical method (p. 38)

operational definition (p. 40)

instrument (p. 40)

validity (p. 41)

reliability (p. 41)

power (p. 41)

demand characteristics (p. 41)

naturalistic observation (p. 41)

double-blind observation (p. 44)

frequency distribution (p. 44)

normal distribution (p. 45)

mode (p. 45)

mean (p. 45)

median (p. 45)

range (p. 46)

standard deviation (p. 47)

variable (p. 48)

correlation (p. 48)

correlation coefficient (p. 49)

natural correlation (p. 50)

third-variable correlation (p. 51)

matched samples technique (p. 52)

matched pairs technique (p. 52)

third-variable problem (p. 53)

experiment (p. 53)

manipulation (p. 54)

independent variable (p. 54)

experimental group (p. 54)

control group (p. 54)

dependent variable (p. 54)

self-selection (p. 55)

random assignment (p. 56)

internal validity (p. 59)

external validity (p. 59)

population (p. 60)

sample (p. 60)

case method (p. 60)

random sampling (p. 60)

direct replication (p. 61)

informed consent (p. 67)

debriefing (p. 67)

CHANGING MINDS

1. Back in Psychology: Evolution of a Science, you read about B. F. Skinner, who studied the principle of reinforcement, which states that the consequences of a behavior determine whether it will be more or less likely to occur in the future. So, for example, a rat's rate of lever pressing will increase if it receives food reinforcement after each lever press. When you tell a classmate about this principle, she only shrugs. "That's obvious. Anyone who's ever owned a dog knows how to train animals. If you ask me, psychology is just common sense. You don't have to conduct scientific experiments to test things that everyone already knows are true." How would you explain the value of studying something that seems like "common sense"?

2. You're watching TV with a friend when a news program reports that a research study has found that people in Europe who work longer hours are less happy than those who work shorter hours, but in the United States it's the other way around: Americans who work long hours are happier (Okulicz-Kozaryn, 2011). "That's an interesting experiment," he says. You point out that the news only said it was a research study, not an experiment. What would have to be true for it to be an experiment? Why aren't all research studies experiments? What can't you learn from this study that you *could* learn from an experiment?

3. After the first exam, your professor says she's noticed a strong positive correlation between the location of students' seats and their exam scores: "The closer students sit to the front of the room, the higher their scores on the exam," she says. After class, your friend suggests that the two of you should sit up front for the rest of the semester to improve your grades. Having read about correlation and causation, should you be skeptical? What are some possible reasons for the correlation between seating position and good grades? Could you design an experiment to test whether sitting up front actually causes good grades?

4. A classmate in your criminal justice class suggests that mental illness is a major cause of violent crimes in the United States. As evidence, he mentions a highly publicized murder trial in which the convicted suspect was diagnosed with schizophrenia. What scientific evidence would he need to support this claim?

5. You ask your friend if he wants to go to the gym with you. "No," he says, "I never exercise." You tell him that regular exercise has all kinds of health benefits, including greatly reducing the risk of heart disease. "I don't believe that," he replies. "I had an uncle who got up at 6 a.m. every day of his life to go jogging, and he still died of a heart attack at age 53." What would you tell your friend? Does his uncle's case prove that exercise really doesn't protect against heart disease after all?

ANSWERS TO KEY CONCEPT QUIZ

1. c; 2. c; 3. b; 4. d; 5. a; 6. b; 7. a; 8. c; 9. a; 10. a.

LaunchPad features the full e-Book of *Psychology*, the LearningCurve adaptive quizzing system, videos, and a variety of activities to boost your learning. Visit LaunchPad at launchpadworks.com.

Neuroscience and Behavior

3

R ay Easterling and Dave Duerson came from different times and places: Easterling, born in 1949, grew up in Richmond, Virginia; Duerson, born in 1960, grew up in Muncie, Indiana. But their lives as young men showed striking parallels. Both loved football and played the position of defensive back well enough to star in college and make it all the way to the National Football League. Easterling played for the Atlanta Falcons during the 1970s, and Duerson played for the Chicago Bears in the 1980s. Unfortunately, the parallels between Easterling and Duerson continued into their retirement years. Both men suffered from significant cognitive decline and depression, and both ended up taking their own lives: Duerson in 2011, Easterling in 2012. Postmortem analyses of their brains revealed the presence of a condition known as *chronic traumatic encephalopathy* (CTE), a form of progressive brain damage that has been linked to repeated concussions (Montenigro, Corp, Stein, Cantu, & Stern, 2015). Duerson and Easterling are just two of many former NFL players who have been diagnosed with CTE, including the Hall of Famer and former *Monday Night Football* broadcaster Frank Gifford, whose death in August 2015 and subsequent CTE diagnosis focused national attention on the problem. CTE has also been observed after repeated head injuries in boxing, wrestling, hockey, and rugby (Costanza et al., 2011; Daneshvar et al., 2011; Lahkan & Kirchgessner, 2012; McKee et al., 2009).

UNCREDITED/AP IMAGES

MICHAEL J. MINARDI/GETTY IMAGES

Ray Easterling (*left*) and Dave Duerson (*right*) had similarly outstanding NFL careers and similarly troubled retirements, perhaps associated with brain damage.

◄ AURORA/GETTY IMAGES

In December 2015, attention to CTE was further heightened by the release of the movie *Concussion*, which focuses on the story of Bennet Omalu (played by Will Smith), the pathologist who first uncovered evidence for CTE in the brain of an NFL player. Although statements by the Omalu character in the movie imply that CTE has caused the decline and death of former NFL players, in fact we don't know whether there is an exact correlation. Indeed, former NFL players are at lower risk for suicide than men in the general population (Iverson, 2015), and scientists are actively debating the nature and consequences of CTE (Castellani, Perry, & Iverson, 2015). However, we do know that CTE is associated with an array of cognitive and emotional deficits in afflicted individuals, including inability to concentrate, memory loss, irritability, and depression, usually beginning within a decade after repeated concussions and worsening with time (McKee et al., 2009; Montenigro et al., 2015). Fortunately, there is growing awareness of CTE and its associated symptoms, which is leading professional sports organizations, as well as colleges, schools, and others involved in youth sports, to take steps to address the problem.

The symptoms of CTE are reminders that our psychological, emotional, and social well-being depend critically on the health and integrity of the brain, and also highlight that understanding neuroscience isn't just an academic exercise confined to scientific laboratories: The more we know about the brain, and the more people who know it, the better our chances of finding solutions to problems such as CTE.

IN THIS CHAPTER, WE'LL CONSIDER HOW THE BRAIN WORKS, what happens when it doesn't, and how both states of affairs determine behavior. First, we'll introduce you to the basic unit of information processing in the brain, the neuron. The electrical and chemical activities of neurons are the starting point of all behavior, thought, and emotion. Next, we'll consider the anatomy of the central nervous system, focusing especially on the brain, including its overall organization, its key structures that perform different functions, and its evolutionary development. Finally, we'll discuss methods that allow us to study the brain and clarify our understanding of how it works. These include methods that examine the damaged brain and methods for scanning the living and healthy brain.

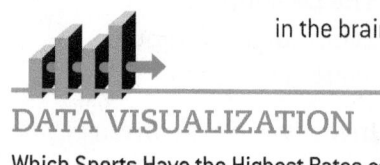

DATA VISUALIZATION

Which Sports Have the Highest Rates of Concussion?
Go to launchpadworks.com.

Neurons: The Origin of Behavior

Learning Outcomes

- ▶ Explain the function of neurons.
- ▶ Outline the components of the neuron.
- ▶ Differentiate the three major types of neurons by their function.

An estimated 1 billion people watch the final game of World Cup soccer every four years. That's a whole lot of people, but to put it in perspective, it's still only a little over 14% of the estimated 7 billion people currently living on earth. A more impressive number might be the 30 billion viewers who tune in to watch any of the World Cup action over the course of the tournament. But a really, really big number is inside your skull right now, helping you make sense of these big numbers you're reading about. There are approximately *100 billion* nerve cells in your brain that perform a variety of tasks to allow you to function as a human being.

Humans have thoughts, feelings, and behaviors that are often accompanied by visible signals. Consider how you might feel on your way to meet a good friend. An observer might see a smile on your face or notice how fast you are walking; internally, you might mentally rehearse what you'll say to your friend and feel a surge of happiness as you approach her. All those visible and experiential signs are coordinated by the activity of your brain cells. The anticipation you have, the happiness you feel, and the speed of your feet are the result of information processing in your brain. In a way, all of your thoughts, feelings, and behaviors spring from cells in the brain that take in information and produce some kind of output trillions of times a day. These cells are **neurons,** *cells in the nervous system that communicate with each other to perform information-processing tasks.*

COMPONENTS OF THE NEURON

During the 1800s, scientists began to turn their attention from studying the mechanics of limbs, lungs, and livers to studying the harder–to-observe workings of the brain. Philosophers wrote poetically about an "enchanted loom" that mysteriously wove a tapestry of behavior, and many scientists confirmed that metaphor (Corsi, 1991). To those scientists, the brain looked as though it were composed of a continuously connected lattice of fine threads, leading them to conclude that it was one big woven web of material. However, in the late 1880s, the Spanish physician Santiago Ramón y Cajal (1852–1934) learned about a new technique for staining neurons in the brain (DeFelipe & Jones, 1988). The stain highlighted the appearance of entire cells, revealing that they came in different shapes and sizes (see **FIGURE 3.1**).

Ramón y Cajal discovered that neurons are complex structures composed of three basic parts: the cell body, the dendrites, and the axon (see **FIGURE 3.2**). Like cells in all organs of the body, neurons have a **cell body** (also called the *soma*), the largest component of the neuron that *coordinates the information-processing tasks and keeps the cell alive.* Functions such as protein synthesis, energy production, and metabolism take place here. The cell body contains a *nucleus*, which houses chromosomes that contain your DNA, or the genetic blueprint of who you are. The cell body is surrounded by a porous cell membrane that allows some molecules to flow into and out of the cell.

Unlike other cells in the body, neurons have two types of specialized extensions of the cell membrane that allow them to communicate: dendrites and axons. **Dendrites** *receive information from other neurons and relay it to the cell body.* The term *dendrite* comes from the Greek word for "tree"; indeed, most neurons have many dendrites that look like tree branches. The **axon** *carries information to other neurons, muscles, or glands.* Axons can be very long, even stretching up to a meter from the base of the spinal cord down to the big toe.

In many neurons, the axon is covered by a **myelin sheath,** *an insulating layer of fatty material.* The myelin sheath is composed of **glial cells** (named for the Greek word for "glue"), which are *support cells found in the nervous system.* Although there are 100 billion neurons busily processing information in your brain, there are 10 to 50 times that many glial cells serving a variety of functions. Some glial cells digest parts of dead neurons, others provide physical and nutritional support for neurons, and others form myelin to help the axon carry information more efficiently. An axon insulated with myelin can more efficiently transmit signals to other neurons, organs, or muscles. In fact, *demyelinating diseases,* such as multiple sclerosis, cause the myelin sheath to deteriorate, slowing the transmission of information from one neuron to another (Schwartz & Westbrook, 2000). This slowdown leads to a variety of problems, including loss of feeling in the limbs, partial blindness, and difficulties in coordinated movement and cognition (Butler, Corboy, & Filley, 2009).

Ramón y Cajal also observed that the dendrites and axons of neurons do not actually touch each other. There's a small gap between the axon of one neuron and the dendrites or cell body of another. This gap is part of the **synapse,** *the junction or region between the axon of one neuron and the dendrites or cell body of another* (see Figure 3.2). Many of the 100 billion neurons in your brain have a few thousand synaptic junctions, so it should come as no shock that most adults have 100 to 500 trillion synapses. As you'll read shortly, the transmission of information across the synapse is fundamental to communication between neurons, a process that allows us to think, feel, and behave.

OXFORD SCIENTIFIC/GETTY IMAGES

▲ Figure 3.1

GOLGI-STAINED NEURONS Santiago Ramón y Cajal used a Golgi stain (like the one shown here) to highlight the appearance of neurons. He was the first to see that each neuron is composed of a body with many threads extending outward toward other neurons. In a surprising finding, he also saw that the threads of each neuron do not actually touch other neurons.

neurons Cells in the nervous system that communicate with one another to perform information-processing tasks.

cell body (or soma) The part of a neuron that coordinates information-processing tasks and keeps the cell alive.

dendrite The part of a neuron that receives information from other neurons and relays it to the cell body.

axon The part of a neuron that carries information to other neurons, muscles, or glands.

myelin sheath An insulating layer of fatty material.

glial cells Support cells found in the nervous system.

synapse The junction or region between the axon of one neuron and the dendrites or cell body of another.

Myelin sheath

Neural impulse

Axon

Cell body — **Nucleus**

Dendrites

Terminal branches of the axon

Dendrites receive information from other neurons and relay it to the cell body.

The **cell body** coordinates the information-processing tasks and keeps the cell alive.

Lying within the cell body, the **nucleus** houses chromosomes that contain DNA.

The **axon** carries information to other neurons, muscles, or glands.

The **synapse** is the small gap between between the axon of one neuron and the dendrites or cell body of another across which information is transmitted.

The **myelin sheath** is an insulating layer of fatty material composed of **glial cells**.

Sending neuron

Receiving neuron

Vesicles

Neurotransmitter

Receptor

▲ **Figure 3.2**

COMPONENTS OF A NEURON A neuron is made up of three parts: a cell body, dendrites, and an axon. Notice that neurons do not actually touch one another: There is a small synaptic space between them across which information is transmitted.

sensory neurons Neurons that receive information from the external world and convey this information to the brain via the spinal cord.

motor neurons Neurons that carry signals from the spinal cord to the muscles to produce movement.

NEURONS SPECIALIZED BY FUNCTION

There are three major types of neurons, each performing a distinct function: sensory neurons, motor neurons, and interneurons.

▶ **Sensory neurons** *receive information from the external world and convey this information to the brain via the spinal cord.* They have specialized endings on their dendrites that receive signals for light, sound, touch, taste, and smell. For example, sensory neurons' endings in our eyes are sensitive to light.

▶ **Motor neurons** *carry signals from the spinal cord to the muscles to produce movement.* These neurons often have long axons that reach to muscles at our extremities.

■ Cell Body
■ Axon
■ Dendrites

Purkinje cell of
cerebellum (brain)

(a)

Hippocampal pyramidal
cell (brain)

(b)

Bipolar neuron

(c)

◄ Figure 3.3

NEURONS SPECIALIZED BY LOCATION Neurons
have a cell body, an axon, and at least one
dendrite. The size and shape of neurons vary
considerably, however. The Purkinje cell has
an elaborate treelike assemblage of dendrites
(a). Pyramidal cells have a triangular cell body
and a single, long dendrite with many smaller
dendrites (b). Bipolar cells have only one
dendrite and a single axon (c).

▶ **Interneurons** *connect sensory neurons, motor neurons, or other interneurons.* Most
of the nervous system is composed of the interneurons. Some carry information
from sensory neurons into the nervous system, others carry information from the
nervous system to motor neurons, and still others perform a variety of information-
processing functions within the nervous system. Interneurons work together in
small circuits to perform simple tasks, such as identifying the location of a sensory
signal, and much more complicated ones, such as recognizing a familiar face.

interneurons Neurons that connect
sensory neurons, motor neurons, or other
interneurons.

NEURONS SPECIALIZED BY LOCATION

Besides specialization for sensory, motor, or connective functions, neurons are also
somewhat specialized, depending on their location (see **FIGURE 3.3**). For example,
Purkinje cells are a type of interneuron that carries information from the cerebellum
to the rest of the brain and the spinal cord. These neurons have dense, elaborate
dendrites that resemble bushes. *Pyramidal cells*, found in the cerebral cortex, have
a triangular cell body and a single, long dendrite among many smaller dendrites.
Bipolar cells, a type of sensory neuron found in the retinas of the eye, have a single
axon and a single dendrite. The brain processes different types of information, so
a substantial amount of specialization at the cellular level has evolved to handle
these tasks.

Build to the Outcomes

1. What do neurons do?

2. What are the three primary components of the neuron?

3. Do neurons actually touch when they communicate?
   Explain.

4. What is the function of the myelin sheath?

5. What are glial cells?

6. How do the three types of neurons work together to
   transmit information?

The Electrochemical Actions of Neurons: Information Processing

Learning Outcomes

▶ Describe how an electric signal moves across a neuron.

▶ Outline the steps in synaptic transmission.

▶ Explain how drugs are able to mimic neurotransmitters.

Our thoughts, feelings, and actions depend on neural communication, but how does it happen? Neurons are electronically excitable cells and communication of information happens in the form of electrical signals within and between neurons. This occurs in two stages:

▶ *Conduction* is the movement of an electric signal within neurons, from the dendrites to the cell body, then throughout the axon.

▶ *Transmission* is movement of electric signals from one neuron to another over the synapse.

Together, these stages are what scientists generally refer to as the *electrochemical action* of neurons.

ELECTRIC SIGNALING: CONDUCTING INFORMATION WITHIN A NEURON

resting potential The difference in electric charge between the inside and outside of a neuron's cell membrane.

The neuron's cell membrane has small pores that act as channels to allow small electrically charged molecules, called *ions*, to flow in and out of the cell. It is this flow of ions across the neuron's cell membrane that creates the conduction of an electric signal within the neuron. How does it happen?

The Resting Potential: The Origin of the Neuron's Electrical Properties

Neurons have a natural electric charge called the **resting potential,** *the difference in electric charge between the inside and outside of a neuron's cell membrane* (Kandel, 2000). When first discovered by biologists in the 1930s, the resting potential was measured at about −70 millivolts. This is a much smaller charge than a typical battery has; for example, a 9-volt battery has 9,000 millivolts (Klein & Thorne, 2007).

The resting potential is caused by the difference in concentrations of ions inside and outside the neuron's cell membrane (see **FIGURE 3.4a**). Ions can carry a positive (+) or a negative (−) charge. In the resting state, there is a high concentration of positively charged potassium ions (K^+), as well as larger, negatively charged protein ions (A^-), *inside* the neuron's cell membrane compared to outside it. By contrast, there is a high concentration of positively charged sodium ions (Na^+) and negatively charged chloride ions (Cl^-) *outside* the neuron's cell membrane. As a result, during the resting potential, the inside of the cell membrane is negatively charged relative to the outside.

Normally, ions from the area of higher concentration move to the area of lower concentration until the concentrations are equal–or in equilibrium–but special channels in the cell membrane restrict the movement of the ions in and out of the cell. An active chemical "pump" in the cell membrane helps maintain the high concentration of K^+ ions inside by pushing Na^+ ions out of the cell and pulling K^+ ions into the cell. This pump and other structures in the cell membrane ensure that during the resting potential excess K^+ ions are built up inside the cell, ready to rush out to create equilibrium with the low concentration of K^+ ions outside the cell. Similarly, excess Na^+ ions outside the cell are ready to rush in to create equilibrium with the low concentration of Na^+ ions within the cell. Special voltage-gated channels specific to the K^+ and Na^+ ions are closed during the resting potential, allowing the inside of the neuron to maintain the electrical charge of −70 millivolts relative to the outside. Like the Hoover Dam, which holds back the Colorado River until the floodgates are released, these channels in the cell membrane hold back the ions, building potential energy that can be released as an electrical impulse in a small fraction of a second.

The biologists Alan Hodgkin and Andrew Huxley discovered the resting potential in the summer of 1939 while studying marine invertebrates—sea creatures that lack a spine, such as clams, squid, and lobsters (Stevens, 1971). Hodgkin and Huxley worked with the squid giant axon because it is 100 times larger than the biggest axon in humans. They inserted a thin wire into the squid axon so that it touched the jellylike fluid inside. Then they placed another wire just outside the axon in the watery fluid that surrounds it. They found a substantial difference between the electric charges inside and outside the axon, which they called the resting potential.

Membrane potential (millivolts)

40

0

−70

(b) The Action Potential
Electric stimulation of the neuron opens the Na⁺ channels, allowing Na⁺ to flow in and increase the positive charge inside the axon relative to the outside.

(c) After the action potential reaches its maximum, the Na⁺ channels become inactive, and the K⁺ channels open. K⁺ ions rush out of the neuron returning the charge of the cell membrane from positive to negative.

Stimulating electrode

(d) The imbalance in ions from the action potential is reversed by an active chemical "pump" that moves Na⁺ outside the axon and moves K⁺ inside the axon. The neuron can now generate another action potential.

Na⁺   K⁺

(−70 millivolts)

Threshold of excitation

(a) The Resting Potential
In the resting state the gated channels for the Na+ and K+ ions are closed. The inside of the neuron has a charge of about −70 millivolts relative to the outside, which is the potential energy that will be used to generate the action potential.

1   2   3

Time (msec)

▲ Figure 3.4

THE RESTING AND ACTION POTENTIALS Neurons have a natural electric charge called a resting potential. Electric stimulation causes an action potential.

The Action Potential: Sending Signals Across the Neuron

The biologists working with the squid giant axon (see accompanying photo) noticed that they could produce an electrical impulse down the length of the axon by stimulating it with a brief electric shock (Hausser, 2000; Hodgkin & Huxley, 1939). This electric impulse is called an **action potential,** *an electric signal that is conducted along the length of a neuron's axon to a synapse.*

The action potential occurred only when the electric shock reached a certain level, or *threshold*. When the shock was below this threshold, the researchers recorded only tiny signals that dissipated rapidly. When the shock reached the threshold, a much larger signal, the action potential, was observed. In an interesting finding, increases in the electric shock above the threshold did *not* increase the strength of the action potential. The action potential is *all or none*: Electric stimulation below the threshold fails to produce an action potential, whereas electric stimulation at or above the threshold always produces the action potential. The action potential always occurs with exactly the same characteristics and at the same magnitude regardless of whether the stimulus is at or above the threshold.

The biologists working with the giant squid axon observed another surprising property of the action potential: They measured it at a charge of about +40 millivolts, which is well above zero. This suggests that the mechanism driving the action potential could not simply be the loss of the −70 millivolt resting potential, because that only would have brought the charge back to zero. So why does the action potential reach a value above zero?

Membrane Channels Change to Allow in Positively Charged Ions

The action potential occurs when there is a change in the state of the axon's membrane channels. Remember, during the resting potential, the special channels for the

action potential An electric signal that is conducted along a neuron's axon to a synapse.

Like the flow of electricity when you turn on a light, the action potential is all or none. Either the switch is turned on or the room remains dark. Similarly, either the electrical stimulation in the neuron reaches the threshold to fire an action potential, or it remains at the resting potential.

refractory period The time following an action potential during which a new action potential cannot be initiated.

the K$^+$ and Na$^+$ ions are closed. However, when an electric charge is raised to the threshold value, the sodium-specific channels open up like the floodgate of a dam, and the Na$^+$ ions rush into the cell (see Figure 3.4b). In less than one millisecond, the rapid influx of Na$^+$ ions raises the charge of the inside membrane from negative to positive relative to the outside and pushes the action potential to its peak of +40 millivolts.

At this point, two events restore the negative charge of the resting potential. First, the Na$^+$ channels inactivate themselves for several milliseconds, blocking the flow of Na$^+$ ions. During this inactivation time, the neuron is said to be in a **refractory period.** *the time following an action potential during which a new action potential cannot be initiated.* In the second event, channels specific to the K$^+$ ions open, allowing the excess K$^+$ ions inside the cell to escape (see Figure 3.4c). The rapid exit of the positively charged K$^+$ ions returns the electrical charge of the membrane to a negative state, after which the K$^+$ channels close. Ion pumps continue to push Na$^+$ ions out of the cell and bring in additional K$^+$ ions. Along with other special channels, they return the concentrations of ions to the resting potential (see Figure 3.4d). The entire process is so fast that some neurons fire more than 100 times in a single second.

The Action Potential Moves Across the Neuron in a Domino Effect

So far we've described how the action potential occurs at one point in the neuron. But how does this electric charge move down the axon? It's a domino effect. When an action potential is generated at the beginning of the axon, it spreads a short distance along the axon's length, which generates an action potential at a nearby location on the axon. That action potential also spreads, initiating an action potential at another nearby location, and so on, thus conducting the charge down the length of the axon. This simple mechanism ensures that the action potential travels the full length of the axon and that it achieves its full intensity at each step, regardless of the distance traveled.

The myelin sheath facilitates the conduction of the action potential. Myelin doesn't cover the entire axon; rather, it clumps around the axon with little break points between clumps, looking kind of like sausage links. These breakpoints are called the *nodes of Ranvier,* after the French pathologist Louis-Antoine Ranvier, who discovered them (see **FIGURE 3.5**). When an electric current passes down the length of a myelinated axon, the charge seems to "jump" from node to node rather than having to traverse the entire axon (Poliak & Peles, 2003). This process is called *saltatory conduction,* and it helps speed the flow of information down the axon.

CHEMICAL SIGNALING: TRANSMISSION BETWEEN NEURONS

When the action potential reaches the end of an axon, you might think that it stops there. After all, the synaptic space between neurons means that the axon of one neuron and the neighboring neuron's dendrites do not actually touch one another. However, the electric charge of the action potential takes a form that can cross the

▶ Figure 3.5

MYELIN AND NODES OF RANVIER Myelin is formed by a type of glial cell. It wraps around a neuron's axon to speed the movement of the action potential along the length of the axon. Breaks in the myelin sheath are called the nodes of Ranvier. The electric impulse jumps from node to node, thereby speeding the conduction of information down the axon.

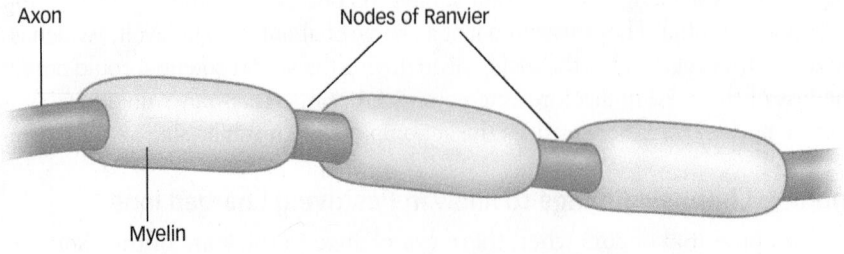

relatively small synaptic gap by relying on a bit of chemistry.

Axons usually end in **terminal buttons,** *knoblike structures that branch out from an axon.* A terminal button is filled with tiny *vesicles,* or "bags," that contain **neurotransmitters,** *chemicals that transmit information across the synapse to a receiving neuron's dendrites.* The dendrites of the receiving neuron contain **receptors,** *parts of the cell membrane that receive neurotransmitters and either initiate or prevent a new electric signal.*

As K^+ and Na^+ ions flow across a cell membrane, they move the sending neuron, or *presynaptic neuron*, from a resting potential to an action potential. The action potential travels down the length of the axon to the terminal buttons, where it stimulates the release of neurotransmitters from vesicles into the synapse. These neurotransmitters float across the synapse and bind to receptor sites on a nearby dendrite of the receiving neuron, or *postsynaptic neuron*. A new action potential is initiated in that neuron, and the process continues down that neuron's axon to the next synapse and the next neuron. This electrochemical action, called *synaptic transmission* (see **FIGURE 3.6**), allows neurons to communicate with each other and ultimately underlies your thoughts, emotions, and behavior.

Now that you understand the basic process of how information moves from one neuron to another, let's refine things a bit. You'll recall that a given neuron may make a few thousand synaptic connections with other neurons, so what tells the dendrites which of the neurotransmitters flooding into the synapse to receive? One answer is that neurons tend to form pathways in the brain that are characterized by specific types of neurotransmitters; one neurotransmitter might be prevalent in one part of the brain, whereas a different neurotransmitter might be prevalent in a different part of the brain.

A second answer is that neurotransmitters and receptor sites act like a lock-and-key system. Just as a particular key will only fit in a particular lock, so too will only some neurotransmitters bind to specific receptor sites on a dendrite. The molecular structure of the neurotransmitter must "fit" the molecular structure of the receptor site.

Another question is what happens to the neurotransmitters left in the synapse after the chemical message is relayed to the postsynaptic neuron? Something must make neurotransmitters stop acting on neurons; otherwise, there'd be no end to the signals that they send. Neurotransmitters leave the synapse through three processes (see Figure 3.6). First, *reuptake* occurs when neurotransmitters are reabsorbed by the terminal buttons of the presynaptic neuron's axon. Second, neurotransmitters can be destroyed by enzymes in the synapse in a process called *enzyme deactivation*; specific enzymes break down specific neurotransmitters. Finally, neurotransmitters can bind to certain receptor sites called *autoreceptors* on the presynaptic neurons. Autoreceptors detect how much of a neurotransmitter has been released into a synapse and signal the neuron to stop releasing the neurotransmitter when an excess is present.

Types and Functions of Neurotransmitters

Given that different kinds of neurotransmitters can activate different kinds of receptors, like a lock and key, you might wonder how many types of neurotransmitters are floating across synapses in your brain right now. Today we know that some 60 chemicals play a role in transmitting information throughout the brain and body

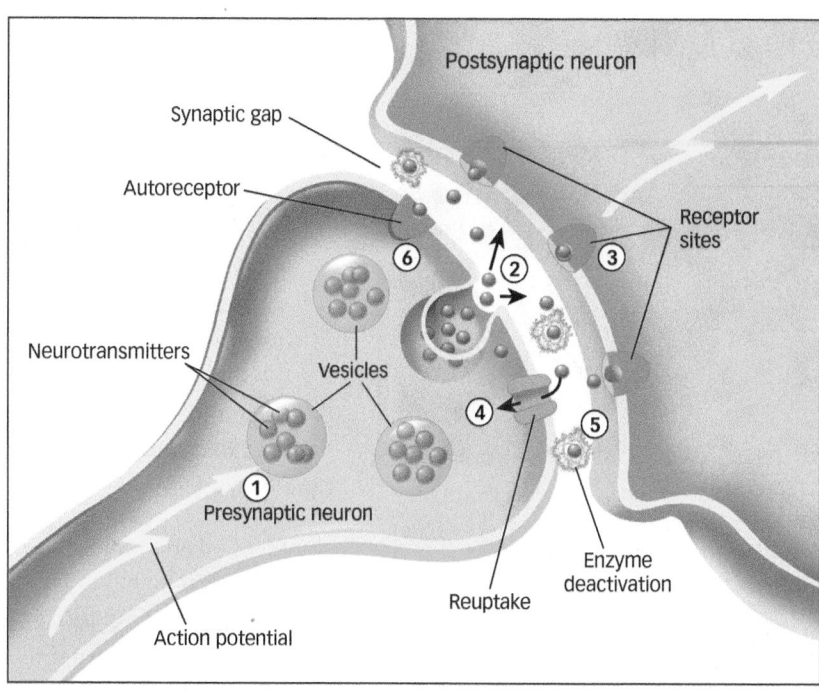

▲ Figure 3.6

SYNAPTIC TRANSMISSION (1) The action potential travels down the axon and (2) stimulates the release of neurotransmitters from vesicles. (3) The neurotransmitters are released into the synapse, where they float to bind with receptor sites on a dendrite of a postsynaptic neuron, initiating a new action potential. The neurotransmitters are cleared out of the synapse by (4) reuptake into the sending neuron, (5) being broken down by enzymes in the synapse, or (6) binding to autoreceptors on the sending neuron.

terminal buttons Knoblike structures that branch out from an axon.

neurotransmitters Chemicals that transmit information across the synapse to a receiving neuron's dendrites.

receptors Parts of the cell membrane that receive the neurotransmitter and initiate or prevent a new electric signal.

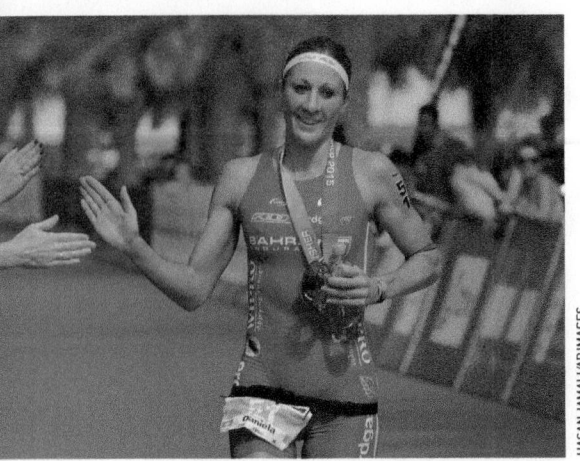

HASAN JAMALI/AP IMAGES

Swiss triathlete Daniela Ryf greets fans after completing the running portion of the 2015 Ironman World Championship in Bahrain. When athletes such as Ryf engage in extreme sports, they may experience the subjective highs that result from the release of endorphins—chemical messengers acting in emotion and pain centers that elevate mood and dull the experience of pain.

acetylcholine (ACh) A neurotransmitter involved in a number of functions, including voluntary motor control.

dopamine A neurotransmitter that regulates motor behavior, motivation, pleasure, and emotional arousal.

glutamate The major excitatory neurotransmitter in the brain.

GABA (gamma-aminobutyric acid) The primary inhibitory neurotransmitter in the brain.

norepinephrine A neurotransmitter that is particularly involved in states of vigilance or heightened awareness of dangers in the environment.

serotonin A neurotransmitter that is involved in the regulation of sleep and wakefulness, eating, and aggressive behavior.

endorphins Chemicals that act within the pain pathways and emotion centers of the brain.

and differentially affect thought, feeling, and behavior, but a few major classes seem particularly important. We'll summarize those here, and you'll meet some of these neurotransmitters again in later chapters.

▶ **Acetylcholine (ACh)** is *a neurotransmitter involved in a number of functions, including voluntary motor control.* Acetylcholine is found in neurons of the brain and in the synapses where axons connect to muscles and body organs, such as the heart. Acetylcholine activates muscles to initiate motor behavior, but it also contributes to the regulation of attention, learning, sleeping, dreaming, and memory (Gais & Born, 2004; Hasselmo, 2006; Wrenn et al., 2006). Alzheimer's disease, a medical condition involving severe memory impairments (Salmon & Bondi, 2009), is associated with the deterioration of ACh-producing neurons.

▶ **Dopamine** is *a neurotransmitter that regulates motor behavior, motivation, pleasure, and emotional arousal.* Because of its role in basic motivated behaviors, such as seeking pleasure or associating actions with rewards, dopamine plays a role in drug addiction (Baler & Volkow, 2006). High levels of dopamine have been linked to schizophrenia (Winterer & Weinberger, 2004), whereas low levels have been linked to Parkinson's disease.

▶ **Glutamate** is the *major excitatory neurotransmitter in the brain,* meaning that it enhances the transmission of information between neurons. **GABA (gamma-aminobutyric acid),** in contrast, is *the primary inhibitory neurotransmitter in the brain*, meaning that it tends to stop the firing of neurons. Too much glutamate, or too little GABA, can cause neurons to become overactive, causing seizures.

▶ Two related neurotransmitters influence mood and arousal: norepinephrine and serotonin. **Norepinephrine** is *particularly involved in states of vigilance, or a heightened awareness of dangers in the environment* (Ressler & Nemeroff, 1999). **Serotonin** is *involved in the regulation of sleep and wakefulness, eating, and aggressive behavior* (Dayan & Huys, 2009; Kroeze & Roth, 1998). Because both neurotransmitters affect mood and arousal, low levels of each have been implicated in mood disorders (Tamminga et al., 2002).

▶ **Endorphins** *are chemicals that act within the pain pathways and emotion centers of the brain* (Keefe et al., 2001). The term *endorphin* is a contraction of *endogenous m*orphine, and that's a pretty apt description. Morphine is a synthetic drug that has a calming and pleasurable effect; an endorphin is an internally produced substance that has similar properties, such as dulling the experience of pain and elevating moods. The "runner's high" experienced by many athletes as they push their bodies to painful limits of endurance can be explained by the release of endorphins in the brain (Boecker et al., 2008).

Each of these neurotransmitters affects thought, feeling, and behavior in different ways, so normal functioning involves a delicate balance of each. Even a slight imbalance—too much of one neurotransmitter or not enough of another—can dramatically affect behavior. These imbalances sometimes occur naturally: Sometimes the brain doesn't produce enough serotonin, for example, which contributes to depressed or anxious moods. Other times a person may actively seek to cause imbalances. People who smoke, drink alcohol, or take drugs, legal or not, are altering the balance of neurotransmitters in their brains. The drug LSD, for example, is structurally very similar to serotonin, so it binds very easily with serotonin receptors in the brain, producing similar effects on thoughts, feelings, or behavior. In the next section, we'll look at how some drugs are able to "trick" receptor sites in just this way.

How Drugs Mimic Neurotransmitters

Many drugs that affect the nervous system operate by increasing, interfering with, or mimicking the manufacture or function of neurotransmitters (Cooper, Bloom, & Roth,

Agonists increase the action of a neurotransmitter

Antagonists block the function of a neurotransmitter

Drugs such as Clonidine bind to autoreceptors and block their inhibitory effect

Autoreceptor

Neurotransmitters

Drugs such as L-dopa increase production of neurotransmitters

Vesicle

Drug molecule

Action potential

Receptor sites

Drugs such as amphetamines increase release of neurotransmitters

Drugs such as Prozac block the deactivation or reuptake of neurotransmitters

Drugs such as nicotine bind to postsynaptic receptor sites and activate them or increase the neurotransmitter effect

Drugs such as caffeine activate autoreceptors so they inhibit release of neurotransmitters

Autoreceptor

Neurotransmitters

Vesicle

Drug molecule

Action potential

Receptor sites

Drugs such as AMPT block production of neurotransmitters

Drugs such as the beta-blocker Propranalol bind to postsynaptic receptors and block neurotransmitter binding

Drugs bind to receptor sites and block neurotransmitters

Drugs such as botulinium toxin block release of neurotransmitters

▲ Figure 3.7

THE ACTIONS OF AGONIST AND ANTAGONIST DRUGS Agonist and antagonist drugs can enhance or interfere with synaptic transmission at every point in the process: in the production of neurotransmitters, in the release of neurotransmitters, at the autoreceptors, in reuptake, in the postsynaptic receptors, and in the synapse itself.

2003; Sarter, 2006). **Agonists** are *drugs that increase the action of a neurotransmitter*. **Antagonists** are *drugs that block the function of a neurotransmitter*. Some drugs alter a step in the production or release of the neurotransmitter, whereas others have a chemical structure so similar to a neurotransmitter that the drug is able to bind to that neuron's receptor. If, by binding to a receptor, a drug activates the neurotransmitter, it is an agonist; if it blocks the action of the neurotransmitter, it is an antagonist (see **FIGURE 3.7**).

For example, the drug L-dopa was developed to treat Parkinson's disease, a movement disorder characterized by tremors and difficulty initiating movement, caused by the loss of neurons that use the neurotransmitter dopamine. Dopamine is created in neurons by a modification of a common molecule called L-dopa. Ingesting L-dopa will elevate the amount of L-dopa in the brain and spur the surviving neurons to produce more dopamine. In other words, L-dopa acts as an agonist for dopamine. The use of L-dopa has been reasonably successful in the alleviation of Parkinson's disease symptoms (Muenter & Tyce, 1971; Schapira et al., 2009). However, the effectiveness of L-dopa typically decreases when used over a long period of time, so that many long-time users experience some symptoms of the disease. The actor Michael J. Fox, who was diagnosed with Parkinson's disease in 1991 and takes L-dopa, described the simple act of trying to brush his teeth in his memoir:

Grasping the toothpaste is nothing compared to the effort it takes to coordinate the two-handed task of wrangling the toothbrush and strangling out a line of paste onto the bristles. By now, my right hand has started up again, rotating at the wrist in a circular motion, perfect for what I'm about to do. My left hand guides my right hand up to my mouth, and once the back of the Oral-B touches the inside of my upper lip, I let go. It's like releasing the tension on a slingshot and compares favorably to

agonists Drugs that increase the action of a neurotransmitter.

antagonists Drugs that block the function of a neurotransmitter.

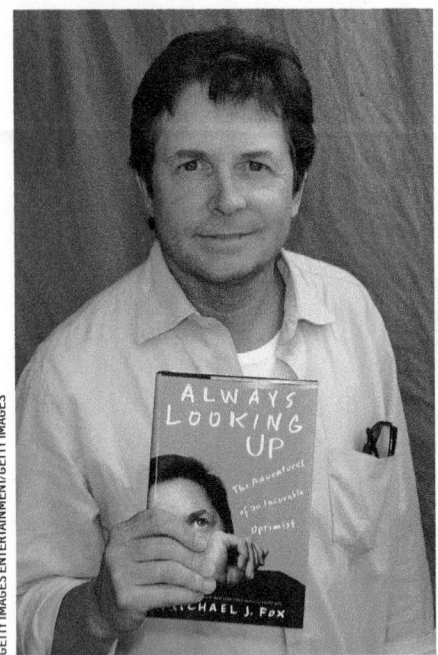

Michael J. Fox vividly described his struggles with Parkinson's disease in his 2009 memoir. Fox's visibility has increased public awareness of the disease and spurred greater efforts toward finding a cure.

the most powerful state-of-the-art electric toothbrush on the market. With no off switch, stopping means seizing my right wrist with my left hand, forcing it down to the sink basin, and shaking the brush loose as though disarming a knife-wielding attacker. (Fox, 2009, pp. 2–3)

Many other drugs, including some street drugs, alter the actions of neurotransmitters. Let's look at a few more examples.

Amphetamine is a popular drug that stimulates the release of norepinephrine and dopamine. In addition, both amphetamine and *cocaine* prevent the reuptake of norepinephrine and dopamine. The combination of increased release of norepinephrine and dopamine and prevention of their reuptake floods the synapse with those neurotransmitters, resulting in increased activation of their receptors. Both of these drugs therefore are strong agonists, although their psychological effects differ somewhat because of subtle distinctions in where and how they act on the brain. Norepinephrine and dopamine play a critical role in mood control, such that increases in either neurotransmitter result in euphoria, wakefulness, and a burst of energy. However, norepinephrine also increases heart rate. An overdose of amphetamine or cocaine can cause the heart to contract so rapidly that heartbeats do not last long enough to pump blood effectively, leading to fainting and sometimes death.

Methamphetamine, a variant of amphetamine, affects pathways for dopamine, serotonin, and norepinephrine at the neuron's synapses, making it difficult to interpret exactly how this drug works. But the combination of its agonist and antagonist effects alters the functions of neurotransmitters that help us perceive and interpret visual images, sometimes resulting in strange hallucinations.

Prozac, a drug commonly used to treat depression, is another example of a neurotransmitter agonist. Prozac blocks the reuptake of the neurotransmitter *serotonin*, making it part of a category of drugs called *selective serotonin reuptake inhibitors*, or *SSRIs* (Wong, Bymaster, & Engelman, 1995). People suffering from clinical depression typically have reduced levels of serotonin in their brains. By blocking reuptake, more of the neurotransmitter remains in the synapse longer and produces greater activation of serotonin receptors. Serotonin elevates mood, which can help relieve depression (Mann, 2005).

An antagonist with important medical implications is a drug called *propranalol*, one of a class of drugs called *beta blockers* that obstruct a receptor site for norepinephrine in the heart. Because norepinephrine cannot bind to these receptors, the heart rate slows down, which is helpful for disorders in which the heart beats too fast or irregularly. Beta blockers are also prescribed to reduce the agitation, racing heart, and nervousness associated with stage fright (Mills & Dimsdale, 1991; for additional discussion of antianxiety and antidepression drug treatments, see the Treatment of Psychological Disorders chapter).

Build to the Outcomes

1. What difference between the inside and outside of the neuron's cell membrane creates the resting potential?

2. How does the neuron's membrane change over the course of an action potential?

3. What is the importance of the "pump" in the last stage of the action potential?

4. What is the role of neurotransmitters in neural communication?

5. Chose two neurotransmitters and compare and contrast their functions?

6. Is L-dopa an agonist for dopamine or an antagonist? Explain.

The Organization of the Nervous System

We've seen how individual neurons communicate with each other. What's the bigger picture? Neurons work by forming circuits and pathways in the brain, which in turn influence circuits and pathways in other areas of the body. Without this kind of organization and delegation, neurons would be churning away with little purpose. Neurons are the building blocks that form *nerves*, or bundles of axons and the glial cells that support them. The **nervous system** is *an interacting network of neurons that conveys electrochemical information throughout the body.* In this section, we'll look at the major divisions and components of the nervous system.

DIVISIONS OF THE NERVOUS SYSTEM

There are two major divisions of the nervous system: the central nervous system and the peripheral nervous system (see **FIGURE 3.8**). The **central nervous system (CNS)** is *composed of the brain and spinal cord.* The central nervous system receives sensory information from the external world, processes and coordinates this information, and sends commands to the skeletal and muscular systems for action. At the top of the CNS rests the brain, which contains structures that support the most complex perceptual, motor, emotional, and cognitive functions of the nervous system. The spinal cord branches down from the brain; nerves that process sensory information and relay commands to the body connect to the spinal cord.

The **peripheral nervous system (PNS)** *connects the central nervous system to the body's organs and muscles.* The peripheral nervous system is itself composed of two major subdivisions, the somatic nervous system and the autonomic nervous system. The **somatic nervous system** is *a set of nerves that conveys information between voluntary muscles and the central nervous system.* Humans have conscious control over

nervous system An interacting network of neurons that conveys electrochemical information throughout the body.

central nervous system (CNS) The part of the nervous system that is composed of the brain and spinal cord.

peripheral nervous system (PNS) The part of the nervous system that connects the central nervous system to the body's organs and muscles.

somatic nervous system A set of nerves that conveys information between voluntary muscles and the central nervous system.

▼ Figure 3.8

THE HUMAN NERVOUS SYSTEM The nervous system is organized into the peripheral and central nervous systems. The peripheral nervous system is further divided into the autonomic and somatic nervous systems.

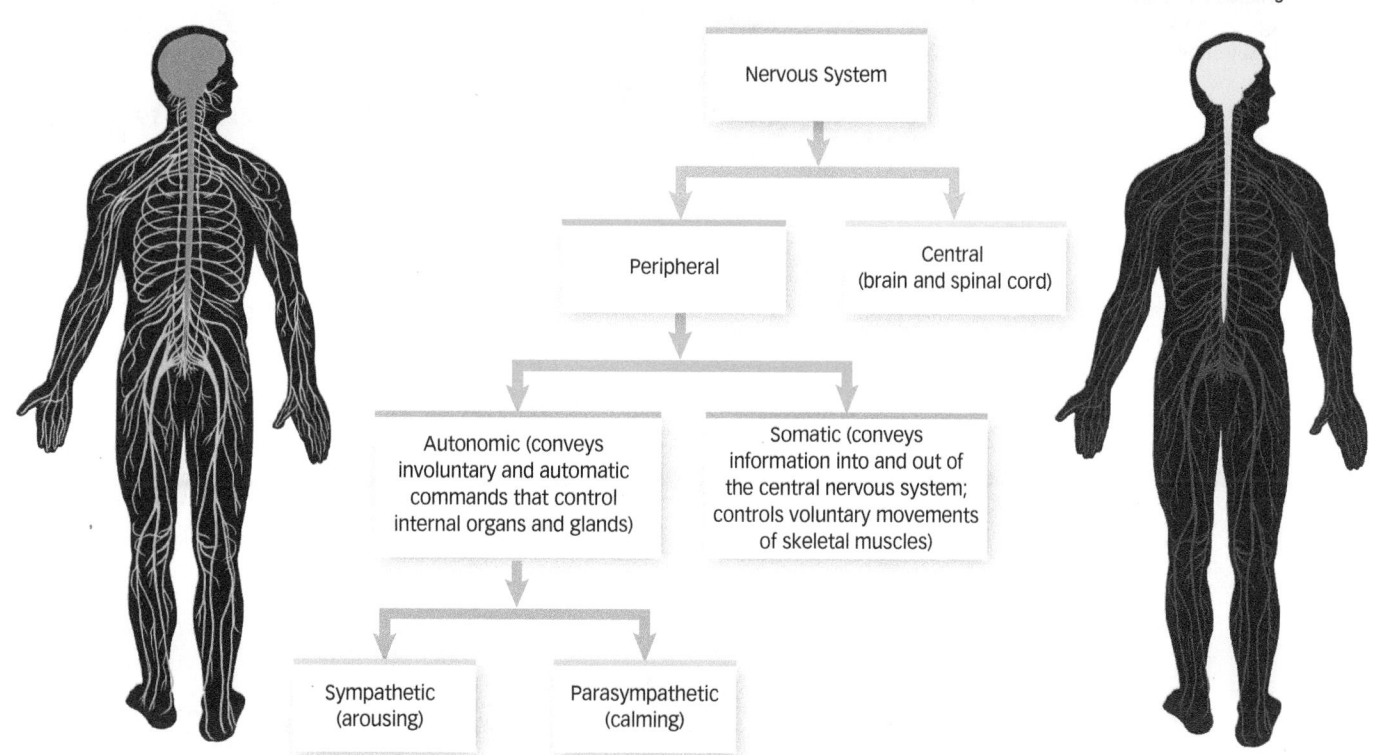

autonomic nervous system (ANS) A set of nerves that carries involuntary and automatic commands that control blood vessels, body organs, and glands.

sympathetic nervous system A set of nerves that prepares the body for action in challenging or threatening situations.

this system and use it to perceive, think, and coordinate their behaviors. For example, reaching for your morning cup of coffee involves the elegantly orchestrated activities of the somatic nervous system: Information from the receptors in your eyes travels to your brain, registering that a cup is on the table; signals from your brain travel to the muscles in your arm and hand; feedback from those muscles tells your brain that the cup has been grasped, and so on.

In contrast, the **autonomic nervous system (ANS)** is *a set of nerves that carries involuntary and automatic commands that control blood vessels, body organs, and glands.* As suggested by its name, this system works on its own to regulate bodily systems, largely outside of conscious control. The ANS has two major subdivisions, the sympathetic nervous system and the parasympathetic nervous system. Each exerts a different type of control on the body. The **sympathetic nervous system** is *a set of nerves that prepares the body for action in challenging or threatening situations* (see **FIGURE 3.9**). For example, imagine that you are walking alone late at night and are frightened by footsteps behind you in a dark alley. Your sympathetic nervous system kicks into action at this point: It dilates your pupils to let in more light, increases your heart rate and respiration to pump more oxygen to your muscles, diverts blood flow to your brain and muscles, and activates sweat glands to cool your body. To conserve energy, the sympathetic nervous system inhibits salivation and bowel movements, suppresses the body's immune responses, and suppresses responses to pain and injury. The sum total of these fast, automatic responses is that they increase the likelihood that you can escape.

▶ Figure 3.9
SYMPATHETIC AND PARASYMPATHETIC SYSTEMS The autonomic nervous system is composed of two subsystems that complement each other. Activation of the sympathetic system serves several aspects of arousal, whereas the parasympathetic nervous system returns the body to its normal resting state.

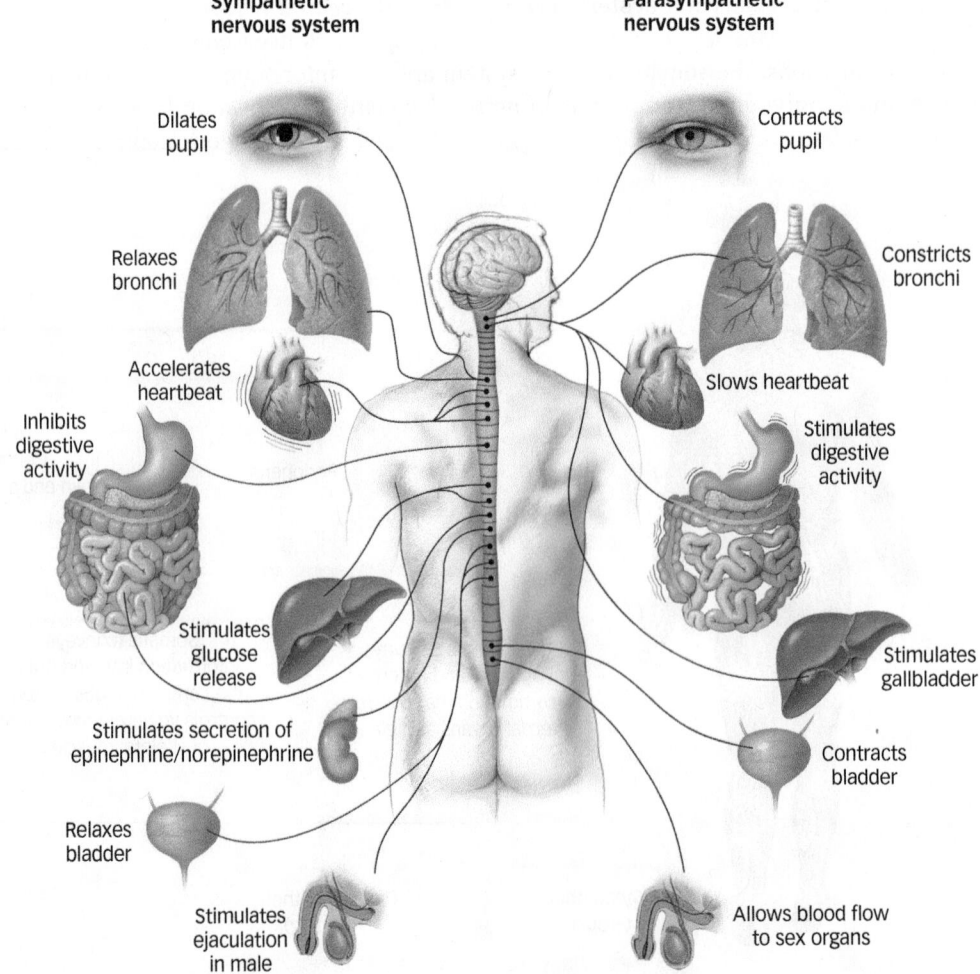

Sympathetic nervous system

Dilates pupil

Relaxes bronchi

Accelerates heartbeat

Inhibits digestive activity

Stimulates glucose release

Stimulates secretion of epinephrine/norepinephrine

Relaxes bladder

Stimulates ejaculation in male

Parasympathetic nervous system

Contracts pupil

Constricts bronchi

Slows heartbeat

Stimulates digestive activity

Stimulates gallbladder

Contracts bladder

Allows blood flow to sex organs

The **parasympathetic nervous system** *helps the body return to a normal resting state*. When you're far away from your would-be attacker, your body doesn't need to remain on red alert. Now the parasympathetic nervous system kicks in to reverse the effects of the sympathetic nervous system and return your body to its normal state. The parasympathetic nervous system generally mirrors the connections of the sympathetic nervous system. For example, the parasympathetic nervous system constricts your pupils, slows your heart rate and respiration, diverts blood flow to your digestive system, and decreases activity in your sweat glands.

As you might imagine, the sympathetic and parasympathetic nervous systems coordinate to control many bodily functions. One example is sexual behavior. In men, the parasympathetic nervous system engorges the blood vessels of the penis to produce an erection, but the sympathetic nervous system is responsible for ejaculation. In women, the parasympathetic nervous system produces vaginal lubrication, but the sympathetic nervous system underlies orgasm. In both men and women, a successful sexual experience depends on a delicate balance of these two systems; in fact, anxiety about sexual performance can disrupt this balance. For example, sympathetic nervous system activation caused by anxiety can lead to premature ejaculation in males and lack of lubrication in females.

COMPONENTS OF THE CENTRAL NERVOUS SYSTEM

Compared with the many divisions of the peripheral nervous system, the central nervous system may seem simple. After all, it has only two elements: the brain and the spinal cord. But those two elements are ultimately responsible for most of what we do as humans.

The spinal cord often seems like the brain's poor relation: The brain gets all the glory, and the spinal cord just hangs around, doing relatively simple tasks. Those tasks, however, are pretty important: They keep you breathing, respond to pain, and move your muscles, allowing you to walk. What's more, without the spinal cord, the brain would not be able to put any of its higher processing into action.

Do you need your brain to tell you to pull your hand away from a hot stove? For some very basic behaviors such as this, the spinal cord doesn't need input from the brain at all. Connections between the sensory inputs and motor neurons in the spinal cord mediate **spinal reflexes,** *simple pathways in the nervous system that rapidly generate muscle contractions.* If you touch a hot stove, the sensory neurons that register pain send inputs directly into the spinal cord (see **FIGURE 3.10**). Through just a few

parasympathetic nervous system A set of nerves that helps the body return to a normal resting state.

spinal reflexes Simple pathways in the nervous system that rapidly generate muscle contractions.

◀ Figure 3.10

THE PAIN WITHDRAWAL REFLEX Many actions of the central nervous system don't require the brain's input. For example, withdrawing from pain is a reflexive activity controlled by the spinal cord. Painful sensations (such as the heat of fire) travel directly to the spinal cord via sensory neurons, which then issue an immediate command to motor neurons to retract the hand.

C1 — CERVICAL NERVES
C2 — Head and neck
C3
C4 — Diaphragm
C5 — Deltoids, biceps
C6
— Wrist extenders
C7 — Triceps
T1
— Hand
T2
T3 — THORACIC NERVES
T4
T5 — Chest muscles
T6
T7
T8
T9 — Abdominal
T10   muscles
T11
T12

L1 — LUMBAR NERVES
L2
L3 — Leg muscles
L4
L5 — SACRAL NERVES
S1
S2 — Bowel, bladder
S3
S4 — Sexual function
S5

◄ **Figure 3.11**

REGIONS OF THE SPINAL CORD The spinal cord is divided into four main sections; each controls different parts of the body. Damage higher on the spinal cord usually means greater impairment.

synaptic connections within the spinal cord, interneurons relay these sensory inputs to motor neurons that connect to your arm muscles and direct you to quickly retract your hand. These spinal reflexes illustrate the operation of a **reflex arc**, *a neural pathway that controls reflex actions.* Reflex arcs can include sensory neurons, interneurons, and motor neurons, but some simple reflex arcs are comprised of only sensory and motor neurons.

Beyond reflexes, more elaborate tasks require the collaboration of the spinal cord and the brain. The peripheral nervous system sends messages from sensory neurons through the spinal cord into the brain. The brain sends commands for voluntary movement through the spinal cord to motor neurons, whose axons project out to skeletal muscles. Damage to the spinal cord severs the connection from the brain to the sensory and motor neurons that are essential to sensory perception and movement. The location of the spinal injury often determines the extent of the abilities that are lost. As you can see in **FIGURE 3.11**, different regions of the spinal cord control different systems of the body. Individuals with damage at a particular level of the spinal cord lose sensations of touch and pain in body parts below the level of the injury, as well as a loss of motor control of the muscles in the same areas. A spinal injury higher up the cord usually predicts a much poorer prognosis, such as quadriplegia (loss of sensation and motor control over all limbs), breathing through a respirator, and lifelong immobility.

The late actor Christopher Reeve, who starred as Superman in four *Superman* movies, damaged his spinal cord in a horseback riding accident in 1995, resulting in loss of sensation and motor control in all of his body parts below the neck. Despite great efforts over several years, Reeve made only modest gains in his motor control and sensation, highlighting the extent to which we depend on communication from the brain through the spinal cord to the body, and showing how difficult it is to compensate for the loss of these connections (Edgerton et al., 2004). Unfortunately, Christopher Reeve died at age 52 in 2004 from complications due to his paralysis. On a brighter note, researchers are making progress in understanding the nature of spinal cord injuries and how to treat them by focusing on how the brain changes in response to injury (Blesch & Tuszynski, 2009; Dunlop, 2008), a process that is closely related to the concept of brain plasticity that we will examine later in this chapter. Progress in constructing brain–machine interfaces could also improve the lives of people who have suffered paralysis from spinal cord injuries (see Hot Science: The Power of Thought: Brain–Machine Interfaces).

reflex arc A neural pathway that controls reflex actions.

Build to the Outcomes

1. What is the neuron's role in the body's nervous system?

2. What are the components of the central nervous system?

3. What are the two divisions of the peripheral nervous system?

4. What triggers the increase in your heart rate when you feel threatened?

5. What important functions does the spinal cord perform on its own?

The Power of Thought: Brain–Machine Interfaces

In the wildly popular James Cameron movie *Avatar*, the paraplegic marine Jake Sully's brain is able to control, via computer, the actions of an avatar body. Though this scenario is seemingly far fetched, scientists recently have been taking steps to bring this type of science-fiction fantasy closer to reality.

Experiments with monkeys conducted a little over a decade ago provided initial evidence that the brain can control mechanical devices through thoughts alone (Carmena et al., 2003). The researchers implanted multiple wires into the monkeys' motor cortices and trained them to obtain a juice reward by moving a joystick that controlled a cursor on a computer screen. Using the activity patterns of many neurons, they created a computer model of the neural activity that corresponded to different directions of joystick movements. Then they disconnected the joystick from the computer, and instead connected the signals that their model extracted from the monkey's motor cortex activity directly to the computer. With just a few days of practice, the monkeys learned to adjust their motor cortex activity patterns to hit the targets successfully. In effect, the monkeys were controlling the cursor with their thoughts.

These findings raised the possibility that cortical recordings and state-of-the-art computer programs could be developed into a kind of neuroprosthesis to help people with brain or spinal injuries that leave them paralyzed. Important recent evidence supports this idea. For example, Hochberg et al. (2012) studied a 58-year-old woman and a 66-year-old man who had suffered strokes to the brainstem that produced tetraplegia: paralysis resulting in the loss of use of all limbs. They examined whether the patients could use a brain–machine interface to control a robotic arm for performing reaching and grasping movements. In order to guide movement, the researchers sent the robotic arm signals that were decoded by a computer program from a small population of neurons in each individual's motor cortex, similar to the earlier experiments with monkeys. The participants' task was to reach for and grasp purple spheres that were elevated above a table. Both participants were able to perform the task with relatively high levels of accuracy and speed, though they were not so accurate or so fast as were able-bodied participants. Using signals decoded from her motor cortex, the female patient was even able to use the robotic arm to drink her coffee (see photo)!

These results are exciting, and researchers continue to develop new ways to improve brain–machine interfaces. One recent study used a computer program that decodes brain signals that convey cognitive information about whether an individual judges that the action being carried out by a robotic arm attempting to touch a target (a square of a particular color) is correct or erroneous (Iturrate et al., 2015). The researchers recorded EEG activity from the scalp in healthy young volunteers as they attempted to control the robotic arm, extracting specific signals that arise when people are aware that they have made a correct response or an error. The researchers found that after a relatively brief training period of about 25 minutes, participants were successful in guiding the robot arm to specific targets on the basis of the brain activity associated with evaluating actions as correct or erroneous. These findings are potentially important because the same kinds of evaluation or monitoring signals used here could potentially be applied to a wide variety of situations.

Although these studies do not quite take us all the way to the world envisioned in *Avatar*, they provide clear evidence that what we once thought of as pure science fiction is well on its way to becoming science fact.

REACH AND GRASP BY PEOPLE WITH TETRAPLEGIA USING A NEURALLY CONTROLLED ROBOTIC ARM. *NATURE, 485, 372–375* (17 MAY 2012) ©2012 MACMILLAN PUBLISHERS LIMITED.

▲ A participant drinking from a bottle using the robotic arm.

Structure of the Brain

The human brain, weighing in at about three pounds, is really not much to look at. You already know that its neurons and glial cells are busy humming away, giving you potentially brilliant ideas, consciousness, and feelings. But which neurons in which parts of the brain control which functions? To answer that question, neuroscientists had to find a way of describing the brain that allows researchers to communicate with one another. It can be helpful to talk about areas of the brain from "bottom to top," noting how the different regions are specialized for different kinds of tasks. In general,

SCIENCE SOURCE

The human brain weighs only three pounds and isn't much to look at, but its accomplishments are staggering.

Learning Outcomes

▶ Differentiate the functions of the major divisions of the brain.

▶ Describe the main glands of the endocrine system.

▶ Explain the functions of the cerebral cortex according to organization across hemispheres, within hemispheres, and within specific lobes.

▶ Define brain plasticity.

hindbrain The area of the brain that coordinates information coming into and out of the spinal cord.

medulla An extension of the spinal cord into the skull that coordinates heart rate, circulation, and respiration.

reticular formation A brain structure that regulates sleep, wakefulness, and levels of arousal.

cerebellum A large structure of the hindbrain that controls fine motor skills.

simpler functions are performed at the "lower" levels of the brain, whereas more complex functions are performed at successively "higher" levels (see **FIGURE 3.12a**). Or, as you'll see shortly, the brain can also be approached in a "side-by-side" fashion: Although each side of the brain is roughly analogous, one half of the brain specializes in some tasks that the other half doesn't. Although these divisions make it easier to understand areas of the brain and their functions, keep in mind that none of these structures or areas in the brain can act alone: They are all part of one big, interacting, interdependent whole.

Let's look first at the divisions of the brain, and the responsibilities of each part, moving from the bottom to the top. Using this view, we can divide the brain into three parts: the hindbrain, the midbrain, and the forebrain (see Figure 3.12a).

THE HINDBRAIN

If you follow the spinal cord from your tailbone to where it enters your skull, you'll find it difficult to determine where your spinal cord ends and your brain begins. That's because the spinal cord is continuous with the **hindbrain,** *an area of the brain that coordinates information coming into and out of the spinal cord.* The hindbrain looks like a stalk on which the rest of the brain sits, and it controls the most basic functions of life: respiration, alertness, and motor skills. The structures that make up the hindbrain include: the medulla, the reticular formation, the cerebellum, and the pons (see Figure 3.12b).

The **medulla** is *an extension of the spinal cord into the skull that coordinates heart rate, circulation, and respiration.* Beginning inside the medulla and extending upward is a small cluster of neurons called the **reticular formation,** which *regulates sleep, wakefulness, and levels of arousal.* In one early experiment, researchers stimulated the reticular formation of a sleeping cat. This caused the animal to awaken almost instantaneously and remain alert. Conversely, severing the connections between the reticular formation and the rest of the brain caused the animal to lapse into an irreversible coma (Moruzzi & Magoun, 1949). The reticular formation maintains the

▼ Figure 3.12
STRUCTURE OF THE BRAIN

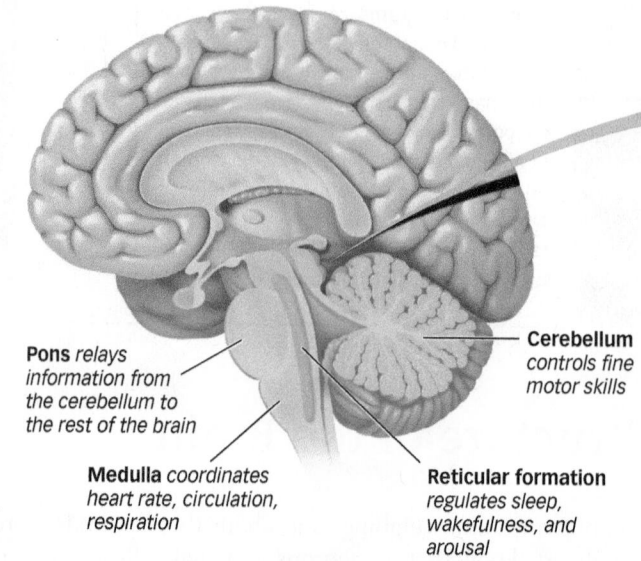

(a)
The Major Divisions of the Brain
The brain can be organized into three parts, moving from the bottom to the top, from simpler functions to the more complex: the hindbrain, the midbrain, and the forebrain.

(b)
The Hindbrain
The hindbrain coordinates information coming into and out of the spinal cord and controls the basic functions of life.

same delicate balance between alertness and unconsciousness in humans. In fact, many general anesthetics work by reducing activity in the reticular formation, rendering the patient unconscious.

Behind the medulla is the **cerebellum**, *a large structure of the hindbrain that controls fine motor skills.* (*Cerebellum* is Latin for "little brain," and this structure does look like a small replica of the brain.) The cerebellum orchestrates the proper sequence of movements when we ride a bike, play the piano, or maintain balance while walking and running. It contributes to the fine-tuning of behavior: smoothing our actions to allow their graceful execution rather than initiating the actions (Smetacek, 2002). The initiation of behavior involves other areas of the brain; as you'll recall, different brain systems interact and are interdependent with each other.

The last major area of the hindbrain is the **pons,** *a structure that relays information from the cerebellum to the rest of the brain.* (*Pons* means "bridge" in Latin.) Although the detailed functions of the pons remain poorly understood, it essentially acts as a relay station or bridge between the cerebellum and other structures in the brain.

THE MIDBRAIN

Sitting on top of the hindbrain is the *midbrain*, which is relatively small in humans. As you can see in Figure 3.12c, the midbrain contains two main structures: the tectum and the tegmentum. The **tectum** *orients an organism in the environment.* The tectum receives stimulus input from the eyes, ears, and skin and moves the organism in a coordinated way toward the stimulus. For example, when you're studying in a quiet room and you hear a *click* behind and to the right of you, your body will swivel and orient to the direction of the sound; this is your tectum in action.

The **tegmentum** is *involved in movement and arousal*; it also helps to orient an organism toward sensory stimuli. The midbrain may be relatively small, but it is a central location of neurotransmitters involved in arousal, mood, and motivation and the brain structures that rely on them (White, 1996). You could survive if you had only

The high-wire artist Freddy Nock relied on his cerebellum to coordinate the movements necessary to walk on the rope of the Corvatsch cable car from more than 10,000 feet over sea level down to the base station in Silvaplana, Switzerland on January 29, 2011. Nock set a new mark that day for the Guinness World Records.

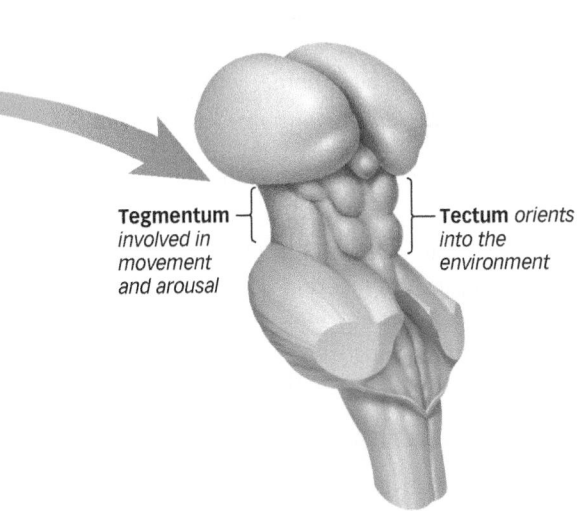

Tegmentum *involved in movement and arousal*

Tectum *orients into the environment*

(c)
The Midbrain
The midbrain is important for orientation and movement.

Cerebral cortex

Subcortical structures:

Basal ganglia *a set of subcortical structures that directs intentional movements*

Thalamus *receives and transmits information from the senses to the cerebral cortex*

Hippocampus *critical for creating and integrating new memories*

Amygdala *plays a role in emotional processes*

Hypothalamus *regulates body temperature, hunger, thirst, and sexual behavior*

Pituitary gland *releases hormones that direct many other glands*

Corpus callosum

(d)
The Forebrain
The forebrain is the highest level of the brain and is critical for complex cognitive, emotional, sensory, and motor functions. The forebrain is divided into two parts: the cerebral cortex and the underlying subcortical structures. The cerebral cortex, the outermost layer of the brain, is divided into two hemispheres, connected by the corpus callosum (see Figure 3.15).

pons A brain structure that relays information from the cerebellum to the rest of the brain.

tectum A part of the midbrain that orients an organism in the environment.

tegmentum A part of the midbrain that is involved in movement and arousal.

cerebral cortex The outermost layer of the brain, visible to the naked eye and divided into two hemispheres.

subcortical structures Areas of the forebrain housed under the cerebral cortex near the very center of the brain.

thalamus A subcortical structure that relays and filters information from the senses and transmits the information to the cerebral cortex.

hypothalamus A subcortical structure that regulates body temperature, hunger, thirst, and sexual behavior.

ISTOCK/GETTY IMAGES

The thalamus receives inputs from all the major senses except smell. You can thank your thalamus when you see the red apple, feel its smoothness in your hand, hear the crunch as you bite into it, and taste its sweetness.

a hindbrain and a midbrain. The structures in the hindbrain would take care of all the bodily functions necessary to sustain life, and the structures in the midbrain would orient you toward or away from pleasurable or threatening stimuli in the environment. But this wouldn't be much of a life. To understand where the abilities that make us fully human come from, we need to consider the last division of the brain.

THE FOREBRAIN

When you appreciate the beauty of a poem, detect the sarcasm in a friend's remark, plan to go skiing next winter, or notice the faint glimmer of sadness on a loved one's face, you are enlisting the forebrain. The *forebrain* is the highest level of the brain— literally and figuratively—and controls complex cognitive, emotional, sensory, and motor functions. The forebrain itself is divided into two main sections: the cerebral cortex and the subcortical structures.

The **cerebral cortex** is *the outermost layer of the brain, visible to the naked eye, and divided into two hemispheres.* The **subcortical structures** are *areas of the forebrain housed under the cerebral cortex near the center of the brain* (see Figure 3.12d). We'll have much more to say about the two hemispheres of the cerebral cortex and the functions they serve in the next section, with the highest level of the brain fittingly saved for last. First, we'll examine the subcortical structures.

Subcortical Structures

The subcortical (beneath the cortex) structures are nestled deep inside the brain, where they are quite protected. If you imagine sticking an index finger in each of your ears and pushing inward until they touch, that's about where you'd find the *thalamus,* three components of the limbic system (the *hypothalamus,* the *hippocampus,* and the *amygdala*), the basal ganglia, and the pituitary gland, which is part of the endocrine system (see Figure 3.12d). Each of these subcortical structures plays an important role in relaying information throughout the brain, as well as performing specific tasks that allow us to think, feel, and behave as humans. Here we'll give you a brief introduction to each, and you'll read more about many of these structures in later chapters.

Thalamus and Hypothalamus. The thalamus and hypothalamus, located in the center of the brain, interact closely with several other brain structures. They relay signals to and from these structures and also help to regulate them.

The **thalamus** *relays and filters information from the senses and transmits the information to the cerebral cortex.* The thalamus receives inputs from all the major senses except smell, which has direct connections to the cerebral cortex. The thalamus acts as a kind of computer server in a networked system, taking in multiple inputs and relaying them to a variety of locations (Guillery & Sherman, 2002). However, unlike the mechanical operations of a computer ("send input A to location B"), the thalamus actively filters sensory information, giving more weight to some inputs and less weight to others. The thalamus also closes the pathways of incoming sensations during sleep, providing a valuable function in *not* allowing information to pass to the rest of the brain.

The **hypothalamus,** located below the thalamus (*hypo-* is Greek for "under"), *regulates body temperature, hunger, thirst, and sexual behavior.* Although the hypothalamus is a tiny area of the brain, clusters of neurons in the hypothalamus oversee a wide range of basic behaviors, keeping body temperature, blood sugar levels, and metabolism within an optimal range for normal human functioning. Lesions to some areas of the hypothalamus result in overeating, whereas lesions to other areas leave an animal with no desire for food at all, highlighting that the hypothalamus plays a key role in regulating food intake (Berthoud & Morrison, 2008). Also, when you think about sex, messages from your cerebral cortex are sent to the hypothalamus to trigger the release of hormones. Finally, electric stimulation of some areas of the hypothalamus in cats can produce hissing and biting, whereas stimulation of other areas in the hypothalamus can produce what appears to be intense pleasure for an animal (Siegel et al., 1999). The researchers James Olds and Peter Milner found that a small electric current delivered to a certain region of a rat's hypothalamus was extremely rewarding for the animal (Olds & Milner, 1954). In fact, when allowed to press a bar attached to the electrode to initiate their own stimulation, rats would do so several thousand times an hour, often to the point of exhaustion!

The Limbic System. The hypothalamus also is part of the **limbic system,** a group of forebrain structures including the hypothalamus, the hippocampus, and the amygdala, which are involved in motivation, emotion, learning, and memory (Maclean, 1970; Papez, 1937). The limbic system is where the subcortical structures meet the cerebral cortex.

The **hippocampus** (from Latin for "sea horse," due to its shape) is *critical for creating new memories and integrating them into a network of knowledge so that they can be stored indefinitely in other parts of the cerebral cortex.* Individuals with damage to the hippocampus can acquire new information and keep it in awareness for a few seconds, but as soon as they are distracted, they forget the information and the experience that produced it (Scoville & Milner, 1957; Squire, 2009). This kind of disruption is limited to everyday memory for facts and events that we can bring to consciousness; memory of learned habitual routines or emotional reactions remains intact (Squire, Knowlton, & Musen, 1993). For example, people with damage to the hippocampus can remember how to drive and talk, but they cannot recall where they have recently driven or a conversation they have just had. You will read more about the hippocampus and its role in creating, storing, and combining memories in the Memory chapter.

The **amygdala** (from Latin for "almond," also due to its shape), *located at the tip of each horn of the hippocampus, plays a central role in many emotional processes, particularly the formation of emotional memories* (Aggleton, 1992). The amygdala attaches significance to previously neutral events that are associated with fear, punishment, or reward (LeDoux, 1992). For example, think of the last time something scary or unpleasant happened to you: A car came barreling toward you as you started walking into an intersection, or a ferocious dog leaped out of an alley as you passed by. Those stimuli—a car or a dog—are fairly neutral; you don't have a panic attack every time you walk by a used car lot. The emotional significance attached to events involving those stimuli is the work of the amygdala (McGaugh, 2006, 2015). When we are in emotionally arousing situations, the amygdala stimulates the hippocampus to remember many details surrounding the situation (Kensinger & Schacter, 2005). For example, people who lived through the terrorist attacks of September 11, 2001 remember vivid details about where they were, what they were doing, and how they felt when they heard the news, even years later (Hirst et al., 2009, 2015). In particular, the amygdala seems to be especially involved in encoding events as *fearful* (Adolphs et al., 1995; Sigurdsson et al., 2007). We'll have more to say about the amygdala in the Emotion and Motivation chapter. For now, keep in mind that a group of neurons the size of a lima bean buried deep in your brain help you to laugh, weep, or shriek in fright when the circumstances call for it.

The Basal Ganglia. There are several other structures in the subcortical area, but we'll consider just one more. The **basal ganglia** are *a set of subcortical structures that directs intentional movements.* The basal ganglia are located near the thalamus and hypothalamus; they receive input from the cerebral cortex and send outputs to the motor centers in the brain stem (Nelson & Kreitzer, 2015). One part of the basal ganglia, the *striatum,* is involved in the control of posture and movement. As we saw in the excerpt from Michael J. Fox's book, people who suffer from Parkinson's disease typically show symptoms of uncontrollable shaking and sudden jerks of the limbs and are unable to initiate a sequence of movements to achieve a specific goal. This happens because the dopamine-producing neurons in the substantia nigra (found

A haunted house is designed to stimulate your amygdala, but only a little.

iSTOCK/GETTY IMAGES

limbic system A group of forebrain structures including the hypothalamus, the hippocampus, and the amygdala, which are involved in motivation, emotion, learning, and memory.

hippocampus A structure critical for creating new memories and integrating them into a network of knowledge so that they can be stored indefinitely in other parts of the cerebral cortex.

amygdala A part of the limbic system that plays a central role in many emotional processes, particularly the formation of emotional memories.

basal ganglia A set of subcortical structures that directs intentional movements.

endocrine system A network of glands that produce and secrete into the bloodstream chemical messages known as hormones, which influence a wide variety of basic functions, including metabolism, growth, and sexual development.

pituitary gland The "master gland" of the body's hormone-producing system, which releases hormones that direct the functions of many other glands in the body.

in the tegmentum of the midbrain) have become damaged (Dauer & Przedborski, 2003). The undersupply of dopamine then affects the striatum in the basal ganglia, which in turn leads to the visible behavioral symptoms of Parkinson's.

So what's the problem in Parkinson's: the jerky movements, the ineffectiveness of the striatum in directing behavior, the botched interplay of the substantia nigra and the striatum, or the underproduction of dopamine at the neuronal level? The answer is all of the above (Weiner, Shulman, & Lang, 2013). This unfortunate disease provides a nice illustration of two themes regarding the brain and behavior. First, invisible actions at the level of neurons in the brain can produce substantial effects at the level of behavior. Second, the interaction of hindbrain, midbrain, and forebrain structures shows how the various regions are interdependent.

The Endocrine System

The **endocrine system** is *a network of glands that produce and secrete into the bloodstream chemical messages known as hormones, which influence a wide variety of basic functions, including metabolism, growth, and sexual development.* The endocrine system is distinct from the nervous system but works closely with it, especially the limbic system, to regulate thoughts, emotions, and behaviors. Some of the main glands in the endocrine system include the thyroid, which regulates bodily functions such as body temperature and heart rate; the adrenals, which regulate stress responses; the pancreas, which controls digestion; and the pineal, which secretes melatonin, influencing the sleep/wake cycle. The overall functioning of the endocrine system is orchestrated by the **pituitary gland,** *the "master gland" of the body's hormone-producing system, which releases hormones that direct the functions of many other glands in the body* (see **FIGURE 3.13**).

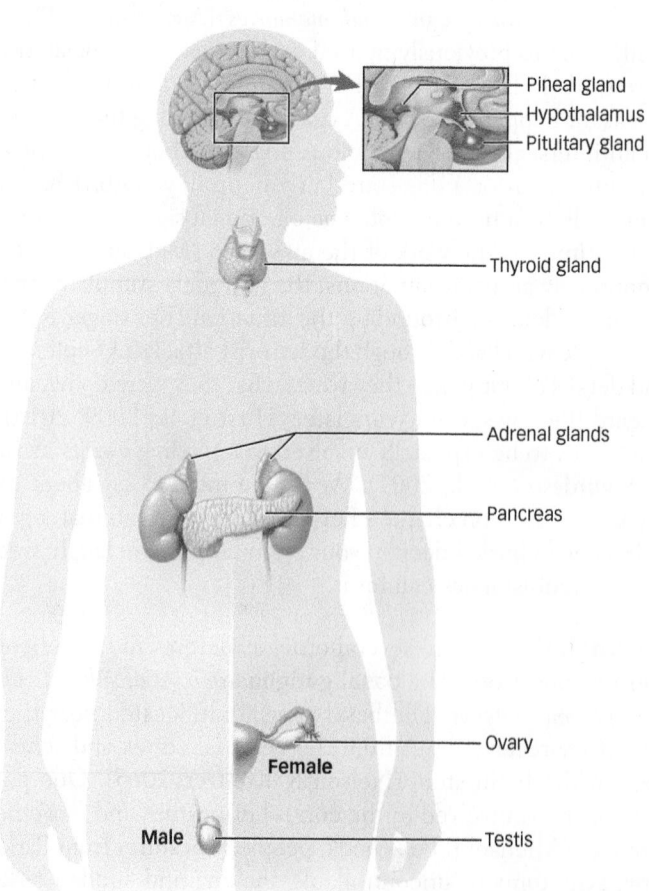

► Figure 3.13

MAJOR GLANDS OF THE ENDOCRINE SYSTEM
The endocrine system is a network of glands that works with the nervous system and impacts many basic functions by releasing hormones into the bloodstream.

The hypothalamus sends hormonal signals to the pituitary gland, which in turn sends hormonal signals to other glands to control stress, digestive activities, and reproductive processes. For example, when a baby suckles its mother's breast, sensory neurons in her breast send signals to her hypothalamus, which then signals her pituitary gland to release a hormone called *oxytocin* into the bloodstream (McNeilly et al., 1983). Oxytocin, in turn, stimulates the release of milk from reservoirs in the breast. The pituitary gland is also involved in the response to stress. When we sense a threat, sensory neurons send signals to the hypothalamus, which stimulates the release of adrenocorticotropic hormone (ACTH) from the pituitary gland. ACTH, in turn, stimulates the adrenal glands to release hormones that activate the sympathetic nervous system (Selye & Fortier, 1950). As you read earlier in this chapter, the sympathetic nervous system prepares the body either to meet the threat head on or to flee from the situation.

The endocrine system also plays a key role in sexual behavior and reproduction. The sexual reproductive glands are the ovaries in females, which make the hormone *estrogen*, and the testes in males, which make the hormone *testosterone* (see Figure 3.13). However, testosterone is not exclusive to males, and estrogen is not exclusive to females: the ovaries generate small amounts of testosterone, and the testes generate small amounts of estrogen (Davis & Wahlin-Jacobsen, 2015; Wibowo & Wassersug, 2014). Although it is widely believed that fluctuations in sexual desire are closely linked to fluctuations in sex hormones, recent research has failed to reveal a strong link between testosterone levels and sexual desire in men or women (Roney & Simmons, 2013; van Anders, 2012), whereas there is evidence for a link between estrogen levels and sexual desire in women (Gangestad & Haselton, 2015; Roney & Simmons, 2013).

The Cerebral Cortex

Our tour of the brain has taken us from the very small (neurons) to the somewhat bigger (major divisions of the brain) to the very large: the cerebral cortex. The cortex is the highest level of the brain, and it is responsible for the most complex aspects of perception, emotion, movement, and thought (Fuster, 2003). It sits over the rest of the brain, like a mushroom cap shielding the underside and stem, and it is the wrinkled surface you see when looking at the brain with the naked eye.

The smooth surfaces of the cortex—the raised part—are called *gyri* (*gyrus* if you're talking about just one), and the indentations or fissures are called *sulci* (*sulcus* when singular). The sulci and gyri are a triumph of evolution. The cerebral cortex occupies roughly the area of a newspaper page. Fitting that much cortex into a human skull is a tough task. But if you crumple a sheet of newspaper, you'll see that the same surface area now fits compactly into a much smaller space. The cortex, with its wrinkles and folds, holds a lot of brainpower in a relatively small package that fits comfortably inside the human skull (see **FIGURE 3.14**). The functions of the cerebral cortex can be understood at three levels: the separation of the cortex into two hemispheres, the functions of each hemisphere, and the role of specific cortical areas.

Organization Across Hemispheres. The first level of organization divides the cortex into the left and right hemispheres. The two hemispheres are more or less symmetrical in their appearance and, to some extent, in their functions. However, each hemisphere controls the functions of the opposite side of the body. This is called *contralateral control*, meaning that your right cerebral hemisphere perceives stimuli from and controls movements on the left side of your body, whereas your left cerebral hemisphere perceives stimuli from and controls movement on the right side of your body.

The cerebral hemispheres are connected to each other by *commissures*, bundles of axons that make possible communication between parallel areas of the cortex in

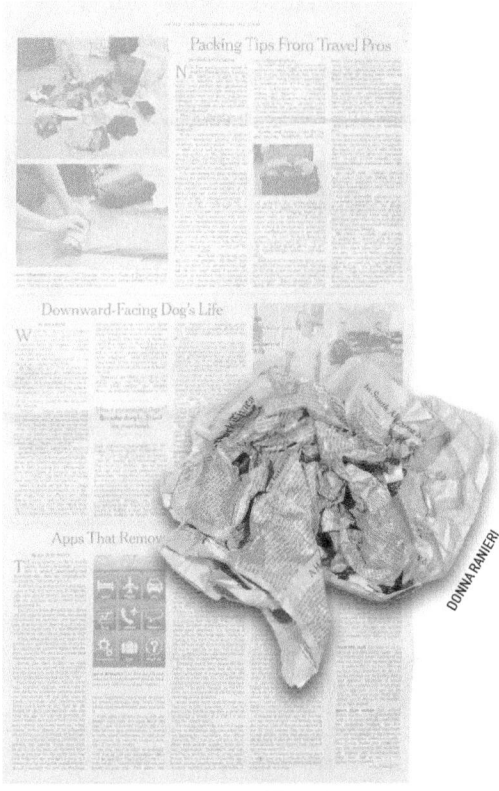

Crumpling a newspaper allows the same amount of surface area to fit into a much smaller space, just as the wrinkles and folds in the cortex allow a great deal of brain power to fit inside the human skull.

▼ Figure 3.14

CEREBRAL CORTEX AND LOBES The four major lobes of the cerebral cortex are the occipital lobe, the parietal lobe, the temporal lobe, and the frontal lobe. The smooth surfaces of the cortex are called gyri, and the indentations are called sulci.

▲ Figure 3.15

CEREBRAL HEMISPHERES The corpus callosum connects the two hemispheres of the brain and supports communication between them.

corpus callosum A thick band of nerve fibers that connects large areas of the cerebral cortex on each side of the brain and supports communication of information across the hemispheres.

occipital lobe A region of the cerebral cortex that processes visual information.

parietal lobe A region of the cerebral cortex whose functions include processing information about touch.

each half. The largest of these commissures is the **corpus callosum,** which *connects large areas of the cerebral cortex on each side of the brain and supports communication of information across the hemispheres* (see **FIGURE 3.15**). This means that information received in the right hemisphere, for example, can pass across the corpus callosum and be registered, virtually instantaneously, in the left hemisphere.

Organization Within Hemispheres. The second level of organization in the cerebral cortex distinguishes the functions of the different regions within each hemisphere of the brain. Each hemisphere of the cerebral cortex is divided into four areas, or *lobes*: From back to front, these are the occipital lobe, the parietal lobe, the temporal lobe, and the frontal lobe, as shown in Figure 3.14. We'll examine the functions of these lobes in more detail in later chapters, noting how scientists have used a variety of techniques to understand the operations of the brain. For now, here's a brief overview of the main functions of each lobe.

The **occipital lobe,** located at the back of the cerebral cortex, *processes visual information*. Sensory receptors in the eyes send information to the thalamus, which in turn sends information to the primary areas of the occipital lobe, where simple features of the stimulus are extracted, such as the location and orientation of an object's edges (see the Sensation and Perception chapter for more details). These features are then processed into a more complex "map" of the stimulus onto the occipital cortex, leading to comprehension of what's being seen. As you might imagine, damage to the primary visual areas of the occipital lobe can leave a person with partial or complete blindness. Information still enters the eyes, which work just fine. But without the ability to process and make sense of the information at the level of the cerebral cortex, the information is as good as lost (Zeki, 2001).

The **parietal lobe,** located in front of the occipital lobe, carries out functions that include *processing information about touch*. The parietal lobe contains the *somatosensory cortex*, a strip of brain tissue running from the top of the brain down to the sides (see **FIGURE 3.16**). Within each hemisphere, the somatosensory cortex represents the skin areas on the contralateral surface of the body. Each part of the somatosensory cortex maps onto a particular part of the body. If a body area is more sensitive, a larger part of the somatosensory cortex is devoted to it. For example, the part of the somatosensory

▶ Figure 3.16

SOMATOSENSORY AND MOTOR CORTICES The motor cortex, a strip of brain tissue in the frontal lobe, represents and controls different skin and body areas on the contralateral side of the body. Directly behind the motor cortex, in the parietal lobe, lies the somatosensory cortex. Like the motor cortex, the somatosensory cortex represents skin areas of particular parts on the contralateral side of the body.

cortex that corresponds to the lips and tongue is larger than the area corresponding to the feet. The somatosensory cortex can be illustrated as a distorted figure, called a *homunculus* ("little man"), in which the body parts are rendered according to how much of the somatosensory cortex is devoted to them (Penfield & Rasmussen, 1950). Directly in front of the somatosensory cortex, in the frontal lobe, is a parallel strip of brain tissue called the *motor cortex*. As in the somatosensory cortex, different parts of the motor cortex correspond to different body parts. The motor cortex initiates voluntary movements and sends messages to the basal ganglia, cerebellum, and spinal cord. The motor and somatosensory cortices, then, are like sending and receiving areas of the cerebral cortex, taking in information and sending out commands, as the case might be.

The **temporal lobe,** located on the lower side of each hemisphere, is *responsible for hearing and language*. The *primary auditory cortex* in the temporal lobe is analogous to the somatosensory cortex in the parietal lobe and the primary visual areas of the occipital lobe: It receives sensory information from the ears based on the frequencies of sounds (Recanzone & Sutter, 2008). Secondary areas of the temporal lobe then process the information into meaningful units, such as speech and words. The temporal lobe also houses the visual association areas that interpret the meaning of visual stimuli and help us recognize common objects in the environment (Martin, 2007).

The **frontal lobe,** which sits behind the forehead, has *specialized areas for movement, abstract thinking, planning, memory, and judgment*. As you just read, it contains the motor cortex, which coordinates movements of muscle groups throughout the body. Other areas in the frontal lobe coordinate thought processes that help us manipulate information and retrieve memories, which we can use to plan our behaviors and interact socially with others. In short, the frontal cortex allows us to do the kind of thinking, imagining, planning, and anticipating that sets humans apart from most other species (Schoenemann, Sheenan, & Glotzer, 2005; Stuss & Benson, 1986; Suddendorf & Corballis, 2007).

Organization Within Specific Lobes. The third level of organization in the cerebral cortex involves the representation of information within specific lobes in the cortex. A hierarchy of processing stages from primary areas handles fine details of information all the way up to **association areas,** which are *composed of neurons that help provide sense and meaning to information registered in the cortex*. For example, neurons in the primary visual cortex are highly specialized: Some detect features of the environment that are in a horizontal orientation, others detect movement, and still others process information about human versus nonhuman forms. Secondary areas interpret the information extracted by these primary areas (shape, motion, etc.) to make sense of what's being perceived; in this case, perhaps a large cat leaping toward your face. Similarly, neurons in the primary auditory cortex register sound frequencies, but it's the association areas of the temporal lobe that allow you to turn those noises into the meaning of your friend screaming, "Look out for the cat!" Association areas, then, help stitch together the threads of information in the various parts of the cortex to produce a meaningful understanding of what's being registered in the brain.

A striking example of this property of association areas comes from the discovery of the mirror-neuron system. **Mirror neurons** are *active when an animal performs a behavior, such as reaching for or manipulating an object, and are also activated when another animal observes that animal performing the same behavior*. Mirror neurons are found in the frontal lobe (near the motor cortex) and in the parietal lobe (Rizzolatti & Craighero, 2004; Rizzolatti & Sinigaglia, 2010). They have been identified in birds, monkeys, and humans, and their name reflects the function they serve. Neuroimaging studies with humans have shown that mirror neurons are active when people watch someone perform a behavior, such as grasping in midair. But they are more highly activated when that behavior has some purpose or context, such as grasping a cup to take a drink (Iacoboni et al., 2005), and seem to be related to recognizing the goal someone has in carrying out an action and the outcome of the action, rather than to

temporal lobe A region of the cerebral cortex responsible for hearing and language.

frontal lobe The region of the cerebral cortex that has specialized areas for movement, abstract thinking, planning, memory, and judgment.

association areas Areas of the cerebral cortex that are composed of neurons that help provide sense and meaning to information registered in the cortex.

mirror neurons Neurons that are active when an animal performs a behavior, such as reaching for or manipulating an object, and are also activated when another animal observes that animal performing the same behavior.

When one animal observes another engaging in a particular behavior, some of the same neurons become active in the observer as well as in the animal exhibiting the behavior. These mirror neurons seem to play an important role in social behavior.

the particular movements a person makes while performing that action (Hamilton & Grafton, 2006, 2008; Iacoboni, 2009; Rizzolatti & Sinigaglia, 2010). In the Learning chapter we'll find out more about the role of mirror neurons in learning.

Finally, neurons in the association areas are usually less specialized and more flexible than neurons in the primary areas. Thus, they can be shaped by learning and experience to do their job more effectively. This kind of shaping of neurons by environmental forces allows the brain flexibility, or plasticity, our next topic.

BRAIN PLASTICITY

The cerebral cortex may seem to be a fixed structure, one big sheet of neurons designed to help us make sense of our external world. It is remarkable, though, sensory cortices are not fixed. They can adapt to changes in sensory inputs, a quality researchers call *plasticity* (i.e., the ability to be molded). As an example, if you lose your middle finger in an accident, the part of the somatosensory area that represents that finger is initially unresponsive (Kaas, 1991). After all, there's no longer any sensory input going from that location to that part of the brain. You might expect the left middle-finger neurons of the somatosensory cortex to wither away. However, over time, that area in the somatosensory cortex becomes responsive to stimulation of the fingers *adjacent* to the missing finger. The brain is plastic: Functions that were assigned to certain areas of the brain may be capable of being reassigned to other areas of the brain to accommodate changing input from the environment (Feldman, 2009). This suggests that sensory inputs "compete" for representation in each cortical area. See the Real World: Brain Plasticity and Sensations in Phantom Limbs for a striking example of phantom limbs.)

Plasticity doesn't occur only to compensate for missing digits or limbs, however. An extraordinary amount of stimulation of one finger can result in that finger's "taking over" the representation of the part of the cortex that usually represents other, adjacent fingers (Merzenich et al., 1990). For example, concert pianists have highly developed cortical areas for finger control: The continued input from the fingers commands a larger area of representation in the somatosensory cortices in the brain. Consistent with this observation, recent research indicates greater plasticity within the motor cortex of professional musicians compared with nonmusicians, perhaps reflecting an increase in the number of motor synapses as a result of extended practice (Rosenkranz, Williamon, & Rothwell, 2007). Similar findings have been obtained with quilters (who have highly developed areas for the thumb and forefinger, which are critical to their profession) and taxi drivers (who have overdeveloped brain areas in the hippocampus that are used during spatial navigation; Maguire, Woollett, & Spiers, 2006).

Plasticity is also related to a question you might not expect to find in a psychology textbook: How much exercise have you been getting lately? Although we expect that you are spending countless happy hours reading this text, we also hope that you've been finding enough time for physical exercise. A large number of studies in rats and other nonhuman animals indicate that physical exercise can increase the number of synapses and even promote the development of new neurons in the hippocampus (Hillman, Erickson, & Kramer, 2008; van Praag, 2009). Recent studies with people have begun to document beneficial effects of cardiovascular exercise on aspects of brain function and cognitive performance (Colcombe et al., 2004, 2006; Prakash et al., 2015). Although these effects tend to be seen most clearly in older adults (okay, so it's time for your textbook authors to get on a treadmill), benefits have also been documented throughout the life span (Hertig & Nagel, 2012; Hillman et al., 2008). Recent evidence indicates that even a single session of moderate-to-intensive exercise can boost aspects of memory and motor skills (Roig et al., 2012; Statton et al., 2015). In fact, some researchers believe that this kind of activity-dependent brain plasticity

Keith Jarrett is a virtuoso who has been playing piano for more than 60 years. Compared with those of a novice, the brain regions that control Jarrett's fingers are relatively *less* active when he plays.

Brain Plasticity and Sensations in Phantom Limbs

Long after a limb is amputated, many patients continue to experience sensations where the missing limb would be, a phenomenon called *phantom limb syndrome*. Patients can feel their missing limbs moving, even in coordinated gestures such as shaking hands. Some even report feeling pain in their phantom limbs (Ramachandran & Brang, 2015). Why does this happen? Some evidence suggests that phantom limb syndrome may arise in part because of plasticity in the brain.

Researchers stimulated the skin surface in various regions around the face, torso, and arms while monitoring brain activity in amputees and nonamputatee volunteers (Ramachandran & Blakeslee, 1998; Ramachandran, Brang, & McGeoch, 2010; Ramachandran, Rodgers-Ramachandran, & Stewart, 1992). Brain imaging techniques displayed the somatosensory cortical areas activated when the skin was stimulated. This allowed the researchers to map how touch is represented in the somatosensory cortex for different areas of the body. For example, when the face was touched, the researchers could determine which areas in the somatosensory cortex were most active; when the torso was stimulated, they could see which areas responded, and so on.

Brain scans of the amputees revealed that stimulating areas of the face and upper arm activated an area in the somatosensory cortex that previously would have been activated by a now-missing hand. The face and arm were represented in the somatosensory cortex in an area adjacent to where the person's hand—now amputated—would have been represented. Stimulating the face or arm produced phantom limb sensations in the amputees; they reported "feeling" a sensation in their missing limbs.

Brain plasticity can explain these results (Pascual-Leone et al., 2005). The cortical representations for the face and the upper arm normally lie on either side of the representation for the hand. The somatosensory areas for the face and upper arm were larger in amputees and had taken over the part of the cortex normally representing the hand. Indeed, the new face and arm representations were now contiguous with each other, filling in the space occupied by the

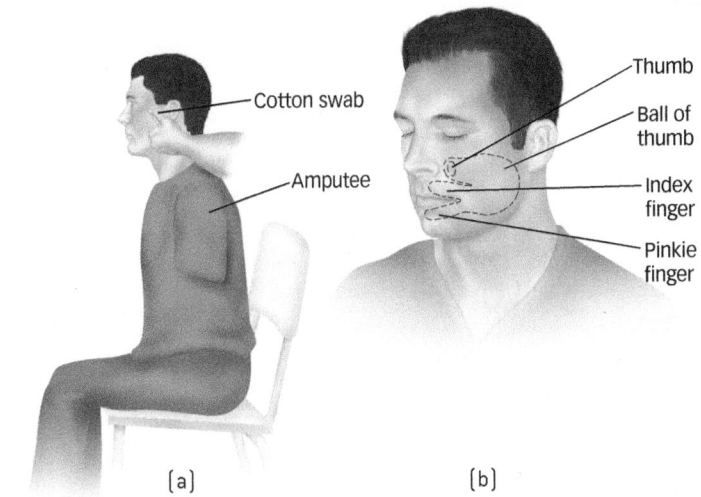

▲ MAPPING SENSATIONS IN PHANTOM LIMBS (a) Researchers lightly touch an amputee's face with a cotton swab, eliciting sensations in the "missing" hand. (b) Touching different parts of the cheek can even result in sensations in particular fingers or the thumb of the missing hand.

hand representation. Some of these new mappings were quite concise. For example, in some amputees, when specific areas of the facial skin were activated, the patient reported sensations in just *one finger* of the phantom hand!

This and related research suggest one explanation for a previously poorly understood phenomenon. How can a person "feel" something that isn't there? Brain plasticity, an adaptive process through which the brain reorganizes itself, offers an answer (Flor, Nikolajsen, & Jensen, 2006). The brain established new mappings that led to novel sensations.

This idea also has practical implications for dealing with the pain that can result from phantom limbs (Ramachandran & Altschuler, 2009). Researchers have used a "mirror box" to teach patients a new mapping to increase voluntary control over their phantom limbs. For example, a patient would place his intact right hand and phantom left hand in the mirror box such that when looking at the mirror, he sees his right hand reflected on the left—where he has placed his phantom hand—creating the illusion that the phantom has been restored. The phantom hand thus appears to respond to motor commands given by

the patient, and with practice the patient can become better at "moving" the phantom in response to voluntary commands. As a result, when feeling the excruciating pain associated with a clenched phantom hand, the patient can now voluntarily unclench the hand and reduce the pain. This therapeutic approach based on brain plasticity has been applied successfully to a variety of patient populations (Ramachandran & Altschuler, 2009). In one of the most striking applications of this approach, researchers used mirror box therapy with survivors of the destructive 2010 earthquake in Haiti who were experiencing phantom limb pain after amputation of lower limbs (Miller, Seckel, & Ramachandran, 2012). Seventeen of the 18 amputees in that study reported a significant reduction in experienced pain following mirror box therapy.

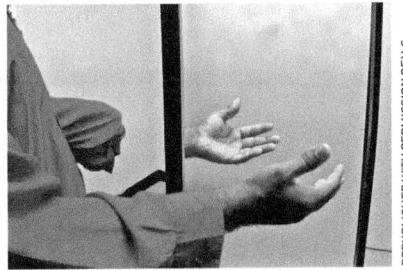

REPUBLISHED WITH PERMISSION OF V. S. RAMACHANDRAN ET AL., 2009. THE USE OF VISUAL FEEDBACK, IN PARTICULAR MIRROR VISUAL FEEDBACK, IN RESTORING BRAIN FUNCTION. *BRAIN* 2009: *132 (7)*; 1693-1719, P. 1693. PERMISSION CONVEYED THROUGH COPYRIGHT CLEARANCE CENTER, INC.

▲ A mirror box creates the illusion that the phantom limb has been restored.

is relevant to treating spinal cord injuries (which, as we have seen, have a devastating impact on people's lives), because understanding how to maximize plasticity through exercise and training may help to guide rehabilitation efforts (Dunlop, 2008). It should be clear by now that the plasticity of the brain is not just an interesting theoretical idea; it has potentially important applications to everyday life (Bryck & Fisher, 2012).

Build to the Outcomes

1. Which part of the brain controls the basic functions of life, such as respiration?

2. Which part of the brain helps with orientation to the environment?

3. How is the thalamus like a computer?

4. Which area of the brain is associated with emotional memories?

5. Why is Parkinson's disease a good example of the interrelationship between the brain and behavior?

6. What is the main function of the pituitary gland?

7. Why is the part of the somatosensory cortex relating to the lips bigger than the area corresponding to the feet?

8. What types of thinking occur in the frontal lobe?

9. Give examples of research that proves that the brain is able to change because of a person's life experience.

The Development and Evolution of Nervous Systems

Learning Outcomes

▶ Explain the stages of development of the embryonic brain.

▶ Explain the progression of the human brain's evolution.

▶ Give examples of the influence of genetics and the environment to human behavior.

Far from being a single, elegant machine, the human brain is instead a system comprising many distinct components that have been added at different times during the course of evolution. The human species has retained what worked best in earlier versions of the brain, then added bits and pieces to get us to our present state through evolution.

To understand the central nervous system, it is helpful to consider two aspects of its development. Prenatal development (growth from conception to birth), reveals how the nervous system develops and changes within each member of a species. Evolutionary development reveals how the nervous system in humans evolved and adapted from other species.

PRENATAL DEVELOPMENT OF THE CENTRAL NERVOUS SYSTEM

The nervous system is the first major bodily system to take form in an embryo (Moore, 1977). It begins to develop within the third week after fertilization, when the embryo is still in the shape of a sphere. Initially, a ridge forms on one side of the sphere and then builds up at its edges to become a deep groove. The ridges fold together and fuse to enclose the groove, forming a structure called the *neural tube*. The tail end of the neural tube will remain a tube, and as the embryo grows larger, it forms the basis of the spinal cord. The tube expands at the opposite end, so that by the 4th week the three basic levels of the brain are visible. During the fifth week, the forebrain and hindbrain further differentiate into subdivisions. During the seventh week and later, the forebrain expands considerably to form the cerebral hemispheres.

As the embryonic brain continues to grow, each subdivision folds onto the next one and begins to form the structures easily visible in the adult brain (see **FIGURE 3.17**).

The hindbrain forms the cerebellum and medulla, the midbrain forms the tectum and the tegmentum, and the forebrain subdivides further, separating the thalamus and hypothalamus from the cerebral hemispheres. Over time, the cerebral hemispheres undergo the greatest development, ultimately covering almost all the other subdivisions of the brain.

The *ontogeny* of the brain (how it develops within a given individual) is pretty remarkable. In about half the time it takes you to complete a 15-week semester, the basic structures of the brain are in place and rapidly developing, eventually allowing a newborn to enter the world with a fairly sophisticated set of abilities. In comparison, the *phylogeny* of the brain (how it developed within a particular species) was a much slower process. However, it, too, has allowed humans to make the most of the available brain structures, enabling us to perform an incredible array of tasks.

EVOLUTIONARY DEVELOPMENT OF THE CENTRAL NERVOUS SYSTEM

The central nervous system evolved from the very basic ones found in simple animals to the elaborate nervous system in humans today. Even the simplest animals have sensory neurons and motor neurons for responding to the environment (Shepherd, 1988). For example, single-celled protozoa have molecules in their cell membrane that are sensitive to food in the water. Those molecules trigger the movement of tiny threads called *cilia*, which help propel the protozoa toward the food source. The first neurons appeared in invertebrates, such as jellyfish; the sensory neurons in the jellyfish's tentacles can feel the touch of a potentially dangerous predator, which prompts the jellyfish to swim to safety. If you're a jellyfish, this simple neural system is sufficient to keep you alive. The first central nervous system worthy of the name, though, appeared in flatworms. The flatworm has a collection of neurons in the head—a primitive kind of brain—that includes sensory neurons for vision and taste and motor neurons that control feeding behavior. Emerging from the brain is a pair of tracts that form a spinal cord.

A Division Forms: Vertebrates and Invertebrates

During the course of evolution, a major split in the organization of the nervous system occurred between invertebrate animals (those without a spinal column) and vertebrate animals (those with a spinal column). In all vertebrates, the central nervous system is organized into a hierarchy: The lower levels of the brain and spinal cord execute simpler functions, while the higher levels of the nervous system perform more complex functions. As you saw earlier, in humans, reflexes are accomplished in the spinal cord. At the next level, the midbrain executes the more complex task of orienting toward an important stimulus in the environment. Finally, a more complex task, such as imagining what your life will be like 20 years from now, is performed in the forebrain (Addis, Wong, & Schacter, 2007; Schacter et al., 2012; Szpunar, Watson, & McDermott, 2007).

The forebrain undergoes further evolutionary advances in vertebrates. In lower vertebrate species such as amphibians (frogs and newts), the forebrain consists only

26 days   40 days   50 days

3 months   5 months   7 months

8 months   9 months

▲ Figure 3.17

PRENATAL BRAIN DEVELOPMENT The more primitive parts of the brain, the hindbrain and midbrain, develop first, followed by successively higher levels. The cerebral cortex with its characteristic fissures doesn't develop until the middle of the pregnancy. The cerebral hemispheres undergo most of their development in the final trimester.

Flatworms don't have much of a brain, but then again, they don't need much of a brain. The rudimentary brain areas found in simple invertebrates eventually evolved into the complex brain structures found in humans.

▲ **Figure 3.18**

DEVELOPMENT OF THE FOREBRAIN Reptiles and birds have almost no cerebral cortex. Mammals such as rats and cats do have a cerebral cortex, but their frontal lobes are proportionately much smaller than the frontal lobes of humans and other primates. How might this explain the fact that only humans have developed complex language, computer technology, and calculus?

of small clusters of neurons at the end of the neural tube. In higher vertebrates, including reptiles, birds, and mammals, the forebrain is much larger, and it evolves in two different patterns. Reptiles and birds have almost no cerebral cortex. By contrast, mammals have a highly developed cerebral cortex consisting of multiple areas that serve a broad range of higher mental functions. This forebrain development has reached its peak—so far—in humans (**FIGURE 3.18**).

The human brain, then, is not so much one remarkable thing; rather, it is a succession of extensions from a quite serviceable foundation. The forebrain of a bullfrog is about as differentiated as it needs to be to survive in a frog's world. The human forebrain, however, shows substantial refinement, which allows for some remarkable, uniquely human abilities: self-awareness, sophisticated language use, abstract reasoning, and imagining, among others.

The Human Brain Evolved on the Fast Track

There is intriguing evidence that the human brain evolved more quickly than the brains of other species (Dorus et al., 2004). Researchers compared the sequences of 200 brain-related genes in mice, rats, monkeys, and humans and discovered a collection of genes that evolved more rapidly among primates. What's more, they found that primate brains not only evolved quickly compared to those of other species, but the brains of the primates who eventually became humans evolved even more rapidly. These results suggest that in addition to the normal adaptations that occur over the process of evolution, the genes for human brains took particular advantage of a variety of mutations (changes in a gene's DNA) along the evolutionary pathway (Vallender, Mekel-Bobrov, & Lahn, 2008). These results also suggest that the human brain is still evolving—becoming bigger and more adapted to the demands of the environment (Evans et al., 2005; Mekel-Bobrov et al., 2005).

Genes may direct the development of the brain on a large, evolutionary scale, but they also guide the development of an individual and, generally, the development of a species. Let's take a brief look at how genes and the environment contribute to the biological bases of behavior.

GENES, EPIGENETICS, AND THE ENVIRONMENT

Is it genetics (nature) or the environment (nurture) that reigns supreme in directing a person's behavior? The emerging picture from current research is that both nature *and* nurture play a role in directing behavior, and the focus has shifted to examining the interaction of the two rather than the absolute contributions of either alone (Gottesman & Hanson, 2005; Rutter & Silberg, 2002; Zhang & Meaney, 2010).

What Are Genes?

A **gene** is *the major unit of hereditary transmission.* Over time, the term *gene* has been used to refer to two distinct but related concepts. The initial, relatively abstract concept of a gene referred to units of inheritance that specify traits such as eye color. More recently, genes have been defined as sections on a strand of DNA (deoxyribonucleic acid) that code for the protein molecules that affect traits. Genes are organized into large threads called **chromosomes,** *strands of DNA wound around each other in a double-helix configuration* (see **FIGURE 3.19a**). The DNA in our chromosomes produces protein molecules through the action of a molecule known as messenger

gene The major unit of hereditary transmission.

chromosomes Strands of DNA wound around each other in a double-helix configuration.

Chromosome

Nucleus

Cell

Chromatin

DNA

(a)

Gene

Methyl group

Gene

DNA

Histone tail

DNA winding around histones

(b)

▲ Figure 3.19

GENES AND EPIGENETICS (a) Genes, Chromosomes, and Their Recombination. The cell nucleus houses chromosomes, which are made up of double-helix strands of DNA. Every cell in our bodies has 23 pairs of chromosomes. Genes are segments on the strand of DNA. **(b) Epigenetics.** Studies suggest that DNA methylation and histone modification play a key role in the long-lasting effects of early life experiences for both rodents and humans.

RNA (ribonucleic acid; mRNA), which communicates a copy of the DNA code to cells that produce proteins. Chromosomes come in pairs, and humans have 23 pairs each. These pairs of chromosomes are similar but not identical: You inherit one of each pair from your father and one from your mother. There's a twist, however: The selection of *which* of each pair is given to you is random.

Perhaps the most striking example of this random distribution is the determination of sex. In mammals, the chromosomes that determine sex are the X and Y chromosomes; females have two X chromosomes, whereas males have one X and one Y chromosome. You inherited an X chromosome from your mother because she has only X chromosomes to give. Your biological sex, therefore, was determined by whether you received an additional X chromosome or a Y chromosome from your father.

As a species, we share about 99% of the same DNA (and almost as much with other apes), but a portion of DNA varies across individuals. Children share more of this variable portion of DNA with their parents than with more distant relatives or with nonrelatives: They share half their genes with each parent, a quarter of their genes with their grandparents, an eighth of their genes with cousins, and so on. The probability of sharing genes is called *degree of relatedness.* The most genetically related people are *monozygotic twins* (also called *identical twins*), who develop from the splitting of a single fertilized egg and therefore share 100% of their genes. *Dizygotic twins* (*fraternal twins*) develop from two separate fertilized eggs and share 50% of their genes, the same as any two siblings born separately.

Many researchers have tried to determine the relative influence of genetics on behavior. One way to do this is to compare a trait shown by monozygotic twins with that same trait among dizygotic twins. This type of research usually enlists twins who were raised in the same household, so that the impact of their environment (their socioeconomic status, access to education, parental child-rearing practices, environmental stressors) remains relatively constant. Finding that monozygotic twins have a higher presence of a specific trait suggests a genetic influence (Boomsma, Busjahn, & Peltonen, 2002).

For example, the likelihood that the dizygotic twin of a person who has schizophrenia (a mental disorder we'll discuss in greater detail in the Psychological Disorders

Monozygotic twins (*left*) share 100% of their genes in common, whereas dizygotic twins (*right*) share 50% of their genes, the same as other siblings. Studies of monozygotic and dizygotic twins help researchers estimate the relative contributions of genes and environmental influences on behavior.

chapter) will *also* develop schizophrenia is 27%. However, this statistic rises to 50% for monozygotic twins. This observation suggests a substantial genetic influence on the likelihood of developing schizophrenia. Monozygotic twins share 100% of their genes, and if one assumes environmental influences are relatively consistent for both members of the twin pair, the 50% likelihood can be traced to genetic factors. That sounds scarily high—until you realize that the remaining 50% probability must be due to environmental influences. In short, genetics can contribute to the development, likelihood, or onset of a variety of traits. But a more complete picture of genetic influences on behavior must always take the environmental context into consideration. Genes express themselves within an environment, not in isolation.

A Role for Epigenetics

The idea that genes are expressed within an environment is central to an important and rapidly growing area of research known as **epigenetics:** *the study of environmental influences that determine whether or not genes are expressed, or the degree to which they are expressed, without altering the basic DNA sequences that constitute the genes themselves.* To understand how epigenetic influences work, it is useful to think about DNA as analogous to a script for a play or a movie. The biologist Nessa Carey (2012) offers the example of Shakespeare's *Romeo and Juliet*, which was made into a movie back in 1936 starring the classic actors Leslie Howard and Norma Shearer, and in 1996 starring Leonardo DiCaprio and Claire Danes. Shakespeare's tragedy formed the basis of both screenplays, but the directors of the two films used Shakespeare's material in different ways, and the actors in the two films gave different performances. Thus, the final products departed from Shakespeare's play and were different from one another, even though Shakespeare's original play still exists. Something similar happens with epigenetics: depending on the environment, a gene can be expressed or not without altering the underlying DNA code.

The environment can influence gene expression through **epigenetic marks,** *chemical modifications to DNA that can turn genes on or off.* You can think of epigenetic marks as analogous to notes that the movie directors made on Shakespeare's play that determined how the play was used in a particular film. There are two widely studied epigenetic marks:

▶ **DNA methylation** involves *adding a methyl group to DNA.* There are special enzymes, referred to as *epigenetic writers,* whose role is to add methyl groups to DNA. Although adding a methyl group doesn't alter the basic DNA sequence, it switches off the methylated gene (see Figure 3.19b). This process is roughly analogous to Claire Danes's director making notes that instruct her to ignore

epigenetics The study of environmental influences that determine whether or not genes are expressed, or the degree to which they are expressed, without altering the basic DNA sequences that constitute the genes themselves.

epigenetic marks Chemical modifications to DNA that can turn genes on or off.

DNA methylation Adding a methyl group to DNA.

a certain portion of the Shakespeare play. That portion of the play—like the switched-off gene—is still there, but its contents are not expressed.

▶ **Histone modification** involves *adding chemical modifications to proteins called histones that are involved in packaging DNA*. We tend to visualize DNA as the free-floating double helix shown in Figure 3.19a, but DNA is actually tightly wrapped around groups of histone proteins, as shown in Figure 3.19b. However, whereas DNA methylation switches genes off, histone modification can either switch genes off or turn them on. But just like DNA methylation, histone modifications influence gene expression without altering the underlying DNA sequence (Carey, 2012).

Okay, so now you have learned a lot of strange new terms and may have wondered whether Claire Danes's performance in *Romeo and Juliet* prepared her to play Carrie in *Homeland*. But what is the relevance of epigenetics to the brain and to psychology? It turns out to be more relevant than anyone suspected until the past decade or so. Experiments with rats and mice have shown that epigenetic marks left by DNA methylation and histone modification play a role in learning and memory (Bredy et al., 2007; Day & Sweatt, 2011; Levenson & Sweatt, 2005). Several studies have linked epigenetic changes with responses to stress (Zhang & Meaney, 2010), including recent research with humans. For example, studies of nurses working in high-stress versus low-stress environments found differences between the two groups in DNA methylation (Alasaari et al., 2012). Subjective levels of stress in a sample of 92 Canadian adults, as well as physiological signs of stress, were correlated with levels of DNA methylation (Lam et al., 2012). Another study reported a link between DNA methylation and early life experience, with differences observed between individuals who grew up in relatively affluent households and others who grew up in poverty, even when controlling for such factors as current socioeconomic status (Lam et al., 2012). Similar findings were reported in a separate study of 40 British adults (Borghol et al., 2012). These observations fit well with an important line of research described in Hot Science: Epigenetics and the Persisting Effects of Early Experiences, showing that DNA methylation and histone modifications play a key role in the long-lasting effects of early experiences for both rats and humans.

The Role of Environmental Factors

Genes set the range of possibilities that can be observed in a population, but the characteristics of any individual within that range are determined by environmental factors and experience. The genetic capabilities that another species might enjoy, such as breathing underwater, are outside the range of *your* possibilities, no matter how much you might desire them.

"The title of my science project is 'My Little Brother: Nature or Nurture.'"

With these parameters in mind, behavioral geneticists use calculations based on relatedness to compute the heritability of behaviors (Plomin et al., 2001). **Heritability** is *a measure of the variability of behavioral traits among individuals that can be accounted for by genetic factors*. Heritability is calculated as a proportion, and its numerical value (index) ranges from 0 to 1.00. A heritability of 0 means that genes do not contribute to individual differences in the behavioral trait; a heritability of 1.00 means that genes are the *only* reason for the individual differences. As you might guess, scores of 0 or 1.00 occur so infrequently that they are theoretical limits rather than realistic values; almost nothing in human behavior is completely due to the environment or owed *completely* to genetic inheritance. Scores between 0 and 1.00, then, indicate that individual differences are caused by varying degrees of genetic and environmental contributions—a little stronger influence of genetics here, a little stronger influence of the environment

histone modification Adding chemical modifications to proteins called histones that are involved in packaging DNA.

heritability A measure of the variability of behavioral traits among individuals that can be accounted for by genetic factors.

Epigenetics and the Persisting Effects of Early Experiences

An exciting series of studies show that epigenetic processes play a critical role in the long-lasting effects of early life experiences. Much of this work has come from the laboratory of Michael Meaney and his colleagues at McGill University, beginning with research on maternal behaviors in rats and recently extending to the persisting effects of childhood abuse.

Let's first consider early work from Meaney's lab that provides critical background (Francis et al., 1999; Liu et al., 1997). This work was based on the finding that there are notable differences in the mothering styles of rats: Some mothers spend a lot of time licking and grooming their young pups (high LG mothers), which rat pups greatly enjoy, whereas others spend little time doing so (low LG mothers). The researchers found that pups of high LG mothers are much less fearful as adults when placed in stressful situations than the adult pups of low LG mothers. Perhaps this simply reflects the effects of a genetic profile shared by the mother and her pups. Not so. Meaney and colleagues demonstrated that the same effects are obtained when the offspring of high LG mothers are raised by low LG mothers, and vice versa. These effects were accompanied by physiological changes. When placed in fear-inducing situations, adult rats raised by the high LG mothers showed lower levels of several stress-related hormones than adult rats that had been raised by low LG mothers. There was also increased evidence of hippocampal serotonin in the adult pups of high LG mothers; as you learned earlier in this chapter, increased levels of serotonin are associated with elevated mood. In other words, the high LG pups grow up to become "chilled out" adults. But exactly how did these effects persist from infancy to adulthood? This is where epigenetics come in. The increased serotonin response

produced by high LG mothers triggers a decrease in DNA methylation of the glucocorticoid receptor gene (see the Stress and Health chapter for a discussion of glucocorticoids and stress), which leads to greater expression of the gene and a corresponding ability to respond more calmly to stress (Weaver et al., 2004).

The rats raised by low LG mothers showed relatively increased DNA methylation of the glucocorticoid receptor gene, which leads to reduced expression of the gene and a corresponding inability to respond calmly to stress. Because DNA methylation can be very stable over time, these studies with rats provide the foundation for more recent studies with humans showing a role for epigenetics in the persisting effects of a highly disturbing experience: childhood abuse.

Meaney's group examined hippocampal samples taken from the brains of 24 men who had committed suicide around the age of 35 (McGowan et al., 2009). (The hippocampus plays a role in response to stress and has the highest concentration of glucocorticoid receptors in the entire brain.) Twelve of those men had a history of childhood abuse, and 12 did not. The researchers compared their hippocampal samples to a separate control group of 12 men who had died suddenly at around the same age but had no history of abuse and had not committed suicide. They found striking evidence for increased levels of DNA methylation at the hippocampal glucocorticoid receptor gene in the 12 men who had suffered childhood abuse and committed suicide compared with the 12 men in the control group. But they found no such differences between the 12 men who committed suicide but had not been abused and the 12 men in the control group. Increased DNA methylation reduced expression of the glucocorticoid receptor gene in the 12 victims of childhood abuse, just as in the adult pups

JUNIORS BILDARCHIV GMBH/ALAMY

▲ Rodent pups raised by mothers who spend a lot of time licking and grooming them are less fearful as adults in stressful situations.

of low LG mothers. Although this research doesn't tell us whether or how differences in DNA methylation were related to the behaviors of the abused and nonabused men when they were alive, it does point toward similar epigenetic effects of adverse early experiences in rats and humans.

Studies suggest that the effects of early experience are not restricted to a single gene, but occur more broadly. A more recent study of rats from Meaney's lab demonstrates hundreds of DNA methylation differences in the hippocampus of the offspring of high and low LG mothers (McGowan et al., 2011). New analyses of hippocampal samples from abused suicide victims also reveal widespread DNA methylation differences between the abused sample and a control group of nonabused individuals (Suderman et al., 2012).

The results of these studies suggest a broad role for epigenetic influences in understanding the effects of early experiences on subsequent development and behavior (Meaney & Ferguson-Smith, 2010), and have led both clinicians and researchers to recognize increasingly the importance of epigenetics for various psychological disorders in which early life stress is a risk factor, including depression, schizophrenia, and posttraumatic stress disorder (Kundakovic et al., 2015; Provencal & Binder, 2015).

there, but each always within the context of the other (Moffitt, 2005; Zhang & Meaney, 2010).

For human behavior, almost all estimates of heritability are in the moderate range, between .30 and .60. For example, a heritability index of .50 for intelligence indicates that half of the variability in intelligence test scores is attributable to genetic influences and the remaining half is due to environmental influences. Smart parents often (but not always) produce smart children; genetics certainly plays a role. But smart and not-so-smart children attend good or not-so-good schools, practice their piano lessons with more or less regularity, study or don't study as hard as they might, have good and not-so-good teachers and role models, and so on. Genetics is only half the story in intelligence. Environmental influences also play a significant role in predicting the basis of intelligence (see the Intelligence chapter).

Heritability has proven to be a theoretically useful and statistically sound concept in helping scientists understand the relative genetic and environmental influences on behavior. However, there are four important points about heritability to bear in mind.

- ▶ *Heritability is an abstract concept*: It tells us nothing about the *specific* genes that contribute to a trait.
- ▶ *Heritability is a population concept*: It tells us nothing about an individual. Heritability provides guidance for understanding differences across individuals in a population rather than abilities within an individual.
- ▶ *Heritability is dependent on the environment.* Just as behavior occurs within certain contexts, so do genetic influences. For example, intelligence isn't an unchanging quality: People are intelligent within a particular learning context, a social setting, a family environment, a socioeconomic class, and so on. Heritability, therefore, is meaningful only for the environmental conditions in which it was computed, and heritability estimates may change dramatically under other environmental conditions.
- ▶ *Heritability is not fate.* It tells us nothing about the degree to which interventions can change a behavioral trait. Heritability is useful for identifying behavioral traits that are influenced by genes, but it is not useful for determining how individuals will respond to particular environmental conditions or treatments.

Build to the Outcomes

1. What is the *ontogeny*, compared with the *phylogeny*, of the brain?

2. Which of the major parts of the brain develop first?

3. What is the structural difference between the brain of a reptile or bird, and the brain of a mammal?

4. Why do dizygotic twins share 50% of their genes, just as do siblings born separately?

5. Are abilities, such as intelligence and memory, inherited through our genes?

6. What do epigenetic studies suggest about how early life experiences may influence whether genes are expressed?

Investigating the Brain

So far, you've read a great deal about the nervous system: how it's organized, how it works, what its components are, and what those components do. But one question remains largely unanswered: *How* do we know all of this? Anatomists can dissect a human brain and identify its structures, but they cannot determine which structures play a role in producing which behaviors by dissecting a nonliving brain.

Scientists use a variety of methods to understand how the brain affects behavior. Let's consider three of the main ones: studying people with brain damage; studying the brain's electrical activity; and using brain imaging to study brain structure and watch the brain in action. Let's examine each of these ways of investigating the brain.

Learning Outcome

- ▶ Identify the three main ways that researchers study the human brain.

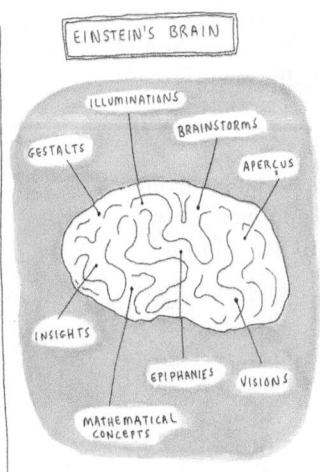

STUDYING THE DAMAGED BRAIN

To understand the normal operation of a process better, it is instructive to understand what happens when that process fails. Much research in neuroscience correlates the loss of specific perceptual, motor, emotional, or cognitive functions with specific areas of brain damage (Andrewes, 2001; Kolb & Whishaw, 2003). By studying these instances, neuroscientists can theorize about the functions those brain areas normally perform. The modern history of neuroscience can be dated to the work of Paul Broca (see the Psychology: Evolution of a Science chapter). In 1861, Broca described a patient who had lost the capacity to produce spoken language (but not the ability to understand language) due to damage in a small area in the left frontal lobe. In 1874, Carl Wernicke (1848–1905) described a patient with an impairment in language comprehension (but not the ability to produce speech) associated with damage to an area in the upper-left temporal lobe. These areas were named, respectively, *Broca's area* and *Wernicke's area* (see Figure 9.3 in the Language and Thought chapter), and they provided the earliest evidence that the brain locations for speech production and speech comprehension are separate and that for most people, the left hemisphere is critical to producing and understanding language (Young, 1990).

The Emotional Functions of the Frontal Lobes

As you've already seen, the human frontal lobes are a remarkable evolutionary achievement. However, psychology's first glimpse at some functions of the frontal lobes came from a rather unremarkable fellow. He was so unremarkable, in fact, that a single event in his life defined his place in the annals of psychology's history (Macmillan, 2000). Phineas Gage was a muscular 25-year-old railroad worker. On September 13, 1848, in Cavendish, Vermont, he was packing an explosive charge into a crevice in a rock when the powder exploded, driving a 3-foot, 13-pound iron rod through his head at high speed (Harlow, 1848). As **FIGURE 3.20** shows, the rod entered through his lower left jaw and exited through the middle top of his head. Incredibly, Gage lived to tell the tale. But his personality underwent a significant change.

Before the accident, Gage had been mild mannered, quiet, conscientious, and a hard worker. After the accident, however, he became irritable, irresponsible, indecisive, and given to profanity. The sad decline of Gage's personality and emotional life nonetheless provided an unexpected benefit to psychology. His case study was the first to allow researchers to investigate the hypothesis that the frontal lobe is involved in emotion regulation, planning, and decision making. Furthermore, because the connections between the frontal lobe and the subcortical structures of the limbic system were affected, scientists were able to understand better how the amygdala, hippocampus, and related brain structures interacted with the cerebral cortex (Damasio, 2005).

▼ **Figure 3.20**

PHINEAS GAGE (a) Phineas Gage's traumatic accident allowed researchers to investigate the functions of the frontal lobe and its connections with emotion centers in the subcortical structures. (b) The likely path of the metal rod through Gage's skull is reconstructed here.

(a)   (b)

The Distinct Roles of the Left and Right Hemispheres

You'll recall that the cerebral cortex is divided into two hemispheres, although typically the two hemispheres act as one integrated unit. Sometimes, though, disorders can threaten the ability of the brain to function, and the only way to stop them is with radical methods. This is sometimes the case for people who suffer from severe, intractable epilepsy. Seizures that begin in one hemisphere cross the corpus callosum (the thick band of nerve fibers that allows the two hemispheres to communicate) to the opposite hemisphere and start a feedback loop that results in a kind of firestorm in the brain. To alleviate the severity of the seizures, surgeons can sever the corpus callosum in an operation called a *split-brain procedure*. The result is that a seizure that starts in one hemisphere is isolated in that hemisphere, because there is no longer a connection to the other side. This procedure helps people with epilepsy but also produces some unusual, if not unpredictable, behaviors.

The Nobel laureate Roger Sperry (1913–1994), shown in the accompanying photo, was intrigued by the observation that the everyday behavior of people who had their corpus collosum severed did not seem to be affected by the operation. Did this mean that the corpus callosum played no role at all in behavior? Sperry thought that this conclusion was premature, reasoning that casual observations of everyday behaviors could easily fail to detect impairments that might be picked up by sensitive tests. To evaluate this idea experimentally, Sperry and his colleagues first showed that when the corpus collosum was severed in cats, learning was not transferred from one hemisphere to the other (Sperry, 1964). Later, Sperry designed several experiments that investigated the behaviors of people with split brains and in the process revealed a great deal about the independent functions of the left and right hemispheres (Sperry, 1964). Normally, any information that initially enters the left hemisphere is also registered in the right hemisphere and vice versa: The information comes in and travels across the corpus callosum, and both hemispheres understand what's going on (see **FIGURE 3.21**). But in a person with a split brain, information entering one hemisphere stays there. Without an intact corpus callosum, there's no way for that information to reach the other hemisphere. Sperry and his colleagues used this understanding of lateralized perception in a series of experiments. For example, they had a person with a split brain look at a spot in the center of a screen and then projected a stimulus either on the left side of the screen (the left visual field) or the right side of the screen (the right visual field), isolating the stimulus to the opposite hemisphere (see Figure 4.10 in the Sensation and Perception chapter for more details about how information from one visual field enters the opposite hemisphere).

The hemispheres themselves are specialized for different kinds of tasks. You've just learned about Broca's and Wernicke's areas, which revealed that language processing is largely a left-hemisphere activity. So imagine that some information came into the left hemisphere of a person with a split brain, and she was asked to describe verbally what it was. No problem: The left hemisphere has the information,

Roger Wolcott Sperry (1913–1994) received the Nobel Prize in Physiology in 1981 for his pioneering work investigating the independent functions of the cerebral hemispheres.

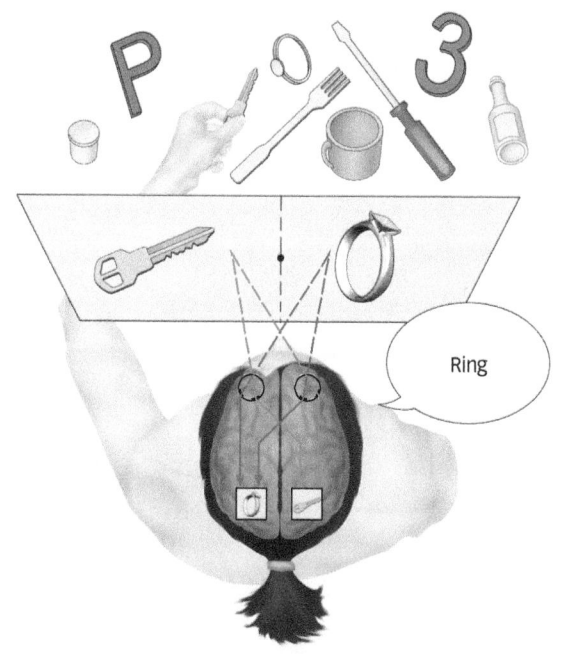

▶ Figure 3.21

SPLIT-BRAIN EXPERIMENT When a person with a split brain is presented with the picture of a ring on the right and that of a key on the left side of a screen, she can verbalize *ring* but not *key* because the left hemisphere "sees" the ring and language is usually located in the left hemisphere. She would be able to choose a key with her left hand from a set of objects behind a screen. She would not, however, be able to pick out a ring with her left hand because what the left hemisphere "sees" is not communicated to the left side of her body.

it's the "speaking" hemisphere, and so she should have no difficulty verbally describing what she saw. But suppose she was asked to reach behind the screen with her left hand and pick up the object she just saw. Remember that the hemispheres exert contralateral control over the body, meaning that the left hand is controlled by the right hemisphere. But this person's right hemisphere has no clue what the object was, because that information was received in the left hemisphere and was unable to travel to the right hemisphere! So even though she saw the object and could verbally describe it, she would be unable to use the right hemisphere to perform other tasks regarding that object, such as correctly selecting it from a group with her left hand (see Figure 3.21).

Of course, information presented to the right hemisphere would produce complementary deficits. In this case, she might be presented with a familiar object in her left hand (e.g., a key), be able to demonstrate that she knew what it was (by twisting and turning the key in midair), yet be unable to verbally describe what she was holding. In this case, the information in the right hemisphere is unable to travel to the left hemisphere, which controls the production of speech.

Furthermore, suppose a person with a split brain was shown the unusual face in **FIGURE 3.22.** This is called a *chimeric face,* and it is assembled from half-face components of the full faces also shown in the figure. When asked to indicate which face was presented, she would indicate that she saw *both* faces because

▶ Figure 3.22

CHIMERIC FACES AND THE SPLIT BRAIN
(a) When a person with a split brain views a chimeric face of Brad Pitt and Leonardo DiCaprio, her left hemisphere is aware only of Leonardo DiCaprio, and her right hemisphere sees only Brad Pitt. (b) When asked whom she sees, she answers, "Leonardo DiCaprio," because speech is controlled by the left hemisphere. (c) When asked to point to the face she saw with her left hand, she points to Brad Pitt, because her right hemisphere is aware only of the left half of the picture.

information about the face on the left is recorded in the right hemisphere and information about the face on the right is recorded in the left hemisphere (Levy, Trevarthen, & Sperry, 1972).

These split-brain studies reveal that the two hemispheres perform different functions and can work together seamlessly as long as the corpus callosum is intact. Without a way to transmit information from one hemisphere to the other, information remains in the hemisphere it initially entered, and we become acutely aware of the different functions of each hemisphere. Of course, a person with a split brain can adapt to this by simply moving her eyes a little so that the same information independently enters both hemispheres. Split-brain studies have continued over the past few decades and continue to play an important role in shaping our understanding of how the brain works (Gazzaniga, 2006).

STUDYING THE BRAIN'S ELECTRICAL ACTIVITY

A second approach to studying the link between brain structures and behavior involves recording the pattern of electrical activity of neurons. An **electroencephalograph (EEG)** is *a device used to record electrical activity in the brain*. Typically, electrodes are placed on the outside of the head, and even though the source of electrical activity in synapses and action potentials is far removed from these wires, the EEG can amplify the electric signals several thousand times. This provides a visual record of the underlying electrical activity, as shown in **FIGURE 3.23.** Using this technique, researchers can determine the amount of brain activity during different states of consciousness. For example, as you'll read in the Consciousness chapter, the brain shows distinctive patterns of electrical activity when awake versus asleep; in fact, different brain-wave patterns are even associated with different stages of sleep. EEG recordings allow researchers to make these fundamental discoveries about the nature of sleep and wakefulness (Dement, 1978). The EEG can also be used to examine the brain's electrical activity when awake individuals engage in a variety of psychological functions, such as perceiving, learning, and remembering.

A different approach to recording electrical activity resulted in a more refined understanding of the brain's division of responsibilities, even at a cellular level. The Nobel laureates David Hubel and Torsten Wiesel used a technique in which they inserted electrodes into the occipital lobes of anesthetized cats and observed the patterns of action potentials of individual neurons (Hubel, 1988). Hubel and Wiesel amplified the action potential signals through a loudspeaker so that they could hear the signals as clicks as well as seen on an oscilloscope. While flashing lights in front of the animal's eye, Hubel and Wiesel recorded the resulting activity of neurons in the occipital cortex. They discovered that neurons in the primary visual cortex are activated whenever a contrast between light and dark occurs in part of the visual field, seen particularly well when the visual stimulus was a thick line of light against a dark background. They then found that each neuron responded vigorously only when presented with a contrasting edge at a particular orientation. Since then, many studies have shown that neurons in the primary visual cortex respond to particular features of visual stimuli, such as contrast, shape, and color (Zeki, 1993).

These neurons in the visual cortex are known as *feature detectors* because they selectively respond to certain aspects of a visual image. For example, some neurons fire only when detecting a vertical line in the middle of the visual field, other neurons fire when a line at a 45° angle is perceived, and still others in response to wider lines, horizontal lines, lines in the periphery of the visual field, and so on (Livingstone & Hubel, 1988). The discovery of this specialized function for neurons was a huge leap forward in our understanding of how the visual cortex works. Feature detectors identify basic dimensions of a stimulus ("slanted line . . . other slanted line . . . horizontal

▲ Figure 3.23
EEG The electroencephalograph (EEG) records electrical activity in the brain. Many states of consciousness, such as wakefulness and stages of sleep, are characterized by particular types of brain waves.

electroencephalograph (EEG) A device used to record electrical activity in the brain.

David Hubel (*left*, b. 1926) and Torsten Wiesel (*right*, b. 1924) received the Nobel Prize in Physiology in 1981 for their work on mapping the visual cortex.

line"); those dimensions are then combined during a later stage of visual processing to allow recognition and perception of a stimulus ("Oh, it's a letter *A*").

Other studies have identified a variety of features that are detected by sensory neurons. For example, some visual processing neurons in the temporal lobe are activated only when detecting faces (Kanwisher, 2000; Perrett, Rolls, & Caan, 1982). Neurons in this area are specialized for processing faces; damage to this area results in an inability to perceive faces. These complementary observations (showing that the type of function that is lost or altered when a brain area is damaged corresponds to the kind of information processed by neurons in that cortical area) provide the most compelling evidence linking the brain to behavior.

USING BRAIN IMAGING TO STUDY STRUCTURE AND TO WATCH THE BRAIN IN ACTION

The third major way that neuroscientists can peer into the workings of the human brain has only become possible within the past several decades. EEG readouts give an overall picture of a person's level of consciousness, and single-cell recordings shed light on the actions of particular clumps of neurons. The ideal of neuroscience, however, has been the ability to see the brain in operation during behavior. This goal has been steadily achieved thanks to a wide range of *neuroimaging techniques* that use advanced technology to create images of the living, healthy brain (Posner & Raichle, 1994; Raichle & Mintun, 2006). *Structural brain imaging* provides information about the basic structure of the brain and allows clinicians or researchers to see abnormalities in brain structure. *Functional brain imaging*, in contrast, provides information about the activity of the brain while people perform various kinds of cognitive or motor tasks.

▲ Figure 3.24

STRUCTURAL IMAGING TECHNIQUES (CT AND MRI) CT (*left*) and MRI (*right*) scans are used to provide information about the structure of the brain and can help to spot tumors and other kinds of damage. Each scan shown here provides a snapshot of a single slice in the brain. Note that the MRI scan provides a clearer, higher-resolution image than the CT scan. (See the text for further discussion of how these images are constructed and what they depict.)

Structural Brain Imaging

One of the first neuroimaging techniques developed was the *computerized axial tomography (CT) scan*. In a CT scan, a scanner rotates a device around a person's head and takes a series of X-ray photographs from different angles. Computer programs then combine these images to provide views from any angle. CT scans show different densities of tissue in the brain. For example, the higher-density skull looks white on a CT scan, the cortex shows up as gray, and the least dense fissures and ventricles in the brain look dark (see **FIGURE 3.24**). CT scans are used to locate lesions or tumors, which typically appear darker because they are less dense than the cortex.

Magnetic resonance imaging (MRI) uses a strong magnetic field to line up the nuclei of specific molecules in the brain tissue. Brief but powerful pulses of radio waves cause the nuclei to rotate out of alignment. When a pulse ends, the nuclei snap back in line with the magnetic field and give off a small amount of energy in the process. Different molecules have unique energy signatures when they snap back in line with the magnetic field, so these signatures can be used to reveal brain structures with different molecular compositions. MRI produces pictures of soft tissue at a better resolution than a CT scan, as you can see in Figure 3.24. These techniques give psychologists a clearer picture of the structure of the brain and can help localize brain damage (as when someone suffers a stroke), but they reveal nothing about the functions of the brain.

Diffusion tensor imaging (DTI) is a relatively recently developed type of MRI that is used to visualize white matter pathways, which are fiber bundles that connect both nearby and distant brain regions to each other. DTI measures the rate and direction of diffusion or movement of water molecules along white matter pathways. Because the diffusion of water molecules follows the direction of the pathway, information about the direction in which water molecules diffuse can be used to determine where a white matter pathway goes. Scientists can use measures based on the rate and direction of diffusion to assess the integrity of a white matter pathway, which is very useful in cases of neurological and psychological disorders (Thomason & Thompson, 2011).

Because DTI provides information about pathways that connect brain areas to one another, it is a critical tool in mapping the connectivity of the human brain and plays a central role in an ambitious undertaking known as the Human Connectome Project. This is a collaborative effort funded by the National Institutes of Health beginning in 2009 that involves a partnership between researchers at Massachusetts General Hospital and UCLA, and another partnership between researchers at Washington University and the University of Minnesota. The main goal of the project is to provide a complete map of the connectivity of neural pathways in the brain: the human connectome (Toga et al., 2012). A unique and exciting feature of the Human Connectome Project is that the researchers have made available some of their results at their Web site (www.humanconnectomeproject.org), which include fascinating colorful images of some of the connection pathways they have discovered.

DTI allows researchers to visualize white matter pathways in the brain, the fiber bundles that play an important role by connecting brain regions to one another.

Functional Brain Imaging

Functional brain imaging techniques show researchers much more than just the structure of the brain by allowing us to watch the brain in action. These techniques rely on the fact that activated brain areas demand more energy for their neurons to work. This energy is supplied through increased blood flow to the activated areas. Functional imaging techniques can detect such changes in blood flow. In *positron emission tomography (PET)*, a harmless radioactive substance is injected into a person's bloodstream. Then the brain is scanned by radiation detectors as the person performs perceptual or cognitive tasks, such as reading or speaking. Areas of the brain that are activated during these tasks demand more energy and greater blood flow, resulting in a higher amount of the radioactivity in that region. The radiation detectors record the level of radioactivity in each region, producing a computerized image of the activated areas (see **FIGURE 3.25**). Note that PET scans differ from CT scans and MRIs in that the image produced shows activity in the brain while the person performs certain tasks. So, for example, a PET scan of a person speaking would show activation in Broca's area in the left frontal lobe.

For psychologists, the most widely used functional brain imaging technique nowadays is *functional magnetic resonance imaging (fMRI)*, which detects the difference between oxygenated hemoglobin and deoxygenated hemoglobin when exposed to magnetic pulses. Hemoglobin is the molecule in the blood that carries oxygen to our tissues, including the brain. When active neurons demand more energy and blood flow, oxygenated hemoglobin concentrates in the active areas; fMRI detects

▼ Figure 3.25

FUNCTIONAL IMAGING TECHNIQUES (PET AND fMRI) PET and fMRI scans provide information about the function of the brain by revealing which brain areas become more or less active in different conditions. The PET scan (*directly below*) shows areas in the left hemisphere (Broca's area, left; lower parietal–upper temporal area, right) that become active when people hold in mind a string of letters for a few seconds. The yellow areas in the fMRI scans (*all views to the left*) indicate activity in the auditory cortex of a person listening to music.

the oxygenated hemoglobin and provides a picture of the level of activation in each brain area (see Figure 3.25). Just as MRI was a major advance over CT scans, *functional* MRI is a similar leap in our ability to record the brain's activity during behavior. Both fMRI and PET allow researchers to localize changes in the brain very accurately. However, fMRI has a couple of advantages over PET. First, fMRI does not require any exposure to a radioactive substance. Second, fMRI can localize changes in brain activity across briefer periods than PET, which makes it more useful for analyzing psychological processes that occur extremely quickly, such as reading a word or recognizing a face. With PET, researchers often have to use experimental designs different from those they would use in the psychology laboratory in order to adapt to the limitations of PET technology. With fMRI, researchers can design experiments that more closely resemble the ones they carry out in the psychology laboratory.

Functional MRI can also be used to explore the relationship of brain regions with each other, using a recently developed technique referred to as *resting state functional connectivity*. As implied by the name, this technique does not require participants to perform a task; they simply rest quietly while fMRI measurements are made. Functional connectivity measures the extent to which spontaneous activity in different brain regions is correlated over time; brain regions whose activity is highly correlated are thought to be functionally connected with each other (Lee, Smyser, & Shimony, 2013). Functional connectivity measures have been used extensively in recent years to identify brain *networks*, that is, sets of brain regions that are closely connected to each other (Yeo et al., 2011). For example, functional connectivity helped to identify the *default network* (Gusnard & Raichle, 2001; Raichle, 2015), a group of interconnected regions in the frontal, temporal, and parietal lobes that is involved in internally focused cognitive activities, such as remembering past events, imagining future events, daydreaming, and mind wandering (Andrews-Hanna, 2012; Buckner, Andrews-Hanna, & Schacter, 2008; see the chapters on Memory and Consciousness). Functional connectivity, along with DTI (which measures structural connectivity), is used in studies conducted by the Human Connectome Project, and will contribute important information to the map of the human connectome. It also has potentially important applications because researchers believe that advances in understanding brain connectivity can enhance our ability to predict and characterize the clinical course of brain disorders, such as Alzheimer's disease (Fornito, Zalesky, & Breakspear, 2015).

Insights from Functional Imaging

PET and fMRI provide remarkable insights into the types of information processing that take place in specific areas of the brain. For example, when a person performs a simple perceptual task, such as looking at a circular checkerboard, the primary visual areas are activated. As you have read, when the checkerboard is presented to the left visual field, the right visual cortex shows activation, and when the checkerboard is presented to the right visual field, the left visual cortex shows activation (Fox et al., 1986). Similarly, when people look at faces, fMRI reveals strong activity in a region located near the border of the temporal and occipital lobes called the *fusiform gyrus* (Kanwisher, McDermott, & Chun, 1997). When this structure is damaged, people experience problems with recognizing faces—even faces of friends and family they've known for years—although they don't have problems with their eyes and can recognize visual objects other than faces (Mestry et al., 2012). Finally, when people perform a task that engages emotional processing (e.g., looking at sad pictures), researchers observe significant activation in the amygdala, which you learned earlier is linked with emotional arousal (McGaugh, 2015; Phelps, 2006). There is also increased activation in parts of the frontal lobe that are involved in emotional regulation—in fact, in the same areas that were most likely damaged in the case of Phineas Gage (Dolcos, 2014; Wang et al., 2005).

Modern Techniques Confirm Some Theories. You'll recall from the Methods chapter that at the heart of the scientific method is the relationship between ideas and evidence. There is no statute of limitations on scientific investigation. In this case, these modern brain imaging techniques confirm the theories derived from studies of brain damage from over 100 years ago. When Broca and Wernicke reached their conclusions about language production and language comprehension, they had little more to go on than some isolated cases and good hunches. PET scans have since confirmed that different areas of the brain are activated when a person is listening to spoken language, reading words on a screen, saying words out loud, or thinking of related words. This suggests that different parts of the brain are activated during these related but distinct functions. Similarly, it was pretty clear to the physician who examined Phineas Gage that the location of Gage's injuries played a major role in his drastic change in personality and emotionality. fMRI scans have since confirmed that the frontal lobe plays a central role in regulating emotion. It's always nice when independent methods (in these instances, very old case studies and very recent technology) arrive at the same conclusions. As you'll also see at various points in the text, brain imaging techniques such as fMRI are also revealing new and surprising findings.

Caution Is Needed Before Jumping to Conclusions. Although the insights that we are obtaining from fMRI are exciting, it is important that we don't get too carried away with them, as sometimes happens in media depictions of fMRI results (Marcus, 2012). Consider as an example the topic of memory accuracy and distortion. Using experimental paradigms that you'll learn about in the chapter on Memory, fMRI studies have shown that activity in some parts of the brain is greater during the retrieval of accurate rather than inaccurate memories (Schacter & Loftus, 2013). Does that mean we are ready to use fMRI in the courtroom to determine whether a witness is recounting an accurate memory or an inaccurate memory? Schacter and Loftus argued that the answer to this question is an emphatic no. For example, we don't yet know whether the results of laboratory fMRI studies of memory, which typically use simple materials like words or pictures, generalize to the kinds of complex everyday events that are relevant in the courtroom. Furthermore, evidence that fMRI can distinguish accurate from inaccurate memories comes from studies in which brain activity is averaged across a *group* of participants. But in the courtroom we need to determine whether an *individual* is remembering accurately or not, and there is little evidence yet that fMRI can do so. More generally, it is important to think carefully about how fMRI evidence is obtained before we leap to conclusions about how that evidence can be used in everyday life.

Transcranial magnetic stimulation (TMS) activates and deactivates regions of the brain with a magnetic pulse, temporarily mimicking brain damage.

Transcranial Magnetic Stimulation

We noted earlier that scientists have learned a lot about the brain by studying the behavior of people with brain injuries. But although brain damage may be related to particular patterns of behavior, that relationship may or may not be causal. Experimentation is the premier method for establishing causal relationships between variables, but scientists cannot ethically cause brain damage in human beings, thus they have not been able to establish causal relationships between particular kinds of brain damage and particular patterns of behavior. Functional neuroimaging techniques such as fMRI don't help on this point, because they do not provide information about when a particular pattern of brain activity causes a particular behavior.

Happily, scientists have discovered a way to mimic brain damage with a benign technique called *transcranial magnetic stimulation* (TMS; Barker, Jalinous, &

Neuromyths

PHOTO BY MATT MILLESS; COURTESY DANIEL J. SIMONS

Christopher Chabris is an associate professor of psychology at Union College. **Daniel Simons** is a professor of psychology at the University of Illinois. Chabris and Simons coauthored *The Invisible Gorilla: And Other Ways Our Intuitions Deceive Us* (2010).

You've no doubt often heard the phrase "we only use 10% of our brains," and perhaps you've wondered whether there is anything to it. Chabris and Simons (2012) discussed this and other statements about the brain that they believe to be merely myths, based in part, on a recent study by Dekker et al. (2012).

Pop quiz: Which of these statements is false?

1. We use only 10% of our brain.

2. Environments rich in stimuli improve the brains of preschool children.

3. Individuals learn better when they receive information in their preferred learning style, whether auditory, visual, or kinesthetic.

If you picked the first one, congratulations. The idea that we use only 10% of our brain is patently false. Yet it so permeates popular culture that, among psychologists and neuroscientists, it is known as the "10% myth." Contrary to popular belief, the entire brain is put to use—unused neurons die and unused circuits atrophy. Reports of neuroimaging research might perpetuate the myth by showing only a small number of areas "lighting up" in a brain scan, but those are just areas that have more than a base line level of activity; the dark regions aren't dormant or unused.

Did you agree with the other two statements? If so, you fell into our trap. All three statements are false—or at least not substantiated by scientific evidence. Unfortunately, if you got any of them wrong, you're hardly alone.

These "neuromyths," along with others, were presented to 242 primary and secondary school teachers in the Netherlands and the United Kingdom as part of a study by Sanne Dekker and colleagues at VU University Amsterdam and Bristol University, and just published in the journal *Frontiers in Psychology*. They found that 47% of the teachers believed the 10% myth. Even more, 76%, believed that enriching children's environments will strengthen their brains.

This belief might have emerged from evidence that rats raised in cages with amenities like exercise wheels, tunnels, and other rats showed better cognitive abilities and improvements in brain structure compared with rats that grew up isolated in bare cages. But such experiments show only that a truly impoverished and unnatural environment leads to poorer developmental outcomes than a more natural environment with opportunities to play and interact. It follows that growing up locked in a closet or otherwise cut off from human contact will impair a child's brain development. It does not follow that "enriching" a child's environment beyond what is already

typical (e.g., by constant exposure to "Baby Einstein"-type videos) will boost cognitive development.

The myth about learning styles was the most popular: 94% of the teachers believed that students perform better when lessons are delivered in their preferred learning style. Indeed, students do have preferences about how they learn; the problem is that these preferences have little to do with how effectively they learn. . . .

Our own surveys of the U.S. population have found even more widespread belief in myths about the brain. About two-thirds of the public agreed with the 10% myth. Many also believed that memory works like a video recording or that they can tell when someone is staring at the back of their head.

Ironically, in the Dekker group's study, the teachers who knew the most about neuroscience also believed in the most myths. Apparently, teachers who are (admirably) enthusiastic about expanding their knowledge of the mind and brain have trouble separating fact from fiction as they learn. Neuromyths have so much intuitive appeal, and they spread so rapidly in fields like business and self-help, that eradicating them from popular consciousness might be a Sisyphean task. But reducing their influence in the classroom would be a good start.

If for some perverse reason you wanted to annoy the instructor of your psychology course, you probably could do no better than to claim that "we use only 10% of our brains." Even though, as pointed out by Chabris and Simons (2012), a surprisingly high proportion of elementary and secondary schoolteachers in the Netherlands and the United Kingdom subscribe to this myth, we don't know any psychologists teaching courses like the one you are taking who would endorse it, and we hope that there aren't any. How did the myth get started? Nobody really knows. Some think it may have arisen from a quotation by the great psychologist William James ("We are making use of only a small part of our possible mental and physical resources") or that it possibly owes to Albert Einstein's attempt to make sense of his own massive intellect (Boyd, 2008).

The key point for our purposes is that when you hear such bold claims made, say, by a friend who heard it from somebody else, it's time for you to put into action the kinds of critical thinking skills that we are focusing on in this text, and start asking questions: What's the evidence for the claim? Is there a specific study or studies that your friend can name to provide evidence in support of the claim? Are any such studies published in peer-reviewed scientific journals? What kind of sample was used in the study? Is it large enough to support a clear conclusion? Has the finding been replicated? Tall tales such as the 10% myth don't stand much chance of surviving for long if claims for their existence are met head on with critical thinking.

Freeston, 1985; Hallett, 2000). If you've ever held a magnet under a piece of paper and used it to drag a pin across the paper's surface, you know that magnetic fields can pass through insulating material. The human skull is no exception. TMS delivers a magnetic pulse that passes through the skull and deactivates neurons in the cerebral cortex for a short period. Researchers can direct TMS pulses to particular brain regions (essentially turning them off) and then measure temporary changes in the way a person moves, sees, thinks, remembers, speaks, or feels. By manipulating the state of the brain, scientists can perform experiments that establish causal relationships.

For example, in an early study using TMS, scientists discovered that magnetic stimulation of the visual cortex temporarily impairs a person's ability to detect the motion of an object without impairing the person's ability to recognize that object (Beckers & Zeki, 1995). This intriguing discovery suggests that motion perception and object recognition are accomplished by different parts of the brain, but moreover, it establishes that activity in the visual cortex *causes* motion perception. More recent research has revealed that applying TMS to the specific part of the visual cortex responsible for motion perception also impairs the accuracy with which people localize and reach for moving objects (Maus et al., 2013; Schenk et al., 2005) or for stationary objects when there is motion in the background of a visual scene (Whitney et al., 2007). These findings indicate that the visual motion area plays a crucial role in guiding actions when we're responding to motion in the visual environment.

Rather than relying solely on observational studies of people with brain injuries or the snapshots provided by fMRI or PET scans, researchers can also manipulate brain activity and measure its effects. Scientists have also begun to combine TMS with fMRI, allowing them to localize precisely where in the brain TMS is having its effect (Parkin, Ekhtiari, & Walsh, 2015). Studies suggest that TMS has no harmful side effects (Anand & Hotson, 2002; Pascual-Leone et al., 1993), and this new tool has changed the study of how our brains create our thoughts, feelings, and actions. Hopefully the picture of human brain activity that emerges from these new methods can help to dispel popular myths about the brain that remain popular even today (see Other Voices: Neuromyths).

In the Methods chapter, you learned about the difference between correlation and causation, and that even if two events are correlated, it does not necessarily mean that one causes the other. Suppose a researcher designs an experiment in which participants view words on a screen and are asked to pronounce each word aloud, while the researcher uses fMRI to examine brain activity. First, what areas of the brain would you expect to show activity on fMRI while participants complete this task? Second, can the researcher now safely conclude that those brain areas are required for humans to perform word pronunciation?

COURTESY VICKI GILLIS, COLORADO STATE UNIVERSITY

Build to the Outcomes

1. How have brain disorders been central to the study of specific areas of the brain?

2. What role does the corpus callosum play in behavior?

3. How does the EEG record electrical activity in the brain?

4. Compare what can be learned from structural brain imaging with results from functional brain imaging.

5. What does an fMRI track in an active brain?

6. Why should we avoid jumping to conclusions based on fMRI results?

Chapter Review

Neurons: The Origin of Behavior

▶ Neurons are the building blocks of the nervous system: They process information received from the outside world, communicate with each other, and send messages to the body's muscles and organs.

▶ Neurons are composed of three major parts: the cell body, dendrites, and the axon. The cell body contains the nucleus, which houses the organism's genetic material. Dendrites receive sensory signals from other neurons and transmit this information to the cell body. Each axon carries signals from the cell body to other neurons or to muscles and organs in the body.

▶ Neurons don't actually touch. They are separated by a small gap, which is part of the synapse across which signals are transmitted from one neuron to another.

▶ Glial cells provide support for neurons, usually in the form of the myelin sheath, which coats the axon to facilitate the transmission of information. In demyelinating diseases, the myelin sheath deteriorates.

▶ Neurons are differentiated according to the functions they perform. The three major types of neurons include sensory neurons (e.g., bipolar neurons), motor neurons, and interneurons (e.g., Purkinje cells).

The Electrochemical Actions of Neurons: Information Processing

▶ The neuron's resting potential is due to differences in the potassium (K^+) concentrations inside and outside the cell membrane, resulting from open channels that allow K^+ to flow outside the membrane while closed channels don't allow sodium ions (Na^+) and other ions to flow into the neuron. The conduction of an electric signal within a neuron happens when the resting potential is reversed by an electric impulse called an action potential.

▶ If electric signals reach a threshold, this initiates an action potential, an all-or-none signal that moves down the entire length of the axon. The action potential occurs when K^+ channels in the axon membrane close and Na^+ channels open, allowing the Na^+ ions to flow inside the axon.

▶ After the action potential has reached its maximum, a chemical pump reverses the imbalance in ions, returning the neuron to its resting potential. For a brief refractory period, the action potential cannot be reinitiated. Once it is initiated, the action potential spreads down the axon, jumping across the nodes of Ranvier to the synapse.

▶ Communication between neurons takes place through synaptic transmission, where an action potential triggers release of neurotransmitters from the terminal buttons of the sending neuron's axon, which travel across the synapse to bind with receptors in the receiving neuron's dendrite. Neurotransmitters bind to dendrites on specific receptor sites. Neurotransmitters leave the synapse through reuptake, through enzyme deactivation, and by binding to autoreceptors.

▶ Some of the major neurotransmitters are acetylcholine (ACh), dopamine, glutamate, GABA, norepinephrine, serotonin, and endorphins.

▶ Drugs can affect behavior by acting as agonists, that is, by facilitating or increasing the actions of neurotransmitters, or as antagonists by blocking the action of neurotransmitters. Recreational drug use can have an effect on brain function.

The Organization of the Nervous System

▶ Neurons make up nerves, which in turn form the human nervous system.

▶ The nervous system is divided into the peripheral and the central nervous systems. The central nervous system is composed of the spinal cord and the brain.

▶ The peripheral nervous system connects the central nervous system with the rest of the body, and it is itself divided into the somatic nervous system and the autonomic nervous system. The somatic nervous system, which conveys information into and out of the central nervous system, controls voluntary muscles, whereas the autonomic nervous system automatically controls the body's organs.

▶ The autonomic nervous system is further divided into the sympathetic and parasympathetic nervous systems, which complement each other in their effects on the body. The sympathetic nervous system prepares the body for action in threatening situations, and the parasympathetic nervous system returns it to its normal state.

▶ The spinal cord can control some basic behaviors such as spinal reflexes without input from the brain.

Structure of the Brain

▶ The brain can be divided into the hindbrain, midbrain, and forebrain.

▶ The hindbrain generally coordinates information coming into and out of the spinal cord with structures such as the medulla, the reticular formation, the cerebellum, and the pons. These structures respectively coordinate breathing and heart rate, regulate sleep and arousal levels, coordinate fine motor skills, and communicate this information to the cortex.

▶ The structures of the midbrain, the tectum and tegmentum, generally coordinate functions such as orientation to the environment and movement and arousal toward sensory stimuli.

▶ The forebrain generally coordinates higher-level functions, such as perceiving, feeling, and thinking. The forebrain houses subcortical structures, such as the thalamus, hypothalamus, limbic system (including the hippocampus and amygdala), and basal ganglia; all these structures perform a variety of functions related to motivation and emotion.

▶ The endocrine system works closely with the nervous system to regulate thoughts, emotions, and behaviors through the release of hormones. The pituitary gland orchestrates the functioning of the endocrine system by releasing hormones that direct the functions of other glands.

▶ Also in the forebrain, the cerebral cortex, composed of two hemispheres with four lobes each (occipital, parietal, temporal, and frontal), performs tasks that help make us fully human: thinking, planning, judging, perceiving, and behaving purposefully and voluntarily.

▶ Neurons in the brain can be shaped by experience and the environment, making the human brain amazingly plastic.

The Development and Evolution of the Nervous System

▶ Examining the development of the nervous system over the life span of an individual (its ontogeny) and across the time within which a species evolves (its phylogeny) presents further opportunities for understanding the human brain.

▶ The nervous system is the first system that forms in an embryo, starting as a neural tube, which forms the basis of the spinal cord. The neural tube expands on one end to form the hindbrain, midbrain, and forebrain, each of which folds onto the next structure. Within each of these areas, specific brain structures begin to differentiate.

▶ Nervous systems evolved from simple collections of sensory and motor neurons in simple animals, such as flatworms, to elaborate centralized nervous systems found in mammals. The evolution of the human nervous system can be thought of as a process of refining, elaborating, and expanding structures present in other species. Reptiles and birds have almost no cerebral cortex. By contrast, mammals have a highly developed cerebral cortex. The human brain appears to have evolved more quickly compared with those of other species to become adapted to a more complex environment.

▶ The gene, or the unit of hereditary transmission, is built from strands of DNA in a double-helix formation that is organized into chromosomes. Humans have 23 pairs of chromosomes; half come from each parent. A child shares 50% of his or her genes with each parent.

▶ Monozygotic twins share 100% of their genes, whereas dizygotic twins share 50%, the same as any other siblings. Because of their genetic relatedness, twins are often participants in genetic research.

▶ The study of genetics indicates that both genes and the environment work together to influence behavior. Genes set the range of variation in populations within a given environment, but they do not predict individual characteristics; experience and other environmental factors play a crucial role as well.

▶ Epigenetics refers to the study of environmental influences that determine whether or not genes are expressed, without altering the basic DNA sequences that constitute the genes themselves. Epigenetic marks such as DNA methylation and histone modification influence whether specific genes are switched on or off. Epigenetic influences have been shown to play a critical role in persisting effects of early experiences in rats and humans.

Investigating the Brain

▶ There are three major approaches to studying the link between the brain and behavior:

▶ Observing how perceptual, motor, intellectual, and emotional capacities are affected following brain damage. By carefully relating specific psychological and behavioral disruptions to damage in particular areas of the brain, researchers can better understand how the brain area normally plays a role in producing those behaviors.

▶ Examining global electrical activity in the brain and the activity patterns of single neurons. The patterns of electrical activity in large brain areas can be examined from outside the skull using the electroencephalograph (EEG). Single-cell recordings taken from specific neurons can be linked to specific perceptual or behavioral events, suggesting that those neurons represent particular kinds of stimuli or control particular aspects of behavior.

▶ Using brain imaging to scan the brain as people perform different perceptual or intellectual tasks. Correlating energy consumption in particular brain areas with specific cognitive and behavioral events suggests that those brain areas are involved in specific types of perceptual, motor, cognitive, or emotional processing.

KEY CONCEPT QUIZ

1. Signals are transmitted from one neuron to another
   a. across a synapse.
   b. through a glial cell.
   c. by the myelin sheath.
   d. in the cell body.

2. Which type of neuron receives information from the external world and conveys this information to the brain via the spinal cord?
   a. sensory neuron
   b. motor neuron
   c. interneuron
   d. axon

3. An electric signal that is conducted along the length of a neuron's axon to the synapse is called
   a. a resting potential.
   b. an action potential.
   c. a node of Ranvier.
   d. an ion.

4. The chemicals that transmit information across the synapse to a receiving neuron's dendrites are called
   a. vesicles.
   b. terminal buttons.
   c. postsynaptic neurons.
   d. neurotransmitters.

5. The _____ automatically controls the organs of the body.
   a. autonomic nervous system
   b. parasympathetic nervous system
   c. sympathetic nervous system
   d. somatic nervous system

6. Which part of the hindbrain coordinates fine motor skills?
   a. the medulla
   b. the cerebellum
   c. the pons
   d. the tegmentum

7. What part of the brain is involved in movement and arousal?
   a. the hindbrain
   b. the midbrain
   c. the forebrain
   d. the reticular formation

8. The _____ regulates body temperature, hunger, thirst, and sexual behavior.
   a. cerebral cortex
   b. pituitary gland
   c. hypothalamus
   d. hippocampus

9. What explains the apparent beneficial effects of cardiovascular exercise on aspects of brain function and cognitive performance?
   a. the different sizes of the somatosensory cortices
   b. the position of the cerebral cortex
   c. specialization of association areas
   d. neuron plasticity

10. Genes set the _____ in populations within a given environment.
   a. individual characteristics
   b. range of variation
   c. environmental possibilities
   d. behavioral standards

 LearningCurve   **Don't stop now! Quizzing yourself is a powerful study tool. Go to LaunchPad to access the LearningCurve adaptive quizzing system and your own personalized learning plan. Visit launchpadworks.com.**

KEY TERMS

neurons (p. 77)

cell body (or soma) (p. 77)

dendrite (p. 77)

axon (p. 77)

myelin sheath (p. 77)

glial cells (p. 77)

synapse (p. 77)

sensory neurons (p. 78)

motor neurons (p. 78)

interneurons (p. 79)

resting potential (p. 80)

action potential (p. 81)

refractory period (p. 82)

terminal buttons (p. 83)

neurotransmitters (p. 83)

receptors (p. 83)

acetylcholine (ACh) (p. 84)

dopamine (p. 84)

glutamate (p. 84)

GABA (gamma-aminobutyric acid) (p. 84)

norepinephrine (p. 84)

serotonin (p. 84)

endorphins (p. 84)

agonists (p. 85)

antagonists (p. 85)

nervous system (p. 87)

central nervous system (CNS) (p. 87)

peripheral nervous system (PNS) (p. 87)

somatic nervous system (p. 87)

autonomic nervous system (ANS) (p. 88)

sympathetic nervous system (p. 88)

parasympathetic nervous system (p. 89)

spinal reflexes (p. 89)

reflex arc (p. 90)

hindbrain (p. 92)

medulla (p. 92)

reticular formation (p. 92)

cerebellum (p. 92)

pons (p. 94)

tectum (p. 94)

tegmentum (p. 94)

cerebral cortex (p. 94)

subcortical structures (p. 94)

thalamus (p. 94)

hypothalamus (p. 94)

limbic system (p. 95)

hippocampus (p. 95)

amygdala (p. 95)

basal ganglia (p. 95)

endocrine system (p. 96)

pituitary gland (p. 96)

corpus callosum (p. 98)

occipital lobe (p. 98)

parietal lobe (p. 98)

temporal lobe (p. 99)

frontal lobe (p. 99)

association areas (p. 99)

mirror neurons (p. 99)

gene (p. 104)

chromosomes (p. 104)

epigenetics (p. 106)

epigenetic marks (p. 106)

DNA methylation (p. 106)

histone modification (p. 107)

heritability (p. 107)

electroencephalograph (EEG) (p. 113)

CHANGING MINDS

1. While watching late-night TV, you come across an infomercial for all-natural BrainGro. "It's a well-known fact that most people use only 10% of their brain," the spokesman promises, "but with BrainGro you can increase that number from 10% to 99%!" Why should you be skeptical of the claim that we use only 10% of our brains? What would happen if a drug actually increased neuronal activity tenfold?

2. Your friend has been feeling depressed and has gone to a psychiatrist for help. "He prescribed a medication that's supposed to increase serotonin in my brain. But my feelings depend on me, not on a bunch of chemicals in my head," she said. What examples could you give your friend to convince her that hormones and neurotransmitters really do influence our cognition, mood, and behavior?

3. A classmate has read the section in this chapter about the evolution of the central nervous system. "Evolution is just a theory," he says. "Not everyone believes in it. And even if it's true that we're all descended from monkeys, that doesn't have anything to do with the psychology of humans alive today." What is your friend misunderstanding about evolution? How would you explain to him the relevance of evolution to modern psychology?

4. A news program reports on a study (Hölzel et al., 2011) in which people who practiced meditation for about 30 minutes a day for 8 weeks showed changes in their brains, including increases in the size of the hippocampus and the amygdala. You tell a friend, who's skeptical. "The brain doesn't change like that. Basically, the brain you're born with is the brain you're stuck with for the rest of your life." Why is your friend's statement wrong? What are several specific ways in which the brain does change over time?

5. A friend of yours announces that he's figured out why he's bad at math. "I read it in a book," he says. "Left-brained people are analytical and logical, but right-brained people are creative and artistic. I'm an art major, so I must be right brained, and that's why I'm not good at math." Why is your friend's view too simplistic?

ANSWERS TO KEY CONCEPT QUIZ

1. a; 2. a; 3. b; 4. d; 5. a; 6. b; 7. b; 8. c; 9. d; 10. b.

LaunchPad features the full e-Book of *Psychology*, the LearningCurve adaptive quizzing system, videos, and a variety of activities to boost your learning. Visit LaunchPad at launchpadworks.com.

Sensation and Perception

4

I N THE 1930S, A YOUNG ARCHITECT and designer named Donald Deskey won a competition to design the interiors of Radio City Music Hall in New York City. His design was met with immediate acclaim and enabled Deskey to create his own graphic design firm. In 1946, he helped to create the box design for Procter & Gamble's revolutionary new laundry detergent, Tide, the first one made with synthetic compounds rather than plain old soap (Hine, 1995). Although extremely familiar to us today, in 1946 the bold, blue "Tide" emblazoned on bull's-eye rings of yellow and orange marked the first use of eye-catching Day-Glo colors on a commercial product, and this mix of type and graphics was unlike any product design that anyone had seen before. This product would be impossible to miss on the shelves of a store, and as admirers of the design observed, "it was the box itself that most dynamically conveyed the new product's extraordinary power" (Dyer, Dalzell, & Olegario, 2004). Tide went to market in 1949, and Procter & Gamble never looked back.

Nowadays we're used to seeing advertisements that feature exciting, provocative, or even sexual images to sell products. In television commercials, these images are accompanied by popular music that advertisers hope will evoke an overall mood favorable to the product. Advertisers hope that viewers will associate the sight and sound of exciting things with what might be an otherwise drab product. This form of advertising is known as *sensory branding* (Lindstrom, 2005). The idea is to exploit all the senses to promote a product or a brand. Sensory branding goes beyond sight and sound by enlisting smell, taste, and touch as well as vision and hearing. That new-car smell you anticipate while you take a test drive? It's a manufactured fragrance sprayed inside the car, carefully tested to evoke positive feelings among

- Sensation and Perception Are Distinct Activities

- Vision I: The Eyes and the Brain Convert Light Waves to Neural Signals

- Vision II: Recognizing What We Perceive

- Audition: More Than Meets the Ear

- The Body Senses: More Than Skin Deep

- The Chemical Senses: Adding Flavor

Donald Deskey recognized the power of perception back in 1946, when he grabbed the attention of consumers by using eye-catching colors and a striking design on the first box of Tide.

◄ ANDREW GEIGER

THE PHOTO WORKS

potential buyers. Bang & Olufsen, a Danish high-end stereo manufacturer, carefully designed its remote-control units to have a certain distinctive "feel" in a user's hand. Singapore Airlines, which frequently has been rated the "world's best airline," has actually patented the smell of its airplane cabins. (It's called Stefan Floridian Waters.)

These companies, just as Procter & Gamble did back in 1946, recognize the power of sensation and perception to shape human experience and behavior.

IN THIS CHAPTER WE'LL EXPLORE KEY INSIGHTS into the nature of sensation and perception. These experiences are basic to survival and reproduction; we wouldn't last long without the ability to accurately make sense of the world around us. Indeed, research on sensation and perception is the basis for much of psychology, a pathway toward understanding more complex cognition and behavior such as memory, emotion, motivation, or decision making. Yet sensation and perception also sometimes reveal various kinds of illusions that you might see at a science fair or in a novelty shop: reminders that the act of perceiving the world is not so simple or straightforward as it might seem.

We'll look at how physical energy in the world around us is encoded by our senses, sent to the brain, and enters our conscious awareness. Vision is predominant among our senses; correspondingly, we'll devote a fair amount of space to understanding how the visual system works. Then we'll discuss how we perceive sound waves as words or music or noise, followed by the body senses, emphasizing touch, pain, and balance. We'll end with the chemical senses of smell and taste, which together allow you to savor the foods you eat. But before doing any of that, we will provide a foundation for examining all of the sensory systems by reviewing how psychologists measure sensation and perception in the first place.

Sensation and Perception Are Distinct Activities

Learning Outcomes

► Explain the interrelationship of sensation and perception.

► Describe the basic process of transduction.

► Give examples of how sensation and perception are measured.

To us, sensation and perception appear to be one seamless event. However, they are two distinct activities.

► **Sensation** is *simple stimulation of a sense organ*. It is the basic registration of light, sound, pressure, odor, or taste as parts of your body interact with the physical world.

► After a sensation registers in your central nervous system, **perception** takes place at the level of your brain: *the organization, identification, and interpretation of a sensation in order to form a mental representation*.

For example, your eyes are coursing across these sentences right now. The sensory receptors in your eyeballs are registering different patterns of light reflecting off the page. Your brain, however, is integrating and processing that light information into the meaningful perception of words, such as *meaningful*, *perception*, and *words*. Your eyes—the sensory organs—aren't really seeing words; they're simply encoding different lines and curves on a page. Your brain—the perceptual organ—is transforming those lines and curves into a coherent mental representation of words and concepts.

If all of this sounds a little peculiar, it's because, from the vantage point of your conscious experience, it *seems* as if you're reading words directly. If you think of the discussion of brain damage in the Neuroscience and Behavior chapter, you'll recall

sensation Simple stimulation of a sense organ.

perception The organization, identification, and interpretation of a sensation in order to form a mental representation.

126

that sometimes a person's eyes can work just fine, yet the individual is still "blind" to faces she has seen for many years (p. 116). Damage to the visual processing centers in the brain can interfere with the interpretation of information coming from the eyes: The senses are intact, but perceptual ability is compromised. Sensation and perception are related—but separate—events.

How do sensory receptors communicate with the brain? It all depends on the process of **transduction,** which occurs *when many sensors in the body convert physical signals from the environment into encoded neural signals sent to the central nervous system*. In vision, light reflected from surfaces provides the eyes with information about the shape, color, and position of objects. In audition, vibrations (from vocal cords or a guitar string, perhaps) cause changes in air pressure that propagate through space to a listener's ears. In touch, the pressure of a surface against the skin signals its shape, texture, and temperature. In taste and smell, molecules dispersed in the air or dissolved in saliva reveal the identity of substances that we may or may not want to eat. In each case physical energy from the world is converted to neural energy inside the central nervous system. We'll discuss in more detail how transduction works with each of the five primary senses—vision, hearing, touch, taste, and smell—in separate sections later in this chapter.

PSYCHOPHYSICS

Knowing that perception takes place in the brain, you might wonder if two people see the same colors in the sunset when looking at the evening sky. It's intriguing to consider the possibility that our basic perceptions of sights or sounds might differ fundamentally from those of other people. How can we measure such a thing objectively? Measuring the physical energy of a stimulus, such as the wavelength of a color, is easy enough: You can probably buy the necessary instruments online to do that yourself. But how do you quantify a person's private, subjective *perception* of that light?

The early structuralist psychologists tried using introspection to measure perceptual experiences (see the Psychology: Evolution of a Science chapter). They failed miserably at this task. After all, two people may both describe their experience of the sunset in the same words ("orange" and "beautiful"), but neither can directly perceive the other's experience of the same event. During the mid-1800s, the German scientist and philosopher Gustav Fechner (1801–1887) developed a new approach to measuring sensation and perception called **psychophysics:** *methods that measure the strength of a stimulus and the observer's sensitivity to that stimulus* (Fechner, 1860/1966). In a typical psychophysics experiment, researchers ask people to make a simple judgment—whether or not they saw a flash of light, for example. The psychophysicist then relates the measured stimulus, such as the brightness of the light flash, to each observer's yes-or-no response.

MEASURING THRESHOLDS

Psychophysicists begin the measurement process with a single sensory signal to determine precisely how much physical energy is required for an observer to become aware of a sensation. The simplest quantitative measurement in psychophysics is the **absolute threshold,** *the minimal intensity needed to just barely detect a stimulus in 50% of the trials*. A *threshold* is a boundary. Just as the doorway that separates the inside from the outside of a house is a threshold, so is the boundary between two psychological states (awareness and unawareness, for example). In finding the absolute threshold for sensation, the two states in question are *sensing* and *not sensing* some stimulus. **TABLE 4.1** lists the approximate sensory thresholds for each of the five senses.

To measure the absolute threshold for detecting a sound, for example, an observer sits in a soundproof room wearing headphones linked to a computer. The experimenter

You can enjoy a tempting ice cream sundae even if you do not know that its sweet taste depends on a complex process of transduction, in which molecules dissolved in saliva are converted to neural signals processed by the brain.

transduction The process that occurs when many sensors in the body convert physical signals from the environment into encoded neural signals sent to the central nervous system.

psychophysics Methods that measure the strength of a stimulus and the observer's sensitivity to that stimulus.

absolute threshold The minimal intensity needed to just barely detect a stimulus in 50% of trials.

TABLE 4.1

Approximate Sensory Thresholds

Sense	Absolute Threshold	
Vision	A candle flame 30 miles away on a clear, dark night	JANOS MISETA FEATUREPICS
Hearing	A clock's tick 20 feet away when all is quiet	KATERYNA MOISEYENKO/ SHUTTERSTOCK
Touch	A fly's wing falling on the cheek from 1 centimeter away	ISTOCK/GETTY IMAGES
Smell	A single drop of perfume diffused through an area equivalent to the volume of six rooms	MARCO ANDRAS EST/ AGE FOTOSTOCK
Taste	A teaspoon of sugar dissolved in two gallons of water	FOODFOLIO/ ALAMY

Research from Galanter (1962).

presents a pure tone (the sort of sound made by striking a tuning fork), using the computer to vary the loudness or the length of time each tone lasts and recording how often the observer reports hearing that tone under each condition. The outcome of such an experiment is graphed in **FIGURE 4.1**. Notice from the shape of the curve that the transition from *not hearing* to *hearing* is gradual rather than abrupt.

If we repeat this experiment for many different tones, we can observe and record the thresholds for tones ranging from very low to very high pitch. It turns out that people tend to be most sensitive to the range of tones corresponding to human conversation. If the tone is low enough, such as the lowest note on a pipe organ, most humans cannot hear it at all; we can only feel it. If the tone is high enough, we likewise cannot hear it, but dogs and many other animals can.

The absolute threshold is useful for assessing how sensitive we are to faint stimuli, but the human perceptual system is better at detecting *changes* in stimulation than the simple onset or offset of stimulation. When parents hear their infant's cry, it's useful to be able to differentiate the "I'm hungry" cry from the "I'm cranky" cry from the "something is biting my toes" cry. The **just noticeable difference (JND)** is *the minimal change in a stimulus that can just barely be detected.*

The JND is not a fixed quantity; rather, it depends on how intense the stimuli being measured are and on the particular sense being measured. Consider measuring the JND for a bright light. An observer in a dark room is shown a light of fixed intensity, called the *standard* (S), next to a comparison light that is slightly brighter or dimmer than the standard. When S is very dim, observers can see even a very small difference in brightness between the two lights: The JND is small. But if S is bright, a much larger increment is needed to detect the difference: The JND is larger.

When calculating a difference threshold, it is the proportion between stimuli that is important. This relationship was first noticed in 1834 by the German physiologist Ernst Weber (Watson, 1978). Fechner applied Weber's insight directly to psychophysics, describing a formal relationship called **Weber's law:** *The just noticeable difference of a stimulus is a constant proportion despite variations in intensity.* As an example, if you picked up a 1-ounce envelope, then a 2-ounce envelope, you'd probably notice the difference between them. But if you picked up a 20-pound package, then a 20-pound, 1-ounce package, you'd probably detect no difference at all between them.

▶ Figure 4.1

ABSOLUTE THRESHOLD Some of us are more sensitive than others, and we may even detect sensory stimulation below our own absolute threshold. Absolute threshold is graphed here as the point where the increasing intensity of the stimulus enables an observer to detect it on 50% of the trials. As its intensity gradually increases, we detect the stimulation more frequently.

Absolute threshold for sound

Percent correct

100

50% respond, "Yes, I hear it."

50

0

Absolute threshold

Physical intensity of stimulus tone

SIGNAL DETECTION

Measuring absolute and difference thresholds requires a critical assumption: that a threshold exists! But much of what scientists know about biology suggests that such a discrete, all-or-none change in the brain is unlikely. Humans don't suddenly and rapidly switch between perceiving and not perceiving; in fact, recall that the transition from *not sensing* to *sensing* is gradual (see Figure 4.1). The very same physical stimulus, such as a dim light or a quiet tone, presented on several different occasions, may be perceived by the same person on some occasions but not on others. Remember, an absolute threshold is operationalized as perceiving the stimulus 50% of the time, which means that the other 50% of the time it might go undetected.

Our accurate perception of a sensory stimulus, then, can be somewhat haphazard. Whether in the psychophysics lab or out in the world, sensory signals face a lot of competition, or *noise,* which refers to all the other stimuli coming from the internal and external environment. Memories, moods, and motives intertwine with what you are seeing, hearing, and smelling at any given time. This internal "noise" competes with your ability to detect a stimulus with perfect, focused attention. Other sights, sounds, and smells in the world at large also compete for attention; you rarely have the luxury of attending to just one stimulus apart from everything else. As a consequence of noise, you may not perceive everything that you sense, and you may even perceive things that you haven't sensed. Think of the last time you had a hearing test. You no doubt missed some of the quiet beeps that were presented, but you also probably said you heard beeps that weren't really there.

Signal Detection Theory

An approach to psychophysics called **signal detection theory** holds that *the response to a stimulus depends both on a person's sensitivity to the stimulus in the presence of noise and on a person's decision criterion.* That is, observers consider the sensory evidence evoked by the stimulus and compare it with an internal decision criterion (Green & Swets, 1966; Macmillan & Creelman, 2005). If the sensory evidence exceeds the criterion, the observer responds by saying, "Yes, I detected the stimulus," and if it falls short of the criterion, the observer responds by saying, "No, I did not detect the stimulus."

Signal detection theory allows researchers to quantify an observer's response in the presence of noise. In a signal detection experiment, a stimulus, such as a dim light, is randomly presented or not. If you've ever taken an eye exam that checks your peripheral vision, you have an idea of this kind of setup: Lights of varying intensity are flashed at various places in the visual field, and your task is to respond any time you see one. Observers in a signal detection experiment must decide whether they saw the light or not. If the light is presented and the observer correctly responds yes, the outcome is a *hit.* If the light is presented and the observer says no, the result is a *miss.* However, if the light is *not* presented and the observer nonetheless says it was, a *false alarm* has occurred. Finally, if the light is *not* presented and the observer responds no, a *correct rejection* has occurred: The observer accurately detected the absence of the stimulus.

Signal detection theory proposes a way to measure *perceptual sensitivity* (how effectively the perceptual system represents sensory events) separately from the observer's decision-making strategy. It explicitly takes into account observers' response tendencies, such as liberally saying yes when there is any hint of a stimulus or conservatively reserving identifications only for obvious instances of the stimulus. Even when one person says yes much more often than another, both may be equally accurate in distinguishing between the presence or absence of a stimulus.

Practical Applications

Signal detection theory has practical applications at home, school, and work, and even while driving. For example, a radiologist may have to decide whether a mammogram shows that a woman has breast cancer. The radiologist knows that certain features, such as a mass of a particular size and shape, are associated with the presence of

just noticeable difference (JND) The minimal change in a stimulus that can just barely be detected.

Weber's law States that the just noticeable difference of a stimulus is a constant proportion despite variations in intensity.

signal detection theory Holds that the response to a stimulus depends on both a person's sensitivity to the stimulus in the presence of noise and the person's response criterion.

Crowds of people such as this one at New York City's Thanksgiving Day Parade present our visual system with a challenging signal detection task.

BLICKWINKEL/ALAMY

cancer. But noncancerous features can have a very similar appearance to cancerous ones. The radiologist may decide on a strictly liberal criterion and check every possible case of cancer with a biopsy. This decision strategy minimizes the possibility of missing a true cancer but leads to many unnecessary biopsies. A strictly conservative criterion will cut down on unnecessary biopsies but will miss some treatable cancers.

For another example, imagine that the police are on the lookout for a suspected felon who they have reason to believe will be at a crowded soccer match. Although the law enforcement agency provided a fairly good description (6 feet tall, sandy brown hair, beard, glasses) there are still thousands of people to scan. Rounding up all men between 5'5" and 6'5" probably would produce a hit (the felon is caught) but at the expense of an extraordinary number of false alarms (many innocent people are detained and questioned).

Scientists must weigh these different types of errors against each other in setting the decision criterion. Signal detection theory offers a practical way to choose among

THE REAL WORLD

Multitasking

By one estimate, using a cell phone while driving makes having an accident four times more likely (McEvoy et al., 2005). In response to highway safety experts and statistics such as this, state legislatures are passing laws that restrict, and sometimes ban, using mobile phones while driving. You might think that's a fine idea . . . for everyone else on the road. But surely *you* can manage to punch in a number on a phone, carry on a conversation, or maybe even text-message while simultaneously driving in a safe and courteous manner. Right? In a word, *wrong*.

The issue here is *selective attention,* or perceiving only what's currently relevant to you. Perception is an active, moment-to-moment exploration for relevant or interesting information, not a passive receptacle for whatever happens to come along. Talking on a cell phone while driving demands that you juggle two independent sources of sensory input—vision and audition—at the same time. This is problematic, because research has found that when attention is directed to audition, activity in visual areas decreases (Shomstein & Yantis, 2004).

This kind of *multitasking* creates problems when you need to react suddenly while driving. Researchers have tested experienced drivers in a highly realistic driving simulator, measuring their response times to brake lights and stop signs while they listened to the radio or carried on phone conversations about a political issue, among other tasks (Strayer, Drews, & Johnston, 2003). These experienced drivers reacted significantly more slowly during phone conversations than during the other tasks. This is because a phone conversation requires memory retrieval, deliberation, and planning what to say and often carries an emotional stake in the conversation topic. Tasks such as listening to the radio require far less attention.

The tested drivers became so engaged in their conversations that their minds no longer seemed to be in the car. Their slower braking response translated into an increased stopping distance that, depending on the driver's speed, would have resulted in a rear-end collision. Whether the phone was handheld or hands free made little difference, and similar results have been obtained in field studies of actual driving (Horrey & Wickens, 2006). This suggests that laws requiring drivers to use hands-free phones may have little effect on reducing accidents. Even after drivers had extensive practice at driving while using a hands-free cell phone in a simulator, the disruptive effects of cell phone use were still observed (Cooper & Strayer, 2008). The situation is even worse when text messaging is involved: Compared with a no-texting control condition, when either sending or receiving a text message in the simulator, drivers spent dramatically less time looking at the road, had a much harder time staying in their lane, missed numerous lane changes, and had greater difficulty maintaining an appropriate distance behind the car ahead of them (Hosking, Young, & Regan, 2009). A recent review concluded that the impairing effect of

Superior temporal lobe   Fusiform gyrus

(a)   (b)

SHOMSTEIN & YANTIS, 2004, CONTROL OF ATTENTION SHIFTS BETWEEN VISION AND AUDITION IN HUMAN CORTEX, *THE JOURNAL OF NEUROSCIENCE, 24 NOVEMBER 2004, 24(47):10702-10706, DOI: 10.1523/JNEUROSCI.2939-04.2004. PERMISSION CONVEYED THROUGH COPYRIGHT CLEARANCE CENTER.*

Shifting attention participants received fMRI scans as they performed tasks that required them to shift their attention between visual and auditory information. (a) When participants focused on auditory information, a region in the superior (upper) temporal lobe involved in auditory processing showed increased activity (yellow/orange). (b) In striking contrast, a visual region, the fusiform gyrus, showed decreased activity when participants focused on auditory information (blue).

texting while driving is comparable with that of alcohol consumption and greater than that of smoking marijuana (Pascual-Ferrá, Liu, & Beatty, 2012).

In an interesting finding, people who report that they multitask frequently in everyday life have difficulty in laboratory tasks that require focusing attention in the face of distractions, compared with individuals who do not multitask much in daily life (Ophir, Nass, & Wagner, 2009). Frequent multitasking in academic settings (via texting or Facebook use) can have a negative impact on learning (Chen & Yan, 2015; Judd, 2014). So how well do we multitask in several thousand pounds of metal hurtling down the highway? Unless you have two heads with one brain each—one to talk and one to concentrate on driving—you would do well to keep your eyes on the road and not on the phone.

criteria that permit decision makers to take into account the consequences of hits, misses, false alarms, and correct rejections (McFall & Treat, 1999; Swets, Dawes, & Monahan, 2000). For an example of a common everyday task that can interfere with signal detection, see The Real World: Multitasking.

SENSORY ADAPTATION

When you walk into a bakery, the aroma of freshly baked bread overwhelms you, but after a few minutes the smell fades. If you dive into cold water, the temperature is shocking at first, but after a few minutes you get used to it. When you wake up in the middle of the night for a drink of water, the bathroom light blinds you, but after a few minutes you no longer squint. These are all examples of **sensory adaptation,** whereby *sensitivity to prolonged stimulation tends to decline over time as an organism adapts to current conditions.*

Sensory adaptation is a useful process for most organisms. Imagine what your sensory and perceptual world would be like without it. When you put on your jeans in the morning, the feeling of rough cloth against your bare skin would be as noticeable hours later as it was in the first few minutes. The stink of garbage in your apartment when you first walk in would never dissipate. If you had to be constantly aware of how your tongue feels while it is resting in your mouth, you'd be driven to distraction. Our sensory systems respond more strongly to changes in stimulation than to constant stimulation. A stimulus that doesn't change usually doesn't require any action; your car probably emits a certain hum all the time that you've gotten used to. But a change in stimulation often signals a need for action. If your car starts making different kinds of noises, you're not only more likely to notice them but you're also more likely to do something about it.

According to the theory of natural selection, inherited characteristics that provide a survival advantage tend to spread throughout the population across generations. Why might sensory adaptation have evolved? What survival benefits might it confer to a small animal trying to avoid predators? To a predator trying to hunt prey?

sensory adaptation The process whereby sensitivity to prolonged stimulation tends to decline over time as an organism adapts to current conditions.

Build to the Outcomes

1. Use the example of the person with healthy eyes, yet who is blind to faces she knows, to differentiate between sensation and perception.

2. By what process do sensory inputs, such as light and sound waves, become messages sent to the brain?

3. Why isn't it enough for a psychophysicist to measure only the strength of a stimulus?

4. What is an absolute threshold?

5. What is the importance of proportion to the measurement of just noticeable difference?

6. What are the two aspects of signal detection theory?

7. What are the benefits of sensory adaptation?

Vision I: The Eyes and the Brain Convert Light Waves to Neural Signals

You might be proud of your 20/20 vision, even if it is corrected by glasses or contact lenses. The term *20/20* refers to a measurement associated with a Snellen chart, named after Hermann Snellen (1834–1908), the Dutch ophthalmologist who developed it as a means of assessing **visual acuity,** *the ability to see fine detail:* it is the smallest line of letters that a typical person can read from a distance of 20 feet. But if you dropped into the Birds of Prey Ophthalmologic Office, your visual pride would wither. Hawks, eagles, owls, and other raptors have much greater visual acuity than humans: in many cases, about 8 times greater, or the equivalent of 20/2 vision (meaning that what the normal human can just see from 2 feet away can be seen by these birds at a distance of 20 feet away). Your sophisticated visual system has evolved to transduce visual energy in the world into neural signals in the brain. Humans have sensory receptors in their eyes that respond to wavelengths of light energy. When we

Learning Outcomes

▶ Describe how the eye converts light waves into neural impulses.

▶ Discuss how we perceive color.

▶ Describe what happens once the neural impulses reach the brain.

visual acuity The ability to see fine detail.

STEVE SKJOLD/ALAMY

Though controversial for other reasons, research has shown that action shooter games improve attention and even basic visual acuity (Green & Bavelier, 2007; Li et al., 2009).

look at people, places, and things, patterns of light and color give us information about where one surface stops and another begins. The array of light reflected from those surfaces preserves their shapes and enables us to form a mental representation of a scene (Rodieck, 1998). Understanding vision, then, starts with understanding light.

SENSING LIGHT

Visible light is simply that portion of the electromagnetic spectrum that we can see, and it is an extremely small slice (see **FIGURE 4.2**). You can think about light as waves of energy. Like ocean waves, light waves vary in height and in the distance between their peaks, or *wavelengths*. There are three properties of light waves, each of which has a physical dimension that produces a corresponding psychological dimension (see **TABLE 4.2**). Length, amplitude, and purity are properties of the light waves themselves, and they exist independent of human observers. What humans perceive from those properties are color, brightness, and saturation.

▶ The *length* of a light wave determines its hue, or what humans perceive as color.

▶ The intensity or *amplitude* of a light wave—how high the peaks are—determines what we perceive as the brightness of light.

▶ *Purity* is the number of distinct wavelengths that make up the light. Purity corresponds to what humans perceive as saturation, or the richness of colors.

▶ Figure 4.2

ELECTROMAGNETIC SPECTRUM The sliver of light waves visible to humans as a rainbow of colors from violet-blue to red is bounded on the short end by ultraviolet rays, which honeybees can see, and on the long end by infrared waves, on which night-vision equipment operates. Someone wearing night-vision goggles, for example, can detect another person's body heat in complete darkness. Light waves are minute, but the scale along the bottom of this chart offers a glimpse of their varying lengths, measured in nanometers (nm; 1 nm = 1 billionth of a meter).

TABLE 4.2		
Properties of Light Waves		
Physical Dimension		**Psychological Dimension**
Length		Hue or what we perceive as color
Amplitude		Brightness
Purity	saturated desaturated	Saturation or richness of color

The Eye Detects and Focuses Light

Eyes have evolved as specialized organs to detect light. **FIGURE 4.3a** shows the human eye in cross-section. Light that reaches the eyes passes first through a clear, smooth outer tissue called the *cornea,* which bends the light wave and sends it through the *pupil,* a hole in the colored part of the eye. This colored part is the *iris,* which is a translucent, doughnut-shaped muscle that controls the size of the pupil and hence the amount of light that can enter the eye.

Immediately behind the iris, muscles inside the eye control the shape of the *lens* to bend the light again and focus it onto the **retina,** *a layer of light-sensitive tissue lining the back of the eyeball.* The muscles change the shape of the lens to focus objects at different distances, making the lens flatter for objects that are far away or rounder for nearby objects. This change is called **accommodation,** *the process by which the eye maintains a clear image on the retina.* Figure 4.3b shows how accommodation works.

If your eyeballs are a little too long or a little too short, the lens will not focus images properly on the retina. If the eyeball is too long, images are focused in front of the retina, leading to nearsightedness (*myopia*). If the eyeball is too short, images are focused behind the retina, and the result is farsightedness (*hyperopia*). Eyeglasses, contact lenses, and surgical procedures can correct either condition. For example, eyeglasses and contacts both provide an additional lens to help focus light more appropriately, and procedures such as LASIK physically reshape the eye's existing lens.

Light Is Converted into Neural Impulses in the Retina

How does a wavelength of light become a meaningful image? The retina is the interface between the world of light outside the body and the world of vision inside the central nervous system. Two types of *photoreceptor cells* in the retina contain light-sensitive pigments that transduce light into neural impulses. **Cones** *detect color, operate under normal daylight conditions, and allow us to focus on fine detail.* **Rods** *become active under low-light conditions for night vision* (see Figure 4.3c).

Rods are much more sensitive photoreceptors than cones, but this sensitivity comes at a cost. Because all rods contain the same photopigment, they provide no information about color and sense only shades of gray. Think about this the next time you wake up in the middle of the night and make your way to the bathroom for a drink of water. Using only the moonlight from the window to light your way, do you see the room in color or in shades of gray? Rods and cones differ in several other ways as well, most notably in their numbers. About 120 million rods are distributed more or less evenly around each retina except in the very center, the **fovea,** *an area of the retina where vision is the clearest and there are no rods at all.* The absence of rods in the fovea decreases the sharpness of vision in reduced light, but that can be overcome. For example, when amateur astronomers view dim stars through their telescopes at night, they know to look a little off to the side of the target so that the image will not fall on the rod-free fovea, but on some other part of the retina that contains many highly sensitive rods.

In contrast to rods, cones are far less numerous. Each retina contains only about 6 million cones, which are densely packed in the fovea and much more sparsely

retina A layer of light-sensitive tissue lining the back of the eyeball.

accommodation The process whereby the eye maintains a clear image on the retina.

cones Photoreceptors that detect color, operate under normal daylight conditions, and allow us to focus on fine detail.

rods Photoreceptors that become active under low-light conditions for night vision.

fovea An area of the retina where vision is the clearest and there are no rods at all.

MIKE SONNENBERG/ISTOCKPHOTO/GETTY IMAGES

The full-color image on the top is what you'd see if your rods and cones are fully at work. The grayscale image on the bottom is what you'd see if only your rods are functioning.

THINKSTOCK/ISTOCK/GETTY IMAGES

The image on the left was taken at a higher resolution than the image on the right. The difference in quality is analogous to light falling on the fovea, rather than on the periphery of the retina.

a. The Eye Captures Light Waves Reflected from an Object's Surface

Light reflected from an object's surface enters the eyes via the transparent **cornea**, bending to pass through the **pupil** at the center of the colored **iris**.

Cornea

Pupil

Iris

Lens

Retina

Fovea

Behind the iris, the thickness and shape of the **lens** adjust to focus light on the **retina**, where the image appears upside down and backward. Vision is clearest at the **fovea**.

b. Muscles Change the Shape of the Lens to Focus Objects at Different Distances, a Process Called Accommodation

People with **normal vision** focus the image on the retina at the back of the eye, both for near and far objects.

Nearsighted people see clearly what's nearby, but distant objects are blurry because light from them is focused in front of the retina.

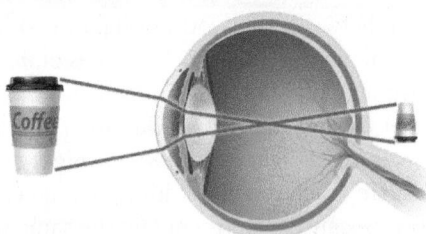

For **farsighted** people, distant objects are clear, but those nearby are blurry because their point of focus falls beyond the surface of the retina.

▲ Figure 4.3
THE EYE TRANSDUCES LIGHT WAVES INTO NEURAL ENERGY

distributed over the rest of the retina, as you can see in Figure 4.3c. This distribution of cones directly affects visual acuity and explains why objects off to the side, in your *peripheral vision,* aren't so clear. The light reflecting from those peripheral objects is less likely to land in the fovea, making the resulting image less sharp. The more fine detail the visual system encodes and represents, the clearer the perceived image. The process is analogous to the quality of photographs taken with a 6-megapixel digital camera versus a 2-megapixel camera.

The retina is thick with cells. As seen in Figure 4.3c, the photoreceptor cells (rods and cones) form the innermost layer, beneath a layer of transparent neurons, the bipolar and retinal ganglion cells. The *bipolar cells* collect neural signals from the rods and cones and transmit them to the outermost layer of the retina, where neurons called *retinal ganglion cells (RGCs)* organize the signals and send them to the brain.

The bundled RGC axons—about 1.5 million per eye—form the *optic nerve,* which leaves the eye through a hole in the retina. Because it contains neither rods nor cones and therefore has no mechanism for sensing light, this hole in the retina creates a

c. The Retina is the Interface Between the Eye and the Brain

The surface of the retina is composed of photoreceptor cells, the rods and cones, beneath a layer of transparent neurons, the bipolar and retinal ganglion cells (RGCs), connected in sequence. The axon of a retinal ganglion cell joins with all other RGC axons to form the **optic nerve**. The optic nerve creates the blind spot.

The **fovea**, the area of greatest visual acuity, is where most color-sensitive cones are concentrated, allowing us to see fine detail as well as color. Rods, the predominant photoreceptors activated in low-light conditions, are distributed everywhere else on the retina.

d. The Optic Nerve Carries the Neural Energy into the Brain

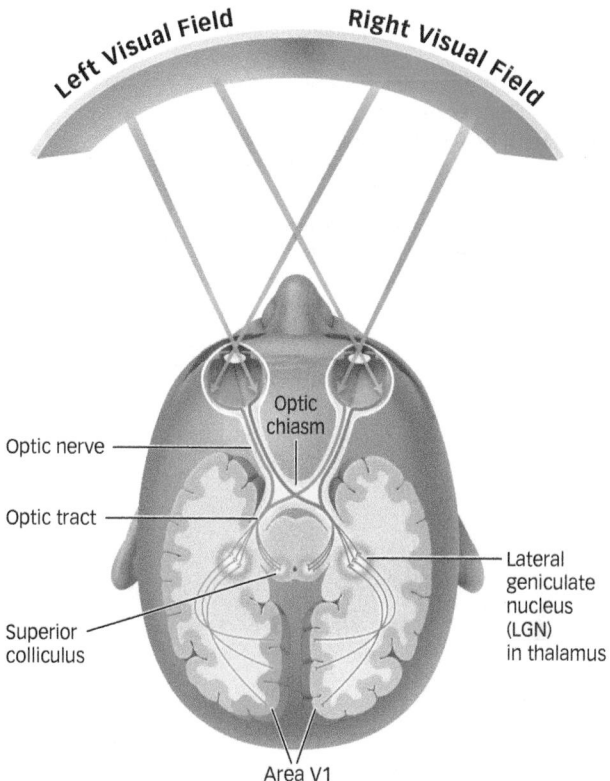

Objects in the right visual field stimulate the left half of each retina, and objects in the left visual field stimulate the right half of each retina. Just before the optic nerves enter the brain at the optic chiasm, about half the nerve fibers from each eye cross. The left half of each optic nerve (representing the right visual field) runs through the brain's left hemisphere via the thalamus, and the right half of each optic nerve (representing the left visual field) travels this route through the right hemisphere. So, information from the right visual field ends up in the left hemisphere and information from the left visual field ends up in the right hemisphere.

---

blind spot, *a location in the visual field that produces no sensation on the retina.* Try the demonstration in **FIGURE 4.4** to find the blind spot in each of your own eyes.

The Optic Nerve Carries Neural Impulses to the Brain

Streams of action potentials (neural impulses) containing information encoded by the retina travel to the brain along the optic nerve. Half of the axons in the optic nerve that leave each eye come from retinal ganglion cells (RGCs) that code information in the right visual field, whereas the other half code information in the left visual field. These two nerve bundles link to the left and right hemispheres of the brain, respectively (see Figure 4.3d). The optic nerve travels from each eye to the *lateral geniculate nucleus (LGN),* located in the thalamus. As you will recall from the Neuroscience and Behavior chapter, the thalamus receives inputs from all of the senses except smell. From there, the visual signal travels to the back of the brain, to a location called **area V1,** the *part of the occipital lobe that contains the primary visual cortex.*

blind spot A location in the visual field that produces no sensation on the retina.

area V1 The part of the occipital lobe that contains the primary visual cortex.

▶ Figure 4.4

BLIND SPOT DEMONSTRATION To find your blind spot, close your left eye and stare at the cross with your right eye. Hold this book 6 to 12 inches (15 to 30 centimeters) away from your eyes and move it slowly toward and away from you until the dot disappears. The dot is now in your blind spot and not visible. At this point the vertical lines may appear as one continuous line, because the visual system fills in the area occupied by the missing dot. To test your left eye's blind spot, turn the book upside down and repeat the experiment with your right eye closed.

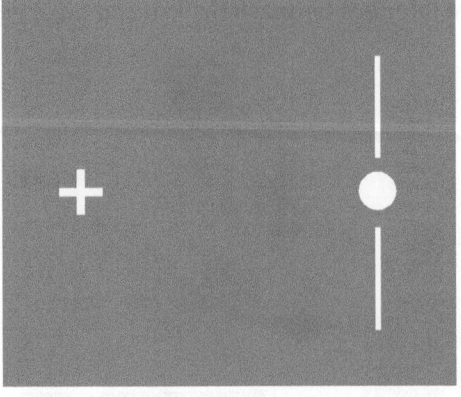

PERCEIVING COLOR

Sir Isaac Newton pointed out around 1670 that color is not something "in" light. In fact, color is nothing but our perception of wavelengths along the spectrum of visible light (see Figure 4.2). We perceive the shortest visible wavelengths as deep purple. As wavelengths become longer, the color we perceive changes gradually and continuously to blue, then green, yellow, orange, and, with the longest visible wavelengths, red. This rainbow of hues and accompanying wavelengths is called the *visible spectrum,* illustrated in **FIGURE 4.5.**

You'll recall that all rods are ideal for low-light vision but bad for distinguishing colors. Cones, by contrast, come in three types; each type is especially sensitive to either long-wavelength (perceived as red), medium-wavelength (perceived as green), or short-wavelength (perceived as blue) light. Red, green, and blue are the primary colors of light; color perception results from different combinations of the three basic elements in the retina that respond to the wavelengths corresponding to the three primary colors of light. For example, lighting designers add primary colors of light together, as when they shine red and green spotlights on a surface to create a yellow light, as shown in **FIGURE 4.6.** Notice that in the center of the figure, where

▶ Figure 4.5

SEEING IN COLOR We perceive a spectrum of color because objects selectively absorb some wavelengths of light and reflect others. Color perception corresponds to the summed activity of the three types of cones. Each type is most sensitive to a narrow range of wavelengths in the visible spectrum—short (bluish light), medium (greenish light), or long (reddish light). Rods, represented by the white curve, are most sensitive to the medium wavelengths of visible light but do not contribute to color perception.

▶ Figure 4.6

COLOR MIXING The millions of shades of color that humans can perceive are products not only of a light's wavelength but also of the mixture of wavelengths a stimulus absorbs or reflects. Colored spotlights work by causing the surface to reflect light of a particular wavelength, which stimulates the red, blue, or green photopigments in the cones. When all visible wavelengths are present, we see white.

THE LIFE PICTURE COLLECTION/GETTY IMAGES

the red, green, and blue lights overlap, the surface looks white. This demonstrates that a white surface actually reflects all visible wavelengths of light. Another example of how color perception depends critically on lighting conditions comes from the Internet phenomenon known as "The Dress," discussed in A World of Difference: The Dress.

The fact that three types of cones in the retina respond preferentially to different wavelengths (corresponding to blue, green, or red light) means that the pattern of responding across the three types of cones provides a unique code for each color. In

A WORLD OF DIFFERENCE

The Dress

On February 25, 2015, a Tumblr user posted a picture of a dress – not an action that you would expect to produce a firestorm on social media. But that is exactly what happened. The user explained that her friends were divided on the color of the dress—some saw it as white and gold, others as blue and black. Who was right? Over the next two days the post attracted over 400,000 notes on Tumblr. Millions responded to a BuzzFeed poll that asked about people's perceptions of the dress: More people claimed that it was white and gold than blue and black. Friends and families across the globe nearly came to blows over the color of the dress, with people typically insisting that their perception was the correct one and failing to believe that others could see it differently. In photos of the dress under different lighting conditions posted by the online retailer that sold it, the dress was unambiguously blue and black, as confirmed by the dress's name: Royal-Blue Lace Detail Bodycon Dress.

Vision scientists have begun to grapple with the mystery of the dress, and though we don't yet fully understand why people see its color so differently, we do have some clues and hypotheses. Consider a study by Lafer-Sousa, Hermann, and Conway (2015). They showed 1,401 people (some in the laboratory, most over the Internet) a smaller version of the photo of the dress posted at Tumblr and asked them to complete the sentence "This is a _____ and _____ dress". The researchers found that 57% called the dress blue/black, 30% called it white/gold, and the remaining participants provided other color combinations. People who had seen the dress before were somewhat more likely to call it white/gold than those who had not, indicating a role for prior experience in shaping color perception. When the researchers increased the size of the image, more people saw the dress as white/gold (perhaps explaining why most

What colors do you see in the dress? Researchers found that perception of the dress as white and gold increased with age.

people saw it as white/gold on Tumblr, where a larger version was posted). Surprisingly, there was a significant correlation between age and color perception: Older people were more likely to see the dress as white/gold than younger people (see accompanying figure). And women were more likely to see it as white/gold than were men.

Lafer-Sousa et al. (2015) and other researchers (Gegenfurter, Bloj, & Toscani, 2015; Winkler et al., 2015) suggest that perception of the dress's color is heavily influenced by how people perceive the lighting of the room where the photo was taken; the lighting is highly ambiguous and thus subject to different interpretations. Daylight has "cool" (bluish) components and "warm" (yellowish) components. If you perceive the lighting in the room as "cool" and "bluish," then your visual system assigns the bluishness of the dress to the lighting, and you end up seeing the dress as white/gold. But if you perceive the room lighting as "warm" and "yellowish," your visual system attributes blue to the dress and you see blue/black. In a result consistent with this idea, changing the illumination of the room had the predicted effects on perception of the dress's color (Lafer-Sousa et al., 2015).

Still, this hypothesis just changes the ultimate question regarding individual differences to a question about why some people see the lighting of the room as "cool," and others see it as "warm." Though we don't have a definitive answer, Lafer-Sousa et al. suggest that people who experience more daylight ("larks") may be more likely to perceive lighting as "cool" (because the sky is blue) and thus perceive the dress as white/gold, whereas "night owls" may be more likely to perceive lighting as "warm" and thus perceive the dress as blue/black. In a finding consistent with this idea, Lafer-Sousa et al. cited evidence that older adults and women are more likely to be "larks," which would fit with their greater tendency to see the dress as white/gold, but more evidence is needed to evaluate this hypothesis.

Though still not fully understood, "the dress" highlights an important lesson: The colors we perceive are not simply inherent properties of an object, but instead represent our visual system's best guess about color on the basis of complex patterns of incoming sensory data as well as our past experiences.

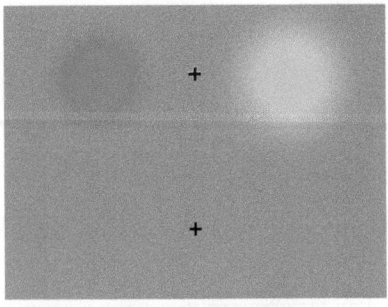

▲ Figure 4.7

COLOR AFTERIMAGE DEMONSTRATION Follow the accompanying instructions in the text, and sensory adaptation will do the rest. When the afterimage fades, you can get back to reading the chapter.

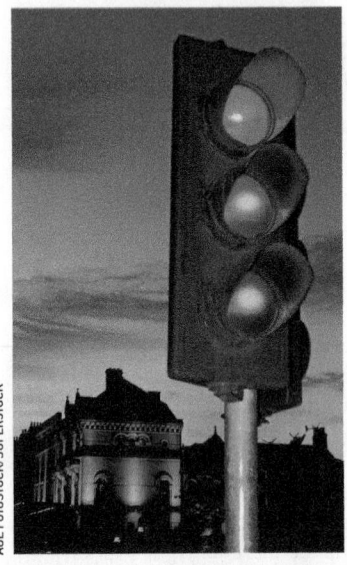

AGE FOTOSTOCK/SUPERSTOCK

Many people (including about 5% of all males) inherit conditions in which either the red or the green photoreceptors do not transduce light properly. Such people have difficulty distinguishing hues that to typical individuals appear as red or green. Unfortunately, in the United States, traffic signals use red and green lights to indicate whether cars should stop or go through an intersection. Why do drivers with red–green blindness not risk auto accidents every time they approach an intersection?

color-opponent system Theory stating that pairs of visual neurons work in opposition.

fact, researchers can "read out" the wavelength of the light entering the eye by working backward from the relative firing rates of the three types of cones (Gegenfurtner & Kiper, 2003). A genetic disorder in which one of the cone types is missing—and, in some very rare cases, two or all three—causes a *color deficiency*. This trait is sex linked, affecting men much more often than women.

Color deficiency is often referred to as *color blindness,* but in fact, people missing only one type of cone can still distinguish many colors, just not as many as someone who has the full complement of three cone types. You can create a kind of temporary color deficiency by exploiting the idea of sensory adaptation. Just like the rest of your body, cones need an occasional break too. Staring too long at one color fatigues the cones that respond to that color, producing a form of sensory adaptation that results in a *color afterimage.* To demonstrate this effect for yourself, follow these instructions for **FIGURE 4.7**:

▶ Stare at the small cross between the two color patches for about 1 minute. Try to keep your eyes as still as possible.

▶ After a minute, look at the lower cross. You should see a vivid color aftereffect that lasts for a minute or more. Pay particular attention to the colors in the afterimage.

Were you puzzled that the red patch produces a green afterimage and the green patch produces a red afterimage? This result reveals something important about color perception. The explanation stems from the **color-opponent system,** in which *pairs of visual neurons work in opposition:* red-sensitive cells against green-sensitive (as in Figure 4.7) and blue-sensitive cells against yellow-sensitive (Hurvich & Jameson, 1957). The color-opponent system explains color aftereffects. When you view a color—let's say, green—the cones that respond most strongly to green become fatigued over time. Now, when you stare at a white or gray patch, which reflects all the colors equally, the green-sensitive cones respond only weakly compared with the still-fresh red-sensitive cones, which fire strongly. The result? You perceive the patch as tinted red.

THE VISUAL BRAIN

The optic nerve carries the neural impulses to area V1 in the brain, as we've seen (Figure 4.3d). Here the information is systematically mapped into a representation of the visual scene.

Neural Systems for Perceiving Shape

One of the most important functions of vision involves perceiving the shapes of objects; our day-to-day lives would be a mess if we couldn't distinguish individual shapes. Imagine not being able to differentiate reliably between a warm doughnut with glazed icing and a straight stalk of celery and you'll get the idea; breakfast could become a traumatic experience if you couldn't distinguish shapes. Perceiving shape depends on the location and orientation of an object's edges. It is not surprising, then, that area V1 (see Figure 4.3d) is specialized for encoding edge orientation. As you also read in the Neuroscience and Behavior chapter, neurons in the visual cortex selectively respond to bars and edges in specific orientations in space (Hubel & Wiesel, 1962, 1998). In effect, area V1 contains populations of neurons, each "tuned" to respond to edges oriented at each position in the visual field. This means that some neurons fire when we perceive an object in a vertical orientation, other neurons fire when we perceive an object in a horizontal orientation, still other neurons fire when we perceive objects in a diagonal orientation of 45°, and so on (see **FIGURE 4.8**). The outcome of the coordinated response of all these feature detectors contributes to a sophisticated visual system that can detect where a doughnut ends and a celery stalk begins.

Pathways for What, Where, and How

Two functionally distinct pathways, or *visual streams,* project from the occipital cortex to visual areas in other parts of the brain (see **FIGURE 4.9**):

Stimulus   Neuron's responses

THE LIFE PICTURE COLLECTION /GETTY IMAGES

◄ Figure 4.8

SINGLE-NEURON FEATURE DETECTORS Area V1 contains neurons that respond to specific orientations of edges. Here a single neuron's responses are recorded (*left*) as the monkey views bars at different orientations (*right*). This neuron fires continuously when the bar is pointing to the right at 45°, less often when it is vertical, and not at all when it is pointing to the left at 45°.

▶ The *ventral* (below) *stream* travels across the occipital lobe into the lower levels of the temporal lobes and includes brain areas that represent an object's shape and identity—in other words, what it is, essentially a "what" pathway (Kravitz et al., 2013; Ungerleider & Mishkin, 1982).

▶ The *dorsal* (above) *stream* travels up from the occipital lobe to the parietal lobes (including some of the middle and upper levels of the temporal lobes), connecting with brain areas that identify the location and motion of an object—in other words, where it is (Kravitz et al., 2011). Because the dorsal stream allows us to perceive spatial relations, researchers originally dubbed it the "where" pathway (Ungerleider & Mishkin, 1982). Neuroscientists later argued that because the dorsal stream is crucial for guiding movements, such as aiming, reaching, or tracking with the eyes, the "where" pathway should more appropriately be called the "how" pathway (Milner & Goodale, 1995).

▲ Figure 4.9

VISUAL STREAMING One interconnected visual system forms a pathway that courses from the occipital visual regions into the lower temporal lobe. This ventral pathway enables us to identify what we see. Another interconnected pathway travels from the occipital lobe through the upper regions of the temporal lobe into the parietal regions. This dorsal pathway allows us to locate objects, to track their movements, and to move in relation to them.

How do we know there are two pathways? The most dramatic evidence comes from studying the impairments that result from brain injuries to each of the areas.

For example, a woman known as D.F. suffered permanent damage to a large region of the lateral occipital cortex, an area in the ventral stream (Goodale et al., 1991). Her ability to recognize objects by sight was greatly impaired, although her ability to recognize objects by touch was normal. This suggests that her *visual representation* of objects, but not her *memory* for objects, was damaged. D.F.'s brain damage belongs to a category called **visual form agnosia,** *the inability to recognize objects by sight* (Goodale & Milner, 1992, 2004). In an odd effect of this damage, although D.F. could not recognize objects visually, she could accurately *guide* her actions by sight, as demonstrated in **FIGURE 4.10.** When D.F. was scanned with fMRI, researchers found that she showed normal activation of regions within the dorsal stream during guided movement (James et al., 2003).

Conversely, other people with brain damage to the parietal lobe, a section of the dorsal stream, have difficulty using vision to guide their reaching and grasping movements (Perenin & Vighetto, 1988). However, their ventral streams are intact, meaning they recognize what objects are.

We can conclude from these two patterns of impairment that the ventral and dorsal visual streams are functionally distinct; it is possible for one to be damaged, whereas the other remains intact. Still, the two streams must work together during visual

visual form agnosia The inability to recognize objects by sight.

▶ **Figure 4.10**

TESTING VISUAL FORM AGNOSIA (*left*) When researchers asked D. F. to turn a handheld card until its orientation matched the orientation of the angle of the slot in the testing apparatus, she was unable to comply. (*right*) However, when asked to insert a card into the slot at various angles, D. F. accomplished the task virtually to perfection.

perception in order to integrate "what" and "where," and researchers are starting to examine how they interact. One intriguing possibility is suggested by recent fMRI research indicating that some regions within the dorsal stream are sensitive to properties of an object's identity, responding differently, for example, to line drawings of the same object in different sizes or viewed from different vantage points (Konen & Kastner, 2008; Sakuraba et al., 2012). This may be what allows the dorsal and ventral streams to exchange information and thus integrate the "what" and the "where" (Farivar, 2009; Konen & Kastner, 2008).

Build to the Outcomes

1. What are the physical and psychological dimensions of the properties of light waves?

2. What is the importance of the process of accommodation in the eye?

3. What is the function of the photoreceptor cells (rods and cones)?

4. What is the function of retinal ganglion cells? What is the relationship between the right and left eyes, and the right and left visual fields?

5. Why does color perception depend on combinations of three primary colors of light?

6. What happens when the cones in your eyes become fatigued?

7. What happens in the brain when an object's shape is perceived? What are the main jobs of the main and dorsal streams?

Vision II: Recognizing What We Perceive

parallel processing The brain's capacity to perform multiple activities at the same time.

binding problem How the brain links features together so that we see unified objects in our visual world rather than free-floating or miscombined features.

Our journey into the visual system has already revealed how it accomplishes some pretty astonishing feats. But the system needs to do much more in order for us to be able to interact effectively with our visual worlds. Let's now consider how the system links together individual visual features into whole objects, allows us to recognize what those objects are, organizes objects into visual scenes, and detects motion and change in those scenes. Along the way we'll see that studying visual errors and illusions provides key insights into how these processes work.

ATTENTION: THE "GLUE" THAT BINDS INDIVIDUAL FEATURES INTO A WHOLE

Specialized feature detectors in different parts of the visual system analyze each of the multiple features of a visible object: orientation, color, size, shape, and so forth. **Parallel processing** is *the brain's capacity to perform many activities at the same time.* Ultimately, though, parallel processing of these different features must somehow be integrated into a single, unified perception of an object (Nassi & Callaway, 2009). What allows us to perceive so easily and correctly that the young man in the photo is wearing a gray shirt and the young woman is wearing a red shirt? Why don't we see free-floating patches of gray and red, or even incorrect combinations, such as the young man wearing a red shirt and the young woman wearing a gray shirt? These questions refer to what researchers call the **binding problem** in perception, *how the brain links features together so that we see unified objects in our visual world rather than free-floating or miscombined features* (Treisman, 1998, 2006).

Illusory Conjunctions: Perceptual Mistakes

In everyday life, we correctly combine features into unified objects so automatically and effortlessly that it may be difficult to appreciate that binding is ever a problem at all. However, researchers have discovered errors in binding that reveal important clues about how the process works. One such error is known as an **illusory conjunction,** *a perceptual mistake whereby the brain incorrectly combines features from multiple objects.* In a pioneering study of illusory conjunctions, Anne Treisman and Hilary Schmidt (1982) briefly showed study participants visual displays in which black digits flanked colored letters, then instructed them first to report the black digits and second to describe the colored letters. Participants frequently reported illusory conjunctions, claiming to have seen, for example, a blue *A* or a red *X* instead of the red *A* and the blue *X* that had actually been shown (see **FIGURE 4.11a** and **b**). These illusory conjunctions were not just the result of guessing; they occurred more frequently than other kinds of errors, such as reporting a letter or color that was not present in the display (see Figure 4.11c). The illusory conjunctions looked real to the participants, who were just as confident they had seen them as they were about the actual colored letters they perceived correctly.

Why do illusory conjunctions occur? Treisman and her colleagues have tried to explain them by proposing a **feature-integration theory** (Treisman, 1998, 2006; Treisman & Gelade, 1980; Treisman & Schmidt, 1982), which holds that *focused attention is not required to detect the individual features that make up a stimulus, such as the color, shape, size, and location of letters, but is required to bind those individual features together.* From this perspective, attention provides the "glue" necessary to bind features together, and illusory conjunctions occur when it is difficult for participants to pay full attention to the features that need to be glued together. For example, in the experiments we just considered, participants were required to process the digits that flanked the colored letters, thereby reducing attention to the letters and allowing illusory conjunctions to occur. When experimental conditions are changed so that participants can pay full attention to the colored letters, and they are able to correctly bind their features together, illusory conjunctions disappear (Treisman, 1998; Treisman & Schmidt, 1982).

The Role of the Parietal Lobe

The binding process makes use of feature information processed by structures within the ventral visual stream, the "what" pathway (Seymour et al., 2010; see Figure 4.9). But because binding involves linking together features processed in distinct parts of the ventral stream at a particular spatial location, it also depends critically on the parietal lobe in the dorsal stream, the "where" pathway (Robertson, 1999). For example, Treisman and others studied a man known as R.M., who had suffered strokes that destroyed both his left and right parietal lobes. Although many aspects of his visual function were intact, he had severe problems attending to spatially distinct objects. When presented with stimuli such as those in Figure 4.11, R.M. perceived an abnormally large number of illusory conjunctions, even when he was given as much as 10 seconds to look at the displays (Friedman-Hill, Robertson, & Treisman, 1995; Robertson, 2003). More recent studies of persons with similar brain injuries suggest that damage to the upper and posterior portions of the parietal lobe is likely to produce

ICONICA/GETTY IMAGES

We correctly combine features into unified objects. Thus, for example, we see that the young man is wearing a gray shirt and the young woman is wearing a red shirt.

Presented

(a)

1　　A　　X　　8

Reported

(b)

A　　X

Illusory conjunction

(c)

A　　T　　　　A　　X

Misreported letter　　　Misreported color

▲ Figure 4.11

ILLUSORY CONJUNCTIONS Illusory conjunctions occur when features such as color and shape are combined incorrectly. For example, when participants are shown a red *A* and a blue *X*, they sometimes report seeing a blue *A* and a red *X*. Other kinds of errors, such as a misreported letter (e.g., reporting *T* when no *T* was presented) or misreported color (reporting green when no green was presented) occur rarely, indicating that illusory conjunctions are not the result of guessing (based on Robertson, 2003).

illusory conjunction A perceptual mistake whereby the brain incorrectly combines features from multiple objects.

feature-integration theory The idea that focused attention is not required to detect the individual features that make up a stimulus but is required to bind those individual features together.

With only a quick glance, you recognize all these letters as G, but their varying sizes, shapes, angles, and orientations ought to make this recognition task difficult. What is it about the process of object recognition that allows us to perform this task effortlessly?

Our visual systems allow us to identify people as the same individuals even when they change such features as hairstyle and skin color. Despite the extreme changes in these two photos, you can probably tell that they both portray Johnny Depp.

perceptual constancy A perceptual principle stating that even as aspects of sensory signals change, perception remains consistent.

similar problems (Braet & Humphreys, 2009; McCrea, Buxbaum, & Coslett, 2006). These same parietal regions are activated in healthy individuals when they perform the kind of visual feature binding that persons with parietal lobe damage are unable to perform (Shafritz, Gore, & Marois, 2002), as well as when they search for conjunction features (Corbetta et al., 1995; Donner et al., 2002).

RECOGNIZING OBJECTS BY SIGHT

Take a quick look at the letters in the accompanying illustration. Even though they're quite different from each other, you probably effortlessly recognized all of them as examples of the letter G. Now consider the same kind of demonstration but using your best friend's face. Your friend might have long hair, but one day she decides to get it cut extremely short. Suppose one day your friend gets a dramatic new haircut—or adds glasses, hair dye, or a nose ring. Even though your friend now looks strikingly different, you still recognize that person with ease. Just like the variability in Gs, you somehow are able to extract the underlying features of the face that allow you to accurately identify your friend.

This thought exercise may seem trivial, but it's no small perceptual feat. If the visual system were somehow stumped each time a minor variation occurred in an object being perceived, the inefficiency of it all would be overwhelming. We'd have to process information effortfully just to perceive our friend as the same person from one meeting to another, not to mention laboring through the process of knowing when a G is really a G. In general, though, object recognition proceeds fairly smoothly, in large part due to the operation of the feature detectors we discussed earlier.

How do feature detectors help the visual system get from a spatial array of light hitting the eye to the accurate perception of an object in different circumstances, such as your friend's face? Some researchers argue for a *modular view*, that specialized brain areas, or modules, detect and represent faces or houses or even body parts. Using fMRI to examine visual processing in healthy young adults, researchers found a subregion in the temporal lobe that responds most strongly to faces compared with just about any other object category, whereas a nearby area responds most strongly to buildings and landscapes (Kanwisher, McDermott, & Chun, 1997). This view suggests we have not only feature detectors to aid in visual perception but also "face detectors," "building detectors," and possibly other types of neurons specialized for particular types of object perception (Downing et al., 2006; Kanwisher & Yovel, 2006). Other researchers argue for a more *distributed representation* of object categories. In this view, it is the pattern of activity across multiple brain regions that identifies any viewed object, including faces (Haxby et al., 2001). Each of these views explains some data better than the other one, and researchers continue to debate their relative merits (Duchaine & Yovel, 2015).

Another perspective on this issue is provided by experiments designed to measure precisely where seizures originate; these experiments have also provided insights on how single neurons in the human brain respond to objects and faces (Quiroga, 2016; Suthana & Fried, 2012). For example, in a study by Quiroga et al. (2005), electrodes were placed in the temporal lobes of people suffering from epilepsy. Then the volunteers were shown photographs of faces and objects as the researchers recorded their neural responses. The researchers found that neurons in the temporal lobe respond to specific objects viewed from multiple angles and to people wearing different clothing and facial expressions and photographed from various angles. In some cases, the neurons also respond to the words for these same objects. For example, a neuron that responded to photographs of the Sydney Opera House also responded when the words *Sydney Opera* were displayed, but not when the words *Eiffel Tower* were displayed.

Taken together, these experiments demonstrate the principle of **perceptual constancy:** *Even as aspects of sensory signals change, perception remains consistent.* Think back once again to our discussion of difference thresholds early in this chapter. Our perceptual systems are sensitive to relative differences in changing stimulation and make allowances for varying sensory input. This general principle helps explain why you still recognize your friend despite changes in hair color or style or the addition of facial jewelry. It's not as though your visual perceptual system responds to a change with, "Here's a new and unfamiliar face to perceive." Rather, it's as though it responds with, "Interesting . . . here's a deviation from the way this face usually looks." Perception is sensitive to changes in stimuli, but perceptual constancies allow us to notice the differences in the first place.

Principles of Perceptual Organization

Before object recognition can even kick in, the visual system must perform another important task: grouping the image regions that belong together into a representation of an object. The idea that we tend to perceive a unified, whole object rather than a collection of separate parts is the foundation of Gestalt psychology, which you read about in the Psychology: Evolution of a Science chapter. Gestalt principles characterize many aspects of human perception. Among the foremost are the Gestalt *perceptual grouping rules,* which govern how the features and regions of things fit together (Koffka, 1935). Here's a sampling:

▶ *Simplicity*: A basic rule in science is that the simplest explanation is usually the best so, when confronted with two or more possible interpretations of an object's shape, the visual system tends to select the simplest or most likely interpretation. In **FIGURE 4.12a** we see an arrow.

▶ *Closure:* We tend to fill in missing elements of a visual scene, allowing us to perceive edges that are separated by gaps as belonging to complete objects. In Figure 4.12b we see an arrow despite the gaps.

▶ *Continuity:* Edges or contours that have the same orientation have what the Gestalt psychologists called *good continuation*, and we tend to group them together perceptually. In Figure 4.12c we perceive two crossing lines instead of two V shapes.

▶ *Similarity:* Regions that are similar in color, lightness, shape, or texture are perceived as belonging to the same object. In Figure 4.12d we perceive three columns—a column of circles flanked by two columns of triangles.

▶ *Proximity:* Objects that are close together tend to be grouped together. In Figure 4.12e we perceive three groups or "clumps" of 5 or 6 dots each, not just 16 dots.

▶ *Common fate:* Elements of a visual image that move together are perceived as parts of a single moving object. In Figure 4.12f the series of flashing lights in the road sign are perceived as a moving arrowhead.

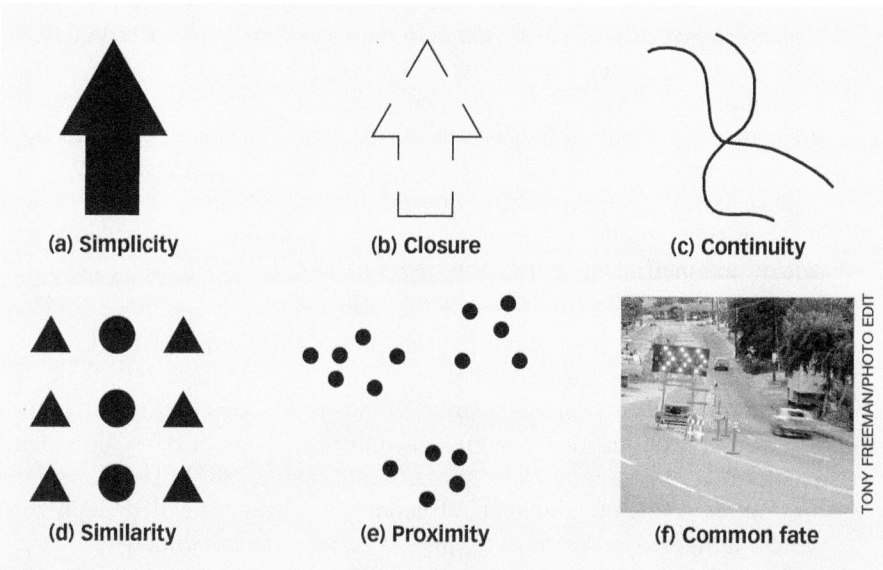

(a) Simplicity (b) Closure (c) Continuity

(d) Similarity (e) Proximity (f) Common fate

TONY FREEMAN/PHOTO EDIT

◀ Figure 4.12
PERCEPTUAL GROUPING RULES Principles first identified by Gestalt psychologists and now supported by experimental evidence demonstrate that the brain is predisposed to impose order on incoming sensations. One neural strategy for perception involves responding to patterns among stimuli and grouping like patterns together.

▲ Figure 4.13

AMBIGUOUS EDGES Here's how Rubin's classic reversible figure–ground illusion works: Fix your eyes on the center of the image. Your perception will alternate between a vase and facing silhouettes, even as the sensory stimulation remains constant.

Separating Figure From Ground

Perceptual grouping is a powerful aid to our ability to recognize objects by sight. Grouping involves visually separating an object from its surroundings. In Gestalt terms, this means identifying a *figure* apart from the (back)*ground* in which it resides. For example, you perceive the words on this page as figural: They stand out from the ground of the sheet of paper on which they're printed. Similarly, you perceive your instructor as the figure against the backdrop of all the other elements in your classroom. You certainly can perceive these elements differently, of course: The words *and* the paper are all part of a thing called *a page*, and your instructor *and* the classroom can all be perceived as *your learning environment*. Typically, though, our perceptual systems focus attention on some objects as distinct from their environments.

Size provides one clue to what's figure and what's ground: Smaller regions are likely to be figures, such as tiny letters on a big sheet of paper. Movement also helps: Your instructor is (we hope) a dynamic lecturer, moving around in a static environment. Another critical step toward object recognition is *edge assignment*. When we see an edge, or boundary, between figure and ground, which region does that edge belong to? If the edge belongs to the figure, it helps define the object's shape, and the background continues behind the edge. Sometimes, though, it's not easy to tell which is which.

Edgar Rubin (1886–1951), a Danish psychologist, capitalized on this ambiguity and developed a famous illusion called the *Rubin vase* or, more generally, a *reversible figure–ground relationship*. You can view this "face–vase" illusion in **FIGURE 4.13** in two ways, either as a vase on a black background or as a pair of silhouettes facing each other. Your visual system settles on one or the other interpretation and fluctuates between them every few seconds. This happens because the edge that would normally separate figure from ground is really part of neither: It equally defines the contours of the vase and the contours of the faces. Evidence from fMRIs shows, quite nicely, that when people are seeing the Rubin image as faces, there is greater activity in the face-selective region of the temporal lobe we discussed earlier than when they are seeing it as a vase (Hasson et al., 2001).

Theories of Object Recognition

Researchers have proposed two broad explanations of object recognition, one based on the object as a whole and the other on its parts.

> ▶ According to *image-based object recognition* theories, an object you have seen before is stored in memory as a **template,** *a mental representation that can be directly compared to a viewed shape in the retinal image* (Tarr & Vuong, 2002). Your memory compares the current retinal image with its templates and selects the template that most closely matches the current image. Image-based theories are widely accepted, yet they do not explain everything about object recognition. For one thing, correctly matching images to templates suggests that you'd have to have one template for cups in a normal orientation, another template for cups on their side, another for cups upside down, and so on. This makes for an unwieldy and inefficient system and therefore one that is unlikely to be effective, yet seeing a cup on its side rarely perplexes anyone for long.

> ▶ *Parts-based object recognition* theories propose instead that the brain deconstructs objects we see into a collection of parts (Marr & Nishihara, 1978). One important parts-based theory contends that objects are stored in memory as structural descriptions: mental inventories of object parts along with the spatial relations among those parts (Biederman, 1987). The parts inventories act as a sort of "alphabet" of geometric elements called *geons* that can be combined to make objects, just as letters are combined to form words

template A mental representation that can be directly compared with a viewed shape in the retinal image.

(a) Geons   **(b) Objects**

◄ Figure 4.14

AN ALPHABET OF GEOMETRIC ELEMENTS Parts-based theory holds that objects such as those shown in (b) are made up of simpler 3-D components called *geons*, shown in (a), much as letters combine to form different words.

(see **FIGURE 4.14**). Parts-based object recognition does not require a template for every view of every object, and so avoids some of the pitfalls of image-based theories. But parts-based object recognition does have major limitations. Most important, it allows for object recognition only at the level of categories and not at the level of the individual object. Parts-based theories offer an explanation for recognizing an object such as a face, for example, but are less effective at explaining how you distinguish between your best friend's face and a stranger's face.

Each set of theories has strengths and weaknesses, making object recognition an active area of study in psychology. Researchers are developing hybrid theories that attempt to exploit the strengths of each approach (Peissig & Tarr, 2007).

PERCEIVING DEPTH AND SIZE

Objects in the world are arranged in three dimensions—length, width, and depth—but the retinal image contains only two dimensions, length and width. How does the brain process a flat, 2-D retinal image so that we perceive the depth of an object and how far away it is? The answer lies in a collection of *depth cues* that change as you move through space. Monocular and binocular depth cues all help visual perception (Howard, 2002).

Monocular Depth Cues

Monocular depth cues are *aspects of a scene that yield information about depth when viewed with only one eye.* These cues rely on the relationship between distance and size. Even when you have one eye closed, the retinal image of an object you've focused on grows smaller as that object moves farther away, and larger as it moves closer. Our brains routinely use these differences in retinal image size, or *relative size,* to perceive distance.

This works particularly well in a monocular depth cue called *familiar size.* Most adults, for example, fall within a familiar range of heights (perhaps 5–7 feet tall), so retinal image size alone is usually a reliable cue to how far away they are. Our visual system automatically corrects for size differences and attributes them to differences in distance. **FIGURE 4.15** demonstrates how strong this mental correction for familiar size is.

monocular depth cues Aspects of a scene that yield information about depth when viewed with only one eye.

▶ Figure 4.15

FAMILIAR SIZE AND RELATIVE SIZE When you view images of people, such as the people in the left-hand photo, or of things you know well, the object you perceive as smaller appears farther away. With a little image manipulation, you can see in the right-hand photo that the relative size difference projected on your retinas is far greater than you perceive. The image of the person in the blue vest is exactly the same size in both photos.

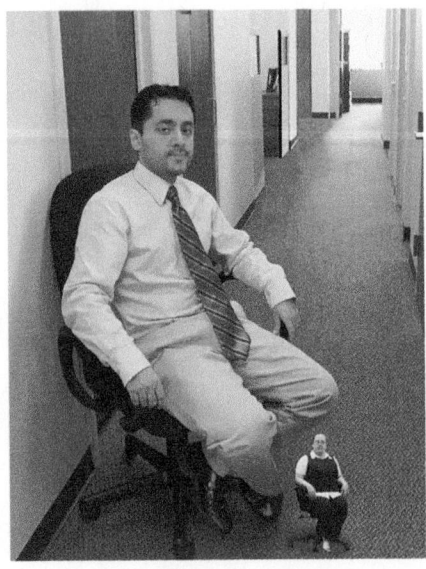

THE PHOTO WORKS

In addition to relative size and familiar size, there are several more monocular depth cues, such as:

▶ *Linear perspective,* which describes the phenomenon that parallel lines seem to converge as they recede into the distance (see **FIGURE 4.16a**).

▶ *Texture gradient,* which arises when you view a more or less uniformly patterned surface because the size of the pattern elements, as well as the distance between them, grows smaller as the surface recedes from the observer (see Figure 4.16b).

▶ *Interposition,* which occurs when one object partly blocks another (see Figure 4.16c). You can infer that the blocking object is closer than the block*ed* object. However, interposition by itself cannot provide information about how far apart the two objects are.

▶ Figure 4.16

PICTORIAL DEPTH CUES Visual artists rely on a variety of monocular cues to make their work come to life. You can rely on cues in an image such as linear perspective (a), texture gradient (b), interposition (c), and relative height (d) to infer distance, depth, and position, even if you're wearing an eye patch.

DC PRODUCTIONS-EXACTOSTOCK-1598

[a]

AGE FOTOSTOCK/AGE FOTOSTOCK

[b]

NPE-ED7-/ISTOCK/GETTY IMAGES PLUS

[c]

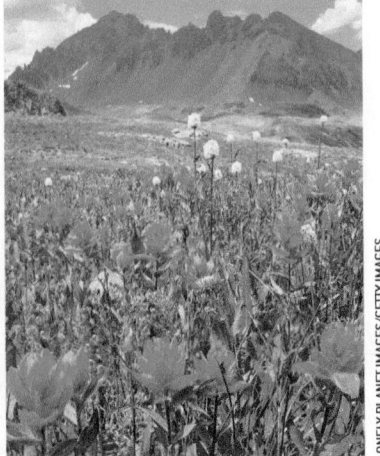

LONELY PLANET IMAGES/GETTY IMAGES

[d]

▶ *Relative height in the image* depends on your field of vision (see Figure 4.16d). Objects that are closer to you are lower in your visual field, whereas faraway objects are higher.

Binocular Depth Cues

We can also obtain depth information through **binocular disparity,** *the difference in the retinal images of the two eyes that provides information about depth.* Because our eyes are slightly separated, each registers a slightly different view of the world. Your brain computes the disparity between the two retinal images to perceive how far away objects are, as shown in **FIGURE 4.17.** Viewed from above in the figure, the images of the more distant square and the closer circle each fall at different points on each retina.

Binocular disparity as a cue to depth perception was first discussed by Sir Charles Wheatstone in 1838. Wheatstone went on to invent the stereoscope, essentially a holder for a pair of photographs or drawings taken from two horizontally displaced locations. (Wheatstone did not lack for original ideas; he also invented the accordion and an early telegraph and coined the term *microphone.*) When viewed, one by each eye, the pairs of images evoked a vivid sense of depth. The View-Master toy is the modern successor to Wheatstone's invention, and 3-D movies are based on this same idea.

Illusions of Depth and Size

We all are vulnerable to *illusions,* which, as you'll remember from the Psychology: Evolution of a Science chapter, are errors of perception, memory, or judgment in which subjective experience differs from objective reality (Wade, 2005). The relation between size and distance has been used to create elaborate illusions that depend on fooling the visual system about how far away objects are. All these illusions depend on the same principle: When you view two objects that project the same retinal image size, the object you perceive as farther away will be perceived as larger. One of the most famous illusions is the *Ames room,* constructed by the American ophthalmologist Adelbert Ames in 1946. The room is trapezoidal in shape rather than square: Only two sides are parallel (see **FIGURE 4.18a**). A person standing in one corner of an Ames room is physically twice as far away from the viewer as a person standing in the other corner. But when viewed with one eye through the small peephole placed in one wall, the Ames room looks square because the shapes of the windows and the flooring tiles are carefully crafted to *look* square from the viewing port (Ittelson, 1952).

The visual system perceives the far wall as perpendicular to the line of sight so that people standing at different positions along that wall appear to be at the same distance, and the viewer's judgments of their sizes are based directly on retinal image size. As a result, a person standing in the right corner appears to be much larger than a person standing in the left corner (see Figure 4.18b).

PERCEIVING MOTION AND CHANGE

You should now have a good sense of how we see what and where objects are, a process made substantially easier when the objects stay in one place. But real life, of course, is full of moving targets. Objects change position over time: Birds fly, and horses gallop; rain and snow fall; and trees bend in the wind. Understanding how we perceive motion and why we sometimes fail to perceive change can bring us closer to appreciating how visual perception works in everyday life.

Motion Perception

To sense motion, the visual system must encode information about both space and time. The simplest case to consider is an observer who does not move trying to perceive an object that does.

binocular disparity The difference in the retinal images of the two eyes that provides information about depth.

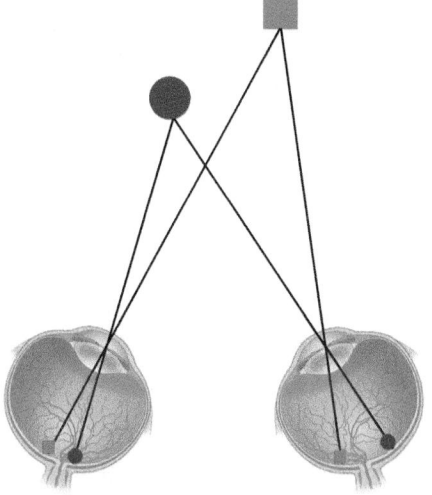

▲ Figure 4.17

BINOCULAR DISPARITY We see the world in three dimensions because our eyes are a distance apart, so the image of an object falls on a slightly different place on the retina of each eye. In this two-object scene, the images of the square and the circle fall on different points of the retina in each eye. The disparity in the positions of the circle's retinal images provides a compelling cue to depth.

The View-Master has been a popular toy for decades. It is based on the principle of binocular disparity: Two images taken from slightly different angles produce a stereoscopic effect.

▶ **Figure 4.18**

THE AMAZING AMES ROOM (a) A diagram showing the actual proportions of the Ames room reveals its secrets. The sides of the room form a trapezoid with parallel sides but a back wall that's way off square. The uneven floor makes the room's height in the far back corner shorter than the other. Add misleading cues such as specially designed windows and flooring and position the room's occupants in each far corner, and you're ready to lure an unsuspecting observer. (b) Looking into the Ames room through the viewing port with only one eye, the observer infers a normal size–distance relationship—that both people are the same distance away. But the different image sizes they project on the retina leads the viewer to conclude, from the monocular cue of familiar size, that one person is very small and the other is very large.

(a)   (b)

Color perception and motion perception both rely partially on opponent processing, which is why we fall prey to illusions such as color aftereffects and the waterfall illusion.

apparent motion The perception of movement as a result of alternating signals appearing in rapid succession in different locations.

As an object moves across a stationary observer's visual field, it first stimulates one location on the retina, and then a little later it stimulates another location on the retina. Neural circuits in the brain can detect this change in position over time and respond to specific speeds and directions of motion (Emerson, Bergen, & Adelson, 1992). A region in the middle of the temporal lobe referred to as *MT* (part of the dorsal stream we discussed earlier) is specialized for the visual perception of motion (Born & Bradley, 2005; Newsome & Paré, 1988), and brain damage in this area causes a deficit in normal motion perception (Zihl, von Cramon, & Mai, 1983).

Of course, in the real world, rarely are you a stationary observer. As you move around, your head and eyes move all the time, and motion perception is not so simple. The motion-perception system must take into account the position and movement of your eyes, and ultimately of your head and body, in order to perceive the motions of objects correctly and allow you to approach or avoid them. The brain accomplishes this by monitoring your eye and head movements and "subtracting" them from the motion in the retinal image.

Motion perception, like color perception, operates in part through opponent processes and is subject to sensory adaptation. A motion aftereffect called the *waterfall illusion* is analogous to color aftereffects. If you stare at the downward rush of a waterfall for several seconds, you'll experience an upward motion aftereffect when you then look at stationary objects near the waterfall, such as trees or rocks. What's going on here?

This process is similar to seeing green after staring at a patch of red. Motion-sensitive neurons are connected to motion detector cells in the brain that encode motion in opposite directions. A sense of motion comes from the difference in the strength of these two opposing sensors. If one set of motion detector cells is fatigued through adaptation to motion in one direction, then the opposing sensor will take over. The net result is that motion is perceived in the opposite direction. Evidence from fMRIs indicates that when people experience the waterfall illusion while viewing a stationary stimulus, there is increased activity in region MT, which plays a key role in motion perception (Tootell et al., 1995).

The movement of objects in the world is not the only event that can evoke the perception of motion. The successively flashing lights of a Las Vegas casino sign can evoke a strong sense of motion because people perceive a series of flashing lights as a whole, moving object (see Figure 4.12f). This *perception of movement as a result of alternating signals appearing in rapid succession in different locations* is called **apparent motion.**

Video technology and animation depend on apparent motion. Motion pictures flash 24 still frames per second (fps). A slower rate would produce a much choppier sense of motion; a faster rate would be a waste of resources because we would not perceive the motion as any smoother than it appears at 24 fps.

Change Blindness and Inattentional Blindness

Motion involves a change in an object's position over time, but objects in the visual environment can change in ways that do not involve motion (Rensink, 2002). You might walk

RESEARCH FROM SIMONS, D. J., & LEVIN, D. T. (1998). FAILURE TO DETECT CHANGES TO PEOPLE DURING A REAL-WORLD INTERACTION. *PSYCHONOMIC BULLETIN & REVIEW, 5(4)*, 644–649.

[a]   [b]   [c]

◄ **Figure 4.19**

CHANGE BLINDNESS The white-haired man was giving directions to one experimenter (a), who disappeared behind the moving door (b), only to be replaced by another experimenter (c). Like many other people, the man failed to detect a seemingly obvious change.

by the same clothing store window every day and notice when a new suit or dress is on display or register surprise when you see a friend's new haircut. Intuitively, we feel that we can easily detect changes to our visual environment. However, our comfortable intuitions have been challenged by experimental demonstrations of **change blindness,** which occurs *when people fail to detect changes to the visual details of a scene* (Rensink, 2002; Simons & Rensink, 2005). It is striking that change blindness occurs even when major details of a scene are changed—changes that we incorrectly believe that we could not miss (Beek, Levin, & Angelone, 2007). In a study that dramatically illustrates this idea, an experimenter asked a person on a college campus for directions (Simons & Levin, 1998). While they were talking, two men walked between them, holding a door that hid a second experimenter (see **FIGURE 4.19**). Behind the door, the two experimenters traded places, so that when the men carrying the door moved on, a different person was asking for directions than the one who had been there just a second or two earlier. In a remarkable finding, only 7 of 15 participants reported noticing this change.

Although it is surprising that people can be blind to such dramatic changes, these findings once again illustrate the importance of focused attention for visual perception (see the discussion of feature-integration theory, p. 141). Just as focused attention is critical for binding together the features of objects, it is also necessary for detecting changes to objects and scenes (Rensink, 2002; Simons & Rensink, 2005). Change blindness is most likely to occur when people fail to focus attention on the changed object (even though the visual system registers the object) and is least likely to occur for items that draw attention to themselves (Rensink, O'Regan, & Clark, 1997).

The role of focused attention in conscious visual experience is also dramatically illustrated by the closely related phenomenon of **inattentional blindness,** *a failure to perceive objects that are not the focus of attention.* Imagine the following scenario: You are watching a circle of people passing around a basketball, somebody dressed in a gorilla costume walks through the circle, and the gorilla stops to beat his chest before moving on. It seems inconceivable that you would fail to notice the gorilla, right? Think again. Simons and Chabris (1999) filmed such a scene, using two teams of three players each who passed the ball to each other as the costumed gorilla made his entrance and exit. Participants watched the film and were asked to track the movement of the ball by counting the number of passes made by one of the teams. With their attention focused on the moving ball, approximately half the participants failed to notice the chest-beating gorilla.

This result has interesting implications for a world in which many of us are busy texting and talking on our cell phones while carrying on other kinds of everyday business. We've already seen that using cell phones has negative effects on driving (see The Real World: Multitasking). Ira Hyman and colleagues (2010) asked whether cell phone use contributes to inattentional blindness in everyday life. They recruited a clown to ride a unicycle in the middle of a large square in the middle of the campus at Western Washington University. On a pleasant afternoon, the researchers asked 151 students who had just walked through the square whether they saw the clown. Seventy-five percent of the students who were using cell phones failed to notice the clown, compared with less than 50% who were not using cell phones. In a more recent study, Hyman, Sarb, and

change blindness Failure to detect changes to the visual details of a scene.

inattentional blindness A failure to perceive objects that are not the focus of attention.

HYMAN ET AL., 2009

College students who were using their cell phones while walking through campus failed to notice the unicycling clown more frequently than students who were not using their cell phones.

Hallucinations and the Visual System

We rely on our perceptual systems to provide reliable information about the world around us. Yet we've already seen that perception is susceptible to various kinds of illusions. Even more striking, our perceptual systems are capable of creating hallucinations: perceptions of sights, sounds, or other sensory experiences that don't exist in the world outside us. As discussed by the perceptual psychologist V. S. Ramachandran in an interview with the *New York Times*, reported in an article written by Susan Kruglinski, vivid visual hallucinations can occur in low-vision or even blind individuals with severe damage to their retinas.

One day a few years ago, Doris Stowens saw the monsters from Maurice Sendak's "Where the Wild Things Are" stomping into her bedroom. Then the creatures morphed into traditional Thai dancers with long brass fingernails, whose furious dance took them from the floor to the walls to the ceiling.

Although shocked to witness such a spectacle, Ms. Stowens, 85, was aware that she was having hallucinations, and she was certain that they had something to do with the fact that she suffered from the eye disease macular degeneration.

"I knew instantly that something was going on between my brain and my eyes," she said.

Ms. Stowens says that ever since she developed partial vision loss, she has been seeing pink walls and early American quilts floating through the blind spots in her eyes several times each week.

In fact, Ms. Stowens's hallucinations are a result of Charles Bonnet syndrome, a strange but relatively common disorder found in people who have vision problems. Because the overwhelming majority of people with vision problems are more than 70 years old, the syndrome, named after its 18th-century Swiss discoverer, is mostly found among the elderly. And because older people are more susceptible to cognitive deterioration, which can include hallucinations or delusions, Charles Bonnet (pronounced bon-NAY) is easily misdiagnosed as mental illness.

Many patients who have it never consult a doctor, out of fear that they will be labeled mentally ill.

"It is not a rare disorder," said Dr. V. S. Ramachandran, a neurologist at the University of California at San Diego, who has written about the syndrome. "It's quite common. It's just that people don't want to talk about it when they have it."

Researchers estimate that 10 to 15 percent of people whose eyesight is worse than 20/60 develop the disorder. Any eye disease that causes blind spots or low vision can be the source, including cataracts, glaucoma, diabetic retinopathy and, most commonly, macular degeneration. The hallucinations can vary from simple patches of color or patterns to lifelike images of people or landscapes to phantasms straight out of dreams. The hallucinations are usually brief and nonthreatening, and people who have the syndrome usually understand that what they are seeing is not real.

In some ways, researchers say, the hallucinations that define the syndrome are similar to the phenomenon of phantom limbs, where patients still vividly feel limbs that have been amputated, or phantom hearing, where a person hears music or other sounds while going deaf. In all three cases, the perceptions are caused by a loss of the sensory information that normally flows unceasingly into the brain.

In the case of sight, the primary visual cortex is responsible for taking in information, and also for forming remembered or imagined images. This dual function, Dr. Ramachandran and other experts say, suggests that normal vision is in fact a fusion of incoming sensory information with internally generated sensory input, the brain filling in the visual field with what it is used to seeing or expects to see. If you expect the person sitting next to you to be wearing a blue shirt, for example, you might, in a quick sideways glance, mistakenly perceive a red shirt as blue. A more direct gaze allows for more external information to correct the misperception.

"In a sense, we are all hallucinating all the time," Dr. Ramachandran said. "What we call normal vision is our selecting the hallucination that best fits reality."

With extensive vision loss, less external information is available to adjust and guide the brain's tendency to fill in sensory gaps. The results may be Thai dancers or monsters from a children's book.

Charles Bonnet syndrome was first described over 250 years ago by Bonnet, a Swiss scientist whose own blind grandfather experienced hallucinations like those reported by Ms. Stowens. However, neurologists and others have only recently begun to study the syndrome. Can you make some sense of this syndrome, applying what you have learned about the visual system? How can someone who sees poorly or who cannot see at all have intense visual experiences? What brain processes could be responsible for these kinds of visual hallucinations? Some clues come from neuroimaging studies of people who experience visual hallucinations. These studies have shown that specific types of hallucinations are accompanied by activity in parts of the brain responsible for the particular content of the hallucinations (Allen, Larøi, McGuire, & Aleman, 2008). For example, facial hallucinations are accompanied by activity in a part of the temporal lobe known to be involved in face processing. Our understanding of the visual system beyond the retina can provide some insight into how and why blind individuals experience visual hallucinations.

Wise-Swanson (2014) found that walkers using cell phones show reduced awareness of obstacles in their path and may even fail to notice a tree with money hanging from it! Using cell phones draws on focused attention, resulting in increased inattentional blindness and emphasizing again that our conscious experience of our visual environment is restricted to those features or objects selected by focused attention. In some extreme cases, conscious visual experience may reflect what we expect to see rather than what exists in the external world (see Other Voices: Hallucinations and the Visual System).

Build to the Outcomes

1. How does the study of illusory conjunctions help us understand the role of attention in feature binding?

2. How do we recognize our friends, even when they're hidden behind sunglasses?

3. What are the perceptual grouping rules for vision?

4. What does the face–vase illusion tell us about perceptual grouping?

5. What is an important difference between template and parts-based theory of object recognition?

6. How do monocular depth cues help us with depth perception?

7. What role does binocular disparity have in perceiving depth?

8. How can flashing lights on a casino sign give the impression of movement?

9. How can a failure of focused attention explain change blindness?

Audition: More Than Meets the Ear

Vision is based on the spatial pattern of light waves on the retina. The sense of hearing, by contrast, is all about *sound waves*: changes in air pressure unfolding over time. Plenty of things produce sound waves: the collision of a tree hitting the forest floor, the impact of two hands clapping, the vibration of vocal cords during a stirring speech, the resonance of a bass guitar string during a thrash metal concert. Understanding auditory experience requires understanding how we transform changes in air pressure into perceived sounds.

SENSING SOUND

Striking a tuning fork produces a *pure tone,* a simple sound wave that first increases air pressure and then creates a relative vacuum. This cycle repeats hundreds or thousands of times per second as sound waves travel outward in all directions from the source. Just as there are three dimensions of light waves corresponding to three dimensions of visual perception, so, too, there are three physical dimensions of a sound wave. Frequency, amplitude, and complexity determine what we hear as the pitch, loudness, and quality of a sound (see **TABLE 4.3**).

▶ The *frequency* of the sound wave, or its wavelength, depends on how often the peak in air pressure passes the ear or a microphone, measured in cycles per second, or hertz (Hz). Changes in the physical frequency of a sound wave are perceived by humans as changes in **pitch,** *how high or low a sound is.*

▶ The *amplitude* of a sound wave refers to its height, relative to the threshold for human hearing (which is set at zero decibels, or dBs). Amplitude corresponds to **loudness,** or *a sound's intensity.* To give you an idea of amplitude and intensity, the rustling of leaves in a soft breeze is about 20 dB, normal conversation is measured at about 40 dB, shouting produces 70 dB, a Slayer concert is about 130 dB, and the sound of the space shuttle taking off 1 mile away registers at 160 dB or more. That's loud enough to cause permanent damage to the auditory system and is well above the pain threshold; in fact, any sounds above 85 dB can be enough to cause hearing damage, depending on the length and type of exposure.

▶ Differences in the *complexity* of sound waves, or their mix of frequencies, correspond to **timbre,** *a listener's experience of sound quality or resonance.* Timbre (pronounced "TAM-ber") offers us information about the nature of sound. The

Learning Outcomes

▶ Relate the properties of a sound wave to how sound is perceived.

▶ Describe how the ear converts sound waves into neural impulses.

▶ Discuss how we perceive pitch.

▶ Compare the two main causes of hearing loss.

pitch How high or low a sound is.

loudness A sound's intensity.

timbre A listener's experience of sound quality or resonance.

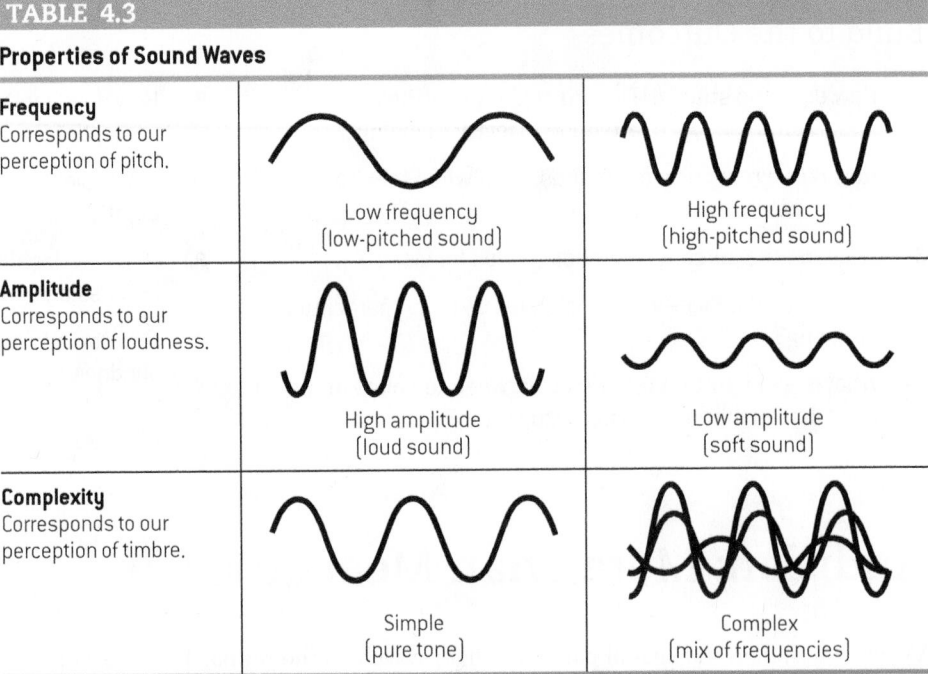

TABLE 4.3

Properties of Sound Waves

Frequency Corresponds to our perception of pitch.	Low frequency (low-pitched sound)	High frequency (high-pitched sound)
Amplitude Corresponds to our perception of loudness.	High amplitude (loud sound)	Low amplitude (soft sound)
Complexity Corresponds to our perception of timbre.	Simple (pure tone)	Complex (mix of frequencies)

same note played at the same loudness produces a perceptually different experience, depending on whether it was played on a flute or a trumpet, a phenomenon due entirely to timbre. Many natural sounds also illustrate the complexity of wavelengths, such as the sound of bees buzzing, the tonalities of speech, or the babbling of a brook. Unlike the purity of a tuning fork's hum, the drone of cicadas is a clamor of many different sound frequencies.

Most sounds—such as voices, music, the sound of wind in trees, the screech of brakes, the purring of a cat—are composed of not one, but many different frequency components. Although you perceive the mixture (the cat's purr, for example, not the 206 Hz component in the purr), the first thing the ear does to a sound is to break it down—to analyze it—into its separate component frequencies. The psychological attributes of pitch, loudness, and timbre are then built up by the brain from the separate frequency components that are represented in the inner ear, just as visual perceptions are built up from the spatial pattern of activity on the retina. The focus in our discussion of hearing, then, is on how the auditory system encodes and represents sound frequency (Kubovy, 1981).

How does the auditory system convert sound waves into neural signals? This process is very different from what happens in the visual system. This is not surprising, given that light is a form of electromagnetic radiation, whereas sound is a physical change in air pressure over time: Different forms of energy require different processes of transduction.

Having Two Ears Helps Us Localize Sound Sources

Just as the different positions of our eyes give us stereoscopic vision, the placement of our ears on opposite sides of the head gives us stereophonic hearing. The sound arriving at the ear closer to the sound source is louder than the sound in the farther ear, mainly because the listener's head partially blocks sound energy. This loudness difference decreases as the sound source moves from a position directly to one side (maximal difference) to straight ahead (no difference).

"The ringing in your ears—I think I can help."

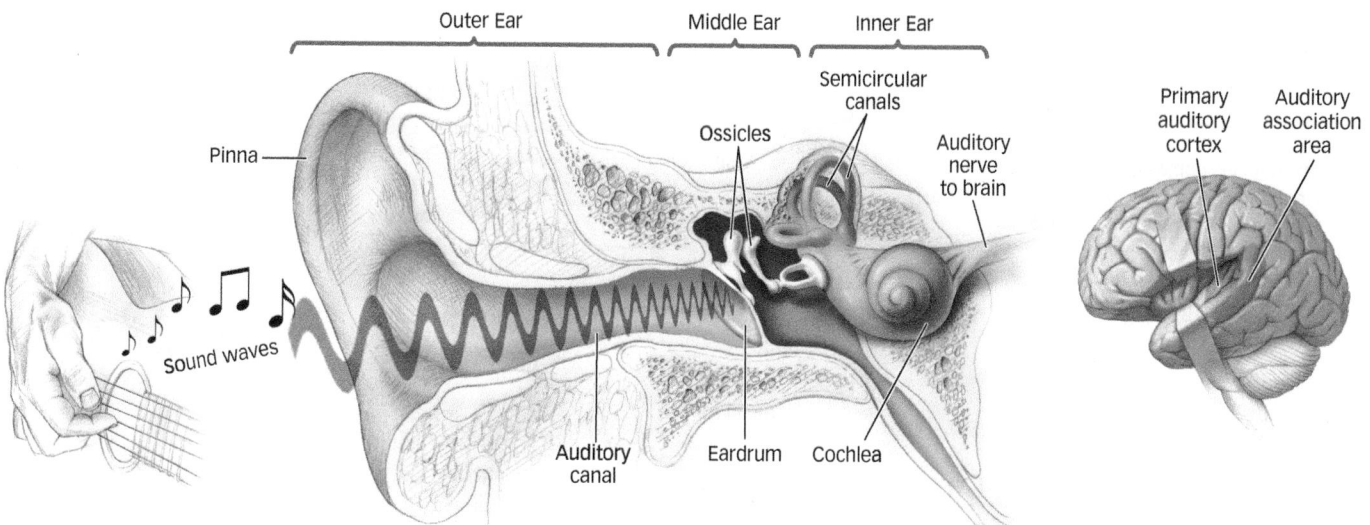

▲ Figure 4.20

ANATOMY OF THE HUMAN EAR The pinna funnels sound waves into the auditory canal, causing the eardrum to vibrate at a rate that corresponds to the sound's constituent frequencies. In the middle ear, the ossicles pick up the eardrum vibrations, amplify them, and pass them along, causing the vibration of a membrane at the surface of the fluid-filled cochlea in the inner ear. Here, fluid carries the wave energy to the auditory receptors that transduce it into electrochemical activity, exciting the neurons that form the auditory nerve, leading to the brain.

Another clue to a sound's location arises from timing: Sound waves arrive a little sooner at the near ear than at the far ear. The timing difference can be as brief as a few microseconds, but together with the intensity difference, it is sufficient to allow us to perceive the location of a sound. When the sound source is ambiguous, you may find yourself turning your head from side to side to localize it. By doing this, you are changing the relative intensity and timing of sound waves arriving in your ears and collecting better information about the likely source of the sound. Turning your head also allows you to use your eyes to locate the source of the sound—and your visual system is much better at pinpointing the location of things than your auditory system is.

The Outer Ear Funnels Sound Waves to the Middle Ear

The human ear is divided into three distinct parts, as shown **FIGURE 4.20.** The *outer ear* collects sound waves and funnels them toward the *middle ear,* which transmits the vibrations to the *inner ear,* embedded in the skull, where they are transduced into neural impulses.

The outer ear consists of the visible part on the outside of the head (called the *pinna*); the auditory canal; and the eardrum, an airtight flap of skin that vibrates in response to sound waves gathered by the pinna and channeled into the canal. The middle ear, a tiny, air-filled chamber behind the eardrum, contains the three smallest bones in the body, called *ossicles*. Named for their appearance as hammer, anvil, and stirrup, the ossicles fit together into a lever that mechanically transmits and intensifies vibrations from the eardrum to the inner ear.

Sound Is Converted Into Neural Impulses in the Inner Ear

The inner ear contains the spiral-shaped **cochlea** (Latin for "snail"), *a fluid-filled tube that is the organ of auditory transduction.* The cochlea is divided along its length by the **basilar membrane,** *a structure in the inner ear that undulates when vibrations from the ossicles reach the cochlear fluid* (see **FIGURE 4.21**). Its wavelike movement stimulates thousands of tiny **hair cells,** *specialized auditory receptor neurons embedded in the basilar membrane.* The hair cells then release neurotransmitter molecules, initiating a neural signal in the auditory nerve that travels to the brain. You might not want to think that the whispered "I love you" that sends chills up your spine got a kick start from lots of little hair cells wiggling around, but the mechanics of hearing are what they are!

cochlea A fluid-filled tube that is the organ of auditory transduction.

basilar membrane A structure in the inner ear that undulates when vibrations from the ossicles reach the cochlear fluid.

hair cells Specialized auditory receptor neurons embedded in the basilar membrane.

▶ Figure 4.21

AUDITORY TRANSDUCTION Inside the cochlea (shown here as though it were uncoiling), the basilar membrane undulates in response to wave energy in the cochlear fluid. Waves of differing frequencies ripple varying locations along the membrane, from low frequencies at its tip to high frequencies at the base, and bend the embedded hair cell receptors at those locations. The hair cell motion generates impulses in the auditory neurons, whose axons form the auditory nerve that emerges from the cochlea.

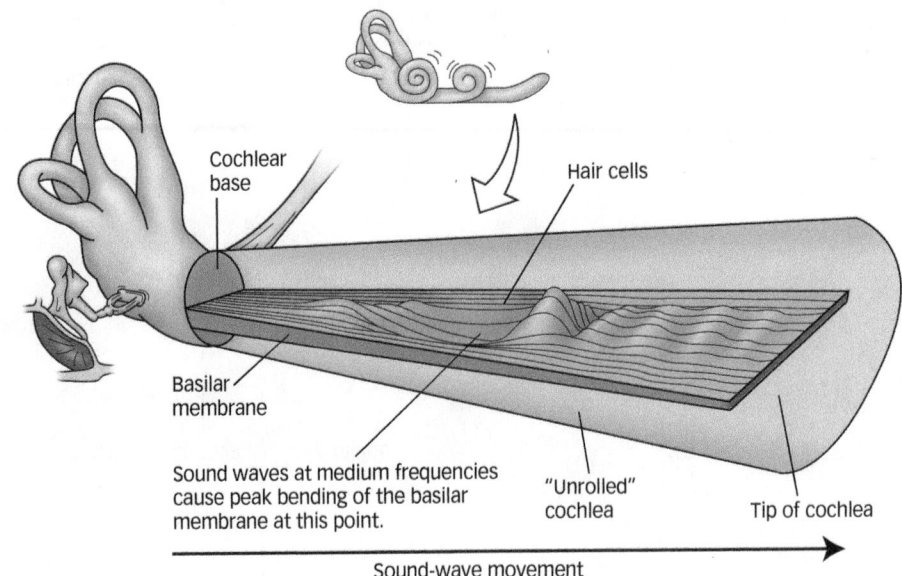

Cochlear base

Hair cells

Basilar membrane

Sound waves at medium frequencies cause peak bending of the basilar membrane at this point.

"Unrolled" cochlea

Tip of cochlea

Sound-wave movement

area A1 A portion of the temporal lobe that contains the primary auditory cortex.

The Auditory Nerve Carries the Neural Impulses to the Brain

From the inner ear, action potentials in the auditory nerve travel to the thalamus and ultimately to an area of the cerebral cortex called **area A1,** *a portion of the temporal lobe that contains the primary auditory cortex* (see **FIGURE 4.22**). For most of us, the auditory areas in the left hemisphere analyze sounds related to language, whereas those in the right hemisphere specialize in rhythmic sounds and music. There is also evidence that the auditory cortex is composed of two distinct streams, roughly analogous to the dorsal and ventral streams of the visual system. Spatial ("where") auditory features, which allow you to locate the source of a sound in space, are handled by areas toward the back (caudal) part of the auditory cortex. Nonspatial ("what") features, which allow you to identify the sound, are handled by areas in the lower (ventral) part of the auditory cortex (Recanzone & Sutter, 2008).

▶ Figure 4.22

PRIMARY AUDITORY CORTEX Area A1 is folded into the temporal lobe beneath the lateral fissure in each hemisphere. The left hemisphere auditory areas govern speech in most people. The Area A1 cortex has a topographic organization (*inset*), with lower frequencies mapping toward the front of the brain and higher frequencies toward the back, mirroring the organization of the basilar membrane along the cochlea (see Figure 4.21).

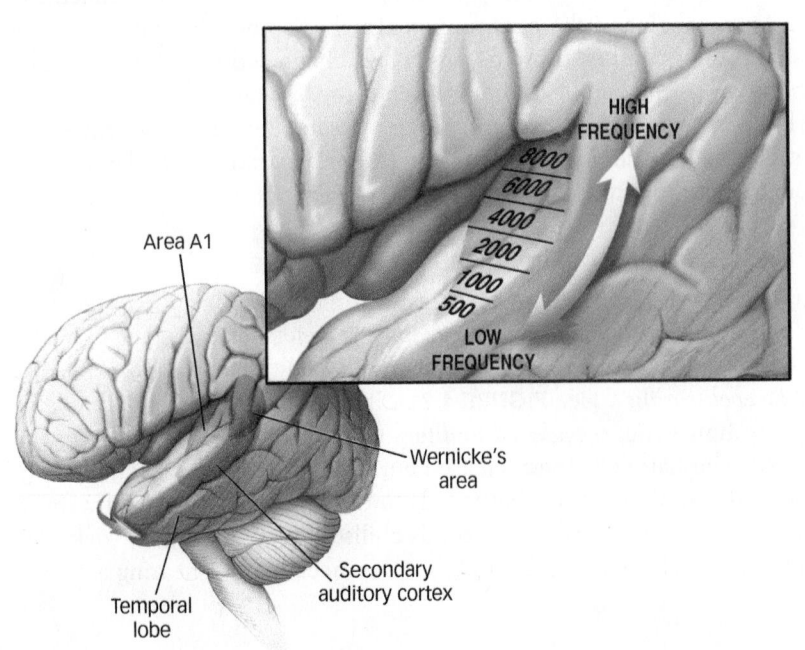

HIGH FREQUENCY

8000
6000
4000
2000
1000
500

LOW FREQUENCY

Area A1

Wernicke's area

Secondary auditory cortex

Temporal lobe

PERCEIVING PITCH

Neurons in area A1 respond well to simple tones, and successive auditory areas in the brain process sounds of increasing complexity (see Figure 4.22, inset; Rauschecker & Scott, 2009; Schreiner, Read, & Sutter, 2000; Schreiner & Winer, 2007). The human ear is most sensitive to frequencies around 1,000 to 3,500 Hz. But how is the frequency of a sound wave encoded in a neural signal? Our ears have evolved two mechanisms to encode sound-wave frequency, one for high frequencies and one for low frequencies.

▶ The **place code,** used mainly for high frequencies, refers to the process by which *different frequencies stimulate neural signals at specific places along the basilar membrane.* In a series of experiments carried out from the 1930s to the 1950s, the Nobel laureate Georg von Békésy (1899–1972) used a microscope to observe the basilar membrane in the inner ears of cadavers that had been donated for medical research (Békésy, 1960). Békésy found that the movement of the basilar membrane resembles a traveling wave (see Figure 4.21). The frequency of the stimulating sound determines the wave's shape. When the frequency is low, the wide, floppy tip (*apex*) of the basilar membrane moves the most; when the frequency is high, the narrow, stiff end (*base*) of the membrane moves the most. The movement of the basilar membrane causes hair cells to bend, initiating a neural signal in the auditory nerve. Axons fire the strongest in the hair cells along the area of the basilar membrane that moves the most, and the brain uses information about which axons are the most active to help determine the pitch you hear.

▶ A complementary process handles lower frequencies. A **temporal code** *registers relatively low frequencies (up to about 5000 Hz) via the firing rate of action potentials entering the auditory nerve.* Action potentials from the hair cells are synchronized in time with the peaks of the incoming sound waves (Johnson, 1980). If you imagine the rhythmic *boom-boom-boom* of a bass drum, you can probably also imagine the *fire-fire-fire* of action potentials corresponding to the beats. This process provides the brain with very precise information about pitch that supplements the information provided by the place code.

place code The process by which different frequencies stimulate neural signals at specific places along the basilar membrane, from which the brain determines pitch.

temporal code The process whereby the cochlea registers low frequencies via the firing rate of action potentials entering the auditory nerve.

HEARING LOSS

In broad terms, hearing loss has two main causes. *Conductive hearing loss* arises because the eardrum or ossicles are damaged to the point that they cannot conduct sound waves effectively to the cochlea. The cochlea itself, however, is normal, making this a kind of "mechanical problem" with the moving parts of the ear: the hammer, anvil, stirrup, or eardrum. In many cases, medication or surgery can correct the problem. Sound amplification from a hearing aid also can improve hearing through conduction via the bones around the ear directly to the cochlea.

Sensorineural hearing loss is caused by damage to the cochlea, the hair cells, or the auditory nerve, and it happens to almost all of us as we age. Sensorineural hearing loss can be heightened in people regularly exposed to high noise levels (such as rock musicians or jet mechanics). Simply amplifying the sound does not help, because the hair cells can no longer transduce sound waves. In these cases a *cochlear implant* may offer some relief.

A cochlear implant is an electronic device that replaces the function of the hair cells (Waltzman, 2006). The external parts of the device include a microphone and a speech processor, about the size of a USB key, worn behind the ear, and a small, flat, external transmitter that sits on the scalp behind the ear. The implanted parts include a receiver just inside the skull and a thin wire containing electrodes inserted into the cochlea to stimulate the auditory nerve. Sound picked up by the microphone is transformed into electric signals by the speech processor, which is essentially a small computer. The signal is transmitted to the implanted receiver, which activates the

A cochlear implant works when a microphone picks up sounds and sends them to a small speech-processing computer worn on the user's belt or behind the ear. The electric signals from the speech processor are transmitted to an implanted receiver, which sends the signals via electrodes to the cochlea, where the signals directly stimulate the auditory nerve.

HOT SCIENCE

Music Training: Worth the Time

Did you learn to play an instrument when you were younger? Maybe for you, music was its own reward (or maybe not). For anyone who practiced mostly to keep Mom and Dad happy, there's good news. Musical training has a range of benefits.

Let's start with the brain. Musicians have greater plasticity in the motor cortex, compared with nonmusicians (Rosenkranz et al., 2007); they have increased grey matter in motor and auditory brain regions, compared with nonmusicians (Gaser & Schlaug, 2003; Hannon & Trainor, 2007), and they show differences in brain responses to musical stimuli, compared with nonmusicians (Pantev et al., 1998). But musical training also extends to auditory processing in nonmusical domains (Kraus & Chandrasekaran, 2010). Musicians, for example, show enhanced brain responses when listening to speech compared with nonmusicians (Parbery-Clark et al., 2012). Musicians also exhibit an improved ability to detect speech when it is presented in a noisy background (Parbery-Clark, Skoe, & Kraus, 2009; Parbery-Clark et al., 2011)

Remembering to be careful not to confuse correlation with causation, you may ask: Do differences between musicians and nonmusicians reflect the effects of musical training? Or do they reflect individual differences, perhaps genetic ones, that lead some people to become musicians in the first place? Maybe people blessed with enhanced brain responses to musical or other auditory stimuli decide to become musicians *because* of their natural abilities. Several experiments support a causal role for musical training. One study demonstrated structural brain differences in auditory and motor areas of elementary schoolchildren after 15 months of musical training (learning to play piano), compared with children who did not receive musical training (Hyde et al., 2009). Another study compared two groups of 8-year-old children, one group with 6 months of musical training and the other with 6 months of painting training. Musical training produced changes in the brain's electrical responses to musical and speech stimuli, and those changes were correlated with enhanced performance on both musical and speech perception tasks (Moreno et al., 2009).

THINKSTOCK/ISTOCK/GETTY IMAGES

▲ The consistency of subcortical responses to speech sounds declined during the course of adolescence in the JROTC training group but not in the music training group (*left*), whereas the ability to process sounds in words showed greater increase in the music training group (*right*).

The foregoing benefits of musical training were observed in studies of elementary school students, but a recent experiment provides striking evidence that these benefits can be observed even in high school students, thus altering the course of auditory processing in adolescence. Tierney, Krizman, and Kraus (2015) compared two groups of students who were just beginning their first year of high school. One group participated in a music training program, whereas another received similar amounts of nonmusical training in a Junior Reserve Officers Training Corp (JROTC) program. Aside from these different training experiences, the high school curriculum was the same for the two groups. Before the training began, the researchers obtained several measures of auditory and language processing, and then reassessed those measures three years later, just before the students began their final year of high school.

The results showed clear effects of musical training. One of the main measures of interest was the brain's electrical response to auditory stimuli, which reflects activity in the primary auditory cortex (see Figure 4.22) as well as in subcortical auditory regions (i.e., the brainstem). The consistency of this response to speech sounds is increased in musicians compared with nonmusicians (Skoe & Kraus, 2013), but declines during adolescence (Skoe, Krizman, Anderson, & Kraus, 2015). As shown in the accompanying figure, this decline was observed in the JROTC training group, but not in the musical training group. The researchers also examined cognitive measures that probed participants' abilities to process sounds in words, known as phonological awareness, which typically increases during adolescence. As shown in the accompanying figure, phonological awareness increased to a greater extent during high school in the musical training group than the JROTC group.

We don't yet know all the reasons that musical training has such broad effects on auditory processing, but one likely contributor is that learning to play an instrument demands attention to precise details of sounds (Kraus & Chandrasekaran, 2010). Future studies will no doubt pinpoint additional factors, but the research to date leaves little room for doubt that your hours of practice were indeed worth the time.

electrodes in the cochlea. Cochlear implants are now in routine use and can improve hearing to the point that the wearer can understand speech.

Marked hearing loss is commonly experienced by people as they grow older, but is rare in an infant. However, infants who have not yet learned to speak are especially vulnerable, because they may miss the critical period for language learning (see the Learning chapter). Without auditory feedback during this time, normal speech is nearly impossible to achieve, but early use of cochlear implants has been associated with improved speech and language skills in deaf children (Hay-McCutcheon et al., 2008). Efforts are under way to introduce cochlear implants to children as young as 12 months old or even younger to maximize their chances of normal language development (DesJardin, Eisenberg, & Hodapp, 2006; Holman et al., 2013). (For research on the importance of music and brain development, see Hot Science: Music Training: Worth the Time).

Build to the Outcomes

1. What are the three properties of sound waves?

2. Why does one note sound so different on a flute and on a trumpet?

3. How do we determine the location of a sound?

4. What are the roles of the outer, middle, and inner parts of the ear in audition?

5. How do hair cells in the ear enable us to hear?

6. How does the frequency of a sound wave relate to what we hear?

7. In which type of hearing loss does sound amplification help?

8. What causes different types of hearing loss?

The Body Senses: More Than Skin Deep

Vision and audition provide information about the world at a distance. By responding to light and sound energy in the environment, these "distance" senses allow us to identify and locate the objects and people around us. In comparison, the body senses, also called *somatosenses* (*soma* from the Greek for "body"), are up close and personal. **Haptic perception** is the *active exploration of the environment by touching and grasping objects with our hands*. We use sensory receptors in our muscles, tendons, and joints as well as a variety of receptors in our skin to get a feel for the world around us (see **FIGURE 4.23**).

Learning Outcomes

▶ Describe how touch receptors transmit messages to the brain.

▶ Discuss why pain is both a physical and psychological perception.

▶ Explain how we use various senses to keep our balance.

haptic perception The active exploration of the environment by touching and grasping objects with our hands.

Somatosensory cortex

Skin surface

Texture and pattern receptors

Pain receptor (free nerve endings)

Pressure receptor

Low-frequency vibrating receptor

Duct of sweat gland

Fat cells

High-frequency vibrator receptor

◀ Figure 4.23

TOUCH RECEPTORS Specialized sensory neurons form distinct groups of haptic receptors that detect pressure, temperature, and vibrations against the skin. Touch receptors respond to stimulation within their receptive fields, and their long axons enter the brain via the spinal or cranial nerves. Pain receptors populate all body tissues that feel pain; they are distributed around bones and within muscles and internal organs as well as under the skin surface. Sensory signals on the body travel to the somatosensory cortex.

This rather unimposing geodesic dome sits on the floor of the Exploratorium, a world-renowned science museum in San Francisco. Called the Tactile Dome, it was created in 1971 by August Coppola (brother of the director Francis Ford Coppola and father of the actor Nicolas Cage) and Carl Day, who wanted to create an environment in which only haptic perception could be used. The inside of the dome is pitch black; visitors must crawl, wiggle, slide, and otherwise navigate the unfamiliar terrain using only their sense of touch. How would you feel being in that environment for an hour or so?

Be warned about your next shopping trip: Touching the merchandise can lead you to value it more highly than just looking at it.

SENSING TOUCH

Touch begins with the transduction of skin sensations into neural signals. Receptors located under the skin's surface enable us to sense pain, pressure, texture, pattern, or vibration against the skin (see Figure 4.23). The receptive fields of these specialized cells work together to provide a rich tactile (from Latin, "to touch") experience when you explore an object by feeling it or attempting to grasp it. In addition, *thermoreceptors,* nerve fibers that sense cold and warmth, respond when your skin temperature changes. All these sensations blend seamlessly together in perception, of course, but detailed physiological studies have successfully isolated the parts of the touch system (Hollins, 2010; Johnson, 2002).

There are three important principles regarding the neural representation of the body's surface. First, the left half of the body is represented in the right half of the brain and vice versa. Second, just as more of the visual brain is devoted to foveal vision, where acuity is greatest, more of the tactile brain is devoted to parts of the skin surface where sensitivity to small spatial differences is greatest. Regions such as the fingertips and lips are very good at discriminating fine spatial detail, whereas areas such as the lower back are quite poor at that task. Refer back to Figure 3.16 in the Neuroscience and Behavior chapter; you'll recall that different locations on the body project sensory signals to different locations in the somatosensory cortex in the parietal lobe. Third, there is mounting evidence for a distinction between "what" and "where" pathways in touch analogous to similar distinctions we've already considered for vision and audition. The "what" system for touch provides information about the properties of surfaces and objects; the "where" system provides information about a location in external space that is being touched or a location on the body that is being stimulated—(Lederman & Klatzky, 2009). Evidence from fMRI suggests that the "what" and "where" touch pathways involve areas in the lower and upper parts of the parietal lobe, respectively (Reed, Klatzky, & Halgren, 2005).

Touch information is not all biological. It also can have a powerful effect on our decisions and judgments. For example, recent research has shown that merely touching an object that we don't already own can increase our feeling of ownership and lead us to value the object more highly than when we view it but don't touch it (Peck & Shu, 2009); the longer we touch an object, the more highly we value it (Wolf, Arkes, & Muhanna, 2008). You might keep this "mere touch" effect in mind next time you are in a shop and considering buying an expensive item. Retailers are probably aware of this effect: During the 2003 holiday shopping season the office of the Illinois state attorney general warned shoppers to be cautious in stores that encouraged them to touch the merchandise (Peck & Shu, 2009).

SENSING PAIN

Does the possibility of a life free from pain seem appealing? Although pain is arguably the least pleasant of sensations, this aspect of touch is among the most important for survival: Pain indicates damage or potential damage to the body. Without the ability to feel pain, we might ignore infections, broken bones, or serious burns. Congenital insensitivity to pain, a rare inherited disorder that specifically impairs pain perception, is more of a curse than a blessing: Children who experience this disorder often mutilate themselves (e.g., biting into their tongues or gouging their skin while scratching) and are at increased risk of dying during childhood (Nagasako, Oaklander, & Dworkin, 2003).

Tissue damage is transduced by pain receptors, the free nerve endings shown in Figure 4.23. In addition, researchers have distinguished between fast-acting *A-delta fibers,* which transmit the initial sharp pain one might feel right away from a sudden

Emotional/Motivational ■
Sensory/Discriminative ■

Spinal cord (section)

◄ Figure 4.24
PAIN TRAVELS TWO PATHWAYS
Neural signals for pain travel two pathways: one to the somatosensory cortex, where the location and type of pain are determined; the other to the motivational and emotional centers of the brain.

injury, and slower C *fibers,* which transmit the longer-lasting, duller pain that persists after the initial injury. If you were running barefoot outside and stubbed your toe against a rock, you would first feel a sudden stinging pain transmitted by A-delta fibers that would die down quickly, only to be replaced by the throbbing but longer-lasting pain carried by C fibers. Both the A-delta and C fibers are impaired in cases of congenital insensitivity to pain, which is one reason that this disorder can be life threatening.

PERCEIVING PAIN

As you'll remember from the chapter on Neuroscience and Behavior, the pain-withdrawal reflex is coordinated by the spinal cord. No brainpower is required when you touch a hot stove; you retract your hand almost instantaneously. But neural signals for pain—such as wrenching your elbow as you brace yourself from falling—travel to two distinct areas in the brain and evoke two distinct psychological experiences (see **FIGURE 4.24;** Treede et al., 1999). One pain pathway sends signals to the so-matosensory cortex, identifying where the pain is occurring and what sort of pain it is (sharp, burning, dull). The second pain pathway sends signals to the motivational and

referred pain Feeling of pain when sensory information from internal and external areas converges on the same nerve cells in the spinal cord.

gate-control theory of pain A theory of pain perception based on the idea that signals arriving from pain receptors in the body can be stopped, or *gated*, by interneurons in the spinal cord via feedback from two directions.

emotional centers of the brain, such as the hypothalamus and amygdala, and to the frontal lobe. This is the aspect of pain that is unpleasant and motivates us to escape from or relieve the pain.

Pain typically feels as if it comes from the site of the tissue damage that caused it. If you burn your finger, you will perceive the pain as originating there. But we have pain receptors in many areas besides the skin: around bones and within muscles and internal organs as well. When pain originates internally, in a body organ, for example, we actually feel it on the surface of the body. This kind of **referred pain** occurs when *sensory information from internal and external areas converges on the same nerve cells in the spinal cord*. One common example is a heart attack: Victims often feel pain radiating from the left arm rather than from inside the chest.

Pain intensity cannot always be predicted solely from the extent of the injury that causes the pain (Keefe, Abernathy, & Campbell, 2005). For example, *turf toe* sounds like the mildest of ailments; it is pain at the base of the big toe as a result of bending or pushing off repeatedly, as a runner or football player might do during a sporting event. This small-sounding injury in a small area of the body can nonetheless sideline an athlete for a month with considerable pain. On the other hand, you've probably heard a story or two about someone treading bone-chilling water for hours on end, or dragging their shattered legs a mile down a country road to seek help after a tractor accident, or performing some other incredible feat despite searing pain and extensive tissue damage. Pain type and pain intensity show a less-than-perfect correlation, a fact that has researchers intrigued.

Some recent evidence indicates that subjective pain intensity may differ among ethnic groups (Campbell & Edwards, 2012). For example, a study that examined responses to various kinds of experimentally induced pain, including heat pain and cold pain, found that compared with White young adults, African American young adults had a lower tolerance for several kinds of pain and rated the same pain stimuli as more intense and unpleasant (Campbell, Edwards, & Fillingim, 2005).

One influential account of pain perception is known as **gate-control theory of pain,** which holds that *signals arriving from pain receptors in the body can be stopped, or gated, by interneurons in the spinal cord via feedback from two directions* (Melzack & Wall, 1965). Pain can be gated by the skin receptors, for example, by rubbing the affected area. Rubbing your stubbed toe activates neurons that "close the gate" to stop pain signals from traveling to the brain. Pain can also be gated from the brain by modulating the activity of pain-transmission neurons. This neural feedback is elicited not by the pain itself but rather by activity deep within the thalamus.

The neural feedback comes from a region in the midbrain called the *periaqueductal gray* (PAG). Under extreme conditions, such as high stress, naturally occurring endorphins can activate the PAG to send inhibitory signals to neurons in the spinal cord that then suppress pain signals to the brain, thereby modulating the experience of pain. The PAG also responds to the action of opiate drugs, such as morphine.

A different kind of feedback signal can *increase* the sensation of pain. This system is activated by events such as infection and learned danger signals. When we are quite ill, what we otherwise might experience as mild discomfort can feel quite painful. This pain facilitation signal presumably evolved to motivate people who are ill to rest and avoid strenuous activity, allowing their energy to be devoted to healing.

Although some details of the gate-control theory of pain have been challenged, a key concept underlying the theory—that perception is a two-way street—has broad implications. The senses feed information such as pain sensations to the brain, a pattern that perceptual psychologists term *bottom-up control*. The brain processes these sensory data into perceptual information at successive levels to support movement, object recognition, and eventually more complex cognitive tasks, such as memory and planning. But there is ample evidence that the brain exerts plenty of control over what we sense as well. Visual illusions and the gestalt principles of filling in, shaping up, and rounding out what isn't really there provide some examples. This kind of *top-down control* also explains how the brain influences the experience of touch and pain (Kucyi & Davis, 2015; Wager & Atlas, 2013).

BODY POSITION, MOVEMENT, AND BALANCE

It may sound odd, but one aspect of sensation and perception is knowing where parts of your body are at any given moment. Your body needs some way to sense its position in physical space other than moving your eyes constantly to see the location of your limbs. Sensations related to position, movement, and balance depend on stimulation produced within our bodies. Receptors in the muscles, tendons, and joints signal the position of the body in space, whereas information about balance and head movement originates in the inner ear.

Sensory receptors provide the information we need to perceive the position and movement of our limbs, head, and body. These receptors also provide feedback about whether we are performing a desired movement correctly and how resistance from held objects may be influencing the movement. For example, when you swing a baseball bat, the weight of the bat affects how your muscles move your arm as well as the change in sensation when the bat hits the ball. You can use muscle, joint, and tendon feedback about how your arms actually moved to improve performance through learning.

Maintaining balance depends primarily on the **vestibular system,** *the three fluid-filled semicircular canals and adjacent organs located next to the cochlea in each inner ear* (see Figure 4.20). The semicircular canals are arranged in three perpendicular orientations and studded with hair cells that detect movement of the fluid when the head moves or accelerates. The bending of the hair cells generates activity in the vestibular nerve that is then conveyed to the brain. This detected motion enables us to maintain our balance, or the position of our bodies relative to gravity (Lackner & DiZio, 2005).

Vision also helps us keep our balance. If you see that you are swaying relative to a vertical orientation, such as the contours of a room, you move your legs and feet to keep from falling over. Psychologists have experimented with this visual aspect of balance by placing people in rooms that can be tilted forward and backward (Bertenthal, Rose, & Bai, 1997; Lee & Aronson, 1974). If the room tilts enough, people—particularly small children—will topple over as they try to compensate for what their visual system is telling them. When a mismatch between the information provided by visual cues and vestibular feedback occurs, motion sickness can result. Remember this discrepancy the next time you try reading in the back seat of a moving car!

RICK RYCROFT/AP IMAGES

Hitting a ball with a bat or racquet provides feedback about where your arms and body are in space, as well as how the resistance of these objects affects your movement and balance. Successful athletes, such as Serena Williams, have particularly well-developed body senses.

vestibular system The three fluid-filled semicircular canals and adjacent organs located next to the cochlea in the inner ear.

Build to the Outcomes

1. What is the difference between the "distance" senses and the somatosenses?

2. Why might discriminating spatial detail be important for fingertips and lips?

3. What is the role of the various parts of the skin in touch and pain?

4. Why does rubbing an injured area sometimes help alleviate pain?

5. What is the vestibular system?

6. Why is it so hard to stand on one foot with your eyes closed?

The Chemical Senses: Adding Flavor

Learning Outcomes

▶ Describe how odorant molecules are converted into neural impulses in the roof of the nose.

▶ Explain the importance of smell in personal and social experiences.

▶ Describe how taste sensations are converted into neural impulses by the tongue.

▶ Explain the importance of taste in personal and social experiences.

Somatosensation is all about physical changes in or on the body: Vision and audition sense energetic states of the world—light and sound waves—and touch is activated by physical changes in or on the body surface. The last set of senses we'll consider share a chemical basis to combine aspects of distance and proximity. The chemical senses of *olfaction* (smell) and *gustation* (taste) respond to the molecular structure of substances floating into the nasal cavity as you inhale or dissolving in saliva. Smell and taste combine to produce the perceptual experience we call *flavor*.

SENSE OF SMELL

Olfaction is the least understood sense and the only one directly connected to the forebrain, with pathways into the frontal lobe, amygdala, and other forebrain structures. (Recall from the Neuroscience and Behavior chapter that the other senses connect first to the thalamus.) This mapping indicates that smell has a close relationship with areas involved in emotional and social behavior. Smell seems to have evolved in animals as a signaling sense for the familiar: a friendly creature, an edible food, or a sexually receptive mate.

Countless substances release odors into the air, and some of their *odorant molecules* make their way into our noses, drifting in on the air we breathe. Situated along the top of the nasal cavity shown in **FIGURE 4.25** is a mucous membrane called the *olfactory epithelium*, which contains about 10 million **olfactory receptor neurons (ORNs)**, *receptor cells that initiate the sense of smell*. Odorant molecules bind to sites on these specialized receptors, and if enough bindings occur, the ORNs send neural impulses into the olfactory nerve (Dalton, 2003).

olfactory receptor neurons (ORNs) Receptor cells that initiate the sense of smell.

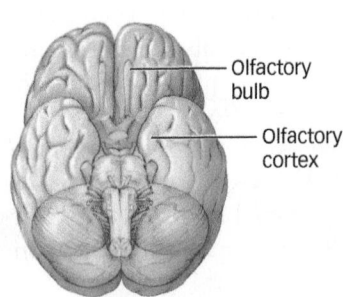

◀ Figure 4.25

ANATOMY OF SMELL Along the roof of the nasal cavity, odorant molecules dissolve in the mucous membrane that forms the olfactory epithelium. Odorants may then bind to olfactory receptor neurons (ORNs) embedded in the epithelium. ORNs respond to a range of odors. Once activated, they relay action potentials to their associated glomeruli in the olfactory bulb, located just beneath the frontal lobes. The glomeruli form synapses on neurons whose axons form the olfactory nerve, which projects directly into the forebrain.

Each olfactory neuron has receptors that bind to some odorants but not to others, as if the receptor is a lock and the odorant is the key (see Figure 4.25). Groups of ORNs send their axons from the olfactory epithelium into the **olfactory bulb,** *a brain structure located above the nasal cavity beneath the frontal lobes*. Humans possess about 350 different ORN types that permit us to discriminate among some 10,000 different odorants through the unique patterns of neural activity each odorant evokes. This setup is similar to our ability to see a vast range of colors through only a small number of retinal receptor cell types or to feel a range of skin sensations through only a handful of touch-receptor cell types.

Some dogs have as many as 100 times more ORNs than humans do; they have a correspondingly sharpened ability to detect and discriminate among millions of odors. Nevertheless, humans are sensitive to the smells of some substances in extremely small concentrations. For example, we can sense a chemical compound that is added to natural gas to help detect gas leaks at a concentration of just 0.0003 part per million. By contrast, acetone (nail polish remover), something most people regard as pungent, can be detected only if its concentration is 15 parts per million or greater.

PERCEIVING SMELL

The olfactory bulb sends outputs to various centers in the brain, including the parts that are responsible for controlling basic drives, emotions, and memories. Odor perception includes both information about the identity of an odor, which involves relating olfactory inputs to information stored in memory (Stevenson & Boakes, 2003), as well as our emotional response to whether it is pleasant or unpleasant (Khan et al., 2007). Which of these processes occurs first? When you walk into a house and encounter the wonderful smell of freshly baked chocolate chip cookies, does your positive emotional response come before you identify the smell or vice versa? According to the *object-centered approach*, information about the identity of the "odor object" is quickly retrieved from memory and then triggers an emotional response (Stevenson & Wilson, 2007). According to the *valence-centered approach*, the emotional response comes first and provides a basis for determining the identity of the odor (Yeshurun & Sobel, 2010). Recent attempts to distinguish between these two views support the idea that odor perception is guided first by memory and then by emotion (Olofsson et al., 2012).

The relationship between smell and emotion explains why smells can have immediate, strongly positive or negative effects on us. If the slightest whiff of an apple pie baking brings back fond memories of childhood, or if the unexpected sniff of vomit mentally returns you to a particularly bad party you once attended, you've got the idea. Fortunately, sensory adaptation is at work when it comes to smell, just as it is with the other senses. Whether the associations are good or bad, after just a few minutes the smell fades. Smell adaptation makes sense: It allows us to detect new odors that may require us to act, but after that initial evaluation has occurred, it may be best to reduce our sensitivity to allow us to detect other smells.

Our experience of smell is determined not only by bottom-up influences, such as odorant molecules binding to sites on ORNs, but also by top-down influences, such as our previous experiences with an odor (Gottfried, 2008; Rolls, 2015). Consistent with this idea, people rate the identical odor as more pleasant when it is paired with an appealing verbal label such as *cheddar cheese* rather than an unappealing one such as *body odor* (de Araujo et al., 2005; Herz & von Clef, 2001). fMRI evidence indicates that brain regions involved in coding the pleasantness of an experience, such as the orbitofrontal cortex, respond more strongly to the identical odor when people think it is cheddar cheese than when they think it is a body odor (de Araujo et al., 2005).

Smell may also play a role in social behavior. Humans and other animals can detect odors from **pheromones,** *biochemical odorants emitted by other members of its species*

olfactory bulb A brain structure located above the nasal cavity beneath the frontal lobes.

pheromones Biochemical odorants emitted by other members of its species that can affect an animal's behavior or physiology.

Taste and smell both contribute to what we perceive as flavor. This is why smelling the bouquet of a wine is an essential part of the wine-tasting ritual. The experience of wine tasting is also influenced by cognitive factors, such as knowledge of a wine's price.

ADAM GREGOR/SHUTTERSTOCK

▶ Figure 4.26

SMELL AND SOCIAL BEHAVIOR In a PET study, heterosexual women, homosexual men, and heterosexual men were scanned as they were presented with each of several odors. During the presentation of a testosterone-based odor (referred to in the figure as AND), there was significant activation in the hypothalamus for heterosexual women (*left*) and homosexual men (*center*) but not for (*right*) heterosexual men (Savic et al., 2005).

Heterosexual women   Homosexual men   Heterosexual men

AND

Hypothalamus

IVANKA SAVIC, HA BERGLUND, AND PER LINDSTROM. PNAS 2005 102 (20) 7356—7361. NATIONAL ACADEMY OF SCIENCES, USA.

that can affect the animal's behavior or physiology. Parents can distinguish the smell of their own children from that of other people's children. An infant can identify the smell of its mother's breast as opposed to the smell of other mothers. Pheromones also play a role in reproductive behavior in insects and in several mammalian species, including mice, dogs, and primates (Brennan & Zufall, 2006). Can the same thing be said of human reproductive behavior?

Studies of people's preference for the odors of individuals of the opposite sex have produced mixed results, with no consistent tendency for people to prefer them over other pleasant odors. Recent research, however, has provided a link between sexual orientation and responses to odors that may constitute human pheromones. Researchers used positron emission tomography (PET) scans to study the brain's response to two odors, one related to testosterone, which is produced in men's sweat, and the other related to estrogen, which is found in women's urine. The testosterone-based odor activated the hypothalamus (a part of the brain that controls sexual behavior; see the Neuroscience and Behavior chapter) in heterosexual women but not in heterosexual men, whereas the estrogen-based odor activated the hypothalamus in heterosexual men but not in women. In a striking finding, homosexual men responded to the two chemicals in the same way as women did: The hypothalamus was activated by the testosterone- but not estrogen-based odor (Savic, Berglund, & Lindstrom, 2005; see **FIGURE 4.26**). Other common odors unrelated to sexual arousal were processed similarly by all three groups. A follow-up study with lesbian women showed that their responses to the testosterone- and estrogen-based odors were largely similar to those of heterosexual men (Berglund, Lindstrom, & Savic, 2006). Taken together, the two studies suggest that some human pheromones are related to sexual orientation.

SENSE OF TASTE

One of the primary responsibilities of the chemical sense of taste is identifying things that are bad for you—as in poisonous and lethal. Many poisons are bitter, and we avoid eating things that nauseate us for good reason, so taste aversions have a clear adaptive significance. Some aspects of taste perception are genetic, such as an aversion to extreme bitterness, and some are learned, such as an aversion to a particular food that once caused nausea. In either case, the direct contact between the tongue and possible foods allows us to anticipate whether something will be harmful or palatable.

The tongue is covered with thousands of small bumps, called *papillae,* which are easily visible to the naked eye. Within each papilla are hundreds of **taste buds,** *the organs of taste transduction* (see **FIGURE 4.27**). The mouth contains 5,000 to 10,000 taste buds fairly evenly distributed over the tongue, the roof of the mouth, and the upper throat (Bartoshuk & Beauchamp, 1994; Halpern, 2002). Each taste bud contains 50 to 100 taste receptor cells. Taste perception fades with age (Methven et al., 2012): On average, people lose half their taste receptors by the time they turn 20. This

taste buds The organ of taste transduction.

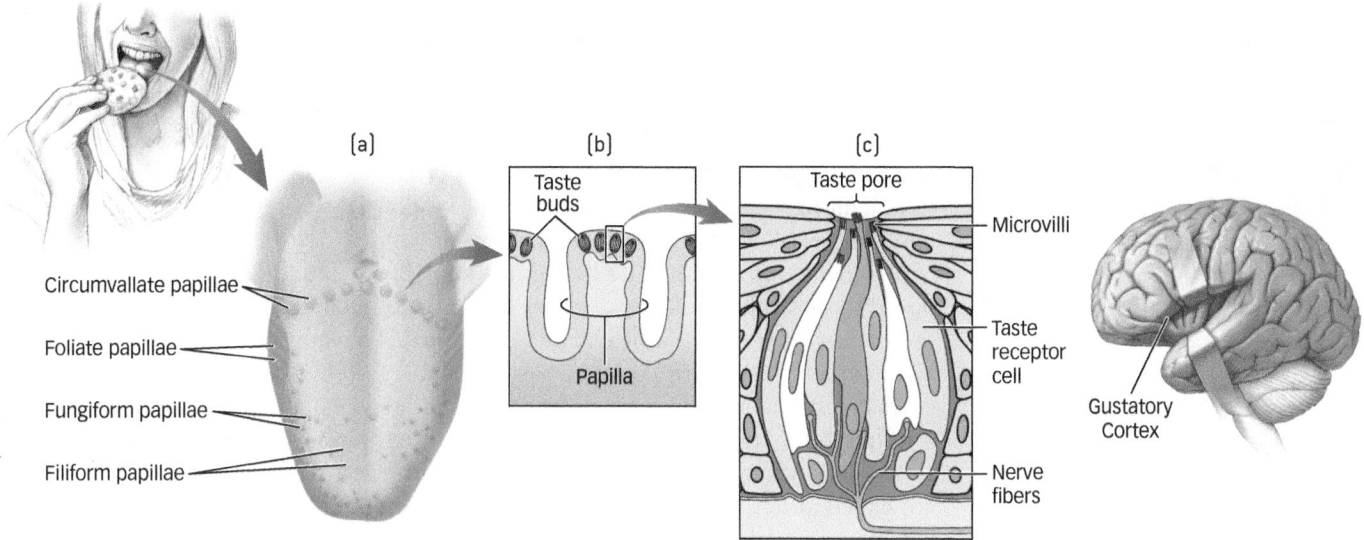

▲ Figure 4.27

A TASTE BUD (a) Taste buds stud the bumps (papillae) on the tongue, shown here, as well as the back, sides, and roof of the mouth. (b) Each taste bud contains a range of receptor cells that respond to varying chemical components of foods called *tastants*. (c) Tastant molecules dissolve in saliva and stimulate the microvilli that form the tips of the taste receptor cells. Each taste bud contacts the branch of a cranial nerve at its base.

may help to explain why young children seem to be "fussy eaters," since their greater number of taste buds brings with it a greater range of taste sensations.

The human eye contains millions of rods and cones, and the human nose contains some 350 different types of olfactory receptors, but the taste system contains just five main types of taste receptors, corresponding to five primary taste sensations: salt, sour, bitter, sweet, and *umami* (savory). The first four are quite familiar, but *umami* may not be. In fact, perception researchers are still debating its existence. The umami receptor was discovered by Japanese scientists who attributed it to the tastes evoked by foods containing a high concentration of protein, such as meats and cheeses (Yamaguchi, 1998). If you're a meat eater and you savor the feel of a steak topped with butter or a cheeseburger as it sits in your mouth, you've got an idea of the umami sensation.

Each taste bud contains several types of taste receptor cells whose tips, called *microvilli,* react with *tastant molecules* in food. Salt receptors are most strongly activated by sodium chloride (table salt). Sour receptor cells respond to acids, such as vinegar or lime juice. Bitter and sweet taste receptors are more complex. Some 50 to 80 distinct binding sites in bitter receptors are activated by an equal number of different bitter-tasting chemicals. Sweet receptor cells likewise can be activated by a wide range of substances in addition to sugars.

Although umami receptor cells are the least well understood, researchers are homing in on their key features (Chandrashekar et al., 2006). They respond most strongly to glutamate, an amino acid in many protein-containing foods. Recall from the Neuroscience and Behavior chapter that glutamate acts as a neurotransmitter; in fact, it's a major excitatory neurotransmitter. The food additive *monosodium glutamate (MSG),* which is often used to flavor Asian foods, particularly activates umami receptors. Some people develop headaches or allergic reactions after eating MSG.

Recent research suggests that there may be a sixth basic taste, fat, that is elicited by fatty acids and is distinct from the five primary taste sensations (Running, Craig, & Mattes, 2015). The researchers noted that the sensation people experience in response to fatty acids is not necessarily consistent with expectations of "fattiness," and so they proposed a new word for this taste sensation: *oleogustus*. (*Oleosus* is Latin for "fatty" or "oily," and *gustus* signifies "taste").

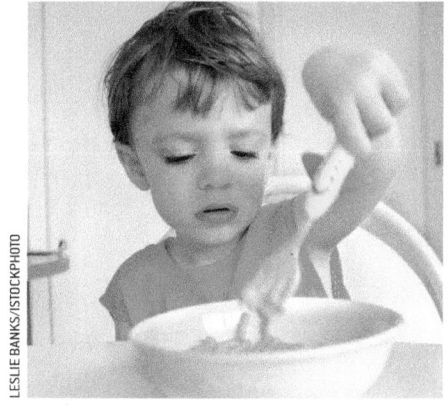

Fussy eater? Or just too many taste buds? Our taste perception declines with age: We lose about half of our taste receptors by the time we're 20 years old. That can make childhood a time of either savory delight or sensory overload of taste.

PERCEIVING TASTE

Of course, the variety of taste experiences greatly exceeds the five basic receptors discussed here. Any food molecules dissolved in saliva evoke specific, combined patterns

"We would like to be genetically modified to taste like Brussels sprouts."

DATA VISUALIZATION

Finding the Best Way to Describe Experimental Data

Go to launchpadworks.com.

of activity in the five taste receptor types. Although we often think of taste as the primary source of flavor, in fact, taste and smell collaborate to produce this complex perception. As any wine connoisseur will attest, the full experience of a wine's flavor cannot be appreciated without a finely trained sense of smell. Odorants from substances outside your mouth enter the nasal cavity via the nostrils, and odorants in the mouth enter through the back of the throat. This is why wine aficionados are taught to pull air in over wine held in the mouth: It allows the wine's odorant molecules to enter the nasal cavity through this "back door."

You can easily demonstrate the contribution of smell to flavor by tasting a few different foods while holding your nose, preventing the olfactory system from detecting their odors. If you have a head cold, you probably already know how this turns out. Your favorite spicy burrito or zesty pasta probably tastes as bland as can be.

Taste experiences also vary widely across individuals. About 50% of people report a mildly bitter taste in caffeine, saccharine, certain green vegetables, and other substances, whereas roughly 25% report no bitter taste. Members of the first group are called *tasters;* members of the second group are called *nontasters*. The remaining 25% of people are *supertasters*, who report that such substances, especially dark green vegetables, are extremely bitter, to the point of being inedible (Bartoshuk, 2000). Children start out as tasters or supertasters, which could help explain their early tendency toward fussiness in food preference. However, some children grow up to become nontasters. Because supertasters tend to avoid fruits and vegetables that contain tastes they experience as extremely bitter, they may be at increased health risk for diseases such as colon cancer. On the other hand, because they also tend to avoid fatty, creamy foods, they tend to be thinner and may have decreased risk of cardiovascular disease (Bartoshuk, 2000). There is evidence that genetic factors contribute to individual differences in taste perception (Kim et al., 2003), but much remains to be learned about the specific genes that are involved (Hayes et al., 2008; Reed, 2008).

It is also clear that cognitive factors can have a strong effect on taste perception. In one study, researchers used fMRI to scan 20 participants while they drank different wines or a control solution (Plassman et al., 2008). The participants were told that they would be sampling five different cabernet sauvignons, that the different wines would be identified by their price, and that they should rate how much they liked each wine. The participants did not know, however, that only three different wines were actually presented, and that two critical wines were presented twice. One critical wine was presented once at its actual price ($5) and once marked up to a high price ($45); the other critical wine was also presented once at its actual price ($90) and once at a marked-down price ($10). This design allowed the researchers to compare ratings and brain activity for the identical wine when participants thought it was expensive or cheap.

Results revealed that during scanning, participants reported liking both wines better when they were accompanied by a high price than by a low price. For the fMRI analysis, the researchers focused on the activity of the medial orbitofrontal cortex (mOFC), a part of the brain located deep inside the frontal lobe that is known to be involved in coding the pleasantness of an experience (Kuhn & Gallinat, 2012). The level of mOFC activity was closely correlated with subjective ratings of taste pleasantness in a previous fMRI study (Kringelbach et al., 2003). There was greater mOFC activity for both wines in the high price condition than in the low price condition. These results and those from related studies that vary whether people expect a liquid to be sweet or tasteless (Veldhuizen et al., 2011) demonstrate clearly that taste experience and associated neural activity can be affected by cognitive influences such as price knowledge.

Build to the Outcomes

1. How do the chemical senses differ from the other senses?

2. What is the role of the various parts of the nose in smell?

3. How many scents can humans smell?

4. How does taste and smell contribute to flavor?

5. What is the relationship between smell and emotion?

6. How does smell contribute to social behavior?

7. Why is the sense of taste an evolutionary advantage?

8. What are the five main types of taste receptors?

9. What are tasters, nontasters, and supertasters?

Chapter Review

Sensation and Perception Are Distinct Activities

▶ Sensation and perception are critical to survival. Sensation is the simple stimulation of a sense organ, whereas perception organizes, identifies, and interprets sensation at the level of the brain.

▶ All of our senses depend on the process of transduction, which converts physical signals from the environment into neural signals carried by sensory neurons into the central nervous system.

▶ In the 19th century, researchers developed psychophysics, an approach to studying perception that measures the strength of a stimulus and an observer's sensitivity to that stimulus. Psychophysicists have developed procedures for measuring an observer's absolute threshold, or the smallest intensity needed to just barely detect a stimulus; and the just noticeable difference (JND), or the smallest change in a stimulus that can just barely be detected.

▶ Signal detection theory allows researchers to distinguish between an observer's perceptual sensitivity to a stimulus and criteria for making decisions about the stimulus.

▶ Sensory adaptation occurs because sensitivity to lengthy stimulation tends to decline over time.

Vision I: The Eyes and the Brain Convert Light Waves to Neural Signals

▶ Light travels in waves that pass through several layers in the eye to reach the retina. In a process called accommodation, the eye muscles change the shape of the lens to focus objects at different distances on the retina.

▶ Two types of photoreceptor cells in the retina transduce light into neural impulses: cones, which operate under normal daylight conditions and sense color; and rods, which are active under low-light conditions for night vision. The neural impulses travel along the optic nerve to the brain.

▶ The retina consists of several layers; the outermost consists of retinal ganglion cells (RGCs) that collect and send signals to the brain. Bundles of RGCs form the optic nerve.

▶ Information encoded by the retina travels to the brain along the optic nerve, which connects to the lateral geniculate nucleus in the thalamus and then to the primary visual cortex, area V1, in the occipital lobe.

▶ Light striking the retina causes a specific pattern of response in each of three cone types that are critical to color perception: short-wavelength (bluish) light, medium-wavelength (greenish) light, and long-wavelength (reddish) light. The overall pattern of response across the three cone types results in a unique code for each color.

▶ The shapes of objects are perceived when different neurons in the visual cortex fire in response to different orientations of the object's edges.

▶ Two functionally distinct pathways project from the occipital lobe to visual areas in other parts of the brain. The ventral stream travels into the lower levels of the temporal lobes and includes brain areas that represent an object's shape and identity. The dorsal stream goes from the occipital lobes to the parietal lobes, connecting with brain areas that identify the location and motion of an object.

Vision II: Recognizing What We Perceive

▶ Illusory conjunctions occur when features from separate objects are mistakenly combined. According to feature-integration theory, attention provides the glue necessary to bind features together. The parietal lobe is important for attention and contributes to feature binding.

▶ Some regions in the occipital and temporal lobes respond selectively to specific object categories, supporting the modular view that specialized brain areas detect particular classes of objects such as faces or houses or body parts.

▶ The principle of perceptual constancy holds that even as sensory signals change, perception remains consistent.

▶ Gestalt principles of perceptual grouping, such as simplicity, closure, and continuity, govern how the features and regions of things fit together.

▶ According to image-based theories, object recognition happens when your memory compares a new object with an object in its store. According to parts-based theories, the brain holds mental inventories of object parts, which become a sort of alphabet that the brain can organize into various combinations. Both theories have limitations, so researchers are developing hybrid theories that incorporate each perspective.

▶ Depth perception depends on monocular cues, such as familiar size and linear perspective; binocular cues, such as retinal disparity; and motion-based cues, which are based on the movement of the head over time.

▶ We experience a sense of motion through the differences in the strengths of output from motion-sensitive neurons. These processes can give rise to illusions such as apparent motion.

▶ Change blindness and inattentional blindness occur when we fail to notice visible and even salient features of our environment, emphasizing that our conscious visual experience depends on focused attention.

Audition: More Than Meets the Ear

▶ Perceiving sound depends on three physical dimensions of a sound wave: The frequency of the sound wave determines the pitch; the amplitude determines the loudness; and differences in the complexity, or mix, of frequencies determine the sound quality, or timbre.

▶ Auditory pitch perception begins in the ear, which consists of an outer ear that funnels sound waves toward the middle ear, which in turn sends the vibrations to the inner ear, which contains the cochlea. Action potentials from the inner ear travel along an auditory pathway through the thalamus to the primary auditory cortex (area A1) in the temporal lobe.

▶ Auditory perception depends on both a place code and a temporal code. Our ability to localize sound sources depends critically on the placement of our ears on opposite sides of the head.

▶ Some hearing loss can be overcome with hearing aids that amplify sound. When hair cells are damaged, a cochlear implant is a possible solution.

The Body Senses: More Than Skin Deep

▶ Sensory receptors on the body send neural signals to locations in the somatosensory cortex, a part of the parietal lobe, which the brain translates as the sensation of touch. Different locations on the body project sensory signal to different locations in the cortex, and some areas are better at discriminating details.

▶ The experience of pain depends on signals that travel along two distinct pathways. One pathway sends signals to the somatosensory cortex to indicate the location and type of pain, and another sends signals to the emotional centers of the brain that result in unpleasant feelings that we wish to escape. The experience of pain varies across individuals, which is explained by bottom-up and top-down aspects of the gate-control theory of pain.

▶ Balance and acceleration depend primarily on the vestibular system but are also influenced by vision.

The Chemical Senses: Adding Flavor

▶ Our experience of smell, or olfaction, is associated with odorant molecules binding to sites on specialized olfactory receptors, which converge at the glomerulus within the olfactory bulb. The olfactory bulb in turn sends signals to parts of the brain that control drives, emotions, and memories, which helps to explain why smells can have immediate and powerful effects on us.

▶ Smell is also involved in social behavior, as illustrated by pheromones, which are related to reproductive behavior and sexual responses in several species.

▶ Sensations of taste depend on taste buds, which are distributed across the tongue, the roof of the mouth, and the upper throat and on taste receptors that correspond to the five primary taste sensations of salt, sour, bitter, sweet, and umami.

▶ Taste experiences vary widely across individuals and, like olfactory experiences, depend in part on cognitive influences.

KEY CONCEPT QUIZ

1. Sensation involves _____ , whereas perception involves _____ .
   a. organization; coordination
   b. stimulation; interpretation
   c. identification; translation
   d. comprehension; information

2. What process converts physical signals from the environment into neural signals carried by sensory neurons into the central nervous system?
   a. representation
   b. identification
   c. propagation
   d. transduction

3. The smallest intensity needed to just barely detect a stimulus is called
   a. proportional magnitude.
   b. the absolute threshold.
   c. the just noticeable difference.
   d. Weber's law.

4. Light striking the retina, causing a specific pattern of response in the three cone types, leads to our ability to see
   a. motion.
   b. colors.
   c. depth.
   d. shadows.

5. Which part of the brain is the location of the primary visual cortex, where encoded information is systematically mapped into a representation of the visual scene?
   a. the thalamus
   b. the lateral geniculate nucleus
   c. the fovea
   d. area V1

6. Our ability to combine visual details so that we perceive unified objects is explained by
   a. feature-integration theory.
   b. illusory conjunction.
   c. synesthesia.
   d. ventral and dorsal streaming.

7. Image-based and parts-based theories both attempt to explain the problem of
   a. motion detection.
   b. object identification.
   c. separating figure from ground.
   d. judging proximity.

8. What kind of cues are relative size and linear perspective?
   a. motion-based
   b. binocular
   c. monocular
   d. template

9. The placement of our ears on opposite sides of the head is crucial to our ability to
   a. localize sound sources.
   b. determine pitch.
   c. judge intensity.
   d. recognize complexity.

10. What best explains why smells can have immediate and powerful effects?
    a. the involvement in smell of brain centers for emotions and memories
    b. the vast number of olfactory receptor neurons we have
    c. our ability to detect odors from pheromones
    d. the fact that different odorant molecules produce varied patterns of activity

LearningCurve Don't stop now! Quizzing yourself is a powerful study tool. Go to LaunchPad to access the LearningCurve adaptive quizzing system and your own personalized learning plan. Visit launchpadworks.com.

KEY TERMS

sensation (p. 126)	cones (p. 133)	template (p. 144)	area A1 (p. 154)
perception (p. 126)	rods (p. 133)	monocular depth cues (p. 145)	place code (p. 155)
transduction (p. 127)	fovea (p. 133)	binocular disparity (p. 147)	temporal code (p. 155)
psychophysics (p. 127)	blind spot (p. 135)	apparent motion (p. 148)	haptic perception (p. 157)
absolute threshold (p. 127)	area V1 (p. 135)	change blindness (p. 149)	referred pain (p. 160)
just noticeable difference (JND) (p. 129)	color-opponent system (p. 138)	inattentional blindness (p. 149)	gate-control theory of pain (p. 160)
Weber's law (p. 129)	visual form agnosia (p. 139)	pitch (p. 151)	vestibular system (p. 161)
signal detection theory (p. 129)	parallel processing (p. 140)	loudness (p. 151)	olfactory receptor neurons (ORNs) (p. 162)
sensory adaptation (p. 131)	binding problem (p. 140)	timbre (p. 151)	olfactory bulb (p. 163)
visual acuity (p. 131)	illusory conjunction (p. 141)	cochlea (p. 153)	pheromones (p. 163)
retina (p. 133)	feature-integration theory (p. 141)	basilar membrane (p. 153)	taste buds (p. 164)
accommodation (p. 133)	perceptual constancy (p. 142)	hair cells (p. 153)	

CHANGING MINDS

1. A friend of yours is taking a class in medical ethics. "We discussed a tough case today," she says. "It has to do with a patient who's been in a vegetative state for several years, and the family has to decide whether to take him off life support. The doctors say he has no awareness of himself or his environment, and he is never expected to recover. But when light is shone in his eyes, his pupils contract. That shows he can sense light, so he has to have some ability to perceive his surroundings, doesn't he?" Without knowing any of the details of this particular case, how would you explain to your friend that a patient might be able to sense light but not perceive it? What other examples from the chapter could you use to illustrate the difference between sensation and perception?

2. In your philosophy class, the professor discusses the proposition that "perception is reality." From the point of view of philosophy, reality is the state of things that actually exists, whereas perception is how they appear to the observer. What does psychophysics have to say about this issue? What are three ways in which sensory transduction can alter perception, causing perceptions that may differ from absolute reality?

3. A friend comes across the story of an American soldier, Sergeant Leroy Petry, who received the Medal of Honor for saving the lives of two of his men. The soldiers were in a firefight in Afghanistan when a live grenade landed at their feet; Petry picked up the grenade and tried to toss it away from the others, but it exploded, destroying his right hand. According to the news report, Petry didn't initially feel any pain; instead, he set about applying a tourniquet to his own arm while continuing to shout orders to his men as the firefight continued. "That's amazingly heroic," your friend says, "but that bit about not feeling the pain—that's crazy. He must just be so tough that he kept going despite the pain." What would you tell your friend? How can the perception of pain be altered?

ANSWERS TO KEY CONCEPT QUIZ

1. b; 2. d; 3. b; 4. b; 5. d; 6. a; 7. b; 8. c; 9. a; 10. a.

 LaunchPad macmillan learning LaunchPad features the full e-Book of *Psychology*, the LearningCurve adaptive quizzing system, videos, and a variety of activities to boost your learning. Visit LaunchPad at launchpadworks.com.

Consciousness

5

U NCONSCIOUSNESS IS SOMETHING YOU DON'T REALLY appreciate until you
need it. Belle Riskin needed it one day on an operating table, when she
awoke just as doctors were pushing a breathing tube down her throat.
She felt she was choking, but she couldn't see, breathe, scream, or move. Unable
even to blink an eye, she couldn't signal to the surgeons that she was conscious.
"I was terrified. Why is this happening to me? Why can't I feel my arms? I could
feel my heart pounding in my head. It was like being buried alive, but with somebody shoving something down your throat," she explained later. "I knew I was
conscious, that something was going on during the surgery. I had just enough
awareness to know I was being intubated" (Groves, 2004).

How could this happen? Anesthesia for surgery is supposed to leave the patient
unconscious, "feeling no pain," and yet in this case—and in about one in every
20,000 surgical procedures (Pandit et al., 2014)—the patient regains consciousness at some point and even remembers the experience. Some patients remember
pain; others remember the clink of surgical instruments in a pan or the conversations of doctors and nurses. This is not how modern surgery is supposed to go, but
the problem arises because muscle-relaxing drugs are used to keep the patient
from moving involuntarily and making unhelpful contributions to the operation. But
when the drugs that are given to induce unconsciousness fail to do their job, the
patient with extremely relaxed muscles is unable to show or tell doctors that there
is a problem.

Waking up in surgery sounds pretty rough all by itself, but it can cause additional
complications. The conscious patient could become alarmed and emotional during
the operation, spiking blood pressure and heart rate to dangerous levels. Awareness also might lead to later emotional problems. Fortunately, new methods of
monitoring wakefulness by measuring the electrical activity of the brain are being
developed. One system uses sensors attached to the patient's head and
gives readings on a scale from 0 (*no electrical activity in the brain*)
to 100 (*fully alert*), providing a kind of "consciousness meter."

MASTERFILE

When it's time for surgery,
it's great to be unconscious.

Anesthesiologists using this index deliver anesthetics to keep the patient in the recommended range of 40 to 60 for general anesthesia during surgery; they have found that this system reduces postsurgical reports of consciousness and memory of the surgical experience (Myles et al., 2004), and that letting patients fall below 45 on this index for prolonged periods increases the risk of negative postoperative outcomes, including death (Kertai et al., 2010). One of these devices in the operating room might have helped Belle Riskin settle into the unconsciousness she so sorely needed.

MOST OF THE TIME, OF COURSE, CONSCIOUSNESS IS SOMETHING we cherish. How else could we experience a favorite work of art, the familiar lyrics of our favorite song, the taste of sweet chocolate, or the touch of a loved one's hand? **Consciousness** is *a person's subjective experience of the world and the mind.* Although you might think of consciousness as simply "being awake," the defining feature of consciousness is *experience,* which you have when you're awake or when you're having a vivid dream. Conscious experience is essential to what it means to be human. The anesthesiologist's dilemma in trying to monitor Belle Riskin's consciousness is a stark reminder, though, that it is impossible for one person to experience another's consciousness. Your consciousness is utterly private, a world of personal experience that only you can know.

How can this private world be studied? We'll begin by examining consciousness directly, trying to understand what it is like and how it compares with the mind's *unconscious* processes. Then we'll examine its departures from normal by exploring altered states: sleep and dreams, intoxication with alcohol and other drugs, and hypnosis. Like the traveler who learns the meaning of *home* by roaming far away, we can learn the meaning of *consciousness* by exploring its exotic variations.

The Mysteries of Consciousness

consciousness A person's subjective experience of the world and the mind.

phenomenology The study of how things seem to the conscious person.

What does it feel like to be you right now? It probably feels as though you are somewhere inside your head, looking out at the world through your eyes. You can notice the position of your body in your chair as you read or the sounds in the room when you orient yourself toward them. If you shut your eyes, you may be able to imagine things in your mind, even though all the while thoughts and feelings come and go, passing through your imagination. But where are "you," really? And how is it that this theater of consciousness gives you a view of some things in your world and your mind but not others? The theater in your mind doesn't have seating for more than one, making it difficult to share what's on your mental screen with your friends, a researcher, or even yourself in precisely the same way a second time.

Other sciences, such as physics, chemistry, and biology, have the great luxury of studying *objects,* things that we all can see. Psychology studies objects, too, looking at people and their brains and behaviors, but it has the unique challenge of also trying to make sense of *subjects.* A physicist is not concerned with what it is like to be a neutron, but psychologists hope to understand what it is like to be a human—that is, they seek to understand the subjective perspectives of the people whom they study.

Psychologists hope to include an understanding of **phenomenology,** *how things seem to the conscious person,* in their understanding of mind and behavior. After all, consciousness is an extraordinary human property. But including phenomenology in psychology brings up mysteries pondered by great thinkers almost since the beginning of thinking. Let's look at two of the more vexing mysteries of consciousness: the problem of other minds and the mind–body problem.

THE PROBLEM OF OTHER MINDS

One great mystery is called the **problem of other minds,** *the fundamental difficulty we have in perceiving the consciousness of others.* How do you know that anyone else is conscious? They tell you that they are conscious, of course, and are often willing to describe in depth how they feel, how they think, what they are experiencing, and how good or how bad it all is. But perhaps they are just *saying* these things. There is no clear way to distinguish a conscious person from someone who might do and say all the same things as a conscious person but who is *not* conscious. Philosophers have called this hypothetical nonconscious person a *zombie,* in reference to the living-yet-dead creatures of horror films (Chalmers, 1996). A philosopher's zombie could talk about experiences ("The lights are so bright!") and even seem to react to them (wincing and turning away) but might not be having any inner experience at all. No one knows whether there could be such a zombie, but then again, because of the problem of other minds, none of us will ever know for sure that another person is *not* a zombie.

Even the consciousness meter used by anesthesiologists falls short. It certainly doesn't give the anesthesiologist any special insight into what it is like to be the patient on the operating table; it only predicts whether patients will *say* they were conscious. We simply lack the ability to directly perceive the consciousness of others. In short, *you* are the only thing in the universe you will ever truly know what it is like to be.

The problem of other minds also means there is no way you can tell if another person's experience of anything is at all like yours. Although you know what the color red looks like to you, for instance, you cannot know whether it looks the same to other people. Maybe they're seeing what you see as blue and just calling it red in a consistent way. If their inner experience "looks" blue, but they say it looks hot and is the color of a tomato, you'll never be able to tell that their experience differs from yours. Of course, most people have come to trust each other in describing their inner lives, reaching the general assumption that other human minds are pretty much like their own. But they don't know this for a fact, and they can't know it firsthand.

How do people perceive other minds? Researchers conducting a large online survey asked people to compare the minds of 13 different targets, such as a baby, chimp, robot, man, and woman, on 18 different mental capacities, such as feeling pain, pleasure, hunger, and consciousness (see **FIGURE 5.1**; Gray, Gray, & Wegner, 2007). Respondents who were judging the mental capacity to feel pain, for example, compared

Luckily these zombies have the standard zombie look. But how do you know those around you are really conscious the same way that you are?

problem of other minds The fundamental difficulty we have in perceiving the consciousness of others.

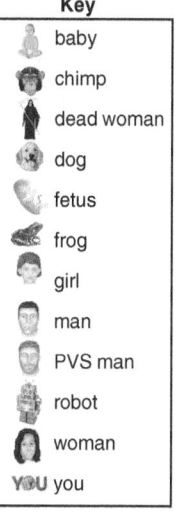

◄ Figure 5.1

DIMENSIONS OF MIND PERCEPTION
When participants judged the mental capacities of 13 targets, two dimensions of mind perception were discovered (Gray et al., 2007). Participants perceived minds as varying in the capacity for experience (such as abilities to feel pain or pleasure) and in the capacity for agency (such as abilities to plan or exert self-control). They perceived normal adult humans (male, female, or "you," the respondent) to have minds on both dimensions, whereas other targets were perceived to have reduced experience or agency. The man in a persistent vegetative state ("PVS man"), for example, was judged to have only some experience and very little agency.

Key

- baby
- chimp
- dead woman
- dog
- fetus
- frog
- girl
- man
- PVS man
- robot
- woman
- YOU you

Experience

Agency

mind–body problem The issue of how the mind is related to the brain and body.

pairs of targets: Is a frog or a dog more able to feel pain? Is a baby or a robot more able to feel pain? When the researchers examined all the comparisons on the different mental capacities with the computational technique of factor analysis (see the Intelligence chapter), they found two dimensions of mind perception. People judge minds according to the capacity for *experience* (such as the ability to feel pain, pleasure, hunger, consciousness, anger, or fear) and the capacity for *agency* (such as the ability for self-control, planning, memory, or thought). As shown in Figure 5.1, respondents rated some targets as having little experience or agency (the dead woman), others as having experiences but little agency (the baby), and yet others as having both experience and agency (adult humans). Still others were perceived to have agency without experiences (the robot, God). The perception of minds, then, involves more than just whether something has a mind. People appreciate that minds both have experiences and lead us to perform actions.

Ultimately, the problem of other minds is a problem for psychological science. As you'll remember from the Methods chapter, the scientific method requires that any observation made by one scientist should, in principle, be available for observation by any other scientist. But if other minds aren't observable, how can consciousness be a topic of scientific study? One radical solution is to eliminate consciousness from psychology entirely and follow the other sciences into total objectivity by renouncing the study of *anything* mental. This was the solution offered by behaviorism, and it turned out to have its own shortcomings, as you saw in the Psychology: Evolution of a Science chapter. Despite the problem of other minds, modern psychology has embraced the study of consciousness. The astonishing richness of mental life simply cannot be ignored.

THE MIND–BODY PROBLEM

Another mystery of consciousness is the **mind–body problem,** *the issue of how the mind is related to the brain and body. The* French philosopher and mathematician René Descartes (1596–1650) is famous for proposing, among other things, that the human body is a machine made of physical matter but that the human mind or soul is a separate entity made of a "thinking substance." He suggested that the mind has its effects on the brain and body through the pineal gland, a small structure located near the center of the brain (see **FIGURE 5.2**). In fact, the pineal gland is not even a nerve structure but rather is an endocrine gland, and so is poorly equipped to serve as a center of human consciousness. We now know that, far from the tiny connection between mind and brain in the pineal gland that Descartes proposed, the mind and brain are connected everywhere to each other. In other words, "the mind is what the brain does" (Minsky, 1986, p. 287).

But Descartes was right in pointing out the difficulty of reconciling the physical body with the mind. Most psychologists assume that mental events are intimately tied to brain events, such that every thought, perception, or feeling is associated with a particular pattern of activation of neurons in the brain (see the Neuroscience and Behavior chapter). Thinking about a particular person, for instance, occurs with a unique array of neural connections and activations. If the neurons repeat that pattern, then you must be thinking of the same person; conversely, if you think of the person, the brain activity occurs in that pattern.

One telling set of studies, however, suggests that the brain's activities *precede* the activities of the conscious mind. Researchers measured the electrical activity in the brains of volunteers by placing sensors on their scalps as they repeatedly decided when to move a hand (Libet, 1985). Participants were also asked to indicate exactly when they consciously chose to move by reporting the position of a dot moving rapidly around the face of a clock just at the point of the decision (**FIGURE 5.3a**). As a rule, the brain begins to show electrical activity around half a second before a voluntary action (535 milliseconds, to be exact). This makes sense, because brain activity certainly seems to be necessary to get an action started.

▼ Figure 5.2

SEAT OF THE SOUL Descartes imagined that the seat of the soul—and consciousness—might reside in the pineal gland located behind the third ventricle of the brain. This original drawing from Descartes (1662) shows the pineal gland (H) nicely situated for a soul, right in the middle of the brain.

Pineal gland

Brain activity begins (EEG)

Conscious wish to act is experienced (clock reading)

Finger movement occurs (EMG)

Time → −535 msec · · · −204 msec · · · 0

(a) · · · (b)

▲ Figure 5.3

THE TIMING OF CONSCIOUS WILL (a) In Benjamin Libet's experiments, the participant was asked to move fingers at will while watching a dot move around the face of a clock to mark the moment at which the action was consciously willed. Meanwhile, EEG sensors timed the onset of brain activation and EMG sensors timed the muscle movement. (b) The experiment showed that brain activity (EEG) precedes the willed movement of the finger (EMG), but that the reported time of consciously willing the finger to move follows the brain activity.

What this experiment revealed, though, was that the brain also started to show electrical activity before the person's conscious decision to move. As shown in Figure 5.3b, these studies found that the brain becomes active more than 300 milliseconds before participants report that they are consciously trying to move. The feeling that you are consciously willing your actions, it seems, may be a result rather than a cause of your brain activity. Although your personal intuition is that you *think* of an action and *then* do it, these experiments suggest that your brain is getting started before *either* the thinking or the doing, preparing the way for both thought and action. Quite simply, it may appear to us that our minds are leading our brains and bodies, but the order of events may be the other way around (Haggard & Tsakiris, 2009; Wegner, 2002).

Consciousness has its mysteries, but psychologists like a challenge. Although researchers may not be able to see the consciousness of others or know exactly how consciousness arises from the brain, this does not prevent them from collecting people's reports of conscious experiences and learning how these reports reveal the nature of consciousness.

Build to the Outcomes

1. How do people perceive other minds?

2. How does the capacity for experience differ from the capacity for agency?

3. Which comes first: brain activity or conscious thinking?

The Nature of Consciousness

How would you describe your own consciousness? Researchers examining people's descriptions suggest that consciousness has four basic properties (intentionality, unity, selectivity, and transience); that it occurs on different levels; and that it includes a range of different contents. Let's examine each of these points in turn.

FOUR BASIC PROPERTIES

Researchers have identified four basic properties of consciousness, based on people's reports of conscious experience.

1. Consciousness has *intentionality,* which is the quality of being directed toward an object. Consciousness is always *about* something. Despite all the lush detail you see in your mind's eye, the kaleidoscope of sights and sounds and feelings and thoughts, the object of your consciousness at any one moment is focused on just a small part of all of this. To describe how this works, psychologists refer to three other properties of consciousness: unity, selectivity, and transience.

Learning Outcomes

▶ Describe the four basic properties of consciousness.

▶ Compare the three levels of consciousness.

▶ Explain why we can't always control our conscious thoughts.

DRESDEN FROM RIGHT BANK OF ELBE UPSTREAM FROM BRIDGE OF AUGUSTUS, CIRCA 1750, BY BERNARDO BELLOTTO, KNOWN AS CANALETTO (1721–1780), OIL ON CANVAS, 50X84 CM, DETAIL / DE AGOSTINI PICTURE LIBRARY / A. DAGLI ORTI / BRIDGEMAN IMAGES

▲ **Figure 5.4**

BELLOTTO'S *DRESDEN* AND CLOSEUP (*left*) The people on the bridge in the distance look very finely detailed in *View of Dresden with the Frauenkirche* by Bernardo Bellotto (1720–1780). However, when you examine the detail closely (*right*), you discover that the people are made of brushstrokes merely *suggesting* people—an arm here, a torso there. Consciousness produces a similar impression of "filling in," as it seems to consist of extreme detail even in areas that are peripheral (Dennett, 1991).

dichotic listening A task in which people wearing headphones hear different messages presented to each ear.

cocktail-party phenomenon A phenomenon in which people tune in one message even while they filter out others nearby.

IMAGE SOURCE PLUS/ALAMY

Participants in a dichotic listening experiment hear different messages played to the right and left ears and may be asked to "shadow" one of the messages by repeating it aloud.

2. Consciousness has *unity*, which is resistance to division, or the ability to integrate information from all of the body's senses into one coherent whole (see **FIGURE 5.4**). As you read this book, your five senses are taking in a great deal of information. Your eyes are scanning lots of black squiggles on a page (or screen) while also sensing an enormous array of shapes, colors, depths, and textures in your periphery; your hands are gripping a heavy book (or computer); your butt and feet may sense pressure from gravity pulling you against a chair or floor; and you may be listening to music or talking in another room while smelling the odor of freshly made popcorn (or your roommate's dirty laundry). Although your body is constantly sensing an enormous amount of information from the world around you, your brain—amazingly—integrates all of this information into the experience of one unified consciousness (or two in the case of the split-brain patients described in the Neuroscience and Behavior chapter).

3. Consciousness has *selectivity*, the capacity to include some objects but not others. While binding the many sensations around you into a coherent whole, your mind must make decisions about which pieces of information to include and which to exclude. This property is shown through studies of **dichotic listening,** *in which people wearing headphones hear different messages in each ear.* Research participants were instructed to repeat aloud the words they heard in one ear while a different message was presented to the other ear (Cherry, 1953). As a result of focusing on the words they were supposed to repeat, participants noticed little of the second message, often not even realizing that at some point it changed from English to German! So consciousness *filters out* some information. At the same time, participants did notice when the voice in the unattended ear changed from a man's to a woman's, suggesting that the selectivity of consciousness can also work to *tune in* other information.

How does consciousness decide what to filter in and what to tune out? The conscious system is most inclined to select information of special interest to the person. For example, in what has come to be known as the **cocktail-party phenomenon,** *people tune in one message even while they filter out others nearby.* In the dichotic listening situation, for example, research participants are especially likely to notice if their own name is spoken into the unattended ear (Moray, 1959). Perhaps you, too, have noticed how abruptly your attention is diverted from whatever conversation you are having when someone else within earshot at the party mentions your name. Selectivity is not only a property of waking consciousness: the mind works this way in other states. People are more sensitive to their own name than others' names, for example, even during sleep (Oswald, Taylor, & Triesman, 1960). This is why, when you are trying to wake someone, it is best to use the person's name.

4. Consciousness has *transience,* or the tendency to change. Consciousness wiggles and fidgets like a toddler in the seat behind you on an airplane. The mind wanders not just sometimes, but incessantly, from one "right now" to the next "right now" and then on to the next (Wegner, 1997). William James, whom you met way back in the Psychology: Evolution of a Science chapter, famously described consciousness as a "stream" (James, 1890). Books, songs, and poems written in the "stream of consciousness" style illustrate the whirling, chaotic, and constantly changing flow of consciousness. Perhaps because it resembles our own experience of consciousness, this style is widely used, appearing in classic books such as James Joyce's *Ulysses,* and in modern music such as Nas's "New York State of Mind Part II" (1999), in which he describes what it is like growing up in his neighborhood in Queens, New York:

> Broken glass in the hallway, bloodstained floors
>
> Neighbors, look at every bag you bring through your doors
>
> Lock the top lock, momma shoulda cuffed me to the radiator,
>
> Why not? It might've saved me later from my block,
>
> N.Y. cops, hookers crawlin' off the stroll, coughin,' stitches in they head,
> Stinkin' and I dread thinkin' they be snitchin' but who else, could it be,
>
> Shook at these, unmarked vans parked in the dark—NARCs,
>
> Where's your heart? Hustlers starve, they bust a U-E, I jog to my buildin'
>
> Come out later wearing camouflage
>
> See the sergeant and the captain, strangle men

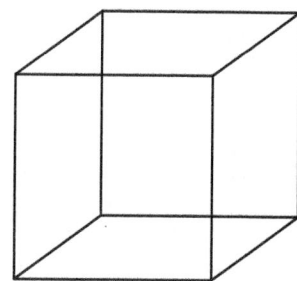

▲ Figure 5.5

THE NECKER CUBE This cube has the property of reversible perspective in that you can bring one or the other of its two square faces to the front in your mind's eye. Although it may take a while to reverse the figure at first, once people have learned to do it, they can reverse it regularly, about once every 3 seconds (Gomez et al., 1995). The stream of consciousness flows even when the target is a constant object.

The stream of consciousness may flow in this way partly because of the limited capacity of the conscious mind. We humans can hold only so much information in mind, after all, so when we select more information, some of what is currently there must disappear. As a result, our focus of attention keeps changing. The stream of consciousness flows so inevitably that it even changes our perspective when we view a constant object such as a Necker cube (see **FIGURE 5.5**).

LEVELS OF CONSCIOUSNESS

Consciousness can also be understood as having levels, ranging from minimal consciousness to full consciousness to self-consciousness. These levels of consciousness would probably all register as "conscious" on that wakefulness meter for surgery patients you read about at the beginning of this chapter. The levels of consciousness that psychologists distinguish among are not a matter of degree of overall brain activity, but instead involve different qualities of awareness of the world and of the self.

In its minimal form, consciousness is just a connection between the person and the world. When you sense the sun coming in through the window, for example, you might turn toward the light. Such **minimal consciousness** is *a low-level kind of sensory awareness and responsiveness that occurs when the mind inputs sensations and may output behavior* (Armstrong, 1980). This kind of sensory awareness and responsiveness could even happen when someone pokes you while you're asleep and you turn over. Something seems to register in your mind, at least in the sense that you experience it, but you may not think at all about having had the experience. It could be that animals or, for that matter, even plants can have this minimal level of consciousness. But because of the problem of other minds and the notorious reluctance of animals and plants to talk to us, we can't know for sure that they *experience* the things that make them respond. At least in the case of humans, we can safely assume that there is something it "feels like" to be them and that when they're awake, they are at least minimally conscious.

Human consciousness is often more than minimal, of course, but what exactly gets added? Consider the glorious feeling of waking up on a spring morning as rays of sun

minimal consciousness A low-level kind of sensory awareness and responsiveness that occurs when the mind inputs sensations and may output behavior.

The Mind Wanders

Yes, the mind wanders. Ideally, it doesn't wander so much that it can't finish this paragraph. But it does tend to come and go over time, not only changing topics as it goes, but sometimes simply "zoning out." You've no doubt had experiences of reading and suddenly realizing that you have not even been processing what you've read. Even while your eyes are dutifully following the lines of print, at some point you begin to think about something else—and only later catch yourself having wandered, perhaps thinking, where was I? Or, why did I come into this room?

Mind wandering, or the experience of "stimulus-independent thoughts," occurs most often when we are engaged in repetitive, undemanding tasks (Buckner, Andrews-Hanna, & Schacter, 2008). This happens a lot. One study revealed that we engage in mind wandering during nearly half of our daily activities (46.9%), regardless of what we are doing (Killingsworth & Gilbert, 2010; see the figure). Indeed, mind wandering occurred at least 30% of the time in every activity recorded. (The one exception is making love, during which it is apparently rare to have stimulus-independent thoughts.) The amount of time spent engaging in different activities, and happiness during those activities, are shown in the figure [to the right]. Although the mind often wanders, this study found that people are significantly less happy when mind wandering compared to when they are thinking about what they are currently doing.

More than that, recent research suggests that many people seriously dislike being alone with their thoughts. In a series of 11 studies, Wilson and colleagues (2014) asked research participants to simply sit and think in a room by themselves for a period of 6 to 15 minutes. That's it. Simple, right? Well it turns out that most people (58%) reported that their minds wandered even though they weren't engaged in any other activity, and approximately half (49%) reported that they did not enjoy sitting alone with their thoughts. Just how unenjoyable is it to sit alone with one's thoughts? In one of the 11 studies, participants were exposed to negative stimuli (e.g., an electric shock) and asked how much they would pay to avoid those stimuli in the future. It was interesting that sitting with one's thoughts for 15 minutes was so aversive that 67% of men and 25% of women elected to self-administer electric shocks rather than sitting quietly alone with their thoughts. It is not clear why sitting alone with one's thoughts is so aversive for some people (that's a question for a future study), but it is clear from this line of research that the mind wanders, and for many people it wanders into places that are not always so pleasant. Our advice is to keep your mind busy by continuing to read this textbook!

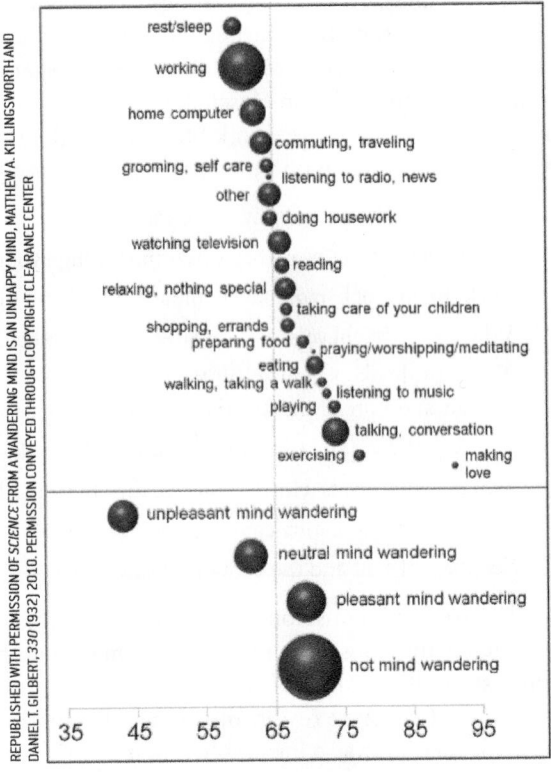

REPUBLISHED WITH PERMISSION OF *SCIENCE* FROM A WANDERING MIND IS AN UNHAPPY MIND, MATHEW A. KILLINGSWORTH AND DANIEL T. GILBERT, 330 (932) 2010. PERMISSION CONVEYED THROUGH COPYRIGHT CLEARANCE CENTER

▲ This figure shows data from Killingsworth and Gilbert's (2010) experiment in which people reported on their level of happiness (from 0–100, shown on the *x*-axis) while engaged in various activities. The size of the bubbles represents the frequency of occurrence. Activities from top to bottom show those associated with the least happiness (rest/sleep) to the most happiness (making love). The bottom part of the figure shows how happy people are while mind wondering—and that they are less happy when mind wandering than not mind wondering.

Full consciousness involves a consciousness of oneself, such as thinking about the act of driving while driving a car. How is this different from self-consciousness?

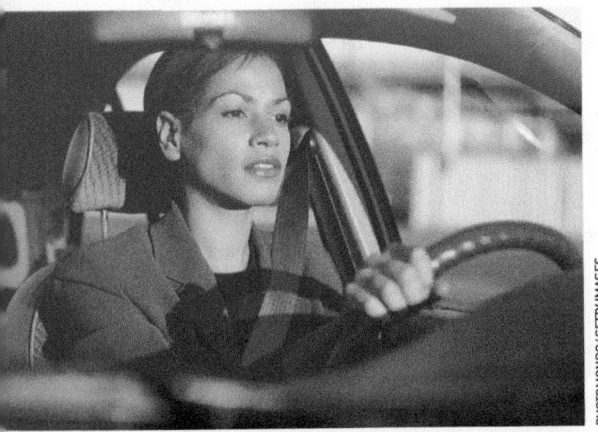

PHOTOMONDO/GETTY IMAGES

stream across your pillow. It's not just that you are having this experience: Being fully conscious means that you are also *aware* that you are having this experience. The critical ingredient that accompanies **full consciousness** is that you *know and are able to report your mental state.* That's a subtle distinction: Being fully conscious means that you are aware of having a mental state while you are experiencing the mental state itself. When you have a hurt leg and mindlessly rub it, for instance, your pain may be minimally conscious. After all, you seem to be experiencing pain because you have acted and are indeed rubbing your leg. It is only when you realize that it hurts, though, that you become fully conscious of the pain. Have you ever been driving a car and suddenly realized that you don't remember the past 15 minutes of driving? Chances are that you were not unconscious, but instead minimally conscious. When you are completely aware and thinking about your driving, you have moved into the realm of full consciousness. Full consciousness involves not only thinking about things but also thinking about the fact that you are thinking about things (Jaynes, 1976; see Hot Science: The Mind Wanders).

Full consciousness involves a certain consciousness of oneself; the person notices the self in a particular mental state. ("Here I am, reading this sentence.") However, this is not quite the same thing as *self*-consciousness. Sometimes consciousness is entirely flooded with the self. ("Not only am I reading this sentence, but I have a blemish on the end of my nose today that makes me feel like I'm guiding a sleigh.") Self-consciousness focuses on the self to the exclusion of almost everything else. William James (1890) and other theorists have suggested that **self-consciousness** is yet another *distinct level of consciousness in which the person's attention is drawn to the self as an object* (Morin, 2006). Most people report experiencing such self-consciousness when they are embarrassed; when they find themselves the focus of attention in a group; when someone focuses a camera on them; or when they are deeply introspective about their thoughts, feelings, or personal qualities.

Self-consciousness brings with it a tendency to evaluate yourself and notice your shortcomings. Looking in a mirror, for example, is all it takes to make people evaluate themselves—thinking not just about their looks, but also about whether they are good or bad in other ways. People go out of their way to avoid mirrors when they've done something they are ashamed of (Duval & Wicklund, 1972). Self-consciousness can certainly spoil a good mood, so much so that a tendency to be chronically self-conscious is associated with depression (Pyszczynski, Holt, & Greenberg, 1987). However, because it makes them self-critical, the self-consciousness that results when people see their own mirror images can make them briefly more helpful, more cooperative, and less aggressive (Gibbons, 1990). Perhaps everyone would be a bit more civilized if mirrors were held up for them to see themselves as objects of their own scrutiny.

Most animals can't follow this path to civilization. The typical dog or cat seems mystified by a mirror, ignoring it or acting as though there is some other critter back there. However, chimpanzees that have spent time with mirrors sometimes behave in ways that suggest they recognize themselves in a mirror. To examine this, researchers painted an odorless red dye over the eyebrow of an anesthetized chimp and then watched when the awakened chimp was presented with a mirror (Gallup, 1977). If the chimp interpreted the mirror image as a representation of some other chimp with an unusual approach to cosmetics, we would expect it just to look at the mirror or perhaps to reach toward it. But the chimp reached toward its *own eye* as it looked into the mirror—not the mirror image—suggesting that it recognized the image as a reflection of itself.

Versions of this experiment have now been repeated with many different animals, and it turns out that, like humans, animals such as chimpanzees and orangutans (Gallup, 1997), possibly dolphins (Reiss & Marino, 2001), and maybe even elephants (Plotnik, de Waal, & Reiss, 2006) and magpies (Prior, Schwartz, & Güntürkün, 2008) recognize their own mirror images. Dogs, cats, crows, monkeys, and gorillas have been tested, too, but don't seem to know they are looking at themselves. Even humans don't have self-recognition right away. Infants don't recognize themselves in mirrors until they've

Self-consciousness is a curse and a blessing. Looking in a mirror can make people evaluate themselves on deeper attributes such as honesty as well as superficial ones such as looks.

full consciousness A level of consciousness in which you know and are able to report your mental state.

self-consciousness A distinct level of consciousness in which the person's attention is drawn to the self as an object.

A chimpanzee tried to wipe off the red dye on its eyebrow in the Gallup experiment. This suggests that some animals recognize themselves in the mirror.

Dilbert

OKAY, LET ME THINK ALOUD FOR A MINUTE.

THE COST WILL BE $3,000...LOSING FOCUS...MONKEYS ARE FUNNY...MY TONGUE IS DIGESTING IN MY MOUTH.

THAT DIDN'T HELP AS MUCH AS I HAD HOPED.

TABLE 5.1

How Was Your Day? Women's Ratings of Level of Positive Affect and Amount of Time in Daily Activities

Activities	Mean Affect Rating	
	Positive Affect	Mean Hours/Day
Intimate relations	5.1	0.2
Socializing	4.6	2.3
Relaxing	4.4	2.2
Pray/worship/meditate	4.4	0.4
Eating	4.3	2.2
Exercising	4.3	0.2
Watching TV	4.2	2.2
Shopping	4.0	0.4
Preparing food	3.9	1.1
On the phone	3.9	2.5
Napping	3.9	0.9
Taking care of my children	3.9	1.1
Computer/e-mail/Internet	3.8	1.9
Housework	3.7	1.1
Working	3.6	6.9
Commuting	3.5	1.6

Data from Kahneman, D., Krueger, A. B., Schkade, D. A., Schwartz, N., & Stone, A. A. (2004). A survey method for characterizing daily life experience: The day reconstruction method (Table 1). *Science, 306,* 1776–1780.

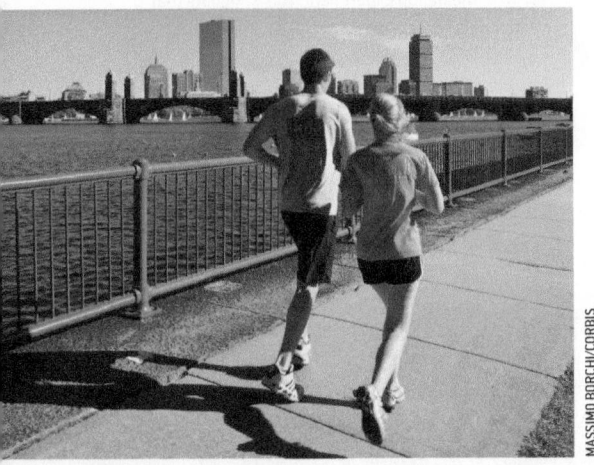

One concern on many students' minds is diet and exercise to keep in shape.

reached about 18 months of age (Lewis & Brooks-Gunn, 1979). The experience of self-consciousness, as measured by self-recognition in mirrors, is limited to a few animals and to humans only after a certain stage of development.

CONSCIOUS CONTENTS

What's on your mind? For that matter, what's on everybody's mind? One way to learn what is on people's minds is to ask them, and much research has called on people simply to *think aloud.* A more systematic approach is the *experience-sampling technique,* in which people are asked to report their conscious experiences at particular times. Equipped with electronic beepers or called on cell phones, for example, participants are asked to record their current thoughts when asked at random times throughout the day (Bolger, Davis, & Rafaeli, 2003).

Experience-sampling studies show that consciousness is dominated by the immediate environment—what we see, feel, hear, taste, and smell. What do you experience while actually carrying out the events of your daily life? Researchers who have begun using experience-sampling methods to record the emotions people experience during everyday activities have found interesting results. One recent study collected data from over 900 working women by asking them to reflect on the events of the past day and record how they felt while engaging in each activity (Kahneman et al., 2004). Some of the results are as expected. For instance, as shown in **TABLE 5.1**, people score lowest on positive affect when commuting, working, and doing housework, and unfortunately this is how we spend a large part of our day. The women in this study reported having the most positive affect while being intimate with another person, although they only did this for 12 minutes of the day. Some less intuitive findings are related to the activities that fell in between the two. In survey studies parents often report that they are happiest when spending time with their children, but when asked about actual events of the prior day, being with one's children ranked just two ticks above housework and well below other activities such as shopping, watching TV, and making more children.

Much of consciousness beyond engaging with one's environment turns to the person's *current concerns,* or what the person is thinking about repeatedly (Klinger, 1975). **TABLE 5.2** shows the results of a Minnesota study in which 175 college students were asked to report their current concerns (Goetzman, Hughes, & Klinger, 1994). The researchers sorted the concerns into the categories shown in the table. Keep in mind that these concerns are ones the students didn't mind reporting to psychologists; their private preoccupations may have been different and probably far more interesting.

Daydreams: The Brain Is Always Active

Current concerns do not seem all that concerning, however, during *daydreaming,* a state of consciousness in which a seemingly purposeless flow of thoughts comes to mind. When thoughts drift along this way, it may seem as if you are just wasting time. The brain, however, is active even when it has no specific task at hand. This mental work done in daydreaming was examined in an fMRI study of people resting in the scanner (Mason et al., 2007). Usually, people in brain-scanning studies don't have

MASSIMO BORCHI/CORBIS

TABLE 5.2

What's on Your Mind? College Students' Current Concerns

Current Concern Category	Example	Frequency of Students Who Mentioned the Concern
Health	Diet and exercise	85%
Household	Clean room	52%
Religious	Attend church more	51%
Education	Go to graduate school	43%
Friends	Make new friends	42%
Family	Gain better relations with immediate family	40%
Social activities	Gain acceptance into a campus organization	34%
Employment	Get a summer job	33%
Roommate	Change attitude or behavior of roommate	29%
Dating	Desire to date a certain person	24%
Sexual intimacy	Abstaining from sex	16%
Government	Change government policy	14%
Financial	Pay rent or bills	8%

Data from: Goetzman, E. S., Hughes, T., & Klinger, E. (1994). *Current concerns of college students in a midwestern sample.* University of Minnesota, Morris.

MASON ET AL., 2007

▲ Figure 5.6

THE DEFAULT NETWORK ACTIVATED DURING DAYDREAMING An fMRI scan shows that many areas, known as the default network, are active when the person is not given a specific mental task to perform during the scan.

[REPUBLISHED WITH PERMISSION OF *SCIENCE* FROM WONDERING MINDS: THE DEFAULT NETWORK AND STIMULUS-INDEPENDENT THOUGHT. MASON, NORTON, VAN HORN, WEGNER, GRAFTON, MACRAE, VOL. 315, JANUARY 19, 2007, PP.393–395. PERMISSION CONVEYED THROUGH COPYRIGHT CLEARANCE CENTER.]

time to daydream much because they are kept busy with mental tasks—scans cost money and researchers want to get as much data as possible for their bucks. But when people are *not* busy, they still show a widespread pattern of activation in many areas of the brain—now known as the *default network* (Gusnard & Raichle, 2001). The study by Mason et al. revealed that this network became activated whenever people worked on a mental task that they knew so well that they could daydream while doing it (see **FIGURE 5.6**). The areas of the default network are known to be involved in thinking about social life, about the self, and about the past and future—all the usual haunts of the daydreaming mind (Mitchell, 2006).

Efforts to Suppress Current Concerns Can Backfire

The current concerns that populate consciousness can sometimes get the upper hand, transforming daydreams or everyday thoughts into rumination and worry. Thoughts that return again and again, or problem-solving attempts that never seem to succeed, can come to dominate consciousness. When this happens, people may exert **mental control,** *the attempt to change conscious states of mind.* For example, someone troubled by a recurring worry about the future ("What if I can't get a decent job when I graduate?") might choose to try *not* to think about this because it causes too much anxiety and uncertainty. Whenever this thought comes to mind, the person engages in **thought suppression,** the *conscious avoidance of a thought.* This may seem like a perfectly sensible strategy because it eliminates the worry and allows the person to move on to think about something else.

Or does it? The great Russian novelist Fyodor Dostoyevsky (1863/1988, p. 49), remarked on the difficulty of thought suppression: "Try to pose for yourself this task: not to think of a polar bear, and you will see that the cursed thing will come to mind every minute." Inspired by this observation, Daniel Wegner and his colleagues (1987) gave people this exact task in the laboratory. Participants were asked to try not to think

mental control The attempt to change conscious states of mind.

thought suppression The conscious avoidance of a thought.

Go ahead, look away from this book for a minute and try not to think about a white bear.

LARRY WILLIAMS/CORBIS

▶ Figure 5.7

REBOUND EFFECT Research participants were first asked to try not to think about a white bear, and to ring a bell whenever it came to mind. Compared to those who were simply asked to think about a bear without prior suppression, those people who *first* suppressed the thought showed a rebound of increased thinking (Wegner et al., 1987).

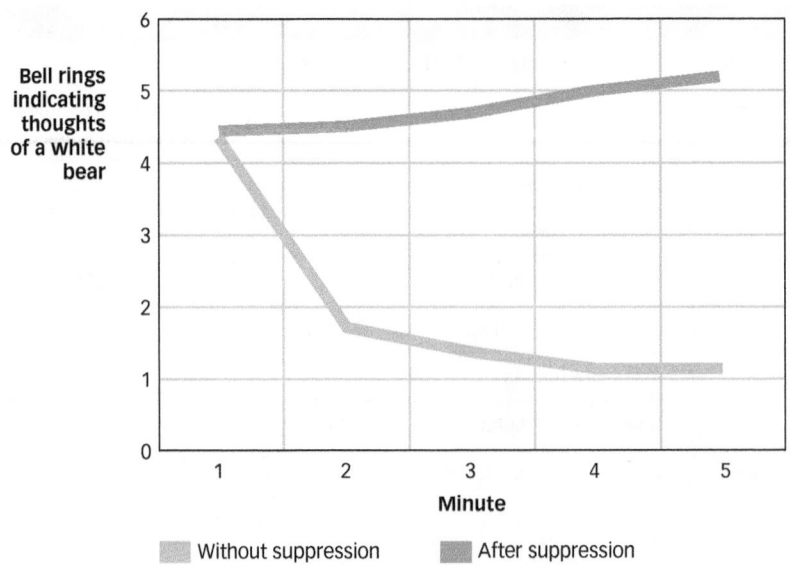

about a white bear for 5 minutes while they recorded all their thoughts aloud into a tape recorder. In addition, they were asked to ring a bell if the thought of a white bear came to mind. On average, they mentioned the white bear or rang the bell (indicating the thought) more than once per minute. Thought suppression simply didn't work and instead produced a flurry of returns of the unwanted thought. What's more, when some research participants later were specifically asked to change tasks and deliberately *think* about a white bear, they became oddly preoccupied with it. A graph of their bell rings in **FIGURE 5.7** shows that for these participants, the white bear came to mind far more often than it did for people who had only been asked to think about the bear from the outset, with no prior suppression. This **rebound effect of thought suppression,** *the tendency of a thought to return to consciousness with greater frequency following suppression,* suggests that attempts at mental control may be difficult indeed. The act of trying to suppress a thought may itself cause that thought to return to consciousness in a robust way.

Processes Outside of Consciousness Can Stymie Attempts at Conscious Control

As with thought suppression, other attempts to steer consciousness in any direction can result in mental states that are precisely the opposite of those desired. How ironic: Trying to consciously achieve one task may produce precisely the opposite outcome! These ironic effects seem most likely to occur when the person is distracted or under stress. People who are distracted while they are trying to get into a good mood, for example, tend to become sad (Wegner, Erber, & Zanakos, 1993), and those who are distracted while trying to relax actually become more anxious than those who are not trying to relax (Wegner, Broome, & Blumberg, 1997). Likewise, an attempt not to overshoot a golf putt, undertaken during distraction, often yields the unwanted overshot (Wegner, Ansfield, & Pilloff, 1998). The theory of **ironic processes of mental control** proposes that such *ironic errors occur because the mental process that monitors errors can itself produce them* (Wegner, 1994a, 2009). The irony about the attempt not to think of a white bear, for instance, is that a small part of the mind is *searching* for the white bear.

This ironic monitoring process is not present in consciousness. After all, trying *not* to think of something would be useless if monitoring the progress of suppression required keeping that target in consciousness. For example, if trying not to think of

rebound effect of thought suppression The tendency of a thought to return to consciousness with greater frequency following suppression.

ironic processes of mental control A mental process that can produce ironic errors because monitoring for errors can itself produce them.

a white bear meant that you consciously kept repeating to yourself, "No white bear! No white bear!" then you've failed before you've begun: That thought is present in consciousness even as you strive to eliminate it. Rather, the ironic monitor is a process of the mind that works *outside* of consciousness, making us sensitive to all the things we do not want to think, feel, or do so that we can notice and consciously take steps to regain control if these things come back to mind. As this unconscious monitoring whirs along in the background, it unfortunately increases the person's sensitivity to the very thought that is unwanted. Ironic processes are mental functions that are needed for effective mental control—they help in the process of banishing a thought from consciousness—but they can sometimes yield the very failure they seem designed to overcome. Ironic effects of mental control arise from processes that work outside of consciousness, so they remind us that much of the mind's machinery may be hidden from our view, lying outside the fringes of our experience.

Build to the Outcomes

1. What are the limitations to the number of objects consciousness can take on at one time?

2. How does your mind know which information to allow into consciousness and which to filter out?

3. Which characteristic of full consciousness distinguishes it from minimal consciousness?

4. When do people go out of their way to avoid mirrors?

5. Which animals are also aware of their own reflection in a mirror?

6. What part of the brain is active during daydreaming?

7. Is consciously avoiding a worrisome thought a sensible strategy?

The Unconscious Mind

Many mental processes are unconscious, in the sense that they occur without our experience of them. When we speak, for instance, "We are not really conscious either of the search for words, or of putting the words together into phrases, or of putting the phrases into sentences. . . . The actual process of thinking . . . is not conscious at all . . . only its preparation, its materials, and its end result are consciously perceived" (Jaynes, 1976, p. 41). Just to put the role of consciousness in perspective, think for a moment about the mental processes involved in simple addition. What happens in consciousness between hearing a problem (what's four plus five?) and thinking of the answer (nine)? Probably nothing—the answer just appears in the mind. But this is a piece of calculation that must take at least a bit of thinking. After all, at a very young age you may have had to solve such problems by counting on your fingers. Now that you don't have to do that anymore (please tell me you don't have to do that anymore), the answer seems to pop into your head automatically, by virtue of a process that doesn't require you to be aware of any underlying steps and, for that matter, doesn't even *allow* you to be aware of the steps. The answer just suddenly appears.

In the early part of the 20th century, when structuralist psychologists such as Wilhelm Wundt believed that introspection was the best method of research (see the Psychology: Evolution of a Science chapter), research volunteers trained in describing their thoughts tried to discern what happens when a simple problem brings to mind a simple answer (e.g., Watt, 1905). They drew the same blank you probably did. Nothing conscious seems to bridge this gap, but the answer comes from somewhere, and this emptiness points to the unconscious mind. To explore these hidden recesses, we can look at the classical theory of the unconscious introduced by Sigmund Freud and then at the modern cognitive psychology of unconscious mental processes.

Learning Outcome

▶ Compare Freud's conception of the unconscious with the modern view.

There are no conscious steps between hearing an easy problem (what's four plus five?) and thinking of the answer—unless you have to count on your fingers.

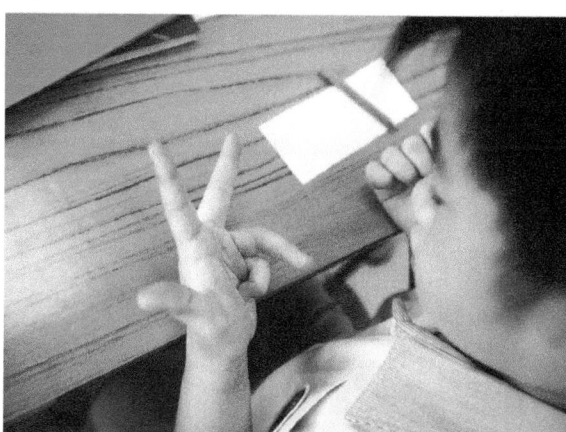

FUSE/GETTY IMAGES

dynamic unconscious An active system encompassing a lifetime of hidden memories, the person's deepest instincts and desires, and the person's inner struggle to control these forces.

repression A mental process that removes unacceptable thoughts and memories from consciousness and keeps them in the unconscious.

cognitive unconscious All the mental processes that give rise to a person's thoughts, choices, emotions, and behavior even though they are not experienced by the person.

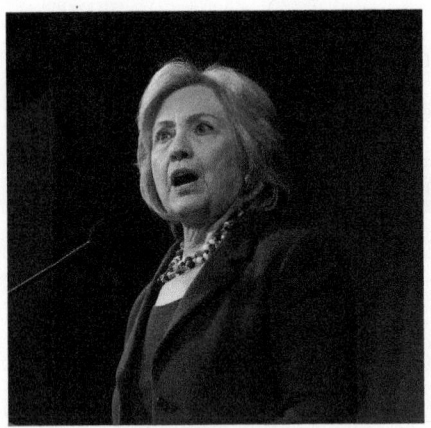

While campaigning for the presidency, Hillary Clinton accidentally mixed up the words "president" and "prisoner" when talking about people having to talk about their past criminal behavior. This is a textbook example of a Freudian slip, which is why we put it you know where.

FREUDIAN UNCONSCIOUS

The true champion of the unconscious mind was Sigmund Freud. As you read in the Psychology: Evolution of a Science chapter, Freud's psychoanalytic theory viewed conscious thought as the surface of a much deeper mind made up of unconscious processes—but far more than just a collection of hidden processes. Freud described a **dynamic unconscious**—*an active system encompassing a lifetime of hidden memories, the person's deepest instincts and desires, and the person's inner struggle to control these forces.* The dynamic unconscious might contain hidden sexual thoughts about one's parents, for example, or destructive urges aimed at a helpless infant—the kinds of thoughts people keep secret from others and may not even acknowledge to themselves. According to Freud's theory, the unconscious is a force to be held in check by **repression**, *a mental process that removes unacceptable thoughts and memories from consciousness and keeps them in the unconscious.* Without repression, a person might think, do, or say every unconscious impulse or animal urge, no matter how selfish or immoral. With repression, these desires are held in the recesses of the dynamic unconscious.

Freud looked for evidence of the unconscious mind in speech errors and lapses of consciousness, or what are commonly called *Freudian slips*. Forgetting the name of someone you dislike, for example, is a slip that seems to have special meaning. Freud believed that errors are not random and instead have some surplus meaning that may appear to have been created by an intelligent unconscious mind, even though the person consciously disavows them. For example, while running for president, Hillary Clinton—the wife of former president Bill Clinton—was proposing that former prisoners should not have to check a box when applying for jobs indicating that they had been to prison. She slipped, however, and said that when she is president: "former presidents (she meant "prisoners") won't have to declare their criminal history at the very start of the hiring process." Oops.

Did Hillary's slip mean anything? One experiment revealed that slips of speech can indeed be prompted by a person's pressing concerns (Motley & Baars, 1979). Research participants in one group were told they might receive minor electric shocks, whereas those in another group heard no mention of this. Each person was then asked to read quickly through a series of word pairs, including *shad bock*. Those in the group warned about shock more often slipped in pronouncing this pair, blurting out *bad shock*.

Unlike errors created in experiments such as this one, many of the meaningful errors Freud attributed to the dynamic unconscious were not predicted in advance and so seem to depend on clever after-the-fact interpretations. Such interpretations can be wrong. Suggesting a pattern to a series of random events is not the same as scientifically predicting and explaining when and why an event should happen. Anyone can offer a reasonable, compelling explanation for an event after it has already happened, but the true work of science is to offer testable hypotheses that are evaluated based on reliable evidence. Freud's (1901/1938) book *The Psychopathology of Everyday Life* suggests not so much that the dynamic unconscious produces errors but that Freud himself was a master at finding meaning in errors that might otherwise have seemed random.

A MODERN VIEW OF THE COGNITIVE UNCONSCIOUS

Modern psychologists share Freud's interest in the impact of unconscious mental processes on consciousness and on behavior. However, rather than seeing Freud's vision of the unconscious as a teeming menagerie of animal urges and repressed thoughts, the current study of the unconscious mind views it as a rapid, automatic information processor that influences our thoughts, feelings, and behaviors. The **cognitive unconscious** includes *all the mental processes that give rise to a person's thoughts, choices, emotions, and behavior even though they are not experienced by the person.*

Our Brains Are Wired for Both Fast and Slow Thinking

Modern views of cognition propose that we have two different types of minds wired into our one little brain. **Dual process theories** suggest that we have two different systems in our brains for processing information: one dedicated to fast, automatic, and unconscious processing; and the other dedicated to slow, effortful, and conscious processing. The first, which is now commonly referred to as System 1 (Stanovich & West, 2000), is at work when you effortlessly engage in activities such as reading these words; solving problems such as 2 + 2 = __; and walking down the street avoiding people, cars, and other obstacles. You use the second, System 2, when you rationally and intentionally work to complete a task, such as answering this chapter's quiz questions, solving problems such as 245 × 32 = __, and placing an order at a restaurant. These systems, and the important roles they play, are outlined in detail in the psychologist and Nobel laureate Daniel Kahneman's book *Thinking Fast and Slow* (Kahneman, 2011).

This dual process perspective is in some ways consistent with Freud's idea of the split between the unconscious and the conscious mind. However, dual process theories do not incorporate all of Freud's beliefs about hidden urges, defense mechanisms, and the like. Instead, they simply propose that we have these two different ways of processing information that draw on different neural pathways. Dual process theories have been used to understand the workings of different cognitive processes such as attention, learning, and memory (for example, see the discussions of implicit and explicit learning and memory in later chapters on these topics), and continue to guide thinking and research in many different areas of psychology.

Behavior Can Be Influenced by Factors Outside of Consciousness

One example of the cognitive unconscious (System 1) at work occurs when a person's thoughts or behaviors are changed by exposure to information outside of consciousness. This happens in **subliminal perception**, when *thought or behavior is influenced by stimuli that a person cannot consciously report perceiving.* As an example, one classic study reported that exposure to information about getting old can make a person walk more slowly. John Bargh and his colleagues had college students complete a survey that called for them to make sentences with various words (1996). The students were not informed that most of the words were commonly associated with aging (*Florida, gray, wrinkled*), and even afterward they didn't report being aware of this trend. In this case, the "aging" idea wasn't presented subliminally, just not very noticeably. As these research participants left the experiment, they were clocked as they walked down the hall. Compared with those not exposed to the aging-related words, these participants walked more slowly! Just as with subliminal perception, a passing exposure to ideas can influence actions without conscious awareness.

THE UNCONSCIOUS MIND: SMART OR NOT SO SMART?

The unconscious mind can be a kind of "mental butler," taking over background tasks that are too tedious, subtle, or bothersome for consciousness to trifle with (Bargh & Chartrand, 1999; Bargh & Morsella, 2008; Bower, 1999). Psychologists have long debated just how smart this mental butler might be. Freud attributed great intelligence to the unconscious, believing that it harbors complex motives and inner conflicts and that it expresses these in an astonishing array of thoughts and emotions, as well as psychological disorders (see the Disorders chapter). Contemporary cognitive psychologists wonder whether the unconscious is so smart, however, and point out that some unconscious processes even seem downright "dumb" (Loftus & Klinger, 1992). For example, the unconscious processes that underlie the perception of subliminal visual stimuli do not seem able to understand the combined meaning of word pairs, although they can understand single words. To the *conscious* mind, for example, a

dual process theories Theories that suggest that we have two different systems in our brains for processing information: one dedicated to fast, automatic, and unconscious processing, and the other dedicated to slow, effortful, and conscious processing.

subliminal perception Thought or behavior that is influenced by stimuli that a person cannot consciously report perceiving.

Choosing a roommate can be like playing the lottery: You win some, you lose some, and then you lose some more.

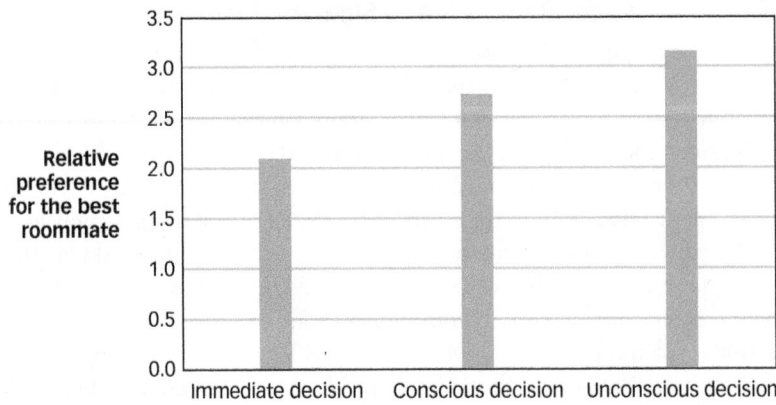

► Figure 5.8

DECISIONS People making roommate decisions who had some time for unconscious deliberation chose better roommates than those who thought about the choice consciously or those who made snap decisions (Dijksterhuis, 2004).

word pair such as *enemy loses* is somewhat positive—it is good to have your enemy lose. However, subliminal presentations of this word pair make people think of negative things, as though the unconscious mind is simply adding together the unpleasantness of the single words *enemy* and *loses* (Greenwald, 1992). So the mental butler is fast, but perhaps not all that bright.

In some cases, however, the unconscious mind can make better decisions than the conscious mind. Participants in an experiment were asked to choose which of three hypothetical people with many different qualities they would prefer to have as a roommate (Dijksterhuis, 2004). One candidate was objectively better, with more positive qualities, and participants who were given 4 minutes to make a *conscious decision* tended to choose that one. A second group was asked for an *immediate decision* as soon as the information display was over, and a third group was encouraged to reach an *unconscious decision*. This group was also given 4 minutes after the display ended to give their answer (as the conscious group had been given), but during this interval their conscious minds were occupied with solving a set of anagrams. As you can see in **FIGURE 5.8**, the unconscious decision group showed a stronger preference for the good roommate than did the immediate decision or conscious decision groups. Unconscious minds seemed *better able* than conscious minds to sort out the complex information and arrive at the best choice. You sometimes can end up more satisfied with decisions you make after just going with your gut than with the decisions you consciously agonize over.

Build to the Outcomes

1. According to Freud, what is the source of unconscious errors in speech?

2. What evidence shows that the unconscious mind can be a good decision maker?

Sleep and Dreaming: Good Night, Mind

Learning Outcomes

▸ Describe the stages of sleep.

▸ Identify the types of sleep disorders.

▸ Compare the two leading theories of why we dream.

What's it like to be asleep? Sometimes it's like nothing at all. Sleep can produce a state of unconsciousness in which the mind and brain apparently turn off the functions that create experience: The theater in your mind is closed. But this is an oversimplification because the theater actually seems to reopen during the night for special shows of bizarre cult films—in other words, dreams. Dream consciousness involves a transformation of experience that is so radical it is commonly considered an **altered state of consciousness:** *a form of experience that departs significantly from the normal subjective experience of the world and the mind.* Such altered states can be accompanied by changes in thinking, disturbances in the sense of time, feelings of the loss of control, changes in emotional expression, alterations in body image and sense of self, perceptual distortions, and changes in meaning or significance (Ludwig, 1966). The world of sleep and dreams, the two topics in this section, provides two unique perspectives on consciousness: a view of the mind without consciousness and a view of consciousness in an altered state.

altered state of consciousness A form of experience that departs significantly from the normal subjective experience of the world and the mind.

circadian rhythm A naturally occurring 24-hour cycle.

SLEEP

Consider a typical night. As you begin to fall asleep, the busy, task-oriented thoughts of the waking mind are replaced by wandering thoughts and images and odd juxtapositions, some of them almost dreamlike. This presleep consciousness is called the *hypnagogic state.* On some rare nights you might experience a *hypnic jerk,* a sudden quiver or sensation of dropping, as though missing a step on a staircase. No one is quite sure why these happen. Eventually, your presence of mind goes away entirely. Time and experience stop, you are unconscious, and in fact there seems to be no "you" there to have experiences. But then come dreams, whole vistas of a vivid and surrealistic consciousness you just don't get during the day, a set of experiences that occur with the odd prerequisite that there is nothing "out there" you are actually experiencing. More patches of unconsciousness may occur, with more dreams here and there. And finally, the glimmerings of waking consciousness return again in a foggy and imprecise form as you enter postsleep consciousness (the *hypnopompic state*) and then awake, often with bad hair.

Dreamers, by Albert Joseph Moore (1879/1882) Although their bodies are in the same room, their minds are probably worlds apart.

Sleep Cycle

The sequence of events that occurs during a night of sleep is part of one of the major rhythms of human life, the cycle of sleep and waking. This **circadian rhythm** is *a naturally occurring 24-hour cycle,* from the Latin *circa* (about) and *dies* (day). Even people sequestered in underground buildings without clocks ("time-free environments") who are allowed to sleep when they want tend to have a rest–activity cycle of about 25.1 hours (Aschoff, 1965). This slight deviation from 24 hours is not easily explained (Lavie, 2001), but it seems to underlie the tendency many people have to want to stay up a little later each night and wake up a little later each day. We're 25.1-hour people living in a 24-hour world.

Research Reveals Five Stages of Sleep The sleep cycle is far more than a simple on–off routine, however, as many bodily and psychological processes ebb and flow in this rhythm. In 1929 researchers made EEG (electroencephalograph) recordings of the human brain for the first time (Berger, 1929; see the Neuroscience and Behavior chapter). Before this, many people had offered descriptions of their nighttime experiences, and researchers knew that there are deeper and lighter periods of sleep, as well as dream periods. But no one had been able to measure much of anything about sleep without waking up the sleeper and ruining it. The EEG recordings revealed a regular pattern of changes in electrical activity in the brain accompanying the circadian cycle. During waking, these changes involve alternation between high-frequency activity (*beta waves*) during alertness and lower-frequency activity (*alpha waves*) during relaxation.

The largest changes in EEG occur during sleep. These changes show a regular pattern over the course of the night that allowed sleep researchers to identify five sleep stages (see **FIGURE 5.9**). In the first stage of sleep, the EEG moves to frequency

▶ Figure 5.9

EEG PATTERNS DURING THE STAGES OF SLEEP The waking brain shows high-frequency beta wave activity, which changes during drowsiness and relaxation to lower-frequency alpha waves. Stage 1 sleep shows lower-frequency theta waves, which are accompanied in stage 2 by irregular patterns called sleep spindles and K complexes. Stages 3 and 4 are marked by the lowest frequencies, delta waves. During REM sleep, EEG patterns return to higher-frequency sawtooth waves that resemble the beta waves of waking.

Awake
Beta waves

50 μv
1 sec.

Drowsy, Relaxed
Alpha waves

Stage 1 Sleep
Theta waves

Theta waves

Stage 2 Sleep
Sleep spindles,
K complexes

Sleep spindle

K complex

Stage 3/Stage 4 Sleep
Delta waves

Delta activity

REM Sleep
Fast, random

Sawtooth waves

REM sleep A stage of sleep characterized by rapid eye movements and a high level of brain activity.

electrooculograph (EOG) An instrument that measures eye movements.

Psychologists learn about what happens when we sleep by collecting EOG, EEG, and other measurements from research volunteers while they sleep in sleep laboratories such as this one.

patterns even lower than alpha waves (*theta waves*). In the second stage of sleep, these patterns are interrupted by short bursts of activity called *sleep spindles* and *K complexes,* and the sleeper becomes somewhat more difficult to awaken. The deepest stages of sleep are stages 3 and 4, known as slow-wave sleep, in which the EEG patterns show activity called *delta waves.*

During the fifth sleep stage, **REM sleep,** *a stage of sleep characterized by rapid eye movements and a high level of brain activity,* EEG patterns become high-frequency sawtooth waves, similar to beta waves, suggesting that the mind at this time is as active as it is during waking (see Figure 5.9). Using an **electrooculograph (EOG)**—*an instrument that measures eye movements*—during sleep, researchers found that sleepers wakened during REM periods reported having dreams much more often than those wakened during non-REM periods (Aserinsky & Kleitman, 1953). During REM sleep, the pulse quickens, blood pressure rises, and there are telltale signs of sexual arousal. At the same time, measurements of muscle movements indicate that the sleeper is very still, except for a rapid side-to-side movement of the eyes. (Watch someone sleeping and you may be able to see the REMs through their closed eyelids. But be careful doing this with strangers down at the bus station.)

Although many people believe that they don't dream much (if at all), some 80% of people awakened during REM sleep report dreams. If you've ever wondered whether dreams actually take place in an instant or whether they take as long to happen as the events they portray might take, the analysis of REM sleep offers an answer. The sleep

◄ Figure 5.10

STAGES OF SLEEP DURING THE NIGHT Over the course of the typical night, sleep cycles into deeper stages early on and then more shallow stages later. REM periods become longer in later cycles, and the deeper slow-wave sleep of stages 3 and 4 disappears halfway through the night.

researchers William Dement and Nathaniel Kleitman (1957) woke volunteers either 5 minutes or 15 minutes after the onset of REM sleep and asked them to judge, on the basis of the events in the remembered dream, how long they had been dreaming. Sleepers in 92 of 111 cases were correct, suggesting that dreaming occurs in "real time." The discovery of REM sleep has offered many insights into dreaming, but not all dreams occur in REM periods. Some dreams are also reported in other sleep stages, but not as many—and the dreams that occur at those times are described as less wild than REM dreams and more like normal thinking.

A Typical Night's Sleep Putting EEG and REM data together produces a picture of how a typical night's sleep progresses through cycles of sleep stages (see **FIGURE 5.10**). In the first hour of the night, you fall all the way from waking to the fourth and deepest stage of sleep, the stage marked by delta waves. These slow waves indicate a general synchronization of neural firing, as though the brain is doing one thing at this time rather than many: the neuronal equivalent of "the wave" moving through the crowd at a stadium as lots of individuals move together in synchrony. You then return to lighter sleep stages, eventually reaching REM and dreamland. Note that although REM sleep is lighter than that of lower stages, it is deep enough that you may be difficult to awaken. You then continue to cycle between REM and slow-wave sleep stages every 90 minutes or so throughout the night. Periods of REM last longer as the night goes on, and lighter sleep stages predominate between these periods, with the deeper slow-wave stages 3 and 4 disappearing halfway through the night. Although you're either unconscious or dream-conscious at the time, your brain and mind cycle through a remarkable array of different states each time you have a night's sleep.

Sleep Needs and Deprivation

How much do people sleep? The answer depends on the age of the sleeper (Dement, 1999). Newborns will sleep 6 to 8 times in 24 hours, often totaling more than 16 hours. Their napping cycle gets consolidated into "sleeping through the night," usually sometime between 9 and 18 months, but occasionally even later. The typical 6-year-old child might need 11 or 12 hours of sleep, and the progression to less sleep then continues into adulthood, when the average is about 7 to 7.5 hours per night. With aging, people can get along with even a bit less sleep than that. Over a whole lifetime, we get about 1 hour of sleep for every 2 hours we are awake.

This is a lot of sleeping. Could we tolerate less? Monitored by William Dement, Randy Gardner stayed up for 264 hours and 12 minutes in 1965 for a science project.

DATA VISUALIZATION
How Does Sleep Affect You?
Go to launchpadworks.com.

Sleep following learning is essential for memory consolidation. Sleep during class, on the other hand, no so much.

When 17-year-old Randy finally did go to sleep, he slept only 14 hours and 40 minutes and awakened essentially recovered (Dement, 1978).

Feats such as this one suggest that sleep might be expendable. This is the theory behind the classic all-nighter that you may have tried just before a rough exam. But it turns out that this theory is mistaken. Robert Stickgold and his colleagues (2000) found that when people learning a difficult perceptual task are kept up all night after they have finished practicing the task, their learning of the task is wiped out. Even after two nights of catch-up sleep, they show little indication of their initial training on the task. Sleep following learning appears to be essential for memory consolidation (see Hot Science: Sleep on It, p. 228 in the Memory chapter). It is as though memories normally deteriorate unless sleep occurs to help keep them in place. Studying all night may help you cram for the exam, but it won't make the material stick, which pretty much defeats the whole purpose.

Sleep turns out to be a necessity rather than a luxury in other ways as well. At the extreme, sleep loss can be fatal. When rats are forced to break Randy Gardner's human waking record and stay awake even longer, they have trouble regulating their body temperature and lose weight although they eat much more than normal. Their bodily systems break down and they die, on average, in 21 days (Rechsthaffen et al., 1983). Shakespeare called sleep "nature's soft nurse," and it is clear that even for healthy young humans, a few hours of sleep deprivation each night can have a cumulative detrimental effect: reducing mental acuity and reaction time, increasing irritability and depression, and increasing the risk of accidents and injury (Coren, 1997).

Some researchers have deprived people of different sleep stages selectively by waking them whenever certain stages are detected. Studies of REM sleep deprivation indicate that this part of sleep is psychologically important. Memory problems and excessive aggression are observed in both humans and rats after only a few days of being wakened whenever REM activity starts (Ellman et al., 1991). The brain must value something about REM sleep, because REM deprivation causes a rebound of more REM sleep the next night (Brunner et al., 1990). Deprivation from slow-wave sleep (in stages 3 and 4), in turn, has more physical effects, with just a few nights of deprivation leaving people feeling tired, fatigued, and hypersensitive to muscle and bone pain (Lentz et al., 1999).

It's clearly dangerous to neglect the need for sleep. But why would we have such a need in the first place? All animals appear to sleep, although the amount of sleep required varies quite a bit (see **FIGURE 5.11**). Giraffes sleep less than 2 hours daily,

▶ Figure 5.11

All animals and insects seem to require sleep, although in differing amounts. Next time you oversleep and someone accuses you of "sleeping like a baby," you might tell them instead that you were sleeping like a tiger, or a brown bat.

whereas brown bats snooze for almost 20 hours. These variations in sleep needs, and the very existence of a need, are hard to explain. Is the restoration that happens during the unconsciousness of sleep something that simply can't be achieved during consciousness? Sleep is, after all, potentially costly in the course of evolution. The sleeping animal is easy prey, so the habit of sleep would not seem to have developed so widely across species unless it had significant benefits that made up for this vulnerability. Theories of sleep have not yet determined why the brain and body have evolved to need these recurring episodes of unconsciousness.

Sleep Disorders

In answer to the question "Did you sleep well?" the comedian Stephen Wright said, "No, I made a couple of mistakes." Sleeping well is something everyone would love to do, but for many people, sleep disorders are deeply troubling. The most common disorders that plague sleep include insomnia, sleep apnea, and somnambulism.

Insomnia, *difficulty in falling asleep or staying asleep,* is perhaps the most common sleep disorder. About 30 to 48% of people report symptoms of insomnia, 9 to 15% report insomnia severe enough to lead to daytime complaints, and 6% of people meet criteria for a diagnosis of insomnia, which involves persistent and impairing sleep problems (Bootzin & Epstein, 2011; Ohayon, 2002). Unfortunately, insomnia often is a persistent problem; most people with insomnia experience it for at least a year (Morin et al., 2009).

Insomnia has many potential causes. In some instances it results from lifestyle choices such as working night shifts (self-induced insomnia), whereas in other cases it occurs in response to depression, anxiety, or some other condition (secondary insomnia). In still other cases there are no obvious causal factors (primary insomnia). Regardless of type, insomnia can be exacerbated by worrying about insomnia (Borkevec, 1982). No doubt you've experienced some nights when sleeping was a high priority, such as before a class presentation or an important interview, and you've found that you were unable to fall asleep. The desire to sleep initiates an ironic process of mental control—a heightened sensitivity to signs of sleeplessness—and this sensitivity interferes with sleep. In fact, participants in an experiment who were instructed to go to sleep quickly became hypersensitive and had more difficulty sleeping than those who were not instructed to hurry (Ansfield, Wegner, & Bowser, 1996). The paradoxical solution for insomnia in some cases, then, may be to give up the pursuit of sleep and instead find something else to do.

Giving up on trying so hard to sleep is probably better than another common remedy—the use of sleeping pills. Although sedatives can be useful for brief sleep problems associated with emotional events, their long-term use is not effective. To begin with, most sleeping pills are addictive. People become dependent on the pills to sleep and may need to increase the dose over time to achieve the same effect. Even in short-term use, sedatives can interfere with the normal sleep cycle. Although they promote sleep, they can reduce the proportion of time spent in REM and slow-wave sleep (Qureshi & Lee-Chiong, 2004), robbing people of dreams and their deepest sleep stages. As a result, the quality of sleep achieved with pills may not be as high as without them, and people may experience side effects such as grogginess and irritability during the day. Finally, stopping the use of sleeping pills suddenly can produce insomnia that is worse than before.

Sleep apnea is *a disorder in which the person stops breathing for brief periods while asleep.* A person with apnea usually snores because apnea involves an involuntary obstruction of the breathing passage. When episodes of apnea occur for over 10 seconds at a time and recur many times during the night, they may cause many awakenings and sleep loss or insomnia. Apnea occurs most often in middle-aged, overweight men (Punjabi, 2008) and may go undiagnosed because it is not easy for the sleeper to notice. Bed partners may be the ones who finally get tired of the snoring and noisy

ROZ CHAST/THE NEW YORKER COLLECTION/WWW.CARTOONBANK.COM

insomnia Difficulty in falling asleep or staying asleep.

sleep apnea A disorder in which the person stops breathing for brief periods while asleep.

PHOTOALTO AGENCY RF COLLECTIONS/GETTY IMAGES

Sleepwalkers in cartoons have their arms outstretched and eyes closed, but that's just for cartoons. A real-life sleepwalker usually walks normally with eyes open, sometimes with a glassy look.

somnambulism (or sleepwalking) Occurs when a person arises and walks around while asleep.

narcolepsy A disorder in which sudden sleep attacks occur in the middle of waking activities.

sleep paralysis The experience of waking up unable to move.

night terrors (or sleep terrors) Abrupt awakenings with panic and intense emotional arousal.

gasping for air when the sleeper's breathing restarts, or the sleeper may eventually seek treatment because of excessive sleepiness during the day. Therapies involving weight loss, drugs, sleep masks that push air into the nasal passage, or surgery may solve the problem.

Somnambulism (or **sleepwalking**), occurs when *a person arises and walks around while asleep.* Sleepwalking is more common in children, peaking between the ages of 4 and 8 years, with 15 to 40% of children experiencing at least one episode (Bhargava, 2011). Sleepwalking tends to happen early in the night, usually during slow-wave sleep. Sleepwalkers may awaken during their walk or return to bed without waking, in which case they will probably not remember the episode in the morning. The sleepwalker's eyes are usually open in a glassy stare. Walking with hands outstretched is uncommon except in cartoons. Sleepwalking is not usually linked to any additional problems and is problematic only in that sleepwalkers sometimes engage in strange or unwise behaviors such as urinating in places other than the toilet and leaving the house while still sleeping. People who walk while they are sleeping do not tend to be very coordinated and can trip over furniture or fall down stairs. After all, they're sleeping. Contrary to popular belief, it is safe to wake sleepwalkers or lead them back to bed.

Other sleep disorders are less common. **Narcolepsy** is *a disorder in which sudden sleep attacks occur in the middle of waking activities.* Narcolepsy involves the intrusion of a dreaming state of sleep (with REM) into waking and is often accompanied by unrelenting excessive sleepiness and uncontrollable sleep attacks lasting from 30 seconds to 30 minutes. This disorder appears to have a genetic basis, because it runs in families, and can be treated effectively with medication. **Sleep paralysis** is *the experience of waking up unable to move* and is sometimes associated with narcolepsy. This eerie experience usually happens as you are awakening from REM sleep but before you have regained motor control. This period typically lasts only a few seconds or minutes and can be accompanied by hypnopompic (when awakening) or hypnagogic (when falling asleep) hallucinations in which dream content may appear to occur in the waking world. A very clever series of recent studies suggests that sleep paralysis accompanied by hypnopompic hallucinations of figures being in one's bedroom seems to explain many perceived instances of alien abductions and recovered memories of sexual abuse (aided by therapists who used hypnosis to help the sleepers [incorrectly] piece it all together; McNally & Clancy, 2005). **Night terrors** (or **sleep terrors**) are *abrupt awakenings with panic and intense emotional arousal.* These terrors, which occur most often in children and in only about 2% of adults (Ohayon, Guilleminault, & Priest, 1999), happen most often in non-REM sleep early in the sleep cycle and do not usually have dream content the sleeper can report.

To sum up, a lot happens when we close our eyes for the night. Humans follow a pretty regular sleep cycle, going through the five stages of sleep during the night. Disruptions to that cycle, either from sleep deprivation or sleep disorders, can produce consequences for waking consciousness. But something else happens during a night's sleep that affects our consciousness, both while asleep and when we wake up.

DREAMS

The pioneering sleep researcher William C. Dement (1959) said, "Dreaming permits each and every one of us to be quietly and safely insane every night of our lives." Indeed, dreams do seem to have a touch of insanity about them. We experience crazy things in dreams, but even more bizarre is the fact that we are the writers, producers, and directors of the crazy things we experience. Just what are these experiences, and how can they be explained?

Dream Consciousness

Dreams depart dramatically from reality. You may dream of being naked in public, of falling from a great height, of sleeping through an important appointment, of your teeth being loose and falling out, or of being chased (Holloway, 2001). These things don't happen much in reality unless you're having a terrible, horrible, no good, very bad day. The quality of consciousness in dreaming is also altered significantly from waking consciousness. Five major characteristics of dream consciousness distinguish it from the waking state (Hobson, 1988).

1. We intensely feel *emotion,* whether it is bliss or terror or love or awe.

2. Dream *thought* is illogical: The continuities of time, place, and person don't apply. You may find you are in one place and then another, for example, without any travel in between—or people may change identity from one dream scene to the next.

3. *Sensation* is fully formed and meaningful; visual sensation is predominant, and you may also deeply experience sound, touch, and movement (although pain is very uncommon).

4. Dreaming occurs with *uncritical acceptance,* as though the images and events are perfectly normal rather than bizarre.

5. We have *difficulty remembering* the dream after it is over. People often remember dreams only if they are awakened during the dream and even then may lose recall for the dream within just a few minutes of waking. If your waking memory were this bad, you'd be standing around half-naked in the street much of the time, having forgotten your destination, clothes, and lunch money.

Not all of our dreams are fantastic and surreal, however. Far from the adventures in nighttime insanity storied by Freud, dreams are often ordinary (Domhoff, 2007). We often dream about mundane topics that reflect prior waking experiences or "day residue." Current conscious concerns pop up (Nikles et al., 1998), along with images from the recent past. A dream may even incorporate sensations experienced during sleep, as when sleepers in one study were led to dream of water when drops were sprayed on their faces during REM sleep (Dement & Wolpert, 1958). The day residue does not usually include episodic memories, that is, complete daytime events replayed in the mind. Instead, dreams that reflect the day's experience tend to single out sensory experiences or objects from waking life. Rather than simply being a replay of that event, dreams often consist of "interleaved fragments of experience" from different times and places that our mind weaves together into a single story (Wamsley & Stickgold, 2011). For instance, after a fun day at the beach with your roommates, your dream that night might include cameo appearances by bouncing beach balls or a flock of seagulls. One study had research participants play the computer game Tetris and found that participants often reported dreaming about the Tetris geometrical figures falling down—even though they seldom reported dreams about being in the experiment or playing the game (Stickgold et al., 2001). Even severely amnesic individuals who couldn't recall playing the game at all reported Tetris-like images appearing in their dreams (Stickgold et al., 2000). The content of dreams takes snapshots from the day rather than retelling the stories of what you have done or seen. This means that dreams often come without clear plots or story lines, so they may not make a lot of sense.

Some of the most memorable dreams are nightmares, and these frightening dreams can wake up the dreamer (Levin & Nielsen, 2009). One set of daily dream logs from college undergraduates suggested that the average student has about 24 nightmares per year (Wood & Bootzin, 1990), although some people may have them as often as every night. Children have more nightmares than adults, and people who have experienced traumatic events are inclined to have nightmares that relive those events.

WARNER BROS/THE KOBAL COLLECTION/ART RESOURCE

Dreams often are quite intense, vivid, and illogical. This can lead to very cool experiences, such as that depicted in this scene from the movie *Inception.*

The Nightmare, by Henry Fuseli (1790). Fuseli depicts not only a mare in this painting but also an incubus—an imp perched on the dreamer's chest that is traditionally associated with especially horrifying nightmares.

GOETHE HOUSE AND MUSEUM/SNARK/ART RESOURCE, NY

Following the 1989 earthquake in the San Francisco Bay area, for example, college students who had experienced the quake reported more nightmares than those who had not and often reported that the dreams were about the quake (Wood et al., 1992). This effect of trauma may not only produce dreams of the traumatic event: When police officers experience "critical incidents" of conflict and danger, they tend to have more nightmares in general (Neylan et al., 2002).

Dream Theories

Dreams are puzzles that cry out to be solved. How could you not want to make sense out of these experiences? Although dreams may be fantastic and confusing, they are emotionally riveting, filled with vivid images from your own life, and they seem very real. The search for dream meaning goes all the way back to biblical figures, who interpreted dreams and looked for prophecies in them. In the Old Testament, the prophet Daniel (a favorite of three of the authors of this book) curried favor with King Nebuchadnezzar of Babylon by interpreting the king's dream. The question of what dreams mean has been burning since antiquity, mainly because the meaning of dreams is usually far from obvious.

Freud's View: Dreams Hold Meaning   In the first psychological theory of dreams, Freud (1900/1965) proposed that dreams are confusing and obscure because the dynamic unconscious creates them precisely *to be* confusing and obscure. According to Freud's theory, dreams represent wishes, and some of these wishes are so unacceptable, taboo, and anxiety producing that the mind can express them only in disguised form. Freud believed that many of the most unacceptable wishes are sexual. For instance, he would interpret a dream of a train going into a tunnel as symbolic of sexual intercourse. According to Freud, the **manifest content** of a dream, *a dream's apparent topic or superficial meaning,* is a smoke screen for its **latent content,** *a dream's true underlying meaning.* For example, a dream about a tree burning down in the park across the street from where a friend once lived (the manifest content) might represent a camouflaged wish for the death of the friend (the latent content). In this case, wishing for the death of a friend is unacceptable, so it is disguised as a tree on fire. The problem with Freud's approach is that any dream has an infinite number of potential interpretations. Finding the correct one is a matter of guesswork—and of convincing the dreamer that one interpretation is superior to the others.

Although dreams may not represent elaborately hidden wishes, there is evidence that they do feature the return of suppressed thoughts. Researchers asked volunteers to think of a personal acquaintance and then to spend five minutes before going to bed writing down whatever came to mind (Wegner, Wenzlaff, & Kozak, 2004). Some participants were asked to suppress thoughts of this person as they wrote, others were asked to focus on thoughts of the person, and yet others were asked just to write freely about anything. The next morning, participants wrote dream reports. Overall, all participants mentioned dreaming more about the person they had named than about other people. But they most often dreamed of the person they named if they were in the group that had been assigned to suppress thoughts of the person the night before. This finding suggests that Freud was right to suspect that dreams harbor unwanted thoughts. Perhaps this is why actors dream of forgetting their lines, travelers dream of getting lost, and football players dream of fumbling the ball.

The Activation–Synthesis Model: The Brain Imposes Meaning on Random Neural Activity   Another key theory of dreaming is the **activation–synthesis model** (Hobson & McCarley, 1977). This theory proposes that dreams are produced when the brain attempts to make sense of random neural activity that occurs during

manifest content A dream's apparent topic or superficial meaning.

latent content A dream's true underlying meaning.

activation–synthesis model The theory that dreams are produced when the brain attempts to make sense of random neural activity that occurs during sleep.

sleep. During waking consciousness, the mind is devoted to interpreting lots of information that arrives through the senses. You figure out that the odd noise you're hearing during class is your cell phone vibrating, for example, or you realize that the strange smell in the hall outside your room must be from burned popcorn. In the dream state, the mind doesn't have access to external sensations, but it keeps on doing what it usually does: interpreting information. Because that information now comes from neural activations that occur without the continuity provided by the perception of reality, the brain's interpretive mechanisms can run free. This might be why, for example, a person in a dream can sometimes change into someone else. No actual person is being perceived to help the mind keep a stable view. In the mind's effort to perceive and give meaning to brain activation, the person you view in a dream about a grocery store might seem to be a clerk, but then change to be your favorite teacher when the dream scene moves to your school. The great interest people have in interpreting their dreams the next morning may be an extension of the interpretive activity they've been doing all night.

The Freudian theory and the activation–synthesis theory differ in the significance they place on the meaning of dreams. In Freud's theory, dreams begin with meaning, whereas in the activation–synthesis theory, dreams begin randomly—but meaning can be added as the mind lends interpretations in the process of dreaming. Dream research has not yet sorted out whether one of these theories or yet another might be the best account of the meaning of dreams.

The Dreaming Brain

What happens in the brain when we dream? Several studies have involved making fMRI scans of people's brains during sleep, focusing on the areas of the brain that show changes in activation during REM periods. These studies show that the brain changes that occur during REM sleep correspond clearly with certain alterations of consciousness that occur in dreaming. **FIGURE 5.12** shows some of the patterns of activation and deactivation found in the dreaming brain (Nir & Tononi, 2010; Schwartz & Maquet, 2002).

In dreams there are heights to look down from, dangerous people lurking, the occasional monster, some minor worries, and at least once in a while that major exam you've forgotten about until you walk into class. These themes suggest that the brain areas responsible for fear or emotion somehow work overtime in dreams, and it turns out that this is clearly visible in fMRI scans. The amygdala is involved in responses to threatening or stressful events, and indeed the amygdala is quite active during REM sleep.

Freud theorized that dreams represent unacceptable wishes that the mind can only express in disguised form. The activation–synthesis model proposes that dreams are produced when the mind attempts to make sense of random neural activity that occurs during sleep. Suppose a man is expecting a visit from his mother-in-law; the night before her arrival, he dreams that a bus is driven through the living room window of his house. How might Freud have interpreted such a dream? How might the activation–synthesis model interpret such a dream?

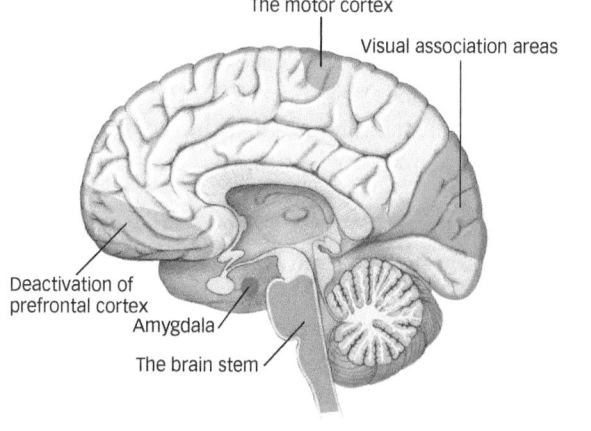

The motor cortex

Visual association areas

Deactivation of prefrontal cortex

Amygdala

The brain stem

(a)

(b)

◄ Figure 5.12

BRAIN ACTIVATION AND DEACTIVATION DURING REM SLEEP Brain areas shaded red are activated during REM sleep; those shaded blue are deactivated. (a) The medial view shows activation of the amygdala, the visual association areas, the motor cortex, and the brain stem and deactivation of the prefrontal cortex. (b) The ventral view shows activation of other visual association areas and deactivation of the prefrontal cortex (Schwartz & Maquet, 2002).

Dreaming Blind

What are your dreams like? Are they mostly visual? Do you hear sounds? Do you experience the sense of touch? taste? smell? We all differ in our experience of dreaming, just as we do in our waking life. Most people have the ability to experience all of their senses during dreaming. But what about people who lack the ability to experience one of their senses? What is the experience of dreaming like for those who are blind? Researchers have examined this question by asking people who are blind to keep dream journals each day for several weeks, and comparing their reports of their dreams with those of people with sight. For instance, a study by Meaidi and colleagues (2014) revealed that 100% of dreams among sighted people contain visual impressions, compared with only about 75% of dreams among those who had sight and then lost it ("late blind") and 20% of dreams among those who were born blind ("congenitally blind"). It is perhaps not surprising that people who could never see are less likely to "see" during

their dreams, but interesting that in 20% of their dreams they can see (although these visual impressions occur only in blind individuals who have at least some amount of light perception).

The lack of visual content in the dreams of people who are blind is made up for by a higher percentage of dreams containing auditory and tactile impressions, as shown in the figure.

Unfortunately, those who are congenitally blind also have a much higher

frequency of nightmares, which occur in nearly 25% of their dreams. These nightmares often have the theme that the blind person is doing something wrong (as a result of their lack of sight), which leads to aggressive responses from others (Maeidi et al., 2014). Virtually all of psychology is focused on understanding the waking mind; however, there appear to be a wide range of important individual differences in the experience of the dreaming mind that are just beginning to be understood.

=O= Sighted   =□= Legally blind   =△= Congenitally blind

The typical dream is also a visual wonderland, with visual events present in almost all dreams. However, there are fewer auditory sensations, even fewer tactile sensations, and almost no smells or tastes. Moreover, people differ dramatically in how much of each sensation they experience in their dreams, as described in A World of Difference: Dreaming Blind. This dream "picture show" doesn't involve actual perception, of course, just the imagination of visual events. It turns out that the areas of the brain responsible for visual perception are *not* activated during dreaming, whereas the visual association areas in the occipital lobe that are responsible for visual imagery *do* show activation (Braun et al., 1998). Your brain is smart enough to realize that it's not really seeing bizarre images but acts instead as though it's imagining bizarre images.

During REM sleep, the prefrontal cortex shows relatively less arousal than it usually does during waking consciousness. What does this mean for the dreamer? As a rule, the prefrontal areas are associated with planning and executing actions, and often dreams seem to be unplanned and rambling. Perhaps this is why dreams often don't have very sensible story lines—they've been scripted by an author whose ability to plan is inactive.

Another odd fact of dreaming is that although the eyes are moving rapidly, the body is otherwise very still. During REM sleep, the motor cortex is activated, but spinal neurons running through the brain stem inhibit the expression of this motor activation (Lai & Siegal, 1999). This turns out to be a useful property of brain activation in dreaming; otherwise, you might get up and act out every dream! Individuals suffering from one rare sleep disorder, in fact, lose the normal muscular inhibition accompanying REM sleep and so act out their dreams, thrashing around in bed or stalking around the bedroom (Mahowald & Schenck, 2000). However, most people who are moving during sleep are probably not dreaming. The brain specifically inhibits movement during dreams, perhaps to keep us from hurting ourselves.

Build to the Outcomes

1. What do EEG recordings tell us about sleep?

2. What are the stages in a typical night's sleep?

3. What is the relationship between sleep and learning?

4. What are some problems caused by sleeping pills?

5. Is it safe to wake a sleepwalker?

6. What distinguishes dream consciousness from the waking state?

7. According to Freud, what do dreams represent?

8. What does the activation–synthesis model propose about the link between the brain and dreams?

9. What do fMRI studies tell us about why dreams don't have coherent story lines?

Drugs and Consciousness: Artificial Inspiration

The author of the dystopian novel *Brave New World,* Aldous Huxley (1932), once wrote of his experiences with the drug mescaline. *The Doors of Perception* described the intense experience that accompanied Huxley's departure from normal consciousness. He described "a world where everything shone with the Inner Light, and was infinite in its significance. The legs, for example, of a chair—how miraculous their tubularity, how supernatural their polished smoothness! I spent several minutes—or was it several centuries?—not merely gazing at those bamboo legs, but actually *being* them" (Huxley, 1954, p. 22).

Being the legs of a chair? This probably is better than being the seat of a chair, but it still sounds like an odd experience. Still, many people seek out such experiences, often through using drugs. **Psychoactive drugs** are *chemicals that influence consciousness or behavior by altering the brain's chemical message system.* You read about several such drugs in the Neuroscience and Behavior chapter when we explored the brain's system of neurotransmitters. And you will read about them in a different light when we turn to their role in the treatment of psychological disorders in the Treatment chapter. Whether these drugs are used for entertainment, for treatment, or for other reasons, they each exert their influence by increasing the activity of a neurotransmitter (the agonists) or decreasing its activity (the antagonists).

Some of the most common neurotransmitters are serotonin, dopamine, gamma-aminobutyric acid (GABA), and acetylcholine. Drugs alter the functioning of neurotransmitters by preventing them from binding to sites on the postsynaptic neuron, by inhibiting their reuptake to the presynaptic neuron, or by enhancing their binding and transmission. Different drugs can intensify or dull transmission patterns, creating changes in brain electrical activities that mimic natural operations of the brain. For example, a drug such as Valium (benzodiazepine) induces sleep but prevents dreaming and so induces a state similar to slow-wave sleep—that is, what the brain naturally develops several times each night. Other drugs prompt patterns of brain activity that do not occur naturally, however, and their influence on consciousness can be dramatic. Like Huxley, who perceived himself becoming the legs of a chair, people using drugs can have experiences unlike any they might find in normal waking consciousness or even in dreams. To understand these altered states, let's explore how people use and abuse drugs, and examine the major categories of psychoactive drugs.

Learning Outcomes

▶ Explain the dangers of addiction.

▶ Identify categories of psychoactive drugs and their effects on the body.

psychoactive drugs Chemicals that influence consciousness or behavior by altering the brain's chemical message system.

Why do kids enjoy spinning around until they get so dizzy that they fall down? Even when we are young, there seems to be something enjoyable about altering states of consciousness.

MATTHEW NOCK

DRUG USE AND ABUSE

Why do children sometimes spin around until they get dizzy and fall down? There is something strangely attractive about states of consciousness that depart from the norm, and people throughout history have sought out these altered states by dancing, fasting, chanting, meditating, and ingesting a bizarre assortment of chemicals to intoxicate themselves (Tart, 1969). People pursue altered consciousness even when there are costs, from the nausea that accompanies dizziness to the life-wrecking obsession with a drug that can come with addiction. In this regard, the pursuit of altered consciousness can be a fatal attraction.

Often, drug-induced changes in consciousness begin as pleasant and spark an initial attraction. Researchers have measured the attractiveness of psychoactive drugs by seeing how hard laboratory animals will work to get them. In one study researchers allowed rats to administer cocaine to themselves intravenously by pressing a lever (Bozarth & Wise, 1985). Rats given free access to cocaine increased their use over the course of the 30-day study. They not only continued to self-administer at a high rate but also occasionally binged to the point of giving themselves convulsions. They stopped grooming themselves and eating until they lost on average almost a third of their body weight. About 90% of the rats died by the end of the study. The picture is not so simple, however, because rats show more attraction to sweets such as sugar or saccharine than they do to cocaine (Lenoir et al., 2007), suggesting that the idea that drugs are more addictive than any other substance is an oversimplification (Hart, 2013).

Rats are not tiny little humans, of course, so such research is not a firm basis for understanding human responses to cocaine. But these results do make it clear that cocaine is addictive and that the consequences of such addiction can be dire. Studies of self-administration of drugs in laboratory animals show that animals will work to obtain not only cocaine but also alcohol, amphetamines, barbiturates, caffeine, opiates (such as morphine and heroin), nicotine, phencyclidine (PCP), MDMA (Ecstasy), and THC (tetrahydrocannabinol, the active ingredient in marijuana). There are some psychoactive drugs that animals won't work for (such as mescaline or the antipsychotic drug phenothiazine), suggesting that these drugs have less potential for causing addiction (Bozarth, 1987).

Dangers of Addiction

People usually do not become addicted to a psychoactive drug the first time they use it. They may experiment a few times, then try again, and eventually find that their tendency to use the drug increases over time. Three primary factors are influential:

1. **Drug tolerance** is *the tendency for larger drug doses to be required over time to achieve the same effect.* Physicians who prescribe morphine to control pain in their patients are faced with tolerance problems, because steadily greater amounts of the drug may be needed to dampen the same pain. With increased tolerance comes the danger of drug overdose; recreational users find they need to use more and more of a drug to produce the same high. But then, if a new batch of heroin or cocaine is more concentrated than usual, the "normal" amount the user takes to achieve the same high can be fatal.

2. *Physical dependence* is the pain, convulsions, hallucinations, or other unpleasant symptoms that accompany withdrawal from drug use. People who suffer from physical dependence may seek to continue drug use to avoid becoming physically ill. A common example is the "caffeine headache" some people complain of when they haven't had their daily jolt of java.

3. *Psychological dependence* is a strong desire to return to the drug even when physical withdrawal symptoms are gone. Drugs can create an emotional need

drug tolerance The tendency for larger doses of a drug to be required over time to achieve the same effect.

over time that continues to prey on the mind, particularly in circumstances that are reminders of the drug. Some ex-smokers report longing wistfully for an after-dinner smoke, for example, even years after they've successfully quit the habit.

Drug addiction reveals a human frailty: our inability to look past the immediate consequences of our behavior to see and appreciate the long-term consequences. Although we would like to think that our behavior is guided by a rational analysis of future consequences, more typically occasions when we "play first, pay later" lead directly to "let's just play a lot right now." There is something intensely inviting about the prospect of a soon-to-be-had pleasure and something pale, hazy, and distant about the costs this act might bring at some future time. For example, given the choice of receiving $1 today or $2 a week later, most people will take the $1 today. However, if the same choice is to be made for some date a year in the future (when the immediate pleasure of today's windfall is not so strong; for instance, $1 in 52 weeks vs. $2 in 53 weeks), people choose to wait and get the $2 (Ainslie, 2001). The immediate satisfaction associated with taking most drugs may outweigh a rational analysis of the later consequences that can result from taking those drugs, such as drug addiction.

The psychological and social problems stemming from drug addiction are immense. For many people, drug addiction becomes a way of life, and for some, it is a cause of death. Like the cocaine-addicted rats in the study noted earlier (Bozarth & Wise, 1985), some people become so attached to a drug that their lives are ruled by it. However, this is not always the end of the story. This ending is best known because the addict becomes a recurrent, visible social problem, "publicized" through repeated crime and repeated appearances in prisons and treatment programs. But a life of addiction is not the only possible end point of drug use.

Most People Who Use Drugs Do Not Become Addicted

Stanley Schachter (1982) suggested that the visibility of addiction is misleading and that in fact, many people overcome addictions. He found that 64% of a sample of people who had a history of cigarette smoking had quit successfully, although many had to try again and again to achieve their success. Indeed, large-scale studies conducted in the 1980s, 1990s, and 2000s consistently show that approximately 75% of those with substance use disorders overcome their addiction, with the biggest drop in use occurring between ages 20 and 30 (Heyman, 2009). One classic study of soldiers who became addicted to heroin in Vietnam found that, years after their return, only 12% remained addicted (Robins et al., 1980). The return to the attractions and obligations of normal life, as well as the absence of the familiar places and faces associated with their old drug habit, made it possible for returning soldiers to quit successfully. Although addiction is dangerous, it is not necessarily incurable. More recent carefully controlled laboratory studies in which people are asked to select between a hit of their drug of choice or a small monetary reward (e.g., $5) show that people addicted to drugs such as crack cocaine and methamphetamine very often choose a small monetary reward over taking the drug, suggesting that addictive drugs often are not so powerfully addictive as the media portrays them to be (Hart, 2013).

What's Considered "Addictive" Can Change

It may not be accurate to view all recreational drug use under the umbrella of "addiction." Many people at this point in the history of Western society, for example, would not call the repeated use of caffeine an addiction, and some do not label the use of alcohol, tobacco, or marijuana in this way. In other times and places, however, each of these has been considered a terrifying addiction worthy of prohibition and public censure. In the early 17th century, for example, tobacco use was punishable by death in Germany, by castration in Russia, and by decapitation in China (Corti, 1931). Not a good time or place to be a smoker. By contrast, cocaine, heroin, marijuana,

Many soldiers serving in Vietnam became addicted to heroin while there. Robins and colleagues (1980) found that after returning home to the United States, the vast majority left their drug habit behind and were no longer addicted.

© SUEDDEUTSCHE ZEITUNG PHOTO/ALAMY

The production, sale, and transportation of alcohol was made illegal in the U.S. in 1920. This period of "prohibition" ended in 1933 due to social and economic pressures. Although most U.S. counties allow the sale of alcohol (shown on the map in blue), there are still many counties where there are laws restricting alcohol sales (shown in yellow) and even some "dry" counties where selling alcohol is illegal (shown in red). Why might the prohibition of alcohol have failed nationally?

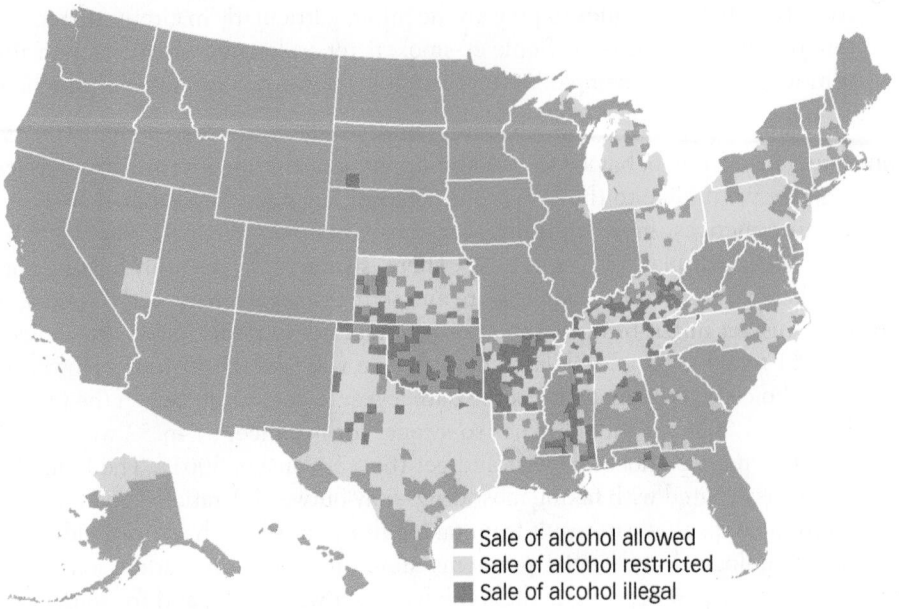

- Sale of alcohol allowed
- Sale of alcohol restricted
- Sale of alcohol illegal

and amphetamines have each been popular and even recommended as medicines at several points throughout history, each without any stigma of addiction attached (Inciardi, 2001).

Although "addiction" as a concept is familiar to most of us, there is no standard clinical definition of what an addiction actually is. The concept of addiction has been extended to many human pursuits, giving rise to such terms as *sex addict*, *gambling addict*, *workaholic*, and, of course, *chocoholic*. Societies react differently at different times, with some uses of drugs ignored, other uses encouraged, others simply taxed, and yet others subjected to intense prohibition (see the Real World: Drugs and the Regulation of Consciousness on p. 205). Rather than viewing *all* drug use as a problem, we need to consider the costs and benefits of such use and to establish ways to help people choose behaviors that are informed by this knowledge (Parrott et al., 2005).

TYPES OF PSYCHOACTIVE DRUGS

Four in five North Americans use caffeine in some form every day, but not all psychoactive drugs are this familiar. To learn how both the well-known and lesser-known drugs influence the mind, let's consider several broad categories of drugs: depressants, stimulants, narcotics, hallucinogens, and marijuana. **TABLE 5.3** summarizes what is known about the potential dangers of these different types of drugs.

Depressants

Depressants are *substances that reduce the activity of the central nervous system*. The most commonly used depressant is alcohol; others include barbiturates, benzodiazepines, and toxic inhalants (such as glue or gasoline). Depressants have a sedative or calming effect, tend to induce sleep in high doses, and can arrest breathing in extremely high doses. Depressants can produce both physical and psychological dependence.

Alcohol

Alcohol is king of the depressants, with its worldwide use beginning in prehistory, its easy availability in most cultures, and its widespread acceptance as a socially approved substance. Fifty-two percent of Americans over 12 years of age report having had a drink in the past month, and 24% have binged on alcohol (over five drinks in succession) in that time. Young adults (ages 18–25) have even higher rates, with 62% reporting a drink the previous month and 42% reporting a binge (National Center for Health Statistics, 2012).

depressants Substances that reduce the activity of the central nervous system.

TABLE 5.3

Dangers of Drugs

Drug	Dangers		
	Overdose (Can taking too much cause death or injury?)	**Physical Dependence** (Will stopping use make you sick?)	**Psychological Dependence** (Will you crave it when you stop using it?)
Depressants			
Alcohol	X	X	X
Benzodiazepines/Barbiturates	X	X	X
Toxic inhalants	X	X	X
Stimulants			
Amphetamines	X	X	X
MDMA (Ecstasy)	X		?
Nicotine	X	X	X
Cocaine	X	X	X
Narcotics (opium, heroin, morphine, methadone, codeine)	X	X	X
Hallucinogens (LSD, mescaline, psilocybin, PCP, ketamine)	X		?
Marijuana		?	?

Alcohol's initial effects, euphoria and reduced anxiety, feel pretty positive. As alcohol is consumed in greater quantities, drunkenness results, bringing slowed reactions, slurred speech, poor judgment, and other reductions in the effectiveness of thought and action. The exact way in which alcohol influences neural mechanisms is still not understood, but like other depressants, alcohol increases activity of the neurotransmitter GABA (De Witte, 1996). As you read in the Neuroscience and Behavior chapter, GABA normally inhibits the transmission of neural impulses, and so one effect of alcohol is as an inhibitor—a chemical that stops the firing of other neurons. But there are many contradictions. Some people using alcohol become loud and aggressive, others become emotional and weepy, others become sullen, and still others turn giddy—and the same person can experience each of these effects in different circumstances. How can one drug do this? Two theories have been offered to account for these variable effects: *expectancy theory* and *alcohol myopia.*

1. **Expectancy theory** suggests that *alcohol effects can be produced by people's expectations of how alcohol will influence them in particular situations* (Marlatt & Rohsenow, 1980). So, for instance, if you've watched friends or family drink at weddings and notice that this often produces hilarity and gregariousness, you could well experience these effects yourself should you drink alcohol on a similarly festive occasion. Seeing people getting drunk and fighting in bars, in turn, might lead to aggression after drinking. The expectancy theory has been tested in experiments using a **balanced placebo design**, in which *behavior is observed following the presence or absence of an actual stimulus and also following the presence or absence of a placebo stimulus.* In such a study, participants are given drinks containing alcohol or a substitute liquid (adjusted for scent and color), and some people in each group are led to believe they had alcohol and others

expectancy theory The idea that alcohol effects can be produced by people's expectations of how alcohol will influence them in particular situations.

balanced placebo design A study design in which behavior is observed following the presence or absence of an actual stimulus and also following the presence or absence of a placebo stimulus.

LISE GAGNE/GETTY IMAGES

Which theory, expectancy theory or alcohol myopia, views a person's response to alcohol as being (at least partially) learned, through a process similar to observational learning?

are led to believe they did not. These experiments often show that the belief that one has had alcohol can influence behavior as strongly as the ingestion of alcohol itself (Goldman, Brown, & Christiansen, 1987).

2. The theory of **alcohol myopia** proposes that *alcohol hampers attention, leading people to respond in simple ways to complex situations* (Steele & Josephs, 1990). This theory recognizes that life is filled with complicated pushes and pulls, and our behavior is often a balancing act. Imagine that you are really attracted to someone who is dating your friend. Do you make your feelings known or focus on your friendship? The myopia theory holds that when you drink alcohol, your fine judgment is impaired. It becomes hard to appreciate the subtlety of these different options, and the inappropriate response is to veer full tilt one way or the other. In one study on the alcohol myopia theory, men (half of whom were drinking alcohol) watched a video showing an unfriendly woman and then were asked how acceptable it would be for a man to act in a sexually aggressive way toward a woman (Johnson, Noel, & Sutter-Hernandez, 2000). The unfriendly woman seemed to remind them that sex was out of the question, and indeed, men who were drinking alcohol and had seen this video were no more likely to think sexual advances were acceptable than were men who were sober. However, when the same question was asked of a group of men who had seen a video of a *friendly* woman, those who were drinking were more inclined to recommend sexual overtures than those who were not, even when these overtures might be unwanted. Apparently, alcohol makes the complicated decisions involved in relationships seem simple ("Gee, she was so friendly")—and potentially open to serious misjudgments.

Both the expectancy and myopia theories suggest that people using alcohol will often go to extremes (Cooper, 2006). In fact, it seems that drinking is a major contributing factor to social problems that result from extreme behavior. Drinking while driving is a major cause of auto accidents. Twenty-two percent of drivers involved in fatal car crashes in 2009 had a blood alcohol level of .08% or higher (U.S. Census Bureau, 2012). Alcohol also has been linked to increased aggression toward others in dozens of studies, including increased likelihood of aggression in general, as well as sexual violence and intimate partner violence (Crane et al., 2015).

Barbiturates, Benzodiazepines, and Toxic Inhalants. Compared to alcohol, the other depressants are much less popular, but still are widely used and abused. Barbiturates such as Seconal or Nembutal are prescribed as sleep aids and as anesthetics before surgery. Benzodiazepines such as Valium and Xanax are also called minor tranquilizers and are prescribed as antianxiety drugs. These drugs are prescribed by physicians to treat anxiety or sleep problems, but they are dangerous when used in combination with alcohol because they can cause respiratory depression. Physical dependence is possible because withdrawal from long-term use can produce severe symptoms (including convulsions), and psychological dependence is common as well. Finally, toxic inhalants are perhaps the most alarming substances in this category (Ridenour & Howard, 2012). These drugs are easily accessible even to children in the vapors of household products such as glue, hair spray, nail polish remover, or gasoline. Sniffing or "huffing" vapors from these products can promote temporary effects that resemble drunkenness, but overdoses can be lethal, and continued use holds the potential for permanent neurological damage (Howard et al., 2011).

Stimulants

Stimulants are *substances that excite the central nervous system, heightening arousal and activity levels.* They include caffeine, amphetamines, nicotine, cocaine, modafinil, and Ecstasy, and sometimes have a legitimate pharmaceutical purpose. Amphetamines

alcohol myopia A condition that results when alcohol hampers attention, leading people to respond in simple ways to complex situations.

stimulants Substances that excite the central nervous system, heightening arousal and activity levels.

(also called *speed*), for example, were originally prepared for medicinal uses and as diet drugs; however, amphetamines such as Methedrine and Dexedrine are widely abused, causing insomnia, aggression, and paranoia with long-term use. Stimulants increase the levels of dopamine and norepinephrine in the brain, thereby inducing higher levels of activity in the brain circuits that depend on these neurotransmitters. As a result, they increase alertness and energy in the user, often producing a euphoric sense of confidence and a kind of agitated motivation to get things done. Stimulants produce physical and psychological dependence, and their withdrawal symptoms involve depressive effects such as fatigue and negative emotions.

Ecstasy (also known as MDMA, "X," or "E"), an amphetamine derivative, is a stimulant, but it has added effects somewhat like those of hallucinogens. (We'll talk about those shortly.) Ecstasy is particularly known for making users feel empathic and close to those around them. It is used often as a party drug to enhance the group feeling at dance clubs or raves, but it has unpleasant side effects, such as causing jaw clenching and interfering with the regulation of body temperature. The rave culture has popularized pacifiers and juices as remedies for these problems, but users remain highly susceptible to heat stroke and exhaustion. Although Ecstasy is not so likely as some other drugs to cause physical or psychological dependence, it nonetheless can lead to some dependence. What's more, the impurities sometimes found in street pills are also dangerous (Parrott, 2001). Ecstasy's potentially toxic effect on serotonin neurons in the human brain is under debate, although mounting evidence from animal and human studies suggests that sustained use is associated with damage to serotonergic neurons and potentially associated problems with mood, attention and memory, and impulse control (Kish et al., 2010; Urban et al., 2012).

Cocaine is derived from leaves of the coca plant, which has been cultivated by indigenous peoples of the Andes for millennia and chewed as a medication. Yes, the urban legend is true: Coca-Cola contained cocaine until 1903 and still may use coca leaves (with cocaine removed) as a flavoring—although the company's not telling. (Pepsi-Cola never contained cocaine and is probably made from something brown.) Sigmund Freud tried cocaine and wrote effusively about it for a while. Cocaine (usually snorted) and crack cocaine (smoked) produce exhilaration and euphoria and are seriously addictive, both for humans and the rats you read about earlier in this chapter. Withdrawal takes the form of an unpleasant crash, and dangerous side effects of cocaine use include both psychological problems such as insomnia, depression, aggression, and paranoia, as well as physical problems such as death from a heart attack or hyperthermia (Marzuk et al., 1998). Although cocaine has enjoyed popularity as a party drug, its extraordinary potential to create dependence and potentially lethal side effects should be taken very seriously.

Nicotine is something of a puzzle. This is a drug with almost nothing to recommend it to the newcomer. It usually involves inhaling smoke that doesn't smell that great, at least at first, and there's not much in the way of a high either—at best, some dizziness or a queasy feeling. So why do people use it? Tobacco use is motivated far more by the unpleasantness of quitting than by the pleasantness of using. The positive effects people report from smoking—relaxation and improved concentration, for example—come chiefly from relief from withdrawal symptoms (Baker, Brandon, & Chassin, 2004). The best approach to nicotine is to never get started.

Narcotics

Opium, which comes from poppy seeds, and its derivatives heroin, morphine, methadone, and codeine (as well as prescription drugs such as Demerol and Oxycontin), are known as **narcotics** (or **opiates**), *highly addictive drugs derived from opium that relieve pain.* Narcotics induce a feeling of well-being and relaxation that is enjoyable but can also induce stupor and lethargy. The addictive properties of narcotics are powerful, and long-term use produces both tolerance and dependence. Because these drugs are

Because of the known dangers of smoking cigarettes, many are turning to electronic cigarettes (e-cigarettes) under the assumption that they are a safe alternative. However, a recent investigation of the chemicals contained in flavored e-cigarettes revealed that 92% of them contain the dangerous chemical diacetyl, which has been linked to severe and irreversible medical problems such as "popcorn lung" (Allen et al., 2016).

People will often endure significant inconveniences to maintain their addictions.

narcotics (or opiates) Highly addictive drugs derived from opium that relieve pain.

hallucinogens Drugs that alter sensation and perception and often cause visual and auditory hallucinations.

marijuana (or cannabis) The leaves and buds of the hemp plant, which contain a psychoactive drug called tetrahydrocannabinol (THC).

often administered with hypodermic syringes, they also introduce the danger of diseases such as HIV when users share syringes. Unfortunately, these drugs are especially alluring because they mimic the brain's own internal relaxation and well-being system.

The brain produces endogenous opioids or endorphins, which are neuropeptides closely related to opiates. As you learned in the Neuroscience and Behavior chapter, endorphins play a role in how the brain copes internally with pain and stress. These substances reduce the experience of pain naturally. When you exercise for a while and start to feel your muscles burning, for example, you may also find that a time comes when the pain eases—sometimes even *during* exercise. Endorphins are secreted in the pituitary gland and other brain sites as a response to injury or exertion, creating a kind of natural remedy, sometimes referred to as "runner's high" that subsequently reduces pain and increases feelings of well-being. (Recent, interesting research suggests that runner's high also seems to be induced in part by activation of the brain's endocannabinoid system—the same one involved in response to smoking marijuana; Fuss et al., 2015.) When people use narcotics, the brain's endorphin receptors are artificially flooded, however, reducing receptor effectiveness and possibly also depressing the production of endorphins. When external administration of narcotics stops, withdrawal symptoms are likely to occur.

Hallucinogens

The drugs that produce the most extreme alterations of consciousness are the **hallucinogens**, *drugs that alter sensation and perception, and often cause visual and auditory hallucinations.* These include LSD (lysergic acid diethylamide, or acid), mescaline, psilocybin, PCP (phencyclidine), and ketamine (an animal anesthetic). Some of these drugs are derived from plants (mescaline from peyote cactus, psilocybin or "shrooms" from mushrooms) and have been used by people since ancient times. For example, the ingestion of peyote plays a prominent role in some Native American religious practices. The other hallucinogens are largely synthetic. LSD was first made by the chemist Albert Hofmann in 1938, leading to a rash of experimentation that influenced popular culture in the 1960s. Timothy Leary, at the time a lecturer in the Department of Psychology at Harvard, championed the use of LSD to "turn on, tune in, and drop out"; the Beatles sang of "*Lucy in the Sky with Diamonds*" (denying, of course, that this might be a reference to LSD); and the wave of interest led many people to experiment with hallucinogens.

The experiment was not a great success. These drugs produce profound changes in perception. Sensations may seem unusually intense, stationary objects may seem to move or change, patterns or colors may appear, and these perceptions may be accompanied by exaggerated emotions ranging from blissful transcendence to abject terror. These are the "I've-become-the-legs-of-a-chair!" drugs. But the effects of hallucinogens are dramatic and unpredictable, creating a psychological roller-coaster ride that some people find intriguing and others find deeply disturbing. Hallucinogens are the main class of drugs that animals won't work to self-administer, so it is not surprising that in humans these drugs are unlikely to be addictive. Hallucinogens do not induce significant tolerance or dependence, and overdose deaths are rare. Although hallucinogens still enjoy a marginal popularity with people interested in experimenting with their perceptions, they have been more a cultural trend than a dangerous attraction.

ANDREW HERXGERS CREATIVE/SUPERSTOCK

Psychedelic art and music of the 1960s were inspired by some visual and auditory effects of drugs such as LSD.

Marijuana

Marijuana (or **cannabis**) *is a plant whose leaves and buds contain a psychoactive drug called tetrahydrocannabinol (THC).* When smoked or eaten, either as is or in concentrated form as *hashish,* this drug produces an intoxication that is mildly hallucinogenic. Users describe the experience as euphoric, with heightened senses of sight and sound and the perception of a rush of ideas. Marijuana affects judgment and short-term memory, and impairs motor skills and coordination—making driving a car or operating heavy equipment a poor choice during its use. ("Dude, where's my bulldozer?") Researchers have found that receptors in the brain that respond to THC (Stephens, 1999) are normally activated by a neurotransmitter called *anandamide* that is naturally produced in the brain (Wiley, 1999). Anandamide is involved in the regulation of mood, memory, appetite, and pain perception and has been found temporarily to stimulate overeating in laboratory animals, much as marijuana does in humans (Williams & Kirkham, 1999). Some chemicals found in dark chocolate also mimic anandamide, although very weakly, perhaps accounting for the well-being some people claim they enjoy after a "dose" of chocolate.

The addiction potential of marijuana is not strong, because tolerance does not seem to develop, and physical withdrawal symptoms are minimal. Psychological dependence is possible, however, and some people do become chronic users. Marijuana use has been widespread throughout the world throughout recorded history, both as a medicine for pain and/or nausea and as a recreational drug, but its use remains controversial. Marijuana abuse and dependence have been linked with increased risk of depression, anxiety, and other forms of psychopathology. Many people also are concerned that marijuana (along with alcohol and tobacco) is a **gateway drug,** *a drug whose use increases the risk of the subsequent use of more harmful drugs*. The gateway

gateway drug A drug whose use increases the risk of the subsequent use of more harmful drugs.

harm reduction approach A response to high-risk behaviors that focuses on reducing the harm such behaviors have on people's lives.

THE REAL WORLD

Drugs and the Regulation of Consciousness

Everyone has an opinion about drug use. Given that we can't experience what happens in anyone else's mind, why does it matter to us what people experience in their own consciousness? Is consciousness something that governments should be able to legislate? Or should people be free to choose their own conscious states? After all, how can a "free society" justify regulating what people do inside their own heads?

Many people suggest that we should answer these questions by considering the costs of drug addiction, both to the addict and to the society that must "carry" unproductive people, pay for their welfare, and often even take care of their children. Drug users appear to be troublemakers and criminals, the culprits behind all those drug-related shootings, knifings, and robberies you see in the news every day. Widespread anger about the drug problem surfaced in the form of the War on Drugs, a federal government program born in the 1970s that focused on drug use as a criminal offense and attempted to stop drug use through the imprisonment of users.

Drug use did not stop with 40 years of the War on Drugs though, and instead, prisons filled with people arrested for drug use. From 1990 to 2007, the number of drug offenders in state and federal prisons increased from 179,070 to 348,736—a jump of 94% (Bureau of Justice Statistics, 2008)—not because of a measurable increase in drug use, but because of the rapidly increasing use of imprisonment for drug offenses. Many people who were being prevented from ruining their lives with drugs were instead having their lives ruined by prison. Like the failed policy of alcohol prohibition from 1920 to 1933, the policy of the drug war seemed to be causing more harm than it was preventing.

What can be done? The policy of the Obama administration is to wind down the war mentality and instead focus on reducing the harm that drugs cause (A drug policy for the 21st century, 2015). This **harm reduction approach** is *a response to high-risk behaviors that focuses on reducing the harm such behaviors have on people's lives* (Marlatt & Witkiewitz, 2010). Harm reduction originated in the Netherlands and Britain with tactics such as eliminating criminal penalties for some drug use or providing intravenous drug users with sterile syringes to help them avoid contracting HIV and other infections from shared

▲ There are many reasons that U.S. prisons are overcrowded: This country has the highest incarceration rate in the world. Treating drug abuse as a crime that requires imprisonment is one of the reasons.

REUTERS/LUCY NICHOLSON/CORBIS

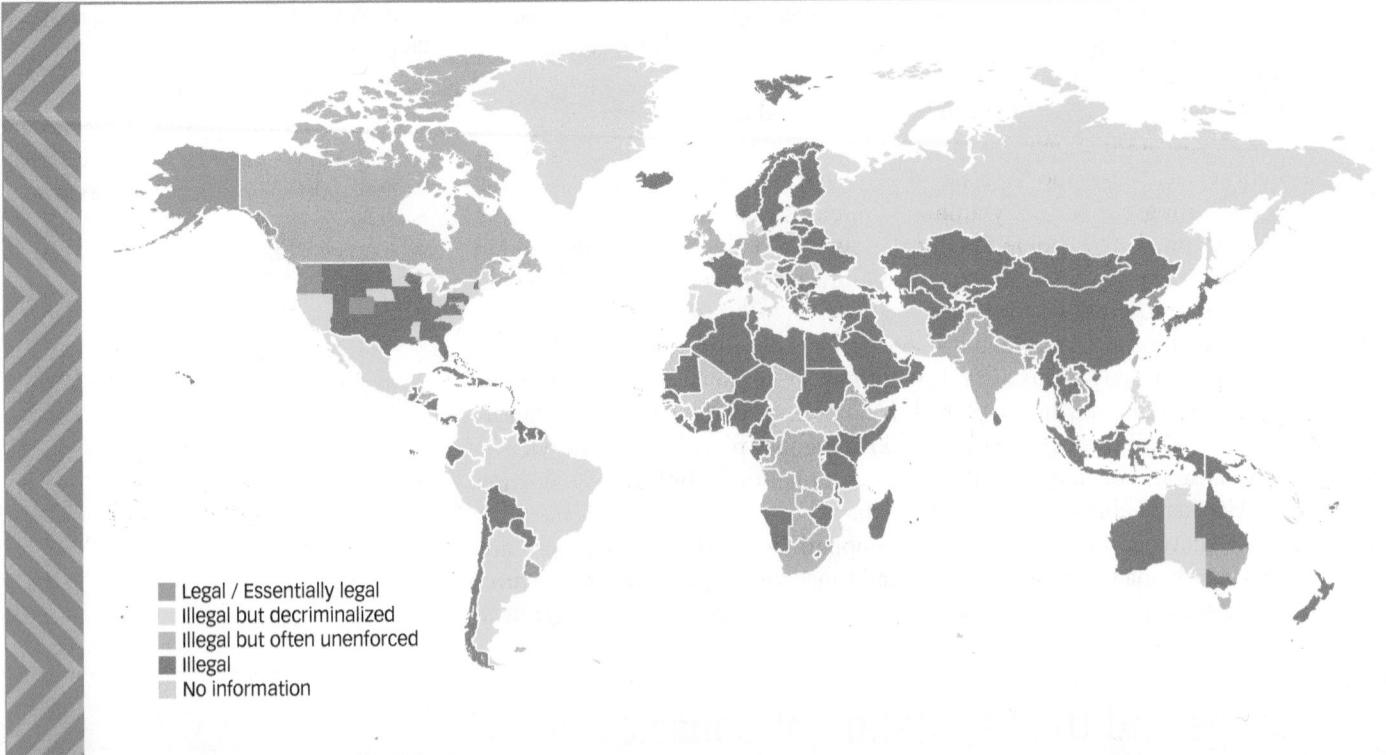

Legend:
- Legal / Essentially legal
- Illegal but decriminalized
- Illegal but often unenforced
- Illegal
- No information

needles (Des Jarlais et al., 2009). Harm reduction may even involve providing drugs for addicts to reduce the risks of poisoning and overdose they face when they get impure drugs of unknown dosage from criminal suppliers. A harm reduction idea for alcoholics, in turn, is to meet people where they are (in terms of their current level of drinking), and not to condemn their drinking behavior but to allow moderate drinking while minimizing the harmful effects of heavy drinking (Marlatt & Witkiewitz, 2010). Harm reduction strategies do not always find public support because they challenge the popular idea that the solution to drug and alcohol problems must always be prohibition: stopping use entirely.

There appears to be increasing support for the idea that people should be free to decide whether they want to use substances to alter their consciousness, especially when use of the substance carries a medical benefit, such as decreased nausea, decreased insomnia, and increased appetite. Since 1996, 18 states and the District of Columbia have enacted laws to legalize the use of marijuana for medical purposes. In 2012, Colorado and Washington became the first two states to legalize marijuana for purely recreational purposes, followed shortly thereafter by Oregon and the District of Columbia. Other U.S. states have taken steps to decriminalize marijuana use, as has been the trend globally. As happened with the prohibition of alcohol in the 1920s and 1930s, public opinion has certainly shifted on this issue. Indeed, whereas only 12% of US citizens in 1969 believed that marijuana should be legal, by 2015 that number had risen to 58% (Gallup, 2015).

theory has gained mixed support, with recent studies challenging this theory and suggesting that early-onset drug use in general, regardless of type of drug, increases the risk of later drug problems (Degenhardt et al., 2008). Because of the harm attributed to marijuana use, the U.S. government classifies marijuana as a Schedule I Controlled Substance, recognizing no medical use and maintaining that marijuana has the same high potential for abuse as other drugs such as heroin. Despite the federal laws against the use of marijuana, approximately 42% of adults in the United States have reported using it at some point in their lives—a rate much higher than that observed in most other countries (Degenhardt et al., 2008). Perhaps due to the perceived acceptability of marijuana among the general public, several states recently have taken steps to permit the sale of marijuana for medical purposes, decriminalize possession of marijuana (so violators pay a fine rather than going to jail), or to legalize its sale and possession outright. The debate about the legal status of marijuana will likely take years to resolve. In the meantime, depending on where you live, the greatest risk of marijuana use may be incarceration (see The Real World: Drugs and the Regulation of Consciousness and Other Voices: A Judge's Plea for Pot).

A Judge's Plea for Pot

The Honorable Gustin L. Reichbach served as a New York State Supreme Court Justice from 1999 until 2012. He died of pancreatic cancer in July 2012.

Should all drugs be illegal? Where should we draw the line between acceptable chemical alteration of one's own consciousness and criminal or pathological behavior? Let's take a specific example—think for a minute about where you stand on the legalization of marijuana. The Honorable Gustin L. Reichbach (2012, p. A27), a New York State Supreme Court Justice, recently wrote a strongly worded piece (slightly condensed here) on this issue, although his position surprised many people.

Three and a half years ago, on my 62nd birthday, doctors discovered a mass on my pancreas. It turned out to be Stage 3 pancreatic cancer. I was told I would be dead in four to six months. Today I am in that rare coterie of people who have survived this long with the disease. But I did not foresee that after having dedicated myself for 40 years to a life of the law, including more than two decades as a New York State judge, my quest for ameliorative and palliative care would lead me to marijuana.

My survival has demanded an enormous price, including months of chemotherapy, radiation hell and brutal surgery. For about a year, my cancer disappeared, only to return. About a month ago, I started a new and even more debilitating course of treatment. Every other week, after receiving an IV booster of chemotherapy drugs that takes three hours, I wear a pump that slowly injects more of the drugs over the next 48 hours.

Nausea and pain are constant companions. One struggles to eat enough to stave off the dramatic weight loss that is part of this disease. Eating, one of the great pleasures of life, has now become a daily battle, with each forkful a small victory. Every drug prescribed to treat one problem leads to one or two more drugs to offset its side effects. Pain medication leads to loss of appetite and constipation. Anti-nausea medication raises glucose levels, a serious problem for me with my pancreas so compromised. Sleep, which might bring respite from the miseries of the day, becomes increasingly elusive.

Inhaled marijuana is the only medicine that gives me some relief from nausea, stimulates my appetite, and makes it easier to fall asleep.

The oral synthetic substitute, Marinol, prescribed by my doctors, was useless. Rather than watch the agony of my suffering, friends have chosen, at some personal risk, to provide the substance. I find a few puffs of marijuana before dinner gives me ammunition in the battle to eat. A few more puffs at bedtime permits desperately needed sleep.

This is not a law-and-order issue; it is a medical and a human rights issue. Being treated at Memorial Sloan Kettering Cancer Center, I am receiving the absolute gold standard of medical care. But doctors cannot be expected to do what the law prohibits, even when they know it is in the best interests of their patients. When palliative care is understood as a fundamental human and medical right, marijuana for medical use should be beyond controversy. . . .

Cancer is a nonpartisan disease, so ubiquitous that it's impossible to imagine that there are legislators whose families have not also been touched by this scourge. It is to help all who have been affected by cancer, and those who will come after, that I now speak. Given my position as a sitting judge still hearing cases, well-meaning friends question the wisdom of my coming out on this issue. But I recognize that fellow cancer sufferers may be unable, for a host of reasons, to give voice to our plight. It is another heartbreaking aporia in the world of cancer that the one drug that gives relief without deleterious side effects remains classified as a narcotic with no medicinal value.

Because criminalizing an effective medical technique affects the fair administration of justice, I feel obliged to speak out as both a judge and a cancer patient suffering with a fatal disease. . . . Medical science has not yet found a cure, but it is barbaric to deny us access to one substance that has proved to ameliorate our suffering.

How should we decide which consciousness-altering substances are OK for members of our society to use, and which should be made illegal? What criteria would you propose? Should this decision be based on negative health consequences associated with use of the substance? What weight should be given to positive consequences, such as those described by Justice Reichbach? Research described in this chapter tested, and failed to support, the gateway theory of drug use. If you had the opportunity to design and conduct a study to answer a key question in this area, what would you do?

Build to the Outcomes

1. What is the allure of altered consciousness?

2. What is the risk associated with increased tolerance to a drug?

3. Identify both physical and psychological drug withdrawal problems.

4. What are the statistics on overcoming addiction?

5. Why do people experience being drunk differently?

6. Do stimulants create dependency?

7. What are some of the dangerous side effects of cocaine use?

8. Why are narcotics especially alluring?

9. What are the effects of hallucinogens?

10. What are the risks of marijuana use?

Hypnosis: Open to Suggestion

You may have never been hypnotized, but you have probably heard or read about it. People often describe its wonders with an air of amazement; demonstrations of stage hypnosis make it seem very powerful and mysterious. When you think of hypnosis, you may envision people completely under the power of a hypnotist, who is ordering them to dance like a chicken or perhaps "regress" to early childhood and talk in child-like voices. Many common beliefs about hypnosis are false. **Hypnosis** refers to *a social interaction in which one person (the hypnotist) makes suggestions that lead to a change in another person's (the subject's) subjective experience of the world* (Kirsch et al., 2011). The essence of hypnosis is in leading people to expect that certain things will happen to them that are outside their conscious will (Wegner, 2002).

INDUCTION AND SUSCEPTIBILITY

To induce hypnosis, a hypnotist may ask the person to be hypnotized to sit quietly and focus on some item, such as a spot on the wall (or a swinging pocket watch), and then make suggestions to the person about what effects hypnosis will have (e.g., "your eyelids are slowly closing" or "your arms are getting heavy"). Even without hypnosis, some suggested behaviors might commonly happen just because a person is concentrating on them—just thinking about their eyelids slowly closing, for instance, may make many people shut their eyes briefly or at least blink. In hypnosis, however, suggestions may be made—and followed by people in a susceptible state of mind—for very unusual behavior that most people would not normally do, such as flapping their arms and making loud clucking sounds.

Not everyone is equally hypnotizable. Susceptibility varies greatly. Some highly suggestible people are very easily hypnotized, most people are only moderately influenced, and some people are entirely unaffected by attempts at hypnosis. Susceptibility is not easily predicted by a person's personality traits. A hypnotist will typically test someone's hypnotic susceptibility with a series of suggestions designed to put a person into a more easily influenced state of mind. One of the best indicators of a person's susceptibility is the person's own judgment. So if you think you might be hypnotizable, you may well be (Hilgard, 1965). People with active, vivid imaginations, or who are easily absorbed in activities such as watching a movie, are also somewhat more likely to be good candidates for hypnosis (Sheehan, 1979; Tellegen & Atkinson, 1974).

HYPNOTIC EFFECTS

From watching stage hypnotism, you might think that the major effect of hypnosis is making people do peculiar things. So what do we actually know to be true about hypnosis? Some impressive demonstrations suggest that real changes occur in those under hypnosis. At the 1849 festivities for Prince Albert of England's birthday, for example, a hypnotized guest was asked to ignore any loud noises and then didn't even flinch when a pistol was fired near his face. These days, hypnotists are discouraged from using firearms during stage shows, but they often have volunteers perform other impressive feats. One common claim for superhuman strength under hypnosis involves asking a hypnotized person to become "stiff as a board" and lie unsupported with shoulders on one chair and feet on another while the hypnotist stands on the hypnotized person's body.

Studies have demonstrated that hypnosis can undermine memory, but with important limitations. People susceptible to hypnosis can be led to experience **posthypnotic amnesia,** *the failure to retrieve memories following hypnotic suggestions to forget.* Ernest Hilgard (1986) taught a hypnotized person the populations of some

hypnosis A social interaction in which one person (the hypnotist) makes suggestions that lead to a change in another person's (the subject's) subjective experience of the world.

posthypnotic amnesia The failure to retrieve memories following hypnotic suggestions to forget.

remote cities, for example, and then suggested that the participant forget the study session; after the session, the person was quite surprised at being able to give the census figures correctly. Asked how he knew the answers, the individual decided he might have learned them from a TV program. Such amnesia can then be reversed in subsequent hypnosis.

Some important research has found that only memories that were lost under hypnosis can be retrieved through hypnosis. The false claim that hypnosis helps people to unearth memories that they are not able to retrieve in normal consciousness seems to have surfaced because hypnotized people often make up memories to satisfy the hypnotist's suggestions. For example, Paul Ingram, a sheriff's deputy accused of sexual abuse by his daughters in the 1980s, was asked by interrogators in session after session to relax and imagine having committed the crimes. He emerged from these sessions having confessed to dozens of horrendous acts of "satanic ritual abuse." These confessions were called into question, however, when the independent investigator Richard Ofshe used the same technique to ask Ingram about a crime that Ofshe had simply made up out of thin air, something of which Ingram had never been accused. Ingram produced a three-page handwritten confession, complete with dialogue (Ofshe, 1992). Still, prosecutors in the case accepted Ingram's guilty plea, and he was only released in 2003 after a public outcry and years of work on his defense. After a person claims to remember something, even under hypnosis, it is difficult to convince others that the memory was false (Loftus & Ketchum, 1994).

Hypnosis can lead to measurable physical and behavioral changes in the body. One well-established effect is **hypnotic analgesia,** *the reduction of pain through hypnosis in people who are susceptible to hypnosis.* For example, one study (see **FIGURE 5.13**) found that for pain induced in volunteers in the laboratory, hypnosis was more effective than morphine, diazepam (Valium), aspirin, acupuncture, or placebos (Stern et al., 1977). For people who are hypnotically susceptible, hypnosis can be used to control pain in surgeries and dental procedures, in some cases more effectively than any form of anesthesia (Druckman & Bjork, 1994; Kihlstrom, 1985).

Hypnosis also has been shown to enable people to control mental processes previously believed to be beyond conscious control. For instance, the Stroop task (Stroop, 1935) is a classic psychological test in which a person is asked to name the color of words on a page (appearing in ink that is red, blue, green, etc.). This is a simple task. However, sometimes the words themselves are the names of colors—but are printed in a different color of the ink. It turns out that people are significantly slower, and make more errors, when naming ink colors that don't match the content of the word (e.g., when the word "green" is written in red ink) than if the content is neutral or

Stage hypnotists often perform an induction on the whole audience and then bring some of the more susceptible members on stage for further demonstrations.

hypnotic analgesia The reduction of pain through hypnosis in people who are susceptible to hypnosis.

Pain Reduction

(Bar graph showing pain reduction values: Hypnosis ≈ 16, Acupuncture ≈ 9, Morphine ≈ 7, Aspirin ≈ 4, Placebo ≈ 1, Diazepam ≈ 0. Y-axis scaled 0 to 18.)

◀ Figure 5.13

HYPNOTIC ANALGESIA The degree of pain reduction (values represent differences between experimental and control conditions on a self-reported pain scale) reported by people using different techniques for the treatment of laboratory-induced pain. Hypnosis wins (Stern et al., 1977).

AMORE RAZ, JIN FAN, AND MICHAEL POSNER. HYPNOTIC SUGGESTION REDUCES CONFLICT IN THE HUMAN BRAIN. PNAS, JULY 12, 2005, VOL. 102, NO. 28. COPYRIGHT 2005, NATIONAL ACADEMY OF SCIENCES, USA.

(a)   (b)

▲ Figure 5.14

BRAIN ACTIVITY DURING HYPNOSIS
(a) Researchers found that the anterior cingulate cortex (shown in the crosshairs), a part of the brain involved in conflict monitoring, is activated in all people *when viewing incongruent trails during the Stroop task* (for instance, when the word *red* appears in blue type). (b) However, under hypnosis, when instructed to ignore the content of the words and just name the font color, highly suggestible people do not show increased activation in this brain region during incongruent trials (Raz et al., 2005).

congruent (e.g., if the word "desk" or "red" is written in red ink). This effect is present no matter how hard we try. In an amazing result, the effect is completely eliminated when highly suggestible people are hypnotized and told to respond to all words the same way (Raz et al., 2002). It is important, though, that follow-up studies have revealed that hypnotic induction is not required to eliminate the Stroop effect. It turns out that simply suggesting to highly suggestible people that they should respond to all words the same way has the same effect as hypnosis (Lifshitz, et al., 2013). This suggests that hypnotic effects may result when highly suggestible people comply with the suggestions of others.

Nevertheless, people under hypnotic suggestion are not merely telling the hypnotist what he or she wants to hear. Instead, they seem to be experiencing what they have been asked to experience. Under hypnotic suggestion, for example, regions of the brain responsible for color vision are activated in highly hypnotizable people when they are asked to perceive color, even when they are really shown gray stimuli (Kosslyn et al., 2000). While engaged in the Stroop task, people who can eliminate the Stroop effect under suggestion show decreased activity in the anterior cingulate cortex (ACC), the part of the brain involved in conflict monitoring (**FIGURE 5.14**; Raz, Fan, & Posner 2005), consistent with the lack of conflict perceived between the color name and ink. Overall, hypnotic suggestion appears to change the subjective perception of those experiencing it, as reflected by changes in their self-report, behavior, and brain activity.

Build to the Outcomes

1. What factors make someone more easily hypnotizable?

2. What type of memory can be retrieved through hypnosis?

3. Can hypnosis be as effective for pain relief as anesthesia?

4. How does hypnosis change the brain activity of someone engaged in the Stroop task?

Chapter Review

The Mysteries of Consciousness

▶ People judge mind perception according to the capacities for experience and agency.

▶ Research suggests that mental activity happens first, preparing the way for both conscious thought and action.

The Nature of Consciousness

▶ Consciousness has four basic properties: intentionality, unity, selectivity, and transience. It can also be understood in terms of levels: minimal consciousness, full consciousness, and self-consciousness.

▶ Conscious contents can include current concerns, daydreams, and unwanted thoughts. Efforts to suppress a thought—such as of a white bear—may backfire as the mind searches for thoughts of that white bear to suppress.

The Unconscious Mind

▶ Unconscious processes are sometimes understood as expressions of the Freudian dynamic unconscious, but they are more commonly viewed as processes of the cognitive unconscious that create our conscious thought and behavior. The cognitive unconscious is at work when subliminal perception and unconscious decision processes influence thought or behavior without the person's awareness.

Sleep and Dreaming: Good Night, Mind

▶ Sleeping and dreaming present a view of the mind in an altered state of consciousness. During a night's sleep, the brain passes in and out of five stages of sleep; most dreaming occurs in the REM sleep stage.

▶ Sleep needs decrease over the life span, but being deprived of sleep and dreams has psychological and physical costs. Sleep can be disrupted through disorders that include insomnia, sleep apnea, somnambulism, narcolepsy, sleep paralysis, and night terrors.

▶ Dream consciousness differs from the waking state in that: we feel emotion intensely, thought is illogical, sensation is fully formed and meaningful; images and events occur with uncritical acceptance; and dreams are difficult to remember.

▶ Theories of dreaming include Freud's psychoanalytic theory and the activation–synthesis model. fMRI studies of the brain while dreaming reveal activations associated with visual imagery, increased sensitivity to emotions such as fear, lessened capacities for planning, and the prevention of motor movement.

Drugs and Consciousness: Artificial Inspiration

▶ Psychoactive drugs influence consciousness by altering the brain's chemical messaging system and intensifying or dulling the effects of neurotransmitters. Drug tolerance can result in overdose, and physical and psychological dependence can lead to addiction.

▶ Depressants reduce activity of the central nervous system (CNS); stimulants excite the CNS; narcotics relieve pain; hallucinogens alter sensation and perception; and marijuana is mildly hallucinogenic.

Hypnosis: Open to Suggestion

▶ Hypnosis is an altered state of consciousness characterized by suggestibility.

▶ Although many claims for hypnosis overstate its effects, hypnosis can create the experience that one's actions are occurring involuntarily, create analgesia, and even change brain activations in ways that suggest that hypnotic experiences are more than imagination.

QUIZ

1. Currently, unconscious processes are understood as
   a. a concentrated pattern of thought suppression.
   b. a hidden system of memories, instincts, and desires.
   c. a blank slate.
   d. unexperienced mental processes that give rise to thoughts and behavior.

2. The _____ unconscious is at work when subliminal and unconscious processes influence thought and behavior.
   a. minimal
   b. repressive
   c. dynamic
   d. cognitive

3. The cycle of sleep and waking is one of the major patterns of human life called
   a. the circadian rhythm.
   b. the sleep stages.
   c. the altered state of consciousness.
   d. subliminal perception.

4. Sleep needs _____ over the life span.
   a. decrease
   b. increase
   c. fluctuate
   d. remain the same

5. During dreaming, the dreamer _____ changes in emotion, thought, and sensation.
   a. is skeptical of
   b. is completely unconscious of
   c. uncritically accepts
   d. views objectively

6. Which explanation of dreams proposes that they are produced when the mind attempts to make sense of random neural activity that occurs in the brain during sleep?
   a. Freud's psychoanalytic theory
   b. the activation–synthesis model
   c. the cognitive unconscious model
   d. the manifest content framework

7. Psychoactive drugs influence consciousness by altering the effects of
   a. agonists.
   b. neurotransmitters.
   c. amphetamines.
   d. spinal neurons.

8. Tolerance for drugs involves
   a. larger doses being required over time to achieve the same effect.
   b. openness to new experiences.
   c. the initial attraction of drug use.
   d. the decrease of the painful symptoms that accompany withdrawal.

9. Alcohol expectancy refers to
   a. alcohol's initial effects of euphoria and reduced anxiety.
   b. the widespread acceptance of alcohol as a socially approved substance.
   c. alcohol leading people to respond in simple ways to complex situations.
   d. people's beliefs about how alcohol will influence them in particular situations.

10. Hypnosis has been proven to have
    a. an effect on physical strength.
    b. a positive effect on memory retrieval.
    c. an analgesic effect.
    d. an age-regression effect.

 LearningCurve   Don't stop now! Quizzing yourself is a powerful study tool. Go to LaunchPad to access the LearningCurve adaptive quizzing system and your own personalized learning plan. Visit launchpadworks.com.

KEY TERMS

consciousness (p. 172)

phenomenology (p. 172)

problem of other minds (p. 173)

mind–body problem (p. 174)

dichotic listening (p. 176)

cocktail-party phenomenon (p. 176)

minimal consciousness (p. 177)

full consciousness (p. 178)

self-consciousness (p. 179)

mental control (p. 181)

thought suppression (p. 181)

rebound effect of thought suppression (p. 182)

ironic processes of mental control (p. 182)

dynamic unconscious (p. 184)

repression (p. 184)

cognitive unconscious (p. 184)

dual process theories (p. 185)

subliminal perception (p. 185)

altered state of consciousness (p. 187)

circadian rhythm (p. 187)

REM sleep (p. 188)

electrooculograph (EOG) (p. 188)

insomnia (p. 191)

sleep apnea (p. 191)

somnambulism (or sleepwalking) (p. 192)

narcolepsy (p. 192)

sleep paralysis (p. 192)

night terrors (or sleep terrors) (p. 192)

manifest content (p. 194)

latent content (p. 194)

activation–synthesis model (p. 194)

psychoactive drugs (p. 197)

drug tolerance (p. 198)

depressants (p. 200)

expectancy theory (p. 201)

balanced placebo design (p. 201)

alcohol myopia (p. 202)

stimulants (p. 202)

narcotics (or opiates) (p. 203)

hallucinogens (p. 204)

marijuana (or cannabis) (p. 204)

gateway drug (p. 205)

harm reduction approach (p. 205)

hypnosis (p. 208)

posthypnotic amnesia (p. 208)

hypnotic analgesia (p. 209)

CHANGING MINDS

1. "I had a really weird dream last night," your friend tells you. "I dreamed that I was trying to fly like a bird but I kept flying into clotheslines. I looked it up online, and dreams where you're struggling to fly mean that there is someone in your life who's standing in your way and preventing you from moving forward. I suppose that has to be my boyfriend, so maybe I'd better break up with him." Applying what you've read in this chapter, what would you tell your friend about the reliability of dream interpretation?

2. During an early-morning class, you notice your friend yawning, and you ask if he slept well the night before. "On weekdays, I'm in class all day, and I work the night shift," he says. "So I don't sleep much during the week. But I figure it's okay because I make up for it by sleeping late on

Saturday mornings." Is it realistic for your friend to assume that he can balance regular sleep deprivation with rebound sleep on the weekends?

3. You and a friend are watching the 2010 movie *Inception*, starring Leonardo DiCaprio as a corporate spy. DiCaprio's character is hired by a businessman named Saito to plant an idea in the unconscious mind of a competitor while he sleeps. According to the plan, when the competitor awakens, he'll be compelled to act on the idea, to the secret benefit of Saito's company. "It's a cool idea," your friend says, "but it's pure science fiction. There's no such thing as an unconscious mind, and no way that unconscious ideas could influence the way you act when you're conscious." What would you tell your friend? What evidence do we have that the unconscious mind exists and can influence conscious behavior?

ANSWERS TO KEY CONCEPT QUIZ

1. d; 2. d; 3. a; 4. a; 5. c; 6. b; 7. b; 8. a; 9. d; 10. c

LaunchPad features the full e-Book of *Psychology*, the LearningCurve adaptive quizzing system, videos, and a variety of activities to boost your learning. Visit LaunchPad at launchpadworks.com.

Memory

6

J ill Price was 12 years old when she began to suspect that she possessed an unusually good memory. While she was studying for a seventh-grade science final on May 30, her mind drifted and she became aware that she could recall vividly everything she had been doing on May 30 of the previous year. A month later, something similar happened: Enjoying vanilla custards at Paradise Cove near Los Angeles with her friend Kathy, Jill recalled that they had done the same thing precisely a year earlier. Expecting that Kathy would recall the episode as easily as she did, Jill was surprised when Kathy replied blankly, "We did?"

Remembering specifics of events that occurred a year ago may not seem so extraordinary—you can probably recall what you did for your last birthday or where you spent last Thanksgiving. But can you recall the details of what you did exactly 1 year ago today? Or what you did a week, a month, 6 months, or 6 years before that day? Probably not, but Jill Price can.

As she grew older, Jill's memory flashes became even more frequent. Now in her early 50s, Jill can recall clearly and in great detail what has happened to her *every single day since early 1980* (Price & Davis, 2008). This is not just Jill's subjective impression. Dr. James McGaugh, a well-known memory researcher based at the University of California—Irvine, and his colleagues tested Jill's memory over a period of a few years and came up with some shocking results (Parker, Cahill, & McGaugh, 2006). For example, they asked Jill to recall the dates of each Easter from 1980 to 2003, which is a pretty tough task considering that Easter can fall on any day between March 22 and April 15. Even though she had no idea that she would be asked this question, Jill recalled the correct dates quickly and easily; nobody else the researchers tested came close. When Jill was asked about the dates of public events that had occurred years earlier (Rodney King beating? O. J. Simpson verdict? bombing at Atlanta Olympics?), she rattled off the correct answers without a hitch (March 3, 1991; October 3, 1995; July 26, 1996). The researchers also asked Jill about the details of what she had been doing on various randomly chosen dates, and they checked Jill's recall against her personal diary.

Jill Price can accurately remember just about everything that has happened to her during the past 30 years, as confirmed by her diary, but Jill's extraordinary memory is more of a curse than a blessing.

Again, Jill answered quickly and accurately: *July 1, 1986?*—"I see it all, that day, that month, that summer. Tuesday. Went with (friend's name) to (restaurant name)." *October 3, 1987?*—"That was a Saturday. Hung out at the apartment all weekend, wearing a sling—hurt my elbow." *April 27, 1994?*— "That was Wednesday. That was easy for me because I knew where I was exactly. I was down in Florida. I was summoned to come down and to say goodbye to my grandmother who they all thought was dying but she ended up living" (E. S. Parker et al., 2006, pp. 39–40).

Jill's memory is a gift we'd all love to have—right? Not necessarily. Here's what Jill has to say about her ability: "Most have called it a gift but I call it a burden. I run my entire life through my head every day and it drives me crazy!!!" (E. S. Parker et al., 2006, p. 35).

Researchers still don't understand all the reasons that Jill Price can remember her past so much more fully than the rest of us, but it turns out that Jill is not alone. Jill's extraordinary memory abilities became widely known after a *60 Minutes* story that featured her and Dr. McGaugh. That story elicited a flurry of inquiries to Dr. McGaugh from other people around the world who thought that they, too, possessed the spectacular memory abilities demonstrated by Jill. Although most of them did not, McGaugh and his colleagues identified 11 other individuals with "highly superior autobiographical memory" abilities that resemble those they had seen in Jill Price (LePort et al., 2012). The researchers discovered differences in the structure of several brain regions known to be involved in memory in the superior autobiographical memory group compared with a control group, suggesting that further study of these unusual individuals might help to understand the nature of memory more generally.

THE EASE WITH WHICH SOMEONE SUCH AS JILL CAN INSTANTLY REMEMBER HER PAST shouldn't blind us to appreciating how complex that act of remembering really is. Because memory is so remarkably complex, it is also remarkably fragile (Schacter, 1996). We all have had the experience of forgetting something we desperately wanted to remember or of remembering something that never really happened. Why does memory serve us so well in some situations and play such cruel tricks on us in other cases? When can we trust our memories, and when should we view them skeptically? Is there just one kind of memory, or are there many? These are among the questions that psychologists have asked and answered, and they're the topics of this chapter. We'll start by answering the fundamental question: What is memory?

What Is Memory?

memory The ability to store and retrieve information over time.

encoding The process of transforming what we perceive, think, or feel into an enduring memory.

storage The process of maintaining information in memory over time.

retrieval The process of bringing to mind information that has been previously encoded and stored.

Memory *is the ability to store and retrieve information over time.* Even though few of us possess the extraordinary memory abilities of Jill Price and the handful of others with highly superior autobiographical memory, each of us has a unique identity that is intricately tied to the things we have thought, felt, done, and experienced. Memories are the residue of those events, the enduring changes that experience makes in our brains and leaves behind when it passes. If an experience passes without leaving a trace, it might just as well not have happened. But as Jill's story suggests, remembering all that has happened is not necessarily a good thing, either—a point we'll explore more fully later in this chapter.

As you've seen in other chapters, the mind's mistakes provide key insights into its fundamental operation, and there is no better illustration of this than in the realm of memory. There are three key functions of memory: **encoding,** *the process of transforming what we perceive, think, or feel into an enduring memory;* **storage,** *the process of maintaining information in memory over time;* and **retrieval,** *the process of bringing to mind information that has been previously encoded and stored.*

Encoding: Transforming Perceptions Into Memories

Bubbles P., a professional gambler with no formal education who spent most of his time shooting craps at local clubs or playing high-stakes poker, had no difficulty rattling off 20 numbers, in either forward or backward order, after just a single glance (Ceci, DeSimone, & Johnson, 1992). Most people can listen to a list of numbers and then repeat them from memory—as long as the list is no more than about seven items long. (Try it for yourself using **FIGURE 6.1**.)

How did Bubbles accomplish his astounding feats of memory? For at least 2,000 years, people have thought of memory as a recording device that makes exact copies of the information that comes in through our senses, and then stores those copies for later use. This idea is simple and intuitive. It is also completely incorrect. We make memories by combining information we *already* have in our brains with new information that comes in through our senses. In this way memory is like cooking; starting from a recipe but improvising along the way, we add old information to new information, mix, shake, and bake, and out pops a memory. Memories are *constructed,* not recorded, and encoding is the process by which we transform what we perceive, think, or feel into an enduring memory. Let's look at three types of encoding processes—semantic encoding, visual imagery encoding, and organizational encoding—and then consider the possible survival value of encoding for our ancestors.

SEMANTIC ENCODING

Memories are a combination of old and new information, so the nature of any particular memory depends as much on the old information already in our memories as it does on the new information coming in through our senses. In other words, how we remember something depends on how we think about it at the time. For example, as a professional gambler, Bubbles found numbers unusually meaningful, so when he saw a string of digits, he tended to think about their meanings. However, when Bubbles was tested with materials other than numbers—faces, words, objects, or locations—his memory performance was no better than average. Most of us, unlike Bubbles, can't remember 20 digits, but we can remember 20 experiences (a favorite camping trip, a 16th birthday party, a first day at college, etc.). One reason is that we often think about the meaning behind our experiences, so we semantically encode them without even trying (Craik & Tulving, 1975). **Semantic encoding** *is the process of relating new information in a meaningful way to knowledge that is already stored in memory* (Brown & Craik, 2000).

In one study, researchers presented participants with a series of words and asked them to make one of three types of judgments (Craik & Tulving, 1975):

▶ *Semantic judgments* required the participants to think about the meaning of the words (Is *hat* a type of clothing?).

▶ *Rhyme judgments* required the participants to think about the sound of the words (Does *hat* rhyme with *cat*?).

▶ *Case judgments* required the participants to think about the appearance of the words (Is *HAT* written in uppercase or lowercase?).

```
        28
       691
       0473
      87454
      902481
     5742296
     64719304
     356718485
    1028834729
   47208274264
  731093435138
```

Learning Outcomes

▶ Explain how memory is a construction and not a recording of new information.

▶ Describe the three main ways that information is encoded into the brain.

▶ Give reasons that we remember survival-related information so well.

Have you ever wondered why you can remember 20 experiences (your favorite camping trip, your 16th birthday party, your first day at college, etc.) but not 20 digits? One reason is that we often think about the meaning behind our experiences, so we semantically encode them without even trying (Craik & Tulving, 1975).

semantic encoding The process of relating new information in a meaningful way to knowledge that is already stored in memory.

◀ Figure 6.1

DIGIT MEMORY TEST How many digits can you remember? Start on the first row and cover the rows below it with a piece of paper. Study the numbers in the row for 1 second and then cover that row back up again. After a couple of seconds, try to repeat the numbers. Then uncover the row to see if you were correct. If so, continue down to the next row, using the same instructions, until you can't recall all the numbers in a row. The number of digits in the last row you can remember correctly is your digit span. Bubbles P. could remember 20 random numbers, or about five rows deep. How did you do?

visual imagery encoding The process of storing new information by converting it into mental pictures.

The type of judgment task influenced how participants thought about each word— what old information they combined with the new—and had a powerful impact on their memories. Those participants who made semantic judgments (i.e., thought about the meaning of the words) had much better memory for the words than did participants who thought about how the word looked or sounded. The results of these and many other studies have shown that long-term retention is greatly enhanced by semantic encoding.

So where does this semantic encoding take place? What's going on in the brain when this type of information processing occurs? Studies reveal that semantic encoding is uniquely associated with increased activity in the lower left part of the frontal lobe and the inner part of the left temporal lobe (**FIGURE 6.2a**; Demb et al., 1995; Kapur et al., 1994; Wagner et al., 1998). In fact, the amount of activity in each of these two regions during encoding is directly related to whether people later remember an item. The more activity there is in these areas, the more likely the person will remember the information.

VISUAL IMAGERY ENCODING

In Athens in 477 BCE, the Greek poet Simonides had just left a banquet when the ceiling collapsed and killed all the people inside. Simonides was able to name every one of the dead simply by visualizing each chair around the banquet table and recalling the person who had been sitting there. Simonides wasn't the first, but he was among the most proficient, to use **visual imagery encoding,** *the process of storing new information by converting it into mental pictures.*

How might you use visual encoding to help store a new fact, such as the date of a friend's birthday that falls on, say, November 24th?

If you wanted to use Simonides' method to create an enduring memory, you could simply convert the information that you wanted to remember into a visual image and then store it in a familiar location. For instance, if you were going to the grocery store and wanted to remember to buy Coke, popcorn, and cheese dip, you could use the rooms in your house as locations and imagine your living room flooded in Coke, your bedroom pillows stuffed with popcorn, and your bathtub as a greasy pond of cheese dip. When you arrived at the store, you could then take a mental walk around your house and "look" into each room to remember the items you needed to purchase.

Numerous experiments have shown that visual imagery encoding can substantially improve memory. In one experiment, participants who studied lists of words by creating visual images of them later recalled twice as many items as participants who just mentally repeated the words (Schnorr & Atkinson, 1969). Why does visual imagery encoding work so well? First, visual imagery encoding does some of the same things that semantic encoding does: When you create a visual image, you relate incoming information to knowledge already in memory. For example, a visual image of a parked car might help you create a link to your memory of your first kiss.

Second, when you use visual imagery to encode words and other verbal information, you end up with two different mental *placeholders* for the items— a visual one and a verbal one—which gives you more ways to remember them than just a verbal placeholder alone (Paivio, 1971, 1986). Visual imagery encoding activates visual processing regions in the occipital lobe (see Figure 6.2b), which suggests that people actually enlist the visual system when forming memories based on mental images (Kosslyn et al., 1993; Pearson & Kosslyn, 2015).

ORGANIZATIONAL ENCODING

Have you ever ordered dinner with a group of friends and watched in amazement as your server took the order without writing anything down? To find out how this is done, one researcher spent 3 months working in a restaurant where servers routinely wrote down orders but then left the check at the customer's table before proceeding to the kitchen and *telling* the cooks what to make (Stevens, 1988). The researcher wired the servers with microphones and asked them to think aloud, that is, to say what they

Ever wonder how a server remembers who ordered the pizza and who ordered the fries without writing anything down? Some have figured out how to use organizational encoding.

a. Semantic Judgments

b. Visual Judgments

c. Organizational Judgments

◀ Figure 6.2

BRAIN ACTIVITY DURING DIFFERENT TYPES OF JUDGMENTS fMRI studies reveal that different parts of the brain are active during different types of judgments: (a) During semantic encoding, the lower left frontal lobe is active; (b) during visual imagery encoding, the occipital lobe is active; and (c) during organizational encoding, the upper left frontal lobe is active.

were thinking as they walked around all day doing their jobs. The researcher found that as soon as the server left a customer's table, he or she immediately began *grouping* or *categorizing* the orders into hot drinks, cold drinks, hot foods, and cold foods. The servers grouped the items into a sequence that matched the layout of the kitchen, first placing drink orders, then hot-food orders, and finally cold-food orders. The servers remembered their orders by relying on **organizational encoding,** *the process of categorizing information according to the relationships among a series of items.*

For example, suppose you had to memorize the words *peach, cow, chair, apple, table, cherry, lion, couch, horse, desk.* The task seems difficult, but if you organize the

organizational encoding The process of categorizing information according to the relationships among a series of items.

▶ Figure 6.3

ORGANIZING WORDS INTO A HIERARCHY
Organizing words into conceptual groups and relating them to each other—as in this example of a hierarchy—makes it easier to reconstruct the items from memory later (Bower et al., 1969). Keeping track of the 17 items in this example can be facilitated by remembering the hierarchical groupings they fall under.

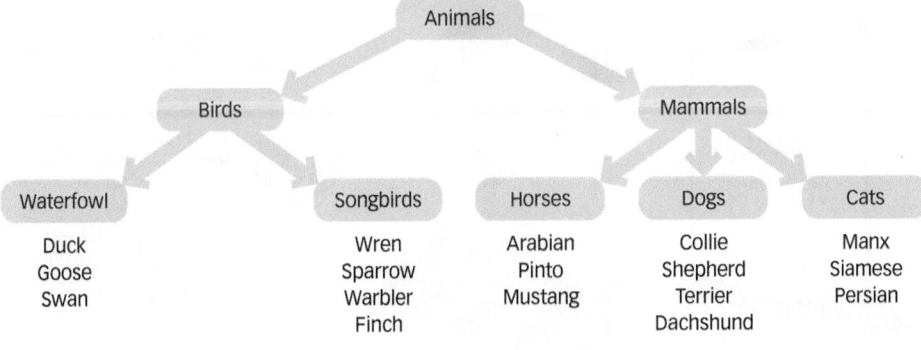

| Animals |
Birds	Mammals
Waterfowl	Songbirds	Horses	Dogs	Cats
Duck Goose Swan	Wren Sparrow Warbler Finch	Arabian Pinto Mustang	Collie Shepherd Terrier Dachshund	Manx Siamese Persian

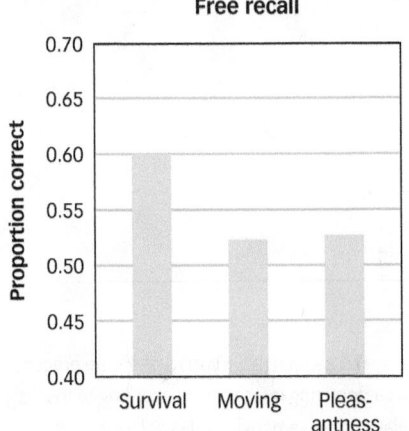

DATA VISUALIZATION

Do Men and Women Differ in the Way They Remember Location Information?
Go to launchpadworks.com.

▼ Figure 6.4

SURVIVAL ENCODING ENHANCES LATER RECALL
People recall more words after survival encoding tasks than after moving or pleasantness-encoding tasks (Nairne et al., 2007). Explain this from an evolutionary perspective.

Free recall

[Bar chart showing Proportion correct on y-axis (0.40 to 0.70). Survival ≈ 0.60, Moving ≈ 0.52, Pleasantness ≈ 0.53.]

items into three categories—fruit (*peach, apple, cherry*), animals (*cow, lion, horse*), and furniture (*chair, table, couch, desk*)—the task becomes much easier. Studies have shown that instructing people to sort items into categories is an effective way to enhance their subsequent recall of those items (Mandler, 1967). Even more complex organizational schemes have been used, such as the hierarchy in **FIGURE 6.3** (Bower et al., 1969). People can improve their recall of individual items by organizing them into multiple-level categories, all the way from a general category such as *animals*, through intermediate categories such as *birds* and *songbirds*, down to specific examples such as *wren* and *sparrow*.

Just as semantic and visual imagery encoding activates distinct regions of the brain, so, too, does organizational encoding. As you can see in Figure 6.2c, organizational encoding activates the upper surface of the left frontal lobe (Fletcher, Shallice, & Dolan, 1998; Savage et al., 2001). Different types of encoding strategies appear to rely on the activation of different areas of the brain.

ENCODING OF SURVIVAL-RELATED INFORMATION

Encoding new information is critical to many aspects of everyday life—prospects for attaining your degree would be pretty slim without this ability. According to the evolutionary perspective, which is based on Darwin's principle of natural selection, features of an organism that help it survive and reproduce are more likely than other features to be passed on to subsequent generations (see the Psychology: Evolution of a Science chapter). Therefore, memory mechanisms that help us to survive and reproduce should be preserved by natural selection. Our memory systems should be built in a way that allows us to remember especially well encoded information that is relevant to our survival, such as sources of food and water and the location of predators.

To test this idea, researchers gave participants three different encoding tasks (Nairne, Thompson, & Pandeirada, 2007). In the first task, a survival-encoding condition, participants were asked to imagine that they were stranded in the grasslands of a foreign land without any survival materials. They were told that over the next few months they would need supplies of food and water and also need to protect themselves from predators. The researchers then showed participants randomly chosen words (e.g., *stone, meadow, chair*) and asked them to rate on a 1–5 scale how relevant each item would be to survival in the hypothetical situation. In a second task, a moving-encoding condition, a second group of participants was asked to imagine that they were planning to move to a new home in a foreign land, and to rate on a 1–5 scale how useful each item might be in helping them to set up a new home. In the third task, the pleasantness-encoding condition, a third group was shown the same words and asked to rate on a 1–5 scale the pleasantness of each word.

The findings, displayed in **FIGURE 6.4**, show that participants recalled more words after the survival-encoding task than after either the moving or pleasantness tasks. In later studies, the researchers found that survival encoding resulted in higher levels of recall than several other non-survival-encoding tasks involving semantic encoding, imagery encoding, or organizational encoding (Nairne, Pandeirada, & Thompson, 2008). Exactly what about survival encoding produces such high levels of memory?

One advantage of survival encoding is that it draws on elements of semantic, visual imagery, and organizational encoding (Burns, Hwang, & Burns, 2011). Also, survival encoding encourages participants to think in detail about the goals they want to achieve and thus engage in extensive planning, which in turn benefits memory and may account for much of the benefit of survival encoding (Bell, Roer, & Buchner, 2015). For example, survival scenarios that *do* involve planning produce superior subsequent memory compared with survival scenarios that do *not* involve planning. It is critical that superior recall is also observed for scenarios that *involve planning but not survival*, such as planning a dinner party (Klein, Robertson, & Delton, 2011). Of course, planning for the future is itself critical for our long-term survival, so these findings are still broadly consistent with the evolutionary perspective that memory is built to enhance our chances of survival (Klein et al., 2011; Schacter, 2012; Suddendorf & Corballis, 2007).

Build to the Outcomes

1. In what way is making a memory like cooking from a recipe?

2. What do we consider when making a semantic judgment?

3. What two factors make visual imagery effective?

4. How might you use organizational encoding to remember material before an exam?

5. What is the evolutionary perspective on encoding survival-related information?

Storage: Maintaining Memories over Time

Encoding is the process of turning perceptions into memories. But one of the hallmarks of a memory is that you can bring it to mind on Tuesday, not on Wednesday, and then bring it to mind again on Thursday. So where are our memories when we aren't using them? Clearly, those memories are stored in some form in your brain. As pointed out earlier, *storage is the process of maintaining information in memory over time*. There are three major kinds of memory storage: sensory, short-term, and long-term. As these names suggest, the three kinds of storage are distinguished primarily by the amount of time over which a memory is retained.

SENSORY STORAGE

Sensory memory is *a type of storage that holds sensory information for a few seconds or less*. In a series of classic experiments, research participants were asked to remember rows of letters (Sperling, 1960). In one version of the procedure, participants viewed three rows of four letters each, as shown in **FIGURE 6.5**. The researcher flashed the letters on a screen for just 1/20th of a second. When asked to remember all 12 of the letters they had just seen, participants recalled fewer than half. There were two possible explanations for this:

▶ People simply couldn't encode all the letters in such a brief period of time.

▶ People encoded the letters but forgot them while trying to recall everything they had seen.

Learning Outcomes

▶ Distinguish sensory memory from short-term memory.

▶ Describe the elements of the model of working memory.

▶ Explain the interrelationship between memory and the hippocampus.

▶ Summarize the role of the neural synapse in long-term memory storage.

sensory memory A type of storage that holds sensory information for a few seconds or less.

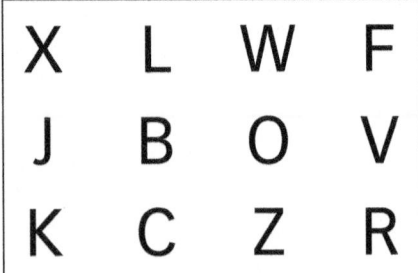

▲ Figure 6.5

ICONIC MEMORY TEST When a grid of letters is flashed on screen for only 1/20th of a second, it is difficult to recall individual letters. But if prompted to remember a particular row immediately after the grid is shown, research participants will do so with high accuracy. Sperling used this procedure to demonstrate that although iconic memory stores the whole grid, the information fades away too quickly for a person to recall everything (Sperling, 1960).

iconic memory A fast-decaying store of visual information.

echoic memory A fast-decaying store of auditory information.

short-term memory A type of storage that holds nonsensory information for more than a few seconds but less than a minute.

rehearsal The process of keeping information in short-term memory by mentally repeating it.

serial position effect The observation that the first few and last few items in a series are more likely to be recalled than the items in the middle.

To test the two ideas, the researcher relied on a clever trick. Just after the letters disappeared from the screen, a tone sounded that cued the participants to report the letters in a particular row. A *high* tone cued participants to report the contents of the top row, a *medium* tone cued participants to report the contents of the middle row, and a *low* tone cued participants to report the contents of the bottom row. When asked to report only a single row, people recalled almost all of the letters in that row! Because the tone sounded after the letters disappeared from the screen, the researchers concluded that people could have recalled the same number of letters from any of the rows, had they been asked. Participants had no way of knowing which of the three rows would be cued, so the researcher inferred that virtually all the letters had been encoded. In fact, if the tone was substantially delayed, participants couldn't perform the task because the information had slipped away from their sensory memories. Like the afterimage of a flashlight, the 12 letters flashed on a screen are visual icons, a lingering trace stored in memory for a very short period.

Because we have more than one sense, we have more than one kind of sensory memory. **Iconic memory** is *a fast-decaying store of visual information.* A similar storage area serves as a temporary warehouse for sounds. **Echoic memory** is *a fast-decaying store of auditory information.* When you have difficulty understanding what someone has just said, you probably find yourself replaying the last few words—listening to them echo in your "mind's ear," so to speak. When you do that, you are accessing information that is being held in your echoic memory store. The hallmark of both the iconic and echoic memory stores is that they hold information for a very short time. Iconic memories usually decay in about 1 second or less, and echoic memories usually decay in about 5 seconds (Darwin, Turvey, & Crowder, 1972).

These two sensory memory stores are a bit like doughnut shops: The products come in, they sit briefly on the shelf, and then they are discarded. If you want one, you have to grab it fast. But how to grab it? If information from sensory memory is quickly lost, how do we recall it at all? The key is attention, and that brings us to short-term memory (see **FIGURE 6.6**).

SHORT-TERM STORAGE AND WORKING MEMORY

A second kind of memory storage is **short-term memory,** which *holds nonsensory information for more than a few seconds but less than a minute.* We need to attend to incoming information for it to enter short-term memory, but as soon as we attend to something else, the information is quickly lost. For example, if someone tells you a telephone number and you pay attention to what they say, you can usually repeat it back with ease—but you will quickly lose the information as soon as your attention focuses on anything else. In one study, research participants were given consonant strings to remember, such as DBX and HLM. After seeing each string, participants were asked to count backward from 100 by 3 for varying amounts of time and were then asked to recall the strings (Peterson & Peterson, 1959). As shown in **FIGURE 6.7,**

► Figure 6.6

THE FLOW OF INFORMATION THROUGH THE MEMORY SYSTEM Information moves through several stages of memory as it gets encoded, stored, and made available for later retrieval.

Maintenance rehearsal

Sensory input → Sensory memory → (Attention) Short-term memory → (Encoding / Retrieval) Long-term memory

Unattended information is lost.   Unrehearsed information is lost.   Some information may be lost over time.

memory for the consonant strings declined rapidly, from approximately 80% after a 3-second delay to less than 20% after a 20-second delay. These results suggest that information can be held in the short-term memory store for about 15 to 20 seconds.

Rehearsal and "Chunking" Strengthen Memory

What if 15 to 20 seconds isn't enough time? What if we need the information for a while longer? We can use a trick that allows us to get around the natural limitations of our short-term memories. **Rehearsal** is *the process of keeping information in short-term memory by mentally repeating it.* If someone gives you a telephone number and you can't immediately enter it into your cell phone or write it down, you say it over and over to yourself until you can. Each time you repeat the number, you are reentering it into short-term memory, giving it another 15 to 20 seconds of shelf life.

Rehearsal can play a role in the **serial position effect,** which refers to the observation that *the first few and last few items in a series are more likely to be recalled than the items in the middle.* Enhanced recall of the first few items in, say, a list of words is called the *primacy effect.* It occurs because these items receive more rehearsals than subsequent items in the middle of the list and thus are more likely to be encoded into long-term storage. Enhanced recall of the last few items is called the *recency effect* and can result from rehearsing items that are still in short-term storage (Atkinson & Shiffrin, 1968). Consistent with this interpretation, classic studies showed that the recency effect—but not the primacy effect—is eliminated when participants count backward by threes after the final list item is presented, which prevents them from relying on short-term storage to rehearse the last few items (Glanzer & Cunitz, 1966). However, both primacy and recency effects can be observed in situations that involve only long-term storage, such as recalling details of opera performances over a period of twenty-five years (Sehulster, 1989) or recalling the order of the seven Harry Potter books (Kelley, Neath, & Suprenant, 2013).

Short-term memory is limited in how *long* it can hold information and also is limited in how *much* information it can hold. Not only can most people keep approximately seven numbers in short-term memory, but if they put more new numbers in, then old numbers begin to fall out (Miller, 1956). Short-term memory isn't limited to numbers, of course. It can also hold about seven letters or seven words—even though those seven words contain many more than seven letters. In fact, short-term memory can hold about seven *meaningful items* at once (Miller, 1956). Therefore, one way to increase storage is to group several letters into a single meaningful item. **Chunking** involves *combining small pieces of information into larger clusters or chunks that are more easily held in short-term memory.* Waitresses who use organizational encoding (see p. 219) to organize customer orders into groups are essentially chunking the information, giving themselves less to remember.

Working Memory Stores and Manipulates Information

Short-term memory was originally conceived of as a kind of "place" where information is kept for a limited amount of time. More recently, researchers developed and refined a more dynamic model of a limited-capacity memory system, **working memory,** which refers to *active maintenance of information in short-term storage* (Baddeley & Hitch, 1974). As illustrated in **FIGURE 6.8**, working memory includes two subsystems that store and manipulate information, one for visual images (*the visuo-spatial sketchpad*) and another for verbal information (*the phonological loop*), and an *episodic buffer* that integrates visual and verbal information from the subsystems into a multidimensional code and a *central executive* that coordinates the subsystems and the episodic buffer (Baddeley, 2001; Baddeley, Allen, & Hitch, 2011). If you wanted to keep the arrangement of pieces on a chessboard in mind as you contemplated your next move,

▼ Figure 6.7

THE DECLINE OF SHORT-TERM MEMORY A 1959 experiment showed how quickly short-term memory fades without rehearsal. On a test for memory of three-letter strings, research participants were highly accurate when tested a few seconds after exposure to each string, but if the test was delayed another 15 seconds, people barely recalled the strings at all (Peterson & Peterson, 1959).

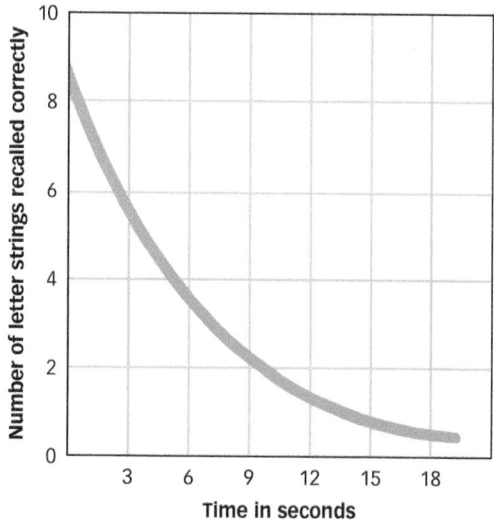

chunking Combining small pieces of information into larger clusters or chunks that are more easily held in short-term memory.

working memory A type of short-term storage that actively maintains information.

"Which of the books in the Harry Potter series are you likely to most easily recall, according to the serial position effect?"

V. RAYMOND

▶ **Figure 6.8**

A REFINED MODEL OF WORKING MEMORY The working memory system consists of a central executive that controls the flow of information through the system, a visuo-spatial sketchpad and phonological loop that temporarily hold visual/spatial images and verbal/auditory information, respectively, and an episodic buffer that integrates the various kinds of information that are maintained by the visuo-spatial sketchpad and phonological loop.

BADDELEY ET AL. (2011). BINDING IN VISUAL WORKING MEMORY: THE ROLE OF THE EPISODIC BUFFER. *NEUROPSYCHOLOGIA, 49,* 1393—1400.

you'd be relying on your visuo-spatial sketchpad to hold the visual representation of the positions of the pieces. You'd also rely on your central executive to control mental manipulation of the possible moves and awareness of the flow of information into and out of memory, all stored for a limited amount of time. In short, the working memory model acknowledges both the limited nature of this kind of memory storage and the activities that are commonly associated with it.

Research conducted in the context of this model has taught us that working memory plays an important role in many aspects of our cognitive lives (Baddeley, 2012). For example, studies of individuals with neurological damage to the phonological loop subsystem of working memory reveal that not only do they have problems holding on to strings of digits and letters for a few seconds, but they also have difficulty learning novel words. This suggests a link between this part of the working memory system and the ability to learn language (Baddeley, 2001; Gathercole, 2008).

Brain imaging studies indicate that the central executive component of working memory depends on regions within the frontal lobe that are important for controlling and manipulating information on a wide range of cognitive tasks (Baddeley, 2001; D'Esposito & Postle, 2015). Children who score low on working memory tasks have difficulty learning new information and performing well in the classroom (Alloway et al., 2009).

Researchers only recently have begun to study the episodic buffer. In a typical experiment, people perform tasks in which they need to combine different kinds of information, such as colors, shapes, and sounds, and hold that information over a brief period of time. Evidence from such experiments suggests that the episodic buffer automatically combines separate items into an integrated whole (Baddeley, Allen, & Hitch, 2011) and is a gateway to long-term memory, which we will discuss at length in the section on explicit memory later in this chapter (see pp. 225–236). The episodic buffer plays a role in learning to recognize words, which requires combining visual and verbal information. A recent study of grade school children and young adults showed that the ability to link together visual and auditory information and hold it in working memory, a task thought to depend on the episodic buffer, shows marked increases with age, even when controlling for the ability to hold the individual items in working memory (Wang, Allen, Lee, & Hsieh, 2015). Baddeley and colleagues have suggested that the episodic buffer also integrates other kinds of sensory information, such as smell and taste (see Figure 6.8), but research is needed to address this suggestion.

Research Is Examining the Link Between Working Memory Training and Cognitive Functioning

Can working memory skills be trained, and can such training enhance cognitive functioning? This question has become a hot research topic over the past few years (Klingberg, 2010; Shipstead, Redick, & Engle, 2012). In typical studies, participants are first given extensive practice in performing working memory tasks that require the maintenance and manipulation of visual or verbal information. They are then tested on new working memory tasks that have not been specifically trained, as well as on other cognitive tasks (reasoning, comprehension, or paying sustained attention). Some encouraging results have been reported. For example, elementary school students trained on several working memory tasks (about 35 minutes/day for at least 20 days over a 5- to 7-week time period) showed improvement on other working memory tasks when compared with untrained children (Holmes, Gathercole, & Dunning, 2009). These gains were evident even when the children were tested 6 months after training. There was also some evidence of improvement on math tasks. However, many working memory training studies are inconclusive as to whether it is the training in particular that is responsible for the effects that are observed (Slagter, 2012). Further, a recent study found that working memory training improved performance on the working memory task that was trained but did not result in improvements on other cognitive tasks (Redick et al., 2013). More research will be needed to determine whether working memory training produces any general improvements in cognitive performance and, if so, whether the improvements are large enough to affect performance on everyday cognitive tasks (Au, Sheehan, Tsai, Duncan, Buschkuehl, & Jaeggi, 2015; Redick, 2015; Shipstead et al., 2012).

LONG-TERM STORAGE

The artist Franco Magnani was born in Pontito, Italy, in 1934. In 1958, he left his village to see the rest of the world and settled in San Francisco in the 1960s. Soon after arriving, Magnani began to suffer from a strange illness. Every night he experienced feverish dreams of Pontito, in which he recalled the village in vivid detail. The dreams soon penetrated his waking life in the form of overpowering recollections, and Magnani decided that the only way to rid himself of these images was to capture them on canvas. For the next 20 years, he devoted much of his time to painting, in exquisite detail, his memories of his beloved village. Many years later, the photographer Susan Schwartzenberg went to Pontito, armed with a collection of Magnani's paintings, and photographed each scene from the perspective of the paintings. As you can see in the images, the correspondence between the paintings and the photographs was striking (Sacks, 1995; Schacter, 1996).

Many years intervened between Magnani's visual perception and his artistic reconstruction of the village, suggesting that very detailed information can sometimes be stored for a very long time. In contrast to the time-limited sensory and short-term storage stores, **long-term memory** is *a type of storage that holds information for hours, days, weeks, or years*. In contrast to both sensory and short-term storage, long-term memory has no known capacity limits (see Figure 6.6). For example, most people can recall 10,000 to 15,000 words in their native language, tens of thousands of facts (The capital of France is Paris, and $3 \times 3 = 9$), and an untold number of personal experiences. Just think of all the song lyrics you can recite by heart, and you'll understand that you've got a lot of information tucked away in your long-term memory!

More amazing, people can recall items from long-term memory even if they haven't thought of them for years. For example, researchers have found that even 50 years after graduation, people can accurately recognize about 90% of their high-school classmates from yearbook photographs (Bahrick, 2000). Such a feat is more remarkable when you consider that the people in the study probably had not accessed most of this information for years before the experiment.

The Hippocampus as Index: Linking Pieces into One Memory

Where is long-term memory located in the brain? The clues to answering this question come from individuals who are unable to store long-term memories. Not everyone has the same ability to encode information into long-term memory. In 1953, a 27-year-old man, known then by the initials HM, suffered from intractable epilepsy (Scoville & Milner, 1957). In a desperate attempt to stop the seizures, HM's doctors removed parts of his temporal lobes, including the hippocampus and some surrounding regions (**FIGURE 6.9**). After the operation, HM could converse easily, use and understand

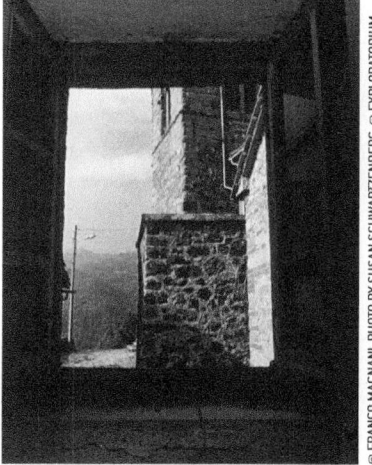

Even years after leaving home in Pontito, Italy, the painter Franco Magnani was able to create a near-perfect reproduction of what he'd seen there. Magnani's painting (*top*), based on a memory of a place he hadn't seen for years, is remarkably similar to the photograph (*bottom*) Susan Schwartzenberg took of the actual scene.

long-term memory A type of storage that holds information for hours, days, weeks, or years.

▶ **Figure 6.9**

THE HIPPOCAMPUS PATIENT HM had his hippocampus and adjacent structures of the medial temporal lobe (indicated by the shaded area) surgically removed to stop his epileptic seizures (*left*). As a result, he could not remember things that happened after the surgery. Henry Molaison (*right*), better known to the world as patient HM, passed away on December 2, 2008, at the age of 82 at a nursing home near Hartford, Connecticut. Molaison participated in countless memory experiments after he became amnesic in 1953, and in so doing made fundamental contributions to our understanding of memory and the brain (Corkin, 2013).

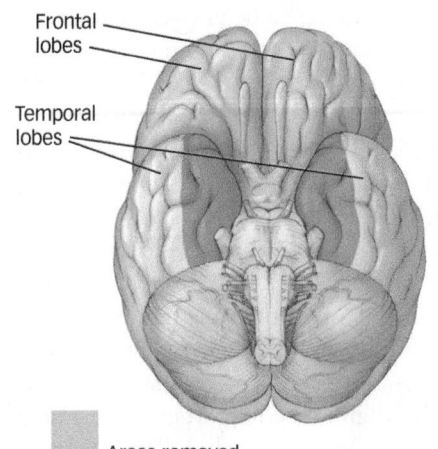

Frontal lobes

Temporal lobes

Areas removed

2016 MACMILLAN LEARNING

language, and perform well on intelligence tests, but he could not remember anything that happened to him after the operation. HM could repeat a telephone number with no difficulty, suggesting that his short-term memory store was just fine (Corkin, 2002, 2013; Hilts, 1995; Squire, 2009). But after information left the short-term store, it was gone forever. For example, he would often forget that he had just eaten a meal or fail to recognize the hospital staff who helped him on a daily basis. Studies of HM and others have shown that the hippocampal region of the brain is critical for putting new information into the long-term store (Clark & Maguire, 2016; Smith, Frascino, Hopkins, & Squire, 2013). When this region is damaged, individuals suffer from a condition known as **anterograde amnesia,** which is *the inability to transfer new information from the short-term store into the long-term store.*

Some individuals with amnesia also suffer from **retrograde amnesia,** which is *the inability to retrieve information that was acquired before a particular date, usually the date of an injury or surgery.* The fact that HM had much worse anterograde than retrograde amnesia suggests that the hippocampal region is not the site of long-term memory. Indeed, research has shown that different aspects of a single memory—its sights, sounds, smells, emotional content—are stored in different places in the cortex (Damasio, 1989; Schacter, 1996; Squire & Kandel, 1999). Some psychologists have argued that the hippocampal region acts as a kind of "index" that links together all of these otherwise separate bits and pieces so that we remember them as one memory (Schacter, 1996; Squire, 1992; Teyler & DiScenna, 1986). Recent fMRI studies support this "index view." The evidence shows that activity in the hippocampus relates to retrieving as a holistic unit the separate elements that an episode comprises, such as a person, location, and an object, which were initially encoded by distinct regions in the cortex (Horner, Bisby, Bush, Lin, & Burgess, 2015).

Over time, however, the hippocampal index may become less necessary. Going back to our cooking analogy, you can think of the hippocampal region index as a printed recipe. The first time you make a pie, you need the recipe to help you retrieve all the ingredients and then mix them together in the right amounts. As you bake more and more pies, though, you don't need to rely on the printed recipe anymore. Similarly, although the hippocampal region index is critical when a new memory is first formed, it may become less important as the memory ages. Another possibility is that the hippocampal index remains involved over long periods of time with some memories (highly detailed recollections of personal experiences, the kinds of memories that give us the feeling that we are almost reliving a past experience), but does not stay involved in less detailed, more general memories (Harand et al., 2012; Winocur, Moscovitch, & Bontempi, 2010). In terms of the cooking analogy, you might need to rely on a recipe each time you cook a complex meal with many details but not

anterograde amnesia The inability to transfer new information from the short-term store into the long-term store.

retrograde amnesia The inability to retrieve information that was acquired before a particular date, usually the date of an injury or surgery.

when you cook a simpler meal with a less detailed recipe. Scientists are still debating the extent to which the hippocampal region helps us to remember details of our old memories (Bayley, Gold, et al., 2005; Kirwan et al., 2008; Moscovitch, Cabeza, Nadel, & Winocur, 2016; Squire & Wixted, 2011; Winocur et al., 2010). However, the notion of the hippocampus as an index explains why people such as HM cannot make new memories and why they can remember many old ones.

Consolidation Stabilizes Memories

The idea that the hippocampus becomes less important over time for maintaining memories is closely related to the concept of **consolidation,** *the process by which memories become stable in the brain* (McGaugh, 2000; McGaugh, 2015). Shortly after encoding, memories exist in a fragile state in which they can be disrupted easily; once consolidation has occurred, they are more resistant to disruption. One type of consolidation operates over seconds or minutes. For example, when someone experiences a head injury in a car crash and later cannot recall what happened during the few seconds or minutes before the crash—but can recall other events normally—the head injury probably prevented consolidation of short-term memory into long-term memory. Another type of consolidation occurs over much longer periods of time— days, weeks, months, and years—and likely involves transfer of information from the hippocampus to more permanent storage sites in the cortex. The operation of this longer-term consolidation process is why individuals with retrograde amnesia with hippocampal damage can recall memories from childhood relatively normally, but are impaired when recalling experiences that occurred just a few years prior to the time they became amnesic (Kirwan et al., 2008; Squire & Wixted, 2011).

How does a memory become consolidated? The act of recalling a memory, thinking about it, and talking about it with others probably contributes to consolidation (Moscovitch et al., 2006). And though you may not be aware of it, consolidation gets a boost from something that you do effortlessly every night: sleep. As explained in Hot Science: Sleep on It, mounting evidence gathered during the past decade indicates that sleep plays an important role in memory consolidation.

Recalled Memories May Be Disrupted During Reconsolidation

Many researchers have long believed that a fully consolidated memory becomes a permanent fixture in the brain, more difficult to get rid of than a computer virus. But another line of research that has developed rapidly in recent years suggests that things are not so simple. Experiments have shown that even seemingly consolidated *memories can become vulnerable to disruption when they are recalled, thus requiring them to be consolidated again.* This process is called **reconsolidation** (Dudai, 2012; Nader & Hardt, 2009). Evidence for reconsolidation mainly comes from experiments with rats showing that when animals are cued to retrieve a new memory that was acquired a day earlier, giving the animal a drug (or an electrical shock) that prevents initial consolidation will cause forgetting (Nader, Shafe, & LeDoux, 2000; Sara, 2000). It is critical that if the animal is not actively retrieving the memory, the same drug (or shock) has no effect when given a day after initial encoding. Researchers have produced similar effects using electrical shocks in studies with people (Schiller et al., 2010). This finding is surprising because it was once thought that when memories are consolidated, drugs or shock that prevent initial consolidation no longer have any impact. On the contrary, it appears that each time they are retrieved, memories become vulnerable to disruption and have to be reconsolidated.

Disrupting Reconsolidation May Reduce Traumatic Memories

Might it be possible one day to eliminate or modify painful memories by disrupting reconsolidation? Recent research suggests it could be. When a traumatic event was

consolidation The process by which memories become stable in the brain.

reconsolidation The process whereby memories can become vulnerable to disruption when they are recalled, thus requiring them to be consolidated again.

Sleep on It

HOT SCIENCE

Thinking about pulling an all-nighter before your next big test? Here's a reason to reconsider: Our minds don't simply shut off when we sleep (see the Consciousness chapter). In fact, sleep may be as important to our memories as wakefulness.

Nearly a century ago, Jenkins and Dallenbach (1924) reported that recall of recently learned information is greater immediately after sleeping than after the same amount of time spent awake. But Jenkins and Dallenbach did not think that sleep played an active role in strengthening or consolidating memory. They argued instead that being asleep passively protects us from encountering information that interferes with our ability to remember. As is explained by retroactive interference (p. 245), that's a valid argument. However, during the past decade, evidence has accumulated that sleep plays an active role in memory consolidation, doing more than simply protecting us from waking interference (Diekelman & Born, 2010; Ellenbogen, Payne, & Stickgold, 2006; Vorster & Born, 2015). Sleep selectively enhances the consolidation of memories that reflect the meaning or gist of an experience (Payne et al., 2009), as well as emotionally important memories (Payne et al., 2008, 2015), suggesting that sleep helps us to remember what's important and to discard what's trivial.

This idea is reinforced by evidence which shows that the beneficial effects of sleep on subsequent memory are observed only when people expect to be tested. In one study (van Dongen et al., 2012), participants studied pictures of either buildings or furniture that were each associated with a particular location on a slide (see at right). Soon after, participants received a memory test for the picture–

location associations. They were then instructed that they would be retested 14 hours later for either the building pictures or the furniture pictures (the relevant category) and would not be retested on the other type of picture (the irrelevant category). Half of the participants were tested after sleep (initial learning was in the afternoon for these individuals) and half after remaining awake (initial learning was in the morning for these individuals). On the retest, there was less forgetting for the relevant than for the irrelevant categories in the sleep group, but there was no such difference in the awake group. Furthermore, participants who slept longer retained more of the relevant but not the irrelevant information.

Another recent line of evidence shows that memory consolidation during sleep can be enhanced by presenting sounds during sleep that reactivate specific memories (Oudiette & Paller, 2013). Before sleep, participants learned to associate an object, such as a kettle, with a particular location on a screen; they saw a picture of the kettle

and also heard its characteristic whistling sound. During a subsequent period of sleep, researchers played the sounds of some of the studied objects to participants in an attempt to reactivate their memories of the object-location associations. In a remarkable result, when tested after awakening, participants showed more accurate memory for the location of the objects whose characteristic sounds were presented during sleep than for the locations of objects whose characteristic sounds were not presented—even though participants were not aware that any sounds had been presented while they slept. Such targeted memory reactivation effects are strongest for those associations that are not well learned initially (Creery et al., 2015). These findings suggest that it may be possible to use targeted memory reactivation during sleep to boost learning.

So when you find yourself nodding off after hours of studying for your exam, the science is on the side of a good night's sleep.

The Picture-Location Task

A. Location Arrays

B. Encoding

1s   1s   2s

C. Retrieval

4s   until response   1s   until response   3–7s

VAN DONGEN EV, THIELEN J-W, TAKASHIMA A, BARTH M, FERNÁNDEZ G (2012) SLEEP SUPPORTS SELECTIVE RETENTION OF ASSOCIATIVE MEMORIES BASED ON RELEVANCE FOR FUTURE UTILIZATION. PLOS ONE 7(8): E43426. DOI:10.1371/JOURNAL.PONE.0043426.
© VAN DONGEN ET AL.

reactivated in traumatized individuals who had been given a drug to reduce anxiety, there was a subsequent reduction in traumatic symptoms (Brunet et al., 2008, 2011). However, drugs are not necessary to disrupt reconsolidation of painful memories. Consider the traumatic events of April 15, 2013, when two bombs exploded near the finish line of the Boston Marathon, killing three people and injuring over 250 others. Several months later, researchers asked undergraduates at Boston University, which is located near the site of the bombing, to recall where they were when they learned of the bombing, what they were doing, and how they felt (Kredlow & Otto, 2015). The students' memories were detailed, and they recalled feeling considerable distress at the time. One minute after this memory reactivation, during the reconsolidation phase when memories are vulnerable to disruption, some students read a negative story, others read either a positive or neutral story, and others (the control group) did nothing. All the students returned a week later and recalled their memories of the bombing again. Compared with the students in the control group, the students who read a negative story shortly after memory reactivation recalled significantly fewer details about the bombing than they had initially, whereas those who read positive or neutral stories showed smaller, nonsignificant reductions in recalled details. Reading the negative story appeared to interfere with reconsolidation of students' negative memories of the bombing.

Related work using fMRI indicates that disrupting reconsolidation can seemingly eliminate a fear memory in a part of the brain called the *amygdala*, which we will learn, later in this chapter, plays a key role in emotional memory (Agren et al., 2012). Reconsolidation thus appears to be a key memory process with many important implications.

The Boston marathon bombings in April 2013 produced detailed and disturbing memories in people at or near the site of the bombings. However, research shows that the amount of detail in these memories can be reduced by interfering with their reconsolidation.

MEMORIES, NEURONS, AND SYNAPSES

We've already discussed parts of the brain that are related to memory storage, but we haven't said much about how or where memories are stored. Research suggests that memory storage depends critically on the *spaces* between neurons. You'll recall from the Neuroscience and Behavior chapter that a *synapse* is the small space between the axon of one neuron and the dendrite of another and that neurons communicate by sending neurotransmitters across these synapses. As it turns out, sending a neurotransmitter across a synapse isn't like sending a toy boat across a pond, because the act of sending actually *changes* the synapse. Specifically, it strengthens the connection between the two neurons, making it easier for them to transmit to each other the next time. This is why researchers sometimes say, "Cells that fire together wire together" (Hebb, 1949).

The idea that the connections between neurons are strengthened by their communication, making communication easier the next time, provides the neurological basis for long-term memory, and much of what we know about this comes from the tiny sea slug *Aplysia* (see **FIGURE 6.10**). The story of *Aplysia* and memory is closely linked with the work of the neuroscientist Eric Kandel, who won the Nobel Prize in 2000 for his work with the creature. When Kandel first became interested in *Aplysia* back in the late 1950s, only two researchers in the entire world were studying the tiny slug. But *Aplysia* was attractive to Kandel because it is relatively uncomplicated and has an extremely simple nervous system consisting of only 20,000 neurons (compared with roughly 100 billion in the human brain), so Kandel followed his intuition and studied *Aplysia* (Kandel, 2006).

When an experimenter stimulates *Aplysia*'s tail with a mild electric shock, the slug immediately withdraws its gill, and if the experimenter does it again a moment later, *Aplysia* withdraws its gill even more quickly. If the experimenter comes back an hour later and shocks *Aplysia*, the withdrawal of the gill happens as slowly as it did the first time, as if *Aplysia* can't "remember" what happened an hour earlier (Abel et al., 1995). But if the experimenter shocks *Aplysia* over and over, it does develop an enduring "memory" that can last for days or even weeks. Research suggests that this long-term storage involves the growth of new synaptic connections between neurons (Abel et al., 1995; Kandel, 2006; Squire & Kandel, 1999). So learning in *Aplysia* is based on changes involving the synapses for both short-term storage (enhanced neurotransmitter release) and long-term storage (growth of new synapses). Any experience

▲ Figure 6.10

APLYSIA By studying the sea slug *Aplysia californica*'s extremely simple nervous system, researchers were able to determine that long-term memory storage depends on the growth of new synaptic connections between neurons.

Nobel Prize–winning neuroscientist Eric Kandel took a risk and studied the tiny sea slug *Aplysia* based in part on a lesson he had learned from his wife regarding their recent marriage, which encouraged him to trust his intuition: "Denise was confident that our marriage would work, so I took a leap of faith and went ahead. I learned from that experience that there are many situations in which one cannot decide on the basis of cold facts alone—because the facts are often insufficient. One ultimately has to trust one's unconscious, one's instincts, one's creative urge. I did this again in choosing *Aplysia*" (Kandel, 2006, p. 149).

SPENCER PLATT/NEWSMAKERS/GETTY IMAGES

long-term potentiation (LTP) A process whereby repeated communication across the synapse between neurons strengthens the connection, making further communication easier.

that results in memory produces physical changes in the nervous system—even if you are a slug.

If you're something more complex than a slug—say, a chimpanzee or your roommate—a similar process of synaptic strengthening happens in the hippocampus, which we've seen is an area crucial for storing new long-term memories. In the early 1970s, researchers applied a brief electrical stimulus to a neural pathway in a rat's hippocampus (Bliss & Lømo, 1973). They found that the electrical current produced a stronger connection between synapses that lay along the pathway and that the strengthening lasted for hours or even weeks. They called this effect **long-term potentiation** (more commonly known as **LTP**), *a process whereby communication across the synapse between neurons strengthens the connection, making further communication easier.* Long-term potentiation has a number of properties that indicate to researchers that it plays an important role in long-term memory storage: It occurs in several pathways within the hippocampus; it can be induced rapidly; and it can last for a long time. In fact, drugs that block LTP can turn rats into rodent versions of patient HM: The animals have great difficulty remembering where they've been recently and become easily lost in a maze (Bliss, 1999; Morris et al., 1986).

Build to the Outcomes

1. What evidence from the iconic memory test suggests that all the letters presented to participants were stored in memory before quickly fading?

2. Define iconic and echoic memory.

3. Why is it helpful to repeat a telephone number you're trying to remember?

4. How does working memory expand on the idea of short-term memory?

5. What did researchers learn about the role of the hippocampus and memory from HM?

6. Define anterograde and retrograde amnesia.

7. How does the process of recalling a memory affect its stability?

8. How does building a memory produce a physical change in the nervous system?

Retrieval: Bringing Memories to Mind

There is something fiendishly frustrating about piggy banks. You can put money in them, you can shake them around to assure yourself that the money is there, but you can't easily get the money out. If memories were like pennies in a piggy bank, stored but inaccessible, what would be the point of saving them in the first place? Retrieval is the process of bringing to mind information that has been previously encoded and stored, and it is perhaps the most important of all memory processes (Roediger, 2000; Schacter, 2001a).

Learning Outcomes

▶ Explain the encoding specificity principle.

▶ Explain how memories can be changed by the act of retrieval.

▶ Describe the difference in brain activity when trying versus successfully recalling information.

RETRIEVAL CUES: REINSTATING THE PAST

One of the best ways to retrieve information from *inside* your head is to encounter information *outside* your head that is somehow connected to it. The information outside your head is called a **retrieval cue,** *external information that is associated with stored information and helps bring it to mind*. Retrieval cues can be incredibly effective. How many times have you said something such as, "I *know* who played Amy Schumer's boyfriend in *Trainwreck,* but I just can't remember his name"?, only to have a friend give you a hint ("He was on *Saturday Night Live* for years"), which instantly brings the answer to mind ("Bill Hader!").

In one experiment, undergraduates studied lists of words, such as *table, peach, bed, apple, chair, grape,* and *desk* (Tulving & Pearlstone, 1966). Later, the students were asked to write down all the words from the list that they could remember. When they were absolutely sure that they had emptied their memory stores of every last word, the experimenters again asked the students to remember the words on the list. This time, however, the experimenters provided retrieval cues, such as "furniture" or "fruit." The students who were sure that they had done all the remembering they possibly could were suddenly able to remember more words. These results suggest that information is sometimes *available* in memory even when it is momentarily *inaccessible* and that retrieval cues help us bring inaccessible information to mind.

External Context Provides Cues

Hints are one kind of retrieval cue, but they are not the only kind. The **encoding specificity principle** states that *a retrieval cue can serve as an effective reminder when it helps re-create the specific way in which information was initially encoded* (Tulving & Thomson, 1973). External contexts often make powerful retrieval cues (Hockley, 2008). For example, in one study divers learned some words on land and some other words underwater; they recalled the words best when they were tested in the same dry or wet environment in which they had initially learned them, because the environment itself was a retrieval cue (Godden & Baddeley, 1975). Recovering alcoholics often experience a renewed urge to drink when visiting places in which they once drank because those places are retrieval cues. There may even be some wisdom to finding a seat in a classroom, sitting in it every day, and then sitting in it again when you take the test. The feel of the chair and the sights you see may help you remember the information you learned while you sat there.

Inner States Also Provide Cues

Retrieval cues need not be external contexts—they can also be inner states. **State-dependent retrieval** is *the process whereby information tends to be better recalled when the person is in the same state during encoding and retrieval*. For example, retrieving information when you are in a sad or happy mood increases the likelihood that you will retrieve sad or happy episodes (Eich, 1995). This is part of the reason it is so hard to "look on the bright side" when you're feeling low. Similarly, you'd probably expect a

Retrieval cues are hints that help bring stored information to mind. How does this explain the fact that most students prefer multiple-choice exams to fill-in-the-blank exams?

retrieval cue External information that is associated with stored information and helps bring it to mind.

encoding specificity principle The idea that a retrieval cue can be an effective reminder when it helps re-create the specific way in which information was initially encoded.

state-dependent retrieval The process whereby information tends to be better recalled when the person is in the same state during encoding and retrieval.

AP PHOTO/*POCONO RECORD*, ADAM RICHINS

transfer-appropriate processing The process whereby memory is more likely to transfer from one situation to another when the encoding and retrieval contexts of the situations match.

fellow student who studied for an exam while drunk to perform poorly, and you would probably be right—but only if he made the mistake of taking the exam while sober! Studies of state-dependent retrieval suggest that if the student studied while drunk, he would probably perform poorly the next day, but he'd perform better if he'd had a six-pack instead of Cheerios for breakfast (Eich, 1980; Weissenborn, 2000). Why should that be? Because a person's physiological or psychological state at the time of encoding is associated with the information that is encoded. For example, being in a good mood affects patterns of electrical activity in parts of the brain responsible for semantic processing, suggesting that mood has a direct influence on semantic encoding (Kiefer et al., 2007). If the person's state at the time of retrieval matches the person's state at the time of encoding, the state itself is a retrieval cue. It is a bridge that connects the moment at which we experience something to the moment at which we remember it. Retrieval cues can even be thoughts themselves, as when one thought calls to mind another, related thought (Anderson et al., 1976).

Matching Encoding and Retrieval Contexts Improves Recall

The encoding specificity principle makes some unusual predictions. For example, you learned earlier that making semantic judgments about a word (e.g., What does *brain* mean?) usually produces a more durable memory for the word than does making rhyme judgments (e.g., What rhymes with *brain*?). Consider this scenario: A friend and you were shown a cue card of the word *brain*. Your friend was asked to think about what *brain* means, whereas you were asked to think of a word that rhymes with *brain*. We would expect your friend to remember the word better the next day if we simply asked you both, "Hey, what was that word you saw yesterday?" However, if instead of asking that question, we asked you both, "What was that word that rhymed with *train*?" the retrieval cue would match your encoding context better than your friend's, and we would expect you to remember it better than your friend did (Fisher & Craik, 1977). This is a fairly astounding finding. The principle of **transfer-appropriate processing** is *the idea that memory is likely to transfer from one situation to another when the encoding and retrieval contexts of the situations match* (Morris, Bransford, & Franks, 1977; Roediger, Weldon, & Challis, 1989).

CONSEQUENCES OF RETRIEVAL

Human memory differs substantially from computer memory. Simply retrieving a file from my computer doesn't have any effect on the likelihood that the file will open again in the future. Not so with human memory. Retrieval doesn't merely provide a readout of what is in memory; it also changes the state of the memory system in important ways.

Retrieval Can Improve Subsequent Memory

Psychologists have known for some time that the act of retrieval can strengthen a retrieved memory, making it easier to remember that information at a later time (Bjork, 1975). Does this finding surprise you? Probably not. Does studying information twice have the same benefit as retrieving information twice? This finding probably *will* surprise you. It turns out that retrieving information from memory has different effects from studying it again. This point was made dramatically in an experiment in which participants studied brief stories and then either studied them again or were given a test that required retrieving the stories (Roediger & Karpicke, 2006). Participants were then given a final recall test for the stories either 5 minutes, 2 days, or 1 week later. As shown in **FIGURE 6.11**, at the 5-minute delay, studying the stories twice resulted in slightly higher recall than did studying paired with retrieval (testing). In a critical finding, the opposite occurred at the 2-day and 1-week delays: Retrieval produced much higher levels of recall than did an extra study exposure. A subsequent

▲ Figure 6.11

MEMORY TESTING BENEFITS LONG-TERM RETENTION With a 5-minute retention interval, the study–study condition results in slightly higher recall. But the results change dramatically with retention intervals of 2 days and 1 week: With these longer delays, the study–test condition yields much higher levels of recall than does the study–study condition (Roediger & Karpicke, 2006).

experiment using foreign vocabulary items also revealed that retrieval of the items produced a much bigger benefit on a delayed vocabulary test than did further study (Karpicke & Roediger, 2008). The benefits of testing on subsequent retention occur not only in adults but also in grade school children (Jaeger, Eisenkraemer, & Stein, 2015). Although there are specific situations in which testing produces little or no benefit for subsequent retention (Van Gog et al., 2015), the benefits of testing have been documented across many different memory tasks, and with both simple and complex materials (Karpicke & Aue, 2015). These findings have potentially important implications for learning in educational contexts (Karpicke, 2012), which we will explore further in the Learning chapter.

Retrieval Can Also Impair Subsequent Memory

As much as retrieval can help memory, that's not always the case. **Retrieval-induced forgetting** is *a process by which retrieving an item from long-term memory impairs subsequent recall of related items* (Anderson, 2003; Anderson, Bjork, & Bjork, 1994; Murayama, Miyatsu, Buchli, & Storm, 2014).

Let's see how a typical experiment on retrieval-induced forgetting works (**FIGURE 6.12**; Anderson et al., 1994). Participants first studied word pairs consisting of a category name and an example of an item from that category (e.g., *fruit–orange, fruit–apple, tree–elm, tree–birch*). Then they practiced recalling some of the items in response to a category cue and the initial letters of the target item. For example, for the fruit category participants would practice recalling *orange* to the cue "fruit or ____," but would not practice recalling *apple*. The general idea was that while they were practicing recall of *orange*, participants suppressed the competitor item *apple*. For other categories (e.g., *trees*), no retrieval practice was given for any of the studied pairs. Later, the participants were given a final test for all the words they initially studied. It was not surprising that on the final test, participants remembered words that they practiced (e.g., *orange*) better than words from categories that they did not practice (e.g., *elm*). But what happened on the final test to the items such as *apple*, which were not practiced, and which participants presumably had to suppress while they practiced recall of related items? Those items were recalled most poorly of all,

	a. study phase		b. retrieval practice phase; only the "fruit" category tested	c. recall phase results
category	FRUIT	TREES	FRUIT: or____	
			FRUIT: ba____	practiced items (orange, banana, lemon) remembered better than items in the unpracticed category (trees)
items:	orange	elm	FRUIT: le____	
	apple	birch		
	banana	cedar		
	lemon	beech		unpracticed items from practiced category (apple, pear, pineapple) – suppressed items – most poor recall of all
	pear	fir		
	pineapple	maple		

▲ Figure 6.12

RECALLING ITEMS FROM MEMORY IMPAIRS RECALL OF RELATED ITEMS (a) Participants first studied word pairs with category names and an example of an item in each of the categories. (b) One category and some of the items were practiced with cues to prompt recall. (c) Practiced items were recalled best, but items not practiced from the same category were more poorly recalled then even the unpracticed category (Anderson et al., 1994).

indicating that retrieving the similar target items (e.g., *orange*) caused subsequent forgetting of the related but suppressed items (e.g., *apple*). In fact, even if you don't successfully retrieve the target item, the act of suppressing the competitors while you attempt to retrieve the target still reduces your ability to retrieve the competitors at a later time (Storm et al., 2006).

Can you think of any examples of how retrieval-induced forgetting could affect memory in everyday life? Here are two. First, retrieval-induced forgetting can occur during conversations: When a speaker selectively talks about some aspects of memories shared with a listener and doesn't mention related information, the listener later has a harder time remembering the omitted events, as does the speaker (Cuc, Koppel, & Hirst, 2007; Hirst & Echterhoff, 2012). This effect occurs even for memories as important as the events of September 11, 2001 (Coman, Manier, & Hirst, 2009). Second, retrieval-induced forgetting can affect eyewitness memory. When witnesses to a staged crime are questioned about some details of the crime scene, their ability to later recall related details that they were not asked about is impaired, compared with that of witnesses who initially were not questioned at all (MacLeod, 2002; Shaw, Bjork, & Handal, 1995). These findings suggest that initial interviews with eyewitnesses should be as complete as possible in order to avoid potential retrieval-induced forgetting of significant details that are not probed during an interview (MacLeod & Saunders, 2008).

Retrieval Can Change Subsequent Memory

In addition to improving and impairing subsequent memory, the act of retrieval also can change what we remember from an experience. Consider an experiment in which participants went on a tour of a museum, where they took some time to view designated exhibits, each of which contained several different stops (St. Jacques & Schacter, 2013). The participants took the tour while wearing a camera that, every 15 seconds, automatically took pictures of what was in front of them. Two days later, the participants visited the memory laboratory (in a separate building) for a "reactivation session." After memories of some of the stops were reactivated by looking at photos of them, participants were asked to rate, on a 1–5 scale, how vividly they reexperienced what had happened at each stop. Next, the participants were shown novel photos of *unvisited* stops within the exhibit, then were asked to judge how closely these novel photos were related to the photos of the stops that they had actually seen in that exhibit. Finally, the participants were given a memory test 2 days after the reactivation session.

Participants sometimes incorrectly remembered that the stop shown in the novel photo had been part of the original tour. Most important, participants who tended to make this mistake also tended to have more vivid recollections during the reactivation session. In other words, retrieving and vividly reexperiencing memories of what participants actually did see at the museum led them to incorporate into their memory information that was not part of their original experience. This finding may be related to the phenomenon of reconsolidation that we discussed earlier (p. 227), where reactivating a memory temporarily makes it vulnerable to disruption and change. At the very least, this finding reinforces the idea that retrieving a memory involves far more than a simple readout of information. Cultural influences on retrieval of early childhood memories, which have been linked with cultural differences in how frequently people retrieve past experiences, make a similar point (see A World of Difference: Childhood Amnesia in Western and Eastern Cultures).

SEPARATING THE COMPONENTS OF RETRIEVAL

Before leaving the topic of retrieval, let's look at how the process actually works. There is reason to believe that *trying* to recall an incident and *successfully* recalling

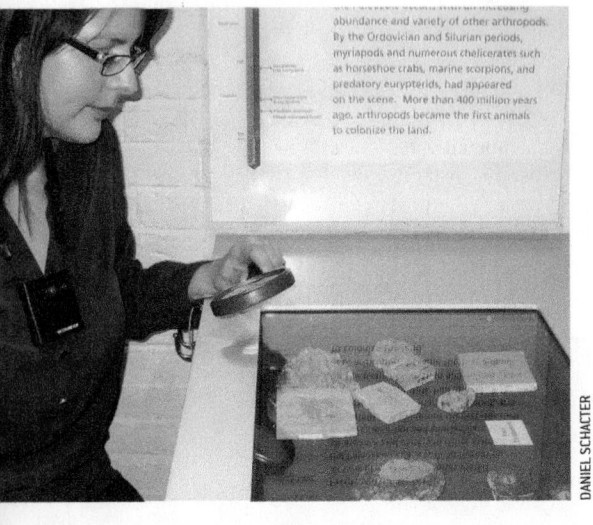

As part of a recent experiment, participants wore cameras that took pictures every 15 seconds as they toured a museum.

DANIEL SCHACTER

Childhood Amnesia in Western and Eastern Cultures

Are there differences in how far back into their infancy children can remember depending on where they grew up? You can easily recall many experiences from different times in your life. However, you probably have few or no memories from the first few years of your life, due to *childhood amnesia,* or *infantile amnesia.* On average, an individual's first memory dates to about 3 to 3 1/2 years of age (Dudycha & Dudycha, 1933; Waldfogel, 1948), with women reporting slightly earlier first memories (3.07 years of age) than men (3.4 years) (Howes, Siegel, & Brown, 1993). But these estimates are based on individuals from Western (i.e., North American and European) cultures, which emphasize talking about the past. First memories are seen at later ages in Asian cultures that place less emphasis on talking about the past, such as Korea and China (MacDonald, Uesiliana, & Hayne, 2000; Mullen, 1994; Peterson, Wang, & Hou, 2009). A comparison of Canadian and Chinese children showed that first memories of

8-year-old children in both cultures come from younger ages than the first memories of 14-year-old children, suggesting that early memories fade or disappear as children age (Peterson et al., 2009). In a critical finding, the first memories of the 14-year-old Chinese children came from

a later age than did the first memories of the 14-year-old Canadians. In fact, the onset of childhood amnesia in the Chinese 14-year-olds was identical to that of North American adults. Culture thus has a significant impact on even our earliest memories.

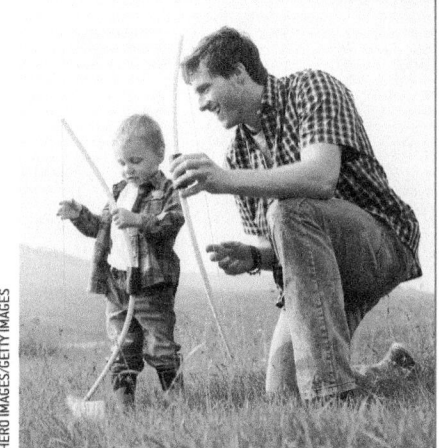

ZHANG BO/GETTY IMAGES

HERO IMAGES/GETTY IMAGES

▲ First memories are seen later in cultures that place less emphasis on talking about the past.

one are fundamentally different processes that occur in different parts of the brain (Moscovitch, 1994; Schacter, 1996). For example, regions in the left frontal lobe show heightened activity when people *try* to retrieve information that was presented to them earlier (Oztekin, Curtis, & McElree, 2009; Tulving et al., 1994). This activity may reflect the mental effort of struggling to dredge up the past event (Lepage et al., 2000). However, *successfully* remembering a past experience tends to be accompanied by activity in the hippocampal region (see **FIGURE 6.13**; Eldridge et al., 2000; Giovanello, Schnyer, & Verfaellie, 2004; Schacter, Alpert, et al., 1996). Furthermore, successful

High recall minus baseline   **Low recall minus baseline**

Left frontal lobe

Hippocampus

(a)   (b)

◄ Figure 6.13

PET SCANS OF SUCCESSFUL AND UNSUCCESSFUL RECALL When people successfully remembered words they saw earlier in an experiment (achieving high levels of recall on a test), the hippocampus showed increased activity. When people tried but failed to recall words they had seen earlier (achieving low levels of recall on a test), the left frontal lobe showed increased activity. SCHACTER ET AL. (1996). CONSCIOUS RECOLLECTION AND THE HUMAN HIPPOCAMPAL FORMATION: EVIDENCE FROM POSITRON EMISSION TOMOGRAPHY. *PROC NATL ACAD SCI USA, 93,* 321–325.

recall also activates parts of the brain that play a role in processing the sensory features of an experience. For instance, recall of previously heard sounds is accompanied by activity in the auditory cortex (the upper part of the temporal lobe), whereas recall of previously seen pictures is accompanied by activity in the visual cortex (in the occipital lobe; Wheeler, Petersen, & Buckner, 2000). Although retrieval may seem like a single process, brain studies suggest that separately identifiable processes are at work.

This finding sheds some light on the phenomenon we just discussed: retrieval-induced forgetting. Recent fMRI evidence indicates that during memory retrieval, regions within the frontal lobe that are involved in retrieval effort play a role in suppressing competitors (Benoit & Anderson, 2012; Kuhl et al., 2007; Wimber et al., 2009). Indeed, repeated attempts to retrieve target items result in a suppression of the specific neural patterns that are uniquely associated with competitors (Wimber et al., 2015). So, for example, when hippocampal activity during retrieval practice signals successful recall of an unwanted competitor, frontal lobe mechanisms are recruited that help to suppress the competitor. Once the competitor is suppressed, the frontal lobe no longer has to work as hard at controlling retrieval, ultimately making it easier to recall the target item (Kuhl et al., 2007). In addition, successful suppression of an unwanted memory causes reduced activity in the hippocampus (Anderson et al., 2004). These findings make sense once we understand the specific roles played by particular brain regions in the retrieval process.

Build to the Outcomes

1. Why are external contexts powerful retrieval cues?

2. How does mood affect memory?

3. Should students spend more time testing themselves on material (retrieval), or studying it over and over?

4. How can retrieval-induced forgetting occur during conversations?

5. How is it possible to remember something you've never seen?

6. How is brain activity different when you are *trying* to recall versus *successfully* recalling?

Forms of Long-Term Memory: More Than One Kind

Learning Outcomes

▶ Distinguish between explicit and implicit memory.

▶ Give examples of both semantic and episodic memories.

▶ Describe the pros and cons of collaborative memory.

In 1977, the neurologist Oliver Sacks interviewed a young man named Greg who had a tumor in his brain that wiped out his ability to remember day-to-day events. One thing Greg could remember was his life during the 1960s in New York's Greenwich Village, years before the tumor formed, when Greg's primary occupation seemed to be attending rock concerts by his favorite band, the Grateful Dead. Greg's memories of those Dead concerts stuck with him over the following years, when he was living in a long-term care hospital and was interviewed regularly by Dr. Sacks. In 1991, Dr. Sacks took Greg to a Dead concert at New York's Madison Square Garden, wondering whether such a momentous event might jolt his memory into action. "That was fantastic," Greg told Dr. Sacks as they left the concert. "I will always remember it. I had the time of my life." But when Dr. Sacks saw Greg the next morning and asked him whether he recalled the previous night's Dead concert at the Garden, Greg drew a blank: "No, I've never been to the Garden" (Sacks, 1995, pp. 76–77).

Although Greg was unable to make new memories, some of the new things that happened to him seemed to leave a mark. For example, Greg did not recall learning that his father had died, but he did seem sad and withdrawn for years after hearing the news. Similarly, HM could not make new memories after his surgery, but if he played a game in which he had to track a moving target, his performance gradually improved with each round (Milner, 1962). Greg could not consciously remember hearing about his father's death, and HM could not consciously remember playing the tracking game, but both showed clear signs of having been permanently changed by experiences that they so rapidly forgot. In other words, they *behaved* as though they were remembering things while claiming to remember nothing at all. This suggests that there must be several kinds of memory, some that are accessible to conscious recall, and some that we cannot consciously access (Eichenbaum & Cohen, 2001; Schacter & Tulving, 1994; Schacter, Wagner, & Buckner, 2000; Squire & Kandel, 1999).

Memories can be broken down into two types. **Explicit memory** occurs *when people consciously or intentionally retrieve past experiences.* Recalling last summer's vacation, incidents from a novel you just read, or facts you studied for a test all involve explicit memory. Indeed, anytime you start a sentence with "I remember . . . ," you are talking about an explicit memory. **Implicit memory** occurs when *past experiences influence later behavior and performance, even without an effort to remember them or an awareness of the recollection* (Graf & Schacter, 1985; Schacter, 1987). Let's look next at both of these.

explicit memory The act of consciously or intentionally retrieving past experiences.

implicit memory The influence of past experiences on later behavior and performance, even without an effort to remember them or an awareness of the recollection.

procedural memory The gradual acquisition of skills as a result of practice, or "knowing how" to do things.

IMPLICIT MEMORY

Implicit memories are not consciously recalled, but their presence is "implied" by our actions. Greg's persistent sadness after his father's death, even though he had no conscious knowledge of the event, is an example of implicit memory. So is HM's improved performance on a tracking task that he didn't consciously remember doing.

The ability to ride a bike or tie your shoelaces or play the guitar are other examples of implicit memory. You may know how to do these things, but you probably can't describe how to do them. Such knowledge reflects a particular kind of implicit memory called **procedural memory,** which refers to *the gradual acquisition of skills as a result of practice, or "knowing how" to do things.*

One of the hallmarks of procedural memory is that the things you remember are automatically translated into actions. Sometimes you can explain how it is done (put one finger on the third fret of the E string, one finger . . .), and sometimes you can't (get on the bike and . . . well, uh . . . just balance). The fact that people who have amnesia can acquire new procedural memories suggests that the hippocampal structures that are usually damaged in these individuals may be necessary for explicit memory, but they aren't needed for implicit procedural memory. In fact, it appears that brain regions outside the hippocampal area (including areas in the motor cortex) are involved in procedural memory. The Learning chapter discusses this evidence further, and you will also see that procedural memory is crucial for learning various kinds of motor, perceptual, and cognitive skills.

Guitarists such as Jack White rely heavily on procedural memory to acquire and use the skills they need to play their music at a high level.

Priming Makes Some Information More Accessible

Not all implicit memories are procedural or "how to" memories. For example, in one experiment, college students were asked to study a long list of words, including items such as *avocado, mystery, climate, octopus,* and *assassin* (Tulving, Schacter, & Stark, 1982). Later, explicit memory was tested by showing participants some of these words along with new ones they hadn't seen and asking them which words were on the list. To test implicit memory, participants received word fragments and were asked to come up with a word that fitted the fragment. Try the test yourself:

c h – – – – n k   o – t – p – –   – o g – y – – –   – l – m – t e

priming An enhanced ability to think of a stimulus, such as a word or object, as a result of a recent exposure to that stimulus.

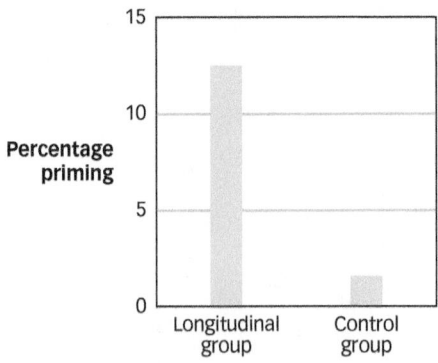

▲ Figure 6.14

LONG-TERM PRIMING OF VISUAL OBJECTS Participants who viewed drawings of common objects, and 17 years later were given a test in which they tried to identify the objects from fragmented drawings (longitudinal group), showed a strong priming effect. In contrast, participants who had not seen the drawings 17 years earlier (control group) showed nonsignificant priming (Mitchell, 2006).

You probably had difficulty coming up with the answers for the first and third fragments (*chipmunk, bogeyman*) but had little trouble coming up with answers for the second and fourth (*octopus, climate*). Seeing *octopus* and *climate* on the original list made those words more accessible later, during the fill-in-the-blanks test. This is an example of **priming,** which refers to *an enhanced ability to think of a stimulus, such as a word or object, as a result of a recent exposure to the stimulus* (Tulving & Schacter, 1990). Just as priming a pump makes water flow more easily, priming the memory system makes some information more accessible. In the fill-in-the-blanks experiment, people showed priming for studied words even when they failed to remember consciously that they had seen them earlier. This suggests that priming is an example of implicit, not explicit, memory.

A truly stunning example of this point comes from a study by Mitchell (2006) in which participants first studied black-and-white line drawings depicting everyday objects. Later, the participants were shown fragmented versions of the drawings that were difficult to identify; some of them depicted objects that they had studied earlier in the experiment, whereas others depicted new objects that they had not studied. Mitchell found that participants correctly identified more fragmented drawings of studied than new objects, and identified more studied objects than did participants in a control group who had never seen the pictures—a clear demonstration of priming (see **FIGURE 6.14**). Here's the stunning part: The fragmented drawing test was given 17 years after presentation of the study list! By that time, participants had little or no explicit memory of having seen the drawings, and some had no recollection that they had ever participated in the experiment! "I'm sorry—I really don't remember this experiment at all," said one 36-year-old man who showed a strong priming effect. A 36-year-old woman who showed even more priming stated simply, "Don't remember anything about it" (Mitchell, 2006, p. 929). These observations confirm that priming is an example of implicit memory, and also that priming can persist over very long periods of time.

Procedural Memory and Priming Do Not Rely on the Hippocampus

Because priming is an example of implicit memory, not explicit memory, you'd expect amnesic individuals such as HM and Greg to show priming. In fact, many experiments have shown that amnesic individuals can show substantial priming effects—often as great as healthy, nonamnesic individuals—even though they have no explicit memory for the items they studied. These and other similar results suggest that priming, like procedural memory, does not require the hippocampal structures that are damaged in cases of amnesia (Schacter & Curran, 2000).

If the hippocampal region isn't required for procedural memory and priming, which parts of the brain are involved? Experiments have revealed that priming is associated with *reduced* activity in various regions of the cortex that are activated when people perform an unprimed task. For instance, when research participants are shown the word stem *mot___* or *tab___* and are asked to provide the first word that comes to mind, parts of the occipital lobe involved in visual processing and parts of the frontal lobe involved in word retrieval become active. But if people perform the same task after being primed by seeing *motel* and *table,* there's less activity in these same regions (Buckner et al., 1995; Schott et al., 2005). Something similar happens when people see pictures of everyday objects on two different occasions. On the second exposure to a picture, there's less activity in parts of the visual cortex that were activated by seeing the picture initially. Priming seems to make it easier for parts of the cortex that are involved in perceiving a word or object to identify the item after a recent exposure to it (Schacter, Dobbins, & Schnyer, 2004; Wiggs & Martin, 1998). This suggests that the brain saves a bit of processing time after priming (see **FIGURE 6.15**).

REPUBLISHED WITH PERMISSION OF SCHACTER & BUCKNER FROM PRIMING AND THE BRAIN, *NEURON 20*, 185–195, ELSEVIER, FIGURE 1. (1998); PERMISSION CONVEYED THROUGH COPYRIGHT CLEARANCE CENTER, INC.

Left frontal lobe

Occipital/ temporal lobe

◄ **Figure 6.15**
PRIMED AND UNPRIMED PROCESSING OF STIMULI Priming is associated with reduced levels of activation in the cortex on a number of different tasks. In each pair of fMRIs, the images on the upper left (A, C) show brain regions in the frontal lobe (A) and occipital/temporal lobe (C) that are active during an unprimed task (in this case, providing a word response to a visual word cue). The images on the lower right within each pair (B, D) show reduced activity in the same regions during the primed version of the same task.

Neuroimaging studies also indicate that different brain systems are involved in two distinct forms of priming: *perceptual priming,* which reflects implicit memory for the sensory features of an item (e.g., the visual characteristics of a word or picture), and *conceptual priming,* which reflects implicit memory for the meaning of a word or how you would use an object. Studies using fMRI indicate that perceptual priming depends primarily on regions toward the back of the brain, such as the visual cortex, whereas conceptual priming depends more on regions toward the front of the brain, such as the frontal lobes (Wig, Buckner, & Schacter, 2009). There is also some evidence that perceptual priming is associated primarily with the right cerebral hemisphere, whereas conceptual priming is associated with the left hemisphere (Schacter, Wig, & Stevens, 2007).

EXPLICIT MEMORY: SEMANTIC AND EPISODIC

Consider these two questions: (1) Why do we celebrate on July 4? and (2) What is the most spectacular Fourth of July celebration you've ever seen? Every American knows the answer to the first question (we celebrate the signing of the Declaration of Independence on July 4, 1776), but we all have our own answers to the second. Both of these are explicit memories, consciously or intentionally retrieved from past experiences. Although both of these questions require you to search your long-term memory and retrieve information that is stored there, one requires you to dredge up a fact that every American schoolchild knows and that is not part of your personal autobiography, and one requires you to revisit a particular time and place—or episode—from your personal past. These memories are called *semantic* and *episodic* memories, respectively (Tulving, 1972, 1983, 1998).

▶ **Semantic memory** is *a network of associated facts and concepts that make up our general knowledge of the world.*

▶ **Episodic memory** is *the collection of past personal experiences that occurred at a particular time and place.*

Episodic memory is special because it is the only form of memory that allows us to engage in mental time travel, projecting ourselves into the past and revisiting events that have happened to us. This ability allows us to connect our pasts and our presents and construct a cohesive story of our lives. People who have amnesia can usually travel back in time and revisit episodes that occurred before they became amnesic, but they are unable to revisit episodes that happened later. For example, Greg couldn't travel back to any time after 1969, because that's when he stopped being able to create new episodic memories. But can people with amnesia create new semantic memories?

semantic memory A network of associated facts and concepts that make up our general knowledge of the world.

episodic memory The collection of past personal experiences that occurred at a particular time and place.

These new Americans are taking the Oath of Allegiance after passing a citizenship test that would have required them to use their semantic memories.

Researchers have studied three young adults who suffered damage to the hippocampus during birth as a result of difficult deliveries that interrupted oxygen supply to the brain (Brandt et al., 2009; Vargha-Khadem et al., 1997). Their parents noticed that the children could not recall what happened during a typical day, had to be constantly reminded of appointments, and often became lost and disoriented. In view of their hippocampal damage, you might also expect that each of the three would perform poorly in school and might even be classified as learning disabled. In a remarkable outcome, however, all three children learned to read, write, and spell; developed normal vocabularies; and acquired other kinds of semantic knowledge that allowed them to perform well in school. On the basis of this evidence, researchers have concluded that the hippocampus is not necessary for acquiring new *semantic* memories.

Episodic Memory Contributes to Imagination and Creativity

We've already seen that episodic memory allows us to travel backward in time, but it turns out that episodic memory also plays a role in allowing us to travel forward in time. An amnesic man known by the initials K.C. provided an early clue. K.C. could not recollect any specific episodes from his past, and when he was asked to imagine a future episode—such as what he might do tomorrow—he reported a complete "blank" (Tulving, 1985). Consistent with this observation, more recent findings from individuals with hippocampal amnesia reveal that some of them have difficulty imagining new experiences, such as sunbathing on a sandy beach (Hassabis et al., 2007), or events that might happen in their everyday lives (Race, Keane, & Verfaellie, 2011). Something similar happens with aging. When asked either to recall episodes that actually occurred in their pasts or to imagine new episodes that might occur in their futures, older adults provided fewer details about what happened, or what might happen, than did college students (Addis, Wong, & Schacter, 2008; Schacter, Gaesser, & Addis, 2013). Consistent with these findings, neuroimaging studies reveal that a network of brain regions known to be involved in episodic memory—including the hippocampus—shows similarly increased activity when people remember the past and imagine the future (Addis, Wong, & Schacter, 2007; Okuda et al., 2003; Schacter et al., 2012; Szpunar, Watson, & McDermott, 2007; see **FIGURE 6.16**).

Taken together, these observations strongly suggest that we rely heavily on episodic memory to envision our personal futures (Schacter, Addis, & Buckner, 2008; Szpunar, 2010). Episodic memory is well suited to the task, because it is a flexible system that allows us to recombine elements of past experience in new ways, so that we can

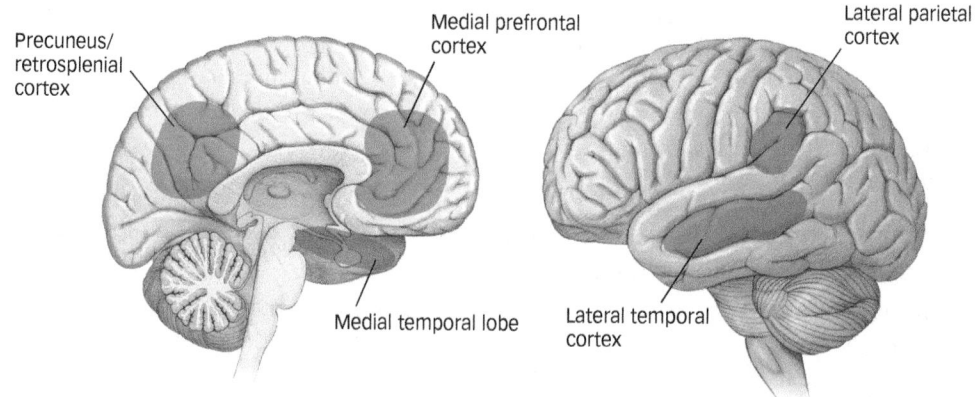

Precuneus/retrosplenial cortex

Medial prefrontal cortex

Lateral parietal cortex

Medial temporal lobe

Lateral temporal cortex

◄ **Figure 6.16**

REMEMBERING THE PAST AND IMAGINING THE FUTURE DEPEND ON A COMMON NETWORK OF BRAIN REGIONS A common brain network is activated when people remember episodes that actually occurred in their personal pasts and when they imagine episodes that might occur in their personal futures. This network includes the hippocampus, a part of the medial temporal lobe long known to play an important role in episodic memory (Schacter, Addis, & Buckner, 2007).

mentally try out different versions of what might happen (Schacter, 2012; Schacter & Addis, 2007; Suddendorf & Corballis, 2007). For example, when you imagine having a difficult conversation with a friend that will take place in a couple of days, you can draw on past experiences to envision different ways in which the conversation might unfold, and hopefully avoid saying things that, based on past experience, are likely to make the situation worse. As we'll discuss later, however, this flexibility of episodic memory might also be responsible for some kinds of memory errors (see p. 256).

Imagining the future by recombining elements of past experiences sounds a lot like what psychologists refer to as *divergent creative thinking*: generating creative ideas by combining different types of information in new ways (Guilford, 1967). One common test of divergent creative thinking, the Alternate Uses Task (AUT; Guilford, 1967) requires participants to generate unusual uses of common objects, such as a brick. How many unusual uses of a brick can you think of? On the AUT, you would receive credit for coming up with novel uses such as a doorstop, paperweight, or even a weapon. When people perform the AUT during an fMRI scan, the brain network that supports episodic memory, including the hippocampus, shows increased activity (Beaty et al., 2016; Benedek et al., 2014), suggesting that episodic memory may contribute to divergent creative thinking. In findings consistent with this idea, amnesic patients with hippocampal damage and episodic memory deficits perform poorly on tests that tap divergent creative thinking (Duff et al., 2013). Finally, a recent study of healthy young adults revealed that brief training in retrieving details from episodic memory enhances divergent creative thinking on the AUT (Madore, Addis, & Schacter, 2015). Training in recalling episodic details led participants to rely more on their episodic memories during the AUT, helping them to recombine information in novel ways and come up with more unusual uses of objects.

COLLABORATIVE MEMORY: SOCIAL INFLUENCES ON REMEMBERING

So far we've focused mainly on memory in individuals functioning on their own. But this is an incomplete picture that is missing something important: other people. Remembering serves important social functions. Getting together with friends or family to talk about memories of shared experiences is a familiar and enjoyable activity for most of us. When we post photos of parties or vacations on Facebook, we are effectively sharing memories with our friends. And we are quick to communicate our memories to others: In a diary study in which college students recorded a memorable event each day for a week, they disclosed 62% of these events to others before the end of the day on which the event occurred (Pasupathi, McLean, & Weeks, 2009). Sharing memories with others can strengthen them (Hirst & Echterhoff, 2012), but we've already seen that talking about some aspects of a memory, but omitting other related events, can also produce retrieval-induced forgetting (see p. 233; Coman et al., 2009; Cuc et al., 2007). Psychologists have become increasingly interested in how people remember in groups, which is now referred to as *collaborative memory* (Rajaram, 2011).

Groups Can Recall More Than a Single Individual, But Less Than Multiple Individuals Working on Their Own

In a typical collaborative memory experiment, participants first encode a set of target materials, such as a list of words, on their own (just as in the traditional memory experiments that we've already considered). Things start to get interesting at the time of retrieval, when participants work together in small groups (usually two or three participants) to try to remember the target items. The number of items recalled by this group can then be compared with the number of items recalled by individuals who are trying to recall items on their own, without any help from others. The collaborative group typically recalls more target items than any individual (Hirst & Echterhoff, 2012; Weldon, 2001), suggesting that collaboration benefits memory. That makes a lot of sense and generally fits with our intuitions about what should happen in such a situation (Rajaram, 2011). For example, Tim might recall an item that Emily forgot, and Eric might remember items that neither Tim nor Emily recalled, so the sum total of the group will exceed what any one person can recall.

But things get really interesting when we compare the performance of the collaborative group with the performance of what is called a *nominal group*: the combined recall of several individuals recalling target items on their own. Let's consider a nominal group of three compared with a collaborative group of three. In the nominal group, let's assume that after studying a list of eight words, Tim recalls items 1, 2, and 8, Emily recalls items 1, 4, and 7, and Eric recalls items 1, 5, 6, and 8. Functioning on their own, Tim, Emily, and Eric recalled in combination seven of the eight items that were presented. (Nobody recalled item 3.) The surprising finding now reported by many studies is that the collaborative group typically recalls fewer items than the nominal group; that is, when they remember together, Tim, Emily, and Eric will come up with fewer total items than when they remember on their own (Basden et al., 1997; Hirst & Echterhoff, 2012; Rajaram, 2011; Rajaram & Pereira-Pasarin, 2010; Weldon, 2001). This negative effect of group recall on memory is known as *collaborative inhibition*: The same number of individuals working together recall fewer items than they would on their own.

What's going on here? Most people believe, on the basis of intuition, that working together should increase rather than decrease recall (Rajaram, 2011). Why does it turn out otherwise? One possibility is that in a group, some individuals are prone to "social loafing": They let others do the work and don't pull their own weight. Although social loafing is well known to occur in groups (Karau & Williams, 1993), memory researchers have tested this account of collaborative inhibition and rejected it (Barber, Rajaram, & Fox, 2012). A more likely explanation is that when recalling items together, the retrieval strategies used by individual members of the group disrupt those used by others (Basden et al., 1997; Hirst & Echterhoff, 2012; Rajaram, 2011). For example, suppose that Tim goes first and recalls items in the order that they were presented. This retrieval strategy may be disruptive to Emily, who prefers to recall the last item first and then work backward through the list. Interesting recent research indicates that the negative effects of collaborative inhibition on memory persist even when individual members of a group later try to recall studied items on their own, without the disruption of retrieval strategies by other group members (Barber, Harris, & Rajaram, 2015). These findings suggest that collaborative inhibition produces a lasting reduction in the accessibility of individuals' memories.

Remembering as a collaborative group leads to greater recall than any single member of the group would achieve, but less than that produced by a nominal group of individuals remembering on their own.

BLEND IMAGES/ALAMY

→ Is Google Hurting Our Memories?

Take some time to try to answer a simple question before returning to reading this box: What country has a national flag that is not rectangular? Now let's discuss what went through your mind as you searched for an answer. (The correct one is Nepal.) Did you start thinking about the shapes of national flags? Take a mental walk through a map of the world? Or did you think instead about computers—more specifically, about typing the question into Google? There probably was a time not too long ago when most people would have tried to conjure up images of national flags or take a mental world tour, but recent research conducted in the lab of one of your textbook authors indicates that nowadays, most of us think about computers and Google searches when confronted with questions of this kind (Sparrow, Liu, & Wegner, 2011).

Sparrow et al. found that after people were given difficult general-knowledge questions, they were slower to name the color in which a computer-related word (e.g., Google, Internet, Yahoo) was printed than the color in which a noncomputer-related word (e.g., Nike, table, Yoplait) was printed. This suggests that after being given difficult questions, these people were thinking about things related to computers, which interfered with their ability to name the color in which the word was printed. The researchers concluded that we are now so used to searching for information on Google when we don't immediately know the answer to a question that we immediately think of computers, rather than searching our memories. Thinking about computers when faced with a tough question makes sense: We will probably come up with the answer more quickly if we do a Google search than if we think about what different flags look like. But this result also raises troubling questions: Is reliance on computers and the Internet having an adverse effect on human memory? If we rely on Google for answers, are we unknowingly making our memories obsolete?

Sparrow et al. conducted additional experiments aimed at addressing these kinds of questions. In one experiment, they found that participants had a harder time remembering bits of trivia ("An ostrich's eye is bigger than its brain") that they typed into a computer when they were told that the computer would save their answers than when they were told that the answers would be erased. They also found that people often were able to remember where they saved the answers even when they did not remember the information itself. People seemed to be using the computer in an efficient way to help remember facts while relying on their own memories to recall where those facts could be found. More recent research has shown that saving information to a computer can take some of the load off people's own memories. When participants saved a PDF file containing a word list to the computer and didn't try to remember the words themselves, they remembered more words from a *second* PDF file presented a few seconds later then they remembered in the first file (Storm & Stone, 2015).

Taken together, the findings from these studies indicate that offloading our memories to computers has both costs and benefits. Sparrow and colleagues suggested that people may be adapting their memories to the demands of new technology, relying on computers in a way that is similar to how we sometimes rely on other people (friends, family members, or colleagues) to remember things that we may not remember ourselves. This is similar to what we discussed as *collaborative memory*, and just as collaborative remembering with other people has both helpful and harmful effects, so does collaborative remembering with our computers.

▲ What does your computer remember for you?

HA PHOTOS/ALAMY

Collaborative Recall Has Other Benefits

Despite the effects of collaborative inhibition, when individuals recall information together in a group, they are exposed to items recalled by others that they may not recall themselves. This exposure improves their memory when they are retested at a later time (Blumen & Rajaram, 2008). And when group members discuss what they have recalled, they can help each other to correct and reduce memory errors (Ross, Blatz, & Schryer, 2008). These observations fit with earlier work showing that couples in close relationships often rely on collaborative remembering (also called *transactive memory*; Wegner, Erber, & Raymond, 1991), whereby each member of the couple remembers certain kinds of information that they can share with the other. (Can you rely on your computer for collaborative remembering? See The Real World: Is Google Hurting Our Memories?) So, next time you are sharing memories of a past activity with friends, you will be shaping your memories for both better and worse.

Build to the Outcomes

1. What is the type of memory in which you just "know how" to do something?

2. How does priming make memory more efficient?

3. What form of memory is like a time machine to our past?

4. How does episodic memory help us imagine our futures?

5. Why does a collaborative group typically recall fewer items than a nominal group?

Memory Failures: The Seven "Sins" of Memory

Learning Outcomes

▶ Identify each of the memory "sins."

▶ Describe possible benefits of each of the memory "sins."

You probably haven't given much thought to breathing today, and the reason is that from the moment you woke up, you've been doing it effortlessly and well. But the moment breathing fails, you are reminded of just how important it is. Memory is like that. Every time we see, think, notice, imagine, or wonder, we are drawing on our ability to use information stored in our brains, but it isn't until this ability fails that we become acutely aware of just how much we should treasure it. We've seen in other contexts how an understanding of the foibles and errors of human thought and action reveals the normal operation of various behaviors. Such memory errors—the seven "sins" of memory—cast similar illumination on how memory normally operates and how often it operates well (Schacter, 1999, 2001b). We'll discuss each of the seven "sins" in detail below.

1. TRANSIENCE

On March 6, 2007, I. Lewis "Scooter" Libby, the former chief of staff to Vice President Dick Cheney, was convicted of perjury, making false statements, and obstruction of justice during an FBI investigation into whether members of the Bush administration had unlawfully disclosed the identity of a CIA agent to the media a couple of years earlier. According to Libby's defense team, any misstatements he might have made in response to FBI questioning were the result of faulty memory, not an intention to deceive. Libby's case received massive media attention and resulted in a national debate: How could Libby forget such important events? Subsequent research has shown that people sometimes mistake the factors that influence the forgetting of important events (Kassam et al., 2009). Despite the controversy over forgetting in the Libby case, one thing is certain: Memories can and do degrade with time. The culprit here is **transience:** *forgetting what occurs with the passage of time.*

Transience occurs during the storage phase of memory, after an experience has been encoded and before it is retrieved. You've already seen the workings of transience—rapid forgetting—in sensory storage and short-term storage. Transience also occurs in long-term storage, as was first illustrated in the late 1870s by Hermann Ebbinghaus, a German philosopher who measured his own memory for lists of nonsense syllables at different delays after studying them (Ebbinghaus, 1885/1964). Ebbinghaus charted his recall of nonsense syllables over time, creating the forgetting curve shown in **FIGURE 6.17**. Ebbinghaus noted a rapid drop-off in retention during the first few tests, followed by a slower rate of forgetting on later tests—a general pattern confirmed by many subsequent memory researchers (Wixted & Ebbensen, 1991). So, for example, when English-speakers were tested for memory of Spanish vocabulary acquired during high school or college courses 1 to 50 years previously, there was a rapid drop-off in memory during the first 3 years after the students' last

transience Forgetting what occurs with the passage of time.

I. Lewis "Scooter" Libby was convicted of perjury and obstructing justice, but he claimed that forgetting and related memory problems were responsible for any misstatements he made.

GETTY IMAGES NEWS/GETTY IMAGES

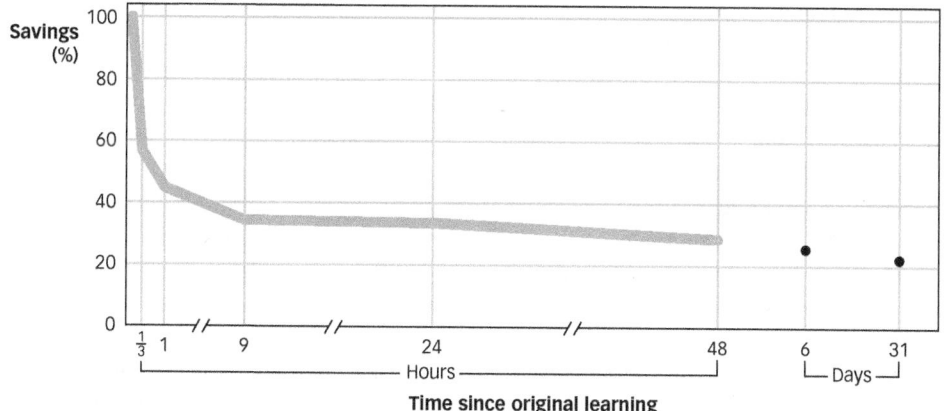

THE CURVE OF FORGETTING Hermann Ebbinghaus measured his retention at various delay intervals after he studied lists of nonsense syllables. He measured retention in percent savings, that is, the percentage of time he needed to relearn the list compared with the time he needed to learn it initially.

class, followed by tiny losses in later years (Bahrick, 1984, 2000). In all these studies, memories didn't fade at a constant rate as time passed; most forgetting happened soon after an event occurred, with increasingly less forgetting as more time passed.

Not only do we forget memories with the passage of time but the quality of our memories also changes. At early time points on the forgetting curve—minutes, hours, and days—memory preserves a relatively detailed record, allowing us to reproduce the past with reasonable if not perfect accuracy. But with the passing of time, we increasingly rely on our general memories for what usually happens and attempt to reconstruct the details by inference and even sheer guesswork. Transience involves a gradual switch from specific to more general memories (Brewer, 1996; Eldridge, Barnard, & Bekerian, 1994; Thompson et al., 1996). In one early study, British research participants read a brief Native American folktale that had odd imagery and unfamiliar plots in it, and then recounted it as best they could after a delay (Bartlett, 1932). The readers made interesting but understandable errors, often eliminating details that didn't make sense to them or adding elements to make the story more coherent. As the specifics of the story slipped away, the general meaning of the events stayed in memory, but usually with elaborations and embellishments that were consistent with the readers' worldview. Because the story was unfamiliar to the readers, they raided their stores of general information and patched together a reasonable recollection of what *probably* happened.

Yet another way that memories can be distorted is by interference from other memories. For example, if you carry out the same activities at work each day, by the time Friday rolls around, it may be difficult to remember what you did on Monday because later activities blend in with earlier ones. This is an example of **retroactive interference,** *situations in which later learning impairs memory for information acquired earlier* (Postman & Underwood, 1973). **Proactive interference,** in contrast, refers to *situations in which earlier learning impairs memory for information acquired later.* If you use the same parking lot each day at work or at school, you've probably gone out to find your car and then stood there confused by the memories of having parked it on previous days.

2. ABSENTMINDEDNESS

The great cellist Yo-Yo Ma put his treasured $2.5 million instrument in the trunk of a taxicab in Manhattan and then rode to his destination. After a 10-minute trip, he paid the driver and left the cab, forgetting his cello. Minutes later, Ma realized what he had done and called the police. Fortunately, they tracked down the taxi and recovered the instrument within hours (Finkelstein, 1999). But how had the celebrated cellist forgotten about something so important that had occurred only 10 minutes earlier?

retroactive interference Situations in which information learned later impairs memory for information acquired earlier.

proactive interference Situations in which information learned earlier impairs memory for information acquired later.

Yo-Yo Ma with his $2.5 million cello. The famous cellist lost the instrument when he absentmindedly forgot that he'd placed it in a taxicab's trunk minutes earlier.

absentmindedness A lapse in attention that results in memory failure.

prospective memory Remembering to do things in the future.

Transience is not a likely culprit. As soon as Mr. Ma realized what he'd done with his instrument, he recalled where he had put it. This information had not disappeared from his memory (which is why he was able to tell the police where the cello was). Instead, Yo-Yo Ma was a victim of **absentmindedness,** *a lapse in attention that results in memory failure.*

What makes people absentminded? One common cause is lack of attention. Attention plays a vital role in encoding information into long-term memory. Without proper attention, material is much less likely to be stored properly and recalled later. In studies of divided attention, research participants are given materials to remember, such as a list of words, a story, or a series of pictures. At the same time, they are required to perform an additional task that draws their attention away from the material. For example, in one study, participants listened to lists of 15 words for a later memory test (Craik et al., 1996). They were allowed to pay full attention to some of the lists, but while they heard other lists, they simultaneously viewed a visual display containing four boxes and pressed different keys to indicate where an asterisk was appearing and disappearing. On a later test, participants recalled far fewer words from the list they had heard while their attention was divided.

There Is Less Activity in the Left Frontal Lobe When Attention Is Divided

What happens in the brain when attention is divided? In one study, volunteers tried to learn a list of word pairs while researchers scanned their brains with positron emission tomography (PET; Shallice et al., 1994). Some people simultaneously performed a task that took little attention (they moved a bar the same way over and over), whereas other people simultaneously performed a task that took a great deal of attention (they moved a bar over and over but in a novel, unpredictable way each time). The researchers observed less activity in the participants' lower left frontal lobe when their attention was divided. As we saw earlier, greater activity in the lower left frontal region during encoding is associated with better memory. Dividing attention, then, prevents the lower left frontal lobe from playing its normal role in semantic encoding, and the result is absentminded forgetting. More recent research using fMRI has shown that divided attention also leads to less hippocampal involvement in encoding (Kensinger, Clarke, & Corkin, 2003; Uncapher & Rugg, 2008). Given the importance of the hippocampus to episodic memory, this finding may help to explain why absentminded forgetting is sometimes so extreme, as when we forget where we put our keys or glasses only moments earlier.

Talking on a cell phone while driving is a common occurrence of divided attention in everyday life; texting is even worse. This can be dangerous, and an increasing number of states have banned the practice.

FSTOP/GETTY IMAGES

We Don't Always Remember to Remember

Another common cause of absentmindedness is forgetting to carry out actions that we plan to do in the future. On any given day, you need to remember the times and places that your classes meet, you need to remember with whom and where you are having lunch, you need to remember which grocery items to pick up for dinner, and you need to remember which page of this book you were on when you fell asleep. In other words, you have to remember to remember, and this is called **prospective memory,** *remembering to do things in the future* (Einstein & McDaniel, 1990, 2005).

Failures of prospective memory are a major source of absentmindedness. Avoiding these problems often requires having a cue available at the moment you need to remember to carry out an action. For example, air traffic controllers must sometimes postpone an action, such as granting a pilot's request to change altitude, but remember to carry out that action a few minutes later when conditions change. In a simulated air traffic control experiment, researchers provided controllers with electronic signals to remind them to carry out a deferred request 1 minute later. The reminders were made available either during the 1-minute waiting period or at the time the controller needed to act on the deferred request. The controllers' memory for the deferred action improved only when the reminder was available at the time needed for retrieval. Providing the reminder during the waiting period did not help (Vortac, Edwards, & Manning, 1995). An early reminder, then, is no reminder at all.

3. BLOCKING

Have you ever tried to recall the name of a famous movie actor or a book you've read—and felt that the answer was on the tip of your tongue, rolling around in your head *somewhere* but just out of reach at the moment? This tip-of-the-tongue experience is a classic example of **blocking,** *a failure to retrieve information that is available in memory even though you are trying to produce it.* The sought-after information has been encoded and stored, and a cue is available that would ordinarily trigger recall of it. The information has not faded from memory, and you aren't forgetting to retrieve it. Rather, you are experiencing a full-blown retrieval failure, which makes this memory breakdown especially frustrating. It seems absolutely clear that you should be able to produce the information you seek, but the fact of the matter is that you can't. Researchers have described the tip-of-the-tongue state, in particular, as "a mild torment, something like [being] on the brink of a sneeze" (Brown & McNeill, 1966, p. 326).

Blocking occurs especially often for the names of people and places (Cohen, 1990; Semenza, 2009; Valentine, Brennen, & Brédart, 1996). Why? Because their links to related concepts and knowledge are weaker than for common names. That somebody's last name is Baker doesn't tell us much about the person, but saying that he *is* a baker does. To illustrate this point, researchers showed people pictures of cartoon and comic strip characters, some with descriptive names that highlight key features of the character (e.g., Grumpy, Snow White, Scrooge) and others with arbitrary names (e.g., Aladdin, Mary Poppins, Pinocchio; Brédart & Valentine, 1998). Even though the two types of names were equally familiar to participants in the experiment, they blocked less often on the descriptive names than on the arbitrary names.

Although it's frustrating when it occurs, blocking is a relatively infrequent event for most of us. However, it occurs more often as we grow older, and it is a very common complaint among people in their 60s and 70s (Burke et al., 1991; Schwartz, 2002). Even more striking, some individuals with brain damage live in a nearly perpetual tip-of-the-tongue state (Semenza, 2009). One such individual could recall the names of only 2 of 40 famous people when she saw their photographs, compared with 25 of 40 for healthy volunteers in the control group (Semenza & Zettin, 1989). Yet she could still recall correctly the occupations of 32 of these people—the same number as healthy people could recall. This case and similar ones have given researchers important clues about what parts of the brain are involved in retrieving proper names. Name blocking usually results from damage to parts of the left temporal lobe on the surface of the cortex, most often as a result of a stroke. In fact, studies that show strong activation of regions within the temporal lobe when people recall proper names support this idea (Damasio et al., 1996; Gorno-Tempini et al., 1998).

4. MEMORY MISATTRIBUTION

Shortly after the devastating 1995 bombing of the federal building in Oklahoma City, police set about searching for two suspects they called John Doe 1 and John Doe 2. John Doe 1 turned out to be Timothy McVeigh, who was quickly apprehended and later convicted of the crime and sentenced to death. John Doe 2, who had supposedly accompanied McVeigh when he rented a van from Elliott's Body Shop two days before the bombing, was never found. In fact, John Doe 2 had never existed; he was a product of the memory of Tom Kessinger, a mechanic at Elliott's Body Shop who was present when McVeigh rented the van. The day after, two other men had also rented a van in Kessinger's presence. The first man, like McVeigh, was tall and fair.

blocking A failure to retrieve information that is available in memory even though you are trying to produce it.

Suppose that, mentally consumed with planning for a psychology test the next day, you place your keys in an unusual spot, and later forget where you put them. Is this more likely to reflect the memory "sin" of transience, absentmindedness, or blocking?

▶ **Figure 6.18**

MEMORY MISATTRIBUTION In 1995 the Murrah Federal Building in Oklahoma City was bombed in an act of terrorism. The police sketch shows John Doe 2, who originally was thought to have been the culprit Timothy McVeigh's partner in the bombing. It was later determined that the witness had confused his memories of different men whom he had encountered at Elliott's Body Shop on different days.

The second man was shorter and stockier, was dark-haired, wore a blue and white cap, and had a tattoo beneath his left sleeve—a match to the description of John Doe 2. Tom Kessinger had confused his recollections of men he had seen on separate days in the same place. He was a victim of **memory misattribution,** *assigning a recollection or an idea to the wrong source* (see **FIGURE 6.18**).

Memory misattribution errors are some of the primary causes of eyewitness misidentifications. The memory researcher Donald Thomson was accused of rape on the basis of the victim's detailed recollection of his face, but he was eventually cleared when it turned out he had an airtight alibi. At the time of the rape, Thomson was giving a live television interview on the subject of distorted memories! The victim had been watching the show just before she was assaulted and misattributed her memory of Thomson's face to that of the rapist (Schacter, 1996; Thomson, 1988). Thomson's case, though dramatic, is not an isolated occurrence: Faulty eyewitness memory was a factor in more than 75% of the first 250 cases in which individuals were shown to be innocent through DNA evidence after being convicted of crimes they did not commit (Garrett, 2011; see Other Voices: Memories Inside Out).

Correct Memories Can Be Attributed to the Wrong Source

Part of memory is knowing where our memories came from. This is known as **source memory,** *recall of when, where, and how information was acquired* (Johnson, Hashtroudi, & Lindsay, 1993; Mitchell & Johnson, 2009; Schacter, Harbluk, & McLachlan, 1984). People sometimes correctly recall a fact they learned earlier or accurately recognize a person or object they have seen before but misattribute the source of this knowledge—just as happened to Tom Kessinger and the rape victim in the Donald Thomson incident (Davies, 1988). Such misattribution could be the cause of déjà vu experiences, when you suddenly feel that you have been in a situation before even though you can't recall any details. A present situation that is similar to a past experience may trigger a general sense of familiarity that is mistakenly attributed to having been in the exact situation previously (Brown, 2004; Reed, 1988).

Individuals with damage to the frontal lobes are especially prone to memory misattribution errors (Schacter et al., 1984; Shimamura & Squire, 1987). This is probably because the frontal lobes play a significant role in effortful retrieval processes, which are required to dredge up the correct source of a memory. These individuals sometimes produce bizarre misattributions. In 1991, a British photographer in his mid-40s known as MR was overcome with feelings of familiarity about people he didn't know. He kept asking his wife whether each new passing stranger was "somebody"—a screen actor, television news announcer, or local celebrity. MR's feelings were so intense that he often could not resist approaching strangers and asking whether they were indeed famous celebrities. When given formal tests, MR recognized the faces

memory misattribution Assigning a recollection or an idea to the wrong source.

source memory Recall of when, where, and how information was acquired.

Memories Inside Out

Karen L. Daniel is the director of the Center on Wrongful Convictions at Northwestern University School of Law.

There's a good chance that sometime during the summer of 2015 you saw and enjoyed the hit Pixar movie *Inside Out*, which portrays the emotional struggles of the 11-year-old Riley after her family moves to a new home by drawing on psychological research that distinguishes among basic emotions (see the chapter on Emotion and Motivation, pp. 308–347). The movie also delved into Riley's memories and provided some realistic insights into how memories can be used to regulate emotions. But as Karen Daniel points out in an opinion piece published when the movie opened, the film's depiction of memory ignored some key findings and ideas from psychological research on memory, with potentially serious consequences:

Let me begin by saying that I love, love, love Pixar movies. Like many adults, I began watching them as part of my parental duties. There was a time when I could recite all the dialogue from *Monsters Inc.* and the first two *Toy Story* films.

It was thus with great anticipation that I tuned in to a radio interview of Pete Docter, the director of the latest Pixar release, *Inside Out*. What a fabulous idea: animating the emotions inside the mind of an 11-year-old child named Riley who is undergoing a major life transition. Docter explained that he researched many aspects of psychology to make the film accurate. When it came to human memory, however, Docter departed from science for the sake of the story line.

As shown in a trailer for *Inside Out*, Riley's memories are portrayed as mini-animations safely preserved inside little globes, which can be pulled out and replayed exactly the way they happened. The character Joy explains that certain of these globes contain "core memories" that form the basis of Riley's personality. This representation of memory is essential to the plot but is not true, as Docter candidly admitted.

I couldn't help but cringe. Given the wide appeal of Pixar movies, a new generation may grow up internalizing the profoundly false notion that memory works like a video recording and that perfect memories of events can be recalled at will. In reality, memory is fallible, malleable, and subject to suggestion and distortion. Docter noted that learning this was a revelation to him, even though he chose not to depict memory that way in *Inside Out*.

One may ask, "Who cares? It's just a movie." In the world of criminal justice, it matters a great deal. One of the most critical moments in a criminal trial is when a victim or witness points at the defendant and declares, "I will never forget that face." The witness usually professes complete certainty, and the prosecutor highlights this as proof of the defendant's guilt—even though experts tell us courtroom certainty does not necessarily correlate to accuracy.

In fact, mistaken identification is a leading cause of conviction of the innocent. Myriad factors that are not necessarily obvious to the average person can affect the reliability of an eyewitness identification, such as distractions at the time of the event, lapse of time, post-event discussions with police, and limitations inherent in cross-racial identifications. Expert witnesses can help explain these factors, but most judges exclude expert testimony on the ground [*sic*] that eyewitness identifications are a matter of "common sense" and expert assistance is not necessary. (The Illinois Supreme Court is now reviewing a case that challenges this approach.)

Which brings us back to *Inside Out*. Absent the input of an expert, jurors are left to draw on personal experiences in evaluating testimony. Today's children (and their parents) may become tomorrow's jurors who believe, incorrectly, that memories are stored intact, and that witnesses can simply compare the pictures within their little memory globes to the person sitting at the defendant's table. Docter explained that this comports with most people's sense of how memory works—which is why relying on "common sense" in criminal trials falls short.

We can never entirely eliminate human error from the justice system, but overconfidence in witnesses and misunderstanding by factfinders leads to many wrongful convictions. Let's enjoy Pixar's new film, but when we return from the movie theater, let's ensure that those charged with deciding guilt or innocence in the courtroom are armed with scientific information about eyewitness identifications rather than with the snow globe concept of memory.

As Daniel and the text point out, faulty eyewitness memories are frequently at work in wrongful convictions. It would be unfortunate if the naive view of memory communicated by *Inside Out* has a lasting influence on any prospective jurors. On a more encouraging note, there are signs that some of the important findings regarding memory's fallibility, such as the seven sins of memory that you learned about in this chapter, are being communicated to participants in the legal system. For example, in 2014 the National Academy of Sciences published a report written by a distinguished committee composed of experts in both psychology and law titled *Identifying the Culprit: Assessing Eyewitness Identification*, which is intended to convey the findings of psychological research on eyewitness memory to participants in the legal system. Though no doubt many more people saw *Inside Out* than will read this important report, it seems likely that accurate characterizations of memory research such as those contained in the National Academy of Sciences' report will ultimately be more influential in the courtroom than the entertaining though misleading depictions of Riley's memory globes.

Daniel, K. (2015, June 16). Pixar movie teaches future jurors wrong lesson on memory. *Chicago Sun-Times*.

false recognition A feeling of familiarity about something that hasn't been encountered before.

of actual celebrities as accurately as did healthy volunteers in the control group. But MR also "recognized" more than 75% of unfamiliar faces, whereas healthy volunteers hardly ever did. Neurological exams revealed that MR suffered from multiple sclerosis, which had caused damage to his frontal lobes (Ward et al., 1999). Psychologists call MR's type of memory misattribution **false recognition,** *a feeling of familiarity about something that hasn't been encountered before.*

The subjective experience for MR, as in everyday déjà vu experiences, is characterized by a strong sense of familiarity without any recall of associated details. Other individuals with neurological damage exhibit a recently discovered type of memory misattribution called *déjà vécu:* They feel strongly—but mistakenly—that they have already lived through an experience and remember the details of what happened (Moulin et al., 2005). For example, when watching television, one such individual was certain that he recalled seeing each show before, even when he was watching an entirely new episode. When he went shopping, he constantly thought it was unnecessary to buy needed items because he remembered having done so already. Although the basis of this strange disorder is not well understood, it probably involves disruption to parts of the temporal lobe that normally generate a subjective feeling of remembering (Moulin et al., 2005) as well as parts of the frontal lobe that are involved in source memory (Craik et al., 2014; Moulin, 2013).

Memory Misattribution Happens to Us All

We are all vulnerable to memory misattribution. Take the following test and there is a good chance that you will experience false recognition for yourself. First, study the two lists of words presented in **TABLE 6.1** by reading each word for about 1 second. When you are done, return to this paragraph for more instructions, but don't look back at the table! Now try to recognize which of the following words appeared on the list you just studied: *taste, bread, needle, king, sweet, thread.* If you think that *taste* and *thread* were on the lists you studied, you're right. And if you think that *bread* and *king* weren't on those lists, you're also right. But if you think that *needle* or *sweet* appeared on the lists, you're dead wrong.

Most people make exactly the same mistake, claiming with confidence that they saw *needle* and *sweet* on the list. This occurs because all the words in the lists are associated with *needle* or *sweet.* Seeing each word in the study list activates related words. Because *needle* and *sweet* are related to all of the associates, they become more activated than other words—so highly activated that only minutes later, people swear that they actually studied the words (Deese, 1959; Gallo, 2006, 2010; Roediger & McDermott, 1995, 2000). This error is extremely powerful: even people with "highly superior autobiographical memory" (see chapter opening), who have an extraordinary ability to recall everyday experiences accurately, are as susceptible to this type of memory misattribution as the rest of us are (Patihis et al., 2013). In fact, brain scanning studies using PET and fMRI show that many of the same brain regions are active during false recognition and true recognition, including the hippocampus (Cabeza et al., 2001; Schacter, Reiman, et al., 1996; see **FIGURE 6.19**). Similar results are obtained when people view a series of common objects (e.g., cars, umbrellas) and then are later shown a new object that looks like one they saw earlier: They often falsely recognize the similar new item, and many of the same brain regions become active during this kind of false recognition as during true recognition (Gutchess & Schacter, 2012; Slotnick & Schacter, 2004).

However, false recognition can be reduced (Schacter, Israel, & Racine, 1999). For example, recent evidence shows that when participants are given a choice between an object that they actually saw (e.g., a car) and a visually similar new object (a different car that looks like the one they saw), they almost always choose the car that they actually saw and thus avoid making a false recognition error (Guerin et al., 2012a, 2012b). This finding suggests that false recognition occurs, at least in part, because

TABLE 6.1	
False Recognition	
sour	thread
candy	pin
sugar	eye
bitter	sewing
good	sharp
taste	point
tooth	prick
nice	thimble
honey	haystack
soda	pain
chocolate	hurt
heart	injection
cake	syringe
tart	cloth
pie	knitting

REPRINTED BY PERMISSION FROM MACMILLAN PUBLISHERS LTD. SLOTNICK & SCHACTER, *NATURE NEUROSCIENCE*, 2004, 7(61), P. 669.

Left hippocampus

(a) (b)

▲ Figure 6.19

HIPPOCAMPAL ACTIVITY DURING TRUE AND FALSE RECOGNITION Many brain regions show similar activation during true and false recognition, including the hippocampus. The figure shows results from an fMRI study of true and false recognition of visual shapes (Slotnick & Schacter, 2004). (a) A plot showing the activity level in the strength of the fMRI signal from the hippocampus over time. This shows that after a few seconds, there is comparable activation for true recognition of previously studied shapes (red line) and false recognition of similar shapes that were not presented (yellow line). Both true and false recognition show increased hippocampal activity compared with correct classification of unrelated shapes as new (purple line). (b) A region of the left hippocampus.

when presented with a similar new object on its own, participants don't recollect specific details about the object they actually studied, but they need to retrieve these details in order to indicate correctly that the similar object is new. Yet this information is available in memory, as shown by the ability of participants to choose correctly between the studied object and the visually similar new object. When people experience a strong sense of familiarity about a person, object, or event but lack specific recollections, a potentially dangerous recipe for memory misattribution is in place, both in the laboratory and also in real-world situations involving eyewitness memory. Understanding this point may be a key to reducing the dangerous consequences of misattribution in eyewitness testimony.

5. SUGGESTIBILITY

On October 4, 1992, an El Al cargo plane crashed into an apartment building in a southern suburb of Amsterdam, killing 39 residents and all 4 members of the airline crew. The disaster dominated news in the Netherlands for days as people viewed footage of the crash scene and read about the catastrophe. Ten months later, Dutch psychologists asked a simple question of university students: "Did you see the television film of the moment the plane hit the apartment building?" Fifty-five percent answered yes (Crombag, Wagenaar, & Van Koppen, 1996). All of this might seem perfectly normal except for one key fact: There was no television film of the moment when the plane actually crashed. The researchers had asked a suggestive question that implied that television film of the crash had been shown. Respondents may have viewed television film of the postcrash scene, and they may have read, imagined, or talked about what might have happened when the plane hit the building, but they most definitely did not see it. The suggestive question led participants to misattribute information from these or other sources to a film that did not exist. **Suggestibility** is the *tendency to incorporate misleading information from external sources into personal recollections.*

© 1979 CHARLES ADDAMS. RENEWED 2004 WITH PERMISSION TEE AND CHARLES ADDAMS FOUNDATION

suggestibility The tendency to incorporate misleading information from external sources into personal recollections.

In 1992, an El Al cargo plane crashed into an apartment building in a suburb of Amsterdam. When Dutch psychologists asked students if they had seen the television film of the plane crashing, a majority said they had. In fact, no such footage exists (Crombag et al., 1996).

If misleading details can be implanted in people's memories, is it also possible to suggest entire episodes that never occurred? The answer seems to be yes (Loftus, 1993, 2003). In one study, the research participant, a teenager named Chris, was asked by his older brother, Jim, to try to remember the time Chris had been lost in a shopping mall at age 5. He initially recalled nothing, but after several days, Chris produced a detailed recollection of the event. He recalled that he "felt so scared I would never see my family again" and remembered that a kindly old man wearing a flannel shirt found him crying (Loftus, 1993, p. 532). But according to Jim and other family members, Chris was never lost in a shopping mall. Of 24 participants in a larger study on implanted memories, approximately 25% falsely remembered being lost as a child in a shopping mall or in a similar public place (Loftus & Pickrell, 1995).

People develop false memories in response to suggestions for some of the same reasons memory misattribution occurs. We do not store all the details of our experiences in memory, making us vulnerable to accepting suggestions about what might have happened or should have happened. In addition, visual imagery plays an important role in constructing false memories (Goff & Roediger, 1998). Asking people to imagine an event like spilling punch all over the bride's parents at a wedding increases the likelihood that they will develop a false memory of it (Hyman & Pentland, 1996). Social pressure can enhance suggestibility, as in cases where people falsely confess to crimes that they did not commit after repeated interrogations by authority figures such as police who are convinced of their guilt and press for a confession (Kassin, 2015). In some instances, these wrongly accused individuals develop false memories of the crime (Kassin, 2007).

All of these factors were operating in a recent study that provides some of the most dramatic evidence for suggested false memories. Consider the following question: Did you ever commit a crime when you were between the ages of 11 and 14 years old? Assuming that you did not, do you think that you could ever be convinced that you did? Shaw and Porter (2015) asked college students about an experience that actually occurred between ages 11 and 14, and also about a crime that they supposedly committed during those years (theft, assault, or assault with a weapon). Although none of the students had actually committed any crimes, during three separate interviews the experimenters required them repeatedly to imagine that they did. The researchers also applied social pressure techniques, such as telling students that their parents or caregivers said they had committed the crime, and stating that most people can retrieve seemingly lost memories if they try hard enough. In a remarkable finding, by the end of the third interview 70% of the students developed a false memory of having committed the crime! A similar percentage of students in a separate group exposed to the same suggestive procedures developed noncriminal false memories of emotional events that they repeatedly imagined (an animal attack, losing a lot of money, or an accident resulting in injury).

Studies such as the one by Shaw and Porter (2015) can help us to understand the key role played by suggestibility in a controversy that arose during the 1980s and 1990s concerning the accuracy of childhood memories that people recalled during psychotherapy. One highly publicized example involved a woman named Diana Halbrooks (Schacter, 1996). After a few months in psychotherapy, she began recalling disturbing incidents from her childhood, for example, that her mother had tried to kill her and that her father had abused her sexually. Although her parents denied that these events had ever occurred, her therapist encouraged her to believe in the reality of her memories. Eventually Diana Halbrooks stopped therapy and came to realize that the "memories" she had recovered were inaccurate.

How could this happen? A number of the techniques used by psychotherapists to try to pull up forgotten childhood memories are clearly suggestive (Poole et al., 1995). In an important finding, recent studies show that memories that people remember spontaneously on their own are corroborated by other people at about the same rate as the memories of individuals who never forgot their abuse, whereas memories recovered in response to suggestive therapeutic techniques are virtually never corroborated by others (McNally & Geraerts, 2009).

6. BIAS

In 2000, the outcome of a very close presidential race between George W. Bush and Al Gore was decided by the Supreme Court 5 weeks after the election had taken place. The day after the election (when the result was still in doubt), supporters of Bush and Gore were asked to predict how happy they would be after the outcome of the election was determined (Wilson, Meyers, & Gilbert, 2003). These same respondents reported how happy they felt with the outcome on the day after Al Gore conceded. And 4 months later, the participants recalled how happy they had been right after the election was decided.

How happy do you think you'd be if the candidate you supported won an election? Do you think you'd accurately remember your level of happiness if you recalled it several months later? Chances are good that bias in the memory process would alter your recollection of your previous happiness. Indeed, 4 months after they heard the outcome of the 2000 presidential election, Bush supporters overestimated how happy they were, whereas Gore supporters underestimated how happy they were.

Bush supporters, who eventually enjoyed a positive result (their candidate took office), were understandably happy the day after the Supreme Court's decision. However, their retrospective accounts *over*estimated how happy they were at the time. Conversely, Gore supporters were not pleased with the outcome. But when polled 4 months after the election was decided, Gore supporters *under*estimated how happy they actually were at the time of the result. In both groups, recollections of happiness were at odds with existing reports of their actual happiness at the time (Wilson et al., 2003).

These results illustrate the problem of **bias,** *the distorting influences of present knowledge, beliefs, and feelings on recollection of previous experiences.* Sometimes what people remember from their pasts says less about what actually happened than about what they think, feel, or believe now. Researchers have also found that our current moods can bias our recall of past experiences (Bower, 1981; Buchanan, 2007; Eich, 1995). So in addition to helping you recall actual sad memories (as you saw earlier in this chapter), a sad mood can also bias your recollections of experiences that may not have been so sad. *Consistency bias* is the bias to reconstruct the past to fit the present. One researcher asked people in 1973 to rate their attitudes toward a variety of controversial social issues, including legalization of marijuana, women's rights, and aid to minorities (Marcus, 1986). They were asked to make the same rating again in 1982 and also to indicate what their attitudes had been in 1973. Researchers found that participants' recollections of their 1973 attitudes in 1982 were more closely related to what they believed in 1982 than to what they had actually said in 1973.

bias The distorting influences of present knowledge, beliefs, and feelings on recollection of previous experiences.

Whereas consistency bias exaggerates the similarity between past and present, *change bias* is the tendency to exaggerate differences between what we feel or believe now and what we felt or believed in the past. In other words, *change biases* also occur. For example, most of us would like to believe that our romantic attachments grow stronger over time. In one study, dating couples were asked, once a year for 4 years, to assess the present quality of their relationships and to recall how they felt in past years (Sprecher, 1999). Couples who stayed together for the 4 years recalled that the strength of their love had increased since they last reported on it. Yet their actual ratings at the time did not show any increases in love and attachment. In an objective sense, the couples did not love each other more today than yesterday. But they did from the subjective perspective of memory.

A special case of change bias is *egocentric bias,* the tendency to exaggerate the change between present and past in order to make ourselves look good in retrospect. For example, students sometimes remember feeling more anxious before taking an exam than they actually reported at the time (Keuler & Safer, 1998), and blood

The way each member of this happy couple recalls earlier feelings toward the other depends on how each currently views their relationship.

donors sometimes recall being more nervous about giving blood than they actually were (Breckler, 1994). In both cases, change biases color memory and make people feel that they behaved more bravely or courageously than they actually did. Similarly, when college students tried to remember high school grades and their memories were checked against their actual transcripts, they were highly accurate for grades of A (89% correct) and extremely inaccurate for grades of D (29% correct; Bahrick, Hall, & Berger, 1996). The same kind of egocentric bias occurs with memory for college grades: 81% of errors inflated the actual grade, and this bias was evident even when participants were asked about their grades soon after graduation (Bahrick, Hall, & DaCosta, 2008). People were remembering the past as they wanted it to be rather than the way it was.

7. PERSISTENCE

The artist Melinda Stickney-Gibson awoke in her apartment to the smell of smoke. She jumped out of bed and saw black plumes rising through cracks in the floor. Raging flames had engulfed the entire building, and she had no chance to escape except by jumping from her third-floor window. Shortly after she crashed to the ground, the building exploded into a brilliant fireball. Although she survived the fire and the fall, Melinda became overwhelmed by memories of the fire. When she sat down in front of a blank canvas to start a new painting, her memories of that awful night intruded. Her paintings, which were previously bright, colorful abstractions, became dark meditations that included only black, orange, and ochre—the colors of the fire (Schacter, 1996).

Melinda Stickney-Gibson's experiences illustrate memory's seventh and most deadly sin, **persistence:** *the intrusive recollection of events that we wish we could forget.* Melinda's experience is far from unique; persistence frequently occurs after disturbing or traumatic incidents, such as the fire that destroyed her home. Although being able to recall memories quickly is usually considered a good thing, in the case of persistence, that ability mutates into an unwelcome burden.

Emotional Experiences Are Easiest to Remember

Controlled laboratory studies have revealed that emotional experiences tend to be better remembered than nonemotional ones. For instance, memory for unpleasant pictures, such as mutilated bodies, or pleasant ones, such as attractive men and women, is more accurate than for emotionally neutral pictures, such as household objects (Ochsner, 2000). Emotional arousal seems to focus our attention on the central features of an event. In one experiment, people who viewed an emotionally arousing sequence of slides involving a bloody car accident remembered more of the central themes and fewer peripheral details than people who viewed a nonemotional sequence (Christianson & Loftus, 1987).

Intrusive memories are undesirable consequences of emotional experiences, because emotional experiences generally lead to more vivid and enduring recollections than nonemotional experiences do. One line of evidence comes from the study of **flashbulb memories,** which are *detailed recollections of when and where we heard about shocking events* (Brown & Kulick, 1977). For example, most Americans can recall exactly where they were and how they heard about the September 11, 2001, terrorist attacks on the World Trade Center and the Pentagon—almost as if a mental flashbulb had gone off automatically and recorded the event in long-lasting and vivid detail (Kvavilashvili et al., 2009). Several studies have shown that flashbulb memories are not always entirely accurate, but they are generally better remembered than mundane news events from the same time (Larsen, 1992; Neisser & Harsch, 1992). Enhanced retention of flashbulb memories is partly attributable to the emotional arousal elicited by events such as the 9/11 terrorist attacks, and partly attributable to the fact that we tend to talk and think a lot about these experiences. Recall that

persistence The intrusive recollection of events that we wish we could forget.

flashbulb memories Detailed recollections of when and where we heard about shocking events.

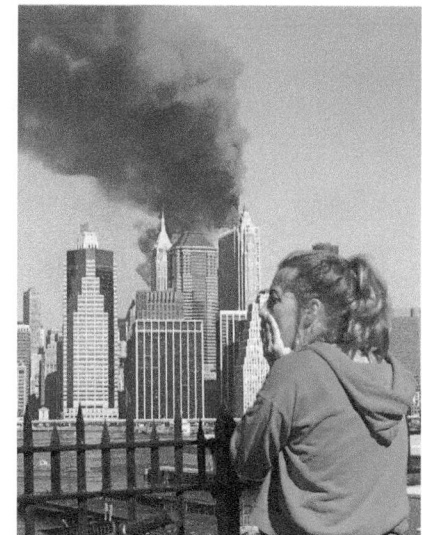

Some events are so emotionally charged—such as President Kennedy's assassination and the terrorist attack on the World Trade Center—that we form unusually detailed memories of when and where we heard about them. These flashbulb memories generally persist much longer than memories for more ordinary events.

semantic encoding enhances memory: When we talk about flashbulb experiences, we elaborate on them and thus further increase the memorability of those aspects of the experience that we discuss (Hirst et al., 2009, 2015).

The Amygdala Plays a Role

Why do our brains succumb to persistence? A key player in the brain's response to emotional events is a small, almond-shaped structure called the *amygdala*, shown in **FIGURE 6.20.** The amygdala influences hormonal systems that kick into high gear when we experience an arousing event; these stress-related hormones, such as adrenaline and cortisol, mobilize the body in the face of threat—and they also enhance memory for the experience. Damage to the amygdala does not result in a general memory deficit. Individuals with amygdala damage, however, do not remember emotional events any better than nonemotional events (Cahill & McGaugh, 1998).

For example, consider what happened when people viewed a series of photographic slides that began with a mother walking her child to school and later included an emotionally arousing event: the child being hit by a car. When tested later, the research participants remembered the arousing event better than the mundane ones. But individuals with amygdala damage remembered the mundane and emotionally arousing events equally well (Cahill & McGaugh, 1998). PET and fMRI scans show that when healthy people view a slide sequence that includes an emotionally arousing event, the level of activity in the amygdala at the time they see it is a good predictor of their subsequent memory for the slide. When there is heightened activity in the amygdala as people watch emotional events, there's a better chance that they will recall those events on a later test (Cahill et al., 1996; Kensinger & Schacter, 2005, 2006). And when people are given a drug that interferes with the amygdala-mediated release of stress hormones, their memory for the emotional sections is no better than their memory for the mundane sections (Lonegran et al., 2013).

In many cases, there are clear benefits to forming strong memories for highly emotional events, particularly those that are life-threatening. In the case of persistence, though, such memories may be too strong—strong enough to interfere with other aspects of daily life.

▼ Figure 6.20

THE AMYGDALA'S INFLUENCE ON MEMORY The amygdala, located next to the hippocampus, responds strongly to emotional events. Individuals with amygdala damage are unable to remember emotional events any better than nonemotional ones (Cahill & McGaugh, 1998).

Amygdala   Hippocampus

ARE THE SEVEN "SINS" VICES OR VIRTUES?

You may have concluded that evolution has burdened us with an extremely inefficient memory system that is so prone to error that it often jeopardizes our well-being. Not so. The seven sins are the price we pay for the many benefits that memory provides, the occasional result of the normally efficient operation of the human memory system (Schacter, 2001b).

Consider transience, for example. Wouldn't it be great to remember all the details of every incident in your life, no matter how much time had passed? Not according to Jill Price (see the chapter opener), who has this ability and says it drives her crazy. If we didn't gradually forget information over time, our minds would be cluttered with details that we no longer need, such as an old phone number (Bjork, 2011; Bjork & Bjork, 1988; Norby, 2015). Information that we use infrequently is less likely to be needed in the future than information that we use more frequently over the same period (Anderson & Schooler, 1991, 2000). Memory, in essence, makes a bet that when we haven't used information recently, we probably won't need it in the future. We win this bet more often than we lose it, making transience an adaptive property of memory.

Similarly, absentmindedness and blocking can be frustrating, but they are side effects of our memory's usually successful attempt to sort through incoming information, preserving details that are worthy of attention and recall, and discarding those that are less worthy.

Memory misattribution and suggestibility both occur because we often fail to recall the details of exactly when and where we saw a face or learned a fact. This is because memory is adapted to retain information that is most likely to be needed in the environment in which it operates. We seldom need to remember all the precise contextual details of every experience. Our memories carefully record such details only when we think we may need them later, and most of the time we are better off for it. Furthermore, we often use memories to anticipate possible future events. As discussed earlier, memory is flexible, allowing us to recombine elements of past experience in new ways, so that we can mentally try out different versions of what might happen. But this very flexibility—a strength of memory—may sometimes produce misattribution errors in which elements of past experience are miscombined (Schacter & Addis, 2007; Schacter, Guerin, & St. Jacques, 2011).

Bias skews our memories so that we depict ourselves in an overly favorable light, but it can produce the benefit of contributing to our overall sense of contentment. Holding positive illusions about ourselves can lead to greater psychological well-being (Taylor, 1989). Although persistence can cause us to be haunted by traumas that we'd be better off forgetting, overall, it is probably adaptive to remember threatening or traumatic events that could pose a threat to survival.

Although each of the seven sins can cause trouble in our lives, each has an adaptive side as well. You can think of the seven sins as costs we pay for benefits that allow memory to work as well as it does most of the time.

Build to the Outcomes

1. How might general memories come to distort specific memories?

2. How is memory affected for someone whose attention is divided?

3. Why is Snow White's name easier to remember than Mary Poppins's?

4. What can explain a déjà vu experience?

5. How can eyewitnesses be misled?

6. How does your current outlook color your memory of a past event?

7. How does emotional trauma affect memory?

8. How are we better off with imperfect memories?

Chapter Review

Encoding: Transforming Perceptions Into Memories

▶ Encoding is the process of transforming the information received through our senses into a lasting memory.

▶ A new memory is made and automatically semantically encoded when new information mixes with old information that already has meaning to us.

▶ Semantic encoding is characterized by relating new information to previous knowledge in a meaningful way.

▶ Visual imagery encoding also relates new information to previous knowledge, but features both a visual and a verbal placeholder.

▶ Organizational encoding is a process of finding relationships between items to make them easier to retrieve.

▶ Encoding information with respect to its survival value is a particularly effective method for increasing subsequent recall, perhaps because our memory systems have evolved in a way that allows us to remember especially well information that is relevant to our survival, and perhaps because survival scenarios used in memory experiments draw on elements of semantic, visual imagery, and organizational encoding, and also require extensive planning.

Storage: Maintaining Memories Over Time

▶ Because research participants could recall the same number of letters from any row of the grid, the iconic memory test suggests that sensory memory holds information for a second or two. "Rehearsal" helps keep memories in short-term storage, and "chunking" combines information into a single, meaningful item.

▶ Working memory is the active maintenance of information in short-term storage, where information is retained for about 15 to 20 seconds. A model of working memory describes the subsystems that store and manipulate visual and verbal information, the episodic buffer that integrates information, and the central executive that coordinates them.

▶ The hippocampus functions as an index to put information into long-term memory, but evidence from amnesiacs indicates that it is not the site of long-term memory storage.

▶ The act of recalling, thinking, and talking about a memory leads to consolidation. Sleep also is an important factor. However, when memories are retrieved, they may also become vulnerable to disruption.

▶ Memory storage depends on changes in synapses, and long-term potentiation (LTP) increases synaptic connections.

Retrieval: Bringing Memories to Mind

▶ Whether we remember a past experience depends on whether retrieval cues are available to trigger recall. Retrieval cues are effective when they are given in the same context as when we encoded an experience. Moods and inner states can become retrieval cues.

▶ Retrieving information from memory has consequences for later remembering. Retrieval improves subsequent memory of the retrieved information, as the benefits of testing on later recall show. However, fMRI evidence shows that regions of the frontal lobe involved with retrieving information also play a role in suppressing related information that is not retrieved. This finding underscores the importance of eyewitness interviews being as complete as possible.

▶ Research shows that retrieving and vividly reexperiencing memories of objects that were seen makes memory vulnerable to disruption, so that unseen objects may be wrongly incorporated into the memory.

▶ Retrieval can be separated into the effort we make while trying to remember what happened in the past and the successful recovery of stored information. Neuroimaging studies suggest that trying to remember activates the left frontal lobe, whereas successful recovery of stored information activates the hippocampus and regions in the brain related to the sensory aspects of an experience.

Forms of Long-Term Memory: More Than One Kind

▶ Long-term memory consists of several different forms.

▶ Implicit memory refers to the unconscious influence of past experiences on later behavior and performance, such as procedural memory and priming. Procedural memory involves the acquisition of skills as a result of practice, and priming is a change in the ability to recognize or identify an object or a word as the result of past exposure to it. People who have amnesia are able to retain implicit memory, including procedural memory and priming, but they lack explicit memory.

▶ Explicit memory is the act of consciously or intentionally retrieving past experiences. Episodic memory is the collection of personal experiences from a particular time and place; it allows us both to recollect the past and imagine the future. Semantic memory is a networked, general, impersonal knowledge of facts, associations, and concepts.

▶ Collaborative memory refers to remembering in groups. Collaborative remembering can both impair memory (collaborative inhibition) and enhance it by exposing people to new information and helping to correct errors.

Memory Failures: The Seven "Sins" of Memory

▶ Memory's mistakes can be classified into seven "sins."

▶ Transience is reflected by a rapid decline in memory followed by more gradual forgetting. With the passing of time, memory switches from detailed to general. Both decay and interference contribute to transience.

▶ Absentmindedness results from failures of attention, shallow encoding, and the influence of automatic behaviors, and is often associated with forgetting to do things in the future.

▶ Blocking occurs when stored information is temporarily inaccessible, as when information is on the tip of the tongue.

▶ Memory misattribution happens when we experience a sense of familiarity but don't recall, or mistakenly recall, the specifics of when and where an experience occurred. Misattribution can result in eyewitness misidentification or false recognition. Individuals suffering from frontal lobe damage are especially susceptible to false recognition.

▶ Suggestibility gives rise to implanted memories of small details or entire episodes. Suggestive techniques such as hypnosis or visualization can promote vivid recall of suggested events, and therapists' use of suggestive techniques may be responsible for some individuals' false memories of childhood traumas. Bias reflects the influence of current knowledge, beliefs, and feelings on memory or past experiences.

▶ Bias can lead us to make the past consistent with the present, exaggerate changes between past and present, or remember the past in a way that makes us look good.

▶ Persistence reflects the fact that emotional arousal generally leads to enhanced memory, whether we want to remember an experience or not. Persistence is partly attributable to the operation of hormonal systems influenced by the amygdala. Although each of

the seven sins can cause trouble in our lives, they have an adaptive side as well.

▶ You can think of the seven "sins" as costs we pay for benefits that allow memory to work as well as it does most of the time.

QUIZ

1. Encoding is the process
   a. by which we transform what we perceive, think, or feel into an enduring memory.
   b. of maintaining information in memory over time.
   c. of bringing to mind information that has been previously stored.
   d. through which we recall information previously learned but forgotten.

2. What is the process of relating new information in a meaningful way to knowledge that is already in memory?
   a. spontaneous encoding
   b. organization encoding
   c. semantic encoding
   d. visual imagery encoding

3. What kind of memory storage holds information for a second or two?
   a. retrograde memory
   b. working memory
   c. short-term memory
   d. sensory memory

4. The process by which memories become stable in the brain is called
   a. consolidation.
   b. long-term memory.
   c. iconic memory.
   d. hippocampal indexing.

5. Long-term potentiation occurs through
   a. the interruption of communication between neurons.
   b. the strengthening of synaptic connections.
   c. the reconsolidation of disrupted memories.
   d. sleep.

6. The increased likelihood of recalling a sad memory when you are in a sad mood is an illustration of
   a. the encoding specificity principle.
   b. state-dependent retrieval.
   c. transfer-appropriate processing.
   d. memory accessibility.

7. Neuroimaging studies suggest that *trying* to remember activates the
   a. left frontal lobe.
   b. hippocampal region.
   c. occipital lobe.
   d. upper temporal lobe.

8. The act of consciously or intentionally retrieving past experiences is
   a. priming.
   b. procedural memory.
   c. implicit memory.
   d. explicit memory.

9. Remembering a family reunion that you attended as a child illustrates
   a. semantic memory.
   b. procedural memory.
   c. episodic memory.
   d. perceptual priming.

10. Eyewitness misidentification or false recognition is most likely a result of
    a. memory misattribution.
    b. suggestibility.
    c. bias.
    d. retroactive interference.

 LearningCurve   **Don't stop now! Quizzing yourself is a powerful study tool. Go to LaunchPad to access the LearningCurve adaptive quizzing system and your own personalized learning plan. Visit launchpadworks.com.**

KEY TERMS

CHANGING MINDS

1. A friend of yours lost her father to cancer when she was a very young child. "I really wish I remembered him better," she says. "I know all the memories are locked in my head. I'm thinking of trying hypnotism to unlock some of those memories." You explain that we don't, in fact, have stored memories of everything that ever happened to us locked in our heads. What examples could you give of ways in which memories can be lost over time?

2. Another friend of yours has a very vivid memory of sitting with his parents in the living room on September 11, 2001, watching live TV as the Twin Towers fell during the terrorist attacks. "I remember my mother was crying," he says, "and that scared me more than the pictures on the TV." Later, he goes home for a visit and discusses the events of 9/11 with his mother—and is stunned when she assures him that he was actually in school on the morning of the attacks and was only sent home at lunchtime, after the towers had fallen. "I don't understand," he tells you afterward. "I think she must be confused, because I have a perfect memory of that morning." Assuming your friend's mother is recalling events correctly, how would you explain to your friend the ways in which his snapshot memory could be wrong? What memory sin might be at work?

3. You ask one of your psychology classmates if she wants to form a study group to prepare for an upcoming exam. "No offense," she says, "but I can study the material best by just reading the chapter eight or nine times, and I can do that without a study group." What's wrong with your classmate's study plan? In what ways might the members of a study group help each other learn more effectively?

4. You and a friend go to a party on campus where you meet a lot of new people. After the party, your friend says, "I liked a lot of the people we met, but I'll never remember all their names. Some people just have a good memory, and some don't, and there's nothing I can do about it." What advice could you give your friend to help him remember the names of people he meets at the next party?

5. A friend of yours who is taking a criminal justice class reads about a case in which the conviction of an accused murderer was later overturned on the basis of DNA evidence. "It's a travesty of justice," she says. "An eyewitness clearly identified the man by picking him out of a lineup and then identified him again in court during the trial. No results from a chemistry lab should count more than eyewitness testimony." What is your friend failing to appreciate about eyewitness testimony? What sin of memory could lead an eyewitness to honestly believe she is identifying the correct man when she is actually making a false identification?

ANSWERS TO KEY CONCEPT QUIZ

1. a; 2. c; 3. d; 4. a; 5. b; 6. b; 7. a; 8. d; 9. a; 10. a.

LaunchPad features the full e-Book of *Psychology*, **the LearningCurve adaptive quizzing system, videos, and a variety of activities to boost your learning. Visit LaunchPad at launchpadworks.com.**

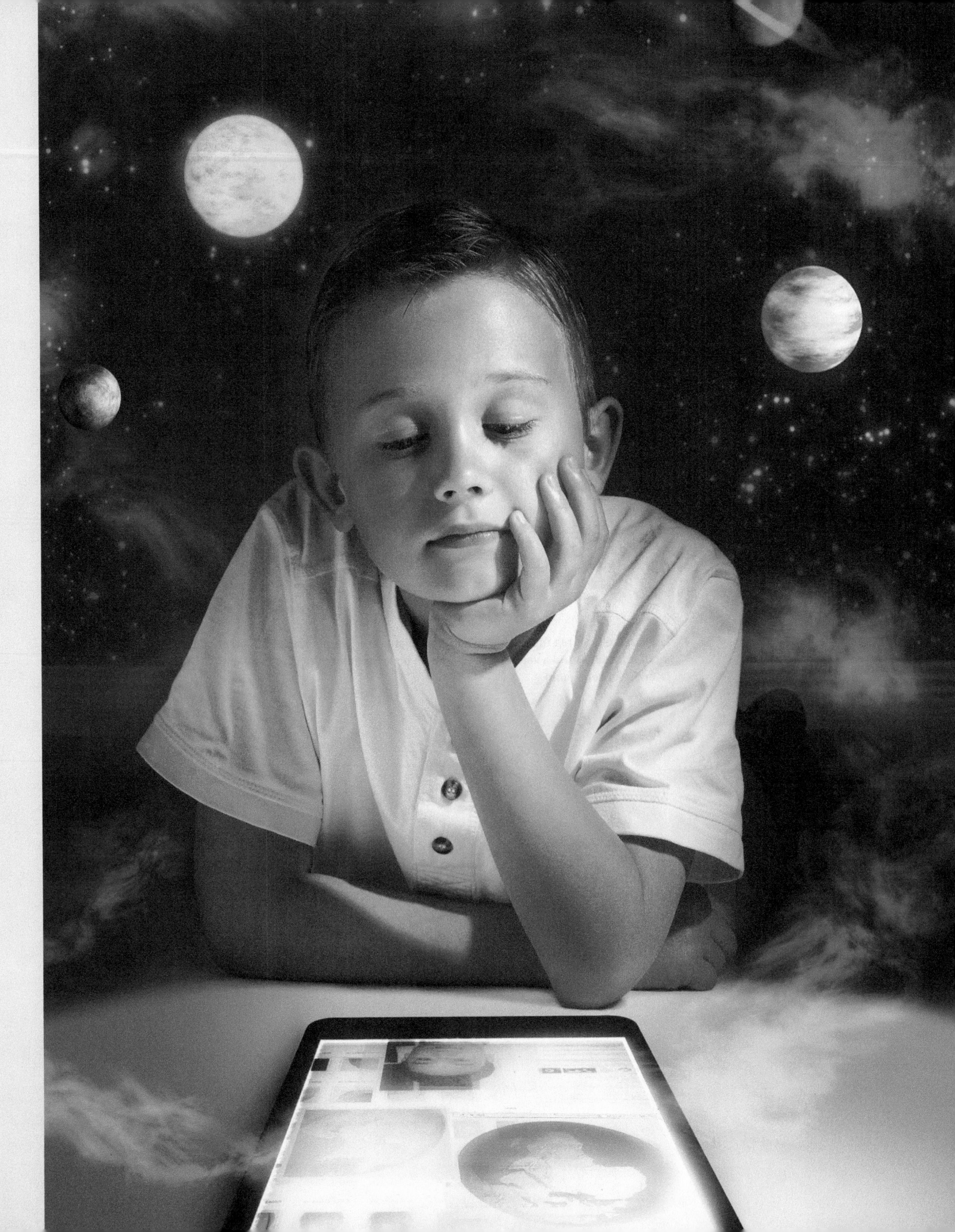

Learning

7

JENNIFER, A 45-YEAR-OLD CAREER MILITARY NURSE, lived quietly in a rural area of the United States with her spouse of 21 years and their two children before she served 19 months abroad during the Iraq war. In Iraq, she provided care to American and international soldiers as well as to Iraqi civilians, prisoners, and militant extremists. Jennifer served 4 months of her assignment in a hospital near Baghdad, where she witnessed many horrifying events. The prison was the target of relentless mortar fire, resulting in numerous deaths and serious casualties, including bloody injuries and loss of limbs. Jennifer worked 12- to 14-hour shifts, trying to avoid incoming fire while tending to some of the most gruesomely wounded cases. She frequently encountered the smell of burned flesh and the sight of "young, mangled bodies" as part of her daily duties (Feczer & Bjorklund, 2009, p. 285).

This repetitive trauma took a toll on Jennifer, and when she returned home, it became evident that she had not left behind her war experiences. Jennifer thought about them repeatedly, and they profoundly influenced her reactions to many aspects of everyday life. The sight of blood or the smell of cooking meat made her sick to her stomach, to the point that she had to stop eating meat. The previously innocent sound of a helicopter approaching, which in Iraq signaled that new wounded bodies were about to arrive, now created in Jennifer heightened feelings of fear and anxiety. She regularly awoke from nightmares concerning the most troubling aspects of her Iraq experiences, such as tending to soldiers with multiple amputations. In the words of the authors who described her case, Jennifer was "forever changed" by her Iraq experiences (Feczer & Bjorklund, 2009). And that is one reason why Jennifer's story is a compelling, though disturbing, introduction to the topic of learning.

During the 4 months that she served at a prison hospital near Baghdad during the Iraq war, Jennifer learned to associate the sound of an arriving helicopter with wounded soldiers. That learned association had a long-lasting influence on her.

◀ ICONICA/GETTY IMAGES

JOHN MOORE/AP IMAGES

Much of what happened to Jennifer after she returned home reflects the operation of a kind of learning based on association. Sights, sounds, and smells in Iraq had become associated with negative emotions in a way that created an enduring bond, so that encountering similar sights, sounds, and smells at home elicited similarly intense negative feelings.

LEARNING IS SHORTHAND FOR A COLLECTION OF DIFFERENT TECHNIQUES, procedures, and outcomes that produce changes in an organism's behavior. Learning psychologists have identified and studied as many as 40 different kinds of learning. In this chapter, we'll discuss the development and basic psychological principles behind two major approaches to learning: classical conditioning and operant conditioning. We'll then move on to see that some important kinds of learning occur when we simply watch others, and that such observational learning plays an important role in the cultural transmission of behavior. Next, we'll discover that some kinds of learning can occur entirely outside of awareness. We'll conclude with a discussion of learning in a context that should matter a lot to you: the classroom. We kick off the chapter, however, with some basics insights and definitions.

What Is Learning?

Despite the many different kinds of learning that psychologists have discovered, there is a basic principle at the core of all of them. **Learning** involves *the acquisition, from experience, of new knowledge, skills, or responses that results in a relatively permanent change in the state of the learner*. This definition emphasizes these key ideas:

► Learning is based on experience.

► Learning produces changes in the organism.

► These changes are relatively permanent.

Think about Jennifer's time in Iraq and you'll see all of these elements: Experiences such as the association between the sound of an approaching helicopter and the arrival of wounded soldiers changed the way Jennifer responded to certain situations in a way that lasted for years.

Learning can also occur in much simpler, nonassociative forms. You are probably familiar with the phenomenon of **habituation**, *a general process in which repeated or prolonged exposure to a stimulus results in a gradual reduction in responding*. If you've ever lived under the flight path of your local airport, near railroad tracks, or by a busy highway, you've probably noticed the deafening roar as a Boeing 737 made its way toward the landing strip, the clatter of a train speeding down the track, or the sound of traffic when you first moved in. You probably also noticed that, after a while, the roar wasn't quite so deafening anymore and that eventually you ignored the sounds of the planes, trains, or automobiles in your vicinity. This welcome reduction in responding reflects the operation of habituation.

Habituation occurs even in the simplest organisms. For example, in the Memory chapter you learned about the sea slug *Aplysia*, studied in detail by the Nobel Prize winner Eric Kandel (2006). Kandel and his colleagues showed clearly that *Aplysia* exhibits habituation: When lightly touched, the sea slug initially withdraws its gill, but the response gradually weakens after repeated light touches. In addition, *Aplysia* also exhibits another simple form of learning known as **sensitization**, which occurs when *presentation of a stimulus leads to an increased response to a later stimulus*. For example, Kandel found that after receiving a strong shock, *Aplysia* showed an increased

learning The acquisition, from experience, of new knowledge, skills, or responses that results in a relatively permanent change in the state of the learner.

habituation A general process in which repeated or prolonged exposure to a stimulus results in a gradual reduction in responding.

sensitization A simple form of learning that occurs when presentation of a stimulus leads to an increased response to a later stimulus.

gill-withdrawal response to a light touch. In a similar manner, people whose houses have been broken into may later become hypersensitive to late-night sounds that wouldn't have bothered them previously.

Although these simple kinds of learning are important, in this chapter we'll focus on more complex kinds of learning that psychologists have studied intensively. As you'll recall from the Psychology: Evolution of a Science chapter, a sizable chunk of psychology's history was devoted to behaviorism, with its insistence on measuring only observable, quantifiable behavior and its dismissal of mental activity as irrelevant and unknowable. Behaviorism was the major outlook of most psychologists working from the 1930s through the 1950s, the period during which most of the fundamental work on learning theory took place.

You might find the intersection of behaviorism and learning theory a bit surprising. After all, at one level learning seems abstract: Something intangible happens to you, and you think or behave differently thereafter. It seems logical that you'd need to explain that transformation in terms of a change in mental outlook. However, most behaviorists argued that learning's "permanent change in experience" could be demonstrated equally well in almost any organism: rats, dogs, pigeons, mice, pigs, or humans. From this perspective, behaviorists viewed learning as a purely behavioral activity requiring no mental activity.

In many ways the behaviorists were right. Much of what we know about how organisms learn comes directly from the behaviorists' observations of behaviors. However, they also overstated their case. We need to address some important cognitive considerations (i.e., elements of mental activity) in order to understand the learning process.

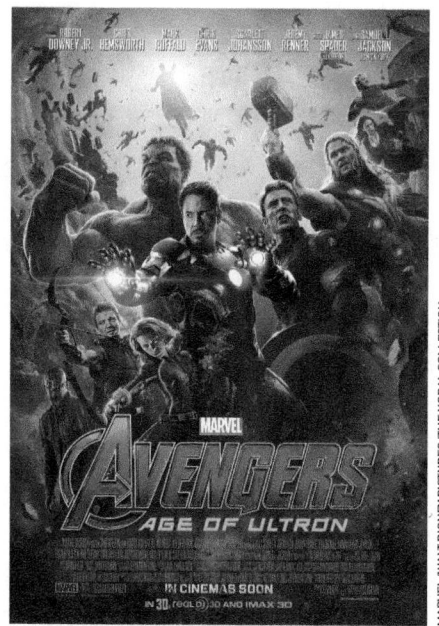

How might psychologists use the concept of habituation to explain the fact that today's action movies, like *Avengers: Age of Ultron*, tend to show much more graphic violence than movies of the 1980s, which in turn tended to show more graphic violence than movies of the 1950s?

Build to the Outcomes

1. What are the key ideas that support the definition of learning?

2. How do habituation and sensitization occur?

Classical Conditioning: One Thing Leads to Another

The American psychologist John B. Watson kick-started the behaviorist movement, arguing that psychologists should "never use the terms *consciousness, mental states, mind, content, introspectively verifiable, imagery*, and the like" (Watson, 1913, p. 166). Watson's firebrand stance was fueled in large part by the work of a Russian physiologist, Ivan Pavlov (1849–1936).

Pavlov was awarded the Nobel Prize in Physiology in 1904 for his work on the salivation of dogs. Pavlov studied the digestive processes of laboratory animals by surgically implanting test tubes into the cheeks of dogs to measure their salivary responses to different kinds of foods. Serendipitously, his explorations into spit and drool revealed the mechanics of one form of learning, which came to be called classical conditioning. **Classical conditioning** occurs *when a neutral stimulus produces a response after being paired with a stimulus that naturally produces a response.* In his classic experiments, Pavlov showed that dogs learned to salivate to neutral stimuli such as a bell or a tone after the dogs had associated that stimulus with another stimulus that naturally evokes salivation, such as food.

When Pavlov's findings first appeared in the scientific and popular literature (Pavlov, 1923a, 1923b), they produced a flurry of excitement because psychologists now had demonstrable evidence of how conditioning produced learned behaviors.

Learning Outcomes

▶ Describe the process of classical conditioning.

▶ Explain how cognitive, neural, and evolutionary aspects influence our understanding of classical conditioning.

classical conditioning A type of learning that occurs when a neutral stimulus produces a response after being paired with a stimulus that naturally produces a response.

This was the kind of behaviorist psychology John B. Watson was proposing: An organism experiences events or stimuli that are observable and measurable, and scientists can directly observe and measure changes in that organism. Dogs learned to salivate to the sound of a buzzer, and there was no need to resort to explanations about why it had happened, what the dog wanted, or how the animal thought about the situation. In other words, there was no need to consider the mind in this classical conditioning paradigm, which appealed to Watson and the behaviorists. Pavlov also appreciated the significance of his discovery and embarked on a systematic investigation of the mechanisms of classical conditioning. Let's take a closer look at some of these principles. (As The Real World: Understanding Drug Overdoses shows, these principles help explain how drug overdoses occur.)

THE BASIC PRINCIPLES OF CLASSICAL CONDITIONING

Pavlov's basic experimental setup involved cradling dogs in a harness to administer the foods and to measure the salivary response, as shown in **FIGURE 7.1**. He noticed that

---

THE REAL WORLD

Understanding Drug Overdoses

All too often, police are confronted with a perplexing problem: the sudden death of addicts from a drug overdose. The problem exists worldwide and has increased substantially during the past decade (Martins et al., 2015). These deaths are puzzling for at least three reasons: The victims are often experienced drug users; the dose taken is usually not larger than what they usually take; and the deaths tend to occur in unusual settings. Experienced drug users are just that: experienced! So, you'd think that the chances of an overdose would be lower than usual.

Classical conditioning provides some insight into how these deaths occur. First, when classical conditioning takes place, the CS is more than a simple bell or tone: It also includes the overall *context* within which the conditioning takes place. Indeed, Pavlov's dogs often began to salivate even as they approached the experimental apparatus. Second, many CRs are compensatory reactions to the US. Heroin, for example, slows down a person's breathing rate, so the body responds with a compensatory reaction that speeds up breathing in order to maintain a state of balance or homeostasis, a critically important CR.

These two finer points of classical conditioning help explain the seeming paradox of fatal heroin overdoses in experienced drug users (Siegel, 1984, 2005). When the drug is injected, the entire setting (the drug paraphernalia, the room, the lighting, the addict's usual companions) functions as the CS, and the addict's brain reacts to the heroin by secreting neurotransmitters

that counteract its effects. Over time, this protective physiological response becomes part of the CR, and like all CRs, it occurs in the presence of the CS but prior to the actual administration of the drug. These compensatory physiological reactions are also what make drug abusers take increasingly larger doses to achieve the same effect. Ultimately, these reactions produce *drug tolerance*, discussed in the Consciousness chapter.

On the basis of these principles of classical conditioning, taking drugs in a new environment can be fatal for a longtime drug user. If an addict injects the usual dose in a setting that is sufficiently novel or where he or she has never taken heroin before, the CS is now altered, so that the physiological compensatory CR that usually has a protective function either does not occur or is substantially decreased (Siegel et al., 2000). As a result, the addict's usual dose becomes an overdose, and death often results. Addicts intuitively may stick with the crack houses, drug dens, or "shooting galleries" with which they're familiar for just this reason. This effect has also been shown experimentally: Rats that have had extensive experience with morphine in one setting were much more likely to survive dose increases in that same setting than in a novel one (Siegel, 1976; Siegel et al., 2000). This same basic effect occurs with a variety of drugs. For example, college students show less tolerance for the intoxicating effects of alcohol when they consume it in the presence of a novel cue (a peppermint-flavored drink) than a familiar one (a beer-flavored drink; Siegel, 2005).

Understanding these principles has also led to treatments for drug addicts. For example, the addict can experience the brain's compensatory response to a drug, when elicited by the familiar contextual cues ordinarily associated with drug taking that constitute the CS, as withdrawal symptoms. In *cue exposure therapies*, an addict is exposed to drug-related cues without being given the usual dose of the drug itself, eventually resulting in extinction of the association between the contextual cues and the effects of the drug. After such treatment, encountering familiar drug-related cues will no longer result in the compensatory response linked to withdrawal symptoms, thereby making it easier for a recovering addict to remain abstinent (Siegel, 2005).

CHRIS GARDNER/AP IMAGES

Although drug dens and crack houses may be considered blights, it is often safer for addicts to use drugs there. The environment becomes part of the addict's CS, so it is ironic that busting crack houses may contribute to more deaths from drug overdoses when addicts are pushed to use drugs in new situations.

◀ **Figure 7.1**

PAVLOV'S APPARATUS FOR STUDYING CLASSICAL CONDITIONING Using a bell or a tuning fork, Pavlov presented auditory stimuli to the dogs. Visual stimuli could be presented on the screen.

unconditioned stimulus (US) Something that reliably produces a naturally occurring reaction in an organism.

unconditioned response (UR) A reflexive reaction that is reliably produced by an unconditioned stimulus.

dogs that had previously been in the experiment began to produce a kind of "anticipatory" salivary response as soon as they were put in the harness, before any food was presented. Pavlov and his colleagues regarded these responses as annoyances at first because they interfered with collecting naturally occurring salivary secretions. In reality, the dogs were behaving in line with the basic elements of classical conditioning:

▶ When the dogs were initially presented with a plate of food, they began to salivate. No surprise here—placing food in front of most animals will launch the salivary process. Pavlov called the presentation of food an **unconditioned stimulus (US),** *something that reliably produces a naturally occurring reaction in an organism* (see **FIGURE 7.2a**). He called the dogs' salivation an **unconditioned response (UR),** *a reflexive reaction that is reliably produced by an unconditioned stimulus.*

▼ **Figure 7.2**

THE ELEMENTS OF CLASSICAL CONDITIONING a) Before conditioning, the dog salivates in response to food, the unconditioned stimulus (US), but not to a ringing bell. b) During conditioning, the food is paired with the ringing bell, which becomes a conditioned stimulus (CS). c) After conditioning, the ringing bell, now a conditioned stimulus (CS) can produce salivation. d) In second-order conditioning, the ringing bell can be used to condition a new stimulus, such as a black square.

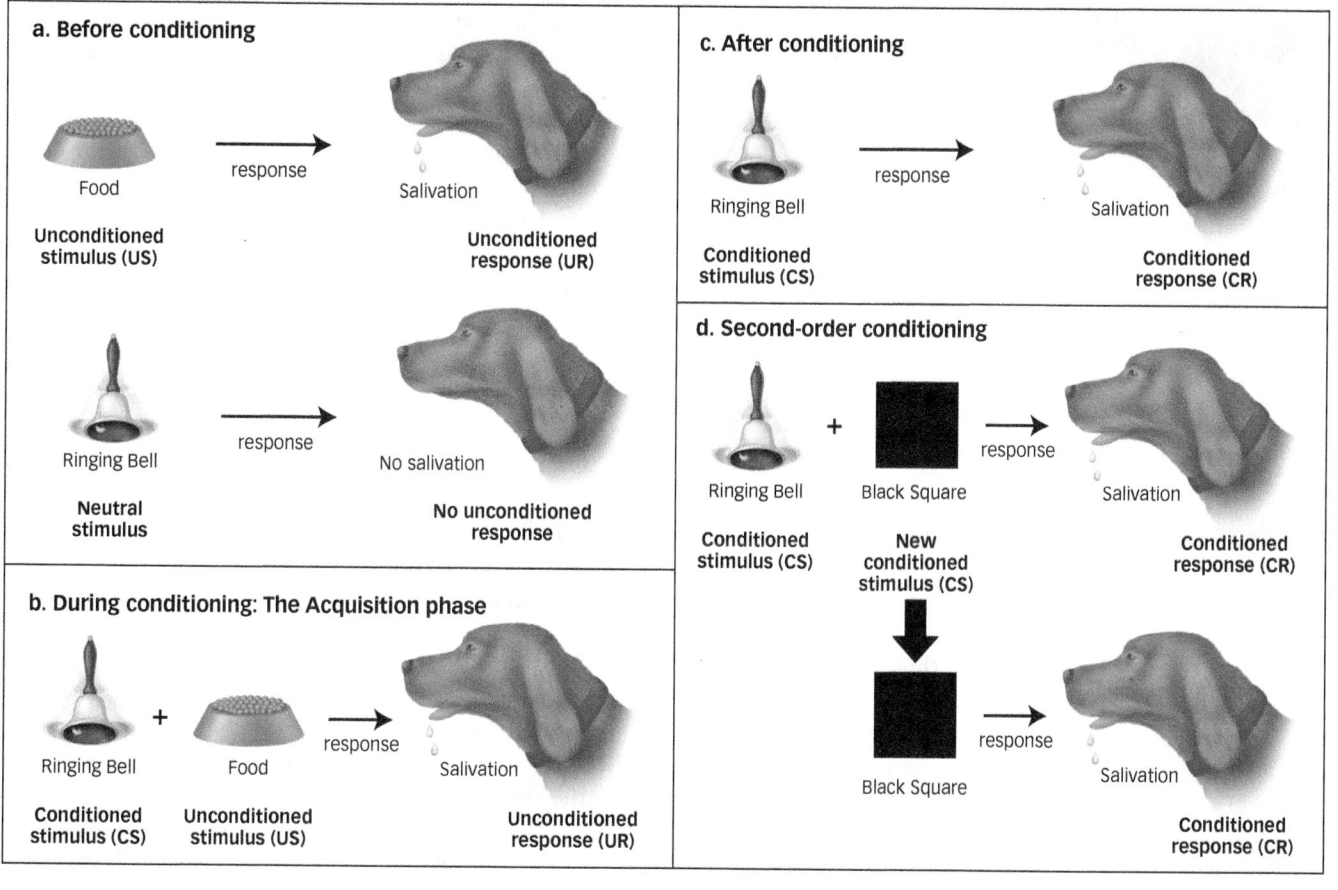

acquisition The phase of classical conditioning when the CS and the US are presented together.

conditioned stimulus (CS) A previously neutral stimulus that produces a reliable response in an organism after being paired with a US.

conditioned response (CR) A reaction that resembles an unconditioned response but is produced by a conditioned stimulus.

second-order conditioning A type of learning where a CS is paired with a stimulus that became associated with the US in an earlier procedure.

extinction The gradual elimination of a learned response that occurs when the CS is repeatedly presented without the US.

"I THINK MOM'S USING THE CAN OPENER."

DENNIS THE MENACE: NORTH AMERICA SYNDICATE, INC.

▶ Then Pavlov paired the presentation of food with the sound of a bell, the ticking of a metronome, the humming of a tuning fork, or the flash of a light (Pavlov, 1927). This period is called **acquisition,** *the phase of classical conditioning when the CS and the US are presented together* (see Figure 7.2b).

▶ Nothing in nature would make a dog salivate to the sound of a bell. However, when the CS (the sound of a bell) is paired over time with the US (the food), the animal will learn to associate food with the sound, and eventually the CS is sufficient to produce a response, or salivation. Sure enough, Pavlov found that the dogs salivated to these sounds and flashes, each of which had become a **conditioned stimulus (CS),** *a previously neutral stimulus that produces a reliable response in an organism after being paired with a US.* This response resembles the UR, but Pavlov called it the **conditioned response (CR),** *a reaction that resembles an unconditioned response but is produced by a conditioned stimulus.* In this example, the dogs' salivation (CR) was eventually prompted by the sound of the bell (CS) alone because the sound of the bell and the food (US) had been associated so often in the past (see Figure 7.2c).

Consider your own dog (or cat). Does your dog always know when dinner's coming, preparing just short of pulling up a chair and tucking a napkin into her collar? It's as though she has one eye on the clock every day, waiting for the dinner hour. Alas, your dog is no clock-watching wonder hound. Instead, for her the presentation of food (the US) has become associated with a complex CS—your getting up, moving into the kitchen, opening the cabinet, working the can opener—such that the CS alone signals to your dog that food is on the way and therefore initiates the CR of her getting ready to eat.

After conditioning has been established, a phenomenon called **second-order conditioning** can be demonstrated: *a type of learning where a CS is paired with a stimulus that became associated with the US in an earlier procedure.* For example, in an early study, Pavlov repeatedly paired a new CS, a black square, with the now reliable tone. After a number of training trials, his dogs produced a salivary response to the black square, even though the square itself had never been directly associated with the food (see Figure 7.2d). Second-order conditioning helps explain why some people desire money to the point that they hoard it and value it even more than the objects it purchases. Money is initially used to purchase objects that produce gratifying outcomes, such as an expensive car. Although money is not directly associated with the thrill of driving a new sports car, through second-order conditioning, money can become linked with this type of desirable reward.

Acquisition, Extinction, and Spontaneous Recovery

Remember when you first got your dog? Chances are she didn't seem too smart, especially the way she stared at you vacantly as you went into the kitchen, not anticipating that food was on the way. During the initial phase of the acquisition period of classical conditioning, typically there is a gradual increase in learning: It starts low, rises rapidly, and then slowly tapers off, as shown on the left side of **FIGURE 7.3**. Pavlov's dogs gradually increased their amount of salivation over several trials of pairing a tone with the presentation of food, and similarly, your dog eventually learned to associate your kitchen preparations with the subsequent appearance of food. After learning has been established, in the second-order phase, the CS by itself will reliably elicit the CR.

After Pavlov and his colleagues had explored the process of acquisition extensively, they turned to the next logical question: What would happen if they continued to present the CS (tone) but stopped presenting the US (food)? Repeatedly presenting the CS without the US produces exactly the result you might imagine. As shown on the right side of the first panel in Figure 7.3, behavior declines abruptly and continues to drop until eventually the dog ceases to salivate to the sound of the tone. This process is called **extinction,** *the gradual elimination of a learned response that occurs when the CS is repeatedly presented without the US.* This term was introduced

◀ **Figure 7.3**
ACQUISITION, EXTINCTION, AND SPONTANEOUS RECOVERY In classical conditioning, the CS is originally neutral and elicits no specific response. After several trials pairing the CS with the US, the CS alone comes to elicit the salivary response (the CR). Learning tends to take place fairly rapidly and then levels off as stable responding develops. In extinction, the CR diminishes quickly until it no longer occurs. A rest period, however, is typically followed by spontaneous recovery of the CR. In fact, a well-learned CR may show spontaneous recovery after more than one rest period even without any additional learning trials.

because the conditioned response is "extinguished" and no longer observed. Having established that he could produce learning through conditioning and then extinguish it, Pavlov wondered if this elimination of conditioned behavior was permanent. Is a single session of extinction sufficient to knock out the CR completely? Or is there some residual change in the dog's behavior such that the CR might reappear?

To explore this question, Pavlov extinguished the classically conditioned salivation response and then allowed the dogs to have a short rest period. When they were brought back to the lab and presented with the CS again, they displayed **spontaneous recovery,** *the tendency of a learned behavior to recover from extinction after a rest period.* This phenomenon is shown in the middle panel in Figure 7.3. Notice that this recovery takes place even though there have not been any additional associations between the CS and US. Some spontaneous recovery of the conditioned response even takes place in what is essentially a second extinction session after another period of rest (see the right-hand panel in Figure 7.3). Clearly, extinction had not completely erased the learning that had been acquired. The ability of the CS to elicit the CR was weakened, but it was not eliminated.

Generalization and Discrimination

Do you think your dog will be stumped, unable to anticipate the presentation of her food, if you get a new can opener? Will you need to establish a whole new round of conditioning with this modified CS?

Probably not. It wouldn't be very adaptive for an organism if each little change in the CS–US pairing required an extensive regimen of new learning. Rather, the phenomenon of **generalization** tends to take place: *The CR is observed even though the CS is slightly different from the CS used during acquisition.* This means that the conditioning generalizes to stimuli that are similar to the CS used during the original training. As you might expect, the more the new stimulus changes, the less conditioned responding is observed. If you replaced a manual can opener with an electric can opener, your dog would probably show a much weaker conditioned response (Pearce, 1987; Rescorla, 2006).

When an organism generalizes to a new stimulus, two things are happening. First, by responding to the new stimulus used during generalization testing, the organism demonstrates that it recognizes the similarity between the original CS and the new stimulus. Second, by displaying a *diminished* response to that new stimulus, it also tells us that it notices a difference between the two stimuli. In the second case, the organism shows **discrimination,** *the capacity to distinguish between similar but distinct stimuli.* Generalization and discrimination are two sides of the same coin. The more organisms show one, the less they show the other, and training can modify the balance between the two.

Your first electric can opener may cause your dog some confusion, but likely only for a little while.

spontaneous recovery The tendency of a learned behavior to recover from extinction after a rest period.

generalization The CR is observed even though the CS is slightly different from the CS used during acquisition.

discrimination The capacity to distinguish between similar but distinct stimuli.

John Watson and Rosalie Rayner show Little Albert an unusual bunny mask. Why isn't the mere presence of these experimenters a conditioned stimulus in itself?

WATSON & RAYNER, 1920

CONDITIONED EMOTIONAL RESPONSES: THE CASE OF LITTLE ALBERT

Before you conclude that classical conditioning is merely a sophisticated way to train your dog, let's revisit the larger principles of Pavlov's work. Classical conditioning demonstrates that scientists can achieve durable, substantial changes in behavior simply by setting up the proper conditions. It was this kind of simplicity that appealed to behaviorists. In fact, Watson and his followers thought that it was possible to develop general explanations of pretty much *any* behavior of *any* organism based on classical conditioning principles. As a step in that direction, Watson embarked on a controversial study with his research assistant Rosalie Rayner (Watson & Rayner, 1920). To support his contention that even complex behaviors were the result of conditioning, Watson enlisted the assistance of 9-month-old "Little Albert." Albert was a healthy, well-developed child, and, by Watson's assessment, "stolid and unemotional" (Watson & Rayner, 1920, p. 1). Watson wanted to see if such a child could be classically conditioned to experience a strong emotional reaction—namely, fear.

Watson presented Little Albert with a variety of stimuli: a white rat, a dog, a rabbit, various masks, and a burning newspaper. Albert reacted in most cases with curiosity or indifference, and he showed no fear of any of the items. Watson also established that something *could* make him afraid. While Albert was watching Rayner, Watson unexpectedly struck a large steel bar with a hammer, producing a loud noise. Predictably, this caused Albert to cry, tremble, and be generally displeased.

Watson and Rayner then led Little Albert through the acquisition phase of classical conditioning. Albert was presented with a white rat. As soon as he reached out to touch it, the steel bar was struck. This pairing occurred again and again over several trials. Eventually, the sight of the rat alone caused Albert to recoil in terror, crying and clamoring to get away from it. In this situation, a US (the loud sound) was paired with a CS (the presence of the rat) such that the CS all by itself was sufficient to produce the CR (a fearful reaction). Little Albert also showed stimulus generalization. The sight of a white rabbit, a seal-fur coat, and a Santa Claus mask produced the same kinds of fear reactions in the infant.

What was Watson's goal in all this? First, he wanted to show that a relatively complex reaction could be conditioned using Pavlovian techniques. Second, he wanted to show that emotional responses such as fear and anxiety could be produced by classical conditioning and therefore need not be the product of deeper unconscious processes or early life experiences as Freud and his followers had argued (see the Psychology: Evolution of a Science chapter). Instead, Watson proposed that fears could be learned, just like any other behavior. Third, Watson wanted to confirm that conditioning could be applied to humans as well as to other animals. This study was controversial in its cavalier treatment of a young child, especially given that Watson and Rayner did not follow up with Albert or his mother during the ensuing years (Harris, 1979). Modern ethical guidelines that govern the treatment of research participants make sure that this kind of study could not be conducted today. At the time, however, it was consistent with a behaviorist view of psychology.

The kind of conditioned fear responses that were at work in Little Albert's case were also important in the chapter-opening case of Jennifer, who experienced fear and anxiety when hearing the previously innocent sound of an approaching helicopter as a result of her experiences in Iraq. Indeed, a therapy that has proven effective in dealing with such trauma-induced fears is based directly on principles of classical conditioning: Individuals are repeatedly exposed to conditioned stimuli associated with their trauma in a safe setting in an attempt to extinguish the conditioned fear response (Bouton, 1988; Rothbaum & Schwartz, 2002). However, conditioned emotional responses include much more than just fear and anxiety responses. Advertisers, for example, understand that conditioned emotional responses can include various kinds of positive emotions

What response do you think the advertisers of Budweiser are looking for when they feature Clydesdale horses in an ad?

KYLE ERICSON/AP IMAGES

that they would like potential customers to associate with their products, which may be why attractive women are commonly involved in ads for products geared toward young males, including beer and sports cars. Even the warm and fuzzy feelings that envelop you when hearing a song on the radio that you used to listen to with a former boyfriend or girlfriend are a type of conditioned emotional response.

A DEEPER UNDERSTANDING OF CLASSICAL CONDITIONING

As a form of learning, classical conditioning could be reliably produced: It had a simple set of principles and applications to real-life situations. In short, classical conditioning offered a good deal of utility for psychologists who sought to understand the mechanisms underlying learning, and it continues to do so today.

Like a lot of strong starters, though, classical conditioning has been subjected to deeper scrutiny in order to understand exactly how, when, and why it works. Let's examine three areas that give us a closer look at the mechanisms of classical conditioning: the cognitive, neural, and evolutionary elements.

The Cognitive Elements of Classical Conditioning

As we've seen, Pavlov's work was a behaviorist's dream come true. In this view, conditioning is something that *happens* to a dog, a rat, or a person, apart from what the organism thinks about the conditioning situation. However, although the dogs salivated when their feeders approached (see the Psychology: Evolution of a Science chapter), they did not salivate when Pavlov did. Eventually someone was bound to ask an important question: *Why not?* After all, Pavlov also delivered the food to the dogs, so why didn't he become a CS? Indeed, if Watson was present whenever the unpleasant US was sounded, why didn't Little Albert come to fear *him?*

Somehow, Pavlov's dogs were sensitive to the fact that Pavlov was not a *reliable* indicator of the arrival of food. Pavlov was linked with the arrival of food, but he was also linked with other activities that had nothing to do with food, including checking on the apparatus, bringing the dog from the kennel to the laboratory, and standing around and talking with his assistants.

Robert Rescorla and Allan Wagner (1972) were the first to theorize that classical conditioning occurs when an animal has learned to set up an *expectation*. The sound of a bell, because of its systematic pairing with food, set up this cognitive state for the laboratory dogs; Pavlov, because of the lack of any reliable link with food, did not. In fact, in situations such as this, many responses are actually being conditioned. When the bell sounds, the dogs also wag their tails, make begging sounds, and look toward the food source (Jenkins et al., 1978). In short, what is really happening is something like the situation shown in **FIGURE 7.4**.

▼ Figure 7.4

EXPECTATION IN CLASSICAL CONDITIONING
In the Rescorla–Wagner model of classical conditioning, a CS sets up an expectation. The expectation in turn leads to an array of behaviors associated with the presence of the CS.

DON MASON/CORBIS

Conditioned stimulus (e.g., tone, bell) → Expectation of food → Salivation / Tail wagging / Looking for food / Begging

The Rescorla–Wagner model introduced a cognitive component that accounted for a variety of classical conditioning phenomena that were difficult to understand from a simple behaviorist point of view. For example, the model predicted that conditioning would be easier when the CS was an *unfamiliar* event than when it was familiar. The reason is that familiar events, being familiar, already have expectations associated with them, making new conditioning difficult. In short, classical conditioning might appear to be a primitive process, but it is actually quite sophisticated and incorporates a significant cognitive element.

The Neural Elements of Classical Conditioning

Pavlov saw his research as providing insights into how the brain works. After all, he was trained in medicine, not psychology, and was a bit surprised when psychologists became excited by his findings. Recent research has clarified some of what Pavlov hoped to understand about conditioning and the brain.

A series of pioneering experiments conducted across several decades by Richard Thompson and his colleagues focused on classical conditioning of eyeblink responses in rabbits. In the most basic type of eyeblink conditioning, the CS (a tone) is immediately followed by the US (a puff of air), which elicits a reflexive eyeblink response. After many CS–US pairings, the eyeblink response occurs in response to the CS alone. Thompson and colleagues showed convincingly that the cerebellum is critical for the occurrence of eyeblink conditioning (Thompson, 2005). Studies of people with lesions to the cerebellum supported these findings by demonstrating impaired eyeblink conditioning (Daum et al., 1993). Rounding out the picture, more recent neuroimaging findings in healthy young adults show activation in the cerebellum during eyeblink conditioning (Cheng et al., 2008). As you learned in the Neuroscience and Behavior chapter, the cerebellum is part of the hindbrain and plays an important role in motor skills and learning.

In addition to eyeblink conditioning, fear conditioning has been extensively studied. Also in the Neuroscience and Behavior chapter, you saw that the amygdala plays an important role in the experience of emotion, including fear and anxiety. So it should come as no surprise that the amygdala, particularly an area known as the *central nucleus*, is also critical for emotional conditioning.

Consider a rat that is conditioned to a series of CS–US pairings where the CS is a tone and the US is a mild electric shock. When rats experience sudden painful stimuli in nature, they show a defensive reaction, known as *freezing*, in which they crouch down and sit motionless. In addition, their autonomic nervous systems go to work: Heart rate and blood pressure increase, and various hormones associated with stress are released. When fear conditioning takes place, these two components—one behavioral and one physiological—occur, except that now they are elicited by the CS.

The central nucleus of the amygdala plays a role in producing both of these outcomes through two distinct connections with other parts of the brain. If connections linking the amygdala to the midbrain are disrupted, the rat does not exhibit the behavioral freezing response. If the connections between the amygdala and the hypothalamus are severed, the autonomic responses associated with fear cease (LeDoux et al., 1988). Hence, the action of the amygdala is an essential element in fear conditioning, and its links with other areas of the brain are responsible for producing specific features of conditioning (Bentz & Schiller, 2015). The amygdala is involved in fear conditioning in people as well as in rats and other animals (Olsson & Phelps, 2007; Phelps & LeDoux, 2005).

The Evolutionary Elements of Classical Conditioning

In addition to this cognitive component, evolutionary mechanisms also play an important role in classical conditioning. As you learned in the Psychology: Evolution of a Science chapter, evolution and natural selection go hand in hand with adaptiveness: Behaviors that are adaptive allow an organism to survive and thrive in its environment. In the case of classical conditioning, psychologists began to appreciate how this type of learning could have adaptive value. Much research exploring this adaptiveness has focused on conditioned food aversions.

Consider this example: A psychology professor was once on a job interview in southern California, and his hosts took him to lunch at a Middle Eastern restaurant. Suffering from a case of bad hummus, he was up all night long, and developed a life-long aversion to hummus.

On the face of it, this looks like a case of classical conditioning, but there are several peculiar aspects to this case. The hummus was the CS, a bacterium or some other source of toxicity was the US, and the resulting nausea was the UR. The UR (the nausea) became linked to the once-neutral CS (the hummus) and became a CR (an aversion to hummus). However, all of the psychologist's hosts also ate the hummus, yet none of them reported feeling ill. It's not clear, then, what the US was; it couldn't have been anything that was actually in the food. What's more, the time between the hummus and the distress was several hours; usually, a response follows a stimulus fairly quickly. Most baffling, this aversion was cemented with a single acquisition trial. Usually it takes several pairings of a CS and US to establish learning.

These peculiarities are not so peculiar from an evolutionary perspective. Any species that forages or consumes a variety of foods needs to develop a mechanism by which it can learn to avoid any food that once made it ill. To have adaptive value, this mechanism should have several properties:

▶ Rapid learning should occur in perhaps one or two trials. If learning takes more trials than this, the animal could die from eating a toxic substance.

▶ Conditioning should be able to take place over very long intervals, perhaps up to several hours. Toxic substances often don't cause illness immediately, so the organism would need to form an association between the food and the illness over a longer term.

▶ The organism should develop the aversion to the smell or taste of the food rather than its ingestion. It's more adaptive to reject a potentially toxic substance based on smell alone than it is to ingest it.

▶ Learned aversions should occur more often with novel foods than familiar ones. It is not adaptive for an animal to develop an aversion to everything it has eaten on the particular day it got sick. Our psychologist friend didn't develop an aversion to the Coke he drank with lunch or the scrambled eggs he had for breakfast that day; however, the sight and smell of hummus do make him uneasy.

A Modern Application

John Garcia and his colleagues illustrated the adaptiveness of classical conditioning in a series of studies with rats (Garcia & Koelling, 1966). They used a variety of CSs (visual, auditory, tactile, taste, and smell) and several different USs (injection of a toxic substance, radiation) that caused nausea and vomiting hours later. The researchers found weak or no conditioning when the CS was a visual, auditory, or tactile stimulus, but a strong food aversion developed with stimuli that had a distinct taste and smell.

This research had an interesting application. It led to the development of a technique for dealing with an unanticipated side effect of radiation and chemotherapy: Cancer patients who experience nausea from their treatments often develop aversions to foods they ate before the therapy. Broberg and Bernstein (1987) reasoned that, if the findings with rats generalized to humans, a simple technique should minimize the negative consequences of this effect. They gave their patients an unusual food (coconut- or root-beer-flavored candy) at the end of the last meal before undergoing treatment. Sure enough, the conditioned food aversions that the patients developed were overwhelmingly for one of the unusual flavors and not for any of the other foods

Under certain conditions, people may develop food aversions. This serving of hummus looks inviting and probably tastes delicious, but at least one psychologist avoids it like the plague.

Rats can be difficult to poison because of learned taste aversions, which are an evolutionarily adaptive element of classical conditioning. Here a worker tries his best in the sewers of Paris.

biological preparedness A propensity for learning particular kinds of associations over others.

in the meal. Other than any root beer or coconut fanatics among the sample, patients were spared developing aversions to common foods that they were more likely to eat.

Studies such as these suggest that evolution has provided each species with a kind of **biological preparedness,** *a propensity for learning particular kinds of associations over others,* so that some behaviors are relatively easy to condition in some species but not others. For example, the taste and smell stimuli that produce food aversions in rats do not work with most species of birds. Birds depend primarily on visual cues for finding food and are relatively insensitive to taste and smell. However, as you might guess, it is relatively easy to produce a food aversion in birds using an unfamiliar visual stimulus as the CS, such as a brightly colored food (Wilcoxon, Dragoin, & Kral, 1971). Indeed, most researchers agree that conditioning works best with stimuli that are biologically relevant to the organism (Domjan, 2005).

Build to the Outcomes

1. Why do some dogs seem to know when it's dinnertime?

2. If both an unconditioned and conditioned stimulus can produce the same effect, what is the difference?

3. What is second-order conditioning?

4. How does a conditioned behavior change when the unconditioned stimulus is removed?

5. Why are generalization and discrimination "two sides of the same coin"?

6. Why did Albert fear the rat?

7. How does the role of expectation in conditioning challenge behaviorist ideas?

8. What is the role of the amygdala in fear conditioning?

9. How has cancer patients' discomfort been eased by our understanding of food aversions?

Operant Conditioning: Reinforcements from the Environment

Learning Outcomes

▶ Describe the process of operant conditioning.

▶ Explain how behavioral, cognitive, neural, and evolutionary aspects influence our understanding of operant conditioning.

The study of classical conditioning is the study of behaviors that are *reactive*. Most animals don't voluntarily salivate or feel spasms of anxiety; rather, they exhibit these responses involuntarily during the conditioning process. Involuntary behaviors make up only a small portion of our behavioral repertoires. The remainder are behaviors that we voluntarily perform. We engage in these voluntary behaviors in order to obtain rewards and avoid punishment; understanding them is essential to developing a complete picture of learning. Because classical conditioning has little to say about these voluntary behaviors, we turn now to a different form of learning: **operant conditioning,** *a type of learning in which the consequences of an organism's behavior determine whether it will repeat that behavior in the future.* The study of operant conditioning is the exploration of behaviors that are *active*.

THE DEVELOPMENT OF OPERANT CONDITIONING: THE LAW OF EFFECT

operant conditioning A type of learning in which the consequences of an organism's behavior determine whether it will repeat that behavior in the future.

The study of how active behavior affects the environment began at about the same time as classical conditioning. In fact, Edward L. Thorndike (1874–1949) first examined active behaviors back in the 1890s, before Pavlov published his findings. Thorndike's

◀ Figure 7.5

THORNDIKE'S PUZZLE BOX In Thorndike's original experiments, food was placed just outside the door of the puzzle box, where the cat could see it. If the cat triggered the appropriate lever, it would open the door and the cat could get out.

research focused on *instrumental behaviors*, that is, behavior that required an organism to *do* something, solve a problem, or otherwise manipulate elements of its environment (Thorndike, 1898). For example, Thorndike completed several experiments using a puzzle box, which was a wooden crate with a door that would open when a concealed lever was moved in the right way (see **FIGURE 7.5**). A hungry cat placed in a puzzle box would try various behaviors to get out—scratching at the door, meowing loudly, sniffing the inside of the box, putting its paw through the openings—but only one behavior opened the door and led to food: tripping the lever in just the right way. After this happened, Thorndike placed the cat back in the box for another round. Don't get the wrong idea. Thorndike probably *really liked* cats. Far from teasing them, he was after an important behavioral principle.

Fairly quickly, the cats became quite skilled at triggering the lever for their release. Notice what's going on. At first, the cat enacts any number of likely (but ultimately ineffective) behaviors, but only one behavior leads to freedom and food. Over time, the ineffective behaviors become less and less frequent, and the one instrumental behavior (going right for the latch) becomes more frequent (see **FIGURE 7.6**). From these

◀ Figure 7.6

THE LAW OF EFFECT Thorndike's cats displayed trial-and-error behavior when trying to escape from the puzzle box. They made lots of irrelevant movements and actions until, over time, they discovered the solution. Once they figured out which behavior was instrumental in opening the latch, they stopped all other ineffective behaviors and escaped from the box faster and faster.

law of effect The principle that behaviors that are followed by a "satisfying state of affairs" tend to be repeated, and those that produce an "unpleasant state of affairs" are less likely to be repeated.

operant behavior Behavior that an organism performs that has some impact on the environment.

reinforcer Any stimulus or event that increases the likelihood of the behavior that led to it.

punisher Any stimulus or event that decreases the likelihood of the behavior that led to it.

▼ Figure 7.7

SKINNER BOX This is a typical Skinner box, or operant conditioning chamber. A rat, pigeon, or other suitably sized animal is placed in this environment and observed during learning trials that apply operant conditioning principles.

observations, Thorndike developed the **law of effect**, the principle that *behaviors that are followed by a "satisfying state of affairs" tend to be repeated, and those that produce an "unpleasant state of affairs" are less likely to be repeated.*

The circumstances that Thorndike used to study learning were very different from those in studies of classical conditioning. Remember that in classical conditioning experiments, the US occurred on every training trial, no matter what the animal did. Pavlov delivered food to the dog whether it salivated or not. But in Thorndike's work, the behavior of the animal determined what happened next. If the behavior was "correct" (i.e., the animal triggered the latch), the animal was rewarded with food. Incorrect behaviors produced no results, and the animal was stuck in the box until it performed the correct behavior. Although different from classical conditioning, Thorndike's work resonated with most behaviorists at the time: It was still observable, quantifiable, and free from explanations involving the mind (Galef, 1998).

B. F. SKINNER: THE ROLE OF REINFORCEMENT AND PUNISHMENT

Several decades after Thorndike's work, B. F. Skinner (1904–1990) coined the term **operant behavior** to refer to *behavior that an organism performs that has some impact on the environment.* In Skinner's system, all of these emitted behaviors "operated" on the environment in some manner, and the environment responded by providing events that either strengthened those behaviors (i.e., they *reinforced* them) or made them less likely to occur (i.e., they *punished* them). Skinner's elegantly simple observation was that most organisms do *not* behave like a dog in a harness, passively waiting to receive food no matter what the circumstances. Rather, most organisms are like cats in a box, actively engaging the environment in which they find themselves to reap rewards (Skinner, 1938, 1953).

In order to study operant behavior scientifically, Skinner developed a variation on Thorndike's puzzle box. The *operant conditioning chamber,* or *Skinner box,* as it is commonly called (shown in **FIGURE 7.7**), allows a researcher to study the behavior of small organisms in a controlled environment.

Skinner's approach to the study of learning focused on *reinforcement* and *punishment.* These terms, which have commonsense connotations, turned out to be rather difficult to define. For example, some people love roller coasters, whereas others find them horrifying; the chance to go on one will be reinforcing for one group but punishing for another. Dogs can be trained with praise and a good belly rub—procedures that are nearly useless for most cats. Skinner settled on a neutral definition that would characterize each term by its effect on behavior. Therefore, a **reinforcer** is *any stimulus or event that increases the likelihood of the behavior that led to it,* whereas a **punisher** is *any stimulus or event that decreases the likelihood of the behavior that led to it*

Whether a particular stimulus acts as a reinforcer or a punisher depends in part on whether it increases or decreases the likelihood of a behavior. Presenting food is usually reinforcing and produces an increase in the behavior that led to it; removing food is often punishing and leads to a decrease in the behavior. Turning on an electric shock is typically punishing (and decreases the behavior that led to it); turning it off is rewarding (and increases the behavior that led to it).

To keep these possibilities distinct, Skinner used the term *positive* for situations in which a stimulus was presented and *negative* for situations in which it was removed. Consequently, as shown in **TABLE 7.1**, there is *positive reinforcement* (a stimulus is presented that increases the likelihood of a behavior) and a *negative reinforcement* (a stimulus is removed that increases the likelihood of a behavior), as well as *positive punishment* (a stimulus is administered that reduces the likelihood of a behavior) and a *negative punishment* (a stimulus is removed that decreases the likelihood of a behavior). Here the words *positive* and *negative* mean, respectively, something that is

SCIENCE SOURCE

TABLE 7.1

Reinforcement and Punishment

	Increases the Likelihood of Behavior	Decreases the Likelihood of Behavior
Stimulus is presented	Positive reinforcement	Positive punishment
Stimulus is removed	Negative reinforcement	Negative punishment

B. F. Skinner with one of his many research participants.

added or something that is *taken away*, but do not mean "good" or "bad" as they do in everyday speech.

These distinctions can be confusing at first; after all, "negative reinforcement" and "punishment" both sound like they should be "bad" and produce the same type of behavior. However, negative reinforcement, for example, does not involve administering something that decreases the likelihood of a behavior; it's the *removal* of something, such as a shock, that increases the likelihood of a behavior.

Reinforcement is generally more effective than punishment in promoting learning. There are many reasons for this (Gershoff, 2002), but one reason is: Punishment signals that an unacceptable behavior has occurred, but it doesn't specify what should be done instead. Spanking a young child for starting to run into a busy street certainly stops the behavior, but it doesn't promote any kind of learning about the *desired* behavior.

Primary and Secondary Reinforcement and Punishment

Reinforcers and punishers often gain their functions from basic biological mechanisms. A pigeon that pecks at a target in a Skinner box is usually reinforced with food pellets, just as an animal that learns to escape a mild electric shock has avoided the punishment of tingly paws. Food, comfort, shelter, and warmth are examples of *primary reinforcers* because they help satisfy biological needs. However, the vast majority of reinforcers or punishers in our daily lives have little to do with biology: Verbal approval, a bronze trophy, or money all serve powerful reinforcing functions, yet none of them taste very good or help keep you warm at night. The point is, we learn to perform a lot of behaviors on the basis of reinforcements that have little or nothing to do with biological satisfaction.

These *secondary reinforcers* derive their effectiveness from their associations with primary reinforcers through classical conditioning. For example, money starts out as a neutral CS that, through its association with primary USs such as acquiring food or shelter, takes on a conditioned emotional element. Flashing lights, originally a neutral CS, acquire powerful negative elements through association with a speeding ticket and a fine.

Immediate versus Delayed Reinforcement and Punishment

A key determinant of the effectiveness of a reinforcer is the amount of time between the occurrence of a behavior and the reinforcer: The more time elapses, the less effective the reinforcer (Lattal, 2010; Renner, 1964). This was dramatically illustrated in experiments with hungry rats in which food reinforcers were given at varying times after a rat pressed the lever (Dickinson, Watt, & Griffiths, 1992). Delaying reinforcement by even a few seconds led to a reduction in the number of times the rat subsequently pressed the lever, and extending the delay to a minute rendered the food reinforcer completely ineffective (see **FIGURE 7.8**). The most likely explanation for this effect is that delaying the reinforcer made it difficult for the rats to figure out exactly what behavior they needed to perform in order to obtain it. In the same way,

Negative reinforcement involves the removal of something unpleasant from the environment. When Daddy stops the car, he gets a reward: His little monster stops screaming. However, from the perspective of the child, this is positive reinforcement. The child's tantrum results in something positive added to the environment—stopping for a snack.

▶ Figure 7.8

DELAY OF REINFORCEMENT Rats pressed a lever in order to obtain a food reward. Researchers varied the amount of time between the lever press and the delivery of food reinforcement. The number of lever presses declined substantially with longer delays.

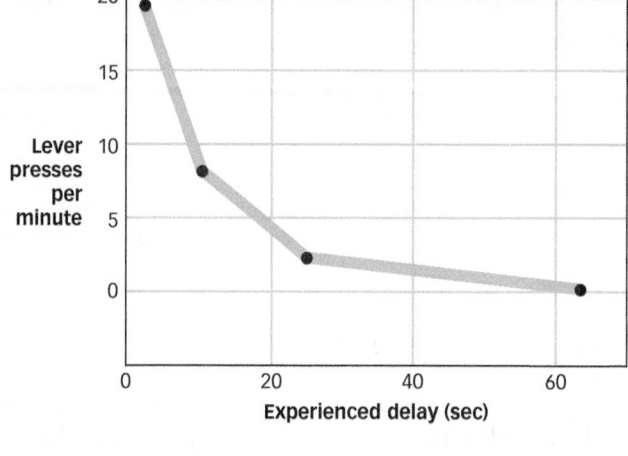

parents who wish to use a piece of candy to reinforce their children for playing quietly should provide the candy while the child is still playing quietly; waiting until later, when the child may be engaging in other behaviors—perhaps making a racket with pots and pans—will make it more difficult for the child to link the reinforcer with the behavior of playing quietly (Powell et al., 2009).

The greater potency of immediate versus delayed reinforcers may help us to appreciate why it can be difficult to engage in behaviors that have long-term benefits. The smoker who desperately wants to quit smoking will be reinforced immediately by the feeling of relaxation that results from lighting up, but may have to wait years to be reinforced with better health that results from quitting; the dieter who sincerely wants to lose weight may easily succumb to the temptation of a chocolate sundae that provides reinforcement now, rather than waiting weeks or months for the reinforcement (looking and feeling better) that would be associated with losing weight.

Similar considerations apply to punishment: As a general rule, the longer the delay between a behavior and the administration of punishment, the less effective the punishment will be in suppressing the targeted behavior (Kamin, 1959; Lerman & Vorndran, 2002). The reduced effectiveness of delayed punishment can be a serious problem in nonlaboratory settings, because in everyday life it is often difficult to administer punishment immediately or even soon after a problem behavior has occurred (Meindl & Casey, 2012). For example, a parent whose child misbehaves at a shopping mall may be unable to punish the child immediately with a time-out because it is impractical in the mall setting. Some problem behaviors, such as cheating, can be difficult to detect immediately, and therefore punishment is necessarily delayed. Research in both the laboratory and everyday settings suggests several strategies for increasing the effectiveness of delayed punishment, including increasing the severity of the punishment or attempting to bridge the gap between the behavior and the punishment with verbal instructions (Meindl & Casey, 2012). The parent in the shopping mall, for example, might tell the misbehaving child exactly when and where a later time-out will occur.

Suppose you are the mayor of a suburban town, and you want to institute some new policies to decrease the number of drivers who speed on residential streets. How might you use punishment to decrease the undesirable behavior (speeding)? How might you use reinforcement to increase the desirable behavior (safe driving)? Thinking about the principles of operant conditioning you read about in this section, which approach do you think might be most fruitful?

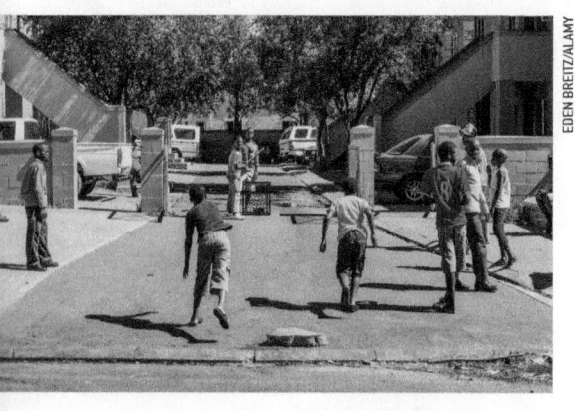

EDEN BREITZ/ALAMY

THE BASIC PRINCIPLES OF OPERANT CONDITIONING

After establishing how reinforcement and punishment produced learned behavior, Skinner and other scientists began to expand the parameters of operant conditioning. This took the form of investigating some phenomena that were well known in classical conditioning (such as discrimination, generalization, and extinction) as well as some practical applications, such as how best to administer reinforcement or how to produce complex learned behaviors in an organism. Let's look at some of these basic principles of operant conditioning.

Discrimination, Generalization, and the Importance of Context

We all take off our clothes at least once a day, but usually not in public. We scream at rock concerts, but not in libraries. We say, "Please pass the gravy," at the dinner table, but not in a classroom. Although these observations may seem like nothing more than common sense, Thorndike was the first to recognize the underlying message: Learning takes place *in contexts*, not in the free range of any plausible situation. As Skinner rephrased it later, most behavior is under *stimulus control*, which develops when a particular response occurs only when an appropriate *discriminative stimulus*, a stimulus that indicates that a response will be reinforced, is present. Skinner (1972) discussed this process in terms of a "three-term contingency": In the presence of a *discriminative stimulus* (classmates drinking coffee together in Starbucks), a *response* (joking comments about a psychology professor's increasing waistline and receding hairline) produces a *reinforcer* (laughter among classmates). The same response in a different context—the professor's office—would most likely produce a very different outcome.

Stimulus control, perhaps not surprisingly, shows both discrimination and generalization effects similar to those we saw with classical conditioning. To demonstrate this, researchers used either a painting by the French impressionist Claude Monet or one of Pablo Picasso's paintings from his cubist period for the discriminative stimulus (Watanabe, Sakamoto, & Wakita, 1995). Participants in the experiment were reinforced only if they responded when the appropriate painting was presented. After training, the participants discriminated appropriately; those trained with the Monet painting responded when other paintings by Monet were presented, and those trained with a Picasso painting reacted when other cubist paintings by Picasso were shown. And as you might expect, Monet-trained participants did not react to Picassos, and Picasso-trained participants did not respond to Monets. What's more, the research participants showed that they could generalize *across* painters as long as they were from the same artistic tradition. Those trained with Monet responded appropriately when shown paintings by Auguste Renoir (another French impressionist), and the Picasso-trained participants responded to artwork by the cubist painter Henri Matisse, despite never having seen those paintings before. If these results don't seem particularly startling to you, it might help to know that the research participants were pigeons that were trained to key-peck to these various works of art. Stimulus control, and its ability to foster stimulus discrimination and stimulus generalization, is effective even if the stimulus has no meaning to the respondent.

Extinction

As in classical conditioning, operant behavior undergoes extinction when the reinforcements stop. Pigeons cease pecking at a key if food is no longer presented following that behavior. You wouldn't put more money into a vending machine if it failed to give you its promised candy bar or soda. Warm smiles that are greeted with scowls and frowns will quickly disappear. On the surface, extinction of operant behavior looks like that of classical conditioning: The response rate drops off fairly rapidly and, if a rest period is provided, spontaneous recovery is typically seen.

However, there is an important difference. As noted, in classical conditioning, the US occurs on every trial, no matter what the organism does. In operant conditioning, the reinforcements occur only when the proper response has been made, and they don't always occur even then. Not every trip into the forest produces nuts for a squirrel, auto salespeople don't sell to everyone who takes a test drive, and researchers run many experiments that do not work out and never get published. Yet these behaviors don't weaken and gradually extinguish. In fact, they typically become stronger and more resilient. Curiously, then, extinction is a bit more complicated in operant conditioning than in classical conditioning because it depends, in part, on how often reinforcement is received. In fact, this principle is an important cornerstone of operant conditioning that we'll examine next.

In research on stimulus control, participants trained with Picasso paintings, such as the one on the top, responded to other paintings by Picasso or even to paintings by other cubists. Participants trained with Monet paintings, such as the one at the bottom, responded to other paintings by Monet or by other French impressionists. An interesting detail: The participants in this study were pigeons.

▲ Figure 7.9

REINFORCEMENT SCHEDULES Different schedules of reinforcement produce different rates of response. These lines represent the number of responses that occur under each type of reinforcement. The black slash marks indicate when reinforcement was administered. Notice that ratio schedules tend to produce higher rates of responding than do interval schedules, as shown by the steeper lines for fixed-ratio and variable-ratio reinforcement.

Schedules of Reinforcement

Skinner was intrigued by the apparent paradox surrounding extinction, and in his autobiography, he described how he began studying it (Skinner, 1979). He was laboriously rolling ground rat meal and water to make food pellets to reinforce the rats in his early experiments. It occurred to him that perhaps he could save time and effort by not giving his rats a pellet for every bar press but instead delivering food on some intermittent schedule. The results of this hunch were dramatic. Not only did the rats continue bar pressing, but they also shifted the rate and pattern of bar pressing depending on the timing and frequency of the presentation of the reinforcers. Unlike in classical conditioning, where the sheer *number* of learning trials was important, in operant conditioning the *pattern* with which reinforcements appeared was crucial.

Skinner explored dozens of what came to be known as *schedules of reinforcement* (Ferster & Skinner, 1957; see **FIGURE 7.9**). The two most important are *interval schedules*, based on the time intervals between reinforcements, and *ratio schedules*, based on the ratio of responses to reinforcements.

Interval Schedules. Under a **fixed-interval schedule (FI)**, *reinforcers are presented at fixed time periods, provided that the appropriate response is made.* For example, on a 2-minute fixed-interval schedule, a response will be reinforced, but only after 2 minutes have expired since the last reinforcement. Rats and pigeons in Skinner boxes produce predictable patterns of behavior under these schedules. They show little responding right after the presentation of the reinforcement, but as the next time interval draws to a close, they show a burst of responding. Many undergraduates behave exactly like this. They do relatively little work until just before the upcoming exam, then engage in a burst of reading and studying.

Under a **variable-interval schedule (VI),** *a behavior is reinforced on the basis of an average time that has expired since the last reinforcement.* For example, on a 2-minute variable-interval schedule, responses will be reinforced every 2 minutes *on average* but not after each 2-minute period. Variable-interval schedules typically produce steady, consistent responding because the time until the next reinforcement is less predictable.

Students cramming for an exam often show the same kind of behavior as pigeons being reinforced under a fixed-interval schedule.

fixed-interval schedule (FI) An operant conditioning principle whereby reinforcers are presented at fixed time periods, provided that the appropriate response is made.

variable-interval schedule (VI) An operant conditioning principle whereby behavior is reinforced on the basis of an average time that has expired since the last reinforcement.

fixed-ratio schedule (FR) An operant conditioning principle whereby reinforcement is delivered after a specific number of responses have been made.

Variable-interval schedules are not encountered that often in real life, although one example might be radio promotional giveaways, such as tickets to rock concerts. The reinforcement—getting the tickets—might average out to once an hour across the span of the broadcasting day, but the presentation of the reinforcement is variable: It might come early in the 10:00 o'clock hour, later in the 11:00 o'clock hour, immediately into the 12:00 o'clock hour, and so on.

Both fixed-interval schedules and variable-interval schedules tend to produce slow, methodical responding because the reinforcements follow a time scale that is independent of how many responses occur. It doesn't matter if a rat on a fixed-interval schedule presses a bar 1 time during a 2-minute period or 100 times: The reinforcing food pellet won't drop out of the shoot until 2 minutes have elapsed, regardless of the number of responses.

Radio station promotions and giveaways often follow a variable-interval schedule of reinforcement.

Ratio Schedules. Under a **fixed-ratio schedule (FR),** *reinforcement is delivered after a specific number of responses have been made.* One schedule might present reinforcement after every fourth response, and a different schedule might present reinforcement after every 20 responses; the special case of presenting reinforcement after each response is called *continuous reinforcement,* and it's what drove Skinner to investigate these schedules in the first place. Notice that, in each example, the ratio of reinforcements to responses, once set, remains fixed.

There are many situations in which people, sometimes unknowingly, find themselves being reinforced on a fixed-ratio schedule: Book clubs often give you a freebie after a set number of regular purchases; pieceworkers get paid after making a fixed number of products; and some credit card companies return to their customers a percentage of the amount charged. When a fixed-ratio schedule is operating, it is possible, in principle, to know exactly when the next reinforcer is due. A laundry pieceworker on a 10-response, fixed-ratio schedule who has just washed and ironed the ninth shirt knows that payment is coming after the next shirt is done.

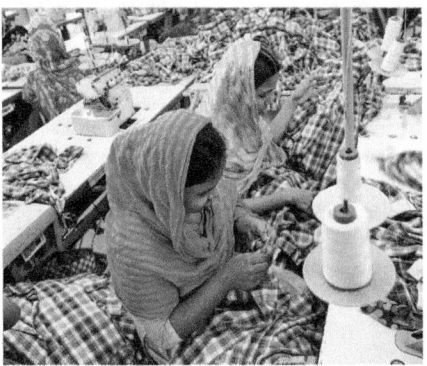

These pieceworkers in a textile factory get paid according to a fixed-ratio schedule: They receive payment after sewing some set number of shirts.

Under a **variable-ratio schedule (VR),** *the delivery of reinforcement is based on a particular average number of responses.* For example, if a laundry worker was following a 10-response variable-ratio schedule instead of a fixed-ratio schedule, she or he would still be paid, on average, for every 10 shirts washed and ironed but not for *each* 10th shirt. Slot machines in a modern casino pay off on variable-ratio schedules that are determined by the random number generator that controls the play of the machines. A casino might advertise that its machines pay off on "every 100 pulls on average," which could be true. However, one player might hit a jackpot after 3 pulls on a slot machine, whereas another player might not hit a jackpot until after 80 pulls. The ratio of responses to reinforcements is variable, which probably helps casinos stay in business.

It should come as no surprise that variable-ratio schedules produce slightly higher rates of responding than fixed-ratio schedules, primarily because the organism never knows when the next reinforcement is going to appear. What's more, the higher the ratio, the higher the response rate tends to be: A 20-response variable-ratio schedule will produce considerably more responding than a 2-response variable-ratio schedule. When schedules of reinforcement provide **intermittent reinforcement,** *whereby only some of the responses made are followed by reinforcement,* they produce behavior that is much more resistant to extinction than does a continuous reinforcement schedule. One way to think about this effect is to recognize that the more irregular and intermittent a schedule is, the more difficult it becomes for an organism to detect when it has actually been placed on extinction.

For example, if you've just put a dollar into a soda machine that, unknown to you, is broken, no soda comes out. Because you're used to getting your sodas on a continuous reinforcement schedule—one dollar produces one soda—this abrupt change in the environment is easy to notice, and you are unlikely to put additional money into the machine: You'd quickly show extinction. However, if you've put your dollar into a slot

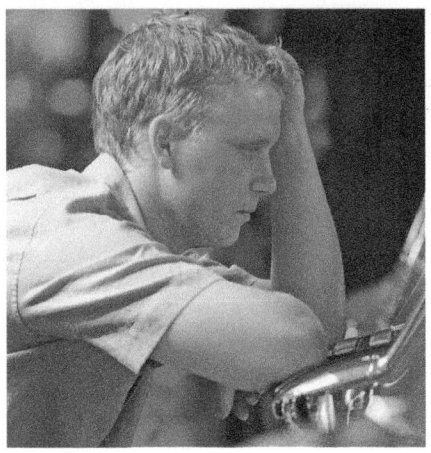

Slot machines in casinos pay out following a variable-ratio schedule. This helps explain why some gamblers feel incredibly lucky, whereas others (like this chap) can't believe they can play a machine for so long without winning a thing.

variable-ratio schedule (VR) An operant conditioning principle whereby the delivery of reinforcement is based on a particular average number of responses.

intermittent reinforcement An operant conditioning principle whereby only some of the responses made are followed by reinforcement.

ISTOCK/GETTY IMAGES

Imagine you own an insurance company, and you want to encourage your salespeople to sell as many policies as possible. You decide to give them bonuses according to the number of policies they sell. How might you set up a system of bonuses using an FR schedule? Using a VR schedule? Which system do you think would encourage your salespeople to work harder, in terms of making more sales?

intermittent reinforcement effect The fact that operant behaviors that are maintained under intermittent reinforcement schedules resist extinction better than those maintained under continuous reinforcement.

shaping Learning that results from the reinforcement of successive steps to a final desired behavior.

machine that, unknown to you, is broken, do you stop after one or two plays? Almost certainly not. If you're a regular slot player, you're used to going for many plays in a row without winning anything, so it's difficult to tell that anything is out of the ordinary. Under conditions of intermittent reinforcement, all organisms will show considerable resistance to extinction and continue for many trials before they stop responding. This effect has been observed even in infants (Weir et al., 2005).

This relationship between intermittent reinforcement schedules and the robustness of the behavior they produce is called the **intermittent reinforcement effect,** *the fact that operant behaviors that are maintained under intermittent reinforcement schedules resist extinction better than those maintained under continuous reinforcement.* In one extreme case, Skinner gradually extended a variable-ratio schedule until he managed to get a pigeon to make an astonishing 10,000 pecks at an illuminated key for one food reinforcer! Behavior maintained under a schedule like this is virtually immune to extinction.

Shaping Through Successive Approximations

Have you ever been to SeaWorld and wondered how the dolphins learn to jump up in the air, twist around, splash back down, do a somersault, and then jump through a hoop, all in one smooth motion? Well, they don't. Wait—of course they do—you've seen them. It's just that they don't learn to do all those complex aquabatics in *one* smooth motion. Rather, elements of their behavior are shaped over time until the final product looks like one smooth motion.

Skinner noted that the trial-by-trial experiments of Pavlov and Thorndike were rather artificial. Behavior rarely occurs in fixed frameworks where a stimulus is presented and then an organism has to engage in some activity or another. We are continuously acting and behaving, and the world around us reacts in response to our actions. Most of our behaviors, then, are the result of **shaping,** *learning that results from the reinforcement of successive steps to a final desired behavior.* The outcomes of one set of behaviors shape the next set of behaviors, whose outcomes shape the next set of behaviors, and so on.

Skinner realized the potential power of shaping one day in 1943 when he was working on a wartime project sponsored by General Mills in a lab on the top floor of a flour mill where pigeons frequently visited (Peterson, 2004). In a lighthearted moment, Skinner and his colleagues decided to see whether they could teach the pigeons to "bowl" by swiping with their beaks at a ball that Skinner had placed in a box along with some pins. Nothing worked until Skinner decided to reinforce any response even remotely related to a swipe, such as merely looking at the ball. "The result amazed us," Skinner recalled. "In a few minutes the ball was caroming off the walls of the box as if the pigeon had been a champion squash player" (Skinner, 1958, p. 974). Skinner applied this insight in his later laboratory research. For example, he noted that if you put a rat in a Skinner box and wait for it to press the bar, you could end up waiting a very long time: Bar pressing just isn't very high in a rat's natural hierarchy of responses. However, it is relatively easy to shape bar pressing. Watch the rat closely: If it turns in the direction of the bar, deliver a food reward. This will reinforce turning toward the bar, making such a movement more likely. Now wait for the rat to take a step toward the bar before delivering food; this will reinforce moving toward the bar. After the rat walks closer to the bar, wait until it touches the bar before presenting the food. Notice that none of these behaviors is the final desired behavior (reliably pressing the bar). Rather, each behavior is a *successive approximation* to the final product, or a behavior that gets incrementally closer to the overall desired behavior. In the dolphin example—and indeed, in many instances of animal training in which relatively simple animals seem to perform astoundingly complex behaviors—you can think through how each smaller behavior is reinforced until the overall sequence of behavior is performed reliably.

B. F. Skinner shaping a dog named Agnes. In the span of 20 minutes, Skinner was able to use reinforcement of successive approximations to shape Agnes's behavior. The result was a pretty neat trick: Agnes wandered in, stood on her hind legs, and jumped.

Superstitious Behavior

Everything we've discussed so far suggests that one of the keys to establishing reliable operant behavior is the correlation between an organism's response and the occurrence of reinforcement. In the case of continuous reinforcement, when every response is followed by the presentation of a reinforcer, there is a one-to-one, or perfect, correlation. In the case of intermittent reinforcement, the correlation is weaker (i.e., not every response is met with the delivery of reinforcement), but it's not zero. As you read in the Methods in Psychology chapter, however, just because two things are correlated (i.e., they tend to occur together in time and space) doesn't imply that there is causality (i.e., the presence of one reliably causes the other to occur).

Skinner (1948) designed an experiment that illustrates this distinction. He put several pigeons in Skinner boxes, set the food dispenser to deliver food every 15 seconds, and left the birds to their own devices. Later he returned and found the birds engaging in odd, idiosyncratic behaviors, such as pecking aimlessly in a corner or turning in circles. He referred to these behaviors as "superstitious" and offered a behaviorist analysis of their occurrence. The pigeons, he argued, were simply repeating behaviors that had been accidentally reinforced. A pigeon that just happened to have pecked randomly in the corner when the food showed up had connected the delivery of food to that behavior. Because this pecking behavior was reinforced by the delivery of food, the pigeon was likely to repeat it. Now pecking in the corner was more likely to occur, and it was more likely to be reinforced 15 seconds later when the food appeared again. For each pigeon, the behavior reinforced would most likely be whatever the pigeon

People believe in many superstitions and engage in all kinds of superstitious behaviors. Players in the National Hockey League do not shave their beards while their team is still alive in the playoffs, and this superstitious behavior was even adopted by a female fan of the Los Angeles Kings during the 2012 NHL playoffs. Skinner thought superstitions resulted from the unintended reinforcement of inconsequential behavior.

happened to be doing when the food was first delivered. Skinner's pigeons acted as though there was a causal relationship between their behaviors and the appearance of food when it was merely an accidental correlation.

Although some researchers questioned Skinner's characterization of these behaviors as superstitious (Staddon & Simmelhag, 1971), later studies have shown that reinforcing adults or children using schedules in which reinforcement is not contingent on their responses can produce seemingly superstitious behavior. It seems that people, like pigeons, behave as though there's a correlation between their responses and reward when in fact the connection is merely accidental (Bloom et al., 2007; Mellon, 2009; Ono, 1987; Wagner & Morris, 1987). Such findings should not be surprising to sports fans. Baseball players who enjoy several home runs on a day when they happened not to have showered are likely to continue that tradition, laboring under the belief that the accidental correlation between poor personal hygiene and a good day at bat is somehow causal. This "stench causes home runs" hypothesis is just one of many examples of human superstitions (Gilbert et al., 2000; Radford & Radford, 1949).

A DEEPER UNDERSTANDING OF OPERANT CONDITIONING

Like classical conditioning, operant conditioning also quickly proved to be a powerful approach to learning. But B. F. Skinner, like Watson before him, was satisfied to observe an organism perform a learned behavior; he didn't look for a deeper explanation of mental processes (Skinner, 1950). In this view, an organism behaved in a certain way in response to stimuli in the environment, not because the animal in question wanted, wished, or willed anything. However, some research on operant conditioning digs deeper into the underlying mechanisms that produce the familiar outcomes of reinforcement. As we did with classical conditioning earlier in this chapter, let's examine three elements that expand our view of operant conditioning: the cognitive, neural, and evolutionary elements of operant conditioning.

The Cognitive Elements of Operant Conditioning

Edward Chace Tolman (1886–1959) was one of the first researchers to question Skinner's strictly behaviorist interpretation of learning and was the strongest early advocate of a cognitive approach to operant learning. Tolman argued that there was more to learning than just knowing the circumstances in the environment (the properties of the stimulus) and being able to observe a particular outcome (the reinforced response). Instead, Tolman proposed that an animal established a means–ends relationship. That is, the conditioning experience produced knowledge or a belief that in this particular situation, a specific reward (the end state) will appear if a specific response (the means to that end) is made.

Tolman's means–ends relationship may remind you of the Rescorla–Wagner model of classical conditioning. Rescorla argued that the CS functions by setting up an expectation about the arrival of a US, and expectations most certainly involve cognitive processes. In both Rescorla's and Tolman's theories, the stimulus does not directly evoke a response; rather, it establishes an internal cognitive state that then produces the behavior. These cognitive theories of learning focus less on the stimulus–response (SR) connection and more on what happens in the organism's mind when faced with the stimulus. During the 1930s and 1940s, Tolman and his students conducted studies that focused on *latent learning* and *cognitive maps,* two phenomena that strongly suggest that simple S–R interpretations of operant learning behavior are inadequate.

Edward Chace Tolman advocated a cognitive approach to operant learning and provided evidence that in maze-learning experiments, rats develop a mental picture of the maze, which he called a cognitive map.

latent learning A process in which something is learned, but it is not manifested as a behavioral change until sometime in the future.

Latent Learning and Cognitive Maps. In **latent learning,** *something is learned, but it is not manifested as a behavioral change until sometime in the future.* Latent learning can easily be established in rats and occurs without any obvious

◄ Figure 7.10
LATENT LEARNING Rats in a control group that never received any reinforcement (green curve) improved at finding their way through the maze over 17 days, but not by much. Rats that received regular reinforcements (blue curve) showed fairly clear learning; their error rate decreased steadily over time. Rats in the latent learning group (orange curve) were treated exactly like the control group rats for the first 10 days and then like the regularly rewarded group for the last 7 days. Their dramatic improvement on day 12 shows that these rats had learned a lot about the maze and the location of the goal box even though they had never received reinforcements. Notice, also, that on the last 7 days, these latent learners actually seem to make fewer errors than their regularly rewarded counterparts.

reinforcement, a finding that posed a direct challenge to the then-dominant behaviorist position that all learning required some form of reinforcement (Tolman & Honzik, 1930a).

Tolman gave three groups of rats access to a complex maze every day for over 2 weeks. The control group never received any reinforcement for navigating the maze. They were simply allowed to run around until they reached the goal box at the end of the maze. In **FIGURE 7.10** you can see that over the 2 weeks of the study, the control group (in green) got a little better at finding their way through the maze, but not by much. A second group of rats received regular reinforcements; when they reached the goal box, they found a small food reward there. Not surprisingly, these rats showed clear learning, as can be seen in blue in Figure 7.10. A third group was treated exactly like the control group for the first 10 days and then rewarded for the last 7 days. This group's behavior (in orange) was quite striking. For the first 10 days, they behaved like the rats in the control group. However, during the final 7 days, they behaved a lot like the rats in the second group, which had been reinforced every day. Clearly, the rats in this third group had learned a lot about the maze and the location of the goal box during those first 10 days even though they had not received any reinforcements for their behavior. In other words, they showed evidence of latent learning.

These results suggested to Tolman that beyond simply learning "start here, end here," his rats had developed a sophisticated mental picture of the maze. Tolman called this a **cognitive map,** *a mental representation of the physical features of the environment.* Tolman thought that the rats had developed a mental picture of the maze, along the lines of "make two lefts, then a right, then a quick left at the corner," and he devised several experiments to test that idea (Tolman & Honzik, 1930b; Tolman, Ritchie, & Kalish, 1946).

Further Support for Cognitive Explanations. One simple experiment provided support for Tolman's theories and wreaked havoc with the noncognitive explanations offered by staunch behaviorists. Tolman trained a group of rats in the maze shown in **FIGURE 7.11a**. As you can see, rats run down a straightaway, take a left, a right, a long right, and then end up in the goal box at the end of the maze. Because we're looking at it from above, we can see that the rat's position at the end of the maze, relative to the starting point, is diagonal to the upper right. Of course, all the rat in the maze sees is the next set of walls and turns until it eventually reaches the goal box. Nonetheless, rats learned to navigate this maze without error or hesitation after about four nights. Clever rats. But they were cleverer than you think.

After the rats had mastered the maze, Tolman changed things around a bit and put them in the maze shown in Figure 7.11b. The goal box was still in the same place relative to the start box. However, many alternative paths now spoked off the main platform, and the main straightaway that the rats had learned to use was blocked.

cognitive map A mental representation of the physical features of the environment.

▶ Figure 7.11

COGNITIVE MAPS (a) Rats trained to run from a start box to a goal box in the maze on the left mastered the task quite readily. When those rats were then placed in the maze on the right (b), in which the main straightaway had been blocked, they did something unusual. Rather than simply backtracking and trying the next closest runway (i.e., one of those labeled 8 or 9 in the figure), which would be predicted by stimulus generalization, the rats typically chose runway 5, which led most directly to where the goal box had been during their training. The rats had formed a cognitive map of their environment and knew where they needed to end up spatially, relative to where they began.

(a) Apparatus used in preliminary training

(b) Apparatus used in test trial

Most behaviorists would predict that the rats in this situation—running down a familiar path only to find it blocked—would show stimulus generalization and pick the next closest path, such as one immediately adjacent to the straightaway. This was not what Tolman observed. When faced with the blocked path, the rats instead ran all the way down the path that led directly to the goal box. The rats had formed a sophisticated cognitive map of their environment and behaved in a way that suggested they were successfully following that map after the conditions had changed. Latent learning and cognitive maps suggest that operant conditioning involves an animal's doing much more than responding to a stimulus. Tolman's experiments strongly suggest that there is a cognitive component, even in rats, to operant learning.

Learning to Trust: For Better or Worse. Cognitive factors also played a key role in an experiment examining learning and brain activity (using fMRI) in people who played a "trust" game with a fictional partner (Delgado, Frank, & Phelps, 2005). On each trial, a participant could either keep a $1 reward or transfer the reward to a partner, who would receive $3. The partner could then either keep the $3 or share half of it with the participant. When playing with a partner who was willing to share the reward, the participant would be better off transferring the money, but when playing with a partner who did not share, the participant would be better off keeping the reward in the first place. Participants in such experiments typically find out who is trustworthy on the basis of trial-and-error learning during the game, transferring more money to partners who reinforce them by sharing.

In the study by Delgado and colleagues, participants were given detailed descriptions of their partners that portrayed the partners as either trustworthy, neutral, or suspect. Even though during the game itself the sharing behavior of the three types of partners did not differ—they each reinforced participants to the same extent through sharing—the participants' cognitions about their partners had powerful effects. Participants transferred more money to the trustworthy partner than to the others, essentially ignoring the trial-by-trial feedback that would ordinarily shape their playing behavior, thus reducing the amount of reward they received. Highlighting the power of the cognitive effect, signals in a part of the brain that ordinarily distinguishes between positive and negative feedback were evident only when participants played with the neutral partner; these feedback signals were absent when participants played with the trustworthy partner and reduced when participants played with the suspect partner.

These kinds of effects might help us to understand otherwise perplexing real-life cases such as that of the con artist Bernard Madoff, who in March 2009 pleaded guilty to swindling numerous investors out of billions of dollars in a highly publicized case that attracted worldwide attention. Madoff had been the chairman of the NASDAQ stock exchange and seemed to his investors an extremely trustworthy figure with whom they could safely invest their money. Those powerful cognitions might have caused investors to miss danger signals that otherwise would have led them to learn about the true nature of Madoff's operation. If so, the result was one of the most expensive failures of learning in modern history.

Bernard Madoff, shown here leaving a court hearing in March 2009, pleaded guilty to fraud after swindling billions of dollars from investors who trusted him.

The Neural Elements of Operant Conditioning

Soon after psychologists came to appreciate the range and variety of things that could function as reinforcers, they began looking for underlying brain mechanisms that might account for these effects. The first hint of how specific brain structures might contribute to the process of reinforcement arose from the discovery of what came to be called *pleasure centers*. James Olds and his associates inserted tiny electrodes into different parts of a rat's brain and allowed the animal to control electric stimulation of its own brain by pressing a bar. They discovered that some brain areas, particularly those in the limbic system (see the Neuroscience and Behavior chapter), produced what appeared to be intensely positive experiences: The rats would press the bar repeatedly to stimulate these structures. The researchers observed that these rats would ignore food, water, and other life-sustaining necessities for hours on end simply to receive stimulation directly in the brain. They then called these parts of the brain *pleasure centers* (Olds, 1956; see **FIGURE 7.12**).

In the years since these early studies, researchers have identified a number of structures and pathways in the brain that deliver rewards through stimulation (Wise, 1989, 2005). The neurons in the *medial forebrain bundle*, a pathway that meanders its way from the midbrain through the *hypothalamus* into the *nucleus accumbens*, are the most susceptible to stimulation that produces pleasure. This is not surprising, because psychologists have identified this bundle of cells as crucial to behaviors that clearly involve pleasure, such as eating, drinking, and engaging in sexual activity. Second, the neurons all along this pathway and especially those in the nucleus accumbens itself

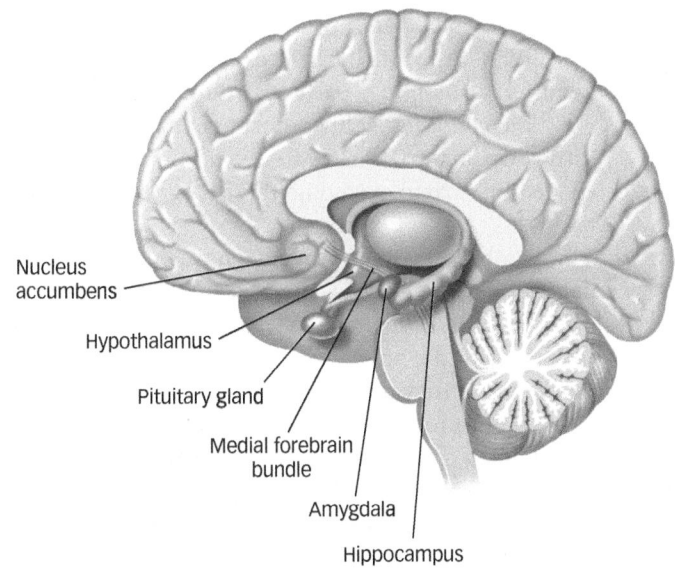

Nucleus accumbens

Hypothalamus

Pituitary gland

Medial forebrain bundle

Amygdala

Hippocampus

◀ Figure 7.12

PLEASURE CENTERS IN THE BRAIN The nucleus accumbens, medial forebrain bundle, and hypothalamus are all major pleasure centers in the brain.

are all *dopaminergic* (i.e., they secrete the neurotransmitter *dopamine*). Remember from the Neuroscience and Behavior chapter that higher levels of dopamine in the brain are usually associated with positive emotions. During recent years, several competing hypotheses about the precise role of dopamine have emerged, including the idea that dopamine is more closely linked with the expectation of reward than with reward itself (Fiorillo, Newsome, & Schultz, 2008; Schultz, 2006, 2007), or that dopamine is more closely associated with wanting or even craving something rather than simply liking it (Berridge, 2007).

Whichever view turns out to be correct, researchers have found good support for a reward center in which dopamine plays a key role. First, as you've just seen, rats will work to stimulate this pathway at the expense of other basic needs (Olds & Fobes, 1981). However, if drugs that block the action of dopamine are administered to the rats, they cease stimulating the pleasure centers (Stellar, Kelley, & Corbett, 1983). Second, drugs such as cocaine, amphetamine, and opiates activate these pathways and centers (Moghaddam & Bunney, 1989), but dopamine-blocking drugs dramatically diminish their reinforcing effects (White & Milner, 1992). Third, fMRI studies show increased activity in the nucleus accumbens in heterosexual men looking at pictures of attractive women (Aharon et al., 2001) and in individuals who believe they are about to receive money (Cooper et al., 2009; Knutson et al., 2001). Finally, rats given primary reinforcers such as food or water, or who are allowed to engage in sexual activity, show increased dopamine secretion in the nucleus accumbens—but only if they are hungry, thirsty, or sexually aroused (Damsma et al., 1992). This last finding is exactly what we might expect given our earlier discussion of the complexities of reinforcement. After all, food tastes a lot better when we are hungry, and sexual activity is more pleasurable when we are aroused. These biological structures underlying rewards and reinforcements probably evolved to ensure that species engaged in activities that helped survival and reproduction. (For more on the relationship between dopamine and Parkinson's, see Hot Science: Dopamine and Reward Learning in Parkinson's Disease.)

The Evolutionary Elements of Operant Conditioning

As you'll recall, classical conditioning has an adaptive value that has been fine-tuned by evolution. Not surprisingly, we can also view operant conditioning from an evolutionary perspective. This viewpoint grew out of a set of curious observations from the early days of conditioning experiments. Several behaviorists who were using simple T mazes such as the one shown in **FIGURE 7.13** to study learning in rats discovered that if a rat found food in one arm of the maze on the first trial of the day, it typically ran down the *other* arm on the very next trial. A staunch behaviorist wouldn't expect the rats to behave this way. After all, the rats in these experiments were hungry, and they had just been reinforced for turning in a particular direction. According to operant conditioning, this should *increase* the likelihood of their turning in that same direction, not reduce it. With additional trials, the rats eventually learned to go to the arm with the food, but they had to learn to overcome this initial tendency to go the wrong way. How can we explain this?

What was puzzling from a behaviorist perspective makes sense when viewed from an evolutionary perspective. Rats are foragers, and like all foraging species, they have evolved a highly adaptive strategy for survival. They move around in their environment, looking for food. If they find it somewhere, they eat it (or store it) and then go look somewhere else for more. If they do not find food, they forage in another part of the environment. So if the rat just found food in the *right* arm of a T maze, the obvious place to look next time is the *left* arm. The rat knows that there isn't any more food in the right arm because it just ate the food it found there! Indeed, foraging animals such as rats have well-developed spatial representations that allow them to search their environment efficiently. If given the opportunity to explore a complex environment

▲ Figure 7.13

A SIMPLE T MAZE When rats find food in the right arm of a typical T maze, on the next trial, they will often run to the left arm of the maze. This contradicts basic principles of operant conditioning: If the behavior of running to the right arm is reinforced, it should be more likely to occur again in the future. However, this behavior is perfectly consistent with a rat's evolutionary preparedness. Like most foraging animals, rats explore their environments in search of food and seldom return to where food has already been found. If the rat already has found food in the right arm of the T maze, it quite sensibly will search the left arm next to see if more food is there.

Dopamine and Reward Learning in Parkinson's Disease

Many of us have relatives or friends who have been affected by Parkinson's disease, which involves movement disorders and loss of neurons that produce dopamine. As you learned in the Neuroscience and Behavior chapter, the drug L-dopa is often used to treat Parkinson's disease because it spurs surviving neurons to produce more dopamine. Dopamine also plays a key role in reward-related learning.

Researchers have focused on the role of dopamine in reward-based learning, especially the *expectation* of reward. A key idea is that dopamine plays an important role in *reward prediction error*, the difference between the actual reward received and the amount of predicted or expected reward. For example, when an animal presses a lever and receives an unexpected food reward, a *positive* prediction error occurs (a better-than-expected outcome), and the animal learns to press the lever again. By contrast, when an animal expects to receive a reward from pressing a lever but does not receive it, a *negative* prediction error occurs (a worse-than-expected outcome), and the animal subsequently will be less likely to press the lever again. Reward prediction error can thus be a kind of "teaching signal" that helps the animal to learn to behave in a way that maximizes reward.

In pioneering studies linking reward prediction error to dopamine, Wolfram Schultz and his colleagues recorded activity in dopamine neurons located in the reward centers of a monkey's brain. They found that those neurons showed increased activity when the monkey received unexpected juice rewards and decreased activity when the monkey did not receive expected juice rewards. This suggests that dopamine neurons play an important role in generating the reward prediction error (Schultz, 2006, 2007; Schultz, Dayan, &

Montague, 1997). Schultz and his colleagues' observations have been backed up by studies using neuroimaging techniques to show that human brain regions involved in reward-related learning also produce reward prediction error signals and that dopamine is involved in generating those signals (O'Doherty et al., 2003; Pessiglione et al., 2006).

So how do these findings relate to people with Parkinson's disease? Several studies report that reward-related learning can be impaired in persons with Parkinson's (Dagher & Robbins, 2009). Other studies provide evidence that when individuals with Parkinson's perform reward-related learning tasks, the reward prediction error signal is disrupted (Schonberg et al., 2009). There is also evidence that Parkinson's treatment drugs can interfere with reward-related learning and the reward prediction error signal (Rutledge et al., 2009).

These results may relate to another intriguing feature of Parkinson's disease: Some individuals develop serious problems with compulsive gambling, shopping, and related impulsive behaviors. Such problems seem to be largely the consequence of Parkinson's drugs that stimulate dopamine receptors (Ahlskog, 2011; Weintraub, Papay, & Siderowf, 2013). Voon et al. (2010) studied individuals who developed gambling and shopping problems only after they had contracted Parkinson's disease and who were receiving treatment with drugs that stimulate dopamine receptors. Those individuals were scanned with fMRI while they performed a reward-learning task in which they chose between stimuli that had a greater or lesser probability of producing a monetary gain or loss. Their performance was compared with that of individuals with Parkinson's but who did not have gambling and shopping problems, either on or off drug

ISTOCK/GETTY IMAGES

treatment. Compared with both of these groups, those who had compulsive gambling and shopping problems showed an increase in the rate of learning from gains. Also important, they showed an increased positive reward prediction error signal in the striatum, a subcortical region in the basal ganglia (see Figure 3.16) that is rich in dopamine receptors and has been linked with the reward prediction error. The researchers suggested that these results likely reflected an effect of the drug treatment on individuals who are susceptible to compulsive behaviors. Their conclusions are supported by other recent neuroimaging studies that have provided evidence of increased dopamine responses to reward cues in Parkinson's patients who develop problems with compulsive gambling as a consequence of drugs that stimulate dopamine receptors (Clark & Dagher, 2014). The care and management of such patients poses major challenges that will require new treatment approaches (Connolly & Fox, 2014).

More studies will be needed to unravel the complex relations among dopamine, reward prediction error, learning, and Parkinson's disease, but the studies to date suggest that such research should have important practical as well as scientific implications.

such as the multi-arm maze shown in **FIGURE 7.14**, rats will systematically go from arm to arm collecting food, rarely returning to an arm they have previously visited (Olton & Samuelson, 1976).

Two of Skinner's former students, Keller Breland and Marian Breland, were among the first researchers to discover that it wasn't just rats in T mazes that presented a problem for behaviorists (Breland & Breland, 1961). The Brelands pointed out that

▶ Figure 7.14

A COMPLEX T MAZE Like many other foraging species, rats placed in a complex T maze such as this one show evidence of their evolutionary preparedness. These rats will systematically travel from arm to arm in search of food, never returning to arms they have already visited.

Start

psychologists and the organisms they study often seemed to "disagree" on what the organisms should be doing. Their argument was simple: When this kind of dispute develops, the animals are always right, and the psychologists had better rethink their theories.

The Brelands, who made a career out of training animals for commercials and movies, often used pigs because pigs are surprisingly good at learning all sorts of tricks. However, they discovered that it was extremely difficult to teach a pig the simple task of dropping coins in a box. Instead of depositing the coins, the pigs persisted in rooting with them as if they were digging them up in soil, tossing them in the air with their snouts and pushing them around. The Brelands tried to train raccoons at the same task, with different but equally dismal results. The raccoons spent their time rubbing the coins between their paws instead of dropping them in the box.

The misbehavior of organisms: Pigs are biologically predisposed to root out their food, just as raccoons are predisposed to wash their food. Trying to train either species to behave differently can prove to be an exercise in futility.

JOHN WILKINSON/CORBIS

MILLARD H. SHARP/SCIENCE SOURCE

Having learned the association between the coins and food, the animals began to treat the coins as stand-ins for food. Pigs are biologically predisposed to root out their food, and raccoons have evolved to clean their food by rubbing it with their paws. That is exactly what each species of animal did with the coins.

The Brelands' work shows that all species, including humans, are biologically predisposed to learn some things more readily than others and to respond to stimuli in ways that are consistent with their evolutionary history (Gallistel, 2000). Such adaptive behaviors, however, evolved over extraordinarily long periods and in particular environmental contexts. If those circumstances change, some of the behavioral mechanisms that support learning can lead an organism astray. Raccoons that associated coins with food failed to follow the simple route to obtaining food by dropping the coins in the box; "nature" took over and they wasted time rubbing the coins together. The point is that, although much of every organism's behavior results from predispositions sharpened by evolutionary mechanisms, these mechanisms sometimes can have ironic consequences.

BY KAZ—LARRY KATZMAN/CARTOONSTOCK.COM

Build to the Outcomes

1. What is the law of effect?

2. What do "positive" and "negative" mean in operant conditioning?

3. Why is reinforcement more constructive than punishment in learning desired behavior?

4. What are primary and secondary reinforcers?

5. How does the concept of delayed reinforcement relate to difficulties with quitting smoking?

6. What does it mean to say that learning takes place in contexts?

7. How is the concept of extinction different in operant conditioning than it is in classical conditioning?

8. How does a radio station use scheduled reinforcements to keep you listening?

9. How do ratio schedules work to keep you spending your money?

10. How can operant conditioning produce complex behaviors?

11. What are cognitive maps? Why are they a challenge to behaviorism?

12. How do specific brain structures contribute to the process of reinforcement?

13. What explains a rat's behavior in a T maze?

Observational Learning: Look at Me

Four-year-old Rodney and his 2-year-old sister Margie had always been told to keep away from the stove, and that's good advice for any child and many an adult. Being a mischievous imp, however, Rodney decided one day to heat up a burner and place his hand over it until the singeing of his flesh led him to recoil, shrieking in pain. Rodney was more scared than hurt, really—and no one hearing this story doubts that he learned something important that day. But little Margie, who stood by, watching these events unfold, *also* learned the same lesson. Rodney's story is a behaviorist's textbook example: The administration of punishment led to a learned change in his behavior. But how can we explain Margie's learning? She received neither punishment nor reinforcement—indeed, she didn't even have direct experience with the wicked appliance—yet it's arguable that she's just as likely to keep her hands away from stoves in the future as Rodney is.

Learning Outcomes

▶ Explain the social, cultural, and evolutionary aspects of observational learning.

▶ Compare evidence of observational learning in animals raised among humans with that in animals raised in the wild.

▶ Explain the neural elements of observational learning.

Observational learning plays an important role in surgical training, as illustrated by the medical students observing the famed German surgeon Vincenz Czerny (beard and white gown) perform stomach surgery in 1907 at a San Francisco hospital.

Margie's is a case of **observational learning,** in which *an organism learns by watching the actions of others.* Observational learning challenges behaviorism's reinforcement-based explanations of classical and operant conditioning, but there is no doubt that this type of learning produces changes in behavior. In all societies, appropriate social behavior is passed on from generation to generation largely through observation (Bandura, 1965). The rituals and behaviors that are a part of our culture are acquired by each new generation, not only through deliberate training of the young but also through young people observing the patterns of behaviors of their elders and each other (Flynn & Whiten, 2008). Tasks such as using chopsticks or operating a TV's remote control are more easily acquired if we watch these activities being carried out before we try them ourselves. Even complex motor tasks, such as performing surgery, are learned in part through extensive observation and imitation of models. And anyone who is about to undergo surgery is grateful for observational learning. Just the thought of a generation of surgeons acquiring their surgical techniques through the trial-and-error methods that Thorndike studied, or the shaping of successive approximations that captivated Skinner, would make any of us very nervous.

OBSERVATIONAL LEARNING IN HUMANS

In a series of studies that have become landmarks in psychology, Albert Bandura and his colleagues investigated the parameters of observational learning (Bandura, Ross, & Ross, 1961; for additional discussion of Bandura's work, see the Social Psychology chapter). The researchers escorted individual preschoolers into a play area, where they found a number of desirable toys that 4-year-olds typically like. An adult *model*—someone whose behavior might be a guide for others—was then led into the room and seated in the opposite corner, where among other toys was a Bobo doll, which is a large, inflatable plastic toy with a weighted bottom that allows it to bounce back upright when knocked down. The adult played quietly for a bit but then started aggressing toward the Bobo doll, knocking it down, jumping on it, hitting it with a toy mallet, kicking it around the room, and yelling "Pow!" and "Kick him!" When the children who observed these actions were later allowed to play with a variety of toys, including a child-size Bobo doll, they were more than twice as likely to interact with it in an aggressive manner as a group of children who hadn't observed the aggressive model.

So what? Kids like to break stuff, and after all, Bobo dolls are made to be punched. Although that's true, as **FIGURE 7.15** shows, the degree of imitation that the children showed was startling. In fact, the adult model purposely used novel behaviors such as hitting the doll with the toy mallet or throwing it up in the air, so that the researchers could distinguish aggressive acts that were clearly the result of observational learning. The children in these studies also showed that they were sensitive to the consequences of the actions they observed. When they saw the adult models being punished for behaving aggressively, the children showed considerably less aggression. When the children observed a model being rewarded and praised for aggressive behavior, they displayed an increase in aggression (Bandura, Ross, & Ross, 1963). The observational learning seen in Bandura's studies has implications for social learning and cultural transmission of behaviors, norms, and values (Bandura, 1977, 1994).

Research with children has shown that observational learning is well suited to seeding behaviors that can spread widely across a culture through a process called a **diffusion chain,** whereby *individuals initially learn a behavior by observing another individual perform that behavior, and then become models from which other individuals learn the behavior* (Flynn, 2008; Flynn & Whiten, 2008). Experiments investigating the operation of diffusion chains in preschool-age children have used a procedure in which a child (B) observes an adult model (A) performing a target act, such as using a

observational learning A condition in which an organism learns by watching the actions of others.

diffusion chain A process in which individuals initially learn a behavior by observing another individual perform that behavior, and then become models from which other individuals learn the behavior.

▲ **Figure 7.15**

BEATING UP BOBO Children who were exposed to an adult model who behaved aggressively toward a Bobo doll were likely to behave aggressively toward it themselves. This behavior occurred in the absence of any direct reinforcement. Observational learning was responsible for producing the children's behaviors.

novel tool to obtain a reward. Then, person B becomes a model for another child, C, who watches B perform the target act, followed by child D observing C perform the target act, and so forth. The evidence to date indicates that children can learn how to use a novel tool by observing an adult model use that tool, and more important, can then become effective models for other children to learn how to use that tool.

Initial studies of diffusion chains showed that behaviors such as novel tool use could be spread accurately across 10 children (Flynn & Whiten, 2008; Horner et al., 2006). More recent work indicates faithful transmission of tool use across a diffusion chain comprising 20 children (Hopper et al., 2010). These findings of transmission across multiple "cultural generations" underscore that observational learning is well suited for transmission through a diffusion chain and thus a potentially powerful means of influencing a culture (Legare & Nielsen, 2015).

Observational learning is important in many domains of everyday life. Sports provide a good example. Coaches in just about all sports rely on observational learning when they demonstrate critical techniques and skills to players, and athletes also have numerous opportunities to observe other athletes perform. Studies of varsity- and recreational-level athletes in both team and individual sports indicate that they all report relying heavily on observational learning to improve their performance of critical skills in their respective sports, with varsity athletes reporting an even greater reliance on observational learning than recreational athletes (Wesch, Law, & Hall, 2007). But can merely observing a skill result in an improvement in performing that skill without actually practicing it? A number of studies have shown that observing someone else perform a motor task, ranging from reaching for a target to pressing a sequence of keys, can produce robust learning in the observer. In fact, observational learning sometimes results in just as much learning as practicing the task itself (Heyes & Foster, 2002; Mattar & Gribble, 2005; Vinter & Perruchet, 2002).

Coaches rely on observational learning when they demonstrate techniques to athletes.

Monkeys can learn to fear snakes through observational learning if they see another monkey reacting with fear to the sight of a snake. But monkeys cannot be trained to fear flowers through observational learning—no matter how many times they watch another monkey who has been conditioned to fear the same flower. How does the principle of biological preparedness account for this finding?

OBSERVATIONAL LEARNING IN ANIMALS

Humans aren't the only creatures capable of learning through observing. A wide variety of species learn by observing. In one study, for example, pigeons watched other pigeons get reinforced for either pecking at the feeder or stepping on a bar. When placed in the box later, the pigeons tended to use whatever technique they had observed other pigeons using earlier (Zentall, Sutton, & Sherburne, 1996).

In an interesting series of studies, researchers showed that laboratory-raised rhesus monkeys that had never seen a snake would develop a fear of snakes simply by observing the fear reactions of other monkeys (Cook & Mineka, 1990; Mineka & Cook, 1988). In fact, the fear reactions of these lab-raised monkeys were so authentic and pronounced that they could be models for still *other* lab-raised monkeys, creating a kind of observational learning "chain." These results also support our earlier discussion of how each species has evolved particular biological predispositions for specific behaviors. Virtually every rhesus monkey raised in the wild has a fear of snakes, which strongly suggests that such a fear is one of this species' predispositions. This research also helps to explain why some phobias that humans suffer from, such as fear of heights (acrophobia) or of enclosed spaces (claustrophobia), are so common, even in people who have never had unpleasant experiences in these contexts (Mineka & Ohman, 2002). The fears may emerge not from specific conditioning experiences but from observing and learning from the reactions of others.

Monkeys and Chimpanzees Can Learn to Use Tools Through Observation

One of the most important questions about observational learning in animals concerns whether monkeys and chimpanzees can learn to use tools by observing tool use in others, which we've already seen young children can accomplish. In one of the first controlled studies to examine this issue, chimpanzees observed a model (the experimenter) use a metal bar shaped like a T to pull items of food toward them (Tomasello et al., 1987). Compared with a group that did not observe any tool use, these chimpanzees showed more learning when later performing the task themselves. However, the researchers noted that the chimpanzees hardly ever used the tool in the exact same way that the model did. So, in a later experiment, they introduced a novel twist (Nagell, Olguin, & Tomasello, 1993). In one condition, a model used a rake in its normal position (with the teeth pointed toward the ground) to capture a food reward—but this method was rather inefficient because the teeth were widely spaced, and the food sometimes slipped between them. In a second condition, the model flipped over the rake, so that the teeth were pointed up and the flat edge of the rake touched the ground—a more effective procedure for capturing the food. Both groups that observed tool use performed better when trying to obtain the food themselves than did a control group that did not observe a model use the tool. However, the chimpanzees who observed the more efficient procedure did not use it any more often than did those who observed the less efficient procedure; the two groups performed identically. By contrast, 2-year-old children exposed to the same conditions used the rake in the exact same way that each of the models did in the two observational learning conditions. The chimpanzees seemed only to be learning that the tool could be used to obtain food, whereas the children learned something specific about how to use the tool.

Chimpanzees Raised with Humans Learn to Imitate Exact Actions

The chimpanzees in these studies had been raised by their mothers in the wild. In a related study, the researchers asked whether chimpanzees who had been raised in environments that also included human contact could learn to imitate the exact actions performed by a model (Tomasello, Savage-Rumbaugh, & Kruger, 1993). The answer was a resounding yes: Chimpanzees raised in a more humanlike environment showed more specific observational learning than did those who had been reared by their mothers and performed similarly to human children. This finding led Tomasello et al. (1993) to put forth what they termed the *enculturation hypothesis*: Being raised in a human culture has a profound effect on the cognitive abilities of chimpanzees, especially their ability to understand the intentions of others when performing tasks such as using tools, which in turn increases their observational learning capacities. Others have criticized this hypothesis (Bering, 2004), noting that there is relatively little evidence in support of it beyond the results of the Tomasello et al. (1993) study.

However, more recent research has found something similar in capuchin monkeys, who are known for their tool use in the wild, such as employing branches or stone hammers to crack open nuts (Boinski, Quatrone, & Swartz, 2000; Fragaszy et al., 2004) or using stones to dig up buried roots (Moura & Lee, 2004). Fredman and Whiten (2008) studied monkeys who had been reared in the wild by their mothers or by human families in Israel as part of a project to train the monkeys to aid quadriplegics. A model demonstrated two ways of using a screwdriver to gain access to a food reward hidden in a box. Some monkeys observed the model poke through a hole in the center of the box, whereas others watched him pry open the lid at the rim of the box (see **FIGURE 7.16**). A control group did not observe any use of the tool. Both mother-reared and human-reared monkeys showed evidence of observational learning compared with those in the control group, but the human-reared monkeys carried out the exact action they had observed more often than did the mother-reared monkeys.

Although this evidence implies that there is a cultural influence on the cognitive processes that support observational learning, the researchers noted that the effects on observational learning could be attributed to any number of influences on the human-reared monkeys, including more experience with tools, more attention to a model's behavior, or as originally suggested by Tomasello et al. (1993), increased sensitivity to the intentions of others. Thus, more work is needed to understand the exact nature of those processes (Bering, 2004; Mesoudi et al., 2015; Tomasello & Call, 2004).

▲ Figure 7.16

OBSERVATIONAL LEARNING Monkeys who had been reared in the wild by their mothers or by human families either (*top*) watched a model poke a screwdriver through a hole in the center of a box to obtain a food reward or (*bottom*) pry open the lid. Both groups showed some evidence of observational learning, but the human-reared monkeys were more likely to carry out the exact action they had watched.

NEURAL ELEMENTS OF OBSERVATIONAL LEARNING

Observational learning involves a neural component as well. As you read in the Neuroscience and Behavior chapter, *mirror neurons* are a type of cell found in the brains of primates (including humans). Mirror neurons fire when an animal performs an action, as when a monkey reaches for a food item. More important, however, mirror neurons also fire when an animal watches someone *else* perform the same specific task (Rizzolatti & Craighero, 2004). Although this "someone else" is usually a fellow member of the same species, some research suggests that mirror neurons in monkeys also fire when they observe humans performing an action (Fogassi et al., 2005). For example, monkeys' mirror neurons fired when they observed humans grasping for a piece of food, either to eat it or to place it in a container.

Mirror neurons, then, may play a critical role in the imitation of behavior as well as the prediction of future behavior (Rizzolatti, 2004). Mirror neurons are thought to be located in specific subregions in the frontal and parietal lobes, and there is evidence that individual subregions respond most strongly to observing certain kinds of actions (see **FIGURE 7.17**). If appropriate neurons fire when an animal sees another animal performing an action, it could indicate an awareness of intentionality, or that the animal is anticipating a likely course of future actions. Although the exact functions of mirror neurons continue to be debated (Hickok, 2009), both of these elements—rote imitation of well-understood behaviors and an awareness of how behavior is likely to unfold—contribute to observational learning.

Studies of observational learning in healthy adults have shown that watching someone else perform a task engages some of the same brain regions that are activated when people actually perform the task themselves. Do you consider yourself a good dancer? Have you ever watched someone who is a good dancer—a friend or maybe a

▼ Figure 7.17

MIRROR NEURON SYSTEM Regions in the frontal lobe (area 44) and parietal lobe (area 40) are thought to be part of the mirror neuron system in humans.

Area 40

Area 44

ADAM TAYLOR/ABC VIA GETTY IMAGES

Observing skilled dancers, such as this energetic pair in *Dancing with the Stars*, engages many of the same brain regions as does actual dance practice, and can produce significant learning.

celebrity on *Dancing with the Stars*—in the hopes of improving your own dance-floor moves? In one fMRI study, participants performed two tasks for several days prior to scanning: practicing dance sequences to unfamiliar techno-dance songs, and watching music videos of other dance sequences accompanied by unfamiliar techno-dance songs (Cross et al., 2009). The participants were then scanned while viewing videos of sequences that they had previously danced or watched, as well as videos of sequences they had not danced or watched (untrained sequences).

Analysis of the fMRI data revealed that in comparison with the untrained sequences, viewing the previously danced or watched sequences recruited largely similar brain networks, including regions considered part of the mirror neuron system, as well as a couple of brain regions that showed more activity for previously danced than watched videos. The results of a surprise dancing test given to participants after the conclusion of scanning showed that performance was better on sequences previously watched than on the untrained sequences, demonstrating significant observational learning, but was best of all on the previously danced sequences (Cross et al., 2009). So although watching *Dancing with the Stars* might indeed improve your dancing skills, practicing on the dance floor should help even more.

Related evidence indicates that observational learning of some motor skills relies on the motor cortex, which is known to be critical for motor learning. For example, when participants watch another individual engage in a task that involves making a complex reaching movement, significant observational learning occurs (Mattar & Gribble, 2005). To examine whether the observational learning depends on the motor cortex, researchers applied transcranial magnetic stimulation (TMS) to the motor cortex just after participants observed performance of the reaching movement. (As you learned in the Neuroscience and Behavior chapter, TMS results in a temporary disruption in the function of the brain region to which it is applied.) In a striking finding, applying TMS to the motor cortex greatly reduced the amount of observational learning, whereas applying TMS to a control region outside the motor cortex had no effect on observational learning (Brown, Wilson, & Gribble, 2009).

These findings indicate that some kinds of observational learning are grounded in brain regions that are essential for action. When one organism patterns its actions on another organism's behaviors, learning is speeded up, and potentially dangerous errors (think of Margie, who won't burn her hand on the stove) are prevented.

Build to the Outcomes

1. What is observational learning?

2. Why might a younger sibling appear to learn faster than a firstborn?

3. What did the Bobo doll experiment show about children and aggressive behavior?

4. What is a diffusion chain?

5. What are the cognitive differences between chimpanzees raised among humans and those raised in the wild?

6. What do mirror neurons do?

Implicit Learning: Under the Radar

Learning Outcomes

▶ Explain why language studies led to studies of implicit learning.

▶ Outline the number of ways that implicit and explicit learning differ.

It's safe to assume that people are sensitive to the patterns of events that occur in the world around them. Most people don't stumble through life, thoroughly unaware of what's going on. Okay, maybe your roommate does. But people usually are attuned to linguistic, social, emotional, or sensorimotor events in the world around them—so much so that they gradually build up internal representations of those patterns that they acquired without explicit awareness. This process is often called **implicit learning,** or *learning that takes place largely independent of awareness of both the process and the products of information acquisition.* Because it occurs without our awareness, implicit learning is knowledge that sneaks in "under the radar."

Habituation, which we discussed at the outset of this chapter, is a very simple kind of implicit learning in which repeated exposure to a stimulus results in a reduced response. Habituation occurs even in a simple organism such as *Aplysia*, which lacks the brain structures necessary for explicit learning, such as the hippocampus (Eichenbaum, 2008; Squire & Kandel, 1999). In contrast, some forms of learning start out explicitly but become more implicit over time. When you first learned to drive a car, for example, you probably devoted a lot of attention to the many movements and sequences that you needed to carry out simultaneously. ("Step lightly on the accelerator while you push the turn indicator, and look in the rearview mirror while you turn the steering wheel.") That complex interplay of motions is now probably quite effortless and automatic for you. Explicit learning has become implicit over time. These distinctions in learning might remind you of similar distinctions in memory, and for good reason. In the Memory chapter, you read about the differences between *implicit* and *explicit* memories. Do implicit and explicit learning mirror implicit and explicit memory? It's not that simple, but it is true that learning and memory are inextricably linked. Learning produces memories, and conversely, the existence of memories implies that knowledge was acquired, that experience was registered and recorded in the brain, or that learning has taken place.

Implicit learning has some characteristics that distinguish it from explicit learning. For example, when asked to carry out implicit tasks, people differ relatively little from each other, but on explicit tasks (such as conscious problem solving), they show large individual-to-individual differences (Reber, Walkenfeld, & Hernstadt, 1991).

implicit learning Learning that takes place largely independent of awareness of both the process and the products of information acquisition.

Ten years ago, no one knew how to type using their thumbs; now just about all teenagers do it automatically.

COGNITIVE APPROACHES TO IMPLICIT LEARNING

Psychologists became interested in implicit learning when researchers began to investigate how children learn language and social conduct (Reber, 1967). Most children, by the time they are 6 or 7 years old, are linguistically and socially fairly sophisticated. Yet most children reach this state with very little explicit awareness that they have learned something, and with equally little awareness of what it was they have actually learned. For example, although children are often given explicit rules of social conduct ("Don't chew with your mouth open"), they learn how to behave in a civilized way through experience. They're probably not aware of when or how they learned a particular course of action and may not even be able to state the general principle underlying their behavior. Yet most kids have learned not to eat with their feet, to listen when they are spoken to, and not to kick the dog.

What Research in the Lab Shows

To investigate implicit learning in the laboratory, in early studies, researchers showed participants 15- or 20-letter strings and asked them to memorize them. The letter strings, which at first glance look like nonsense syllables, were actually formed using a complex set of rules called an *artificial grammar* (see **FIGURE 7.18**). Participants were not told anything about the rules, but with experience, they gradually developed a vague, intuitive sense of the "correctness" of particular letter groupings. Once these letter groups became familiar to the participants, they processed them more rapidly and efficiently than the "incorrect" letter groupings (Reber, 1967, 1996).

Take a look at the letter strings shown in Figure 7.18. Those on the left are correct and follow the rules of the artificial grammar; those on the right all violate the rules. The differences are pretty subtle, and if you haven't been through the learning phase of the experiment, both sets look a lot alike. In fact, each nongrammatical string only

▼ Figure 7.18

ARTIFICIAL GRAMMAR AND IMPLICIT LEARNING These are examples of letter strings formed by an artificial grammar. Research participants are exposed to the rules of the grammar and are later tested on new letter strings. Participants show reliable accuracy at distinguishing the valid, grammatical strings from the invalid, nongrammatical strings—even though they usually can't explicitly state the rule they are following when making such judgments. Using an artificial grammar is one way of studying implicit learning (Reber, 1996).

Grammatical Strings	Nongrammatical Strings
VXJJ	VXTJJ
XXVT	XVTVVJ
VJTVXJ	VJTTVTV
VJTVTV	VJTXXVJ
XXXXVX	XXXVTJJ

has a single letter violation. Research participants were asked to classify new letter strings according to whether they follow the rules of the grammar. People turn out to be quite good at this task (usually they get 60–70% correct), but they are unable to provide much in the way of explicit awareness of the rules and regularities that they are using. The experience is similar to coming across a sentence with a grammatical error. You are immediately aware that something is wrong, and you can certainly make the sentence grammatical, but unless you are a trained linguist, you'll probably find it difficult to articulate which rules of English grammar were violated or which rules you used to repair the sentence.

Other studies of implicit learning have used a *serial reaction time* task (Nissen & Bullemer, 1987). Here, research participants are presented with five small boxes on a computer screen. Each box lights up briefly, and when it does, the participant is asked to press the button that is just underneath that box as quickly as possible. Like the artificial grammar task, the sequence of lights appears to be random, but in fact it follows a pattern. Research participants eventually get faster with practice as they learn to anticipate which box is most likely to light up next. But if asked, they are generally unaware that there is a pattern to the lights.

Implicit learning has some characteristics that distinguish it from explicit learning. For example, when asked to carry out implicit tasks, people differ relatively little from one another, but on explicit tasks (such as conscious problem solving), they show large individual-to-individual differences (Reber, Walkenfeld, & Hernstadt, 1991). Implicit learning also seems to be unrelated to IQ: People with high scores on standard intelligence tests are no better at implicit learning tasks, on average, than those whose scores are more modest (Reber & Allen, 2000). Perhaps even more striking, recent evidence indicates that at least one form of implicit learning is *enhanced* in autistic adults whose IQs are matched to those of nonautistic adults (see A World of Difference: Implicit Learning in Autism Spectrum Disorder). Implicit learning changes little across the life span. Researchers discovered well-developed implicit learning of complex, rule-governed auditory patterns in 8-month-old infants (Saffran, Aslin, & Newport, 1996). Infants heard streams of speech that contained experimenter-defined nonsense words. For example, the infants might hear a sequence such as "bidakupadotigolabubidaku," which contains the nonsense word *bida*. The infants weren't given any explicit clues as to which sounds were "words" and which were not, but after several repetitions, the infants showed signs that they had learned the novel words. Infants tend to prefer novel information, and they spent more time listening to novel nonsense words that had not been presented earlier than to the nonsense words such as *bida* that had been presented. It was remarkable that the infants in this study were as good at learning these sequences as college students. At the other end of the life span, researchers have found that implicit learning abilities extend well into old age and that they decline more slowly than explicit learning abilities (Howard & Howard, 1997).

Implicit Learning Is Resistant to Some Disorders That Affect Explicit Learning

Implicit learning is remarkably resistant to various disorders that are known to affect explicit learning. A group of patients suffering from various psychoses were so severely impaired that they could not solve simple problems that college students had little difficulty with. Yet those patients were able to solve an artificial grammar learning task about as well as college students (Abrams & Reber, 1988). Other studies have found that profoundly amnesic patients not only show normal implicit memories but also display virtually normal implicit learning of artificial grammar (Knowlton, Ramus, & Squire, 1992). In fact, they made accurate judgments about novel letter strings even though they had essentially no explicit memory of having been in the learning phase of the experiment! In contrast, several studies have shown that dyslexic children who fail to acquire reading skills despite normal intelligence and good educational opportunities

Implicit learning, which is involved in acquiring and retaining the skills needed to ride a bicycle, tends to be less affected by age than explicit learning.

CAIAIMAGE/ROBERT DALY/GETTY IMAGES

MIKE KEMP/GETTY IMAGES

Implicit Learning in Autism Spectrum Disorder

As pointed out elsewhere in this chapter, implicit learning generally doesn't differ much among individuals. But recent research has uncovered a striking exception. In the Psychological Disorders chapter, you will become acquainted with a condition known as Autism Spectrum Disorder (ASD).

People with ASD have communication problems and engage in repetitive and restricted behaviors. But they also have some intriguing strengths, such as normal or even superior visuo-spatial abilities relative to impaired verbal abilities (Caron et al., 2006). This pattern is clearest in situations where the task is to focus on parts or local details of a visual display, as opposed to the "big picture" of how all the parts fit together (Happé & Frith, 2006; Rondan & Deruelle, 2007). Roser and colleagues (2015) recently sought to test this in an implicit learning experiment. Participants viewed a nine-box grid containing visual shapes in some of the boxes, as in the figure above. Unknown to the participants, the grid contained pairs of visual shapes that always appeared in a particular spatial relationship to one another: shapes 1 and 2 always side by side; shapes 3 and 4 always diagonally apart; and shape 5 always above shape 6 (see top row). The target shapes could appear in different boxes in different displays, but they always appeared in the same spatial relationship to one another (see bottom row). During the learning phase of the experiment, participants were shown hundreds of grids containing different combinations of these shapes and were instructed simply to look at the shapes in the grids, which appeared for about 3 seconds each.

After viewing the grids, participants were asked a series of questions designed to probe their *explicit* awareness of the spatial relationships among the shapes they had seen:

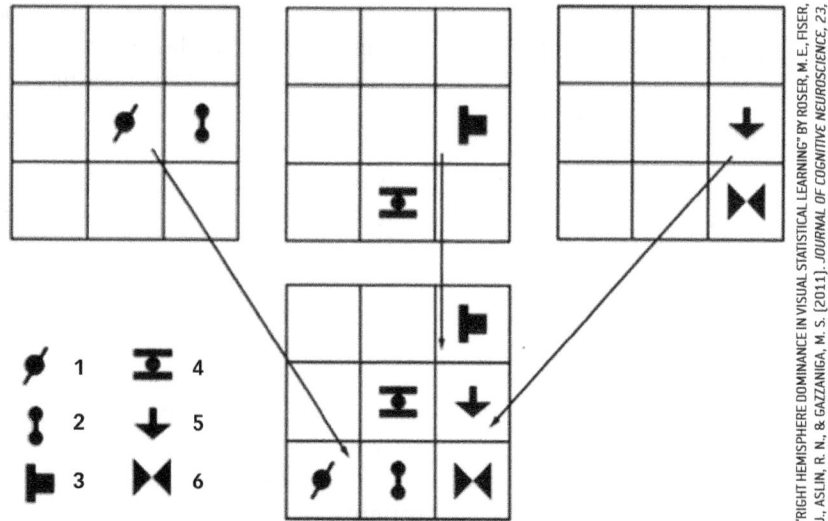

"RIGHT HEMISPHERE DOMINANCE IN VISUAL STATISTICAL LEARNING" BY ROSER, M. E., FISER, J., ASLIN, R. N., & GAZZANIGA, M. S. (2011). *JOURNAL OF COGNITIVE NEUROSCIENCE*, 23, 1091. ©2011, BY THE MIT PRESS. HTTP://WWW.MITPRESSJOURNALS.ORG/DOI/ABS/10.1162/JOCN.2010.21.508#.VZDMI9DLR28. REPRINTED BY PERMISSION OF MIT PRESS JOURNALS.

1. Can you tell me anything about the things you have just seen?

2. Did you notice anything about the arrangement of the shapes in the grid?

3. Did you notice any regularity in the arrangement of the shapes?

4. Did you notice any shapes that were associated in any way with any other shapes?

5. Did you notice that shapes always appeared in pairs in the same spatial arrangement?

Almost all of the ASD and control participants said "no" to all five questions; only a couple were aware that some shapes appeared consistently with others, and none were aware of the exact spatial relationships in any shape pairs.

To test whether participants showed *implicit* learning of the spatial relationships within target pairs, the experimenters gave a test consisting of grids that contained pairs of objects, some in the same spatial relationship as during the learning phase, and others in a different spatial relationship. On this test, all participants showed evidence of implicit learning, that is, they chose the shapes depicted in the correct spatial relationships significantly more often than would be expected on the basis of chance. In a striking finding, adults with ASD performed at a significantly higher level than adults without ASD, whereas 13-year-old children with ASD performed at about the same level as 13-year-old children without ASD.

Roser and colleagues (2015) suggest that adults with ASD outperformed adults without ASD because when they viewed the grids during the learning phase of the experiment, they naturally focused more on the local relationships between individual pairs of objects, rather than taking in the entire display; thus, they implicitly learned more about the recurring spatial relationships of the object pairs. The authors believe that the ASD children have this same tendency but did not show superior implicit learning, because this tendency is not yet as fully developed in them as in the ASD adults. An intriguing question for future research concerns whether spared or enhanced capacities for implicit learning could be exploited to help individuals with ASD in everyday life.

exhibit deficits in implicit learning of artificial grammars (Pavlidou, Williams, & Kelly, 2009) and motor and spatial sequences on the serial reaction time task (Bennett et al., 2008; Orban, Lungu, & Doyon, 2008; Stoodley et al., 2008). These findings suggest that problems with implicit learning play an important role in developmental dyslexia and need to be taken into account in the development of remedial programs (Stoodley et al., 2008).

IMPLICIT AND EXPLICIT LEARNING USE DISTINCT NEURAL PATHWAYS

The fact that individuals suffering amnesia show intact implicit learning strongly suggests that the brain structures that underlie implicit learning are distinct from those that underlie explicit learning. As we learned in the Memory chapter, amnesic individuals are characterized by lesions to the hippocampus and nearby structures in the medial temporal lobe; thus, researchers have concluded that these regions are not necessary for implicit learning (Bayley, Frascino, & Squire, 2005). What's more, it appears that distinct regions of the brain may be activated depending on how people approach a task (Reber, 2013).

For example, in one study, participants saw a series of dot patterns, each of which looked like an array of stars in the night sky (Reber et al., 2003). Actually, all the stimuli were constructed to conform to an underlying prototypical dot pattern. The dots, however, varied so much that it was virtually impossible for a viewer to guess that they all had this common structure. Before the experiment began, half of the participants were told about the existence of the prototype; in other words, they were given instructions that encouraged explicit processing. The others were given standard implicit learning instructions: They were told nothing other than to attend to the dot patterns.

The participants were then scanned as they made decisions about new dot patterns, attempting to categorize them according to whether or not they conformed to the prototype. Interestingly, both groups performed equally well on this task, correctly classifying about 65% of the new dot patterns. However, the brain scans revealed that the two groups made these decisions using very different parts of their brains (see **FIGURE 7.19**). Participants who were given the explicit instructions showed *increased* brain activity in the prefrontal cortex, parietal cortex, hippocampus, and a variety of other areas known to be associated with the processing of explicit memories. Those given the implicit instructions showed *decreased* brain activation primarily in the occipital region, which is involved in visual processing. This finding suggests that participants recruited distinct brain structures in different ways, depending on whether they were approaching the task using explicit or implicit learning.

▶ Figure 7.19

IMPLICIT AND EXPLICIT LEARNING ACTIVATE DIFFERENT BRAIN AREAS Research participants were scanned with fMRI while engaged in either implicit or explicit learning about the categorization of dot patterns. The occipital region (in blue) showed decreased brain activity after implicit learning. The areas in yellow, orange, and red showed increased brain activity during explicit learning, including the left temporal lobe (*far left*), the right frontal lobe (*second from left and second from right*), and the parietal lobe (*second from right and far right*; Reber et al., 2003).

© REBER, P. J., GITELMAN, D. R., PARRISH, T. B., & MESULAM, M. M. (2003). DISSOCIATING EXPLICIT AND IMPLICIT CATEGORY KNOWLEDGE WITH fMRI. *JOURNAL OF COGNITIVE NEUROSCIENCE, 15,* 574–583. PERMISSION CONVEYED THROUGH COPYRIGHT CLEARANCE CENTER, INC.

Other studies have begun to pinpoint the brain regions that are involved in two of the most commonly tested implicit learning tasks: artificial grammar learning and sequence learning on the serial reaction time task. Several fMRI studies have shown that Broca's area—which, as you learned in the Neuroscience and Behavior chapter, plays a key role in language production—is turned on during artificial grammar learning (Forkstam et al., 2006; Petersson, Forkstam, & Ingvar, 2004). Furthermore, activating Broca's area by applying electrical stimulation to the overlying scalp enhances implicit learning of artificial grammar, most likely by facilitating acquisition of grammatical rules (De Vries et al., 2010). In contrast, the motor cortex appears critical for sequence learning on the serial reaction time task. When the motor cortex was temporarily disabled by the application of a recently developed type of TMS that lasts for a long time (so that participants can perform the task without having TMS constantly applied while they are doing so), sequence learning was abolished (Wilkinson et al., 2010).

Build to the Outcomes

1. What is the difference between implicit and explicit learning?

2. How are learning and memory linked?

3. How can you learn something without being aware of it?

4. Why are tasks learned implicitly difficult to explain to others?

5. What technology shows that implicit and explicit learning are associated with separate structures of the brain?

Learning in the Classroom

In this chapter we've considered several different types of learning from behavioral, cognitive, evolutionary, and neural perspectives. Yet it may seem strange to you that we haven't discussed the kind of learning to which you are currently devoting much of your life: learning in educational settings such as the classroom. Way back in the first chapter of this book (Psychology: Evolution of a Science), we reviewed some techniques that we think are useful for studying the material in this course and others (see The Real World: Improving Study Skills, pp. 8–9). But we didn't say much about the actual research that supports these suggestions. During the past several years, psychologists have published a great deal of work specifically focused on enhancing learning in educational settings. Let's consider what some of this research says about learning techniques, and then turn to the equally important topic of exerting control over learning processes.

Learning Outcomes

▶ Explain why distributed practice and practice testing are effective study techniques.

▶ Describe how judgments of learning (JOLs) impact learning.

TECHNIQUES FOR LEARNING

Students use a wide variety of study techniques in attempts to improve their learning. Popular techniques—ones that you might use yourself—include highlighting and underlining, rereading, summarizing, and visual imagery mnemonics (Annis & Annis, 1982; Wade, Trathen, & Schraw, 1990). How effective are these and other techniques? A team of psychologists who specialize in learning published a comprehensive analysis of research concerning 10 learning techniques that students use (Dunlosky et al., 2013). They considered the usefulness of each technique across four main variables: learning conditions (e.g., how often and in what context the technique is used),

TABLE 7.2

Effectiveness of Study Techniques

High Effectiveness	Moderate Effectiveness	Low Effectiveness
Practice testing	Elaborative interrogation	Summarization
Distributed practice	Self-explanation Interleaved practice	Highlighting/Underlining Keyword mnemonic
		Imagery for text
		Rereading

materials to be learned (e.g., texts, math problems, concepts), student characteristics (e.g., age and ability level), and outcome measures (e.g., rote retention, comprehension, problem solving). On the basis of the picture that emerged across these four variables, Dunlosky and colleagues evaluated the overall usefulness of each technique and classified it as high, moderate, or low utility (**TABLE 7.2**).

Despite their popularity, highlighting, rereading, summarizing, and visual imagery mnemonics (which encompasses keyword mnemonic and imagery for the text) all received a low utility assessment. That doesn't mean that these techniques have no value whatsoever for improving learning, but it does indicate that each one has significant limitations and that students could better spend their time using other approaches—a reason that none of these techniques appeared in the Improving Study Skills box. The Improving Study Skills box did review strategies roughly corresponding to two of the techniques in Table 7.2 that received a moderate utility assessment—elaboration interrogation and self-explanation. We also discussed some material related to these techniques in the Memory chapter (pp. 217–220). Although the Improving Study Skills box also highlighted strategies that underlie distributed practice, interleaved practice, and practice testing, let's take a deeper look at them now (see Other Voices: Learning at Jiffy Lube University).

Distributed Practice

Cramming for exams (neglecting to study for an extended period of time and then studying intensively just before an exam; Vacha & McBride, 1993) is a common occurrence in educational life. Surveys of undergraduates across a range of colleges and universities indicate that anywhere from about 25% to as many as 50% of students report relying on cramming (McIntyre & Munson, 2008). Although cramming is better than not studying at all, when students cram for an exam, they repeatedly study the information to be learned with little or no time between repetitions, a procedure known as *massed practice*. Such students are thus denying themselves the benefits of *distributed practice*, which involves spreading out study activities so that more time intervenes between repetitions of the information to be learned. (Furthermore, students who rely on cramming are also inviting some of the health and performance problems associated with procrastination that we will address in the Stress and Health chapter).

The benefits of distributed practice relative to massed practice have been known for a long time; in fact, Ebbinghaus (1885/1964) first reported them in his classic studies concerning retention of nonsense syllables (see the Memory chapter). What's most impressive is just how widespread the benefits of distributed practice are: They have been observed for numerous different kinds of materials, including foreign vocabulary, definitions, and face–name pairs, and have been demonstrated not only in undergraduates but also in children, older adults, and individuals with memory

Learning at Jiffy Lube University

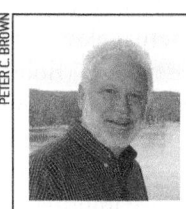

PETER C. BROWN

Peter C. Brown is a writer in St. Paul, Minnesota. **Henry L. Roediger III** and **Mark A. McDaniel** are both professors of psychology at Washington University in St. Louis.

The study techniques we reviewed in this chapter on learning in the classroom can help to improve academic performance. But these techniques also have broader applications outside the classroom, in situations where people need to acquire new knowledge and skills. One of the most important everyday applications of learning techniques involves training to perform a job. In an excellent 2014 book called *Make It Stick: The Science of Successful Learning*, which elaborates on several of the key techniques and ideas we have discussed in this section, the writer Peter C. Brown and the cognitive psychologists Henry L. Roediger III and Mark A. McDaniel tell the story of Jiffy Lube University. This is an educational program where the well-known service-garage business has incorporated practice testing, distributed practice, and other learning techniques to aid the training of employees:

If you don't expect innovations in training to spring from your local service garage, Jiffy Lube may surprise you. An integrated suite of educational course under the felicitous name Jiffy Lube University is helping the company's franchises win customers, reduce employee turnover, broaden their service offerings, and boost sales.

Jiffy Lube is a network of more than two thousand service centers in the United States and Canada that provide oil changes, tire rotation, and other automotive services. Although the company is a subsidiary of Shell Oil Company, every outlet is owned and operated by an independent franchisee, who hires employees to serve customers.

The rapid-oil-change business, like most others, has had to adjust to changes in the marketplace and advances in technology. Synthetic lubricants have made oil changes less frequent, and because cars have become more complicated, garage employees need higher levels of training to understand diagnostic codes and provide appropriate services.

No employee may work on a customer's car until he or she has been certified as proficient. For this, they enter Jiffy Lube University, a Web-based learning platform. Certification starts with interactive e-learning, with frequent quizzing and feedback to learn what a particular job entails and how it's to be performed. When employees score 80 percent or better on an exam, they are eligible to begin training on the job, practicing new skills by following a written guide that breaks each service activity into its component steps. The steps may number as many as thirty and are performed as part of a team, often involving call and response (for example, between a technician working from the top side of an engine and another underneath). A supervisor coaches the employee and rates his or her performance on each step. When the technician demonstrates mastery, certification is recorded in his or her permanent file, signed by the supervisor. Technicians must recertify every two years to keep their mastery up to snuff and adapt to operational and technical changes. Higher-level jobs for advanced services

like brake repair or running engine diagnostics are trained in the same manner.

The e-learning and on-the-job training are active learning strategies that incorporate various forms of quizzing, feedback, and spaced and interleaved practice. All progress is displayed by computer on a virtual "dashboard" that provides an individualized learning plan, enabling an employee to track his or her performance, focus on skills that need to be raised, and monitor his or her progress against the company's completion schedule. Jiffy Lube employees are typically eighteen to twenty-five years old and filing for their first jobs. As a technician is certified in one job, he or she begins training in another, until he or she has trained in all store positions, including management.

Ken Barber, Jiffy Lube International's manager of learning and development, says training has to be engaging in order to hold employees' attention. At the time we spoke, Barber was putting the finishing touches on a computer-based simulation game for company managers called "A Day in the Life of a Store Manager." The service center manager is confronted with various challenges and is required to select among a range of possible strategies for resolving them. The manager's choices determine how the game unfolds, providing feedback and the opportunity to strive for better outcomes, sharpening decision-making skill.

In the six years since Jiffy Lube University was launched, it has received many accolades from the training profession and earned accreditation by the American Council on Education. Employees who progress through training in all job certifications can enroll at a postsecondary institution with seven hours of college credit under their belts. Since the program's beginning, employee turnover has dropped and customer satisfaction has increased.

"For most employees of a Jiffy Lube franchisee, this is a way into the workforce, and the training curriculum helps them to grow and expand their knowledge," Barber says. "It helps them find a path to success."

From the results thus far, Jiffy Lube University appears to be a big success. It is notable that in addition to incorporating learning techniques that we've described in this chapter, Jiffy Lube University combines e-learning based on a Web platform with actual on-the-job training. The use of e-learning, also referred to as online learning, has expanded rapidly in recent years, and debates about its effectiveness have been spirited (Brooks, 2012; Koller, 2011). Jiffy Lube's successful combination of e-learning and live learning fits with earlier evidence indicating that combining these two formats may be especially effective (Means et al., 2010). And Jiffy Lube isn't the only company to make use of effective learning techniques. Brown, Roediger, and McDaniel also summarize successful training programs developed by Farmers Insurance, Andersen Window and Doors, and other companies. So after you complete your studies and enter the workforce, don't be surprised if you find yourself applying practice testing, distributed practice, and related study techniques and principles that promote effective learning.

Peter C. Brown, Henry L. Roediger III, and Mark A. McDaniel, *Make It Stick: The Science of Successful Learning* (Cambridge, MA: Harvard University Press), 245–246.

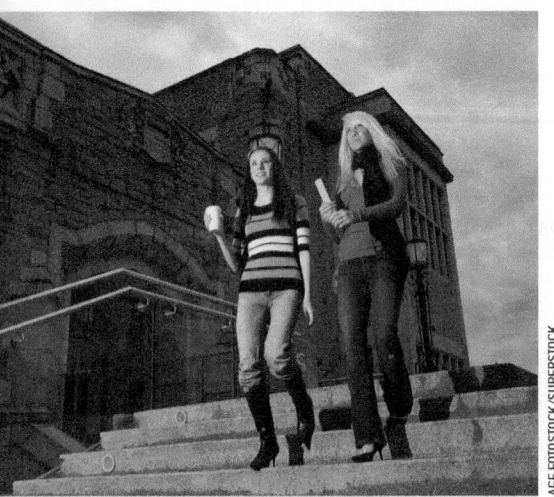

Studying well in advance of an exam, so that you can take breaks and distribute study time, will generally produce a better outcome than cramming at the last minute.

problems due to brain damage (Dunlosky et al., 2013). A review of 254 separate studies involving more than 14,000 participants concluded that on average, participants retained 47% of studied information after distributed practice compared with 37% after massed practice (Cepeda et al., 2006). Several recent studies have also shown that distributed practice can improve long-term retention of actual classroom learning in student populations, including eighth-graders and college students (Rohrer, 2015).

Despite all the evidence indicating that distributed practice is an effective learning strategy, we still don't fully understand why that is so. One promising idea is that when we engage in massed practice, retrieving recently studied information is relatively easy, whereas during distributed practice, it is more difficult to retrieve information that we studied less recently. More difficult retrievals benefit subsequent learning more than easy retrievals, in line with the idea of "desirable difficulties" (Bjork & Bjork, 2011), introduced in the Improving Study Skills box. Whatever the explanation for the effects of distributed practice, there is no denying its benefits for students.

Interleaved Practice

Researchers have also discovered some novel benefits of the closely related technique of *interleaved practice*, a practice schedule that mixes different kinds of problems or materials within a single study session. Dunlosky et al. (2013) assigned interleaved practice a moderate utility assessment, but recent research suggests that it may be particularly effective for learning mathematics. Rohrer, Dedrick, and Stershic (2015) gave seventh-grade students practice math problems over a three-month period. The researchers presented some students problems in the traditional blocked form; the students practiced a group of similar problems that all required the same solution. They presented other students problems in interleaved form; these students practiced a mixture of different kinds of problems that each required distinct strategies. The interleaved practice group scored higher than the blocked practice group on surprise tests given 1 day or 30 days after the conclusion of practice. The researchers suggested that interleaved practice was more effective because it requires students to choose a strategy according to the nature of individual problems (as students must do on a test), whereas during blocked practice, students could repeatedly apply the same strategy without having to select among possible strategies.

Practice Testing

Practice testing, like distributed practice, has proven useful across a wide range of materials, including learning of stories, facts, vocabulary, and lectures (Dunlosky et al., 2013; Karpicke & Aue, 2015; see also the LearningCurve system associated with this text, which uses practice testing). As you learned in the Memory chapter, practice testing is effective, in part, because actively retrieving an item from memory during a test improves subsequent retention of that item more efficiently than simply studying it again (Roediger & Karpicke, 2006). Yet when asked about their preferred study strategies, students indicated by a wide margin that they prefer rereading materials to testing themselves (Karpicke, 2012). The benefits of testing tend to be greatest when the test is difficult and requires considerable retrieval effort (Pyc & Rawson, 2009), also consistent with the desirable difficulties hypothesis (Bjork & Bjork, 2011). Not only does testing increase verbatim learning of the exact material that is tested but it also enhances the *transfer* of learning from one situation to another (Carpenter, 2012). For example, if you are given practice tests with short-answer questions, such testing improves later performance on both short-answer and multiple-choice questions more than restudying (Kang, McDermott, & Roediger, 2007). Testing also improves the ability to draw conclusions from the studied material, which is an important part of learning and often critical to performing well in the classroom (Karpicke & Blunt, 2011). Also important, studies of students' performance in actual classrooms reveal benefits of practice testing that are similar to those observed in the laboratory (McDaniel et al., 2013; McDermott et al., 2014).

TESTING AIDS ATTENTION

Recent research conducted in the laboratory of one of your textbook authors highlights yet another benefit of testing: Including brief tests during a lecture can improve learning by reducing the mind's tendency to wander (Szpunar, Khan, & Schacter, 2013). How often have you found your mind wandering—thinking about your evening plans, recalling a scene from a movie, or texting a friend—in the midst of a lecture that you know that you ought to be attending to carefully? It's probably happened more than once. Research indicates that students' minds wander frequently during classroom lectures (Bunce, Flens, & Neiles, 2011; Lindquist & McLean, 2011; Wilson & Korn, 2007). Such mind wandering critically impairs learning of the lecture material (Risko et al., 2012). In the study by Szpunar and colleagues (2013), participants watched a videotaped statistics lecture that was divided into four segments. All of the participants were told that they might or might not be tested after each segment; they were also encouraged to take notes during the lectures.

▶ Participants in the *tested* group received brief tests on each segment.

▶ Participants in the *nontested* group did not receive a test until after the final segment. (They worked on arithmetic problems after each of the earlier segments.)

▶ Participants in a *restudy* group were shown, but not tested on, the same material as the tested group after each segment.

At random times during the lectures, participants in all groups were asked about whether they were paying attention to the lecture or whether their minds were wandering off to other topics. Participants in the nontested and restudy groups indicated that they were mind wandering in response to about 40% of the inquiries, but the incidence of mind wandering was cut in half, to about 20%, in the tested group. Participants in the tested group took significantly more notes during the lectures and retained significantly more information from the lecture on a final test than did participants in the other two groups, who performed similarly on this test. Participants in the tested group were also less anxious about the final test than those in the other groups. These results indicate that part of the value of testing comes from encouraging people to sustain attention to a lecture in a way that discourages task-irrelevant activities such as mind wandering and encourages task-relevant activities such as note taking. Because these benefits of testing were observed in response to a videotaped lecture, they apply most directly to online learning, where taped lectures are the norm (Breslow et al., 2013; Schacter & Szpunar, 2015), but there is every reason to believe that the results would apply to live classroom lectures as well, especially in light of the evidence we just discussed that practice testing enhances classroom performance.

CONTROL OF LEARNING

It's the night before the final exam in your introductory psychology course. You've put in a lot of time reviewing your course notes and the material in this textbook, and you feel that you have learned most of it pretty well. You are coming down the home stretch with little time left, and you've got to decide whether to devote those precious remaining minutes to studying psychological disorders or social psychology. How do you make that decision? What are its potential consequences? An important part of learning involves assessing how well we know something and how much more time we need to devote to studying it.

Recent research has shown that people's judgments about what they have learned play a critical role in guiding further study and learning (Dunlosky & Thiede, 2013;

Metcalfe, 2009). Experimental evidence reveals that these subjective assessments, which psychologists refer to as *judgments of learning* (JOLs), have a causal influence on learning: People typically devote more time to studying items that they judge they have not learned well (Metcalfe & Finn, 2008; Son & Metcalfe, 2000).

The finding that JOLs are causally related to decisions about how much to study a particular item is important because JOLs are sometimes inaccurate (Castel, McCabe, & Roediger, 2007). For example, after you read and reread a chapter or article in preparation for a test, the material will likely feel quite familiar, and that feeling may convince you that you've learned the material well enough that you don't need to study it further. However, the feeling of familiarity can be misleading: It may be the result of a low-level process such as perceptual priming (see the Memory chapter) and not the kind of learning that will be required to perform well on an exam (Bjork & Bjork, 2011). Similarly, recent research has shown that students are sometimes overconfident in judging how well they have learned definitions of new terms and fail to study them effectively (Dunlosky & Rawson, 2012). Practice testing can help to reduce this kind of overconfidence (Soderstrom & Bjork, 2014). Therefore, one way to avoid being fooled by misleading subjective impressions is to test yourself from time to time when studying for an exam under examlike conditions; in the case of learning definitions, carefully compare your answers to the actual definitions.

So if you are preparing for the final exam in this course and need to decide whether to devote more time to studying psychological disorders or social psychology, try to exert control over your learning by testing yourself on material from those two chapters; you can use the results of those tests to help you decide which chapter requires further work. Heed the conclusion from researchers (Bjork, Dunlosky, and Kornell, 2013) that becoming a more sophisticated and effective learner requires understanding: (1) key features of learning and memory; (2) effective learning techniques; (3) how to monitor and control one's own learning; and (4) biases that can undermine judgments of learning.

DATA VISUALIZATION

Do People Differ in How They Learn?
Go to launchpadworks.com.

Build to the Outcomes

1. What are the most and least effective study techniques?

2. What are the benefits of distributed practice?

3. Why does a difficult practice test have the greatest benefit?

4. How does taking practice tests help focus a wandering mind?

5. In what ways can JOLs be misleading?

Chapter Review

What Is Learning?

▶ Learning involves the acquisition of new knowledge, skills, and responses. It is based on experience and produces a change in the organism, and that change is relatively permanent.

▶ Even the simplest organisms exhibit simple forms of learning known as habituation and sensitization.

Classical Conditioning: One Thing Leads to Another

▶ Classical conditioning can be thought of as an exercise in pairing a neutral stimulus with a meaningful event or stimulus. Ivan Pavlov's initial work paired a neutral tone (a conditioned stimulus) with a meaningful act: the presentation of food to a hungry animal (an unconditioned stimulus). As he and others demonstrated, the pairing of a CS and a US during the acquisition phase of classical conditioning eventually allows the CS, all by itself, to elicit a response called a conditioned response (CR).

- In second-order conditioning, the CS can be paired with a new neutral stimulus to elicit a response.
- The conditioned response will decline in a process called extinction if the CS is repeatedly presented without the US, although spontaneous recovery can occur after a rest period.
- Conditioning generalizes to similar stimuli, which indicates an ability to discriminate between them.

▶ Classical conditioning was embraced by behaviorists such as John B. Watson, who believed that higher-level functions, such as thinking or awareness, did not need to be invoked to understand behavior. Later researchers showed, however, that the underlying mechanism of classical conditioning is more complex (and more interesting) than the simple association between a CS and a US.

▶ Classical conditioning involves setting up expectations and is sensitive to the degree to which the CS is a genuine predictor of the US, indicating that classical conditioning can involve some degree of cognition. The cerebellum plays an important role in eyeblink conditioning, whereas the amygdala is important for fear conditioning.

▶ The evolutionary aspects of classical conditioning show that each species is biologically predisposed to acquire particular CS–US associations on the basis of its evolutionary history. In short, classical conditioning is not an arbitrary mechanism that merely forms associations. Rather, it is a sophisticated mechanism that evolved precisely because it has adaptive value.

Operant Conditioning: Reinforcements from the Environment

▶ Operant conditioning has at its root the law of effect and is a process by which behaviors are reinforced and therefore become more likely to occur. Positive and negative reinforcement increase the likelihood of behavior; positive and negative punishment decrease the likelihood of behavior.

- Secondary reinforcers can derive their effectiveness from associations with primary reinforcers.
- Delayed reinforcement or punishment is less effective than immediate reinforcement or punishment.
- Reinforcements occur only when the proper response has been made, but not every time, as evidenced by varying schedules of reinforcement.
- Complex behaviors are shaped through reinforcement of successive steps.

▶ Like Watson, B. F. Skinner tried to explain behavior without considering cognitive, neural, or evolutionary mechanisms. However, as with classical conditioning, this approach turned out to be incomplete.

- Operant conditioning has clear cognitive components: Organisms behave as though they have expectations about the outcomes of their actions and adjust their actions accordingly. Cognitive influences can sometimes override the trial-by-trial feedback that usually influences learning.

- Studies with both animals and people highlight the operation of a neural reward center that affects learning.
- The associative mechanisms that underlie operant conditioning have their roots in evolutionary biology. Some things are relatively easy to learn, whereas others are difficult; the history of the species is usually the best clue as to which will be which.

Observational Learning: Look at Me

▶ Observational learning is based on cognitive mechanisms such as attention, perception, memory, and reasoning. But observational learning also has roots in evolutionary biology and for the most basic of reasons: It has survival value. Observational learning is an important process by which species gather information about the world around them.

▶ Observational learning has important social and cultural consequences, because it appears to be well suited to transmission of novel behaviors across individuals.

▶ Chimpanzees and monkeys can benefit from observational learning, supporting the idea that each species evolved particular biological predispositions.

▶ The mirror neuron system becomes active during observational learning, and many of the same brain regions are active during both observation and performance of a skill. Observational learning is closely tied to parts of the brain that are involved in action.

Implicit Learning: Under the Radar

▶ Children are generally linguistically and socially sophisticated by age 6 or 7, but without awareness of how they have learned.

▶ Implicit learning is a process that detects, learns, and stores patterns without the application of explicit awareness by the learner. Simple behaviors such as habituation can reflect implicit learning, but complex behaviors, such as language use or socialization, can also be learned through an implicit process.

▶ Tasks that have been used to document implicit learning include artificial grammar and serial reaction time tasks.

▶ Implicit and explicit learning differ from each other in a number of ways: There are fewer individual differences in implicit than explicit learning; psychotic and amnesic patients with explicit learning problems can exhibit intact implicit learning; and neuroimaging studies indicate that implicit and explicit learning recruit different brain structures, sometimes in different ways.

Learning in the Classroom

▶ Research on learning techniques indicates that some popular study methods, such as highlighting, underlining, and rereading, have low utility, whereas other techniques, such as practice testing and distributed practice, have high utility.

▶ Practice testing improves retention and transfer of learning and can also enhance learning and reduce mind wandering during lectures.

▶ Judgments of learning play a causal role in determining what material to study, but they can be misleading.

KEY CONCEPT QUIZ

1. In classical conditioning, a conditioned stimulus is paired with an unconditioned stimulus to produce
   a. a neutral stimulus.
   b. a conditioned response.
   c. an unconditioned response.
   d. another conditioned stimulus.

2. What occurs when a conditioned stimulus is no longer paired with an unconditioned stimulus?
   a. generalization
   b. spontaneous recovery
   c. extinction
   d. acquisition

3. What did Watson and Rayner seek to demonstrate about behaviorism through the Little Albert experiment?
   a. Conditioning involves a degree of cognition.
   b. Classical conditioning has an evolutionary component.
   c. Behaviorism alone cannot explain human behavior.
   d. Even sophisticated behaviors such as emotion are subject to classical conditioning.

4. Which part of the brain is involved in the classical conditioning of fear?
   a. the amygdala
   b. the cerebellum
   c. the hippocampus
   d. the hypothalamus

5. After having a bad experience with a particular type of food, people can develop a lifelong aversion to that food. This suggests that conditioning has a(n) ____ aspect.
   a. cognitive
   b. evolutionary
   c. neural
   d. behavioral

6. Which of the following mechanisms have no role in Skinner's approach to behavior?
   a. cognitive
   b. neural
   c. evolutionary
   d. all of the above

7. Latent learning provides evidence for a cognitive element in operant conditioning because
   a. it occurs without any obvious reinforcement.
   b. it requires both positive and negative reinforcement.
   c. it points toward the operation of a neural reward center.
   d. it depends on a stimulus–response relationship.

8. Neural research indicates that observational learning is closely tied to brain areas that are involved in
   a. memory.
   b. vision.
   c. action.
   d. emotion.

9. What kind of learning takes place largely independent of awareness of both the process and the products of information acquisition?
   a. latent learning
   b. implicit learning
   c. observational learning
   d. conscious learning

10. Which study strategy has been shown to be the most effective?
    a. highlighting text
    b. rereading
    c. summarizing
    d. taking practice tests

 LearningCurve   Don't stop now! Quizzing yourself is a powerful study tool. Go to LaunchPad to access the LearningCurve adaptive quizzing system and your own personalized learning plan. Visit launchpadworks.com.

KEY TERMS

learning (p. 262)

habituation (p. 262)

sensitization (p. 262)

classical conditioning (p. 263)

unconditioned stimulus (US) (p. 265)

unconditioned response (UR) (p. 265)

acquisition (p. 266)

conditioned stimulus (CS) (p. 266)

conditioned response (CR) (p. 266)

second-order conditioning (p. 266)

extinction (p. 266)

spontaneous recovery (p. 267)

generalization (p. 267)

discrimination (p. 267)

biological preparedness (p. 272)

operant conditioning (p. 272)

law of effect (p. 274)

operant behavior (p. 274)

reinforcer (p. 274)

punisher (p. 274)

fixed-interval schedule (FI) (p. 278)

variable-interval schedule (VI) (p. 278)

fixed-ratio schedule (FR) (p. 278)

variable-ratio schedule (VR) (p. 279)

intermittent reinforcement (p. 279)

intermittent reinforcement effect (p. 280)

shaping (p. 280)

latent learning (p. 282)

cognitive map (p. 283)

observational learning (p. 290)

diffusion chain (p. 290)

implicit learning (p. 295)

CHANGING MINDS

1. A friend is taking a class in childhood education. "Back in the old days," she says, "teachers used physical punishment, but of course that's not allowed anymore. Now, a good teacher should only use reinforcement. When children behave, teachers should provide positive reinforcement, like praise. When children misbehave, teachers should provide negative reinforcement, like scolding or withholding privileges." What is your friend misunderstanding about reinforcement? Can you give better examples of how negative reinforcement could be applied productively in an elementary school classroom?

2. A friend of your family is trying to train her daughter to make her bed every morning. You suggest trying positive reinforcement. A month later, the woman reports back to you. "It's not working very well," she says. "Every time she makes her bed, I put a gold star on the calendar, and at the end of the week, if there are seven gold stars, I give Vicky a reward— a piece of licorice. But so far, she's earned the licorice only twice." How could you explain why the desired behavior—bed making—might not increase as a result of this reinforcement procedure?

3. While studying for the psych exam, you ask your study partner to provide a definition of classical conditioning. "In classical conditioning," she says, "there's a stimulus, the CS, that predicts an upcoming event, the US. Usually, it's something bad, like an electric shock, nausea, or a frightening, loud noise. The learner makes a response, the CR, in order to prevent the US. Sometimes, the US is good, like food for Pavlov's dogs, and then the learner makes the response in order to earn the US." What's wrong with this definition?

4. One of your classmates announces that he liked the last chapter (on memory) better than the current chapter on learning. "I want to be a psychiatrist," he says, "so I mostly care about human learning. Conditioning might be a really powerful way to train animals to push levers or perform tricks, but it really doesn't have much relevance to how humans learn things." How similar is learning in humans and other animals? What real-world examples can you provide to show that conditioning does occur in humans?

ANSWERS TO KEY CONCEPT QUIZ

1. b; 2. c; 3. d; 4. a; 5. b; 7. d; 7. a; 8. c; 9. b; 10. d.

 LaunchPad
macmillan learning

LaunchPad features the full e-Book of *Psychology*, the LearningCurve adaptive quizzing system, videos, and a variety of activities to boost your learning. Visit LaunchPad at launchpadworks.com.

Emotion and Motivation

L EONARDO IS 5 YEARS OLD and cute as a button. He can do many of the things that other 5-year-olds can do: solve puzzles, build towers of blocks, and play guessing games with grown-ups. But unlike other 5-year-olds, Leonardo has never been proud of his abilities, angry with his mother, or bored with his lessons. That's because Leonardo has a condition that makes him unable to experience emotions of any kind. He has never felt joy or sorrow, delight or despair, shame, envy, annoyance, excitement, gratitude, or regret. He has never laughed or cried.

As you might expect, Leonardo's condition has had a profound impact on his life. For example, because he doesn't experience emotions, he isn't motivated to do the things that bring most children pleasure, such as eating cookies or playing hide-and-seek. And because he doesn't feel, he can't really tell what others are feeling, which makes social interaction a challenge. Luckily, his mother cares a lot about him and has spent years teaching Leonardo how to make the facial expressions that indicate emotions such as surprise and sadness, and how to detect the meaning of those facial expressions when others make them. So Leonardo knows that he is supposed to smile when someone says something nice to him and that he is supposed to raise his eyebrow every once in a while to show interest in what other people are saying. So when Leonardo's mother smiles at him, he always smiles back. She is glad he can do that trick, but she is also keenly aware that Leonardo is simply making the faces he was taught to make and that he doesn't feel any love for her at all.

A typical 5-year-old can experience emotions such as pride, anger, and boredom.

Leonardo and his "mom," MIT Professor Cynthia Breazeal.

But she doesn't mind. Because even though he cannot return her affection, Dr. Cynthia Breazeal still considers Leonardo one of the greatest robots she's ever designed (Breazeal, 2009).

YES, LEONARDO IS A ROBOT—A MACHINE WITH A FURRY FACE. He can see and hear, remember and reason. But despite his adorable smile and knowing wink, he cannot feel a thing, and that makes him infinitely different from us. Our ability to love and to hate, to be amused and annoyed, to feel elated and devastated, is an essential element of our humanity, and a person who could not feel these things would seem a lot like a robot to the rest of us. But what exactly are these things we call feelings? And why are they so essential? In this chapter we will explore these questions. We'll start by discussing the nature of emotions and seeing how they relate to the states of our bodies and our brains. Next, we'll see how people express their emotions, and how they use those expressions to communicate with each other. Finally, we'll examine the essential role that emotions play in motivation—how they inform us, and how they compel us to do everything from making war to making love.

Emotional Experience: The Feeling Machine

It is almost impossible not to feel something when you look at this photograph, but it is almost impossible to say exactly what you are feeling.

Leonardo doesn't know what love feels like and there's no way to teach him, because trying to describe the feeling of love to someone who has never experienced it is a bit like trying to describe the color green to someone who was born blind. We could tell Leonardo what causes the feeling ("It happens whenever I see Marilynn") and we could tell him about its consequences ("I breathe hard and say goofy stuff"), but in the end these descriptions would miss the point because the essential feature of love—like the essential feature of all emotions—is the *experience*. It *feels* like something to love someone, and what it feels like is love's defining attribute (Heavey, Hurlburt, & Lefforge, 2012).

WHAT IS EMOTION?

How can we scientifically study something whose defining attribute defies description? One way is by using a technique that capitalizes on the fact that even though people can't always say what their emotional experiences feel like ("Love is . . . um . . . uh . . ."), they can say how similar one emotional experience is to another ("Love is more like happiness than like anger"). By asking people to rate the similarity of dozens of emotional experiences, psychologists have been able to use a technique known as *multidimensional scaling* to create a map of those experiences. The mathematics behind this technique is complex, but the logic is simple.

If you handed your friend a list of the distances between a half dozen U.S. cities and then asked her to draw a map in which each city was exactly the right distance from every other city, your friend would be forced to draw a map that looked just like the United States (see **FIGURE 8.1**). Why? Because this is the one and only map that allows every city to appear at precisely the right distance from every other. If you don't believe it, just try moving Chicago. Multidimensional scaling is a mathematical technique that creates maps from nothing more than a list of distances. Why is that useful? When people estimate the similarity of a list of emotional experiences, they are essentially describing the "distance" between them. This means that psychologists can

	Chicago	LA	SF	Omaha	Phoenix	Boston
Chicago	0	1749	1863	433	1447	856
LA	1749	0	344	1318	367	2605
SF	1863	344	0	1432	658	2708
Omaha	433	1318	1432	0	1029	1288
Phoenix	1447	367	658	1029	0	2290
Boston	856	2605	2708	1288	2299	0

◀ Figure 8.1

FROM DISTANCES TO MAPS Knowing the distances between things—like cities, for example—allows us to draw a map that reveals the dimensions on which they vary.

take these distances and use multidimensional scaling to draw a map of the emotional landscape. That map is shown in **FIGURE 8.2**. It is the one and only map that allows every emotional experience to be plotted precisely the right distance from every other.

Fine. But what good is a map of the emotional landscape? Maps don't just show us how close things are to each other, which is something we already knew anyway. Maps also reveal the *dimensions* on which those things vary. For example, the map in

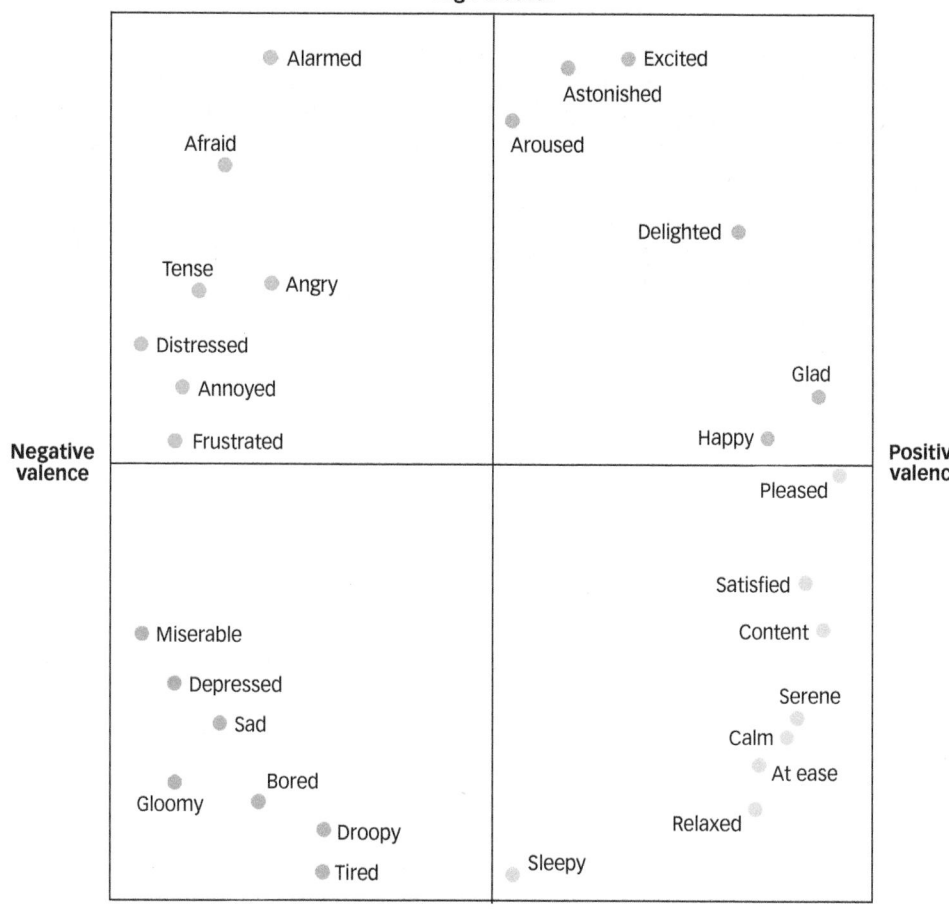

◀ Figure 8.2

TWO DIMENSIONS OF EMOTION Just as the locations of cities vary on two dimensions called longitude and latitude, emotions vary on two dimensions called valence and arousal.

emotion A positive or negative experience that is associated with a particular pattern of physiological activity.

James–Lange theory The theory that a stimulus triggers activity in the body, which in turn produces an emotional experience in the brain.

Figure 8.1 shows that cities vary on exactly two dimensions that we call longitude (the east-west dimension) and latitude (the north-south dimension). As you can see from this map, one dimension is not enough to describe how cities vary, and three dimensions are too many. Now look at Figure 8.2. That map shows that emotional experiences also vary on two dimensions—a dimension called *valence* (how positive or negative the experience is) and a dimension called *arousal* (how active or passive the experience is). Decades of research have shown that all the emotional experiences that human beings have can be described by their unique location on this two-dimensional map (Russell, 1980; Watson & Tellegen, 1985; Yik, Russell, & Steiger, 2011).

This map can also help us say what an emotion is. Any definition of emotion must include the fact that emotional experiences have different amounts of positivity and negativity and different amounts of physiological arousal. With these facts in mind, we can define **emotion** as *a positive or negative experience that is associated with a particular pattern of physiological activity*. As you are about to see, the first step in understanding emotion involves understanding how the experience part of this definition and the physiological activity part of this definition are related.

THE EMOTIONAL BODY

You may think that if you walked into your kitchen right now and saw a bear nosing through the trash, you would feel afraid. Then your muscles would tense and your heart would start to pound. And then your legs would do everything legs can do to get your butt out of the kitchen. That's how it *feels* to be afraid. But more than a century ago, psychologists began to suspect that how it feels isn't exactly how it is, and that these particular responses don't actually happen in this particular order.

Early Theories

In the late 19th century, William James suggested that your feeling of fear does not cause your body to respond, but rather, it's the other way around: "Bodily changes follow directly the perception of the exciting fact," he wrote, "and feeling of the same changes as they occur *is* the emotion" (1884, pp. 189–190). According to James, you first see the bear (the "exciting fact"), and then your heart starts pounding and your leg muscles contract (the "bodily changes"), and *then* you experience fear, which is nothing more or less than your perception of your body's response. James argued that different emotional experiences are simply the perception of different patterns of bodily responses, and without all that heart pounding and muscle clenching, we would have no experience of emotion at all. The psychologist Carl Lange suggested something similar at about the same time, so this idea became known as the **James–Lange theory** of emotion, which states that a *stimulus triggers activity in the body, which in turn produces an emotional experience in the mind*. According to this theory, our emotional experiences are the consequence and not the cause of our body's reactions to events in the world. Such as bears.

Not everyone thought this theory made sense. The physiologists Walter Cannon and Philip Bard argued that the James–Lange theory had four major problems.

▶ First, emotional experiences sometimes happen more rapidly than bodily responses do. For example, people typically feel embarrassed within a few seconds of noticing that their pants have fallen off in public, and yet the bodily response known as blushing takes a full 15 to 30 seconds to occur. So how could the feeling of embarrassment be the "perception of blushing" if blushing only happens after we feel embarrassed?

▶ Second, people are not always aware of their bodily responses. For example, most people cannot tell when their hearts start beating faster. If people can't detect changes in their bodies, and if emotions are nothing more than the perception of bodily changes, then why do they experience emotions at all?

Did the Duchess of Cambridge just make her husband, Prince William, blush by embarrassing him, or did she embarrass him by making him blush? The experience of embarrassment precedes blushing by up to 30 seconds, so it is unlikely that blushing is the cause of the emotional experience.

GETTY IMAGES NEWS/GETTY IMAGES

▶ Third, all sorts of utterly unemotional events can cause the body to respond. When the room gets hot, for example, the heart starts to beat faster. If fear is just the perception of a rapid heartbeat, then why don't people feel afraid when they are in a warm room?

▶ Fourth, physiologists know that there are far fewer unique patterns of bodily activity than there are unique emotional experiences. That means that several different emotional experiences must be associated with the same pattern of bodily activity. So how do people who are in a particular physiological state decide which of several emotions they are experiencing?

As you can probably tell, Cannon and Bard didn't think much of the James–Lange theory. But they really liked the hyphen, so they developed the **Cannon–Bard theory** of emotion, which states that *a stimulus simultaneously triggers activity in the body and emotional experience in the mind* (Bard, 1934; Cannon, 1929). According to this theory, the bear in your kitchen makes your heart race *and* it makes you feel afraid. But those two things happen independently and simultaneously—the first is not the cause of the second.

Modern Theories

So what do modern psychologists make of these two early theories? Most agree that both theories made good points but that neither got it right. In the early 1960s, the psychologists Stanley Schachter and Jerome Singer argued that James and Lange were right to suggest that our experience of emotion is based on our perception of our bodily reactions, but that Cannon and Bard were right to claim that we do not have nearly enough unique bodily reactions to account for the wide variety of emotions that we experience (Schachter & Singer, 1962). So Schachter and Singer developed a new theory that took the best bits and pieces of the two theories that came before it, as well as the hyphen (see **FIGURE 8.3**). Their **two-factor theory of emotion** states that *a stimulus triggers a general state of arousal in the body, which the mind then interprets as a specific emotion*.

According to this theory, when you see a bear in your kitchen, your body becomes aroused—your heart pounds, your muscles tense, and you start breathing hard. Your mind notices all this activity and immediately starts looking around for an explanation. And what does it see? A bear! So what does it conclude? "I'm afraid!" Having noticed both a thumping heart and a growling grizzly in the same room, your mind comes to the logical conclusion that you must be afraid. According to the two-factor theory, when you find yourself physiologically aroused in the presence of something that really

Cannon–Bard theory The theory that a stimulus simultaneously triggers activity in the body and emotional experience in the brain.

two-factor theory of emotion The theory that emotions are based on inferences about the causes of physiological arousal.

◀ Figure 8.3

CLASSIC THEORIES OF EMOTION Classic theories make different claims about the origins of emotion. (a) The James–Lange theory suggests that stimuli trigger specific physiological states that are then experienced as emotions. (b) The Cannon–Bard theory suggests that stimuli trigger both specific physiological states and emotional experiences independently. (c) The two-factor theory suggests that stimuli trigger general physiological arousal whose cause the brain interprets, and this interpretation leads to emotional experience.

(a) James–Lange → Specific physiological state → Experience of fear

(b) Cannon–Bard → Specific physiological state / Experience of fear

(c) Two-factor → General physiological arousal → Experience of fear

JIM ZUCKERMAN/CORBIS

PHOTOINKE/ALAMY STOCK PHOTO

The fact that people can mistake physical arousal for romantic attraction may help explain why so many first dates involve roller coasters.

ought to scare you, you interpret that arousal as *fear*. But if you had precisely the same bodily response in the presence of something that really ought to delight you, such as a pair of skydiving kittens or a mile-high stack of pancakes, then you might call that arousal *excitement*. The two-factor theory suggests that people have just one bodily reaction to all emotional stimuli, but they interpret that reaction differently on different occasions—and that is what gives rise to the experience of different emotions.

How has the two-factor theory fared in the last half century? One of the theory's key claims has fared quite well: People do indeed make inferences about the causes of their physiological arousal, and those inferences determine their emotional experiences (Lindquist & Barrett, 2008). For instance, participants in one study (Schachter & Singer, 1962) were injected with epinephrine, which causes physiological arousal, and were then exposed to either a goofy or a nasty confederate. Just as the two-factor theory predicted, when the confederate acted goofy, participants concluded that they were feeling *happy*, but when the confederate acted nasty, participants concluded that they were feeling *angry*. Research has shown that when people are aroused in other ways—for example, by riding an exercise bike in the laboratory—they subsequently find attractive people more attractive, annoying people more annoying, and funny cartoons funnier, as if they were interpreting their exercise-induced arousal as attraction, annoyance, or amusement (Byrne et al., 1975; Dutton & Aron, 1974; Zillmann, Katcher, & Milavsky, 1972).

On the other hand, research has not been so kind to the two-factor theory's claim that different emotional experiences are merely different interpretations of a single bodily state called "arousal." When researchers measure people's physiological reactions as they experience different emotions, they find that anger, fear, and sadness produce a higher heart rate than disgust does; that fear and disgust produced higher galvanic skin response (sweating) than sadness or anger do; and that anger produces a larger increase in finger temperature than fear does (Ekman, Levenson, & Friesen, 1983; Levenson, Ekman, & Friesen, 1990; Levenson et al., 1991, 1992; see **FIGURE 8.4**). In other words, a single bodily response does not underlie all emotions. Indeed, we now know that certain bodily responses are associated with just a single emotion. Embarrassment, for example, is uniquely associated with blushing (Leary et al., 1992), and prosocial emotions such as compassion are associated with a specific pattern of activity in the parasympathetic nervous system that does not seem to occur in other instances (Oately, Keltner, & Jenkins, 2006). This does not mean that every emotion has its own individual "physiological fingerprint"

▼ **Figure 8.4**

THE PHYSIOLOGY OF EMOTION Contrary to the claims of the two-factor theory, different emotions do seem to have different underlying patterns of physiological arousal. (a) Anger, fear, and sadness all produce higher heart rates than do happiness, surprise, and disgust. (b) Anger produces a much greater increase in finger temperature than any other emotion.

(a)

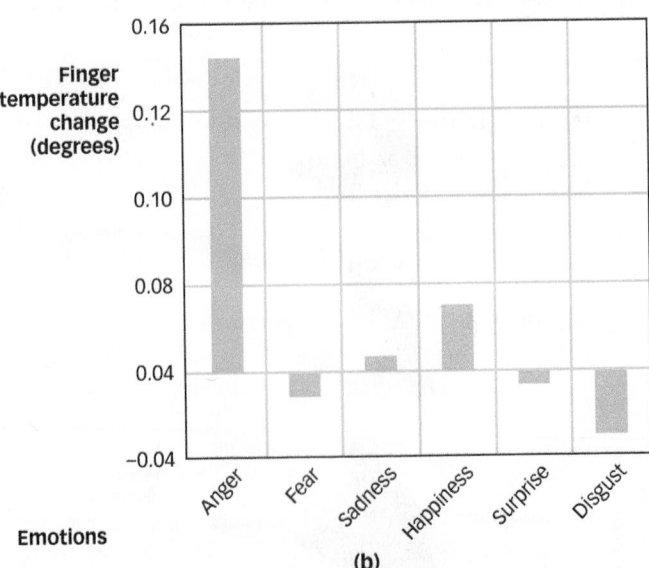

Emotions

(b)

(Clark-Polner, Johnson, & Barrett, 2016; Siegel et al., 2016), but it does mean that the bodily responses associated with different emotions are not always identical—a finding that is at odds with the two-factor theory.

Where does that leave us? A lot has changed since the days of William James, Walter Cannon, and Stanley Schachter. The relationship between the mind and the body, and the way they work together to produce emotional experience, has turned out to be much more complicated than any of their models suggested. We know this because new technologies have given us access to something that previous generations of psychologists could merely imagine: the emotional brain.

THE EMOTIONAL BRAIN

In the late 1930s, two researchers made an accidental discovery (Kluver & Bucy, 1937, 1939). A few days after performing brain surgery on a monkey named Aurora, they noticed that she was acting strangely. First, she would eat just about anything and have sex with just about anyone—as though she could no longer distinguish between good and bad food, or between good and bad mates. Second, she was absolutely fearless and unflappable, remaining perfectly calm when she was handled by researchers or even when confronted by snakes, both of which monkeys generally don't much like. What had happened to Aurora?

The Amygdala

As it turned out, during the surgery, the researchers had accidentally damaged a structure in Aurora's brain called the *amygdala*. Subsequent studies have confirmed that the amygdala plays a special role in producing emotions such as fear (Cunningham & Brosch, 2012). For example, researchers performed surgery on a monkey so that the visual information that entered the monkey's left eye was transmitted to its amygdala, but the visual information entering its right eye was not (Downer, 1961). When the monkey saw a threatening stimulus with only its left eye, it responded with fear and alarm; but when it saw a threatening stimulus with only its right eye, it remained calm and unruffled. Studies of human beings have shown similar effects. For example, most people have better memory for emotionally evocative words such as *death* or *vomit* than for ordinary words such as *box* or *chair*, but this is not true of people whose amygdalae have been damaged (LaBar & Phelps, 1998) or who have been given drugs that temporarily impair neurotransmission in the amygdala (van Stegeren et al., 1998; see **FIGURE 8.5**). Although people with amygdala damage do not feel fear when they *see* a threat, they do feel fear when they *experience* a threat, for example, when they suddenly find they can't breathe (Feinstein et al., 2013).

DAVID LONGSTREATH/AP IMAGES

The tourist and the tiger have something in common: each has an amygdala that is working at lightning speed to decide whether the other is a threat. Let's hope the tourist's is working a little faster.

▼ Figure 8.5

EMOTION RECOGNITION AND THE AMYGDALA Facial expressions of emotion were morphed into a continuum that ran from happiness to surprise to fear to sadness to disgust to anger and back to happiness. This sequence was shown to a patient with amygdala damage and to a control group of 10 people without brain damage. Although the patient's recognition of happiness, sadness, and surprise was generally in line with that of the control group, her recognition of anger, disgust, and fear was impaired (Calder et al., 1996).

CALDER, A. J., YOUNG, A.W., ROWLAND, D., PERRETT, D. I., HODGES, J. R., & ETCOFF, N. L. (1996). FACIAL EMOTION RECOGNITION AFTER BILATERAL AMYGDALA DAMAGE: DIFFERENTLY SEVERE IMPAIRMENT OF FEAR. *COGNITIVE NEUROPSYCHOLOGY*, 13, 699–745. (FIGURE 1 PP. 713–714; FIGURE 2A PP. 718–719). TAYLOR & FRANCIS GROUP: WWW.TANDFONLINE.COM

appraisal An evaluation of the emotion-relevant aspects of a stimulus.

Together, these findings provide clues about what the amygdala does. Before an animal can feel fear, it must know that there is something to be afraid of. A real bear is fear-worthy but Winnie-the-Pooh probably is not. Psychologists use the word **appraisal** to mean *an evaluation of the emotion-relevant aspects of a stimulus* (Arnold, 1960; Ellsworth & Scherer, 2003; Lazarus, 1984; Roseman, 1984; Roseman & Smith, 2001; Scherer, 1999, 2001), and it appears that the amygdala's primary function is to make those appraisals. In a sense, the amygdala is an extremely fast and sensitive detector whose primary job is to decide whether a stimulus is or is not a threat (Whalen et al., 1998). As you're about to see, the speed with which the amygdala makes its appraisals is very important.

The Fast and Slow Pathways

In the waning years of the twentieth century, the psychologist Joseph LeDoux decided that it might be interesting to map the route that information about a stimulus takes as it moves through the brain. In a series of careful experiments, LeDoux discovered that information is transmitted simultaneously along two distinct routes: the "fast pathway," which goes from the thalamus directly to the amygdala, and the "slow pathway," which goes from the thalamus to the cortex and *then* to the amygdala (see **FIGURE 8.6**).

LeDoux showed that when you see a bear, the information about the bear goes from your eye to your thalamus and then to your cortex, which uses that information to answer a rather complicated question: What in the world is that thing? The cortex uses all the information at its disposal to conduct a full-scale investigation of the stimulus in order to determine its identity ("This seems to be an animal, probably a mammal, maybe a member of the genus *Ursus*. . . ."). But while all this is happening, the thalamus has also sent the information directly to your amygdala, which uses it to answer a much simpler question: Is this a threat? If your amygdala's answer to that question is yes, then it initiates the processes that produce the bodily reactions that—when your cortex is finally done with all that investigating—you will call *fear*.

In short, LeDoux showed how we get scared. So how do we stop? As Figure 8.6 shows, your amygdala receives information directly from your thalamus via the fast pathway, but it also receives information from your cortex via the slow pathway. This latter connection allows your cortex to "talk" to your amygdala—and one of the things it often says is this: "Hey, amygdala, chill out!" Once the cortex has finished its full-scale investigation of the stimulus, this connection allows it to *downregulate* the amygdala, which is a fancy way of saying that it sends a signal to the amygdala telling it to reduce its activity. In a sense, the amygdala's job is to hit the emotional gas pedal and the cortex's job is to hit the brakes. That's why adults who have cortical damage, and children (whose cortices are not well developed), often have trouble inhibiting their emotional responses (Cohen et al., 2016; Stuss & Benson, 1986). When experimental participants are asked to feel sad, afraid, or angry, they show increased activity in the amygdala and decreased activity in the cortex (Damasio et al., 2000), but when they are asked to *not* feel these same emotions, they show increased cortical activity and decreased amygdala activity (Ochsner et al., 2002).

Does this mean that the amygdala is the brain's "fear center?" If only the brain were so simple! Research shows that there are times when the amygdala is activated and people feel no fear, and times when people feel fear and the amygdala is not activated (Feinstein et al., 2013). In other words, we do not yet fully understand what the amygdala does. But what we do know is that the cortex and the amygdala (as well as other limbic structures) work together in complex ways to produce our emotional reactions and experiences, and that's a lot more than William James ever dreamed of.

Thalamus

Cortex

Amygdala

Stimulus

Experience of fear

JIM ZUCKERMAN/CORBIS

PARAMOUNT PICTURES/THE KOBAL COLLECTION

▲ Figure 8.6

THE FAST AND SLOW PATHWAYS OF FEAR Information about a stimulus takes two routes simultaneously through the brain: the "fast pathway" (shown in pink), which runs from the thalamus directly to the amygdala, and the "slow pathway" (shown in green), which runs from the thalamus to the cortex and then to the amygdala. Because the amygdala receives information from the thalamus before it receives information from the cortex, a person can be afraid of something before he or she knows what it is.

THE REGULATION OF EMOTION

You may or may not care about hedgehogs, earwax, or the War of 1812, but if you are human, you almost certainly care about what you are feeling. **Emotion regulation** refers to *the strategies people use to influence their own emotional experience*. Nine out of 10 people report that they attempt to regulate their emotional experience at least once a day (Gross, 1998), and they describe more than a thousand different strategies for doing so (Parkinson & Totterdell, 1999).

Some of these strategies are behavioral (e.g., avoiding situations that trigger unwanted emotions) and some are cognitive (e.g., recruiting memories that trigger the desired emotion; Webb, Miles, & Sheeran, 2012), but regardless of how they work, people seem to have a poor understanding of which are most effective (Heiy & Cheavens, 2014). For example, most people think that *suppression*, which involves inhibiting the outward signs of an emotion, is an effective way to regulate it. But they are wrong (Gross, 2002; Kalokerinos, Greenaway, & Denson, 2015). Not only is suppression ineffective but it may actually have deleterious consequences (Franchow & Suchy, 2015). On the other hand, most people think that *affect labeling,* which involves putting one's feelings into words, will have little or no impact on their emotions. But in fact, affect labeling is an effective way to reduce the intensity of emotional states (Lieberman et al., 2011).

Research also suggests that one of the best strategies for emotion regulation is **reappraisal**, which involves *changing one's emotional experience by changing the way one thinks about the emotion-eliciting stimulus* (Ochsner et al., 2009). In one study, participants who watched a video of a circumcision that was described as a joyous religious ritual had slower heart rates and reported less distress than did participants who watched the same video but did not hear that description (Lazarus & Alfert, 1964). In another study, participants' brains were scanned as they saw photos that induced negative emotions, such as a photo of a woman crying during a funeral. Some participants were then asked to reappraise the picture, for example, by imagining that the woman in the photo was at a wedding rather than a funeral. The results showed that when participants initially saw the photo their amygdalae were activated, but when they reappraised the picture, their cortices were activated and moments later their amygdalae were deactivated (Ochsner et al., 2002). In other words, participants were able to downregulate the activity of their own amygdalae simply by thinking about the photo in a different way.

Reappraisal is a skill. Like most skills, it can be learned (Denny & Ochsner, 2014), and like most skills, some people are naturally better at it than others (Malooly, Genet, & Siemer, 2013). People who are especially good at reappraisal tend to be both mentally and physically healthier (Davidson, Putnam, & Larson, 2000; Gross & Muñoz, 1995), and to have better relationships (Bloch, Haase, & Levenson, 2014). This should not be surprising, given that reappraisal is one of the skills that therapists commonly try to teach people who are dealing with emotional problems (Jamieson, Mendes, & Nock, 2013). On the other hand, this skill has a dark side: People who are good at changing how they see things in order to feel better about the things they see can be less compassionate toward those who are suffering (Cameron & Payne, 2011). Given how effective reappraisal is, you might expect people to do it all the time, but you'd be wrong (Heiy & Cheavens, 2014). People tend to underutilize reappraisal, in part because it takes some effort (Suri, Whittaker, & Gross, 2015), which also explains why people are even less inclined to use reappraisal as they age (Scheibe, Sheppes, & Staudinger, 2015).

emotion regulation The strategies people use to influence their own emotional experiences.

reappraisal Changing one's emotional experience by changing the way one thinks about the emotion-eliciting stimulus.

RICK BOWMER/AP IMAGES

Emotion regulation can be difficult. In 2011, the city of Portland, Oregon, flushed 8 million gallons of drinking water simply because a man was seen urinating into this reservoir. Although the minuscule amount of urine posed no health threat, it made people feel disgusted—and the inability to regulate that emotion cost the citizens of Portland nearly $30,000.

Build to the Outcomes

1. What is multidimensional scaling used for?

2. What are the two dimensions on which emotions vary?

3. How did the Cannon–Bard theory challenge the James–Lange theory?

4. How did the two-factor theory build on earlier theories?

5. How do the amygdala and cortex interact to produce emotion?

6. What are the best ways to regulate emotion?

Emotional Communication: Msgs w/o Wrds

Learning Outcomes

▸ Describe evidence for and against the universality hypothesis.

▸ Explain the facial feedback hypothesis.

▸ Describe how people use emotional expressions to deceive and how they detect such deception.

Leonardo the robot may not be able to feel, but he sure can smile. And wink. And nod. Indeed, people who interact with Leonardo find it hard to think of him as a machine precisely because Leonardo *expresses* emotions that he doesn't actually have. An **emotional expression** is *an observable sign of an emotional state*, and although robots can be taught to exhibit them, human beings do so quite naturally.

Emotional states express themselves in a variety of ways. For example, they change the way we talk—from our intonation and inflection to the volume and duration of our speech—and research shows that listeners can infer emotional states from vocal cues alone with better-than-chance accuracy (Banse & Scherer, 1996; Cordaro et al., 2016; Frick, 1985). Observers can also estimate a person's emotional state from the direction of the person's gaze, the rhythm of their gait, or even from the way they touch another person's arm (Dael, Mortillaro, & Scherer, 2012; Dittrich et al., 1996; Hertenstein et al., 2009; Keltner & Shiota, 2003; Wallbott, 1998). In some sense, people are walking, talking advertisements for what's going on inside them.

Of course, no part of a person's body is more exquisitely designed for communicating their emotional state than the face. Underneath your face lie 43 muscles that are capable of creating more than 10,000 unique configurations that enable you to convey information about your emotional state with an astonishing degree of subtlety and specificity (Ekman, 1965). The psychologists Paul Ekman and Wallace Friesen (1971) spent years cataloguing the muscle movements that the human face is capable "of making." They isolated 46 unique *action units* and gave each one a name, such as "cheek puffer," "dimpler," and "nasolabial deepener." Research shows that some (though not all) of these action units are reliably associated with specific emotional states (Davidson et al., 1990; Mehu & Scherer, 2015). For example, when we feel happy, our *zygomatic major* (a muscle that pulls our lip corners up) and our *obicularis oculi* (a muscle that crinkles the outside edges of our eyes) produce a unique facial expression that psychologists describe as "action units 6 and 12" but that the rest of us simply call smiling (Ekman & Friesen, 1982; Frank, Ekman, & Friesen, 1993; Steiner, 1986).

COMMUNICATIVE EXPRESSION

Why are our emotions written all over our faces? In 1872, Charles Darwin published *The Expression of the Emotions in Man and Animals*, in which he speculated about the evolutionary significance of emotional expression. Darwin noticed that human and nonhuman animals share certain postures and facial expressions, and he suggested that they were meant to communicate information about internal states. It isn't hard to see how such communications might be useful (Shariff & Tracy, 2011; Tracy, Randles, & Steckler, 2015). For example, if a dominant animal can bare his teeth and communicate the message "I am angry" and if a subordinate male animal can lower his head and communicate the message "I am afraid" then the two can establish a pecking order without any actual pecking. Darwin suggested that emotional expressions are a convenient way for one animal to let another animal know how it is feeling and therefore how it is prepared to act. In this sense, emotional expressions are a bit like the words of a nonverbal language.

According to Charles Darwin (1872/1998), both human and nonhuman animals use facial expressions to communicate information about their internal states.

emotional expression An observable sign of an emotional state.

universality hypothesis The theory that emotional expressions have the same meaning for everyone.

The Universality of Expression

Of course, language works only when everybody speaks the same one, and that's what led Darwin to advance the **universality hypothesis,** which suggests that *emotional expressions have the same meaning for everyone.* Darwin believed that every human being naturally expresses happiness with a smile, and that as a result, every human being naturally understands that a smile signifies happiness. Emotional expression is a language that is universally spoken and universally understood.

Evidence suggests that Darwin was mainly right. For example, people who have never seen a human face make the same facial expressions as those who have: Congenitally blind people smile when they are happy (Galati, Scherer, & Ricci-Bitt, 1997; Matsumoto & Willingham, 2009), and 2-day-old infants make a disgust face when bitter chemicals are put in their mouths (Steiner, 1973, 1979). Not only are people good at identifying the emotional expressions of members of cultures with which they are familiar (Ekman & Friesen, 1971; Elfenbein & Ambady, 2002; Frank & Stennet, 2001; Haidt & Keltner, 1999) but they are also good at identifying the emotional expressions of members of cultures they have never seen before. In the 1950s, researchers took photographs of Westerners expressing anger, disgust, fear, happiness, sadness, and surprise and showed them to members of the South Fore, a people who lived a Stone Age existence in the highlands of Papua New Guinea and who at that point had had little contact with the modern world. When the researchers asked these participants to match each photograph to a word (such as "happy" or "afraid"), they found that the South Fore made matches that were essentially the same as those made by Americans.

A majority of psychologists believe that facial displays of at least five emotions—*anger, disgust, fear, happiness,* and *sadness*—are universal (Ekman, 2016), and that a few other emotions such as *embarrassment, surprise, amusement, guilt, shame,* and *pride* may have universal patterns of facial expression as well (Keltner, 1995; Keltner & Buswell, 1996; Keltner & Haidt, 1999; Keltner & Harker, 1998; Tracy et al., 2013). But not all psychologists are convinced. Recent research shows that members of an isolated tribe called the Himba can match faces to emotion words just as Americans do. But when the Himba are instead asked to match faces that are "feeling the same way" to each other, they produce matches that are quite unlike those produced by their American counterparts (Gendron et al., 2014). Studies such as these suggest that the universality hypothesis may turn out to have been overstated. For now we can safely say that humans show considerable agreement about the emotional meaning of facial expressions but that this agreement is less than perfect.

The Cause and Effect of Expression

Members of different cultures seem to express their emotions in much the same way. But why? They don't all speak the same language, so why do they all smile the same smile and frown the same frown? The answer is that words are *symbols,* and facial expressions are *signs.* Symbols are arbitrary designations that have no causal relationship with the things they symbolize. English speakers use the word *cat* to indicate a particular animal, but there is nothing about felines that actually causes this particular sound to pop out of our mouths, and we aren't surprised when other human beings make entirely different sounds—such as *popoki* or *gatto*—to indicate a furry pet that generally thinks it is better than you. But facial expressions are not arbitrary symbols of the emotions they convey. They are signs of those emotions because unlike symbols, signs are *caused* by the things they signify. The feeling of happiness *causes* the contraction of the zygomatic major, so that contraction is a sign of that feeling in the same way that a footprint in the snow is a sign that someone walked there.

Of course, just as a symbol (*cat*) can have more than one meaning ("a small domesticated carnivorous mammal" or "a woman given to spiteful gossip"), so too can a sign. Is the man in **FIGURE 8.7** feeling joy or sorrow? It is hard to tell because these two emotions often produce the same facial expression. So how do we tell them apart? Research suggests that one answer is *context*. When a man says, "My cat ate a mouse," the context of the sentence suggests that he is referring to his pet and not

Nobuyuki Tsujii (*middle*) won the prestigious Van Cliburn International Piano Competition. Although he was born blind and has never seen a facial expression, winning a million-dollar prize immediately gave rise to a million-dollar smile.

On September 19, 1982, Scott Fahlman posted a message to an Internet user's group that read, "I propose the following character sequence for joke markers: :-) Read it sideways." And so the emoticon was born. Fahlman's smile (*above right*) is a sign of happiness, whereas his emoticon is a symbol.

▲ Figure 8.7

TWO EMOTIONS, ONE EXPRESSION Without any context, it is difficult to know if this man is feeling sorrow or joy.

facial feedback hypothesis The theory that emotional expressions can cause the emotional experiences they signify.

▲ Figure 8.8

THE FACIAL FEEDBACK HYPOTHESIS When Jonathan Kalb, a theater professor at Hunter College, contracted Bell's palsy in 2002, part of his face became paralyzed, and he lost the ability to smile. "For the past thirteen years, my smile has been an incoherent tug-of-war between a grin on one side and a frown on the other: an expression of joy spliced to an expression of horror. . . . The worst effect of my damaged smile is that it can dampen my experience of joy. . . . my brain doesn't receive the same feedback messages that normal people receive from their smiles, which reinforce their happy feelings as well as relaying them. I've been devastated by the loss" (Kalb, 2015).

his wife. Similarly, the context in which a facial expression occurs often tells us what that expression means (Aviezer et al., 2008; Barrett, Mesquita, & Gendron, 2011; Kayyal, Widen, & Russell, 2015; Meeren, Heijnsbergen, & de Gelder, 2005). It may be difficult to tell what the man in Figure 8.7 is feeling, but if you turn to **FIGURE 8.12** on page 324 and see his face in context, you will have no trouble identifying his emotion. Indeed, when you return to this page, you may wonder how you could *ever* have thought he was feeling the opposite emotion.

Our emotional experiences cause our emotional expressions, but it also works the other way around. The **facial feedback hypothesis** (Adelmann & Zajonc, 1989; Izard, 1971; Tomkins, 1981) suggests that *emotional expressions can cause the emotional experiences they signify*. For instance, studies show that people feel happier when they are asked to make the sound of a long *e* or to hold a pencil in their teeth (both of which cause contraction of the zygomatic major) than when they are asked to make the sound of a long *u* or to hold a pencil in their lips (Rummer et al., 2015; Strack, Martin, & Stepper, 1988; Zajonc, 1989). Similarly, when people are instructed to arch their brows they find facts more surprising, and when instructed to wrinkle their noses they find odors less pleasant (Lewis, 2012). These things happen because facial expressions and emotional states become strongly associated with each other over time (Ding! Remember Pavlov?), and eventually each can bring about the other (see **FIGURE 8.8**). These effects are not limited to the face. For example, people feel more assertive when instructed to make a fist (Schubert & Koole, 2009) and more confident when instructed to stand with their legs apart (Carney, Cuddy, & Yap, 2010). They even rate others as more hostile when instructed to extend their middle fingers (Chandler & Schwarz, 2009).

The fact that emotional expressions can cause the emotional experiences they signify may explain why people are so good at recognizing the emotional expressions of others. When people interact, they unconsciously mimic their interaction partner's body postures and facial expressions (Chartrand & Bargh, 1999; Dimberg, 1982). When our interaction partners smile, we smile too (Foroni & Semin, 2009). Indeed, the tendency to ape the facial expressions of our interaction partners is so natural that, yes, even apes do it (Davila Ross, Menzler, & Zimmermann, 2008). This mimicry may have a hidden benefit: Because facial expressions and body postures can cause people to experience the emotions they signify, mimicking an interaction partner's expressions can cause people to *feel* what their partners are feeling, which makes it easy for them to identify their partner's emotions. If your friend's frown makes you frown, and your frown makes you feel sad, then you don't have to think very hard to know what your friend is feeling.

Is there any evidence to suggest that people do, in fact, use their own emotions to identify the emotions of others? There is. First, people find it difficult to identify other people's emotions when they are unable to make facial expressions of their own, for example, if their facial muscles are paralyzed with Botox (Niedenthal et al., 2005). People also find it difficult to identify other people's emotions when they are unable to *experience* emotions of their own (Hussey & Safford, 2009; Pitcher et al., 2008). For example, some people with amygdala damage don't feel fear and anger, and as a result, they are typically poor at recognizing the expressions of those emotions in others (Adolphs, Russell, & Tranel, 1999). On the flip side, the people who are naturally talented at figuring out what others are feeling also tend to be natural mimics (Sonnby-Borgstrom, Jonsson, & Svensson, 2003). And their mimicry seems to pay off: Negotiators who mimic the facial expressions of their opponents earn more money than those who don't (Maddux, Mullen, & Galinsky, 2008).

DECEPTIVE EXPRESSION

Our emotional expressions can communicate our true feelings—or not. When a stranger makes a snarky remark about our taste in music, we express our contempt with an arched brow and a reinforcing hand gesture; but when our grandmother makes the same remark, we swallow hard and fake a smile. Our knowledge that it is permissible to show contempt for a stranger but not for a grandparent is a **display rule,** which is a *norm for the appropriate expression of emotion* (Ekman, 1972; Ekman & Friesen, 1968). Obeying a display rule requires several techniques:

- ▶ *Intensification* involves exaggerating the expression of one's emotion, as when a person pretends to be pleased by an unwanted gift. ("A bow tie! Wow! It's just what I always wanted!")

- ▶ *Deintensification* involves muting the expression of one's emotion, as when the loser of a contest tries to look a bit disappointed rather than totally devastated. ("No, really, I'm fine with the silver medal. It matches my belt buckle.")

- ▶ *Masking* involves expressing one emotion while feeling another, as when a judge tries not to betray contempt for lawyers as they make their cases. ("I'm impartially considering your idiotic argument, so please go on.")

- ▶ *Neutralizing* involves showing no expression of the emotion one is feeling, as when a card player tries to keep a "poker face" despite having been dealt a winning hand. ("Four aces. Ho hum. Nice weather today.") (see **FIGURE 8.9**).

Although people in different cultures use all of these same techniques, they use them in the service of different display rules. For example, in one study, Japanese and American college students watched an unpleasant video of car accidents and amputations (Ekman, 1972; Friesen, 1972). When the students didn't know that the experimenters were observing them, Japanese and American students showed similar facial expressions of disgust, but when they knew they were being observed, the Japanese students masked their disgust with pleasant expressions, but the American students did not. In many eastern cultures it is considered rude to display negative emotions in the presence of a respected person, and so members of these cultures tend to mask or neutralize their expressions. The fact that different cultures have different display rules may be one of the reasons that people are generally better at recognizing the facial expressions of members of their own cultures (Elfenbein & Ambady, 2002; see A World of Difference: Say Cheese).

Of course, our attempts to obey our culture's display rules don't always work out. Anyone who has ever watched the loser of a beauty pageant congratulate the winner

display rule A norm for the appropriate expression of emotion.

A popular form of cosmetic enhancement is the Botox injection, which paralyzes certain facial muscles. The reality TV judge Simon Cowell gets them regularly and says, "Botox is no more unusual than toothpaste.... It works, you do it once a year—who cares?" Well, maybe he should. Some evidence suggests that Botox injections can impair both the experience of emotion (Davis, 2008; Davis et al., 2010) and the ability to process emotional information (Havas et al., 2010). Also, toothpaste once a year? Eeew.

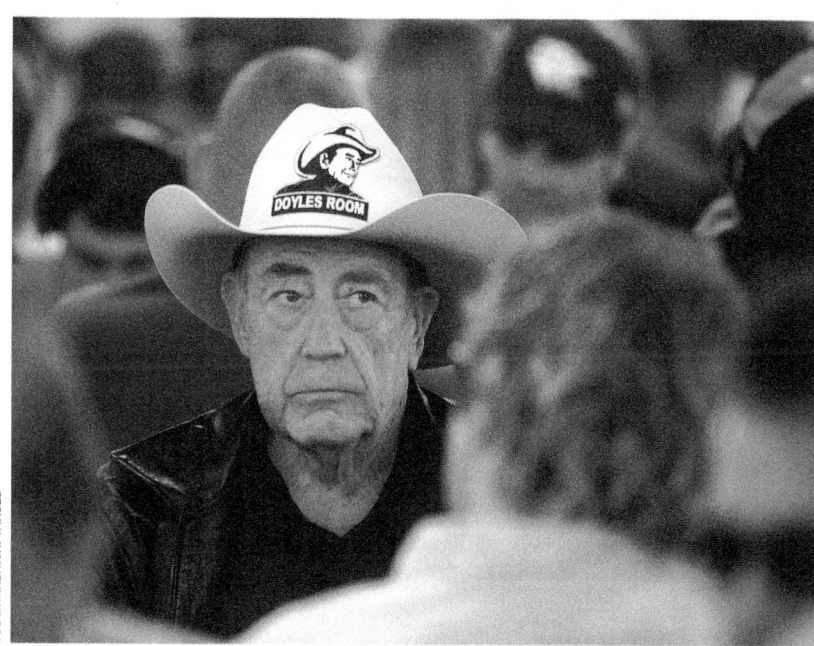

◀ Figure 8.9

NEUTRALIZING Can you tell what this man is feeling? He hopes not. Doyle Brunson is a champion poker player who does not want other players to know how he feels about his cards. So far, it seems to be working. Brunson has won more than $6 million.

Say Cheese

Americans come from such a wide range of cultures that one of the few things they share is a need for hyphenation. African-Americans, Asian-Americans, European-Americans, and many other kinds of Americans live and work side by side, making the United States one of the most culturally diverse nations on earth. But diversity creates challenges, and one of those is communication. Different cultures have different display rules—different ways of nonverbally expressing emotions—which suggests that Americans with different backgrounds should have trouble "reading" their neighbors. And yet, they don't seem to. How come?

Wood, Rychlowska, and Niedenthal (2016) analyzed data from 92 scientific papers that had measured the accuracy with which people from 82 different cultures could recognize the emotional expressions of people from other cultures. First, the researchers used historical, genetic, and sociological data to compute the cultural diversity of each of the 82 cultures. Nations such as Brazil and the United States scored high in diversity, whereas nations such as Japan and Ethiopia scored low (see the map above). Second, they computed how easily the facial expressions of people from each of these cultures could be recognized by people from other cultures. When they compared these two measures, they found a positive correlation (see the graph to the right). The more diverse a culture is, the more easily the facial expressions of its members can be understood by members of other cultures. Why might that be the case?

The researchers suggest that in nations with little cultural diversity, people can communicate with subtle expressions—a slightly raised eyebrow or the fleeting flare of a nostril—because everyone knows and follows the same display rules. But in diverse nations, people of different backgrounds follow different sets of rules, so to communicate with each other they have learned to use expressions that are so perfectly clear

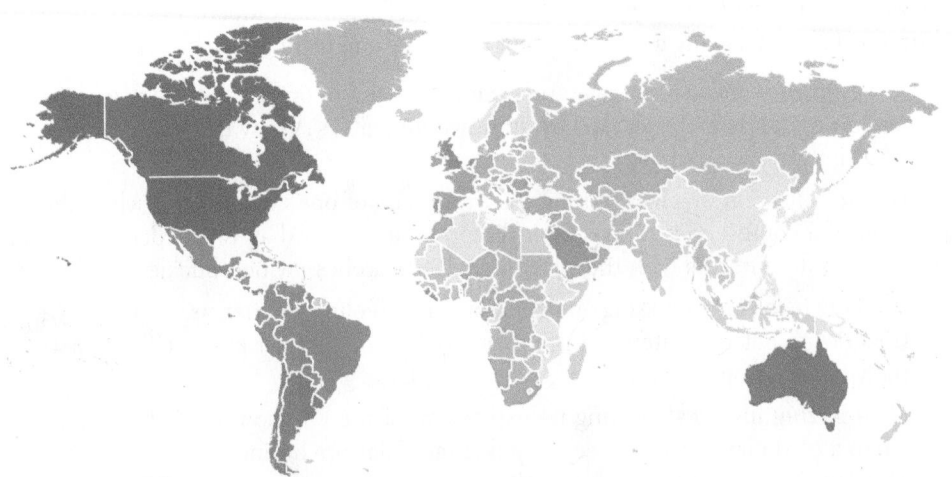

▲ The diversity of cultures: Darker colors indicate greater cultural diversity.

that they can be accurately recognized by any human on the planet. This fact may help explain a common stereotype about Americans. As one blogger noted:

> Fellow Americans, did you know that your smile is famous? I sure did not until I came to Europe. Traveling from country to country, locals would tell me that I have THE American-girl smile. It took me actually moving here to see what they meant. Americans just have this smile. It's unique and it's huge. The

phrase "grinning from ear to ear" came from somewhere (Butts, 2013).

Although people all over the world seem to believe that the big, toothy American smile is an indicator of our optimism, our phoniness, or our naiveté, this study suggests that it may instead be a clever solution to a knotty communication problem that results from our diversity. In a land where every face speaks a different language, it has to learn to shout.

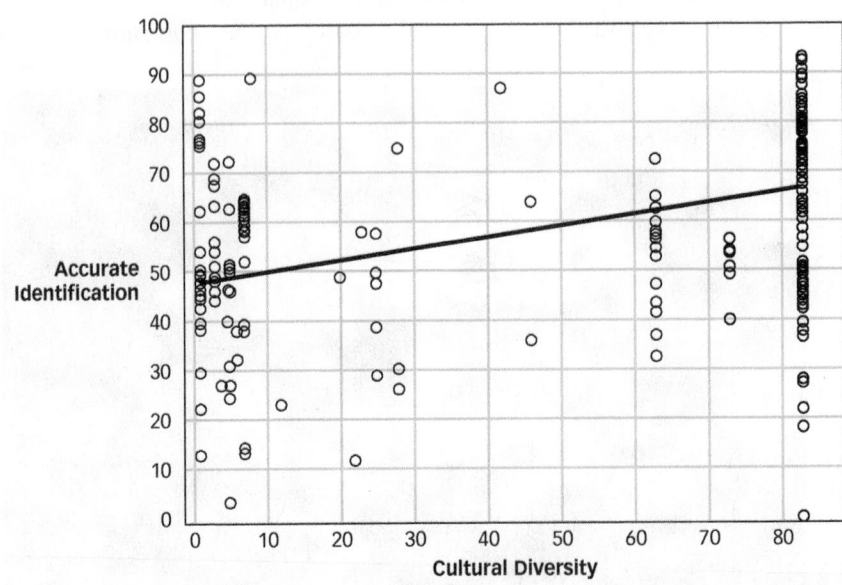

▲ Diversity and accuracy: Each circle in this figure represents one of the 82 cultures.

knows that voices, bodies, and faces often betray a person's true emotional state. Darwin (1899/2007, p. 64) noted that "those muscles of the face which are least obedient to the will, will sometimes alone betray a slight and passing emotion," and once again Darwin was right. Even when people smile bravely to mask their disappointment, for example, their faces tend to express small bursts of disappointment that last just 1/5 to 1/25 of a second (Porter & ten Brinke, 2008). These *micro-expressions* happen so quickly that they are almost impossible to detect with the naked eye. But a few features that distinguish between sincere and insincere facial expressions are a bit easier to observe (Ekman, 2003).

▶ *Morphology*: Sincere expressions involve the so-called *reliable muscles*, which are those that people cannot easily control. For example, people can easily control the *zygomatic major* muscles that raise the corners of their mouths, but not the *obicularis oculi* muscles that crinkle the corners of their eyes. That's why smiles are not necessarily sincere expressions of happiness but eye crinkles are (see **FIGURE 8.10**).

▶ *Symmetry*: Sincere expressions tend to be a bit more symmetrical than insincere expressions, which is why a slightly lopsided smile suggests insincerity.

▶ *Duration*: Sincere expressions tend to last between a half second and 5 seconds; expressions of much longer duration tend to be insincere.

▶ *Temporal patterning*: Sincere expressions appear and disappear smoothly over the course of a few seconds, whereas insincere expressions tend to have abrupt onsets and offsets.

Our emotions don't just leak on our faces. They leak all over the place. Research shows that many aspects of our verbal and nonverbal behavior are altered when we tell a lie (DePaulo et al., 2003). For example, liars tend to speak more slowly, take longer to respond to questions, and respond in less detail than do people who are telling the truth. Liars are also less fluent, less engaging, more uncertain, tenser, and less pleasant than truth-tellers. Oddly enough, one of the telltale signs of a liar is that his or her performances tend to be just a little too good. A liar's speech will often lack the small imperfections that a truth-teller's speech contains, such as superfluous details ("I noticed that the robber was wearing the same shoes that I saw on sale last week at Bloomingdale's and I found myself wondering what he paid for them"), spontaneous correction ("He was six feet tall . . . well, no, actually more like six-two"), and expressions of self-doubt ("I think he had blue eyes, but I'm really not sure").

Given the reliable differences between sincere and insincere expressions and between truth-tellers and liars, you might think that people would be quite good at distinguishing between them. In fact, people are fairly dreadful at this, and under most circumstances they don't perform much better than chance (DePaulo, Stone, & Lassiter, 1985; Ekman, 1992; Zuckerman, DePaulo, & Rosenthal, 1981; Zuckerman & Driver, 1985). One reason for this is that people have a strong bias toward believing that others are expressing sincere emotions or telling the truth, which explains why people tend to mistake liars for truth-tellers more often than they mistake truth-tellers for liars (Gilbert, 1991). A second reason is that people don't know what to look for when they try to detect insincerity and dishonesty (Vrij et al., 2011). For instance, people think that fast talking is a sign of lying when it actually isn't, and that slow talking is not a sign of lying when it actually is. Decades of research show that people are bad lie detectors who don't know they are bad lie detectors. Indeed, the correlation between a person's ability to detect lies and the person's confidence in that ability is essentially zero (DePaulo et al., 1997).

When people can't do something well, such as adding 87-digit numbers or picking up 10-ton rocks, they typically turn the job over to a machine. Can machines detect lies better than we can? The answer is yes, but that's not saying very much.

RAUL DEMOLINA/AP IMAGES

▲ Figure 8.10

DARN THOSE RELIABLE MUSCLES! If you want to know which of the two contestants in the 1986 Miss America pageant just won the crown, check out their eyes. Only one of the women has the telltale "corner crinkles" that signify genuine happiness, and that's the one on the right. But don't feel too bad for the one on the left. That loser is named Halle Berry, and she went on to become a seriously famous movie star.

The Canadian prime minister Justin Trudeau wipes away tears after delivering an emotional speech. Crying is very difficult to control and thus provides reliable information about the intensity of a person's emotions.

REUTERS/CHRIS WATTIE

▶ **Figure 8.11**

LIE DETECTION MACHINES Some researchers hope to replace the polygraph with machines that measure changes in blood flow in the brain and the face. As the top panel shows, some areas of the brain are more active when people tell lies than when they tell the truth (shown in red), and some are more active when people tell the truth than when they tell lies (shown in blue; Langleben et al., 2005). The bottom panel shows images taken by a thermal camera that detects the heat caused by blood flow to different parts of the face. The images show a person's face before (*left*) and after (*right*) telling a lie (Pavlidis, Eberhardt, & Levine, 2002). Although neither of these new lie-detection techniques is yet extremely accurate, that could soon change.

Right side   Left side   Anterior

REPUBLISHED WITH PERMISSION OF LANGLEBEN, D. D., LOUGHEAD, J. W., BILKER, W. B., RUPAREL, K., CHILDRESS, A. R., BUSCH, S. I., GUR, R. C. FROM (2005). TELLING TRUTH FROM LIE IN INDIVIDUAL SUBJECTS WITH FAST EVENT-RELATED FMRI. *HUMAN BRAIN MAPPING* 26, PP. 262–272. PERMISSION CONVEYED THROUGH COPYRIGHT CLEARANCE CENTER, INC.

REPUBLISHED WITH PERMISSION OF PAVLIDIS, EBERHARDT, AND LEVINE, 2002. FROM HUMAN BEHAVIOUR: SEEING THROUGH THE FACE OF DECEPTION, *NATURE*, 415, 35. PERMISSION CONVEYED THROUGH COPYRIGHT CLEARANCE CENTER, INC.

REUTERS/FAYAZ AZIZ

▲ **Figure 8.12**

WHAT DO YOU THINK NOW? This Pakastani man is being led away from the scene of the suicide bombing that killed his father. Now can you see the pain and sorrow in his face? Is it hard to imagine how this expression could ever have been mistaken for joy?

The most widely used lie detection machine is the *polygraph*, which measures a variety of physiological responses that are associated with stress, which people often feel when they are afraid of being caught in a lie. A polygraph can detect lies with better-than-chance accuracy, but its error rate is still too high to make it a useful lie detector. For example, imagine that 10 of the 10,000 people coming through a particular airport are terrorists and that when hooked up to a polygraph, they all claim to be innocent. A polygraph that is set to *maximum* sensitivity would catch 8 of the 10 terrorists in a lie, but it would also mistakenly catch 1,598 innocent people. If the polygraph was instead set to *minimum* sensitivity, then it would mistakenly catch just 39 innocent people, but it would only catch 2 of the 10 real terrorists. And these numbers assume that terrorists don't know how to fool a polygraph, which is something that people can, in fact, be trained to do! No wonder the National Research Council (2003) warned, "Given its level of accuracy, achieving a high probability of identifying individuals who pose major security risks in a population with a very low proportion of such individuals would require setting the test to be so sensitive that hundreds, or even thousands, of innocent individuals would be implicated for every major security violator correctly identified" (p. 6). In short, neither people nor machines are particularly good at lie detection, which is probably why lying remains such a popular human sport (see **FIGURE 8.11**).

Build to the Outcomes

1. What is the difference between a sign and a symbol?

2. What evidence suggests that facial expressions of emotion are or are not universal?

3. How do emotional expressions cause emotional experiences?

4. What are display rules?

5. What features distinguish between sincere and insincere facial expressions?

6. What is the problem with lie-detecting machines?

Motivation: Being Moved

Leonardo is a robot, so he does what he is programmed to do and nothing more. Because he doesn't have wants and urges—doesn't crave friendship or desire chocolate or hate homework—he doesn't initiate his own behavior. He can learn but he cannot yearn, and therefore he isn't *motivated* to act in the same way we are. A **motivation** is *the psychological cause of an action*, and it is no coincidence that the words *emotion* and *motivation* share a common linguistic root that means "to move." Unlike robots, human beings act because their emotions move them, and they do this in two ways. First, emotions provide people with *information* about the world, and second, emotions are the *objectives* toward which people strive. Let's examine each of these in turn.

THE FUNCTION OF EMOTION

In the film *Invasion of the Body Snatchers*, a young boy suspects that his parents have been kidnapped by aliens and replaced with replicas. This bizarre belief is a common symptom of bad science fiction movies, but it is also a common symptom of Capgras syndrome. People who suffer from this syndrome typically believe that one or more of their family members are imposters. As one Capgras sufferer told her doctor, "He looks exactly like my father, but he really isn't. He's a nice guy, but he isn't my father . . . . Maybe my father employed him to take care of me, paid him some money so he could pay my bills" (Hirstein & Ramachandran, 1997, p. 438). But this woman's father had not been body-snatched, nor had he hired a doppelgänger to pay off her credit cards. Rather, the neural connections between this woman's temporal lobe (where faces are identified) and limbic system (where emotions are generated) had been damaged. So when she saw her father's face she could identify him as "Dad," but because the visual information was not also transmitted to her limbic system, she didn't feel the warm emotions that her real dad could be expected to produce. Her father "looked right" but didn't "feel right," and so she concluded that the man before her was an imposter (see **FIGURE 8.13**). The woman used her emotional experience as information about the world, and as you will see, so do the rest of us.

Emotions Are Information

Why do people report being more satisfied with their lives when they are asked about them on a sunny day rather than a rainy day (Schwarz & Clore, 1983)? Because people tend to feel happier on sunny days, and if they don't stop to think about the fact that the sunshine is what is making them happy, they may mistakenly take their emotional experience as information about the quality of their lives. After all, a satisfying life makes you happy, so if you feel happy . . . why then, you must have a satisfying life! Because events in the world can influence our emotions, our emotions can provide information about events in the world (Schwarz, 2012; Schwarz, Mannheim, & Clore, 1988). Sometimes that information leads us astray, but more often than not it is quite useful (Mikels et al., 2011; Pham, Lee, & Stephen, 2012).

Indeed, without the information that emotions provide, we would be utterly lost (Lerner et al., 2015). When a neurologist was asked to see a patient who had an unusual form of brain damage, he asked the patient to choose between two dates for an appointment. It sounds like a simple decision, but for the next half hour, the patient enumerated reasons for and against each of the two possible dates, completely unable to decide in favor of one option or the other (Damasio, 1994). The patient was unable to make a simple decision—not because he couldn't think, but because he couldn't feel. His brain injury had left him unable to experience emotion, so when he entertained one option ("If I come next Tuesday, I'll have to cancel my lunch with Fred"), he didn't feel any better or any worse than when he entertained another

Learning Outcomes

▶ Identify the two basic functions of emotion.

▶ Explain the concepts of instinct and drive

motivation The psychological cause of an action.

In the 1956 film *Invasion of the Body Snatchers*, little Jimmy Grimaldi tells the nurse and the doctor that his mother has been replaced by a replica. Their response? Give him a chill pill and send him home to be eaten by aliens. Nice.

Strength of emotional response

▲ Figure 8.13

CAPGRAS SYNDROME This graph shows the emotional responses (as measured by skin conductance) of a participant with Capgras syndrome and a group of control participants to a set of familiar and unfamiliar faces. Although the controls have stronger emotional responses to the familiar than to the unfamiliar faces, the Capgras patient has similar emotional responses to both (Hirstein & Ramachandran, 1997).

When we try to make a decision, we often ask how we "feel" about it. If we couldn't feel, then we wouldn't know which alternative to choose. Without emotions, Rihanna would probably just stand there until someone came along and gave her a Grammy for Best Orange Stiletto.

("If I come next Wednesday, I'll have to get up early to catch the bus"). And because he *felt* nothing when he thought about each option, he couldn't decide which was best. Studies show that when individuals with this particular form of brain damage are given the opportunity to gamble, they tend to make very risky bets because they don't feel that little twinge of anxiety that tells most of us that we are about to do something dangerous (Shiv et al., 2005).

Emotions Are Goals

If the first function of emotion is to provide us with information about the world, then the second function is to tell us what to do with that information. The **hedonic principle** is *the claim that people are motivated to experience pleasure and avoid pain*. That claim has a very long history. The ancient Greek philosopher Aristotle argued that the hedonic principle could explain everything there was to know about human motivation: "It is for the sake of this that we all do all that we do." We want many things, from peace and prosperity to health and security, but we want them for just one reason, and that is that they make us feel good. "Are these things good for any other reason except that they end in pleasure, and get rid of and avert pain?" asked Plato. "Are you looking to any other standard but pleasure and pain when you call them good?" Plato and Aristotle were suggesting that pleasure isn't just good—it is what the word *good* actually *means*.

According to the hedonic principle, our emotional experience can be thought of as a gauge that ranges from bad to good, and our primary motivation—perhaps even our *sole* motivation—is to keep the needle on the gauge as close to *good* as possible. Even when we voluntarily do things that tilt the needle in the opposite direction, such as letting the dentist drill our teeth or waking up early for a boring class, we are doing these things because we believe that they will nudge the needle toward *good* in the future and keep it there longer. Although there are occasionally times when people want to be angry or worried or sad (Michaela et al., 2009; Miyamoto, Ma, & Petermann, 2014; Tamir & Ford, 2012; Tamir et al., 2015), it seems fairly obvious that most people would rather feel good than bad most of the time.

INSTINCTS AND DRIVES

If our primary motivation is to keep the needle on *good*, then which things push the needle in that direction and which things push it away? And where do these things get the power to push our needle around, and exactly how do they do the pushing? The answers to such questions lie in two concepts that have played unusually important roles in the history of psychology: *instincts* and *drives*.

Instincts

When a newborn baby is given a drop of sugar water, it smiles, and when it is given a check for $10,000, it acts like it couldn't care less. By the time the baby goes to college, these responses pretty much reverse. It seems clear that nature endows us with certain motivations and that experience endows us with others. William James (1890) called the natural tendency to seek a particular goal an *instinct*, which he defined as "the faculty of acting in such a way as to produce certain ends, without foresight of the ends, and without previous education in the performance" (p. 383). According to James, nature hardwired people, penguins, parrots, and puppies to want certain things without being taught to want them, and to execute the behaviors that produce these things without ever thinking about it. He and other psychologists of his time tried to make a list of what those things were.

They were a little too successful. In just a few decades of list-making, their list of instincts had grown to contain nearly 6,000 instincts, including some rather exotic ones such as "the instinct to be secretive" and "the instinct to grind one's teeth." Some

All animals are born with instincts. In the annual running of the bulls in Pamplona, Spain, no one has to teach the bulls to chase the runners, and no one has to teach the runners to flee.

hedonic principle The claim that people are motivated to experience pleasure and avoid pain.

researchers complained that the term suffered from "a great variety of usage and the almost universal lack of critical standards" (Bernard, 1924, p. 21), and others worried that attributing the tendency for people to befriend each other to an "affiliation instinct" was more of a description than an explanation (Ayres, 1921; Dunlap, 1919; Field, 1921). By 1930, the term had fallen out of fashion, in part because it didn't really seem to explain anything, but also because it flew in the face of American psychology's hot new trend: behaviorism.

Behaviorists rejected the concept of instinct on two grounds. First, they believed that behavior should be explained by the external stimuli that evoke it and not by the hypothetical internal states on which it presumably depends. The father of behaviorism, John Watson, had written that "the time seems to have come when psychology must discard all reference to consciousness" (1913, p. 163), and behaviorists saw instincts as just the sort of unnecessary "mind blather" that Watson forbade. The second reason that behaviorists rejected the concept of instinct was that instincts are inherited, and behaviorists believed that complex behaviors were learned, not hard wired. So what did the behaviorists replace instincts with?

Drives

Although Watson's younger followers agreed in principle with his ban on mind blather, they also realized that certain phenomena were difficult to explain without some reference to an organism's internal state. For example, if all behavior is a response to an external stimulus, then why does a rat that is sitting still in its cage at 9:00 a.m. start wandering around and looking for food by noon? Nothing in the cage has changed, so why has the rat's behavior changed? What visible, measurable, external stimulus is the wandering rat responding to? The obvious answer is that the rat is responding to something inside itself, which meant that Watson's young followers (the "new behaviorists" as they called themselves) were forced to look inside the rat to explain its wandering. But how could they do that without talking about the "thoughts" and "feelings" that Watson had forbidden them to mention?

They did it by talking about **drives,** which are *internal states caused by physiological needs.* Bodies, it seems, are a bit like thermostats. When a thermostat detects that the room is too cold, it sends a signal that initiates corrective actions, such as turning on a furnace. Similarly, when bodies detect that they are underfed, they send signals that initiate corrective actions such as eating. According to Clark Hull, one of the leaders of the new behaviorists, "When conditions deviate from the optimum, equilibrium may as a rule be restored by some sort of action on the part of the organism" (1943, p. 384). Hull was talking about **homeostasis** which is *the tendency for a system to take action to keep itself in an optimal state.* To survive, an organism needs to maintain precise levels of nutrition, warmth, and so on. When these levels deviate too much from the optimum, the brain sends a signal to the organism to take corrective action. That signal is called a drive, and Hull's **drive-reduction theory** is *a theory suggesting that organisms are motivated to reduce their drives.* According to this theory, it isn't food per se that organisms find rewarding; it is the reduction of the drive for food. A reinforcement, then, is any "substance or commodity in the environment which satisfies a need, i.e., which reduces a drive" (Hull, 1943, p. 131).

You will be relieved to know that the words *instinct* and *drive* are no longer widely used in psychology. But both concepts have something to teach us. The concept of instinct reminds us that nature endows organisms with a tendency to seek certain things, and the concept of drive reminds us that this seeking is initiated by an internal state. The psychologist William McDougall (1930) called the study of motivation *hormic psychology.* The term *hormic* is derived from the Greek word for "urge," and people clearly do have urges—some of which they acquire through experience and some of which they do not—that motivate them to take certain actions. So what kinds of urges do they have, and what kinds of actions do they take to satisfy them?

Aristotle claimed that water had "gravity" and fire had "levity" and that these properties made them go downward and upward, respectively. It now seems obvious that Aristotle was merely describing the motion of these elements and not really explaining it—much as William James did when he attributed behavior to instinct. By the way, that's Plato and Aristotle standing together under the arch in Raphael's 1509 masterpiece *The School of Athens,* which has allowed us to mention four really famous guys in just one caption.

drive An internal state caused by physiological needs.

homeostasis The tendency for a system to take action to keep itself in an optimal state.

drive-reduction theory A theory suggesting that organisms are motivated to reduce their drives.

Wanting: The Body's Desires

Learning Outcomes

▶ Describe the biological signals that turn hunger on and off.

▶ Identify the common eating disorders.

▶ Understand what causes obesity and how it can be prevented.

▶ Describe the biological mechanisms underlying sexual interest and activity.

Abraham Maslow (1954) attempted to organize the list of human urges—or, as he preferred to call them, *needs*—in a meaningful way (see **FIGURE 8.14**). He noticed that some needs are more pressing than others, and that the pressing needs (such as the need to eat) must be satisfied before the less pressing needs (such as the need to have friends). So Maslow built a "hierarchy of needs" that had the most pressing ones at the bottom and the least pressing ones at the top. Maslow suggested that as a rule, people are more likely to experience a need when the needs below it are met. So when people are hungry or thirsty or exhausted, for example, they are less likely to seek intellectual fulfillment or moral clarity (see **FIGURE 8.15**). According to Maslow, our most pressing needs are those we share with other animals, such as the need to eat and mate. Let's explore these two needs in detail.

HUNGER

Animals convert matter into energy by eating, and they are driven to do this by an internal state called *hunger*. But what is hunger and where does it come from? At every moment, your body is sending signals to your brain about its current energy state. If your body needs energy, it sends an *orexigenic* signal to your brain telling it to switch the experience of hunger on, and if your body has sufficient energy it sends an *anorexigenic* signal to your brain telling it to switch the experience of hunger off (Gropp et al., 2005). No one knows precisely what these signals are or how they are sent and received, but research has identified a few candidates.

Ghrelin is a hormone that is produced in the stomach and appears to be one of the orexigenic signals that tells the brain to switch hunger on (Inui, 2001; Nakazato et al., 2001). When people are injected with ghrelin, they become intensely hungry

binge eating disorder An eating disorder characterized by recurrent and uncontrolled episodes of eating a large number of calories in a short time.

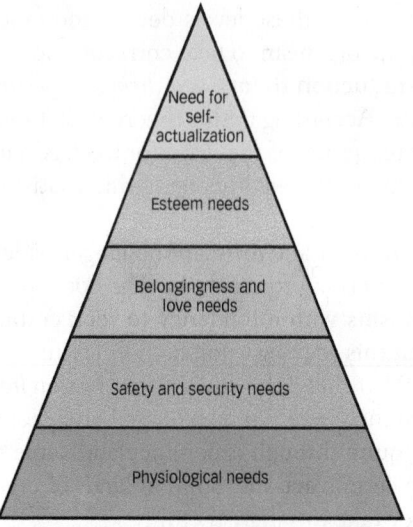

◀ Figure 8.14

MASLOW'S HIERARCHY OF NEEDS
The psychologist Abraham Maslow believed that needs form a hierarchy, with physiological needs at the bottom and self-actualization needs at the top.

Need for self-actualization

Esteem needs

Belongingness and love needs

Safety and security needs

Physiological needs

and eat about 30% more than usual (Wren et al., 2001). Interestingly, ghrelin also binds to neurons in the hippocampus and temporarily improves learning and memory (Diano et al., 2006), perhaps so that we become just a little bit better at locating food when our bodies need it most. *Leptin* is a chemical secreted by fat cells, and it is an anorexigenic signal that tells the brain to switch hunger off. It seems to do this by making food less rewarding (Farooqi et al., 2007). People who are born with a leptin deficiency have trouble controlling their appetites (Montague et al., 1997). For example, in 2002, medical researchers reported on the case of a 9-year-old girl who weighed 200 pounds, but after just a few leptin injections, she reduced her food intake by 84% and attained normal weight (Farooqi et al., 2002). Some researchers think the idea that chemicals turn hunger on and off is far too simple. They argue that there is no general state called *hunger*, but rather that there are many different hungers, each of which is a response to a unique nutritional deficit and each of which is switched on by a unique chemical messenger (Rozin & Kalat, 1971). For example, rats that are deprived of protein will seek proteins while turning down fats and carbohydrates, suggesting that they are experiencing a specific "protein hunger" and not a general hunger (Rozin, 1968).

We do not know whether hunger is one signal or many, but we do know that the primary receiver of these signals is the hypothalamus. Different parts of the hypothalamus receive different signals (see **FIGURE 8.16**). The *lateral hypothalamus* receives orexigenic signals, and when it is destroyed, animals sitting in a cage full of food will starve themselves to death. The *ventromedial hypothalamus* receives anorexigenic signals, and when it is destroyed, animals will gorge themselves to the point of illness and obesity (Miller, 1960; Steinbaum & Miller, 1965). These two structures were once thought to be the "hunger center" and the "satiety center" of the brain, but this view turned out to be far too simple (Woods et al., 1998). Hypothalamic structures clearly play an important role in turning hunger on and off, but the precise way in which they execute these functions remains poorly understood (Stellar & Stellar, 1985).

EATING DISORDERS

Feelings of hunger tell most of us when to start and stop eating. But for the 10 to 30 million Americans who have eating disorders, eating is a much more complicated affair (Hoek & van Hoeken, 2003). Let's take a quick look at some of the better known disorders.

BED, Bulimia, and Anorexia

Binge Eating Disorder (or BED) is *an eating disorder characterized by recurrent and uncontrolled episodes of consuming a large number of calories in a short time*. People with BED quickly consume large quantities of food over a period of just a few hours, often times at night. They often report feeling a lack of control over their own behavior—a sense that they "just can't stop eating." **Bulimia nervosa** is *an eating disorder characterized by binge eating followed by compensatory behavior*. People with bulimia also binge, but then they take actions to compensate for their eating, such as fasting, excessive exercising, taking diuretics or laxatives, or even inducing vomiting to purge the food from their bodies. People with BED or bulimia are caught in a cycle: They eat to ease negative emotions such as sadness and anxiety, but then concern about weight gain leads them to experience negative emotions such as guilt and self-loathing (Sherry & Hall, 2009; cf. Haedt-Matt & Keel, 2011). **Anorexia nervosa** is *an eating disorder characterized by an intense fear of being overweight and a severe restriction of food intake*. People with anorexia tend to have a distorted body image that leads them to believe they are overweight when they may actually be emaciated.

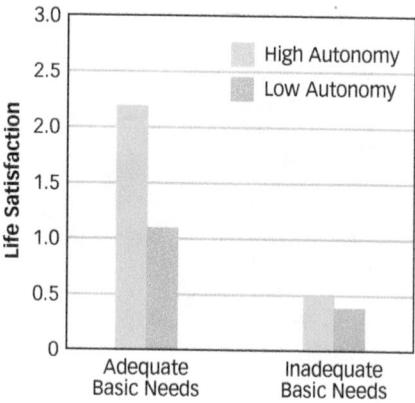

▲ Figure 8.15

WHEN DO HIGHER NEEDS MATTER? A study of 77,000 people in the world's 51 poorest nations (Martin & Hill, 2012) showed that if people have their basic needs met, then autonomy (i.e., freedom to make their own decisions) increases their satisfaction with their lives. But when people do not have their basic needs met, autonomy makes little difference.

▲ Figure 8.16

HUNGER, SATIETY, AND THE HYPOTHALAMUS The hypothalamus comprises many parts. In general, the lateral hypothalamus receives the signals that turn hunger on and the ventromedial hypothalamus receives the signals that turn hunger off.

bulimia nervosa An eating disorder characterized by binge eating followed by compensatory behavior.

anorexia nervosa An eating disorder characterized by an intense fear of being overweight and a severe restriction of food intake.

Bar Refaeili is Israel's best known supermodel. In 2012, Israel enacted a law banning models whose body mass index is under 18.5 from appearing in advertisements. So a 5-foot, 8-inch model must weigh at least 119 pounds.

They tend to be high-achieving perfectionists who see their severe control of eating as a triumph of will over impulse. Anorexia is often fatal, leading people to literally starve themselves to death.

What causes these eating disorders? Their origins appear to be genetic (Zerwas & Bulik, 2011), experiential (Inniss, Steiger, & Bruce, 2011), and psychological (Klump et al., 2004), but they may be cultural as well (Hogan & Strasburger, 2008). For example, women with anorexia typically believe that thinness equals beauty, and it isn't hard to understand why. The average American woman is 5 feet, 4 inches tall and weighs 140 pounds, but the average American fashion model is 5 feet, 11 inches tall and weighs 117 pounds. So perhaps it is not surprising that most college-age women report wanting to be thinner than they are (Rozin, Trachtenberg, & Cohen, 2001), and nearly 20% report being *embarrassed* to be seen buying chocolate (Rozin, Bauer, & Catanese, 2003). But anorexia is not just "vanity run amok" (Striegel-Moore & Bulik, 2007). Most researchers believe that there are biological and genetic components to this illness as well. For example, although anorexia primarily affects women, men have a sharply increased risk of becoming anorexic if they have a female twin who has the disorder (Procopio & Marriott, 2007), suggesting that anorexia may have something to do with prenatal exposure to female hormones.

OBESITY

Bulimia and anorexia are serious problems that affect about 0.01% of the population (Hoek, 2006). The most pervasive eating-related problem is obesity. In the last 15 years, Americans have collectively gained more than a billion pounds (Kolbert, 2009). The average American man is now 17 pounds heavier and the average American woman is now 19 pounds heavier than they were in the 1970s. The proportion of overweight children has doubled, the proportion of overweight teens has tripled, and a full 40% of American women are now too heavy to enlist in the military. In 1991, no U.S. state had an obesity rate *higher* than 20%, but by 2012, only one state (Colorado) had an obesity rate *lower* than 20% (see **FIGURE 8.17**). The problem is not unique to America: Nearly 30% of the world's population is overweight or obese, and not one country has reduced its obesity rate in the last 33 years (Ng et al., 2014). In fact, it is the citizens of Middle Eastern countries, including Egypt and Saudi Arabia, who have gained the most weight over the last three decades.

▼ Figure 8.17
THE GEOGRAPHY OF OBESITY
As this 2014 map shows, obesity is a problem everywhere in the United States, but ironically, it is most prevalent in the nation's . . . um, midsection.

Least obese

Most obese

Times have changed. Although modern ads promise to help young women lose weight, ads from the 1960s promised to help them gain it.

Obesity is defined as having a body mass index (BMI) of 30 or greater. **TABLE 8.1** allows you to compute your BMI, and the odds are that you won't like what you learn. Although BMI is a better predictor of mortality for some people than for others (Romero-Corral et al., 2006; van Dis et al., 2009), most researchers agree that an extremely high BMI is unhealthy. Every year, obesity-related illnesses cost the

TABLE 8.1

Body Mass Index Table

	Normal						Overweight					Obese									Extreme Obesity															
BMI	19	20	21	22	23	24	25	26	27	28	29	30	31	32	33	34	35	36	37	38	39	40	41	42	43	44	45	46	47	48	49	50	51	52	53	54
Height (Inches)													Body Weight (pounds)																							
58	91	96	100	105	110	115	119	124	129	134	138	143	148	153	158	162	167	172	177	181	186	191	196	201	205	210	215	220	224	229	234	239	244	248	253	258
59	94	99	104	109	114	119	124	128	133	138	143	148	153	158	163	169	173	178	183	188	193	198	203	308	212	217	222	227	232	237	242	247	252	257	262	267
60	97	102	107	112	116	123	128	133	138	143	148	153	156	163	168	174	179	184	189	194	199	204	209	215	220	225	230	235	240	245	250	256	261	266	271	278
61	100	108	111	116	122	127	132	137	143	148	153	156	164	169	174	180	186	190	195	201	206	211	217	222	227	232	238	243	248	254	259	264	269	275	280	285
62	104	109	115	120	126	131	138	142	147	153	158	164	169	175	180	186	191	196	202	207	213	218	224	229	235	240	248	251	258	262	267	273	278	264	289	295
63	107	113	118	124	130	135	141	148	152	158	163	169	175	180	188	191	197	203	208	214	220	225	231	237	242	248	254	260	265	270	278	282	287	293	299	304
64	110	118	122	128	134	140	145	151	157	163	169	174	180	188	192	197	204	209	215	221	227	232	238	244	250	258	262	267	273	279	285	291	298	302	308	314
65	114	120	128	132	138	144	150	156	162	168	174	180	186	192	193	204	210	218	222	228	234	240	246	252	258	264	270	278	282	288	294	300	308	312	318	324
66	118	124	130	138	142	148	155	161	167	173	179	186	192	198	204	210	216	223	229	235	241	247	253	260	266	272	278	284	291	297	303	309	315	322	328	334
67	121	127	134	140	146	153	159	166	172	178	185	191	198	204	211	217	223	230	238	242	249	256	261	268	274	280	287	293	299	308	312	319	325	331	338	344
68	125	131	138	144	151	158	164	171	177	184	190	197	203	210	216	223	230	236	243	249	256	262	269	278	282	289	295	302	303	315	322	328	335	341	348	354
69	128	135	142	149	155	162	169	178	182	189	195	203	209	218	223	230	236	243	250	257	263	270	277	284	291	297	304	311	318	324	331	338	345	351	358	365
70	132	139	146	153	160	167	174	181	188	195	202	209	216	222	229	236	243	250	257	264	271	278	285	292	299	308	313	320	327	334	341	348	355	362	369	378
71	138	143	150	157	166	172	179	186	193	200	208	215	222	229	235	243	250	257	265	272	279	288	293	301	308	315	322	329	338	343	351	358	365	372	379	388
72	140	147	154	162	169	177	184	191	199	208	213	221	228	235	242	250	258	265	272	279	287	294	302	309	316	324	331	338	346	353	361	368	375	383	390	397
73	144	151	159	166	174	182	189	197	204	212	219	227	236	242	250	257	266	272	280	288	295	302	310	318	326	333	340	348	355	363	371	378	388	393	401	408
74	148	155	163	171	179	188	194	202	210	218	225	233	241	249	258	264	272	280	287	295	303	311	319	328	334	342	350	358	365	373	381	389	398	404	412	420
75	152	160	166	178	184	192	200	208	216	224	232	240	248	256	264	272	279	287	295	303	311	319	327	335	343	351	359	367	375	383	391	399	407	415	423	431
76	158	164	172	180	189	197	205	213	221	230	238	246	254	263	271	279	287	295	304	312	320	328	338	344	353	361	369	377	385	394	402	410	418	428	436	443

Information from: National Institutes of Health, 1998, *Clinical Guidelines on the Identification, Evaluation, and Treatment of Overweight and Obesity in Adults: The Evidence Report.* This and other information about overweight and obesity can be found at www.nhlbi.nih.gov/guidelines/obesity/ob_home.htm.

A Feast for the Eyes

In 1923, a reporter for the *New York Times* asked the British mountaineer George Leigh Mallory why he wanted to climb Mount Everest. Mallory replied, "Because it's there."

Apparently, that's also the reason why we eat. Brian Wansink and colleagues (2005) wondered whether the amount of food people eat is influenced by the amount of food they see in front of them. So they invited participants to their laboratory, sat them down in front of a large bowl of tomato soup, and told them to eat as much as they wanted. In one condition of the study, a server came to the table and refilled each participant's bowl whenever it got down to about a quarter full. In another condition, the bowls were not refilled by a server. Rather, unbeknownst to the participants, the bottom of the bowl was connected by a long tube to a large vat of soup, so whenever a participant ate from the bowl it would slowly and almost imperceptibly refill itself.

What the researchers found was sobering. Participants who unknowingly ate from a "bottomless bowl" consumed a whopping 73% more soup than those who ate from normal bowls—and yet, they didn't think they had consumed more and they didn't report feeling any more full.

It seems that we find it easier to keep track of *what* we are eating than *how much*, and this can cause us to overeat even when we are trying our best to do just the opposite. For instance, one study showed that diners at an Italian restaurant often chose to eat butter on their bread rather than dipping it in olive oil because they thought that doing so would reduce the number of calories per slice. And they were right. What they didn't realize, however, is that they would unconsciously compensate for this reduction in calories by eating 23% more bread during the meal (Wansink & Linder, 2003).

▲ The researcher Brian Wansink and his bottomless soup bowl.

BOB FILA/CHICAGO TRIBUNE/NEWSCOM

This and other research suggests that one of the best ways to reduce our waists is simply to count our bites.

United States about $150 billion (Finkelstein et al., 2009) and upward of about 300,000 lives (Mokdad et al., 2003). In addition to these physical risks, obese people tend to have lower psychological well-being, lower self-esteem, and lower quality of life, and are viewed negatively by others (Gallup, 2014; Hebl & Heatherton, 1997; Kolotkin, Meter, & Williams, 2001; Sutin, Stephan, & Terracciano, 2015). Obese women earn about 7% less than their nonobese counterparts (Lempert, 2007), and the stigma of obesity is so powerful that average-weight people are viewed negatively if they have a relationship with someone who is obese (Hebl & Mannix, 2003). All of this is true, but sad. As one scientist noted, we need "a war on obesity, not the obese" (Friedman, 2003).

Obesity's Causes Obesity seems to have many causes. For example, obesity is highly heritable (Allison et al., 1996) and may have a genetic component, which may explain why a disproportionate amount of the weight gained by Americans in the past few decades has been gained by those who were already the heaviest (Flegal & Troiano, 2000). Some studies suggest that "obesogenic" toxins in the environment can disrupt the functioning of the endocrine system and predispose people to obesity (Grün & Blumberg, 2006; Newbold et al., 2005), whereas other studies suggest that obesity can be caused by a dearth of "good bacteria" in the gut (Liou et al., 2013). Whatever the cause, obese people are often leptin-resistant (i.e., their brains do not respond to the chemical signal that tells the brain to shut hunger off), and even leptin injections don't seem to help (Friedman & Halaas, 1998; Heymsfield et al., 1999).

Genes, pollutants, and bacteria all have been implicated, but in most cases the cause of obesity isn't much of a mystery: We simply eat too much. We eat when we are hungry, of course, but we also eat when we are sad or anxious, or when everyone else is eating (Herman, Roth, & Polivy, 2003). Sometimes we eat simply because the clock tells us to, which is why people with amnesia will happily eat a second lunch shortly after finishing an unremembered first one (Rozin et al., 1998; see The Real World: A Feast for the Eyes). Why does this happen? After all, most of us don't breathe ourselves sick or sleep ourselves sick, so why do we eat ourselves sick?

DATA VISUALIZATION

Have BMI and Food Consumption Changed over Time? Go to launchpadworks.com.

HOT SCIENCE

The Nutritionist Behind Your Eyes

Are there more calories in an avocado or a Snickers bar? If you are like most people, you aren't really sure. But you know that an avocado is a fruit (healthy healthy!) and that a Snickers bar is a candy (naughty naughty!), so you'd probably guess that the latter has more calories. But you'd be wrong, because an avocado has about 50% more calories than a Snickers bar. Holy guacamole!

Don't feel bad. When it comes to estimating the caloric content of foods, most people haven't got a clue. But recent research suggests that people's brains may know things that the people who own them don't.

Tang, Fellows, and Dagher (2014) showed participants photos of a variety of food items and measured three things. First, they asked the participants to estimate how many calories each of the food items contained. Second, they asked the participants how much they would pay to eat each of the food items. And third, they used fMRI to measure the activity in the participants' brains as they stared at the food item. What did the researchers find?

Panel A of the figure below shows the correlation between the actual caloric density (the number of calories per gram) of each food item and the participants' estimates of caloric density. If that line looks flat, then you've got good eyes. That utterly flat line indicates that the correlation between these two measures was zero. In other words, the participants were completely unable to say which foods were calorie rich and which were calorie poor. But now look at Panel B. That's the correlation between the actual caloric density of the food item and how much the participants wanted to eat it, as measured by their willingness to part with their hard-earned cash in order to get a bite. That line has a positive slope, which means that participants were willing to pay more for the opportunity to eat foods that were calorie rich than calorie poor.

Finally, when the researchers examined the data from the brain scans, they discovered that neural activity in one of the brain's "reward regions" (the ventromedial prefrontal cortex) was (1) uncorrelated with participants' guesses about caloric content; but (2) positively correlated with actual caloric content. In other words, the participants wanted to eat calorie-rich food, and their brains responded positively to calorie-rich food, and yet, the participants themselves could not say which foods were rich in calories!

People have been counting the calories in food for just a few decades, but their brains have been wanting and valuing and enjoying food forever. It appears that evolution has wired our brains to detect and delight in the calorie-rich foods that can best fuel them, even if we do not consciously know which foods those are. So if you want to know how many calories are in that bagel or banana, just ask yourself how much you'd pay to have a bite.

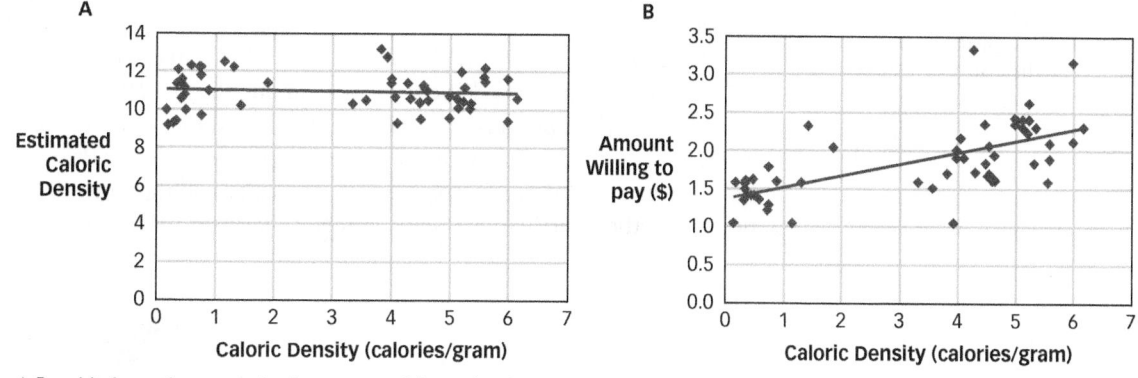

▲ Panel A shows the correlation between participants' estimates of the caloric density and the actual caloric density of the food items. Panel B shows the correlation between the amount participants were willing to pay to eat the food items and the actual caloric density of the food items.

Blame evolution. Hundreds of thousands of years ago, the main food-related problem facing our ancestors was starvation, and so humans evolved two strategies to avoid it. First, we developed a strong attraction to foods that provide large amounts of energy per bite (in other words, foods that are calorie-rich), which is why most of us prefer cheeseburgers and milkshakes to spinach and tea (see Hot Science: The Nutritionist Behind Your Eyes). Second, we developed an ability to store excess food energy in the form of fat, which enabled us to eat more than we needed when food was plentiful and then live off our reserves when food was scarce. These two adaptations allowed us to survive in a world in which calorie-rich food was scarce, but the problem is that we don't live in that world anymore. Instead, we live in a world in which the calorie bombs of modern technology—from chocolate cupcakes to sausage pizzas—are both inexpensive and readily available (Simpson & Raubenheimer, 2014). "We evolved on the savannahs of Africa; we now live in Candyland" (Power & Schulkin, 2009).

metabolism The rate at which energy is used by the body.

Idris Lewis and his wife both fit into the pants he used to wear when he weighed 364 pounds. Unfortunately, dieting rarely works. Most people who lose significant amounts of weight regain most or all of it within a year (Polivy & Herman, 2002).

To make matters worse, many of Candyland's foods tend to be high in saturated fat, which has the paradoxical effect of making the brain *less* sensitive to some of the chemical messengers that tell it to shut hunger off (Benoit et al., 2009).

Conquering Obesity Our brains and bodies were engineered for a very different world, which is why it is so easy to bulk up and so hard to slim down. Just as our bodies seek weight gain, they resist weight loss, and they do this in two ways.

▶ First, when we gain weight, we experience an increase in both the size and the number of fat cells in our bodies (usually in our abdomens if we are male and in our thighs and buttocks if we are female). When we lose weight, the size of our fat cells decreases, but the number does not. Once our bodies have added a fat cell, that cell is with us pretty much forever. It may become smaller when we lose weight, but it is unlikely to die.

▶ Second, our bodies respond to dieting by decreasing our **metabolism,** which is *the rate at which energy is used by the body.* When our bodies sense that we are living through a famine (which is what they conclude when we refuse to feed them), they find more efficient ways to turn food into fat. This was a great trick for our ancestors, but it is a real nuisance for us. When rats are overfed, then put on diets, then overfed again and put on diets again, they gain weight faster and lose it more slowly the second time around, which suggests that with each round of dieting, their bodies become increasingly efficient at converting food to fat (Brownell et al., 1986).

Clearly, avoiding obesity is easier than overcoming it (Casazza et al., 2013). And avoiding it is exactly what some psychologists are trying to help people do by using small interventions that have a big impact. For instance, one study showed that placing hard-boiled eggs just a few inches away from the more healthful ingredients in a salad bar led people to eat 10% fewer eggs (Rozin et al., 2011). Now, 10% of an egg may not sound like much, but if you eat two eggs every day, cutting that amount by just 10% would cause you to lose about one and a half pounds every year, which would make you the skinniest person at your 25th high school reunion. In another study, people ate fewer Pringles when every 7th chip had been colored red, simply because the color coding allowed them to keep track of how much they were eating (Geier, Wansink, & Rozin, 2012). In another study, people

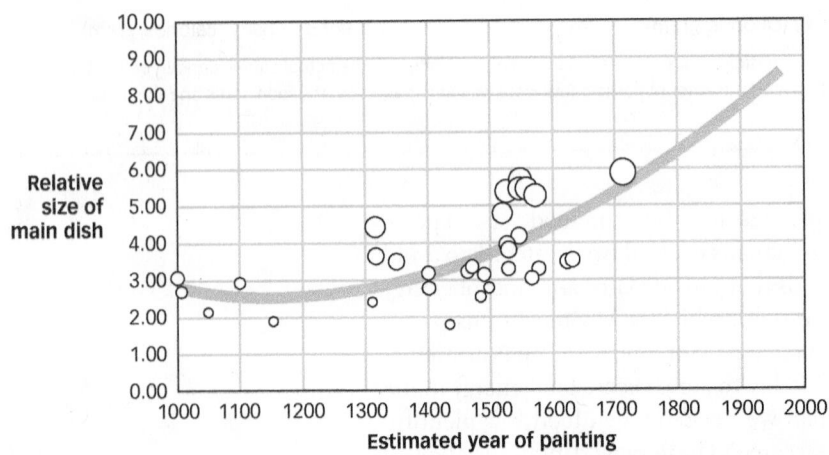

One reason that obesity rates are rising is that "normal portions" keep getting larger. When researchers analyzed 52 depictions of *The Last Supper* that were painted between the years 1000 and 1800, they found that the average plate size had increased by 66% (Wansink & Wansink, 2010).

ate 22% less pasta with tomato sauce when they used a white plate instead of a red plate, simply because the white plate provided a stark contrast that allowed them to see what they were eating (van Ittersum & Wansink, 2012). These and many other studies show that small "nudges" can make big differences to our waistlines.

SEXUAL DESIRE

Food motivates us because we die without it. Although sex is not essential to our individual survival, it is essential to the survival of our DNA, and that's why evolution has wired sexual desire into almost everybody's brain. The general wiring scheme is simple: Glands secrete hormones that travel through the blood to the brain and stimulate our sexual interest. But the details of the wiring scheme are complicated: Which hormones trigger which parts of the brain, and what triggers the launch in the first place?

Three hormones play key roles. The hormone *dihydroepiandosterone* (DHEA) seems to be involved in the initial onset of sexual desire. Both boys and girls begin producing this slow-acting hormone at about the age of 6, which may explain why boys and girls both experience their initial sexual interest at about the age of 10, despite the fact that boys reach puberty much later than girls do. Two other hormones have more gender-specific effects. Both males and females produce *testosterone* and *estrogen*, but males produce more of the former and females produce more of the latter. As you will learn in the Development chapter, these two hormones are largely responsible for the physical and psychological changes that characterize puberty. But are they also responsible for sexual desire in adults?

The answer is yes—as long as those adults are rats. Testosterone increases the sexual desire of male rats by acting on a particular area of the hypothalamus, and estrogen increases the sexual desire of female rats by acting on a different area of the hypothalamus. Lesions to these areas reduce sexual motivation in the respective sexes, and when testosterone or estrogen is applied to these areas, sexual motivation increases. In short, testosterone regulates sexual desire in male rats, and estrogen regulates both sexual desire and fertility in female rats.

The story for human beings is far more interesting. The females of most mammalian species (e.g., dogs, cats, and rats) have little or no interest in sex except when their estrogen levels are high, which happens when they are ovulating, or "in estrus." In other words, estrogen regulates both ovulation and sexual interest in these mammals. But female humans can be interested in sex at any time. Although the level of estrogen in a woman's body changes dramatically over the course of her monthly menstrual cycle, studies suggest that sexual desire changes little. Somewhere in the course of our evolution, it seems, women's sexual interest became independent of ovulation. Why might that have happened?

Some scientists speculate that this independence gave women an evolutionary advantage, because it made it more difficult for men to know whether a woman was in the fertile phase of her monthly cycle. Most male mammals guard their mates jealously when their mates are ovulating, but then go off in search of other receptive females when their mates are not. But if a male could not use his female mate's sexual receptivity as information about when she was ovulating, then he would have no choice but to hang around and guard her all the time. This is a considerable advantage for females who are trying to keep their male mates at home so that they can contribute to the rearing of children. No one knows if this is actually the reason that human females are interested in sex even when they are not fertile, but at least it suggests a way in which this adaptation might have evolved.

Hormonally, then, female humans are a lot more complicated than female rats. But if estrogen is not the hormonal basis of a woman's sex drive, then what is? Two pieces of evidence suggest that the answer is testosterone—the same hormone that drives male sexuality. First, men naturally have more testosterone than women do, and they generally have stronger sex drives. Men are more likely than women to think about

NATIONAL GEOGRAPHIC/GETTY IMAGES

STOCKBYTE/GETTY IMAGES

The red coloration on the female gelada's chest (*top*) indicates that she is in estrus and amenable to sex. The sexual interest of a female human being (*bottom*) is not limited to a particular time in her monthly cycle, and is not so easily gauged.

human sexual response cycle The stages of physiological arousal during sexual activity.

sex, have sexual fantasies, seek sex and sexual variety (whether positions or partners), masturbate, want sex at an early point in a relationship, sacrifice other things for sex, have permissive attitudes toward sex, and complain about low sex drive in their partners (Baumeister, Cantanese, & Vohs, 2001). Second, when women are given testosterone, their sex drives increase. These facts suggest that testosterone may be the hormonal basis of sexual motivation in both men and women.

SEXUAL ACTIVITY

Men and women may have different levels of sexual drive, but their physiological responses during sex are fairly similar. Prior to the 1960s, data on human sexual behavior consisted primarily of people's answers to questions about their sex lives, and you may have noticed that this is a topic about which people don't always tell the truth. William Masters and Virginia Johnson changed all that by conducting groundbreaking studies in which they actually measured the physical responses of hundreds of volunteers as they masturbated or had sex in a laboratory (Masters & Johnson, 1966). Their work was controversial at the time, but it led to a much deeper scientific understanding of the **human sexual response cycle,** which comprises *the stages of physiological arousal during sexual activity* (see **FIGURE 8.18**). Human sexual response has four phases:

▶ During the *excitement phase*, muscle tension and blood flow increase in and around the sexual organs, heart and respiration rates increase, and blood pressure rises. Both men and women may experience erect nipples and a "sex flush" on the skin of the upper body and face. A man's penis typically becomes erect or partially erect and his testicles draw upward, while a woman's vagina typically becomes lubricated and her clitoris becomes swollen.

▶ During the *plateau phase*, heart rate and muscle tension increase further. A man's urinary bladder closes to prevent urine from mixing with semen, and muscles at the base of his penis begin a steady rhythmic contraction. A man's Cowper gland may secrete a small amount of lubricating fluid (which, by the way, often contains enough sperm to cause pregnancy). A woman's clitoris may withdraw slightly, and her vagina may become more lubricated. Her outer vagina may swell, and her muscles may tighten and reduce the diameter of the opening of the vagina.

▶ During the *orgasm* phase, breathing becomes extremely rapid and the pelvic muscles begin a series of rhythmic contractions. Both men and women experience quick cycles of muscle contraction of the anus and lower pelvic muscles, and women often experience uterine and vaginal contractions as well. During this phase, men ejaculate about 2 to 5 milliliters of semen (depending on how long it has been since their last orgasm and how long they were aroused prior to ejaculation). Ninety-five percent of heterosexual men and 69% of heterosexual women reported having an orgasm during their last sexual encounter (Richters

▶ Figure 8.18

THE HUMAN SEXUAL RESPONSE CYCLE
The pattern of the sexual response cycle is quite similar for men and for women. Both men and women go through the excitement, plateau, orgasm, and resolution phases, though the timing of their responses may differ.

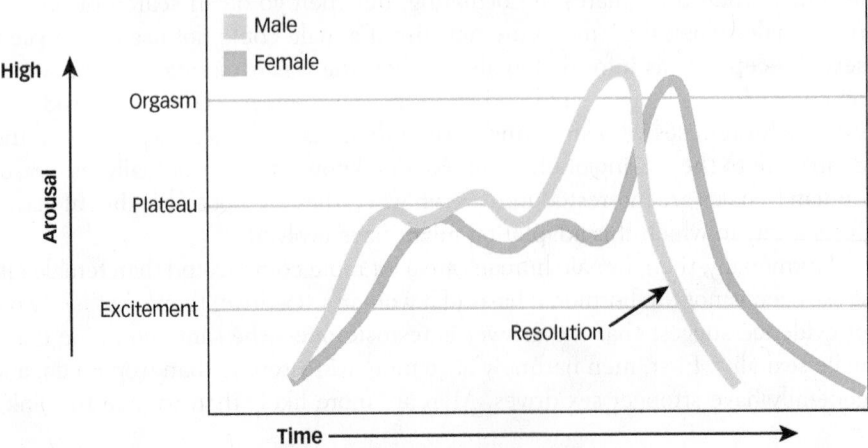

TABLE 8.2

Reasons for Sex

Top Ten Reasons Why Men and Women Report Having Sex

	Women	Men
1	I was attracted to the person.	I was attracted to the person.
2	I wanted to experience the physical pleasure.	It feels good.
3	It feels good.	I wanted to experience the physical pleasure.
4	I wanted to show my affection to the person.	It's fun.
5	I wanted to express my love for the person.	I wanted to show my affection to the person.
6	I was sexually aroused and wanted the release.	I was sexually aroused and wanted the release.
7	I was "horny."	I was "horny."
8	It's fun.	I wanted to express my love for the person.
9	I realized I was in love.	I wanted to achieve an orgasm.
10	I was "in the heat of the moment."	I wanted to please my partner.

Information from: Meston & Buss, 2007.

et al., 2006). However, roughly 15% of women never experience orgasm, fewer than half experience orgasm from intercourse alone, and roughly half report having "faked" an orgasm at least once (Wiederman, 1997). The frequency with which women have orgasms seems to have a genetic component (Dawood et al., 2005). And it probably goes without saying that when men and women have orgasms, they typically experience them as intensely pleasurable.

▶ During the *resolution phase*, muscles relax, blood pressure drops, and the body returns to its resting state. Most men and women experience a *refractory period*, during which further stimulation does not produce excitement. This period may last from minutes to days and is typically longer for men than for women.

Although sex is generally a prerequisite for reproduction, the vast majority of sexual acts are not intended to produce babies. College students, for example, are rarely aiming to get pregnant, but they often do aim to have sex, either because of *physical attraction* ("The person had beautiful eyes"), as a *means to an end* ("I wanted to be popular"), to increase *emotional connection* ("I wanted to communicate at a deeper level"), to *alleviate insecurity* ("It was the only way my partner would spend time with me"), or more than one of the above (Meston & Buss, 2007). Although men are more likely than women to report having sex for purely physical reasons, **TABLE 8.2** shows that men and women don't differ dramatically in their most frequent reasons. It is worth noting that not all sex is motivated by any of these reasons: About 1 in 15 U.S. adults report having been forced to have sex at some time in their lives (Basile et al., 2007). We will have much more to say about sexual attraction and relationships in the Social Psychology chapter.

Build to the Outcomes

1. Why do some motivations take precedence over others?
2. What purpose does hunger serve?
3. What causes BED, bulimia, and anorexia?
4. What causes obesity?
5. Why is dieting so difficult and ineffective?
6. Which hormones regulate sexual interest in men and women?
7. What is the human sexual response cycle?
8. Why do people have sex?

Wanting: The Mind's Desires

AFP/GETTY IMAGES

Mohamed Bouazizi was a fruit seller. In 2010 he set himself on fire to protest his treatment by the Tunisian government, and his dramatic suicide ignited the revolution that came to be known as the "Arab Spring." Clearly, psychological needs—such as the need for justice—can be even more powerful than biological needs.

intrinsic motivation A motivation to take actions that are themselves rewarding.

extrinsic motivation A motivation to take actions that lead to reward.

Survival and reproduction are every animal's first order of business, so it is no surprise that we are strongly motivated by food and sex. But humans are motivated by other things too. Yes, we crave kisses of both the chocolate and romantic variety, but we also crave friendship and respect, security and certainty, wisdom and meaning, and a whole lot more. Our psychological motivations can be every bit as powerful as our biological motivations, but they differ in two important ways.

First, although we share our biological motivations with most other animals, our psychological motivations appear to be unique. Chimps and rabbits and robins and turtles are all motivated to have sex, but only human beings seem motivated to imbue the act with deeper meaning. Second, although our biological motivations are of a few basic kinds—food, sex, oxygen, sleep, and a handful of other things—our psychological motivations are virtually limitless. The things we care about feeling and thinking, knowing and believing, having and being are just so numerous and varied that no psychologist has ever been able to make a complete list of them (Hofmann, Vohs, & Baumeister, 2012). Nonetheless, even if you looked at an incomplete list, you'd quickly notice that psychological motivations vary on three key dimensions: Some are extrinsic and others are intrinsic, some are conscious and others are unconscious, and some lead us to approach while others lead us to avoid. Let's examine each of these dimensions in turn.

INTRINSIC VERSUS EXTRINSIC

Eating a potato chip and taking a psychology exam are different in many ways. One makes you chubby and the other makes you crabby, one requires that you move your lips and the other requires that you don't, and so on. But one of the most important differences between these activities is that the first is a means to an end and the second is an end in itself. An **intrinsic motivation** is *a motivation to take actions that are themselves rewarding*. When we eat a potato chip because it tastes good, exercise because it feels good, or listen to music because it sounds good, we are intrinsically motivated. These activities don't *have* a payoff because they *are* a payoff. Conversely, an **extrinsic motivation** is *a motivation to take actions that lead to reward*. When we floss our teeth so we can avoid gum disease, when we work hard for money so we can pay our rent, and when we take an exam so we can get a college degree (which allows us to earn more money and buy more dental floss), we are extrinsically motivated. None of these things is a source of pleasure in and of itself, but all can increase pleasure in the long run.

Extrinsic Motivation

Extrinsic motivation gets a bad rap. Americans tend to believe that people should "follow their hearts" and "do what they love," and we feel sorry for students who choose courses just to please their parents and for parents who choose jobs just to earn a pile of money. But the fact is that our ability to engage in behaviors that are unrewarding in the present because we believe they will bring greater rewards in the future is one of our species' most significant talents, and no other species can do it quite as well as we can (Gilbert, 2006). Researchers who study how well people can put off pleasure or "delay gratification" (Ayduk et al., 2007; Mischel et al., 2004) typically give participants a choice between getting something they want right now (e.g., a scoop of ice cream today) or getting more of what they want later (e.g., two scoops of ice cream tomorrow). Waiting for ice cream in a study like this is a lot like taking an exam or flossing: It isn't much fun, but you might do it because you know that if you are

Should We Pay People to Vote?

Stephen L. Carter is the William Nelson Cromwell Professor of Law at Yale University. His novels include *The Emperr of Ocean Park*, and his nonfiction books include *The Violence of Peace: America's Wars in the Age of Obama*.

Some people think that citizens of democracies should vote because they *want* to, that they should be proud to exercise a right for which others have fought and died. But some people think that voting is too important to be voluntary, and they have called for making it compulsory in America, as it is in many other nations. Stephen Carter, a law professor and novelist, has a different idea. Instead of either leaving citizens to their own devices or forcing them to vote, why not just pay them?

President Barack Obama recently mooted the idea of making voting mandatory, as a means of increasing turnout. It's true that U.S. citizens are less likely to go to the polls than those of many (not all) other democracies. Nevertheless, with all due respect to the president, I don't much like his idea. And if getting more people to the polls is the goal, I have a better suggestion.

Let me spell out my biases. I'm a happy nonvoter. More to the point, I find that I am more at peace when I don't bother following electoral politics than when I do. Staying away from the polls helps me to focus on my work, to take a relaxed attitude toward life, even to be a better husband and father than I otherwise might. So naturally I'm distressed at the thought that my government would even consider using coercion to disturb my peace of mind.

This isn't apathy. And it's not that I'm uninformed. But given that my vote can't possibly make any difference to the outcome, I'm hard-pressed to come up with a reason to go to the polls. . . .

Still, the debate over whether voting should be compulsory has a great deal of academic currency. Supporters often argue that those who are staying away from the polls tend to be political outsiders whose views policy rarely reflects. Others contend that low information voters, if required to go to the polls, might be transformed into high information voters. President Obama put the case that mandatory voting could reduce the influence of money in politics.

These seemingly strong arguments have equally strong rejoinders. For example, as the law professor Ilya Somin has pointed out, forcing low-information voters to the polls might actually heighten the influence of money in politics—at least if, as I suspect, low-information voters tend to watch a lot of television.

As to the claim that the outsiders who stay away from the polls would make a crucial policy difference, the philosopher Jason Brennan offers a sharp riposte: "The argument seems to presume that voter[s] vote for their self-interest. But we have overwhelming empirical evidence, drawn from hundreds of studies, that they don't vote their self-interest. Instead, they vote altruistically, for what they perceive to be in the national interest."

You won't be surprised to learn that I'm with the dissenters. . . . If I'd rather spend Election Day reading a good book, I think my government should let me.

Besides, if increasing turnout is really so important, why signal that fact by punishing people who don't go to the polls? Maybe we'd do better to reward them instead. If voting is such an unadorned good, let's pay people to show up. Surely paying people to do a good thing isn't a bad thing.

Social scientists have understood for some time that cash payments alter people's incentives, sometimes drastically. For example, paying people money to quit smoking greatly enhances the chances of success. Paying students to keep a certain grade-point average seems to make a difference. Paying teenage girls not to get pregnant greatly decreases the chance that they'll get pregnant.

These are all behavioral changes we want to encourage. Why not treat voting the same way? It's likely to work. An experiment conducted by Fordham political scientist Costas Panagopoulos found that paying cash rewards of $25 raised turnout in a municipal election from 14.9 percent to 19.2 percent—no small increase. . . .

I've long been mystified by our bipartisan national determination to achieve what we think is best by punishing people who won't go along. Rewards for good behavior are better than punishments for bad. They force us to discover how much we really value what we claim to want. If increasing turnout is really as important as supporters say, let's give nonvoters a real incentive to go the polls: cash.

Most of us think it is perfectly fine to pay someone to paint our house or wash our car, but not to give us their kidney or tell us they love us. Some things should just be intrinsically motivated. So what about voting? Would paying citizens be an effective way to get them to vote? Even if it is, might there be unanticipated consequences of turning an intrinsically motivated behavior into an extrinsically motivated one?

Adapted from Stephen L. Carter, "Want More Voters? Pay Them," *Bloomberg View*, April 2, 2015. https://www.bloomberg.com/view/articles/2015-04-02/want-more-voters-pay-them

patient, you will reap greater rewards in the end. Studies show that 4-year-old children who can delay gratification are judged to be more intelligent and socially competent 10 years later and have higher SAT scores when they enter college (Mischel, Shoda, & Rodriguez, 1989). In fact, the ability to delay gratification is a better predictor of a child's grades in school than is the child's IQ (Duckworth & Seligman, 2005). Apparently there is something to be said for extrinsic motivation (see Other Voices: Should We Pay People to Vote?).

Intrinsic Motivation

There is a lot to be said for intrinsic motivation too (Patall, Cooper, & Robinson, 2008). People work harder when they are intrinsically motivated, they enjoy what they do more, and they do it more creatively. Both kinds of motivation have advantages, which is why many of us try to build lives in which we are both intrinsically and extrinsically motivated by the same activity—lives in which we are paid the big bucks for doing exactly what we like to do best. Who hasn't fantasized about becoming an artist or an athlete or Beyoncé's personal party planner? Alas, research suggests that it is difficult to get paid for doing what you love and still end up loving what you do because rewards can undermine intrinsic motivation (Deci, Koestner, & Ryan, 1999; Henderlong & Lepper, 2002). For example, in one study, college students who were intrinsically motivated to complete a puzzle either were paid to complete it or completed it for free. Those who received money were less likely to play with the puzzle later on (Deci, 1971). In a similar study, children who were intrinsically motivated to draw with colored markers were either promised or not promised a reward. Those who were promised the reward were less likely to use the markers later (Lepper, Greene, & Nisbett, 1973). It appears that under some circumstances, then, people interpret rewards as information about the goodness of an activity ("If they had to pay me to do that puzzle, it couldn't have been a very fun one"), which means that rewards can sometimes undermine intrinsic motivation.

Just as the promise of a reward can undermine intrinsic motivation, the threat of punishment can create it. In one study, children who had no intrinsic motivation to play with a toy suddenly gained one when the experimenter threatened to punish them if they touched the toy (Aronson, 1963). College students who had no intrinsic motivation to cheat on a test were more likely to do so if the experimenter explicitly warned against it (Wilson & Lassiter, 1982). Just as the presence of a reward can suggest that an activity is undesirable, the presence of a threat can suggest the opposite. That's why threats sometimes promote the very behaviors they are meant to discourage. For example, when a group of day care centers got fed up with parents who picked up their children late, some instituted a small financial penalty for tardiness. As **FIGURE 8.19** shows, the financial penalty did not decrease tardiness—it *increased* it (Gneezy & Rustichini, 2000). Why? Because most parents were intrinsically motivated to pick up their kids on time. But when the day care centers started punishing them for their tardiness, the parents became *extrinsically* motivated to pick up their children on time—and because the price of tardiness wasn't particularly high, they decided to pay a small financial penalty in order to leave their children in day care for an extra hour. When threats and rewards change intrinsic motivation into extrinsic motivation, unexpected consequences can follow.

▶ Figure 8.19

WHEN THREATS BACKFIRE Threats can cause behaviors that were once intrinsically motivated to become extrinsically motivated. Day care centers that instituted fines for late-arriving parents saw an increase in the number of parents who arrived late.

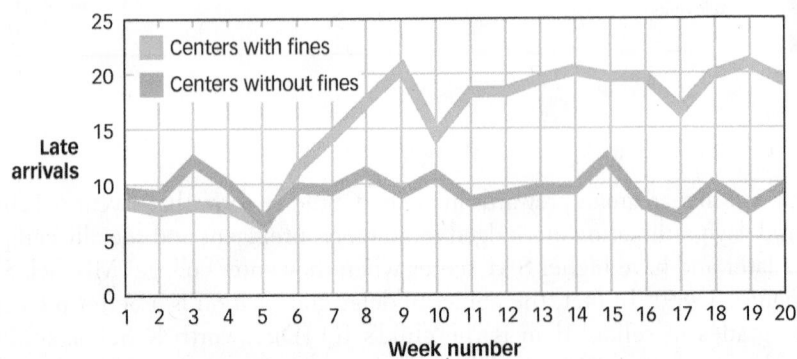

CONSCIOUS VERSUS UNCONSCIOUS

When prizewinning artists and scientists are asked to explain how they achieved greatness, they typically say things such as, "I wanted to liberate color from form" or "I wanted to cure diabetes." They almost never say things such as, "I wanted to exceed my father's accomplishments, thereby proving to my mother that I was worthy of her love." Prizewinners can articulate their **conscious motivations,** which are *motivations of which people are aware*, but by definition they have trouble articulating their **unconscious motivations,** which are *motivations of which people are not aware* (Aarts, Custers, & Marien, 2008; Bargh et al., 2001; Hassin, Bargh, & Zimerman, 2009).

For example, people vary in their **need for achievement,** which is *the motivation to solve worthwhile problems* (McClelland et al., 1953). This basic motivation is unconscious and thus must be measured with special techniques such as the Thematic Apperception Test, which presents people with a series of drawings and asks them to tell stories about them. The amount of "achievement-related imagery" in the person's story ostensibly reveals the person's unconscious need for achievement. (You'll learn more about these sorts of tests in the Personality chapter.) Although there has been much controversy about the validity and reliability of measures such as these (Lilienfeld, Wood, & Garb, 2000; Tuerlinckx, De Boeck, & Lens, 2002), research shows that a person's responses on this test do reliably predict the person's behavior in certain circumstances (Khalid, 1991). Research also suggests that this motivation can be primed in much the same way that thoughts and feelings can be primed. For example, when words such as *achievement* are presented on a computer screen so rapidly that people cannot consciously perceive them, those people will work especially hard to solve a puzzle (Bargh et al., 2001) and will feel especially unhappy if they fail (Chartrand & Kay, 2006).

What determines whether we are conscious of our motivations? Most actions have more than one motivation, and the ease or difficulty of performing the action sometimes determines which of these motivations we will be aware of (Vallacher & Wegner, 1985; 1987). When actions are easy (e.g., screwing in a light bulb), we are aware of our most *general motivations* (e.g., to be helpful), but when actions are difficult (e.g., wrestling with a light bulb that is stuck in its socket), we are aware of our more specific motivations (e.g., to get the threads aligned). People usually are aware of the general motivations for their behavior and become aware of their more specific motivations only when they encounter problems. For example, participants in one experiment drank coffee either from a normal mug or from a mug that had a heavy weight attached to the bottom, which made the mug difficult to manipulate. When asked what they were doing, those who were drinking from the normal mug explained that they were "satisfying needs," whereas those who were drinking from the weighted mug explained that they were "swallowing" (Wegner et al., 1984). The ease with which we can execute an action is one of many factors that determine which of our motivations we are conscious of.

APPROACH VERSUS AVOIDANCE

The poet James Thurber (1956) wrote: "All men should strive to learn before they die / What they are running from, and to, and why." As these lines remind us, the hedonic principle actually describes two distinct motivations: one that makes us "run to" pleasure and another that makes us "run from" pain. Psychologists—being a bit less poetic and a lot more precise—call these **approach motivation,** which is *the motivation to experience positive outcomes*, and **avoidance motivation,** which is *the*

Michael Phelps is clearly high—in need for achievement, that is—which is one of the reasons he remains the most decorated Olympic athlete of all time.

conscious motivations Motivations of which people are aware.

unconscious motivations Motivations of which people are not aware.

need for achievement The motivation to solve worthwhile problems.

approach motivation The motivation to experience a positive outcome.

avoidance motivation The motivation not to experience a negative outcome.

loss aversion The tendency to care more about avoiding losses than about achieving equal-size gains.

motivation to avoid experiencing negative outcomes. Pleasure and pain may be two sides of the same coin, but they *are* two sides. Pleasure is not just the lack of pain, and pain is not just the lack of pleasure. Pleasure and pain are distinct experiences, each of which is associated with distinct patterns of activity in different regions of the brain (Davidson et al., 1990; Gray, 1990).

But which is more powerful? Research suggests that, all else being equal, avoidance motivation tends to be the stronger of the two. This is easy to illustrate: Would you bet on a coin flip that will pay you $100 if it comes up heads but will require you to pay $80 if it comes up tails? Mathematically speaking, this should be an extremely attractive wager, because the potential gain is larger than the equally likely potential loss. And yet most people refuse a bet such as this because they expect the pain of losing $80 to be stronger than the pleasure of winning $100. **Loss aversion** is *the tendency to care more about avoiding losses than about achieving equal-size gains* (Kahneman & Tversky, 1979, 1984), and its effects can be dramatic. Grocery stores in the Washington, DC, area tried to motivate their customers to reuse their shopping bags by giving them a 5-cent bonus whenever they did (a financial gain), or by taxing them whenever they didn't (a financial loss), or by doing neither or both of these things. As **FIGURE 8.20** shows, the prospect of losing money had a large impact on shoppers' behavior, but the prospect of gaining the same amount of money had no impact at all (Homonoff, 2013). People, it seems, are unusually anxious about losing what they have, which is why they display reduced loss aversion after taking drugs that reduce fear and anxiety (Sokol-Hessner et al., 2015) and increased loss aversion after being exposed to stimuli that increase fear and anxiety (Schulreich, Gerhardt, & Heekeren, 2015).

Because people expect the pain of a loss to outweigh the pleasure of a gain, they typically take more risks to avoid the former than to achieve the latter. For instance, what would you do if you knew that a terrible disease was going to kill 600 students at your school, and you were the one who was in charge of deciding whether to administer Vaccine A (which would save exactly 200 students) or Vaccine B (which has a one-third chance of saving everybody and a two-thirds chance of saving nobody)? When people are asked this question, about three-quarters of them decide to play it safe and select Vaccine A. And yet, when people are given a choice between Vaccine C (which would allow exactly 400 students to die) and Vaccine D (which has a one-third chance of allowing no one to die and a two-thirds chance of allowing everyone to die), about three quarters of them decide to take the risk and select Vaccine D (Tversky & Kahneman, 1981). As **FIGURE 8.21** shows, Vaccines A and C are actually identical, as are Vaccines B and D. Indeed, the only difference is that A and B are described in terms of lives gained, whereas C and D are described in terms of lives lost. And yet those descriptions matter quite a lot, leading people to take risks in one case but not

▶ Figure 8.20

THE POWER OF LOSS Avoidance motivation is typically more powerful than approach motivation. Shoppers in the Washington, DC, area were highly motivated to reuse their bags to avoid a 5-cent tax but were entirely unmotivated to reuse their bags to get a 5-cent bonus. (Homonoff, 2013).

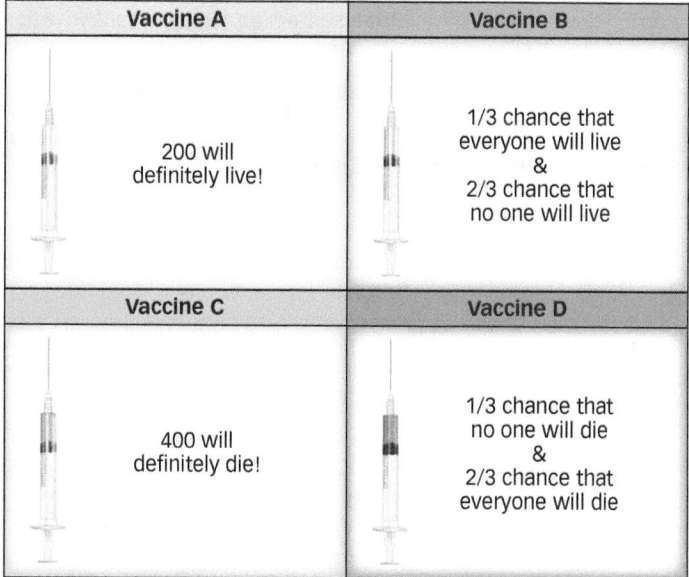

Without vaccine, 600 students will die...

Vaccine A	Vaccine B
200 will definitely live!	1/3 chance that everyone will live & 2/3 chance that no one will live

Vaccine C	Vaccine D
400 will definitely die!	1/3 chance that no one will die & 2/3 chance that everyone will die

◄ Figure 8.21

WHEN DO WE TAKE RISKS? Loss aversion leads people to take risks to avoid losses (most people choose Vaccine D over C) but not to achieve gains (most people choose Vaccine A over B).

in another. By the way, monkeys also take risks to avoid losses but not to achieve gains (Lakshminarayanan, Chen, & Santos, 2011), which suggests that you probably should not put one in charge of your major medical decisions.

Although avoidance motivation is stronger than approach motivation on average, the relative strength of these two tendencies does differ from person to person. **TABLE 8.3** shows a series of questions that have been used to measure the relative strength of an individual's approach and avoidance tendencies (Carver & White, 1994). Research shows that people who are described by the high-approach items are happier when rewarded than those who are not, whereas those who are described by the high-avoidance items are more anxious when threatened than those who are not (Carver, 2006). Just as some people seem to be more responsive to rewards than to punishments (and vice versa), some people tend to think about their behaviors as attempts to get rewards rather than to avoid punishment (and vice versa). People who have a *promotion focus* tend to think in terms of achieving gains, whereas people who have a *prevention focus* tend to think in terms of avoiding losses (Higgins, 1997). In one study, participants were given an anagram task. Some were told that they would be paid $4 for the experiment, but they could earn an extra dollar by finding 90% or more of all the possible words. Others were told that they would be paid $5 for the experiment, but they could avoid losing a dollar by not missing more than 10% of all the possible words. People who had a promotion focus performed better in the first case than in the second, but people who had a prevention focus performed better in the second case than in the first (Shah, Higgins, & Friedman, 1998). Similarly, people with a high need for achievement tend to be somewhat more motivated by their hope for success, whereas people with a low need for achievement tend to be somewhat more motivated by their fear of failure.

So what is the one thing that virtually every human being wants to avoid? Death, of course. All animals strive to stay alive, but only human beings know that all that striving is ultimately in vain, because no matter what you do, eventually you will die. Some psychologists have suggested that this knowledge creates a uniquely human "existential terror" that much of human behavior is an attempt to manage. **Terror management theory** is *a theory about how people respond to knowledge of their own*

terror management theory The theory that people cope with their existential terror by developing a cultural worldview.

TABLE 8.3

Scale for Measuring the Behavioral Inhibition System and Behavioral Activation System

To what extent do each of these items describe you? The items in red measure the strength of your avoidance tendency, and the items in green measure the strength of your approach tendency.

- Even if something bad is about to happen to me, I rarely experience fear or nervousness. (LOW AVOIDANCE)

- I go out of my way to get things I want. (HIGH APPROACH)

- When I'm doing well at something, I love to keep at it. (HIGH APPROACH)

- I'm always willing to try something new if I think it will be fun. (HIGH APPROACH)

- When I get something I want, I feel excited and energized. (HIGH APPROACH)

- Criticism or scolding hurts me quite a bit. (HIGH AVOIDANCE)

- When I want something, I usually go all-out to get it. (HIGH APPROACH)

- I will often do things for no other reason than that they might be fun. (HIGH APPROACH)

- If I see a chance to get something I want, I move on it right away. (HIGH APPROACH)

- I feel pretty worried or upset when I think or know somebody is angry at me. (HIGH AVOIDANCE)

- When I see an opportunity for something I like, I get excited right away. (HIGH APPROACH)

- I often act on the spur of the moment. (HIGH APPROACH)

- If I think something unpleasant is going to happen, I usually get pretty "worked up." (HIGH AVOIDANCE)

- When good things happen to me, it affects me strongly. (HIGH APPROACH)

- I feel worried when I think I have done poorly at something important. (HIGH AVOIDANCE)

- I crave excitement and new sensations. (HIGH APPROACH)

- When I go after something, I use a "no holds barred" approach. (HIGH APPROACH)

- I have very few fears compared to my friends. (LOW AVOIDANCE)

- It would excite me to win a contest. (HIGH APPROACH)

- I worry about making mistakes. (HIGH AVOIDANCE)

Information from: Carver & White, 1994.

mortality, and it suggests that one of the ways that people cope with existential terror is by developing a *cultural worldview,* which is a shared set of beliefs about what is good and right and true (Greenberg, Solomon, & Arndt, 2008; Solomon et al., 2004). These beliefs allow people to see themselves as more than mortal animals because they inhabit a world of meaning in which they can achieve symbolic immortality (e.g., by leaving a great legacy or having children) and perhaps even literal immortality (e.g., by being pious and earning a spot in the afterlife). According to this theory, a cultural worldview is a kind of shield that buffers people against the overwhelming anxiety that certain knowledge of their own deaths elicits.

If that's true, then people who are reminded of their mortality should be especially motivated to hang on to their cultural worldviews. In the last 20 years, this *mortality salience hypothesis* has been supported by the results of nearly 400 studies. Those results show that when people are reminded of death (often in very subtle ways, such as by flashing the word *death* for just a few milliseconds in a laboratory, or by stopping people on a street corner that happens to be near a graveyard), they are more likely to praise and reward those who share their cultural worldviews, derogate and punish those who don't, value their spouses and defend their countries, feel disgusted by "animalistic" behaviors such as breast-feeding, and so on. All of these responses are presumably ways of shoring up their cultural worldviews, thereby protecting themselves from the existential terror that reminders of mortality create.

Build to the Outcomes

1. What are intrinsic and extrinsic motivations?

2. Why should people delay gratification?

3. Why do rewards sometimes backfire?

4. What makes people conscious of their motivations?

5. What is loss aversion?

6. What are the consequences of mortality salience?

Chapter Review

8

Emotional Experience: The Feeling Machine

▶ Emotional experiences are difficult to describe, but psychologists have identified their two underlying dimensions: arousal and valence.

▶ Psychologists have spent more than a century trying to understand how emotional experience and physiological activity are related. The James–Lange theory suggests that a stimulus triggers a specific bodily reaction that produces an emotional experience; the Cannon–Bard theory suggests that a stimulus triggers both a specific bodily reaction and an emotional experience at the same time; and the two-factor theory suggests that a stimulus triggers general bodily arousal, which people then interpret as a specific emotion. None of these theories is entirely right, but each has elements that are supported by research.

▶ Emotions are produced by the complex interaction of the cortex and limbic structures such as the amygdala. Information about a stimulus is sent simultaneously to the amygdala (which makes a quick appraisal of the stimulus) and the cortex (which does a slower and more comprehensive analysis of the stimulus). Sometimes, the cortex downregulates the amygdala.

▶ People care about their emotional experiences, but they do not always use the most effective strategies for regulating them. Reappraisal involves changing the way one thinks about an emotional event, and it is one of the most effective but underutilized ways to regulate emotion.

Emotional Communication: Msgs w/o Wrds

▶ The voice, the body, and the face all communicate information about a person's emotional state. Research suggests that some emotional expressions may be universal.

▶ Emotions cause expressions, but expressions can also cause emotions. Emotional mimicry allows people to experience and hence identify the emotions of others.

▶ People follow display rules that tell them when and how to express emotion. Different cultures have different display rules, but people follow them by using the same basic techniques.

▶ There are reliable differences between honest and dishonest expressions, both verbal and nonverbal, but people are generally quite poor at telling them apart. The polygraph does a better job than most humans, but its error rate is troublingly high.

Motivation: Being Moved

▶ Emotions motivate us by providing information about the world, and by serving as goals. The hedonic principle suggests that people approach pleasure and avoid pain and that this basic motivation underlies all others. All organisms are born with some motivations and acquire others through experience.

▶ William James called the natural tendency to pursue a particular goal an *instinct*.

▶ Clark Hull suggested that departures from homeostasis produce *drives* that organisms are motivated to reduce.

Wanting: The Body's Desires

▶ Biological motivations generally take precedence over psychological motivations in the "hierarchy of needs."

▶ Hunger is the result of complex physiological processes by which the body informs the brain about its current energy state.

▶ Eating disorders and obesity have genetic, experiential, psychological, and cultural origins, and all are difficult to overcome. It is easier to prevent obesity than to remedy it. Dieting is generally ineffective because our bodies store excess food energy as fat as a defense against times of food scarcity, and our metabolisms slow as a response to reduced calories.

▶ Men and women have sex drives that are regulated by testosterone, experience roughly the same physiological sequence of events during sex, and engage in sex for mostly the same reasons.

Wanting: The Mind's Desires

▶ People have many psychological motivations that vary on three key dimensions. Intrinsic motivations can be undermined by extrinsic rewards and punishments.

▶ People tend to be conscious of their most general motivations and become conscious of their specific motivations only when they encounter difficulty carrying out their actions.

▶ The fact that avoidance motivations generally are more powerful than approach motivations leads to loss aversion. The ultimate loss is death, and people develop cultural worldviews to protect themselves against the anxiety that foreknowledge of death elicits.

KEY CONCEPT QUIZ

1. Emotions can be described by their location on the two dimensions of
   a. motivation and scaling.
   b. arousal and valence.
   c. stimulus and reaction.
   d. pain and pleasure.

2. Which theorists claimed that a stimulus simultaneously causes both an emotional experience and a physiological reaction?
   a. Cannon and Bard
   b. James and Lange
   c. Schacter and Singer
   d. Maslow and Hull

3. Which brain structure is most directly involved in the rapid appraisal of whether a stimulus is good or bad?
   a. the cortex
   b. the lateral hypothalamus
   c. the amygdala
   d. the ventromedial hypothalamus

4. Through _____, we change an emotional experience by changing the meaning of the emotion-eliciting stimulus.
   a. deactivation   c. valence
   b. appraisal   d. reappraisal

5. _____ is the idea that emotional expressions can cause emotional experiences.
   a. A display rule
   b. Expressional deception
   c. The universality hypothesis
   d. The facial feedback hypothesis

6. Two friends have asked you to help them settle a disagreement. You hear each side of the story and have an emotional response to

one viewpoint, but you don't express it. This is an example of which display rule?
   a. deintensification
   b. masking
   c. neutralizing
   d. intensification

7. The hedonic principle states that
   a. emotions provide people with information.
   b. people are motivated to experience pleasure and avoid pain.
   c. people use their moods as information about the likelihood of succeeding at a task.
   d. motivations are acquired solely through experience.

8. According to the early psychologists, an unlearned tendency to seek a particular goal is called
   a. an instinct.
   b. a drive.
   c. a motivation.
   d. a corrective action.

9. According to Maslow, our most basic needs are
   a. self-actualization and self-esteem.
   b. biological.
   c. unimportant until other needs are met.
   d. belongingness and love.

10. Which of the following statements is true?
    a. Men and women engage in sex for many of the same reasons.
    b. Boys and girls experience initial sexual interest at very different ages.
    c. The sequence of physiological arousal for men and women differs dramatically.
    d. The human male sex drive is regulated by testosterone, whereas the human female sex drive is regulated by estrogen.

 LearningCurve   **Don't stop now! Quizzing yourself is a powerful study tool. Go to LaunchPad to access the LearningCurve adaptive quizzing system and your own personalized learning plan. Visit launchpadworks.com.**

KEY TERMS

emotion (p. 312)

James–Lange theory (p. 312)

Cannon–Bard theory (p. 313)

two-factor theory of emotion (p. 313)

appraisal (p. 316)

emotion regulation (p. 317)

reappraisal (p. 317)

emotional expression (p. 318)

universality hypothesis (p. 318)

facial feedback hypothesis (p. 320)

display rule (p. 321)

motivation (p. 325)

hedonic principle (p. 326)

drive (p. 327)

homeostasis (p. 327)

drive-reduction theory (p. 327)

binge eating disorder (p. 329)

bulimia nervosa (p. 329)

anorexia nervosa (p. 329)

metabolism (p. 334)

human sexual response cycle (p. 336)

intrinsic motivation (p. 338)

extrinsic motivation (p. 338)

conscious motivations (p. 341)

unconscious motivations (p. 341)

need for achievement (p. 341)

approach motivation (p. 341)

avoidance motivation (p. 341)

loss aversion (p. 342)

terror management theory (p. 343)

CHANGING MINDS

1. A friend is nearing graduation and has received a few job offers. "I went on the first interview," she says, "and I really liked the company, but I know you shouldn't go with your first impressions on difficult decisions. You should be completely rational and not let your emotions get in the way." Are emotions always barriers to rational decision making? In what ways can emotions help guide our decisions?

2. While watching TV, you and a friend hear about a celebrity who punched a fan in a restaurant. "I just lost it," the celebrity said. "I saw what I was doing, but I just couldn't control myself." According to the TV report, the celebrity was sentenced to anger management classes. "I'm not excusing the violence," your friend says, "but I'm not sure anger management classes are any use either. You can't control your emotions; you just feel them." What example could you give your friend of ways in which people can control their emotions?

3. One of your friends has just been dumped by her boyfriend, and she's devastated. She's spent days in her room, refusing to go out. You and your roommate decide to keep a close eye on her during this tough time.

"Negative emotions are so destructive," your roommate says. "We'd all be better off without them." What would you tell your roommate? In what ways are negative emotions critical for our survival and success?

4. A friend is majoring in education. "We learned today about several cities, including New York and Chicago, that tried giving cash rewards to students who passed their classes or did well on achievement tests. That's bribing kids to get good grades, and as soon as you stop paying them, they'll stop studying." Your friend is assuming that extrinsic motivation undermines intrinsic motivation. In what ways is the picture more complicated?

5. One of your friends is a gym rat who spends all his free time working out and is very proud of his ripped abs. His roommate, though, is very overweight. "I keep telling him to diet and exercise," your friend says, "but he never loses any weight. If he just had a little more willpower, he could succeed." What would you tell your friend? When an individual has difficulty losing weight, what factors may contribute to this difficulty?

ANSWERS TO KEY CONCEPT QUIZ

1. b; 2. a; 3. c; 4. d; 5. d; 6. c; 7. b; 8. a; 9. b; 10. a.

 LaunchPad
macmillan learning

LaunchPad features the full e-Book of *Psychology,* **the LearningCurve adaptive quizzing system, videos, and a variety of activities to boost your learning. Visit LaunchPad at launchpadworks.com.**

Language and Thought

9

A N ENGLISH BOY NAMED CHRISTOPHER showed an amazing talent for languages. By the age of 6, he had learned French from his sister's schoolbooks; he acquired Greek from a textbook in only 3 months. His talent was so prodigious that grown-up Christopher could converse fluently in 16 languages. When tested on English–French translations, he scored as well as a native French-speaker. Presented with a made-up language, he figured out the complex rules easily, even though advanced language students found them virtually impossible to decipher (Smith & Tsimpli, 1995).

If you've concluded that Christopher is extremely smart, perhaps even a genius, you're wrong. His scores on standard intelligence tests are far below normal. He fails simple cognitive tests that 4-year-old children pass with ease, and he cannot even learn the rules for simple games like tic-tac-toe. Despite his dazzling talent, Christopher lives in a halfway house because he does not have the cognitive capacity to make decisions, reason, or solve problems in a way that would allow him to live independently.

Christopher absorbed languages quickly from textbooks, yet he completely failed simple tests of other cognitive abilities.

CHRISTOPHER'S STRENGTHS AND WEAKNESSES offer compelling evidence that cognition is composed of distinct abilities. People who learn languages with lightning speed are not necessarily gifted at decision making or problem solving. People who excel at reasoning may have no special ability to master languages. In this chapter, you will learn about five key higher cognitive functions: acquiring and using language, forming concepts and categories, making decisions, solving problems, and reasoning. We excel at these functions compared with other animals, and they help define who we are as a species. We'll learn about each of these abilities by examining evidence that reveals their unique psychological characteristics, and we'll learn about their distinct neural underpinnings by considering individuals with brain lesions as well as neuroimaging studies. But despite clear differences among them, these five cognitive abilities have something important in common: They are critical to our functioning in just about all aspects of our everyday existence—including work, school, and personal relationships—and as we've just seen with Christopher, impairment of these cognitive abilities can result in major and lasting disruptions to our lives.

Language and Communication: From Rules to Meaning

Learning Objectives

- Describe the basic characteristics of language.
- Explain the milestones of language development.
- Compare the behaviorist, nativist, and interactionist theories of language development.

Most social species have systems of communication that allow them to transmit messages to each other. Honeybees communicate the location of food sources by means of a "waggle dance" that indicates both the direction and distance of the food source from the hive (Kirchner & Towne, 1994; Von Frisch, 1974). Vervet monkeys have three different warning calls that uniquely signal the presence of their main predators: a leopard, an eagle, and a snake (Cheney & Seyfarth, 1990). A leopard call provokes them to climb higher into a tree; an eagle call makes them look up into the sky. Each different warning call conveys a particular meaning and functions like a word in a simple language.

Honeybees communicate with each other about the location of food by doing a waggle dance that indicates the direction and distance of food from the hive.

Language is *a system for communicating with others using signals that are combined according to rules of grammar and that convey meaning.* **Grammar** is *a set of rules that specify how the units of language can be combined to produce meaningful messages.* Language allows individuals to exchange information about the world, coordinate group action, and form strong social bonds.

Human language may have evolved from signaling systems used by other species. However, three striking differences distinguish human language from vervet monkey yelps, for example. First, the complex structure of human language distinguishes it from simpler signaling systems. Most humans can express a wide range of ideas and concepts as well as generate an essentially infinite number of novel sentences. Second, humans use words to refer to intangible things, such as *unicorn* or *democracy.* These words could not have originated as simple alarm calls. Third, we use language to name, categorize, and describe things to ourselves when we think, which influences how knowledge is organized in our brains. It's doubtful that honeybees consciously think, "I'll fly north today to find more honey so the queen will be impressed!"

In this section, we'll examine the elements of human language that contribute to its complex structure. We'll consider the ease with which we acquire language despite this complexity, and how both biological and environmental influences shape language acquisition and use.

THE COMPLEX STRUCTURE OF HUMAN LANGUAGE

Compared with other forms of communication, human language is a relatively recent evolutionary phenomenon, emerging as a spoken system no more than 1 to 3 million years ago and as a written system as recently as 6,000 years ago. There are approximately 4,000 human languages, which linguists have grouped into about 50 language families (Nadasdy, 1995). Despite their differences, all of these languages share a basic structure involving a set of sounds and rules for combining those sounds to produce meanings.

Basic Characteristics

The smallest units of sound that are recognizable as speech rather than as random noise are called **phonemes.** These building blocks of spoken language differ in how they are produced. For example, when you say *ba,* your vocal cords start to vibrate as soon as you begin the sound, but when you say *pa,* there is a 60-millisecond lag between the time you start the *p* sound and the time your vocal cords start to vibrate. *B* and *p* are classified as separate phonemes in English because they differ in the way they are produced by the human speaker.

Every language has **phonological rules** that *indicate how phonemes can be combined to produce speech sounds.* For example, the initial sound *ts* is acceptable in German but not in English. Typically, people learn these phonological rules without instruction, and if the rules are violated, the resulting speech sounds so odd that we describe it as speaking with an accent.

Phonemes are combined to make **morphemes,** *the smallest meaningful units of language* (see **FIGURE 9.1**). For example, your brain recognizes the *p* sound you make at the beginning of *pat* as a speech *sound,* but it carries no particular meaning. The morpheme *pat,* on the other hand, is recognized as an element of speech that carries meaning.

All languages have grammar rules that generally fall into two categories: rules of morphology and rules of syntax. **Morphological rules** *indicate how morphemes can be combined to form words.* Some morphemes—content morphemes and function morphemes—can stand alone as words. *Content morphemes* refer to things and events (e.g., "cat," "dog," "take"). *Function morphemes* serve grammatical functions, such as tying sentences together ("and," "or," "but") or indicating time ("when"). About half of the morphemes in human languages are function morphemes, and it is the function morphemes that make

language A system for communicating with others using signals that are combined according to rules of grammar and that convey meaning.

grammar A set of rules that specify how the units of language can be combined to produce meaningful messages.

phoneme The smallest unit of sound that is recognizable as speech rather than as random noise.

phonological rules A set of rules that indicate how phonemes can be combined to produce speech sounds.

morphemes The smallest meaningful units of language.

morphological rules A set of rules that indicate how morphemes can be combined to form words.

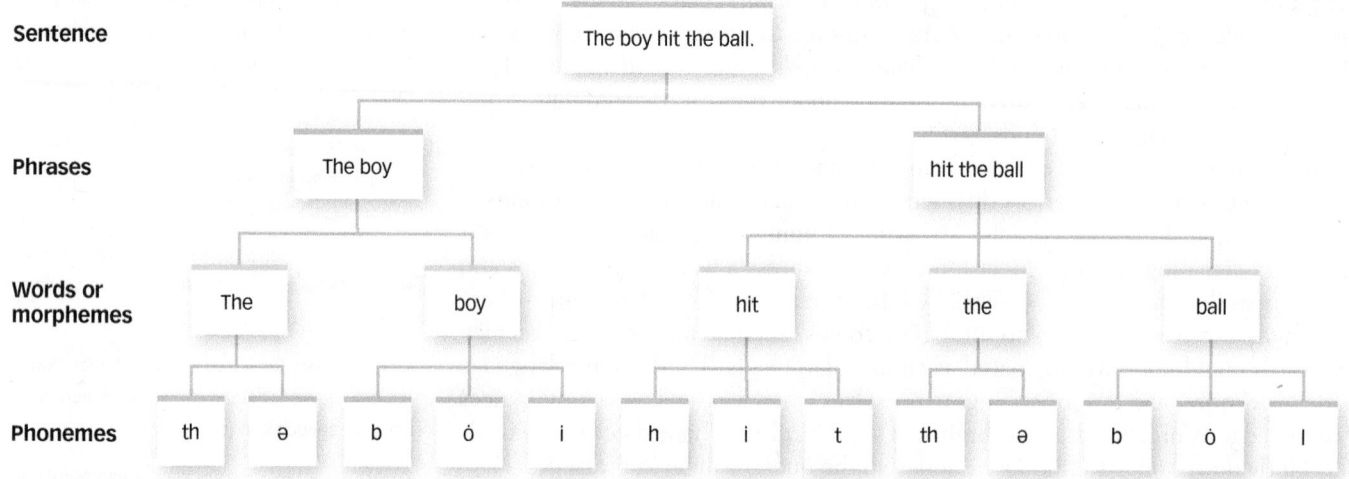

Sentence	The boy hit the ball.
Phrases	The boy / hit the ball
Words or morphemes	The / boy / hit / the / ball
Phonemes	th ə b ȯ i / h i t / th ə b ȯ l

▲ Figure 9.1

UNITS OF LANGUAGE

A sentence—the largest unit of language—can be broken down into progressively smaller units: phrases, morphemes, and phonemes. In all languages, phonemes and morphemes form words, which can be combined into phrases and ultimately into sentences.

human language grammatically complex enough to permit us to express abstract ideas rather than simply to point verbally to real objects in the here and now.

Content and function morphemes can be combined and recombined to form an infinite number of new sentences, which are governed by syntax. **Syntactical rules** *indicate how words can be combined to form phrases and sentences.* A simple syntactical rule in English is that every sentence must contain one or more nouns, which may be combined with adjectives or articles to create noun phrases (see **FIGURE 9.2**). A sentence also must contain one or more verbs, which may be combined with adverbs or articles to create verb phrases. So the utterance "dogs bark" is a full sentence, but "the big gray dog over by the building" is not.

Meaning: Deep Structure versus Surface Structure

Sounds and rules are critical ingredients of human language that allow us to convey meaning. A sentence can be constructed in a way that obeys syntactical and other rules, yet be entirely lacking in meaning or *semantics,* as in the famous example provided by linguist Noam Chomsky (1957, p. 15), "Colorless green ideas sleep furiously." Though we wouldn't be breaking any grammatical rules by uttering such a sentence, we could expect to elicit head scratches and strange looks from any nearby listeners. Language usually conveys meaning quite well, but everyday experience shows us that misunderstandings can occur. These errors sometimes result from differences between the deep structure of sentences and their surface structure (Chomsky, 1957). **Deep structure** refers to *the meaning of a sentence.* **Surface structure** refers to *how a sentence is worded.* "The dog chased the cat" and "The cat was chased by the dog" mean the same thing (they have the same deep structure), even though on the surface their structures are different.

To generate a sentence, you begin with a deep structure (the meaning of the sentence) and create a surface structure (the particular words) to convey that meaning. When you comprehend a sentence, you do the reverse, processing the surface structure in order to extract the deep structure. After the deep structure is extracted, the surface structure is usually forgotten (Jarvella, 1970, 1971). In one study, researchers played tape-recorded stories to volunteers and then asked them to pick the sentences they had heard (Sachs, 1967). Participants frequently confused sentences they heard with sentences that had the same deep structure but a different surface structure. For example, if they heard the sentence "He struck John on the shoulder," they often mistakenly claimed they had heard "John was struck on the shoulder by him." In contrast, they rarely misidentified "John struck him on the shoulder" because this sentence has a different deep structure from the original sentence.

syntactical rules A set of rules that indicate how words can be combined to form phrases and sentences.

deep structure The meaning of a sentence.

surface structure How a sentence is worded.

◄ **Figure 9.2**
SYNTACTICAL RULES
Syntactical rules indicate how words can be combined to form sentences. Every sentence must contain one or more nouns, which can be combined with adjectives or articles to create a noun phrase. A sentence also must contain one or more verbs, which can be combined with noun phrases, adverbs, or articles to create a verb phrase.

LANGUAGE DEVELOPMENT

Language is a complex cognitive skill, yet we can carry on complex conversations with playmates and family before we begin school. Three characteristics of language development are worth bearing in mind. First, children learn language at an astonishingly rapid rate. The average 1-year-old has a vocabulary of 10 words. This tiny vocabulary expands to over *10,000* words in the next 4 years, requiring the child to learn, on average, about 6 or 7 new words *every day.* Second, children make few errors while learning to speak, and as we'll see shortly, the errors they do make usually result from applying, but overgeneralizing, grammatical rules they've learned. This is an extraordinary feat. There are over *3 million* ways to rearrange the words in any 10-word sentence, but only a few of these arrangements will be both grammatically correct and meaningful (Bickerton, 1990). Third, children's *passive mastery* of language develops faster than their *active mastery.* At every stage of language development, children understand language better than they speak.

Distinguishing Speech Sounds

At birth, infants can distinguish among all of the contrasting sounds that occur in all human languages. Within the first 6 months of life, they lose this ability, and, like their parents, can only distinguish among the contrasting sounds in the language they hear being spoken around them. For example, two distinct sounds in English are the *l* sound and the *r* sound, as in *lead* and *read.* These sounds are not distinguished in Japanese; instead, the *l* and *r* sounds fall within the same phoneme. Japanese adults cannot hear the difference between these two phonemes, but American adults can distinguish between them easily—and so can Japanese infants.

In one study, researchers constructed a tape of a voice saying "la-la-la" or "ra-ra-ra" repeatedly (Eimas et al., 1971). They rigged a pacifier so that whenever an infant sucked on it, a tape player that broadcast the "la-la" tape was activated. When the "la-la" sound began playing in response to their sucking, the infants were delighted and kept sucking on the pacifier to keep the "la-la" sound playing. After a while, they began to lose interest, and sucking frequency declined to about half of its initial rate. At this

Why are we able to communicate effectively when we quickly forget the surface structure of sentences? Why might this be an evolutionary benefit?

In this videotaped test, the infant watches an animated toy animal while a single speech sound is repeated. After a few repetitions, the sound changes and then the display changes, and then they both change again. If the infant switches her attention when the sound changes, she is anticipating the new display, which demonstrates that she can discriminate between the sounds.

point, the experimenters switched the tape so that "ra-ra" was repeatedly played. The Japanese infants began sucking again with vigor, indicating that they could hear the difference between the old, boring "la" sound and the new, interesting "ra" sound.

Infants can distinguish among speech sounds, but they cannot produce them reliably, relying mostly on cooing (i.e, simple vowel-like sounds, such as *ah-ah*), cries, laughs, and other vocalizations to communicate. Between the ages of about 4 and 6 months, they begin to babble speech sounds. Babbling involves combinations of vowels and consonants that sound like real syllables but are meaningless. Regardless of the language they hear spoken, all infants go through the same babbling sequence. For example, *d* and *t* appear in infant babbling before *m* and *n*. Even deaf infants babble sounds they've never heard, and they do so in the same order as hearing infants do (Ollers & Eilers, 1988). This is evidence that infants aren't simply imitating the sounds they hear and suggests that babbling is a natural part of the language development process. Recent research has shown that babbling serves as a signal that the infant is in a state of focused attention and ready to learn (Goldstein et al., 2010). Deaf infants don't babble as much, however, and their babbling starts later than that of hearing infants (at 11 months rather than 6 months).

In order for vocal babbling to continue, however, infants must be able to hear themselves. In fact, delayed babbling or the cessation of babbling merits testing for possible hearing difficulties. Babbling problems can lead to speech impairments, but they do not necessarily prevent language acquisition. Deaf infants whose parents communicate using American Sign Language (ASL) begin to babble with their hands at the same age that hearing children begin to babble vocally—between 4 and 6 months (Petitto & Marentette, 1991). Their babbling consists of sign language syllables that are the fundamental components of ASL.

Language Milestones

At about 10 to 12 months of age, infants begin to utter (or sign) their first words. By 18 months, they can say about 50 words and can understand several times more than that. Toddlers generally learn nouns before verbs, and the nouns they learn first are names for everyday, concrete objects (e.g., chair, table, milk) (see **TABLE 9.1**). At about this time, their vocabularies undergo explosive growth. By the time the average

Deaf infants who learn sign language from their parents start babbling with their hands around the same time that hearing infants babble vocally.

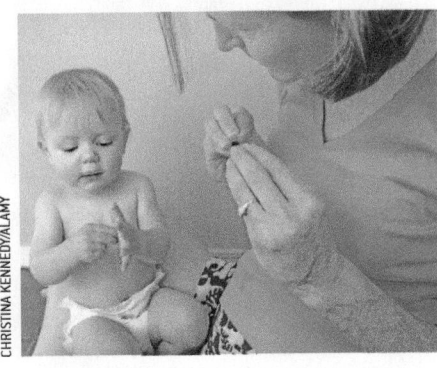

TABLE 9.1	
Language Milestones	
Average Age	**Language Milestones**
0–4 months	Can tell the difference between speech sounds (phonemes). Cooing, especially in response to speech.
4–6 months	Babbles consonants.
6–10 months	Understands some words and simple requests.
10–12 months	Begins to use single words.
12–18 months	Vocabulary of 30–50 words (simple nouns, adjectives, and action words).
18–24 months	Two-word phrases ordered according to syntactic rules. Vocabulary of 50–200 words. Understands rules.
24–36 months	Vocabulary of about 1,000 words. Production of phrases and incomplete sentences.
36–60 months	Vocabulary grows to more than 10,000 words. Production of full sentences. Mastery of grammatical morphemes (such as *-ed* for past tense) and function words (such as *the, and, but*). Can form questions and negations.

child begins school, a vocabulary of 10,000 words is not unusual. (These averages may differ for children in low- and high-income families, as discussed in A World of Difference: Exploring the 30-Million-Word Gap). By fifth grade, the average child knows the meanings of 40,000 words. By college, the average student's vocabulary is about 200,000 words. **Fast mapping,** *the process whereby children map a word onto an underlying concept after only a single exposure,* enables them to learn at this rapid pace (Kan & Kohnert, 2008; Mervis & Bertrand, 1994). This astonishingly easy process contrasts dramatically with the effort required later to learn other concepts and skills, such as arithmetic or writing.

Around 24 months, children begin to form two-word sentences, such as "more milk" or "throw ball." Such sentences are referred to as **telegraphic speech** because they are *devoid of function morphemes and consist mostly of content words.* Yet despite the absence of function words, such as prepositions or articles, these two-word sentences tend to be grammatical; the words are ordered in a manner consistent with the syntactical rules of the language children are learning to speak. So, for example, toddlers will say "throw ball" rather than "ball throw" when they want you to throw the ball to them, and "more milk" rather than "milk more" when they want to give them more milk. With these seemingly primitive expressions, 2-year-olds show that they have already acquired an appreciation of the syntactical rules of the language they are learning.

The Emergence of Grammatical Rules

Evidence of the ease with which children acquire grammatical rules comes from some interesting errors that children make while forming sentences. If you listen to average 2- or 3-year-old children speaking, you may notice that they use the correct past-tense versions of common verbs, as in the expressions "I ran" and "you ate." By the age of 4 or 5, the same children will be using incorrect forms of these verbs, saying such things as "I runned" or "you eated," forms most children are unlikely ever to have heard (Prasada & Pinker, 1993). The reason is that very young children memorize the particular sounds (i.e., words) that express what they want to communicate. But as children acquire the grammatical rules of their language, they tend to *overgeneralize.* For example, if a child overgeneralizes the rule that past tense is indicated by *-ed,* then *run* becomes *runned* or even *ranned* instead of *ran.*

These errors show that language acquisition is not simply a matter of imitating adult speech. Instead, children acquire grammatical rules by listening to the speech around them and using those rules to create verbal forms they've never heard. They manage this without explicit awareness of the grammatical rules they've learned. In fact, few children or adults can articulate the grammatical rules of their native language, yet the speech they produce obeys these rules.

By about 3 years of age, children begin to generate complete simple sentences that include function words (e.g., "Give me *the* ball" and "That belongs *to* me"). The sentences increase in complexity over the next 2 years. By the time children are 4 to 5 years of age, many aspects of the language acquisition process are complete. As children continue to mature, their language skills become more refined, with added appreciation of subtler communicative uses of language, such as humor, sarcasm, or irony.

Language Development and Cognitive Development

Language development typically unfolds as a sequence of steps in which children achieve one milestone before moving on to the next. Nearly all infants begin with one-word utterances before progressing to telegraphic speech and then to simple sentences that include function morphemes. It's hard to find solid evidence of infants launching immediately into speaking in sentences—even though you may occasionally

fast mapping The process whereby children can map a word onto an underlying concept after only a single exposure.

telegraphic speech Speech that is devoid of function morphemes and consists mostly of content words.

Exploring the 30-Million-Word Gap

In 1995, the psychologists Betty Hart and Todd Risley published a book that described their research concerning the language development of 1- to 2-year-old children in families at different levels of socioeconomic status (SES), ranging from families on welfare (low SES) to working class (middle SES) and professional (high SES; Hart & Risley, 1995). They studied 42 families and observed each of them for one hour per month over 2½ years. Hart and Risley's results were stunning: By the time they reached age 3, children in high-SES families were exposed to millions more words than were children in lower-SES families, which came to be known as the "30 million word gap." The researchers also found that these early language differences were highly predictive of how these children performed as third graders on various language and cognitive tests. (For further discussion of the effects of SES on various aspects of intellectual function, see the chapter on Intelligence.)

Since that time, the 30 million word gap has become widely known. Awareness of the gap has led to increased appreciation of the importance of SES differences in early language development as well as attempts to increase language exposure in low-SES children. Psychologists have continued to carry out research in an attempt to learn more about the origins and nature of the gap, which is critical to devising effective methods to reduce it, and they have made some important discoveries during the past few years. Fernald, Marchman, and Weisleder (2013) studied 48 young, English-learning children of lower- and higher-SES families from 18 months of age to 24 months of age. During this time, parents completed checklists that assess words that their children understand and say. The children also performed a language task in the laboratory that probed how quickly they could call to mind and use individual words. For this task, each child sat in his or her caregiver's arms and watched a screen where separate images of two common objects appeared. At the same time, a recorded voice asked about one of the objects. For example, if the child saw a dog on the left and a flower on the right, the voice would ask "Where is the

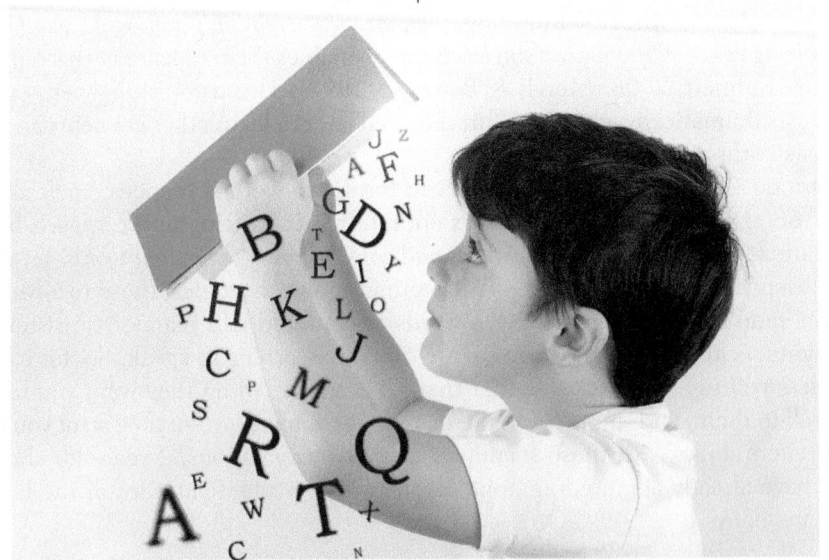

Quantity and quality of communication between a parent and a child is an essential factor in language development.

ESTHERMM/GETTY IMAGES

doggy?" The researchers measured how quickly the child's eyes moved to the correct object. (The caregiver was wearing sunglasses in order to avoid cueing the child.) Fernald et al. found significant differences between low- and high-SES children as young as 18 months of age: low-SES children had smaller vocabularies than high-SES children, and they were also slower and less accurate in moving their eyes to the object named by the speaker than were high-SES children. By the age of 24 months, language abilities in the low-SES children were already about six months behind those in the high-SES children.

What exactly is it that produces these troubling lags in low SES children? A recent study by Hirsh-Pasek and colleagues (2015) provides evidence that in addition to the sheer number of words that low-SES children are exposed to, the *quality* of early communications makes an important contribution. Hirsh-Pasek et al. focused on 24-month-old children from low-SES families, using video records of mother-child interactions while they played with items from three different boxes (a storybook, toy stove/cooking accessories, and a dollhouse). The researchers assessed the quantity of words used during these interactions and also the quality of the communications, such as how coordinated the mother-child interactions were (e.g., taking turns), and how often they were jointly engaged in a task (e.g., when playing with the dollhouse, the child produced the word "baby" with a gesture indicating sleep, and the mother placed the figure on the bed).

A year later, the researchers assessed the children's language abilities using scales that were developed to detect changes in language development in young children. Consistent with earlier studies, Hirsh-Pasek and colleagues found that the quantity of words used by the mother during the play task was associated with her child's language performance a year later. (More words from the mother predicted higher performance by the child.) Importantly, though, they also found that the rated quality of communication during the play task was an even stronger predictor of language performance a year later. The findings thus suggest that to counter some of the negative consequences associated with the 30 million word gap, it will be important to take into account and improve the quality of communications between parents and children in low-SES families.

hear reports of such feats from proud parents, including possibly your own! There are two possible explanations for this:

▶ The orderly progression could result from general cognitive development that is unrelated to experience with a specific language (Shore, 1986; Wexler, 1999). For example, perhaps infants begin with one- and then two-word utterances because their short-term memories are so limited that initially they can hold in mind only a word or two; additional cognitive development might be necessary before they have the capacity to put together a simple sentence.

▶ By contrast, the orderly progression might depend on experience with a specific language, reflecting a child's emerging knowledge of that language (Bates & Goodman, 1997; Gillette et al., 1999).

These two possibilities are difficult to tease apart, but recent research has begun to do so using a novel strategy: examining the acquisition of English by internationally adopted children who did not know any English prior to adoption (Snedeker, Geren, & Shafto, 2007, 2012). Although most of those adoptees were infants or toddlers, a significant proportion were preschoolers. Studying the acquisition of English in such an older population provides a unique opportunity to explore the relationship between language development and cognitive development. If the orderly sequence of milestones that characterizes the acquisition of English by infants is a by-product of general cognitive development, then different patterns should be observed in older internationally adopted children, who are more advanced cognitively than infants. However, if the milestones of language development are critically dependent on experience with a specific language—English—then language learning in older adopted children should show the same orderly progression as seen in infants.

Snedeker and colleagues (2007) examined preschoolers ranging from 2½ to 5½ years old, 3 to 18 months after they were adopted from China. They did so by mailing materials to parents, who periodically recorded language samples in their homes and also completed questionnaires concerning specific features of language observed in their children. These data were compared with similar data obtained from monolingual infants. The main result was clear cut: Language acquisition in preschool-age adopted children showed the same orderly progression of milestones that characterizes infants. These children began with one-word utterances before moving on to simple word combinations. Furthermore, their vocabulary, just like that of infants, was initially dominated by nouns, and they produced few function morphemes.

These results indicate that some of the key milestones of language development depend on experience with English. However, the adopted children did add new words to their vocabularies more quickly than infants did, perhaps reflecting an influence of general cognitive development. Overall, though, the main message from this study is that observed shifts in early language development reflect specific characteristics of language learning rather than general limitations of cognitive development. A later study by Snedeker and colleagues (2012) provided additional support for this general conclusion, but also produced new evidence for a role of cognitive development in specific aspects of language. For example, adopted preschoolers acquire words that refer to the past or the future—such as *tomorrow*, *yesterday*, *before*, or *after*—much more quickly than do infants, perhaps reflecting that infants have difficulty representing these abstract concepts and therefore take longer to learn the words than more cognitively sophisticated preschoolers.

THEORIES OF LANGUAGE DEVELOPMENT

We know a good deal about how language develops, but what underlies the process? The language acquisition process has been the subject of considerable controversy and (at times) angry exchanges among scientists coming from three different approaches: behaviorist, nativist, and interactionist.

Chinese preschoolers who are adopted by English-speaking parents progress through the same sequence of linguistic milestones as do infants born into English-speaking families, suggesting that these milestones reflect experience with English rather than general cognitive development.

THE WASHINGTON POST/GETTY IMAGES

Behaviorist Explanations

According to B. F. Skinner's behaviorist explanation of language learning, we learn to talk in the same way we learn any other skill: through reinforcement, shaping, extinction, and the other basic principles of operant conditioning that you read about in the Learning chapter (Skinner, 1957). As infants mature, they begin to vocalize. Those vocalizations that are not reinforced gradually diminish, and those that are reinforced remain in the developing child's repertoire. So, for example, when an infant gurgles "prah," most parents are pretty indifferent. However, a sound that even remotely resembles "da-da" is likely to be reinforced with smiles, whoops, and cackles of "Goooood baaaaaby!" by doting parents. Maturing children also imitate the speech patterns they hear. Then parents or other adults shape the children's speech patterns by reinforcing those that are grammatical and ignoring or punishing those that are ungrammatical. "I no want milk" is likely to be squelched by parental clucks and titters, whereas "No milk for me, thanks" will probably be reinforced.

The behavioral explanation is attractive because it offers a simple account of language development, but this theory cannot account for many fundamental characteristics of language development (Chomsky, 1986; Pinker, 1994; Pinker & Bloom, 1990).

> ▶ First, parents don't spend much time teaching their children to speak grammatically. In one well-documented study, researchers found that parents typically respond more to the truth content of their children's statements than to the grammar (Brown & Hanlon, 1970). So, for example, when a child expresses a sentiment such as "Nobody like me," his or her mother will respond with something like "Why do you think that?" or "I like you!" rather than "Now, listen carefully and repeat after me: Nobody likes me."

> ▶ Second, children generate many more grammatical sentences than they ever hear. This shows that children don't just imitate, they learn the rules for generating sentences. You'll recall that the same deep structure can generate a multitude of surface structures. It's highly unlikely that the developing child heard, reinforced, and learned each of those separate surface structures; it's much more likely that children simply acquire the ability to generate grammatical sentences.

> ▶ Third, as you read earlier in this chapter, the errors children make when learning to speak tend to be overgeneralizations of grammatical rules. The behaviorist explanation would not predict these overgeneralizations if children were learning through trial and error or simply imitating what they hear.

Nativist Explanations

The study of language and cognition underwent an enormous change in the 1950s, when the linguist Noam Chomsky (1957, 1959) published a blistering reply to the behaviorist approach. According to Chomsky, language-learning capacities are built into the brain, which is specialized to acquire language rapidly through simple exposure to speech. This **nativist theory** holds that *language development is best explained as an innate, biological capacity.* According to Chomsky, the human brain is equipped with a **language acquisition device (LAD),** *a collection of processes that facilitate language learning.* Language processes naturally emerge as the infant matures, provided the infant receives adequate input to maintain the acquisition process.

Language Ability Is Separate From General Intelligence Christopher's story is consistent with the nativist view of language development: His genius for language acquisition, despite his low overall intelligence, indicates that language capacity can be distinct from other mental capacities. Other individuals show the opposite pattern:

nativist theory The view that language development is best explained as an innate, biological capacity.

language acquisition device (LAD) A collection of processes that facilitate language learning.

Some people with normal or nearly normal intelligence can find certain aspects of human language difficult or impossible to learn. This condition is known as **genetic dysphasia,** a syndrome characterized by an inability to learn the grammatical structure of language despite having otherwise normal intelligence. Genetic dysphasia tends to run in families, and a single dominant gene has been implicated in its transmission (Gontier, 2008; Gopnik, 1990a, 1990b; Vargha-Khadem et al., 2005). Consider some sentences generated by children with the disorder:

> *She remembered when she hurts herself the other day.*
> *Carol is cry in the church.*

Notice that the ideas these children are trying to communicate are intelligent. Their problems with grammatical rules persist even if they receive special language training. When asked to describe what she did over the weekend, one child wrote, "On Saturday I watch TV." Her teacher corrected the sentence to "On Saturday, I watch*ed* TV," drawing attention to the *-ed* rule for describing past events. The following week, the child was asked to write another account of what she did over the weekend. She wrote, "On Saturday I wash myself and I watched TV and I went to bed." Notice that although she had memorized the past-tense forms *watched* and *went,* she could not generalize the rule to form the past tense of another word (*washed*).

As predicted by the nativist view, studies of people with genetic dysphasia suggest that normal children learn the grammatical rules of human language with ease in part because they are "wired" to do so. This biological predisposition to acquire language explains why newborn infants can distinguish contrasts among phonemes that occur in all human languages—even phonemes they've never heard spoken. If we learned language through imitation, as behaviorists theorized, infants would distinguish only the phonemes they'd actually heard. The nativist theory also explains why deaf infants babble speech sounds they have never heard and why the pattern of language development is similar in children throughout the world. These characteristics of language development are just what would be expected if our biological heritage provided us with the broad mechanics of human language.

Language Is Harder to Learn After Puberty Sets In   Also consistent with the nativist view is evidence that language can be acquired only during a restricted period of development, as has been observed with songbirds. If young songbirds are prevented from hearing adult birds sing during a particular period in their early lives, they do not learn to sing. A similar mechanism seems to affect human language learning, as illustrated by the tragic case of Genie (Curtiss, 1977). At the age of 20 months, Genie was tied to a chair by her parents and kept in virtual isolation. Her father forbade Genie's mother and brother to speak to her, and he himself only growled and barked at her. She remained in this brutal state until the age of 13 when her mother finally sought help for Genie. Genie's life improved substantially, and she received years of language instruction, but it was too late. Her language skills remained extremely primitive. She developed a basic vocabulary and could communicate her ideas, but she could not grasp the grammatical rules of English.

Similar cases have been reported, with a common theme: Once puberty is reached, acquiring language becomes extremely difficult (Brown, 1958). Data from studies of language acquisition in immigrants support this conclusion. In one study, researchers found that the proficiency with which immigrants spoke English depended not on how long they'd lived in the United States but on their age at immigration (Johnson & Newport, 1989). Those who arrived as children were the most proficient, whereas among those who immigrated after puberty, proficiency showed a significant decline regardless of the number of years immigrants were in their new country. More recent work using fMRI shows that acquiring a second language early in childhood (between 1 and 5 years of age) results in very different representation of that language in the

genetic dysphasia A syndrome characterized by an inability to learn the grammatical structure of language despite having otherwise normal intelligence.

"GOT IDEA. TALK BETTER. COMBINE WORDS. MAKE SENTENCES."

SPENCER GRANT/PHOTOEDIT

Immigrants who learn English as a second language are more proficient if they start to learn English before puberty rather than after.

brain than does acquiring that language much later (after 9 years of age; Bloch et al., 2009).

Interactionist Explanations

Nativist theories are often criticized because they do not explain *how* language develops; they merely explain why. A complete theory of language acquisition requires an explanation of the processes by which the innate, biological capacity for language combines with environmental experience. The interactionist approach is that although infants are born with an innate ability to acquire language, social interactions play a crucial role in language. Interactionists point out that parents tailor their verbal interactions with children in ways that simplify the language acquisition process: They speak slowly, enunciate clearly, and use simpler sentences than they do when speaking with adults (Bruner, 1983; Farrar, 1990).

Further evidence of the interaction of biology and experience comes from a fascinating study of deaf children's creation of a new language (Senghas, Kita, & Ozyurek, 2004). Prior to about 1980, deaf children in Nicaragua stayed at home and usually had little contact with other deaf individuals. In 1981, some deaf children began to attend a new vocational school. At first, the school did not teach a formal sign language, and none of the children had learned to sign at home, but the children gradually began to communicate using hand signals that they invented.

Over the past 30 years, their sign language has developed considerably (Pyers et al., 2010), and researchers have studied this new language for the telltale characteristics of languages that have evolved over much longer periods. For instance, mature languages typically break down experience into separate components. When we describe something in motion, such as a rock rolling down a hill, our language separates the type of movement (rolling) and the direction of movement (down). If we simply made a gesture, however, we would use a single continuous downward movement to indicate this motion. This is exactly what the first children to develop the Nicaraguan sign language did. But younger groups of children, who have developed the sign language further, use separate signs to describe the direction and the type of movement—a defining characteristic of mature languages. That the younger children did not merely copy the signs from the older users suggests that a predisposition exists to use language to dissect our experiences. Thus, their acts of creation nicely illustrate

How does the evolution of the Nicaraguan deaf children's sign language support the interactionist explanation of language development?

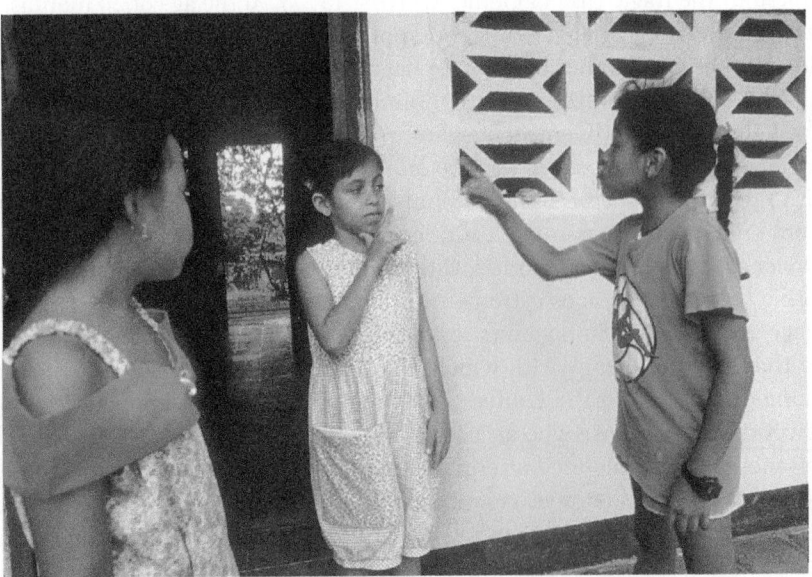

SUSAN MEISELAS/MAGNUM

the interplay of nativism (the predisposition to use language) and experience (growing up in an insulated deaf culture).

Build to the Outcomes

1. What are language and grammar?

2. What are the distinctions between human language and animal communication?

3. Is the meaning of a sentence more memorable than how the sentence is worded?

4. What language ability do infants have that adults do not?

5. What are the language milestones?

6. How do children learn and use grammatical rules?

7. What is the role of cognitive development in acquiring language?

8. How do behaviorists, nativists, and interactionists explain language development?

Language Development and the Brain

As the brain matures, specialization of specific neurological structures takes place, and this allows language to develop (Kuhl, 2010; Kuhl & Rivera-Gaxiola, 2008). Where, then, are the language centers of the brain?

BROCA'S AREA AND WERNICKE'S AREA OF THE BRAIN

In early infancy, language processing is distributed across many areas of the brain. But language processing gradually becomes more and more concentrated in two areas, Broca's area and Wernicke's area, sometimes referred to as the language centers of the brain. As the brain matures, these areas become increasingly specialized for language, so much so that damage to them results in a serious condition called **aphasia,** *difficulty in producing or comprehending language.*

Broca's area is located in the left frontal cortex and is involved in the production of the sequential patterns in vocal and sign languages (see **FIGURE 9.3**). As you saw in the Psychology: Evolution of a Science chapter, Broca's area is named after the French physician Paul Broca, who first reported on speech problems resulting from damage to a specific area of the left frontal cortex (Broca, 1861, 1863). Individuals with damage to this area, which results in *Broca's aphasia*, understand language relatively well, although they have increasing comprehension difficulty as grammatical structures get more complex. But their real struggle is with speech production. Typically, they speak in short, staccato phrases that consist mostly of content morphemes (e.g., *cat, dog*). Function morphemes (e.g., *and, but*) are usually missing, and grammatical structure is impaired. A person with Broca's aphasia might say something like "Ah, Monday, uh, Casey park. Two, uh, friends, and, uh, 30 minutes."

Wernicke's area, located in the left temporal cortex, is involved in language comprehension (whether spoken or signed). The German neurologist Carl Wernicke first described the area that bears his name after observing speech difficulty in patients who had sustained damage to the left posterior temporal cortex (Wernicke, 1874). Individuals with *Wernicke's aphasia* differ from those with Broca's aphasia in two ways: They can produce grammatical speech, but it tends to be meaningless, and they have considerable difficulty comprehending language. A person suffering from Wernicke's aphasia might say something like "Feel very well. In other words, I used to be able to work cigarettes. I don't know how. Things I couldn't hear from are here."

In normal language processing, Wernicke's area is highly active when we make judgments about word meaning, and damage to this area impairs comprehension of

Learning Outcomes

▸ Describe the language centers of the brain.

▸ Identify cognitive advantages and disadvantages for bilingual children.

▸ Explain what has been learned from language studies with nonhuman primates.

aphasia Difficulty in producing or comprehending language.

▼ Figure 9.3

BROCA'S AND WERNICKE'S AREAS Neuroscientists study people with brain damage in order to better understand how the brain normally operates. When Broca's area is damaged, people have a hard time producing sentences. When Wernicke's area is damaged, people can produce sentences, but they tend to be meaningless.

Broca's area

Wernicke's area

Japanese individuals who suffer from Wernicke's aphasia can still understand pictographs like these, even though they have difficulty understanding speech sounds.

spoken and signed language, although the ability to identify nonlanguage sounds is unimpaired. For example, Japanese can be written using symbols that, like the English alphabet, represent speech sounds, or by using pictographs that, like Chinese pictographs, represent ideas. Japanese persons who suffer from Wernicke's aphasia encounter difficulties in writing and understanding the symbols that represent speech sounds but not pictographs (Sasanuma, 1975).

INVOLVEMENT OF THE RIGHT CEREBRAL HEMISPHERE

As important as Broca's and Wernicke's areas are for language, they are not the entire story. Four kinds of evidence indicate that the right cerebral hemisphere also contributes to language processing, especially to language comprehension (Jung-Beeman, 2005). First, when words are presented to the right hemisphere of healthy participants using divided visual field techniques (see the Neuroscience and Behavior chapter), the right hemisphere shows some capacity for processing meaning. Second, individuals with damage to the right hemisphere sometimes have subtle problems with language comprehension. Third, a number of neuroimaging studies have revealed evidence of right-hemisphere activation during language tasks. Fourth, and most directly related to language development, some children who have had their entire left hemispheres removed during adolescence as a treatment for epilepsy can recover many of their language abilities.

BILINGUALISM AND THE BRAIN

Early studies of bilingual children seemed to suggest that bilingualism slows or interferes with normal cognitive development. When compared with monolingual children, bilingual children performed more slowly when processing language, and their IQ scores were lower. A reexamination of these studies, however, revealed several crucial flaws. First, the tests were given in English even when that was not the children's primary language. Second, the bilingual participants were often first- or second-generation immigrants whose parents were not proficient in English. Finally, the bilingual children came from lower socioeconomic backgrounds than the monolingual children (Andrews, 1982).

Later studies controlled for these factors, revealing a very different picture of bilingual children's cognitive skills. The available evidence concerning language acquisition indicates that bilingual and monolingual children do not differ significantly in the course and rate of many aspects of their language development (Nicoladis & Genesee, 1997). In fact, middle-class children who are fluent in two languages have been found to score higher than monolingual children on several measures of cognitive functioning, including executive control capacities such as the ability to prioritize information and flexibly focus attention (Bialystok, 1999, 2009; Bialystok, Craik, & Luk, 2012). The idea here is that bilingual individuals benefit from exerting executive control in their daily lives when they attempt to suppress the language that they don't want to use. Recent evidence indicates that bilingualism also can have benefits much later in life: Bilingual individuals tend to have a later onset of Alzheimer's disease than monolingual individuals, perhaps reflecting the fact that during their lives they have built up a greater amount of back-up cognitive ability, or "cognitive reserve" (Schweizer et al., 2012; Woumans et al., 2015; this finding and some other benefits of bilingualism are noted in Other Voices: Americans' Future Has to Be Bilingual). These findings are consistent with research showing that learning a second language produces lasting changes in the brain (Mechelli et al., 2004; Stein et al., 2009). For example, the gray matter in a part of the left parietal lobe that is involved in language is denser in bilingual than in monolingual individuals, and the increased density is most pronounced in those who are most proficient in using their second language (Mechelli et al., 2004; see **FIGURE 9.4**).

Lower left parietal region

(a)

Gray matter density

Proficiency in second language

(b)

◄ **Figure 9.4**

BILINGUALISM ALTERS BRAIN STRUCTURE Learning a second language early in life increases the density of gray matter in the brain. (a) A view of the lower left parietal region, which has denser gray matter in bilingual relative to monolingual individuals. (b) As proficiency in a second language increases, so does the density of gray matter in the lower parietal region. People who acquired a second language earlier in life were also found to have denser gray matter in this region. Interestingly, this area corresponds to the same area that is activated during verbal fluency tasks (Mechelli et al., 2004).

Some studies have revealed disadvantages, however. Bilingual children tend to have a smaller vocabulary in each language than their monolingual peers (Portocarrero, Burright, & Donovick, 2007); they also process language more slowly than monolingual children and can sometimes take longer to formulate sentences (Bialystok, 2009; Taylor & Lambert, 1990). Thus, learning a second language brings a number of benefits along with some costs (Bialystok, Abutalebi, Bak, Burke, & Kroll, 2016).

CAN OTHER SPECIES LEARN HUMAN LANGUAGE?

The human vocal tract and the extremely nimble human hand are better suited to human language than are the throats and paws of other species. Nonetheless, attempts have been made to teach nonhuman animals, particularly apes, to communicate using human language.

Early attempts to teach apes to speak failed dismally because their vocal tracts cannot accommodate the sounds used in human languages (Hayes & Hayes, 1951). Later attempts to teach apes human language have met with more success, including teaching them to use American Sign Language and computer-monitored keyboards that display geometric symbols that represent words. Allen and Beatrix Gardner were the first to use ASL with apes (Gardner & Gardner, 1969). The Gardners worked with a young female chimpanzee named Washoe as though she were a deaf child, signing to her regularly, rewarding her correct efforts at signing, and assisting her acquisition of signs by manipulating her hands in a process referred to as *molding*. In 4 years, Washoe learned approximately 160 words and could construct simple sentences, such as "More fruit." She also formed novel word constructions such as "water bird" for "duck." After a fight with a rhesus monkey, she signed, "dirty monkey!" This constituted a creative use of the term because she had only been taught the use of *dirty* to refer to soiled objects.

Other chimpanzees were immersed in ASL in a similar fashion, and Washoe and her companions were soon signing to each other, creating a learning environment conducive to language acquisition. One of Washoe's cohorts, a chimpanzee named Lucy, learned to sign "drink fruit" for watermelon. When Washoe's second infant died, her caretakers arranged for her to adopt an infant chimpanzee named Loulis.

In a few months, young Loulis, who was not exposed to human signers, learned 68 signs simply by watching Washoe communicate with the other chimpanzees. People who have observed these interactions and are themselves fluent in ASL report little difficulty in following the conversations (Fouts & Bodamer, 1987). One such observer, a *New York Times* reporter who spent some time with Washoe, reported, "Suddenly I realized I was conversing with a member of another species in my native tongue."

Other researchers have taught bonobo chimpanzees to communicate using a geometric keyboard system (Savage-Rumbaugh, Shanker, & Taylor, 1998). Their star pupil, Kanzi, learned the keyboard system by watching researchers try to teach his

Allen and Beatrix Gardner used sign language to teach the female chimpanzee Washoe about 160 words. Washoe could also construct simple sentences and combine words in novel ways.

Americans' Future Has to Be Bilingual

Linda Moore is the founder and executive director of the Elsie Whitlow Stokes Community Freedom Public Charter School in Washington, DC.

We discuss in this chapter some benefits of bilingualism that have been documented in recent research. Linda Moore (2012) noted several such benefits in the following article from the *Washington Diplomat* and argued that the American educational system should teach students foreign languages earlier than is commonly done.

We Americans must confront a stark disadvantage we face when it comes to the global economy. Some eight in 10 Americans speak only English, and the number of schools teaching a foreign language is in decline, according to a new study by the Council on Foreign Relations. But the opposite is true among our economic competitors.

While some 200 million Chinese students are learning English, only 24,000 Americans are studying Chinese, U.S. Department of Education statistics say. Foreign language degrees account for only 1 percent of all U.S. undergraduate degrees. And fewer than 2 percent of U.S. undergraduates study abroad in a given year, the Education Department says.

Our nation is largely monolingual but is entering an increasingly multilingual world. More than half of European Union citizens speak a language other than their mother tongue, and more than a quarter speak at least three languages. This is because additional languages are studied in European primary and secondary schools, and are taken up by European college students in much larger numbers than in the United States.

The Council on Foreign Relations—sponsored task force report, headed by former New York City Schools Chancellor Joel Klein and former Secretary of State Condoleezza Rice, concluded: "Education failure puts the United States' future economic prosperity, global position, and physical safety at risk." It warned that the country "will not be able to keep pace—much less lead—globally unless it moves to fix the problems it has allowed to fester for too long."

For decades, our children were deprived of bilingual or multilingual education out of a mistaken belief that it took time away from other subjects, hindering students' academic development. But recent research has shown that learning another language is a wise investment, rather than a waste. Research from the University of Georgia found that bilingual school children perform better on standardized tests including the Scholastic Aptitude Test (SAT) than their monolingual peers. A George Mason University study discovered that younger students who had enrolled in a second language immersion program outperformed those who did not in coursework, as well as on standardized tests, throughout their scholastic careers.

Educators now conclude that learning additional languages improves one's ability to focus, plan and solve problems. Among other benefits, this means that such students are better able to move efficiently from one subject to another. The D.C.-based Center for Applied Linguistics has ascertained that the earlier we learn a foreign language, the greater the benefits. Moreover, these benefits can last a lifetime. Learning another language can help people stave off the effects of aging, including preventing the onset of dementia and other age-related conditions like Alzheimer's, according to research done by University of California neuroscientists.

I believe that teaching students foreign languages in pre-kindergarten to sixth-grade classes is a worthwhile investment. Our school educates 350 students in Northeast Washington, D.C., to think, speak, read, write and learn in two languages, either English and French, or English and Spanish.

Exposure to a new language and the skills it helps develop is a key reason that our school, where 80 percent of our students come from low-income households, was ranked as high performing by D.C.'s Public Charter School Board in December. The ranking system was based on several factors, including test scores, attendance and re-enrollment rates.

The benefits of learning a new language go beyond the classroom. When students graduate, being fluent in a second language improves their career prospects. The Bureau of Labor Statistics reports that a number of emerging occupations need workers who can speak and write in more than one language. A University of Florida study revealed that in large, linguistically diverse cities such as Miami and San Antonio, the ability to speak a second language translates into more than $7,000 of increased annual income. We want our students to have access to these opportunities and more.

The economic importance of being bilingual is highlighted by the fact that 31 percent of company executives can speak at least two languages, according to international executive search firm Korn/Ferry.

Using multilingualism, we are expanding the scope of children's learning at a time when public policy limits school accountability to math and reading. Most policymakers want their children to have global skill sets but do not encourage this in our public schools.

Other countries have learned this lesson and have made the necessary commitments to teach their students additional languages. Their students' exposure to additional languages is paying dividends. I would like to see the U.S. Department of Education encourage local education authorities to invest in bilingual and multilingual education. Given the global competition for good jobs, this is not a luxury, but a necessity. It will help our children, and our nation, to succeed in the economy of tomorrow.

Are you convinced by Moore's argument? If not, why not? And if so, how far do you think that the educational system should go in promoting multilingual education? What about the possible impact on other subjects of devoting more time in early grades to teaching languages? What kinds of research would you want to see done to evaluate the effects of early instruction in foreign languages?

mother. Like Loulis, young Kanzi picked up the language relatively easily (his mother never did learn the system), suggesting that like humans, birds, and other species, apes experience a critical period for acquiring communicative systems.

Kanzi has learned hundreds of words and has combined them to form thousands of word combinations. Also as in human children, his passive mastery of language

linguistic relativity hypothesis The proposal that language shapes the nature of thought.

appears to exceed his ability to produce language. In one study, researchers tested 9-year-old Kanzi's understanding of 660 spoken sentences. These grammatically complex sentences asked him to perform simple actions, such as "Go get the balloon that's in the microwave" and "Pour the Perrier into the Coke." Some sentences were also potentially misleading, such as "Get the pine needles that are in the refrigerator," when there were pine needles in clear view on the floor. Impressively, Kanzi correctly carried out 72% of the 660 requests (Savage-Rumbaugh & Lewin, 1996).

These results indicate that apes can acquire sizable vocabularies, string words together to form short sentences, and process sentences that are grammatically complex. Their skills are especially impressive because human language is hardly their normal means of communication. Research with apes also suggests that the neurological "wiring" that allows us to learn language overlaps to some degree with theirs (and perhaps with other species').

Equally informative are the limitations apes exhibit when learning, comprehending, and using human language:

- *Limited vocabularies.* As mentioned, Washoe's and Kanzi's vocabularies number in the hundreds, but an average 4-year-old human child has a vocabulary of approximately 10,000 words.

- *Limited conceptual repertoire.* Apes primarily sign and respond to names for concrete objects and simple actions. Apes (and several other species) have the ability to map arbitrary sounds or symbols onto objects and actions, but learning, say, the meaning of the word *economics* would be difficult for Washoe or Kanzi. In other words, apes can learn signs for concepts they understand, but the words they can master are smaller and simpler than those that humans understand.

- *Limited understanding of grammar.* The third and perhaps most important limitation is the complexity of grammar that apes can use and comprehend. Apes can string signs together, but their constructions rarely exceed three or four words, and when they do, they are rarely grammatical. Comparing the grammatical structures produced by apes with those produced by human children highlights the complexity of human language as well as the ease and speed with which we generate and comprehend it.

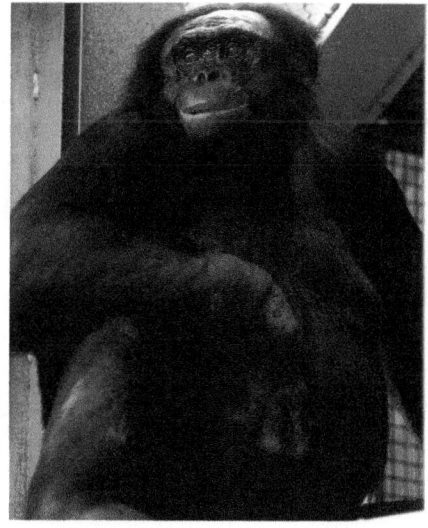

Kanzi, a young male bonobo chimpanzee, learned hundreds of words and word combinations through a keyboard system as he watched researchers try to teach his mother.

"He says he wants a lawyer."

Build to the Outcomes

1. How does language processing change the brain as the child matures?

2. What are the Broca's and Wernicke's areas?

3. How does bilingualism influence brain structure?

4. What do studies of apes and language teach us about humans and language?

Language and Thought: How Are They Related?

Language is such a dominant feature of our mental world that it is tempting to equate language with thought. Some theorists have even argued that language is simply a means of expressing thought. Benjamin Whorf (1956), on the other hand, championed the **linguistic relativity hypothesis,** the idea that *language shapes the nature of thought.* Whorf was an engineer who studied language in his spare time and was especially interested in Native American languages. The most frequently cited example of linguistic relativity comes from the Inuit in Canada. Their language has

Learning Outcome

- Describe the evidence that both supports and discounts the linguistic relativity hypothesis.

The Inuit of Canada use many different terms for snow, leading Benjamin Whorf (1956) to propose that they think about snow differently than do English-speakers.

many different terms for frozen white flakes of precipitation, for which we use the word *snow*. Whorf believed that because they have so many terms for snow, the Inuit perceive and think about snow differently than do English speakers. However, Whorf has been criticized for the anecdotal nature of his observations (Pinker, 1994).

LANGUAGE AND COLOR PROCESSING: DIFFERING RESULTS

Eleanor Rosch (1973) cast doubt on Whorf's hypothesis with studies of the Dani, an isolated agricultural tribe living in New Guinea. They have only two terms for colors, which roughly refer to "dark" and "light." If Whorf's hypothesis were correct, you would expect the Dani to have problems perceiving and learning different shades of color. But in Rosch's experiments, they learned shades of color just as well as people who have many more color terms in their first language.

However, more recent evidence shows that language may indeed influence color processing (Roberson et al., 2004). Researchers compared English children with African children from a cattle-herding tribe in Namibia known as the Himba. The English have 11 basic color terms, but the Himba, who are largely isolated from the outside world, have only five. For example, they use the term *serandu* to refer to what English speakers would call red, pink, or orange. Researchers showed a series of colored tiles to each child and then asked the child to choose one color from an array of 22 different colors. The youngest children, both English and Himba, who knew few or no color names, tended to confuse similar colors. But as the children grew and acquired more names for colors, their choices increasingly reflected the color terms they had learned. English children made fewer errors matching tiles that had English color names; Himba children made fewer errors for tiles with color names in Himba. These results reveal that language can indeed influence how children think about colors.

Similar effects have been observed in adults. Consider the 20 blue rectangles shown in **FIGURE 9.5**, which you'll easily see change gradually from lightest blue on the left to darkest blue on the right. What you might not know is that in Russian, there are different words for light blue (*goluboy*) and dark blue (*siniy*). Researchers investigated whether Russian speakers would respond differently to patches of blue when they fell into different linguistic categories rather than into the same linguistic category (Winawer et al., 2007). Both Russian- and English-speakers on average classified rectangles 1 through 8 as light blue and 9 through 20 as dark blue, but only Russian speakers used different words to refer to the two classes of blue. In the experimental task, participants were shown three blue squares, as in the lower part of Figure 9.5, and were asked to pick which of the two bottom squares matched the colors of the top square. Russian speakers responded more quickly when one of the bottom squares

▶ Figure 9.5

LANGUAGE AFFECTS HOW WE THINK ABOUT COLOR Unlike English, the Russian language has different words for light blue and dark blue. Russian-speakers asked to pick which of the two bottom squares matched the color of the single square above responded more quickly when one of the bottom squares was called *goluboy* (light blue) and the other was called *siniy* (dark blue) than when both were referred to by the same name. English-speakers took about the same amount of time.

01 02 03 04 05 06 07 08 09 10 11 12 13 14 15 16 17 18 19 20

WINAWER ET AL., RUSSIAN BLUES REVEAL EFFECTS OF LANGUAGE ON COLOR DISCRIMINATION. PNAS V 104-19 2007. 7780-7785. COPYRIGHT 2007 NATIONAL ACADEMY OF SCIENCES, USA.

was *goluboy* and the other was *siniy* than when both bottom squares were *goluboy* or both were *siniy*, whereas English speakers took about the same amount of time to respond in the two conditions (Winawer et al., 2007). As with children, language can affect how adults think about colors.

LANGUAGE AND THE CONCEPT OF TIME: RESULTS IMPLY A LINK

In another study exploring the relationship between language and thought, researchers looked at the way people think about time. In English, we often use spatial terms: We look *forward* to a promising future or move a meeting *back* to fit our schedule (Casasanto & Boroditsky, 2008). We also use these terms to describe horizontal spatial relations, such as taking three steps *forward* or two steps *back* (Boroditsky, 2001). In contrast, speakers of Mandarin (Chinese) often describe time using terms that refer to a vertical spatial dimension: Earlier events are referred to as *up*, and later events as *down*. To test the effect of this difference, researchers showed English-speakers and Mandarin-speakers either a horizontal or vertical display of objects and then asked them to make a judgment involving time, such as whether March comes before April (Boroditsky, 2001). English-speakers were faster to make the time judgments after seeing a horizontal display, whereas for Mandarin-speakers the opposite was true. When English speakers learned to use Mandarin spatial terms, their time judgments were also faster after seeing the vertical display! More recent evidence indicates that Mandarin-speakers are more likely than English-speakers to think about time along a vertical dimension when making judgments such as whether a photo of a famous person comes from an earlier or later stage of their life: Mandarin-speakers but not English-speakers responded more quickly when the "earlier" response key was on the top than on the bottom of a display (Boroditsky, Fuhrman, & McCormick, 2011). These results nicely show another way in which language can influence thought.

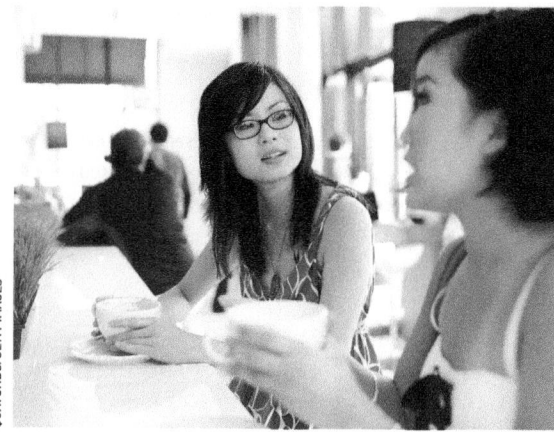

Westerners have a horizontal concept of time and see themselves as moving forward in time. Speakers of Mandarin have a vertical concept of time and see future events as down.

WAS WHORF "HALF RIGHT"?

Bear in mind, though, that either thought or language ability can be severely impaired while the capacity for the other is spared, as illustrated by the dramatic case of Christopher, which you read earlier in this chapter—and as we'll see again in the next section. These kinds of observations have led some researchers to suggest that Whorf was only "half right" in his claims about the effect of language on thought (Regier & Kay, 2009). Others suggest that, consistent with this idea, it is overly simplistic to talk in general terms about whether language influences thought, and that researchers need to be more specific about the exact ways in which language influences thought. For example, Wolff & Holmes (2011) rejected the idea that language entirely determines thought. But they also pointed out that there is considerable evidence that language can influence thought both by highlighting specific properties of concepts and by allowing us to formulate verbal rules that help to solve problems. Thus, recent research has started to clarify the ways in which the linguistic relativity hypothesis is right and the ways in which it is wrong.

DATA VISUALIZATION
How Do Subtle Language Changes Influence Decisions?
Go to launchpadworks.com.

Build to the Outcomes

1. What is the linguistic relativity hypothesis?

2. How does language influence our understanding of color?

3. How does a horizontal concept of time contrast with a vertical concept of time?

4. What does the fact that impaired language does not mean impaired thought suggest about the relationship between the two?

Concepts and Categories: How We Think

Learning Outcomes

▶ Identify why concepts are fundamental to our ability to think.

▶ Compare the family resemblance, prototype, and exemplar theories of concepts.

▶ Describe the involvement of the brain in organizing and processing concepts.

In October 2000, a 69-year-old man known by the initials JB went for a neurological assessment because he was having difficulty understanding the meaning of words, even though he still performed well on many other perceptual and cognitive tasks. In 2002, as his problems worsened, he began participating in a research project concerned with the role of language in naming, recognizing, and classifying colors (Haslam et al., 2007). As the researchers observed JB over the next 15 months, they documented that his color language deteriorated dramatically; he had great difficulty naming colors and could not even match objects with their typical colors (e.g., strawberry and red, banana and yellow). Yet even as his language deteriorated, JB could still classify colors normally, sorting color patches into groups of green, yellow, red, and blue in the exact same manner that healthy participants did. JB retained an intact concept of colors despite the decline of his language ability—a finding that suggests that we need to look at factors in addition to language in order to understand concepts (Haslam et al., 2007).

concept A mental representation that groups or categorizes shared features of related objects, events, or other stimuli.

"Attention, everyone! I'd like to introduce the newest member of our family."

JEFF KAUFMAN/THE NEW YORKER COLLECTION/CARTOONBANK.COM

There is family resemblance between family members despite the fact that there is no defining feature that they all have in common. Instead, there are shared common features. Someone who also shares some of those features may be categorized as belonging to the family.

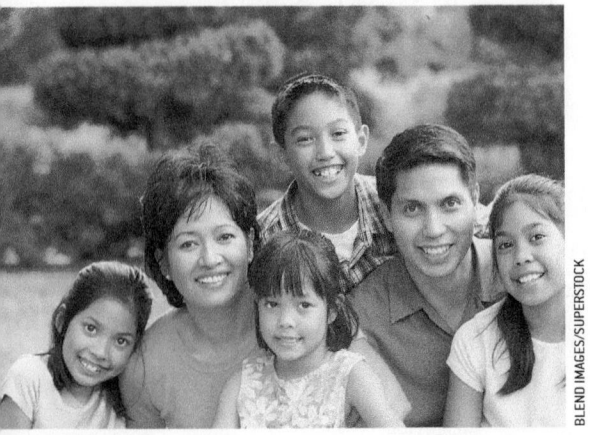

BLEND IMAGES/SUPERSTOCK

Concept refers to a *mental representation that groups or categorizes shared features of related objects, events, or other stimuli.* A concept is an abstract representation, description, or definition that designates a class or category of things. The brain organizes our concepts about the world, classifying them into categories based on shared similarities. Our category for *dog* may be something like "small, four-footed animal with fur that wags its tail and barks." Our category for *bird* may be something like "small, winged, beaked creature that flies." We form these categories in large part by noticing similarities among objects and events that we experience in everyday life. For example, your concept of a chair might include such features as sturdiness, relative flatness, and an object that you can sit on. That set of attributes defines a category of objects in the world—desk chairs, recliner chairs, flat rocks, bar stools, and so on—that can all be described in that way.

Concepts are fundamental to our ability to think and make sense of the world. We'll first compare various theories that explain the formation of concepts and then consider studies that link the formation and organization of concepts to the brain. As with other aspects of cognition, we can gain insight into how concepts are organized by looking at some instances in which they are rather disorganized. We'll encounter some unusual disorders that help us understand how concepts are organized in the brain.

PSYCHOLOGICAL THEORIES OF CONCEPTS AND CATEGORIES

Early psychological theories described concepts as rules that specify the necessary and sufficient conditions for membership in a particular category. A *necessary condition* is something that must be true of the object in order for it to belong to the category. For example, suppose you were trying to determine whether an unfamiliar animal was a dog. It is necessary that the creature be a mammal; otherwise it doesn't belong to the category *dog* because all dogs are mammals. A *sufficient condition* is something that, if it is true of the object, proves that it belongs to the category. Suppose someone told you that the creature was a German shepherd and you know that a German shepherd is a type of dog. *German shepherd* is a sufficient condition for membership in the category *dog*.

Most natural categories, however, cannot be so easily defined in terms of this classical approach of necessary and sufficient conditions. For example, what is your definition of *dog*? Can you come up with a rule of "dogship" that includes all dogs and excludes all non-dogs? Most people can't, but they still use the term *dog* intelligently, easily classifying objects as dogs or non-dogs. Three theories seek to explain how people perform these acts of categorization.

Family resemblance theory puts aside necessity and sufficiency to focus on *features that appear to be characteristic of category members but may not be possessed by every member* (Rosch, 1973, 1975; Rosch & Mervis, 1975; Wittgenstein, 1953/1999). For example, you and your brother may have your mother's eyes, although you and your sister may have your father's high cheekbones. There is a strong family resemblance among you, your parents, and your siblings despite the fact that there is no necessarily defining feature that you all have in common. Similarly, many members of the *bird* category have feathers and wings, so these are the characteristic features. Anything that has these features is likely to be classified as a bird because of this "family resemblance" to other members of the *bird* category. **FIGURE 9.6** illustrates family resemblance theory.

Prototype theory is based on *the "best" or "most typical" member of a category*. A prototype possesses most (or all) of the most characteristic features of the category. For North Americans, the prototype of the *bird* category would be something like a wren: a small animal with feathers and wings that flies through the air, lays eggs, and migrates (see **FIGURE 9.7**). If you lived in Antarctica, your prototype of a bird might be a penguin: a small animal that has flippers, swims, and lays eggs. According to *prototype*

▲ Figure 9.6

FAMILY RESEMBLANCE THEORY The family resemblance here is unmistakable, even though no two Smith brothers share all the family features. The prototype is brother 9. He has it all: brown hair, large ears, large nose, mustache, and glasses.

family resemblance theory The concept that members of a category have features that appear to be characteristic of category members but may not be possessed by every member.

prototype The "best" or "most typical" member of a category.

Properties	Generic bird	Wren	Blue heron	Golden eagle	Domestic goose	Penguin
Flies regularly	✔	✔	✔	✔		
Sings	✔	✔	✔			
Lays eggs	✔	✔	✔	✔	✔	✔
Is small	✔	✔				
Nests in trees	✔	✔				

◀ Figure 9.7

CRITICAL FEATURES OF A CATEGORY We tend to think of a generic bird as possessing a number of critical features, but not every bird possesses all of those features. In North America, a wren is a better example of a bird than a penguin or an ostrich.

▶ Figure 9.8

PROTOTYPE THEORY AND EXEMPLAR THEORY According to prototype theory, we classify new objects by comparing them to the "prototype" (or most typical) member of a category. According to exemplar theory, we classify new objects by comparing them with all category members.

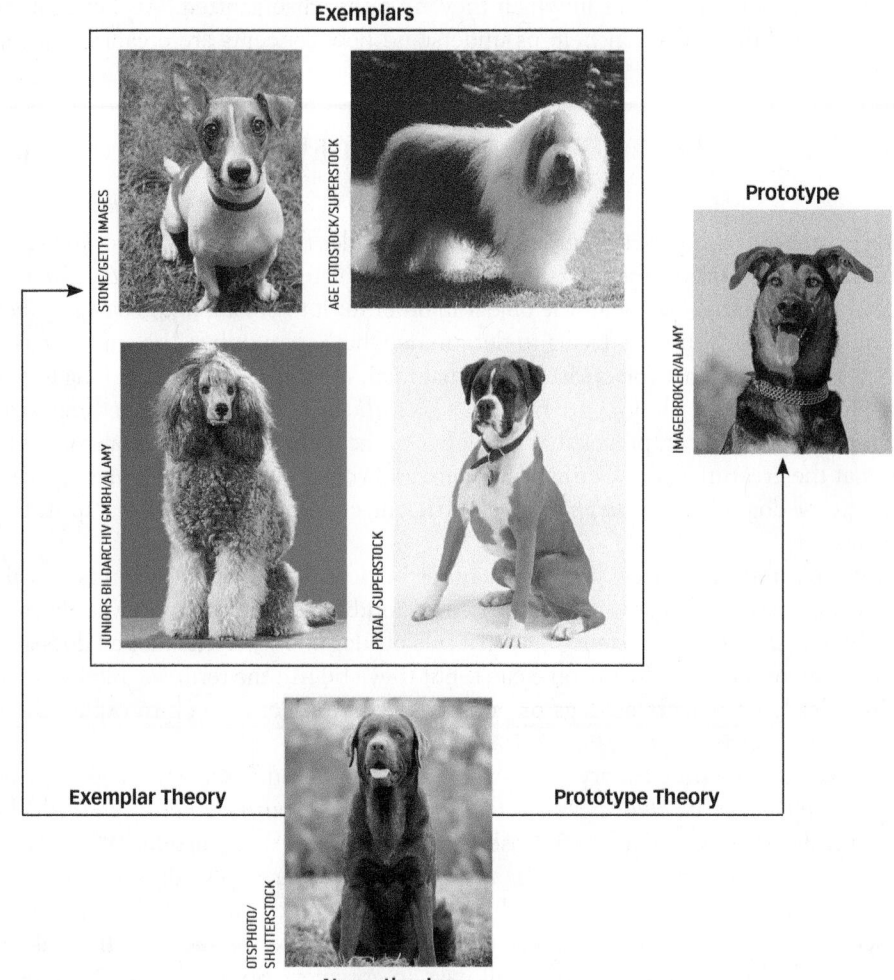

Exemplars

Prototype

Exemplar Theory

Prototype Theory

New stimulus

theory, if your prototypical bird is a robin, then a canary would be considered a better example of a bird than would an ostrich, because a canary has more features in common with a robin than an ostrich does. People make category judgments by comparing new instances with the category's prototype. This contrasts with the classical approach to concepts in which something either is or is not an example of a concept (i.e., it either does or does not belong in the category *dog* or *bird*).

Exemplar theory holds that *we make category judgments by comparing a new instance with stored memories for other instances of the category* (Medin & Schaffer, 1978). Imagine that you're out walking in the woods, and from the corner of your eye you spot a four-legged animal that might be a wolf or a coyote but that reminds you of your cousin's German shepherd. You figure it must be a dog and continue to enjoy your walk rather than fleeing in a panic. You probably categorized this new animal as a dog because it bore a striking resemblance to other dogs you've encountered; in other words, it was a good example (or an *exemplar*) of the category *dog*. Exemplar theory does a better job than prototype theory of accounting for certain aspects of categorization, especially in that we recall not only what a *prototypical* dog looks like but also what *specific* dogs look like. **FIGURE 9.8** illustrates the difference between prototype theory and exemplar theory.

exemplar theory A theory of categorization that argues that we make category judgments by comparing a new instance with stored memories of other instances of the category.

CONCEPTS, CATEGORIES, AND THE BRAIN

Studies that have attempted to link concepts and categories to the brain have helped to make sense of the theories we have just considered. For example, in one set of studies (Marsolek, 1995), participants classified prototypes faster when the stimuli were presented to the right visual field, meaning that the left hemisphere received the input first. (See the Neuroscience and Behavior chapter for a discussion of how the two hemispheres of the brain receive input from the outside world.) In contrast, participants classified previously seen exemplars faster when images were presented to the left visual field (meaning that the right hemisphere received the input first). These results suggest a role for both exemplars and prototypes: The left hemisphere is primarily involved in forming prototypes, and the right hemisphere is mainly active in recognizing exemplars.

"Don't panic. It's only a prototype."

More recently, researchers using neuroimaging techniques have also concluded that we use both prototypes and exemplars when forming concepts and categories. The visual cortex is involved in forming prototypes, whereas the prefrontal cortex and basal ganglia are involved in learning exemplars (Ashby & Ell, 2001; Ashby & O'Brien, 2005). This evidence suggests that exemplar-based learning involves analysis and decision making (prefrontal cortex), whereas prototype formation is a more holistic process involving image processing (visual cortex).

Some of the most striking evidence linking concepts and categories with the brain originated in a pioneering study of an odd case. Two neuropsychologists (Warrington & McCarthy, 1983) described a man with brain damage who could not recognize a variety of human-made objects or retrieve any information about them, but whose knowledge of living things and foods was perfectly normal. In the following year, neuropsychologists (Warrington & Shallice, 1984) reported on four individuals with brain damage who exhibited the reverse pattern: They could recognize information about human-made objects, but their ability to recognize information about living things and foods was severely impaired. Over 100 similar cases have since been reported (Martin & Caramazza, 2003). These unusual cases became the basis for a syndrome called **category-specific deficit,** *an inability to recognize objects that belong to a particular category, although the ability to recognize objects outside the category is undisturbed.*

Category-specific deficits like these have been observed even when the brain trauma that produces them occurs shortly after birth. Two researchers reported the case of Adam, a 16-year-old boy who suffered a stroke a day after he was born (Farah & Rabinowitz, 2003). Adam has severe difficulty recognizing faces and other biological objects. When shown a picture of a cherry, he identified it as "a Chinese yo-yo." When shown a picture of a mouse, he identified it as an owl. He made

category-specific deficit A neurological syndrome that is characterized by an inability to recognize objects that belong to a particular category, although the ability to recognize objects outside the category is undisturbed.

errors like these on 79% of the animal pictures and 54% of the plant pictures he was shown. In contrast, he made errors only 15% of the time when identifying pictures of nonliving things, such as spatulas, brooms, and cigars. What's so important about this case? The fact that 16-year-old Adam exhibited category-specific deficits despite suffering a stroke when he was only 1 day old strongly suggests that the brain is "prewired" to organize perceptual and sensory inputs into broad-based categories, such as living and nonliving things.

The type of category-specific deficit suffered depends on where the brain is damaged. Deficits usually result when an individual suffers a stroke or other trauma to areas in the left hemisphere of the cerebral cortex (Mahon & Caramazza, 2009). Damage to the front part of the left temporal lobe results in difficulty identifying humans; damage to the lower left temporal lobe results in difficulty identifying animals; damage to the region where the temporal lobe meets the occipital and parietal lobes impairs the ability to retrieve names of tools (Damasio et al., 1996). Similarly, when healthy people undertake the same task, imaging studies have demonstrated that the same regions of the brain are more active during naming of tools than during naming of animals and vice versa, as shown in **FIGURE 9.9** (Martin, 2007; Martin & Chao, 2001).

How do particular brain regions develop category preferences for objects such as tools or animals? One possibility is that these preferences develop from the specific visual experiences that individuals have during the course of their lives. An alternative possibility is suggested by the study of Adam that we just considered: The brain may be prewired such that particular regions respond more strongly to some categories than to others. A recent study tested these ideas by examining the activity of category-preferential regions in adults who have been blind since birth (Mahon et al., 2009). While in the fMRI scanner, blind and sighted individuals each heard a series of words, including some words that referred to animals and others that referred to tools. For each word, participants made a judgment about the size of the corresponding object. The critical finding was that category-preferential regions showed highly similar patterns of activity in the blind and sighted individuals. In both groups, for example, regions in the visual cortex and temporal lobe responded to animals and tools in much the same manner as shown in Figure 9.9.

These results provide compelling evidence that category-specific organization of visual regions does not depend on an individual's visual experience. The category-specific organization conceivably could have arisen from interactions with objects that blind individuals have had involving senses other than vision, such as touch (Peelen & Kastner, 2009). However, when these results are combined with the observations of Adam, the simplest explanation may be that category-specific brain organization is innately determined (Bedny & Saxe, 2012; Mahon et al., 2009).

▶ Figure 9.9

BRAIN AREAS INVOLVED IN CATEGORY-SPECIFIC PROCESSING Participants were asked to silently name pictures of animals and tools while they underwent fMRI scanning. The fMRIs revealed greater activity in the areas in white when participants named animals, and areas in black showed greater activity when participants named tools. Specific regions indicated by numbers include areas within the visual cortex (1, 2), parts of the temporal lobe (3, 4), and the motor cortex (5). Note that the images are left/right reversed.

Build to the Outcomes

1. What are concepts?

2. Why are concepts useful to us?

3. What are necessary and sufficient conditions in forming concepts?

4. How do the family resemblance, prototype, and exemplar theories differ?

5. How do prototypes and exemplars relate to each other?

6. What evidence suggests that the brain is "prewired" to organize perceptual and sensory inputs?

7. What is the role of vision in category-specific organization?

Decision Making: Rational and Otherwise

We use categories and concepts to guide the hundreds of decisions and judgments we make during the course of an average day. Some decisions are easy (what to wear; what to eat for breakfast; whether to walk, ride a bicycle, or drive to class) and some are more difficult (which car to buy, which apartment to rent, who to hang out with on Friday night, and even which job to take after graduation). Some decisions are based on sound judgments. Others are not.

THE RATIONAL IDEAL

Economists contend that if we are rational and are free to make our own decisions, we will behave as predicted by **rational choice theory**: *We make decisions by determining how likely something is to happen, judging the value of the outcome, and then multiplying the two* (Edwards, 1955). This means that our judgments will vary depending on the value we assign to the possible outcomes. Suppose, for example, you were asked to choose between a 10% chance of gaining $500 and a 20% chance of gaining $2,000. The rational person would choose the second alternative because the expected payoff is $400 ($2,000 × 20%), whereas the first offers an expected gain of only $50 ($500 × 10%). Selecting the option with the highest expected value seems so straightforward that many economists accept the basic ideas in rational choice theory. But how well does this theory describe decision making in our everyday lives? In many cases, the answer is not very well.

THE IRRATIONAL REALITY

Is the ability to classify new events and objects into categories always a useful skill? Alas, no. These strengths of human decision making can turn into weaknesses when certain tasks inadvertently activate these skills. In other words, the same principles that allow cognition to occur easily and accurately can pop up to bedevil our decision making.

Judging Frequencies and Probabilities

Consider the following list of words:

block table block pen telephone block disk glass table block
telephone block watch table candy

You probably noticed that the words *block* and *table* occur more frequently than the other words do. In fact, studies have shown that people are quite good at estimating

Learning Outcomes

▶ Explain why people sometimes fail to make rational decisions.

▶ Summarize the ideas underlying prospect theory.

▶ Describe the role of the brain in decision making.

People don't always make rational choices. When a lottery jackpot is larger than usual, more people will buy lottery tickets, thinking that they might well win big. However, more people buying lottery tickets reduces the likelihood of any one person winning the lottery. Ironically, people have a better chance at winning a lottery with a relatively small jackpot.

rational choice theory The classical view that we make decisions by determining how likely something is to happen, judging the value of the outcome, and then multiplying the two.

frequency, simply the number of times something will happen. This skill matters quite a bit when it comes to decision making. In contrast, we perform poorly on tasks that require us to think in terms of *probabilities,* or the likelihood that something will happen.

Even with probabilities, however, performance varies depending on how the problem is described. In one experiment, 100 physicians were asked to predict the incidence of breast cancer among women whose mammogram screening tests showed possible evidence of breast cancer. The physicians were told to take into consideration the rarity of breast cancer (1% of the population at the time the study was done) and radiologists' record in diagnosing the condition (correctly recognized only 79% of the time and falsely diagnosed almost 10% of the time). Of the 100 physicians, 95 estimated the probability that cancer was present to be about 75%! The correct answer was 8%. The physicians apparently experienced difficulty taking so much information into account when making their decision (Eddy, 1982). Similar dismal results have been reported with a number of medical screening tests (Hoffrage & Gigerenzer, 1996; Windeler & Kobberling, 1986).

However, dramatically different results were obtained when the study was repeated using *frequency* information instead of *probability* information. Stating the problem as "10 out of every 1,000 women actually have breast cancer" instead of "1% of women actually have breast cancer" led 46% of the physicians to derive the right answer, compared with only 8% who came up with the right answer when the problem was presented using probabilities (Hoffrage & Gigerenzer, 1998). This finding suggests, at a minimum, that when seeking advice (even from a highly skilled decision maker), make sure your problem is described using frequencies rather than probabilities.

Availability Bias

Take a look at the list of names in **FIGURE 9.10.** Now look away from the book and estimate the number of male names and female names in the figure. Did you notice that some of the women on the list are famous and none of the men are? Was your estimate off because you thought the list contained more women's than men's names (Tversky & Kahneman, 1973, 1974)? The reverse would have been true if you had looked at a list with the names of famous men and unknown women because people typically fall prey to **availability bias**: *Items that are more readily available in memory are judged as having occurred more frequently.*

The availability bias affects our estimates because memory strength and frequency of occurrence are directly related. Frequently occurring items are remembered more easily than *in*frequently occurring items, so you naturally conclude that items for which you have better memory must also have been more frequent. Unfortunately, better memory in this case was not due to greater *frequency,* but to greater *familiarity.*

Shortcuts such as the availability bias are sometimes referred to as **heuristics**, *fast and efficient strategies that may facilitate decision making but do not guarantee that a solution will be reached.* Heuristics are mental shortcuts, or rules of thumb, that are often—but not always—effective when approaching a problem (Swinkels, 2003). In contrast, an **algorithm** is *a well-defined sequence of procedures or rules that guarantees a solution to a problem.* Consider, for example, two approaches to constructing a PowerPoint presentation involving features you rarely use, such as inserting movies and complex animations: (1) you try to remember what you did the last time you tried to do a similar presentation; and (2) you follow a set of step-by-step directions that you wrote down the last time you did something similar, which tells you exactly how to insert movies and build complex animations.

The first procedure is an intelligent heuristic that may be successful, but you could continue searching your memory until you finally run out of time or patience. The second strategy is a series of well-defined steps that, if properly executed, will guarantee a solution.

Jennifer Aniston	Robert Kingston
Judy Smith	Gilbert Chapman
Frank Carson	Gwyneth Paltrow
Elizabeth Taylor	Martin Mitchell
Daniel Hunt	Thomas Hughes
Henry Vaughan	Michael Drayton
Agatha Christie	Julia Roberts
Arthur Hutchinson	Hillary Clinton
Jennifer Lopez	Jack Lindsay
Allen Nevins	Richard Gilder
Jane Austen	George Nathan
Joseph Litton	Britney Spears

▲ Figure 9.10

AVAILABILITY BIAS Looking at this list of names, estimate the number of women's and men's names.

availability bias The concept that items that are more readily available in memory are judged as having occurred more frequently.

heuristic A fast and efficient strategy that may facilitate decision making but does not guarantee that a solution will be reached.

algorithm A well-defined sequence of procedures or rules that guarantees a solution to a problem.

The Conjunction Fallacy

The availability bias illustrates a potential source of error in human cognition. Unfortunately, it's not the only one. Consider the following description:

> Linda is 31 years old, single, outspoken, and very bright. In college, she majored in philosophy. As a student, she was deeply concerned with issues of discrimination and social justice and also participated in antinuclear demonstrations.

Which state of affairs is more probable?

a. Linda is a bank teller.

b. Linda is a bank teller and is active in the feminist movement.

In one study, 89% of participants rated option b as more probable than option a (Tversky & Kahneman, 1983), although that's logically impossible. Let's say there's a 20% chance that Linda is a bank teller; after all, there are plenty of occupations she might hold. Independently, let's say there's also a 20% chance that she's active in the feminist movement; she probably has lots of interests. The joint probability that *both* things are true simultaneously is the product of their separate probabilities. In other words, the 20% chance that she's a teller multiplied by the 20% chance that she's in the feminist movement produces a 4% chance that both things are true at the same time (.20 × .20 = .04, or 4%). The combined probability of events is always less than the independent probability of each event; therefore, it's always *more* probable that any one state of affairs is true than is a set of events simultaneously.

This situation is called the **conjunction fallacy** because *people think that two events are more likely to occur together than either individual event.* The fallacy is that when they have more and more pieces of information, people think there's a higher probability that all are true. Actually, the probability diminishes rapidly. Judging by her description, do you think Linda also voted for the liberal candidate in the last election? Do you think she also writes poetry? Do you think she's also signed her name to fair-housing petitions? With each additional bit of information, you probably think you're getting a better and better description of Linda, but as you can see in **FIGURE 9.11**, the likelihood of all those events being true *at the same time* is very small.

Representativeness Heuristic

Think about the following situation:

A panel of psychologists wrote 100 descriptions based on interviews with engineers and lawyers. THE DESCRIPTIONS WERE OF 70 ENGINEERS AND 30 LAWYERS. You will be shown a random selection of these descriptions. Read each and then pause and decide if it is more likely that the person is an engineer or a lawyer. Note your decision and read on.

1. Jack enjoys reading books on social and political issues. During the interview, he displayed particular skill at argument.

2. Tom is a loner who enjoys working on mathematical puzzles during his spare time. During the interview, his speech remained fairly abstract and his emotions were well controlled.

3. Harry is a bright man and an avid racquetball player. During the interview, he asked many insightful questions and was very well spoken.

Research participants were shown a series of descriptions like these and asked after reading each one to judge the likelihood that the person described was a lawyer or an engineer (Kahneman & Tversky, 1973). Remember, of the descriptions, 70 were engineers and 30 were lawyers. If participants took this proportion into consideration, their judgments should have reflected the fact that there were more than twice as many engineers as lawyers. But researchers found that people didn't use this

conjunction fallacy When people think that two events are more likely to occur together than either individual event.

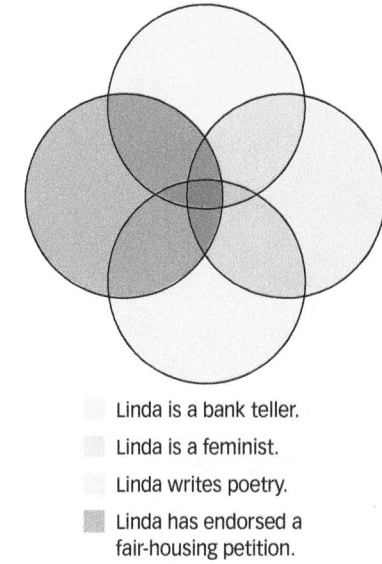

☐ Linda is a bank teller.
☐ Linda is a feminist.
☐ Linda writes poetry.
■ Linda has endorsed a fair-housing petition.

▲ Figure 9.11

THE CONJUNCTION FALLACY People often think that with each additional bit of information, the probability that all the facts are simultaneously true of a person increases. In fact, the probability decreases dramatically. Notice how the intersection of all these possibilities is much smaller than the area of any one possibility alone.

representativeness heuristic A mental shortcut that involves making a probability judgment by comparing an object or event with a prototype of the object or event.

framing effects A bias whereby people give different answers to the same problem depending on how the problem is phrased (or framed).

sunk-cost fallacy A framing effect in which people make decisions about a current situation on the basis of what they have previously invested in the situation.

Worth the cost? Sports teams sometimes try to justify their investment in an expensive player who is underperforming, an example of a sunk-cost effect. Ömer Aşik is a highly paid basketball player, but his recent performance has not lived up to his salary.

JOE ROBBINS/GETTY IMAGES

information and based their judgments solely on how closely the description matched their own concepts of lawyers and engineers. So the majority of participants thought descriptions such as 1 were more likely to be lawyers, those like 2 were more likely to be engineers, and those like 3 could be either.

Consider participants' judgments about Harry. His description doesn't sound like a lawyer's or an engineer's, so most people said he was *equally likely* to hold either occupation. But the pool contains more than twice as many engineers as lawyers, so it is far *more* likely that Harry is an engineer. People seem to ignore information about *base rate,* or the existing probability of an event, basing their judgments on similarities to categories. Researchers call this the **representativeness heuristic**: *making a probability judgment by comparing an object or event with a prototype of the object or event* (Kahneman & Tversky, 1973). Thus, the probability judgments were skewed toward the participants' prototypes of lawyer and engineer. The greater the similarity, the more likely they were judged to be members of that category despite the existence of much more useful base rates.

Heuristics such as availability, representativeness, or the conjunction fallacy highlight both the strengths and weaknesses of the way we think. We are very good at forming categories based on prototypes and making classification judgments on the basis of similarity to prototypes. Judging probabilities is not our strong suit. As we saw earlier in this chapter, the human brain easily processes frequency information, and decision-making performance can usually be improved if probability problems are reframed using frequencies.

Framing Effects

You've seen that, according to rational choice theory, our judgments will vary depending on the value we place on the expected outcome. So how effective are we at assigning value to our choices? Studies show that **framing effects,** which occur when *people give different answers to the same problem depending on how the problem is phrased (or framed),* can influence the assignment of value.

For example, if people are told that a particular drug has a 70% effectiveness rate, they're usually pretty impressed: getting what ails you cured 70% of the time by the drug sounds like a good deal. Tell them instead that a drug has a 30% failure rate—30% of the time it does no good—and they typically perceive it as risky, potentially harmful, and something to be avoided. Notice that the information is the same: A 70% effectiveness rate means that 30% of the time, it's ineffective. The way the information is framed, however, leads to substantially different conclusions (Tversky & Kahneman, 1981).

One of the most striking framing effects is the **sunk-cost fallacy,** which occurs when *people make decisions about a current situation on the basis of what they have previously invested in the situation.* Imagine waiting in line for 3 hours, paying $100 for a ticket to the Warped Tour to see your favorite bands, and waking on the day of the outdoor concert to find that it's bitterly cold and rainy. If you go, you'll feel miserable. But you go anyway, reasoning that the $100 you paid for the ticket and the time you spent in line will have been wasted if you stay home.

Notice that you have two choices: (1) spend $100 and stay comfortably at home; or (2) spend $100 and endure many uncomfortable hours in the rain. The $100 is gone in either case: It's a sunk cost, irretrievable at the moment of your decision. But the way you framed the problem created a problem: Because you invested time and money, you feel obligated to follow through, even though it's something you no longer want. If you can turn off this feeling and ask, Would I rather spend $100 to be comfortable or spend it to be miserable? the smart choice is clear: Stay home and listen to the podcast!

Even the National Basketball Association (NBA) is guilty of a sunk-cost fallacy. Coaches should play their most productive players and keep them on the team longer, but they don't. The most *expensive* players are given more time on court and are kept on the team longer than cheaper players, even if the costly players are not performing up to par (Staw & Hoang, 1995). Coaches act to justify their team's investment in an expensive player rather than recognize the loss. Framing effects can be costly!

Optimism Bias

In addition to heuristics and the biases we've just considered, human decision making often reflects the effects of **optimism bias**: *People believe that, compared with other people, they are more likely to experience positive events and less likely to experience negative events in the future* (Sharot, 2011). For example, compared with others, people believe that they are more likely to own their own homes and live a long life, and that they are less likely to have a heart attack or a drinking problem (Weinstein, 1980). Although optimism about the future is often a good thing for our mental and physical health—optimistic individuals are usually well adjusted psychologically and are able to handle stress well (Nes & Sergerstrom, 2006)—too much optimism can be detrimental because it may prevent us from taking the necessary steps to achieve our goals. Thus, overly optimistic individuals may think that they can attain a goal even when they lack the ability to achieve it, as exemplified by the finding that higher levels of optimism can be associated with lower levels of academic achievement (Sweeny, Carroll, & Shepperd, 2006).

Several studies have found that optimism bias is greater in North Americans than in individuals from eastern cultures such as Japan (Heine & Lehman, 1995; Klein & Helwig-Larsen, 2002). One study examined optimism bias concerning the risk of natural disasters and terrorist attacks in American, Japanese, and Argentinean mental health workers who had received training in responding to such events (Gierlach, Blesher, & Beutler, 2010). Although participants in all three countries judged that they were at lower risk of experiencing a disaster than others in their country, optimism bias was strongest in the American sample. Cultural differences such as these may eventually help us understand why optimism bias occurs.

WHY DO WE MAKE DECISION-MAKING ERRORS?

As you have seen, everyday decision making seems riddled with errors and shortcomings. Our decisions vary wildly, depending on how a problem is presented (e.g., framed in terms of frequencies vs. probabilities or in terms of losses rather than savings). We also seem to be prone to fallacies, such as the sunk-cost fallacy, the conjunction fallacy, or optimism bias. Psychologists have developed several theories to explain why everyday decision making suffers from these failings. We'll review the most influential theory, known as prospect theory.

According to a totally rational model of inference, people should make decisions that maximize value; in other words, they should seek to increase what psychologists and economists call *expected utility.* We face decisions like this every day. If you are making a decision that involves money, and if money is what you value, then you should choose the outcome that is likely to bring you the most money. When deciding which of two apartments to rent, you'd compare the monthly expenses for each and choose the one that leaves more money in your pocket.

As you have seen, however, people often make decisions that are inconsistent with this simple principle. The question is, why? To explain these effects, Amos Tversky and Daniel Kahneman (1992) developed **prospect theory**: *People choose to take on risks when evaluating potential losses and avoid risks when evaluating potential gains.* These decision processes take place in two phases:

▶ First, people simplify available information. So in a task such as choosing an apartment, they tend to ignore a lot of potentially useful information because apartments differ in so many ways (the closeness of restaurants, the presence of a

optimism bias A bias whereby people believe that, compared with other people, they are more likely to experience positive events and less likely to experience negative events in the future.

prospect theory The theory that people choose to take on risk when evaluating potential losses and avoid risks when evaluating potential gains.

swimming pool, the color of the carpet, and so forth). Comparing each apartment on each factor is simply too much work; focusing only on differences that matter is more efficient.

▶ In the second phase, people choose the prospect that they believe offers the best value. This value is personal and may differ from an objective measure of "best value." For example, you might choose the apartment with higher rent because you can walk to eight great bars and restaurants.

Prospect theory makes other assumptions that account for people's choice patterns. One assumption, called the *certainty effect*, suggests that when making decisions, people give greater weight to outcomes that are a sure thing. When deciding between playing a lottery with an 80% chance of winning $4,000 or receiving $3,000 outright, most people choose the $3,000, even though the expected value of the first choice is $200 more ($4,000 × 80% = $3,200)! Apparently, people weigh certainty much more heavily than expected payoffs when making choices.

Prospect theory also assumes that in evaluating choices, people compare them with a reference point. For example, suppose you're still torn between two apartments. The $400 monthly rent for apartment A is discounted $10 if you pay before the fifth of the month. A $10 surcharge is tacked onto the $390 per month rent for apartment B if you pay after the fifth of the month. Although the apartments are objectively identical in terms of cost, different reference points may make apartment A seem psychologically more appealing than apartment B.

Prospect theory also assumes that people are more willing to take risks to avoid losses than to achieve gains. Given a choice between a definite $300 rebate on your first month's rent or spinning a wheel that offers an 80% chance of getting a $400 rebate, you'll most likely choose the lower sure payoff over the higher potential payoff ($400 × 80% = $320). However, given a choice between a sure fine of $300 for damaging an apartment or spinning a wheel that has an 80% chance of a $400 fine, most people will choose the higher potential loss over the sure loss. This asymmetry

Bernie Sanders

Ted Cruz

According to rational choice theory, people evaluate all options when making a decision and choose the alternative with the greatest benefit to them. However, psychological research shows us that this is not always the case. How might some political candidates use the conjunction fallacy, framing effects, or prospect theory to influence voters' evaluations of their opponents or their opponents' views?

Carly Fiorina

Elizabeth Warren

in risk preferences shows that we are willing to take on risk if we think it will ward off a loss, but we're risk averse if we expect to lose some benefits.

DECISION MAKING AND THE BRAIN

A man identified as Elliot was a successful businessman, husband, and father prior to developing a brain tumor. After surgery, his intellectual abilities seemed intact, but he was unable to differentiate between important and unimportant activities and would spend hours at mundane tasks. He lost his job and got involved in several risky financial ventures that bankrupted him. He had no difficulty discussing what had happened, but his descriptions were so detached and dispassionate that it seemed as though his abstract intellectual functions had become dissociated from his social and emotional abilities.

Research confirms that this interpretation of Elliot's downfall is right on track. In one study, researchers looked at how healthy volunteers differed from people with prefrontal lobe damage on a gambling task that involves risky decision making (Bechara et al., 1994, 1997). Four decks of cards were placed face down, and participants were required to make 100 selections of cards that specified an amount of play money they could win or lose. Two of the decks usually provided large payoffs or large losses, whereas the other two provided smaller payoffs and losses. While playing the game, the participants' galvanic skin responses (GSRs) were recorded to measure heightened emotional reactions.

The performance of players with prefrontal lobe damage mirrored Elliot's real-life problems: They selected cards equally from the riskier and the safer decks, leading most to eventually go bankrupt. At first, the healthy volunteers also selected from each deck equally, but they gradually shifted to choosing primarily from the safer decks. This difference in strategy occurred even though both groups showed strong emotional reactions to big gains and losses, as measured by their comparable GSR scores. The two groups differed in one important way. As the game progressed, the healthy participants began to show anticipatory emotional reactions when they even *considered* choosing a card from the risky deck. Their GSR scores jumped dramatically even before they were able to say that some decks were riskier than others (Bechara et al., 1997). The participants with prefrontal damage didn't show these anticipatory feelings when they were thinking about selecting a card from the risky deck. Apparently, their emotional reactions did not guide their thinking, so they continued to make risky decisions, as shown in **FIGURE 9.12**.

Further studies of the participants with prefrontal damage suggest that their risky decision making grows out of insensitivity to the future consequences of their behavior (Naqvi, Shiv, & Bechara, 2006). Unable to think beyond immediate consequences, they could not shift their choices in response to a rising rate of losses or a declining rate of rewards (Bechara, Tranel, & Damasio, 2000).[1] Interestingly, substance-dependent individuals, such as alcoholics and cocaine addicts, act the same way. Most perform as poorly on the gambling task as do individuals with prefrontal damage (Bechara et al., 2001). More recent work has extended these impairments on the gambling task across cultures to Chinese adolescents with binge-drinking problems (Johnson, Xiao, et al., 2008). These findings have potentially important implications for such everyday issues as road safety. A recent study focused on people who had been convicted of driving while impaired with alcohol (DWI). Offenders who performed poorly on the gambling task were much more likely to commit repeated DWI offenses than those who performed well on the gambling task (Bouchard, Brown, & Nadeau, 2012). Related recent work has documented gambling-task impairments in binge eaters, another group in which there is an insensitivity to the future consequences of behavior (Danner et al., 2012).

▶ **Figure 9.12**

THE NEUROSCIENCE OF RISKY DECISION MAKING In a study of risky decision making, researchers compared healthy controls' choices to those made by people with damage to the prefrontal cortex. Participants played a game in which they selected a card from one of four decks. Two of the decks were made up of riskier cards, that is, cards that provided large payoffs or large losses. The other two contained safer cards—those with much smaller payoffs and losses. At the beginning of the game, both groups chose cards from the two decks with equal frequency. Over the course of the game, the healthy controls avoided the bad decks and showed large emotional responses (SCRs, or skin conductance responses) when they even considered choosing a card from a risky deck. Participants with prefrontal brain damage, on the other hand, continued to choose cards from the two decks with equal frequency and showed no evidence of emotional learning and eventually went bankrupt (data from Bechara et al., 1997).

Neuroimaging studies of healthy individuals have provided evidence that fits well with the earlier studies of individuals with damage to the prefrontal cortex: During the gambling task, an area in the prefrontal cortex is activated when participants make risky decisions as compared to safe decisions. Indeed, the activated region is in the part of the prefrontal cortex that is typically damaged in participants who perform poorly on the gambling task, and greater activation in this region is correlated with better task performance in healthy individuals (Fukui et al., 2005; Lawrence et al., 2009). Taken together, the neuroimaging and lesion studies show clearly that aspects of risky decision making depend critically on the contributions of the prefrontal cortex.

Build to the Outcomes

1. What is the importance of rational choices in decision making?

2. Why is a better decision more likely when we consider frequency, rather than the likelihood that something will happen?

3. How are memory strength and frequency of occurrence related?

4. How can more information sometimes lead people to wrong conclusions?

5. What can cause people to ignore the base rate of an event?

6. How does framing a problem differently influence one's answer?

7. Why will most people take more risks to avoid losses than to make gains?

8. What role does the prefrontal cortex play in risky behavior?

Problem Solving: Working It Out

You have a problem when you find yourself in a place where you don't want to be. In such circumstances, you try to find a way to change the situation so that you end up in a situation you *do* want. Let's say that it's the night before a test, and you are trying to study but just can't settle down and focus on the material. This is a situation you don't want, so you try to think of ways to help yourself focus. You might begin with the material that most interests you, or provide yourself with rewards, such as a music break or a trip to the refrigerator. If these activities enable you to get down to work, your problem is solved.

Two major types of problems complicate our daily lives. The first and most frequent is the *ill-defined problem,* one that does not have a clear goal or well-defined solution paths. Your study block is an ill-defined problem: Your goal isn't clearly defined (i.e., somehow get focused), and the solution path for achieving the goal is even less clear (i.e., there are many ways to gain focus). Most everyday problems (being a better person, finding that special someone, achieving success) are ill defined. In contrast, a *well-defined problem* is one with clearly specified goals and clearly defined solution paths. Examples include following a clear set of directions to get to school, solving simple algebra problems, or playing a game of chess.

MEANS—ENDS ANALYSIS

In 1945, the German psychologist Karl Duncker reported some important studies of the problem-solving process. He presented people with ill-defined problems and asked them to "think aloud" while solving them (Duncker, 1945). On the basis of what people said about how they solve problems, Duncker described problem solving in terms of **means—ends analysis,** *a process of searching for the means or steps to reduce the differences between the current situation and the desired goal.* This process usually took the following steps:

1. Analyze the goal state (i.e., the desired outcome you want to attain).
2. Analyze the current state (i.e., your starting point, or the current situation).
3. List the differences between the current state and the goal state.
4. Reduce the list of differences by
   - ▶ Direct means (a procedure that solves the problem without intermediate steps).
   - ▶ Generating a subgoal (an intermediate step on the way to solving the problem).
   - ▶ Finding a similar problem that has a known solution.

Consider, for example, one of Duncker's problems:

A patient has an inoperable tumor in his abdomen. The tumor is inoperable because it is surrounded by healthy but fragile tissue that would be severely damaged during surgery. How can the patient be saved?

The *goal state* is a patient without the tumor and with undamaged surrounding tissue. The *current state* is a patient with an inoperable tumor surrounded by fragile tissue. The *difference* between these two states is the tumor. A *direct-means solution* would be to destroy the tumor with X-rays, but the required X-ray dose would destroy the fragile surrounding tissue and possibly kill the patient. A *subgoal* would be to modify the X-ray machine to deliver a weaker dose. After this subgoal is achieved, a direct-means solution could be to deliver the weaker dose to the patient's abdomen. But this solution won't work either: The weaker dose wouldn't damage the healthy tissue but also wouldn't kill

- ▶ Compare the means-ends analysis and analogical problem-solving approaches.
- ▶ Explain the factors that lead to, or inhibit, creativity and insight.

Even though it may not be easy to put together this model, having instructions for assembly makes it a well-defined problem.

means—ends analysis A process of searching for the means or steps to reduce differences between the current situation and the desired goal.

analogical problem solving The process of solving a problem by finding a similar problem with a known solution and applying that solution to the current problem.

the tumor. So, what to do? Find a similar problem that has a known solution. Let's see how this can be done.

ANALOGICAL PROBLEM SOLVING

When we engage in **analogical problem solving,** we attempt to *solve a problem by finding a similar problem with a known solution and applying that solution to the current problem.* Consider the following story:

> An island surrounded by bridges is the site of an enemy fortress. The massive fortification is so strongly defended that only a very large army could capture it. Unfortunately, the bridges would collapse under the weight of such a huge force. So a clever general divides the army into several smaller units and sends the units over different bridges, timing the crossings so that the many streams of soldiers converge on the fortress at the same time, and the fortress is taken.

Does this story suggest a solution to the tumor problem? It should. Removing a tumor and attacking a fortress are very different problems, but the two problems are analogous because they share a common structure: The *goal state* is a conquered fortress with undamaged surrounding bridges. The *current state* is an occupied fortress surrounded by fragile bridges. The *difference* between the two states is the occupying enemy. The *solution* is to divide the required force into smaller units that are light enough to spare the fragile bridges and send them down the bridges simultaneously so that they converge on the fortress. The combined units will form an army strong enough to take the fortress (see **FIGURE 9.13**).

This analogous problem of the island fortress suggests the following direct-means solution to the tumor problem:

> Surround the patient with X-ray machines and simultaneously send weaker doses that converge on the tumor. The combined strength of the weaker X-ray doses will be sufficient to destroy the tumor, but the individual doses will be weak enough to spare the surrounding healthy tissue.

Did this solution occur to you after reading the fortress story? In studies that have used the tumor problem, only 10% of participants spontaneously generated the correct solution. This percentage rose to 30% if participants read the island fortress problem or another analogous story. However, the success rate climbed dramatically to 75%

▶ Figure 9.13

ANALOGICAL PROBLEM SOLVING Just as smaller, lighter battalions can reach the fortress without damaging the bridges, many small X-ray doses can destroy the tumor without harming the delicate surrounding tissue. In both cases, the additive strength achieves the objective.

among participants who had a chance to read more than one analogous problem or were given a deliberate hint to use the solution to the fortress story (Gick & Holyoak, 1980).

Why was the fortress problem so ineffective by itself? Problem solving is strongly affected by superficial similarities between problems, and the relationship between the tumor and fortress problems lies deep in their structure (Catrambone, 2002).

CREATIVITY AND INSIGHT

Analogical problem solving shows us that successfully solving a problem often depends on learning the principles underlying a particular type of problem and also that solving lots of problems improves our ability to recognize certain problem types and generate effective solutions. Some problem solving, however, seems to involve brilliant flashes of insight and creative solutions that have never before been tried (see Hot Science: Creative Problem Solving: Insiders and Outsiders). Creative and insightful solutions often rely on restructuring a problem so that it turns into a problem you already know how to solve (Cummins, 2012).

Genius and Insight

Consider the exceptional mind of the mathematician Friedrich Gauss (1777–1855). One day, Gauss's elementary schoolteacher asked the class to add up the numbers 1 through 10. While his classmates laboriously worked their sums, Gauss had a flash of insight that caused the answer to occur to him immediately. Gauss imagined the numbers 1 through 10 as weights lined up on a balance beam, as shown in **FIGURE 9.14**. Starting at the left, each "weight" increases by 1. In order for the beam to balance, each weight on the left must be paired with a weight on the right. You can see this by starting at the middle and noticing that $5 + 6 = 11$, then moving outward, $4 + 7 = 11$, $3 + 8 = 11$, and so on. This produces five number pairs that add up to 11. Now the problem is easy: Multiply. Gauss's genius lay in restructuring the problem in a way that allowed him to notice a very simple and elegant solution to an otherwise tedious task—a procedure, by the way, that generalizes to series of any length.

According to Gestalt psychologists, insights such as these reflect a spontaneous restructuring of a problem. A sudden flash of insight contrasts with incremental problem-solving procedures whereby one gradually gets closer and closer to a solution. Early researchers studying insight found that people were more likely to solve a non-insight problem if they felt they were gradually getting "warmer" (incrementally closer to the solution). But whether someone felt "warm" did not predict the likelihood of

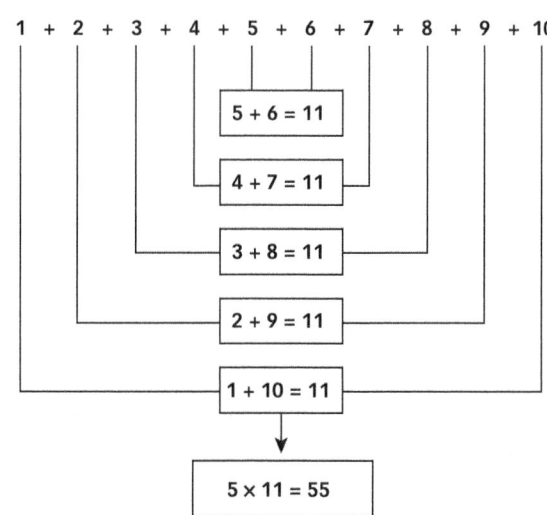

◀ Figure 9.14

GENIUS AND INSIGHT Young Friedrich Gauss imagined the scheme shown here and quickly reduced a laborious addition problem to an easy multiplication task. Gauss's early insight later led him to realize an intriguing truth: This simple solution generalizes to number series of any length (information from Wertheimer, 1945/1982).

Creative Problem Solving: Insiders and Outsiders

When it comes to creative problem solving, knowledge can be both a blessing and a curse: a blessing because when we know a lot about a particular topic, we may be able to use that knowledge to generate associations that help us to come up with a creative solution (Weisberg, 1999); a curse because knowing a lot about a topic may prevent us from considering novel solutions and lead us to rely on old, familiar ideas (Bilalić, McLeod, & Gobet, 2008), similar to the "functional fixedness" effect described in this chapter (pp. 386–387). In professions where creative problem solving is prized, such as science, we can see evidence for both the blessing and the curse of knowledge. On the one hand, Nobel prizes are typically awarded to "insiders"—experts with extensive knowledge of their chosen fields. On the other hand, there are many cases in which creative ideas and major advances come from "outsiders"—a physicist, for example, who generates a novel solution to a long-standing problem in biology (Harman & Dietrich, 2013). These observations raise intriguing questions about the processes whereby insiders and outsiders generate creative solutions to problems.

Acar and Ende (2016) addressed this issue in a fascinating study that drew on problems and solutions posted at InnoCentive.com, a crowd-sourcing Web site that brings together clients (typically companies) who have difficult, unsolved problems and individuals who try to propose solutions to those problems in exchange for a cash reward from the client. A look at the website in April 2016 revealed problems ranging from "Downstream Fish Passage at Tall Dams" for a $20,000 reward to "Design and Synthesis of a Small Molecule Glucose Binder" for $200,000. (Anyone can join, so check out the site and see whether any of the currently posted problems appeal to you!)

Acar and Ende sent out email surveys to people who had participated in InnoCentive.com contests, and analyzed responses from 230 contest participants who had submitted problem solutions during the previous 2.5 years. To assess the extent to which an individual was an insider or outsider with respect to the problem that they tried to solve, the researchers asked them to rate their expertise on a 1-to-7 scale, where 1 indicated "inside my field of expertise" (*low knowledge distance*), and 7 indicated "outside my field of expertise" (*high knowledge distance*). Acar and Ende were particularly interested in two aspects of how individuals came up with their solutions. The first involved *search variation*, measured with a 1-to-7 scale where a "1" response indicated that they drew on knowledge from a single domain (e.g., physics), and "7" indicated that they drew on knowledge from a variety of domains (e.g., physics, biology, and neuroscience). The second involved *search effort*: how much cognitive effort participants exerted to generate a solution, as assessed by participants' estimates of how many hours they had devoted to thinking and reading about the solution. Acar and Ende sought to determine how high and low levels of search variation and search effort related to the odds of a winning solution by insiders (low knowledge distance) and outsiders (high levels of knowledge distance).

As shown in the figure below, the odds of submitting a winning solution are slim when search effort is low, regardless of search variation or knowledge distance (blue and orange curves in the figure); apparently there is no shortcut to achieving prize-winning creativity. The most striking finding was that when search effort was high, low search variation was associated with much greater odds of winning for outsiders (high knowledge distance) than for insiders (low knowledge distance; green curve in the figure). In other words, when they engaged in a focused search that didn't draw on lots of different kinds of knowledge, outsiders stood a good chance of coming up with a creative, winning solution. In contrast, when search effort was high, the odds of winning for insiders (low knowledge distance) were better with high than with low search variation (red curve). In other words, people who were closer to the knowledge domain did well when they combined different kinds of knowledge, perhaps allowing them to break free from being overly familiar with the domain and to see the problem in a novel light.

So these results suggest that it is too simplistic to claim that knowledge of a domain is either a blessing or a curse for creative problem solving. It can be both, depending on what kinds of problem solving strategies people apply. Keeping that in mind could pay off next time you visit InnoCentive.com.

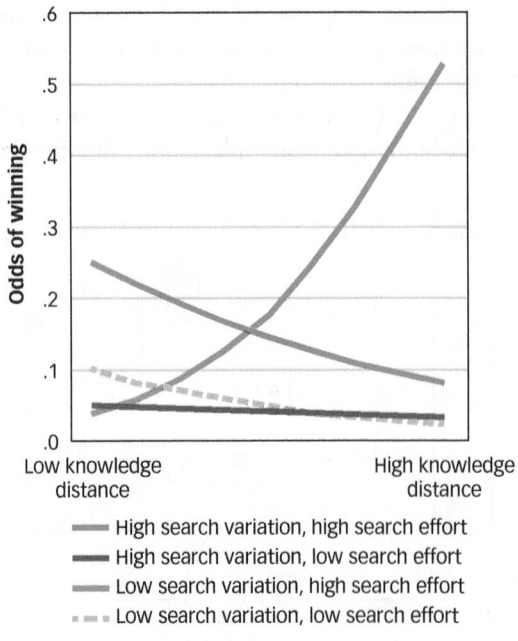

- ―― High search variation, high search effort
- ―― High search variation, low search effort
- ―― Low search variation, high search effort
- ----- Low search variation, low search effort

their solving an insight problem (Metcalfe & Wiebe, 1987). The solution for an insight problem seemed to appear out of the blue, regardless of what the participant felt.

Later research, however, suggests that sudden, insightful solutions may actually result from unconscious incremental processes (Bowers et al., 1990). In one study, research participants were shown paired, three-word series like those in **FIGURE 9.15** and asked to find a fourth word that was associated with the three words in each series. However, only one series in each pair had a common associate. Solvable series were termed *coherent,* whereas those with no solution were called *incoherent.*

Even if participants couldn't find a solution, they could reliably decide, more than by chance alone, which of the pairs was coherent. However, if insightful solutions actually occur in a sudden, all-or-nothing manner, their performance should have been no better than chance. Thus, the findings suggest that even insightful problem solving is an incremental process—one that occurs outside of conscious awareness. The process works something like this: The pattern of clues that constitute a problem unconsciously activates relevant information in memory. Activation then spreads through the memory network, recruiting additional relevant information (Bowers et al., 1990). When sufficient information has been activated, it crosses the threshold of awareness, and we experience a sudden flash of insight into the problem's solution.

Finding a connection between the words *strawberry* and *traffic* might take some time, even for someone motivated to figure out how they are related. But if the word *strawberry* activates *jam* in long-term memory (see the Memory chapter), and the activation spreads from *strawberry* to *traffic,* the solution to the puzzle may suddenly spring into awareness without the thinker's knowing how it got there. What might seem like a sudden insight would really result from an incremental process that consists of activation spreading through memory, adding new information as more knowledge is activated. Nonetheless, we will next consider studies of brain activity during problem solving that reveal striking differences between problems solved by sudden insight and those solved by using more deliberate strategies.

Sudden Insight and the Brain

The "aha!" moment that accompanies a sudden flash of insight highlights that solving a problem based on insight *feels* radically different from solving it through step-by-step analysis or trial and error. This difference in subjective experience suggests that something different is going on in the brain when we solve a problem using insight instead of analytic strategies (Kounios & Beeman, 2009).

To examine brain activity associated with insight, researchers used a procedure called *compound remote associates* that is similar in some respects to the three-word problems displayed in Figure 9.15. Each compound remote associates problem consists of three words, such as *crab*, *pine*, and *sauce*. Sometimes people solve these problems with a flash of insight: The solution word (*apple!*) suddenly pops into their minds, seemingly out of nowhere. Other times, people solve the problem by using analytic strategies that involve trying out different alternatives by generating a compound word for *crab* and then assessing whether that word fits *pine* and *sauce*. *Crabgrass* works, but *grass* doesn't work with *pine* and *sauce*. *Crabapple*? Problem solved.

Participants are instructed to press a button the moment a solution comes to mind, then describe whether they arrived at the solution via insight or through an analytic strategy. In an initial study, researchers used the electroencephalograph (EEG; see the Neuroscience and Behavior chapter) to measure brain electrical activity as participants attempted to solve the problems. What they observed was striking: Beginning about one-third of a second before participants came up with a solution, there was a sudden and dramatic burst of high-frequency electrical activity (40 cycles per second, or gamma band) for problems solved via insight, but not for problems solved via analytic strategies (Jung-Beeman et al., 2004). This activity was centered over the front part of the right temporal lobe, slightly above the right ear. When the researchers performed a

Coherent	Incoherent
Playing	Still
Credit	Pages
Report	Music
Blank	Light
White	Folk
Lines	Head
ticket	Town
Shop	Root
Broker	Car
Magic	House
Plush	Lion
Floor	Butter
Base	Swan
Snow	Army
Dance	Mask
Gold	Noise
Stool	Foam
Tender	Shade

INFORMATION FROM BOWERS ET AL., 1990.

Solutions:
Card, paper, pawn, carpet, ball, bar

▲ Figure 9.15

INSIGHTFUL SOLUTIONS ARE REALLY INCREMENTAL Participants were asked to find a fourth word that was associated with the other three words in each series. Even if they couldn't find a solution, they could reliably choose which series of three words were solvable and which were not. Try to solve these.

Louis Pasteur realized that sudden scientific insights don't just happen out of the blue; they depend on a prepared mind to take advantage of opportunity.

functional fixedness The tendency to perceive the functions of objects as unchanging.

similar study using fMRI to measure brain activity, they found that this right temporal area was the only region in the entire brain that showed greater activity for insight solutions than for solutions based on analytic strategies.

The great French scientist Louis Pasteur once stated, "Chance favors only the prepared mind." Inspired by this observation, researchers asked whether brain activity occurring just before presentation of a problem influenced whether that problem was solved via insight or analytic strategies (Kounios et al., 2006). It did. In the moments before a problem was solved with an insight solution, there was increased activity deep in the frontal lobes, in a part of the brain known as the anterior cingulate, which controls cognitive processes, such as the ability to switch attention from one thing to another. The researchers suggested that this increased activity in the anterior cingulate allowed participants to attend to and detect associations that were only weakly activated, perhaps at a subconscious level, and that facilitated sudden insight.

The results of these studies suggest that the familiar image of a light bulb turning on in your head when you experience an "aha!" moment is on the mark. Those moments are accompanied by something like an electrical power surge in the brain, and the increasing amount of research on creative insight and the brain (Beaty et al., 2016; Kounios & Beeman, 2015) should tell us much more about how to turn on the mental light bulb and keep it burning bright.

Functional Fixedness

Sudden insights occur relatively infrequently. One reason for their rarity is that problem solving (like decision making) suffers from framing effects. In problem solving, framing tends to limit the types of solutions that occur to us. **Functional fixedness**—*the tendency to perceive the functions of objects as unchanging*—is a process that constricts our thinking. Look at **FIGURES 9.16** and **9.17** and see if you can solve the problems before reading on. In Figure 9.16, your task is to illuminate a dark room using the following objects: some thumbtacks, a box of matches, and a candle. In Figure 9.17, your task is to use the items on the table to find a way to hold on to a string hanging from the ceiling and at the same time reach a second string that is too far away to grasp.

Difficulty with solving these problems derives from our tendency to think of the objects only in terms of their normal, typical, or "fixed" functions. We don't think to use the matchbox for a candleholder because boxes typically hold matches, not

▶ Figure 9.16

FUNCTIONAL FIXEDNESS AND THE CANDLE PROBLEM How can you use these objects—a box of matches, thumbtacks, and a candle—to mount the candle on the wall so that it illuminates the room? Give this problem some thought before you check the answer in Figure 9.19 on page 388.

◄ Figure 9.17
FUNCTIONAL FIXEDNESS AND THE STRING PROBLEM The strings hanging from hooks on either side of the ceiling are long enough to be tied together, but they are positioned too far apart to reach one while holding on to the other. Using the tools shown on the table (nails, matches, and a hammer), how can you accomplish the task? Compare your answer with that in Figure 9.20 on page 388.

candles. Similarly, using the hammer as a pendulum weight doesn't spring to mind because hammers are typically used to pound things. Did functional fixedness prevent you from solving these problems? (The solutions are shown in **FIGURES 9.19** and **9.20**.)

Sometimes framing limits our ability to generate a solution. Before reading on, look at **FIGURE 9.18**. Without lifting your pencil from the page, try to connect all nine dots with only four straight lines. To solve this problem, you must allow the lines you draw to extend outside the imaginary box that surrounds the dots (see **FIGURE 9.21**). This constraint does not reside in the problem but in the mind of the problem solver (Kershaw & Ohlsson, 2004). Despite the apparent sudden flash of insight that seems to yield a solution to problems of this type, research indicates that the thought processes people apply when solving even this type of insight problem are best described as an incremental, means–ends analysis (MacGregor, Ormerod, & Chronicle, 2001).

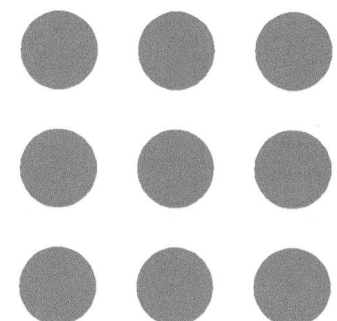

▲ Figure 9.18
THE NINE-DOT PROBLEM Connect all nine dots with four straight lines without lifting your pencil from the paper. Compare your answer with those in Figure 9.21 on page 388.

▲ Figure 9.19

THE SOLUTION TO THE CANDLE PROBLEM What makes this problem difficult is that the usual function of the box (to hold matches) interferes with recognizing that it can be tacked to the wall to serve as a candleholder.

▲ Figure 9.20

THE SOLUTION TO THE STRING PROBLEM The usual function of the hammer (to pound things) interferes with recognizing that it can also serve as a weighted pendulum to swing the string into the person's grasp.

▲ Figure 9.21

TWO SOLUTIONS TO THE NINE-DOT PROBLEM Solving this problem requires "thinking outside the box," that is, going outside the imaginary box implied by the dot arrangement. The limiting box isn't really there; it is imposed by the problem solver's perceptual set.

Build to the Outcomes

1. What is the difference between an ill-defined and a well-defined problem?

2. What are the steps in the means–ends analysis process of problem solving?

3. What is analogical problem solving?

4. What is the role of the unconscious in flashes of insight?

5. What is functional fixedness?

Transforming Information: How We Reach Conclusions

Learning Outcome

▶ Compare practical, theoretical, and syllogistic reasoning.

Reasoning is *a mental activity that consists of organizing information or beliefs into a series of steps in order to reach conclusions.* We rely on logic to assess the results of the reasoning process. Logic is a system of rules that specifies which conclusions follow from a set of statements. To put it another way, if you know that a given set of statements is true, logic will tell you which other statements *must* also be true. If the statement "Jack and Jill went up the hill" is true, then according to the rules of logic, the statement "Jill went up the hill" must also be true. Accepting the truth of the first statement while denying the truth of the second statement would be a contradiction. Logic is a tool for evaluating reasoning, but it should not be confused with the process of reasoning itself. Equating logic and reasoning would be like equating carpenter's tools (logic) with building a house (reasoning).

Earlier in this chapter, we discussed decision making, which often depends on reasoning with probabilities. Practical reasoning and theoretical reasoning also allow us to make decisions (Walton, 1990). **Practical reasoning** is *figuring out what to do, or reasoning directed toward action.* Means–ends analysis is one kind of practical reasoning. An example is figuring out how to get to a concert across town if you don't have a car. In contrast, **theoretical reasoning** (also called *discursive reasoning*) is *reasoning directed toward arriving at a belief.*

We use theoretical reasoning when we try to determine which beliefs follow logically from other beliefs. Suppose you asked your friend Bruce to take you to a concert, and he said that his car wasn't working. You'd undoubtedly find another way to get to the concert. If you then spied him driving into the concert parking lot, you might reason: "Bruce told me his car wasn't working. He just drove into the parking lot. If his car wasn't working, he couldn't drive it here. So either he suddenly fixed it, or he was lying to me. If he was lying to me, he's not much of a friend." Notice the absence of an action-oriented goal. Theoretical reasoning is just a series of inferences concluding in a belief—in this case, about your so-called friend's unfriendliness!

If you concluded from these examples that we are equally adept at both types of reasoning, experimental evidence suggests you're wrong. People generally find figuring out what to do easier than deciding which beliefs follow logically from other beliefs. In cross-cultural studies, this tendency to respond practically when theoretical reasoning is sought has been demonstrated in individuals without schooling. Consider, for example, this dialogue between a Nigerian rice farmer, a member of the preliterate Kpelle people, and an American researcher (Scribner, 1975, p. 155):

Experimenter:	All Kpelle men are rice farmers. Mr. Smith (this is a Western name) is not a rice farmer. Is he a Kpelle man?
Farmer:	I don't know the man in person. I have not laid eyes on the man himself.
Experimenter:	Just think about the statement.
Farmer:	If I know him in person, I can answer that question, but since I do not know him in person, I cannot answer that question.
Experimenter:	Try and answer from your Kpelle sense.
Farmer:	If you know a person, if a question comes up about him, you are able to answer. But if you do not know a person, if a question comes up about him, it's hard for you to answer it.

As this excerpt shows, the farmer does not seem to understand that the problem can be resolved with theoretical reasoning. Instead, he is concerned with retrieving and verifying facts, a strategy that does not work for this type of task.

reasoning A mental activity that consists of organizing information or beliefs into a series of steps in order to reach conclusions.

practical reasoning The process of figuring out what to do, or reasoning directed toward action.

theoretical reasoning (or discursive reasoning) Reasoning directed toward arriving at a belief.

A very different picture emerges when members of preliterate cultures are given tasks that require practical reasoning. One well-known study of rural Kenyans illustrates a typical result (Harkness, Edwards, & Super, 1981). The problem describes a dilemma in which a boy must decide whether to obey his father and give the family some of the money he has earned, even though his father previously promised that the boy could keep it all. After hearing the dilemma, the participants were asked what the boy should do. Here is a typical response from a villager:

> A child has to give you what you ask for just in the same way as when he asks for anything you give it to him. Why then should he be selfish with what he has? A parent loves his child and maybe the son refused without knowing the need of helping his father. . . . By showing respect to one another, friendship between us is assured, and as a result this will increase the prosperity of our family.

This preliterate individual had little difficulty understanding this practical problem. His response is intelligent, insightful, and well reasoned. A principal finding from this kind of cross-cultural research is that the appearance of competency on reasoning tests depends more on whether the task makes sense to participants than on their problem-solving ability.

THE REAL WORLD

From Zippers to Political Extremism: An Illusion of Understanding

Zippers are extremely helpful objects, and we have all used them more times than we could possibly recall. Most of us also think that we have a pretty good understanding of how a zipper works—at least until we are asked to provide a step-by-step explanation. In experiments by Rozenblit and Keil (2002), participants initially rated the depth of their understanding of various everyday objects (e.g., zippers, flush toilets, sewing machines) or procedures (e.g., how to make chocolate cookies from scratch), tried to provide detailed, step-by-step explanations, viewed expert descriptions and diagrams, and then re-rated their depth of understanding. The second set of ratings was significantly lower than the first. Attempting to explain the workings of the objects and procedures, and then seeing the much more detailed expert description, led participants to realize that they had greatly overestimated the depth of their understanding, which Rozenblit and Keil referred to as the *illusion of explanatory depth*.

Recent research suggests that the illusion of explanatory depth applies to a very different domain of everyday life: political extremism. Many pressing issues of our times, such as climate change and health care, share two features: They involve complex policies, and they tend to generate extreme views at either end of the political spectrum. Fernbach et al. (2013) asked whether political views become polarized because people think that they understand

the relevant policies in greater depth than they actually do. To investigate this hypothesis, the researchers asked participants to rate their positions regarding six contemporary political policies (sanctions on Iran for its nuclear program, raising the retirement age for social security, single-payer health care system, cap-and-trade system for carbon emissions, national flat tax, and merit-based pay for teachers) on a 7-point scale ranging from strongly against to strongly in favor. Next, the participants rated their understanding of each of the six policies on the 7-point scale used previously by Rozenblit and Keil (2002). Participants were then asked to generate detailed explanations of two of the six policies, followed in each case by a second set of ratings concerning their positions and their level of understanding of all the policies.

Fernbach et al. (2013) found that after attempting to generate detailed explanations, participants provided lower ratings of understanding and less extreme positions concerning all six policies than they had expressed previously. Furthermore, those participants who exhibited the largest decreases in their pre- versus post-explanation understanding ratings also exhibited the greatest moderation of their positions as a result of explaining them. Were these changes simply a result of thinking more deeply about the policies? Or were they specifically attributable to generating explanations? To address this issue, the researchers conducted an

additional experiment in which some participants provided explanations of policies, whereas others listed reasons that they held their positions. Once again, generating explanations led to lower understanding ratings and less extreme positions. However, no such changes were observed in participants who listed reasons that they held their views. A final experiment showed that after generating explanations, participants indicated that they would be less likely to make donations to relevant advocacy groups, reflecting moderation of their positions.

The overall pattern of results supports the idea that extreme political views are enabled, at least in part, by an illusion of explanatory depth: Once people realize that they don't understand the relevant policy issues in as much depth as they had thought, their views moderate. There probably aren't too many psychological phenomena that are well-illustrated by both political policies and the workings of zippers, but the illusion of explanatory depth is one of them.

STEVE MILLER/AGE FOTOSTOCK

Educated individuals in industrial societies are prone to similar failures in reasoning, as illustrated by **belief bias:** *People's judgments about whether to accept conclusions depend more on how believable the conclusions are than on whether the arguments are logically valid* (Evans, Barston, & Pollard, 1983; see also The Real World: From Zippers to Political Extremism: An Illusion of Understanding). For example, **syllogistic reasoning** assesses *whether a conclusion follows from two statements that are assumed to be true.* Consider the two following syllogisms, evaluate the argument, and ask yourself whether or not the conclusions must be true if the statements are true:

belief bias The idea that people's judgments about whether to accept conclusions depend more on how believable the conclusions are than on whether the arguments are logically valid.

syllogistic reasoning Determining whether a conclusion follows from two statements that are assumed to be true.

Syllogism 1

Statement 1: No cigarettes are inexpensive.

Statement 2: Some addictive things are inexpensive.

Conclusion: Some addictive things are not cigarettes.

Syllogism 2

Statement 1: No addictive things are inexpensive.

Statement 2: Some cigarettes are inexpensive.

Conclusion: Some cigarettes are not addictive.

If you're like most people, you probably concluded that the reasoning is valid in Syllogism 1 but flawed in Syllogism 2. Indeed, researchers found that nearly 100% of participants accepted the first conclusion as valid, but fewer than half accepted the second (Evans, Barston, & Pollard, 1983). But notice that the syllogisms are in exactly the same form. This form of syllogism is valid, so both conclusions are valid. Evidently, the believability of the conclusions influences people's judgments.

Build to the Outcomes

1. What is reasoning?

2. Define practical reasoning.

3. Define theoretical reasoning.

4. What have cross-cultural studies shown us about reasoning tests?

5. What is the role of belief bias in syllogistic reasoning?

Chapter Review

Language and Communication: From Rules to Meaning

▶ Human language is characterized by a complex organization—from phonemes to morphemes to phrases and finally to sentences. The deep structure of sentences is typically more memorable than the surface structure.

▶ Children can distinguish between all contrasting sounds of human language, but lose that ability within the first six months. Vocal babbling occurs at about 4 to 6 months, and first words are uttered or signed by 10 to 12 months. Sentences emerge around 24 months.

▶ Children acquire grammatical rules in development, even without being taught explicitly.

▶ The behaviorist explanation for language learning is based on operant conditioning, whereas nativists hold that humans are biologically predisposed to process language. Interactionists explain it as both a biological and a social process.

Language Development and the Brain

▶ Our abilities to produce and comprehend language depend on distinct regions of the brain, with Broca's area critical for language production and Wernicke's area critical for comprehension.

▶ Bilingual and monolingual children show similar rates of language development. Some bilingual children show greater executive control capacities, such as the ability to prioritize information and flexibly focus attention, and they tend to have a later onset of Alzheimer's disease. However, bilingual children may have smaller vocabularies and may process language more slowly.

▶ Nonhuman primates can learn new vocabulary and construct simple sentences, but there are significant limitations on the size of their vocabularies and the grammatical complexity they can handle.

Language and Thought: How Are They Related?

▶ The linguistic relativity hypothesis maintains that language shapes the nature of thought.

▶ Recent studies on color processing and time judgments point to an influence of language on thought.

▶ However, either language or thought may be impaired while the other is not, suggesting that language and thought are to some extent separate.

Concepts and Categories: How We Think

▶ We organize knowledge about objects, events, or other stimuli by creating concepts, prototypes, and exemplars.

▶ We acquire concepts using three theories: family resemblance theory, which states that items in the same category share certain features, if not all; prototype theory, which uses the most typical member of a category to assess new items; and exemplar theory, which states that we compare new items with stored memories of other members of the category.

▶ Neuroimaging studies have shown that prototypes and exemplars are processed in different parts of the brain.

▶ Studies of people with cognitive and visual deficits have shown that the brain organizes concepts into distinct categories, such as living things and human-made things, and also suggest that visual experience is not necessary for the development of such categories.

Decision Making: Rational and Otherwise

▶ Human decision making often departs from a completely rational process. The mistakes that accompany this departure tell us a lot about how the human mind works.

▶ The values we place on outcomes weigh so heavily in our judgments that they sometimes overshadow objective evidence. When people are asked to make probability judgments, they will turn the problem into something they know how to solve, such as judging memory strength, judging similarity to prototypes, or estimating frequencies. This can lead to errors of judgment.

▶ When a problem fits their mental algorithms, people show considerable skill at making appropriate judgments. In making a judgment about the probability of an event, performance can vary dramatically.

▶ Because we feel that avoiding losses is more important than achieving gains, framing effects can affect our choices. Emotional information also strongly influences our decision making, even when we are not aware of it. Although this influence can lead us astray, it often is crucial for making decisions in everyday life.

▶ The prefrontal cortex plays an important role in decision making, and patients with prefrontal damage make more risky decisions than do non-brain-damaged individuals.

Problem Solving: Working It Out

▶ Like concept formation and decision making, problem solving is a process in which new inputs (in this case, problems) are interpreted in terms of old knowledge. Problems may be ill defined or well defined, leading to more or less obvious solutions.

▶ The solutions we generate depend as much on the organization of our knowledge as they do on the objective characteristics of the problems. Means–ends analysis and analogical problem solving offer pathways to effective solutions, although we often frame things in terms of what we already know and already understand.

▶ Sometimes, as in the case of functional fixedness, that knowledge can restrict our problem-solving processes, making it difficult to find solutions that should be easy to find.

Transforming Information: How We Reach Conclusions

▶ The success of human reasoning depends on the content of the argument or scenario under consideration. People seem to excel at practical reasoning directed toward figuring out what to do or toward an action, but stumble when theoretical reasoning requires evaluation of the truth of a set of arguments.

▶ Belief bias describes a distortion of judgments about conclusions of arguments, causing people to focus on the believability of the conclusions rather than on the logical connections between the premises.

KEY CONCEPT QUIZ

1. The combining of words to form phrases and sentences is governed by
   a. phonological rules.
   b. morphological rules.
   c. structural rules.
   d. syntactical rules.

2. Language development as an innate, biological capacity is explained by
   a. fast mapping.
   b. behaviorism.
   c. nativist theory.
   d. interactionist explanations.

3. Damage to the brain region called Broca's area results in
   a. failure to comprehend language.
   b. difficulty in producing grammatical speech.
   c. the reintroduction of infant babbling.
   d. difficulties in writing.

4. The linguistic relativity hypothesis maintains that
   a. language and thought are separate cognitive phenomena.
   b. words have different meanings to different cultures.
   c. human language is too complex for nonhuman animals to acquire.
   d. language shapes the nature of thought.

5. The "most typical" member of a category is a(n)
   a. prototype.
   b. exemplar.
   c. concept.
   d. definition.

6. Which theory of how we form concepts is based on our judgment of features that appear to be characteristic of category members but may not be possessed by every member?
   a. prototype theory
   b. family resemblance theory
   c. exemplar theory
   d. heuristic theory

7. The inability to recognize objects that belong to a particular category, although the ability to recognize objects outside the category is undisturbed, is called
   a. category-preferential organization.

b. cognitive-visual deficit.

c. category-specific deficit.

d. aphasia.

8. People give different answers to the same problem, depending on how the problem is phrased, because of

a. the availability bias.

b. the conjunction fallacy.

c. the representativeness heuristic.

d. framing effects.

9. Miranda decides on a goal, analyzes her current situation, lists the differences between her current situation and her goal, then settles on

strategies to reduce those differences. Miranda is engaging in

a. means–ends analysis.

b. analogical problem solving.

c. capitalizing on insight.

d. functional fixedness.

10. What kind of reasoning is aimed at deciding on a course of action?

a. theoretical

b. belief

c. syllogistic

d. practical

 LearningCurve Don't stop now! Quizzing yourself is a powerful study tool. Go to LaunchPad to access the LearningCurve adaptive quizzing system and your own personalized learning plan. Visit launchpadworks.com.

KEY TERMS

language (p. 351)

grammar (p. 351)

phoneme (p. 351)

phonological rules (p. 351)

morphemes (p. 351)

morphological rules (p. 351)

syntactical rules (p. 352)

deep structure (p. 352)

surface structure (p. 352)

fast mapping (p. 355)

telegraphic speech (p. 355)

nativist theory (p. 358)

language acquisition device (LAD) (p. 358)

genetic dysphasia (p. 359)

aphasia (p. 361)

linguistic relativity hypothesis (p. 364)

concept (p. 368)

family resemblance theory (p. 369)

prototype (p. 369)

exemplar theory (p. 370)

category-specific deficit (p. 371)

rational choice theory (p. 373)

availability bias (p. 374)

heuristic (p. 374)

algorithm (p. 374)

conjunction fallacy (p. 375)

representativeness heuristic (p. 376)

framing effects (p. 376)

sunk-cost fallacy (p. 376)

optimism bias (p. 377)

prospect theory (p. 377)

means–ends analysis (p. 381)

analogical problem solving (p. 382)

functional fixedness (p. 386)

reasoning (p. 389)

practical reasoning (p. 389)

theoretical reasoning (or discursive reasoning) (p. 389)

belief bias (p. 391)

syllogistic reasoning (p. 391)

CHANGING MINDS

1. You mention to a friend that you've just learned that the primary language we learn can shape the way that we think. Your friend says that people are people everywhere and that this can't be true. What evidence could you describe to support your point?

2. In September 2011, *Wired* magazine ran an article discussing the fourth-down decisions of NFL coaches. On fourth down, a coach can choose to play aggressively and go for a first down (or even a touchdown), or the coach can settle for a punt or a field goal, which are safer options but

result in fewer points than a touchdown. Statistically, the riskier play results in greater point gain, on average, than playing it safe. But in reality, coaches choose the safer plays over 90% of the time. Reading this article, one of your friends is incredulous. "Coaches aren't stupid, and they want to win," he says. "Why would they always make the wrong decision?" Your friend is assuming that humans are rational decision makers. In what ways is your friend wrong? What might be causing the football coaches to make irrational decisions?

ANSWERS TO KEY CONCEPT QUIZ

1. d; 2. c; 3. b; 4. d; 5. a; 6. b; 7. c; 8. d; 9. a; 10. d.

 LaunchPad macmillan learning

LaunchPad features the full e-Book of *Psychology*, the LearningCurve adaptive quizzing system, videos, and a variety of activities to boost your learning. Visit LaunchPad at launchpadworks.com.

Intelligence

10

W HEN ANNE MCGARRAH DIED at the age of 57, she had lived more years than she could count. That's because Anne couldn't count at all. Like most people with Williams syndrome, she couldn't add 3 and 7, couldn't make change for a dollar, and couldn't distinguish right from left. Her cognitive ability was so impaired that she was unable to care for herself or hold a full-time job. So what did she do with her time?

> I love to read. Biographies, fiction, novels, different articles in newspapers, articles in magazines, just about anything. I just read a book about a young girl—she was born in Scotland—and her family who lived on a farm. . . . I love listening to music. I like a little bit of Beethoven, but I specifically like Mozart and Chopin and Bach. I like the way they develop their music—it's very light, it's very airy, and it's very cheerful music. I find Beethoven depressing. (Finn, 1991, p. 54)

People with Williams syndrome are often unable to tie their own shoes or make their own beds, but as Anne's words demonstrate, they often have an unusual flair for language and music. Williams syndrome is caused by the absence of just a few genes on a single chromosome, and no one knows how this tiny genetic glitch can so profoundly impair people's general cognitive abilities and yet leave them with a few extraordinary talents.

BONNIE WELLER/*PHILADELPHIA INQUIRER*/NEWSCOM

People with Williams syndrome have a distinct "elfin" facial appearance and diminished cognitive abilities, but they often have unusual gifts for music and language.

SO WAS ANNE MCGARRAH INTELLIGENT? IT SEEMS ODD TO SAY that someone is intelligent when she can't do simple addition, but it seems equally odd to say that someone is unintelligent when she knows the difference between baroque counterpoint and 19th-century romanticism. In a world of Albert Einsteins and Homer Simpsons, we'd have no trouble distinguishing the geniuses from the dullards. But ours is a world of people like Anne McGarrah and people like us: people who are sometimes brilliant, often bright, usually competent, and occasionally dimmer than broccoli. So what is this elusive thing that distinguishes us from each other?

About 20 years ago, a large group of scientific experts came together to answer this question. They concluded that intelligence...

> involves the ability to reason, plan, solve problems, think abstractly, comprehend complex ideas, learn quickly, and learn from experience. It is not merely book learning, a narrow academic skill, or test-taking smarts. Rather it reflects a broader and deeper capability for comprehending our surroundings—"catching on," "making sense" of things, or "figuring out" what to do. (Gottfredson, 1997, p. 13)

In short, **intelligence** is *the ability to use one's mind to solve novel problems and learn from experience*, and for more than a century, psychologists have been asking four questions about this remarkable ability: *How* can intelligence be measured? *What* exactly is intelligence? *Where* does intelligence come from? *Why* are some people more intelligent than others? As you will see, we now have good answers to all of these questions, but they did not come without controversy.

How Can Intelligence Be Measured?

Learning Outcomes

▶ Define intelligence.

▶ Explain how and why intelligence tests were developed.

▶ Explain why intelligence matters.

Few things are more dangerous than a man with a mission. In the 1920s, the psychologist Henry Goddard administered intelligence tests to arriving immigrants at Ellis Island and concluded that the overwhelming majority of Jews, Hungarians, Italians, and Russians were "feebleminded." Goddard also used his tests to identify feebleminded American families (whom, he claimed, were largely responsible for the nation's social problems) and suggested that the government should segregate them in isolated colonies and "take away from these people the power of procreation" (Goddard, 1913, p. 107). The United States subsequently passed laws restricting the immigration of people from southern and eastern Europe, and the majority of U.S. states passed laws requiring the sterilization of "mental defectives."

From Goddard's day to our own, intelligence tests have been used to rationalize prejudice and discrimination against people of different races, religions, and nationalities. Although intelligence testing has achieved many notable successes, its history is marred by more than its share of fraud and disgrace (Chorover, 1980; Lewontin, Rose, & Kamin, 1984). The fact that intelligence tests have sometimes been used for detestable purposes is especially ironic because, as you are about to see, those tests were originally developed for the noblest of purposes: to help underprivileged children succeed in school.

MEANS PROPOSED FOR CUTTING OFF THE SUPPLY OF
HUMAN DEFECTIVES AND DEGENERATES

I. LIFE SEGREGATION

II. STERILIZATION

III. RESTRICTIVE MARRIAGE

IV. EUGENIC EDUCATION

V. SYSTEM OF MATINGS

VI. GENERAL ENVIRONMENTAL

VII. POLYGAMY

VIII. EUTHANASIA

IX. NEO-MALTHUSIAN DOCTRINE

X. LAISSEZ-FAIRE

Which of these remedies shall be applied?
Shall one, two, several or all be made to operate.

What are the limitations and possibilities of each remedy?

Shall one class of the socially unfit be treated with one remedy and another with a different one?

Shall the specifically selected remedy be applied to the class or to the individual?

What are the principles and the limits of compromise between conservation and elimination in cases of individuals bearing a germ-plasm with a mixture of the deter-miners for both defective and sterling traits

What are the criteria for the identification of individuals bearing defective germ-plasm

What can be hoped from the application of some definite elimination program?

What practical difficulties stand in the way? How can they be overcome?

THE HARRY H. LAUGHLIN PAPERS, TRUMAN STATE UNIVERSITY

During the early 20th century, laws required the involuntary sterilization of people with low intelligence. These laws were widely supported, and the U.S. Supreme Court upheld their constitutionality. As Chief Justice Oliver Wendell Holmes declared in 1927, "Three generations of imbeciles are enough."

THE INTELLIGENCE QUOTIENT

Toward the end of the 19th century, France instituted a sweeping set of social reforms that for the first time required all boys and girls between the ages of 6 and 13 to attend school. This was nice in theory but difficult in practice because, as it turned out, not all children of the same age were equally prepared to learn. So the government appointed a small group of experts to figure out how mandatory public education might actually work. Some of the experts argued that psychiatrists should examine every French child and that the government should build special schools for the "slow-witted" ones—or better yet, send them to asylums. But one of the experts, the psychologist Alfred Binet, had a different idea. He believed that the government should use an objective method to determine how capable of learning each child was, and that those who needed some extra help should be placed in remedial classrooms alongside their peers (Nicolas et al., 2013).

To make this possible, Binet and his student, Théodore Simon, created a series of tasks that "bright" children could perform well and that "slow" children could not.

CORBIS

THE DRS. NICHOLAS AND DOROTHY CUMMINGS CENTER FOR THE HISTORY OF PSYCHOLOGY, THE UNIVERSITY OF AKRON

Alfred Binet (1857–1911; *left*) and Theodore Simon (1872–1961; *right*) developed the first intelligence test to identify children who needed remedial education.

ratio IQ A statistic obtained by dividing a person's mental age by the person's physical age and then multiplying the quotient by 100.

deviation IQ A statistic obtained by dividing an adult's test score by the average adult's test score and then multiplying the quotient by 100.

These tasks included solving logic problems, remembering words, copying pictures, distinguishing edible and inedible foods, making rhymes, and answering questions such as "Before deciding something important, what should you do?" Binet and Simon assembled 30 of these tasks into a test that they suggested could measure a child's "natural intelligence." What did they mean by that phrase?

> We here separate natural intelligence and instruction . . . by disregarding, insofar as possible, the degree of instruction which the subject possesses. . . . We give him nothing to read, nothing to write, and submit him to no test in which he might succeed by means of rote learning. In fact, we do not even notice his inability to read if a case occurs. It is simply the level of his natural intelligence that is taken into account. (Binet, 1905).

In other words, Binet and Simon designed their test to measure a child's *aptitude* for learning, independent of the child's prior educational *achievement*. Moreover, they designed it to allow psychologists to estimate a student's "mental level" simply by computing the average test score of many students in different age groups, and then finding the age group whose average test score best matched the test score of the particular student. For example, a 10-year-old child whose test score was about the same as the average test score of all 8-year-olds was said to have the mental level of an 8-year-old and thus to need remedial education.

About a decade later, the German psychologist William Stern (1914) suggested that this *mental level* could actually be thought of as the child's *mental age*, and that the best way to determine whether a child was developing normally was simply to compute the ratio of the child's mental age to the child's physical age. Thus was born the *intelligence quotient* or what most of us just call IQ. Initially, psychologists computed **ratio IQ**, which is *a statistic obtained by dividing a person's mental age by the person's physical age and then multiplying the quotient by 100*. According to this formula, a 10-year-old child whose test score is about the same as the average 10-year-old child's test score has a ratio IQ of 100 because (10/10) × 100 = 100. But a 10-year-old child whose test score is about the same as the average 8-year-old child's test score has a ratio IQ of 80 because (8/10) × 100 = 80.

This computation sounds simple, and it is. But there's a problem with it. Intelligence increases dramatically in the first decade or so of life and then levels off. As you probably know from your own experience, the intellectual difference between a 10-year-old and a 5-year-old is quite dramatic, but the intellectual difference between a 40-year-old and a 35-year-old is not. This makes ratio IQ scores problematic. For example, a 7-year-old who performs on an intelligence test like a 14-year-old does will have a whopping ratio IQ score of 200—and that's okay, because any 7-year-old who can do algebra is probably pretty smart. But a 20-year-old who performs like a 40-year-old isn't necessarily super smart, and yet he will also have a ratio IQ of 200, which doesn't make sense at all.

Psychologists quickly realized that comparing mental age to chronological age works fairly well for kids, but it doesn't work for adults because adults of different ages just don't have remarkably different intellectual capacities. To solve this problem, psychologists began to measure intelligence by computing **deviation IQ,** which is *a statistic obtained by dividing an adult's test score by the average adult's test score and then multiplying the quotient by 100*. Instead of comparing a person's mental age to her physical age, the deviation IQ score compares her performance to the performance of others. An adult who scores the same as the average adult has a deviation IQ of 100. The nice thing about the deviation IQ is that a 20-year-old whose test performance is like that of the average 40-year-old is no longer mistakenly labeled a genius. When you hear people talk about IQ scores today, they are almost always talking about deviation IQ.

THE INTELLIGENCE TEST

Most modern intelligence tests have their roots in the test that Binet and Simon developed more than a century ago. For instance, the *Stanford–Binet Intelligence Scale*

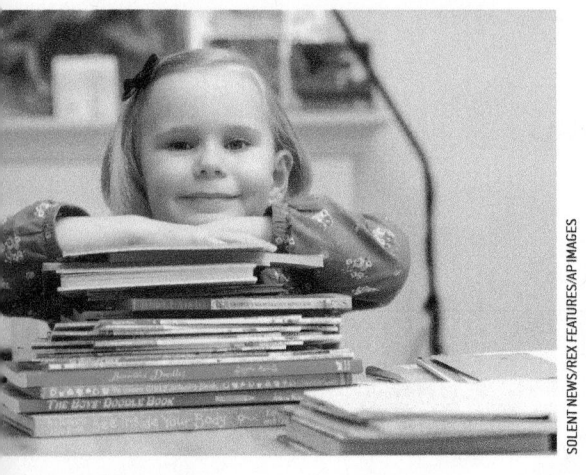

In 2012, 4-year-old Heidi Hankins became one of the youngest people ever admitted to Mensa, an organization for people with unusually high IQs. Heidi's IQ is 159—about the same as Albert Einstein's.

SOLENT NEWS/REX FEATURES/AP IMAGES

is based on Binet and Simon's original test and was initially updated by Lewis Terman and his colleagues at Stanford University. The most widely used modern intelligence tests are the *Wechsler Adult Intelligence Scale* (WAIS) and the *Wechsler Intelligence Scale for Children* (WISC), both of which are named after their originator, psychologist David Wechsler. Wechsler worked with the army during World War I to develop tests to screen new recruits and later became the chief psychologist at Bellevue Psychiatric Hospital. Like Binet and Simon's original test, the WAIS and the WISC measure intelligence by asking people to answer questions and solve problems. Test takers are required to see similarities and differences between ideas and objects, to draw inferences from evidence, to work out and apply rules, to remember and manipulate material, to construct shapes, to articulate the meaning of words, to recall general knowledge, to explain practical actions in everyday life, to use numbers, to attend to details, and so forth. In the spirit of Binet and Simon's early test, none of the tests requires writing words. Some sample problems from the WAIS are shown in **TABLE 10.1**.

TABLE 10.1

The Tests and Core Subtests of the Wechsler Adult Intelligence Scale IV

WAIS-IV Test	Core Subtest	Questions and Tasks
Verbal Comprehension Test	Vocabulary	The test taker is asked to tell the examiner what certain words mean. For example: *chair* (easy), *hesitant* (medium), and *presumptuous* (hard).
	Similarities	The test taker is asked what 19 pairs of words have in common. For example: In what way are an apple and a pear alike? In what way are a painting and a symphony alike?
	Information	The test taker is asked several general knowledge questions. These cover people, places, and events. For example: How many days are in a week? What is the capital of France? Name three oceans. Who wrote *The Inferno?*
Perceptual Reasoning Test	Block Design	The test taker is shown 2-D patterns made up of red and white squares and triangles and is asked to reproduce these patterns using cubes with red and white faces.
	Matrix Reasoning	The test taker is asked to add a missing element to a pattern so that it progresses logically. For example: Which of the four symbols at the bottom goes in the empty cell of the table?
	Visual Puzzles	The test taker is asked to complete visual puzzles like this one: "Which three of these pictures go together to make this puzzle?"
Working Memory Test	Digit Span	The test taker is asked to repeat a sequence of numbers. Sequences run from two to nine numbers in length. In the second part of this test, the sequences must be repeated in reversed order. An easy example is to repeat 3-7-4. A harder one is 3-9-1-7-4-5-3-9.
	Arithmetic	The test taker is asked to solve arithmetic problems, progressing from easy to difficult ones.
Processing Speed Test	Symbol Search	The test taker is asked to indicate whether one of a pair of abstract symbols is contained in a list of abstract symbols. There are many of these lists, and the test taker does as many as he or she can in 2 minutes.
	Coding	The test taker is asked to write down the number that corresponds to a code for a given symbol (e.g., a cross, a circle, and an upside-down T) and does as many as he or she can in 90 seconds.

► Figure 10.1

INCOME AND INTELLIGENCE AMONG SIBLINGS
This graph shows the average annual salary of a person who has an IQ of 90–109 (shown in pink) and of his or her siblings who have higher or lower IQs (shown in blue).

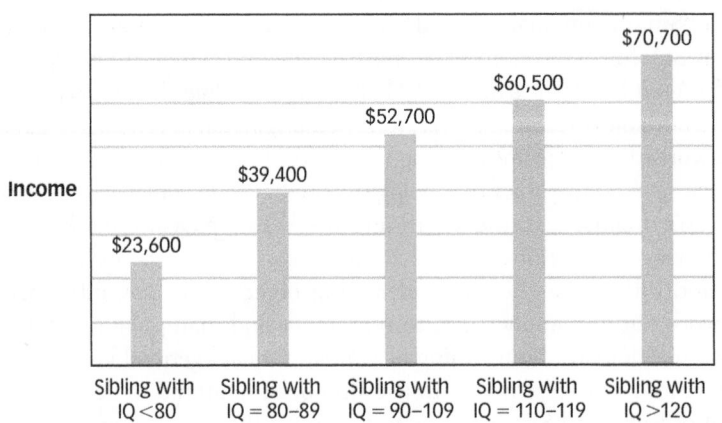

Income

| $23,600 | $39,400 | $52,700 | $60,500 | $70,700 |

| Sibling with IQ<80 | Sibling with IQ = 80–89 | Sibling with IQ = 90–109 | Sibling with IQ = 110–119 | Sibling with IQ >120 |

Intelligence is a good predictor of success. Thomas Jefferson is considered the most intelligent of all U.S presidents, and Calvin Coolidge is considered the least intelligent (Simonton, 2006). Jefferson gave us the Declaration of Independence and Coolidge gave us the Great Depression.

These sample problems may look to you like fun and games (perhaps without the fun part), but decades of research show that a person's performance on tests like the WAIS predict an astonishing number of important life outcomes (Deary, Batty, & Gale, 2008; Deary, Batty, Pattie, & Gale, 2008; Der, Batty, & Deary, 2009; Gottfredson & Deary, 2004; Leon et al., 2009; Richards et al., 2009; Rushton & Templer, 2009; Whalley & Deary, 2001).

For example, intelligence test scores are excellent predictors of income. One study compared siblings who had significantly different IQs and found that the less intelligent sibling earned roughly half of what the more intelligent sibling earned over the course of their lifetimes (Murray, 2002; see **FIGURE 10.1**). One reason for this is that intelligent people have a variety of traits that promote economic success. For example, they are more patient, they are better at calculating risk, and they are better at predicting how other people will act and how they should respond (Burks et al., 2009). But the main reason that intelligent people earn much more money than their less intelligent counterparts (or siblings!) is that they get more education (Deary et al., 2005; Nyborg & Jensen, 2001). In fact, a person's IQ is a better predictor of the amount of education he or she will receive than is that person's social class (Deary, 2012; Deary et al., 2005). Intelligent people not only spend more time in school but also perform better when they're there (Roth et al., 2015). The correlation between IQ and academic performance is roughly $r = .50$ across a wide range of people and situations. The relationship between IQ and performance continues after school ends. Intelligent people perform so much better at their jobs that one pair of researchers concluded that "for hiring employees without previous experience in the job, the most valid measure of future performance and learning is general mental ability" (Schmidt & Hunter, 1998, p. 262).

Intelligent people aren't just wealthier, they are healthier as well. Researchers who have followed millions of people over decades have found a strong correlation between intelligence and both health and longevity (Calvin et al., 2011; Wraw et al., 2015). Intelligent people are less likely to smoke and drink alcohol and are more likely to exercise and eat well (Batty et al., 2007; Ciarrochi, Heaven, & Skinner, 2012; Weiser et al., 2010). Not surprisingly, they also live longer. In fact, every 15-point increase in a young person's IQ is associated with a 24% decrease in his or her ultimate risk of death from a wide variety of causes, including cardiovascular disease, suicide, homicide, and accidents (Calvin et al., 2010). Health and wealth are related, of course, and some data suggest that intelligence promotes longevity by allowing people to succeed in school, which allows them to get better jobs, which allows them to earn more money, which allows them to avoid illnesses such as cardiovascular disease (Deary, Weiss, & Batty, 2011; Jokela et al., 2009). However it happens, the bottom line is clear: Intelligence matters for almost everything people value (see A World of Difference: Equality in Smartland).

Equality in Smartland

Being smart and being happy are pretty nice things, so it doesn't seem fair that the people who have a whole lot of one should also have more than their fair share of the other. But (sigh) they do. Smart people have better health, better jobs, and better relationships, and so predictably, they tend to be happier as well. What's true at the individual level is also true at the national level. Scientists have long known that nations' average IQ scores and average happiness scores are positively correlated: Happy nations have smart citizens and smart nations have happy citizens. Go, Denmark!

But recently, scientists have discovered that the relation between national happiness and national intelligence is more interesting than anyone had realized. Nikolaev and Salahodjaev (2016) gathered data on the intelligence and happiness of the citizens of 81 countries. As expected, they found that there was a positive correlation between a nation's average IQ and its average happiness. But in addition to calculating the mean of each nation's happiness scores, they also calculated the standard deviation, which (as you know from the Methods in Psychology chapter) measures the dispersion of scores around a mean. Just as the mean of a set of happiness scores provides a rough index of a nation's

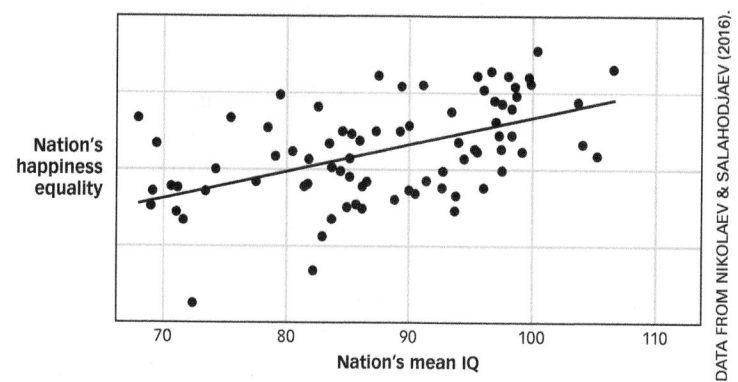

▲ Each dot represents a nation. The positive correlation indicates that the smarter a nation is, the more "happiness equality" it has.

happiness, the standard deviation provides a rough index of a nation's "happiness equality." If most citizens are about equally happy, then the standard deviation is low, and happiness equality is high. But if many citizens are ecstatic and many are despondent, then the standard deviation is high, and happiness equality is low.

When the researchers computed the correlation between IQ and happiness equality, they discovered something that no one had noticed before: Nations with smart citizens do not just have more happiness, they also have more happiness equality (see the graph

above). In other words, if two nations have the same average happiness, the smarter one tends to distribute that happiness more equally among its citizens. Correlations must always be interpreted with caution, of course, but this one is intriguing and begs for explanation. One possible explanation is that intelligent people spread happiness to others. Another explanation is that the social policies that give rise to happiness equality also foster intelligence. Whether either, both, or neither of these explanations turns out to be right, it seems clear that smart people are about as happy as their neighbors.

Build to the Outcomes

1. Why were intelligence tests originally developed?

2. What is an intelligence quotient (IQ)?

3. How do ratio and deviation IQs differ?

4. What important life outcomes do intelligence test scores predict?

What Is Intelligence?

Many people assume that Michael Jordan is some guy who works in Nike's Extremely Expensive Shoe Department. In fact, during the 1990s, Michael Jordan won the National Basketball Association's Most Valuable Player award five times, led the Chicago Bulls to six league championships, and had the highest regular-season scoring average in the history of the game. The Associated Press named him the second greatest athlete of the century, and ESPN named him the first. So when Jordan quit professional basketball in 1993 to join professional baseball, he was as surprised as

Learning Outcomes

▶ Describe the three-level hierarchy of intelligence.

▶ Compare the data-based and theory-based approaches to measuring abilities.

Michael Jordan was an extraordinary basketball player and a mediocre baseball player. So was he or wasn't he a great athlete?

two-factor theory of intelligence
Spearman's theory suggesting that a person's performance on a test is due to a combination of general ability and skills that are specific to the test.

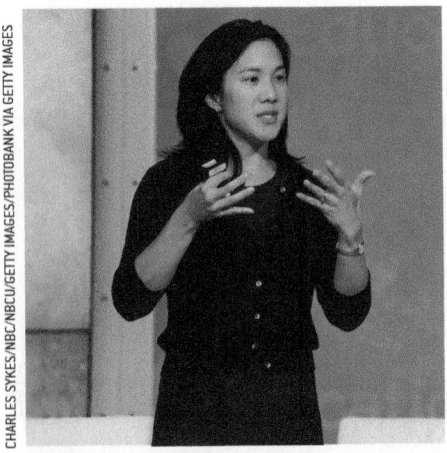

The psychologist Angela Duckworth received a so-called genius award from the MacArthur Foundation for her research on how traits other than intelligence enable people to succeed. Spearman's notion of *g* suggests that because she's *really* good at psychology, she's probably *pretty* good at most other things too.

anyone to find that he—well, there's really no way to say this nicely—sucked. One of his teammates lamented that Jordan "couldn't hit a curveball with an ironing board," and a major-league manager called him "a disgrace to the game" (Wulf, 1994). Given his lackluster performance, it's no wonder that Jordan gave up baseball after just one season and returned to basketball, where he led his team to three consecutive championships.

Michael Jordan's brilliance on the basketball court and his mediocrity on the baseball field proved beyond all doubt that these two sports require different abilities that are not necessarily possessed by the same individual. But if basketball and baseball require different abilities, then what does it mean to say that someone is the greatest athlete of the century? Is *athleticism* a meaningless abstraction? Or does it refer to a real ability? The science of intelligence has grappled with a similar question for more than a hundred years. Intelligence test scores predict important outcomes, from academic success to longevity, but is that because they measure a real ability? Or is intelligence just a meaningless abstraction?

A HIERARCHY OF ABILITIES

If there really is a single, general ability called *intelligence* that enables people to perform a variety of intelligent behaviors, then those who have this ability should do well at just about everything, and those who lack it should do well at just about nothing. In other words, if intelligence is a single, general ability, then there should be a very strong positive correlation between people's performances on many different kinds of tests. This is precisely the hypothesis that the psychologist Charles Spearman (1904) set out to examine. He began by measuring how well school-age children could discriminate small differences in color, auditory pitch, and weight, and he then computed the correlation between these scores and the children's grades in different academic subjects. He immediately noticed two things.

First, Spearman noticed that performances on these different tests were positively correlated, which is to say that children who performed well on one test (e.g., distinguishing the musical notes C# and D) tended to perform well on other tests (e.g., solving algebraic equations). Some psychologists have called this finding "the most replicated result in all of psychology" (Deary, 2000, p. 6), and it may well be. Indeed, there is even a strong positive correlation between performances on different kinds of cognitive tests in mice (Matzel et al., 2003) and in dogs (Arden & Adams, 2016)! Second, Spearman noticed that although performances on different tests were positively correlated, they were not *perfectly* correlated. In other words, the child who had the very highest score on one test didn't necessarily have the very highest score on *every* test. Spearman combined these two facts into his **two-factor theory of intelligence**, which suggests that *a person's performance on a test is due to a combination of general ability and skills that are specific to the test*. Spearman referred to general ability as *g* and to specific ability as *s*.

As sensible as Spearman's theory was, not everyone agreed with it. Louis Thurstone (1938) noticed that although the correlations between performances on different tests were all *positive*, they were much *stronger* when the tests had something in common. For example, performances on a verbal test were more strongly correlated with scores on another verbal test than they were with scores on a perceptual test. Thurstone took this "clustering of correlations" to mean that there was actually no such thing as general ability, but that instead there were a few stable and independent mental abilities—such as perceptual ability, verbal ability, and numerical ability. Thurstone called these the *primary mental abilities* and argued that they were neither general like *g* (e.g., a person might have strong verbal abilities and weak numerical abilities), nor specific like *s* (e.g., a person who had strong verbal abilities tended both to speak and

TABLE 10.2

Thurstone's Primary Mental Abilities

Primary Mental Ability	Description
Word Fluency	Ability to solve anagrams and to find rhymes, etc.
Verbal Comprehension	Ability to understand words and sentences
Numerical Ability	Ability to make mental and other numerical computations
Spatial Visualization	Ability to visualize a complex shape in various orientations
Associative Memory	Ability to recall verbal material, learn pairs of unrelated words, etc.
Perceptual Speed	Ability to detect visual details quickly
Reasoning	Ability to induce a general rule from a few instances

read well). In essence, Thurstone argued that just as we have games called *baseball* and *basketball* but no game called *athletics,* so we have abilities such as verbal ability and perceptual ability but no general ability called intelligence. **TABLE 10.2** shows the primary mental abilities that Thurstone identified.

For more than half a century, psychologists debated the existence of *g*. And then, in the 1980s, a new mathematical technique called *confirmatory factor analysis* brought the debate to a quiet close by revealing that Spearman and Thurstone had both been right, but each in his own way. Specifically, this new technique showed that the correlations between scores on different tests are best described by a three-level hierarchy (see **FIGURE 10.2**) with a *general factor* (much like Spearman's *g*) at the top, *specific factors* (much like Spearman's *s*) at the bottom, and a set of factors called *group factors* (much like Thurstone's *primary mental abilities*) in the middle (Gustafsson, 1984). A reanalysis of massive amounts of data collected over 60 years from more than 130,000 people has shown that almost every study done since the early 1900s can be described by a three-level hierarchy of this kind (Carroll, 1993). This hierarchy suggests that people have a very general ability called intelligence, which is made up of a small set of middle-level abilities, which are made up of a large set of specific abilities that are unique to particular tasks. Although this resolution to a half century of debate is not particularly exciting, it appears to have the compensatory benefit of being true.

▼ Figure 10.2

A THREE-LEVEL HIERARCHY
Most intelligence test data are best described by a three-level hierarchy with general intelligence (g) at the top, specific abilities (s) at the bottom, and a small number of middle-level abilities (m) (sometimes called group factors) in the middle.

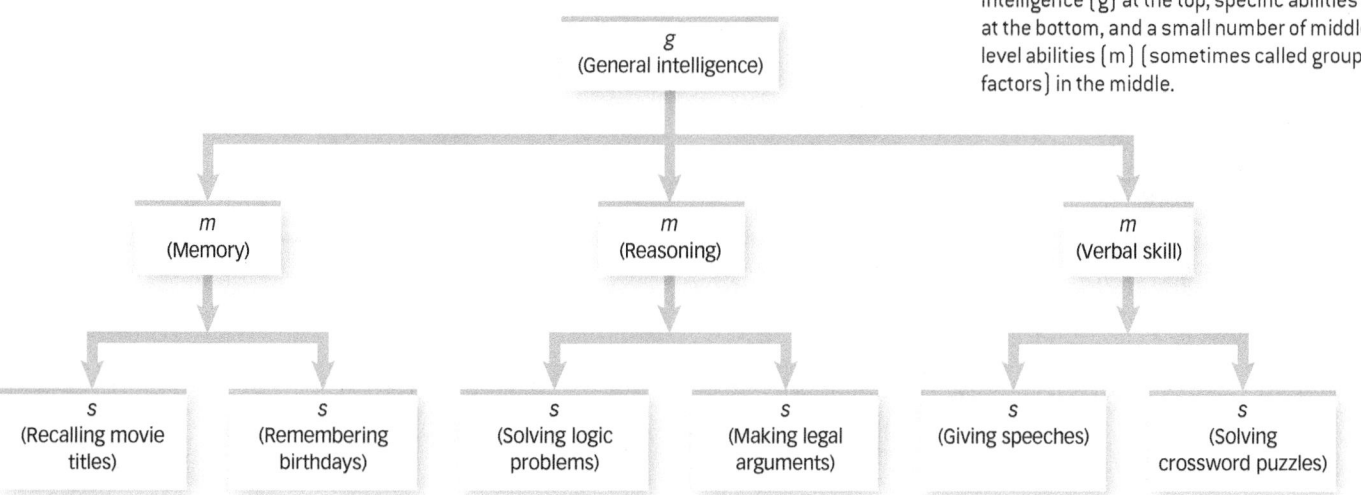

THE MIDDLE-LEVEL ABILITIES

Michael Jordan played basketball much better than baseball, but he played both sports much better than most people can. His specific abilities allowed him to be more successful at one sport than another, but his general ability allowed him to outperform 99.9% of the world's population on both the court and the field. It is easy to see that Michael Jordan had both specific abilities (dribbling) and a general ability (athleticism), but it is not so easy to say precisely what his middle-level abilities were. Should we draw a distinction between speed and power, between guile and patience, or between the ability to work with a team or perform as an individual? Should we describe his athleticism as a function of 3 middle-level abilities, or 4 or 6 or 92.5?

Similar questions arise when we consider intelligence. Most psychologists agree that there are very specific mental abilities as well as a very general mental ability and that the really hard problem is to characterize accurately the middle-level abilities that lie between them. Some psychologists have taken a data-based approach to this problem by starting with people's responses on intelligence tests and then looking to see what kinds of independent clusters these responses form. Other psychologists have taken a theory-based approach to this problem by starting with a broad survey of human abilities and then looking to see which of these abilities intelligence tests measure—or fail to measure. These approaches have led to rather different suggestions about the best way to characterize the middle-level abilities that constitute intelligence.

The Data-Based Approach

One way to determine the nature of the middle-level abilities is to start with the data and go where they lead us. Just as Spearman and Thurstone did, we could compute the correlations between a large number of people's performances on a large number of tests and then see how those correlations cluster. For example, imagine that we tested how well a large group of people could (1) balance teacups, (2) understand Shakespeare, (3) swat flies, and (4) sum the whole numbers between 1 and 1,000. Now imagine that we computed the correlations between scores on each of these tests and observed a pattern of correlations like the one shown in **FIGURE 10.3a**. What would this pattern tell us?

This pattern suggests that a person who can swat flies well can also balance teacups well and that a person who can understand Shakespeare well can also sum numbers well. But it also suggests that a person who can swat flies well and balance teacups well may or may not be able to sum numbers or understand Shakespeare well. From this pattern, we could conclude that there are two-middle-level abilities (shown in Figure 10.3b), which we might call *physical coordination* (the ability that allows people to swat flies and balance teacups) and *academic skill* (the ability that allows

▼ Figure 10.3

PATTERNS OF CORRELATION CAN REVEAL MIDDLE-LEVEL ABILITIES.
The pattern of correlations shown in (a) suggests that these four specific abilities can be thought of as instances of the two middle-level abilities, physical coordination and academic skill, as shown in (b).

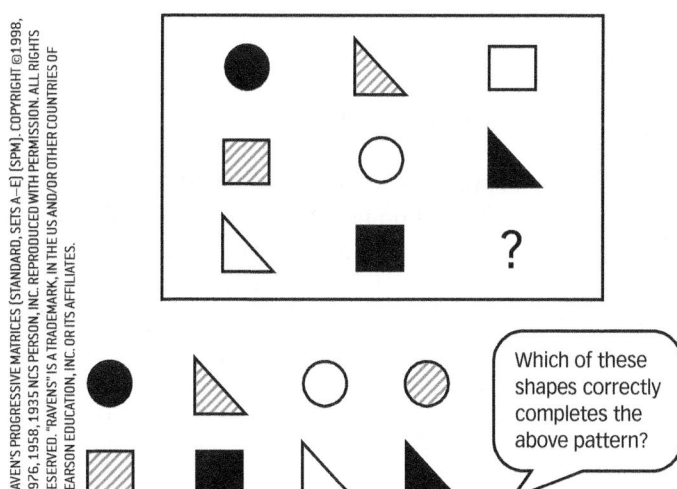

◀ Figure 10.4

MEASURING FLUID INTELLIGENCE
Problems like this one from Raven's Progressive Matrices Test (Raven, Raven, & Court, 2004) measure fluid intelligence rather than crystallized intelligence.

people to understand Shakespeare and sum numbers). In other words, some people are really good at the specific tasks of fly swatting and teacup balancing because they have a middle-level ability called physical coordination, but this middle-level ability is unrelated to the other middle-level ability, academic skill, which is why these people are not necessarily good when it comes to summing numbers or understanding Shakespeare. As this example shows, simply by examining the pattern of correlations between different tests, we can discover the nature and number of the middle-level abilities.

Of course, in the real world there are far more than four specific skills measured by four specific tests. So what kinds of patterns do we observe when we compute the correlations between all the many tests of mental ability that psychologists actually use? This is precisely what the psychologist John Carroll (1993) set out to discover in his landmark analysis of intelligence test scores from nearly 500 studies conducted over a half century. And what Carroll discovered was that there are not 3 middle-level abilities—nor 4 nor 6 nor 92.5. Rather, there are 8, and they are: *memory and learning, visual perception, auditory perception, retrieval ability, cognitive speediness, processing speed, crystallized intelligence,* and *fluid intelligence.*

Although most of the abilities on this list are self-explanatory, the last two are not (Horn & Cattell, 1966). **Crystallized intelligence** refers to the *ability to apply knowledge that was acquired through experience,* and it is generally measured with tests of vocabulary and factual information. **Fluid intelligence** refers to the *ability to solve and reason about novel problems,* and it is generally measured with tests that present people with abstract problems in new domains that must be solved under time pressure (see **FIGURE 10.4**). Problems that require crystallized or fluid intelligence appear to activate different regions of the brain, which may explain why impairment of one kind of intelligence does not always lead to impairment of the other. For example, both autism and Alzheimer's disease impair crystallized intelligence more than fluid intelligence, whereas damage to the prefrontal cortex impairs fluid intelligence more than crystallized intelligence (Blair, 2006).

The Theory-Based Approach

Not everyone agrees that there are precisely eight middle-level abilities, though you will be pleased to know that the reasons have nothing to do with math. The data-based approach discovers middle-level abilities by analyzing the correlation between performances on intelligence tests. The good thing about this approach is that its conclusions are based on hard evidence, but the bad thing about this approach is that it is incapable of discovering any middle-level ability that the hard evidence doesn't happen to provide (Stanovich, 2009). For example, if no intelligence test asks people

crystallized intelligence The ability to apply knowledge that was acquired through experience.

fluid intelligence The ability to solve and reason about novel problems.

emotional intelligence The ability to reason about emotions and to use emotions to enhance reasoning.

to find three new uses for an origami fish or to answer the question "What is the question you thought you'd be asked but weren't?" then no analysis of those tests' scores can ever reveal a middle-level ability called imagination. Are there any middle-level abilities to which the data-based approach has been blind?

The psychologist Robert Sternberg (1999, 2006) thinks so. He has argued that because standard intelligence tests present clearly defined problems that have one right answer and then supply all the information needed to solve them, they can measure only *analytic intelligence,* which is the ability to identify and define problems and to find strategies for solving them. But in everyday life, people find themselves in situations in which they must formulate the *problem,* find the information needed to solve it, and then choose among multiple right answers. These situations require *creative intelligence,* which is the ability to generate solutions that other people do not, and *practical intelligence,* which is the ability to implement these solutions in everyday settings. In one study, workers at milk-processing plants developed complex strategies for efficiently combining partially filled cases of milk. Not only did they outperform highly educated white-collar workers, but their performance was unrelated to their scores on intelligence tests, suggesting that practical and analytic intelligence are not the same thing (Scribner, 1984). Sternberg has argued that tests of practical intelligence are actually better than tests of analytic intelligence at predicting a person's job performance (cf. Brody, 2003; Gottfredson, 2003).

Of course, not all of the problems that intelligence enables us to solve are analytical, practical, or creative. For instance, how do you tell a friend that she talks too much without hurting her feelings? How do you cheer yourself up after failing a test? How do you know whether you are feeling anxious or angry? The psychologists John Mayer and Peter Salovey define **emotional intelligence** as *the ability to reason about emotions and to use emotions to enhance reasoning* (Mayer, Roberts, & Barsade, 2008; Salovey & Grewal, 2005). Emotionally intelligent people know what kinds of emotions a particular event will trigger; they can identify, describe, and manage their emotions; they know how to use their emotions to improve their decisions; and they can identify other people's emotions from facial expressions and tones of voice. Furthermore, they do all this quite easily, which is why emotionally intelligent people show *less* neural activity when solving emotional problems than emotionally unintelligent people do (Jausovec & Jausovec, 2005; Jausovec, Jausovec, & Gerlic, 2001).

Emotional intelligence is also quite important for social relationships. Emotionally intelligent people have better social skills and more friends (Eisenberg et al., 2000; Mestre et al., 2006; Schultz, Izard, & Bear, 2004), they are judged to be more competent in their interactions (Brackett et al., 2006), and they have better romantic relationships (Brackett, Warner, & Bosco, 2005) and workplace relationships (Elfenbein et al., 2007; Lopes et al., 2006). Given all this, it isn't surprising that emotionally intelligent people tend to be happier (Brackett & Mayer, 2003; Brackett et al., 2006), healthier (Mikolajczak et al., 2015), and more satisfied with their lives (Ciarrochi, Chan, & Caputi, 2000; Mayer, Caruso, & Salovey, 1999). Accumulating evidence suggests that emotional intelligence is indeed one of the middle-level abilities that the data-based approach missed (MacCann et al., 2014).

The data-based approach is also blind to middle-level abilities that are valued in cultures where intelligence tests are not common. For instance, Westerners regard people as intelligent when they speak quickly and often (see The Real World: Look Smart), but Africans regard people as intelligent when they are deliberate and quiet (Irvine, 1978). The Confucian tradition emphasizes the ability to behave

Two items from a test of emotional intelligence. Item 1 measures the accuracy with which a person can read emotional expressions (*left*). Item 2 measures the ability to predict emotional responses to events (*right*). The correct answer on both items is a.

PHOTO COURTESY OF DANIEL GILBERT

RESEARCH FROM MAYER ET AL., 2008.

1.

Emotion	Select one:
a. Happy	O
b. Angry	O
c. Fearful	O
d. Sad	O

2.

Tom felt worried when he thought about all the work he needed to do. He believed he could handle it—if only he had the time. When his supervisor brought him an additional project, he felt _____. (Select the best choice.)

Emotion	Select one:
a. Frustrated and anxious	O
b. Content and calm	O
c. Ashamed and accepting	O
d. Sad and guilty	O

The Hungarian chess grandmaster Judit Polgar (*left*) and the Korean actress Ryu Si-Hyeon (*right*) both have genius-level IQs. But their cultures construe intelligence differently. Westerners tend to think of intelligence as an individual's ability to engage in rational thinking, but Easterners tend to think of it as the ability to recognize contradictions and complexities.

→ THE REAL WORLD

Look Smart

Your interview is in 30 minutes. You've checked your hair twice, eaten your weight in breath mints, combed your résumé for typos, and rehearsed your answers to all the standard questions. Now you have to dazzle them with your intelligence—whether you've got it or not. Because intelligence is one of the most valued of all human traits, we are often in the business of trying to make others think we're smart regardless of whether that's true. So we make clever jokes and drop the names of some of the longer books we've read in the hope that prospective employers, prospective dates, prospective customers, and prospective in-laws will be appropriately impressed.

But are we doing the right things? If so, are we getting the credit we deserve? Research shows that ordinary people are, in fact, reasonably good judges of other people's intelligence (Borkenau & Liebler, 1995). For example, observers can look at a pair of photographs and reliably determine which of the two people in them is smarter (Zebrowitz et al., 2002). When observers watch 1-minute videotapes of different people engaged in social interactions, they can accurately estimate which

person has the highest IQ—even if they see the videos without sound (Murphy, Hall, & Colvin, 2003).

People base their judgments of intelligence on a wide range of cues, from physical features (being tall and attractive) to dress (being well groomed and wearing glasses) to behavior (walking and talking quickly). And yet, none of these cues is actually a reliable indicator of a person's

intelligence. The reason that people are such good judges of intelligence is that in addition to all these useless cues, they also take into account one very useful cue: eye contact. As it turns out, intelligent people hold the gaze of their conversation partners both when they are speaking and when they are listening. Observers know this, which is what enables them to estimate a person's intelligence accurately, despite their mythical beliefs about the informational value of spectacles and neckties (Murphy et al., 2003). All of this is especially true when the observers are women (who tend to be better judges of intelligence) and the people being observed are men (whose intelligence tends to be easier to judge).

The bottom line? Breath mints are fine and a little gel on the cowlick certainly can't hurt, but when you get to the interview, don't forget to stare.

◄ Wahad Mehood is interviewing for a job as a petroleum engineer with EPC Global. Studies show that when a job candidate holds an interviewer's gaze, the interviewer is more likely to consider the candidate to be intelligent. And the interviewer is right!

properly, the Taoist tradition emphasizes humility and self-knowledge, and the Buddhist tradition emphasizes determination and mental effort (Yang & Sternberg, 1997). Unlike Western societies, many African and Asian societies conceive of intelligence as including social responsibility and cooperativeness (Azuma & Kashiwagi, 1987; Serpell, 1974; White & Kirkpatrick, 1985). In Zimbabwe, the word for "intelligence" is *ngware,* which means to be wise and cautious in social relationships (Sternberg & Grigorenko, 2004). Some researchers take all this to mean that different cultures have radically different conceptualizations of intelligence, but others are convinced that what appear to be differences in the conceptualization of intelligence are really just differences in language. They argue that every culture values the ability to solve important problems and that what really distinguishes cultures is the *kinds* of problems that are considered important.

Build to the Outcomes

1. What was the debate between Spearman and Thurstone and how was it resolved?

2. What approaches have been used to assess middle-level abilities?

3. What are fluid and crystallized intelligences?

4. What is emotional intelligence?

5. How does the concept of intelligence differ across cultures?

Where Does Intelligence Come From?

Learning Outcomes

▸ Describe the influence of genes on intelligence.

▸ Explain how environmental factors influence intelligence.

No one is born knowing calculus, and no one has to be taught how to blink. Some things are learned, others are not. But almost all of the really *interesting* things about people are a joint product of the experiences they have had and the characteristics with which they were born. Intelligence is one of those really interesting things, and it is influenced both by nature and by nurture. Let's examine them in turn.

NATURE: GENETIC INFLUENCES ON INTELLIGENCE

The notion that intelligence is somehow "in the blood" has been with us for a very long time. As early as 380 BCE, the philosopher Plato suggested that people are born with innate aptitudes that make them good rulers, good soldiers, or good tradesmen. But it wasn't until late in the 19th century that this idea became the subject of scientific

These photos, taken from the "Genetic Portraits" series by artist Ulric Collette, were made by blending the face of a 32-year-old woman with the face of her mother (*left*) and the face of her father (*right*). Because physical appearance is highly heritable, the resemblance between family members can often be quite striking.

ULRIC COLLETTE

inquiry. Sir Francis Galton was a half cousin of Charles Darwin, and his contributions to science ranged from meteorology to fingerprinting. Late in life, Galton (1869) became interested in the origins of intelligence. He did careful genealogical studies of eminent families and collected measurements from over 12,000 people that ranged from head size to the ability to discriminate tones. As the title of his book *Hereditary Genius* suggests, he concluded that intelligence was largely inherited. Was he right?

Do People Who Share More Genes Have More Similar IQs?

The fact that intelligence appears to "run in families" isn't very good evidence of genetic influence, because although family members often share genes, they also share experiences. Parents and children typically live in the same house and eat the same foods. Siblings often go to the same schools, watch the same TV shows and movies, and have many of the same friends. Family members may have similar levels of intelligence because they share genes, because they share environments, or both. If we want to study the influence of genes and environments separately, we need to study the intelligence of (1) people who share genes but not environments (e.g., biological siblings who were separated at birth and raised by different families); (2) people who share environments but not genes (e.g., adopted siblings who are raised together); and (3) people who share both (e.g., biological siblings who are raised together). And that's precisely what psychologists have been doing for the last several decades.

To understand what they've discovered, we must first understand that different kinds of siblings have different degrees of genetic relatedness. Two siblings who have the same biological parents but different birthdays will share on average about 50% of their genes. Twins are siblings who share a birthday and they come in two kinds: **Fraternal twins** (or **dizygotic twins**) are *twins who develop from two different eggs that were fertilized by two different sperm,* and **identical twins** (or **monozygotic twins**) are *twins who develop from the splitting of a single egg that was fertilized by a single sperm.* Fraternal twins are simply siblings who happened to share a womb, and so, like all siblings, they share on average about 50% of their genes. But identical twins are the result of a single fertilized egg that then divided in two, so they are genetic duplicates who share 100% of their genes.

These different degrees of genetic relatedness allow psychologists to assess the influence that genes have on intelligence, and that influence turns out to be quite powerful. For example, the IQs of identical twins are positively correlated—that is, if one twin has a high (or low) IQ, then his or her co-twin is likely to have a high (or low) IQ as well. Moreover, this correlation is observed even among identical twins who were adopted at birth by different families and raised in different households. Indeed, if you look at **TABLE 10.3**, you'll see that identical twins who are raised apart have more similar IQs ($r = .78$) than do fraternal twins who are raised together ($r = .60$)!

What this means is that people who share genes have similar IQs regardless of whether they share environments. In fact, the correlation between the intelligence test scores of identical twins who have never met is about the same as the correlation between the intelligence test scores of a single person who has taken the test twice! By comparison, the intelligence test scores of unrelated people raised in the same household (e.g., two siblings, one or both of whom were adopted) are only modestly correlated (Bouchard & McGue, 2003). These patterns of correlation suggest that genes play an important role in determining intelligence, and that shouldn't surprise you. After all, intelligence is influenced by the structure and function of the brain, and the structure and function of the brain are influenced by the genes that designed it. So it would really be remarkable if genes *didn't* play a role in determining a person's intelligence—especially given that genes play a role in determining just about every other human trait (Polderman et al., 2015). Indeed, the only thing that separates you from a person with Williams syndrome is 20 genes on a single chromosome. Clearly, genes influence intelligence.

Tamara Rabi and Adriana Scott were 20 years old when they met in a McDonald's parking lot in New York. "I'm just standing there looking at her," Adriana recalled. "It was a shock. I saw me" (Gootman, 2003). The two soon discovered that they were twins who had been separated at birth and adopted by different families.

fraternal twins (or dizygotic twins) Twins who develop from two different eggs that were fertilized by two different sperm.

identical twins (or monozygotic twins) Twins who develop from the splitting of a single egg that was fertilized by a single sperm.

heritability coefficient A statistic (commonly denoted as h^2) that describes the proportion of the difference between people's IQ scores that can be explained by differences in their genes.

TABLE 10.3

Intelligence Test Correlations Between People With Different Relationships

Relationship	Shared Environment	Shared Genes [%]	Correlation Between Intelligence Test Scores [r]
Twins			
Identical twins ($n = 4,672$)	yes	100	.86
Identical twins ($n = 93$)	no	100	.78
Fraternal twins ($n = 5,533$)	yes	50	.60
Parents and Children			
Parent–biological child ($n = 8,433$)	yes	50	.42
Parent–biological child ($n = 720$)	no	50	.24
Nonbiological parent–adopted child ($n = 1,491$)	yes	0	.19
Siblings			
Biological siblings (2 parents in common) ($n = 26,473$)	yes	50	.47
Nonbiological siblings (no parents in common) ($n = 714$)	yes	0	.32
Biological siblings (2 parents in common) ($n = 203$)	no	50	.24

Information from: Plomin et al., 2001, p. 168.

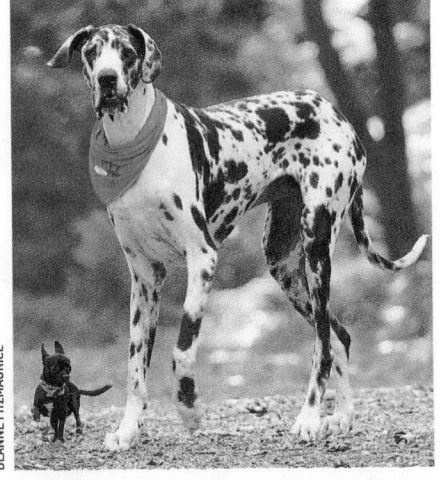

Small genetic differences can make a big difference. A single gene on chromosome 15 determines whether a dog will be too small for your pocket or too large for your garage.

▶ **Figure 10.5**

SOME QUESTIONS CAN'T BE ANSWERED
These rectangles differ in area. The question "How much of the difference in their areas is due to differences in their widths, and how much is due to differences in their heights?" has an answer. But the question "How much of rectangle A's area is due to width and how much is due to height?" does not.

The Heritability Coefficient: Measuring the Influence of Genes on IQ

But exactly how powerful is that influence? The **heritability coefficient** (commonly denoted as h^2) is *a statistic that describes the proportion of the difference between people's IQ scores that can be explained by differences in their genes.* When the data from numerous studies of children and adults are analyzed together, the heritability of intelligence is somewhere between .5 and .7, which is to say that roughly 50% to 70% of the difference between people's intelligence test scores is due to genetic differences between them (Plomin & Spinath, 2004; Plomin et al., 2013; cf. Chabris et al., 2012).

Most people misunderstand the heritability coefficient, so let's make sure you aren't one of them. First, the heritability coefficient h^2 is *not* the same as the correlation coefficient r. Yes, both are quite efficient, but that's where the similarity ends. Second, many people who hear that "the heritability of intelligence is roughly .5" think this means that half of *their* intelligence is due to their genes and half is due to their experiences. That is utterly incorrect, and to understand why, consider the rectangles in **FIGURE 10.5**. These rectangles have the same heights but different widths, and so they have different areas. (Remember high school geometry? A = H × W). So if you were asked how much of the difference in their areas was due to differences in their widths, you would say all of it—one hundred percent—and if you were asked to say how much of the difference in their areas was due to differences in their heights you would say none of it—zero percent. Well done. Your answers about the *differences between the rectangles* are right. Now try to answer a different question: How much of rectangle A's area is due to its height, and how much is due to its width? The right

A	B	C	D

answer to that question is "What are you smoking?" because an individual rectangle's area is a product of *both* its height and its width, so it can't be "due to" one of these more or less than it is "due to" the other.

Now apply all this good thinking to intelligence. If you measured the intelligence of every person at a basketball game and were then asked to say how much of the difference in their intelligence scores was due to differences in their genes and how much was due to differences in their experiences, the fact that h^2 is between .5 and .7 would allow you to guess that about 50% to 70% of the difference was due to genes and about 30% to 50% was due to the environment. But if someone pointed to the annoying guy with the bad haircut in Row 17, Seat 4 and asked how much of *his* intelligence was due to his genes and how much was due to his experiences, the right answer is, "You didn't read the textbook very carefully, did you?" This question is nonsense because the intelligence of a particular person is a joint product of both genes and experience—just as the area of a particular rectangle is a joint product of its height and width—and so it cannot be "due to" one of these things more than another.

The heritability coefficient tells us how big a role genes play in interpersonal differences in intelligence, and so its value changes depending on the particular persons we measure. For example, the heritability of intelligence among high-income children in the United States is about .72 and among low-income children about .10 (Turkheimer et al., 2003). Why should that be? High-income children in America have fairly similar environments—they all have pretty nice homes with lots of books, plenty of free time, ample nutrition—and so differences in their intelligence must be due to the one and only factor that distinguishes them from each other, namely, their genes. Conversely, poor children in America have very different environments—some have books and free time and ample nutrition, but others have little or none of these—and so differences in their intelligence may be due to either of the two factors that distinguish them from each other, namely, their genes and their environments (Tucker-Drob et al., 2010). This may be why intelligence is equally heritable among high- and low-income children in Western Europe and Australia, where people at many different levels of income have roughly equal nutrition, amounts of leisure, access to books, and so on (Bates et al., 2016; Tucker-Drob & Bates, 2016).

The value of the heritability coefficient also changes depending on the age of the people being measured. For example, the heritability of intelligence is higher among adults than among children (see **FIGURE 10.6**), and higher among older children than younger children. Indeed, in infancy, genes account for less than 25% of the interpersonal differences in intelligence, but by adolescence they account for about 70% (Haworth et al., 2010). Why? One possibility is that the environments of older people are more similar than the environments of younger people, and when environments don't differ much across people, then differences in their intelligence scores must be due to the one thing that does differ, namely, their genes. The bottom line is that the heritability coefficient is simply the percentage of the observed differences in a particular group of people that can be attributed to differences in their genes. It may seem paradoxical, but in a science-fictional world of clones, in which all humans were genetically identical, the heritability of intelligence would be zero.

Does that mean that in a science-fictional world in which humans were genetically different but lived in identical houses and received identical meals, educations, parental care, and so on, the heritability coefficient would be 1.00? Not likely, and that's because two unrelated people who live in the same household will have *some* of their experiences but not *all* of their experiences in common. The **shared environment** refers to *features of the environment that are experienced by all relevant members of a household.* For example, siblings raised in the same household usually get about the same nutrition, have about the same access to books, and so on. The **nonshared environment** refers to *features of the environment that are not experienced by all relevant members of a household.* Siblings raised in the same household may have the

Some research suggests that IQ is more heritable among higher-income children, perhaps because their environments are so similar. If there are fewer differences in their environments, then differences in their IQs are more likely to be due to differences in their genes.

shared environment Features of the environment that are experienced by all relevant members of a household.

nonshared environment Features of the environment that are not experienced by all relevant members of a household.

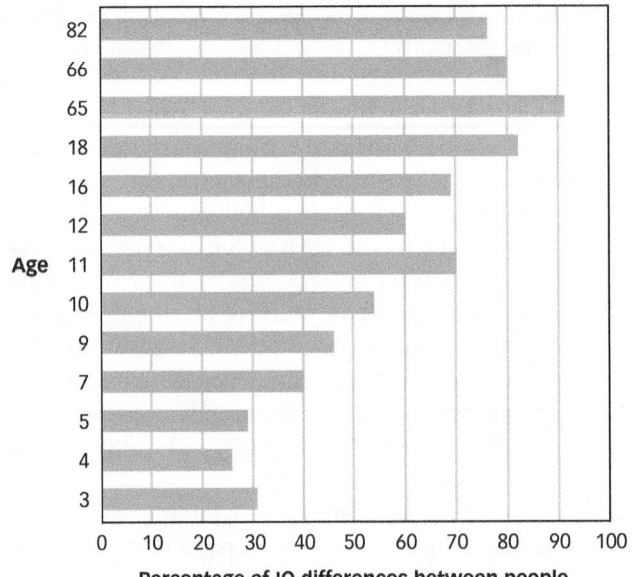

◀ **Figure 10.6**
AGE AND HERITABILITY OF INTELLIGENCE
The heritability of intelligence generally increases with the age of the sample measured.

same access to books, but they have different friends and different teachers, they contract different illnesses, and so on. This may explain why the correlation between the IQ scores of siblings is greater if they are close to each other in age. Similar-aged siblings are more likely to have the same teacher, go on the same vacations, and so on (Sundet, Eriksen, & Tambs, 2008).

NURTURE: ENVIRONMENTAL INFLUENCES ON INTELLIGENCE

Americans believe that every individual should have an equal chance to succeed in life, and one of the reasons that some people get nervous when they hear about genetic influences on intelligence is that they mistakenly believe that our genes are our destinies—that "genetic" is a synonym for "unchangeable" (Pinker, 2003). This is yet another case of utter wrongness, because traits that are strongly influenced by genes may also be strongly influenced by the environment. For example, height is a highly heritable trait, which is why short parents tend to have short children. But that doesn't mean that height is unchangeable: The average height of Korean boys has increased by more than 7 inches in the last 50 years simply because of changes in nutrition (Nisbett, 2009). In 1848, 25% of all Dutch men were rejected by the military because they were less than 5 feet, 2 inches tall, but today the average Dutch man is over 6 feet tall (Max, 2006). Genes may explain why two people who have the same diet differ in height—that is, why Chang-sun is taller than Kwan-ho and why Thijs is taller than Daan—but they do not dictate how tall any of these boys will actually grow up to be. Is intelligence like height? Alfred Binet (1909) thought so:

> A few modern philosophers . . . assert that an individual's intelligence is a fixed quantity that cannot be increased. We must protest and react against this brutal pessimism. . . . With practice, training, and above all method, we manage to increase our attention, our memory, our judgment, and literally to become more intelligent than we were before (p. 141).

It turns out that Binet was right. As **FIGURE 10.7** shows, intelligence clearly changes over time (Owens, 1966; Schaie, 1996, 2005; Schwartzman, Gold, & Andres, 1987). For most people, the direction of this change is upward between adolescence and middle age, and downward thereafter (cf. Ackerman, 2014). The sharpest decline occurs in old age (Kaufman, 2001; Salthouse, 1996a, 2000; Schaie, 2005), and may be

First-born children tend to be more intelligent than their later-born siblings. But when a first-born child dies in infancy and the second-born child becomes the oldest child in the family, that second-born child ends up being just as intelligent as the average first-born child (Kristensen & Bjerkedal, 2007). This suggests that first-borns are smarter than their siblings not for biological reasons but because they experience a different family environment.

SONYA ETCHISON/GETTY IMAGES

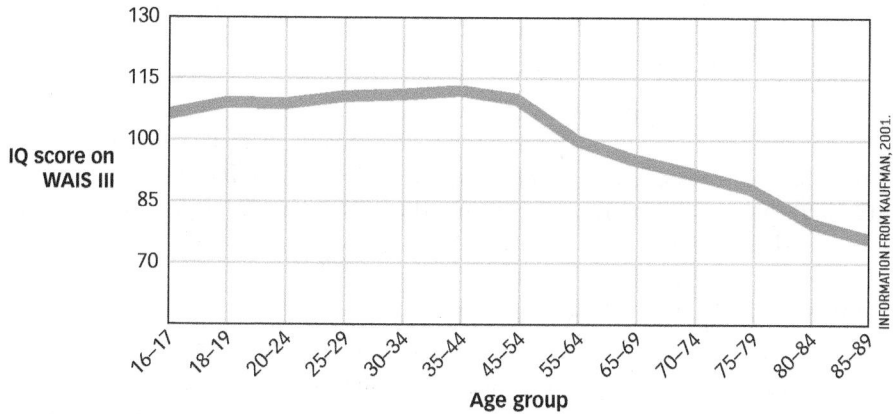

due to a general decrease in the brain's processing speed (Salthouse, 1996b; Zimprich & Martin, 2002). Age-related declines are more evident in some domains than in others. For example, on tests that measure vocabulary, general information, and verbal reasoning, people show only small changes from the ages of 18 to 70, but on tests that are timed, have abstract material, involve making new memories, or require reasoning about spatial relationships, most people show marked declines in performance after middle age (Avolio & Waldman, 1994; Lindenberger & Baltes, 1997; Rabbitt et al., 2004; Salthouse, 2001). Um, did we already tell you that in the Memory chapter?

Not only does intelligence change over the life span but it also changes over generations (see **FIGURE 10.8**). The *Flynn effect* refers to the fact that the average IQ score today is roughly 30 points higher than it was a century ago (Dickens & Flynn, 2001; Flynn, 2012; cf. Lynn, 2013). This is a striking number. It means that the average person today is smarter than 95% of the people who were alive in 1900! Why is each generation outscoring the one before it? Some researchers give the credit to improved nutrition, schooling, and parenting (Baker et al., 2015; Lynn, 2009; Neisser, 1998), whereas others suggest that the least intelligent people got left out of the mating game (Mingroni, 2007). But most scientists believe that the industrial and technological revolutions have changed the nature of daily living such that people now spend more and more time solving precisely the kinds of abstract problems that intelligence tests include—and as we all know, practice makes perfect (Bordone, Scherbov, & Steiber, 2015; Flynn, 2012). This suggestion could explain why these generational increases are nearly twice as large for fluid intelligence as they are for crystalized intelligence (Pietschnig & Voracek, 2015). By the way, research on how well people can estimate other people's IQs shows that people tend to think their

DATA VISUALIZATION

How do Nature and Nurture Influence Intelligence?
Go to launchpadworks.com.

▼ Figure 10.8
THE FLYNN EFFECT
Khatijah (front row, second from right), 105 years old, sits with five generations of her family. As the graph shows, intelligence has been increasing across generations for at least the last century (adapted from Pietschnig & Voracek, 2015).

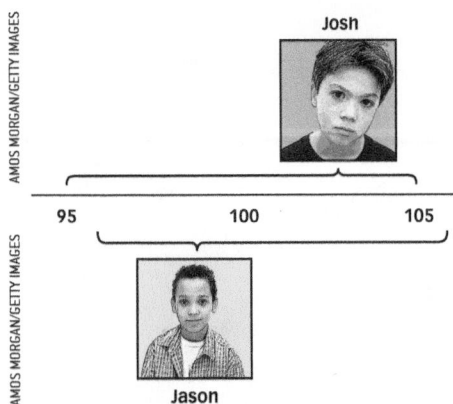

▲ Figure 10.9

GENES AND ENVIRONMENT
Genes establish the range in which a person's intelligence *may* fall, but environment determines the point in that range at which the person's intelligence *will* fall. Although Jason's genes give him a better chance to be smart than Josh's genes do, differences in their diets could easily cause Josh to have a higher IQ than Jason.

To encourage low-SES parents to talk more to their children, the city of Providence, Rhode Island created a program called "Providence Talks." Once a month, a child wears a small recording device for the day, which allows a computer to calculate how many words she spoke, how many were spoken by adults in her vicinity, and how many conversational exchanges she experienced. A caseworker then visits her parent and provides a progress report.

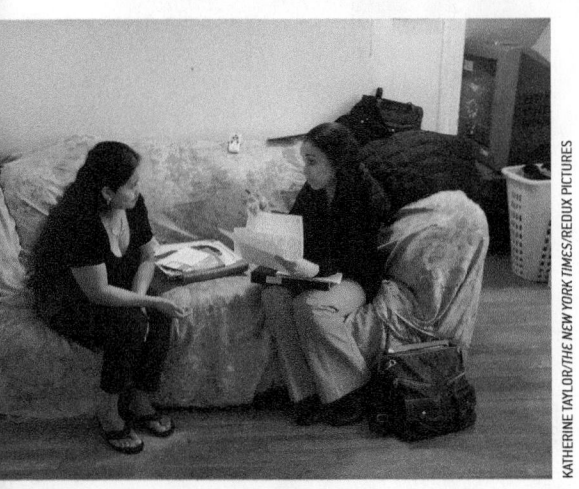

children are smarter than their grandparents—and the Flynn effect suggests that they are right (Furnham, 2001)!

The fact that intelligence changes over the life span and across generations shows that it is by no means a "fixed quantity that cannot be increased" (Binet, 1909, p. 141). Our genes may determine the *range* in which our IQ is likely to fall, but our experiences determine the exact *point* in that range at which it does fall (Hunt, 2011; see **FIGURE 10.9**). As you are about to see, two of the most powerful experiences involve economics and education.

Economics: Poverty Is Intelligence's Enemy

Maybe money can't buy love, but it sure appears to buy intelligence. One of the best predictors of a person's intelligence is the material wealth of the family in which he or she was raised—what scientists call *socioeconomic status* (SES). Studies suggest that being raised in a high-SES family rather than a low-SES family is worth between 12 and 18 IQ points (Nisbett, 2009; van Ijzendoorn, Juffer, & Klein Poelhuis, 2005). For example, one study compared pairs of siblings who were born to low-SES parents. In each case, one of the siblings was raised by his or her low-SES parents, and the other was adopted and raised by a high-SES family. On average, the child who had been raised by high-SES parents had an IQ that was 14 points higher than his or her sibling (Schiff et al., 1978). Although these siblings had similar genes, they ended up with dramatically different IQs simply because one was raised by wealthier parents. High-SES and low-SES children have different IQs at the age of 2, and by the age of 16 the difference between them nearly triples (von Stumm & Plomin, 2015).

Exactly how does SES influence intelligence? One way is by influencing the brain itself. Low-SES children have poorer nutrition and medical care, they experience greater daily stress, and they are more likely to be exposed to environmental toxins such as air pollution and lead—all of which can impair brain development (Chen, Cohen, & Miller, 2010; Evans, 2004; Hackman & Farah, 2008). The fact that low SES can impair a child's brain development may explain why children who experience poverty in early childhood are less intelligent than those who experience poverty in middle or late childhood (Duncan et al., 1998).

SES affects the brain, and it also affects the environment in which that brain lives and learns. Intellectual stimulation increases intelligence (Nelson et al., 2007), and research shows that high-SES parents are more likely to provide it (Nisbett, 2009). For instance, high-SES parents are more likely to read to their children and to connect what they are reading to the outside world ("Billy has a rubber ducky. Who do you know who has a rubber ducky?"; Heath, 1983; Lareau, 2003). When high-SES parents talk to their children, they tend to ask stimulating questions ("Do you think a ducky likes to eat grass?"), whereas low-SES parents tend to give instructions ("Please put your ducky away"; Hart & Risley, 1995). By the age of 3, the average high-SES child has heard 30 million different words, whereas the average low-SES child has heard only 10 million different words. As a result, the high-SES child knows 50% more words than his or her low-SES counterpart. These differences in the intellectual richness of the home environment may explain why children from low-SES families show a decrease in intelligence during the summer when school is not in session, whereas children from the very highest SES families actually show an increase (Burkham et al., 2004; Cooper et al., 1996). Clearly, poverty is the enemy of intelligence (Evans & Kim, 2012).

Education: School Is Intelligence's Friend

Alfred Binet believed that if poverty was intelligence's enemy, then education was its friend. And he was right about that, too. The correlation between the amount of formal education a person receives and his or her intelligence is quite large, somewhere in the range of $r = .55$ to .90 (Ceci, 1991; Neisser et al., 1996). One reason this correlation is so large is that smart people tend to stay in school, but the other reason is that school makes people smarter (Ceci & Williams, 1997). When schooling is delayed because of war, political strife, or the simple lack of qualified teachers, children show a measurable decline in intelligence (Nisbett, 2009). Indeed, children born in the first 9 months of a calendar year typically start school an entire year earlier than those born in the last 3 months of the same year. Sure enough, people with late birthdays tend to have lower intelligence-test scores than people with early birthdays (Baltes & Reinert, 1969).

Does this mean that anyone can become a genius just by showing up for class? Unfortunately not. Although education increases intelligence, its impact tends to be small, and its effects tend to vanish when it stops (Protzko, 2015, 2016). For example, prekindergarten programs for low-SES children tend to raise their IQs, but the effects fade once these children leave their intellectually enriched environments and go to elementary school. A few intensive programs have produced longer-lasting gains. For example, an experiment conducted in the 1970s allowed low-SES children to enroll in a full-time preschool program that focused on developing their cognitive, linguistic, and social skills in small classes of about six (Campbell et al., 2002). Compared with a control group, those children showed IQ gains that were still measurable at the age of 21 (though it appears that girls benefited far more than boys; Anderson, 2008). But so far, very few educational interventions have been shown to produce large and long-lasting increases in intelligence. That doesn't mean education is unimportant. Even when it does not produce long-lasting increases in intelligence, it does produce long-lasting increases in other important skills: In terms of just about every important outcome—from health to wealth to happiness—the difference between an illiterate person with an IQ of 100 and a literate person with an IQ of 101 is much larger than a single IQ point would suggest.

THE NATURE–NURTURE DISTINCTION

Both nature and nurture influence intelligence. But that shouldn't lead you to think of genes and environments as two separate ingredients that are somehow blended together like flour and sugar in a recipe for IQ. The fact is that genes and environments interact in complex ways that make the distinction between them a bit murky.

For example, imagine that there was a gene that made people enjoy the smell of library dust, or that made them unusually sensitive to the glare produced by television sets. People who had such a gene might well read more books, watch less television, and end up being smarter. Would their increased intelligence be due to their genes or to their environments? Well, if they hadn't had those genes, then they wouldn't have turned off the TV and gone to the library, but if they hadn't done those things, then they wouldn't have gotten smarter. The fact is that genes may exert some of their most powerful influence not by determining the structure of a person's brain, but by determining the person's attraction to certain environments (Dickens & Flynn, 2001; Nisbett, 2009; Plomin et al., 2001; Tucker-Drob, Briley, & Harden, 2013). A gene that made someone sociable might lead her to have good relationships with peers, which might lead her to stay in school longer, which might lead her to become smarter—but would we call such a gene a "sociability gene" or an "intelligence gene" (Posthuma & de Geus, 2006)? Would we attribute that person's intelligence to her genes or to the environment that her genes enabled her to create? As these questions suggest, genes and environments are not independent influences on intelligence, and the clear difference between nature and nurture is not nearly so clear as it first appears (see Hot Science: Brains Wide Open).

Roundworms that have the NPR-1 gene get fewer infections than those that don't. Does this gene affect the functioning of the immune system? No, it simply causes roundworms to dislike environments where bacteria hang out. Similarly, genes may increase our intelligence not by amping up our raw brainpower, but by causing us to gravitate toward the environments that do.

Brains Wide Open

One of the things that makes our species so smart is that our brains are designed to be programmed by our environments. Turtles, lizards, and houseflies are all prewired by evolution to react in very specific ways to very specific stimuli. But mammalian brains—and especially human brains—are built to be *environmentally sensitive*, which means that humans are born with the minimal amount of hardwiring and are instead wired by their experiences in the world in which they find themselves. This is what allows human beings to function so effectively in a wide variety of physical and cultural environments.

But the brain's remarkable openness to experiences doesn't last forever. By the age of 18 or so, the cerebral cortex has thickened, and the brain is never again as environmentally sensitive as it was in childhood. If the brain's environmental sensitivity is one of the things that makes our species so smart, it stands to reason that the smartest people among us might have brains that remain environmentally sensitive for longer than usual. Is that true?

That's what Brant and colleagues (2013) set out to discover. They examined data from nearly 11,000 sets of MZ and DZ twins who had taken IQ tests sometime between infancy and adulthood. Using sophisticated mathematical techniques, they computed the extent to which differences in IQ scores at each age had been influenced by genes or by the environment.

What they found was fascinating. Children's brains were relatively open to environmental influence, and adult's brains were relatively closed—but the point at which the closing happened was different for high-IQ and low-IQ people. Whereas the brains of low-IQ people closed by early adolescence, the brains of high-IQ people remained open to influence well into adolescence. The graph shows the magnitude of both environmental and genetic influences at different ages. As it indicates, the brains of high-IQ adolescents remained as sensitive as the brains of children, but the brains of low-IQ adolescents were as insensitive as the brains of adults. Whether you look at the effect of genes (in orange) or the effect of environment (in purple), you'll notice that the high- and low-IQ people start in the same place and end in the same place, but they get there at different speeds—specifically, low-IQ people get there faster.

No one knows why the brains of high-IQ people remain sensitive to the environment for longer, and no one knows if this is a cause or a consequence of their intelligence. All we know is that the longer the brain retains its childlike openness to experience, the more effectively it functions for the rest of its life.

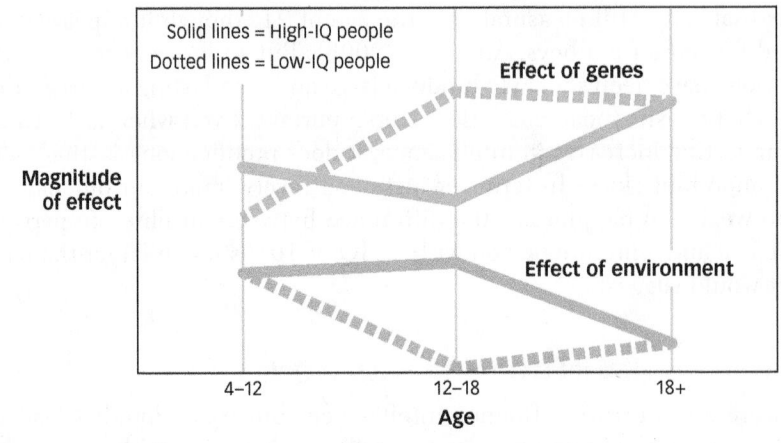

Solid lines = High-IQ people
Dotted lines = Low-IQ people

Effect of genes

Effect of environment

Magnitude of effect

4–12   12–18   18+

Age

Who Is Most Intelligent?

Learning Outcomes

▶ Describe myths about the intellectually gifted and the intellectually disabled.

▶ Explain what is and is not known about between-group differences in intelligence.

▶ Identify ways that intelligence can be enhanced.

INDIVIDUAL DIFFERENCES IN INTELLIGENCE

The average IQ is 100, and 68% of us have IQs between 85 and 115 (see **FIGURE 10.10**). The people who score well above this large middle range are said to be *intellectually gifted*, and the people who score well below it are said to be *intellectually disabled*. Although these people live at opposite ends of the intelligence continuum, they do have one thing in common: They are more likely to be male than female. Males and females have the same average IQ, but the distribution of males' IQ scores is wider and more variable than the distribution of females' IQ scores, which means that there are more males than females

Percentage of individuals scoring in each interval

0.1% 2% 14% 34% 34% 14% 2% 0.1%

40 55 70 85 100 115 130 145 160

IQ score

◀ Figure 10.10

THE NORMAL CURVE OF INTELLIGENCE
Deviation IQ scores produce a normal curve. This graph shows the percentage of people who score in each range of IQ.

at both the very top and the very bottom of the IQ range (Hedges & Nowell, 1995; Lakin, 2013; Wai, Putallaz, & Makel, 2012). Some of this difference is due to the different ways in which boys and girls are socialized, and whether any of this difference is due to innate biological differences between males and females remains a hotly debated issue in psychology (Ceci, Williams, & Barnett, 2009; Nisbett et al., 2012; Spelke, 2005).

Those of us who occupy the large middle of the intelligence spectrum often embrace a number of myths about those who live at the extremes. For example, movies typically portray the "tortured genius" as a person (usually a male person) who is brilliant, creative, misunderstood, despondent, and more than a little bit weird. Although some psychologists do think there is a link between creative genius and certain forms of psychopathology (Gale et al., 2012; Jamison, 1993; cf. Schlesinger, 2012; Simonton, 2014), for the most part Hollywood has the relationship between intelligence and mental illness backward: People with very high intelligence are *less* susceptible to mental illness than are people with very low intelligence (Dekker & Koot, 2003; Didden et al., 2012; Walker et al., 2002). Indeed, a 15-point *decrease* in IQ at age 20 is associated with a 50% *increase* in the risk of later hospitalization for schizophrenia, mood disorder, and alcohol-related disorders (Gale et al., 2010) as well as for personality disorders (Moran et al., 2009). Just as intelligence seems to buffer people against physical illness, so it seems to buffer people against mental illness as well.

Another staple of Hollywood's vivid imagination is the "maladjusted child braniac." In fact, research suggests that very-high-IQ children are about as well adjusted as their peers, and any special social or emotional problems they have seem to stem largely from a lack of appropriate scholastic opportunities (Garland & Zigler, 1999; Neihart, 1999). Being intellectually gifted doesn't necessarily make a child's life worse, but it also doesn't necessarily make it better. For instance, profoundly gifted children are no more likely than moderately intelligent children to become major contributors to the fields in which they work (Richert, 1997; Terman & Oden, 1959). No one knows why the gifts of childhood don't always ripen into the fruits of adulthood: Perhaps there is a natural limit on how much intelligence can improve one's outcomes, or perhaps the educational system fails to help gifted children make the best use of their talents (Robinson & Clinkenbeard, 1998; Winner, 2000).

It is worth noting that gifted children are rarely gifted in all departments, but instead have gifts in a single domain such as math, language, or music. More than 95% of gifted children show a sharp disparity between their mathematical and verbal abilities (Achter, Lubinski, & Benbow, 1996). Because gifted children tend to be "single gifted," they also tend to be single minded, displaying a "rage to master" the domain in which they excel. As one expert noted, "one cannot tear these children away from activities in their area of giftedness, whether they involve an instrument, a computer, a sketch pad, or a math book. These children . . . can focus so intently on work in this domain that they lose sense of the outside world" (Winner, 2000, p. 162). Indeed, some research suggests that the one thing that most clearly distinguishes gifted children from their less gifted peers is the sheer amount of time they spend engaged in their domain of excellence (Ericsson & Charness, 1999). A large part of nature's gift may be the capacity for passionate devotion to a single activity (Mayer et al., 1989; cf. Hambrick et al., 2013).

LEE FOSTER/ALAMY

The artist Vincent van Gogh was the iconic "tortured genius." But data suggest that low intelligence, not high intelligence, is most strongly associated with mental illness.

The artist Judith Scott, who died in 2005, had Down syndrome. Her remarkable textile sculptures have been the subjects of articles, books, and films, and can be seen in galleries and museums all over the world.

VICENTE FRANCO

On the other end of the intelligence spectrum are people with intellectual disabilities, which can range from mild (50 < IQ < 69) to moderate (35 < IQ < 49) to severe (20 < IQ < 34) to profound (IQ < 20). About 70% of people with IQs in this range are male. Two of the most common causes of intellectual disability are *Down syndrome* (caused by the presence of a third copy of chromosome 21) and *fetal alcohol syndrome* (caused by a mother's excessive alcohol use during pregnancy). These intellectual disabilities are quite general, and people who have them typically show impaired performance on most or all cognitive tasks. Perhaps the greatest myth about the intellectually disabled is that they are unhappy. A recent survey of people with Down syndrome revealed that more than 96% are happy with their lives, like who they are, and like how they look (Skotko, Levine, & Goldstein, 2011). People with intellectual disabilities face many challenges, and being misunderstood is one of the most difficult.

GROUP DIFFERENCES IN INTELLIGENCE

In the early 1900s, Professor Lewis Terman of Stanford University improved on Binet and Simon's work and produced the intelligence test now known as the Stanford–Binet Intelligence Scale. Among the things his test revealed was that Whites performed better than non-Whites. "Are the inferior races really inferior, or are they merely unfortunate in their lack of opportunity to learn?" he asked, and then answered unequivocally: "Their dullness seems to be racial, or at least inherent in the family stocks from which they come." He went on to suggest that "children of this group should be segregated into separate classes . . . [because] they cannot master abstractions but they can often be made into efficient workers" (Terman, 1916, pp. 91–92).

A century later, these sentences make most of us cringe. But exactly which parts are cringe-worthy? Terman was making three independent claims: (1) intelligence is influenced by genes; (2) members of some racial groups score better than others on intelligence tests; and (3) the reason members of some racial groups score better than others on intelligence tests is due to differences in their genes. Virtually all modern scientists agree that Terman's first two claims are clearly true: Intelligence *is* influenced by genes,

ARCHIVE PHOTOS/GETTY IMAGES

Men tend to outperform women on abstract mathematical and scientific tests, and women tend to outperform men on verbal tests. So you won't be surprised that actress Hedy Lamarr spoke beautifully in dozens of hit movies of the 1940s. But you might be surprised to learn that in her spare time, she designed torpedo guidance systems for the U.S. Navy and invented (and patented!) the "spread spectrum" technology that is used today in Wi-Fi, Bluetooth, and cellphones. By the way, her co-star Clark Gable invented the pencil mustache, which today is used approximately never.

and some groups *do* perform better than others on intelligence tests. But Terman's third claim—that differences in genes are the *reason* why some groups outperform others—is not a fact. It is a provocative conjecture that has been the subject of both passionate and acrimonious debate. What does science have to tell us about it?

Before answering that question, let's be clear about one thing: Between-group differences in intelligence are not inherently troubling. No one is troubled by the possibility that this year's winners of the Nobel Prize are on average more intelligent than this year's winners of the Super Bowl, or that people who graduate from college are on average more intelligent than people who do not. On the other hand, most of us *are* troubled by the possibility that people of one gender, race, or nationality may be more intelligent than people of another, because intelligence is a valuable commodity, and it doesn't seem fair for a few groups to corner the market by accidents of birth or geography.

But fair or not, they do. Whites routinely outscore Blacks on standard intelligence tests (Neisser et al., 1996; Nisbett et al., 2012). Women routinely outscore men on tests that require rapid access to and use of semantic information, production and comprehension of complex prose, fine motor skills, and perceptual speed of verbal intelligence. Men routinely outscore women on tests that require transformations in visual or spatial memory, certain motor skills, spatiotemporal responding, and fluid reasoning in abstract mathematical and scientific domains (Halpern et al., 2007; Nisbett et al., 2012). Indeed, group differences in performance on intelligence tests "are among the most thoroughly documented findings in psychology" (Suzuki & Valencia, 1997, p. 1104). Although the average difference between groups is considerably less than the average difference within groups, Terman was right when he noted that some groups perform better than others on intelligence tests. The question is: Why?

Tests and Test Takers

One possibility is that there is something wrong with the tests. In fact, there is now little doubt that the earliest intelligence tests asked questions whose answers were more likely to be known by members of one group (usually White Europeans) than by members of another. For example, when Binet and Simon asked students, "When anyone has offended you and asks you to excuse him, what ought you to do?" they were looking for

These high school juniors in South Carolina are taking the SAT. When people are asked about their race or gender before taking a test, their performance can be affected. Why?

MARY ANN CHASTAIN/AP IMAGES

answers such as "accept the apology graciously." Answers such as "demand three goats" would have been counted as wrong. But intelligence tests have come a long way in a century, and one would have to look hard to find questions on a modern intelligence test that have the same blatant cultural bias that Binet and Simon's test did (Suzuki & Valencia, 1997). Moreover, group differences emerge even on those portions of intelligence tests that measure nonverbal skills, such as Raven's Progressive Matrices Test (see Figure 10.4). It would be difficult to argue that the differences between the average scores of different groups is due entirely—or even largely—to a cultural bias in IQ tests.

Of course, even when test *questions* are unbiased, testing *situations* may not be. For example, studies show that African American students (but not European American students) perform more poorly on tests if they are asked to report their race at the top of the answer sheet, presumably because doing so leads them to feel anxious about confirming racial stereotypes (Steele & Aronson, 1995), and anxiety naturally interferes with test performance (Reeve, Heggestad, & Lievens, 2009). **Stereotype threat** is *the fear of confirming the negative beliefs that others may hold* (Aronson & Steele, 2004; Schmader, Johns, & Forbes, 2008; Walton & Spencer, 2009), and it can exert a powerful influence on people's test performance. When Asian American women are reminded of their gender, they perform unusually poorly on tests of mathematical skill, presumably because they are aware of stereotypes suggesting that women can't do math. But when the same women are instead reminded of their ethnicity, they perform unusually well on such tests, presumably because they are aware of stereotypes suggesting that Asians are especially good at math (Shih, Pittinsky, & Ambady, 1999). Indeed, when women read an essay suggesting that mathematical ability is strongly influenced by genes, they perform more poorly on subsequent math tests (Dar-Nimrod & Heine, 2006). Findings such as these remind us that the situations in which intelligence tests are administered can affect members of different groups differently and may cause group differences in performance that do not reflect group differences in actual intelligence.

Environments and Genes

Biases in the testing situation may explain some of the between-group differences in intelligence test scores, but probably not all. If we assume that some of these differences reflect real differences in the abilities that intelligence tests are meant to measure, then what accounts for these ability differences?

There is broad agreement among scientists that environment plays a major role. For example, African American children have lower birth weights, poorer diets, higher

stereotype threat The fear of confirming the negative beliefs that others may hold.

rates of chronic illness, and poorer medical care; attend worse schools; and are three times more likely than European American children to live in single-parent households (Acevedo-Garcia et al., 2007; National Center for Health Statistics, 2016a). African-American households have lower incomes, and studies show that children in families earning more than $100,000 per year are nearly 50% more likely to be in excellent health than are children in families earning less than $35,000 per year (National Center for Health Statistics, 2016b). Given the vast differences between the SES of European Americans and African Americans, it isn't very surprising that African Americans score on average 10 points lower on IQ tests than do European Americans.

Do genes play any role in this difference? So far, scientists have not found a single fact that requires such a conclusion, but they have found several facts that make it unlikely. For example, the average African American has about 20% European genes, but those who have more are no smarter than those who have fewer, which is not what we'd expect if European genes made people smart (Loehlin, 1973; Nisbett et al., 2012; Scarr et al., 1977). Similarly, African American children and mixed-race children have different amounts of European genes, and yet, when they are adopted into middle-class families, their IQs don't differ (Moore, 1986). These facts do not rule out the possibility that between-group differences in intelligence are caused by genetic differences, but they do make that possibility less plausible.

What would it take to prove that behavioral and psychological differences between groups have a genetic origin? It would probably take the kind of evidence that scientists often find when they study the *physical* differences between groups. For example, people who have hepatitis C are often given a prescription for antiviral drugs, and European Americans typically benefit more from this treatment than African Americans do. Physicians once thought that this was because European Americans were more likely to *take* the medicine they were given. Then scientists discovered a gene that makes people unresponsive to these antiviral drugs—and guess what? African Americans are *more* likely than European Americans to have that gene (Ge et al., 2009). This kind of clear-cut evidence of genetic differences between groups is exactly what's lacking in the debate on the causes of between-group differences in intelligence. As Ian Deary, one of the world's leading experts on the science of intelligence, recently noted, "No individual genetic variants are conclusively related to intelligence or its change with age in healthy individuals" (Deary, 2012, p. 463). This may mean that intelligence is influenced by many very tiny genetic effects rather than by a few major "intelligence genes" (Davies et al., 2011), but until researchers can locate those genes, and until they can show that those genes are more prevalent in one group than another, most scientists are unlikely to embrace a genetic explanation of between-group differences in intelligence. Indeed, some experts, such as the psychologist Richard Nisbett, believe the debate is over: "Genes account for none of the difference in IQ between blacks and whites; measurable environmental factors plausibly account for all of it" (Nisbett, 2009, p. 118).

IMPROVING INTELLIGENCE

Intelligence can be improved—by money, for example, and by education. But most people can't just snap their fingers and become wealthier, and education takes time. Is there anything that the average parent can do to raise their child's IQ? Researchers recently analyzed the data from all the high-quality scientific studies on this question that have been performed over the last few decades (Protzko, Aronson, & Blair, 2013), and they found that four things reliably raise a child's intelligence. First, supplementing the diets of pregnant women and neonates with long-chain polyunsaturated fatty acids (substances found in breast milk) appears to raise children's IQ by about 4 points. Second, enrolling low-SES infants in so-called early educational interventions tends to raise their IQ by about 6 points (though enrolling them at a younger age seems to be no better than enrolling them at an older age). Third, reading to children in an interactive manner raises their IQ by about 6 points (and in this case, the earlier the parent starts

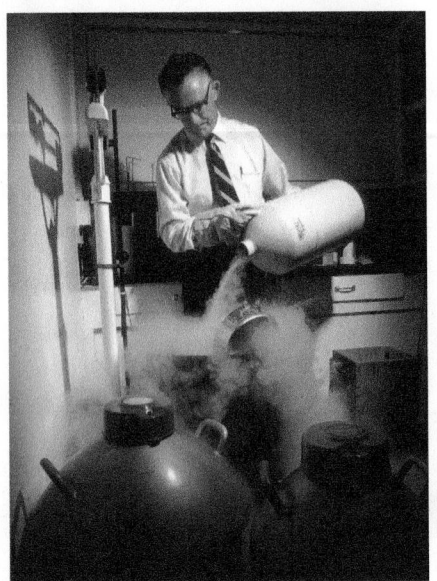

PAUL HARRIS/GETTY IMAGES

The millionaire Robert Graham opened the Repository for Germinal Choice in 1980 to collect sperm from Nobel laureates and mathematical prodigies and allow healthy young women to be inseminated with it. His "genius factory" produced more than 200 children but closed after his death in 1999. No records survived, so no one knows if his experiment was a success.

cognitive enhancers Drugs that improve the psychological processes that underlie intelligent performance.

reading the better). Fourth, sending children to preschool raises their IQ by about 6 points. Clearly, there are some things that parents can do to make their kids smarter.

And there are things parents can do to make themselves smarter as well. Research suggests that various kinds of "mental exercises" can increase intelligence. For example, the *n*-back task involves showing people letters one at a time and then asking them whether the letter they are currently seeing is the same as the letter they saw *n* letters ago. The 1-back version is fairly easy, because the person simply has to say whether the current letter is the same as the letter she just saw. But the 3-back version is quite challenging, because the person has to say whether the current letter is the same as the one she saw three letters ago, which means she must keep a constantly updated record of the three most recent letters she saw in memory. Research shows that people who train for long periods of time with complex high-*n* versions of this task show gains in fluid intelligence (Jaeggi et al., 2008). A variety of other memory-training and attention-training tasks that are similarly long and joyless appear to produce similar improvements in fluid intelligence, in both children and adults (e.g., Mackey et al., 2011; Tranter and Koutstaal, 2007) and may even slow cognitive decline among the elderly (Salthouse, 2015).

But improving intelligence does not always take so much work. **Cognitive enhancers** are *drugs that improve the psychological processes that underlie intelligent performance*. For example, stimulants such as Ritalin (methylphenidate) and Adderall (mixed amphetamine salts) have been shown to enhance cognitive performance (Elliott et al., 1997; Halliday et al., 1994; McKetin et al., 1999), which is why there has been an alarming increase in their use by healthy students over the past few years. Surveys suggest that nearly 7% of students in U.S. universities have used prescription stimulants for cognitive enhancement. On some campuses the number is as high as 25% (McCabe et al., 2005). These drugs improve people's ability to focus their attention, manipulate information in working memory, and flexibly control their responses (Sahakian & Morein-Zamir, 2007). Cognitive performance can also be enhanced by a class of drugs called ampakines (Ingvar et al., 1997). Modafinil is one such drug, and it has been shown to improve both short-term memory and planning abilities (Turner et al., 2003). All of these drugs can have damaging side effects and can lead to abuse, but their effects on cognitive performance are clear.

In the near future, cognitive enhancement may not be achieved with chemicals that temporarily alter the brain's function but rather with techniques that permanently alter its structure. By manipulating the genes that guide hippocampal development, for instance, scientists have created a strain of "smart mice" that have extraordinary memory and learning abilities, leading the researchers to conclude that "genetic enhancement of mental and cognitive attributes such as intelligence and memory in mammals is feasible" (Tang et al., 1999, p. 64). And new "gene-editing" techniques such as CRISPR/Cas9 may allow animals to pass these genetic modifications to their young. Although no one has yet developed a safe and powerful "smart pill" or a gene-editing technique that enhances intelligence in mammals, many experts believe that both of these things will happen in the next few years (Farah et al., 2004; Rose, 2002; Turner & Sahakian, 2006).

At that point, we will have some tough choices to make, because there is no bright line between technological enhancements and the more traditional kinds. As one distinguished group of scientists (Greely et al., 2008, p. 703) recently concluded, "Drugs may seem distinctive among enhancements in that they bring about their effects by altering brain function, but in reality so does any intervention that enhances cognition. Recent research has identified beneficial neural changes engendered by exercise, nutrition and sleep, as well as instruction and reading." If Adderall and the *n*-back task both enhance cognition by altering the way the brain functions, then what is the difference between them? Some think the answer is more ethical than biological: Both drugs and memory-training games can enhance fluid intelligence, but one requires hard work and commitment, whereas the other requires only a prescription. Do we want to live in a world in which a highly prized human achievement such as intelligence can be purchased, rather than being earned or endowed by nature? That's a question we will all soon be asking, and we will need a whole lot of intelligence to answer it (see Other Voices: How Science Can Build a Better You).

How Science Can Build a Better You

David Ewing Duncan is an award-winning author and journalist whose most recent book is *When I'm 164: The New Science of Radical Life Extension, and What Happens If It Succeeds.*

Intelligence is a highly prized commodity that buys people a lot of the good things in life. It can be increased by a solid education and a healthy diet, and everyone is in favor of those things. But it can also be increased by drugs—and there is little doubt that in the near future it will be increased by other even more powerful technologies. Is this a bad idea or a moral imperative? How will we decide who gets to use these technologies and who gets left behind? The author David Ewing Duncan thinks these are critically important questions that we must answer now—*before* the "Age of Enhancement" begins.

Over the last couple of years during talks and lectures, I have asked thousands of people a hypothetical question that goes like this: "If I could offer you a pill that allowed your child to increase his or her memory by 25 percent, would you give it to them?"

The show of hands in this informal poll has been overwhelming, with 80 percent or more voting no.

Then I asked a follow-up question. "What if this pill was safe and increased your kid's grades from a B average to an A average?" People tittered nervously, looked around to see how others were voting as nearly half said yes. (Many didn't vote at all.)

"And what if all of the other kids are taking the pill?" I asked. The tittering stopped and nearly everyone voted yes.

No pill now exists that can boost memory by 25 percent. Yet neuroscientists tell me that pharmaceutical companies are testing compounds in early stage human trials that may enable patients with dementia and other memory-stealing diseases to have better recall. No one knows if these will work to improve healthy people, but it's possible that one will work in the future.

More intriguing is the notion that a supermemory or attention pill might be used someday by those with critical jobs like pilots, surgeons, police officers—or the chief executive of the United States. In fact, we may demand that they use them, said the bioethicist Thomas H. Murray. "It might actually be immoral for a surgeon not to take a drug that was safe and steadied his hand," said Mr. Murray, the former president of the Hastings Center, a bioethics research group. "That would be like using a scalpel that wasn't sterile.". . .

For years, scientists have been manipulating genes in animals to make improvements in neural performance, strength and agility, among other augmentations. Directly altering human DNA using "gene therapy" in humans remains dangerous and fraught with ethical challenges. But it may be possible to develop drugs that alter enzymes and other proteins associated with genes for, say, speed and endurance or dopamine levels in the brain connected to improved neural performance.

Synthetic biologists contend that re-engineering cells and DNA may one day allow us to eliminate diseases; a few believe we will be able to build tailor-made people. Others are convinced that stem cells might one day be used to grow fresh brain, heart or liver cells to augment or improve cells in these and other organs.

Not all enhancements are high-tech or invasive. Neuroscientists are seeing boosts from neuro-feedback and video games designed to teach and develop cognition and from meditation and improvements in diet, exercise and sleep. "We may see a convergence of several of these technologies," said the neurologist Adam Gazzaley of the University of California at San Francisco. He is developing brain-boosting games with developers and engineers who once worked for Lucas Arts, founded by the "Star Wars" director George Lucas. . . .

Ethical challenges for the coming Age of Enhancement include, besides basic safety questions, the issue of who would get the enhancements, how much they would cost, and who would gain an advantage over others by using them. In a society that is already seeing a widening gap between the very rich and the rest of us, the question of a democracy of equals could face a critical test if the well-off also could afford a physical, genetic or bionic advantage. It also may challenge what it means to be human.

Still, the enhancements are coming, and they will be hard to resist. The real issue is what we do with them once they become irresistible.

David Ewing Duncan sees a brave new world on the not-too-distant horizon. The possibility of using technology to increase human intelligence is very exciting because intelligence can bring great rewards to those who have it, as well as to those around them. But how wisely will we seize this opportunity? Will all of humankind reap the harvest and become brighter, more peaceful, and more productive? Or will we end up with a Master Class of highly intelligent people who run the world for their own benefit? We will probably know the answer to this question in your lifetime.

Build to the Outcomes

1. What are the most common misconceptions about the intellectually gifted and the intellectually disabled?

2. What one thing most clearly distinguishes gifted children from others?

3. How can the testing situation affect a person's performance on an IQ test?

4. What is the current best guess about the cause(s) of between-group differences in intelligence?

5. How can intelligence be enhanced? What ethical questions are raised?

Chapter Review

How Can Intelligence Be Measured?

▶ *Intelligence* is the ability to use one's mind to solve novel problems and learn from experience. Binet and Simon developed a test that was meant to measure a child's natural aptitude for learning independent of previous experience.

▶ Intelligence tests produce a score known as an *intelligence quotient,* or IQ. *Ratio IQ* is the ratio of a person's mental to physical age. *Deviation IQ* is the deviation of an adult's test score from the average adult's test score.

▶ Intelligence test scores predict a variety of important life outcomes, such as scholastic performance, job performance, health, and wealth.

What Is Intelligence?

▶ People who score well on one test of mental ability *tend to* score well on others, which suggests that each person has a particular level of general intelligence *(g).*

▶ The person who scores highest on one test doesn't necessarily score highest on every other test, which suggests that different people have different specific abilities *(s).*

▶ Research reveals that between *g* and *s* are several *middle-level abilities.*
   o The *data-based approach* suggests that there are eight middle-level abilities.
   o The *theory-based approach* suggests that there may be middle-level abilities that standard intelligence tests don't measure, such as practical, creative, and emotional intelligence.

▶ Non-Western cultures may include measures of social responsibility and cooperation in their definitions of intelligence.

Where Does Intelligence Come From?

▶ The IQs of MZ twins (who share 100% of their genes) are more highly correlated than are the IQs of DZ twins (who share 50% of their genes), suggesting that genes have a powerful influence on intelligence.

▶ The heritability coefficient (h^2) tells us how much of the difference between the IQ scores of different people is due to differences in their genes, but it does not tell us anything about individuals.

▶ Environments can influence intelligence. SES and education can both be powerful influences on IQ, but the effects of education are often short lived.

▶ Education has only a moderate influence, which may be because it enhances test-taking ability rather than cognitive ability.

Who Is Most Intelligent?

▶ Intelligence is correlated with mental health, and gifted children are as well adjusted as their peers. Despite the myth, people with intellectual disabilities are not necessarily unhappy.

▶ Some groups outscore others on intelligence tests. There is good evidence to suggest that this happens in part because testing situations can impair the performance of some groups more than others, and in part because low-SES environments have an adverse impact on intelligence.

▶ Some groups outscore others on intelligence tests. There is no compelling evidence to suggest that this is due to the genetic differences between the groups.

▶ Human intelligence can be increased by a variety of means, from preschool to mental exercise to pharmaceuticals. Some of these methods carry greater risks and raise more difficult ethical questions than others.

KEY CONCEPT QUIZ

1. Intelligence tests
   a. were first developed to help children who lagged behind their peers.
   b. were developed to measure aptitude rather than educational achievement.
   c. have been used for detestable ends.
   d. all of the above

2. Intelligence tests have been shown to be predictors of
   a. academic performance.
   b. mental health.
   c. physical health.
   d. all of the above.

3. People who score well on one test of mental ability usually score well on others, suggesting that
   a. tests of mental ability are perfectly correlated.
   b. intelligence cannot be measured meaningfully.
   c. there is a general ability called intelligence.
   d. intelligence is genetic.

4. Most scientists now believe that intelligence is best described
   a. as a set of group factors.
   b. by a two-factor framework.
   c. as a single, general ability.
   d. by a three-level hierarchy.

5. Standard intelligence tests typically measure
   a. analytic intelligence.
   b. practical intelligence.
   c. creative intelligence.
   d. all of the above.

6. Intelligence is influenced by
   a. genes alone.
   b. genes and environment.
   c. environment alone.
   d. neither genes nor environment.

7. The heritability coefficient is a statistic that describes how much of the difference between different people's intelligence scores can be explained by
   a. the nature of the specific test.
   b. differences in their environment.
   c. differences in their genes.
   d. their age at the time of testing.

8. Intelligence changes
   a. over the life span and across generations.
   b. over the life span but not across generations.
   c. across generations but not over the life span.
   d. neither across generations nor over the life span.

9. A person's socioeconomic status has a(n) _____ effect on intelligence.

   a. powerful
   b. negligible
   c. unsubstantiated
   d. unknown

10. On which of the following statements does broad agreement exist among scientists?

   a. Differences in the intelligence test scores of different ethnic groups are clearly due to genetic differences between those groups.

   b. Differences in the intelligence test scores of different ethnic groups are caused in part by factors such as low birth weight and poor diet, which are more prevalent in some groups than in others.
   c. Differences in the intelligence test scores of different ethnic groups always reflect real differences in intelligence.
   d. Genes that are strongly associated with intelligence have been found to be more prevalent in some ethnic groups than in others.

 LearningCurve Don't stop now! Quizzing yourself is a powerful study tool. Go to LaunchPad to access the LearningCurve adaptive quizzing system and your own personalized learning plan. Visit launchpadworks.com.

KEY TERMS

intelligence (p. 396)

ratio IQ (p. 398)

deviation IQ (p. 398)

two-factor theory of intelligence (p. 402)

crystallized intelligence (p. 405)

fluid intelligence (p. 405)

emotional intelligence (p. 406)

fraternal twins (or dizygotic twins) (p. 409)

identical twins (or monozygotic twins) (p. 409)

heritability coefficient (p. 410)

shared environment (p. 411)

nonshared environment (p. 411)

stereotype threat (p. 420)

cognitive enhancers (p. 422)

CHANGING MINDS

1. In biology class, the topic turns to genetics. The professor describes how scientists used gene editing to make a smarter mouse. Your classmate turns to you. "I knew it," she said. "There's a 'smart gene' after all. Some people have it, and some people don't, and that's why some people are intelligent, and some people aren't." What would you tell her about the role genetics plays in intelligence and about the way in which genes affect it?

2. One of your friends tells you about his sister. "We're very competitive," he says. "But she's smarter. We both took IQ tests when we were kids, and she scored 104, but I only scored 102." What would you tell your friend about the relationship between IQ scores and intelligence?

3. A new survey shows that in mathematics departments all over the country, tenured male professors outnumber tenured female professors by about 9 to 1. One of your friends says, "But it's a fact—girls just don't do as well as boys at math, so it's not surprising that fewer girls choose math-related careers." Thinking about what you've read in this chapter about group differences in intelligence, how might you explain this fact to your friend?

4. One of your cousins has a young son, and she's very proud of the boy's accomplishments. "He's very smart," she says. "I know this because he has a great memory: He gets 100% on all his vocabulary tests." What kind of intelligence do vocabulary tests measure? Although these skills are important for intelligence, what other abilities contribute to an individual's overall intelligence?

ANSWERS TO KEY CONCEPT QUIZ

1. d; 2. d; 3. c; 4. d; 5. a; 6. b; 7. c; 8. a; 9. a; 10. b.

 LaunchPad macmillan learning LaunchPad features the full e-Book of *Psychology*, the LearningCurve adaptive quizzing system, videos, and a variety of activities to boost your learning. Visit LaunchPad at launchpadworks.com.

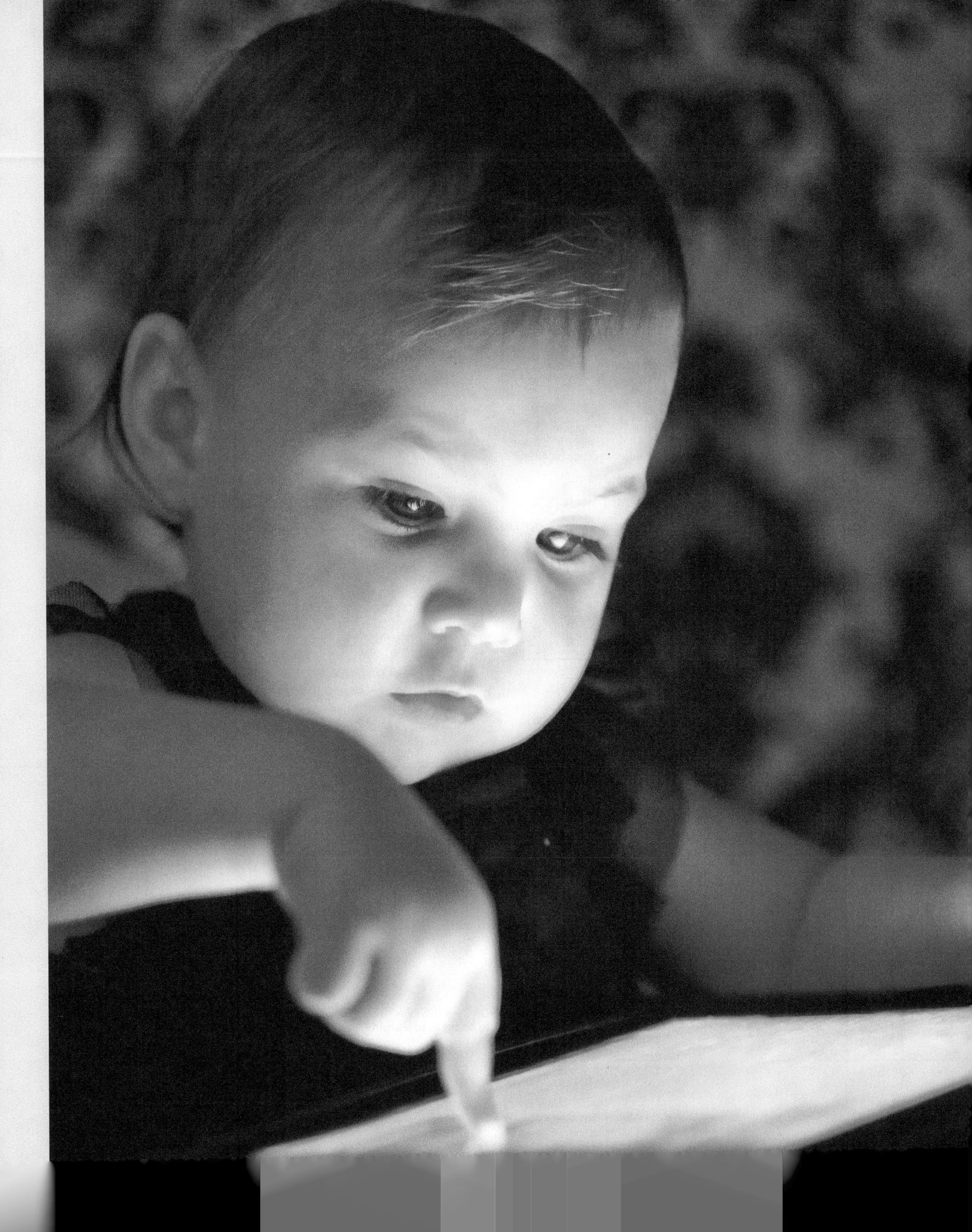

Development

11

HIS MOTHER CALLED HIM ADI and showered him with affection, but his father was not so kind. As his sister later recalled, Adi "got his sound thrashing every day. . . . How often on the other hand did my mother caress him and try to obtain with her kindness where the father could not succeed with harshness." Although his father wanted him to become a civil servant, Adi's true love was art, and his mother quietly encouraged that gentle interest. Adi was just 18 years old when his mother was diagnosed with terminal cancer. His sister recalled that he "spoiled my mother during this time of her life with overflowing tenderness. He was indefatigable in his care for her, wanted to comply with any desire she could possibly have and did all to demonstrate his great love for her."

Adi was heartbroken when his mother died, but he had little time for grieving. As he later wrote, "Poverty and hard reality compelled me to make a quick decision. I was faced with the problem of somehow making my own living." Adi decided to defy his father's wishes and make his living as an artist. But when he applied to art school, he was flatly rejected. So motherless, homeless, and penniless, Adi wandered the streets for years, sleeping on park benches, living in shelters, and eating in soup kitchens, all the while trying desperately to sell his sketches and watercolors. What became of him?

In just ten years, Adi achieved a degree of fame that few artists ever dream of. Today, art collectors all over the world compete at auctions to buy his paintings, which rarely come up for sale. The largest collection of his work, however, is not in the hands of any private citizen or museum. Rather, it is owned by the U.S. government, which keeps the collection under lock and key, in a windowless room in Washington, DC, where few people have ever been allowed to visit. Marylou Gjernes, the longtime curator of the government's collection, once remarked, "I often looked at them and wondered, 'What if? What if he had been accepted into art school? Would World War II have happened?'" Why would the curator ask such a question? Because the artist's mother called him Adi, but the rest of us know him as Adolf Hitler.

Adi painted in many styles, including the precise and well-structured watercolor shown here. In 2013, one of his paintings sold at auction for $ 40,000.

WHY IS IT SO DIFFICULT TO IMAGINE ONE OF THE GREATEST mass murderers of the 20th century as a gentle child who loved to draw, as a compassionate adolescent who cared for his ailing mother, or as a dedicated young adult who endured cold and hunger for the sake of his art? After all, *you* didn't begin as the person you are today, and odds are that you aren't yet in finished form. From birth to infancy, from childhood to adolescence, from young adulthood to old age, human beings change over time. Their development includes both dramatic transformations and striking consistencies in the way they look, think, feel, and act. **Developmental psychology** is *the study of continuity and change across the life span,* and in the last century, developmental psychologists have discovered some truly amazing things about this metamorphosis.

From infancy to childhood to adolescence to adulthood, people exhibit both continuity and change.

ALL PHOTOS COURTESY OF DANIEL GILBERT

The story starts where people do: at conception. First we'll examine the 9-month period between conception and birth and see how prenatal events set the stage for everything to come. Then we'll examine infancy and childhood, the period during which children must learn how to think about the world and their relationship to it, to understand and bond with others, and to tell the difference between right and wrong. Next, we'll examine a relatively new invention called adolescence, which is the stage at which children become both independent and sexual creatures. Finally, we'll examine adulthood, the stage at which people typically leave their parents, find mates, and have children of their own.

Prenatality: A Womb With a View

Learning Outcomes

▶ Describe the three prenatal stages of development.

▶ Explain how the prenatal environment influences the fetus's development.

developmental psychology The study of continuity and change across the life span.

You probably calculate your age by counting your birthdays, but the fact is that on the day you were born, you were already 9 months old. The *prenatal stage* of development ends with birth and begins 9 months earlier when about 200 million sperm set out on a pilgrimage from a woman's vagina, through her uterus, and to her fallopian tubes. Many are called, but few are chosen. Some of the sperm don't swim vigorously enough to make any progress, and others get stuck in a kind of spermatozoidal traffic jam in which too many sperm head in the same direction at the same time. Of those that do manage to make their way through the uterus, many sperm take the wrong turn and end up in the fallopian tube that does not contain an egg. When all is said and done, only one out of every million sperm manages to find the correct fallopian tube, get close to an egg, and release digestive enzymes that erode the egg's protective outer coating. The moment the first sperm does this, the egg releases a chemical that seals its coating back up and keeps all the other sperm from entering. After triumphing over 199,999,999 of its fellow travelers, this single successful sperm sheds its tail and fertilizes the egg. About 12 hours later, the egg merges with the nuclei of the sperm, and the prenatal development of a unique human being begins.

PRENATAL DEVELOPMENT

That unique human being has a name. A **zygote** is *a fertilized egg that contains chromosomes from both an egg and a sperm*, and from the first moment of its existence, the zygote has one thing in common with the person it will soon become: sex. Each human sperm and each human egg contain 23 *chromosomes*. One of these chromosomes (the 23rd, in fact) comes in two varieties known as X and Y. An egg's 23rd chromosome is always of the X variety, but a sperm's 23rd chromosome can be of either the X or Y variety. If the egg is fertilized by a sperm whose 23rd chromosome is Y, then the zygote is a male (also called an XY). If the egg is fertilized by a sperm whose 23rd chromosome is an X, then the zygote is a female (also called an XX).

The brief lifetime of a zygote is called the **germinal stage**, which is *the 2-week period that begins at conception*. During this stage, the one-celled zygote divides into two cells that then divide into four cells that then divide into eight, and so on. By the time an infant is born, its body contains trillions of cells, each of which came from the original zygote, and each of which contains exactly one set of 23 chromosomes from the sperm and one set of 23 chromosomes from the egg. During the germinal stage, the zygote migrates down the fallopian tube and implants itself in the wall of the uterus. This too is a difficult journey, and about half of zygotes do not complete it, either because they are defective or because they implant themselves in an inhospitable part of the uterus. Male zygotes are especially unlikely to complete this journey, but no one understands why (though several comedians have suggested it's because male zygotes are unwilling to stop and ask for directions).

The moment the zygote successfully implants itself in the uterine wall, it loses its old name and earns a new one: *embryo*. The **embryonic stage** is *a period that starts around the 2nd week after conception and lasts until about the 8th week* (see **FIGURE 11.1**). During this stage, the implanted embryo continues to divide, and its cells begin to differentiate. Although it is only an inch long, the embryo already has arms, legs, and a beating heart. It also has the beginnings of female reproductive organs, and if it is a male embryo, it begins to produce a hormone called testosterone which masculinizes those organs.

The embryo doesn't have a lot of time to get used to its new name because at about 9 weeks it is called a *fetus*. The **fetal stage** is *a period that lasts from about the 9th week after conception until birth*. The fetus has a skeleton and muscles that make it capable

This electron micrograph shows several human sperm, one of which is fertilizing an egg. Contrary to what many people think, fertilization does not happen right away. It typically happens 1 to 2 days after intercourse, but can happen as much as 5 days later.

zygote A fertilized egg that contains chromosomes from both a sperm and an egg.

germinal stage The 2-week period of prenatal development that begins at conception.

embryonic stage The period of prenatal development that lasts from the 2nd week until about the 8th week.

fetal stage The period of prenatal development that lasts from the 9th week until birth.

◄ Figure 11.1

Human beings undergo amazing changes during the 9 months of prenatal development. These images show an embryo at 30 days (about the size of a poppy seed), an embryo at 8 to 9 weeks (about the size of an olive), and a fetus at 5 months (about the size of a pomegranate).

This chimp and boy share a deep interest in dirt, bugs, and leaves. But one big difference between them is that the chimp was born with an almost adult-size brain, whereas the boy was born with a brain that ultimately will nearly quadruple in size.

of movement. It develops a layer of insulating fat beneath its skin, and its digestive and respiratory systems mature. During the fetal stage, brain cells begin to generate axons and dendrites (which allow them to communicate with other brain cells). They also begin to undergo a process (described in the Neuroscience and Behavior chapter) known as **myelination,** which is *the formation of a fatty sheath around the axons of a neuron.* Just as plastic sheathing insulates a wire, myelin insulates a brain cell and prevents the leakage of neural signals that travel along the axon. Myelination starts during the fetal stage, but it doesn't end until adulthood.

The human brain grows rapidly during the fetal period, but unlike the brains of other primates, it does not come close to achieving its adult size. A newborn chimpanzee's brain is nearly 60% of its adult size, but a newborn human's brain is only 25% of its adult size, which is to say that 75% of a human's brain development occurs after birth. Why are humans born with such underdeveloped brains? First, humans have really big heads, and if a newborn baby's head were 60% of its adult size (as a newborn chimp's head is), then the baby could never pass through its mother's birth canal. Second, one of our species' greatest talents is its ability to adapt to a wide range of novel environments that differ in climate, social structure, and so on. So rather than arriving in the world with a highly developed brain that may or may not meet the requirements of its environment, human beings arrive with underdeveloped brains that do much of their developing *within* the very environments in which they ultimately must function, thereby gaining the unique capacities that each environment requires.

PRENATAL ENVIRONMENT

The word *environment* probably makes you think of green fields and blue skies. But the womb is also an environment, and it has a powerful impact on development (Coe & Lubach, 2008; Glynn & Sandman, 2011; Wadhwa, Sandman, & Garite, 2001). For example, a woman's bloodstream is physically connected to the bloodstream of her unborn child, and therefore the foods she eats can affect it. Studies show that infants tend to like the foods and spices that their mothers ate while they were in the womb (Mennella, Johnson, & Beauchamp, 1995). More importantly, the children of women who don't receive enough nutrition during pregnancy are at increased risk for a variety of illnesses, such as schizophrenia and antisocial personality disorder (Neugebauer, Hoek, & Susser, 1999; Susser, Brown, & Matte, 1999). Indeed, almost anything a woman eats, drinks, inhales, injects, sniffs, snorts, or rubs on her skin can enter the unborn child's bloodstream. A **teratogen** is *any substance that passes from mother to unborn child and impairs development.* Teratogens include the mercury in fish, the lead in water, and the paint dust in air. But the most common teratogens can be purchased at the convenience store. **Fetal alcohol syndrome (FAS)** is *a developmental disorder that stems from heavy alcohol use by the mother during pregnancy,* and children with FAS have a variety of brain abnormalities and cognitive deficits (Carmichael Olson et al., 1997; Streissguth et al., 1999). One study that followed children born with FAS for 25 years found that by the age of 14, a stunning 60% had been suspended or expelled from school (Streissguth, 2007). Although some studies suggest that light drinking does not harm the fetus, there is little consensus about how much drinking is light (Warren & Hewitt, 2009). On the other hand, everyone agrees that "none" is a perfectly safe amount.

Tobacco is the other common teratogen, and there is no debate about its effects. About 20% of American mothers admit to smoking during pregnancy (Substance Abuse and Mental Health Services Administration, 2005), and the half million infants to which they annually give birth are smaller (Horta et al., 1997) and more likely to have perceptual and attentional problems in both infancy (Wiebe et al., 2014) and childhood (Espy et al., 2011; Fried & Watkinson, 2000). Even secondhand

myelination The formation of a fatty sheath around the axons of a neuron.

teratogens Any substances that pass from mother to unborn child and impair development.

fetal alcohol syndrome (FAS) A developmental disorder that stems from heavy alcohol use by the mother during pregnancy.

KAREN HUNT/CORBIS

smoke can lead to reduced birth weight and deficits in attention and learning (Makin, Fried, & Watkinson, 1991; Windham, Eaton, & Hopkins, 1999). The embryo is more vulnerable to teratogens than is the fetus, but structures such as the central nervous system are vulnerable throughout the entire prenatal period. Some researchers estimate that if all pregnant women in America quit smoking, there would be an 11% reduction in stillbirths and a 5% reduction in newborn deaths (March of Dimes, 2010).

The prenatal environment is rich with chemicals that affect the unborn child, but it is also rich with auditory information. Wombs are dark because only the brightest light can filter through the mother's abdomen, but they are not quiet. The fetus can hear its mother's heartbeat, the gastrointestinal sounds associated with her digestion, and her voice. Newborns will suck a nipple more vigorously when they hear the sound of their mother's voice than when they hear the voice of a female stranger (Querleu et al., 1984), demonstrating that even at birth they are already more familiar with the former. Newborns who listen to strangers speaking two languages will suck more vigorously when they hear words from their mother's native language—unless their mother happens to be bilingual, in which case they suck equally vigorously to both languages (Byers-Heinlein, Burns, & Werker, 2010). What unborn children hear in the womb even influences the sounds they make at birth: French newborns cry with a rising melody and German newborns with a falling melody, mimicking the cadence of their mother's native tongue (Mampe et al., 2009). Clearly, the fetus is listening.

RICK'S PHOTOGRAPHY/SHUTTERSTOCK

This child has some of the telltale facial features associated with fetal alcohol syndrome (FAS): short eye openings, a flat midface, a flat ridge under the nose, a thin upper lip, and an underdeveloped jaw.

Build to the Outcomes

1. What are the three prenatal stages?

2. Why are human beings born with underdeveloped brains?

3. How does the uterine environment affect the unborn child?

4. What are teratogens?

5. What can a fetus see and hear?

Infancy and Childhood: Doing and Thinking

Newborns may appear to be capable of little more than sleeping, squalling, and squirming, but in the last two decades, researchers have discovered that they are much more sophisticated than they appear. **Infancy** is *the stage of development that begins at birth and lasts between 18 and 24 months,* and as you will see, a lot more happens during this stage than meets the untrained eye.

PERCEPTUAL DEVELOPMENT

New parents like to stand around the crib and make goofy faces at the baby because they think the baby will be amused. But newborns have a fairly limited range of vision: The amount of detail that a newborn can see at a distance of 20 feet is roughly equivalent to the amount of detail that an adult can see at 600 feet (Banks & Salapatek, 1983), which is to say that infants are missing a whole lot of the cribside shenanigans. On the other hand, newborns can see things that are 8 to 12 inches away, which happens to be roughly the distance between a mother's face and her nursing infant's eyes. How do psychologists know what a newborn can and can't see? Experiments! For example, in one study, newborns were shown a circle with diagonal stripes over and over again. The newborns stared a lot at first, and then less and less on each subsequent

Learning Outcomes

▶ Describe the evidence for visual perception in newborns.

▶ Explain the two rules of motor development.

▶ Explain the stages of Piaget's theory of cognitive development.

▶ Explain egocentrism and theory of mind.

▶ Describe the key skills that allow infants to learn from others.

infancy The stage of development that begins at birth and lasts between 18 and 24 months.

Infants mimic the facial expressions of adults—and vice versa, of course!

motor development The emergence of the ability to execute physical action.

motor reflexes Specific motor responses that are triggered by specific patterns of sensory stimulation.

cephalocaudal rule The "top-to-bottom" rule that describes the tendency for motor skills to emerge in sequence from the head to the feet.

proximodistal rule The "inside-to-outside" rule that describes the tendency for motor skills to emerge in sequence from the center to the periphery.

cognitive development The process by which infants and children gain the ability to think and understand.

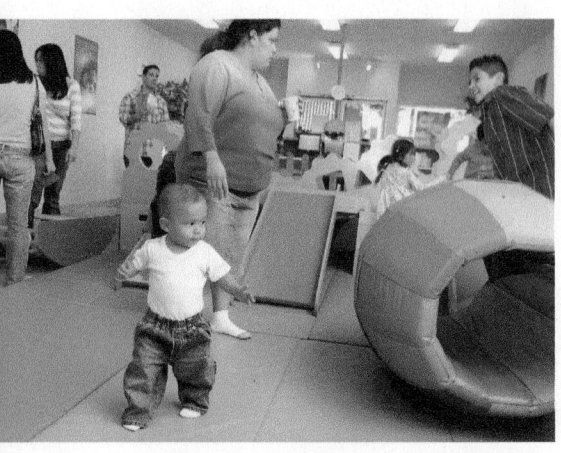

Motor skills develop through practice. In just 1 hour in a playroom, the average 12- to 19-month-old infant takes 2,368 steps, travels 0.4 miles, and falls 17 times (Adolph et al., 2012).

presentation. You'll recall from the Learning chapter that *habituation* is the tendency for organisms to respond less intensely to a stimulus each time it is presented, and infants habituate just as mice do. So what happened when the researchers rotated the circle 90°? The newborns started staring at it again, indicating that they had noticed the change in the circle's orientation (Slater, Morison, & Somers, 1988). By measuring whether changes in a stimulus can reverse habituation, researchers can tell whether a newborn did or didn't see that stimulus.

Newborns can see squares and triangles and diagonal lines, but they are especially attentive to social stimuli (Biro et al., 2014). For example, newborns in one study were shown either a circle, a circle with scrambled facial features, or a circle with a regular face. When the circle was moved across their fields of vision, the newborns tracked the circle by moving their heads and eyes—but they tracked the circle with the regular face longer than they tracked the others (Johnson et al., 1991; cf. Kwon et al., 2016). In another study, researchers stood close to some newborns while sticking out their tongues and stood close to other newborns while pursing their lips. Newborns in the first group stuck out their own tongues more often than those in the second group did, and newborns in the second group pursed their lips more often than those in the first group did (Meltzoff & Moore, 1977). Indeed, newborns have been shown to mimic facial expressions in their very first *hour* of life (Reissland, 1988) and to mimic speech sounds as early as 12 weeks (Kuhl & Meltzoff, 1996). Clearly, the newborn is watching—and what she's watching most closely is us!

MOTOR DEVELOPMENT

Infants can use their eyes and ears right away, but they have to spend a considerable amount of time learning how to use their other parts. **Motor development** is *the emergence of the ability to execute physical actions* such as reaching, grasping, crawling, and walking. Infants can do a bit of this at birth because they are born with a small set of **motor reflexes,** which are *specific motor responses that are triggered by specific patterns of sensory stimulation.* For example, the *rooting reflex* causes infants to move their mouths toward any object that touches their cheek, and the *sucking reflex* causes them to suck any object that enters their mouth. Together, these two reflexes allow newborn infants to find their mother's nipple and begin feeding—a behavior so vitally important that nature took no chances and hard-wired it into every one of us. Interestingly, these and other reflexes that are present at birth seem to disappear in the first few months as infants learn to execute more sophisticated motor behavior.

The development of these more sophisticated behaviors tends to obey two general rules. The first is the **cephalocaudal rule** (or the "top-to-bottom" rule), which describes *the tendency for motor skills to emerge in sequence from the head to the feet.* Infants tend to gain control over their heads first, their arms and trunks next, and their legs last. A young infant who is placed on her stomach may lift her head and her chest by using her arms for support, but she typically has little control over her legs. The second rule is the **proximodistal rule** (or the "inside-to-outside" rule), which describes *the tendency for motor skills to emerge in sequence from the center to the periphery.* Infants learn to control their trunks before their elbows and knees, which they learn to control before their hands and feet (see **FIGURE 11.2**). Although motor skills develop in an orderly sequence, they do not develop on a strict timetable. Rather, the timing of these skills is influenced by many factors, such as the infant's incentive for reaching, body weight, muscular development, and general level of activity.

COGNITIVE DEVELOPMENT

So infants can hear and see and move their bodies. But can they think? In the first half of the 20th century, a Swiss biologist named Jean Piaget became interested in this question. **Cognitive development** is *the process by which infants and*

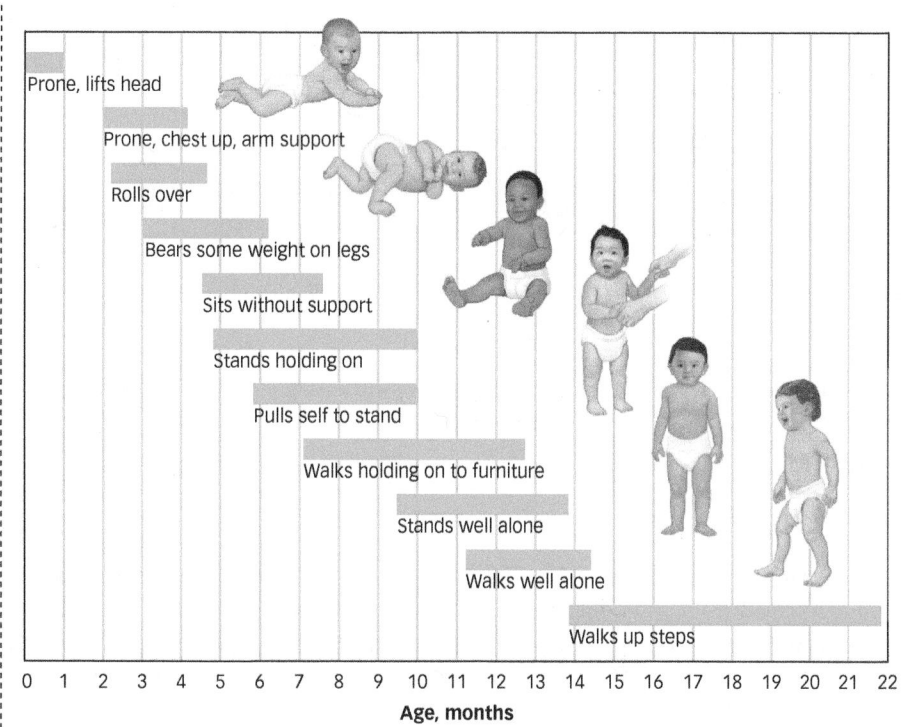

◀ **Figure 11.2**
MOTOR DEVELOPMENT Infants learn to control their bodies from head to feet and from center to periphery. These skills do not emerge on a strict timetable, but they do emerge in a strict sequence.

Jean Piaget (1896–1980) was the father of modern developmental psychology, as well as the last man who actually looked cool wearing a beret.

children gain the ability to think and understand. Piaget suggested that during this process, infants and children learn how the physical world works, how their own minds work, and how other people's minds work. Let's see how they achieve these essential understandings.

Discovering the World

Piaget (1954) suggested that cognitive development occurs in four discrete stages: the *sensorimotor* stage, the *preoperational* stage, the *concrete operational* stage, and the *formal operational* stage (see **TABLE 11.1**). The **sensorimotor stage** is *a stage of cognitive development that begins at birth and lasts through infancy.* As the word *sensorimotor* suggests, infants at this stage are mainly busy using their ability to *sense* and their ability to *move* to acquire information about the world.

By actively exploring their environments with their eyes, mouths, and fingers, infants begin to construct **schemas**, which are *theories about the way the world works.* As every scientist knows, the good thing about theories is that they allow us to predict what will happen next. If an infant learns that tugging at a stuffed animal brings the toy closer, then that observation is incorporated into the infant's theory about how physical objects behave ("Things come closer if I pull them"), and the infant can later use that theory when she wants a different object to come closer, such as a rattle or a ball. Piaget called this **assimilation**, which happens when *infants apply their schemas in novel situations.* Of course, if the infant applies this theory to the family cat, the cat is likely to sprint in the opposite direction. Infants' theories about the world are occasionally disconfirmed by experience, which causes infants to take special notice (Stahl & Feigenson, 2015) and to adjust their theories ("Inanimate things come closer when I pull them, but animate things just hiss and run"). Piaget called this **accommodation**, which happens when *infants revise their schemas in light of new information.*

What kinds of schemas do infants develop, apply, and adjust? Piaget suggested that infants are surprisingly clueless about some of the most basic properties of the physical world and must acquire information about those properties through experience. For example, when you put your shoes in the closet, you know that they are

sensorimotor stage A stage of cognitive development that begins at birth and lasts through infancy, during which infants acquire information about the world by sensing it and moving around within it.

schemas Theories about the way the world works.

assimilation The process by which infants apply their schemas in novel situations.

accommodation The process by which infants revise their schemas in light of new information.

object permanence The fact that objects continue to exist even when they are not visible.

TABLE 11.1	
Piaget's Four Stages of Cognitive Development	
Stage	**Characteristic**
Sensorimotor (Birth–2 years)	Infant experiences world through movement and senses, develops schemas, begins to act intentionally, and shows evidence of understanding object permanence.
Preoperational (2–6 years)	Child acquires motor skills but does not understand conservation of physical properties. Child begins this stage by thinking egocentrically but ends with a basic understanding of other minds.
Concrete operational (6–11 years)	Child can think logically about physical objects and events and understands conservation of physical properties.
Formal operational (11 years and up)	Child can think logically about abstract propositions and hypotheticals.

MICHAEL HAGEDORN/CORBIS

During the sensorimotor stage, infants explore with their hands and mouths, learning important lessons about the physical world such as, "If you smear enough jelly on your face, someone will probably take your picture."

still there even after you close the closet door, and you would be kind of surprised if you opened the door a moment later and found the closet empty. But according to Piaget, this wouldn't surprise an infant because infants do not have a theory of **object permanence**, which refers to *the fact that objects exist even when they are not visible.* Piaget noted that in the first few months of life, infants act as though objects stop existing the moment they are out of sight. For instance, he observed that a 2-month-old infant will track a moving object with her eyes, but once the object leaves her visual field, she will not search for it. Put the shoes in the closet and—poof!—the infant acts as if they no longer exist.

But does that really mean that infants don't realize that objects have permanence? To answer that question definitively, of course, we'd have to know what infants are thinking, which Piaget thought was impossible: "The child's first year of life is unfortunately still an abyss of mysteries for the psychologist. If only we could know what is going on in a baby's mind while observing him in action, we could certainly understand everything there is to psychology" (1927/1977, p. 199). But there's nothing scientists love more than an abyss of mysteries, and during the 1960s, the psychologist Robert Fantz (1964) developed an ingenious technique for finding out what is "going on in a baby's mind." The logic of his *preferential looking time* technique is simple. Check out the objects in **FIGURE 11.3**. The odds are very good that you looked longer at A than at B. Why? Because A is an "impossible object." You found it interesting precisely because it violates your beliefs about how the physical world works. Now, here's the cool part: Because you naturally stare longer at things that violate your beliefs, psychologists can use the duration of your stare to figure out what those beliefs must be! Your mind is no longer an abyss of mysteries. It is open to investigation.

When psychologists used this simple technique with infants, they quickly discovered that infants know more about object permanence than Piaget ever suspected. For instance, in one study, infants were shown a miniature drawbridge that flipped up and down (see **FIGURE 11.4**). Once the infants got used to this, they watched as a solid box was placed behind the drawbridge—in the path of the drawbridge, but out of the infant's sight. Some infants then saw a *possible* event: The drawbridge began to flip and then it suddenly stopped, as if its motion was being impeded by the unseen solid box. Other infants saw an *impossible* event: The drawbridge began to flip—and then it didn't stop, as if its motion was unimpeded by the unseen solid box. So what did infants do? Four-month-old infants stared longer at the impossible event than at the possible event (Baillargeon, Spelke, & Wasserman, 1985). Of course, the only thing that made the impossible event impossible was the fact that an unseen box should have—but didn't—impede the motion of the drawbridge. Clearly, infants realized that

(a)   (b)

◄ Figure 11.3

BUT...THAT'S IMPOSSIBLE! Which of these pictures did you look at longer? What does that reveal about your theory of the physical world?

a box continues to exist even when it can no longer be seen. These and other studies show that infants acquire a theory of object permanence much earlier than Piaget suspected (Shinskey & Munakata, 2005; Wang & Baillargeon, 2008).

Discovering the Mind

The long period following infancy is called **childhood**, which is *the period that begins at about 18 to 24 months and lasts until about 11 to 14 years*. According to Piaget, children enter childhood at one stage of cognitive development and leave at another. They enter at the **preoperational stage**, which is *the stage of cognitive development that begins at about 2 years and ends at about 6 years, during which children develop a preliminary understanding of the physical world*. They exit at the **concrete operational stage**, which is *the stage of cognitive development that begins at about 6 years and ends at about 11 years, during which children learn how actions, or operations, can transform the concrete objects of the physical world*.

The difference between these stages is nicely illustrated by one of Piaget's clever experiments in which he showed children a row of cups and asked them to place an egg in each. Preoperational children were able to do this, and afterward they readily agreed that there were just as many eggs as there were cups. Then Piaget removed the eggs and spread them out in a long line that extended beyond the row of cups.

childhood The stage of development that begins at about 18 to 24 months and lasts until adolescence, which begins between 11 and 14 years.

preoperational stage The stage of cognitive development that begins at about 2 years and ends at about 6 years, during which children develop a preliminary understanding of the physical world.

concrete operational stage The stage of cognitive development that begins at about 6 years and ends at about 11 years, during which children learn how various actions, or *operations*, can affect or transform *concrete* objects.

(a)

Habituation   Possible event   Impossible event

(b)

◄ Figure 11.4

THE IMPOSSIBLE EVENT (a) During the initial trials, infants watch a drawbridge flip back and forth with nothing in its path until they grow bored. During the test trials, a box is placed behind the drawbridge, and the infants are shown either a possible event (in which the motion of the drawbridge is impeded) or an impossible event (in which the motion of the drawbridge is not impeded). (b) The graph shows the infants' looking times during the initial trials and the test trials. During the test trials, their interest was reawakened by the impossible event but not by the possible event (Baillargeon, Spelke, & Wasserman, 1985).

conservation The notion that the quantitative properties of an object are invariant despite changes in the object's appearance.

formal operational stage The final stage of cognitive development that begins around the age of 11, during which children learn to reason about abstract concepts.

egocentrism The failure to understand that the world appears different to different people.

When preoperational children are shown two equal-size glasses filled with equal amounts of liquid, they correctly say that neither glass "has more." But when the contents of one glass are poured into a taller, thinner glass, they incorrectly say that the taller glass now "has more." Concrete operational children don't make this mistake, because they recognize that operations such as pouring change the appearance of the liquid but not its actual volume.

People who reach the formal operational stage can reason about abstract concepts such as freedom and justice. These two protesters are taking part in a demonstration in front of the White House, calling for the closing of the U.S. military prison at Guantánamo Bay, Cuba.

Preoperational children incorrectly claimed that there were now more eggs than cups, pointing out that the row of eggs was longer than the row of cups and hence there must be more of them. Concrete operational children, on the other hand, correctly reported that the number of eggs did not change when they were spread out in a longer line. They understood that *quantity* is a property of a set of concrete objects that does not change when an operation such as *spreading out* alters the set's appearance (Piaget, 1954). Piaget called the child's insight **conservation**, which is *the notion that the quantitative properties of an object are invariant despite changes in the object's appearance.*

Why don't preoperational children grasp the notion of conservation? Adults naturally distinguish between the subjective and the objective, between appearances and realities, between the way things look and the way things are. We know that a wagon can *be* red but *look* gray at dusk, and that a highway can *be* dry but *look* wet in the heat. Visual illusions delight us precisely because we know that they look one way when they are really another. But preoperational children don't make this distinction. They assume that things are as they seem, that what's in their minds is also in the world, and that when something *looks* gray or wet it must *be* gray or wet. As they move from the preoperational to the concrete operational stage, they come to realize that the way the world *appears* and the way the world *is* are sometimes very different things.

Once children have this epiphany, they can suddenly solve problems that require them to ignore an object's subjective appearance (Lane et al., 2014; cf. Deák, 2006). They can understand that when a ball of clay is rolled, stretched, or flattened, it is still the same amount of clay despite the fact that it looks larger in one form than in another. They can understand that when water is poured from a short, wide beaker into a tall, thin cylinder, it is still the same amount of water despite the fact that the water level in the cylinder is higher. They can understand that when a sponge is painted gray to look like a rock, it is still a sponge despite its appearance. In short, they understand that certain operations—such as squishing, pouring, and spreading out—can change what an object *looks* like without changing what the object *is* like.

Children learn to solve physical problems at the concrete operational stage, and they learn to solve nonphysical problems at the **formal operational stage**, which is *the final stage of cognitive development that begins around the age of 11, during which children learn to reason about abstract concepts.* Childhood ends when formal operations begin, and people who move on to this stage (and Piaget believed that some people never do) are able to reason systematically about abstract concepts such as *liberty* and *love* and about hypotheticals and counterfactuals—about events that have not yet happened, and about events that might have happened but didn't. There are no concrete objects in the world to which words such as *liberating* or *loving* refer, and yet people at the formal operational stage can think and reason about such concepts in the same way that a concrete operational child can think and reason about squishing and folding. The ability to generate, consider, reason about, or mentally "operate on" abstract objects, is the hallmark of formal operations.

Discovering Other Minds

As children develop, they discover their own minds. But they also discover the minds of others. Because preoperational children don't fully grasp the fact that they have minds that mentally represent objects, they also don't fully grasp the fact that other people have minds that may mentally represent the same objects in different ways. That's why preoperational children mistakenly expect others to see the world as they do. When 3-year-old children are asked what a person on the opposite side of a table is seeing, they typically claim that the other person sees what they see. **Egocentrism** is *the failure to understand that the world appears different to different people.* Egocentrism is a hallmark of the preoperational stage and it reveals itself in a variety of interesting ways.

Perceptions and Beliefs. Just as 3-year-old children don't realize that other people don't see what they see, they also don't realize that other people don't know what they know. This fact has been demonstrated in hundreds of studies using *the false-belief task* (Wimmer & Perner, 1983). In the standard version of this task, children see a puppet named Maxi deposit some chocolate in a cupboard and then leave the room. A second puppet arrives a moment later, finds the chocolate, and moves it to a different cupboard. The children are then asked where Maxi will look for the chocolate when he returns: in the first cupboard where he initially put it, or in the second cupboard, where the children know it currently is? Most 5-year-olds realize that Maxi will search the first cupboard because Maxi did not see what the children saw, namely, that the chocolate was moved. But 3-year-olds typically claim that Maxi will look in the second cupboard. Why? Because that's where *the children* know the chocolate is—and they assume that what they know, everyone knows! Children are able to give the right answer in the false-belief task somewhere between the ages of 4 to 6 (Callaghan et al., 2005), and children in some cultures are able to give it earlier than children in others (Liu et al., 2008).

But some researchers think that the false-belief task, like Piaget's test for object permanence, doesn't allow very young children to demonstrate their true abilities, and several recent studies have shown that much younger children perform surprisingly well in modified versions of the false-belief task (Baillargeon, Scott, & He, 2010; Onishi & Baillargeon, 2005; Rubin-Fernandez & Geurts, 2012; Senju et al., 2011; Southgate, Senju, & Csibra, 2007). Still, it isn't clear whether very young children arrive at the right answer the same way that older children do, namely, by truly understanding that other people can have beliefs that differ from their own (Apperly & Butterfill, 2009; Low & Watts, 2013). Nonetheless, whatever very young children are doing, their performances are impressive, and it seems clear that children begin to understand the nature of other minds earlier than Piaget suspected.

Just as egocentrism affects children's understandings of others' minds, so too does it affect their understanding of their own minds. Researchers showed young children an M&M box and then opened it, revealing that it contained pencils instead of candy. Then the researchers closed the box and asked, "When I first showed you the box all closed up like this, what did you think was inside?" Although most 5-year-olds said M&Ms, most 3-year-olds said pencils (Gopnik & Astington, 1988). To a 3-year-old child, a past self is like another person, and he assumes that his past self must have known then what his present self knows now.

Desires and Emotions. Different people have different perceptions and beliefs. They also have different desires and emotions. Do children understand that these aspects of other people's mental lives may also differ from their own? Surprisingly, even very young children who do not yet fully understand that others have different perceptions or beliefs do seem to understand that other people have different desires. For example, a 2-year-old who likes dogs can understand that other children don't like dogs and can correctly predict that other children will avoid dogs that the child herself would approach. When 18-month-old toddlers see an adult express disgust while eating a food that the toddlers enjoy, they hand the adult a different food, as if they understand that different people have different tastes (Repacholi & Gopnik, 1997). Interestingly, young children understand other people's desires best when their own desires have already been fulfilled and are not competing for their attention (Atance, Bélanger, & Meltzoff, 2010).

In contrast, children take a much longer time to understand that other people may have emotional reactions unlike their own. When 5-year-olds hear a story in which Little Red Riding Hood knocks on her grandmother's door, unaware that a wolf is inside waiting to devour her, they realize that Little Red Riding Hood does not know what they know; nonetheless, they expect Little Red Riding Hood to feel what they

COURTESY OF DANIEL GILBERT

When small children are told to hide, they sometimes cover their eyes. Because they can't see you, they assume that you can't see them (Russell, Gee, & Bullard, 2012).

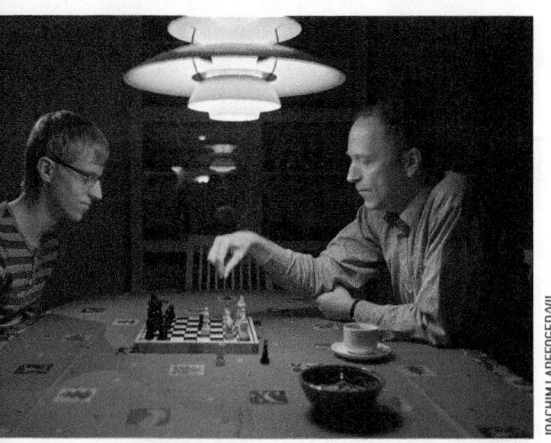

People with autism often have an unusual ability to concentrate on small details, words, and numbers for extended periods of time. Thorkil Sonne (*right*) started a company called Specialisterne.com, which places people with autism—such as his son Lars (*left*)—at jobs that they can do better than more "neurotypical" people can.

feel, namely, fear (Bradmetz & Schneider, 2004; de Rosnay et al., 2004; Harris et al., 1989). When asked where Maxi will look for the chocolate that was moved while Maxi was out of the room, they correctly say that Maxi will look in the original location, but they incorrectly say that Maxi feels sad. It is only at about 6 years of age that children come to understand that because they and others have different knowledge, they and others may also experience different emotions in the same situation.

Theory of Mind. Clearly, children have a whole lot to learn about how the mind works—and most of them eventually do. The vast majority of children ultimately come to understand that they and others have minds and that these minds represent the world in different ways. Once children understand these things, they are said to have acquired a **theory of mind**, which is *the understanding that the mind produces representations of the world and that these representations guide behavior.*

The age at which most children acquire a theory of mind appears to be influenced by a variety of factors, such as the number of siblings the child has, the frequency with which the child engages in pretend play, whether the child has an imaginary companion, the socioeconomic status of the child's family, and even culture (see A World of Difference: That's the Dumbest Thing I Never Heard!). But of all the factors researchers have studied, language seems to be the most important (Astington & Baird, 2005). Children's language skills are an excellent predictor of how well they perform on false-belief tasks (Happé, 1995). The way that caregivers talk to children is also a good predictor of how well children perform on these tasks. Perhaps not surprisingly, children whose caregivers frequently talk about thoughts and feelings tend to be good at understanding beliefs and belief-based emotions. Some psychologists speculate that children benefit from hearing psychological words such as *want, think, know,* and *sad.* Others suggest that children benefit from the grammatically complex sentences that typically contain these psychological words. Yet other psychologists believe that caregivers who use psychological words are also more effective in getting children to reflect on mental states. Whatever the explanation, it is clear that language—and especially language about thoughts and feelings—is an important tool for helping children make sense of their own and others' minds (Harris, de Rosnay, & Pons, 2005). This fact also helps explain why deaf children whose parents do not know sign language are slow to acquire a theory of mind (DeVilliers, 2005; Peterson & Siegal, 1999; Peterson et al., 2016; Pyers & Senghas, 2009).

Another group of people who are slow to acquire a theory of mind are children with *autism*, a disorder we'll cover in more depth in the Disorders chapter. Although children with autism are typically normal on most intellectual dimensions—and sometimes far better than normal—they have difficulty understanding the inner lives of other people (Dawson et al., 2007; Peterson et al., 2016). They do not seem to understand that other people can have false beliefs (Baron-Cohen, Leslie, & Frith, 1985; Senju et al., 2009), and they have special trouble understanding belief-based emotions such as embarrassment and shame (Baron-Cohen, 1991; Heerey, Keltner, & Capps, 2003). Autistic children typically have difficulty communicating with other people and making friends, and some psychologists have suggested that this is because they have trouble acquiring a theory of mind (Frith, 2003). Interestingly, children with autism and other children who have not yet acquired a theory of mind are not susceptible to the phenomenon of "contagious yawning," which apparently requires one to imagine what the yawner is experiencing (Platek et al., 2003; Senju et al., 2007).

Piaget Remixed. Cognitive development is a strange and complex journey, and Piaget's ideas about it were nothing short of groundbreaking. Few psychologists have had such a profound impact on their fields. Many of his ideas have held up quite well, but in the last few decades, psychologists have discovered two general ways in which Piaget got it wrong. First, Piaget thought that children graduated from one stage to another in the same way that they graduated from kindergarten to first grade: A child

theory of mind The understanding that the mind produces representations of the world and that these representations guide behavior.

That's the Dumbest Thing I Never Heard!

Everyone sees the world a bit differently. That's obvious to you. But it isn't obvious to a 2-year-old child, who naturally assumes that her view is everyone else's view as well. As children develop, they acquire a theory of mind, and one component of that theory is the realization that other people may believe things that the child doesn't, and may not believe things that the child does.

But where does that realization come from? Does a light bulb just switch on at some point, leaving the child permanently illuminated? Piaget didn't think so. He thought children came to this realization in the course of their social interactions, where they inevitably encountered disagreement. A child says, "That dog is mean," and his father replies, "No, he's very nice." A playmate says, "My house is red," and another responds, "You're nuts. It's blue!" All of the disagreeable talk that children hear eventually leads them to understand that different people have different beliefs about the world.

Although being disagreeable is a popular pastime in Western societies, not all cultures appreciate a good shouting match as much as Americans do. For instance, many Eastern cultures encourage respect for one's elders and family harmony, and encourage people to avoid arguments and conflicts. In these cultures, if a person doesn't have something agreeable to say, they often say nothing at all. Thus, children who grow up in these cultures do not normally hear people challenging each other's beliefs—so how do they come to understand that different people *have* different beliefs?

The answer seems to be: s-l-o-w-l-y! For example, in one study, 77% of Australian preschoolers understood that different people have different beliefs, but only 47% of Iranian preschoolers understood the same (Shahaeian et al., 2011). Were the Iranian children just slow learners? Nope. In fact, they were just as likely as the Australian children to have acquired other components of a theory of mind—for example, the realization that different people *like* different things—and they were even *more* likely than the Australian children to realize that people know what they see and not what they don't. Iranian preschoolers appear to learn just as fast as Australian preschoolers do. It just takes them a bit longer to understand that people have different beliefs because they are exposed to fewer debates about them. The pattern seen in Australia is also seen in the United States, and the pattern seen in Iran is also seen in China, suggesting that this is a stable difference between Western and Eastern cultures (Wellman et al., 2006).

In the end, of course, everyone comes to realize that human beings don't always see eye to eye. But people who live in places where they are encouraged to speak their minds and debate their differences in public seem to figure that out a bit earlier than most. At least that's what research suggests. Do you agree? Well, why not? What's the matter with you anyway?

▲ When parents debate the best way to get a bike into a car, their children learn that people have different beliefs. For example, Mom believes that Dad should shut up, and Dad doesn't believe that. Yet.

PHOTOALTO/LAURENCE MOUTON/GETTY IMAGES

---

is in kindergarten *or* first grade, he is never in both, and there is an exact moment of transition to which anyone with a calendar can point. Modern psychologists see development as a more fluid, continuous, and less steplike progression than Piaget believed it was. Children who are making the transition between stages may perform more mature behaviors one day and less mature behaviors the next. In a sense, cognitive development is more like the gradual change of seasons than it is like graduation day.

The second thing about which Piaget was mistaken was the ages at which these transitions occur. By and large, they happen *earlier* than he realized (Gopnik, 2012). For example, Piaget suggested that infants had no sense of object permanence because they did not actively search for objects that were moved out of their sight. But when researchers use experimental procedures that allow infants to "show what they know," even 4-month-olds display a sense of object permanence. Piaget suggested that it takes many years until children can overcome their egocentrism enough to realize that others do not know what they know, but new experimental procedures have detected some evidence of this understanding in 13-month-old infants (Baillargeon et al., 2010). Every year, clever researchers find new ways of testing infants and children, and every year, textbook authors must lower the age at which cognitive milestones are achieved. Don't be too surprised if in the coming years, someone discovers that zygotes can do algebra.

Development is not the steplike progression that Piaget imagined. Children who are making the transition between stages may act more mature one day and less mature the next.

KOLOBO4EK/GETTY IMAGES

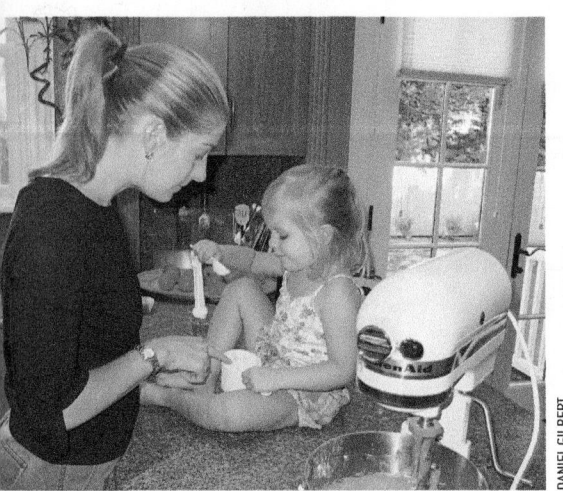

As Vygotsky pointed out, children are not lone explorers who discover the world for themselves but members of families, communities, and societies that teach them much of what they need to know.

DANIEL GILBERT

Discovering Our Cultures

Piaget saw the child as a lone scientist who went out into the world and made observations, developed theories, and then revised those theories in light of new observations. But scientists rarely go it alone. Rather, they receive training from more experienced scientists, inherit the theories and methods of their forebears, and seek each other's opinions. According to the Russian psychologist Lev Vygotsky, children do the same thing. Vygotsky was born in 1896, the same year as Piaget, but unlike Piaget, he believed that cognitive development was largely the result of the child's interaction with members of his or her own culture rather than his or her interaction with rocks, paper, scissors, and other concrete objects. Vygotsky noted that cultural tools, such as language and counting systems, exert a strong influence on cognitive development (Vygotsky, 1978).

Consider one example. In both English and Chinese, the numbers beyond 20 are named by a decade (twenty) that is followed by a digit (one), and their names follow a logical pattern (twenty-one, twenty-two, twenty-three, etc.). In Chinese, the numbers from 11 to 19 are constructed the same way (ten-one, ten-two, ten-three . . .). But in English, the names of the numbers between 11 and 19 either reverse the order of the decade and the digit (sixteen, seventeen) or are just plain arbitrary (eleven, twelve). The difference in the regularity of these two systems makes a big difference to the children who must learn them. The fact that 12 is a 10 plus a 2 is obvious to the Chinese child, who actually calls the number "ten-two," but not so obvious to the English-speaking child, who calls it "twelve." In one study, children from many countries were asked to hand an experimenter a certain number of bricks. Some of the bricks were single, and some were glued together in strips of 10. When Asian children were asked to hand the experimenter 26 bricks, they tended to hand over two strips of 10 plus six singles. Non-Asian children used the clumsier strategy of counting out 26 single bricks (Miura et al., 1994). Results such as these suggest that the regularity of the counting system that children inherit can promote or discourage their discovery of basic mathematical facts (Gordon, 2004; Imbo & LeFevre, 2009).

Human children can take advantage of the accumulated wisdom of their species because unlike most animals, they have three essential skills that allow them to learn from others (Meltzoff et al., 2009; Striano & Reid, 2006):

▶ If an adult turns her head to the left, young infants (3 months) and older infants (9 months) will look to the left. But if the adult first closes her eyes and then looks to the left, the young infant will look to the left, but the older infant will not (Brooks & Meltzoff, 2002). This suggests that younger infants are following the adult's head movements, but that older infants are following her gaze. They are trying to see what they think she is seeing. If older infants can hear but not see an adult, they will use auditory cues to determine which way the adult must be looking and will then look in that direction (Rossano, Carpenter, & Tomasello, 2012). The ability to focus on what another person is focused on is known as *joint attention* and is a prerequisite for learning what others have to teach (Sodian & Kristen-Antonow, 2015; see **FIGURE 11.5**).

▶ Infants are natural mimics who often do what they see adults do (Jones, 2007). But very early on, infants begin to mimic adults' *intentions* rather than their actions per se. When an 18-month-old sees an adult's hand slip as the adult tries to pull the lid off a jar, the infant won't copy the slip, but will instead perform the *intended* action of removing the lid (Meltzoff, 1995, 2007; Yu & Kushnir, 2014). The tendency to do what an adult does—or what an adult meant to do—is known as *imitation*. By the age of 3, children begin to copy adults so precisely that they will even copy parts of actions that they know to be pointless, a phenomenon called *overimitation* (Lyons, Young, & Keil, 2007; Simpson & Riggs, 2011).

(a)

(b)

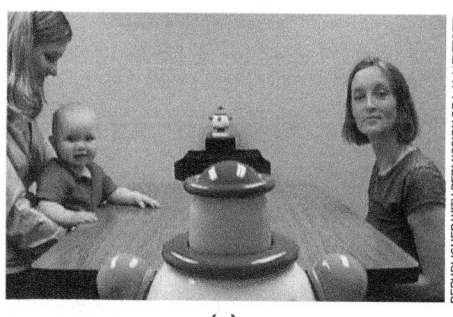
(c)

REPUBLISHED WITH PERMISSION OF A. N. MELTZOFF, P. K. KUHL, T. J. SENJOWSKI, & J. MOVELLAN. "FOUNDATIONS FOR A NEW SCIENCE OF LEARNING" PUBLISHED IN *SCIENCE*, 2009, VOL. 325, JULY 17, PP. 284–288; PERMISSION CONVEYED THROUGH COPYRIGHT CLEARANCE CENTER.

▶ An infant who approaches a new toy will often stop and look back to examine her mother's face for cues about whether Mom thinks the toy is or isn't danger-ous. The ability to use another person's reactions as information about how we should think about the world is known as *social referencing* (Kim, Walden, & Knieps, 2010; Walden & Ogan, 1988).

Joint attention ("I see what you see"), imitation ("I do what you do"), and social refer-encing ("I think what you think") are three of the basic abilities that allow infants to learn from other members of their species (Heyes, 2016).

▲ Figure 11.5

JOINT ATTENTION Joint attention allows children to learn from others. When a 12-month-old infant interacts with an adult (a) who then looks at an object (b), the infant will typically look at the same object (c)—but only when the adult's eyes are open (Meltzoff et al., 2009)

Build to the Outcomes

1. Why are infants born with reflexes?

2. What happens at each of Piaget's stages of cognitive development?

3. What does the false-belief task demonstrate?

4. Do children understand emotions better or worse than they understand beliefs?

5. Which children have special difficulty acquiring a theory of mind?

6. How does culture affect cognitive development?

Infancy and Childhood: Caring and Belonging

Unlike baby turtles, baby humans cannot survive without their caregivers. But what exactly do caregivers provide? Some obvious answers are warmth, safety, and food, and those obvious answers are right. But caregivers also provide something that is far less obvious but every bit as essential to an infant's development.

SOCIAL DEVELOPMENT

During World War II, psychologists studied infants who were living in orphanages while awaiting adoption. Although these children were warm, safe, and well fed, many were developmentally impaired, both physically and psychologically, and nearly 40% died before they could be adopted (Spitz, 1949). A few years later, the psychologist Harry Harlow (1958; Harlow & Harlow, 1965) discovered that infant rhesus monkeys that were warm, safe, and well fed, but were not allowed any social contact for the first 6 months of their lives, developed a variety of behavioral abnormalities. They compulsively rocked back and forth while biting themselves, and if they were intro-duced to other monkeys, they avoided them entirely. These socially isolated monkeys

Learning Outcomes

▶ Describe attachment and its four styles.

▶ Compare Piaget's and Kohlberg's theories of moral development.

▶ Explain the moral intuitionist perspective.

Harlow's monkeys preferred the comfort and warmth of a soft cloth mother (*left*) to the wire mother (*right*), even when the wire mother was associated with food.

PHOTO RESEARCHERS, INC.

PHOTO RESEARCHERS, INC.

turned out to be incapable of communicating with or learning from others of their kind, and when the females matured and became mothers, they ignored, rejected, and sometimes even attacked their own infants. Harlow also discovered that when socially isolated monkeys were put in a cage with two "artificial mothers"—one that was made of wire and dispensed food and one that was made of cloth and dispensed no food—they spent most of their time clinging to the soft cloth mother despite the fact that the wire mother was the source of their nourishment. Clearly, these infants required something more from their caregivers than mere sustenance. But what?

Becoming Attached

When Konrad Lorenz was a child, he became the proud owner of a duck, and he quickly noticed something very interesting. Several decades later, the thing he had noticed helped him win the Nobel Prize. As he explained in his acceptance speech, "From a neighbor, I got a one-day-old duckling and found, to my intense joy, that it transferred its following response to my person." Ducklings normally follow their mother everywhere she goes, and what Lorenz discovered as a child (and then proved scientifically as an adult) is that new hatchlings will faithfully follow the first moving object to which they are exposed. If that object is a human being or a tennis ball, then the hatchling will ignore its mother and follow that object instead. Lorenz theorized that nature designed birds so that the first moving object they saw was *imprinted* on their brains as "the thing I must always stay near" (Lorenz, 1952).

The psychiatrist John Bowlby was fascinated by Lorenz's work, as well as by Harlow's studies of rhesus monkeys reared in isolation and the work on children reared in orphanages, and he sought to understand how human infants form attachments to their caregivers (Bowlby, 1969, 1973, 1980). Bowlby began by noting that from the moment they are born, ducks waddle after their mothers, and monkeys cling to their mothers' furry chests, because the newborns of both species must stay close to their caregivers to survive. Human infants, he suggested, have a similar need, but because they are much less physically developed than ducks or monkeys, they can neither waddle nor cling. So what they do instead is smile and cry. Because they do not have webbed feet or furry hands that allow them to stay close to their caregivers, they use what they do have to keep their caregivers close to them. When an infant cries, gurgles, coos, makes eye contact, or smiles, most adults reflexively move toward the infant. Smiles and cries are signals to which adults respond.

According to Bowlby, infants initially send these signals to anyone within visual or auditory range, and they keep a "mental tally" of who responds most often and most promptly to their signals. Then, at about six months, they begin to target the best and fastest responder, also known as the *primary caregiver*. This person quickly becomes

JOHN ST. GERMAIN/ALAMY

PETER BURIAN/CORBIS

Like hatchlings, human infants need to stay close to their mothers to survive. Unlike hatchlings, human infants know how to get their mothers to come to them rather than the other way around.

the emotional center of the infant's universe. Infants feel secure in the primary caregiver's presence and will happily crawl around, exploring their environments with their eyes, ears, fingers, and mouths. But if their primary caregiver gets too far away, infants begin to feel insecure, and they take action to decrease the distance between themselves and their primary caregiver, perhaps by crawling toward their caregiver or perhaps by crying until their caregiver moves toward them. Bowlby believed that all of this happens because evolution has equipped human infants with a social reflex that is every bit as basic as the physical reflexes that cause them to suck and to grasp. Human infants, Bowlby suggested, are predisposed to form an **attachment**—that is, *an emotional bond*—with a primary caregiver.

Infants who are deprived of the opportunity to become attached experience a variety of negative consequences (Gillespie & Nemeroff, 2007; O'Connor & Rutter, 2000; Rutter, O'Connor, & the English and Romanian Adoptees Study Team, 2004). And even when attachment does happen, it can happen more or less successfully (Ainsworth et al., 1978). The **Strange Situation**, *a behavioral test used to determine a child's attachment style,* involves bringing a child and his or her primary caregiver (usually the child's mother) to a laboratory room and then staging a series of episodes in which the primary caregiver briefly leaves the room and then returns. Infants tend to react to this in one of four ways that are known as *attachment styles.*

> ▶ About 60% of American infants have a *secure* attachment style. When the caregiver leaves, the infant may or may not be distressed. When she returns, the nondistressed infant acknowledges her with a glance or greeting, and the distressed infant goes to her and is calmed by her presence.

> ▶ About 20% of American infants have an *avoidant* attachment style. When the caregiver leaves, the infant is not distressed, and when she returns, the infant does not acknowledge her.

> ▶ About 15% of American infants have an *ambivalent* attachment style. When the caregiver leaves, the infant is distressed, and when she returns, the infant rebuffs her, refusing any attempt at calming while arching his back and squirming to get away.

> ▶ About 5% or fewer American infants have a *disorganized* attachment style. These infants show no consistent pattern of response to their caregiver's leaving and returning.

Research has shown that an infant's behavior in the Strange Situation correlates fairly well with his or her behavior at home (Solomon & George, 1999; see **FIGURE 11.6**). Nonetheless, it is not unusual for an infant's attachment style to change over time (Lamb, Sternberg, & Prodromidis, 1992). And although some aspects of attachment styles appear to be stable across cultures (e.g., secure attachment is the most common style all over the world; van IJzendoorn & Kroonenberg, 1988), other aspects of attachment styles vary across cultures. For example, German children are more likely to have avoidant than ambivalent attachment styles, whereas Japanese children are more likely to have ambivalent than avoidant attachment styles (Takahashi, 1986).

The Origin of Attachment Styles

A child's attachment style is determined in part by the child's biology. Different children are born with different **temperaments**, or *characteristic patterns of emotional reactivity* (Thomas & Chess, 1977). Whether measured by parents' reports or by physiological indices such as heart rate or cerebral blood flow, very young children vary in their tendency toward fearfulness, irritability, activity, positive affect, and other emotional traits (Rothbart & Bates, 1998). About 40% can be classified as *easy babies* who adjust easily to new situations, quickly establish routines, and are generally cheerful and easy to calm; about 10% can be classified as *difficult babies* who are slow to adjust

Children are naturally social creatures who readily develop relationships with caregivers and peers. Toddlers who spend time with a responsive robot will begin to treat it like a classmate instead of like a toy (Tanaka, Cicourel, & Movellan, 2007).

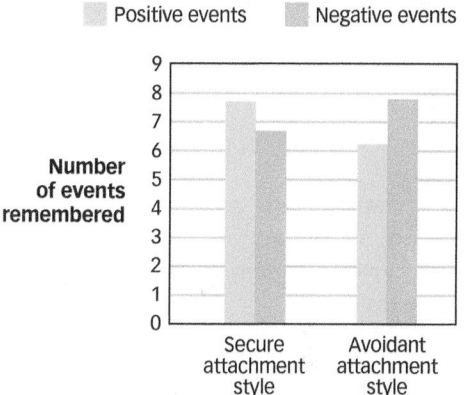

▲ **Figure 11.6**

ATTACHMENT STYLE AND MEMORY We often remember best those events that fit our view of the world. Researchers assessed 1-year-old children's attachment styles with the Strange Situation task. Two years later, the same group of children were shown a puppet show in which some happy events (e.g., the puppet got a present) or unhappy events (e.g., the puppet spilled his juice) occurred. Securely attached children later remembered more of the happy events than the unhappy ones, but insecurely attached children showed the opposite pattern (Belsky, Spritz, & Crnic, 1996).

attachment The emotional bond that forms between newborns and their primary caregivers.

Strange Situation A behavioral test that is used to determine a child's attachment style.

temperaments Characteristic patterns of emotional reactivity.

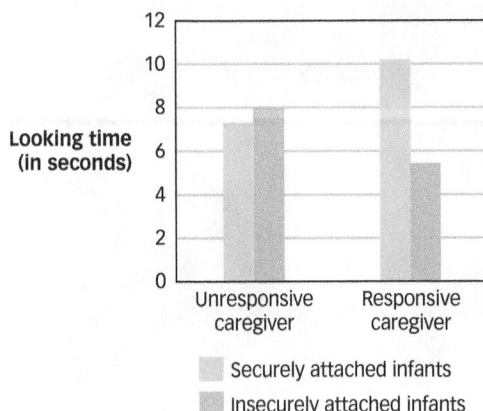

▲ Figure 11.7

WORKING MODELS Do infants really have internal working models? It appears they do. Psychologists know that infants stare longer when they see something they don't expect. Securely attached infants stare longer at a cartoon of a mother ignoring rather than comforting her child, whereas insecurely attached infants do just the opposite (Johnson, Dweck, & Chen, 2007).

internal working model of relationships A set of beliefs about the self, the primary caregiver, and the relationship between them.

Does spending time in day care impair the attachment process? A massive long-term study by the National Institute for Child Health and Human Development showed that attachment style is strongly influenced by maternal sensitivity and responsiveness, but not by the quality, amount, stability, or type of day care (Friedman & Boyle, 2008).

to new experiences and are likely to react negatively and intensely to novel stimuli and events; and about 15% can be classified as *slow-to-warm-up babies*, who are somewhat difficult at first but become easier over time (Thomas & Chess, 1977). These differences are quite stable over time. For example, infants who react fearfully to novel stimuli—such as sudden movements, loud sounds, or unfamiliar people—tend to be more subdued, less social, and less positive at 4 years old (Kagan, 1997). They eventually become children who tend to avoid novel people, objects, and situations, and then adults who are quiet, cautious, and shy (Schwartz et al., 2003). These temperamental differences among infants appear to result from innate biological differences (Baker et al., 2013).

An infant's biologically based temperament plays some role in determining his or her attachment style, but for the most part, attachment style is determined by an infant's social interactions with his or her caregiver. Studies have shown that mothers of securely attached infants tend to be especially sensitive to signs of their child's emotional state, especially good at detecting their infant's "request" for reassurance, and especially responsive to that request (Ainsworth et al., 1978; De Wolff & van IJzendoorn, 1997). Mothers of infants with an ambivalent attachment style tend to respond inconsistently, only sometimes attending to their infants when they show signs of distress. Mothers of infants with an avoidant attachment style are typically indifferent to their child's need for reassurance and may even reject the child's attempts at physical closeness (Isabelle, 1993). As a result of all their interactions, infants develop an **internal working model of relationships**, which is *a set of beliefs about the self, the primary caregiver, and the relationship between them* (Bretherton & Munholland, 1999). Infants with different attachment styles appear to have different working models of relationships (see **FIGURE 11.7**). Specifically:

▶ Infants with a secure attachment style act as though they are *certain that their primary caregiver will respond* when they feel insecure.

▶ Infants with an avoidant attachment style act as though they are *certain that their primary caregiver will not respond*.

▶ Infants with an ambivalent attachment style act as though they are *uncertain about whether their primary caregiver will respond*.

▶ Infants with a disorganized attachment style seem to be confused about their caregivers, which has led some psychologists to speculate that this style primarily characterizes children who have been abused (Carolson, 1998; Cicchetti & Toth, 1998).

If the caregiver's responsiveness determines the child's working model, and if the child's working model determines the child's attachment style, then what determines the caregiver's responsiveness? Differences in how caregivers respond are due in large part to differences in their ability to read their infant's emotional states. Caregivers who are highly sensitive to these signs are almost twice as likely to have a securely attached child as are mothers who are less sensitive (van IJzendoorn & Sagi, 1999). Mothers who think of their infants as unique individuals with emotional lives and not just as creatures with urgent physical needs are more likely to have infants who are securely attached (Meins, 2003; Meins et al., 2001). Although such data are merely correlational, there is reason to suspect that a mother's sensitivity and responsiveness are a *cause* of the infant's attachment style. For instance, researchers studied a group of young mothers whose infants were particularly irritable or difficult. When the infants were about 6 months old, half the mothers participated in a training program designed to sensitize them to their infants' emotional signals and to encourage them to be more responsive. The results showed that when the children were 18 months, 24 months, and 3 years old, those whose mothers had received the training were considerably more likely to have a secure attachment style than were those whose mothers did not receive the training (van den Boom, 1994, 1995).

The Effects of Attachment Styles

Does an infant's attachment style have any influence on the child and adult he or she will become? Yes, it does. Children who were securely attached as infants do better than children who were not securely attached on a wide variety of measures, from their academic achievement (Jacobson & Hoffman, 1997) and cognitive functioning (Bernier et al., 2015) to their psychological well-being (Madigan et al., 2013) and social relationships (McElwain, Booth-LaForce, & Wu, 2011; Schneider, Atkinson, & Tardif, 2001; Simpson, Collins, & Salvatore, 2011; Sroufe, Egeland, & Kruetzer, 1990; Steele et al., 1999; Vondra et al., 2001). Similarly, securely attached infants become more successful adults. In one study that tracked people from infancy to adulthood, researchers found that 1-year-old infants who displayed insecure attachment during the Strange Situation experienced more negative emotions when trying to resolve major relationship conflicts with their romantic partners at age 21 (Simpson et al., 2007). And 1-year-old infants who displayed secure attachment styles in the Strange Situation went on to become adults who rebounded more quickly from conflicts with their romantic partners (Salvatore et al., 2011). Some research suggests that adults continue to apply the working models they developed as infants to their relationships with teachers, friends, and lovers (Waters et al., 2015).

MORAL DEVELOPMENT

From the moment of birth, human beings can make one distinction quickly and well, and that's the distinction between pleasure and pain. Before their bottoms hit their very first diapers, infants can tell when something feels good or bad, and can demonstrate to anyone within earshot that they strongly prefer the former. Over the next few years, they begin to notice that their pleasures ("Throwing food is fun") are often someone else's pains ("Throwing food makes Mom mad"), which is a bit of a problem because infants need these other people to survive. So they start to learn how to balance their needs and the needs of those around them, and they do this in part by developing a distinction between *right* and *wrong*.

According to Piaget, young children do not realize that moral rules can vary across persons and cultures. For instance, most Americans think it is immoral to eat a dog, but most Vietnamese disagree.

Knowing What's Right

How do children think about right and wrong? Piaget had something to say about this, too. He spent time playing games with children and quizzing them about how they came to know the rules of these games and what they thought should happen to children who broke those rules. By listening carefully to what children said, Piaget concluded that the child's moral thinking develops in three important ways (Piaget, 1932/1965).

▶ First, Piaget noticed that children's moral thinking tends to shift *from realism to relativism*. Very young children regard moral rules as real, inviolable truths about the world. For the young child, right and wrong are like day and night: They exist in the world and do not depend on what people think or say. That's why young children generally don't think that a bad action (such as hitting someone) can ever be good, even if everyone agreed to allow it. As they mature, children begin to realize that some moral rules (e.g., wives should obey their husbands) are inventions and not discoveries and that people can therefore agree to adopt them, change them, or abandon them entirely.

▶ Second, Piaget noticed that children's moral thinking tends to shift *from prescriptions to principles*. Young children think of moral rules as guidelines for specific actions in specific situations. ("Each child can play with the iPad for 5 minutes and must then pass it to the child sitting to their left.") As they mature, children come to see that rules are expressions of more general principles, such as fairness and equity, which means that specific rules can be abandoned or

preconventional stage A stage of moral development in which the morality of an action is primarily determined by its consequences for the actor.

conventional stage A stage of moral development in which the morality of an action is primarily determined by the extent to which it conforms to social rules.

postconventional stage A stage of moral development in which the morality of an action is determined by a set of general principles that reflect core values.

During World War II, many Albanian Muslims shielded their Jewish neighbors from the Nazis. "There was no government conspiracy; no underground railroad; no organized resistance of any kind. Only individual Albanians, acting alone, to save the lives of people whose lives were in immediate danger," wrote Norman Gershman, who photographed Muslims such as Baba Haxhi Dede Reshatbardhi (pictured) who saved so many Jewish lives.

modified when they fail to uphold the general principle. ("If Jason missed his turn with the iPad, then he should get two turns now.")

▶ Third, Piaget noticed that children's moral thinking tends to shift *from outcomes to intentions*. For the young child, an unintentional action that causes great harm ("Josh accidentally broke Dad's iPad") seems "more wrong" than an intentional action that causes slight harm ("Josh got mad and broke Dad's pencil"), because young children tend to judge the morality of an action by its outcome rather than by the actor's intentions. As they mature, children begin to see that the morality of an action is critically dependent on the actor's state of mind.

Piaget's observations about the development of moral thinking have generally held up quite well, although he once again seems to have overestimated the ages at which some of these transitions take place. For example, research shows that children as young as 3 years old do sometimes consider people's intentions when judging the morality of their actions (Yuill & Perner, 1988).

The psychologist Lawrence Kohlberg used Piaget's insights as the basis of a detailed theory of the development of moral reasoning (Kohlberg, 1963, 1986). According to Kohlberg, moral reasoning proceeds through three basic stages. Kohlberg (1958) based his theory on people's responses to a series of dilemmas such as this one:

> A woman was near death from a special kind of cancer. There was one drug that the doctors thought might save her. It was a form of radium that a druggist in the same town had recently discovered. The drug was expensive to make, but the druggist was charging ten times what the drug cost him to make. He paid $200 for the radium and charged $2,000 for a small dose of the drug. The sick woman's husband, Heinz, went to everyone he knew to borrow the money, but he could only get together about $1,000, which is half of what it cost. He told the druggist that his wife was dying and asked him to sell it cheaper or let him pay later. But the druggist said: "No, I discovered the drug and I'm going to make money from it." So Heinz got desperate and broke into the man's store to steal the drug for his wife. Should the husband have done that?

On the basis of their responses, Kohlberg concluded that most children are at the **preconventional stage**, which is *a stage of moral development in which the morality of an action is primarily determined by its consequences for the actor.* Immoral actions are simply those for which one is punished, and the appropriate resolution to any moral dilemma is to choose the behavior with the least likelihood of punishment. For example, children at this stage often base their moral judgment of Heinz on the relative costs of one decision ("It would be bad if he got blamed for his wife's death") and another ("It would be bad if he went to jail for stealing").

Kohlberg argued that children are preconventional, but somewhere around adolescence they move to the **conventional stage**, which is *a stage of moral development in which the morality of an action is primarily determined by the extent to which it conforms to social rules.* People at this stage believe that everyone should uphold the generally accepted norms of their cultures, obey the laws of society, and fulfill their civic duties and familial obligations. They argue that Heinz must weigh the dishonor he will bring on himself and his family by stealing (i.e., breaking a law) against the guilt he will feel if he allows his wife to die (i.e., failing to fulfill a duty). People at this stage are concerned not just about spankings and prison sentences but also about the approval of others. Immoral actions are those for which one is condemned.

Finally, Kohlberg believed that in adulthood, some adults (but not all) move to the **postconventional stage**, which is *a stage of moral development in which the morality of an action is determined by a set of general principles that reflect core values,* such as the right to life, liberty, and the pursuit of happiness. When a behavior violates these principles, it is immoral, and if a law requires these principles to be violated, then it should be disobeyed. For a person who has reached the postconventional stage, a woman's life is always more important than a shopkeeper's profits. Thus, stealing the drug is not only a moral behavior, it is a moral obligation.

Research supports Kohlberg's general claim that moral reasoning shifts from an emphasis on punishment to an emphasis on social rules and finally to an emphasis on ethical principles (Walker, 1988). But research also suggests that these stages are not quite so discrete as Kohlberg thought. For instance, a single person might apply preconventional, conventional, and postconventional thinking in different circumstances, which suggests that the developing person does not "reach a stage" so much as he "acquires a skill" that he may or may not use on a particular occasion.

The use of the male pronoun here is intentional. Because Kohlberg developed his theory by studying a sample of American boys, some critics have suggested that it does not describe the development of moral thinking in girls (Gilligan, 1982) or in non-Westerners (Simpson, 1974). The first of these criticisms has received little scientific support (Jaffee & Hyde, 2000; Turiel, 1998), but the second has received quite a bit. For example, some non-Western societies value obedience and community over liberty and individuality; thus, the moral reasoning of people in those societies may *appear* to reflect a conventional devotion to social norms when it *actually* reflects a postconventional consideration of ethical principles. Other critics have noted that although a child's level of moral reasoning is positively correlated with his or her moral behavior (Blasi, 1980; Eisenberg et al., 2014), the correlation is not strong, and this is particularly true when the moral behavior involves doing a good deed rather than refraining from doing a bad deed (Haidt, 2001; Thoma et al., 1999). These critics suggest that how people reason about morality may be interesting in and of itself, but it doesn't tell us very much about how people will behave in their everyday lives. So if moral reasoning doesn't determine moral behavior, then what does?

Feeling What's Right

Research on moral reasoning suggests that people are like judges in a court of law, using rational analysis—sometimes simple and sometimes sophisticated—to distinguish between right and wrong. But moral dilemmas don't just make us think; they also make us *feel*. Consider this one:

> You are standing on a bridge. Below you can see a runaway trolley hurtling down the track toward five people who will be killed if it remains on its present course. You are sure that you can save these people by flipping a lever that will switch the trolley onto a different track, where it will kill just one person instead of five. Is it morally permissible to divert the trolley and prevent five deaths at the cost of one?

Now consider a slightly different version of this problem:

> You and a large man are standing on a bridge. Below you can see a runaway trolley hurtling down the track toward five people who will be killed if it remains on its present course. You are sure that you can save these people by pushing the large man onto the track, where his body will be caught up in the trolley's wheels and stop it before it kills the five people. Is it morally permissible to push the large man and prevent five deaths at the cost of one?

These scenarios are illustrated in **FIGURE 11.8**. If you are like most people, you concluded that it is morally permissible to pull a switch but not to push a man (Greene et al., 2001). In both cases you had to decide whether to sacrifice one human life in order to save five, and in one case you said yes and in another you said no. How can moral reasoning yield such inconsistent conclusions?

Moral Intuitions. It can't, and the odds are that you didn't reach these conclusions by moral reasoning at all. Rather, you simply had a strong negative emotional reaction to the thought of pushing another human being into the path of an oncoming trolley and watching him get sliced and diced, and that reaction instantly led you to

(a)

(b)

▲ Figure 11.8

THE TROLLEY PROBLEM Why does it seem okay to trade one life for five lives by pulling a switch, but not by pushing a man from a bridge? Research suggests that the scenario shown in (b) elicits a more negative emotional response than does the scenario shown in (a), and this emotional response may be the basis for our moral intuitions.

adolescence The period of development that begins with the onset of sexual maturity (about 11 to 14 years of age) and lasts until the beginning of adulthood (about 18 to 21 years of age).

puberty The onset of bodily changes associated with sexual maturity.

primary sex characteristics Bodily structures that are directly involved in reproduction.

secondary sex characteristics Bodily structures that change dramatically with sexual maturity but that are not directly involved in reproduction.

conclude that pushing him was wrong. Sure, you may have come up with a few good arguments to support this conclusion ("What if he turned around and bit me?" or "I'd hate to get spleen on my new shoes"), but those arguments probably followed rather than preceded your conclusion (Greene, 2013).

The way people respond to cases such as these has convinced some psychologists that moral judgments are the consequences—and not the causes—of emotional reactions (Haidt, 2001; Ongley & Malti, 2014). According to this *moral intuitionist* perspective, we have evolved to react emotionally to a small family of events that are particularly relevant to reproduction and survival, and we have developed the distinction between right and wrong as a way of labeling and explaining these emotional reactions (Hamlin, Wynn, & Bloom, 2007). For instance, most of us think that incest disgusts us because it is wrong, but another possibility is that we consider it wrong because it disgusts us. Incest is a poor method for producing genetically viable offspring, and so nature may have selected for people who are disgusted by it. Our reasoning about the immorality of incest may be the *consequence* of that disgust and not its *cause*.

Some research supports the moral intuitionist perspective. For example, in one study, people who had brain damage that prevented them from experiencing normal emotions treated the two situations shown in Figure 11.8 identically, choosing in both cases to sacrifice one life to save five (Koenigs et al., 2007). In another study (Wheatley & Haidt, 2005), participants were hypnotized and told that whenever they heard the word *take,* they would experience "a brief pang of disgust . . . a sickening feeling in your stomach." After they came out of the hypnotic state, the participants were asked to rate the morality of several actions. Sometimes the description of the action contained the word *take* ("How immoral is it for a police officer to *take* a bribe") and sometimes it did not ("How immoral is it for a police officer to *accept* a bribe?"). Participants rated the action as less moral when it contained the word *take,* suggesting that their negative feelings were causing—rather than being caused by—their moral reasoning.

Moral Compassion. All of this suggests that we consider it immoral to push someone onto the tracks simply because the idea of watching someone suffer makes us feel bad (Greene et al., 2001). In fact, research has shown that watching someone suffer activates the very same brain regions that are activated when we suffer ourselves (Carr et al., 2003; see the discussion of mirror neurons in the Neuroscience and Behavior chapter). In one study, women received a shock or watched their romantic partners receive a shock on different parts of their bodies. The regions of the women's brains that processed information about the location of the shock were activated only when the women experienced the shock themselves, but the regions that processed emotional information were activated whether the women received the shock or observed it (Singer et al., 2004). Similarly, the emotion-relevant brain regions that are activated when a person smells a foul odor are also activated when the person sees someone else smelling the foul odor (Wicker et al., 2003). Studies such as these suggest that our brains respond to other people's *expressions* of suffering by creating within us the *experience* of suffering, and this mechanism may have evolved because it allows us to know instantly what others are feeling (de Waal, 2012). The fact that we can actually *feel* another person's suffering may explain why even a small child who is incapable of sophisticated moral reasoning still considers it wrong when someone hurts someone else, especially when the person being hurt is similar to the child (Hamlin et al., 2013).

This may also explain why our aversion to watching others suffer begins so early in childhood (Hamlin & Steckler, 2015; Warneken & Tomasello, 2009). When adults pretend to hit their thumbs with a hammer, even very young children seem alarmed and will attempt to comfort them (Zahn-Waxler et al., 1992). Indeed, even very young children distinguish between actions that are wrong because they violate a social rule and actions that are wrong because they cause suffering. When asked whether it would be okay to leave toys on the floor in a school that allowed such behavior, young children tend to say it would. But when asked whether it would be okay to hit another child in a school that allowed such behavior, young children tend to say it would not (Smetana, 1981; Smetana & Braeges, 1990). Young children say that hitting is wrong, even when an adult instructs someone to do it (Laupa & Turiel, 1986). It appears that from a very early age, other people's suffering can become our suffering, and this leads us to conclude that the actions that caused the suffering are immoral.

Most people are upset by the suffering of others, and research suggests that even young children have this response, which may be the basis of their emerging morality.

Build to the Outcomes

1. How is attachment assessed?

2. How do caregivers influence an infant's attachment style?

3. According to Piaget, what three shifts characterize moral development?

4. What are Kohlberg's three stages of moral development?

5. Do moral judgments come before or after emotional reactions?

6. What happens when we see others suffer?

Adolescence: Minding the Gap

Between childhood and adulthood is an extended developmental stage that may not qualify for a "hood" of its own, but that is clearly distinct from the stages that come before and after. **Adolescence** is *the period of development that begins with the onset of sexual maturity (about 11 to 14 years of age) and lasts until the beginning of adulthood (about 18 to 21 years of age).* Unlike the transition from embryo to fetus or from infant to child, this transition is sudden and clearly marked. In just 3 or 4 years, the average adolescent gains about 40 pounds and grows about 10 inches. For girls, all this growing starts at about the age of 10 and ends when they reach their full heights at about the age of 15.5. For boys it starts at about the age of 12 and ends at about the age of 17.5.

The beginning of this growth spurt signals the onset of **puberty**, which is *the onset of bodily changes associated with sexual maturity.* These changes involve the **primary sex characteristics**, which are *bodily structures that are directly involved in reproduction.* For example, girls undergo the onset of menstruation; boys undergo enlargement of the testes, scrotum, and penis and acquire the capacity for ejaculation. These changes also involve the **secondary sex characteristics**, which are *bodily structures that change dramatically with sexual maturity but that are not directly involved in reproduction.* For example, girls' breasts become enlarged and their hips widen.

Learning Outcomes

▶ Explain why the protraction of adolescence matters.

▶ Describe the determinants of sexual orientation and behavior.

▶ Explain how adolescents are influenced by their peers.

Adolescents are often described as gawky because different parts of their faces and bodies mature at different rates. But as the musician and actor Justin Timberlake can attest, the gawkiness generally clears up.

Facial hair, pubic hair, underarm hair, and the lowering of the voice appear in both sexes. This pattern of changes is caused by increased production of estrogen in girls and testosterone in boys.

Just as the body changes during adolescence, so too does the brain. For example, there is a marked increase in the growth rate of tissue connecting different regions of the brain just before puberty (Thompson et al., 2000). Between the ages of 6 and 13, the connections between the temporal lobe (the brain region specialized for language) and the parietal lobe (the brain region specialized for understanding spatial relations) multiply rapidly and then stop—just about the time that the critical period for learning a language ends (see **FIGURE 11.9**).

But the most important neural changes occur in the prefrontal cortex. An infant's brain forms many more new synapses than it actually needs, and by the time children

▶ Figure 11.9

YOUR BRAIN ON PUBERTY The development of neurons peaks in the frontal and parietal lobes at about age 12 (a, b) and in the temporal lobe at about age 16 (c), and continues to increase in the occipital lobe through age 20 (d).

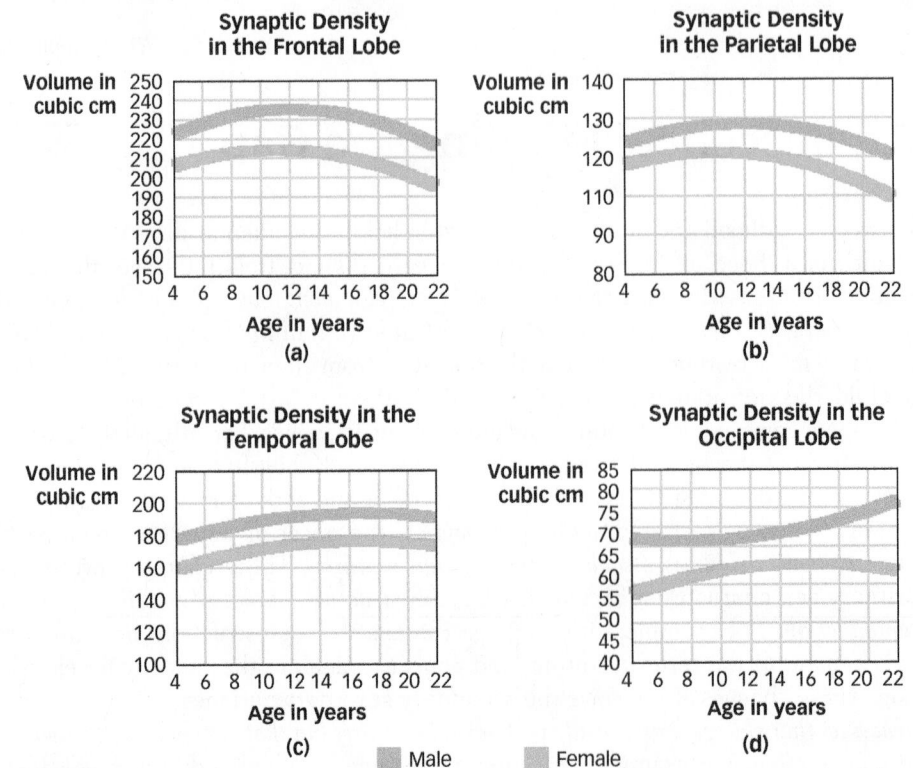

are 2 years old they have about 15,000 synapses per neuron, which is roughly twice as many as the average adult (Huttenlocher, 1979). This early period of *synaptic proliferation* is followed by a period of *synaptic pruning* in which the connections that are not frequently used are eliminated. This clever system allows the brain's wiring to be influenced by its experience in the world, and some studies suggest that if pruning doesn't happen properly, brain function can be permanently impaired (Tang et al., 2014). Scientists used to think that this process ended early in life, but recent evidence suggests that the prefrontal cortex undergoes a second wave of synaptic proliferation just before puberty, and a second wave of synaptic pruning during adolescence (Giedd et al., 1999). Clearly, the adolescent brain is a work in progress.

THE PROTRACTION OF ADOLESCENCE

The age at which puberty begins varies across individuals (e.g.,, people tend to reach puberty at about the same age as their same-sexed parent did) and across ethnic groups (e.g., African American girls tend to reach puberty before European American girls do). It also varies across generations (Malina, Bouchard, & Beunen, 1988). During the 19th century, girls in Scandinavia, the United Kingdom, and the United States had their first menstrual periods when they were about 17 years old, but by 1960, that age had fallen to about 13 years. A recent study found that the average age of breast development for girls in Denmark has decreased by an entire year since 1992 alone (Aksglaede et al., 2009). The average age at which American boys reach puberty has now fallen to between 9 and 10 years old (Herman-Giddens et al., 2012).

Why is puberty happening so much earlier now than it did just a few decades ago? For girls, at least, the main reason appears to be diet (Ellis & Garber, 2000). Young women have more body fat today than ever before, and body fat secretes estrogen, which hastens puberty. Some evidence suggests that exposure to environmental toxins that mimic estrogen may also play a role (Buck Louis et al., 2008). Another surprising cause of early puberty in girls appears to be stress (Belsky, 2012; Belsky et al., 2015). Studies show that girls reach puberty earlier if they grow up in unpredictable households with high levels of conflict, or households without a biological father, or if they are victims of early sexual abuse (Greenspan & Deardorff, 2014).

Whatever its causes, early puberty has important psychological consequences. Just two centuries ago, the gap between childhood and adulthood was relatively brief in Western societies because people became physically mature at roughly the same time that they were ready to accept adult roles in society—that is, to marry and get a job. But today, people get married and get jobs much later, because they typically spend 3 to 10 extra years in school. Thus, although the age at which people become physically adult has decreased, the age at which they are prepared or allowed to take on adult responsibilities has increased, and so the period between childhood and adulthood has become *protracted*.

What are the consequences of a protracted adolescence? Adolescence is often characterized as a time of internal turmoil and external recklessness, and some psychologists have speculated that the protraction of adolescence is partly to blame for its sorry reputation (Moffitt, 1993). According to these theorists, adolescents are adults who have temporarily been denied a place in adult society. American teenagers are subjected to 10 times as many restrictions as older adults, and twice as many restrictions as active-duty U.S. marines or incarcerated felons (Epstein, 2007a). As such, they feel especially compelled to do things to protest these restrictions and demonstrate their adulthood, such as smoking, drinking, using drugs, having sex, and committing crimes. In a sense, adolescents are people who are forced to live in a strange gap between two worlds, and the pathologies of adolescence are partly a result of this predicament. As one researcher noted, "Trapped in the frivolous world of peer culture, they learn virtually everything they know from one another rather than from

The famous Leipzig Boy's Choir is in trouble. Boys enter the choir at the age of 9 and sing soprano until their voices change. Back in 1723, when Johann Sebastian Bach was the choirmaster, that happened at about the age of 17. Today it happens at about the age of 12. As a result, by the time a soprano learns to sing well, he isn't a soprano anymore.

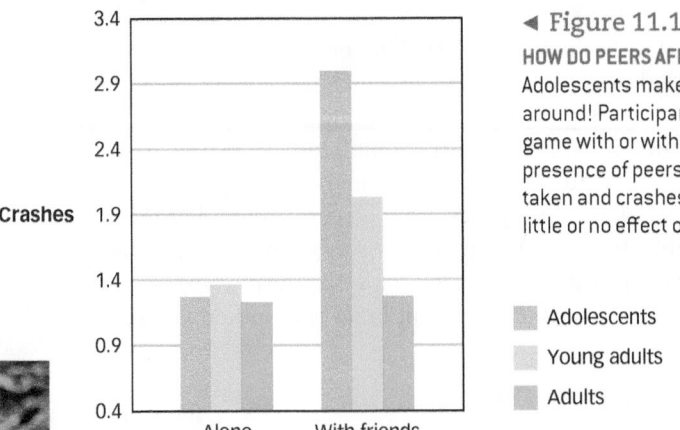

◀ **Figure 11.10**

HOW DO PEERS AFFECT DECISION MAKING?
Adolescents make better decisions when no one is around! Participants in one study played a video driving game with or without their peers in the room. The presence of peers greatly increased the number of risks taken and crashes experienced by adolescents, but had little or no effect on adults (Gardner & Steinberg, 2005).

■ Adolescents
■ Young adults
■ Adults

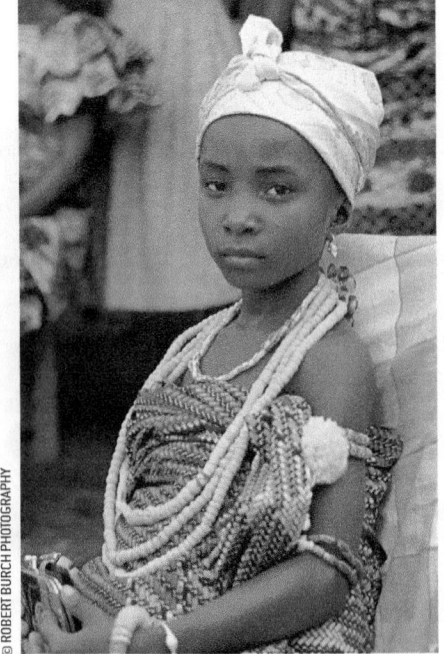

About 60 percent of preindustrial societies don't have a word for adolescence because there is no such stage. When a Krobo girl menstruates for the first time, older women take her into seclusion for two weeks and teach her about sex, birth control, and marriage. Afterward, a public ceremony is held, and the young woman who was regarded as a child just days earlier is forever regarded as an adult.

These students (*left*) may be experimenting with reckless behavior, but they are unlikely to become reckless adults. Of course, the Vermont state trooper (*right*) who is inspecting the car in which four teens died after a night of drinking would probably like to remind them that this rule applies only to those who survive.

the people they are about to become. Isolated from adults and wrongly treated like children, it is no wonder that some teens behave, by adult standards, recklessly or irresponsibly" (Epstein, 2007b).

But the storm and stress of adolescence is neither as prevalent nor as inevitable as HBO would have us believe (Steinberg & Morris, 2001). Research suggests that the "moody adolescent" who is a victim of "raging hormones" is largely a myth. Adolescents are no moodier than children (Buchanan, Eccles, & Becker, 1992), and fluctuations in their hormone levels have a very small impact on their moods (Brooks-Gunn, Graber, & Paikoff, 1994). Although they can be more impulsive and susceptible to peer influence than adults (see **FIGURE 11.10**), they are just as capable of making wise decisions based on good information (Steinberg, 2007). Yes, most adolescents dabble in misbehavior, but they don't seem to major in it. For example, most adolescents in the United States get drunk at least once before they graduate from high school, but few develop drinking problems or allow alcohol to impair their academic success or personal relationships (Hughes, Power, & Francis, 1992; Johnston, Bachman, & O'Malley, 1997). Most adolescent experiments have no long-term consequences (Warren et al., 2016), and the vast majority of adolescents who try drugs or break the law end up becoming sober, law-abiding adults (Steinberg, 1999). In short, the hijinks of adolescence that adults so often lament are actually fairly minor and typically temporary, and in some cultures they barely occur at all (Epstein, 2007b). The fact is that adolescence is not a terribly troubled time for most people, and most adolescents "age out" of the troubles they manage to get themselves into (Martin et al., 2014; Sampson & Laub, 1995; see Other Voices: What Time Leaves Behind).

SEXUALITY

Puberty can be a difficult time, but it is especially difficult for girls who reach it earlier than their peers. These girls are more likely to experience a range of negative consequences, from distress and depression to delinquency and disease (Mendle,

What Time Leaves Behind

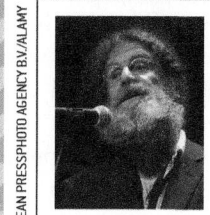

EPA EUROPEAN PRESSPHOTO AGENCY B.V./ALAMY

Robert Sapolsky is a professor of biology, neurology, and neurosurgery at Stanford University.

Much has been written about the teenage brain, and most of it isn't very nice. Teenagers, we are told time and time again, don't yet have a mature frontal cortex, and so they do all sorts of stupid, embarrassing, and dangerous things that they regret—if they manage to live long enough. This is the truth, but it isn't the whole truth. According to the neurobiologist Robert Sapolsky, the highly developed frontal cortex of which adults are so proud may well keep them sober, safe, and sound, but it may also cost them a small piece of their humanity.

The teenage brain is unique. It's not merely an adult brain that is half-cooked or a child's brain left unrefrigerated for too long. Its distinctiveness arises from a key region, the frontal cortex, not being fully developed. . . .

The frontal cortex is the most recently evolved part of the human brain. It's where the sensible mature stuff happens: long-term planning, executive function, impulse control, and emotional regulation. It's what makes you do the right thing when it's the harder thing to do. But its neurons are not fully wired up until your mid-20s. . . .

The delayed maturation of the frontal cortex . . . helps explain the defining feature of adolescence, namely the weird predilection for bungee jumping. During risky decision-making, adolescents show less activation of some key sub-regions of the frontal cortex than do adults, and among adolescents, the less activity in these regions, the poorer the risk assessment. . . .

Ask test subjects to estimate the likelihood of some event happening to them and then tell them the actual likelihood of it happening. . . . Both adults and teens are likely to adjust their assessments when asked again about the likelihood of good news. But teens alone don't get the picture about bad news.

Researcher: "What do you think the odds are of your having a car accident if you're driving drunk?" Adolescent: "One chance in a gazillion." Researcher: "Actually, the risk for people in general is 50 percent; now what do you think your chances are?" Adolescent: "Hey, we're talking about me; one chance in a gazillion." This helps explain why adolescents have 2 to 4 times the rate of pathological gambling than adults. . . .

But adolescence isn't always as dark as it's made out to be. There's a feature of adolescence that makes up for the stupid risk-taking and hideous fashion decisions. And that's an adolescent's frenzied, agitated, incandescent ability to feel someone else's pain, to feel the pains of the entire world, to want to right all its wrongs. Adolescents are nature's most wondrous example of empathy, where the forcefulness of feeling *as* the other can border on nearly *being* the other. . . .

A few years ago, I saw a magnificent example of the empathy that a sluggish frontal cortex can produce in teenagers. My daughter is seriously into theater and at the time she was in a production of a superb, searing play about the Bosnian genocide, Stefanie Zadravec's *Honey Brown Eyes*. She played a 12-year-old Bosnian girl for whom things don't go so great, and whose life-or-death fate is ambiguous as the play ends.

Some high school kids had come to a performance as a group outing for an English class. About halfway through the play, my daughter's character appears for the first time, cautiously emerging from a ventilation duct in her kitchen where she'd been hiding, unaware that the soldier who had just left the apartment after killing her mother was going to return. Up until that point, she had only been hinted at as a character. The soldier had his ethnic-cleansing to-do list of names of Bosnians in the building to kill, and kept demanding of the mother, "Where's your daughter? It says you have a daughter." "I don't have a daughter," the mother repeated up until her death. So as the girl begins to emerge from the ventilation duct, the realization sweeps through the audience: there *is* a daughter. As my daughter began to crawl out, the teenagers in the audience did something you're not supposed to do in a theater, something no adult with a developed frontal cortex would do. After a moment of hushed silence, two or three voices called out, "No!" Another called, "Go back in, it's not safe!," another, "He's coming back!" After the play, the teenagers clustered around my little girl when she came out of the stage door, hugging her, reassuring themselves that both she and her character were OK.

This is the picture of adolescents with their hearts on their sleeves, limbic systems going full blast, and their frontal cortices straining to catch up with some emotional self-regulation. When I see the best of my university students in that agitated, optimistic state, I always have the same thought: It used to be so much easier to be like this. Having this adult frontal cortex of mine probably enables me to do good in a more efficacious, detached way. The trouble, though, is the same detachment makes it so much easier to decide that it's really not my problem.

Sapolsky believes that shouting in a crowded theater is not a sign of childish impulsivity but of untamed compassion, and he laments the ease with which adults can mute those feelings and turn away from human suffering. His essay is a good reminder that as time moves us forward, it leaves something behind, and that the things we gain as we develop are not always better than the things we lose. What other things do people lose as they age? Are the gains worth the losses?

Excerpt from Robert Sapolsky, "Dude, Where's My Frontal Cortex?" *Nautilus*, July 24, 2014. http://nautil.us/issue/15/turbulence/dude-wheres-my-frontal-cortex

Turkheimer, & Emery, 2007). This happens for several reasons (Ge & Natsuaki, 2009). First, early bloomers don't have as much time as their peers do to develop the skills necessary to cope with adolescence (Petersen & Grockett, 1985), but because they look so mature, people expect them to act like adults. In other words, early puberty creates unrealistic expectations that the adolescent may have trouble fulfilling.

Second, early blooming girls draw the attention of older men, who may lead them into a variety of unhealthy activities (Ge, Conger, & Elder, 1996). Some research suggests that for girls, the *timing* of puberty has a greater influence on emotional and behavioral problems than does the occurrence of puberty itself (Buchanan et al., 1992). The timing of puberty does not have such consistent effects on boys: Some studies suggest that early maturing boys do better than their peers, some suggest they do worse, and some suggest that there is no difference at all (Ge, Conger, & Elder, 2001). Interestingly, recent research shows that for boys, the *tempo* or speed with which they make the transition from the first to the last stages of puberty may be a better predictor of negative outcomes than is the timing (Mendle et al., 2010; Mendle, 2014).

Sexual Orientation: A Matter of Biology

For some adolescents, puberty is additionally complicated by the fact that they are attracted to members of the same sex. Why does this make puberty complicated? Roughly 1 to 2% of adolescents identify themselves as gay or lesbian, and about 4 to 7% report having had a same-sex relationship or attraction (Coker, Austin, & Schuster, 2010). This means that lesbian, gay, and bisexual adolescents are different from the vast majority of their peers, and as you probably remember, adolescents care a whole lot about "fitting in" (Somerville et al., 2013). Not only are lesbian, gay, and bisexual adolescents in a minority, but they are in a minority that is often subject to the disdain and disapproval of family, friends, and community. Engaging in sexual activity with members of the same sex is illegal in 75 nations and punishable by death in 11 (Bailey et al., 2016). Although Americans are rapidly becoming more accepting of gay, lesbian, and bisexual people (see **FIGURE 11.11**), many still disapprove to varying degrees, and social disapproval naturally makes an adolescent's life difficult.

What determines whether a person's sexuality is primarily oriented toward the same or the opposite sex? For a long time, psychologists thought the answer was upbringing. For example, during the 1940s and 1950s, psychoanalytic theorists suggested that boys who grow up with domineering mothers and cold, distant fathers are less likely to identify with their fathers and are therefore more likely to be gay. The only trouble with this theory is that research has so far failed to identify *any* aspect of parenting that has a significant impact on a child's ultimate sexual orientation (Bell, Weinberg, & Hammersmith, 1981). Indeed, researchers have not even been able to find evidence that a parent's sexual orientation has any influence on the sexual orientation of his or her child (Patterson, 2013). Although peers do have a measurable influence on both the decision to engage in sexual activity and the desire for romantic relationships, they appear to have no influence on an adolescent's sexual orientation (Brakefield et al., 2014).

▶ Figure 11.11

CHANGING ATTITUDES TOWARD SAME-SEX MARRIAGE In 1965, homosexuality was illegal in America, and most Americans thought it was a mental illness. Things have changed dramatically in the last few years, as witnessed by the near complete turnaround of Americans' attitudes toward same-sex marriage.

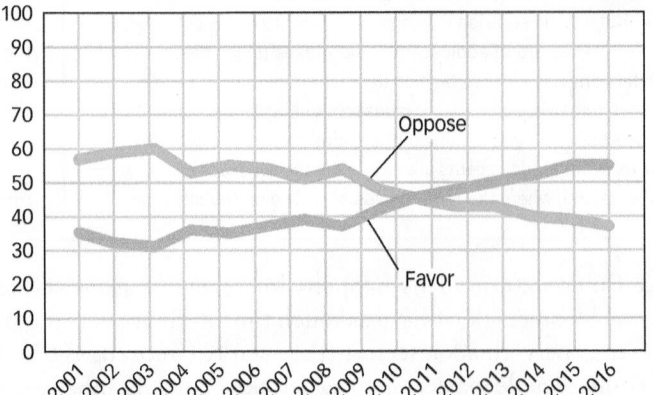

% of U.S. Adults Who Favor/Oppose Same-Sex Marriage (2001–2016)

PEW RESEARCH CENTER, HTTP://WWW.PEWFORUM.ORG/2016/05/12/CHANGING-ATTITUDES-ON-GAY-MARRIAGE/

BOSTON GLOBE/GETTY IMAGES

In 2004, Massachusetts became the first U.S. state to legalize same-sex marriage. On May 17, Marcia Kadish (*left*) and Tanya McCloskey became the first couple to make good use of the new law. A decade later, the Supreme Court ruled that same-sex marriage was legal in all 50 states.

So what *does* determine a person's sexual orientation? There is now considerable evidence to suggest that biology plays the major role. First, same-sex sexual activity is observed in almost all mammals, and in humans it appears to predate civilization itself (Nash, 2001). Second, sexual orientation varies in the same way that many other heritable traits do. For instance, the brother or fraternal twin of a gay man (with whom he shares 50% of his genes) has only a 15% chance of being gay, but the identical twin of a gay man (with whom he shares 100% of his genes) has about a 50% chance of being gay (Bailey & Pillard, 1991; Gladue, 1994). A similar pattern has emerged in studies of women (Bailey et al., 1993). In some ways, the brains of gay and lesbian people tend to look like the brains of opposite-gendered heterosexual people (Savic & Lindstrom, 2008). For example, the cerebral hemispheres of straight men and gay women (both of whom are *gynephilic*, or attracted to women) tend to be of different sizes, whereas the hemispheres of straight women and gay men (both of whom are *androphilic*, or attracted to men) tend to be the same size. Some evidence suggests that high levels of androgens in the womb may predispose a fetus—whether male or female—to become an androphilic adult (Ellis & Ames, 1987; Meyer-Bahlberg et al., 1995).

Another striking piece of evidence for the role of biology is the fact that a child's behavior is a surprisingly good predictor of his or her adult sexual orientation (Bailey & Zucker, 1995). Most children go through a period in which they adamantly refuse to do anything that is stereotypically associated with the opposite gender (Halim et al., 2014). But a few children are eager to engage in what researchers call "gender nonconforming behavior," which for boys includes dressing like a girl and playing with dolls, and for girls includes dressing like a boy and engaging in rough play. These behaviors usually emerge by the time the child is 2 to 4 years old, despite the fact that parents typically discourage them (Cohen-Kettenis & Pfäfflin, 2003). As it turns out, children who engage in gender nonconforming behavior are significantly more likely to become gay, lesbian, or bisexual adults. In one study, participants who watched family videos of children were able to predict the child's ultimate sexual orientation with surprising accuracy (Rieger et al., 2010). This does not mean that every boy who likes pigtails will become a gay man or that every girl who likes pigskin will become a lesbian, but it does mean that some signs of adult sexual orientation are observable long before people begin to experience sexual attraction, around the age of 10.

It is worth noting that men and women differ in how they experience their sexual orientations. For example, a man's sexual orientation is a good predictor of his physiological arousal to erotic stimuli. For example, straight men are aroused by erotic pictures of women but not of men, and gay men are aroused by erotic pictures of men but not of women. But a woman's sexual orientation is not. For example, straight women are equally aroused by erotic pictures of women and men, and lesbians are only slightly more aroused by erotic pictures of women than of men (Chivers et al., 2004; Chivers, Seto, & Blanchard, 2007). Men's sexual orientations also appear to be less fluid than women's. For instance, men are more likely than women to report being either exclusively heterosexual or exclusively homosexual, whereas women are more likely than men to report being either "mostly heterosexual" or bisexual (Savin-Williams & Vrangalova, 2013). Women's sexual orientations are also more likely than men's to depend on circumstances and to shift over time (Baumeister, 2000; Bailey et al., 2016). Of course, the fact that people's sexual orientations *can* change does not mean that they can *be* changed: There is no evidence to suggest that "conversion" or "reparative" therapies can transform gay, lesbian, or bisexual people into heterosexuals (American Psychological Association, 2009).

The science of sexual orientation is still young and fraught with conflicting findings, but at least two conclusions are noncontroversial. First, whatever the complete story of its determinants turns out to be, sexual orientation clearly has a biological component and is not just a "lifestyle choice." Second, human sexual orientation is far more complex and diverse than labels such as "straight" and "gay" seem to suggest. Physiological arousal, psychological attraction, sexual behavior, biological sex, and gender identity are different things that combine in seemingly endless variations that defy simple categorization (see The Real World: Coming to Terms). Indeed, in a recent survey of U.S. adults, the percent who identified as gay or lesbian was only slightly larger than the percent who identified as "something else" or who said they didn't know the answer (Ward et al., 2014). Human beings are sexual creatures who still have a great deal to learn about themselves.

Sexual Behavior: A Matter of Choice

Sexual orientation may not be a choice, but sexual behavior is—and many teenagers choose it. Although the percentage of American high school students who have had sex has been steadily declining in recent years (see **FIGURE 11.12**), it is still nearly half. The problem with this is that teenagers' interest in sex typically surpasses their knowledge about it. Most American parents never talk in depth with their children about sex (Ansuini, Fiddler-Woite, & Woite, 1996), and those who do tend to start late because they overestimate the age at which their children become sexually active (Jaccard, Dittus, & Gordon, 1998). Ignorance has consequences. Almost half of American high school students report having had sexual intercourse, but only 59% of those students report using a condom during their last encounter (Kann et al.,

▶ Figure 11.12

TEENAGERS ARE DELAYING SEX The age at which young Americans have sex for the first time has dropped considerably over the last 25 years.

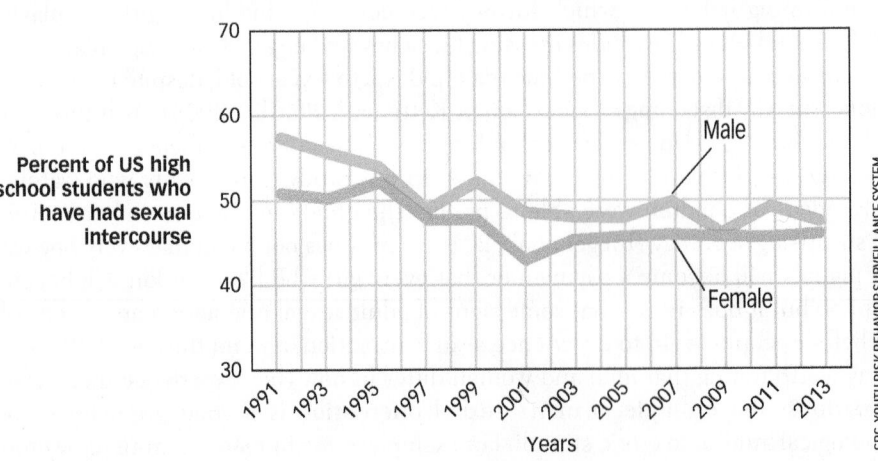

THE REAL WORLD

Coming to Terms

Sexuality is about both the body and the mind. But people's bodies are hidden beneath their clothes, and people's minds are hidden behind their eyes, so the diversity of sexuality in the real world is all too easy to miss. Understanding it requires understanding three distinct but related concepts.

Sex refers to the bodies we are born with. Most (though not all) human bodies are either male (i.e., they have XY chromosomes and a penis) or female (i.e., they have XX chromosomes and a vagina). *Gender* refers to our identities—how we see ourselves, how we want others to see us, and how it feels to be inside our own skins. Most (though not all) adults identify themselves as men or women. Last, *sexual orientation* refers to the kinds of people to whom we find ourselves attracted. Most (though not all) adults are attracted to people of the opposite sex.

These three dimensions don't capture every important aspect of human sexuality, of course, but they do allow us to build a classification scheme that helps us understand and talk to each other. The table shows the terms that typically are used to refer to people who differ on these dimensions. (For more on this topic, go to http://www.glaad.org/reference/transgender).

In Latin, the prefix *trans-* means "on the other side of," and the prefix *cis-* means "on this side of." So the term *transgender* refers to anyone whose gender and sex do not match, and the term *cisgender* refers to anyone whose gender and sex do match. Notice also that the terms *male* and *female* refer to a person's sex, whereas the terms *man* and *woman* refer to a person's gender. Most people prefer to be described in terms of their gender rather than their sex, so both transgender and cisgender women typically prefer to be called *she*, and both cisgender and transgender men typically prefer to be called *he*. It makes sense to think of people as they think of themselves.

It also makes sense to talk about them that way. Over time, descriptors of human categories often take on pejorative connotations for the people they describe. The word *homosexual,* for example, has traditionally been used to describe people with same-sex orientations, but it is quickly becoming an unflattering way to refer to gay and lesbian people. Conversely, terms that were once pejorative are sometimes reclaimed by the people whom they were initially meant to demean. For example, in some communities, *queer* is now a positive description of anyone who is not cisgender and straight. The National Queer Arts Festival has been thriving in San Francisco since 1998, but its name would have been an unthinkable slur just twenty years earlier.

The majority of people are cisgender and straight, and all these new categories and changing terms can make them long for simpler times. But there never were simpler times—just times in which the complexity of human sexuality was a secret, hidden from our view. Those times have passed, and the full range of our diversity is now on display. For those who hope to understand it scientifically, this is a welcome change.

		SEX			
		Male		Female	
		Gender		**Gender**	
		Man	Woman	Man	Woman
	Males	Cisgender Gay Man	Transgender Straight Woman	Transgender Gay Man	Cisgender Straight Woman
Sexual orientation Toward...	Females	Cisgender Straight Man	Transgender Lesbian	Transgender Straight Man	Cisgender Lesbian
	Males & Females	Cisgender Bisexual Man	Transgender Bisexual Woman	Transgender Bisexual Man	Cisgender Bisexual Woman

2014). Although teen birth rates have been falling in the United States for about 20 years, they are still the highest in the developed world, and consequently, so is the rate of abortion.

What can be done? Sex education leads teens to delay having sex for the first time, increases the likelihood they will use birth control when they do have sex, and lowers the likelihood that they will get pregnant or catch a sexually transmitted disease (Mueller, Gavin, & Kulkarni, 2008; Satcher, 2001). But despite these documented benefits, sex education in American schools is often absent, sketchy, or based on the goal of abstinence rather than harm prevention. Alas, there is little evidence to suggest that abstinence-only programs are effective (Kohler, Manhart, & Lafferty, 2008), and some studies suggest that teens who take abstinence pledges are just as likely to have sex as those who don't, but are less likely to use birth control (Rosenbaum, 2009). That's too bad, because teenage mothers fare more poorly than teenage women without children on almost every measure of academic and economic achievement, and their children fare more poorly on most measures of educational success and emotional well-being than do the children of older mothers (Olausson et al., 2001).

The human papilloma virus is a sexually transmitted disease that can lead to cervical cancer. Luckily, there is a vaccine that can prevent it. Some parents worry that being vaccinated will encourage their daughters to have sex early, but studies show that young women who have been vaccinated do not have sex earlier than those who have not been vaccinated.

BLEND IMAGES/ERPRODUCTIONS LTD/GETTY IMAGES

TABLE 11.2

Erikson's Stages of Psychosocial Development

According to Erikson, at each "stage" of development a "key event" creates a challenge or "crisis" that a person can resolve positively or negatively.

Ages	Key Event	Crisis	Positive Resolution
1. Birth to 12–18 months	Feeding	Trust vs. mistrust	Child develops a belief that the environment can be counted on to meet his or her basic physiological and social needs.
2. 18 months to 3 years	Toilet training	Autonomy vs. shame/doubt	Child learns what he or she can control and develops a sense of free will and a corresponding sense of regret and sorrow for inappropriate use of self-control.
3. 3–6 years	Independence	Initiative vs. guilt	Child learns to begin action, to explore, to imagine, and to feel remorse for actions.
4. 6–12 years	School	Industry vs. inferiority	Child learns to do things well or correctly in comparison to a standard or to others.
5. 12–18 years	Peer relationships	Identity vs. role confusion	Adolescent develops a sense of self in relationship to others and to own internal thoughts and desires.
6. 19–40 years	Love relationships	Intimacy vs. isolation	Person develops the ability to give and receive love; begins to make long-term commitment to relationships.
7. 40–65 years	Parenting	Generativity vs. stagnation	Person develops interest in guiding the development of the next generation.
8. 65 to death	Reflection on and acceptance of one's life	Ego integrity vs. despair	Person develops a sense of acceptance of life as it was lived and the importance of the people and relationships that the individual developed over the life span.

FROM PARENTS TO PEERS

Children's views of themselves and their world are tightly tied to the views of their parents, but puberty creates a new set of needs that begins to snip away at those bonds by orienting adolescents toward peers rather than parents. The psychologist Erik Erikson (1959) characterized each stage of life by the major task confronting the individual at that stage. His *stages of psychosocial development* (shown in **TABLE 11.2**) suggest that the major task of adolescence is the development of an adult identity. Whereas children define themselves almost entirely in terms of their relationships with parents and siblings, adolescence marks a shift in emphasis from family relations to peer relations (Roisman, Masten, Coatsworth, & Tellegen, 2004).

Two things can make this shift difficult. First, children cannot choose their parents, but adolescents can choose their peers. As such, adolescents have the power to shape themselves by joining groups that will lead them to develop new values, attitudes, beliefs, and perspectives (Shin & Ryan, 2014). In a sense, the adolescent has the opportunity to invent the adult he or she will soon become, and the responsibility this opportunity entails can be overwhelming (Tarantino et al., 2014). Second, as adolescents strive for greater autonomy, their parents naturally rebel. For instance, parents and adolescents tend to disagree about the age at which certain adult behaviors—such as staying out late or having sex—are permissible, and you don't need a scientist to tell you which position each party in this conflict tends to

"You're free-range when I say you're free-range."

Adolescents form same-sex cliques that meet opposite-sex cliques in public places. Eventually, most of them will form mixed-sex cliques, pair off into romantic relationships, get married, have children, and then worry about them when they do all the same things.

hold (Holmbeck & O'Donnell, 1991). Because adolescents and parents often have different ideas about who should control the adolescent's behavior, their relationships become more conflictive and less close, their interactions become briefer and less frequent (Larson & Richards, 1991), and their parents become less happy about it (Luthar & Ciciolla, 2016). Even so, most adolescents don't have a particularly large number of conflicts with their parents (Chung, Flook, & Fuligni, 2009), and when they do, they tend to be conflicts over relatively minor issues, such as dress and language (which may explain why teenagers argue more with their mothers, who are typically in charge of such issues, than with their fathers; Caspi et al., 1993).

When adolescents pull away from their parents, they move toward their peers. Studies show that across a wide variety of cultures, historical epochs, and even species, peer relations evolve in a similar way (Dunphy, 1963; Weisfeld, 1999). Most young adolescents initially form groups or "cliques" with same-sex peers, many of whom were friends during childhood (Brown, Mory, & Kinney, 1994). Next, male cliques and female cliques begin to meet in public places, such as town squares or shopping malls, and they begin to interact—but only in groups and only in public. After a few years, the older members of these same-sex cliques peel off and form smaller, mixed-sex cliques, which may assemble in private as well as in public, but usually assemble as a group (Molloy, Gest, Feinberg, & Osgood, 2014). Finally, couples (typically but not always, a male and a female) peel off from the small, mixed-sex clique and begin romantic relationships.

Studies show that throughout adolescence, people spend increasing amounts of time with opposite-sex peers while maintaining the amount of time they spend with same-sex peers (Richards et al., 1998), and they accomplish this by spending less time with their parents (Larson & Richards, 1991). Although peers exert considerable influence on the adolescent's beliefs and behaviors, this influence generally occurs because adolescents like their peers and want to impress them, and not because the peers exert pressure (Smith, Chein, & Steinberg, 2014; Susman et al., 1994). In fact, as they age, adolescents show an increasing tendency to resist peer pressure (Steinberg & Monahan, 2007). Acceptance by peers is of tremendous importance to adolescents, and those who are rejected by their peers tend to be withdrawn, lonely, and depressed (Pope & Bierman, 1999). Fortunately for those of us who were seventh-grade nerds, individuals who are unpopular in early adolescence can become popular in later adolescence as their peers become less rigid and more tolerant (Kinney, 1993).

Build to the Outcomes

1. How does the brain change at puberty?

2. What is the importance of an earlier onset of puberty?

3. Are adolescent problems inevitable?

4. What makes adolescence especially difficult?

5. Is sexual orientation a matter of choice?

6. Why do many adolescents make unwise choices about sex?

7. How do family and peer relationships change during adolescence?

8. What are Erikson's stages of psychosocial development?

Adulthood: Change We Can't Believe In

Learning Outcomes

▶ Describe the physical and psychological changes that occur in adulthood.

▶ Describe the effects of children on parental happiness.

In fewer than 7,000 days, a single-celled zygote can become a registered voter. **Adulthood** is *the stage of development that begins around 18 to 21 years and ends at death*. Because physical change slows from a gallop to a crawl, many of us think of adulthood as the destination to which the process of development finally delivers us, and that once we've arrived, our journey is pretty much complete. Nothing could be further from the truth because a whole host of physical, cognitive, and emotional changes take place between our first legal beer and our last legal breath.

CHANGING ABILITIES

The early 20s are the peak years for health, stamina, vigor, and prowess, and because our psychology is so closely tied to our biology, these are also the years during which many of our cognitive abilities are at their sharpest. If you are a typical college student, then at this very moment you see farther, hear better, remember more, and weigh less than you ever will again. Enjoy it while you can. This glorious moment at your physical peak will last for just a few dozen months more—and then, somewhere between the ages of 26 and 30, you will begin the slow and steady decline that will not end until you do. Just 10 or 15 years after puberty, your body will begin to break down in almost every way. Your muscles will be replaced by fat, your skin will become less elastic, your hair will thin and your bones will weaken, your sensory abilities will become less acute, and your brain cells will die at an accelerated rate. Eventually, if you are a woman, your ovaries will stop producing eggs and you will become infertile. Eventually, if you are a man, your erections will be fewer and farther between. Indeed, other than being more resistant to colds and less sensitive to pain, your elderly body just won't work as well as your youthful body does.

As these physical changes accumulate, they will begin to have measurable psychological consequences (Hartshorne & Germine, 2015; Salthouse, 2006). For instance, as your brain ages, your prefrontal cortex and its associated subcortical connections will deteriorate more quickly than the other areas of your brain (Raz, 2000), and you will experience a noticeable decline on many cognitive tasks that require effort, initiative, or strategy. Your memory will get worse overall, though some kinds will get worse than others. For instance, you will experience a greater decline in working memory (the ability to hold information "in mind") than in long-term memory (the ability to retrieve information), a greater decline in episodic memory (the ability to remember particular past events) than in semantic memory (the ability to remember general information such as the meanings of words), and a greater decline in retrieval accuracy than in recognition accuracy.

Is the news all bad? Not really. Even though some of your cognitive machinery will get creakier and rustier as you age, you will learn to use it more skillfully (Bäckman

adulthood The stage of development that begins around 18 to 21 years and ends at death.

One week before his 58th birthday, US Airways pilot Chesley "Sully" Sullenberger made a perfect emergency landing in the Hudson River and saved the lives of everyone on board. None of the passengers wished they'd had a younger pilot.

& Dixon, 1992; Salthouse, 1987). Older chess players *remember* chess positions more poorly than younger players do, but they *play* just as well because they learn to search the board more efficiently (Charness, 1981). Older typists *react* more slowly than younger typists do, but they *type* just as quickly and accurately because they are better at anticipating the next word in spoken or written text (Salthouse, 1984). Older airline pilots are worse than younger pilots when it comes to keeping a list of words in short-term memory, but this age difference disappears when those words are the heading commands that pilots receive from the control tower every flight (Morrow et al., 1994). As **FIGURE 11.13** shows, performance on some cognitive tasks peaks when people are young, but performance on other tasks doesn't peak until people are in their 30s, their 40s, and even their 50s (see Hot Science: I Won't Make *That* Mistake Again!)

How do older adults compensate for age-related declines in memory and attention (Park & McDonough, 2013)? As you know from the Neuroscience and Behavior chapter, young brains are highly differentiated—that is, they have different parts that do different things. But as the brain ages, it becomes *de-differentiated* (Lindenberger & Baltes, 1994). For example, regions of the visual cortex that specialize in face and scene perception in younger people are much less specialized in older people (Grady et al., 1992; Park et al., 2004). The brain is like a bunch of specialists who work independently when they are young and able, but who pull together as a team when

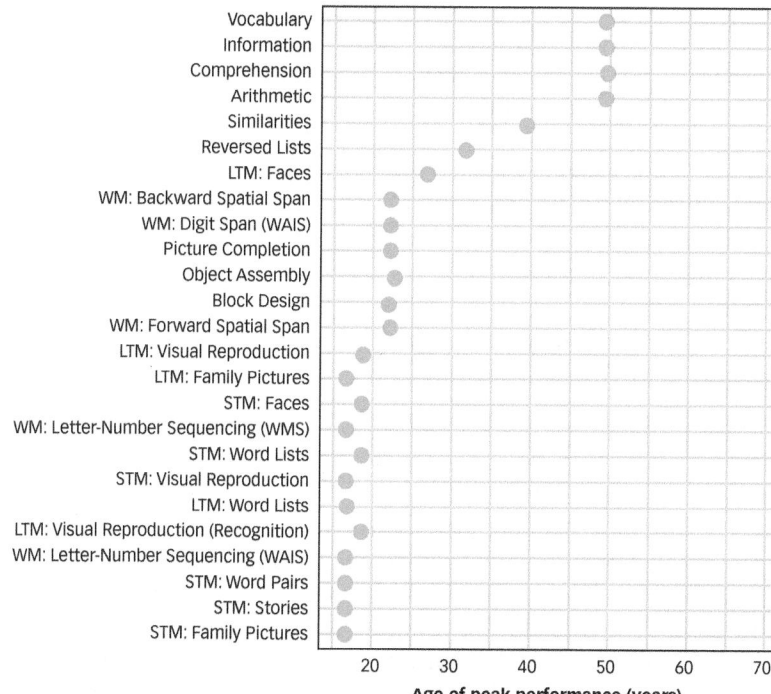

◄ Figure 11.13

AGE-RELATED CHANGES IN COGNITIVE PERFORMANCE This chart shows the age of peak performances on a wide variety of cognitive tests, some of which measure working memory (WM), short-term memory (STM), and long-term memory (LTM). Data from Hartshorne & Germine (2015).

I Won't Make *That* Mistake Again!

What was the name of the woman who founded the Red Cross? If you don't know, then ask your parents. Although younger adults outperform older adults on a wide variety of cognitive tasks, answering general-knowledge questions is an exception to this rule. The reason seems obvious: Older adults have had more time to accumulate facts about the world, which explains why they typically clobber their children and grandchildren when playing Trivial Pursuit. But what seems obvious may not be entirely correct. A recent study suggests that older adults don't outperform younger ones simply because they've had more time to get the facts right, but because they pay closer attention when they get the facts wrong.

Metcalfe and colleagues (2015) gave a group of young adults (24 years old on average) and a group of older adults (74 years old on average) a long series of trivia questions. They asked the participants to answer each question and to say how confident they were in their answers. Next, the researchers gave the participants a chance to learn from their mistakes by showing them the correct answers to the trivia questions. No mat-

ter how much they knew, all participants naturally made some *surprising mistakes* (i.e., they were wrong about answers in which they'd expressed great confidence) and some *unsurprising mistakes* (i.e., they were wrong about answers in which they'd expressed little confidence). After the participants finished studying the right answers, the researchers measured how much participants had learned by asking them to answer all the trivia questions a second time.

The results were fascinating. As expected, older adults got more of the trivia questions right on the very first round. That is, they made fewer mistakes. But in addition, they learned more from the mistakes they made! The *y*-axis in the graph shows the percentage of incorrectly answered questions from the first round that participants answered correctly in the second round. This is a measure of how much participants learned from seeing the right answers between rounds. As the leftmost bars show, all participants learned about the same amount from their surprising mistakes: Discovering that you were completely, totally, and utterly mistaken makes a pretty big impression on people of any age ("I was absolutely *sure* the Red Cross

was founded by Florence Nightingale—and man, was I wrong!"). But as the rightmost bars show, older adults learned much more than younger adults did from their unsurprising mistakes ("I had a vague hunch that it might be Florence Nightingale, but I guess it wasn't"). Apparently, older people pay close attention whenever they are wrong, but younger people only pay close attention when they are *surprised* to be wrong. Grandma may know more about the world than you do because she's been in it longer, but it looks like she's also better at learning from the mistakes she made along the way.

And oh by the way—the founder of the Red Cross was Clara Barton. Someday you'll remember that.

DATA VISUALIZATION

Is There a Cognitive Decline with Age Regardless of Cognitive Stimulation? Go to launchpadworks.com.

each specialist gets older and slower (Park & McDonough, 2013). For example, when young adults try to keep verbal information in working memory, the left prefrontal cortex is more strongly activated than the right, and when young adults try to keep spatial information in working memory, the right prefrontal cortex is more strongly activated than the left (Smith & Jonides, 1997). But this *bilateral asymmetry* pretty much disappears in older adults, which suggests that the older brain is compensating for the declining abilities of each individual neural structure by calling on its other neural structures to help out (Cabeza, 2002; see **FIGURE 11.14**). The physical machinery breaks down as time passes, and one of the ways in which the brain rises to that challenge is by changing its division of labor.

CHANGING GOALS

One reason that Grandpa can't find his car keys is that his prefrontal cortex doesn't work as well as it used to. But another reason is that the location of car keys just isn't the sort of thing that grandfathers want to spend their precious time memorizing (Haase, Heckhausen, & Wrosch, 2013). According to *socioemotional selectivity theory* (Carstensen & Turk-Charles, 1994), younger adults are largely oriented toward the acquisition of information that will be useful to them in the future (e.g., reading restaurant reviews), whereas older adults are generally oriented toward information that

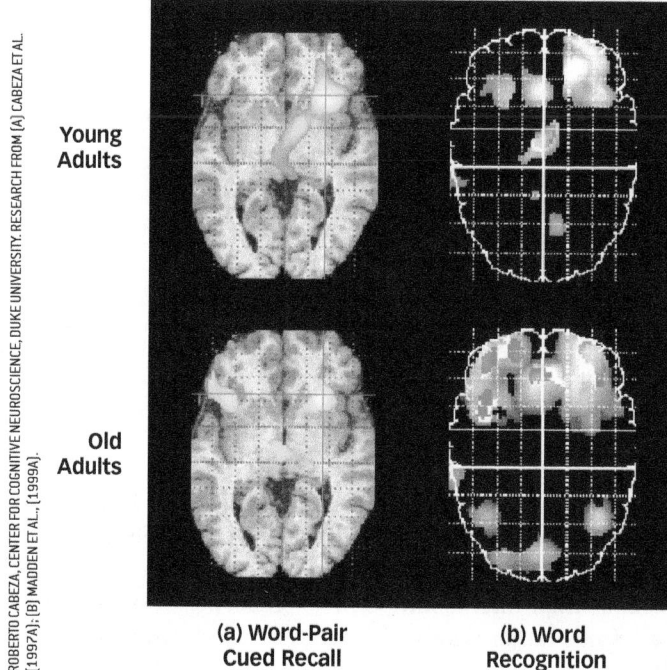

ROBERTO CABEZA, CENTER FOR COGNITIVE NEUROSCIENCE, DUKE UNIVERSITY. RESEARCH FROM (A) CABEZA ET AL. (1997A); (B) MADDEN ET AL., (1999A).

Young Adults

Old Adults

(a) Word-Pair Cued Recall   **(b) Word Recognition**

◄ Figure 11.14

BILATERALITY IN OLDER AND YOUNGER BRAINS Across a variety of tasks, older adult brains show bilateral activation, and young adult brains show unilateral activation. One explanation for this is that older brains compensate for the declining abilities of one neural structure by calling on other neural structures for help.

brings emotional satisfaction in the present (e.g., reading detective novels). Because young people have such long futures, they invest their time attending to, thinking about, and remembering potentially useful information that may fill their informational needs well tomorrow. Because older people have much shorter futures, they spend their time attending to, thinking about, and remembering positive information that fills their emotional needs today (see **FIGURE 11.15**).

For example, older people perform *much* more poorly than younger people when they are asked to remember a series of unpleasant faces, but only *slightly* more poorly when they are asked to remember a series of pleasant faces (Mather & Carstensen, 2003). Whereas younger adults show equal amounts of amygdala activation when they see very pleasant or very unpleasant pictures, older adults show much more activation when they see very pleasant than very unpleasant pictures, suggesting that older adults just aren't attending to information that doesn't make them happy (Mather et al., 2004; Mikels & Shuster, 2016). Indeed, compared with younger adults, older adults are generally better at sustaining positive emotions and curtailing negative ones (Isaacowitz, 2012; Isaacowitz & Blanchard-Fields, 2012; Lawton et al., 1992; Mather & Carstensen, 2005). They also experience fewer negative emotions (Carstensen et al., 2000; Charles, Reynolds, & Gatz, 2001; Mroczek & Spiro, 2005; Schilling, Wahl, & Wiegering, 2013), and are more accepting of them when they do (Shallcross et al., 2013).

Given all this, you shouldn't be surprised to learn that people find late adulthood to be one of the happiest and most satisfying periods of life (see **FIGURE 11.16**). You *shouldn't* be surprised, but you probably are because young adults vastly overestimate the problems of aging (Pew Research Center for People & the Press, 2009; Sneed, 2005; see **FIGURE 11.17**). Indeed, young people predict that they will be happier at 30 than at 70, and yet 70-year-olds typically report greater happiness than 30-year-olds do (Lacey, Smith, & Ubel, 2006). Not only do older adults report being happier, they also report being hotter. Yes, you read that right. When people are asked whether they feel good about their physical appearance, they are more likely to say yes if they are over 65 than if they under 34 (Gallup, 2014)!

Having a short future makes people feel, think, and act differently. For example, because they are not concerned about "saving for tomorrow," older people are more

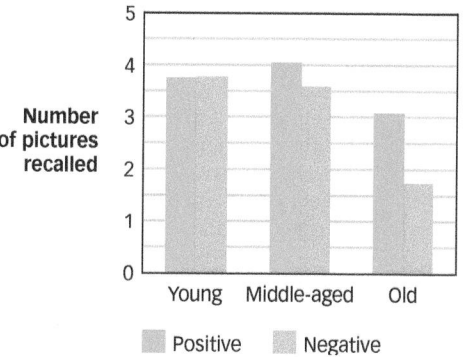

Number of pictures recalled

■ Positive   ■ Negative

▲ Figure 11.15

MEMORY FOR PICTURES Memory generally declines with age, but the ability to remember negative information—such as unpleasant pictures—declines much more quickly than the ability to remember positive information (Carstensen et al., 2000).

▶ Figure 11.16

EMOTIONS AND AGE Older adults experience much lower levels of stress, worry, and anger than younger adults do (Stone et al., 2010).

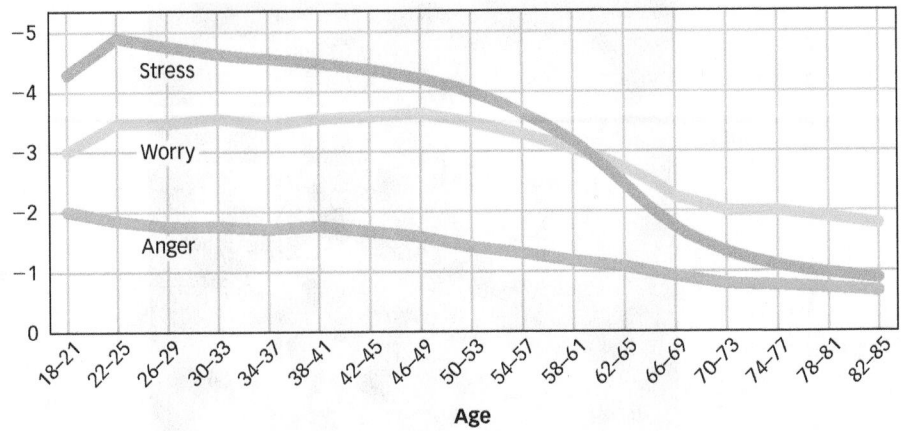

As people age, they prefer to spend time with family and a few close friends rather than large circles of acquaintances.

willing than younger people to forego personal financial gain and instead contribute to the public good (Freund & Blanchard-Fields, 2014). And because they are oriented toward emotionally satisfying rather than profitable experiences, older adults become more selective about their interaction partners, choosing to spend time with family and a few close friends rather than with a large circle of acquaintances (Chui et al, 2014). One study monitored a group of people from the 1930s to the 1990s and found that their rate of interaction with acquaintances declined from early to middle adulthood, but their rate of interaction with spouses, parents, and siblings remained stable or increased (Carstensen, 1992). A study of older adults who ranged in age from 69 to 104 found that the oldest adults had fewer peripheral social partners than the younger adults did, but they had just as many emotionally close partners whom they identified as members of their "inner circle" (Lang & Carstensen, 1994). "Let's go meet some new people" isn't something that most 60-year-olds tend to say, but "Let's go hang out with some old friends" is. It is sad but instructive to note that many of these same cognitive and emotional changes can be observed among younger people who have discovered that their futures will be short because of a terminal illness (Carstensen & Fredrickson, 1998).

CHANGING ROLES

The psychological separation from parents that begins in adolescence usually becomes a physical separation in adulthood. In virtually all human societies, young

▶ Figure 11.17

IT'S BETTER THAN YOU THINK Perhaps it is our youth-obsessed culture, or perhaps it is just their lack of direct experience, but in either case, young adults consistently overestimate the problems of aging (Pew Research Center for the People & the Press, 2009).

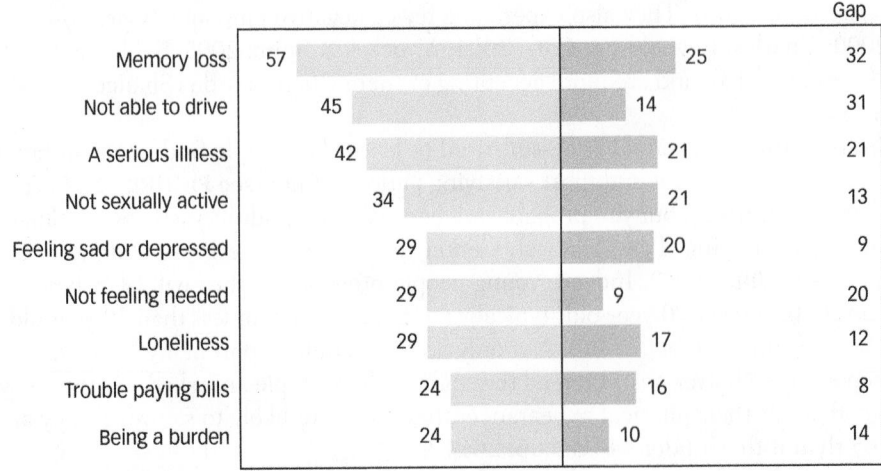

adults leave home, get married, and have children of their own. Marriage and parenthood are two of the most significant aspects of adult life. Census statistics suggest that if you are right now a college-age American, then you are likely to get married at around the age of 27, have approximately 1.8 children, and consider both your partner and your children to be your greatest sources of joy. Indeed, a whopping 93% of American mothers say that their children are a source of happiness all or most of the time (Pew Research Center, 1997).

But do marriage and children really make us happy? Married people do indeed report being somewhat happier than unmarried people—whether those unmarried people are single, widowed, divorced, or cohabiting (Johnson & Wu, 2002; Dion, 2005; Lucas & Dyrenforth, 2005). That's why some researchers consider marriage to be a good investment in one's happiness. But other researchers suggest that married people may be happier simply because happy people are more likely to get married, and that marriage may be the consequence—and not the cause—of happiness (Lucas et al., 2003). The general consensus among scientists seems to be that both of these positions have some merit: Even before marriage, people who will end up married tend to be happier than those who will never marry, but marriage does seem to confer some further happiness benefit, particularly when the members of the couple regard each other as their "best friend" (Helliwell & Grover, 2014). It is worth noting that marriage has become less popular over the last few decades in most Western nations and being single has become an increasingly attractive and satisfying option for many (DePaulo & Morris, 2005). If these trends continue, the happiness boost that marriage seems to provide may soon be a thing of the past.

Children are another story. In general, research suggests that children do not increase their parents' happiness, and more often than not they decrease it (Stanca, 2016). For example, parents typically report lower marital satisfaction than do nonparents—and the more children they have, the less satisfaction they report (Twenge, Campbell, & Foster, 2003). Studies of marital satisfaction at different points in the life span reveal an interesting pattern of peaks and valleys (Van Laningham, Johnson, & Amato, 2001). As **FIGURE 11.18** shows, marital satisfaction starts out high, plummets at about the time that the children are in diapers, begins to recover, plummets again when the children are in adolescence, and returns to its premarital levels only when children leave home. Given that mothers typically do much more child care than fathers, it is not surprising that the negative impact of parenthood is stronger for women than for men. Women with young children are especially likely to experience role conflicts ("How am I supposed to manage being a full-time lawyer and a full-time mother?") and restrictions of freedom ("I never get to play tennis anymore"). A study that measured the moment-to-moment happiness of American women as they went about their daily activities found that women were less happy

Research suggests that marriage has a positive impact on happiness. Especially in the first five minutes.

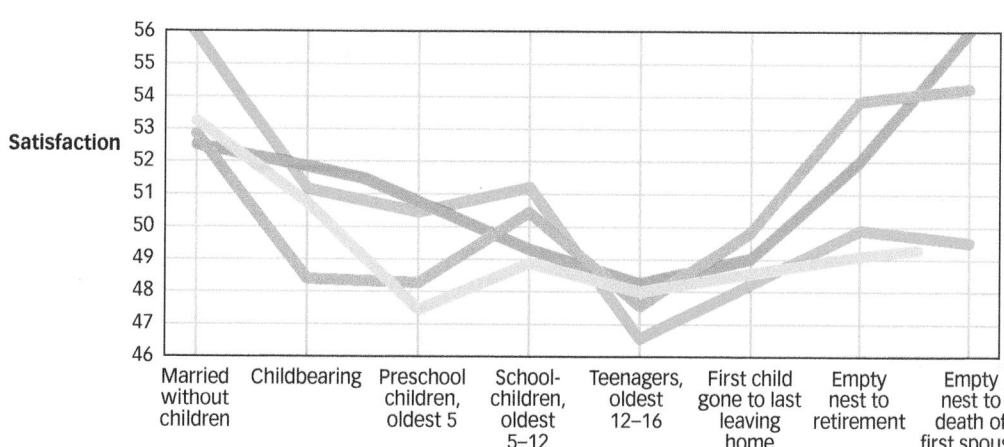

Satisfaction

| | Married without children | Childbearing | Preschool children, oldest 5 | School-children, oldest 5–12 | Teenagers, oldest 12–16 | First child gone to last leaving home | Empty nest to retirement | Empty nest to death of first spouse |

◄ Figure 11.18

MARITAL SATISFACTION OVER THE LIFE SPAN This graph shows the results of four independent studies of marital satisfaction among men and women. All four studies suggest that marital satisfaction is highest before children are born and after they leave home (Walker, 1977).

People with children tend to be less happy than people without them. But this effect is stronger in some countries than in others, and in a few countries, people with children are actually happier than those without them. In 2015, parents in Macedonia (*left*) experienced the largest "happiness penalty" and parents in Montenegro (*right*) experienced the largest "happiness premium."

when taking care of their children than when eating, exercising, shopping, napping, or watching television—and only slightly happier than when they were doing housework (Kahneman et al., 2004).

Does all of this mean that people would be happier if they didn't have children? Not necessarily. Because researchers cannot randomly assign people to be parents or nonparents, studies of the effects of parenthood are necessarily correlational. People who want children and have children may be somewhat less happy than people who neither want them nor have them, but it is possible that people who want children would be even less happy if they didn't have them. What does seem clear is that raising children is a challenging job that people find most rewarding when they're not in the middle of doing it.

Build to the Outcomes

1. What physical and psychological changes are associated with adulthood?

2. How do adults compensate for their declining abilities?

3. How do informational goals change in adulthood?

4. Why is late adulthood such a happy time for most people?

5. What does research say about children and happiness?

Chapter Review

Prenatality: A Womb with a View

▶ Developmental psychology studies continuity and change across the life span.

▶ The prenatal stage of development begins when a sperm fertilizes an egg, producing a zygote. The zygote, which contains chromosomes from both the egg and the sperm, develops into an embryo at 2 weeks and then into a fetus at 8 weeks.

▶ The fetal environment has important physical and psychological influences on the fetus. In addition to the food a pregnant woman eats, teratogens—agents that impair fetal development—can affect the fetus. The most common teratogens are tobacco and alcohol.

▶ Although the fetus cannot see much in the womb, it can hear sounds and become familiar with those it hears often, such as its mother's voice.

Infancy and Childhood: Doing and Thinking

▶ Infants have a limited range of vision, but they can see and remember objects that appear within it. They learn to control their bodies from the top down and from the center out.

▶ Infants slowly develop theories about how the world works. Piaget believed that these theories developed through four stages in which children learn basic facts about the world, such as the fact that objects continue to exist even when they are out of sight, and the fact that objects have enduring properties that are not changed by superficial transformations. Children also learn that their minds represent objects; hence objects may not be as they appear, and others may not see them as the child does.

▶ Cognitive development also comes about through social interactions in which children are given tools for understanding that have been developed over millennia by members of their cultures.

Infancy and Childhood: Caring and Belonging

▶ At a very early age, human beings develop strong emotional ties to their primary caregivers. The quality of these ties—which are indexed by either secure, avoidant, ambivalent, or disorganized attachment styles—is determined both by the caregiver's behavior and the child's temperament.

▶ People get along with each other by learning and obeying moral principles.

▶ Piaget concluded that children's reasoning about right and wrong develops in three ways. It is initially based on inviolable truths about the world, but expands to include concepts of fairness and equity. As they mature, children begin to consider the actor's intentions as well as the extent to which the action obeys abstract moral principles. Kohlberg outlined a theory of morality that progresses from evaluation of an action's consequences, to determination of how it aligns with social rules, and finally to core values.

▶ Moral judgments may be the consequences of our emotional reactions to the suffering of others.

Adolescence: Minding the Gap

▶ Adolescence is a stage of development that is distinct from those stages that come before and after it. It begins with puberty, the onset of sexual maturity of the human body. Puberty now occurs earlier than ever before, and the entrance of young people into adult society occurs later.

▶ Adolescents are somewhat more likely to do things that are risky or illegal, but they rarely inflict serious or enduring harm on themselves or others.

▶ Although most people are attracted to members of the opposite sex, some are not, and research suggests that biology plays a key role in determining a person's sexual orientation. Sex education has been shown to reduce risky sexual behavior.

▶ As adolescents seek to develop their adult identities, they seek increasing autonomy from their parents and become more peer oriented, forming single-sex cliques, followed by mixed-sex cliques. Finally, they pair off as couples.

Adulthood: Change We Can't Believe In

▶ Performance on most cognitive tasks peaks when people are in their 20s, but performance on other tasks peaks when people are in their 30s, 40s, and even 50s. Older people develop a variety of strategies to compensate for their cognitive declines.

▶ Older people are more oriented toward emotional satisfaction which influences the way they attend to and remember information, the size and structure of their social networks, and their happiness.

▶ For most people, adulthood means leaving home, getting married, and having children. The responsibilities that parenthood entails present a significant challenge to people's happiness.

KEY CONCEPT QUIZ

1. Learning begins
   a. in the womb.
   b. at birth.
   c. in the newborn stage.
   d. in infancy.

2. The proximodistal rule states that
   a. motor skills emerge in sequence from the center to the periphery.
   b. motor skills emerge in sequence from the top to the bottom.
   c. motor skills such as rooting are hard wired by nature.
   d. simple motor skills disappear as more sophisticated motor skills emerge.

3. Piaget believed that infants construct _____, which are theories about the way the world works.
   a. assimilations
   b. accommodations
   c. schemas
   d. habituations

4. Once children understand that human behavior is guided by mental representations, they are said to have acquired
   a. joint attention.
   b. a theory of mind.
   c. formal operational ability.
   d. egocentrism.

5. When infants in a new situation examine their mother's face for cues about what to do, they are demonstrating an ability known as
   a. joint attention.
   b. social referencing.
   c. imitation.
   d. all of the above.

6. The capacity for attachment may be innate, but the quality of attachment is influenced by
   a. the child's temperament.
   b. the primary caregiver's ability to read the child's emotional state.
   c. the interaction between the child and the primary caregiver.
   d. all of the above.

7. According to Kohlberg, each stage in the development of moral reasoning is characterized by a specific focus. What is the correct sequence of these stages?
   a. focus on consequences, focus on ethical principles, focus on social rules
   b. focus on ethical principles, focus on social rules, focus on consequences
   c. focus on consequences, focus on social rules, focus on ethical principles
   d. focus on social rules, focus on consequences, focus on ethical principles

8. Scientific evidence suggests that _____ play(s) a key role in determining a person's sexual orientation.
    a. personal choices
    b. parenting styles
    c. sibling relationships
    d. biology

9. Adolescents place the greatest emphasis on relationships with
    a. peers.
    b. parents.
    c. siblings.
    d. nonparental authority figures.

10. Data suggest that, for most people, the last decades of life are
    a. characterized by an increase in negative emotions.
    b. spent attending to the most useful information.
    c. extremely satisfying.
    d. a time during which they begin to interact with a much wider circle of people.

 LearningCurve   **Don't stop now! Quizzing yourself is a powerful study tool. Go to LaunchPad to access the LearningCurve adaptive quizzing system and your own personalized learning plan. Visit launchpadworks.com.**

KEY TERMS

developmental psychology (p. 428)

zygote (p. 429)

germinal stage (p. 429)

embryonic stage (p. 429)

fetal stage (p. 429)

myelination (p. 430)

teratogens (p. 430)

fetal alcohol syndrome (FAS) (p. 430)

infancy (p. 431)

motor development (p. 432)

motor reflexes (p. 432)

cephalocaudal rule (p. 432)

proximodistal rule (p. 432)

cognitive development (p. 432)

sensorimotor stage (p. 433)

schemas (p. 433)

assimilation (p. 433)

accommodation (p. 433)

object permanence (p. 434)

childhood (p. 435)

preoperational stage (p. 435)

concrete operational stage (p. 435)

conservation (p. 436)

formal operational stage (p. 436)

egocentrism (p. 436)

theory of mind (p. 438)

attachment (p. 443)

Strange Situation (p. 443)

temperaments (p. 443)

internal working model of relationships (p. 444)

preconventional stage (p. 446)

conventional stage (p. 446)

postconventional stage (p. 446)

adolescence (p. 448)

puberty (p. 448)

primary sex characteristics (p. 448)

secondary sex characteristics (p. 448)

adulthood (p. 460)

CHANGING MINDS

1. One of your friends recently got married, and she and her husband are planning to have children. You mention to your friend that once this happens she'll have to stop drinking. She scoffs. "They make it sound as though a pregnant woman who drinks alcohol is murdering her baby. Look, my mom drank wine every weekend when she was pregnant with me, and I'm just fine." What is your friend failing to understand about the effects of alcohol on prenatal development? What other teratogens might you tell her about?

2. You are at the grocery store when you spot a crying child in a stroller. The mother picks up the child and cuddles it until it stops crying. A grocery clerk is standing next to you, stocking the shelves. He leans over and says, "Now, that's bad parenting. If you pick up and cuddle a child every time it cries, you're reinforcing the behavior, and the result will be a very spoiled child." Do you agree? What do studies of attachment suggest about the effects of picking up and holding children when they cry?

3. You and your roommate are watching a movie in which a young man tells his parents that he's gay. The parents react badly and decide that they should send him to a "camp" where he can learn to change his sexual orientation. Your roommate turns to you: "Do you know anything about this? Can people really be changed from gay to straight?" What would you tell your friend about "conversion therapy" and about the factors that determine sexual orientation?

4. One of your cousins has just turned 30 and, to his horror, has discovered a gray hair. "This is the end," he says. "Soon I'll start losing my eyesight, growing new chins, and forgetting how to use a cell phone. Aging is just one long, slow, agonizing decline." What could you tell your cousin to cheer him up? Does everything in life get worse with age?

ANSWERS TO KEY CONCEPT QUIZ

1. a; 2. a; 3. c; 4. b; 5. b; 6. d; 7. c; 8. d; 9. a; 10. c.

LaunchPad features the full e-Book of *Psychology*, the LearningCurve adaptive quizzing system, videos, and a variety of activities to boost your learning. Visit LaunchPad at launchpadworks.com.

Personality

12

GROWING UP, STEFANI JOANNE ANGELINA GERMANOTTA seemed to have personality. As a child, she was said to have shown up at the occasional family gathering naked. As the pop star now known as Lady Gaga, she continues the tradition of being different. Her first albums, *The Fame* and *The Fame Monster,* and the fact that she calls her fans "Little Monsters" and herself the "Mother Monster," hinted she might have issues. But she, like most of us, is not one-dimensional. Yes, her style is eccentric and seems silly to many (we're looking at you, raw meat dress), but she also is a serious supporter of humanitarian and personal causes, including equality for people who are gay, bisexual, lesbian, or transgender (as in her song "Born This Way"). Lady Gaga is one of a kind. She has personality in an important sense—she has qualities that make her psychologically different from other people.

The singer Lady Gaga in her meat dress at the MTV Video Music Awards, September 2010.

PA WIRE/AP IMAGES

personality An individual's characteristic style of behaving, thinking, and feeling.

THE FORCES THAT CREATE ANY ONE PERSONALITY ARE ALWAYS something of a mystery. Your personality is different from anyone else's and expresses itself pretty consistently across settings—at home, in the classroom, and elsewhere. But how and why do people differ psychologically? By studying many unique individuals, psychologists seek to gather enough information to answer these central questions of personality psychology scientifically.

Personality is *an individual's characteristic style of behaving, thinking, and feeling.* Whether Lady Gaga's quirks are real or merely put on for publicity, they certainly are hers and they show her distinct personality. In this chapter, we will explore personality, first by looking at what it is and how it is measured, and then by focusing on each of four main approaches to understanding personality: trait–biological, psychodynamic, humanistic–existential, and social–cognitive. Psychologists have personalities, too (well, *most* of them), so their different approaches, even to the topic of personality, shouldn't be that surprising. At the end of the chapter, we discuss the psychology of self to see how our views of what we are like can shape and define our personality.

Personality: What It Is and How It Is Measured

Learning Outcomes

▶ Explain how prior and anticipated events explain personality differences.

▶ Compare personality inventories and projective techniques.

Howard Stern   Hillary Clinton

Kim Kardashian   Chris Rock

How would you describe each of these personalities?

If someone said, "You have no personality," how would you feel? Like a cookie-cutter person, a boring, grayish lump who should go out and get a personality as soon as possible? As a rule, people don't strive for a personality—one seems to develop naturally as we travel through life. As psychologists have tried to understand the process of personality development, they have pondered questions of description (*how* do people differ?), explanation (*why* do people differ?), and the more quantitative question of measurement (how can personality be *assessed*?).

DESCRIBING AND EXPLAINING PERSONALITY

As the first biologists earnestly attempted to classify all plants and animals (whether lichens or ants or fossilized lions), personality psychologists began by labeling and describing different personalities. And just as biology came of age with Darwin's theory of evolution, which *explained* how differences among species arose, the maturing study of personality also has developed explanations of the basis for psychological differences among people.

Most personality psychologists focus on specific, psychologically meaningful individual differences, characteristics such as honesty, anxiety, or moodiness. Still, personality is often in the eye of the beholder. When one person describes another as a "conceited jerk," for example, you may wonder whether you have just learned more about the describer or the person being described. It is interesting that studies that ask acquaintances to describe each other find a high degree of similarity among any one individual's descriptions of many different people ("Jason thinks that Carlos is considerate, Renata is kind, and Jean Paul is nice to others"). In contrast, resemblance is quite low when many people describe one person ("Carlos thinks Jason is smart, Renata thinks he is competitive, and Jean Paul thinks he has a good sense of humor"; Dornbusch et al., 1965).

What leads Lady Gaga to all of her entertaining extremes? Many psychologists attempt to study and explain personality differences by thinking about them in terms of *prior events* that may have shaped an individual's personality or *anticipated events* that motivate the person to reveal particular personality characteristics. In a biological prior event, Stefani Germanotta received genes from her parents that may have led her to develop into the sort of person who loves putting on a display (not to mention putting on raw meat) and stirring up controversy. Researchers interested in events that happen prior to our behavior study our genes, brains, and other aspects of our biological makeup, and also delve into our subconscious and into our circumstances

472

and interpersonal surroundings. The consideration of *anticipated events* emphasizes the person's own, subjective perspective and often seems intimate and personal in its reflection of the person's inner life (hopes, fears, and aspirations).

Of course, our understanding of how the baby named Stefani Germanotta grew into the adult Lady Gaga (or of the life of any woman or man) also depends on insights into the interaction between the prior and anticipated events: We need to know how her history may have shaped her motivations.

MEASURING PERSONALITY

Of all the things psychologists have set out to measure, personality may be one of the toughest. How do you capture the uniqueness of a person? What aspects of people's personalities are important to know about? How should we quantify them? The general personality measures can be classified broadly into personality inventories and projective techniques.

Personality Inventories Rely on Self-reporting

To learn about an individual's personality, you could follow the person around and, clipboard in hand, record every single thing the person does, says, thinks, and feels (including how long this goes on before the person calls the police). Some observations might involve your own impressions (Day 5: seems to be getting irritable); others would involve objectively observable events that anyone could verify (Day 7: grabbed my pencil and broke it in half, then bit my hand).

Psychologists have figured out ways to obtain objective data on personality without driving their subjects to violence. The most popular technique is **self-report,** *a method in which people provide subjective information about their own thoughts, feelings, or behaviors, typically via questionnaire or interview.* In most self-report measures, respondents are asked to circle a number on a scale indicating the degree to which they endorse that item as being self-descriptive (e.g., reporting on a scale of 0–5 to what extent they believe they are a "worrier") or to indicate whether an item is true or false in describing them. The researcher then combines the answers to get a general sense of the individual's personality with respect to a particular domain. **TABLE 12.1** shows the 10 items from a self-report test of different personality traits (Gosling, Rentfrow & Swann, 2003). In this case, the respondent is asked to indicate whether each personality trait applies to him or her. To score the measure, you simply add up the two items for each of the five traits listed at the bottom of the table.

How is a self-report scale created? The usual strategy is to collect sets of self-descriptive statements that indicate different degrees of a personality characteristic. To measure friendliness, for example, you could ask people to rate their agreement with statements ranging from "I am somewhat friendly" to "I am very outgoing," or even to "I love being around people every minute of the day." Adding up the number of statements the person endorses that indicate friendliness (and subtracting endorsements of those who indicate unfriendliness) yields a measure of the person's self-reported friendliness. Scales based on the content of self-reports have been devised to assess a whole range of personality characteristics, all the way from general tendencies such as overall happiness (Lyubomirsky, 2008; Lyubomirsky & Lepper, 1999) to specific ones such as responding rapidly to insults (Swann & Rentfrow, 2001) or complaining about poor service (Lerman, 2006).

One of the most commonly used personality tests is the **Minnesota Multiphasic Personality Inventory (MMPI),** *a well-researched clinical questionnaire used to assess personality and psychological problems.* The MMPI was developed in 1939 and has been revised several times over the years, leading up to the current version, the MMPI–2–RF (restructured form; Ben-Porath & Tellegen, 2008). The MMPI–2–RF consists of 338 self-descriptive statements to which the respondent answers "true," "false," or "cannot say." The MMPI–2–RF measures a wide range of psychological constructs: clinical problems (e.g., antisocial behavior, thought dysfunction), somatic problems (e.g., head pain, cognitive

---

TABLE 12.1

Ten-Item Personality Inventory (TIPI)

Here are a number of personality traits that may or may not apply to you. Please write a number next to each statement to indicate the extent to which *you agree or disagree with that statement.* You should rate the extent to which the pair of traits applies to you, even if one characteristic applies more strongly than the other.

1 = Disagree strongly
2 = Disagree moderately
3 = Disagree a little
4 = Neither agree nor disagree
5 = Agree a little
6 = Agree moderately
7 = Agree strongly

I see myself as:

1. ____ Extraverted, enthusiastic
2. ____ Critical, quarrelsome
3. ____ Dependable, self-disciplined
4. ____ Anxious, easily upset
5. ____ Open to new experiences, complex
6. ____ Reserved, quiet
7. ____ Sympathetic, warm
8. ____ Disorganized, careless
9. ____ Calm, emotionally stable
10. ____ Conventional, uncreative

TIPI scale scoring (R = reverse-scored items): Extraversion (1, 6R); Agreeableness (2R, 7); Conscientiousness (3, 8R); Emotional Stability (4R, 9); Openness to Experience (5, 10R).

Information from Gosling, Rentfrow, & Swann, 2003.

self-report A method in which a person provides subjective information about his or her own thoughts, feelings, or behaviors, typically via questionnaire or interview.

Minnesota Multiphasic Personality Inventory (MMPI) A well-researched clinical questionnaire used to assess personality and psychological problems.

Personality inventories ask people to report what traits they possess. Think about how you would rate yourself according to the items in Table 12.2. Can we rely on people to accurately report on their personality?

SCIENCE SOURCE

▲ Figure 12.1

SAMPLE RORSCHACH INKBLOT Test takers are shown a card such as this sample and asked, "What might this be?" What they perceive, where they see it, and why they believe it looks that way are assumed to reflect unconscious aspects of their personality.

projective tests Tests designed to reveal inner aspects of individuals' personalities by analysis of their responses to a standard series of ambiguous stimuli.

Rorschach Inkblot Test A projective technique in which respondents' inner thoughts and feelings are believed to be revealed by analysis of their responses to a set of unstructured inkblots.

Thematic Apperception Test (TAT) A projective technique in which respondents' underlying motives, concerns, and the way they see the social world are believed to be revealed through analysis of the stories they make up about ambiguous pictures of people.

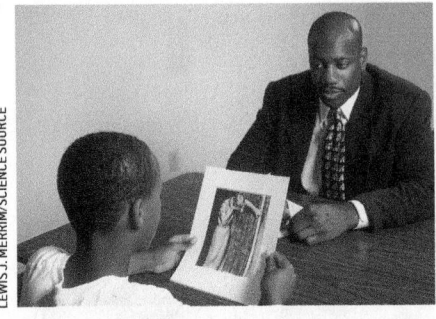

LEWIS J. MERRIM/SCIENCE SOURCE

▲ Figure 12.2

SAMPLE TAT CARD Test takers are shown cards with ambiguous scenes such as this sample and are asked to tell a story about what is happening in the picture. The main themes of the story, the thoughts and feelings of the characters, and how the story develops and resolves are considered useful indices of unconscious aspects of an individual's personality (Murray, 1943).

complaints), internalizing problems (e.g., anxiety, self-doubt), externalizing problems (e.g., aggression, substance abuse), and interpersonal problems (e.g., family problems, avoidance). The MMPI–2–RF also includes *validity scales* that assess a person's attitudes toward test taking and any tendency to try to distort the results by faking answers.

Personality inventories such as the MMPI–2–RF are easy to administer: All that is needed is the test and a pencil (or a computer-based version). The respondent's scores are then calculated and compared with the average ratings of thousands of other test takers. Because no human interpretation of the responses is needed (i.e., "true" means true, "false" means false, etc.), any potential biases of the person giving the test are minimized. Of course, an accurate measurement of personality will only occur if people provide accurate responses. Although self-report test results are easy to obtain, critics of this approach highlight several limitations. One problem is that many people have a tendency to respond in a socially desirable way, such that they underreport things that are unflattering or embarrassing. Perhaps even more problematic is that there are many things we don't know about ourselves and so are unable to report! Studies show that people often are inaccurate in their self-report about what they have experienced in the past, what factors are motivating their behaviors in the present, or how they will feel or behave in the future (Wilson, 2009).

Projective Techniques Rely on Analysis of Ambiguous Information

A second, somewhat controversial, class of tools for evaluating personality designed to circumvent the limitations of self-report mentioned above, is **projective tests,** which are *tests designed to reveal inner aspects of individuals' personalities by analysis of their responses to a standard series of ambiguous stimuli.* The developers of projective tests assume that people will project personality factors that are below awareness—wishes, concerns, impulses, and ways of seeing the world—onto the ambiguous stimuli and will not censor these responses. Probably the best known is the **Rorschach Inkblot Test,** *a projective technique in which respondents' inner thoughts and feelings are believed to be revealed by analysis of their responses to a set of unstructured inkblots.* An example inkblot is shown in **FIGURE 12.1.** Responses are scored according to complicated systems (derived in part from research with people with psychological disorders) that classify what people see (Exner, 1993; Rapaport, 1946). For example, most people who look at Figure 12.1 report seeing birds or people. Someone who reports seeing something very unusual (e.g., "I see two purple tigers eating a velvet cheeseburger") may be experiencing thoughts and feelings that are very different from those of most other people.

The **Thematic Apperception Test (TAT)** is *a projective technique in which respondents' underlying motives and concerns and the way they see the social world are believed to be revealed through analysis of the stories they make up about ambiguous pictures of people.* To get a sense of the test, look at **FIGURE 12.2.** The test administrator shows the respondent the card and asks him or her to tell a story about the picture, asking questions such as: Who is the woman shown on the card? What is happening? What led her to this moment? What will happen next? Many of the TAT drawings tend to elicit a consistent set of themes, such as successes and failures, competition and jealousy, conflict with parents and siblings, feelings about intimate relationships, aggression, and sexuality. Different people tell very different stories about the images. In creating the stories, the respondent is thought to identify with the main characters and to project his or her view of others and the world onto the other details in the drawing. Thus, any details that are not obviously drawn from the picture are believed to be projected onto the story from the respondent's own desires and internal conflicts.

The value of projective tests is debated by psychologists. Although they continue to be widely used by practicing clinicians, critics argue that tests such as the Rorschach and the TAT are open to the biases of the examiner. A TAT story such as the one above may *seem* revealing; however, the examiner must always add an interpretation (Was this about the respondent's actual father, about his own concerns about his academic failures, or about trying to be funny or provocative?), and that interpretation could well be the scorer's *own* projection into the mind of the test taker. Thus, despite the rich picture of a personality and the insights into an individual's motives that these tests offer, we should understand projective tests primarily as a way in which a psychologist can get to know someone personally and intuitively (McClelland et al., 1953). When measured by rigorous scientific criteria, projective tests such as the TAT and the Rorschach have not been found to be reliable or valid in predicting behavior (Lilienfeld, Lynn, & Lohr, 2003).

Methods Utilizing Technology

Newer personality measurement methods are moving beyond both self-report inventories and projective tests (Robins, Fraley, & Krueger, 2007). High-tech methods such as wireless communication, real-time computer analysis, and automated behavior identification open the door to personality measurements that are leaps beyond following the person around with a clipboard—and can lead to surprising findings. The stereotype that women are more talkative than men, for example, was challenged by findings when 396 college students in the United States and Mexico each spent several days wearing an EAR (electronically activated recorder) that captured random snippets of their talk (Mehl et al., 2009). The result? Women and men were *equally* talkative, each averaging about 16,000 words per day. The advanced measurement of how people differ (and how they do not) is a key step in understanding personality.

Psychologists also are using new forms of social media to better understand personality traits and how people express themselves in different ways. An important advantage of this approach, as with the EAR mentioned above, is that it allows psychologists to study people as they actually behave out in the world while interacting with others (vs. in the lab under experimental conditions). For example, one recent study analyzed over 700 million words and phrases that 75,000 people posted on their Facebook pages and compared them to the results from personality tests given to the same people (Schwartz et al., 2013). The results revealed significant differences in how males and females express themselves, as well as differences by age and by personality. For instance, females use more words about emotions, whereas males use more words about objects and more swear words. People posting about going out and partying were those who scored high on extraversion, people posting about being "sick of" things were those who scored high on neuroticism, and people posting about computers and Pokémon cards were those who scored high on introversion. As the world creates newer forms of communicating, psychologists benefit by having newer ways of studying personality.

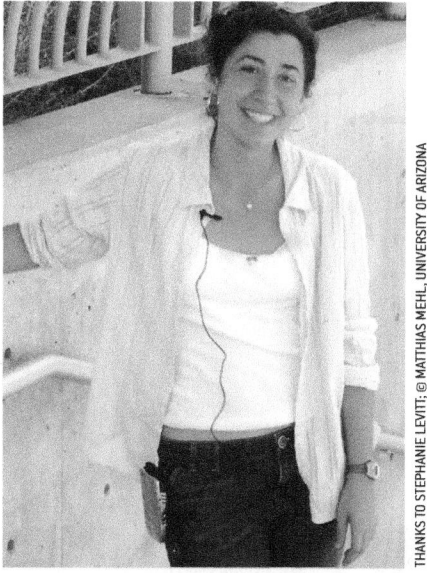

The EAR (electronically activated recorder) sampled conversations of hundreds of participants and found that women and men are equally talkative (Mehl et al., 2009).

Build to the Outcomes

1. What does it mean to say that personality is in the eye of the beholder?

2. Compare the reliability of personality inventories and projective tests.

3. What is the advantage of measurements taken with the EAR and other new technologies?

The Trait Approach: Identifying Patterns of Behavior

Imagine writing a story about the people you know. To capture their special qualities, you might describe their traits: Keesha is *friendly, aggressive,* and *domineering;* Seth is *flaky, humorous,* and *superficial.* With a thesaurus and a free afternoon, you might even be able to describe William as *perspicacious, flagitious,* and *callipygian.* The trait approach to personality uses such trait terms to characterize differences among individuals. In attempting to create manageable and meaningful sets of descriptors, trait theorists face two significant challenges: narrowing down the almost infinite set of

Learning Outcomes

▸ Describe how the trait approach to personality has changed over time.

▸ Describe the traits in the Big Five Factor Model.

▸ Explain the biological basis for personality traits.

trait A relatively stable disposition to behave in a particular and consistent way.

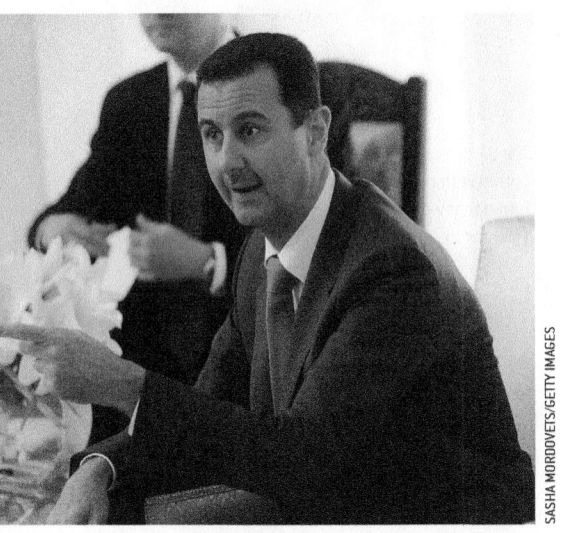

By many accounts, Bashar al-Assad is a despotic ruler who imprisons, tortures, and kills those who oppose him. Why would anyone want to follow such a dictator? The study of the authoritarian personality was inspired by the idea that some people might follow most anyone because their personalities make them adhere to hierarchies of authority, submitting to those above them and dominating those below them.

adjectives and answering the more basic question of why people have particular traits and whether those traits arise from biological or hereditary foundations.

TRAITS AS BEHAVIORAL DISPOSITIONS AND MOTIVES

One way to think about personality is as a combination of traits. This was the approach of Gordon Allport (1937), one of the first trait theorists, who believed people could be described in terms of traits just as an object could be described in terms of its properties. He saw a **trait** as *a relatively stable disposition to behave in a particular and consistent way.* For example, a person who keeps his books organized alphabetically in bookshelves, hangs his clothing neatly in the closet, knows the schedule for the local bus, keeps a clear agenda in a smartphone or daily planner, and lists birthdays of friends and family in his calendar can be said to have the trait of *orderliness.* This trait consistently manifests itself in a variety of settings.

The orderliness trait *describes* a person but doesn't *explain* his or her behavior. Why does the person behave in this way? A trait might provide an explanation for behavior in two basic ways: The trait may be a preexisting disposition of the person that causes the person's behavior, or it may be a motivation that guides the person's behavior. Allport saw traits as preexisting dispositions, causes of behavior that reliably trigger that behavior. The person's orderliness, for example, is an inner property of the person that will cause the person to straighten things up and be tidy in a wide array of situations. Other personality theorists, such as Henry Murray (the creator of the TAT), suggested instead that traits reflect motives. Just as a hunger motive might explain someone's many trips to the snack bar, a need for orderliness might explain the neat closet, organized calendar, and familiarity with the bus schedule (Murray & Kluckhohn, 1953). Researchers examining traits as causes have used personality inventories to measure them, whereas those examining traits as motives have more often used projective tests.

Researchers have described and measured hundreds of different personality traits over the past several decades. Back in the late 1940s, in the wake of World War II, psychologists were very interested in right-wing *authoritarianism,* the tendency toward political conservatism, obedience to authority, and conformity. At that time, researchers were trying to understand what had made people support the rise of Nazi Germany and fascism (Adorno et al., 1950). Although research on the personality traits that lead to authoritarianism continues (Perry & Sibley, 2012), the topic became less focal for researchers once World War II receded into history. Other traits that have come into vogue over the years include cognitive complexity, defensiveness, sensation seeking, and optimism. Like television shows and hairstyles, fashions in trait dimensions come and go over time.

THE SEARCH FOR CORE TRAITS

Picking a fashionable trait and studying it in depth doesn't get us very far in the search for the core of human character: the basic set of traits that defines how humans differ from each other. People may differ strongly in their choice of Coke versus Pepsi, or dogs versus cats, but are these differences important? How have researchers tried to discover the core personality traits?

Early Research Focused on Adjectives That Describe Personality

The study of core traits began with an exploration of how personality is represented in the store of wisdom we call *language*. Generation after generation, people have described people with words, so early psychologists proposed that core traits could be discerned by finding the main themes in all the adjectives used to describe personality. In one such analysis, a painstaking count of relevant words in a dictionary of English resulted in a list of over 18,000 potential traits (Allport & Odbert, 1936)! Attempts to narrow down the list to a more manageable set depend on the idea that traits might

▲ Figure 12.3

HIERARCHICAL STRUCTURE OF TRAITS Traits may be organized in a hierarchy in which many specific behavioral tendencies are associated with a higher-order trait (Eysenck, 1990).

be related in a hierarchical pattern (see **FIGURE 12.3**), with more general or abstract traits at higher levels than more specific or concrete traits. Perhaps the more abstract traits represent the core of personality.

To identify this core, researchers have used the computational procedure called *factor analysis,* described in the Intelligence chapter, which sorts trait terms or self-descriptions into a small number of underlying dimensions, or *factors,* based on how people use the traits to rate themselves. In a typical study using factor analysis, hundreds of people rate themselves on hundreds of adjectives, indicating how accurately each one describes their personality. The researcher then performs calculations to determine similarities in the raters' usage, for example, whether people who describe themselves as *ambitious* also describe themselves as *active* but not *laid-back* or *contented.* Factor analysis also can reveal which adjectives are unrelated. For example, if people who describe themselves as *ambitious* are neither more nor less likely to describe themselves as *creative* or *innovative,* the factor analysis would reveal that *ambitiousness* and *creativity/innovativeness* represent different factors. Each factor is typically presented as a continuum, ranging from one extreme trait (such as *ambitious*) to its opposite (in this case, *laid-back*).

Different factor analysis techniques have yielded different views of personality structure. Cattell (1950) proposed a 16-factor theory of personality (way down from 18,000, but still a lot), whereas others proposed theories with far fewer basic dimensions (John, Naumann, & Soto, 2008). Hans Eysenck (1967) simplified things nicely with a model of personality with only two major traits (although he later expanded it to three). Eysenck's two-factor analysis identified one dimension that distinguished people who are sociable and active (extraverts) from those who are more introspective and quiet (introverts). His analysis also identified a second dimension ranging from the tendency to be very neurotic or emotionally unstable to the tendency to be more emotionally stable. He believed that many behavioral tendencies could be understood in terms of their relation to the core traits of Extraversion and Neuroticism. The third factor he proposed was Psychoticism, which refers to the extent to which a person is impulsive or hostile. (Note that nowadays, the term *psychotic* refers to an abnormal mental state marked by detachment from reality. This is discussed further in the Disorders chapter.)

TABLE 12.2

The Big Five Factor Model

	High on trait .... Low on trait	
Openness to experience	imaginative	down-to-earth
	variety	routine
	independent	conforming
Conscientiousness	organized	disorganized
	careful	careless
	self-disciplined	weak-willed
Extraversion	social	retiring
	fun loving	sober
	affectionate	reserved
Agreeableness	softhearted	ruthless
	trusting	suspicious
	helpful................................	uncooperative
Neuroticism	worried	calm
	insecure	secure
	self-pitying	self-satisfied

DATA VISUALIZATION

Does Personality Remain Stable over Time?
Go to launchpadworks.com.

Big Five The traits of the five-factor model: openness to experience, conscientiousness, extraversion, agreeableness, and neuroticism.

A Consensus Is Reached: The Big Five Dimensions of Personality

Today most researchers agree that personality is best captured by 5 factors rather than 2, 3, 16, or 18,000 (John & Srivastava, 1999; McCrae & Costa, 1999). The **Big Five,** as they are affectionately called, are *the traits of the five-factor personality model: openness to experience, conscientiousness, extraversion, agreeableness, and neuroticism* (see **TABLE 12.2;** remember them by the initials O.C.E.A.N.) The five-factor model, which overlaps with the pioneering work of Cattell and Eysenck, is now widely preferred for several reasons. First, modern factor analysis techniques confirm that this set of five factors strikes the right balance between accounting for as much variation in personality as possible while avoiding overlapping traits. Second, in a large number of studies using different kinds of data (people's descriptions of their own personalities, other people's descriptions of their personalities, interviewer checklists, and behavioral observation) the same five factors have emerged. Third, and perhaps most important, the basic five-factor structure seems to show up across a wide range of participants, including children, adults in other cultures, and even among those who use other languages, suggesting that the Big Five may be universal (John & Srivastava, 1999).

In fact, the Big Five dimensions are so universal that they show up even when people are asked to evaluate the traits of complete strangers (Passini & Norman, 1966). This finding suggests that these dimensions of personality might reside in the eye of the beholder: categories that people use to evaluate others regardless of how well they know them. However, it's not all perception. The reality of these traits has been clearly established in research showing that self-reports on the Big Five are associated with predictable patterns of behavior and social outcomes. People identified as high in extraversion, for example, tend to spend time with lots of other people and are more likely than introverts to look people in the eye. People high in conscientiousness generally perform well at work and tend to live longer. People low on conscientiousness and low in agreeableness are more likely than average to be juvenile delinquents (John & Srivastava, 1999). It turns out that the Big Five personality traits also predict people's online behavior on social networking sites such as Facebook (see Hot Science: Personality on the Surface).

Research on the Big Five has shown the interesting result that people's personalities tend to remain fairly stable through their lifetime: Scores at one time in life correlate strongly with scores at later dates, even decades later (Caspi, Roberts, & Shiner, 2005). William James offered the opinion that "in most of us, by the age of thirty, the character has set like plaster, and will never soften again" (James, 1890, p. 121), but this turns out to be too strong a view. Some variability is typical in childhood, and though there is less in adolescence, some personality change can even occur in adulthood for some people (Srivistava et al., 2003). In general, people become slightly more conscientious in their 20s (got to keep that job!) and a bit more agreeable in their 30s (got to keep those friends!). Neuroticism decreases with age, but only among women (Srivastava et al., 2003). So enjoy the personality you have now, because it may be changing soon.

TRAITS AS BIOLOGICAL BUILDING BLOCKS

Can we explain *why* a person has a stable set of personality traits? Many trait theorists have argued that unchangeable brain and biological processes produce the remarkable stability of traits over the life span. Allport viewed traits as characteristics of the

Personality on the Surface

When you judge someone as friend or foe, interesting or boring, worth hiring or firing, how do you do it? It's nice to think that your impressions of personality are based on solid foundations—something deep. You wouldn't judge personality based on something as shallow as someone's looks, would you? You wouldn't form an impression of them from looking at what pops up on Google images, or on their Facebook page, would you? These criteria may seem to be flimsy bases for understanding personality, but it turns out that some valid personality judgments can be made from exactly such superficial cues. And in certain cases, such judgments are remarkably accurate.

It turns out that you *can* get some accurate information about a book by judging its cover. Studies have shown that extraverts tend to talk faster than others and to subtly mimic other people's behavior as a means of building rapport with them (Duffy & Chartrand, 2015), and people high in openness to experience are more likely to have tattoos (Swami et al., 2012). Find-

ings such as these suggest that people can manipulate their surface identities to try to make desired impressions on others, and that surface signs of personality might therefore be false or misleading. However, one recent study of people's Facebook pages, which are clearly surface expressions of personality intended for others to see, found that the personalities people project online are similar to their own scores on traditional personality tests (Schwartz et al., 2013). The signs

PABLO MARTINEZ MONSIVAIS/AP IMAGES

▲ They say you can't judge a book by its cover, but some new research suggests you can judge a person by their Facebook page.

of personality that appear on the surface may be more than skin deep.

If we go one step further, it turns out that people's Facebook activity is significantly associated with their self-reported personality traits. People high in extraversion report having more Facebook friends as well as making more status updates and comments. People high in agreeableness make more comments on their friends' posts, whereas those high on sensation seeking and openness to experience report playing a lot of games. And as you might have guessed, people high on narcissism post lots of comments, especially about their ideal self, as well as lots of pictures of themselves (Seidman, 2013; Wang et al., 2012). Beyond Facebook, studies of personality have more recently shown that extraverts spend more time messaging friends via apps such as WhatsApp, whereas people high on conscientiousness spend much less time messaging (Montag et al., 2015). We can hope that those conscientious people are using the time they save doing other important things, such as their assigned Intro Psych reading.

brain that influence the way people respond to their environment. And, as you will see, Eysenck searched for a connection between his trait dimensions and specific individual differences in the workings of the brain.

Brain damage certainly can produce personality change, as the classic case of Phineas Gage so vividly demonstrates (see the Neuroscience and Behavior chapter). You may recall that after the blasting accident that blew a steel rod through his frontal lobes, Gage showed a dramatic loss of social appropriateness and conscientiousness (Damasio, 1994). In fact, when someone experiences a profound change in personality, testing often reveals the presence of such brain pathologies as Alzheimer's disease, stroke, or brain tumor (Feinberg, 2001). The administration of antidepressant medication and other pharmaceutical treatments that change brain chemistry also can trigger personality changes, making people, for example, somewhat more extraverted and less neurotic (Bagby et al., 1999; Knutson et al., 1998).

Genes, Traits, and Personality

Some of the most compelling evidence for the importance of biological factors in personality comes from the domain of behavioral genetics. Like researchers studying genetic influences on intelligence (see the Intelligence chapter), personality psychologists have looked at correlations between the traits in monozygotic, or identical, twins, who share the same genes; and dizygotic, or fraternal, twins, who on average share only half of their genes. The evidence has been generally

TABLE 12.3

Heritability Estimates for the Big Five Personality Traits

Trait Dimension	Heritability
Openness	.45
Conscientiousness	.38
Extraversion	.49
Agreeableness	.35
Neuroticism	.41

Information from Loehlin, 1992.

consistent: In one review of studies involving over 24,000 twin pairs, for example, identical twins proved markedly more similar to each other in personality than did fraternal twins (Loehlin, 1992).

Simply put, the more genes you have in common with someone, the more similar your personalities are likely to be. Genes seem to influence most personality traits, and current estimates place the average genetic component of personality at about .40 (Vukasović & Bratko, 2015). These heritability coefficients, as you learned in the Intelligence chapter, indicate that roughly 40% of the variability among individuals results from genetic factors, and the other 60% is from environmental influences. Of course, genetic factors do not account for everything; the remaining half of the variability in personality remains to be explained by differences in life experiences and other factors.

Twin Studies Underscore the Importance of Genetics

Studies of twins suggest that the extent to which the Big Five traits derive from genetic differences ranges from .35 to .49 (see **TABLE 12.3**).

As in the study of intelligence, potential confounding factors must be ruled out to ensure that effects are truly due to genetics and not to environmental experiences. Are identical twins treated more similarly, and do they have a greater *shared environment,* than fraternal twins? As children, were they dressed in the same snappy outfits and placed on the same Little League teams? Could this somehow have produced similarities in their personalities? Studies of identical twins reared far apart in adoptive families—an experience that pretty much eliminates the potential effect of shared environmental factors—suggest that shared environments have little impact: Reared-apart identical twins end up just as similar in personality as those who grow up together (McGue & Bouchard, 1998; Tellegen et al., 1988).

Indeed, one provocative related finding is that such shared environmental factors as parental divorce or parenting style may have little direct impact on personality (Plomin & Caspi, 1999). According to these researchers, simply growing up in the same family does not make people very similar. In fact, when two siblings are similar, this is thought to be due primarily to genetic similarities.

Researchers also have assessed specific behavioral and attitude similarities in twins, and the evidence for heritability in these studies is often striking. One study that examined 3,000 pairs of identical and fraternal twins found evidence for the genetic transmission of conservative views regarding topics such as socialism, church authority, the death penalty, and interracial marriage (Martin et al., 1986). It is very unlikely that a specific gene is directly responsible for a complex psychological outcome such as beliefs about social or political issues. Rather, a set of genes (or, more likely, many sets of interacting genes) may produce specific characteristics or tendencies to think in a conservative or a liberal manner. One recent study examined the DNA of 13,000 people and measured the extent to which they reported conservative versus liberal attitudes. The researchers found associations between conservatism–liberalism and chromosomal regions linked to mental flexibility, or the extent to which a person changes their thinking in response to shifts in their environment, which could be one of the factors influencing our views on social and political issues (Hatemi et al., 2011). Current research by psychological scientists is aimed at better understanding how variations in our genetic code may contribute to the development of personality.

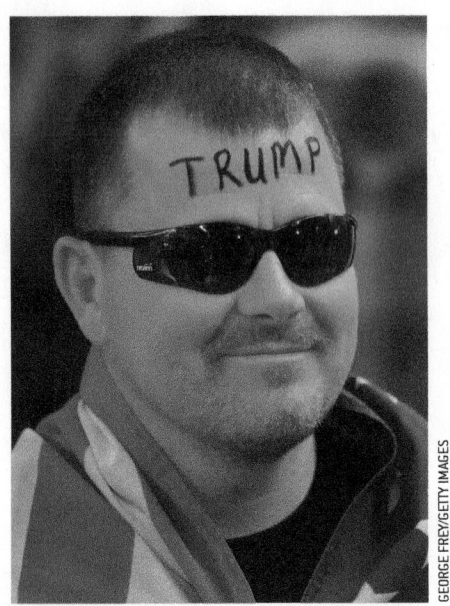

GEORGE FREY/GETTY IMAGES

Our genes influence our personality in various ways. For instance, genetic factors can affect how rigidly versus flexibly we think about things such as religion and politics. This Trump supporter probably shares the same religious and political leanings as other members of his family.

Gender Differences: Biology or Culture?

Do you think there is a typical female personality or a typical male personality? On a variety of personality characteristics, including helpfulness, men and women on average show no reliable differences. Overall, men and women seem to be far more

Why Do Males and Females Have Different Personality Traits?

Although the gender differences in personality are quite small, they tend to get a lot of attention. The debate about the origins of gender differences in personality often involves contrasting an evolutionary biological perspective with a social–cognitive perspective known as *social role theory*. The evolutionary perspective holds that men and women have evolved different personality characteristics, in part because their reproductive success depends on different behaviors. For instance, aggressiveness in men may have an adaptive value in intimidating sexual rivals; women who are agreeable and nurturing may have evolved to protect and ensure the survival of their offspring (Campbell, 1999) as well as to secure a reliable mate and provider (Buss, 1989).

According to social role theory, personality characteristics and behavioral differences between men and women result from cultural standards and expectations that assign them: socially permissible jobs, activities, and family positions (Eagly & Wood, 1999). Because of their physical size and their freedom from childbearing, men historically have taken roles of greater power—roles that in postindustrial society don't necessarily require physical strength. These differences then snowball, with men generally taking roles that require assertiveness and aggression (e.g., executive, school principal, surgeon) and women pursuing roles that emphasize greater supportiveness and nurturance (e.g., nurse, day-care worker, teacher).

Regardless of the source of gender differences in personality, the degree to which people identify personally with

ARDHANARISHVARA, UNIVERSITY OF CALIFORNIA, BERKELEY ART MUSEUM AND PACIFIC FILM ARCHIVE, GIFT OF JEAN AND FRANCIS MARSHALL, 1999.15.10. PHOTOGRAPHED BY BEN BLACKWELL.

◀ Cultures differ in their appreciation of male and female characteristics, but the Hindu deity Ardhanarishwara represents the value of combining both parts of human nature. Male on one side and female on the other, this god is symbolic of the dual nature of the sacred. The only real problem with such side-by-side androgyny comes in finding clothes that fit.

masculine and feminine stereotypes may tell us about important personality differences between individuals. Sandra Bem (1974) designed a scale (the Bem Sex Role Inventory) that assesses the degree of identification with stereotypically masculine and feminine traits. Bem suggested that psychologically *androgynous* people (those who adopt the best of both worlds and identify with positive feminine traits such as kindness and positive masculine traits such as assertiveness) might be better adjusted than people who identify strongly with only one sex role or low on both. So far, the data seem to support this idea. For instance, those who endorse an androgynous sex role report fewer symptoms of depression than those with a masculine or feminine role, regardless of their biological sex (Vafaei et al., 2016). This is also good news for the Hindu deity pictured above.

Bem Sex Role Inventory Sample Items

Respondents taking the Bem Sex Role Inventory rate themselves on each of the items without seeing the gender categorization. Then the scale is scored for masculinity (use of stereotypically masculine items), femininity (use of stereotypically feminine items), and androgyny (the tendency to use both the stereotypically masculine and feminine adjectives to describe oneself) (Bem, 1974).

Masculine items	Feminine items
Self-reliant	Yielding
Defends own beliefs	Affectionate
Independent	Flatterable
Assertive	Sympathetic
Forceful	Sensitive to the needs of others

similar in personality than they are different (Hyde, 2005). However, researchers have found some reliable differences between men and women with respect to their self-reported traits, attitudes, and behaviors. Some of these findings conform to North American stereotypes of masculine and feminine. For example, researchers have found women to be more verbally expressive, more sensitive to nonverbal cues, and more nurturing than are men. Males are more physically aggressive than females, but females engage in more relational aggression (e.g., using relationships to harm someone, such as intentionally excluding them from a social group) than do males, even from a very young age (Crick & Grotpeter, 1995; Leff, Waasdorp, & Crick, 2010; see A World of Difference: Why Do Males and Females Have Different Personality Traits?).

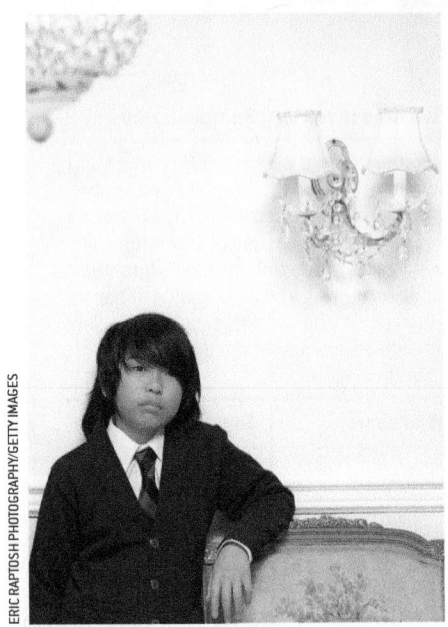

ERIC RAPTOSH PHOTOGRAPHY/GETTY IMAGES

Research has shown that there are small differences in the personalities of men vs. women; however, these differences are largely absent during childhood and don't emerge until adolescence, suggesting that they may be learned based on cultural expectations. This brother and sister seem to have the same personality. Their dog looks happy though.

Other gender differences include males having more assertiveness, slightly higher self-esteem, a more casual approach to sex, and greater sensation seeking than females. On the Big Five, studies across dozens of cultures around the world show that women are higher on neuroticism, extraversion, agreeableness, and conscientiousness; in terms of openness, women report greater openness to feelings and men greater openness to ideas (Costa, Terracciano, & McCrae, 2001; Schmitt et al., 2008).

Many of the gender differences that do exist among adults are much less pronounced during childhood. For instance, one recent review of over 150 previous studies that included more than 20,000 participants found that gender differences in the expression of emotion are detectable, with girls showing more internalizing emotions such as sadness and anxiety, and boys showing more externalizing emotions like anger (Chaplin & Aldao, 2013). However, these differences were much more pronounced as children aged into adolescence, suggesting that cultural factors may play a role in how children learn to express their emotions. Context also seems to play a role, because the observed gender differences were less pronounced when kids were with their parents and more pronounced when with their friends. The finding that gender differences in personality do not begin to emerge until adolescence also has been reported in studies conducted across dozens of different cultures around the world, suggesting that this is a universal phenomenon (De Bolle et al., 2015).

Another factor that may contribute to the emergence of personality differences in adolescence, however, is the simultaneous emergence of differences in sex hormones during puberty. As you know, a lot of things change during adolescence (e.g., more hormones, more interactions with friends, less time spent with parents), and it can be difficult to know what changes are causing what other changes. Interestingly, however, the effect of hormones on personality can be studied experimentally. One recent study followed a sample of transgender men over a three-month period during which they were undergoing testosterone treatment (in an effort to make their bodies more masculine). Personality tests administered before and after testosterone treatment revealed that significant changes occurred, with the transgender men viewing themselves as being more masculine and their scores more closely matching those of nontransgender men (Keo-Meier et al., 2015).

Do Animals Have Personalities?

Another source of evidence for the biological basis of human personality comes from the study of nonhuman animals. Any dog owner, zookeeper, or cattle farmer can tell you that individual animals have characteristic patterns of behavior. One Missouri woman who reportedly enjoyed raising chickens in her suburban home said that the "best part" was "knowing them as individuals" (Tucker, 2003). As far as we know, this pet owner did not give her feathered companions a personality test, though the researcher Sam Gosling (1998) used this approach in a study of a group of spotted hyenas. Well, not exactly. He recruited four human observers to use personality scales to rate the different hyenas in the group. When he examined ratings on the scales, he found five dimensions; three closely resembled the Big Five traits of neuroticism (i.e., fearfulness, emotional reactivity), openness to experience (i.e., curiosity), and agreeableness (i.e., absence of aggression).

In similar studies of guppies and octopi, individual differences in traits resembling extraversion and neuroticism were reliably observed (Gosling & John, 1999). In each study, researchers identified particular behaviors that they felt reflected each trait, based on their observation of the animals' normal repertoire of activities. Octopi, for example, seldom get invited to parties, so they cannot be assessed for their socializing tendencies ("He was all hands!"), but they do vary in terms of whether they prefer to eat in the safety of their den or are willing to venture out at feeding time, and so a behavior that corresponds to extraversion can reasonably be assessed (Gosling & John, 1999). Because different observers seem to agree on where an animal falls on a given dimension, the findings do not simply reflect a particular observer's imagination or tendency to *anthropomorphize* (attribute human characteristics to nonhuman animals). Such findings of cross-species commonality in behavioral styles help support the idea that biological mechanisms underlie personality traits shared by many species.

From an evolutionary perspective, differences in personality reflect alternative adaptations that have evolved in species—human and nonhuman—to deal with the challenges of survival and reproduction. For example, if you were to hang around a bar for an evening or two, you would soon see that evolution has provided humans with more than one way to attract and keep a mate. People who are extraverted would probably show off to attract attention, whereas you'd be likely to see people high in agreeableness displaying affection and nurturance (Buss, 1996). Both approaches might work well for attracting mates and reproducing successfully—depending on the environment. Through this process of natural selection, those characteristics that have proved successful in our evolutionary struggle for survival have been passed on to future generations.

Not only do animals have personalities but they also show consistency in these traits over time. For instance, one recent study examined 31 prior studies that measured the consistency of personality traits in dogs over time. It turns out that personality characteristics present during puppyhood tend to persist into dogs' adult years (Fratkin et al., 2013). Consistency in dog personality is important for working dogs (e.g., bomb-sniffing dogs, service dogs, etc.), as well as for pet owners who sometimes select their pets for their apparent personality. Beyond that, studying personality in nonhuman animals offers several serious benefits: improved ability to measure physiology, more opportunities for naturalistic observation (e.g., observing aggression and social hierarchies), and an accelerated life span (e.g., making longitudinal and life-span studies much more efficient) (Gosling, 2008).

How would you rate this honey badger? Is it antagonistic or agreeable? Neurotic or emotionally stable? Researchers have found that even animals appear to have personalities. Or should they be called "animalities"?

Traits Are Wired in the Brain

What neurophysiological mechanisms might influence the development of personality traits? Much of the thinking on this topic has focused on the extraversion–introversion dimension. In his personality model, Eysenck (1967) speculated that extraversion and introversion might arise from individual differences in cortical arousal. Eysenck suggested that extraverts pursue stimulation because their *reticular formation* (the part of the brain that regulates arousal or alertness, as described in the Neuroscience and Behavior chapter) is not easily stimulated. To achieve greater cortical arousal and feel fully alert, Eysenck argued, extraverts seek out social interaction, parties, and other activities to achieve mental stimulation. In contrast, introverts may prefer reading or quiet activities because their cortex is very easily stimulated to a point higher than optimal alertness.

Behavioral and physiological research generally supports Eysenck's view. When introverts and extraverts are presented with a range of intense stimuli, introverts respond more strongly, including salivating more when a drop of lemon juice is placed on their tongues and reacting more negatively to electric shocks or loud noises (Bartol & Costello, 1976; Stelmack, 1990). This reactivity has an impact on the ability to concentrate: Extraverts tend to perform well at tasks that are done in a noisy, arousing context (such as bartending or teaching), whereas introverts are better at tasks that require concentration in tranquil contexts (such as the work of a librarian or nighttime security guard; Geen, 1984; Lieberman & Rosenthal, 2001; Matthews & Gilliland, 1999).

In a refined version of Eysenck's ideas about arousability, Jeffrey Gray (1970) proposed that the dimensions of extraversion–introversion and neuroticism reflect two basic brain systems. The *behavioral activation system* (BAS), essentially a "go" system,

Extraverts pursue stimulation in the form of people, loud noise, and bright colors. Introverts tend to prefer softer, quieter settings. Pop quiz: Miley Cyrus: introvert or extravert?

activates approach behavior in response to the anticipation of reward. The extravert has a highly reactive BAS and will actively engage the environment, seeking social reinforcement and being on the go. The *behavioral inhibition system* (*BIS*), a "stop" system, inhibits behavior in response to stimuli signaling punishment. The anxious or introverted person, in turn, has a highly reactive BIS and will focus on negative outcomes and be on the lookout for stop signs. Because these two systems operate independently, it is possible for someone to be both a go and a stop person (simultaneously activated and inhibited), caught in a constant conflict between these two traits. An introverted person might be low on BAS (being less motivated to seek out potentially rewarding social situations) and high on BIS (being more likely to steer clear of others for fear of some form of punishment, such as criticism from others). Studies of brain electrical activity (EEG) and functional brain imaging (fMRI) suggest that individual differences in activation and inhibition arise through the operation of distinct brain systems underlying these tendencies (DeYoung & Gray, 2009). Even more recently, studies have suggested that the core personality traits described above may arise from individual differences in the volume of the different brain regions associated with each trait. For instance, self-reported neuroticism is correlated with the volume of brain regions involved in sensitivity to threat; agreeableness with areas associated with processing information about the mental states of other people; conscientiousness with regions involved in self-regulation; and extraversion with areas associated with processing information about reward (DeYoung et al., 2010). Research aimed at understanding how the structure and activity of our brains can contribute to the formation of our personality traits is still in its early stages but is a growing area of the field that many believe holds great promise for helping us better understand how we each develop into the unique people that we are.

Build to the Outcomes

1. How might traits explain behavior?

2. How do psychologists identify the core personality traits?

3. What role has factor analysis played in identifying different traits?

4. What are the strengths of the five-factor model?

5. What do studies of twins tell us about personality?

6. Are there significant personality differences between the genders?

7. Why study animal behavioral styles?

8. What neurological differences explain why extraverts pursue more stimulation that introverts?

The Psychodynamic Approach: Forces That Lie Beneath Awareness

Learning Outcomes

▶ Differentiate the id, ego, and superego.

▶ Explain how defense mechanisms reduce anxiety.

▶ Describe how Freud's theory of psychosexual stages contributes to personality.

Rather than trying to understand personality in terms of broad theories for describing individual differences, Freud looked for personality in the details: the meanings and insights revealed by careful analysis of the tiniest blemishes in a person's thought and behavior. Working with patients who came to him with disorders that did not seem to have any physical basis, he began by interpreting the origins of their everyday mistakes and memory lapses, errors that have come to be called *Freudian slips*.

Freud used the term *psychoanalysis* to refer to both his theory of personality and his method of treating patients. Freud's ideas were the first of many theories building on his basic idea that personality is a mystery to the person who "owns" it because we can't know our own deepest motives. The theories of Freud and his followers (discussed in the Treatment chapter) are referred to as the **psychodynamic approach,** *an approach that regards personality as formed by needs, strivings, and desires largely operating outside of awareness—motives that can produce emotional disorders.* The real engines of personality, in this view, are forces of which we are largely unaware.

THE STRUCTURE OF THE MIND: ID, EGO, AND SUPEREGO

To explain the emotional difficulties that beset his patients, Freud proposed that the mind consists of three independent, interacting, and often conflicting systems: the id, the superego, and the ego.

The most basic system, the **id,** is *the part of the mind containing the drives present at birth; it is the source of our bodily needs, wants, desires, and impulses, particularly our sexual and aggressive drives.* The id operates according to the *pleasure principle,* the psychic force that motivates the tendency to seek immediate gratification of any impulse. If governed by the id alone, you would never be able to tolerate the buildup of hunger while waiting to be served at a restaurant but would simply grab food from tables nearby.

Opposite the id is the **superego,** *the mental system that reflects the internalization of cultural rules, mainly learned as parents exercise their authority.* The superego consists of a set of guidelines, internal standards, and other codes of conduct that regulate and control our behaviors, thoughts, and fantasies. It acts as a kind of conscience, punishing us when it finds we are doing or thinking something wrong (by producing guilt or other painful feelings) and rewarding us (with feelings of pride or self-congratulation) for living up to ideal standards.

The final system of the mind, according to psychoanalytic theory, is the **ego,** *the component of personality, developed through contact with the external world, that enables us to deal with life's practical demands.* The ego operates according to the *reality principle,* the regulating mechanism that enables us to delay gratifying immediate needs and function effectively in the real world. It is the mediator between the id and the superego. The ego helps you resist the impulse to snatch others' food and also finds the restaurant and pays the check.

Freud believed that the relative strength of the interactions among the three systems of mind (i.e., which system is usually dominant) determines an individual's basic personality structure. Together the id force of personal needs, the superego force of pressures to quell those needs, and the ego force of reality's demands are in constant internal conflict. Freud believed that the dynamics among the id, superego, and ego are largely governed by *anxiety,* an unpleasant feeling that arises when unwanted thoughts or feelings occur, such as when the id seeks a gratification that the ego thinks

Sigmund Freud was the first psychology theorist to be honored with his own bobblehead doll. Let's hope he's not the last.

"I'm sorry, I'm not speaking to anyone tonight. My defense mechanisms seem to be out of order."

psychodynamic approach An approach that regards personality as formed by needs, strivings, and desires largely operating outside of awareness—motives that also can produce emotional disorders.

id The part of the mind containing the drives present at birth; it is the source of our bodily needs, wants, desires, and impulses, particularly our sexual and aggressive drives.

superego The mental system that reflects the internalization of cultural rules, mainly learned as parents exercise their authority.

ego The component of personality, developed through contact with the external world, that enables us to deal with life's practical demands.

TABLE 12.4

Defense Mechanisms

Repression is the first defense the ego tries, but if it is inadequate, then other defense mechanisms may come into play.

Defense Mechanism	Description	Example
Repression	Removing painful experiences and unacceptable impulses from the conscious mind: "motivated forgetting."	Not lashing out physically in anger; putting a bad experience out of your mind.
Rationalization	Supplying a reasonable sounding explanation for unacceptable feelings and behavior to conceal (mostly from oneself) one's underlying motives or feelings.	Dropping calculus, allegedly because of poor ventilation in the classroom.
Reaction formation	Unconsciously replacing threatening inner wishes and fantasies with an exaggerated version of their opposite.	Being rude to someone you're attracted to.
Projection	Attributing one's own threatening feelings, motives, or impulses to another person or group.	Judging others as being dishonest because you believe that you are dishonest.
Regression	Reverting to an immature behavior or earlier stage of development, a time when things felt more secure, to deal with internal conflict and perceived threat.	Using baby talk, even though able to use appropriate speech, in response to distress.
Displacement	Shifting unacceptable wishes or drives to a neutral or less threatening alternative.	Slamming a door; yelling at someone other than the person you're mad at.
Identification	Dealing with feelings of threat and anxiety by unconsciously taking on the characteristics of another person who seems more powerful or better able to cope.	A bullied child becoming a bully.
Sublimation	Channeling unacceptable sexual or aggressive drives into socially acceptable and culturally enhancing activities.	Diverting anger to the football or rugby field, or other contact sport.

will lead to real-world dangers or that the superego sees as leading to punishment. When the ego receives an "alert" signal in the form of anxiety, it launches into a defensive position in an attempt to ward off the anxiety. According to Freud, it does so using one of several different **defense mechanisms,** *unconscious coping mechanisms that reduce anxiety generated by threats from unacceptable impulses* (see **TABLE 12.4**). Psychodynamically oriented psychologists believe that defense mechanisms help us overcome anxiety and engage effectively with the outside world and that our characteristic style of defense becomes our signature in dealing with the world—and an essential aspect of our personality.

PSYCHOSEXUAL STAGES AND THE DEVELOPMENT OF PERSONALITY

Freud also proposed that a person's basic personality is formed before 6 years of age during a series of sensitive periods, or life stages, when experiences influence all that will follow. Freud called these periods **psychosexual stages,** *distinct early life stages through which personality is formed as children experience sexual pleasures from specific body areas and caregivers redirect or interfere with those pleasures.* He argued that as a result of adult interference with pleasure-seeking energies, the child experiences conflict. At each stage, a different bodily region, or *erotogenic* zone, dominates the child's subjective experience. (For example, during the oral stage, pleasure centers on the mouth.) Each region is a battleground between the child's id impulses and the adult external world.

Problems and conflicts encountered at any psychosexual stage, Freud believed, will influence personality in adulthood. Conflict resulting from a person's being deprived or, paradoxically, overindulged at a given stage could result in **fixation,** *a phenomenon in which a person's pleasure-seeking drives become psychologically stuck, or arrested, at*

defense mechanisms Unconscious coping mechanisms that reduce anxiety generated by threats from unacceptable impulses.

psychosexual stages Distinct early life stages through which personality is formed as children experience sexual pleasures from specific body areas and caregivers redirect or interfere with those pleasures.

fixation A phenomenon in which a person's pleasure-seeking drives become psychologically stuck, or arrested, at a particular psychosexual stage.

a particular psychosexual stage. Freud described particular personality traits as being derived from fixations at the different psychosexual stages. Here's how he explained each stage and the effects of fixation at each stage:

▶ In the first year and a half of life, the infant is in the **oral stage,** *the first psychosexual stage, in which experience centers on the pleasures and frustrations associated with the mouth, sucking, and being fed.* Infants who are deprived of pleasurable feeding or indulgently overfed are believed to have a personality style in which they are focused on issues related to fullness and emptiness and what they can "take in" from others.

▶ Between 2 and 3 years of age, the child moves on to the **anal stage,** *the second psychosexual stage, in which experience is dominated by the pleasures and frustrations associated with the anus, retention and expulsion of feces and urine, and toilet training.* Individuals who have had difficulty negotiating this conflict are believed to develop a rigid personality and remain preoccupied with issues of control.

▶ Between the ages of 3 and 5 years, the child is in the **phallic stage,** *the third psychosexual stage, in which experience is dominated by the pleasure, conflict, and frustration associated with the phallic–genital region as well as coping with powerful incestuous feelings of love, hate, jealousy, and conflict.* According to Freud, children in the phallic stage experience the **Oedipus conflict,** *a developmental experience in which a child's conflicting feelings toward the opposite-sex parent are (usually) resolved by identifying with the same-sex parent.*

▶ A more relaxed period in which children are no longer struggling with the power of their sexual and aggressive drives occurs between the ages of 5 and 13, when children experience the **latency stage,** *the fourth psychosexual stage, in which the primary focus is on the further development of intellectual, creative, interpersonal, and athletic skills.* Because Freud believed that the most significant aspects of personality development occur before the age of 6, psychodynamic psychologists do not speak of fixation at the latency period. Simply making it to the latency period relatively undisturbed by conflicts of the earlier stages is a sign of healthy personality development.

▶ At puberty and thereafter, the fifth and final stage of personality development occurs. The **genital stage** is *the time for the coming together of the mature adult personality with a capacity to love, work, and relate to others in a mutually satisfying and reciprocal manner.* Freud believed that people who are fixated in a prior stage fail to develop healthy adult sexuality and a well-adjusted adult personality.

What should we make of all this? On the one hand, the psychoanalytic theory of psychosexual stages offers an intriguing picture of early family relationships and the extent to which they allow the child to satisfy basic needs and wishes. On the other hand, critics argue that psychodynamic explanations lack any real evidence and tend to focus on provocative after-the-fact interpretation rather than testable prediction. The psychosexual stage theory offers a compelling set of story lines for interpreting lives once they have unfolded, but it has not generated clear-cut predictions supported by research.

oral stage The first psychosexual stage, in which experience centers on the pleasures and frustrations associated with the mouth, sucking, and being fed.

anal stage The second psychosexual stage, in which experience is dominated by the pleasures and frustrations associated with the anus, retention and expulsion of feces and urine, and toilet training.

phallic stage The third psychosexual stage, in which experience is dominated by the pleasure, conflict, and frustration associated with the phallic-genital region as well as coping with powerful incestuous feelings of love, hate, jealousy, and conflict.

Oedipus conflict A developmental experience in which a child's conflicting feelings toward the opposite-sex parent are (usually) resolved by identifying with the same-sex parent.

latency stage The fourth psychosexual stage, in which the primary focus is on the further development of intellectual, creative, interpersonal, and athletic skills.

genital stage The fifth and final psychosexual stage, the time for the coming together of the mature adult personality with a capacity to love, work, and relate to others in a mutually satisfying and reciprocal manner.

One of the id's desires is to make a fine mess (a desire that is often frustrated early in life, perhaps during the anal stage). The famous painter Jackson Pollock found a way to make extraordinarily fine messes—behavior that at some level all of us envy.

Build to the Outcomes

1. According to Freud, how is personality shaped by the interaction of the id, superego, and ego?

2. What are the various defense mechanisms we use to reduce anxiety?

3. How can fixation influence adult personality?

4. What is believed to occur in each psychosexual stage?

5. Why do critics say Freud's psychosexual stages are more interpretation than explanation?

The Humanistic–Existential Approach: Personality as Choice

Learning Outcomes

▶ Describe the humanistic–existential approach to personality.

▶ Explain the role of self-actualization and angst in personality development.

During the 1950s and 1960s, psychologists began to try to understand personality from a viewpoint quite different from trait theory's biological determinism and Freud's focus on unconscious drives from unresolved childhood experiences. These new humanistic and existential theorists turned attention to how humans make *healthy choices* that create their personalities. *Humanistic psychologists* emphasized a positive, optimistic view of human nature that highlights people's inherent goodness and their potential for personal growth. *Existentialist psychologists* focused on the individual as a responsible agent who is free to create and live his or her life while negotiating the issue of meaning and the reality of death. The *humanistic–existential approach* integrates these insights with a focus on how a personality can become optimal.

HUMAN NEEDS AND SELF-ACTUALIZATION

Humanists see the **self-actualizing tendency,** *the human motive toward realizing our inner potential,* as a major factor in personality. The pursuit of knowledge, the expression of one's creativity, the quest for spiritual enlightenment, and the desire to give to society all are examples of self-actualization. As you saw in the Emotion and Motivation chapter, the noted humanistic theorist Abraham Maslow (1943) proposed a *hierarchy of needs,* a model of essential human needs arranged according to their priority, in which basic physiological and safety needs must be satisfied before a person can afford to focus on higher-level psychological needs. Only when these basic needs are met can one pursue higher needs, culminating in *self-actualization*: the need to be good, to be fully alive, and to find meaning in life.

Humanist psychologists explain individual personality differences as arising from the various ways that the environment facilitates—or blocks—attempts to satisfy psychological needs. For example, someone with the inherent potential to be a great scientist, artist, parent, or teacher might never realize these talents if his or her energies and resources are instead directed toward meeting basic needs of security, belongingness, and the like. Research indicates that when people shape their lives around goals that do not match their true nature and capabilities, they are less likely to be happy than those whose lives and goals do match (Ryan & Deci, 2000).

It feels great to be doing exactly what you are capable of doing. Mihaly Csikszentmihalyi (1990) found that engagement in tasks that exactly match one's abilities creates a mental state of energized focus that he called *flow* (see **FIGURE 12.4**). Tasks that are below our abilities cause boredom, those that are too challenging cause anxiety, and those that are "just right" lead to the experience of flow. If you know how to play the piano, for example, and are playing a Chopin prelude that you know well enough that it just matches your abilities, you are likely to experience this optimal state. People report being happier at these times than at any other times. Humanists believe that such peak experiences, or states of flow, reflect the realization of one's human potential and represent the height of personality development.

PERSONALITY AS EXISTENCE

Existentialists agree with humanists about many of the features of personality but focus on challenges to the human condition that are more profound than the lack of a nurturing environment. Rollo May (1983) and Victor Frankl (2000), for example, argued that specific aspects of the human condition, such as awareness of our own existence and the ability to make choices about how to behave, have a double-edged quality: They bring an extraordinary richness and dignity to human life, but they also

Decades of research have shown that growing up in a distressed neighborhood is associated with worse educational, occupational, and health outcomes. Humanistic psychologists would suggest that people in such settings must struggle to meet their basic daily needs and so do not have opportunities for self-actualization.

self-actualizing tendency The human motive toward realizing our inner potential.

force us to confront realities that are difficult to face, such as the prospect of our own death. The **existential approach** is *a school of thought that regards personality as governed by an individual's ongoing choices and decisions in the context of the realities of life and death.*

According to the existential perspective, the difficulties we face in finding meaning in life and in accepting the responsibility of making free choices provoke a type of anxiety existentialists call *angst* (the anxiety of fully being). The human ability to consider limitless numbers of goals and actions is exhilarating, but it can also open the door to profound questions such as Why am I here? What is the meaning of my life?

Thinking about the meaning of existence also can evoke an awareness of the inevitability of death. What, then, should we do with each moment? What is the purpose of living if life as we know it will end one day, perhaps even today? Alternatively, does life have more meaning, given that it is so temporary? Existential theorists do not suggest that people consider these profound existential issues on a day-to-day and moment-to-moment basis. Rather than ruminating about death and meaning, people typically pursue superficial answers that help them deal with the angst and dread they experience, and the defenses they construct form the basis of their personalities (Binswanger, 1958; May, 1983). Some people organize their lives around obtaining material possessions; others may immerse themselves in drugs or addictive behaviors such as compulsive Web browsing, video gaming, or television watching in order to numb the mind to existential realities.

For existentialists, a healthier solution is to face the issues head on and learn to accept and tolerate the pain of existence. Indeed, being fully human means confronting existential realities rather than denying them or embracing comforting illusions. This requires the courage to accept the inherent anxiety and the dread of nonbeing that is part of being alive. Such courage may be bolstered by developing supportive relationships with others who can supply unconditional positive regard. Something about being loved helps take away the angst.

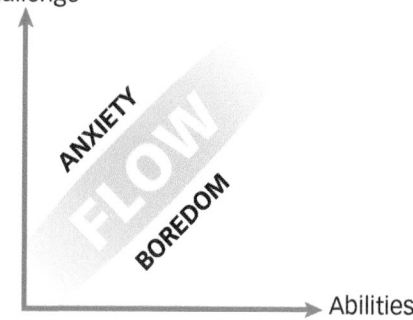

▲ Figure 12.4

FLOW EXPERIENCE It feels good to do things that challenge your abilities but that don't challenge them too much. Mihaly Csikszentmihalyi (1990) described this feeling between boredom and anxiety as the "flow experience."

existential approach A school of thought that regards personality as governed by an individual's ongoing choices and decisions in the context of the realities of life and death.

social–cognitive approach An approach that views personality in terms of how the person thinks about the situations encountered in daily life and behaves in response to them.

Build to the Outcomes

1. How does the humanistic–existential approach differ from the trait and psychodynamic approaches?

2. What does it mean to be self-actualized?

3. How is "flow" created?

4. What is the existential approach to personality?

5. What is angst? How is it created?

The Social–Cognitive Approach: Personalities in Situations

What is it like to be a person? The **social–cognitive approach** *views personality in terms of how the person thinks about the situations encountered in daily life and behaves in response to them.* Bringing together insights from social psychology, cognitive psychology, and learning theory, this approach emphasizes how the person experiences and interprets situations (Bandura, 1986; Mischel & Shoda, 1999; Ross & Nisbett, 1991; Wegner & Gilbert, 2000).

Researchers in social cognition believe that both the current situation and learning history are key determinants of behavior, and focus on how people *perceive* their environments. People think about their goals, the consequences of their behavior,

Learning Outcomes

▶ Describe the social–cognitive approach to personality.

▶ Explain how personal constructs are key to personality differences.

▶ Identify how one's perception of control influences behavior.

"He's not very exciting in social situations but on the net he's a wildman."

MICK STEVENS ©THE NEW YORKER COLLECTION/WWW.CARTOONBANK.COM

and how they might achieve certain things in different situations (Lewin, 1951). The social–cognitive approach looks at how personality and situation interact to cause behavior, how personality contributes to the way people construct situations in their own minds, and how people's goals and expectancies influence their responses to situations.

CONSISTENCY OF PERSONALITY ACROSS SITUATIONS

Although social–cognitive psychologists attribute behavior both to the individual's personality and to his or her situation, situation can often trump personality. For example, a person would have to be pretty strange to act exactly the same way at a memorial service and at a keg party. In their belief that the strong push and pull of situations can influence almost everyone, social–cognitive psychologists are somewhat at odds with the basic assumptions of classic personality psychology; that is, that personality characteristics (such as traits, needs, unconscious drives) cause people to behave in the same way across situations and over time. At the core of the social–cognitive approach is a natural puzzle, the **person–situation controversy,** which focuses on *the question of whether behavior is caused more by personality or by situational factors.*

This controversy began in earnest when Walter Mischel (1968) argued that measured personality traits often do a poor job of predicting individuals' behavior. Mischel reviewed decades of research that compared scores on standard personality tests with actual behavior, looking at evidence from studies asking questions such as "Does a person with a high score on a test of introversion actually spend more time alone than someone with a low score?" Mischel's disturbing conclusion: The average correlation between trait and behavior is only about .30. This is certainly better than zero (i.e., no relation at all) but not very good when you remember that a perfect prediction is represented by a correlation of 1.0.

Mischel also noted that knowing how a person will behave in one situation is not particularly helpful in predicting that person's behavior in another situation. For example, in classic studies, Hugh Hartshorne and M. A. May (1928) assessed children's honesty by examining their willingness to cheat on a test and found that such dishonesty was not consistent from one situation to another. The assessment of a child's trait of honesty in a cheating situation was of almost no use in predicting whether that child would act honestly in a different situation, such as when given the opportunity to steal money. Mischel proposed that measured traits do not predict behaviors very

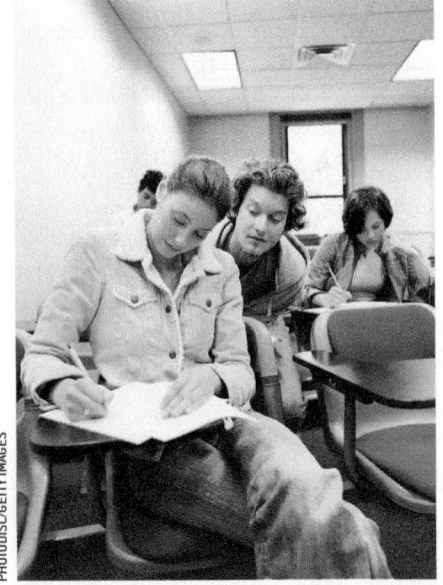

PHOTODISC/GETTY IMAGES

Is a student who cheats on a test more likely than others to steal candy or lie to his grandmother? Social–cognitive research indicates that behavior in one situation does not necessarily predict behavior in a different situation.

person–situation controversy The question of whether behavior is caused more by personality or by situational factors.

Does Your Personality Change Depending on Who You're With?

Social–cognitive psychologists suggest that how you behave is influenced by both your personality and the situations you are in. For instance, you act differently when sitting in a classroom than you do when dancing at a club (unless it's a really fun class). But do your personality and behavior also change when you're talking to different people regardless of context? For instance, do things such as your language, tone of voice, and level of warmth change depending on whom you are talking to?

For most people, the answer is yes. For example, we speak and act differently when interacting with our parents (*"Hello mother, hello father"*) than with our friends (*"Yo! Sup, punk?!"*). Many people change their language and personality when interacting with

people from their own race or cultural group as opposed to those from other groups (e.g., Coates, 2015). And there is evidence from studies of bilingual speakers that people's personality traits shift slightly when they are speaking in one language versus another (Ramirez-Esparza et al., 2004). These are notably subtle shifts rather than complete personality transplants.

Why would our personality characteristics change when we are interacting with one person versus another? One possibility is that we shift our personality and language to match the people with whom we are interacting in order to signal closeness or affiliation with them. Another possibility is that we do this to influence what other people think about us. For instance, one

recent study found that people in positions of power tend to downplay their competence when interacting with subordinates in order to appear warmer and more likeable, whereas subordinates tend to conceal their warmth in order to appear more competent (Swencionis & Fiske, 2016). The authors suggest that in both situations, the participants are attempting to increase the perceived similarity between them and the person with whom they are interacting. The fact that things such as personality, similarity, and perceived competence can influence decisions about hiring and promotions (Rivera, 2012; Tews, Stafford, & Tracey, 2011) means that personality actually has a huge impact on the experiences you have in the real world.

well because behaviors are determined more by situational factors than personality theorists were willing to acknowledge.

Is there no personality, then? Do we all just do what situations require? The person–situation controversy has inspired many studies in the years since Mischel's critique, and it turns out that information about both personality and situation are necessary to predict behavior accurately (Fleeson, 2004; Mischel, 2004). Some situations are particularly powerful, leading most everyone to behave similarly regardless of personality (Cooper & Withey, 2009). At a funeral, almost everyone looks somber, and during an earthquake, almost everyone shakes. But in more moderate situations, personality can come forward to influence behavior (Funder, 2001). Among the children in Hartshorne and May's (1928) studies, cheating versus not cheating on a test was actually a fairly good predictor of cheating on a test later—as long as the situation was similar. Personality consistency, then, appears to be a matter of when and where a certain kind of behavior tends to be shown (see the Real World: Does Your Personality Change Depending on Who You're With?). Social–cognitive theorists believe these patterns of personality consistency arise from the way different people interpret situations and from the ways different people pursue goals within situations.

PERSONAL CONSTRUCTS: THE KEY TO THE PERCEIVER'S PERSONALITY

How can we understand differences in how situations are interpreted? Recall our notion that personality often exists in the eye of the beholder. Situations may exist in the eye of the beholder as well. One person's gold mine may be another person's useless hole in the ground. George Kelly (1955) long ago realized that these differences in perspective could be used to understand the *perceiver's* personality. He suggested that people view the social world from differing perspectives and that these different views arise through the application of **personal constructs,** *dimensions people use in making sense of their experiences.* Consider, for example, different individuals' personal constructs of a clown: One person may see him as a source of fun, another as a tragic figure, and yet another as so frightening that McDonald's must be avoided at all costs.

personal constructs Dimensions people use in making sense of their experiences.

Are two of these people taller and one shorter? Are two bareheaded while one wears a hood? Or are two the daughters and one the mom? George Kelly held that the personal constructs we use to distinguish among people in our lives are basic elements of our own personalities.

Kelly assessed personal constructs about social relationships by asking people to (1) list the people in their life; (2) consider three of the people and state a way in which two of them are similar to each other and different from the third; and (3) repeat this for other triads of people to produce a list of the dimensions that respondents used to classify friends and family. One respondent might focus on the degree to which people (self included) are lazy or hardworking, for example; someone else might attend to the degree to which people are sociable or unfriendly.

Kelly proposed that different personal constructs (*construals*) are the key to personality differences; that is, different construals lead people to engage in different behaviors. Taking a long break from work for a leisurely lunch might seem lazy to you. To your friend, the break might seem an ideal opportunity for catching up with friends and for wondering why you always choose to eat at your desk. Social–cognitive theory explains different responses to situations with the idea that people experience and interpret the world in different ways.

PERSONAL GOALS AND EXPECTANCIES LEAD TO A CHARACTERISTIC STYLE OF BEHAVIOR

Social–cognitive theories also recognize that a person's unique perspective on situations is reflected in his or her personal goals, which are often conscious. In fact, people can usually tell you their goals, whether to find a date for this weekend, get a good grade in psych, establish a fulfilling career, or just get this darn bag of chips open. These goals often reflect the tasks that are appropriate to the person's situation and, in a larger sense, fit the person's role and stage of life (Cantor, 1990; Klinger, 1977; Little, 1983; Vallacher & Wegner, 1985). For instance, common goals for adolescents include being popular, achieving greater independence from parents and family, and getting into a good college. Common goals for adults include developing a meaningful career, finding a mate, securing financial stability, and starting a family.

People translate goals into behavior in part through **outcome expectancies,** *a person's assumptions about the likely consequences of a future behavior.* Just as a laboratory rat learns that pressing a bar releases a food pellet, we learn that "if I am friendly toward people, they will be friendly in return," and "if I ask people to pull my finger, they will withdraw from me." So we learn to perform behaviors that we expect will have the outcome of moving us closer to our goals. We learn outcome expectancies through direct experience, both bitter and sweet, and through merely observing other people's actions and their consequences.

outcome expectancies A person's assumptions about the likely consequences of a future behavior.

TABLE 12.5

Rotter's Locus-of-Control Scale

For each pair of items, choose the option that most closely reflects your personal belief. Then check the answer key below to see if you have more of an internal or external locus of control.

1. a. Many of the unhappy things in people's lives are partly due to bad luck.

    b. People's misfortunes result from the mistakes they make.

2. a. I have often found that what is going to happen will happen.

    b. Trusting to fate has never turned out as well for me as making a decision to take a definite course of action.

3. a. Becoming a success is a matter of hard work; luck has little or nothing to do with it.

    b. Getting a good job depends mainly on being in the right place at the right time.

4. a. When I make plans, I am almost certain that I can make them work.

    b. It is not always wise to plan too far ahead because many things turn out to be a matter of good or bad fortune anyhow.

Information from Rotter, 1966.

Answers: A more internal locus of control would be reflected in choosing options 1b, 2b, 3a, and 4a.

Some days you feel like a puppet on a string. If you have an external locus of control and believe you are at the mercy of other people, or of fate, you may feel that way most days.

Outcome expectancies combine with a person's goals to produce that person's characteristic style of behavior. An individual with the goal of making friends and the expectancy that being kind will produce warmth in return is likely to behave very differently from an individual whose goal is to achieve fame at any cost and who believes that shameless self-promotion is the route to fame. We do not all want the same things from life, clearly, and our personalities largely reflect the goals we pursue and the expectancies we have about the best ways to pursue them.

People differ in their generalized expectancy for achieving goals. Some people seem to feel that they are fully in control of what happens to them in life, whereas others feel that the world doles out rewards and punishments to them irrespective of their actions. Julian Rotter (1966) developed a questionnaire (see **TABLE 12.5**) to measure *a person's tendency to perceive the control of rewards as internal to the self or external in the environment,* a disposition he called **locus of control.** People whose answers suggest that they believe they control their own destiny are said to have an *internal* locus of control, whereas those who believe that outcomes are random, determined by luck, or controlled by other people are described as having an *external* locus of control. These beliefs translate into individual differences in emotion and behavior. For example, people with an internal locus of control tend to be less anxious, achieve more, and cope better with stress than do people with an external orientation (Lefcourt, 1982). To get a sense of your standing on this trait dimension, choose one of the options for each of the sample items from the locus-of-control scale in Table 12.5.

locus of control A person's tendency to perceive the control of rewards as internal to the self or external in the environment.

Build to the Outcomes

1. Do researchers in social cognition think that personality arises from past experiences or from the current environment?

2. How well do measured personality traits predict behavior, according to the social—cognitive approach?

3. Does personality or the current situation predict a person's behavior?

4. What are personal constructs?

5. How do outcome expectancies and personal goals combine to form personality?

6. What is the advantage of an internal, over an external, locus of control?

The Self: Personality in the Mirror

Imagine that you wake up tomorrow morning, drag yourself into the bathroom, look into the mirror, and don't recognize the face looking back at you. This was the plight of a patient studied by the neurologist Todd Feinberg (2001). The woman, married for 30 years and the mother of two grown children, one day began to respond to her mirror image as if it were a different person. She talked to and challenged the person in the mirror. When she got no response, she tried to attack it as if it were an intruder. Her husband, shaken by this bizarre behavior, brought her to the neurologist, who was gradually able to convince her that the image in the mirror was in fact herself.

Most of us are pretty familiar with the face that looks back at us from every mirror. We develop the ability to recognize ourselves in mirrors by 18 months of age (as discussed in the Consciousness chapter), and we share this skill with chimpanzees and other apes that have been raised in the presence of mirrors. Self-recognition in mirrors signals our amazing capacity for reflexive thinking, for directing attention to our own thoughts, feelings, and actions—an ability that enables us to construct ideas about our own personality. Unlike a cow, which will never know that it has a poor sense of humor, or a cat, which will never know that it is awfully friendly, humans have rich and detailed self-knowledge.

Admittedly, none of us knows all there is to know about our own personality. In fact, sometimes others may know us better than we know ourselves (Vazire & Mehl, 2008). But we do have enough self-knowledge to respond reliably to personality inventories and report on our traits and behaviors. These observations draw on what we think about ourselves (our *self-concept*) and on how we feel about ourselves (our *self-esteem*). Self-concept and self-esteem are critically important facets of personality, not just because they reveal how people see their own personalities but because they also guide how people think others will see them.

What do these self-portraits of Frida Kahlo, Vincent van Gogh, Pablo Picasso, Salvador Dali, Wanda Wulz, and Jean-Michel Basquiat reveal about each artist's self-concept?

SELF-CONCEPT

In his renowned psychology textbook, William James (1890) included a theory of self in which he pointed to the self's two facets, the *I* and the *Me*. The *I* is the self that thinks, experiences, and acts in the world; it is the self as a *knower*. The *Me* is the self that is an object in the world; it is the self that is *known*. The *I* is much like consciousness, then, a perspective on all of experience (see the Consciousness chapter), but the *Me* is less mysterious: It is just a concept of a person.

If asked to describe your *Me,* you might mention your physical characteristics (male or female, tall or short, dark-skinned or light); your activities (listening to hip-hop, alternative rock, jazz, or classical music); your personality traits (extraverted or introverted, agreeable or independent); or your social roles (student, son or daughter, member of a hiking club, krumper). These features make up the **self-concept,** *a person's explicit knowledge of his or her own behaviors, traits, and other personal characteristics.* A person's self-concept is an organized body of knowledge that develops from social experiences and has a profound effect on a person's behavior throughout life.

Self-Concept Organization

Almost everyone has a place for memorabilia, a drawer or box somewhere that holds all those sentimental keepsakes—photos, yearbooks, cards and letters, maybe that scrap of the old security blanket—all memories of "life as *Me*." Perhaps you've wanted to organize these things sometime but have never gotten around to it. Fortunately, the knowledge of ourselves that we store in our *autobiographical memory* seems to be organized naturally in two ways: as narratives about episodes in our lives and in terms of traits (as would be suggested by the distinction between episodic and semantic memory discussed in the Memory chapter).

Self-Narratives Are Stories We Tell About Ourselves

The aspect of the self-concept that is a *self-narrative* (a story that we tell about ourselves) can be brief or very lengthy. Your life story could start with your birth and upbringing, describe a series of defining moments, and end where you are today. You could select specific events and experiences, goals and life tasks, and memories of places and people that have influenced you. Self-narrative organizes the highlights (and low blows) of your life

self-concept A person's explicit knowledge of his or her own behaviors, traits, and other personal characteristics.

Think about your own self-narrative (what you have done) and self-concept (how you view yourself). Are there areas that don't match up? Are there things that you've done, good or bad, that are not part of your self-concept? How might you explain that?

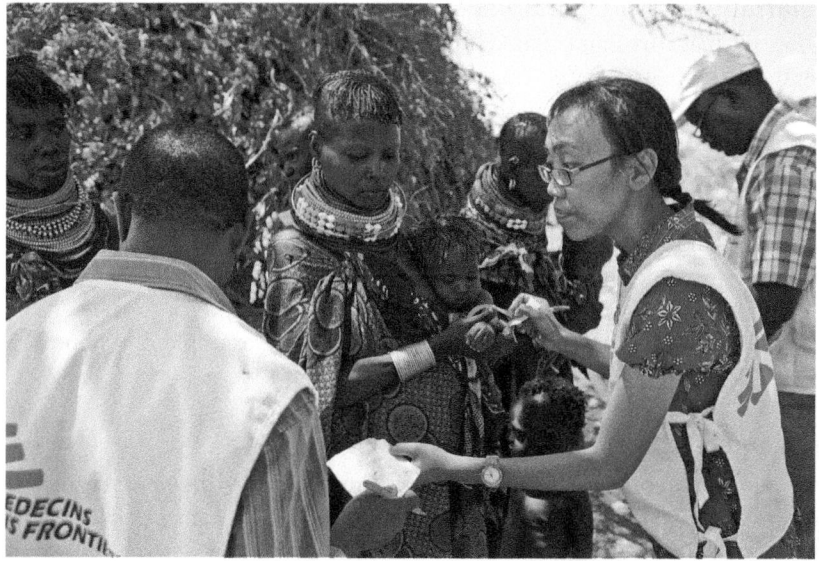

DAVID BATHGATE/CORBIS

into a story in which you are the leading character and binds them together into your self-concept (McAdams, 1993; McLean, 2008). Psychodynamic and humanistic–existential psychologists suggest that people's self-narratives reflect their fantasies and thoughts about core motives and approaches to existence.

Self-Schemas Are Sets of Traits We Use to Define Ourselves Self-concept is also organized in a more abstract way, in terms of personality traits. Just as you can judge an object on its attributes (Is this apple green?), you can judge yourself on any number of traits—whether you are considerate or smart or lazy or active or, for that matter, green—and do so quite reliably, making the same rating on multiple occasions. Hazel Markus (1977) observed that each person finds certain unique personality traits particularly important for conceptualizing the self. One person might define herself as independent, for example, whereas another might not care much about her level of independence but instead emphasize her sense of style. Markus called the traits people use to define themselves *self-schemas,* emphasizing that they draw information about the self into a coherent scheme. Markus asked people to indicate whether they had a trait by pressing response buttons labeled *me* or *not me.* She found that participants' judgment reaction times were faster for self-schemas than for other traits. It's as though some facets of the self-concept have almost a knee-jerk quality—letting us tell quickly who we are and who we are not.

Research also shows that the traits people use to judge the self tend to stick in memory. When people make judgments of themselves on traits, they later recall the traits better than when they judge other people on the same traits (Rogers, Kuiper, & Kirker, 1977). For example, answering a question such as "Are you generous?"—no matter what your answer—is likely to enhance your memory for the trait generous. In studies of this effect of *self-relevance* on memory, researchers using brain imaging technologies have found that the simple activity of making judgments about the trait self-concept is accompanied by activation of the medial prefrontal cortex (MPFC), a brain area involved in understanding people (Mitchell, Heatherton, & Macrae, 2002). This activation is stronger, however, when people are judging their own standing on traits (see **FIGURE 12.5**) than when they are judging the standing of someone else (Kelley et al., 2002). Such stronger activation, then, is linked with better memory for the traits being judged (Macrae et al., 2004). Studies have not been entirely conclusive about which brain areas are most involved in the processing of self-information (Morin, 2002), but they do show that memory for traits is strengthened when the MPFC is activated during self-judgments.

Self-Narratives, Traits, and Behavior Don't Always Match Up How do our behavior self-narratives and trait self-concepts compare? These two methods of self-conceptualization don't always match up. You may think of yourself as an honest person, for example, but also recall that time you nabbed a handful of change from your parents' dresser and conveniently forgot to replace it. The traits we use to describe ourselves are generalizations, and not every episode in our life stories may fit them. In fact, research suggests that the stores of knowledge about our behaviors and traits are not very well integrated (Kihlstrom, Beer, & Klein, 2002). In people who develop amnesia, for example, memory for behaviors can be lost even though the trait self-concept remains stable (Klein, 2004). People can have a pretty strong sense of who they are even though they may not remember a single example of when they acted that way.

Causes and Effects of Self-Concept

How do self-concepts arise, and how do they affect us? In some sense, you learn something about yourself every day. Although we can gain self-knowledge in private moments of insight, we more often arrive at our self-concepts through

Medial prefrontal cortex

REPUBLISHED WITH PERMISSION OF KELLEY, W. M., MACRAE, C. N., WYLAND, C. L., CAGLAR, S., INATI, S., & HEATHERTON, T. F. (2002). FINDING THE SELF? AN EVENT-RELATED FMRI STUDY. *JOURNAL OF COGNITIVE NEUROSCIENCE, 14,* 785–794. FIGURE 4. PERMISSION CONVEYED THROUGH COPYRIGHT CLEARANCE CENTER, INC.

▲ **Figure 12.5**

SELF-CONCEPT IN THE BRAIN fMRI scans reveal that the medial prefrontal cortex (MPFC) is activated (shown here in red and yellow) when people make judgments about whether they possess certain personality traits compared with when they are judging whether those traits apply to someone else (from Kelley et al., 2002.)

interacting with others. Young children in particular receive plenty of feedback from their parents, teachers, siblings, and friends about their characteristics, and this helps them to form an idea of who they are. Even adults would find it difficult to hold a view of the self as "kind" or "smart" if no one else ever shared this impression. The sense of self, then, is largely developed and maintained in relationships with others.

Over the course of a lifetime, however, we become less and less impressed with what others have to say about us. The social theorist George Herbert Mead (1934) observed that all the things people have said about us accumulate after a while into what we see as a kind of consensus held by the "generalized other." We typically adopt this general view of ourselves and hold on to it stubbornly. As a result, the person who says you're a jerk may upset you momentarily, but you bounce back, secure in the knowledge that you actually are not a jerk. And just as we might argue vehemently with someone who tried to tell us a refrigerator is a pair of underpants, we are likely to defend our self-concept against anyone whose view of us departs from our own.

Because it is so stable, a major effect of the self-concept is to promote consistency in behavior across situations (Lecky, 1945). We tend to engage in what William Swann (1983, 2012) called **self-verification,** *the tendency to seek evidence to confirm the self-concept,* and we find it disconcerting if someone sees us quite differently from the way we see ourselves. In one study, Swann (1983) gave people who considered themselves submissive feedback that they seemed very dominant and forceful. Rather than accepting this discrepant information, they went out of their way to act in an extremely submissive manner. As existential theorists emphasize, people derive a comforting sense of familiarity and stability from knowing who they are.

self-verification The tendency to seek evidence to confirm the self-concept.

self-esteem The extent to which an individual likes, values, and accepts the self.

SELF-ESTEEM

When you think about yourself, do you feel good and worthy? Do you like yourself? Or do you feel bad and have negative, self-critical thoughts? **Self-esteem** is *the extent to which an individual likes, values, and accepts the self.* Thousands of studies have examined differences between people with high self-esteem (who generally like themselves) and those with relatively low self-esteem (who are less keen on, and may actively dislike, themselves). Researchers who study self-esteem typically ask participants to fill out a self-esteem questionnaire such as the one shown in **TABLE 12.6** (Rosenberg, 1965). This widely used measure of self-esteem asks people to evaluate themselves

"I don't want to be defined by who I am."

P. C. VEY/THE NEW YORKER COLLECTION/CARTOONBANK.COM

TABLE 12.6

Rosenberg Self-Esteem Scale

Consider each statement and circle SA for strongly agree, A for agree, D for disagree, and SD for strongly disagree.

1. On the whole, I am satisfied with myself.	SA	A	D	SD
2. At times, I think I am no good at all.	SA	A	D	SD
3. I feel that I have a number of good qualities.	SA	A	D	SD
4. I am able to do things as well as most other people.	SA	A	D	SD
5. I feel I do not have much to be proud of.	SA	A	D	SD
6. I certainly feel useless at times.	SA	A	D	SD
7. I feel that I'm a person of worth, at least on an equal plane with others.	SA	A	D	SD
8. I wish I could have more respect for myself.	SA	A	D	SD
9. All in all, I am inclined to feel that I am a failure.	SA	A	D	SD
10. I take a positive attitude toward myself.	SA	A	D	SD

Information from Rosenberg, 1965.

Scoring: For items 1, 3, 4, 7, and 10, SA = 3, A = 2, D = 1, SD = 0; for items 2, 5, 6, 8, and 9, the scoring is reversed, with SA = 0, A = 1, D = 2, SD = 3. The higher the total score, the higher one's self-esteem.

in terms of each statement. People who strongly agree with the positive statements about themselves and strongly disagree with the negative statements are considered to have high self-esteem.

Although some personality psychologists have argued that self-esteem determines virtually everything about a person's life (from a tendency to engage in criminal activity and violence to professional success), the accumulated evidence shows that the benefits of high self-esteem are less striking and all-encompassing but still significant. In general, compared with people with low self-esteem, those with high self-esteem tend to live happier and healthier lives, cope better with stress, and be more likely to persist at difficult tasks. In contrast, individuals with low self-esteem are more likely, for example, to perceive rejection in ambiguous feedback from others and develop eating disorders than those with high self-esteem (Baumeister et al., 2003). How does this aspect of personality develop? And why does everyone—whether high or low in self-esteem—seem to *want* high self-esteem?

Sources of Self-Esteem

Some psychologists contend that high self-esteem arises primarily from being accepted and valued by significant others (Brown, 1993). Other psychologists focus on the influence of specific self-evaluations: judgments about one's value or competence in specific domains such as appearance, athletics, or scholastics.

An important factor is whom people choose for comparison. For example, James (1890) noted that an accomplished athlete who is the second best in the world should feel pretty proud, but this athlete might not if the standard of comparison involves being best in the world. In fact, athletes in the 1992 Olympics who had won silver medals looked less happy during the medal ceremony than those who had won bronze medals (Medvec, Madey, & Gilovich, 1995). If people see the actual self as falling short of the ideal self (the person that they would like to be), they tend to feel sad or dejected. When they become aware that the actual self is inconsistent with the self they have a duty to be, they are likely to feel anxious or agitated (Higgins, 1987).

These are the men's 1,500-meter speed-skating medalists at the 2014 Winter Olympics. From left, Denny Morrison of Canada, bronze; Zbigniew Brodka of Poland, gold; and Koen Verweij of the Netherlands, silver, pose with their medals. Notice the expression on Verweij's face compared with those of the gold- and bronze-medal winners.

AP PHOTO/MORRY GASH

Unconscious perspectives we take on feedback also can affect our sense of self-worth. In one study, researchers looked at the effect of an authority figure's disapproval on self-esteem. They examined the self-esteem of young, Catholic, female undergraduates who had read an article from *Cosmopolitan*, which described a woman's sexual dream (in PG-13 language), and who had either seen a photo of a disapproving-looking pope or a photo of an unfamiliar disapproving person. The photos were shown subliminally, that is, in such brief flashes that the women could not consciously recognize whom they had seen. In self-ratings made afterward, the women in the disapproving-pope group showed a marked reduction in self-esteem compared with the other women: They rated themselves as less competent, more anxious, and less moral. In the words of the researchers, self-esteem can be influenced when an important authority figure is "watching you from the back of your mind" (Baldwin, Carrell, & Lopez, 1989, p. 435).

Self-esteem is also affected by what kinds of domains we consider most important in our self-concept. One person's self-worth might be entirely contingent on, for example, how well she does in school, whereas another's self-worth might be based on her physical attractiveness (Crocker & Wolfe, 2001; Pelham, 1985). The first person's self-esteem might receive a big boost when she gets an A on an exam, but much less of a boost when she's complimented on her new hairstyle, and this effect might be exactly reversed in the second person.

The Desire for Self-Esteem

What's so great about self-esteem? Why do people want to see themselves in a positive light and avoid seeing themselves negatively?

Self-Esteem May Reflect High Social Status Does self-esteem feel good because it reflects our degree of social dominance or status? People with high self-esteem seem to carry themselves in a way that is similar to how high-status animals of other social species carry themselves. Dominant male gorillas, for example, appear confident and comfortable, not anxious or withdrawn. Perhaps high self-esteem in humans reflects high social status or suggests that the person is worthy of respect, and this perception triggers natural affective responses (Barkow, 1980; Maslow, 1937).

Self-Esteem May Have Played a Role in Evolution Could the desire for self-esteem come from a basic need to belong or to be related to others? Evolutionary theory holds that early humans who managed to survive and pass on their genes were those able to maintain good relations with others rather than being cast out to fend for themselves. Clearly, belonging to groups is adaptive, as is knowing whether you are accepted. Thus, self-esteem could be a kind of "sociometer," an inner gauge of how

TIMOTHY KURATEK/CBS VIA GETTY IMAGES

Survivor, The Bachelor, Big Brother. Why are shows in which everyone is fighting to remain a part of the group so popular today? Is it because these shows exploit the evolutionary desire to belong? (Or do people just like to see other people get kicked out of the club?)

much a person feels included by others at any given moment (Leary & Baumeister, 2000). According to evolutionary theory, then, we seek higher self-esteem because we have evolved to seek out belongingness in our families, work groups, and culture, and higher self-esteem indicates that we are being accepted.

Self-Esteem Provides a Sense of Security Consistent with the existential and psychodynamic approaches to personality, self-esteem can be a matter of security. The studies of mortality salience discussed in the Emotion and Motivation chapter suggest that the source of distress underlying negative self-esteem is ultimately the fear of death (Solomon, Greenberg, & Pyszczynski, 1991). In this view, humans find it anxiety provoking—in fact, terrifying—to contemplate their own mortality, and so they try to defend against this awareness by immersing themselves in activities (such as earning money or dressing up to appear attractive) that their culture defines as meaningful and valuable. The desire for self-esteem may stem from a need to find value in ourselves as a way of escaping the anxiety associated with recognizing our mortality. The higher our self-esteem, the less anxious we feel with the knowledge that someday we will no longer exist. (See Other Voices: Does the Study of Personality Lack... Personality? for more on interesting ideas about self-esteem, security, and personality.)

But Can We All Be Above Average? Whatever the reason that low self-esteem feels so bad and high self-esteem feels so good, people are generally motivated to see themselves positively. In fact, we often process information in a biased manner in order to feel good about the self. Research on the **self-serving bias** shows that people tend to take credit for their successes but downplay responsibility for their failures. You may have noticed this tendency in yourself, particularly in terms of the attributions you make about exams when you get a good grade (I studied really intensely, and I'm good at that subject) or a bad grade (The test was ridiculously tricky, and the professor is unfair).

On the whole, most people satisfy the desire for high self-esteem and maintain a reasonably positive view of self by engaging in the self-serving bias (Miller & Ross, 1975; Shepperd, Malone, & Sweeny, 2008). In fact, if people are asked to rate themselves across a range of characteristics, they tend to see themselves as better than the average person in most domains (Alicke et al., 1995). For example, 90% of drivers describe their driving skills as better than average, and 86% of workers rate their performance on the job as above average. Even among university professors, 94% feel they are above average in teaching ability compared with other professors (Cross, 1977). These kinds of judgments simply cannot be accurate, statistically speaking, because the average of a group of people has to be the average, not better than average! This particular error may be adaptive, however. People who do not engage in this self-serving bias to boost their self-esteem tend to be more at risk for depression, anxiety, and related health problems (Taylor & Brown, 1988).

On the other hand, a few people take positive self-esteem to the extreme. Unfortunately, seeing yourself as way, way better than average—a trait called **narcissism,** *a*

self-serving bias People's tendency to take credit for their successes but downplay responsibility for their failures.

narcissism A trait that reflects a grandiose view of the self combined with a tendency to seek admiration from and exploit others.

ARIEL MOLVIG/THE NEW YORKER COLLECTION/CARTOONBANK.COM

"I suffer from accurate self-esteem."

Does the Study of Personality Lack . . . Personality?

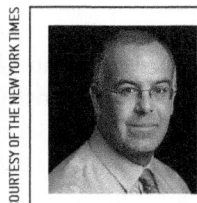

David Brooks is a columnist for the *New York Times,* a commentator on CNN, and the author of several popular books on behavioral science.

As described in this chapter, some of the field's older ideas about personality (such as those described in the sections on psychodynamic and humanistic–existential approaches) are very intriguing but lacking in evidence, and so are not widely studied these days. Instead, personality researchers today are aiming to understand what aspects of our personalities are passed through which genes, and how the Big Five might map onto brain structure and functioning. The old approaches lacked evidence, but is something lacking in the newer approaches to studying personality? David Brooks seems to think so.

.... In the 20th century, psychoanalysts were a big deal. There were a number of best-selling authors spinning theories about the psyche, which had a large impact on how people saw the world and themselves. This includes not only Freud and Jung, but also people like Erick Erikson, Erich Fromm, Carl Rogers, Viktor Frankl and Philip Rieff. Today we're more into cognition and the brain. Over the years, attention has shifted from the soul to the personality to decision-making. Preoccupations have migrated from salvation to psychic security to success.

When it comes to treating mental illness, I guess I'm glad we've made this shift. I put more faith in medications and cognitive therapies than in Freudian or Jungian analysis. But something has been lost as well as gained. We're less adept at talking about personalities and neuroses than we were when psychoanalysts held center stage.

For example, in the middle of the 20th century, a woman named Karen Horney (pronounced HOR-nigh) crafted a series of influential theories about personality. Like many authors of these intellectually ambitious theories, she was raised in Europe and migrated to the United States before World War II. More than most of her male counterparts, Horney felt that people were driven by anxiety and the desire for security. People who have been seriously damaged, she argued, tend to react in one of three ways.

Some people respond to their wounds by moving against others. These domineering types seek to establish security by conquering and outperforming other people. They deny their own weaknesses. They are rarely plagued by self-doubt. They fear dependence and helplessness. They use their children and spouses as tools to win prestige for themselves....

Other people respond to anxiety by moving toward others. These dependent types try to win people's affections by being compliant. They avoid conflict. They become absorbed by their relationships, surrendering their individual opinions. They regard everyone else as essentially good, even people who have been cruel....

Other people move away from others. These detached types try to isolate themselves and adopt an onlooker's attitude toward life. As Terry D. Cooper summarizes the category in his book, *Sin, Pride and Self-Acceptance,* "To guarantee peace, it is necessary to leave the battleground of interpersonal relationships, where there is constant threat of being captured."...

The domineering person believes that, if he wins life's battles, nothing can hurt him. The dependent person believes that, if he shuns private gain and conforms to the wishes of others, then the world will treat him nicely. The detached person believes that, if he asks nothing of the world, the world will ask nothing of him. These are ideal types, obviously, conceptual categories. They join a profusion of personality types that were churned out by various writers in the mid-20th century: the inner directed, the outer directed, the Organization Man, the anal retentive, the narcissist, the outsider.

The books that explained these theories were good bad books. The good bad book (I'm deriving the category from a phrase from Orwell) makes sweeping claims, and lumps people into big groups. Sometimes these claims are not really defensible intellectually. But they are thought-provoking and useful. They provide categories and handles the rest of us can use to understand the people around us, seeing where the category fits and thinking more precisely about where it doesn't.

We're probably poorer now that people like Horney have sunk to near oblivion—less adept at analyzing personality. We probably have less practice analyzing personalities....

Is David Brooks right? As the study of personality has moved away from big picture explanations like those of Freud, Maslow, and Frankl, which attempt to explain why we behave the way we do with one overarching theory, and toward efforts to break down personality into smaller constructs and understand how nature and nurture produce these core traits, have we actually gotten worse at understanding personality? On balance, should interesting theories that make intriguing assumptions about people's personalities, but have no data to support their accuracy, be retained simply because they tell a more interesting story? If you are reading this book, you represent the future of psychology. How can we better understand and measure human personality? What are the most important future steps?

grandiose view of the self combined with a tendency to seek admiration from and exploit others—brings some costs. In fact, at its extreme, narcissism is considered a personality disorder (see the Psychological Disorders chapter). Research has documented disadvantages of an overinflated view of self, most of which arise from the need to defend that grandiose view at all costs. For example, when highly narcissistic adolescents were given reason to be ashamed of their performance on a task, their aggressiveness increased in the form of willingness to deliver loud blasts of noise to punish their opponents in a laboratory game (Thomaes et al., 2008).

Implicit Egotism

What's your favorite letter of the alphabet? About 30% of people answer by picking what just happens to be the first letter of their first name. Could this choice indicate that some people think so highly of themselves that they base judgments of seemingly unrelated topics on how much those topics remind them of themselves?

This *name-letter effect* was discovered some years ago (Nuttin, 1985), but more recently researchers have gone on to discover how broad the egotistic bias in preferences can be. Brett Pelham and his colleagues have found subtle yet systematic biases toward this effect when people choose their home cities, streets, and even occupations (Pelham, Mirenberg, & Jones, 2002). When the researchers examined the rolls of people moving into several southern states, for example, they found that people named George were more likely than those with other names to move to Georgia. The same was true for Florences (Florida), Kenneths (Kentucky), and Louises (Louisiana). You can guess where the Virginias tended to relocate. People whose last name is Street seem biased toward addresses ending in *street,* whereas Lanes like lanes. The name effect seems to work for occupations as well: Slightly more people named Dennis and Denise chose dentistry, and Lauras and Lawrences chose law, compared with other occupations. Although the biases are small, they are consistent across many tests of this hypothesis.

These biases have been called expressions of *implicit egotism* because people are not typically aware that they are influenced by the wonderful sound of their own names (Pelham, Carvallo, & Jones, 2005). When Buffy moves to Buffalo, she is not likely to volunteer that she did so because it matched her name. Yet people who show this egotistic bias in one way also tend to show it in others: People who strongly prefer their own name letter also are likely to pick their birth date as their favorite number (Koole, Dijksterhuis, & van Knippenberg, 2001). And people who like their name letter were also found to evaluate themselves positively on self-ratings of personality traits. This was especially true when the self-ratings were made in response to instructions to work *quickly.* The people who preferred their name letter made snap judgments about themselves that leaned in a positive direction, suggesting that their special self-appreciation was an automatic response. At some level, a bit of egotism is probably good for us, yet implicit egotism is a curiously subtle error: a tendency to make biased judgments of what we will do and where we will go in life just because we happen to have a certain name.

Which one of your authors would be least likely to want to move to Danville? Why?

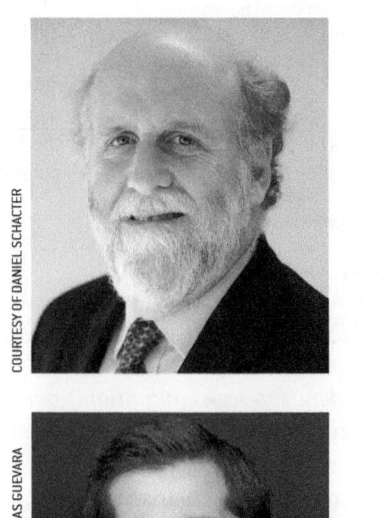

COURTESY OF DANIEL SCHACTER

MATTHEW NOCK PHOTO COURTESY OF NICOLAS GUEVARA

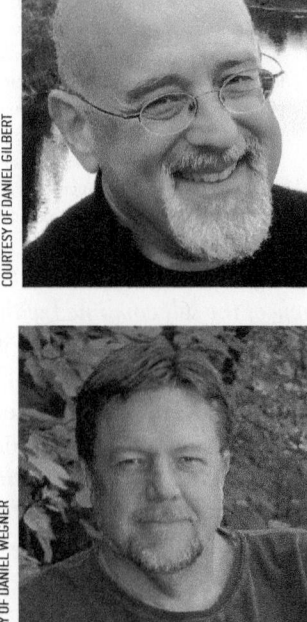

COURTESY OF DANIEL GILBERT

THE FAMILY OF DANIEL WEGNER

The self is the part of personality that the person knows and can report about. Some of the personality measures we have seen in this chapter (such as personality inventories based on self-reports) are really no different from measures of self-concept. Both depend on the person's perceptions and memories of the self's behavior and traits. But personality runs deeper than this as well. The unconscious forces identified in psychodynamic approaches provide themes for behavior and sources of mental disorder that are not accessible for self-report. The humanistic and existential approaches remind us of the profound concerns we humans face and the difficulties we may have in understanding all the forces that shape our self-views. Finally, in emphasizing how personality shapes our perceptions of social life, the social–cognitive approach brings the self back to center stage. The self, after all, is the hub of each person's social world.

Build to the Outcomes

1. What is the difference between *I* and *me*?
2. What makes up our self-concept?
3. How does our self-narrative contribute to our self-concept?
4. What is a self-schema?
5. Why don't traits always reflect knowledge of behavior?
6. How does self-concept influence behavior?
7. What impact does self-verification have on our behaviors?
8. What is self-esteem? Why do we want to be high in it?
9. How do comparisons with others affect self-esteem?
10. How might self-esteem have played a role in evolution?
11. Why is it possible to have too much self-esteem?

Chapter Review

Personality: What It Is and How It Is Measured

▶ In psychology, *personality* refers to a person's characteristic style of behaving, thinking, and feeling. Personality differences can be studied from two points of view: *prior events*, such as biological makeup, life circumstances, and culture; and *anticipated events*, as reflected in a person's hopes, dreams and fears.

▶ Personality inventories, such as the MMPI–2–RF, are easy to administer, but people are often inaccurate in their self-reporting. Projective techniques, such as the Rorschach Inkblot Test and the TAT, provide richer information for a one-to-one relationship but are subject to interpreter bias.

▶ Newer, high-tech methods are proving to be even more effective.

The Trait Approach: Identifying Patterns of Behavior

▶ The trait approach tries to identify personality dimensions that can be used to characterize an individual's behavior. Researchers have attempted to boil down into some core personality dimensions the potentially huge array of things people do, think, and feel.

▶ Researchers use factor analysis to study relationships between the adjectives that people use to self-report traits.

▶ Many personality psychologists currently focus on the Big Five personality factors: openness to experience, conscientiousness, extraversion, agreeableness, and neuroticism. These traits account for variation in personality and appear universal, on the basis of results from many different studies and cultures.

▶ Twin studies indicate that the more genes you have in common with someone else, the more similar your personalities will be. Studies with animals further support the idea that biological mechanisms underlie personality traits.

▶ Research indicates that the part of the brain that regulates arousal and alertness (the reticular formation) is more easily stimulated in introverts than in extraverts, who may need to seek out more interaction and activity to achieve mental stimulation.

The Psychodynamic Approach: Forces That Lie Beneath Awareness

▶ Freud believed that the personality results from forces that are largely unconscious, shaped by the interplay among id, superego, and ego.

▶ Defense mechanisms are techniques the mind may use to reduce anxiety generated by unacceptable impulses.

► Freud also believed that the developing person passes through a series of psychosexual stages and that failing to progress beyond one of the stages results in fixation, which is associated with corresponding personality traits.

► Critics argue that psychodynamic explanations lack real evidence and are after-the-fact interpretations.

The Humanistic–Existential Approach: Personality as Choice

► The humanistic–existential approach to personality grew out of philosophical traditions that are at odds with most of the assumptions of the trait and psychoanalytic approaches. It focuses on how people make healthy choices that form their personalities.

► Humanists see personality as directed by an inherent striving toward self-actualization and development of our unique human potentials.

► Existentialists focus on angst and the defensive response people often have to questions about the meaning of life and the inevitability of death.

The Social–Cognitive Approach: Personalities in Situations

► The social–cognitive approach focuses on personality as arising from individuals' behavior in situations. According to social–cognitive personality theorists, the same person may behave differently in different situations but should behave consistently in similar situations.

► Personal constructs are dimensions people use to make sense of their experiences and that reveal the perceiver's personality.

► People translate their goals into behavior through outcome expectancies. People differ in whether they believe they control their own destiny (internal locus of control) or are at the mercy of fate or other people (external locus of control). Those with an internal locus of control tend to be better able to cope with stress and achieve more.

The Self: Personality in the Mirror

► The self-concept is a person's knowledge of self, including both specific self-narratives and more abstract personality traits or self-schemas. People's self-concept develops through social feedback, and people often act to try to confirm these views through a process of self-verification.

► Self-esteem is a person's evaluation of self; it is derived from being accepted by others, as well as by how we evaluate ourselves by comparison to others. Theories proposed to explain why we seek positive self-esteem suggest that we do so to achieve perceptions of status, or belonging, or of being symbolically protected against mortality.

► People strive for positive self-views through self-serving biases and implicit egotism.

KEY CONCEPT QUIZ

1. From a psychological perspective, personality refers to
   a. a person's characteristic style of behaving, thinking, and feeling.
   b. physiological predispositions that manifest themselves psychologically.
   c. past events that have shaped a person's current behavior.
   d. choices people make in response to cultural norms.

2. Projective techniques to assess personality involve
   a. personal inventories.
   b. self-reporting.
   c. responses to ambiguous stimuli.
   d. actuarial methodology.

3. A relatively stable disposition to behave in a particular and consistent way is a
   a. motive.
   b. goal.
   c. trait.
   d. reflex.

4. Compelling evidence for the importance of biological factors in personality is best seen in studies of
   a. parenting styles.
   b. identical twins reared apart.
   c. brain damage.
   d. factor analysis.

5. After performing poorly on an exam, you drop a class, saying that you and the professor are just a poor match. According to Freud, what defense mechanism are you employing?
   a. regression
   b. rationalization
   c. projection
   d. reaction formation

6. Humanists see personality as directed toward the goal of
   a. existentialism.
   b. self-actualization.
   c. ego control.
   d. sublimation.

7. According to the existential perspective, the difficulties we face in finding meaning in life and in accepting the responsibility for making free choices provoke a type of anxiety called
   a. angst.
   b. flow.
   c. the self-actualizing tendency.
   d. mortality salience.

8. According to social–cognitive theorists, _____ are the dimensions people use in making sense of their experiences.
   a. personal constructs
   b. outcome expectancies
   c. loci of control
   d. personal goals

9. What we think about ourselves is referred to as our _____, and how we feel about ourselves is referred to as our _____ .
   a. self-narrative; self-verification
   b. self-concept; self-esteem
   c. self-concept; self-verification
   d. self-esteem; self-concept

10. When people take credit for their successes but downplay responsibility for their failures, they are exhibiting
   a. narcissism.
   b. implicit egotism.
   c. the self-serving bias.
   d. the name-letter effect.

LearningCurve   Don't stop now! Quizzing yourself is a powerful study tool. Go to LaunchPad to access the LearningCurve adaptive quizzing system and your own personalized learning plan. Visit launchpadworks.com.

KEY TERMS

personality (p. 472)

self-report (p. 473)

Minnesota Multiphasic Personality Inventory (MMPI) (p. 473)

projective tests (p. 474)

Rorschach Inkblot Test (p. 474)

Thematic Apperception Test (TAT) (p. 474)

trait (p. 476)

Big Five (p. 478)

psychodynamic approach (p. 485)

id (p. 485)

superego (p. 485)

ego (p. 485)

defense mechanisms (p. 486)

psychosexual stages (p. 486)

fixation (p. 486)

oral stage (p. 487)

anal stage (p. 487)

phallic stage (p. 487)

Oedipus conflict (p. 487)

latency stage (p. 487)

genital stage (p. 488)

self-actualizing tendency (p. 488)

existential approach (p. 489)

social–cognitive approach (p. 489)

person–situation controversy (p. 490)

personal constructs (p. 491)

outcome expectancies (p. 492)

locus of control (p. 493)

self-concept (p. 495)

self-verification (p. 497)

self-esteem (p. 497)

self-serving bias (p. 500)

narcissism (p. 500)

CHANGING MINDS

1. A presidential candidate makes a Freudian slip on live TV, calling his mother "petty"; he corrects himself quickly and says he meant to say "pretty." The next day the video has gone viral, and the morning talk shows discuss the possibility that the candidate has an unresolved Oedipal conflict. If so, he's stuck in the phallic stage and is likely a relatively unstable person preoccupied with issues of seduction, power, and authority (which may be why he wants to be president). Your roommate knows you're taking a psychology class and asks for your opinion: "Can we really tell that a person is sexually repressed, and maybe in love with his own mother, just because he stumbled over a single word?" How would you reply? How widely are Freud's ideas about personality accepted by modern psychologists?

2. While reading a magazine, you come across an article on the nature–nurture controversy in personality. The magazine describes several adoption studies in which adopted children (who share no genes with each other, but grow up in the same household) are no more like each other than complete strangers. This suggests that family environment—and the influence of parental behavior—on personality is very weak. You show the article to a friend, who has trouble believing the results: "I always thought parents who don't show affection produce kids who have

trouble forming lasting relationships." How would you explain to your friend the relationship between nature, nurture, and personality?

3. One of your friends has found an online site that offers personality testing. He takes the test and reports that the results prove he's an "intuitive" rather than a "sensing" personality, who likes to look at the big picture rather than focusing on tangible here-and-now experiences. "This explains a lot," he says, "like why I have trouble remembering details like other people's birthdays, and why it's hard for me to finish projects before the deadline." Aside from warning your friend about the dangers of self-diagnosis via Internet quizzes, what would you tell him about the relationship between personality types and behavior? How well do scores on personality tests predict a person's actual behavior?

4. One of your friends tells you that her boyfriend cheated on her, so she will never date him or anyone who has ever been unfaithful because "once a cheat, always a cheat." She goes on to explain that personality and character are stable over time, so people will always make the same decisions and repeat the same mistakes over time. What do we know about the interaction between personality and situations that might confirm or deny her statements?

ANSWERS TO KEY CONCEPT QUIZ

1. a; 2. c; 3. c; 4. b; 5. b; 6. b; 7. a; 8. a; 9. b; 10. c.

 LaunchPad macmillan learning   LaunchPad features the full e-Book of *Psychology*, the LearningCurve adaptive quizzing system, videos, and a variety of activities to boost your learning. Visit LaunchPad at launchpadworks.com.

Social Psychology

THE SENIOR SENATOR FROM ARIZONA AND THE FORMER PRESIDENT OF SOUTH AFRICA were different in many ways. One was a White man; one was a Black man. One was a right-wing conservative; one was a left-wing socialist. But both were victims of torture. Senator John McCain was an American navy pilot when he was shot down and captured by the North Vietnamese, and President Nelson Mandela was a political activist when he was imprisoned for 27 years in South Africa. Both men experienced a variety of tortures at the hands of their captors, and both agreed about which was the worst. It has nothing to do with electric shock or waterboarding. It does not require rope or razor blades. It is a remarkably simple technique that has been used for millennia to break the body and destroy the mind. It is called solitary confinement. John McCain spent two years in a cell by himself, and Nelson Mandela spent six. "It crushes your spirit and weakens your resistance more effectively than any other form of mis-treatment," said McCain. "Nothing is more dehumanizing," said Mandela.

Torture often causes pain by depriving people of something they desperately need, such as oxygen, water, food, or sleep. As it turns out, the need for social interaction is just as vital. "I found solitary confinement the most forbidding aspect of prison life," Mandela wrote. "I have known men who took half a dozen lashes in preference to being locked up alone." Indeed, studies of prisoners show that extensive periods of isolation can induce symptoms of psychosis (Grassian, 2006), and even in smaller doses, social isolation takes a toll. Ordinary people who are socially isolated are more likely to become depressed, to become ill, and to die prematurely. In fact, being socially isolated is as bad for your health as being obese or smoking (Cacioppo & Patrick, 2008; Holt-Lunstad et al., 2015).

John McCain and Nelson Mandela each spent years in isolation and described it as the worst form of torture.

▲ Figure 13.1

SOCIAL NETWORKS Human beings build large social networks. A recent analysis of the mobile phone calls of 3.2 million people revealed that the size of a person's social network peaks around the age of 25 and decreases thereafter (data from Bhattacharya et al., 2016).

Learning Objectives

▶ Identify biological and cultural influences on aggression.

▶ Explain why cooperation is risky.

▶ Describe the costs and benefits of groups.

▶ Distinguish between apparent and genuine altruism.

DATA VISUALIZATION

Do Humans Have a "Social Brain"?
Go to launchpadworks.com.

social psychology The study of the causes and consequences of sociality.

aggression Behavior whose purpose is to harm another.

frustration–aggression hypothesis A principle stating that animals aggress when their goals are frustrated.

WHAT KIND OF ANIMAL GETS SICK OR GOES CRAZY when left alone? Our kind. That's because of the 8.7 million species on our planet, human beings are the most social. A few other species—ants, bees, wasps, termites, and naked mole rats—build complex societies in which large numbers of individuals divide labor and cooperate for mutual benefit, but only humans build complex societies of genetically *un*related individuals (see **FIGURE 13.1**). Indeed, some scientists believe that the challenges of living and working in complex societies is the main reason that our brains have gotten so much bigger in the last 2 million years (Sallet et al., 2011; Shultz & Dunbar, 2010; Smith et al., 2010).

Social psychology is *the study of the causes and consequences of sociality.* Every animal faces the twin problems of survival and reproduction, and as you'll see in the first two sections of this chapter, sociality is how our species solved those problems. In the third section, you'll see how social creatures like us learn to influence and control each other's behavior by appealing to each other's basic motives. Finally, in the fourth section, you'll see how we gather and use information to make judgments about each other—sometimes for better and often for worse.

The Survival Game

To survive, all animals must obtain resources such as food, water, and shelter. The problem is that these resources are always scarce, because if they weren't, then the population would increase until they were. Animals often solve this problem by hurting each other or helping each other. *Hurting* and *helping* are antonyms, so you might expect them to have little in common, but as you are about to see, these disparate behaviors are actually two solutions to the same problem (Hawley, 2002).

AGGRESSION

What is the simplest way to solve the problem of scarce resources? Take what you want and kick the stuffing out of anyone who tries to stop you. **Aggression** is *behavior whose purpose is to harm another* (Anderson & Bushman, 2002; Bushman & Huesmann, 2010), and it is a strategy used by just about every animal on the planet. Aggression is not something that animals do for sport but rather as a way of achieving their goals. The **frustration–aggression hypothesis** suggests that *animals aggress when their goals are frustrated* (Dollard et al., 1939). The chimp wants the banana (*goal*), but the pelican is about to take it (*frustration*), so the chimp threatens the pelican with its fist (*aggression*). The robber wants the money (*goal*), but the teller has it all locked up in a vault (*frustration*), so the robber threatens the teller with a gun (*aggression*). Frustrated goals don't cause aggression directly. Rather, they induce negative affect (commonly known as *feeling bad*), and negative affect is what triggers aggression (Berkowitz, 1990). That's why rats that are given painful electric shocks will attack anything in their cage, including other animals, stuffed dolls, or even tennis balls (Kruk et al., 2004). And that's why experimental participants who are required to immerse their hands in ice water or to sit in a very hot room are more likely to blast others with noise weapons or make others eat hot chili (Anderson, 1989; Anderson, Bushman, & Groom, 1997). The idea that negative affect causes aggression may help

**Number of Team A Batters
Previously Hit By Team B Pitcher**

Probability
that Team A
Pitcher will
hit Team B
Batter

3 or More

2

1

0

Temperature (°F)

≤59   0–69   70–79   80–89   ≥90

(a)

(b)

NEW YORK DAILY NEWS/GETTY IMAGES

DATA FROM LARRICK ET AL., 2011

explain why so many acts of violence—from murders to brawls—are more likely to occur on hot days when people are feeling irritated and uncomfortable (Van Lange, Rinderu, & Bushman, 2016; see **FIGURE 13.2**). It is worth noting that not every kind of negative affect gives rise to aggression; for example, when people feel disgusted, they actually become less likely to aggress (Pond et al., 2012).

How Biology Influences Aggression

People aggress when they feel bad. But not everyone does, and no one does all the time. So who does, and when, and why? If you want to know whether someone is likely to behave aggressively and you can ask them just one question, it should be this: "Are you a man?" (Wrangham & Peterson, 1997). Violence is one of the most gender specific of all phenomena. Crimes such as assault, battery, and murder are almost exclusively perpetrated by men (and especially by young men), who are responsible for about 90% of the murders and 80% of the violent crimes in the United States (Strueber, Lueck, & Roth, 2006). Although socialization practices all over the world encourage males to be more aggressive than females (more on that shortly), male aggressiveness is not merely the product of playing with toy soldiers or watching football as a child. Studies show that aggression is strongly correlated with the presence of a hormone called *testosterone*, which is typically higher in men than in women, in younger men than in older men, and in violent criminals than in nonviolent criminals (Dabbs et al., 1995).

Testosterone appears to promote aggression not by making people feel negative affect, but by making them feel powerful and confident in their ability to prevail in interpersonal conflicts (Eisenegger et al., 2010; Eisenegger, Haushofer, & Fehr, 2011). Male chimpanzees with high testosterone tend to stand tall and hold their chins high (Muller & Wrangham, 2004); human beings with high testosterone walk more purposefully, focus more directly on the people they are talking to, and speak in a more forward and independent manner (Dabbs et al., 2001). Testosterone also makes people more sensitive to provocation (Ronay & Galinsky, 2011) and less sensitive to signs of retaliation. Participants in one experiment watched a face as its expression changed from neutral to threatening and were asked to respond as soon as the expression became threatening (see **FIGURE 13.3**). Participants who were given a small dose of testosterone were slower to recognize the threatening expression (van Honk & Schutter, 2007; see also Olsson et al., 2016). As you can imagine, failing to recognize that the guy you are arguing with over a parking space is getting really, really mad is a fairly good way to end up in a fight.

▲ Figure 13.2

HOT AND BOTHERED (a) Professional pitchers have awfully good aim, so when they hit batters with the baseball, it's safe to assume it wasn't an accident. (b) This graph shows data from nearly 60,000 major-league baseball games. As you can see, as the temperature on the field increases, so does the likelihood that Team A batters will be hit by Team B pitchers. This effect becomes even stronger when Team B batters have previously been hit by Team A pitchers, suggesting that the Team B pitcher is seeking revenge (Larrick et al., 2011).

▶ **Figure 13.3**

I SPY THREAT Subjects who were given testosterone needed to see a more threatening expression before they were able to recognize it as such (van Honk & Schutter, 2007).

Testosterone (51%)

Placebo (43%)

0   50   100

Percentage morph change

RESEARCH FROM VAN HONK, J.; SCHUTTER, D. J. (2007).

One of the most reliable methods for eliciting aggression in men is to challenge their status or dominance. Indeed, three quarters of all murders can be classified as "status competitions" or "contests to save face" (Daly & Wilson, 1988). Contrary to popular wisdom, it isn't men with low self-esteem who are most prone to aggression but men with unrealistically *high* self-esteem, because those men are especially likely to perceive others' actions as a challenge to their inflated sense of their own worth (Baumeister, Smart, & Boden, 1996). Men seem especially sensitive to these challenges when they are competing for the attention of women (Ainsworth & Maner, 2012), and losing those competitions can be deadly—for women. The rate at which women in their reproductive years die at the hands of a current or former partner is about as high as the rate at which they die of cancer (Garcia-Moreno et al., 2006).

So are women all sweetness and light? Hardly. Women can be just as aggressive as men, but their aggression tends to be more premeditated than impulsive, and more likely to be focused on obtaining or protecting an actual resource rather than status. Women are much less likely than men to aggress without provocation or to aggress in ways that cause physical injury, but they are only slightly less likely than men to aggress when provoked or to aggress in ways that cause psychological injury (Bettencourt & Miller, 1996; Eagly & Steffen, 1986). Indeed, women may even be more likely than men to aggress by causing social harm, for example, by ostracizing others (Benenson et al., 2011) or by spreading malicious rumors about them (Richardson, 2014).

How Culture Influences Aggression

"Our ancestors have bred pugnacity into our bone and marrow," wrote William James, "and thousands of years of peace won't breed it out of us" (1911, p. 272). Is that true? If James was saying that aggression is part of our biological heritage and that humans will always be capable of it, then yes, he was probably right. But if he was saying that our biological heritage means that we are destined to rape, pillage, and plunder our way through the rest of history, then he was clearly wrong. Indeed, human beings have

Men often aggress in response to status threats. In 2005, John Anderson (*right*) called Russell Tavares (*left*) a "nerd" on a social networking site. So Tavares got in his car, drove 1,300 miles, and burned down Anderson's trailer. "I didn't think anybody was stupid enough to try to kill anybody over an Internet fight," said Anderson. Tavares was later sentenced to 7 years in prison.

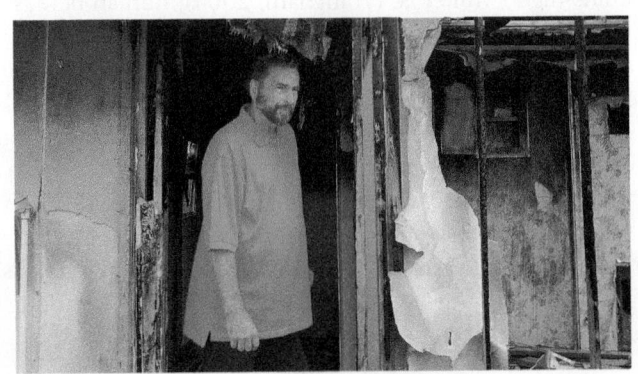

JERRY LARSON/AP IMAGES

become remarkably less aggressive in just the last century alone. As the psychologist Steven Pinker (2007) noted:

> We have been getting kinder and gentler. Cruelty as entertainment, human sacrifice to indulge superstition, slavery as a labor-saving device, conquest as the mission statement of government, genocide as a means of acquiring real estate, torture and mutilation as routine punishment, the death penalty for misdemeanors and differences of opinion, assassination as the mechanism of political succession, rape as the spoils of war, pogroms as outlets for frustration, homicide as the major form of conflict resolution—all were unexceptionable features of life for most of human history. But, today, they are rare to nonexistent in the West, far less common elsewhere than they used to be, concealed when they do occur, and widely condemned when they are brought to light.

Just as levels of aggression can change over time, so too can they differ across geographical boundaries. For example, violent crime in the United States is far more prevalent in the South, where men are taught to react aggressively when they feel their status has been challenged, than in the North, where men are taught to resolve conflicts by appealing to authority (Brown, Osterman, & Barnes, 2009; Nisbett & Cohen, 1996). In one set of experiments, researchers insulted American volunteers from northern and southern states and found that southerners were more likely to experience a surge of testosterone and to feel that their status had been diminished by the insult (Cohen et al., 1996). When a large man walked directly toward them as they were leaving the experiment, the insulted southerners got "right up in his face" before giving way, whereas northerners just stepped aside. On the other hand, in the control condition in which participants were *not* insulted, southerners stepped aside *before* northerners did, which is to say that when they aren't being insulted, southerners are generally more polite!

Variation over time and geography shows that culture can play an important role in determining whether our innate capacity for aggression will result in aggressive behavior (Leung & Cohen, 2011; see **FIGURE 13.4**). People learn by example, which is why some researchers believe that watching violent television shows and playing violent video games can make people more aggressive (Anderson et al., 2010) and less cooperative (Sheese & Graziano, 2005; cf. Ferguson, 2010). But cultures can discourage aggression as well as promote it. (Fry, 2012). For example, the Inuit people of the Canadian Arctic resolve conflicts not with guns or knives, but with song contests in

Baseball pitchers born in southern states are 40% more likely than those born in northern states to hit batters with their pitches (Timmerman, 2007).

▼ Figure 13.4

THE GEOGRAPHY OF VIOLENCE As this map shows, some places are more violent than others. In 2016, Iceland was the least violent nation on Earth, and Syria was the most violent.

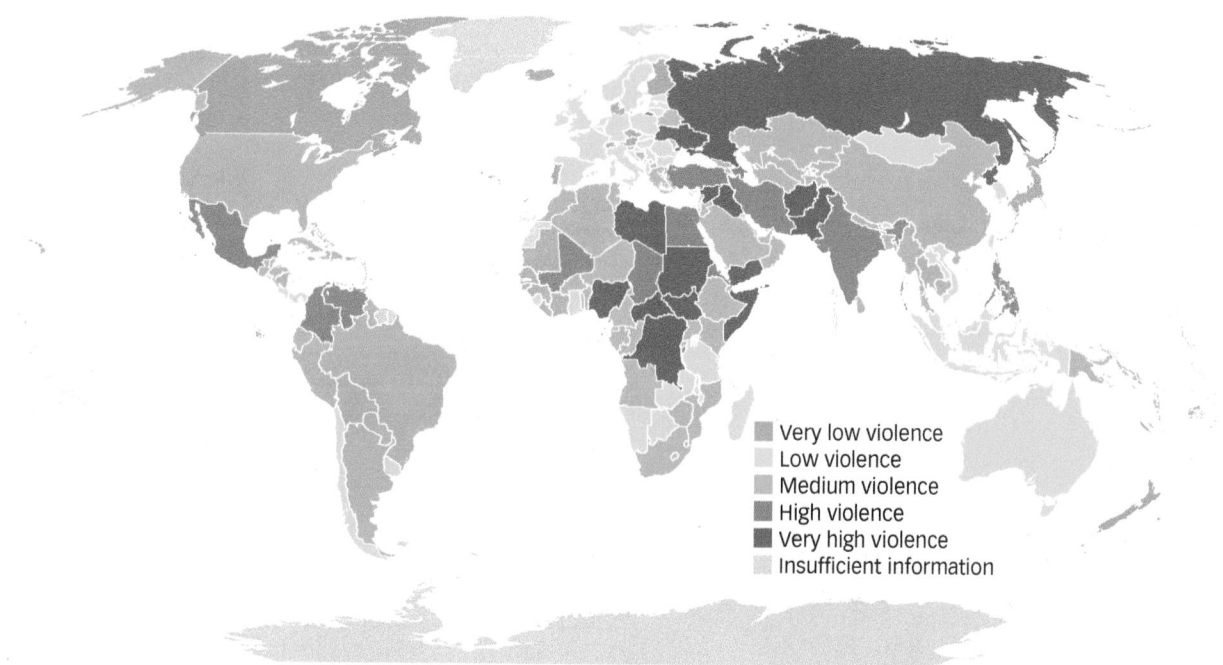

Very low violence
Low violence
Medium violence
High violence
Very high violence
Insufficient information

Depending on where you live, violence may be normal, or it may be unthinkable. In Iraq, where children are exposed to the brutality of extremist groups such as ISIS on a daily basis, boys stage a mock execution as part of their daily play. In India, where Jain children are taught that every form of life is sacred, a girl wears a mask at all times so that she will not harm insects or microbes by inhaling them.

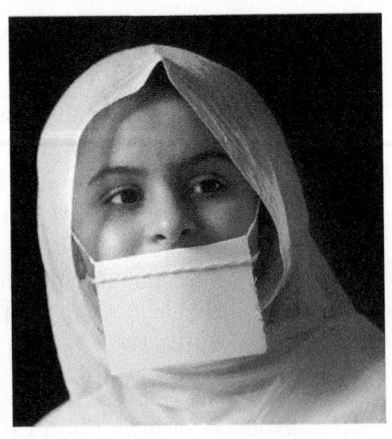

which the person who delivers the most effective verbal put-down of his opponent is declared the winner (Briggs, 2000).

COOPERATION

Two wolves can fight over a dead rabbit, or they can work together to bring down a gazelle. Aggression may be the simplest way to solve the problem of scarce resources, but it is rarely the most effective way, because when individuals work together they can often each get more resources than either could get alone. **Cooperation** is *behavior by two or more individuals that leads to mutual benefit* (Rand & Nowak, 2016), and it is one of our species' greatest achievements—right up there with language, fire, and dental floss (Axelrod, 1984; Axelrod & Hamilton, 1981; Nowak, 2006). Every roadway and supermarket, every iPad and cell phone, every ballet and surgery is the result of cooperation, and it is difficult to think of an important human achievement that could have occurred without it. But if the benefits of cooperation are clear, then why don't we cooperate all the time?

cooperation Behavior by two or more individuals that leads to mutual benefit.

Cooperation Is Risky

Although cooperation is potentially beneficial, it is also risky, and a simple game called the *prisoner's dilemma* shows how. Imagine that you and your friend Tucker have been arrested for hacking into a bank's mainframe and directing a few million dollars to your personal accounts. The police have found some stolen bank codes on your laptops but they don't know which of you actually did the hacking. You and Tucker are now being interrogated in separate rooms, and the detectives ask each of you to sign a statement saying that the other was the actual hacker. They explain that if you both sign, then you'll both get 2 years in prison for hacking, and if you both refuse to sign, then you'll both get 1 year in prison for possession of the stolen codes. However, if one of you signs and the other refuses, then the one who signs will go free, and the one who refuses will get 3 years in prison. What should you do (other than math)? As **FIGURE 13.5** shows, it would be great if you and Tucker cooperated

▶ Figure 13.5

THE PRISONER'S DILEMMA GAME The prisoner's dilemma game illustrates the risk of cooperation. Mutual cooperation leads to a moderate benefit to both players, but if one player cooperates and the other one doesn't, the cooperator gets no benefit and the noncooperator gets a large benefit.

	Tucker refuses to sign (i.e., he cooperates with you)	Tucker signs (i.e., he does not cooperate with you)
You refuse to sign (i.e., you cooperate with Tucker)	You both serve 1 year	You serve 3 years Tucker goes free
You sign (i.e., you do not cooperate with Tucker)	You go free Tucker serves 3 years	You both serve 2 years

and agreed not to sign, because you'd both get off with a very light sentence. But if you agree to cooperate and then Tucker gets sneaky and decides to sign, you'll serve a long sentence while Tucker goes free. So should you cooperate with Tucker or not? Oh my. What a dilemma!

The prisoner's dilemma is not just a game (which is good, because compared with Grand Theft Auto V, it sort of sucks). It is a metaphor for the potential costs and benefits of cooperation in everyday life. For example, consider the dilemma Americans face at tax time. If everyone pays their taxes, then the government can afford to maintain the roads and bridges and everyone can use them. If no one pays their taxes, then the streets will buckle, the bridges will fall down, and everyone will be stranded. So there is a *moderate* benefit to everyone if everyone cooperates and pays their taxes. Alas, there is a *huge* benefit to any sneaky individual who doesn't cooperate because that person pays nothing and gets to use all the roads and bridges free of charge. So should you pay your fair share and risk being a chump, or cheat on your taxes and risk having the bridges collapse? If you are like most citizens, you are willing to cooperate in this situation, but you worry that others won't do the same—and *that's* the dilemma that cooperation so often produces.

Because so much of social life is essentially a prisoner's dilemma game, it is not surprising that people in all cultures value and reward those who play it honorably, and despise and sanction those who don't (Feinberg, Willer, & Shultz, 2014). When people are asked what single quality they most want those around them to have, the answer is *trustworthiness* (Cottrell, Neuberg, & Li, 2007), and when those around us fail to demonstrate that quality we react bitterly. For example, the *ultimatum game* requires one player (the divider) to divide a monetary prize into two parts and offer one of the parts to a second player (the decider) who can either accept or reject the offer. If the decider rejects the offer, then both players get nothing and the game is over. Studies show that deciders typically reject offers that they consider unfair because they'd rather get nothing than get cheated (Fehr & Gaechter, 2002; Thaler, 1988). In other words, people dislike unfairness so much that they will actually give up money in order to punish someone who has treated them unfairly. And it isn't just people who hate unfairness. In one study, monkeys were willing to work for a slice of cucumber until they saw the experimenter give another monkey a more delicious food for doing less work (Brosnan & DeWaal, 2003). At that point the first set of monkeys went on strike and refused to participate further.

How Groups Minimize the Risks of Cooperation

Cooperation requires that we take a risk by benefiting those who have not yet benefited us and then *trusting* them to do the same. But whom can we trust? A **group** is *a collection of people who have something in common that distinguishes them from others.* Every one of us is a member of many groups—from families and teams to religions and nations. Although these groups are quite different, they all have one thing in common, which is that the people in them tend to be especially nice to each other. **Prejudice** is *an evaluation of another person based solely on their group membership* (Dovidio & Gaertner, 2010), and although most people use this word to denote negative evaluations, psychologists use it to denote both positive and negative evaluations (Allport, 1954). Research suggests that although people are not always negatively prejudiced against members of other groups, they are almost always positively prejudiced toward members of their own groups (Brewer, 1999; DiDonato, Ullrich, & Krueger, 2011). This tendency—known as *in-group favoritism*—is evolutionarily ancient (Fu et al., 2012; Mahajan et al., 2011), arises early in development (Dunham, Chen, & Banaji, 2013), and is easily elicited (Efferson, Lalive, & Fehr, 2008). Even when people are randomly assigned to be members of meaningless groups such as "Group 1" or "Group 2," they still favor members of their own group (Hodson & Sorrentino, 2001; Locksley, Ortiz, & Hepburn, 1980). It appears that simply knowing that "I'm one of *us* and not one of *them*" is sufficient to create

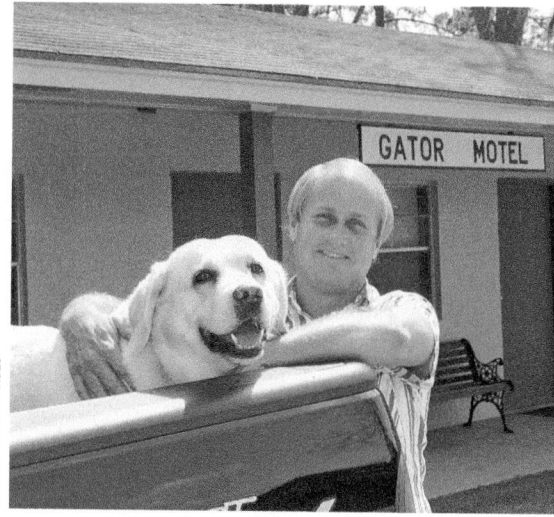

Kevin Hart owns the Gator Motel in Fargo, Georgia, which he runs on an honor system: Guests arrive, stay as long as they like, and leave their payment on the dresser. If just a few people cheated, it would not affect the room rates, but if too many cheated, then prices would have to rise. How would you decide whether to pay or to cheat? Before answering this question, please notice the large dog.

group A collection of people who have something in common that distinguishes them from others.

prejudice A positive or negative evaluation of another person based on their group membership.

common knowledge effect The tendency for group discussions to focus on information that all members share.

group polarization The tendency for groups to make decisions that are more extreme than any member would have made alone.

groupthink The tendency for groups to reach consensus in order to facilitate interpersonal harmony.

in-group favoritism (Tajfel et al., 1971). Because group members can be relied on to favor each other, group membership makes cooperation less risky.

But if groups have benefits, they also have costs. For example, when groups try to make decisions, they rarely do better than the best member would have done alone—and they often do worse (Minson & Mueller, 2012). There are at least four reasons that this happens:

▶ Groups usually don't capitalize fully on the expertise of their members (Hackman & Katz, 2010). For instance, groups (such as a school board) often give too little weight to the opinions of members who are experts (the professor) and too much weight to the opinions of members who happen to be high in status (the mayor) or especially talkative (the mayor).

▶ The **common knowledge effect** is *the tendency for group discussions to focus on information that all members share* (Gigone & Hastie, 1993; Kerr & Tindale, 2004). What makes this a problem is that the information everyone shares (the size of the gymnasium) is often relatively unimportant, whereas the truly important information (how a school in a different district solved its budget crisis) is known to just a few.

▶ A group whose members come to the table with moderate opinions ("We should probably just renovate the auditorium") can end up making an extreme decision ("Let's build a new high school!") simply because, in the course of discussion, each member was exposed to many different arguments in favor of a single position (Isenberg, 1986). **Group polarization** is *the tendency for groups to make decisions that are more extreme than any member would have made alone* (Myers & Lamm, 1975).

▶ Group members usually care about how other members feel and are sometimes reluctant to "rock the boat" even when it needs a good rocking. **Groupthink** is *the tendency for groups to reach consensus in order to facilitate interpersonal harmony* (Janis, 1982). Harmony is important (especially if the group is a choir), but studies show that groups often sacrifice the soundness of their decisions in order to achieve it (Turner & Pratkanis, 1998).

For all of these reasons, then, groups underperform individuals in a wide variety of tasks. But the costs of groups go beyond making some suboptimal decisions. People in groups sometimes do truly terrible things that none of their members would do alone (Yzerbyt & Demoulin, 2010). Lynching, rioting, gang-raping—why do human beings sometimes behave so badly when they assemble in groups? Individuals are especially likely to behave well when they consider their personal values. You may want to steal the Rolex you've had your eye on for weeks or plant a kiss on the attractive

When are people most and least likely to cheat? Researchers posted a picture above an office coffee pot, and found that people were less likely to take coffee without paying when the picture showed eyes than when it showed flowers (Bateson, Nettle, & Roberts, 2006). Other researchers paid people to sit alone in a room and complete puzzles for cash and found that people were less likely to cheat when the lights was bright than when the lights were low (Zhong, Bohns, & Gino, 2010).

stranger you've had your eye on for months, but then you consider the fact that felony theft and sexual assault conflict with your personal values, and so you refrain. But research shows that when individuals assemble in groups, they stop thinking about what is going on inside and instead pay attention to what is going on outside. Their attention is drawn toward others and away from themselves, which makes them less likely to consider their personal values when they take action (Wicklund, 1975). **Deindividuation** occurs *when immersion in a group causes people to become less concerned with their personal values* (Postmes & Spears, 1998) and can lead them to do things they might not do on their own (Baumeister, Ainsworth, & Vohs, 2015).

A second reason that people in groups sometimes behave so badly is **diffusion of responsibility**, which refers to *the tendency for individuals to feel diminished responsibility for their actions when they are surrounded by others who are acting the same way.* Diffusion of responsibility is the main culprit behind something you've probably observed many times—a phenomenon that psychologists call **social loafing**, which is *the tendency for people to expend less effort when in a group than when alone.* For example, individuals in large groups are less likely than individuals in small groups to clap loudly after a performance (Latané, Williams, & Harkins, 1979), exert effort in a team sport (Williams et al.,1989), leave good tips at restaurants (Freeman et al., 1975), donate money to charity (Wiesenthal, Austrom, & Silverman, 1983), and even say hello to passersby (Jones & Foshay, 1984). But the diffusion of responsibility has much more pernicious effects. For example, studies of **bystander intervention**—which is *the act of helping strangers in an emergency situation*—reveal that people are less likely to help an innocent person in distress when there are many other bystanders present, simply because they assume that the other bystanders are collectively more responsible than they are (Darley & Latané, 1968; Fischer et al., 2011). If you saw a fellow student cheating on an exam, you'd probably feel more responsible for reporting the incident if you were taking the exam in a group of 3 than in a group of 3,000 because you'd have a greater share of the responsibility in the first instance than in the second (see **FIGURE 13.6**).

If groups make bad decisions and foster bad behavior, then might we be better off without them? Probably not. Not only do groups minimize the risks of cooperation, but they also contribute to our general well-being (Myers & Diener, 1995). People who are excluded from groups are typically anxious, lonely, depressed, and at increased risk for illness and premature death (Cacioppo & Patrick, 2008; Cohen, 1988; Leary, 1990). Belonging to groups is not just a source of psychological and physical well-being but also a source of identity (Ellemers, 2012; Leary, 2010; Tajfel & Turner, 1986), which is why people typically describe themselves by listing the groups of which they are members ("I'm a Canadian architect"). Groups may sometimes cause us to misjudge and misbehave, but they are also key to our cooperativeness, our health, and our happiness.

deindividuation A phenomenon that occurs when immersion in a group causes people to become less aware of their individual values.

diffusion of responsibility The tendency for individuals to feel diminished responsibility for their actions when they are surrounded by others who are acting the same way.

social loafing The tendency for people to expend less effort when in a group than when alone.

bystander intervention The act of helping strangers in an emergency situation.

◄ Figure 13.6

MOB SIZE AND LEVEL OF ATROCITY Groups are capable of horrible things. These two men were rescued by police just as residents of their town prepared to lynch them for stealing a car. Because larger groups provide more opportunity for diffusion of responsibility, their atrocities become more horrible as the ratio of mob members to victims becomes larger (Leader, Mullen, & Abrams, 2007).

In 2013, a customer at a Tim Horton's drive-through in Winnipeg, Canada decided to perform a random act of kindness and pay for the order of the car behind him. This caused a chain reaction of altruism as 228 consecutive cars received free orders and, in turn, decided to pay for the order of the folks in the next car. The cascade ended when a customer who received four free coffees refused to pay for the car behind him, which had ordered just three coffees.

Wesley Autrey jumped onto the subway tracks to save a stranger's life. Would you have done what he did? Are you sure?

altruism Behavior that benefits another without benefiting oneself.

kin selection The process by which evolution selects for individuals who cooperate with their relatives.

reciprocal altruism Behavior that benefits another with the expectation that those benefits will be returned in the future.

ALTRUISM

Cooperation solves the problem of scarce resources. But is that the only reason we cooperate with others? Aren't we ever just . . . well, *nice*? **Altruism** is *intentional behavior that benefits another at a cost to oneself*, and for centuries, scientists and philosophers have argued about whether people are ever truly altruistic. That may seem like an odd argument to have. After all, people give their blood to the injured, their food to the homeless, and their time to the elderly. We volunteer, donate, contribute, and tithe. People do nice things like these all the time—so why is there any debate about whether people are altruistic?

Because behaviors that appear to be altruistic often have hidden benefits for those who do them. Consider some examples in the animal world. Squirrels emit alarm calls when they see a predator, which puts them at increased risk of being eaten but allows their fellow squirrels to escape. Honeybees spend their lives caring for the offspring of the queen rather than bearing offspring of their own. These behaviors appear to be altruistic, but in fact they are not, because the animals who give help are *genetically related* to the animals who receive it. The squirrels most likely to emit alarm calls are those most closely related to the other squirrels in the den (Maynard-Smith, 1965), and although honeybees do raise their queen's offspring, an odd genetic quirk causes honeybees to be more closely related to those offspring than they would be to their own. When an animal promotes the survival of its relatives, it is actually promoting the survival of its own genes (Hamilton, 1964). **Kin selection** is *the process by which evolution selects for individuals who cooperate with their relatives*, and although cooperating with related individuals may look altruistic, it's actually just selfishness in disguise.

So what about cooperating with unrelated individuals? Well, that isn't necessarily altruistic either. Male baboons will sometimes risk injury to help an unrelated male baboon win a fight, and monkeys will spend time grooming unrelated monkeys when they could be doing something else. Are these examples of altruism? Not really, because as it turns out, the animal that gives favors today tends to get favors tomorrow. **Reciprocal altruism** is *behavior that benefits another with the expectation that those benefits will be returned in the future*, and despite the second word in this term, there's nothing altruistic about it (Trivers, 1972). Indeed, reciprocal altruism is merely cooperation extended over time.

The behavior of nonhuman animals provides little if any evidence of genuine altruism (cf. Bartal, Decety, & Mason, 2011). So what about us? Are we any different? Like other animals, we tend to help our kin more than strangers (Burnstein, Crandall, & Kitayama, 1994; Komter, 2010), and we tend to expect those we help to help us in return (Burger et al., 2009). But unlike other animals, we *do* sometimes provide benefits to complete strangers who have no chance of repaying us (Batson, 2002; Warneken & Tomasello, 2009). We hold the door for people who share precisely none of our genes and tip waiters in restaurants to which we will never return. We give strangers directions, advice, and sometimes even our parking spots (see A World of Difference: Do Me a Favor?). And we do much more than that (see **FIGURE 13.7**). In 2007, Wesley Autrey noticed a student who was having an epileptic seizure at the 137th Street subway station in New York City. The student stumbled and fell onto the tracks just as a train was approaching. So Autrey jumped onto the tracks and lay on top of the student, allowing the train to pass over both of them with only an inch to spare. "I had a split-second decision to make," Autrey said. "I don't feel like I did something spectacular; I just saw someone who needed help. I did what I felt was right" (Buckley, 2007). Clearly, human beings sometimes help others even when the personal costs are potentially staggering. We are capable of genuine altruism, and some studies suggest that we are even more altruistic than we realize (Gerbasi & Prentice, 2013; Miller & Ratner, 1998).

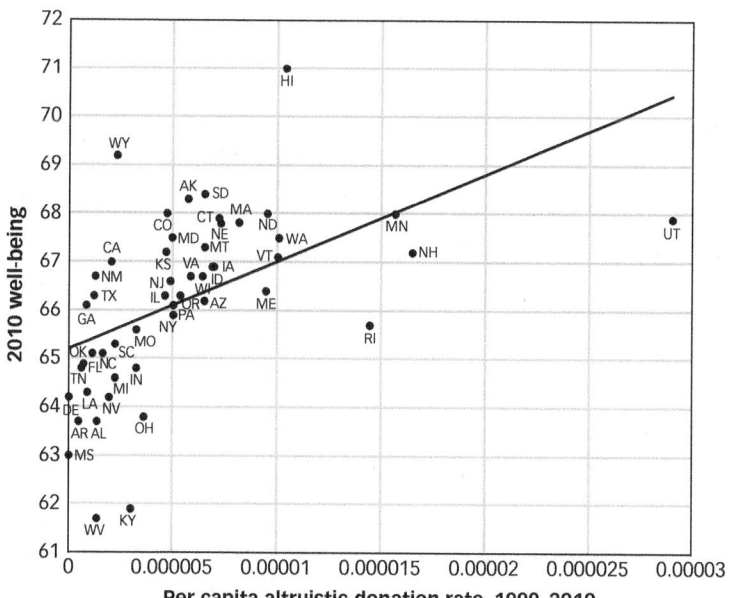

◄ Figure 13.7

ALTRUISM Every year, roughly a hundred Americans donate a kidney to a complete stranger. As this graph shows, these altruists are most likely to live in states that are high in well-being, suggesting that feeling happy and satisfied with one's life may play a role in the decision to help others at a cost to oneself (data from Brethel-Haurwitz & Marsh, 2014).

A WORLD OF DIFFERENCE

Do Me a Favor?

One of the many things that distinguish human beings from other animals is that we often do favors for strangers. Often, but not always. If a stranger walked up to you on the street and asked for directions, you'd tell him; but if he asked to borrow your credit card or move into your spare bedroom, you'd tell him to keep walking. Some requests are reasonable, and some are outrageous. So which are which?

The answer, it seems, depends on your cultural background. In one study (Jonas et al., 2009), researchers approached college students in a campus parking lot and asked them for one of two favors. Some students were asked to give up their parking privileges for a week ("Could I borrow your parking card this week so I can participate in a research project in a nearby building?") and others were asked to give up *everyone's* parking privileges for a week ("Would you mind if we closed the entire parking lot this week for a tennis tournament?"). Both of these requests required the students to relinquish their parking spots for a stranger, so both were a bit irritating. But which one was more irritating?

As the figure shows, European American students were more irritated when the researchers asked them—but *only* them—

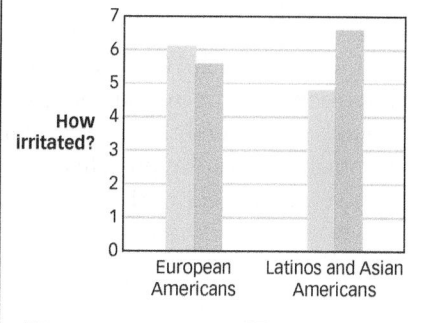

to give up their parking privileges. As members of an individualistic culture in which every person is expected to look out for his own interests, these students were especially annoyed when the researcher singled them out and asked them to give up something that everyone else would be allowed to keep. European American students didn't mind suffering as long as they weren't the only ones to suffer. But Latino students and Asian American students had precisely the opposite reactions. As members of collectivist cultures in which the needs of the many outweigh the needs of the few, these students were especially annoyed when the researcher suggested that many students should give up their parking privileges so that a few students

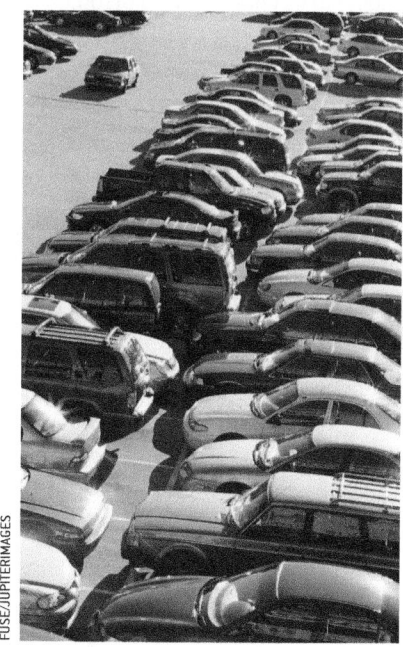

could participate in a tennis tournament. Latino and Asian American students didn't mind suffering as long as everyone didn't have to.

Social life involves favors—soliciting them, offering them, doing them, and denying them. When is a request too big to grant? It all depends on who you ask.

Build to the Outcomes

1. How does the frustration-aggression hypothesis explain aggressive behaviors?

2. How and why does gender influence aggression?

3. What evidence suggests that culture can influence aggression?

4. What are the potential costs and benefits of cooperation?

5. How do groups lower the risks of cooperation?

6. How and why do individuals behave differently when they are in groups?

7. How can we explain selfish behaviors that appear to be altruistic?

The Mating Game

Learning Outcomes

▶ Explain the biological and cultural factors that influence selectivity in mate choice.

▶ Describe the situational, physical, and psychological factors that determine feelings of attraction.

▶ Describe the factors that cause people to get married and divorced.

Among sea horses, it is the male that carries the young, and not coincidentally, males are more selective than are females. If human males could become pregnant, how might their behavior change?

CREATAS/GETTY IMAGES

DR. PAUL ZAHL/SCIENCE SOURCE

All animals must survive and reproduce. As you have seen, social behavior can be very beneficial for survival. But it is an absolute prerequisite for reproduction, which doesn't happen until two people get very, very social with each other. The first step on the road to reproduction is finding someone who wants to travel that road with us, so let's start by seeing how humans do that.

SELECTIVITY

With the exception of a few well-known celebrities, most people don't mate randomly. Rather, they *select* their sexual partners, and as anyone who has lived on earth for more than a few minutes knows, women tend to be more selective than men (Feingold, 1992a; Fiore et al., 2010). When researchers arranged for an attractive man or woman to approach opposite-sex strangers on a college campus and ask, "Would you go out with me?" they found that roughly half of the men who were approached and half of the women who were approached agreed to the request. On the other hand, when the attractive person said to the stranger, "Would you go to bed with me?" exactly *none* of the women and *three quarters* of the men agreed to the request (Clark & Hatfield, 1989). There are many reasons that a woman might turn down a sexual offer from a strange man under such circumstances (Conley, 2011), but research suggests that women tend to be choosier than men under most other circumstances as well (Buss & Schmitt, 1993; Schmitt et al., 2012).

Why are women choosier? One reason is biology. Men produce billions of sperm in their lifetimes, their ability to conceive a child tomorrow is not inhibited by having conceived one today, and conception has no significant physical costs. Therefore, if a man makes a "mating error" and selects a woman who does not produce healthy offspring or who won't do her part to raise them, he's lost nothing but a few minutes and a teaspoon of bodily fluid. But women produce a small number of eggs in their lifetimes, conception eliminates their ability to conceive for at least 9 months, and pregnancy produces physical changes that increase their nutritional requirements and put them at risk of illness and death. So if a woman makes a mating error, she has lost a precious egg, borne the costs of pregnancy, risked her life in childbirth, and missed at least 9 months of other reproductive opportunities. Basic biology makes sex a riskier proposition for women than for men.

But culture and personal experience also play an important role in determining how selective a person will be (Petersen & Hyde, 2010; Zentner & Mitura, 2012). For example, women are typically approached by men more often than men are approached by women (Conley et al., 2011), which means that women can afford to be more selective simply because they have a larger selection to choose from! Another reason that women are more selective is that in most cultures, the reputational costs of promiscuity are higher for women than for men (Eagly & Wood, 1999; Kasser &

Making the Move

Women are generally choosier about their romantic partners than men are, and most scientists believe this has a lot to do with differences in their reproductive biology. But psychologists Eli Finkel and Paul Eastwick (2009) thought that it might also have something to do with the nature of the courtship dance itself.

When it comes to approaching a potential romantic partner, the person with the most interest should be most inclined to "make the first move." Of course, in most cultures, men are *expected* to make the first move, which led the researchers to wonder whether making the first move might *cause* men to think that they have more interest in a woman than she has in them. In other words, could the rule about first moves be one of the *reasons* that women are choosier?

To find out, the researchers teamed up with a local speed-dating service and created two kinds of speed-dating events. In the traditional event, the women stayed in their seats and the men moved around the room, stopping to spend a few minutes chatting with each woman. In the nontraditional event, the men stayed in their seats and the women moved around the room, stopping to spend a few minutes chatting with each man. When the event was over,

the researchers asked each man and woman privately to indicate whether they wanted to exchange phone numbers with any of the potential partners they'd met.

The results were striking (see the accompanying figure). When men made the move (as they traditionally do), women were the choosier gender. That is, men wanted to get a lot more phone numbers than women wanted to give. But when women made the move, men were the choosier gender, and women asked for more numbers than men were willing to hand over. Apparently, approaching someone makes us eager, and being approached makes us cautious. One reason that women are so often the choosier gender may simply be that in most

cultures, men are expected to make the first move. All of this suggests that if you'd like to meet the attractive person at the next table at Starbucks, you should probably avoid saying, "Can I sit with you?" and instead try saying, "Would you like to sit with me?"

GREG GILBERT KRT/NEWSCOM

Sharma, 1999). Indeed, when the potential costs of mating errors are high for men (e.g., when they are choosing a long-term mate rather than a short-term date), they can be every bit as choosy as women (Kenrick et al., 1990). In fact, as The Real World: Making the Move explains, relatively minor changes in the courtship ritual can actually cause men to be *choosier* than women. The point is that biology makes sex a riskier proposition for women than for men, but other factors can exaggerate, equalize, or even reverse those risks. The higher the risk, the more selective people of both sexes tend to be.

ATTRACTION

For most of us, there is a very small number of people with whom we are willing to have sex, an even smaller number of people with whom we are willing to have children, and a staggeringly large number of people with whom we are unwilling to have either. So when we meet someone new, how do we decide which of these categories they belong in? Many things go into choosing a date, a lover, or a partner for life, but perhaps none is more important than the simple feeling we call *attraction* (Berscheid & Reis, 1998). Research suggests that this feeling is the result of situational, physical, and psychological factors.

Attraction Depends on Situational Factors

We tend to think that we select our romantic partners on the basis of their personalities, appearances, and so on—and we do. But we get to select only from the pool of

mere exposure effect The tendency for liking to increase with the frequency of exposure.

people we've met, and the likelihood of meeting a potential partner naturally increases with proximity. Before you ever start ruling out potential romantic partners, geography has already ruled out more than 99.99% of the world's population for you (Festinger, Schachter, & Back, 1950). Proximity not only provides the opportunity for attraction, it also provides the motivation. When you are assigned a roommate or an office mate, you know that your day-to-day existence will be a whole lot easier if you like them than if you don't, so you go out of your way to notice their good qualities and ignore their bad ones. When research participants are told that they will later interact with another person, they immediately like that person more, even before the interaction begins (Darley & Berscheid, 1967).

Proximity breeds attraction for another reason as well. The **mere exposure effect** is *the tendency for liking to increase with the frequency of exposure* (Bornstein, 1989; Zajonc, 1968). Every time we encounter a person, that person becomes a bit more familiar to us, and research shows that people generally prefer familiar to unfamiliar stimuli. For instance, in some experiments, geometric shapes, faces, or alphabetical characters were flashed on a computer screen so quickly that participants were unaware of having seen them. Participants were then shown some of the "old" stimuli that had been flashed across the screen as well as some "new" stimuli that had not. Although they could not reliably say which stimuli were old and which were new, they *liked* the old stimuli more than the new ones (Monahan, Murphy, & Zajonc, 2000). The fact that mere exposure leads to liking may explain why college students who were randomly assigned to seats during a brief psychology experiment were likely to be friends with the person they sat next to a full year later (Back, Schmukle, & Egloff, 2008). Although there are some circumstances under which "familiarity breeds contempt" (Norton, Frost, & Ariely, 2007), for the most part, familiarity seems to breed liking (Reis et al., 2011).

Attraction can be the result of geographical accidents that put people in the same place at the same time, but some places and times are clearly better than others. In one study, researchers observed men as they crossed a swaying suspension bridge. An attractive female researcher approached the men, either when they were in the middle of the bridge or after they had finished crossing it, and asked them to complete a survey. After they did so, she gave each man her telephone number and offered to explain her project in greater detail if he called. Results showed that the men were more likely to call the woman when they had met her in the middle of the swaying bridge (Dutton & Aron, 1974). Why? You may recall from the Emotion and Motivation chapter that people can misinterpret physiological arousal as a sign of attraction (Byrne et al., 1975; Schachter & Singer, 1962). The men were presumably more aroused when they were in the middle of a swaying bridge, and some of those men mistook their arousal for attraction. (By the way, it is worth noting that because researchers can't control who does or does not participate in a field study, it is likely that some of the men in this study were never even *potentially* attracted to the woman—perhaps because they were gay, or happily married, or much older than she was. And yet, the men who were stopped in the middle of the bridge were on average more likely to call the women later. When a study produces an effect on average despite the fact that some of the participants were unlikely to show that effect, then we know that those participants who did show the effect must have showed it quite strongly).

Attraction Depends on Physical Factors

Once people are in the same place at the same time, they can begin to learn about each other's personal qualities, and in most cases, the first quality they learn about is the other person's appearance. The influence of appearance on attraction is remarkably strong. In one study, researchers arranged a "slow dance" for first-year university students and randomly assigned each student to an opposite-sex partner. Midway through the dance, the students confidentially reported how much they liked their partner, how

"I'm a beast, I'm an animal, I'm that monster in the mirror." Like it or not, the mirror is the place where Usher most often sees himself. As a result, he probably prefers pictures of himself that are horizontally reversed (*above left*), whereas his fans probably prefer pictures of him that are not (*above right*). One consequence of the mere exposure effect is that people tend to like the photographic images with which they are most familiar (Mita, Dermer, & Knight, 1977).

PETER KRAMER/NBC/NBC NEWSWIRE VIA GETTY IMAGES

Ben Bostic and Laura Zych were strangers when their US Airways flight crash-landed in the Hudson River in 2009. And then they fell in love. Research shows that when people are in arousing situations together, they often may become attracted to one another.

attractive they thought their partner was, and how much they would like to see their partner again. The researchers measured many of the students' attributes—from their attitudes to their personalities—and they found that the partner's physical appearance was the *only* attribute that reliably influenced the students' feelings of attraction (Walster et al., 1966). (Once again, the fact that some of the students in this field study were almost surely not straight suggests that the results are even stronger than they appear.) Other studies confirm this finding. For instance, one study found that a man's height and a woman's weight were among the best predictors of how many responses a personal ad received (Lynn & Shurgot, 1984), and another study found that physical attractiveness was the *only* factor that predicted the online dating choices of both women and men (Green, Buchanan, & Heuer, 1984).

But beauty gets us more than dates (Etcoff, 1999; Langlois et al., 2000). Beautiful people have more sex, more friends, and more fun than the rest of us do (Curran & Lippold, 1975). They even earn about 10% more money over the course of their lives (Hamermesh & Biddle, 1994; see **FIGURE 13.8**). We tend to think that beautiful people also have superior personal qualities (Dion, Berscheid, & Walster, 1972; Eagly et al., 1991), and in some cases they do. For instance, because beautiful people have more friends and more opportunities for social interaction, they tend to have better social skills than less beautiful people (Feingold, 1992b). Appearance is so powerful that it even influences non-romantic relationships. For example, mothers are more affectionate and playful when their children are attractive than when they are unattractive (Langlois et al., 1995). In fact, the only known disadvantages of being beautiful are that people sometimes feel threatened by beauty (Agthe, Spörrle, & Maner, 2010) and can be unsympathetic to beautiful people's problems (Fisher & Ma, 2014).

▼ Figure 13.8

HEIGHT MATTERS The NFL quarterback Tom Brady is 6′4″ tall, and his wife, the supermodel Gisele Bundchen, is 5′10″ tall. Research shows that tall people earn $789 more per inch per year. The graph shows the average hourly wage of adult White men in the United States classified by height (Mankiw & Weinzierl, 2010).

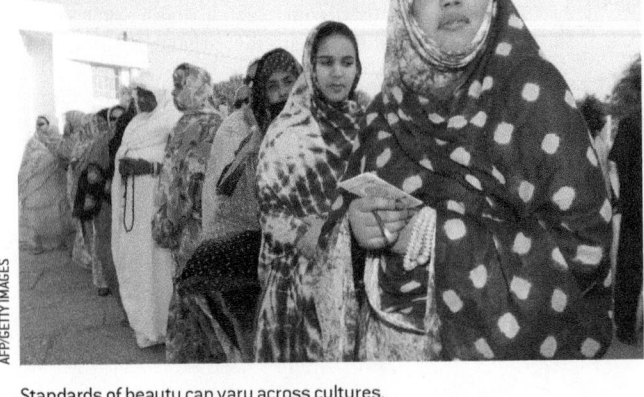

Standards of beauty can vary across cultures. Mauritanian women long to be heavy (*left*), and Ghanian men are grateful to be short (*right*).

Research suggests that men and women are both powerfully and equally influenced by the physical appearance of their partners in the early stages of a relationship (Eastwick et al., 2011) but that this influence may fade more quickly for women than for men (Li et al., 2013; Meltzer et al., 2014).

So yes, it pays to be beautiful. But what exactly constitutes beauty? The answer to that question varies across cultures. In the United States, for example, most women want to be slender, but in Mauritania, young girls are encouraged to drink up to 5 gallons of high-fat milk every day so that someday they will be heavy enough to attract a husband. As one Mauritanian woman noted, "Men want women to be fat, and so they are fat" (LaFraniere, 2007). In the United States, most men want to be tall, but in Ghana, most men are short and consider height a curse. "To be a tall person can be quite embarrassing," said one particularly altitudinous Ghanaian man. "When you are standing in a crowd, the short people start to jeer at you," said another (French, 1997).

But beauty is not entirely in the eye of the beholder. Although different cultures have different standards of beauty, those standards have a surprising amount in common (Cunningham et al., 1995):

▶ *Body shape*. In most cultures, male bodies are considered attractive when they are shaped like a triangle (i.e., broad shoulders with a narrow waist and hips), and female bodies are considered attractive when they are shaped like an hourglass (i.e., broad shoulders and hips with a narrow waist). The most attractive female body in most cultures seems to be the "perfect hourglass," in which a woman's waist is about 70% the size of her hips (Singh, 1993). Culture may determine whether straight men prefer women who are heavy or thin, but in all cultures, straight men seem to prefer this particular waist-to-hip ratio.

▶ *Symmetry*. People in all cultures seem to prefer faces and bodies that are *bilaterally symmetrical*—that is, faces and bodies whose left half is a mirror image of the right half (Perilloux, Webster, & Gaulin, 2010; Perrett et al., 1999).

▶ *Age*. Characteristics such as large eyes, high eyebrows, and a small chin make people look immature or "baby faced" (Berry & McArthur, 1985). As a general rule, female faces are considered more attractive when they have immature features, whereas male faces are considered more attractive when they have mature features (Cunningham, Barbee, & Pike, 1990; Zebrowitz & Montepare, 1992). In every culture, straight women tend to prefer older men, and straight men tend to prefer younger women (Buss, 1989).

Is there any rhyme or reason to this list of scenic attractions? Some psychologists think so. They suggest that nature has designed us to be attracted to people who have good genes and will be good parents (Gallup & Frederick, 2010; Neuberg,

Straight women think men are sexier when they look proud rather than happy, but straight men think women are sexier when they look happy rather than proud. [Tracy & Beall, 2011].

Kenrick, & Schaller, 2010). As it turns out, the features we all seem to find so attractive tend to be fairly reliable indicators of these things. For example:

▶ *Body shape*. Testosterone causes male bodies to become "triangles" and men who are high in testosterone tend to be socially dominant and therefore have more resources to devote to their offspring. Estrogen causes female bodies to become "hourglasses" and women who are high in estrogen tend to be especially fertile and potentially have more offspring to make use of those resources (Singh, 1993). In other words, body shape is an indicator of male dominance and female fertility.

▶ *Symmetry*. Symmetry is a sign of health, which may explain why people are so good at detecting it (Jones et al., 2001; Thornhill & Gangestad, 1993). Indeed, women can distinguish between symmetrical and asymmetrical men by smell alone, and their preference for symmetrical men is especially pronounced when they are ovulating (Thornhill & Gangestad, 1999).

▶ *Age*. Younger women are generally more fertile than older women, whereas older men generally have more resources than younger men. Thus, a youthful appearance is a signal of a woman's ability to bear children, just as a mature appearance is a signal of a man's ability to care for them.

If the feeling we call *attraction* is simply nature's way of telling us that we are in the presence of a person who has good genes and a propensity to be a good parent, then it isn't any wonder that straight people in different cultures appreciate so many of the same features in the opposite sex.

Interestingly, the same seems to be true of people who are not straight. (We have much more to say about the origins and consequences of sexual orientation in the Development chapter). Although research on this topic is still sparse (Amos & McCabe, 2015), studies suggest that gay and straight people generally agree on what features make men and women attractive (Legenbauer et al., 2009; Swami & Tovée, 2008). For example, gay men and straight women agree about which male faces and voices are the most and least attractive (Valentová, Roberts, & Havlíček, 2013). Both gay men and straight men find younger faces more attractive than older ones, but this tendency is particularly pronounced when straight men are looking at women and gay men are looking at men (Teuscher & Teuscher, 2007). It is also important to note that attraction isn't action. Studies show that although everyone may *desire* the most attractive person in the room, most people tend to approach, date, and marry someone who is about as attractive as they are (Berscheid et al., 1971; Lee et al., 2008).

Attraction Depends on Psychological Factors

If attraction is all about big biceps and high cheekbones, then why don't we just skip the small talk and pick our life partners from photographs? Because for human

Similarity is a very strong source of attraction.

beings, attraction is about much more than that. Physical appearance is assessed easily, early, and from across a crowded room (Lenton & Francesconi, 2010), and it definitely determines who draws our attention and quickens our pulse. But once people begin interacting, they move beyond appearances (Cramer, Schaefer, & Reid, 1996; Regan, 1998), which is why physical attractiveness matters less when people have known each other for a long time (Hunt, Eastwick, & Finkel, 2015). People's *inner* qualities—their personalities, points of view, attitudes, beliefs, values, ambitions, and abilities—play an important role in determining their sustained interest in each other, and there isn't much mystery about the kinds of inner qualities that most people find attractive. Intelligence, ambitiousness, loyalty, trustworthiness, and kindness seem to be high on just about everybody's list (Daniel et al., 1985; Farrelly, Lazarus, & Roberts, 2007; Fletcher et al., 1999).

Exactly how much wit and wisdom do we want our mates to have? You might think the answer is "As much as humanly possible!" but research suggests that people are actually most attracted to those who are similar to them on these and almost all other dimensions (Byrne, Ervin, & Lamberth, 1970; Hatfield & Rapson, 1992; Neimeyer & Mitchell, 1988). We marry people of a similar age with similar levels of education, similar religious backgrounds, similar ethnicities, similar socioeconomic statuses, similar personalities, and so on (Botwin, Buss, & Shackelford, 1997; Buss, 1985; Caspi & Herbener, 1990). We even marry people with similar genes (Domingue et al., 2014). When researchers measured 88 distinct characteristics of 1,000 couples, they found that the couples were more similar than one would expect by chance on 66 of those characteristics, and less similar than one would expect by chance on precisely none (Burgess & Wallin, 1953). Indeed, of all the characteristics psychologists have measured, there is just one for which the majority of people have a consistent preference for dissimilarity, and that's gender.

Why is similarity so attractive? There are at least three reasons. First, it's easy to interact with people who are similar to us because we can instantly agree on a wide range of issues, such as what to eat, where to live, how to raise children, and how to spend our money. Second, when someone shares our attitudes and beliefs, we feel validated, and we become more confident that our attitudes and beliefs are right (Byrne & Clore, 1970). Indeed, research shows that when a person's attitudes or beliefs are challenged, they become even more attracted to similar others (Greenberg et al., 1990; Hirschberger, Florian, & Mikulincer, 2002). Third, because we like people who share our attitudes and beliefs, we can reasonably expect them to like us for exactly the same reason, and *being liked* is a powerful source of attraction (Aronson & Worchel, 1966; Backman & Secord, 1959; Condon & Crano, 1988), especially when the people who like us don't seem to like anyone else (Eastwick et al., 2007).

Our desire for similarity goes beyond attitudes and beliefs and extends to abilities as well. For example, we may admire extraordinary skill in quarterbacks and saxophone players, but when it comes to friends and lovers, extraordinary people can threaten our self-esteem and make us feel a bit nervous about our own competence (Tesser, 1991). This seems to be especially true when the extraordinary person is a woman and the nervous person is a man (Ratliff & Oishi, 2013). This may explain why people are attracted to those who have small pockets of incompetence. A minor flaw can make a highly competent person seem a bit more human—and therefore a bit more similar to us (Aronson, Willerman, & Floyd, 1966).

RELATIONSHIPS

The vast majority of human beings eventually become parents, and they typically do this in the context of committed, long-term relationships (Clark & Lemay, 2010). Most animals have relationships that end approximately thirty seconds after sex is over. So why do people have relationships that often last for their entire lives?

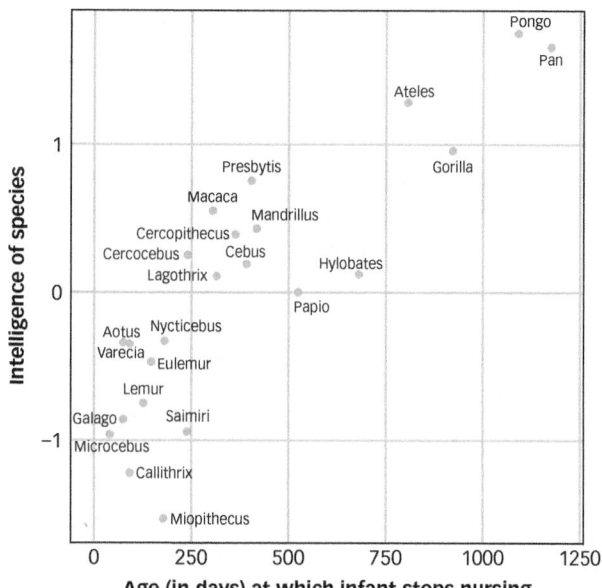

◄ Figure 13.9

BIG BRAIN BABY Smart animals tend to have helpless infants. This figure shows the relationship between the intelligence of different primate species and the age at which their offspring stop nursing. As you can see, the smarter a species is, the longer its infants remain reliant on their parents (data from Piantadosi & Kidd, 2016).

One (slightly weird) answer is that we're born half-baked. Because human beings have large heads to house their large brains, a fully developed human infant could not pass through its mother's birth canal, so human mothers must give birth while their babies are relatively underdeveloped—and underdeveloped babies need a lot more care than one parent can provide. If human infants were more like tadpoles—ready at birth to swim, find food, and escape predators—then their parents might not need to form enduring relationships. But human infants are among the most helpless creatures on earth. They require years and years of nurturing before they can even begin to fend for themselves, and that's one reason that human adults tend to do their parenting in the context of committed, long-term relationships (see **FIGURE 13.9**).

Marriage: Making the Commitment

In most cultures, committed, long-term relationships are signified by marriage, and ours is no exception. About 80% of all 40-year-old Americans have been married, and although marriage has become less popular over the last few decades, the best estimate is that about 75% of current 20-year-olds will eventually get married too (Wang & Parker, 2014). The median age at which Americans get married for the first time is currently 27 for women and 29 for men, which is considerably higher than it was a half century ago, when half of all American women were married by the age of 20. In 2012, 78% of all 25-year-old American men had never married, but 50 years earlier, only 28% had never married. The bottom line is that Americans are increasingly likely to marry late or not at all. Gay and lesbian Americans are, of course, an exception to this rule, because until very recently, the law kept their marriage rate at exactly zero percent. They now have nowhere to go but up!

People get married for many reasons, and love is one of the biggies. About 85% of Americans say that they would not marry without love (Kephart, 1967; Simpson, Campbell, & Berscheid, 1986); the vast majority say they would sacrifice their other life goals to attain it (Hammersla & Frease-McMahan, 1990); and most list love as one of the two most important sources of happiness in life (Freedman, 1978). The fact that people marry for love seems so obvious that you may be surprised to learn that this obvious fact is a rather recent invention. Throughout history, marriage has traditionally served a variety of economic, practical, and decidedly unromantic functions ranging from cementing agreements between clans to paying back debts. Marriage

▶ Figure 13.10

PASSIONATE AND COMPANIONATE LOVE
Companionate and passionate love have different time courses and trajectories. Passionate love begins to cool within just a few months, but companionate love can grow slowly but steadily over years.

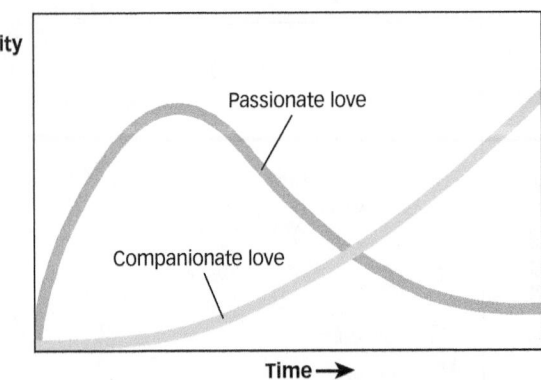

was traditionally regarded as an alliance that helped people fulfill basic needs, such as growing food, building shelter, and protecting each other from violence. Although people have experienced love for ages, it wasn't until the 20th century that Westerners began to think of it as a reason to get married (Finkel et al., 2015).

So what is this thing that modern people marry for? Psychologists distinguish two basic kinds of love: **passionate love**, which is *an experience involving feelings of euphoria, intimacy, and intense sexual attraction*, and **companionate love**, which is *an experience involving affection, trust, and concern for a partner's well-being* (Acevedo & Aron, 2009; Hatfield, 1988; Rubin, 1973; Sternberg, 1986). The ideal romantic relationship gives rise to both types of love, but the speeds, trajectories, and durations of the two experiences are markedly different (see **FIGURE 13.10**). Passionate love is what brings people together: It has a rapid onset, reaches its peak quickly, and begins to diminish within just a few months (Aron et al., 2005). Companionate love is what keeps people together: It takes some time to get started, grows slowly, and need never stop growing (Gonzaga et al., 2001).

Divorce: Unmaking the Commitment

Although the divorce rate in America has fallen in the past few decades, more than a third of those Americans who are currently married will eventually decide to terminate that relationship. Marriage offers benefits (such as love, sex, and financial security), but it also imposes costs (such as additional responsibility, loss of personal freedom, and the potential for interpersonal conflict), and people tend to remain in relationships only as long as they perceive a favorable ratio of costs to benefits (Homans, 1961; Thibaut & Kelley, 1959). But whether a person considers a particular cost-benefit ratio to be favorable depends on at least two things (Le & Agnew, 2003; LeMay, 2016; Rusbult & Van Lange, 2003).

First, it depends on the person's **comparison level**, which is *the cost–benefit ratio that a person believes he or she could attain in another relationship*. A cost–benefit ratio that seems favorable to two people stranded on a desert island may seem unfavorable to two people who live in a large city filled with other potential partners. Indeed, people often accept relationships that have many costs simply because they believe that being single would have even more (Spielmann et al., 2013). Second, the favorability of a cost–benefit ratio depends on how much the person has already invested in the relationship. A ratio that seems favorable to people who have been married for many years may seem unfavorable to people who have been married for just a few months, which is one of the reasons why new marriages are more likely to end than old ones are (Bramlett & Mosher, 2002; Cherlin, 1992). It is also worth noting that people care about their partners' cost–benefit ratio as well as their own. **Equity** is *a state of affairs in which the cost–benefit ratios of two partners are roughly equally favorable* (Bolton & Ockenfels, 2000; Messick & Cook, 1983; Walster, Walster, & Berscheid, 1978), and research suggests that although people are naturally distressed when their ratio is less favorable than their partner's, they are also distressed when it is more favorable (Schafer & Keith, 1980).

passionate love An experience involving feelings of euphoria, intimacy, and intense sexual attraction.

companionate love An experience involving affection, trust, and concern for a partner's well-being.

comparison level The cost–benefit ratio that people believe they deserve or could attain in another relationship.

equity A state of affairs in which the cost–benefit ratios of two partners are roughly equal.

Build to the Outcomes

1. Why are women generally more selective in choosing mates than men?

2. What situational factors play a role in attraction?

3. Why is physical appearance so important?

4. What kind of information does physical appearance convey?

5. Why is similarity such a powerful determinant of attraction?

6. What are the two basic kinds of love?

7. How do people weigh the costs and benefits of their relationships?

Controlling Others

Those of us who grew up reading comics or watching cartoons have usually thought a bit about which of the standard superpowers we'd most like to have. Super strength and super speed have obvious benefits, invisibility and X-ray vision could be interesting as well as lucrative, and there's a lot to be said for flying. But when it comes down to it, the ability to control other people would probably be the most useful of all. Why get in a death match with an alien overlord or rescue orphans from a burning building when you can convince someone else to do these things for you? The things we want from life—gourmet food, interesting jobs, big houses, fancy cars—can all be given to us by others, and the things we want most—loving families, loyal friends, admiring children, appreciative employers—cannot be gotten in any other way.

Social influence is *the ability to change or direct another person's behavior* (Cialdini & Goldstein, 2004). But how does it work? If you want someone to give you their time, money, allegiance, or affection, you'd be wise to consider first what it is *they* want. People have three basic motivations that make them susceptible to social influence (Bargh, Gollwitzer, & Oettingen, 2010; Fiske, 2010). First, people are motivated to experience pleasure and to avoid experiencing pain (the *hedonic motive*). Second, people are motivated to be accepted and to avoid being rejected (the *approval motive*). Third, people are motivated to believe what is right and to avoid believing what is wrong (the *accuracy motive*). As you will see, most attempts at social influence appeal to one or more of these motives.

Learning Outcomes

▶ Describe the hedonic motive and explain how appeals to it can backfire.

▶ Describe the approval motive and distinguish normative influence, conformity, and obedience.

▶ Describe the accuracy motive and distinguish informational influence, persuasion, and consistency.

social influence The ability to change or direct another person's behavior.

THE HEDONIC MOTIVE

If there is an animal that prefers pain to pleasure it must be very good at hiding, because no one has ever seen it. Pleasure seeking is the most basic of all motives, and social influence often involves creating situations in which others can achieve more pleasure by doing what we want them to do than by doing something else. Parents, teachers, governments, and businesses influence our behavior by offering rewards and

According to a group of eminent historians, the civil rights leader Martin Luther King, Jr. (1929–1968) and the suffragist and feminist Susan B. Anthony (1820–1906) are among the 50 most influential Americans who have ever lived. In what ways did these two people "change or direct" your behavior?

▶ Figure 13.11

THE COST OF SPEEDING The penalty for speeding in Massachusetts used to be a modest fine. Then the legislature changed the law so that drivers under 18 who are caught speeding lose their licenses for 90 days—and to get them back, they have to pay $500, attend 8 hours of training classes, and retake the state's driving exam. Guess what? Deaths among drivers under 18 fell by 38% in just 3 years. In other words, more than 8,000 young lives were saved by appealing to the hedonic motive.

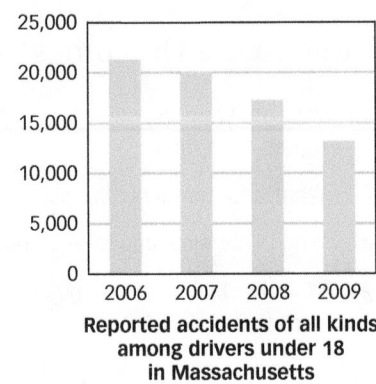

Reported accidents of all kinds among drivers under 18 in Massachusetts

threatening punishments (see **FIGURE 13.11**). There's nothing mysterious about how these influence attempts work, and they are often quite effective. When the Republic of Singapore warned its citizens that anyone caught chewing gum in public would face a year in prison and a $5,500 fine, the rest of the world was outraged; but when the outrage subsided, it was hard to ignore the fact that gum chewing in Singapore had fallen to an all-time low. A good caning will get your attention every time.

You'll recall from the Memory chapter that even a sea slug will repeat behaviors that are followed by rewards and avoid behaviors that are followed by punishments. Although the same is generally true of human beings, in some instances, rewards and punishments can backfire. For example, children in one study were allowed to play with colored markers, and then some were given a "Good Player Award." When the children were given markers the next day, those who had received an award the previous day were *less* likely to play with the markers than were those who had not received an award (Lepper, Greene, & Nisbett, 1973). Why? Because children who had received an award the first day came to think of drawing as something one does to receive rewards, and if no one was going to give them an award the second day, then why the heck should they do it (Deci, Koestner, & Ryan, 1999)? Similarly, rewards and punishments can backfire simply because people resent being bribed and threatened. Researchers placed signs in two restrooms on a college campus: "Please don't write on these walls" and "Do not write on these walls under any circumstances." Two weeks later, the walls in the second restroom had more graffiti, presumably because students didn't appreciate the threatening tone of the second sign and wrote on the walls just to show that they could (Pennebaker & Sanders, 1976).

THE APPROVAL MOTIVE

Other people stand between us and starvation, predation, loneliness, and all the other things that make getting shipwrecked such a bad idea. We depend on others for safety, sustenance, and solidarity, and being rejected or excluded by others is one of the most painful of all human experiences (Eisenberger, Lieberman, & Williams, 2003; Uskul & Over, 2014; Williams, 2007). We are powerfully motivated to have others accept us, like us, and approve of us (Baumeister & Leary, 1995; Leary, 2010), and that motive leaves us vulnerable to social influence.

Normative Influence: We Do What's Appropriate

Consider the many things you know about elevators. When you get on an elevator you are supposed to face forward and not talk to the person next to you even if you were talking to that person before you got on the elevator unless you are the only two people on the elevator in which case it's okay to talk and face sideways but still not backward. Although no one ever taught you this long-winded rule, you probably picked it up somewhere along the way. The unwritten rules that govern social behavior are called **norms**, which are *customary standards for behavior that are widely shared by*

norms Customary standards for behavior that are widely shared by members of a culture.

On average, your risk of becoming obese increases by ...

... **57%**
if someone you
consider a friend
becomes obese.

... **37%**
if your spouse
becomes obese.

... **171%**
if a very close friend
becomes obese.

... **40%**
if one of your siblings
becomes obese.

... **100%**
if you are a man and
your male friend
becomes obese.

... **67%**
if you are a woman
and your sister
becomes obese.

... **38%**
if you are a woman
and your female friend
becomes obese.

... **44%**
if you are a man
and your brother
becomes obese.

FRANCIS DEAN/DEAN PICTURES/THE IMAGE WORKS

◄ Figure 13.12

THE PERILS OF CONNECTION Other people's behavior defines what is normal, and so we tend to do the things we see others doing. Overeating is one of those things. Research shows that if someone you know becomes obese, your chances of becoming obese can increase dramatically (Christakis & Fowler, 2007).

members of a culture (Cialdini, 2013; Miller & Prentice, 1996). We learn norms with exceptional ease, and we obey them with exceptional fidelity, because we know that if we don't, others won't approve of us (Centola & Baronchelli, 2015). For example, every human culture has a **norm of reciprocity**, which is *the unwritten rule that people should benefit those who have benefited them* (Gouldner, 1960). When a friend buys you lunch, you return the favor; and if you don't, your friend gets miffed. Indeed, the norm of reciprocity is so strong that when researchers randomly pulled the names of strangers from a telephone directory and sent them all Christmas cards, they received Christmas cards back from most (Kunz & Woolcott, 1976).

Norms are a powerful weapon in the game of social influence. **Normative influence** occurs when *another person's behavior provides information about what is appropriate* (see **FIGURE 13.12**). For example, waiters and waitresses know all about the norm of reciprocity, which is why they often give customers a piece of candy along with the bill. Studies show that customers who receive a candy feel obligated to do "a little extra" for the waiter who did "a little extra" for them (Strohmetz et al., 2002). Indeed, people will sometimes refuse small gifts precisely because they don't want to feel indebted to the gift giver (Shen, Wan, & Wyer, 2011).

The norm of reciprocity involves swapping, but the thing being swapped doesn't have to be a favor. The **door-in-the-face technique** is *an influence strategy that involves getting someone to deny an initial request*. Here's how it works: You ask someone for something more valuable than you really want, you wait for that person to refuse (to "slam the door in your face"), and then you ask the person for what you really wanted in the first place. For example, when researchers asked college students to volunteer to supervise adolescents who were going on a field trip, only 17% of the students agreed. But when the researchers first asked students to commit to spending 2 hours per week for 2 years working at a youth detention center (to which every one of the students said no) and *then* asked them to supervise a field trip, 50% of the students agreed (Cialdini et al., 1975). Why? The norm of reciprocity! The researchers began by asking for a large favor, which the students refused. Then the researchers made a concession by asking for a smaller favor. Because the researchers made a concession, the norm of reciprocity demanded that the students make one too—and half of them did.

Conformity: We Do What Others Do

People can influence us by invoking familiar norms, such as the norm of reciprocity. But if you've ever found yourself at a fancy dinner, sneaking a peek at the person next

DON PAULSON PHOTOGRAPHY/PURESTOCK/SUPERSTOCK

Have you ever wondered which big spender left the bill as a tip? In fact, the bills are often put there by the very people you are tipping because they know that the presence of paper money will suggest to you that others are leaving big tips and that it would be socially appropriate for you to do the same. By the way, the customary gratuity for someone who writes a textbook for you is 15%. But most students send more.

norm of reciprocity The unwritten rule that people should benefit those who have benefited them.

normative influence A phenomenon that occurs when another person's behavior provides information about what is appropriate.

door-in-the-face technique An influence strategy that involves getting someone to deny an initial request.

A perplexed participant (*center*), flanked by trained actors, is on the verge of conforming in one of Solomon Asch's line-judging experiments.

to you in the hopes of discovering whether the little fork is supposed to be used for the shrimp or the salad, then you know that other people can influence us by defining *new* norms in ambiguous, confusing, or novel situations. **Conformity** is *the tendency to do what others do simply because others are doing it*, and it results in part from normative influence.

In a classic study, the psychologist Solomon Asch had participants sit in a room with seven other people who appeared to be ordinary participants, but who were actually trained actors (Asch, 1951, 1956). An experimenter explained that the participants would be shown cards with three printed lines and their job was simply to say which of the three lines matched a "standard line" that was printed on another card (see **FIGURE 13.13**). The experimenter held up a card and then asked each person to answer in turn. The real participant was among the last to be called on. Everything went well on the first two trials, but then on the third trial, something really strange happened: The actors all began giving the same wrong answer! What did the real participants do? Although most participants gave the right answer on most trials, 75% conformed and announced the wrong answer on at least one trial. Subsequent research has shown that these participants didn't actually misperceive the length of the lines, but were instead succumbing to normative influence (Asch, 1955; Nemeth & Chiles, 1988). Giving the wrong answer was apparently the "right thing to do," and so participants did it.

The behavior of others can tell us what is proper, appropriate, expected, and accepted (in other words, it can define a norm), and once a norm is defined, we feel obliged to honor it. When a Holiday Inn in Tempe, Arizona, left a variety of different "message cards" in guests' bathrooms in the hopes of convincing those guests to reuse their towels rather than laundering them every day, it discovered that the single most effective message was the one that simply read: "Seventy-five percent of our guests use their towels more than once" (Cialdini, 2005). When the Sacramento Municipal Utility District randomly selected 35,000 customers and sent them electric bills showing how their energy consumption compared with that of their neighbors, consumption fell by 2% (Kaufman, 2009). Clearly, normative influence can be a force for good (see Other Voices: Ninety-One Percent of All Students Read This Box and Love It).

conformity The tendency to do what others do simply because others are doing it.

▶ Figure 13.13

ASCH'S CONFORMITY STUDY If you were asked which of the lines on the right (A, B, or C) matches the standard line on the left, what would you say? Research on conformity suggests that your answer would depend, in part, on how other people in the room answered the same question.

Standard

A B C

NORMATIVE INFLUENCE AT HOME In 2008, the Sacramento Municipal Utility District randomly selected 35,000 of its customers and sent them electric bills like the one above. The bill showed not only how much electricity the customer had used, it also showed how much electricity was used by neighbors who lived in similar-sized homes. When the utility crunched the numbers, they discovered that customers who had received this "compare with the neighbors" bill had reduced their electricity consumption by 2%, compared with customers who had received a traditional bill (Kaufman, 2009). Clearly, normative influence can be a force for good.

OTHER VOICES

Ninety-One Percent of All Students Read This Box and Love It

Tina Rosenberg is an editorial writer for the *New York Times*. Her 1995 book *The Haunted Land: Facing Europe's Ghosts After Communism* won both the Pulitzer Prize and the National Book Award.

Binge drinking is a problem on college campuses across America (Wechsler & Nelson, 2001). About half of all students report doing it, and those who do are much more likely to miss classes, fall behind in their school work, drive drunk, and have unprotected sex. So what to do?

Colleges have tried a number of remedies—from education to abstinence—and none of them has worked particularly well. But lately, some schools have taken a new approach called "social norming." Although this approach is surprisingly effective, it is also controversial. Tina Rosenberg's most recent book is *Join the Club: How Peer Pressure Can Transform the World*. In the following essay, she describes both the technique and the controversy.

Like most universities, Northern Illinois University in DeKalb has a problem with heavy drinking. In the 1980s, the school was trying to cut down on student use of alcohol with the usual strategies. One campaign warned teenagers of the consequences of heavy drinking. "It was the 'don't run with a sharp stick you'll poke your eye out' theory of behavior change," said Michael Haines, who was the coordinator of the school's Health Enhancement Services. When that didn't work, Haines tried combining the scare approach with information on how to be well: "It's O.K. to drink if you don't drink too much—but if you do, bad things will happen to you."

That one failed, too. In 1989, 45 percent of students surveyed said they drank more than five drinks at parties. This percentage was slightly higher than when the campaigns began. And students thought heavy drinking was even more common; they believed that 69 percent of their peers drank that much at parties.

But by then Haines had something new to try. In 1987 he had attended a conference on alcohol in higher education sponsored by the United States Department of Education. There Wes Perkins, a professor of sociology at Hobart and William Smith Colleges, and Alan Berkowitz, a psychologist in the school's counseling center, presented a paper that they had just published on how student drinking is affected by peers. "There are decades of research on peer influence—that's nothing new," Perkins said at the meeting. What was new was their survey showing that when students were asked how much their peers drank, they grossly overestimated the amount. If the students were responding to peer pressure, the researchers said, it was coming from imaginary peers.

The "aha!" conclusion Perkins and Berkowitz drew was this: maybe students' drinking behavior could be changed by just telling them the truth.

Haines surveyed students at Northern Illinois University and found that they also had a distorted view of how much their peers drink. He decided to try a new campaign, with the theme "most students drink moderately." The centerpiece of the campaign was a series of ads in the *Northern Star*, the campus newspaper, with pictures of students and the caption "two thirds of Northern Illinois University students (72%) drink 5 or fewer drinks when they 'party.'" . . .

Haines's staff also made posters with campus drinking facts and told students that if they had those posters on the wall when an inspector came around, they would earn $5. (35 percent of the students did have them posted when inspected.) Later they made buttons for students in the fraternity and sorority system—these students drank more heavily—that said "Most of Us," and offered another $5 for being caught wearing one. The buttons were deliberately cryptic, to start a conversation.

After the first year of the social norming campaign, the perception of heavy drinking had fallen from 69 to 61 percent. Actual heavy drinking fell from 45 to 38 percent. The campaign went on for a decade, and at the end of it NIU students believed that 33 percent of their fellow students were episodic heavy drinkers, and only 25 percent really were—a decline in heavy drinking of 44 percent. . . .

Why isn't this idea more widely used? One reason is that it can be controversial. Telling college students "most of you drink moderately" is very different than saying "don't drink." (It's so different, in fact, that the National Social Norms Institute, with headquarters at the University of Virginia, gets its money from Anheuser Busch—a decision that has undercut support for the idea of social norming.) The approach angers people who lobby for a strong, unmuddied message of disapproval—even though, of course, disapproval doesn't reduce bad behavior, and social norming does.

Rosenberg's essay suggests that social norming is a powerful tool for changing behavior, but its use raises important questions. When we tell students about drinking on campus, should we tell them what's true—even if the truth is a bit ugly? Or should we tell them what's best—even if they are unlikely to do it? There are no easy or obvious answers to this question, but as a society, we have no choice but to choose.

obedience The tendency to do what powerful people tell us to do.

Obedience: We Do What We're Told

Other people's behavior can provide information about norms, but in most situations there are a few people whom we all recognize as having special authority both to define the norms and to enforce them. The guy who works at the movie theater may be some high-school fanboy with a bad haircut and a 10:00 p.m. curfew, but in the context of the theater, he is the authority. So when he asks you to put away your cell and stop texting in the middle of the movie, you do as you are asked. **Obedience** is *the tendency to do what powerful people tell us to do.*

Why do we obey powerful people? Well, yes, sometimes they have guns. But while powerful people are often capable of rewarding and punishing us, research shows that much of their influence is *normative* (Tyler, 1990). The psychologist Stanley Milgram (1963) demonstrated this in one of psychology's most infamous experiments. The participants in this experiment met a middle-aged man who was introduced as another participant but who was actually a trained actor. An experimenter in a lab coat explained that the participant would play the role of *teacher* and the actor would play the role of *learner*. The teacher and the learner would sit in different rooms, the teacher would read words to the learner over a microphone, and the learner would then repeat the words back to the teacher. If the learner made a mistake, the teacher would press a button that delivered an electric shock to the learner (see **FIGURE 13.14**). The shock-generating machine (which was totally fake) offered 30 levels of shock, ranging from 15 volts (labeled *slight shock*) to 450 volts (labeled *Danger: severe shock*).

After the learner was strapped into his chair, the experiment began. When the learner made his first mistake, the participant dutifully delivered a 15-volt shock. As the learner made more mistakes, he received more shocks. When the participant delivered the 75-volt shock, the learner cried out in pain. At 150 volts, the learner screamed, "Get me out of here. I told you I have heart trouble. . . . I refuse to go on. Let me out!" With every shock, the learner's screams became more agonized as he pleaded pitifully for his freedom. Then, after receiving the 330-volt shock, the learner stopped responding altogether. Participants were naturally upset by all this and typically asked the experimenter to stop, but the experimenter simply replied, "You have no choice. You must go on." The experimenter never threatened the participant with punishment of any kind. Rather, he just stood there with his clipboard in hand and calmly instructed the participant to continue. So what did the participants do? Eighty percent of the participants continued to shock the learner even after he screamed, complained, pleaded, and then fell silent. And 62% went all the way, delivering the highest possible voltage. Although Milgram's study was conducted nearly half a century ago, a recent replication revealed about the same rate of obedience (Burger, 2009).

Were these people psychopathic sadists? Would normal people electrocute a stranger just because some guy in a lab coat told them to? The answer, it seems, is *yes*—as long as *normal* means being sensitive to social norms (Zimbardo, 2007). The participants in this experiment knew that hurting others is *often* wrong but not *always*

▶ Figure 13.14

MILGRAM'S OBEDIENCE STUDIES The learner (*left*) is being hooked up to the shock generator (*right*) that was used in Stanley Milgram's obedience studies.

wrong: Doctors give painful injections, and teachers give painful exams. There are many situations in which it is permissible—and even desirable—to cause someone to suffer in the service of a higher goal. The experimenter's calm demeanor and persistent instruction suggested that he, and not the participants, knew what was appropriate in this particular situation, and so the participants did as ordered. Subsequent research confirmed that participants' obedience was due to normative pressure. When the experimenter's authority to define the norm was undermined (e.g., when a second experimenter appeared to disagree with the first or when the instructions were given by a person who wasn't wearing a lab coat), the participants rarely obeyed the instructions (Milgram, 1974; Miller, 1986).

THE ACCURACY MOTIVE

When you are hungry, you open the refrigerator and grab an apple because you know that apples (a) taste good and (b) are in the refrigerator. This action, like most actions, relies on both an **attitude**, which is *an enduring positive or negative evaluation of an object or event*, and a **belief**, which is *an enduring piece of knowledge about an object or event*. In a sense, our attitudes tell us what we should do (*eat an apple*) and our beliefs tell us how to do it (*start by opening the fridge*). If our attitudes or beliefs are inaccurate—that is, if we can't tell good from bad or true from false—then our actions are likely to be fruitless. Because we rely so much on our attitudes and beliefs, it isn't surprising that we are motivated to have the right ones, and that motivation leaves us vulnerable to social influence.

Informational Influence: We Do What's Right

If everyone in the mall suddenly ran screaming for the exit, you'd probably join them—not because you were afraid that they would disapprove of you if you didn't, but because their behavior would suggest to you that there was something worth running from. **Informational influence** occurs when *another person's behavior provides information about what is true*. You can observe the power of informational influence yourself just by standing in the middle of the sidewalk, tilting back your head, and staring at the top of a tall building. Research shows that within just a few minutes, other people will stop and stare too (Milgram, Bickman, & Berkowitz, 1969). Why? They will assume that if you are looking, then there must be something worth looking at.

You are the constant target of informational influence. When a salesperson tells you that "most people buy the iPad with extra memory," she is artfully suggesting that you should take other people's behavior as information about the product. Advertisements

attitude An enduring positive or negative evaluation of an object or event.

belief An enduring piece of knowledge about an object or event.

informational influence A phenomenon that occurs when another person's behavior provides information about what is true.

Why do publishers go out of their way to tell readers that a book is a "national bestseller?" Because publishers know that when people who are browsing books see that others have bought one, they become more inclined to buy it too.

It is now common during political debates for broadcasters to display real-time information about people's reactions to the candidates. But recent studies show that this information influences viewers' opinions about who won the debate as well as their voting decisions (Davis, Bowers, & Memon, 2011).

persuasion A phenomenon that occurs when a person's attitudes or beliefs are influenced by a communication from another person.

systematic persuasion The process by which attitudes or beliefs are changed by appeals to reason.

heuristic persuasion The process by which attitudes or beliefs are changed by appeals to habit or emotion.

that refer to soft drinks as "popular" or books as "best sellers" are reminding you that other people are buying these particular drinks and books, which suggests that they know something you don't and that you'd be wise to follow their example. Situation comedies provide laugh tracks because the producers know that when you hear other people laughing, you will mindlessly assume that something must be funny (Fein, Goethals, & Kugler, 2007; Nosanchuk & Lightstone, 1974). Bars and nightclubs make people stand in line outside even when there is plenty of room inside, because they know that passersby will see the line and assume that the club is worth waiting for. In short, the world is full of objects and events that we know little about, and we can often cure our ignorance by paying attention to the way in which others are acting toward them. Alas, the very thing that makes us open to information leaves us open to manipulation as well.

Persuasion: Changing Behavior by Changing Minds

When the next presidential election rolls around, two things will happen. First, the candidates will say that they intend to win your vote by making arguments that focus on the issues. Second, the candidates will then avoid arguments, ignore issues, and attempt to win your vote with a variety of cheap tricks and emotional appeals. What the candidates promise to do and what they actually do reflect two basic forms of **persuasion**, which occurs when *a person's attitudes or beliefs are influenced by a communication from another person* (Albarracín & Vargas, 2010; Petty & Wegener, 1998). The candidates will promise to persuade you by demonstrating that their positions on the issues are the most practical, intelligent, fair, and beneficial. Having made that promise, they will then devote most of their financial resources to persuading you by other means: for example, by dressing nicely and smiling a lot, by surrounding themselves with famous athletes and movie stars, by repeatedly pairing their opponent's picture with Osama bin Laden's, and so on. In other words, the candidates will promise to engage in **systematic persuasion**, *the process by which attitudes or beliefs are changed by appeals to reason*, but they will spend most of their time and money engaged in **heuristic persuasion**, *the process by which attitudes or beliefs are changed by appeals to habit or emotion* (Chaiken, 1980; Petty & Cacioppo, 1986).

How do these two forms of persuasion work? Systematic persuasion appeals to logic and reason and assumes that people will be more persuaded when evidence and arguments are strong rather than weak. Heuristic persuasion appeals to habit and

Does Kim Kardashian know more about toilet paper than you do? Probably not. So why do advertisers hire celebrities like her to endorse their products? (If the phrase "heuristic persuasion" doesn't come to mind, go back and reread this section.)

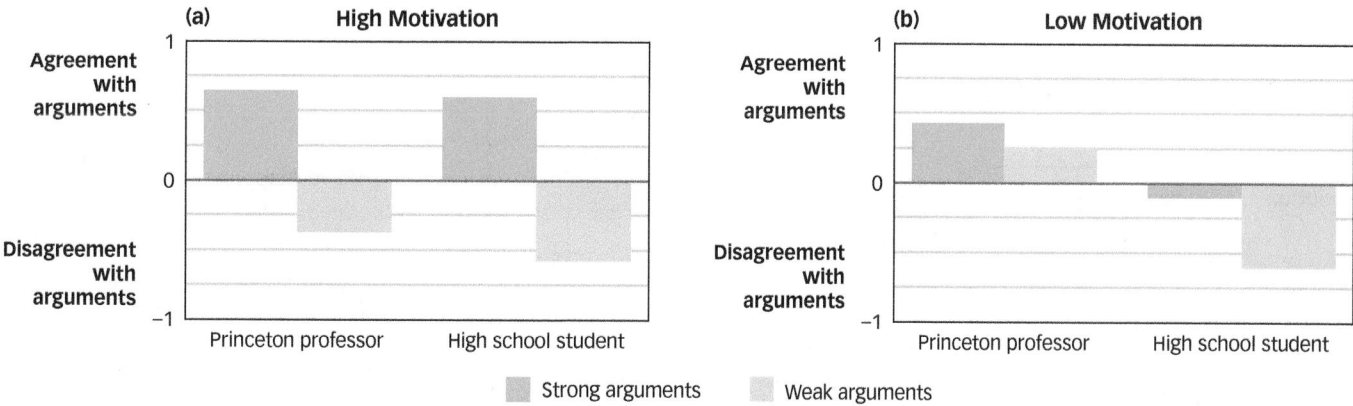

emotion and assumes that rather than weighing evidence and analyzing arguments, people will often use *heuristics* (simple shortcuts or "rules of thumb") to help them decide whether to believe a communication (see the Language and Thought chapter). Which form of persuasion will be more effective depends on whether the person is willing and able to weigh evidence and analyze arguments.

In one study, students heard a speech that contained either strong or weak arguments in favor of instituting comprehensive exams at their school (Petty, Cacioppo, & Goldman, 1981). Some students were told that the speaker was a Princeton University professor, and others were told that the speaker was a high school student—a bit of information that the students could use as a heuristic or shortcut to decide whether to believe the speech. Some students were told that their university was considering implementing these exams right away, whereas others were told that their university was considering implementing these exams in 10 years—a bit of information that made students feel motivated or unmotivated to analyze the evidence. As **FIGURE 13.15** shows, when students were motivated to analyze the evidence, they were systematically persuaded—that is, their attitudes and beliefs were influenced by the strength of the arguments but not by the status of the speaker. But when students were not motivated to analyze the evidence, they were heuristically persuaded—that is, their attitudes and beliefs were influenced by the status of the speaker but not by the strength of the arguments.

Consistency: Changing Minds by Changing Behavior

If a friend told you that rabbits had just staged a coup in Antarctica and were halting all carrot exports, you probably wouldn't turn on CNN. You'd know right away that your friend was either joking or really, really gullible because the statement is logically inconsistent with other things that you know are true, for example, that rabbits do not foment revolution and that Antarctica does not export carrots. People evaluate the accuracy of new beliefs by assessing their *consistency* with old beliefs. Although this is not a foolproof method for determining whether something is true, it provides a pretty good approximation. We are motivated to be accurate, and because consistency is a rough measure of accuracy, we are motivated to be consistent as well (Cialdini, Trost, & Newsom, 1995).

That motivation leaves us vulnerable to social influence. For example, the **foot-in-the-door** technique involves *making a small request and then following it with a larger request* (Burger, 1999). In one study (Freedman & Fraser, 1966), experimenters went to a neighborhood and knocked on doors to see if they could convince homeowners to agree to have a big ugly "Drive Carefully" sign installed in their front yards. One group of homeowners was simply asked to install the sign, and only 17% said yes. A second group of homeowners was first asked to sign a petition urging the state legislature to promote safe driving (which almost all agreed to do) and was *then* asked to install

▲ **Figure 13.15**

SYSTEMATIC AND HEURISTIC PERSUASION
(a) *Systematic persuasion.* When students were motivated to analyze arguments because they would be personally affected by them, their attitudes were influenced by the strength of the arguments (strong arguments were more persuasive than weak arguments) but not by the status of the communicator (the Princeton professor was not more persuasive than the high school student). (b) *Heuristic persuasion.* When students were not motivated to analyze arguments because they would not be personally affected by them, their attitudes were influenced by the status of the communicator (the Princeton professor was more persuasive than the high school student) but not by the strength of the arguments (strong arguments were no more persuasive than weak arguments; Petty, Cacioppo, & Goldman, 1981).

foot-in-the-door technique A technique that involves making a small request and following it with a larger request.

Problem: Cognitive Dissonance

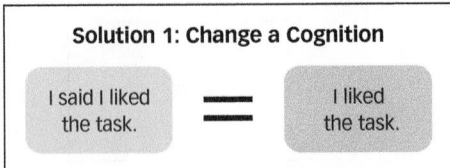

Solution 1: Change a Cognition

Solution 2: Add a Justifying Cognition

▲ Figure 13.16

ALLEVIATING COGNITIVE DISSONANCE Telling a lie can produce an uncomfortable feeling known as cognitive dissonance. One way to reduce that dissonance is to believe the lie (Solution 1). Another is to justify having told it (Solution 2).

Members of Michigan Tech University's Sigma Tau Gamma fraternity brave subzero wind chill to participate in the group's annual "Grundy Run" through the campus. Painful rituals like these often breed group loyalty.

cognitive dissonance An unpleasant state that arises when a person recognizes the inconsistency of his or her actions, attitudes, or beliefs.

the ugly sign. And 55% said yes! Why would homeowners be more likely to grant two requests than one?

Just imagine how the homeowners in the second group felt. They had just signed a petition stating that they thought safe driving was important, yet they knew they didn't want to install an ugly sign in their front yards. As they wrestled with this inconsistency, they probably began to experience **cognitive dissonance**, which is *an unpleasant state that arises when a person recognizes the inconsistency of his or her actions, attitudes, or beliefs* (Festinger, 1957). When people experience cognitive dissonance, they naturally try to alleviate it. Although there are many ways to do this (Randles et al., 2015), one perfectly ordinary way is to put your money where your mouth is—that is, to act in ways that are consistent with your beliefs (Aronson, 1969; Cooper & Fazio, 1984; Harmon-Jones, Harmon-Jones, & Levy, 2015). Agreeing to install a yard sign was just such an action. Indeed, one of the best ways to get people to take an action is to first get them to express an attitude with which that action is consistent. If hotel guests are subtly induced at check-in to call themselves "Friends of the Earth," they are 25% more likely to reuse their towels during their stay (Baca-Motes et al., 2013).

Just as people take actions that are consistent with their attitudes, so too do they adopt attitudes that are consistent with their actions. In a classic study, female college students applied to join a weekly discussion on "the psychology of sex." Women in the control group were allowed to join the discussion, but women in the experimental group were allowed to join the discussion only after first passing an embarrassing test that involved reading pornographic fiction to a strange man. Although the carefully staged discussion was as dull as possible, women in the experimental group found it more interesting than did women in the control group (Aronson & Mills, 1958). Why? Women in the experimental group knew that they had paid a steep price to join the group ("I read all that porn out loud!"), but that belief was inconsistent with the belief that the discussion was worthless. Thus, the women experienced cognitive dissonance, which they alleviated by changing their beliefs about the value of the discussion (see the top half of **FIGURE 13.16**.). We normally think that people pay for things because they value them, but as this study shows, people sometimes value things because they've paid for them—with money, time, attention, blood, sweat, or tears. It is little wonder that some fraternities use hazing to instill loyalty, that some religions require their adherents to make large personal or monetary sacrifices, that some gourmet restaurants charge outrageous amounts to keep their patrons coming back, or that some men and women play hard to get to maintain their suitors' interest.

We are motivated to be consistent, but inevitably there are times when we just can't—for example, when we tell a friend that her new hairstyle is "daring" when it actually resembles a wet skunk after an unfortunate encounter with a snow blower. Why don't we experience cognitive dissonance under such circumstances and come to believe our own lies? Because whereas telling a friend that her hairstyle is daring is inconsistent with the belief that her hairstyle is hideous, it is perfectly consistent with the belief that one should be nice to one's friends. When small inconsistencies are *justified* by large consistencies, cognitive dissonance is reduced.

For example, participants in one study were asked to perform a dull task that involved turning knobs one way, then the other way, and then back again. After the participants were sufficiently bored, the experimenter explained that he desperately needed a few more people to volunteer for the study, and he asked the participants to go into the hallway, find another person, and tell that person that the knob-turning task was great fun. The experimenter offered some participants $1 to tell this lie, and he offered other participants $20. All participants agreed to tell the lie, and after they did so, they were asked to report their true enjoyment of the knob-turning task. The results showed that participants liked the task *more* when they were paid $1 than $20 to lie about it (Festinger & Carlsmith, 1959). Why? Because the belief *this knob-turning task is dull* was inconsistent with the belief *I recommended the task to that person in the hallway*, but the latter belief was perfectly consistent with the belief that *$20 is a lot of money*. For some participants, the large payment justified the lie, so only those people who received the small payment experienced cognitive dissonance. As such, only the participants who received $1 felt the need to restore consistency by changing their beliefs about the enjoyableness of the task (see the bottom half of Figure 13.16).

Build to the Outcomes

1. What are the three basic motives that social influence involves?

2. Why do attempts to influence others with rewards and punishments sometimes backfire?

3. How can the norm of reciprocity be used to influence people?

4. Why do people sometimes do what they see others doing?

5. When and why do people obey authority?

6. What is the difference between normative and informational influence?

7. When is it more effective to engage in systematic persuasion rather than heuristic persuasion?

8. Why does the accuracy motive lead to a desire for consistency?

9. What is cognitive dissonance? How do people alleviate it?

Understanding Others

Kanye West is a creative genius—or at least that's what he tells anyone who will listen. Whether or not you agree with his assessment, reading about it almost surely activated your medial prefrontal cortex, an area of your brain that becomes especially active when you think about other human beings but not when you think about inanimate objects such as houses or tools (Mitchell, Heatherton, & Macrae, 2002). Although most of your brain shows diminished activity when you are at rest, this area remains active all the time (Buckner, Andrews-Hanna, & Schacter, 2008; Spunt, Meyer, & Lieberman, 2015). Why does your brain have specific areas that seem specialized for processing information about just *one* of the millions of objects you might encounter? And why is this area constantly switched on?

Because of the millions of objects you might encounter, other human beings are the single most important. **Social cognition** is *the processes by which people come to understand others*, and your brain is doing it all day long. Whether you know it or not, your brain is constantly making inferences about other people's thoughts and feelings, beliefs and desires, abilities and aspirations, intentions, needs, and characters. It bases these inferences on two kinds of information: the categories to which people belong, and the things they do and say.

STEREOTYPING: DRAWING INFERENCES FROM CATEGORIES

You'll recall from the Language and Thought chapter that categorization is the process by which people identify a stimulus as a member of a class of related stimuli. Once we have identified a novel stimulus as a member of a category ("That's a textbook"), we can then use our knowledge of the category to make educated guesses about the properties of the novel stimulus ("It's probably expensive") and act accordingly ("I think I'll download it illegally").

Learning Outcomes

▶ Explain how stereotypes cause people to draw inaccurate conclusions about others.

▶ Explain why stereotypes are so difficult to overcome.

▶ Explain what an attribution is and what kinds of errors attributions entail.

Thinking about the musician Kanye West activates your medial prefrontal cortex. Do you think about him now and then? Because he's coming home again, loyee oyeee oh.

social cognition The processes by which people come to understand others.

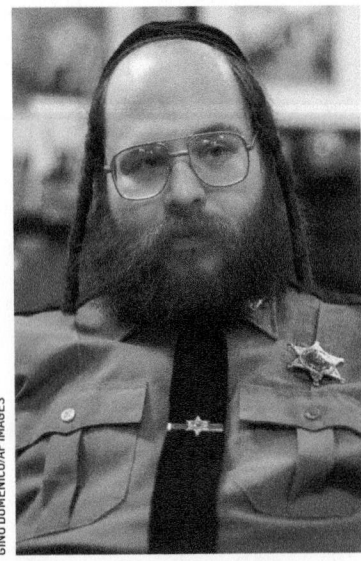

Stereotypes can be inaccurate. Shlomo Koenig does not fit most people's stereotype of a police officer or a rabbi, but he is both.

stereotyping The process by which people draw inferences about others based on their knowledge of the categories to which others belong.

What we do with textbooks we also do with people. No, not the illegal downloading part. The educated guessing part. **Stereotyping** is *the process by which people draw inferences about others based on their knowledge of the categories to which others belong.* The moment we categorize a person as an adult, a male, a baseball player, and a Russian, we can use our knowledge of those categories to make some educated guesses about him—for example, that he shaves his face but not his legs, that he understands the infield fly rule, and that he knows more about Vladimir Putin than we do. When we offer children candy instead of beer or ask gas-station attendants for directions instead of financial advice, we are making inferences about people whom we have never met before based solely on their category membership. As these examples suggest, stereotyping is a very helpful process (Allport, 1954). And yet, ever since the word was coined by the journalist Walter Lippmann in 1936, it has had a distasteful connotation. Why? Because stereotyping is a helpful process that can often produce harmful results, and it does so because stereotypes tend to have four properties: They can be inaccurate, overused, self-perpetuating, and automatic. Let's examine each of them.

Stereotypes Can Be Inaccurate

Americans have a wide range of stereotypes that appear to vary on two important dimensions: warmth ("Are these people nice?") and competence ("Are these people capable?"; Cuddy, Fiske, & Glick, 2007). As **FIGURE 13.17** shows, Americans see some categories of people as warm and competent (women), others as warm but incompetent (the elderly), others as cold and competent (the rich), and others as cold and incompetent (the homeless). Some of these stereotypes are probably right on average (educated professionals are generally more capable than people with intellectual disabilities), but others are surely wrong (Whites are not generally warmer than Hispanics). So where do these inaccurate stereotypes come from?

Much of what we think we know about human categories is hearsay—stuff we picked up from watching television, listening to pop songs, or just hearing people talk. But inaccurate beliefs about human categories can also be produced by direct observation of their members. For example, research participants in one study were shown a long series of positive and negative behaviors and were told that each behavior had been performed by a member of one of two groups: Group A or Group B (see **FIGURE 13.18**). The behaviors were carefully arranged so that each group behaved negatively exactly one third of the time. However, there were more positive than negative behaviors in the series, and there were more members of Group A than of Group B. Thus, negative behaviors were rarer than positive behaviors, and Group B members were rarer than Group A members. After seeing the behaviors,

▶ Figure 13.17

STEREOTYPE CONTENT Stereotypes tend to vary on the dimensions of warmth and competence. This figure shows how Americans see a variety of different groups (data from Cuddy, Fiske, & Glick, 2007).

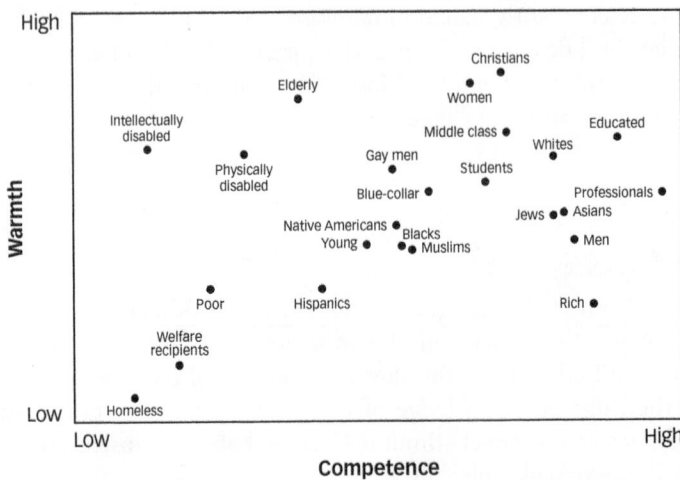

participants correctly reported that Group A had behaved negatively one third of the time. However, they incorrectly reported that Group B had behaved negatively more than *half* the time (Hamilton & Gifford, 1976).

Why did this happen? Bad behavior was rare, and being a member of Group B was rare. Thus, participants were especially likely to notice when the two co-occurred ("Aha! There's one of those unusual Group B people doing an unusually awful thing again"). These findings help explain why members of majority groups tend to overestimate the number of crimes (which are relatively rare events) committed by members of minority groups (who are relatively rare people, hence the word *m-i-n-o-r-i-t-y*). The point here is that even when we directly observe people, we can end up with inaccurate beliefs about the groups to which they belong.

Stereotypes Can Be Overused

Because all thumbtacks are pretty much alike, our stereotypes about thumbtacks (small, cheap, painful when chewed) are quite useful. We will rarely be mistaken if we generalize from one thumbtack to another. But human categories are so variable that our stereotypes may offer only the vaguest of clues about the individuals who populate those categories. You probably believe that men have greater upper body strength than women do, and this belief is right *on average*. But the upper body strength of individuals *within* each of these categories is so varied that you cannot easily predict how much weight a particular person can lift simply by knowing that person's gender. The inherent variability of human categories makes stereotypes much less useful than they seem.

Alas, we don't always recognize this because the mere act of categorizing a stimulus tends to warp our perceptions of that category's variability. For instance, participants in some studies were shown a series of lines of different lengths (see **FIGURE 13.19**; McGarty & Turner, 1992; Tajfel & Wilkes, 1963). For one group of participants, the longest lines were labeled *Group A* and the shortest lines were labeled *Group B*, as they are on the right side of Figure 13.20. For the second group of participants, the lines were shown without these category labels, as they are on the left side of Figure 13.20. Interestingly, those participants who saw the category labels *overestimated* the similarity of the lines that shared a label and *underestimated* the similarity of lines that did not.

You've probably experienced this phenomenon yourself when looking at a rainbow. Because we identify colors as members of categories such as *blue* or *green*, we overestimate the similarity of colors that share a category label and underestimate the similarity of colors that do not. That's why we see discrete *bands* of color when we look at rainbows, which are actually a smooth chromatic continuum (see **FIGURE 13.20**). The same thing happens when we try to estimate distances. Memphis, Tennessee is about the same distance from Pierre, South Dakota as it is from Toronto, Canada, but people underestimate its distance from Pierre because the two towns are in the same nation, and overestimate its distance from Toronto because the two towns are in different nations. (Burris & Branscombe, 2005). Indeed, people believe that they are

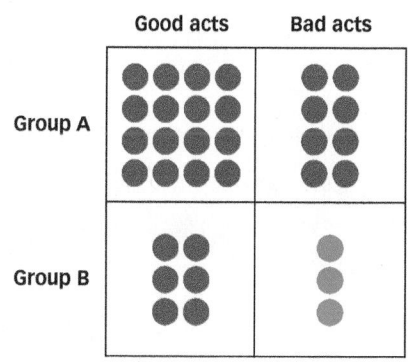

▲ Figure 13.18

SEEING CORRELATIONS THAT AREN'T REALLY THERE Group A and Group B each perform two thirds good acts and one third bad acts. However, Group B and bad acts are both rare, leading people to notice and remember their co-occurrence, which leads them to perceive a correlation between group membership and behavior that isn't really there.

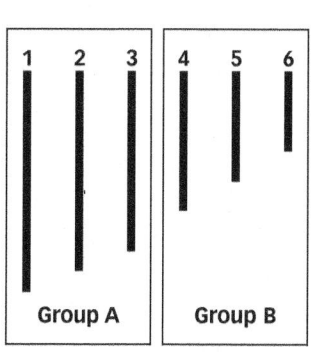

◄ Figure 13.19

HOW CATEGORIZATION WARPS PERCEPTION People who see the lines on the right tend to *overestimate the similarity* of lines 1 and 3 and *underestimate the similarity* of lines 3 and 4. Simply labeling lines 1–3 *Group A* and lines 4–6 *Group B* causes the lines within a group to seem more similar to each other than they really are and the lines in different groups to seem more different from each other than they really are.

► Figure 13.20
PERCEIVING CATEGORIES
Categorization can influence how we see colors and estimate distances.

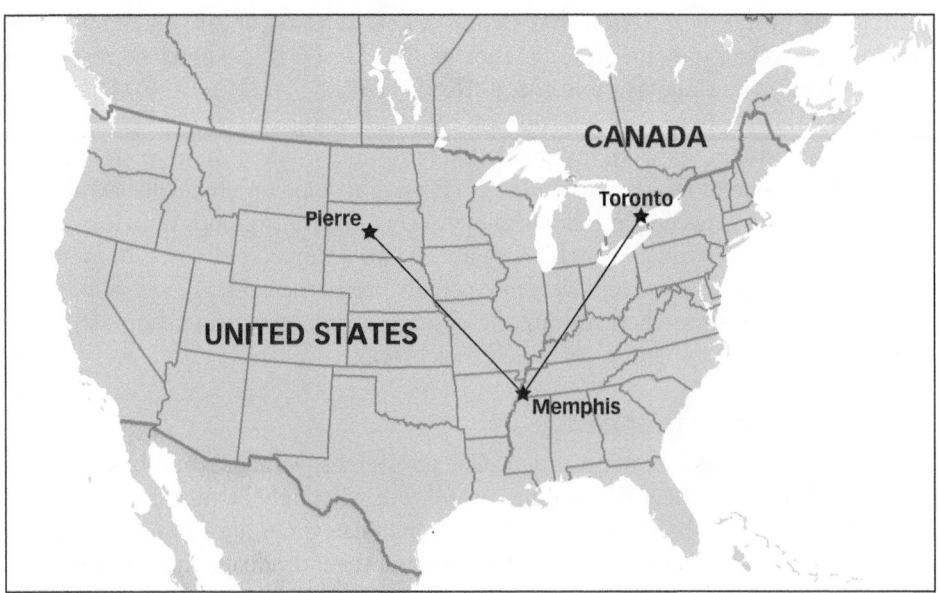

more likely to feel an earthquake whose epicenter is 230 miles away when that spot is in their state rather than in a neighboring state (Mishra & Mishra, 2010).

What's true of colors and cities is true of people as well. The mere act of categorizing people as Blacks or Whites, Jews or Gentiles, artists or accountants, can cause us to underestimate the variability within those categories ("All artists are wacky") and to overestimate the variability between them ("Artists are much wackier than accountants"). When we underestimate the variability of a human category, we naturally overestimate how useful our stereotypes about it will be (Park & Hastie, 1987; Rubin & Badea, 2012).

Stereotypes Can Be Self-Perpetuating

When we meet a truck driver who likes ballet more than football or a senior citizen who likes Drake more than Bach, why don't we simply abandon our stereotypes of these groups? The answer is that stereotypes tend to be self-perpetuating. Like viruses and parasites, once they take up residence inside us, they resist even our most concerted efforts to eradicate them. There are three reasons why:

> ► **Self-fulfilling prophecy** is *the tendency for people to behave as they are expected to behave.* When people know that observers have a negative stereotype about them, they may experience **stereotype threat**, which is *the fear of confirming the negative beliefs that others may hold* (Aronson & Steele, 2004; Schmader, Johns, & Forbes, 2008; Walton & Spencer, 2009). Ironically, this fear may cause them to behave in ways that confirm the very stereotype that threatened them. In one study (Steele & Aronson, 1995), African American and White students took a test, and half the students in each group were asked to list their race at the top of the exam. When students were not asked to list their race, they performed at their academic level, but when students were asked to list their race, African American students became anxious about confirming a negative stereotype of their group, which caused them to perform well below their academic level (see **FIGURE 13.21**). Stereotypes perpetuate themselves in part by causing the stereotyped individual to behave in ways that confirm the stereotype.

> ► Even when people do *not* confirm stereotypes, observers often think they have. **Perceptual confirmation** is *the tendency for people to see what they expect to see,* and this tendency helps perpetuate stereotypes. In one study, participants listened to a radio broadcast of a college basketball game and were asked to

self-fulfilling prophecy The tendency for people to behave as they are expected to behave.

stereotype threat The fear of confirming the negative beliefs that others may hold.

perceptual confirmation The tendency for people to see what they expect to see.

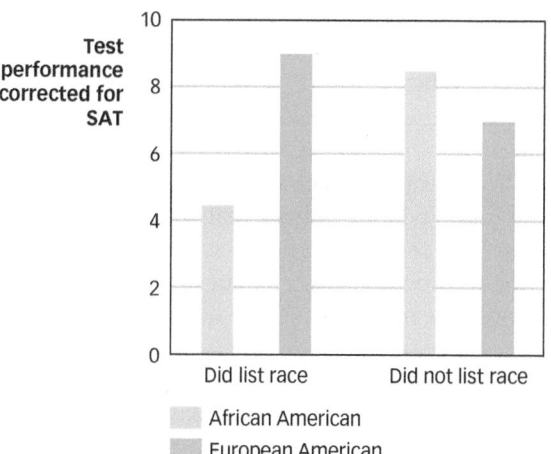

STEREOTYPE THREAT When asked to indicate their race before taking an exam, African American students performed below their academic level (as determined by their SAT scores), but European American students did not.

evaluate the performance of one of the players. Although all participants heard the same prerecorded game, some were led to believe that the player was African American, and others were led to believe that the player was White. Participants' stereotypes led them to expect different performances from athletes of different ethnic origins—and the participants perceived just what they expected. Those who believed the player was African American thought he had demonstrated greater athletic ability but less intelligence than did those who thought he was White (Stone, Perry, & Darley, 1997). Stereotypes perpetuate themselves in part by biasing our perception of individuals, leading us to believe that those individuals have confirmed our stereotypes even when they have not (Fiske, 1998).

▶ So what happens when people clearly *dis*confirm our stereotypes? **Subtyping** is *the tendency for people who receive disconfirming evidence to modify their stereotypes rather than abandon them* (Weber & Crocker, 1983). For example, most of us think of people who work in public relations as sociable. In one study, participants learned about a PR agent who was *slightly* unsociable, and the results showed that their stereotypes about PR agents shifted a bit to accommodate this new information. So far, so good. But when participants learned about a PR agent who was *extremely* unsociable, their stereotypes did not change at all (Kunda & Oleson, 1997). Instead, they decided that the extremely unsociable PR agent was "an exception to the rule," which allowed them to keep their stereotypes intact. Subtyping is a powerful method of preserving our stereotypes in the face of contradictory evidence.

The former First Lady of the United States, Michelle Obama, understands the nature of stereotype threat. "That's a burden that President Obama and I proudly carry every single day in the White House, because we know that everything we do and say can either confirm the myths about folks like us—or it can change those myths" (Baker, 2015).

Stereotyping Can Be Unconscious and Automatic

If we recognize that our stereotypes are inaccurate and self-perpetuating, then why don't we just make a firm resolution to stop using them? The answer is that stereotyping often happens *unconsciously* (which means that we don't always know we are doing it) and *automatically* (which means that we often cannot avoid doing it even when we try; Banaji & Heiphetz, 2010; Greenwald, McGhee, & Schwartz, 1998; Greenwald & Nosek, 2001).

For example, in one study, participants played a video game in which photos of Black or White men holding either guns or cameras were flashed on the screen for less than 1 second each. Participants earned money by shooting men with guns and lost money by shooting men with cameras. The results showed that participants made two kinds of mistakes: They tended to shoot Black men holding cameras and tended not to shoot White men holding guns (Correll et al., 2002). Although the photos appeared on the screen so quickly that participants did not have enough time to consciously consider their stereotypes, those stereotypes worked unconsciously, causing them to mistake a camera for a gun when it was in the hands of a Black man and a gun for a

subtyping The tendency for people who receive disconfirming evidence to modify their stereotypes rather than abandon them.

The Implicit Association Test measures how easily people can learn to associate two things (Greenwald, McGhee, & Schwartz, 1998). Studies using the test show that 70 percent of White Americans find it easier to associate White faces with positive concepts, such as "peace," and Black faces with negative concepts, such as "bomb," than the other way around. Surprisingly, 40 percent of African Americans show this same pattern. You can take the IAT yourself at https://implicit.harvard.edu/implicit/

Major League Baseball umpires try to be objective, but when they mistakenly call a strike, it benefits the pitcher's team. A recent study showed that umpires are 10 percent less likely to make this "helpful error" when the pitcher is African American than when he is European American (Kim & King, 2014). Because stereotypes are automatic, they can influence the judgments of even those who work hard not to apply them.

camera when it was in the hands of a White man (Correll et al., 2015). It is instructive to note that Black participants were just as likely to make this pattern of errors as were White participants. Why did these errors happen?

Stereotypes comprise all the information about human categories that we have absorbed over the years from friends and uncles, books and blogs, jokes and movies and late-night television. When we see Black men holding guns in rap videos, our minds associate these two things, and although we realize that we are watching art and not news, our brains make and remember the association. We cannot later *decide* that we just won't be influenced by it any more than we can *decide* that we just won't be influenced by our knowledge of English or the smell of French fries.

In fact, some research suggests that trying not to use our stereotypes can make matters worse instead of better. Participants in one study were shown a photograph of a tough-looking male "skinhead" and were asked to write an essay describing a typical day in his life. Some of the participants were told that they should not allow their stereotypes about skinheads to influence their essays, and others were given no such instructions. Next, the experimenter brought each participant to a room with eight empty chairs. The first chair had a jacket draped over it, and the experimenter explained that it belonged to a skinhead, who had gone to use the restroom. Where did participants choose to sit? Participants who had earlier been told not to use their stereotypes sat farther away from the jacket than did participants who had been given no instructions (Macrae et al., 1994). As you know from reading the Consciousness chapter, thought suppression is an ironic business that often causes us to do the very thing we were trying to avoid doing (Wegner et al., 1987), and this appears to apply to stereotypes as well.

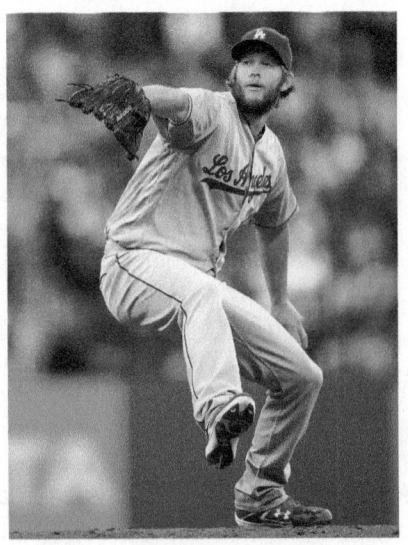

Are the Consequences of Stereotyping Inevitable?

Although stereotyping is unconscious and automatic, that does not mean that its undesirable consequences—bias and prejudice—are inevitable (Blair, 2002; Kawakami et al., 2000; Milne & Grafman, 2001; Rudman, Ashmore, & Gary, 2001). For instance, police officers who receive special training before playing the camera-or-gun video game described earlier do not show the same biases that ordinary people do (Correll et al., 2007). Like ordinary people, they take a few milliseconds longer to decide not to shoot a Black man than a White man, indicating that their stereotypes are unconsciously and automatically influencing their perception. But unlike ordinary people, they don't actually *shoot* Black men more often than White men, indicating that they have learned how to keep those stereotypes from influencing their behavior (Phills et al., 2011; Todd et al., 2011). Other studies suggest that because stereotypes reflect all the information to which people are chronically exposed through music

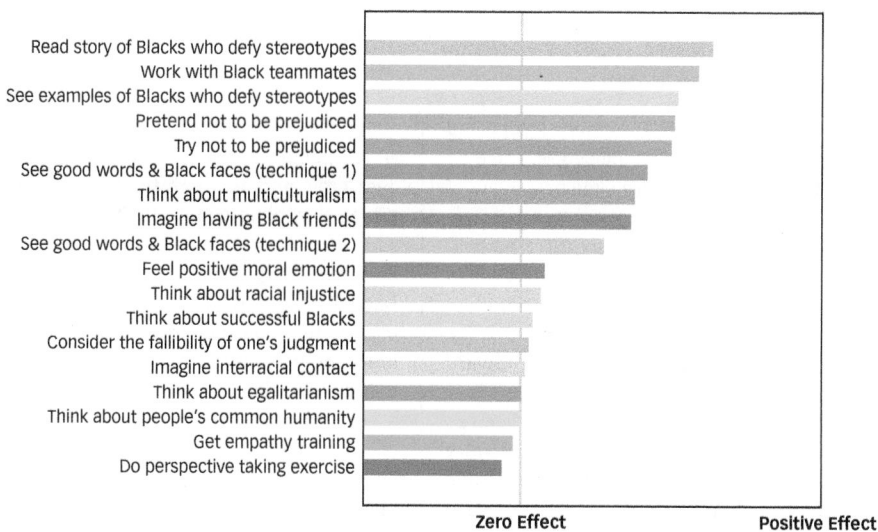

◀ Figure 13.22
STEREOTYPE CONTEST Results of a study
that compared 18 techniques for reducing
unconscious stereotyping of Blacks by Whites
(data from Lai et al., 2014).

videos, advertisements, newscasts, and social media, changing that information can change the stereotypes. In laboratory experiments, for example, White participants who are exposed to positive examples of African-Americans (e.g., Michael Jordan and Denzel Washington) show a reduction in automatic anti-Black bias (Dasgupta, 2013).

So which techniques are most effective? In 2014, a team of psychologists held a contest in which they invited researchers to submit techniques for reducing unconscious stereotyping of Blacks, and then tested each of the techniques against the other. As **FIGURE 13.22** shows, about half the techniques had some effect, and these tended to be techniques that exposed Whites to examples of Blacks who defy their stereotypes. For example, the most effective technique asked participants to imagine in gory detail that they were being assaulted by a White man and then to image being rescued by a Black man. The least effective techniques were those that simply encouraged people to feel compassion toward or take the perspective of a Black person (see Hot Science: Through Other Eyes). One troubling finding was that many of the failed techniques look a lot like the techniques that are often used in schools, businesses, and other organizations. Indeed, when a team of psychologists conducted a thorough examination of the scientific literature on "multicultural education, anti-bias instruction more generally, workplace diversity initiatives, dialogue groups, cooperative learning, moral and values education, intergroup contact, peace education, media interventions, reading interventions, intercultural and sensitivity training, cognitive training, and a host of miscellaneous techniques and interventions," they reluctantly concluded that "we currently do not know whether a wide range of programs and policies tend to work on average, and we are quite far from having an empirically grounded understanding of the conditions under which these programs work best" (Paluck & Green, 2009, p. 357). Eliminating the prejudice that stereotyping can produce in everyday settings is a worthwhile goal, but not one that scientists are very close to achieving.

ATTRIBUTION: DRAWING INFERENCES FROM ACTIONS

In 1963, Dr. Martin Luther King Jr. gave a speech in which he described his vision for America: "I have a dream that my four children will one day live in a nation where they will not be judged by the color of their skin but by the content of their character." Research on stereotyping demonstrates that Dr. King's concern was well-justified. We do judge others by the color of their skin—as well as by their gender, nationality, religion, age, and occupation—and in so doing, we sometimes make consequential mistakes. But are we any better at judging people by the content of their character? If we could somehow turn off our stereotypes and treat each person as a unique individual, would we judge them more accurately?

Through Other Eyes

Every human being sees the world through the lens of his or her own personal experience. Each of us has just one ethnicity, one gender, and one sexual orientation, and we don't really know what it would be like to have different ones. So how can we best understand people whose experiences are unlike our own? In 1895, Mary T. Lathrap wrote a poem entitled "Judge Softly." It wasn't very good, but it did contain a line that is quoted to this day:

Pray, don't find fault with the man
  that limps,
Or stumbles along the road.
Unless you have worn the moccasins
  he wears,
Or stumbled beneath the same load.

Just walk a mile in his moccasins
Before you abuse, criticize and accuse.
If just for one hour, you could find a way
To see through his eyes, instead of your
  own muse.

Lathrap's poem is a call for compassion, and it suggests that the best way to generate compassion for someone is to "walk a mile in his moccasins" if "just for one hour." That suggestion certainly rings true—but is it? To find out, Silverman, Gwinn, and van Boven (2015) gave sighted people the opportunity to experience blindness, and then measured how well they understood those who are actually blind. Participants reported to the laboratory, were blindfolded, and were then asked to perform a variety of ordinary tasks ranging from filling a glass with water to finding the stairwell in a hallway. Participants in a control condition merely watched the first group of participants perform these tasks. After either performing these tasks or watching others

perform them, all participants reported their feelings toward blind people, and then estimated how capable blind people are of working and living independently.

Wearing the blindfold did precisely what Lathrop's poem suggested it would do: It made participants feel more compassionate—more empathetic, friendly, open, sympathetic, and warm toward blind people. But it also had a side effect that the poet did not anticipate. Compared with observers, participants who wore the blindfold thought that blind people were much less competent and capable—less able to get around a city, to cook, to own their own business, to teach school or become an accountant, and so on. In other words, walking in a blind person's moccasins for a few minutes led participants to conclude that walking was pretty much impossible.

But it isn't. Most blind people are perfectly capable of performing ordinary tasks, such as pouring water and finding a stairwell, and perfectly capable of performing jobs from schoolteacher to

accountant. Blindness is a disability to which people adapt extraordinarily well over time, and although there are a few things that blind people can't do as well as sighted people can (e.g., drive), there are other things they can do even better (e.g., hear). Participants in this study had enough time to experience blindness but not enough time to adapt to it. And yet, being blindfolded for a few minutes led them to mistakenly believe that they understood what a lifetime of blindness was like. Rather than becoming more accurate about what it is like to have this particular disability, they became less accurate.

All of us are forever trapped inside our own skins. We can never really know what another person's experience of the world is like, and well-meaning exercises that are designed to expand our horizons can actually do the opposite. If we listen carefully to people, we can gain some appreciation of their perspectives. But we should not be fooled into thinking that we have ever seen the world through someone else's eyes.

▲ Paul Scruggs is blind, but that doesn't prevent him from working as a machine operator in a factory that makes military uniforms. You could probably run this machine with your eyes closed—but not in the first hour of trying.

Not necessarily. Treating people as individuals means judging them by their own words and deeds. This is more difficult than it sounds because the relationship between what a person *is* and what a person *says or does* is not always straightforward. An honest person may lie to save a friend from embarrassment, and a dishonest person may tell the truth to bolster her credibility. Happy people have some weepy moments, polite people can be rude in traffic, and people who despise us can be flattering when they need a favor. In short, people's behavior sometimes tells us about the kinds of people they are, but sometimes it simply tells us about the kinds of situations they happen to be in.

To understand people, we need to know not only *what* they did but also *why* they did it. Is the batter who hit the home run a talented slugger, or was the wind blowing in just the right direction at just the right time? Is the politician who gave the pro-life

Low Consistency + High Consensus + High Distinctiveness =
Situational Attribution

| **Consistency**
Does the person perform this action regularly? | **Consensus**
Do most people perform this action? | **Distinctiveness**
Does the person perform similar actions? |

High Consistency + Low Consensus + Low Distinctiveness =
Dispositional Attribution

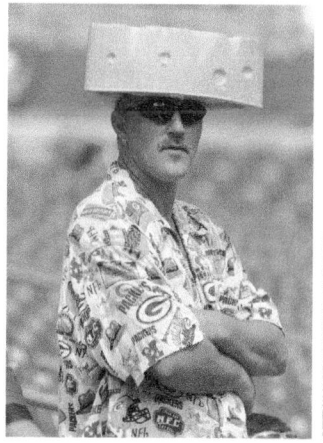

◀ **Figure 13.23**
THE COVARIATION MODEL OF ATTRIBUTION The covariation model tells us whether to make a dispositional or situational attribution for a person's action.

speech really opposed to abortion, or was she just trying to win the conservative vote? When we answer questions such as these, we are making **attributions**, which are *inferences about the causes of people's behaviors* (Epley & Waytz, 2010; Gilbert, 1998). We make *situational attributions* when we decide that a person's behavior was caused by some temporary aspect of the situation in which it happened ("He was lucky that the wind carried the ball into the stands"), and we make *dispositional attributions* when we decide that a person's behavior was caused by a relatively enduring tendency to think, feel, or act in a particular way ("He's got a great eye and a powerful swing").

How do we know whether to make a dispositional or a situational attribution? According to the *covariation model* (Kelley, 1967), the consistency, consensuality, and distinctiveness of an action can tell us what kind of attribution to make. For example, why did the man in **FIGURE 13.23** decide to wear a cheese-shaped hat? Is it because he has a goofy personality (*dispositional attribution*)? Or is he a non-goofy guy who happens to be on his way to a Wisconsin football game (*situational attribution*)? According to the covariation model, you can answer this question by asking whether his behavior is *consistent* (does he usually wear this hat?), *consensual* (are other people wearing this hat?), and *distinctive* (does he do other goofy things?). If it turns out that he wears this hat every day (*high consistency*), and if no one else is wearing a cheese hat today (*low consensus*), and if he tends to do other goofy things—such as wearing clown shoes and saying "Honk, honk" to passersby (*low distinctiveness*)—then you should probably make a dispositional attribution ("He's a certified goofball"). On the other hand, if he rarely wears this hat (*low consistency*), if lots of other people are wearing cheese hats today (*high consensus*), and if he doesn't tend to do other goofy things (*high distinctiveness*), then you should probably make a situational attribution ("He's a Green Bay Packers fan on game day"). As Figure 13.23 shows, patterns of consistency, consensus, and distinctiveness provide useful information about the cause of a person's behavior.

As sensible as this seems, research suggests that people don't always use this information as they should. The **correspondence bias** is *the tendency to make a dispositional attribution when we should instead make a situational attribution* (Gilbert & Malone, 1995; Jones & Harris, 1967; Ross, 1977). This bias is so common and so basic that it is often called the *fundamental attribution error*. For example, volunteers in one experiment played a trivia game in which one participant acted as the quizmaster and made up a list of unusual questions, another participant acted as the contestant and tried to answer those questions, and a third participant acted as the observer and simply watched the game. The quizmasters tended to ask tricky questions based on their own idiosyncratic knowledge, and contestants were generally unable to answer them. After watching the game, the observers were asked to decide how knowledgeable the quizmaster and the contestant were. Although the quizmasters had asked good questions and the contestants had given bad answers, it should have been clear to the observers

attribution An inference about the cause of a person's behavior.

correspondence bias The tendency to make a dispositional attribution even when we should instead make a situational attribution.

"I think success is all perspiration. You make your own luck," said Robert Herjavec, a successful businessman and a judge on *Shark Tank*. But research on the correspondence bias suggests that it is dangerously easy to credit success to intelligence and tenacity, and to blame failure on stupidity and laziness.

actor–observer effect The tendency to make situational attributions for our own behaviors while making dispositional attributions for the identical behavior of others.

that all this asking and answering was a product of the roles they had been assigned to play and that the contestant would have asked equally good questions and the quizmaster would have given equally bad answers had their roles been reversed. And yet observers tended to rate the quizmaster as more knowledgeable than the contestant (Ross, Amabile, & Steinmetz, 1977) and were more likely to choose the quizmaster as their own partner in an upcoming game (Quattrone, 1982). Even when we know that a successful athlete had a home-field advantage or that a successful entrepreneur had family connections, we tend to attribute their success to talent and tenacity.

What causes the correspondence bias? First, the situational causes of behavior are often invisible (Ichheiser, 1949). For example, professors tend to assume that fawning students really do admire them in spite of the strong incentive for students to kiss up to those who control their grades. The problem is that professors can actually *see* students laughing at witless jokes and applauding after boring lectures, but they cannot *see* "control over grades." Situations are not as tangible or visible as behaviors, so it is all too easy to ignore them (Taylor & Fiske, 1975). Second, situational attributions tend to be more complex than dispositional attributions and require more time and attention. When participants in one study were asked to make attributions while performing a mentally taxing task (keeping a seven-digit number in mind), they had no difficulty making dispositional attributions, but they found it quite difficult to make situational attributions (Gilbert, Pelham, & Krull, 1988; Winter & Uleman, 1984). In short, information about situations is hard to get and hard to use, so we tend to believe that other peoples' actions are caused by their dispositions even when there is a perfectly reasonable situational explanation.

The correspondence bias is stronger in some cultures than in others (Choi, Nisbett, & Norenzayan, 1999), among some people than others (D'Agostino & Fincher-Kiefer, 1992; Li et al., 2012), and under some circumstances than others. For example, we seem to be more prone to correspondence bias when judging other people's behavior than when judging our own. The **actor–observer effect** is *the tendency to make situational attributions for our own behaviors while making dispositional attributions for the identical behavior of others* (Jones & Nisbett, 1972). When college students are asked to explain why they and their friends chose their majors, they tend to explain their own choices in terms of situations ("I chose economics because my parents told me I have to support myself as soon as I'm done with college") and their friends' choices in terms of dispositions ("Leah chose economics because she's materialistic"; Nisbett et al., 1973). The actor–observer effect occurs because people typically have more information about the situations that caused their own behavior than about the situations that caused other people's behavior. We will always remember getting the please-major-in-something-practical lecture from our parents, but we weren't at Leah's house to see her get the same lecture. As observers, we are naturally focused on another person's behavior, but as actors, we are quite literally focused on the situations in which our behavior occurs. Indeed, when people are shown videotapes of their conversations that allow them to see themselves from their partner's point of view, they tend to make dispositional attributions for their own behavior and situational attributions for their partner's (Storms, 1973; Taylor & Fiske, 1975).

Build to the Outcomes

1. Where do stereotypes come from? What purpose do they serve?

2. When are stereotypes most and least likely to be useful?

3. Why do stereotypes sometimes seems more accurate than they really are?

4. Why is it difficult not to use stereotypes?

5. What are the three kinds of information that determine whether a dispositional or situational attribution is warranted?

6. Why do people tend to make dispositional attributions even when they should not?

Chapter Review

The Survival Game

▶ Survival and reproduction require scarce resources; aggression and co-operation are two ways to acquire them.

▶ Aggression often results from negative affect. The likelihood that people will aggress when they experience negative affect is determined both by biological and cultural factors.

▶ Cooperation can be beneficial, but it also is risky. One strategy for reducing those risks is to form groups whose members show in-group favoritism.

▶ Groups can be beneficial, but they also have costs. They make poor deci-sions because they overemphasize information that all members share, and they allow people to behave unethically by causing them to lose focus on their personal values.

▶ Many behaviors that appear to be altruistic have hidden benefits for the person who performs them, but there is no doubt that humans some-times do exhibit genuine altruism.

The Mating Game

▶ Both biology and culture tend to make the costs of reproduction higher for women than for men, which is one reason that women tend to be choosier when selecting potential mates.

▶ Attraction is determined by situational factors (such as proximity), physical factors (such as symmetry), and psychological factors (such as similarity).

▶ Human reproduction usually occurs within the context of a long-term relationship. People weigh the costs and benefits of their relationships and are least likely to end them when they do not believe they can do better, when they and their partners have similar cost–benefit ratios, and/or when they have invested a lot of time in the relationship.

Controlling Others

▶ People are motivated to experience pleasure and avoid pain (the hedonic motive), and thus can be influenced by rewards and punishments. These influence attempts can sometimes backfire by changing how people think about their own behavior or by making them feel as though they are being manipulated.

▶ People are motivated to attain the approval of others (the approval mo-tive), and thus can be influenced by social norms, such as the norm of reciprocity. People often look to the behavior of others to determine what kinds of behavior are normative. People tend to obey authorities even when they should not.

▶ People are motivated to know what is true (the accuracy motive). People often look to the behavior of others to determine what is true.

▶ People can be persuaded by appeals to reason or emotion. Each is effec-tive under different circumstances.

▶ People feel bad when they notice inconsistency among their attitudes, beliefs, and actions, and they will often change one of these things in order to achieve consistency.

Understanding Others

▶ We make inferences about others based on the categories to which they belong (stereotyping). This sometimes leads us to misjudge others because stereotypes are often inaccurate, overused, self-perpetuating, unconscious, and automatic.

▶ Some techniques may reduce stereotyping, but so far, none has proved powerful and long-lasting.

▶ We sometimes make mistakes when drawing inferences about people from their behaviors. We tend to attribute those behaviors to the person's dispositions even when we should attribute them to the person's situation.

KEY CONCEPT QUIZ

1. Why are acts of aggression—from violent crime to athletic brawls—more likely to occur on hot days when people are feeling irritated and uncomfortable?
   a. frustration
   b. negative affect
   c. resource scarcity
   d. the prisoner's dilemma

2. What is the single best predictor of aggression?
   a. temperament
   b. age
   c. gender
   d. status

3. The prisoner's dilemma game illustrates
   a. in-group favoritism.
   b. the diffusion of responsibility.
   c. group polarization.
   d. the benefits and costs of cooperation.

4. Which of the following best describes reciprocal altruism?
   a. the ultimatum game
   b. diminished responsibility in groups
   c. cooperation extended over time
   d. cooperation with relatives

5. Which of the following is a situational factor that influences attraction?
   a. proximity
   b. similarity
   c. appearance
   d. personality

6. The fact that people in relationships want their cost–benefit ratio to be about the same as their partners' is known as
   a. companionate love.
   b. bilateral symmetry.
   c. equity.
   d. comparison level.

7. The _____ motive explains the fact that people prefer to experience pleasure rather than pain.
   a. altruistic
   b. accuracy
   c. approval
   d. hedonic

8. The tendency to do what authorities tell us to do is known as
   a. persuasion.
   b. obedience.
   c. conformity.
   d. the self-fulfilling prophecy.

9. What is the process by which people come to understand others?
   a. heuristic processing
   b. reciprocal altruism
   c. social cognition
   d. cognitive dissonance

10. The tendency to make a dispositional attribution even when a person's behavior was caused by the situation is referred to as
    a. comparison leveling.
    b. stereotyping.
    c. covariation.
    d. correspondence bias.

 LearningCurve Don't stop now! Quizzing yourself is a powerful study tool. Go to LaunchPad to access the LearningCurve adaptive quizzing system and your own personalized learning plan. Visit launchpadworks.com.

KEY TERMS

social psychology (p. 508)
aggression (p. 508)
frustration–aggression hypothesis (p. 508)
cooperation (p. 512)
group (p. 513)
prejudice (p. 513)
common knowledge effect (p. 514)
group polarization (p. 514)
groupthink (p. 514)
deindividuation (p. 515)
diffusion of responsibility (p. 515)

social loafing (p. 515)
bystander intervention (p. 515)
altruism (p. 516)
kin selection (p. 516)
reciprocal altruism (p. 516)
mere exposure effect (p. 520)
passionate love (p. 526)
companionate love (p. 526)
comparison level (p. 526)
equity (p. 526)
social influence (p. 527)
norms (p. 528)

norm of reciprocity (p. 529)
normative influence (p. 529)
door-in-the-face technique (p. 529)
conformity (p. 530)
obedience (p. 532)
attitude (p. 533)
belief (p. 533)
informational influence (p. 533)
persuasion (p. 534)
systematic persuasion (p. 534)
heuristic persuasion (p. 534)

foot-in-the-door technique (p. 535)
cognitive dissonance (p. 536)
social cognition (p. 537)
stereotyping (p. 538)
self-fulfilling prophecy (p. 540)
stereotype threat (p. 540)
perceptual confirmation (p. 540)
subtyping (p. 541)
attribution (p. 545)
correspondence bias (p. 545)
actor–observer effect (p. 546)

CHANGING MINDS

1. One of the senators from your state is supporting a bill that would impose heavy fines on aggressive drivers who run red lights. One of your class-mates thinks this is a good idea. "The textbook taught us a lot about punish-ment and reward. It's simple. If we punish aggressive driving, its frequency will decline." Is your classmate right? Might the new law backfire? Might another policy be more effective in promoting safe driving?

2. One of your friends is outgoing, funny, and a star athlete on the women's basketball team. She has started to date a man who is introverted and prefers playing computer games to attending parties. You tease her about the contrast in personalities, and she replies, "Well, opposites attract." Is she right?

3. A large law firm is found guilty of discriminatory hiring practices. Your friend reads about the case and scoffs, "People are always so quick to claim racism. Sure, there are still a few racists out there, but if you do surveys and ask people what they think about people of other races, they generally say they feel fine about them." What would you tell your friend?

4. One of your friends has a very unique fashion sense and always wears a neon orange track suit with a battered fedora. "Most people follow the crowd," he explains. "I don't. I'm an individual, and I make my own choices, without influence from anyone else." Could he be right? What examples might you provide for or against your friend's claim?

5. A classmate learns about the Milgram (1963) study, in which partici-pants were willing to obey orders to administer painful electric shocks to a learner who begged them to stop. "Some people are such sheep!" she says. "I know that I wouldn't behave like that." Is she right? What evidence would you give her to support or oppose her claim?

6. Your family gathers for a holiday dinner, and your cousin Wendy brings her fiancée, Amanda. It's the first time Amanda has met the whole family, and she seems nervous. She talks too much, laughs too loud, and rubs everyone the wrong way. Later, an uncle says to you, "It's hard to imagine Wendy wanting to spend the rest of her life married to someone so annoying." How can you explain to your uncle that you think he has fallen prey to the correspondence bias?

Chapter Review

ANSWERS TO KEY CONCEPT QUIZ

1. b; 2. c; 3. d; 4. c; 5. a; 6. c; 7. d; 8. b; 9. c; 10. d

LaunchPad features the full e-Book of *Psychology*, the LearningCurve adaptive quizzing system, videos, and a variety of activities to boost your learning. Visit LaunchPad at launchpadworks.com.

Stress and Health

14

"I HAVE A KNIFE TO YOUR NECK. Don't make a sound. Get out of bed and come with me or I will kill you and your family." These are the words that awoke 14-year-old Elizabeth Smart in the middle of the night of June 5, 2002, while she was sleeping in her bedroom next to her 9-year-old sister Mary Katherine. Fearing for her life, and the lives of her family, she kept quiet and left with her abductor. Her little sister, terrified, hid in her bedroom for several hours before waking the girls' parents, who awoke to their daughter saying, "She's gone. Elizabeth is gone." Elizabeth was kidnapped by Brian David Mitchell, a man Elizabeth's parents had hired previously to do some roof work on their home. Mitchell broke into the family's home in Salt Lake City through an open window and abducted Elizabeth. He and his wife, Wanda Ileen Barzee, held her in captivity for nine months, during which time Mitchell repeatedly raped her and threatened to kill her and her entire family. Mitchell, Barzee, and Smart were spotted walking down the street by a couple who recognized them from a recent episode of the television show *America's Most Wanted* and called the police. Mitchell and Barzee were apprehended and Elizabeth was returned to her family.

Elizabeth suffered under unimaginable circumstances for a prolonged period of time in what can be thought of as one of the most stressful situations possible. So

Left: SLCPD/NEWSCOM/UNITED PRESS INTERNATIONAL (UPI)/WASHINGTON D.C. USA
Right: GETTY IMAGES ENTERTAINMENT/GETTY IMAGES

This smiling young face is that of Elizabeth Smart, who, between the times of these two photographs, was kidnapped, raped, and tortured for nearly a year. Stressful life events often affect us in ways that cannot be seen from the outside. Fortunately, there are things that we can do in response to even the most stressful of life events that can get us smiling again.

◀ FOTOSEARCH/AGE FOTOSTOCK

stressors Specific events or chronic pressures that place demands on a person or threaten the person's well-being.

stress The physical and psychological response to internal or external stressors.

health psychology The subfield of psychology concerned with ways psychological factors influence the causes and treatment of physical illness and the maintenance of health.

what became of Elizabeth? Fortunately, she is now safe and sound, happily married, and working as an activist. She endured life-threatening stressors for months, and those experiences undoubtedly affected her in ways that will last her entire lifetime. At the same time, hers is a story of resilience. Despite the very difficult hand she was dealt, she appears to have bounced back and to be leading a happy, productive, and rewarding life. Hers is a story of both stress and health.

FORTUNATELY, VERY FEW OF US WILL EVER HAVE TO ENDURE the type of stress that Elizabeth Smart lived through. But life can present a welter of frights, bothers, and looming disasters that can be quite difficult to manage. A reckless driver may nearly run you over; you may be discriminated against, threatened, or intimidated in some way; or a fire may leave you out on the street. Life has its **stressors**, *specific events or chronic pressures that place demands on a person or threaten the person's well-being*. Although such stressors rarely involve threats of death, they do have both immediate and cumulative effects that can influence health.

In this chapter, we'll look at what psychologists and physicians have learned about the kinds of life events that produce **stress**, *the physical and psychological response to internal or external stressors;* typical responses to such stressors; and ways to manage stress. Stress has such a profound influence on health that we consider stress and health together in this chapter. And because sickness and health are not merely features of the physical body, we then consider the more general topic of **health psychology**, *the subfield of psychology concerned with ways psychological factors influence the causes and treatment of physical illness and the maintenance of health*. You will see how perceptions of illness can affect its course and how health-promoting behaviors can improve the quality of people's lives.

Sources of Stress: What Gets to You

Learning Outcomes

► Compare the impact of stressful events and chronic stress.

► Identify the importance of perceived control.

What are the sources of stress in our lives? A natural catastrophe, such as a hurricane, earthquake, or volcanic eruption, is an obvious source. But for most of us, stressors are personal events that affect the comfortable pattern of our lives and little annoyances that bug us day after day. Let's look at the life events that can cause stress, chronic sources of stress, and the relationship between lack of perceived control and the impact of stressors.

STRESSFUL EVENTS

People often seem to get sick after major life events. In pioneering work, Thomas Holmes and Richard Rahe (1967) followed up on this observation, proposing that major life changes cause stress and that increased stress causes illness. To test their idea, they asked people to rate the magnitude of readjustment required by each of many events found to be associated with the onset of illness (Rahe et al., 1964). The resulting list of life events is remarkably predictive: Simply adding up the stress ratings of each life change experienced is a significant indicator of a person's likelihood of future illness (Miller, 1996). Someone who becomes divorced, loses a job, and has a friend die all in the same year, for example, is more likely to get sick than someone who escapes the year with only a divorce.

As the movie *Bridesmaids* showcased perfectly, although weddings are positive events, they also can be stressful due to the often overwhelming amount of planning and decision making involved (and occasionally because of the difficulties in managing the interactions of friends and family).

UNIVERSAL PICTURES/THE KOBAL COLLECTION/HANOVER, SUZANNE

A version of this list adapted for the life events of college students (and sporting the snappy acronym CUSS, for College Undergraduate Stress Scale) is shown in **TABLE 14.1**. To assess your stressful events, check off any events that have happened to you in the past year and sum your point total. In a large sample of students in an introductory psychology class, the average was 1,247 points, ranging from 182 to 2,571 (Renner & Mackin, 1998).

Looking at the list, you may wonder why positive events are included. Stressful life events are unpleasant, right? Why would getting married be stressful? Isn't a wedding supposed to be fun? Research has shown that compared with negative events, positive

TABLE 14.1

College Undergraduate Stress Scale

Event	Stress Rating	Event	Stress Rating
Being raped	100	Lack of sleep	69
Finding out that you are HIV positive	100	Change in housing situation (hassles, moves)	69
Being accused of rape	98	Competing or performing in public	69
Death of a close friend	97	Getting in a physical fight	66
Death of a close family member	96	Difficulties with a roommate	66
Contracting a sexually transmitted disease (other than AIDS)	94	Job changes (applying, new job, work hassles)	65
Concerns about being pregnant	91	Declaring a major or concerns about future plans	65
Finals week	90	A class you hate	62
Concerns about your partner being pregnant	90	Drinking or use of drugs	61
Oversleeping for an exam	89	Confrontations with professors	60
Flunking a class	89	Starting a new semester	58
Having a boyfriend or girlfriend cheat on you	85	Going on a first date	57
Ending a steady dating relationship	85	Registration	55
Serious illness in a close friend or family member	85	Maintaining a steady dating relationship	55
Financial difficulties	84	Commuting to campus or work or both	54
Writing a major term paper	83	Peer pressures	53
Being caught cheating on a test	83	Being away from home for the first time	53
Drunk driving	82	Getting sick	52
Sense of overload in school or work	82	Concerns about your appearance	52
Two exams in one day	80	Getting straight A's	51
Cheating on your boyfriend or girlfriend	77	A difficult class that you love	48
Getting married	76	Making new friends; getting along with friends	47
Negative consequences of drinking or drug use	75	Fraternity or sorority rush	47
Depression or crisis in your best friend	73	Falling asleep in class	40
Difficulties with parents	73	Attending an athletic event	20
Talking in front of class	72		

Note: To compute your personal life change score, sum the stress ratings for all events that have happened to you in the last year.

Information from: Renner & Mackin (1998).

City life can be fun, but the higher levels of noise, crowding, and violence can also be sources of chronic stress.

events produce less psychological distress and fewer physical symptoms (McFarlane et al., 1980), and that happiness can sometimes even counteract the effects of negative events (Fredrickson, 2000). However, positive events often require readjustment and preparedness that many people find extremely stressful (e.g., Brown & McGill, 1989), so these events are included in computing life-change scores.

CHRONIC STRESSORS

Life would be simpler if an occasional stressful event such as a wedding or a lost job were the only pressure we faced. At least each event would be limited in scope, with a beginning, a middle, and, ideally, an end. But unfortunately, life brings with it continued exposure to **chronic stressors,** *sources of stress that occur continuously or repeatedly.* Strained relationships, discrimination, bullying, overwork, money troubles—small stressors that may be easy to ignore if they happen only occasionally— can accumulate to produce distress and illness. People who report being affected by daily hassles also report more psychological symptoms (LaPierre et al., 2012) and physical symptoms (Piazza et al., 2013), and these effects often have a greater and longer-lasting impact than major life events.

Many chronic stressors are linked to social relationships. For instance, as described in the Social Psychology chapter, people often form different social groups on race, culture, interests, popularity, and so on. Being outside the in-group can be stressful. Being actively targeted by members of the in-group can be even more stressful, especially if this happens repeatedly over time (see A World of Difference: Can Discrimination Cause Stress and Illness?). Chronic stressors also can be linked to particular environments. For example, features of city life—noise, traffic, crowding, pollution, and even the threat of violence—provide particularly insistent sources of chronic stress (Evans, 2006). Rural areas have their own chronic stressors, of course, especially isolation and lack of access to amenities such as health care. The realization that

chronic stressors Sources of stress that occur continuously or repeatedly.

A WORLD OF DIFFERENCE

Can Discrimination Cause Stress and Illness?

Have you ever been discriminated against because of your race, gender, sexual orientation, or some other characteristic? If so, then you know that this can be a pretty stressful experience. Discrimination that occurs repeatedly over time can be an especially powerful stressor for anyone. But what exactly does it *do* to people?

Recent research has shown that there are a number of ways that discrimination can lead to elevated stress and negative health outcomes. People from socially disadvantaged groups who experience higher levels of stress as a result of discrimination engage more frequently in maladaptive behaviors (e.g., drinking, smoking, and overeating) in efforts to cope with stress. They also can experience difficulties in their interactions with health care professionals (e.g., clinician biases, patient suspiciousness about treatment; Major, Mendes & Dovidio, 2013). Taken together, these factors may help to explain why members of

socially disadvantaged groups have significantly higher rates of health problems than do members of socially advantaged groups (Penner et al., 2010).

Recent research is revealing how discrimination can literally "get under the skin" to cause negative health outcomes. One study by Wendy Mendes and colleagues (Jamieson, Koslov, et al., 2013) exposed Black and White participants to social rejection by a person of the same race or by a person of a different race to test whether there is something particularly harmful about discrimination, compared with social rejection in general. To test this hypothesis, they had research participants deliver a speech to two confederates in different rooms via a video chat program, after which the confederates provided negative feedback about the participant's speech. The confederates were not seen by the participant but were represented by computer avatars that either matched the participant's race or did

not. In an interesting finding, although the nature of the rejection was the same in all cases, participants responded very differently if the people rejecting them were of a different race than if they were of the same race. Specifically, whereas being rejected by people of your own race was associated with greater displays of shame and physiological changes associated with an avoidance state (increased cortisol), being rejected by members of a different race was associated with displays of anger, greater vigilance for danger, physiological changes associated with an approach state (i.e., higher cardiac output and lower vascular resistance), and higher risk taking.

Studies such as this one help to explain some of the health disparities that currently exist across different social groups. The results suggest that discrimination can lead to physiological, cognitive, and behavioral changes that in the short term prepare a person for action, but in the long-term could lead to negative health outcomes.

chronic stressors are linked to environments has spawned the subfield of *environmental psychology*, the scientific study of environmental effects on behavior and health.

In one study of the influence of noise on children, environmental psychologists looked at the impact of attending schools under the flight path to Heathrow Airport in London, England. Did the noise of more than 1,250 jets flying overhead each day have an influence beyond making kids yell to be heard? Compared with children from matched control schools in low-noise areas, children going to school under the flight path reported higher levels of noise annoyance and showed poorer reading comprehension (Haines et al., 2001). Next time you fly into an airport, please try to do so more quietly. For the children.

PERCEIVED CONTROL OVER STRESSFUL EVENTS

What do catastrophes, stressful life changes, and daily hassles have in common? Right off the bat, of course, their threat to the person or the status quo is easy to see. Stressors challenge you to *do something*—to take some action to eliminate or overcome the stressors.

Paradoxically, events are most stressful when there is *nothing to do*—no way to deal with the challenge. Expecting that you will have control over what happens to you is associated with effectiveness in dealing with stress. The researchers David Glass and Jerome Singer (1972), in classic studies of *perceived control,* looked at the aftereffects of loud noise on people who could or could not control it. Participants were asked to solve puzzles and proofread in a quiet room or in a room filled with loud noise. Glass and Singer found that bursts of such noise hurt people's performance on the tasks after the noise was over. However, this dramatic decline in performance did not occur among participants who were told during the noise period that they could stop the noise just by pushing a button. They didn't actually take this option, but just having access to the "panic button" shielded them from the detrimental effects of the noise.

Subsequent studies have found that a lack of perceived control underlies other stressors too. The stressful effects of crowding, for example, appear to stem from the feeling that you can't control getting away from the crowded conditions (Evans & Stecker, 2004). Being jammed into a crowded dormitory room may be easier to handle, after all, the moment you realize you could take a walk and get away from it all.

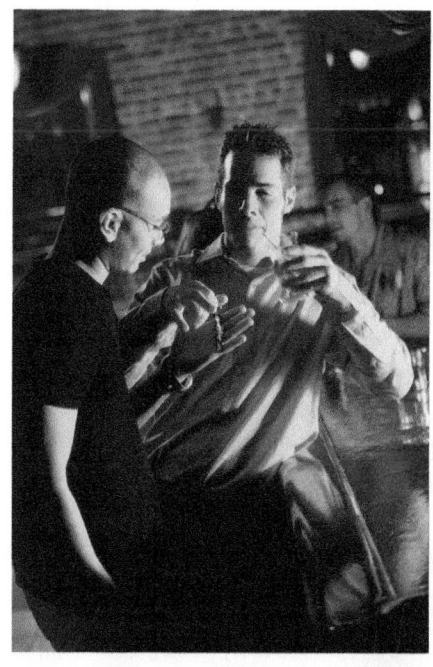

Some stressful life events, such as those associated with drunk driving, are within our power to control. We gain control when we give away the car keys to a designated driver.

Build to the Outcomes

1. Which of the events on the stress rating scale relate to you? Do any of the ratings surprise you?

2. How can positive events be stressful?

3. Give examples of chronic stressors.

4. What are some examples of environmental factors that cause chronic stress?

5. What makes events most stressful?

Stress Reactions: All Shook Up

It was a regular Tuesday morning in New York City. College students were sitting in their morning classes. People were arriving at work and the streets were beginning to fill with shoppers and tourists. Then, at 8:46 a.m., American Airlines Flight 11 crashed into the North Tower of the World Trade Center. People watched in horror. How could this have happened? This seemed like a terrible accident. Then at 9:03 a.m., United Airlines Flight 175 crashed into the South Tower of the World Trade Center. There were then reports of a plane crashing into the Pentagon. And another somewhere in

Learning Outcomes

▶ Explain physical responses to stress.

▶ Identify possible psychological responses to stress.

The threat of death or injury, such as many in New York City experienced at the time of the 9/11 attacks, can cause significant and lasting physical and psychological stress reactions.

fight-or-flight response An emotional and physiological reaction to an emergency that increases readiness for action.

Pennsylvania. America was under attack, and no one knew what would happen next on this terrifying morning of September 11, 2001. The terrorist attacks on the World Trade Center were an enormous stressor that had a lasting impact on many people, physically and psychologically. People living in close proximity to the World Trade Center (within 1.5 miles) on 9/11 were found to have less gray matter in the amygdala, hippocampus, insula, anterior cingulate, and medial prefrontal cortex than those living more than 200 miles away during the attacks, suggesting that the stress associated with the attacks may have reduced the size of these parts of the brain that play an important role in emotion, memory, and decision making (Ganzel et al., 2008). Children who watched more television coverage of 9/11 had higher symptoms of posttraumatic stress disorder than children who watched less coverage (Otto et al., 2007). People around the country who had a stronger acute stress response to the events of 9/11 had a 53% increased incidence of heart problems over the next 3 years (Holman et al., 2008). Stress can produce changes in every system of the body and mind, stimulating both physical reactions and psychological reactions. Let's consider each in turn.

PHYSICAL REACTIONS

You are at a party, and a guy jumps in front of you with his hands up ready to punch you in the face. What do you do?! Walter Cannon (1929) coined a phrase to describe the body's response to any threatening stimulus: the **fight-or-flight response**, *an emotional and physiological reaction to an emergency that increases readiness for action.* The mind asks, "Should I stay and fight this guy? Or should I flee this situation?" And the body prepares to react. Cannon recognized this common response across species and suspected that it might be the body's first mobilization to any threat.

Research conducted since Cannon's discovery has revealed what is happening in the brain and body during this reaction. Brain activation in response to threat occurs in the hypothalamus, stimulating the nearby pituitary gland, which in turn releases a hormone known as ACTH (short for adrenocorticotropic hormone). ACTH travels through the bloodstream and stimulates the adrenal glands atop the kidneys (see **FIGURE 14.1**). In this cascading response of the HPA (hypothalamic–pituitary–

▶ Figure 14.1

HPA AXIS Just a few seconds after a fearful stimulus is perceived, the hypothalamus activates the pituitary gland to release adrenocorticotropic hormone (ACTH). The ACTH then travels through the bloodstream to activate the adrenal glands to release catecholamines and cortisol, which energize the fight-or-flight response.

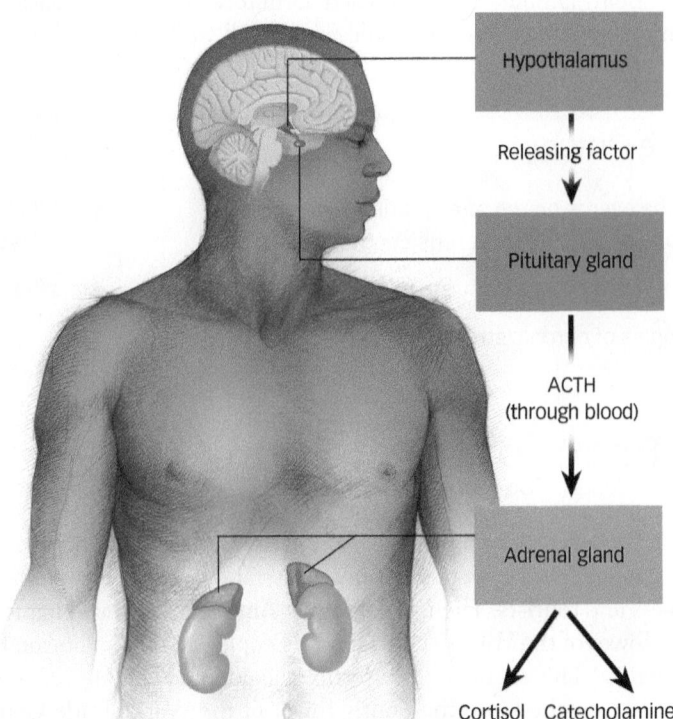

Hypothalamus

Releasing factor

Pituitary gland

ACTH (through blood)

Adrenal gland

Cortisol   Catecholamines

adrenocortical) axis, the adrenal glands are stimulated to release hormones, including the *catecholamines* (epinephrine and norepinephrine), which increase sympathetic nervous system activation (and therefore increase heart rate, blood pressure, and respiration rate) and decrease parasympathetic activation (see the Neuroscience and Behavior chapter). The increased respiration and blood pressure make more oxygen available to the muscles to energize attack or to initiate escape. The adrenal glands also release *cortisol*, a hormone that increases the concentration of glucose in the blood to make fuel available to the muscles. Everything is prepared for a full-tilt response to the threat.

General Adaptation Syndrome

What might have happened if the terrorist attacks of 9/11 were spaced out over a period of days or weeks? Starting in the 1930s, Hans Selye, a Canadian physician, undertook a variety of experiments that looked at the physiological consequences of severe threats to well-being. He subjected rats to heat, cold, infection, trauma, hemorrhage, and other prolonged stressors, making few friends among the rats or their sympathizers, but learning a lot about stress. His stressed-out rats developed physiological responses that included enlargement of the adrenal cortex, shrinking of the lymph glands, and ulceration of the stomach. Noting that many different kinds of stressors caused similar patterns of physiological change, he called the reaction the **general adaptation syndrome (GAS)**, which he defined as a *three-stage physiological stress response that appears regardless of the stressor that is encountered*. The GAS is *nonspecific*; that is, the response doesn't vary, no matter what the source of the repeated stress.

None of this is very good news. Although Friedrich Nietzsche once said, "What does not kill me makes me stronger," Selye found that severe stress takes a toll on the body. He saw the GAS as occurring in three phases (see **FIGURE 14.2**):

▶ First comes the *alarm phase*, in which the body rapidly mobilizes its resources to respond to the threat. Energy is required, and the body calls on its stored fat and muscle. The alarm phase is equivalent to Cannon's fight-or-flight response.

▶ Next, in the *resistance phase*, the body adapts to its high state of arousal as it tries to cope with the stressor. Continuing to draw on resources of fat and muscle, it shuts down unnecessary processes: Digestion, growth, and sex drive stall; menstruation stops; production of testosterone and sperm decreases. The body is being taxed to generate resistance, and all the fun stuff is put on hold.

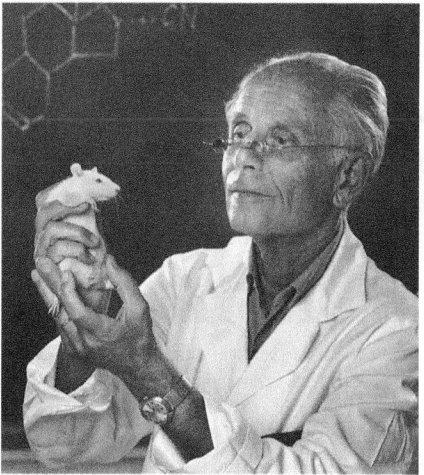

Hans Selye with rat. Given all the stress Selye put rats under, this one looks surprisingly calm.

general adaptation syndrome (GAS) A three-stage physiological response that appears regardless of the stressor that is encountered.

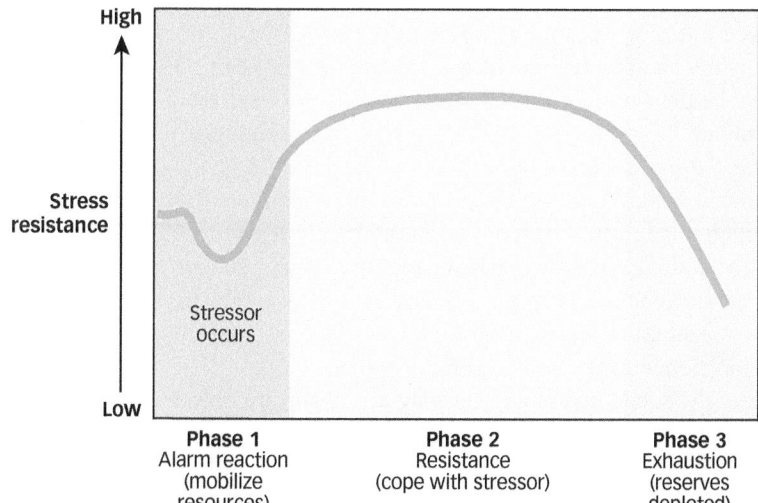

◀ Figure 14.2
SELYE'S THREE PHASES OF STRESS RESPONSE In Selye's theory, resistance to stress builds over time, but then can only last so long before exhaustion sets in.

Chronic stress can actually speed the aging process. Just look at how much each of our last three presidents aged while in office. College can be stressful too, but hopefully not so much so that you have gray hair by graduation.

▶ If the GAS continues long enough, the *exhaustion phase* sets in. The body's resistance collapses. Many of the resistance-phase defenses cause gradual damage as they operate, leading to costs for the body that can include susceptibility to infection, tumor growth, aging, irreversible organ damage, or death.

Stress Negatively Affects Health and Speeds Aging

Right now, you are (we hope!) enjoying years of healthy living. Unfortunately, as people age, the body slowly begins to break down. (Just ask any of the authors of this textbook.) Interestingly, recent research has revealed that stress significantly accelerates the aging process. Elizabeth Smart's parents noted that, on being reunited with her after 9 months of separation, they almost did not recognize her because she appeared to have aged so much (Smart, Smart, & Morton, 2003). Theirs is an extreme example; you can see examples of the effects of stress on aging around you in everyday life. People exposed to chronic stress, whether due to their relationships or jobs, or something else, experience actual wear and tear on their bodies and accelerated aging. Take a look at the pictures of the past three presidents before and after their terms as president of the United States (arguably, one of the most stressful jobs in the world). As you can see, they appear to have aged much more than the 4 to 8 years that passed between their first and second photographs. How exactly can stressors in the environment speed up the aging process?

Understanding this process requires knowing a little bit about how aging occurs. The cells in our bodies are constantly dividing, and as part of this process, our chromosomes are repeatedly copied so that our genetic information is carried into the new cells. This process is facilitated by the presence of **telomeres**, *caps at the ends of the chromosomes that prevent the chromosomes from sticking to each other.* They are kind of like the metal or plastic sheaths at the end of your shoelaces that keep them from being frayed and not working as efficiently. Each time a cell divides, the telomeres become slightly shorter. If they become too short, cells can no longer divide, and this can lead to the development of tumors and a range of diseases. Fortunately, our bodies fix this problem by producing a substance called **telomerase**, *an enzyme that rebuilds telomeres at the tips of chromosomes.* As cells repeatedly divide over the course of our lives, telomerase does its best to re-cap our chromosomes with telomeres. Ultimately, though, telomerase cannot keep up telomere repair at a sufficient pace, and over time cells lose their ability to divide, causing aging and in the end, cell death. The recent discovery of the function of telomeres and telomerase and their relation to aging and disease by Elizabeth Blackburn and colleagues has been one of the most exciting advances in science in the past several decades.

Interestingly, social stressors can play an important role in this process. People exposed to chronic stress have shorter telomere length and lower telomerase activity (Epel et al., 2004). Laboratory studies suggest that cortisol can reduce the activity of telomerase, which in turn leads to shortened telomeres, with downstream negative

telomeres Caps at the ends of the chromosomes that prevent the chromosomes from sticking to each other.

telomerase An enzyme that rebuilds telomeres at the tips of chromosomes.

effects in the form of accelerated aging and increased risk of a wide range of diseases including cancer, cardiovascular disease, diabetes, and depression (Blackburn, Epel & Lin, 2015). This sounds dire, but there are things that you can do to combat this process and potentially live a healthier and longer life! Activities such as exercise and meditation seem to prevent chronic stress from shortening telomere length, providing a potential explanation of how these activities may convey health benefits such as longer life and lower risk of disease (Epel et al., 2009; Puterman et al., 2010)(see Hot Science: Stress, Health, and Money).

HOT SCIENCE

Stress, Health, and Money

Many of us are motivated by money. But why? There has always been a general assumption that money will bring happiness. But does it? In a recent landmark study of 450,000 survey responses, Daniel Kahneman and Angus Deaton (2010), a pair of Nobel Prize winners, showed that as your income increases, your self-reported happiness goes up, and stress goes down. But this is true only up until a point. And that point is approximately $75,000 (which is about the 66th percentile). Beyond that point, higher income is not associated with happiness or stress.

One way to think about findings such as this is that although at a certain point money doesn't make you happier or less stressed, for most people having less money is associated with less happiness and more stress. More recent research has shown more alarmingly that those with less money also are at risk for the most serious outcome: death.

In a new study using data from 1.4 billion U.S. tax and death records, researchers found that people with higher incomes live significantly longer than those with lower incomes (Chetty et al., 2016). How much longer? It turns out that the difference between the wealthiest 1% and the poorest 1% is approximately 15 years for men and 10 years for women, as shown in the figure. Even more concerning is that the difference in life expectancy has been increasing over time, with life expectancy rising 2 to 3 years for the wealthiest, but only <.5 years for the poorest from 2001 to 2014.

Lower income contributes to increased rates of sickness and death through many pathways. The greater levels of stress among those with less money can shorten telomeres, compromise immune functioning, and increase the risk of heart disease and other illnesses (as described in this chapter). Recent research also has suggested that economic stress may be contributing to climbing rates of death due to drugs, alcohol, and suicide among certain subgroups in the United States (Case & Deaton, 2015).

But income is not destiny, and even among the poorest in society, behavioral and environmental factors can make a huge difference. For instance, Chetty and colleagues (2016) found that smoking and obesity are associated with a significantly higher death rate, whereas exercise is associated with a significantly lower rate of death. Moreover, if you are poor but you live in a place with higher population density, a higher percentage of immigrants and college graduates, higher government expenditures, and higher home values, you will live significantly longer. More specifically, the poorest 5% of people live 5 years longer in places such as New York and San Francisco than they would if they lived in Detroit. Why might this be? It turns out that poor people who live in wealthier cities (e.g., New York and San Francisco) also engage in healthier behaviors and in addition may benefit from better government services and policies.

Overall, the data suggest that poverty can affect a person's stress and health in serious ways, ranging from lower levels of happiness to shorter life expectancy. However, the picture is not as simple as this. Having an ever-increasing amount of money will not make you happier, and even those living in the poorest conditions can behave in ways that may increase their health and life expectancy. (On balance, however, many aspects of living in low-income communities can make this quite difficult due to factors such as lack of access to healthy food, parks, and doctor's offices; Woolf & Purnell, 2016). Recent research has taught us a great deal about the associations between stress, health, and money, but we still have a lot to learn about the full nature of these associations and about how we can use psychological science to mitigate stress and increase health among all members of society.

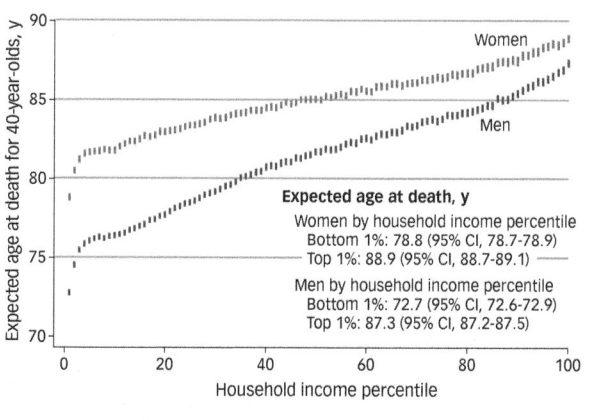

Expected age at death, y

Women by household income percentile
Bottom 1%: 78.8 (95% CI, 78.7-78.9)
Top 1%: 88.9 (95% CI, 88.7-89.1)

Men by household income percentile
Bottom 1%: 72.7 (95% CI, 72.6-72.9)
Top 1%: 87.3 (95% CI, 87.2-87.5)

DATA FROM CHETTY ET AL (2016). *JOURNAL OF THE AMERICAN MEDICAL ASSOCIATION*.

Dr. Elizabeth Blackburn was awarded a Nobel Prize in Physiology or Medicine in 2009 for her groundbreaking discoveries on the functions of telomeres (shown here in yellow) and telomerase.

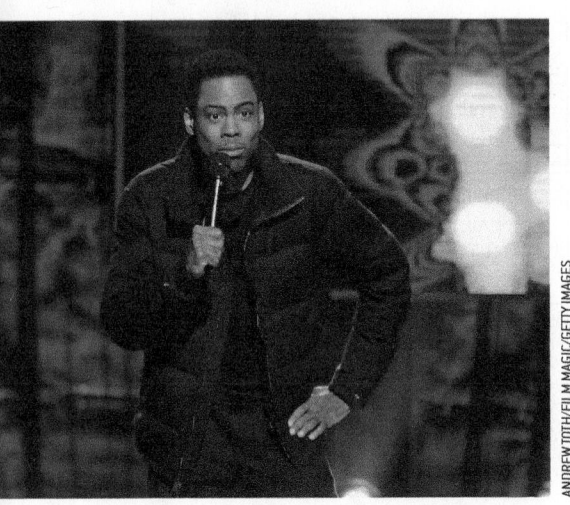

Chris Rock's joke that "rich 50 is like poor 35!" matches up with data suggesting that wealthier people tend to be healthier and younger looking than poorer people.

immune system A complex response system that protects the body from bacteria, viruses, and other foreign substances.

lymphocytes White blood cells that produce antibodies that fight infection, including T cells and B cells.

Chronic Stress Affects the Immune Response

The **immune system** is *a complex response system that protects the body from bacteria, viruses, and other foreign substances.* The system includes white blood cells, such as **lymphocytes** (including T cells and B cells), *white blood cells that produce antibodies that fight infection.* The immune system is remarkably responsive to psychological influences. *Psychoneuroimmunology* is the study of how the immune system responds to psychological variables, such as the presence of stressors. Stressors can cause hormones known as *glucocorticoids* (such as cortisol) to flood the brain (described in the Neuroscience and Behavior chapter), wearing down the immune system and making it less able to fight invaders (Webster, Marketon, & Glaser, 2008).

For example, in one study, medical student volunteers agreed to receive small wounds to the roof of the mouth. Researchers observed that these wounds healed more slowly during exam periods than during summer vacation (Marucha, Kiecolt-Glaser, & Favagehi, 1998). In another study, a set of selfless, healthy volunteers permitted researchers to swab the common cold virus in their noses (Cohen et al., 1998). You might think that a direct application of the virus would be like exposure to a massive full-facial sneeze and that all the participants would catch colds. The researchers observed, though, that some people got colds, but others didn't—and stress helped account for the difference. Volunteers who had experienced chronic stressors (lasting a month or longer) were especially likely to suffer from colds. In particular, participants who had lost a job or who were going through extended interpersonal problems with family or friends were most susceptible to the virus. Brief stressful life events (those lasting less than a month) had no impact. So if you're fighting with your friends or family, best to get it over with quickly; it's better for your health.

The effect of stress on immune response may help to explain why social status is related to health. Studies of British civil servants beginning in the 1960s found that mortality varied precisely with civil service grade: the higher the classification, the lower the death rate, regardless of cause (Marmot et al., 1991). One explanation is that people in lower-status jobs more often engage in unhealthy behavior such as smoking and drinking alcohol, and there is evidence of this. But there is also evidence that the stress of living life at the bottom levels of society increases the risk of infection by weakening the immune system. People who perceive themselves as low in social status are more likely to suffer from respiratory infections, for example, than those who do not bear this social burden—and the same holds true for low-status male monkeys (Cohen, 1999).

Stress Affects Cardiovascular Health

The heart and circulatory system also are sensitive to stress. For example, for several days after Iraq's 1991 missile attack on Israel, heart attack rates went up markedly among citizens in Tel Aviv (Meisel et al., 1991). The full story of how stress affects the cardiovascular system starts earlier than the occurrence of a heart attack: Chronic stress creates changes in the body that increase later vulnerability.

The main cause of coronary heart disease is *atherosclerosis,* a gradual narrowing of the arteries that occurs as fatty deposits, or plaque, build up on the inner walls of the arteries. Narrowed arteries reduce blood supply and, eventually, when an artery is blocked by a blood clot or detached plaque, result in a heart attack. Although smoking, a sedentary lifestyle, and a diet high in fat and cholesterol can cause coronary heart disease, chronic stress also is a major contributor (Silvani et al., 2016). As a result of stress-activated arousal of the sympathetic nervous system, blood pressure goes up and stays up, gradually damaging the blood vessels. The damaged vessels accumulate plaque, and the more plaque, the greater the likelihood of coronary heart disease. For example, a large study of Finnish men aged 42 to 60 found that those who exhibited elevated blood pressure in response to stress and who reported that their work environment was especially stressful showed progressive atherosclerosis of a major artery in the neck during the 4-year study (Everson et al., 1997).

During the 1950s, the cardiologists Meyer Friedman and Ray Rosenman (1974) conducted a revolutionary study that demonstrated a link between work-related stress and coronary heart disease. They interviewed and tested 3,000 healthy middle-aged men and then tracked their subsequent cardiovascular health. From their research, Friedman and Rosenman developed the concept of the **Type A behavior pattern**, which is characterized by *a tendency toward easily aroused hostility, impatience, a sense of time urgency, and competitive achievement strivings.* They compared Type A individuals with those with a less driven behavior pattern (sometimes called *Type B*). The Type A men were identified not only by their answers to questions in the interview (agreeing that they walk and talk fast, work late, set goals for themselves, work hard to win, and easily get frustrated and angry at others) but also by the pushy and impatient way in which they answered the questions. They watched the clock, barked back answers, and interrupted the interviewer, at some points even slapping him with a fish. Okay, the part about the fish is wrong, but you get the idea: These people were intense. The researchers found that of the 258 men who had heart attacks in the 9 years following the interview, over two thirds had been classified as Type A, and only one third had been classified as Type B.

A later study of stress and anger tracked medical students for up to 48 years to see how their behavior while they were young related to their later susceptibility to coronary problems (Chang et al., 2002). Students who responded to stress with anger and hostility were found to be 3 times more likely later to develop premature heart disease and 6 times more likely to have an early heart attack than were students who did not respond with anger. Hostility, particularly in men, predicts heart disease better than any other major causal factor, such as smoking, high caloric intake, or even high levels of LDL cholesterol (Niaura et al., 2002; see also **FIGURE 14.3**). Stress affects the cardiovascular system to some degree in everyone but is particularly harmful in those people who respond to stressful events with hostility.

PSYCHOLOGICAL REACTIONS

The body's response to stress is intertwined with responses of the mind. Perhaps the first thing the mind does is try to sort things out—to interpret whether an event is threatening or not—and if it is, whether something can be done about it.

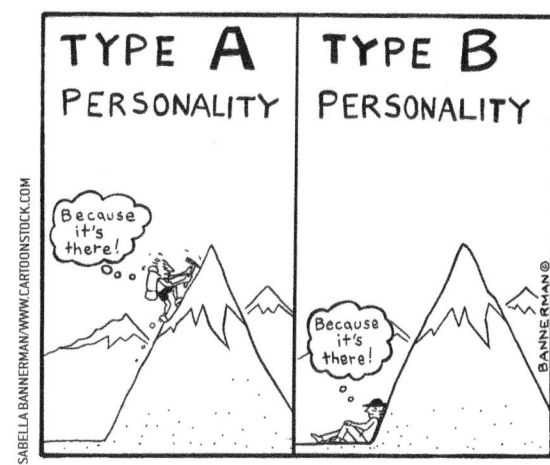

Type A behavior pattern The tendency toward easily aroused hostility, impatience, a sense of time urgency, and competitive achievement strivings.

▶ **Figure 14.3**

HOSTILITY AND CORONARY HEART DISEASE
Of 2,280 men studied over the course of 3 years, 45 suffered coronary heart disease (CHD) incidents, such as heart attack. Many more of these incidents occurred in the men who had initially scored above the 80th percentile in hostility (Niaura et al., 2002).

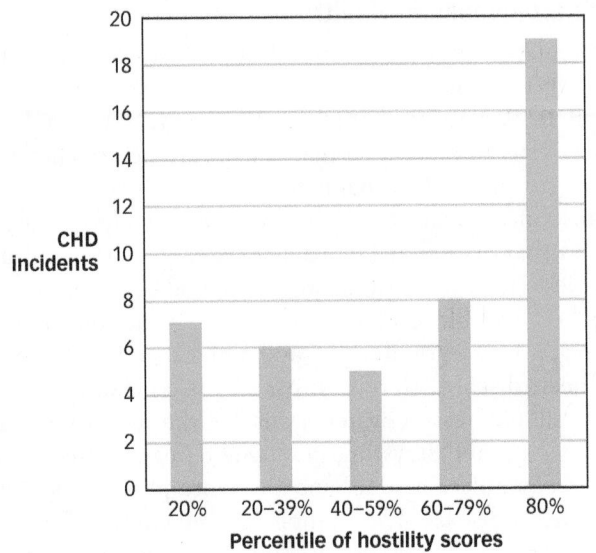

Stress Interpretation Is a Two-step Process

The interpretation of a stimulus as stressful or not is called *primary appraisal* (Lazarus & Folkman, 1984). Primary appraisal allows you to realize that a small, dark spot on your shirt is a stressor (spider!) or that a 70-mile-per-hour drop from a great height in a small car full of screaming people may not be (roller coaster!). In a demonstration of the importance of interpretation, researchers used a gruesome film of a subincision of the penis (a kind of genital surgery that is part of some tribal initiation rites) to severely stress volunteer participants (Speisman et al., 1964). Self-reports and participants' autonomic arousal (heart rate and skin conductance level) were used as measures of stress. Before viewing the film, one group heard an introduction that downplayed the pain and emphasized the coming-of-age aspect of the initiation. This interpretation markedly reduced the film viewers' stress compared with the stress of another group whose viewing was preceded by a lecture accentuating the pain and trauma.

The next step in interpretation is *secondary appraisal*, determining whether the stressor is something you can handle or not; that is, whether you have control over the event (Lazarus & Folkman, 1984). Interestingly, the body responds differently depending on whether the stressor is perceived as a *threat* (a stressor you believe you might *not* be able to overcome) or a *challenge* (a stressor you feel fairly confident you can control; Blascovich & Tomaka, 1996). The same midterm exam is seen as a challenge if you are well prepared, but a threat if you didn't study.

Fortunately, interpretations of stressors can change them from threats to challenges. One study (Jamieson et al., 2010) showed that instructing students to reframe their anxiety about an upcoming exam as arousal that would help them on the test actually boosted their sympathetic arousal (signaling a challenge orientation) and improved test performance. Remember this technique next time you are feeling anxious about a test or presentation: Increased arousal can improve your performance!

Although both threats and challenges raise the heart rate, threats increase vascular reactivity (such as constriction of the blood vessels, which can lead to high blood pressure; see A World of Difference: Can Discrimination Cause Stress and Illness?). In one study, researchers found that even interactions as innocuous as conversations can produce threat or challenge responses, depending on the race of the conversation partner. Asked to talk with another, unfamiliar student, White students showed a challenge reaction when the student was White and a threat reaction when the student was African American (Mendes et al., 2002). Similar threat responses were

Nervous about a class presentation or performance? Reframing that anxiety as arousal, which can help you perform better, can actually improve your performance. Get out there and reframe!

Is there anything worse than taking a horribly boring class? How about being the teacher of that class? What techniques would prevent burnout from stress in people in helping professions (teachers, doctors, nurses, etc.)?

found when White students interacted with an unexpected partner, such as an Asian student with a southern U.S. accent (Mendes et al., 2007). It's as if social unfamiliarity creates the same kind of stress as lack of preparedness for an exam. Interestingly, previous interaction with members of an unfamiliar group tempers the threat reaction (Blascovich et al., 2001).

Chronic Stress Can Lead to Burnout

Did you ever take a class from an instructor who had lost interest in the job? The syndrome is easy to spot: The teacher looks distant and blank, almost robotic, giving predictable and humdrum lessons each day, as if it doesn't matter whether anyone is listening. Now imagine being this instructor. You decided to teach because you wanted to shape young minds. You worked hard, and for a while things were great. But one day, you looked up to see a room full of students who were bored and didn't care about anything you had to say. They updated their Facebook pages while you talked and started shuffling papers and putting things away long before the end of class. You're happy at work only when you're not in class. When people feel this way, especially about their jobs or careers, they are suffering from **burnout**, *a state of physical, emotional, and mental exhaustion resulting from long-term involvement in an emotionally demanding situation and accompanied by lowered performance and motivation.*

Burnout is a particular problem in the helping professions (Fernandez Nievas & Thaver, 2015). Teachers, nurses, clergy, doctors, dentists, psychologists, social workers, police officers, and others who repeatedly encounter emotional turmoil on the job may only be able to work productively for a limited time. Eventually, many succumb to symptoms of burnout: overwhelming exhaustion, a deep cynicism and detachment from the job, and a sense of ineffectiveness and lack of accomplishment (Maslach, 2003). Their unhappiness can even spread to others; people with burnout tend to become disgruntled employees who revel in their coworkers' failures and ignore their coworkers' successes (Brenninkmeijer, Vanyperen, & Buunk, 2001).

What causes burnout? One theory suggests that the culprit is using your job to give meaning to your life (Pines, 1993). If you define yourself only by your career and gauge your self-worth by success at work, you risk having nothing left when work fails. For example, a teacher in danger of burnout might do well to invest time in family, hobbies, or other self-expressions. Others argue that some emotionally stressful jobs lead to burnout no matter how they are approached and that active efforts to overcome the stress before burnout occurs are important. The stress management techniques discussed in the next section may be lifesavers for people in such jobs.

burnout A state of physical, emotional, and mental exhaustion resulting from long-term involvement in an emotionally demanding situation and accompanied by lowered performance and motivation.

Build to the Outcomes

1. How does the body react to a fight-or-flight situation?

2. What are the three phases of GAS?

3. What is a telomere? What do telomeres do for us?

4. How does stress affect the immune system?

5. How does chronic stress increase the chance of a heart attack?

6. What causal factor most predicts heart attacks?

7. What is the difference between a threat and a challenge?

8. Why is burnout a problem, especially in the helping professions?

Stress Management: Dealing With It

Learning Outcomes

▶ Explain techniques for coping with psychological stress.

▶ Identify physical activities that reduce stress.

▶ Define and give examples of situation management.

Most college students (92%) say they occasionally feel overwhelmed by the tasks they face, and over a third say they have dropped courses or received low grades in response to severe stress (Duenwald, 2002). No doubt you are among the lucky 8% who are entirely cool and report no stress. But just in case you're not, you may be interested in our exploration of stress management techniques: ways to counteract psychological and physical stress reactions directly by managing your mind and body, and ways to sidestep stress by managing your situation.

MIND MANAGEMENT

Stressful events are magnified in the mind. If you fear public speaking, for example, just the thought of an upcoming presentation to a group can create anxiety. And if you do break down during a presentation (going blank, for example, or blurting out something embarrassing), intrusive memories of this stressful event could echo in your mind afterward. A significant part of stress management, then, is control of the mind.

repressive coping Avoiding feelings, thoughts, or situations that are reminders of a stressor and maintaining an artificially positive viewpoint.

Repressive Coping: Holding an Artificially Positive Viewpoint

Controlling your thoughts is not easy, but some people do seem to be able to banish unpleasant thoughts from the mind. This style of dealing with stress, called **repressive coping**, is characterized by *avoiding feelings, thoughts, or situations that are reminders of a stressor and maintaining an artificially positive viewpoint*. Everyone has some problems, of course, but repressors are good at deliberately ignoring them (Barnier, Levin, & Maher, 2004). So, for example, when repressors suffer a heart attack, they are less likely than other people to report intrusive thoughts of their heart problems in the days and weeks that follow (Ginzburg, Solomon, & Bleich, 2002).

Like Elizabeth Smart, who for years after her rescue focused in interviews on what was happening in her life now, rather than repeatedly discussing her past in captivity, people often rearrange their lives in order to avoid stressful situations. Many victims of rape, for example, not only avoid the place where the rape occurred but may move away from their home or neighborhood (Ellis, 1983). Anticipating and attempting to avoid reminders of the traumatic experience, they become wary of strangers, especially men who resemble the assailant, and they check doors, locks, and windows more frequently than before. It may make sense to try to avoid stressful thoughts and situations if you're the kind of person who is good at putting unpleasant thoughts and emotions out of mind (Coifman et al., 2007). For some people, however, the avoidance of unpleasant thoughts and situations is so difficult that it can turn into a grim preoccupation (Parker & McNally, 2008; Wegner & Zanakos, 1994). For those who

Terrorist attacks in Paris in November 2015 left 130 people dead and hundreds more wounded. People deal with major stressful life events such as this in different ways. Repressive copers use avoidance; rational copers use acceptance, exposure, and understanding; and reframers try to think about the situation in more positive ways.

CHRISTOPHER FURLONG/GETTY IMAGES

can't avoid negative emotions effectively, it may be better to come to grips with them. This is the basic idea of rational coping.

Rational Coping: Working to Overcome

Rational coping involves *facing the stressor and working to overcome it.* This strategy is the opposite of repressive coping, so it may seem to be the most unpleasant and unnerving thing you could do when faced with stress. It requires approaching, rather than avoiding, a stressor in order to diminish its longer-term negative impact (Hayes, Strosahl, & Wilson, 1999). Rational coping is a three-step process: *acceptance,* coming to realize that the stressor exists and cannot be wished away; *exposure,* attending to the stressor, thinking about it, and even seeking it out; and *understanding,* working to find the meaning of the stressor in your life.

When the trauma is particularly intense, rational coping may be difficult to undertake. In rape trauma, for example, even accepting that the rape happened takes time and effort; the initial impulse is to deny the event and try to live as though it had never occurred. Psychological treatment may help during the exposure step by aiding victims in confronting and thinking about what happened. Using a technique called *prolonged exposure*, rape survivors relive the traumatic event in their imaginations by recording a verbal account of the event and then listening to the recording daily. In one study, rape survivors were instructed to seek out objectively safe situations that caused them anxiety or that they had avoided. This sounds like bitter medicine indeed, but it is remarkably effective, producing significant reductions in anxiety and symptoms of posttraumatic stress disorder compared with no therapy and compared with other therapies that promote more gradual and subtle forms of exposure (Foa & McLean, 2016).

The third element of rational coping involves coming to an understanding of the meaning of the stressful events. A trauma victim may wonder again and again: Why me? How did it happen? Why? Survivors of incest frequently voice the desire to make sense of their trauma (Weiss & Curcio Alexander, 2013), a process that is difficult, even impossible, during bouts of suppression and avoidance.

Reframing: Changing Your Thinking

Changing the way you think is another way to cope with stressful thoughts. **Reframing** involves *finding a new or creative way to think about a stressor that reduces its threat.* If you experience anxiety at the thought of public speaking, for example, you might

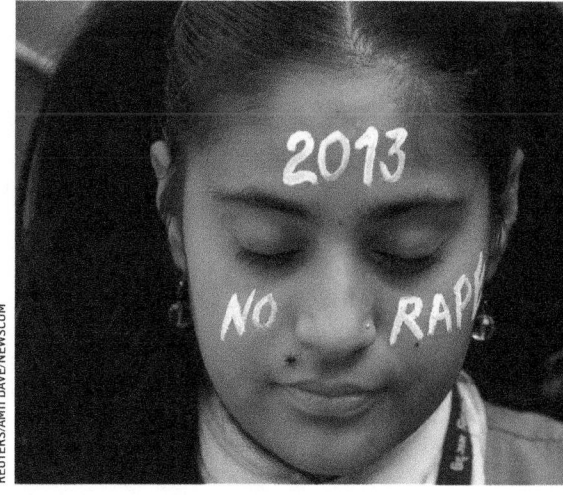

This young woman is praying during a vigil held for the victim of a gang rape in New Delhi. Extremely stressful events, such as rape, are not only acute stressors but often have lasting psychological consequences. Fortunately, there are effective techniques for learning to cope with such events that can lead to improved psychological health.

rational coping Facing a stressor and working to overcome it.

reframing Finding a new or creative way to think about a stressor that reduces its threat.

Stress can affect the body, and it often shows. This guy had a stressful day of trading at the New York Stock Exchange. Looks like he could use a little body management.

stress-inoculation training (SIT) A reframing technique that helps people cope with stressful situations by developing positive ways to think about the situations.

meditation The practice of intentional contemplation.

reframe by shifting from thinking of an audience as evaluating you to thinking of yourself as evaluating them, and this might make speech giving easier.

Reframing can be an effective way to prepare for a moderately stressful situation, but if something like public speaking is so stressful that you can't bear to think about it until you absolutely must, you may not be able to apply this technique. **Stress-inoculation training (SIT)** is *a reframing technique that helps people cope with stressful situations by developing positive ways to think about the situations.* For example, in one study, people who had difficulty controlling their anger were trained to rehearse and reframe their thoughts with phrases such as these: "Just roll with the punches, don't get bent out of shape"; "You don't need to prove yourself"; "I'm not going to let him get to me"; "It's really a shame he has to act like this"; and "I'll just let him make a fool of himself." Anger-prone people who practiced these thoughts were less likely to become physiologically aroused in response to laboratory-based provocations, both imaginary and real. Subsequent research on SIT has revealed that it can be useful, too, for helping people who have suffered prior traumatic events to become more comfortable living with those events (Foa & Meadows, 1997).

Reframing can take place spontaneously if people are given the opportunity to spend time thinking and writing about stressful events. In an important series of studies, Jamie Pennebaker (1989) found that the physical health of college students improved after they spent a few hours writing about their deepest thoughts and feelings. Compared with students who had written about something else, members of the self-disclosure group were less likely in subsequent months to visit the student health center; they also used less aspirin and achieved better grades (Pennebaker & Chung, 2007). In fact, engaging in such expressive writing was found to improve immune function (Pennebaker, Kiecolt-Glaser, & Glaser, 1988), whereas suppressing emotional topics weakened it (Petrie, Booth, & Pennebaker, 1998). The positive effect of self-disclosing writing may reflect its usefulness in reframing trauma and reducing stress.

BODY MANAGEMENT

Stress can express itself as tension in your neck muscles, back pain, a knot in your stomach, sweaty hands, or the harried face you glimpse in the mirror. Because stress so often manifests itself through bodily symptoms, bodily techniques such as meditation, relaxation therapy, biofeedback, and aerobic exercise are useful in managing it.

Meditation: Turning Inward

Meditation is *the practice of intentional contemplation.* Techniques of meditation are associated with a variety of religious traditions and are also practiced outside religious contexts. The techniques vary widely. Some forms of meditation call for attempts to clear the mind of thought; others involve focusing on a single thought (e.g., thinking about a candle flame); still others involve concentration on breathing or on a *mantra* (a repetitive sound such as *om*). At a minimum, these techniques have in common a period of quiet.

Time spent meditating can be restful and revitalizing. Beyond these immediate benefits, many people also meditate in an effort to experience deeper or transformed consciousness. Whatever the reason, meditation does appear to have positive psychological effects (Hölzel et al., 2011). Many believe it does so, in part, by improving control over attention. The focus of many forms of meditation, such as mindfulness meditation, is on teaching ourselves how to remain focused on, and to accept, our immediate experience. Interestingly, experienced meditators show deactivation in the default mode network (which is associated with mind wandering; see Figure 5.6 in the Consciousness chapter) during meditation relative to nonmeditators (Brewer et al., 2011). Even short-term meditation training administered to college undergraduates has been shown to improve the connectivity between parts of the brain involved in conflict monitoring and cognitive and emotional control, and to do so via increased myelination (perhaps due to increased neuron firing) and other axonal changes (see the Neuroscience and Behavior chapter; Tang et al., 2012). Moreover, recent research suggests that those engaging in several weeks of intensive meditation actually show lengthening of their telomeres, suggesting a slight reversal of the effects of stress and aging described above (Conklin et al., 2015). Taken together, these findings suggest that meditators may be better able to regulate their thoughts and emotions, which may translate to a better ability to manage interpersonal relations, anxiety, and a range of other activities that require conscious effort (Sedlmeier et al., 2012).

Relaxation: Picturing Peace

Imagine for a moment that you are scratching your chin. Don't actually do it; just think about it and notice that your body participates by moving ever so slightly, tensing and relaxing in the sequence of the imagined action. Edmund Jacobson (1932) discovered these effects with *electromyography* (EMG), a technique used to measure the subtle activity of muscles. A person asked to imagine rowing a boat or plucking a flower from a bush would produce slight levels of tension in the muscles involved in performing the act. Jacobson also found that thoughts of relaxing the muscles sometimes reduced EMG readings when people didn't even report feeling tense. Our bodies respond to all the things we think about doing every day. These thoughts create muscle tension even when we think we're doing nothing at all.

These observations led Jacobson to develop **relaxation therapy**, *a technique for reducing tension by consciously relaxing muscles of the body.* A person in relaxation therapy may be asked to relax specific muscle groups one at a time or to imagine warmth flowing through the body or to think about a relaxing situation. This activity draws on a **relaxation response**, *a condition of reduced muscle tension, cortical activity, heart rate, breathing rate, and blood pressure* (Benson, 1990). Basically, as soon as you get in a comfortable position, quiet down, and focus on something repetitive or soothing that holds your attention, you relax.

Relaxing on a regular basis can reduce symptoms of stress (Carlson & Hoyle, 1993) and even reduce blood levels of cortisol, the biochemical marker of the stress response (McKinney et al., 1997). For example, in individuals who are suffering from tension headache, relaxation reduces the tension that causes the headache; in people with cancer, relaxation makes it easier to cope with stressful treatments; in people with stress-related cardiovascular problems, relaxation can reduce the high blood pressure that puts the heart at risk (Mandle et al., 1996).

Biofeedback: Enlisting the Help of an External Monitor

Wouldn't it be nice if, instead of having to learn to relax, you could just flip a switch and relax as fast as possible? **Biofeedback**, *the use of an external monitoring device to obtain information about a bodily function and possibly gain control over that function,* was developed with the goal of high-tech relaxation in mind. You might not be aware right now of whether your fingers are warm or cold, for example, but with an electronic thermometer displayed before you, the ability to sense your temperature might allow you (with a bit of practice) to make your hands warmer or cooler at will (e.g., Roberts & McGrady, 1996).

Biofeedback can help people control physiological functions they are not likely to become aware of in other ways. For example, you probably have no idea right now what brain-wave patterns you are producing. In the late 1950s, Joe Kamiya (1969), a psychologist using the electroencephalograph (also called the EEG and discussed in the Neuroscience and Behavior chapter), initiated a brain-wave biofeedback revolution when he found that people could change their brain waves from alert beta patterns to relaxed alpha patterns and back again when they were permitted to monitor their own EEG readings.

Aung San Suu Kyi, the leader of the Myanmar opposition party who was awarded the Nobel Peace Prize in 1991, endured house arrest from 1989 until 2010. She has said that daily meditation helped her through this difficult time by improving her mood, awareness, and clarity.

relaxation therapy A technique for reducing tension by consciously relaxing muscles of the body.

relaxation response A condition of reduced muscle tension, cortical activity, heart rate, breathing rate, and blood pressure.

biofeedback The use of an external monitoring device to obtain information about a bodily function and possibly gain control over that function.

Biofeedback gives people access to visual or audio feedback showing levels of psychophysiological functions such as heart rate, breathing, brain electrical activity, or skin temperature that they would otherwise be unable to sense directly.

MATT DUNHAM/AP IMAGES

Exercise helps reduce stress—unless, as for John Stibbard, your exercise involves carrying the Olympic torch on a wobbly suspension bridge over a 70-meter gorge.

Recent studies suggest that EEG biofeedback (or neurofeedback) is moderately successful in treating brain-wave abnormalities in disorders such as epilepsy (Yucha & Gilbert, 2004) and in teaching people to down-regulate activity in regions of the brain involved in the strong emotional responses seen in some forms of psychopathology (Hamilton et al., 2010). Often, however, the use of biofeedback to produce relaxation in the brain turns out to be a bit of technological overkill and may not be much more effective than simply having the person stretch out in a hammock and hum a happy tune. Although biofeedback is not a magic bullet that gives people control over stress-induced health troubles, it has proven to be a useful technique for increasing relaxation and decreasing chronic pain (Palermo et al., 2011). People who do not benefit from relaxation therapy may find that biofeedback provides a useful alternative.

Aerobic Exercise: Boosting Mood

A jogger nicely decked out in a neon running suit bounces in place at the crosswalk and then springs away when the signal changes. It is tempting to assume that this jogger is the picture of psychological health: happy, unstressed, and even downright exuberant. As it turns out, this stereotype is true: Studies indicate that *aerobic exercise* (exercise that increases heart rate and oxygen intake for a sustained period) is associated with psychological well-being (Hassmen, Koivula, & Uutela, 2000). But does exercise *cause* psychological well-being, or does psychological well-being cause people to exercise? Perhaps general happiness is what inspires the jogger's bounce. Or could some unknown third factor (neon pants?) cause both the need to exercise and the sense of well-being? As we've mentioned many times, correlation does not always imply causation.

To try to tease apart causal factors, researchers have randomly assigned people to aerobic exercise activities and no-exercise comparison groups and have found that exercise actually does promote stress relief and happiness. One recent meta-analysis (a quantitative review of existing studies) compiled data from 90 studies including over 10,000 people with chronic illness who were randomly assigned either to an exercise or a no-exercise condition. People assigned to the aerobic exercise condition experienced a significant reduction in depressive symptoms (Herring et al., 2012). Other recent meta-analyses have come to similar conclusions, showing, for instance, that exercise is as effective as the most effective psychological interventions for depression (Rimer et al., 2012), and that exercise even shows positive physical and mental health benefits for individuals with schizophrenia (Gorczynski & Faulkner, 2011). Pretty good effects for a simple, timeless intervention with no side effects!

The reasons for these positive effects are unclear. Researchers have suggested that the effects result from increases in the body's production of neurotransmitters such as serotonin, which can have a positive effect on mood (as discussed in the Neuroscience and Behavior chapter) or from increases in the production of endorphins (the endogenous opioids discussed in the Neuroscience and Behavior and Consciousness chapters; Jacobs, 1994).

Beyond boosting positive mood, exercise also stands to keep you healthy into the future. Current U.S. government recommendations suggest that 30 minutes of moderately vigorous exercise per day will reduce the risk of chronic illness (Dietary Guidelines Advisory Committee, 2005). Perhaps the simplest thing you can do to improve your happiness and health, then, is to participate regularly in an aerobic activity. Pick something you find fun: Sign up for a dance class, get into a regular basketball game, or start paddling a canoe—just not all at once.

SITUATION MANAGEMENT

After you have tried to manage stress by managing your mind and managing your body, what's left to manage? Look around and you'll notice a whole world out there.

Perhaps that could be managed as well. Situation management involves changing your life situation as a way of reducing the impact of stress on your mind and body. Ways to manage your situation can include seeking out social support, religious or spiritual practice, and finding a place for humor in your life.

Social Support: "Swimming With a Buddy"

The wisdom of the National Safety Council's first rule—"Always swim with a buddy"— is obvious when you're in water over your head, but people often don't realize that the same principle applies whenever danger threatens. Other people can offer help in times of stress. **Social support** is *aid gained through interacting with others.* One of the more self-defeating things you can do in life is fail to connect to people in this way. Just failing to get married, for example, is bad for your health. Unmarried individuals have an elevated risk of mortality from cardiovascular disease, cancer, pneumonia and influenza, chronic obstructive pulmonary disease, and liver disease and cirrhosis (Johnson, Backlund, et al., 2000). More generally, good ongoing relationships with friends and family and participation in social activities and religious groups can be as healthy for you as exercising and avoiding smoking (Umberson et al., 2006). Social support is helpful on many levels:

▶ An intimate partner can help you remember to get your exercise and follow your doctor's orders, and together you'll probably follow a healthier diet than you would all alone with your snacks.

▶ Talking about problems with friends and family can offer many of the benefits of professional psychotherapy, usually without the hourly fees.

▶ Sharing tasks and helping each other when times get tough can reduce the amount of work and worry in each other's lives.

The helpfulness of strong social bonds, though, transcends mere convenience. Lonely people are more likely than others to be stressed and depressed (Baumeister & Leary, 1995), and they can be more susceptible to illness because of lower-than-normal levels of immune functioning (Kiecolt-Glaser et al., 1984). Many first-year college students experience something of a crisis of social support. No matter how outgoing and popular they were in high school, newcomers typically find the task of developing satisfying new social relationships quite daunting. New friendships can seem shallow, connections with teachers may be perfunctory and even threatening, and social groups that are encountered can seem like islands of lost souls. ("Hey, we're forming a club to investigate the lack of clubs on campus—want to join?") It's not surprising that research shows that students reporting the greatest feelings of isolation also show reduced immune responses to flu vaccinations (Pressman et al., 2005). Time spent getting to know people in new social situations can be an investment in your own health.

The value of social support in protecting against stress may be very different for women and men: Whereas women seek support under stress, men are less likely to do so. The fight-or-flight response to stress may be largely a male reaction, according to research on sex differences by Shelley Taylor (2002). Taylor suggested that the female response to stress is to *tend-and-befriend* by taking care of people and bringing them together. This is believed by some to be due at least in part to the release of *oxytocin,* a hormone secreted by the pituitary gland when women are pregnant or nursing, as well as in a range of other contexts. In the presence of estrogen, oxytocin triggers social responses: a tendency to seek out social contacts, nurture others, and create and maintain cooperative groups. After a hard day at work, a man may come home frustrated and worried about his job and end up drinking a beer and fuming alone. A woman under the same type of stress may be more likely to instead play with her kids or talk to friends on the phone. The tend-and-befriend response to stress may help to

social support The aid gained through interacting with others.

Women are more likely than men to seek support when under stress.

explain why women are healthier and have a longer life span than do men. The typical male response amplifies the unhealthy effects of stress, whereas the female response takes less of a toll on a woman's mind and body and provides social support for the people around her as well.

Religious Experiences: Reaping Earthly Rewards

Many people spend a significant amount of time in quiet prayer, reflection, and contemplation. National polls indicate that over 90% of Americans believe in God and that most who do pray at least once per day. Although many who believe in a higher power believe that their faith will be rewarded in an afterlife, it turns out that there may be some benefits here on earth as well. An enormous body of research has examined the associations between *religiosity* (affiliation with or engagement in the practices of a particular religion) and *spirituality* (having a belief in and engagement with some higher power, not necessarily linked to any particular religion) and positive health outcomes. The helpful effects of religiosity and spirituality have been observed in a wide range of areas, including lower rates of heart disease, decreases in chronic pain, and improved psychological health (Seybold & Hill, 2001).

Why do people who endorse religiosity or spirituality have better mental and physical health? Is it divine intervention? Several testable ideas have been proposed. Engagement in religious or spiritual practices, such as attendance at weekly religious services, may lead to the development of a stronger and more extensive social network, which has well-known health benefits. Those who are religious or spiritual also may fare better psychologically and physically as a result of following the healthy recommendations offered in many religious or spiritual teachings. That is, they may be more likely to observe dietary restrictions, abstain from the use of drugs or alcohol, or endorse a more hopeful and optimistic perspective of daily life events, all of which can lead to more positive health outcomes (Seeman, Dubin, & Seeman, 2003; Seybold & Hill, 2001). However, many claims made by some religious groups have not been supported, such as the beneficial effects of intercessory prayer (see **FIGURE 14.4**).

▶ Figure 14.4

PRAY FOR ME? To test whether praying for someone in their time of need actually helped them, researchers randomly assigned 1,802 patients about to undergo cardiac bypass surgery to one of three conditions: those told that they might be prayed for and were; those told that they might be prayed for and weren't; and those told that they definitely would be prayed for and were. Unfortunately, there were no differences in the presence of complications between those who were or were not prayed for. To make matters worse, those who knew they would be prayed for and were experienced significantly more complications than the other two groups (Benson et al., 2006).

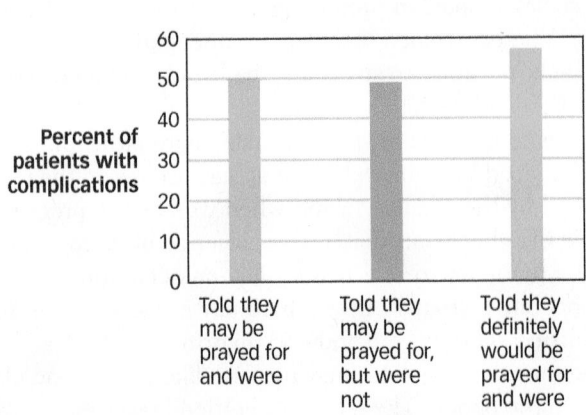

Psychologists are actively testing the effectiveness of various religious and spiritual practices with the goal of better understanding how they might help to explain, and improve, the human condition.

Humor: Laughing It Off

Wouldn't it be nice to laugh at your troubles and move on? Most of us recognize that humor can defuse unpleasant situations and bad feelings, and it makes sense that bringing some fun into your life could help to reduce stress. The extreme point of view on this topic is staked out in self-help books with titles such as *Health, Healing, and the Amuse System* and *How Serious Is This? Seeing Humor in Daily Stress*. Is laughter truly the best medicine? Should we close down the hospitals and send in the clowns?

There is a kernel of truth to the theory that humor can help us cope with stress. For example, humor can reduce sensitivity to pain and distress, as researchers found when they subjected volunteers to an overinflated blood pressure cuff. Participants were more tolerant of the pain during a laughter-inducing comedy audiotape than during a neutral tape or guided relaxation (Cogan et al., 1987).

Humor can also reduce the time needed to calm down after a stressful event. For example, men viewing a highly stressful film about three industrial accidents were asked to narrate the film aloud, either by describing the events seriously or by making their commentary as funny as possible. Although men in both groups reported feeling tense while watching the film and showed increased levels of sympathetic nervous arousal (increased heart rate and skin conductance, decreased skin temperature), those looking for humor in the experience bounced back to normal arousal levels more quickly than did those in the serious story group (Newman & Stone, 1996).

If laughter and fun can alleviate stress quickly in the short term, do the effects accumulate to improve health and longevity? Sadly, the evidence suggests not (Provine, 2000). A study titled "Do Comics Have the Last Laugh?" tracked the longevity of comedians in comparison to other entertainers and nonentertainers (Rotton, 1992). It was found that the comedians died younger—perhaps after too many nights on stage thinking, *I'm dying out here.*

When Andrew Mason, CEO of the Internet company Groupon, left his position, his resignation letter read: "After four and a half intense and wonderful years as CEO of Groupon, I've decided that I'd like to spend more time with my family. Just kidding—I was fired today." He went on to add, "I am so lucky to have had the opportunity to take the company this far with all of you. I'll now take some time to decompress (FYI I'm looking for a good fat camp to lose my Groupon 40, if anyone has a suggestion), and then maybe I'll figure out how to channel this experience into something productive." This seems like a textbook case of using humor to mitigate stress, which is why we put it, um, you know where.

Scheduling and Activating: Getting It Done

At one time or another, most of us have avoided carrying out a task or put it off to a later time. The task may be unpleasant, difficult, or just less entertaining than other things we could be doing at the moment. For college students, procrastination can affect a range of academic activities, such as writing a term paper or preparing for a test. Academic procrastination is not uncommon: Over 70% of college students report that they engage in some form of procrastination (Schouwenburg, 1995), and report engaging in academic procrastination between 30% and 60% of the time (Rabin, Fogel, & Nutter-Upham, 2011). Although it's fun to hang out with your friends tonight, it's not so much fun to worry for three days about your impending history exam or try to study at 4:00 A.M. the day of the test. Studying now, or at least a little bit each day, robs procrastination of its power over you.

Some procrastinators defend this practice by claiming that they tend to work best under pressure or by noting that as long as a task gets done, it doesn't matter all that much if it is completed just before the deadline. Is there any merit to such claims? Or are they just feeble excuses for counterproductive behavior?

A study of 60 undergraduate psychology college students provided some intriguing answers (Tice & Baumeister, 1997). At the beginning of the semester, the instructor announced a due date for the term paper and told students that if they could not meet the date, they would receive an extension to a later date. About a month later, students completed a scale that measures tendencies toward procrastination. At that same time, and then again during the last week of class, students recorded health

Are you a procrastinator?

symptoms they had experienced during the past week, the amount of stress they had experienced during that week, and the number of visits they had made to a health care center during the previous month.

Students who scored high on the procrastination scale tended to turn in their papers late. One month into the semester, these procrastinators reported less stress and fewer symptoms of physical illness than did nonprocrastinators. But at the end of the semester, the procrastinators reported more stress and more health symptoms than did the nonprocrastinators, and they reported more visits to the health center. The procrastinators also received lower grades on their papers and on course exams. More recent studies have found that higher levels of procrastination are associated with poorer academic performance (Moon & Illingworth, 2005) and higher levels of psychological distress (Rice, Richardson, & Clark, 2012). In fact, recent evidence indicates that habitual procrastinators show higher levels of self-reported hypertension and cardiovascular disease, even when controlling for other personality traits associated with these health problems (Sirois, 2015). Although there is no proven method of eliminating procrastination, there is some evidence that procrastination in college students can be reduced by interventions that use training in time management or behavioral methods that target processes that are believed to be responsible for procrastination (Glick & Orsillo, 2015). If you tend toward procrastination, we hope that the research discussed here can alert you to its pitfalls.

Build to the Outcomes

1. When is it useful to avoid stressful thoughts? When is avoidance a problem?

2. What are the three steps in rational coping?

3. What is the difference between repressive and rational coping?

4. How has writing about stressful events been shown to be helpful?

5. What are some positive outcomes of meditation?

6. How does biofeedback work?

7. What are the benefits of exercise?

8. What are the benefits of social support?

9. Why are religiosity and spirituality associated with health benefits?

10. How does humor mitigate stress?

11. How do good study habits support good health?

The Psychology of Illness: Mind Over Matter

Learning Outcome

▶ Describe the interrelationship between the mind and body relating to illness.

One of the mind's most important influences on the body's health and illness is the mind's sensitivity to bodily symptoms. Noticing what is wrong with the body can be helpful when it motivates a search for treatment, but sensitivity can also lead to further problems when it snowballs into a preoccupation with illness that itself can cause harm.

PSYCHOLOGICAL EFFECTS OF ILLNESS

Why does it feel so bad to be sick? You notice scratchiness in your throat or the start of sniffles, and you think you might be coming down with something. And in just a few short hours, you're achy all over, energy gone, no appetite, feverish, feeling dull and listless. You're sick. The question is, why does it have to be like this? Why couldn't it feel good? As long as you're going to have to stay at home and miss out on things anyway, couldn't sickness be less of a pain?

Sickness makes you miserable for good reason. Misery is part of the *sickness response,* a coordinated, adaptive set of reactions to illness organized by the brain (Hart, 1988;

Watkins & Maier, 2005). Feeling sick keeps you home, where you'll spread germs to fewer people. More important, the sickness response makes you withdraw from activity and lie still, conserving the energy for fighting illness that you'd normally expend on other behavior. Appetite loss is similarly helpful: The energy spent on digestion is conserved. Thus, the behavioral changes that accompany illness are not random side effects; they help the body fight disease. These responses become prolonged and exaggerated with aging—subtle signs that we are losing the fight (Barrientos et al., 2009).

How does the brain know it should do this? The immune response to an infection begins with one of the components of the immune response, the activation of white blood cells that "eat" microbes and also release *cytokines,* proteins that circulate through the body and communicate with the other white blood cells and also communicate the sickness response to the brain (Maier & Watkins, 1998). Administration of cytokines to an animal can artificially induce the sickness response, and administration of drugs that oppose the action of cytokines can block the sickness response even during an ongoing infection. Cytokines do not enter the brain, but they activate the vagus nerve, which runs from the intestines, stomach, and chest to the brain and convey the "I am infected" message (Goehler et al., 2000; Klarer et al., 2014). Perhaps this is why we often feel sickness in the "gut," a gnawing discomfort in the very center of the body.

Interestingly, the sickness response can be prompted without any infection at all, merely by the introduction of stress. The stressful presence of a predator's odor, for instance, can trigger the sickness response of lethargy in an animal, along with symptoms of infection such as fever and increased white blood cell count (Maier & Watkins, 2000). In humans, the connection among sickness response, immune reaction, and stress is illustrated in depression, a condition in which all the sickness machinery runs at full speed. So in addition to fatigue and malaise, depressed people show signs characteristic of infection, including high levels of cytokines circulating in the blood (Maes, 1995). Just as illness can make you feel a bit depressed, severe depression seems to recruit the brain's sickness response and make you feel ill (Watkins & Maier, 2005).

RECOGNIZING ILLNESS AND SEEKING TREATMENT

You probably weren't thinking about your breathing a minute ago, but now that you're reading this sentence, you notice it. Sometimes we are very attentive to our bodies. At other times, the body seems to be on "automatic," running along unnoticed until specific symptoms announce themselves or are pointed out by an annoying textbook writer.

Directing attention toward the body or away from it can influence the symptoms we perceive. When people are bored, for example, they have more attention available to direct toward their bodies, so they focus more on their physical symptoms. Pennebaker (1980) audiotaped classrooms and found that people are more likely to cough when someone else has just coughed, but that such psychological contagion is much more likely at boring points in a lecture. Interestingly, coughing is not

If you have been reading this very exciting textbook, there is no chance you have been yawning. However, seeing this guy yawning may cause your brain to initiate a yawn response as well.

How much does it hurt? Pain is a psychological state that can be difficult to measure. One way to put a number on a pain is to have people judge with reference to the external expression of the internal state.

Wong-Baker FACES® Pain Rating Scale

0	2	4	6	8	10
No Hurt	Hurts Little Bit	Hurts Little More	Hurts Even More	Hurts Whole Lot	Hurts Worst

▶ **Figure 14.5**

THE BRAIN IN PAIN These fMRI scans show brain activation in high- (*left*) and low-pain-sensitive (*right*) individuals during painful stimulation. The anterior cingulate cortex and primary somatosensory areas show greater activation in high-pain-sensitive individuals. Levels of activation are highest in yellow and red, then light blue and dark blue (Coghill, McHaffie, & Yen, 2003).

High Pain Sensitivity — Low Pain Sensitivity

something people do on purpose (as Pennebaker found when he recorded clusters of coughs among sleeping firefighters). Thus, awareness and occurrence of physical symptoms can be influenced by psychological factors beyond our control.

People differ substantially in the degree to which they attend to and report bodily symptoms. People who report many physical symptoms tend to be negative in other ways as well, describing themselves as anxious, depressed, and under stress (Watson & Pennebaker, 1989). Do people with many symptom complaints truly have a lot of problems? Or are they just high-volume complainers? To answer this question, researchers used fMRI brain scans to compare the severity of reported sensation of pain with the degree of activation in brain areas usually associated with pain experience. Volunteers underwent several applications of a thermal stimulus (110–120° F) to the leg; as you might expect, some of the participants found it more painful than did others. Scans during the painful events revealed that the anterior cingulate cortex, somatosensory cortex, and prefrontal cortex (areas known to respond to painful body stimulation) were particularly active in those participants who reported higher levels of pain experience (see **FIGURE 14.5**), suggesting that people can report accurately on the extent to which they experience pain (Coghill, McHaffie, & Yen, 2003; see The Real World: This Is Your Brain on Placebos).

In contrast to complainers, other people underreport symptoms and pain or ignore or deny the possibility that they are sick. Insensitivity to symptoms comes with costs: It can delay the search for treatment, sometimes with serious repercussions. Of 2,404 patients in one study who had been treated for a heart attack, 40% had delayed going to the hospital for over 6 hours from the time they first noticed suspicious symptoms (Gurwitz et al., 1997). Severe chest pain or a history of prior heart surgery did send people to the hospital in a hurry. Those with more subtle symptoms often waited around for hours, however, not calling an ambulance or their doctor, just hoping the problem would go away. This is not a good idea, because many of the treatments that can reduce the damage of a heart attack are most useful when provided early. When it comes to your own health, protecting your mind from distress through the denial of illness can result in exposing your body to great danger.

SOMATIC SYMPTOM DISORDERS

psychosomatic illness An interaction between mind and body that can produce illness.

somatic symptom disorders The set of psychological disorders in which a person with at least one bodily symptom displays significant health-related anxiety, expresses disproportionate concerns about their symptoms, and devotes excessive time and energy to their symptoms or health concerns.

The flip side of denial is excessive sensitivity to illness, and it turns out that sensitivity also has its perils. Indeed, hypersensitivity to symptoms or to the possibility of illness underlies a variety of psychological problems and can also undermine physical health. Psychologists studying **psychosomatic illness**, *an interaction between mind and body that can produce illness,* explore ways in which mind (*psyche*) can influence body (*soma*) and vice versa. The study of mind–body interactions focuses on psychological disorders called **somatic symptom disorders**, in which *a person with at least*

This Is Your Brain on Placebos

There is something miraculous about Band-Aids. Your standard household toddler typically *requires* one for any injury at all, expecting and often achieving immediate relief. It is not unusual to find a child who reports that aches or pains are "cured" if a Band-Aid has been applied by a helpful adult. Of course, the Band-Aid is not *really* helping the pain—or is it?

Physicians and psychologists have long puzzled over the *placebo effect,* a clinically significant psychological or physiological response to a therapeutically inert substance or procedure. The classic placebo is the sugar pill, but Band-Aids, injections, heating pads, neck rubs, homeopathic remedies, and kind words can have placebo effects (Diederich & Goetz, 2008). Even sham brain surgery can be more effective than no treatment at all (McRae et al., 2004). The effect is most marked, however, when the patient knows that a treatment is taking place (Stewart-Williams, 2004). This is also true of active treatments: A morphine injection works much better if you know you're getting it (Benedetti, Maggi, & Lopiano, 2003). Knowledge effects can be remarkably specific, mirroring in detail what patients believe about the nature of medicine: for example, that two pills work better than one or that an injection works better than just a pill (de Craen et al., 1999).

How do placebos operate? Do people being treated for pain really feel the pain but distort their report of the experience to make it fit their beliefs about treatment? Or does the placebo actually reduce the pain a patient experiences? Howard Fields and Jon Levine (1984) discovered that placebos trigger the release of endorphins (or *endogenous opioids*), painkilling chemicals similar to morphine that are produced by the brain (see the Consciousness chapter). In their experiments, they found that an injection of naloxone, an opioid-blocking drug, typically reduces the benefit of both an opioid such as morphine and a placebo injection, suggesting that the placebo has

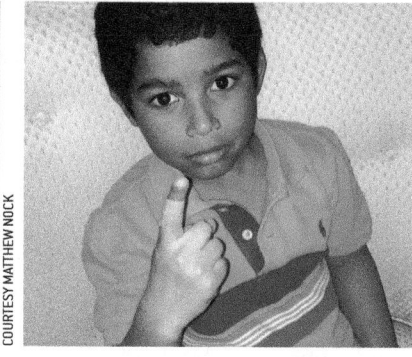

▲ Can a Band-Aid cure all of your aches and pains? Many children, like this little guy, report immediate pain relief following application of a Band-Aid to whatever spot hurts. Although most adults know that Band-Aids don't treat pain, the placebo effect remains powerful throughout the life span.

its painkilling effects because it triggers the release of endorphins.

In another advance in the study of these effects, placebos were found to lower the activation of specific brain areas associated with pain. One set of fMRI studies examined brain activation as volunteers were exposed to electric shock or heat (Wager et al., 2004). In preparation for some exposures to these painful stimuli, a placebo cream was applied to the skin, and the participant was told it was an analgesic that

would reduce the pain. Other participants merely experienced the pain. As you can see in the accompanying images, the fMRI scans showed decreased activation during placebo analgesia in the *thalamus, anterior cingulate cortex,* and *insula,* pain-sensitive brain regions that were activated during untreated pain. These findings suggest that placebos do not lead people to misreport their pain experience but rather reduce brain activity in areas that normally are active during pain experience.

Such findings don't mean that next time your stomach aches, you can break out a Band-Aid and heal yourself. Part of the placebo effect depends on the conscious expectation that the placebo will work, and it could be a challenge to make yourself believe you will feel better when you don't. Part of the placebo effect is unconscious, though, a tendency to feel better that is learned through classical conditioning. When you've been healed in the past by a particular doctor or form of treatment, or when you've been in a particular setting, unconscious learning mechanisms may lead to improvement if you simply encounter a similar doctor, treatment, or setting again, even if you don't consciously expect to improve (Benedetti, Pollo, et al., 2003). There's something comforting about returning to things that have given you comfort in the past.

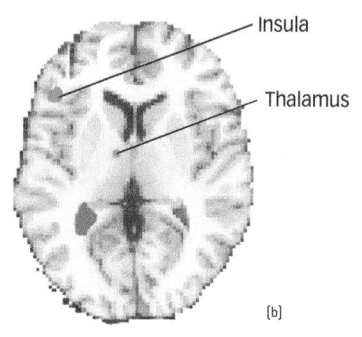

Insula

Thalamus

Anterior cingulate cortex

[a]   [b]

▲ **THE BRAIN'S RESPONSE TO PLACEBO** These fMRI scans reveal that some brain regions normally activated when individuals report pain in response to shocks are deactivated when those individuals are given a placebo analgesic during the shock. These regions include (a) the anterior cingulate cortex and (b) the insula and thalamus (Wager et al., 2004).

one bodily symptom displays significant health-related anxiety, expresses disproportionate concerns about their symptoms, and devotes excessive time and energy to their symptoms or health concerns. These are disorders such as those that will be discussed in the Psychological Disorders chapter, but their association with symptoms in the body makes them relevant to this chapter's concern with stress and health. Disorders focused on concerns about physical illness used to be called *somatoform disorders* and included

Have you ever ridden on a crowded train next to a person with a hacking cough or aggressive sneeze? We are bombarded by advertisements for medicines designed to suppress symptoms of illness so we can keep going. Is staying home with a cold socially acceptable? Or is it considered malingering? How does this jibe with the concept of the *sick role*?

categories such as hypochondriasis. Somatoform disorders were those in which people experienced unexplained medical symptoms believed to be generated by the mind. However, the focus on psychosomatic illness has shifted from concerns about mentally generated physical symptoms to excessive psychological concerns about explainable medical symptoms, with the idea that the latter are serious and could benefit from psychological intervention. Some believe this shift in focus is problematic and will lead psychologists and psychiatrists to label normal concern about one's health as a psychological disorder. The interesting and somewhat complicated question of what should be considered a psychological disorder and what should not is something we tackle more directly in the next chapter on Psychological Disorders.

ON BEING A PATIENT

Getting sick is more than a change in physical state: It can involve a transformation of identity. This change can be particularly profound with a serious illness: A kind of cloud settles over you, a feeling that you are now different, and this transformation can influence everything you feel and do in this new world of illness. You even take on a new role in life, a **sick role**: *a socially recognized set of rights and obligations linked with illness* (Parsons, 1975). The sick person is absolved of responsibility for many everyday obligations and enjoys exemption from normal activities. For example, in addition to skipping school and homework and staying on the couch all day, a sick child can watch TV and avoid eating anything unpleasant at dinner. At the extreme, the sick person can get away with being rude, lazy, demanding, and picky. In return for these exemptions, the sick role also incurs obligations. The properly "sick" individual cannot appear to enjoy the illness or reveal signs of wanting to be sick and must also take care to pursue treatment to end this "undesirable" condition. Parsons observed that illness has psychological, social, and even moral components. You may recall times when you have felt the conflict between sickness and health as though it were a moral decision: Should you drag yourself out of bed and try to make it to the chemistry exam or just slump back under the covers and wallow in your "pain"?

Some people feign medical or psychological symptoms to achieve something they want, a type of behavior called *malingering*. Because many symptoms of illness cannot be faked (even facial expressions of pain are difficult to simulate; Williams, 2002), malingering is possible only with a small number of illnesses. Faking illness is suspected when the secondary gains of illness, such as the ability to rest, to be freed from performing unpleasant tasks, or to be helped by others, outweigh the costs. Such gains can be very subtle, as when a child stays in bed because of the comfort provided by an otherwise distant parent, or they can be obvious, as when insurance benefits turn out to be a cash award for best actor. Some behaviors that may lead to illness may not be under the patient's control; for example, self-starvation may be part of an uncontrollable eating disorder (see the Emotion and Motivation chapter). For this reason, malingering can be difficult to diagnose and treat (Bass & Halligan, 2014).

PATIENT–PRACTITIONER INTERACTION

Medical care usually occurs through a strange interaction. On one side is a patient, often miserable, who expects to be questioned and examined and possibly prodded, pained, or given bad news. On the other side is a health care provider, who comes in knowing nothing about what brings the patient in but who hopes to quickly obtain information from the patient by asking lots of extremely personal questions (and examining extremely personal parts of the body); to identify the problem and a potential solution; to help in some way; and to achieve all of this as efficiently as possible because more patients are waiting. It seems less like a time for healing than an occasion for major awkwardness. One of the keys to an effective medical care interaction is

sick role A socially recognized set of rights and obligations linked with illness.

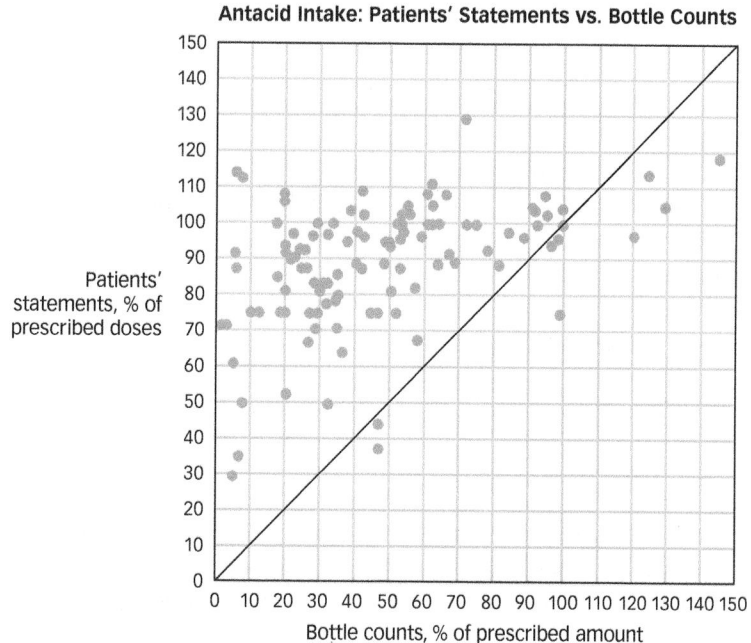

Antacid Intake: Patients' Statements vs. Bottle Counts

Patients' statements, % of prescribed doses

Bottle counts, % of prescribed amount

◄ **Figure 14.6**

ANTACID INTAKE A scatterplot of antacid intake measured by bottle count plotted against patient's stated intake for 116 patients. When the actual and stated intakes are the same, the point lies on the diagonal line; when stated intake is greater than actual, the point lies above the line. Most patients exaggerated their intake (Roth & Caron, 1978).

physician empathy (Kelm et al., 2014). To offer successful treatment, the clinician must simultaneously understand the patient's physical state *and* psychological state. Physicians often err on the side of failing to acknowledge patients' emotions, focusing instead on technical issues of the case (Suchman et al., 1997). This is particularly unfortunate, because a substantial percentage of patients who seek medical care do so for treatment of psychological and emotional problems (Wiegner et al., 2015). As the Greek physician Hippocrates wrote in the 4th century B.C.E.: "Some patients, though conscious that their condition is perilous, recover their health simply through their contentment with the goodness of the physician." The best physician treats the patient's mind as well as the patient's body.

Another important part of the medical care interaction is motivating the patient to follow the prescribed regimen of care (Miller & Rollnick, 2012). When researchers check compliance by counting the pills remaining in a patient's bottle after a prescription has been started, they find that patients often do an astonishingly poor job of following doctors' orders (see **FIGURE 14.6**). Compliance deteriorates when the treatment must be frequent, as when eye drops for glaucoma are required every few hours, or inconvenient or painful, such as drawing blood or performing injections in managing diabetes. Finally, compliance decreases *as the* number *of* treatments increases. This is a worrisome problem, especially for older patients, who may have difficulty remembering when to take which pill. Failures in medical care may stem from the failure of health care providers to recognize the psychological challenges that are involved in self-care. Helping people follow doctors' orders involves psychology, not medicine, and is an essential part of promoting health.

Doctor and patient have two modes of interaction, the technical and the interpersonal. Medical training with robot patients may help doctors learn the technical side of health care, but it is likely to do little to improve the interpersonal side.

Build to the Outcomes

1. What are the physical benefits of the sickness response?

2. What is the relationship between pain and activity in the brain?

3. How can hypersensitivity to symptoms undermine health?

4. What benefits might come from being ill?

5. Why is it important that a physician express empathy?

The Psychology of Health: Feeling Good

Learning Outcome

▶ Explain the attitudes and behaviors that lead to good health.

"Whoa—way too much information."

Adrianne Haslet was approximately 4 feet away from one of the bombs that exploded at the Boston Marathon in 2013. Although the explosion caused her to lose her left foot, Adrianne vowed that she would continue her career as a dancer—and she actually ran in the Boston Marathon in 2016. She is an optimist, and optimism can lead to positive health outcomes.

Two kinds of psychological factors influence personal health: health-relevant personality traits and health behavior. Personality can influence health through relatively enduring traits that make some people particularly susceptible to health problems or stress while sparing or protecting others. The Type A behavior pattern is an example. Because personality is not typically something we choose ("I'd like a bit of that sense of humor and extraversion over there, please, but hold the whininess"), this source of health can be beyond personal control. In contrast, engaging in positive health behaviors is something anyone can do, at least in principle.

PERSONALITY AND HEALTH

Different health problems seem to plague different social groups. For example, men are more susceptible to heart disease than are women, and African Americans are more susceptible to asthma than are Asian or European Americans. Beyond these general social categories, personality turns out to be a factor in wellness, with individual differences in optimism and hardiness being important influences.

Optimism

Pollyanna is one of literature's most famous optimists. Eleanor H. Porter's 1913 novel portrayed Pollyanna as a girl who greeted life with boundless good cheer, even when she was orphaned and sent to live with her cruel aunt. Her response to a sunny day was to remark on the good weather, of course, but her response to a gloomy day was to point out how lucky it is that not every day is gloomy! Her crotchety Aunt Polly had exactly the opposite attitude, somehow managing to turn every happy moment into an opportunity for strict correction. A person's level of optimism or pessimism tends to be fairly stable over time, and research comparing the personalities of twins reared together with those of twins reared apart suggests that this stability arises because these traits are moderately heritable (Plomin et al., 1992). Perhaps Pollyanna and Aunt Polly were each "born that way."

An optimist who believes that "in uncertain times, I usually expect the best" is likely to be healthier than a pessimist who believes that "if something can go wrong for me, it will." One recent review of dozens of studies including tens of thousands of participants concluded that of all of the measures of psychological well-being examined, optimism is the one that most strongly predicted a positive outcome for cardiovascular health (Boehm & Kubzansky, 2012). It is important to note that the association between optimism and cardiovascular health remains even after statistically controlling for traditional risk factors for heart disease including depression and anxiety, suggesting that it is not merely the absence of psychopathology but the presence of positive expectancies for the future that predicts positive health outcomes. Does just having positive thoughts about the future make it so? Unfortunately not.

Rather than improving physical health directly, optimism seems to aid in the maintenance of *psychological* health in the face of physical health problems. When sick, optimists are more likely than pessimists to maintain positive emotions, avoid negative emotions such as anxiety and depression, stick to the medical regimens their caregivers have prescribed, and keep up their relationships with others. Among women who have surgery for breast cancer, for example, optimists are less likely to experience distress and fatigue after treatment than are pessimists, largely because they keep up social contacts and recreational activities during their treatment (Carver, Lehman, & Antoni, 2003). Optimism also seems to aid in the maintenance of physical health. For instance, optimism appears to be associated with cardiovascular health because optimistic people tend to engage in healthier behaviors such as eating a balanced diet and exercising, which in turn leads to a healthier lipid profile, which decreases the risk of heart disease (Boehm et al., 2013). (Higher levels of high-density lipoprotein cholesterol help to prevent buildup in your arteries and lower triglycerides, which are the chemical form of fat storage in the body.) So being optimistic is a positive asset, but it takes more than just hope to obtain positive health benefits.

The benefits of optimism raise an important question: If the traits of optimism and pessimism are stable over time—even resistant to change—can pessimists ever hope to gain any of the advantages of optimism (Heatherton & Weinberger, 1994)? Research has shown that even die-hard pessimists can be trained to become significantly more optimistic and that this training can improve their psychosocial health outcomes. For example, pessimistic breast cancer patients who received 10 weeks of training in stress management techniques became more optimistic and were less likely than those who received only relaxation exercises to suffer distress and fatigue during their cancer treatments (Antoni et al., 2001).

Hardiness

Some people seem to be thick-skinned, somehow able to take stress or abuse that could be devastating to others. Are there personality traits that contribute to such resilience and offer protection from stress-induced illness? To identify such traits, Suzanne Kobasa (1979) studied a group of stress-resistant business executives. These individuals reported high levels of stressful life events but had histories of relatively few illnesses compared with a similar group who succumbed to stress by getting sick. The stress-resistant group (Kobasa labeled them *hardy*) shared several traits, all conveniently beginning with the letter C. They showed a sense of *commitment,* an ability to become involved in life's tasks and encounters rather than just dabbling. They exhibited a belief in *control,* the expectation that their actions and words have a causal influence over their lives and environment. And they were willing to accept *challenge,* undertaking change and accepting opportunities for growth.

Can just anyone develop hardiness? Researchers have attempted to teach hardiness with some success. In one such attempt, participants attended 10 weekly hardiness-training sessions, in which they were encouraged to examine their stresses, develop action plans for dealing with them, explore their bodily reactions to stress, and find ways to compensate for unchangeable situations without falling into self-pity. Compared with control groups (who engaged in relaxation and meditation training or in group discussions about stress), the hardiness-training group reported greater reductions in their perceived personal stress as well as fewer symptoms of illness (Maddi, Kahn, & Maddi, 1998). Hardiness training can have similar positive effects in college students, for some even boosting their GPA (Maddi et al., 2009).

Sometimes hardiness tips over the edge into foolhardiness. Members of the Coney Island Polar Bear Club take the plunge every Sunday of winter.

HEALTH-PROMOTING BEHAVIORS AND SELF-REGULATION

Even without changing our personalities at all, we can do certain things to be healthy. The importance of healthy eating, safe sex, and giving up smoking are common knowledge. But we don't seem to be acting on the basis of this knowledge. Sixty-nine percent of Americans over 20 are overweight or obese (National Center for Health Statistics, 2012). The prevalence of unsafe sex is difficult to estimate, but 65 million Americans currently suffer from an incurable sexually transmitted disease (STD), and 20 million contract one or more new STDs each year (Satterwhite et al., 2013). Another million people live with human immunodeficiency virus/acquired immune deficiency syndrome (HIV/AIDS). Of these, 18.1% are unaware of their infection, which is usually contracted through unprotected sex with an infected partner (Centers for Disease Control and Prevention [CDC], 2012). And despite endless warnings, 17% of U.S. adults still smoke cigarettes (CDC, 2015). What's going on?

self-regulation The exercise of voluntary control over the self to bring the self into line with preferred standards.

Self-regulation

Doing what is good for you is not necessarily easy. Mark Twain once remarked, "The only way to keep your health is to eat what you don't want, drink what you don't like, and do what you'd rather not." Engaging in health-promoting behaviors involves **self-regulation**, *the exercise of voluntary control over the self to bring the self into line with preferred standards*. When you decide on a salad rather than a cheeseburger, for instance, you control your impulse and behave in a way that will help to make you the kind of person you would prefer to be—a healthy one. Self-regulation often involves putting off immediate gratification for longer-term gains.

Self-regulation requires a kind of inner strength or willpower. One theory suggests that self-control is a kind of strength that can be fatigued (Baumeister, Vohs, & Tice, 2007). In other words, trying to exercise control in one area may exhaust self-control, leaving behavior in other areas unregulated. To test this theory, researchers seated hungry volunteers near a batch of fresh, hot, chocolate chip cookies. They asked some participants to leave the cookies alone but help themselves to a healthy snack of radishes, whereas others were allowed to indulge. When later challenged with an impossibly difficult figure-tracing task, the self-control group was more likely than the self-indulgent group to abandon the difficult task—behavior interpreted as evidence that they had depleted their pool of self-control (Baumeister et al., 1998). The take-home message from this experiment is that to control behavior successfully, we need to choose our battles, exercising self-control mainly on the personal weaknesses that are most harmful to health. Most important, however, the exact nature of this effect is still being debated; several research teams have failed to replicate this earlier work (e.g., Lurquin et al., 2016).

Sometimes self-regulation is less a matter of brute force than of strategy. Martial artists claim that anyone can easily overcome a large attacker with the right moves, and overcoming our own unhealthy impulses may also be a matter of finesse. Let's look carefully at healthy approaches to some key challenges for self-regulation—eating, safe sex, and smoking—to learn which "smart moves" can aid us in our struggles.

Nobody ever said self-control was easy. Probably the only reason you're able to keep yourself from eating this cookie is that it's just a picture of a cookie. Really. Don't eat it.

Eating Wisely

In many Western cultures, the weight of the average citizen is increasing alarmingly. One explanation is based on our evolutionary history: In order to ensure their survival, our ancestors found it useful to eat well in times of plenty to store calories for leaner times. In 21st-century postindustrial societies, however, there are no leaner times, and people can't burn all of the calories they consume (Pinel, Assanand, & Lehman, 2000). But why, then, isn't obesity endemic throughout the Western world? Why are people in France leaner on average than Americans, even though their foods are high in fat? One reason has to do with the fact that activity level in France is higher. Research by Paul Rozin and his colleagues also finds that portion sizes in France are significantly smaller than in the United States, but at the same time, people in France take longer to finish their smaller meals. At a McDonald's in France, diners take an average of 22 minutes to consume a meal, whereas in the United States, they take under 15 minutes (Rozin, Kabnick, et al., 2003). Right now, Americans seem to be involved in some kind of national eating contest, whereas in France people are eating less food more slowly, perhaps leading them to be more conscious of what they are eating. This, ironically, probably leads to lower French fry consumption.

Short of moving to France, what can you do? Studies indicate that dieting doesn't always work because the process of conscious self-regulation can easily be undermined by stress, causing people who are trying to control themselves to lose control by overindulging in the very behavior they had been trying to overcome. This may remind you of a general principle we discussed in the Consciousness chapter: Trying hard not to do something can often directly result in the unwanted behavior (Wegner, 1994a, 1994b).

One of the reasons that people in France are leaner than people in the United States is that the average French diner spends 22 minutes to consume a fast-food meal, whereas the average American diner spends only 15 minutes. How could the length of the average meal influence an individual's body weight?

The restraint problem may be inherent in the very act of self-control (Polivy & Herman, 1992). Rather than dieting, then, heading toward normal weight should involve a new emphasis on exercise and nutrition (Prochaska & Sallis, 2004). In emphasizing what is good to eat, a person can think freely about food rather than trying to suppress thoughts about it. A focus on increasing activity rather than reducing food intake, in turn, gives people another positive and active goal to pursue. Self-regulation is more effective when it focuses on what to do rather than on what *not* to do (Molden, Lee, & Higgins, 2009; Wegner & Wenzlaff, 1996).

Avoiding Sexual Risks

People put themselves at risk when they have unprotected vaginal, oral, or anal intercourse. Sexually active adolescents and adults are usually aware of such risks, not to mention the risk of unwanted pregnancy, and yet many behave in risky ways nonetheless. Why doesn't awareness translate into avoidance? Risk takers harbor an *illusion of unique invulnerability,* a systematic bias toward believing that they are less likely to fall victim to the problem than are others (Perloff & Fetzer, 1986). For example, a study of sexually active female college students found that respondents judged their own likelihood of getting pregnant in the next year as less than 10%, but estimated the average for other women at the university to be 27% (Burger & Burns, 1988). Paradoxically, this illusion was even stronger among women in the sample who reported using inadequate or no contraceptive techniques. The tendency to think "It won't happen to me" may be most pronounced when it probably will.

Unprotected sex often is the impulsive result of last-minute emotions. When thought is further blurred by alcohol or recreational drugs, people often fail to use the latex condoms that can reduce their exposure to the risks of pregnancy, HIV, and many other STDs. Like other forms of self-regulation, the avoidance of sexual risk requires the kind of planning that can easily be undone by circumstances that hamper the ability to think ahead. One approach to reducing sexual risk taking, then, is simply finding ways to help people plan ahead. Sex education programs offer adolescents just such a chance by encouraging them, at a time when they have not had much sexual experience, to think about what they might do when they need to make decisions. Although sex education is sometimes criticized as increasing adolescents' awareness of and interest in sex, the research evidence is clear: Sex education reduces the likelihood that adolescents will engage in unprotected sexual activity and benefits their health (American Psychological Association, 2005). The same holds true for adults.

Not Smoking

One in two smokers dies prematurely from smoking-related diseases such as lung cancer, heart disease, emphysema, and cancer of the mouth and throat. Lung cancer alone kills more people than any other form of cancer, and smoking causes 80% of lung cancers. Although the overall rate of smoking in the United States is declining,

DATA VISUALIZATION

How Are Stress and Eating Habits Related?
Go to launchpadworks.com.

"Boy, I'm going to pay for this tomorrow at yoga class."

ALEX GREGORY/THE NEW YORKER COLLECTION/WWW.CARTOONBANK.COM

new smokers abound, and many can't seem to stop. College students are puffing away along with everyone else, with 20% of college students currently smoking (Thompson et al., 2007). In the face of all the devastating health consequences, why don't people quit?

Nicotine, the active ingredient in cigarettes, is addictive, so smoking is difficult to stop once the habit is established (as discussed in the Consciousness chapter). As with other forms of self-regulation, the resolve to quit smoking is fragile and seems to break down under stress. In the months following 9/11, for example, cigarette sales jumped 13% in Massachusetts (Phillips, 2002). And for some time after quitting, ex-smokers remain sensitive to cues in the environment: Eating or drinking, a bad mood, anxiety, or just seeing someone else smoking is enough to make them want a cigarette (Shiffman et al., 1996). The good news is that the urge diminishes, and people become less likely to relapse the longer they've been away from nicotine.

OTHER VOICES

The Dangers of Overparenting

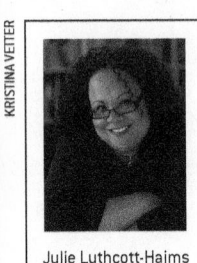

KRISTINA VETTER

Julie Lythcott-Haims

Many parents want to protect their children from experiencing any stress or hardship. This is only natural; we want to protect the ones we love from being hurt, and we want to ensure that they have the best life possible. But is there a downside to doing so? Julie Lythcott-Haims, who for a decade served as Stanford University's Dean of Freshman, believes that "overparenting" can cause significant harm by depriving children of opportunities to learn creativity, competence, and confidence, and to develop a true sense of who they really are. In her new book, "How to raise an adult," Lythcott-Haims describes how overbearing "helicopter parenting" can backfire among college students.

I became a university dean because I'm interested in supporting humans in growing to become who they're meant to become, unfettered by circumstances or other people's expectations. I expected that the kids who would need my help would be first-generation college students or low-income kids, and these populations certainly benefited from the mentorship and support that a dean could provide. But it was my solidly middle- or upper-middle-class students who had the most bewildered looks on their faces, looks that turned to relief when Mom or Dad handled the situations, what it was. These parents seemed involved in their college students' lives in ways that held their kids back instead of propelling them forward.

In 2013 the news was filled with worrisome statistics about the mental health crisis on college campuses, particularly the number of students medicated for depression. Charlie Gofen, the retired chairman of the board at the Latin School of Chicago, a private school serving about 1,100 students, emailed the statistics off to a colleague at another school and asked, "Do you think parents at your school would rather their kid be depressed at Yale or happy at University of Arizona?" The colleague quickly replied, "My guess is 75 percent of the parents would rather see their kids depressed at Yale. They figure that the kid can straighten the emotional stuff out in his/her 20's, but no one can go back and get the Yale undergrad degree."

In 2013 the American College Health Association surveyed close to 100,000 college students from 153 different campuses about their health. When asked about their experiences, at some point over the past 12 months:

- 84.3 percent felt overwhelmed by all they had to do

- 60.5 percent felt very sad
- 57.0 percent felt very lonely
- 51.3 percent felt overwhelming anxiety
- 8.0 percent seriously considered suicide

You're right to be thinking *Yes, but do we know whether overparenting causes this rise in mental health problems?* The answer is that we don't have studies proving causation, but a number of recent studies show *correlation*.

In 2010, psychology professor Neil Montgomery of Keene State College in New Hampshire surveyed 300 college freshmen nationwide and found that students with helicopter parents were less open to new ideas and actions and more vulnerable, anxious, and self-conscious. "[S]tudents who were given responsibility and not constantly monitored by their parents—so-called 'free rangers'—the effects were reversed," Montgomery's study found. A 2011 study by Terri LeMoyne and Tom Buchanan at the University of Tennessee at Chattanooga looking at more than 300 students found that students with "hovering" or "helicopter" parents are more likely to be medicated for anxiety and/or depression.

When parents have tended to do the stuff of life for kids—the waking up, the transporting, the reminding about deadlines and obligations, the bill-paying, the question-asking, the decision-making, the responsibility-taking, the talking to strangers, and the confronting of authorities, kids may be in for quite a shock when parents turn them loose in the world of college or work. They will experience setbacks, which will feel to them like failure. Lurking beneath the problem of whatever thing needs to be handled is the student's inability to differentiate the self from the parent.

Here's the point—and this is so much more important than I realized until rather recently when the data started coming in: The research shows that figuring out for themselves is a critical element to people's mental health. Your kids have to be there for *themselves*. That's a harder truth to swallow when your kid is in the midst of a problem or worse, a crisis, but taking the long view, it's the best medicine for them.

Is being exposed to stressful situations necessarily a bad thing? How else will we learn how to cope with difficult situations? If we never learn to do so, we may be more likely to experience some of the bad outcomes that Lythcott-Haims writes about. So get out there, get stressed, and manage it!

Psychological programs and techniques to help people kick the habit include nicotine replacement systems such as gum and skin patches, counseling programs, and hypnosis, but these programs are not always successful. Trying again and again in different ways is apparently the best approach (Schachter, 1982). After all, to quit smoking forever, you need to quit only one more time than you start up. But like the self-regulation of eating and sexuality, the self-regulation of smoking can require effort and thought. The ancient Greeks blamed self-control problems on *akrasia* (weakness of will). Modern psychology focuses less on blaming a person's character for poor self-regulation and points instead toward the difficulty of the task. Keeping healthy by behaving in healthy ways is one of the great challenges of life (see Other Voices: The Dangers of Overparenting).

Build to the Outcomes

1. Why do optimists tend to have better health?

2. What is hardiness?

3. Why is it difficult to achieve and maintain self-control?

4. Why is exercise a more effective weight-loss choice than dieting?

5. Why does planning ahead reduce sexual risk-taking?

6. To quit smoking forever, how many times do you need to quit?

Chapter Review

Sources of Stress: What Gets to You

▶ Stressors are events and threats that place specific demands on a person or threaten well-being.

▶ Sources of stress include negative life events, but even happy ones require readjustment and preparedness. Chronic stress involves triggers that occur repeatedly, some that are social and some that can be traced to a particular environment.

▶ Events are most stressful when we perceive that there is no way to control or deal with the challenge.

Stress Reactions: All Shook Up

▶ The body responds to stress with an initial fight-or-flight reaction, which activates the hypothalamic–pituitary–adrenocortical (HPA) axis and prepares the body to face the threat or run away from it.

▶ The general adaptation syndrome (GAS) outlines three phases of stress response that occur regardless of the type of stressor: alarm, resistance, and exhaustion.

▶ Chronic stress can wear down the immune system, causing susceptibility to infection, aging, tumor growth, organ damage, and death. People who respond to stress with anger are most at risk of heart disease.

▶ The response to stress will vary depending on whether it's interpreted as something that can be overcome or not.

▶ If prolonged, the psychological response to stress can lead to burnout. It is a particular problem in professions where emotional turmoil is part of the job.

Stress Management: Dealing With It

▶ The management of stress involves strategies for influencing the mind, the body, and the situation.

▶ People try to manage their minds by suppressing stressful thoughts or avoiding the situations that produce them, by rationally coping with the stressor, and by reframing.

▶ Body management strategies involve attempting to reduce stress symptoms through meditation, relaxation, biofeedback, and aerobic exercise.

▶ Overcoming stress by managing your situation can involve seeking out social support, engaging in religious experiences, or attempting to find humor in stressful events.

▶ The Learning chapter details reasons why it's important to avoid procrastinating studying for a test, and there are health reasons as well.

The Psychology of Illness: Mind Over Matter

▶ The psychology of illness concerns how sensitivity to the body leads people to recognize illness and seek treatment.

▶ Somatic symptom disorders can stem from excessive sensitivity to physical problems.

▶ The sick role is a set of rights and obligations linked with illness; some people fake illness in order to accrue those rights.

▶ Successful health care providers interact with their patients to understand both the physical state and the psychological state.

The Psychology of Health: Feeling Good

▶ The connection between mind and body can be revealed through the influences of personality and self-regulation of behavior on health.

▶ The personality traits of optimism and hardiness are associated with reduced risk for illnesses, perhaps because people with these traits can fend off stress.

▶ The self-regulation of behaviors such as eating, sexuality, and smoking is difficult for many people because self-regulation is easily disrupted by stress; strategies for maintaining self-control can pay off with significant improvements in health and quality of life.

KEY CONCEPT QUIZ

1. What kinds of stressors are you likely to be exposed to if you live in a dense urban area with considerable traffic, noise, and pollution?
   a. cultural stressors
   b. intermittent stressors
   c. chronic stressors
   d. positive stressors

2. In an experiment, two groups are subjected to distractions while attempting to complete a task. Those in group A are told they can quiet the distractions by pushing a button. This information is withheld from group B. Why will group A's performance at the task likely be better than group B's?
   a. Group B is working in a different environment.
   b. Group A has perceived control over a source of performance-impeding stress.
   c. Group B is less distracted than group A.
   d. The distractions affecting group B are now chronic.

3. According to the general adaptation syndrome, during the _____ phase, the body adapts to its high state of arousal as it tries to cope with a stressor.
   a. exhaustion
   b. alarm
   c. resistance
   d. energy

4. Which of the following statements most accurately describes the physiological response to stress?
   a. Type A behavior patterns have psychological but not physiological ramifications.
   b. The link between work-related stress and coronary heart disease is unfounded.
   c. Stressors can cause hormones to flood the brain, strengthening the immune system.
   d. The immune system is remarkably responsive to psychological influences.

5. Engaging in aerobic exercise is a way of managing stress by managing the
   a. environment.
   b. body.
   c. situation.
   d. intake of air.

6. Finding a new or creative way to think about a stressor that reduces its threat is called
   a. stress inoculation.
   b. repressive coping.
   c. reframing.
   d. rational coping.

7. Faking an illness is a violation of
   a. malingering.
   b. somatoform disorder.
   c. the sick role.
   d. the Type B pattern of behavior.

8. Which of the following describes a successful health care provider?
   a. displays empathy
   b. pays attention to both the physical and psychological states of the patient
   c. uses psychology to promote patient compliance
   d. all of the above

9. When sick, optimists are more likely than pessimists to
   a. maintain positive emotions.
   b. become depressed.
   c. ignore their caregiver's advice.
   d. avoid contact with others.

10. Stress _____ the self-regulation of behaviors such as eating and smoking.
   a. strengthens
   b. has no effect on
   c. disrupts
   d. normalizes

 LearningCurve Don't stop now! Quizzing yourself is a powerful study tool. Go to LaunchPad to access the LearningCurve adaptive quizzing system and your own personalized learning plan. Visit launchpadworks.com.

KEY TERMS

stressors (p. 552)

stress (p. 552)

health psychology (p. 552)

chronic stressors (p. 554)

fight-or-flight response (p. 556)

general adaptation syndrome (GAS) (p. 557)

telomeres (p. 558)

telomerase (p. 558)

immune system (p. 560)

lymphocytes (p. 560)

Type A behavior pattern (p. 561)

burnout (p. 563)

repressive coping (p. 564)

rational coping (p. 565)

reframing (p. 565)

stress inoculation training (SIT) (p. 566)

meditation (p. 566)

relaxation therapy (p. 567)

relaxation response (p. 567)

biofeedback (p. 567)

social support (p. 569)

psychosomatic illness (p. 574)

somatic symptom disorders (p. 574)

sick role (p. 576)

self-regulation (p. 580)

CHANGING MINDS

1. In 2002, researchers compared severe acne in college students during a relatively stress-free period with acne during a highly stressful exam period. After adjusting for other variables such as changes in sleep or diet, the researchers concluded that increased acne severity was strongly correlated with increased levels of stress. Learning about the study, your roommate is surprised. "Acne is a skin disease," your roommate says. "I don't see how it could have anything to do with your mental state." How would you weigh in on the role of stress in medical diseases? What other examples could you give of ways in which stress can affect health?

2. A friend of yours who is taking a heavy course load confides that he's feeling overwhelmed. "I can't take the stress," he says. "Sometimes I daydream of living on an island somewhere, where I can just lie in the sun and have no stress at all." What would you tell your friend about stress? Is all stress bad? What would a life with no stress really be like?

3. One of your classmates spent the summer interning in a neurologist's office. "One of the most fascinating things," she says, "was the patients with psychosomatic illness. Some had seizures or partial paralysis of an arm, and there were no neurological causes—so it was all psychosomatic. The neurologist tried to refer these patients to psychiatrists, but a lot of the patients thought he was accusing them of faking their symptoms, and were very insulted." What would you tell your friend about psychosomatic illness? Could a disease that's "all in the head" really produce symptoms such as seizures or partial paralysis, or are these patients definitely faking their symptoms?

ANSWERS TO KEY CONCEPT QUIZ

1. c; 2. b; 3. c; 4. d; 5. b; 6. c; 7. c; 8. d; 9. a; 10. c.

LaunchPad features the full e-Book of *Psychology*, the LearningCurve adaptive quizzing system, videos, and a variety of activities to boost your learning. Visit LaunchPad at launchpadworks.com.

Psychological Disorders

15

R OBIN WILLIAMS WAS ONE OF THE FUNNIEST and most beloved comedians in history. Over the course of his nearly 40-year career, Williams was an amazingly successful stand-up comedian, television star, movie star, and philanthropist. He was best known for his fun and zany improvisational style and his ability to consistently make others laugh. He appeared as an actor in over 100 films and television shows, including four major movies released in 2014. On August 11, 2014, Williams locked himself in his bedroom and hanged himself with his belt, dying by suicide. Why would a person who appeared to be so happy, and who was so successful, active, and beloved purposely end his life?

What many people familiar with Robin Williams's professional career did not know was that he had suffered from mental illness for years. Throughout his life, Williams struggled with drug- and alcohol-use disorders that impaired his ability to function and led to multiple hospitalizations. Williams also suffered from major depressive disorder, a condition characterized by long periods of depressed mood, diminished interest in pleasurable activities, feelings of worthlessness, and problems with eating and sleeping. Shortly before his death, he also was diagnosed with Parkinson's disease and dementia, conditions associated with a progressive decline of physical and mental abilities. Many people who are suicidal say that their motivation to die is to escape from some seemingly intolerable situation, such as a long-term struggle with mental illness. That may have been the reason for Williams's suicide, although we will never know for sure.

Williams's case highlights several important facts about mental disorders. They can affect anyone, regardless of the amount of perceived happiness or success one has had. They are characterized by extreme distress and impairment, often limiting a person's ability to carry out their daily activities. But at the same time, many people suffer from them silently, unknown to those around them. And finally, in extreme cases, they can be lethal, leading to severe self-injury or death by suicide. Thus, there is a great need for us to better understand what mental disorders are and what causes them.

MARARTEN DE BOER/SAGF/CONTOUR BY GETTY IMAGES

The actor and comedian Robin Williams (1951–2014) in 2009. Williams was a brilliant performer who had audiences laughing for over 40 years. In his personal life, however, he suffered with bouts of addiction, depression, and dementia, ending with his suicide in 2014.

◄ EASYFOTOSTOCK/AGE FOTOSTOCK

IN THIS CHAPTER, WE FIRST CONSIDER THE QUESTION, What is abnormal? Robin Williams's bouts of addiction, depression, and dementia, along with his eventual suicide, certainly are abnormal in the sense that most people do not have these experiences. However, at times, he led a perfectly normal and happy life. The enormously complicated human mind can produce behaviors, thoughts, and emotions that change radically from moment to moment. How do psychologists decide when a person's thoughts, emotions, and behaviors are "disordered"? We will first examine the key factors that must be weighed in making such a decision. We'll then focus on several major forms of *mental disorder:* depressive and bipolar disorders; anxiety, obsessive-compulsive, and trauma-related disorders; schizophrenia; disorders that begin in childhood and adolescence; and self-harm behaviors. As we view each type of disorder, we will examine how they manifest and what is known about their prevalence and causes.

The disorders examined in this chapter represent a tragic loss of human potential. The contentment, peace, and love that people could be enjoying are crowded out by pain, suffering, and impairment. A new scientific approach to mental disorders considers the biological, psychological, and social factors that combine to cause disorders. Appropriately called the *biopyschosocial model*, this approach is beginning to sort out the symptoms and causes of mental disorders. As we will see in the next chapter, this approach already offers remarkably effective treatments for some disorders; for other disorders, it offers hope that pain and suffering can be alleviated in the future.

Defining Mental Disorders: What Is Abnormal?

Learning Outcomes

► Explain why the *DSM* has become a more credible diagnostic tool over the course of revisions to each edition.

► Identify the fundamental ideas behind the medical model, the biopsychosocial perspective, and the diathesis–stress model.

► Relate how the RDoC expands on the *DSM*.

► Explain why labeling someone with a disorder can be problematic.

The concept of a mental disorder is one of those things that seems simple at first glance, but turns out to be very complex and quite tricky (similar to clearly defining "consciousness," "stress," or "personality"). Any extreme variation in your thoughts, feelings, or behaviors is not a mental disorder. For instance, severe anxiety before a test, sadness after the loss of a loved one, or a night of excessive alcohol consumption—although unpleasant—is not necessarily pathological. Similarly, a persistent pattern of deviating from the norm does not qualify as a mental disorder. If it did, we would diagnose mental disorders in the most creative and visionary people—anyone whose ideas deviate from those of people around them.

So what *is* a mental disorder? Perhaps surprisingly, there is no universal agreement on a precise definition of the term *mental disorder*. However, there is general agreement that a **mental disorder** can be broadly defined as *a persistent disturbance or dysfunction in behavior, thoughts, or emotions that causes significant distress or impairment* (Stein et al., 2010; Wakefield, 2007). One way to think about mental disorders is as dysfunctions or deficits in the normal human psychological processes you have learned about throughout this textbook. People with mental disorders have problems with their perception, memory, learning, emotions, motivation, thinking, and social processes. Of course, this definition leaves many questions unanswered. What kinds of disturbances count as mental disorders? How long must they last to be considered "persistent"? And how much distress or impairment is required? These are all still hotly debated questions in the field.

CONCEPTUALIZING MENTAL DISORDERS

Since ancient times, there have been reports of people acting strangely or reporting bizarre thoughts or emotions. Until fairly recently, such difficulties were conceptualized

mental disorder A persistent disturbance or dysfunction in behavior, thoughts, or emotions that causes significant distress or impairment.

Although mental disorders are deviations from normal behavior, not all deviations from the norm are disordered. Indeed, people thinking differently about the world, and behaving in ways that deviated from the norm, have brought remarkable advances, such as Mickey Mouse, iPhones, and racial equality.

as the result of religious or supernatural forces. In some cultures, psychopathology is still interpreted as possession by spirits or demons, as enchantment by a witch or sha-man, or as God's punishment for wrongdoing. In many societies, including our own, people with psychological disorders have been feared and ridiculed, and often treated as criminals: punished, imprisoned, or put to death for their "crime" of deviating from the normal.

Over the past 200 years, these ways of looking at psychological abnormalities have largely been replaced in most parts of the world by a **medical model**, an *approach that conceptualizes abnormal psychological experiences as illnesses that, like physical ill-nesses, have biological and environmental causes, defined symptoms, and possible cures.* Conceptualizing abnormal thoughts and behaviors as illness suggests that a first step is to determine the nature of the problem through *diagnosis.*

In diagnosis, clinicians seek to determine the nature of a person's mental disorder by assessing *signs* (objectively observed indicators of a disorder) and *symptoms* (subjec-tively reported behaviors, thoughts, and emotions) that suggest an underlying illness. So, for example, just as self-reported sniffles and a cough are symptoms of a cold, Robin Williams's depressed mood and struggles to control his use of mind-altering substances can be seen as symptoms of his depressive and substance-use disorders. It is important to note the differences among three related general medical and clas-sification terms:

- ▶ A *disorder* is a common set of signs and symptoms.
- ▶ A *disease* is a known pathological process affecting the body.
- ▶ A *diagnosis* is a determination as to whether a disorder or disease is present (Kraemer, Shrout, & Rubio-Stipec, 2007).

It is important to note that knowing that a disorder is present (i.e., diagnosed) does not necessarily mean that we know the underlying disease process in the body that gives rise to the signs and symptoms of the disorder.

medical model An approach that conceptualizes abnormal psychological experiences as illnesses that, like physical illnesses, have biological and environmental causes, defined symptoms, and possible cures.

WISE   IGNORANT   INSANE   IDIOTIC

According to the theory of physiognomy, mental disorders could be diagnosed from facial features. This fanciful theory is now considered superstition, but it was popular from antiquity until the early 20th century.

Some critics of the medical model of mental disorders suggest that such an approach "pathologizes" normal human behavior, such as calling shyness social phobia. However, proponents are quick to note that conditions such as social phobia are not merely normal shyness, but serious problems that can impair a person's functioning and ability to carry out a normal life. Here's just one example: The professional baseball player Zack Greinke was unable to play baseball in 2006, early in his professional career, due to social phobia. Fortunately, through effective treatment, he was able to return to the game and has gone on to a very successful professional career.

Diagnostic and Statistical Manual of Mental Disorders (DSM) A classification system that describes the features used to diagnose each recognized mental disorder and indicates how that disorder can be distinguished from other, similar problems.

Viewing mental disorders as medical problems reminds us that people who are suffering deserve care and treatment, not condemnation. Nevertheless, there are some criticisms of the medical model. Some psychologists argue that it is inappropriate to use clients' subjective self-reports, rather than physical tests of pathology (as in other areas of medical diagnostics), to determine underlying illness. Others argue that the model often "medicalizes" or "pathologizes" normal human behavior. For instance, extreme sadness can be considered to be an illness called *major depressive disorder*; extreme shyness can be diagnosed as an illness called *social anxiety disorder*; and trouble concentrating in school is called *attention-deficit/hyperactivity disorder*. Although there are some valid concerns about the current method of defining and classifying mental disorders, it is a huge advance over older alternatives, such as viewing mental disorders as the product of witchcraft or as punishment for sin. Moreover, psychologists keep these concerns in mind as they work to improve the diagnostic procedures.

CLASSIFYING DISORDERS: THE *DSM*

So how is the medical model used to classify the wide range of abnormal behaviors that occur among humans? Psychologists, psychiatrists (physicians concerned with the study and treatment of mental disorders) and most other people working in the area of mental disorders use a standardized system for classifying mental disorders. In 1952, recognizing the need to have a consensual diagnostic system for clinicians and researchers, the American Psychiatric Association published the first version of the ***Diagnostic and Statistical Manual of Mental Disorders (DSM)***. The *DSM* is *a classification system that describes the symptoms used to diagnose each recognized mental disorder and indicates how the disorder can be distinguished from other, similar problems.* Each disorder is named and classified as a distinct illness. The initial version of the *DSM* and its revision, *DSM–II,* published in 1968, provided a common language for talking about disorders. This was a major advance in the study of mental disorders; however, the diagnostic criteria listed in these early volumes were quite vague and based on thin theoretical assumptions. For instance, people who were extremely depressed or anxious for long periods of time might be given the general diagnosis of "neurosis reaction."

The next two editions of the *DSM* (*DSM–III*, published in 1980, and *DSM–IV*, published in 1994) moved from vague descriptions of disorders to very detailed lists of symptoms (or *diagnostic criteria*) that had to be present in order for a disorder to be diagnosed. For instance, in addition to being extremely sad or depressed (for at least 2 weeks), a person must have at least five of nine agreed-on symptoms of depression—for example, diminished interest in normally enjoyable activities, significant weight loss or gain, significantly increased or decreased sleep, loss of energy, feelings of worthlessness or guilt, trouble concentrating. The use of these detailed lists of symptoms for each of more than 200 disorders described in the *DSM* led to a dramatic increase in the reliability, or consistency, of diagnoses of mental disorders. Two clinicians interviewing the same individual were now much more likely to agree on what mental disorders were present, greatly increasing the credibility of the diagnostic process (and the fields of psychiatry and clinical psychology) and improving psychologists' ability to talk to each other, and to people suffering from these conditions, about the disorders being experienced.

In May 2013, the American Psychiatric Association released an updated manual, the *DSM–5*. The *DSM–5* describes 22 major categories containing more than 200 different mental disorders (see **TABLE 15.1**). Along with the disorders listed in these 22 categories, the *DSM–5* describes conditions that could be included as formal disorders but that, for now, require additional research. In addition, one section is devoted to cultural considerations in diagnosing mental disorders. Why the switch from roman

TABLE 15.1

Main *DSM–5* Categories of Mental Disorders

1. **Neurodevelopmental Disorders:** These are conditions that begin early in development and cause significant impairments in functioning, such as intellectual disability (formerly called "mental retardation"), Autism Spectrum Disorder (ASD), and attention-deficit/hyperactivity disorder (ADHD).

2. **Schizophrenia Spectrum and Other Psychotic Disorders:** This is a group of disorders characterized by major disturbances in perception, thought, language, emotion, and behavior.

3. **Bipolar and Related Disorders:** These disorders include major fluctuations in mood—from mania to depression—and also can include psychotic experiences, which is why they are placed between the psychotic and depressive disorders in *DSM–5*.

4. **Depressive Disorders:** These are conditions characterized by extreme and persistent periods of depressed mood.

5. **Anxiety Disorders:** These are disorders characterized by excessive fear and anxiety that are extreme enough to impair a person's functioning, such as panic disorder, generalized anxiety disorder, and specific phobias.

6. **Obsessive-Compulsive and Related Disorders:** These are conditions characterized by the presence of obsessive thinking followed by compulsive behavior in response to that thinking.

7. **Trauma- and Stressor-Related Disorders:** These are disorders that develop in response to a traumatic event, such as posttraumatic stress disorder.

8. **Dissociative Disorders:** These are conditions characterized by disruptions or discontinuity in consciousness, memory, or identity, such as dissociative identity disorder (formerly called "multiple personality disorder").

9. **Somatic Symptom and Related Disorders:** These are conditions in which a person experiences bodily symptoms (e.g., pain, fatigue) associated with significant distress or impairment.

10. **Feeding and Eating Disorders:** These are problems with eating that impair health or functioning, such as anorexia nervosa and bulimia nervosa.

11. **Elimination Disorders:** These involve inappropriate elimination of urine or feces (e.g., bedwetting).

12. **Sleep–Wake Disorders:** These are problems with the sleep–wake cycle, such as insomnia, narcolepsy, and sleep apnea.

13. **Sexual Dysfunctions:** These are problems related to unsatisfactory sexual activity, such as erectile disorder and premature ejaculation.

14. **Gender Dysphoria:** This is a single disorder characterized by incongruence between a person's experienced/expressed gender and assigned gender.

15. **Disruptive, Impulse-Control, and Conduct Disorders:** These are conditions involving problems controlling emotions and behaviors, such as conduct disorder, intermittent explosive disorder, and kleptomania.

16. **Substance-Related and Addictive Disorders:** This collection of disorders involves persistent use of substances or some other behavior (e.g., gambling) despite the fact that it leads to significant problems.

17. **Neurocognitive Disorders:** These are disorders of thinking caused by conditions such as Alzheimer's disease or traumatic brain injury.

18. **Personality Disorders:** These are enduring patterns of thinking, feeling, and behaving that lead to significant life problems.

19. **Paraphilic Disorders:** These are conditions characterized by inappropriate sexual activity, such as pedophilic disorder.

20. **Other Mental Disorders:** This is a residual category for conditions that do not fit into one of the above categories but are associated with significant distress or impairment, such as an unspecified mental disorder due to a medical condition.

21. **Medication-Induced Movement Disorders and Other Adverse Effects of Medication:** These are problems with physical movement (e.g., tremors, rigidity) that are caused by medication.

22. **Other Conditions That May Be the Focus of Clinical Attention:** These include disorders related to abuse, neglect, relationship, and other problems.

Information from *DSM–5* (American Psychiatric Association, 2013).

to arabic numerals? The hope is that with more rapid advances in our understanding of mental disorders, rather than waiting another 20 years to update the *DSM*, we can make revisions as we learn more (*DSM–5.1, 5.2, 5.3,* and so on).

Each of the 22 chapters in the main body of the *DSM–5* lists the specific criteria that must be met in order for a person to be diagnosed with each disorder. Studies of large, representative samples of the U.S. population reveal that approximately half

comorbidity The co-occurrence of two or more disorders in a single individual.

DATA VISUALIZATION

Comorbidity: How Often Do Multiple Disorders Occur? Go to launchpadworks.com.

of Americans report experiencing at least one mental disorder during the course of their lives (Kessler, Berglund, et al., 2005). And most of those with a mental disorder (greater than 80%) report **comorbidity**, *the co-occurrence of two or more disorders in a single individual* (Gadermann et al., 2012).

DISORDERS APPEAR IN ALL CULTURES

Are the mental disorders that we see in the United States also experienced by people in other parts of the world? In an effort to better understand the *epidemiology* (the study of the distribution and causes of health and disease) of mental disorders, Ronald Kessler and colleagues launched the World Health Organization World Mental Health Surveys, a large-scale study in which people from nearly two dozen countries around the world were assessed for the presence of mental disorders (Kessler & Üstün, 2008). The results of this study (see **FIGURE 15.1**) reveal that the major mental disorders seen in the United States appear similarly in countries and cultures all around the world. For instance, depression, anxiety, attention-deficit/hyperactivity disorder, and substance use disorders occur all over the globe. They are reported at different rates in different countries (people in the United States reported the highest rates of mental disorders), but depression and anxiety are always the most common, followed by impulse-control and substance use disorders (Kessler et al., 2007).

Although all countries appear to have the common mental disorders described above, it is clear that cultural context can influence how mental disorders are experienced, described, assessed, and treated (see A World of Difference: The Impact of Culture on Mental Disorders). To address this issue, the *DSM–5* includes a section containing a Cultural Formulation Interview (CFI). The CFI includes 16 questions that the clinician asks a client during a mental health assessment in order to help the clinician understand how the client's culture might influence the experience, expression, and explanation of his or her mental disorder.

Although the *DSM* is the preferred diagnostic system in the United States, many other countries use the World Health Organization's *International Classification of Diseases* (ICD), which is similar to the *DSM* in many ways. In fact, U.S. hospitals and insurance companies use *ICD* codes (that is, each disorder is assigned a specific number) rather than *DSM* codes in documenting which medical or psychological disorder a patient may be experiencing. The reason for this is that it allows all countries to work together to track the incidence and treatment of various conditions around the world.

► Figure 15.1
LIFETIME PREVALENCE OF DSM-IV/CIDI DISORDERS ACROSS WHO REGIONS [Data from Kessler et al., 2007]

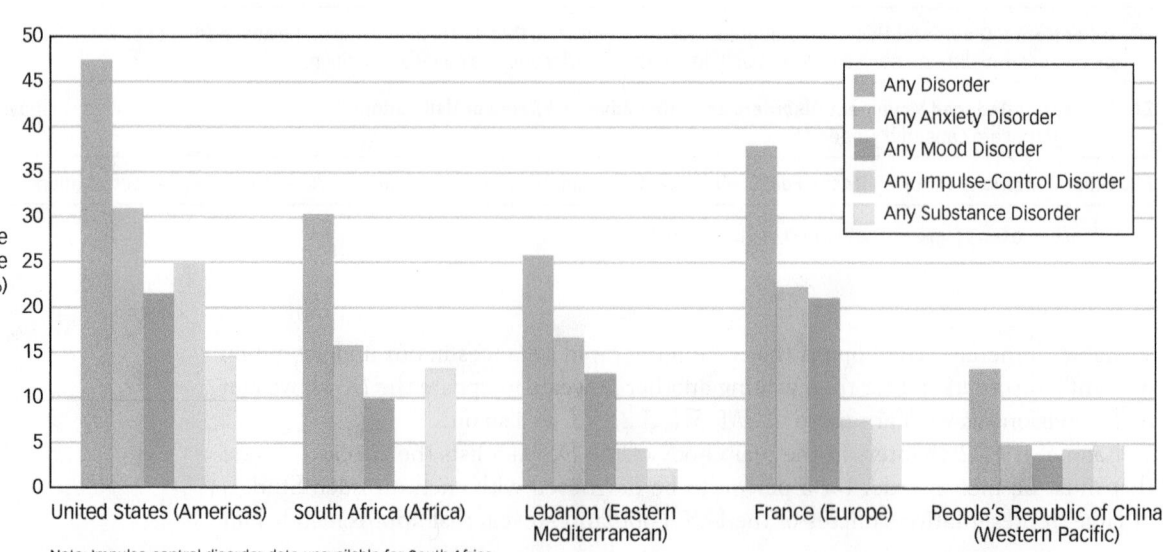

Note: Impulse-control disorder data unavailable for South Africa

The Impact of Culture on Mental Disorders

Just as language, traditions, customs, and other factors differ across cultures, so does the manifestation of mental disorders. The disorders you learn about in this chapter (anxiety disorders, depressive disorders, psychotic disorders, etc.) appear in every culture, but cultural factors often influence the way that these disorders are experienced, talked about, and explained. The *DSM-5* provides a framework for thinking about differences in cultural concepts of distress. It distinguishes among three important concepts:

- *Cultural syndromes* are groups of symptoms that tend to cluster together in specific cultures. For instance, *taijin kyofusho* is a cultural syndrome seen in Japan that is a combination of two *DSM-5* conditions: social anxiety disorder (in which a person fears negative feedback from others) and body dysmorphic disorder (in which a person is preoccupied with perceived flaws in his or her own physical appearance).

- *Cultural idioms of distress* are ways of talking about or expressing distress that can differ across cultures. For instance, *kufungisisa*, or "thinking too much," is an idiom of distress in Zimbabwe (and many other countries/cultures, but by different names) that is

▲ *Taijin kyofusho* is a Japanese syndrome in which a person fears and avoids contact with others due to the belief that they are inadequate or offensive in some way. This syndrome appears to be a combination of two *DSM-5* conditions: social anxiety disorder and body dysmorphic disorder.

associated with a number of depressive and anxiety disorders.

- *Cultural explanations* are culturally recognized descriptions of what causes the symptoms, distress, or disorder. For example, in many South Asian cultures mental disorder is believed to be caused by the loss of *dhat* or *dhatu*, a white substance believed to be in the body and essential for health that can exit the body in the form of semen or during urination or defecation.

So in addition to individual differences (across all people) in how we think, feel, and behave, the cultural context in which we are living can have an impact on how we experience, talk about, and explain mental disorders. This is an important thing to keep in mind when trying to understand mental disorders within your own cultures, and also when trying to understand mental disorders among those from cultures other than yours.

CAUSATION OF DISORDERS

The medical model of mental disorder suggests that knowing a person's diagnosis is useful because any given category of mental illness is likely to have a distinctive cause. In other words, just as different viruses, bacteria, or genetic abnormalities cause different physical illnesses, a specifiable pattern of causes (or *etiology*) may exist for different psychological disorders. The medical model also suggests that each category of mental disorder is likely to have a common *prognosis*, a typical course over time and susceptibility to treatment and cure. Unfortunately, this basic medical model is usually an oversimplification; it is rarely useful to focus on a *single cause* that is *internal* to the person and that suggests a *single cure*.

To understand what factors might cause mental disorders, most psychologists take an integrated **biopsychosocial perspective** that *explains mental disorders as the result of interactions among biological, psychological, and social factors (see* **FIGURE 15.2a**). On the biological side, the focus is on genetic and epigenetic (see Figure 3.19) influences, biochemical imbalances, and abnormalities in brain structure and function. The psychological perspective focuses on maladaptive learning and coping, cognitive biases, dysfunctional attitudes, and interpersonal problems. Social factors include poor socialization, stressful life experiences, and cultural and social inequities. The complexity of causation suggests that different individuals can experience a similar psychological disorder (e.g., depression) for different reasons. A person might fall

biopsychosocial perspective Explains mental disorders as the result of interactions among biological, psychological, and social factors.

▶ Figure 15.2

PROPOSED MODELS OF HOW DISORDERS DEVELOP (a) The biopsychosocial model suggests that biological, psychological, and social factors all interact to produce mental health or mental illness. (b) The diathesis–stress model suggests that mental illness develops when a person who has some predisposition or vulnerability to mental illness (the "diathesis") experiences a major life stressor (the "stress").

(a)

(b)

TERRY SCHMIDBAUER/GETTY IMAGES

Mental disorders can be caused by biological, psychological, and environmental factors. The diathesis–stress model suggests that a person may be predisposed for a psychological disorder that remains unexpressed until triggered by stress. Suppose that identical twins (with the same genetic profile) grow up in the same household (sharing the same parents, the same basic diet, the same access to television, and so on). When they are teenagers, one twin but not the other develops a mental disorder such as schizophrenia. How might this happen?

diathesis–stress model Suggests that a person may be predisposed to a psychological disorder that remains unexpressed until triggered by stress.

into a depression as a result of biological causes (e.g., genetics, hormones), psychological causes (e.g., faulty beliefs, hopelessness, poor strategies for coping with loss),. environmental causes (e.g., stress or loneliness), or more likely as a result of some combination of these factors. And, of course, multiple causes mean there may not be a single cure.

The observation that most disorders have both internal (biological/psychological) *and* external (environmental) causes has given rise to a theory known as the **diathesis–stress model,** which suggests that *a person may be predisposed to a psychological disorder that remains unexpressed until triggered by stress* (see Figure 15.2b). The diathesis is the internal predisposition, and the stress is the external trigger. For example, most people were able to cope with their strong emotional reactions to the terrorist attacks of September 11, 2001. However, for some who had a predisposition to negative emotions, the horror of the events may have overwhelmed their ability to cope, thereby precipitating a psychological disorder. Although diatheses can be inherited, it's important to remember that heritability is not destiny. A person who inherits a diathesis may never encounter the precipitating stress, whereas someone with little genetic propensity to a disorder may come to suffer from it, given the right pattern of stress. The tendency to oversimplify mental disorders by attributing them to single, internal causes is nowhere more evident than in the interpretation of the role of the brain in psychological disorders. Brain scans of people with and without disorders can give rise to an unusually strong impression that psychological problems are internal and permanent, inevitable, and even untreatable. Brain influences and processes are fundamentally important for knowing the full story of psychological disorders, but they are not the only chapter in that story.

A NEW APPROACH TO UNDERSTANDING MENTAL DISORDERS: RDoC

Although the *DSM* and *ICD* provide a useful framework for classifying disorders, concern has been growing over the fact that the findings from scientific research on the biopsychosocial factors that appear to cause psychopathology do not map neatly onto individual *DSM/ICD* diagnoses. Succinctly characterizing the current state of affairs, Thomas R. Insel, the director of the National Institute of Mental Health (NIMH, a federal agency that is the primary funder of research on mental disorders in the United States), noted that although many people describe the *DSM* as a bible, it is more accurate to think of it as a dictionary that provides labels and

How Are Mental Disorders Defined and Diagnosed?

Who decides what goes in the *DSM*? How are these decisions made? In psychology and psychiatry, as in the early days of most areas of the study of human health and behavior, these decisions currently are made by consensus among leaders in the research field. These leaders meet repeatedly over several years to make decisions about which disorders should be included in the new revision of the *DSM* and how they should be defined. Over the years, these decisions have been based on descriptive research reporting in which clinical symptoms tend to cluster together. Everyone agrees that we need a system for classifying and defining mental disorders; however, as the currently available body of knowledge about mental disorders grows, the field is moving beyond

simple descriptive diagnostic categories toward others based on underlying biopsychosocial processes, such as the Research Domain Criteria Project. Future decisions about how mental disorders are defined will likely continue to be reached by consensus among leaders in the field but will be driven more directly by research on the underlying causes of these disorders.

Who decides whether someone actually has a diagnosable disorder? And how are these decisions made? Over the years, researchers have developed structured clinical interviews that convert the lists of symptoms included in the *DSM* into sets of interview questions through which the clinician (psychologist, psychiatrist, social worker) makes a determination about whether or not a given person meets the

criteria for a given disorder (Nock et al., 2007). For instance, according to *DSM–5*, a person must have at least five of the nine symptoms of major depressive disorder in order to meet the criteria for this disorder. Structured clinical interviews typically include nine questions about depression (one per symptom), and if the person reports having at least five of these symptoms, the clinician may conclude that this person is suffering from major depression. Right now, diagnoses are determined primarily by client self-reporting of symptoms. With increasing attention to the underlying causes of mental disorders, many hope that in the future we will have biological and behavioral tests to help us make decisions about who has a mental illness and who does not.

current definitions: "People think that everything has to match *DSM* criteria, but you know what? Biology never read that book" (Insel, quoted in Belluck & Carey, 2013, p. A13). In order to better understand what actually causes mental disorders, researchers at the NIMH have proposed a new framework for thinking about mental disorders, focused not on the currently defined *DSM/ICD* categories of disorders but on the more basic biological, cognitive, and behavioral constructs that are believed to be the building blocks of mental disorders. This new system is called the **Research Domain Criteria Project (RDoC),** *a new initiative that aims to guide the classification and understanding of mental disorders by revealing the basic processes that give rise to them.* The RDoC is not intended to immediately replace the *DSM/ICD* but to inform future revisions to it in the coming years (see The Real World: How Are Mental Disorders Defined and Diagnosed?).

Using the RDoC, researchers study the causes of abnormal functioning by focusing on units (or levels) of analysis that include biological factors from genes to cells to brain circuits; psychological domains, such as learning, attention, memory; and various social processes and behavior (see **TABLE 15.2** for a list of domains). Through the RDoC approach, the NIMH would like to shift researchers away from studying currently defined *DSM/ICD* categories and toward the study of the dimensional biopsychosocial processes believed, at the extreme end of the continuum, to lead to mental disorders. These processes (e.g., fear, anxiety, attention, perception) are referred to as *constructs*, which are themselves grouped into broader categories referred to as *domains*. The five domains included in the RDoC are Negative Valence Systems, Positive Valence Systems, Cognitive Systems, Systems for Social Processes, and Arousal/Regulatory Systems. The long-term goal is to better understand which abnormalities cause different disorders and to classify disorders on the basis of those underlying causes rather than on observed symptoms. This approach would bring the study of mental disorders in line with the study of other medical disorders. For example, if you are experiencing chest pain, severe headaches, fatigue, and difficulty breathing, it is unlikely that you are experiencing four separate disorders (*chest pain disorder, headache disorder*, etc.). Instead, we now know that these are all symptoms of an underlying disease process called hypertension. The RDoC approach similarly aims to shift the focus away from classifications based on surface symptoms and toward

Research Domain Criteria Project (RDoC) A new initiative that aims to guide the classification and understanding of mental disorders by revealing the basic processes that give rise to them.

TABLE 15.2				
Research Domain Criteria (RDoC)				
Domains / Constructs				
Negative Valence Systems	**Positive Valence Systems**	**Cognitive Systems**	**Systems for Social Processes**	**Arousal and Regulatory Systems**
acute threat ("fear")	approach motivation	attention	affiliation and attachment	arousal
potential threat ("anxiety")	initial responsiveness to reward	perception	social communication	circadian rhythms
sustained threat	sustained responsiveness to reward	working memory	perception and understanding of self	sleep and wakefulness
loss	reward learning	declarative memory	perception and understanding of others	
frustrative nonreward	habit	language behavior cognitive (effortful) control		
Units of Analysis				
genes molecules cells circuits physiology behavior self-reports paradigms				

an understanding of the processes that give rise to disordered behavior. For instance, rather than studying cocaine addiction as a distinct disorder, from the RDoC perspective researchers might try to understand what causes abnormalities in "responsiveness to reward," a factor seen in those with excessive cocaine use as well as in those with other addictive behaviors. Indeed, recent research has shown that variations in a gene (*DRD2*) that codes for dopamine D2 receptors are associated with abnormalities in connectivity between parts of the frontal lobe and the striatum (described in the Neuroscience and Behavior chapter). This atypical connectivity is, in turn, related to the impulsiveness and responsiveness to rewards associated with a range of addictive behavior disorders (Buckholtz & Meyer-Lindenberg, 2012). This may help explain why some people seem to have addictive personalities and have trouble inhibiting their reward-seeking behavior. Importantly, understanding what processes cause problems such as addiction will help us to develop more effective treatments, a topic we address in more detail in the next chapter.

You might have noticed that the list of domains in Table 15.2 looks like a slightly more detailed version of the table of contents for this textbook! The RDoC approach has an overall emphasis on neuroscience (Chapter 3), and specific focuses on abnormalities in emotional and motivational systems (Chapter 8), cognitive systems such as memory (Chapter 6), learning (Chapter 7), language and cognition (Chapter 9), social processes (Chapter 13), and stress and arousal (Chapter 14). From the RDoC perspective, mental disorders can be thought of as the result of abnormalities or dysfunctions in normal psychological processes. By learning about many of these processes in this textbook, you will likely have a good understanding of new definitions of mental disorders as they are developed in the years ahead.

DANGERS OF LABELING

An important complication in the diagnosis and classification of psychological disorders is the effect of labeling. Psychiatric labels can have negative consequences because many carry the baggage of negative stereotypes and stigma, such as the idea that a mental disorder is a sign of personal weakness or the idea that all psychiatric patients are dangerous. The stigma associated with mental disorders may explain why most people with diagnosable psychological disorders (approximately 60%) do not seek treatment (Kessler, Demler, et al., 2005; Wang, Berglund, et al., 2005).

The new Research Domain Criteria (RDoC) are intended to help us better understand why some people seem to have addictive personalities and have trouble limiting their engagement in pleasurable experiences.

ISTOP/SUPERSTOCK

Unfortunately, educating people about mental disorders does not dispel the stigma borne by those with these conditions (Phelan et al., 1997). In fact, expectations created by psychiatric labels can sometimes even compromise the judgment of mental health professionals (Garb, 1998). In a classic demonstration of this phenomenon, the psychologist David Rosenhan and six associates reported to different mental hospitals complaining of "hearing voices," a symptom sometimes found in people with schizophrenia. Each was admitted to a hospital, and each promptly reported that the symptom had ceased. Even so, hospital staff were reluctant to identify these people as normal: It took an average of 19 days for these "patients" to secure their release, and even then they were released with the diagnosis of "schizophrenia in remission" (Rosenhan, 1973). Apparently, once hospital staff had labeled these patients as having a psychological disease, the label stuck.

These effects of labeling are particularly disturbing in light of evidence that hospitalizing people with mental disorders is seldom necessary. One set of studies in Vermont followed the lives of patients who were thought to be too dangerous to release and therefore had been kept in the back wards of institutions for years. Their release resulted in no harm to the community (Harding et al., 1987), and further studies have shown that those with a mental disorder are no more likely to be violent than those without a disorder (Elbogen & Johnson, 2009; Monahan, 1992).

Labeling may even affect how labeled individuals view themselves; persons given such a label may come to view themselves not just as mentally disordered but as hopeless or worthless. Such a view may cause them to develop an attitude of defeat and, as a result, to fail to work toward their own recovery. As one small step toward counteracting such consequences, clinicians have adopted the important practice of applying labels to the disorder and not to the person with the disorder. For example, an individual might be described as "a person with schizophrenia," not as "a schizophrenic." You'll notice that we follow this convention in the text.

Although we label mental disorders, we should not apply those labels to people. For instance, rather than saying someone "is ADHD," we would say that the person currently meets diagnostic criteria for ADHD.

Build to the Outcomes

1. What is a mental disorder?

2. How does the medical model explain abnormal behavior?

3. What is the first step in helping someone with a mental disorder?

4. What are the differences among disorder, disease, and diagnosis?

5. What is the *DSM*? How has it changed over time?

6. How do the biopsychosocial perspective and the diathesis–stress model explain disorders?

7. Why does assessment require looking at a number of factors?

8. What are the limitations of using brain scans for diagnosis?

9. What is the RDoC? How does it differ from the *DSM*?

10. Why might someone avoid seeking help for a disorder?

11. What are the dangers of labeling?

Anxiety Disorders: Excessive Fear, Anxiety, and Avoidance

"Okay, time for a pop quiz that will be half your grade for this class." If your instructor had actually said that, you would probably have experienced a wave of anxiety and dread. Your reaction would be appropriate and—no matter how intense the feeling— would not be a sign that you have a mental disorder. In fact, situation-related anxiety is normal and adaptive: in this case, perhaps by reminding you to keep up with your textbook assignments so you are prepared for pop quizzes. When anxiety arises that is out of proportion to real threats and challenges, however, it is maladaptive: It can take

Learning Outcomes

► Explain the major symptoms of anxiety disorders, including phobias, panic disorder, and GAD.

► Describe factors that contribute to phobias, panic disorder, and GAD.

anxiety disorder The class of mental disorders in which anxiety is the predominant feature.

phobic disorders Disorders characterized by marked, persistent, and excessive fear and avoidance of specific objects, activities, or situations.

specific phobia A disorder that involves an irrational fear of a particular object or situation that markedly interferes with an individual's ability to function.

social phobia A disorder that involves an irrational fear of being publicly humiliated or embarrassed.

hold of people's lives, stealing their peace of mind and undermining their ability to function normally. Pathological anxiety is expressed as an **anxiety disorder,** *the class of mental disorders in which anxiety is the predominant feature.* People commonly experience more than one type of anxiety disorder at a given time, and there is significant comorbidity between anxiety and depression (Beesdo et al., 2010; Brown & Barlow, 2002). Among the anxiety disorders recognized in the *DSM–5* are phobic disorders, panic disorder, and generalized anxiety disorder.

PHOBIC DISORDERS

Consider Mary, a 47-year-old mother of three, who sought treatment for *claustrophobia*—an intense fear of enclosed spaces. She traced her fear to her childhood, when her older siblings would scare her by locking her in closets and confining her under blankets. Her own children grown, she wanted to find a job but could not because of a terror of elevators and other confined places that, she felt, shackled her to her home (Carson, Butcher, & Mineka, 2000). Many people feel a little anxious in enclosed spaces, but Mary's fears were abnormal and dysfunctional because they were disproportionate to any actual risk and impaired her ability to carry out a normal life. The *DSM–5* describes **phobic disorders** as characterized by *marked, persistent, and excessive fear and avoidance of specific objects, activities, or situations.* An individual with a phobic disorder recognizes that the fear is irrational but cannot prevent it from interfering with everyday functioning.

A **specific phobia** is *an irrational fear of a particular object or situation that markedly interferes with an individual's ability to function.* Specific phobias fall into five categories: (1) animals (e.g., dogs, cats, rats, snakes, spiders); (2) natural environments (e.g., heights, darkness, water, storms); (3) situations (e.g., bridges, elevators, tunnels, enclosed places); (4) blood, injections, and injury; and (5) other phobias, including choking or vomiting; and in children, loud noises or costumed characters. Approximately 12% of people in the United States will develop a specific phobia during their lives (Kessler, Berglund, et al., 2005), with rates slightly higher among women than men (Kessler et al., 2012).

Social phobia involves *an irrational fear of being publicly humiliated or embarrassed.* Social phobia can be restricted to situations such as public speaking, eating in public, or urinating in a public bathroom or generalized to a variety of social situations that involve being observed or interacting with unfamiliar people. Individuals with social phobia try to avoid situations where unfamiliar people might evaluate them, and they

The preparedness theory explains why most merry-go-rounds carry children on beautiful horses. This mom might have some trouble getting her daughter to ride on a big spider or snake.

COURTESY OF DANIEL WEGNER

experience intense anxiety and distress when public exposure is unavoidable. Social phobia can develop in childhood, but it typically emerges between early adolescence and early adulthood (Kessler, Berglund, et al., 2005). Many people experience social phobia, with about 12% of men and 14% of women qualifying for a diagnosis at some time in their lives (Kessler et al., 2012).

Why are phobias so common? The high rates of both specific and social phobias suggest a predisposition to be fearful of certain objects and situations. Indeed, most of the situations and objects of people's phobias could pose a real threat, for example, falling from a high place or being attacked by a vicious dog or a poisonous snake or spider. Social situations have their own dangers. A roomful of strangers may not attack or bite, but they could form impressions that affect your prospects for friends, jobs, or marriage. And of course, in some very rare cases, they could attack or bite.

Observations such as these are the basis for the **preparedness theory** of phobias, which maintains that *people are instinctively predisposed toward certain fears*. The preparedness theory, proposed by Martin E. P. Seligman (1971), is supported by research showing that both humans and monkeys can quickly be conditioned to have a fear response for stimuli such as snakes and spiders, but not for neutral stimuli such as flowers or toy rabbits (Cook & Mineka, 1989; Öhman, Dimberg, & Öst, 1985). Similarly, research on facial expressions has shown that people are more easily conditioned to fear angry facial expressions than other types of expressions (Öhman, 1996; Woody & Nosen, 2008). Phobias are particularly likely to form for objects that evolution has predisposed us to avoid. This idea is also supported by studies of the heritability of phobias. Family studies of specific phobias indicate greater concordance rates for identical than for fraternal twins (Kendler, Myers, & Prescott, 2002; O'Laughlin & Malle, 2002). Other studies have found that over 30% of first-degree relatives (parents, siblings, or children) of individuals with specific phobias also have a phobia (Fryer et al., 1990).

Temperament may also play a role in vulnerability to phobias. Researchers have found that infants who display excessive shyness and inhibition are at an increased risk for developing a phobic behavior later in life (Morris, 2001; Stein, Chavira, & Jang, 2001). Neurobiological factors may also play a role. Abnormalities in the neurotransmitters serotonin and dopamine are more common in individuals who report phobias than they are among people who don't (Stein, 1998). In addition, individuals with phobias sometimes show abnormally high levels of activity in the amygdala, an area of the brain linked with the development of emotional associations (discussed in the chapter on Emotion and Motivation and in Stein et al., 2001). Interestingly, although people with social phobia report feeling much more distressed than those without social phobia during tasks involving social evaluation (such as giving a speech), they are actually no more physiologically aroused than others (Jamieson, Nock, & Mendes, 2013). This suggests that social phobia may be due to a person's subjective experience of the situation, rather than an abnormal physiological stress response to such situations.

This evidence does not rule out the influence of environments and upbringing on the development of phobic overreactions. As the learning theorist John Watson (1924) demonstrated many years ago, phobias can be classically conditioned (see the discussion of Little Albert and the white rat in the Learning chapter). Similarly, the discomfort of a dog bite could create a conditioned association between dogs and pain, resulting in an irrational fear of all dogs. The idea that phobias are learned from emotional experiences with feared objects, however, is not a complete explanation for the occurrence of phobias. Most studies find that people with phobias are no more likely than people without phobias to recall personal experiences with the feared object that could have provided the basis for classical conditioning (Craske, 1999; McNally & Steketee, 1985). Moreover, many people are bitten by dogs, but few develop phobias. Despite its shortcomings, however, the idea that this is a matter of learning provides a useful model for therapy (see the Treatment chapter).

preparedness theory The idea that people are instinctively predisposed toward certain fears.

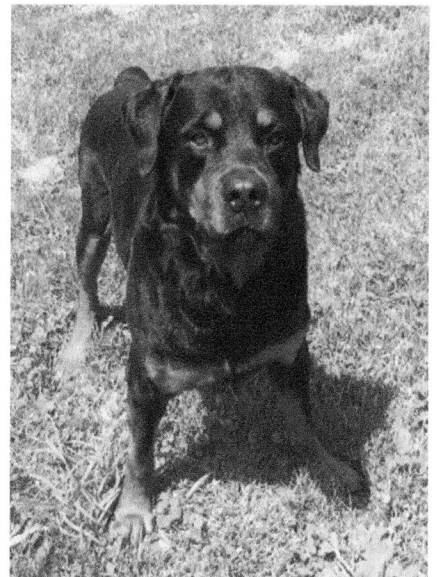

MATTHEW NOCK

Phobias are anxiety disorders that involve excessive and persistent fear of a specific object, activity, or situation. Some phobias may be learned through classical conditioning, in which a conditioned stimulus (CS) that is paired with an anxiety-evoking unconditioned stimulus (US) itself comes to elicit a conditioned fear response (CR). Suppose your friend has a phobia of dogs that is so intense that he is afraid to go outside in case one of his neighbors' dogs barks at him. Applying the principles of classical conditioning you studied in the Learning chapter, how might you help him overcome his fear?

panic disorder A disorder characterized by the sudden occurrence of multiple psychological and physiological symptoms that contribute to a feeling of stark terror.

agoraphobia A specific phobia involving a fear of public places.

PANIC DISORDER AND AGORAPHOBIA

If you suddenly found yourself in danger of death (that lion is headed straight for us!), a wave of panic might wash over you. People who suffer panic attacks are frequently overwhelmed by such intense fears and by powerful physical symptoms of anxiety, even in the complete absence of actual danger. Wesley, a 20-year-old college student, began having panic attacks with increasing frequency, often two or three times a day, when he finally sought help at a clinic. The attacks began with a sudden wave of "intense, terrifying fear" that seemed to come out of nowhere, often accompanied by dizziness, a tightening of the chest, and the thought that he was going to pass out or possibly die. Wesley's attacks had started a few years earlier and had occurred intermittently ever since. Wesley decided to come in for treatment because he had begun to avoid buses, trains, and public places for fear that he would have an attack like this and not be able to escape.

Wesley's condition, called **panic disorder,** is characterized by *the sudden occurrence of multiple psychological and physiological symptoms that contribute to a feeling of stark terror.* The acute symptoms of a panic attack typically last only a few minutes and include shortness of breath, heart palpitations, sweating, dizziness, depersonalization (a feeling of being detached from one's body) or derealization (a feeling that the external world is strange or unreal), and a fear that one is going crazy or about to die. Not surprisingly, panic attacks often send people rushing to emergency rooms or their physicians' offices for what they believe are heart attacks. Unfortunately, because many of the symptoms mimic various medical disorders, a correct diagnosis may take years in spite of costly medical tests that produce normal results (Katon, 1994). According to the *DSM–5* diagnostic criteria, a person has panic disorder only if they experience recurrent unexpected attacks and report significant anxiety about having another attack.

A disorder that sometimes co-occurs with panic disorder is **agoraphobia,** *a specific phobia involving a fear of public places.* Many people with agoraphobia, including Wesley, are not frightened of public places in themselves; instead, they are afraid that something terrible will happen (including having panic symptoms) while they are in a public place and that they will not be able to escape or get help. In severe cases, people who have agoraphobia are unable to leave home, sometimes for years.

Approximately 22% of the U.S. population reports having had at least one panic attack (Kessler, Chiu, et al., 2005), typically during a period of intense stress (Telch, Lucas, & Nelson, 1989). An occasional episode is not sufficient for a diagnosis of panic disorder: The individual also has to experience significant dread and anxiety

Agoraphobia, the fear of being in public because something bad is going to happen and escape will not be possible, may prevent a person from going outside at all.

about having another attack. When this criterion is applied, approximately 5% of people will have diagnosable panic disorder sometime in their lives (Kessler, Berglund, et al., 2005). Panic disorder is more prevalent among women (7%) than men (3%; Kessler et al., 2012). Family studies suggest some hereditary component to panic disorder, with 30 to 40% of the variance in liability for developing panic disorder attributed to genetic influence (Hettema, Neale, & Kendler, 2001).

In an effort to understand the role that physiological arousal plays in panic attacks, researchers have compared the responses of experimental participants with and without panic disorder to *sodium lactate,* a chemical that produces rapid, shallow breathing and heart palpitations. Those with panic disorder were found to be acutely sensitive to the drug; within a few minutes after administration, 60 to 90% experienced a panic attack. Participants without the disorder rarely responded to this substance with a panic attack (Liebowitz et al., 1985).

The difference in responses to this chemical may be due to differing interpretations of physiological signs of anxiety; that is, people who experience panic attacks may be hypersensitive to physiological signs of anxiety, which they interpret as having disastrous consequences for their well-being. Supporting this cognitive explanation is research showing that people who are high in anxiety sensitivity (i.e., they believe that bodily arousal and other symptoms of anxiety can have dire consequences) have an elevated risk for experiencing panic attacks (Olatunji & Wolitzky-Taylor, 2009). Thus, panic attacks may be conceptualized as a "fear of fear" itself.

GENERALIZED ANXIETY DISORDER

Gina, a 24-year-old woman, began to experience debilitating anxiety during her first year of graduate school for clinical psychology. At first she worried about whether she was sufficiently completing all of her assignments, then she worried about whether her clients were improving or if she was actually making them worse. Soon her concerns spread to focus on her health (did she have an undiagnosed medical problem?) as well as that of her boyfriend (he smokes cigarettes . . . perhaps he is currently giving himself cancer?). She worried incessantly for a year and ultimately took time off from school to get treatment for her worries, extreme agitation, fatigue, and feelings of sadness and depression.

Gina's symptoms are typical of **generalized anxiety disorder (GAD)**—called *generalized* because the unrelenting worries are not focused on any particular threat; they are, in fact, often exaggerated and irrational. GAD is *chronic excessive worry accompanied by three or more of the following symptoms: restlessness, fatigue, concentration problems, irritability, muscle tension, and sleep disturbance.* In people suffering from GAD, the uncontrollable worrying produces a sense of loss of control that can so erode self-confidence that simple decisions seem fraught with dire consequences. For example, Gina struggled to make everyday decisions as basic as which vegetables to buy at the market and how to prepare her dinner.

Approximately 6% of people in the United States suffer from GAD at some time in their lives (Kessler, Berglund, et al., 2005), with women experiencing GAD at higher rates (8%) than men (5%; Kessler et al., 2012). Research suggests that both biological and psychological factors contribute to the risk of GAD. Family studies indicate a mild to modest level of heritability (Norrholm & Ressler, 2009). Although identical twin studies of GAD are rare, some evidence suggests that compared with fraternal twins, identical twins have modestly higher *concordance rates* (the percentage of pairs that share the characteristic; Hettema et al., 2001). Moreover, teasing out environmental versus personality influences on concordance rates is quite difficult.

Biological explanations of GAD suggest that neurotransmitter imbalances may play a role in the disorder. The precise nature of this imbalance is not clear. *Benzodiazepines* (a class of sedative drugs discussed in the Treatment chapter; e.g., Valium,

generalized anxiety disorder (GAD) A disorder characterized by chronic excessive worry accompanied by three or more of the following symptoms: restlessness, fatigue, concentration problems, irritability, muscle tension, and sleep disturbance.

The experience of major stressful life events, such as losing a job or a home, can lead to generalized anxiety disorder, a condition characterized by chronic, excessive worry.

JOHN HENLEY/GETTY IMAGES

Librium) that appear to stimulate the neurotransmitter *gamma-aminobutyric acid (GABA)* can sometimes reduce the symptoms of GAD, suggesting a potential role for this neurotransmitter in the occurrence of GAD. However, other drugs that do not directly affect GABA levels (e.g., buspirone and antidepressants such as Prozac) can also be helpful in the treatment of GAD (Gobert et al., 1999; Michelson et al., 1999; Roy-Byrne & Cowley, 1998). To complicate matters, these different prescription drugs do not help all individuals and, in some cases, can produce serious side effects and dependency.

Psychological explanations focus on anxiety-provoking situations in explaining high levels of GAD. The condition is especially prevalent among people who have low incomes, are living in large cities, and/or are in environments rendered unpredictable by political and economic strife. The relatively high rates of GAD among women may also be related to stress because women are more likely than men to live in poverty, experience discrimination, or be subjected to sexual or physical abuse (Koss, 1990; Strickland, 1991). Research shows that unpredictable traumatic experiences in childhood increase the risk of developing GAD, and this evidence also supports the idea that stressful experiences play a role (Torgensen, 1986). Risk of GAD also increases following the experience of a loss or situation associated with future perceived danger (Kendler et al., 2003), such as loss of a home due to foreclosure (McLaughlin et al., 2012). Still, many people who might be expected to develop GAD don't, supporting the diathesis–stress notion that personal vulnerability must also be a key factor in this disorder.

Build to the Outcomes

1. What is an anxiety disorder?

2. When is it helpful? When is anxiety harmful?

3. What is a phobic disorder? What are the different types?

4. Why might we be predisposed to certain phobias?

5. What is a panic disorder?

6. What is it about public places that many people with agoraphobia fear?

7. What is generalized anxiety disorder (GAD)? What factors contribute to it?

Obsessive-Compulsive Disorder: Persistent Thoughts and Repetitive Behaviors

Learning Outcome

▶ Describe the symptoms and potential causes of OCD.

You may have had an irresistible urge to go back to check whether you actually locked the door or turned off the oven, even when you're pretty sure that you did. Or you may have been unable to resist engaging in some superstitious behavior, such as not walking under a ladder or stepping on a crack. For some people, such thoughts and actions spiral out of control and become a serious problem.

Karen, a 34-year-old with four children, sought treatment after several months of experiencing intrusive, repetitive thoughts in which she imagined that one or more of her children was having a serious accident. In addition, an extensive series of protective counting rituals hampered her daily routine. For example, when grocery shopping, Karen had the feeling that if she selected the first item (say, a box of cereal) on a shelf, something terrible would happen to her oldest child. If she selected the second item, some unknown disaster would befall her second child, and so on for all four children. The children's ages were also important. The sixth item in a row, for example, was associated with her youngest child, who was 6 years old.

Karen's preoccupation with numbers extended to other activities, most notably, the pattern in which she smoked cigarettes and drank coffee. If she had one cigarette, she felt that she had to smoke at least four in a row or one of her children would be harmed in some way. If she drank one cup of coffee, she felt compelled to drink four more to protect her children from harm. She acknowledged that her counting rituals were irrational, but she became extremely anxious when she tried to stop (Oltmanns, Neale, & Davison, 1991).

Karen's symptoms are typical of **obsessive-compulsive disorder (OCD),** in which *repetitive, intrusive thoughts (obsessions) and ritualistic behaviors (compulsions) designed to fend off those thoughts interfere significantly with an individual's functioning.* Anxiety plays a role in this disorder because the obsessive thoughts typically produce anxiety, and the compulsive behaviors are performed to reduce it. In OCD, these obsessions and compulsions are intense, frequent, and experienced as irrational and excessive. Attempts to cope with the obsessive thoughts by trying to suppress or ignore them are of little or no benefit. In fact (as discussed in the Consciousness chapter), thought suppression can backfire, increasing the frequency and intensity of the obsessive thoughts (Wegner, 1989; Wenzlaff & Wegner, 2000). Despite anxiety's role, *DSM–5* classifies OCD separately from anxiety disorders, because researchers believe that this disorder has a distinct cause and is maintained via different neural circuitry in the brain than the anxiety disorders.

Although 28% of adults in the United States report experiencing obsessions or compulsions at some point in their lives (Ruscio et al., 2010), only 2% will develop actual OCD (Kessler, Berglund, et al., 2005). Similar to anxiety disorders, rates of OCD are higher among women than men (Kessler et al., 2012). Among those with OCD, the most common obsessions and compulsions involve checking (79% of those with OCD), ordering (57%), moral concerns (43%), and contamination (26%; Ruscio et al., 2010). Although compulsive behavior is always excessive, it can vary considerably in intensity and frequency. For example, fear of contamination may lead to 15 minutes of hand washing in some individuals, whereas others may need to spend hours with disinfectants and extremely hot water, scrubbing their hands until they bleed.

The obsessions that plague individuals with OCD typically derive from concerns that could pose a real threat (such as contamination or disease), which supports preparedness theory. Thinking repeatedly about whether we've left a stove burner on when we leave the house makes sense, after all, if we want to return to a house that is

obsessive-compulsive disorder (OCD) A disorder in which repetitive, intrusive thoughts (obsessions) and ritualistic behaviors (compulsions) designed to fend off those thoughts interfere significantly with an individual's functioning.

Howie Mandel is a successful comedian, but his struggle with OCD is no laughing matter. Like approximately 2% of people in the United States, Mandel struggles with extreme fears of being contaminated by germs and engages in repeated checking and cleaning behaviors that often interfere with his daily life. He has spoken publicly about his struggles with OCD and about the importance of seeking effective treatment for this condition.

CHARLES SYKES/AP IMAGES

posttraumatic stress disorder (PTSD) A disorder characterized by chronic physiological arousal, recurrent unwanted thoughts or images of the trauma, and avoidance of things that call the traumatic event to mind.

not "well done." The concept of preparedness places OCD in the same evolutionary context as phobias (Szechtman & Woody, 2006). However, as with phobias, we need to consider other factors to explain why fears that may have served an evolutionary purpose can become so distorted and maladaptive.

Family studies indicate a moderate genetic heritability for OCD: Identical twins show a higher concordance than do fraternal twins. Relatives of individuals with OCD may not have the disorder themselves, but they are at greater risk for other types of anxiety disorders than are members of the general public (Billet, Richter, & Kennedy, 1998). Researchers have not determined the biological mechanisms that may contribute to OCD (Friedlander & Desrocher, 2006), but one hypothesis implicates heightened neural activity in the caudate nucleus of the brain, a portion of the basal ganglia (discussed in the Neuroscience and Behavior chapter) known to be involved in the initiation of intentional actions (Rappoport, 1990). Drugs that increase the activity of the neurotransmitter serotonin in the brain can inhibit the activity of the caudate nucleus and relieve some of the symptoms of obsessive-compulsive disorder (Hansen et al., 2002). However, this finding does not indicate that overactivity of the caudate nucleus is the cause of OCD. It could also be an effect of the disorder: People with OCD often respond favorably to psychotherapy and show a corresponding reduction in activity in the caudate nucleus (Baxter et al., 1992).

Build to the Outcomes

1. What is obsessive-compulsive disorder (OCD)?

2. How effective is willful effort in curing OCD?

3. What factors may contribute to OCD?

Posttraumatic Stress Disorder: Distress and Avoidance After a Trauma

Learning Outcome

▸ Describe the symptoms and potential causes of PTSD.

The traumatic events of war leave many debilitated by PTSD. But because, unlike other war-related injuries, PTSD does not leave any visible wounds, it can be difficult to diagnose with certainty. Because of this, the Pentagon has decided that psychological casualties of war are not eligible for the Purple Heart—the hallowed medal given to those wounded or killed in action (Alvarez & Eckholm, 2009).

Psychological reactions to traumatic or stressful events can lead to stressor-related disorders. For example, a person who lives through a terrifying and uncontrollable experience may develop **posttraumatic stress disorder (PTSD)**, a disorder characterized by *chronic physiological arousal, recurrent unwanted thoughts or images of the trauma, and avoidance of things that call the traumatic event to mind.*

Psychological disorders following exposure to traumatic events are perhaps nowhere more apparent than in war. Many soldiers returning from combat experience symptoms of PTSD, including flashbacks of battle, exaggerated anxiety and startle reactions, and even medical conditions that do not arise from physical damage (e.g., paralysis or chronic fatigue). Most of these symptoms are normal, appropriate responses to horrifying events, and for most people, the symptoms subside with time. In PTSD, however, the symptoms can last much longer. For example, approximately 12% of U.S. veterans of recent operations in Iraq met the criteria for PTSD after their deployment; and the observed rates of PTSD are even higher in non-Western and developing countries (Keane, Marshall, & Taft, 2006). The effects of PTSD are now recognized not only among victims, witnesses, and perpetrators of war but also among ordinary people who are traumatized by terrible events in civilian life. At some time over the course of their lives, about 7% of Americans are estimated to suffer from PTSD (Kessler, Berglund, et al., 2005).

Not everyone who is exposed to a traumatic event develops PTSD, suggesting that people differ in their degree of sensitivity to trauma. Research using brain imaging techniques to examine brain structure and function has identified important neural correlates of PTSD. Specifically, those with PTSD show heightened activity in the

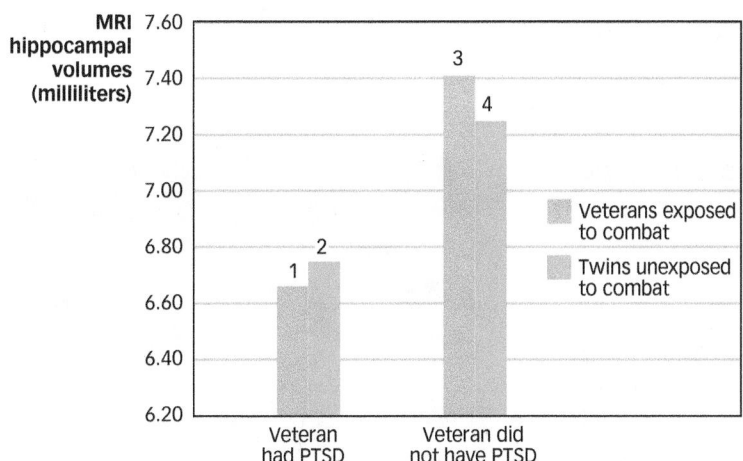

◄ Figure 15.3
HIPPOCAMPAL VOLUMES OF VIETNAM VETERANS AND THEIR IDENTICAL TWINS Average hippocampal volumes for four groups of participants: (1) combat-exposed veterans who developed PTSD; (2) their combat-unexposed twins with no PTSD themselves; (3) combat-exposed veterans who never developed PTSD; and (4) their unexposed twins, also with no PTSD. Smaller hippocampal volumes were found for both the combat-exposed veterans with PTSD (Group 1) and their twins who had not been exposed to combat (Group 2), in contrast to veterans without PTSD (Group 3) and their twins (Group 4). This pattern of findings suggests that an inherited smaller hippocampus may make some people sensitive to conditions that cause PTSD (Gilbertson et al., 2002).

amygdala (a region associated with the evaluation of threatening information and fear conditioning), decreased activity in the medial prefrontal cortex (a region important in the extinction of fear conditioning), and a smaller-size hippocampus (the part of the brain most linked with memory, as described in the Neuroscience and Behavior and Memory chapters; Shin, Rauch, & Pitman, 2006). Of course, an important question is whether people whose brains have these characteristics are at greater risk for PTSD if traumatized, or if these characteristics are the consequences of trauma in some people. For instance, does reduced hippocampal volume reflect a preexisting condition that makes the brain sensitive to stress? Or does the traumatic stress itself somehow kill nerve cells? One important study suggests that although a group of combat veterans with PTSD showed reduced hippocampal volume, so did the identical (monozygotic) twins of those men (see **FIGURE 15.3**), even though the twins had never had any combat exposure or developed PTSD (Gilbertson et al., 2002). This suggests that the veterans' reduced hippocampal volumes weren't caused by the combat exposure; instead, both these veterans and their twin brothers might have had a smaller hippocampus to begin with, a preexisting condition that made them susceptible to developing PTSD when they were later exposed to trauma.

Build to the Outcomes

1. What is posttraumatic stress disorder (PTSD)?

2. How might brain structure and functioning be related to susceptibility to PTSD?

Depressive and Bipolar Disorders: Extreme Highs and Lows

You're probably in a mood right now. Maybe you're happy that it's almost time to get a snack or saddened by something you heard from a friend—or you may feel good or bad without having a clue why. As you learned in the Emotion and Motivation chapter, moods are relatively long-lasting, nonspecific emotional states—and *nonspecific* means we often may have no idea what has caused a mood. Changing moods lend variety to our experiences, like different-colored lights shining on the stage as we play out our lives. However, for people like Robin Williams and others with mood disorders, moods can become so intense that they are pulled or pushed into life-threatening actions.

Learning Outcomes

▶ Describe the symptoms of mood disorders, including depressive and bipolar disorders.

▶ Identify genetic and environmental factors that research indicates may be an influence in mood disorders.

The Blue Devils—!! George Cruikshank (1792–1878) portrayed a depressed man tormented by demons suggesting methods of suicide, harassing him as bill collectors, and forming a funeral procession.

"THE BLUE DEVILS—!!" PUBLISHED BY HANNAH HUMPHREY, 10TH JANUARY 1823 (COLOURED ENGRAVING)/CRUIKSHANK, GEORGE (1792–1878)/INDIVISION CHARMET/BIBLIOTHEQUE NATIONALE, PARIS, FRANCE/BRIDGEMAN IMAGES

Mood disorders are *mental disorders that have mood disturbance as their predominant feature* and take two main forms: *depression* (also called *unipolar depression*) and *bipolar disorder* (so named because people go from one end of the emotional pole [extreme depression] to the other [extreme mania]).

DEPRESSIVE DISORDERS

Everyone feels sad, pessimistic, and unmotivated from time to time. For most people these periods are relatively short lived and mild, but depression is much more than typical sadness. The experience of Mark, a 34-year-old man who visited his primary-care physician complaining of chronic fatigue, is fairly typical. During the visit, he mentioned difficulties falling asleep and staying asleep that left him chronically tired, so much so that he feared that maybe he had some kind of medical problem. He complained that over the past 6 months, he no longer had the energy to exercise and had gained 10 pounds. He also lost all interest in going out with his friends or even talking to other people. Nothing he normally enjoyed, even sexual activity, gave him pleasure anymore; he had trouble concentrating and was forgetful, irritable, impatient, and frustrated. Mark's change in mood and behavior, and the sense of hopelessness and weariness he felt goes far beyond normal sadness. Instead, depressive disorders are dysfunctional and chronic, and fall outside the range of socially or culturally expected responses.

Major depressive disorder (or unipolar depression), which we refer to here simply as "depression," is characterized by *a severely depressed mood and/or inability to experience pleasure that lasts 2 or more weeks and is accompanied by feelings of worthlessness, lethargy, and sleep and appetite disturbance.* In a related condition called **persistent depressive disorder,** *the same cognitive and bodily problems as in depression are present, but they are less severe and last longer, persisting for at least 2 years.* When both types co-occur, the resulting condition is called **double depression,** defined as *a moderately depressed mood that persists for at least 2 years and is punctuated by periods of major depression.*

Some people experience *recurrent depressive episodes in a seasonal pattern* that is commonly known as **seasonal affective disorder (SAD).** In most cases, SAD episodes begin in fall or winter and remit in spring, in a pattern that is due to reduced levels of light over the colder seasons (Westrin & Lam, 2007). Nevertheless, recurrent summer depressive episodes have been reported. A winter-related pattern of depression appears to be more prevalent in higher latitudes.

mood disorders Mental disorders that have mood disturbance as their predominant feature.

major depressive disorder (or unipolar depression) A disorder characterized by a severely depressed mood and/or inability to experience pleasure that lasts 2 or more weeks and is accompanied by feelings of worthlessness, lethargy, and sleep and appetite disturbance.

persistent depressive disorder The same cognitive and bodily problems as in depression are present, but they are less severe and last longer, persisting for at least 2 years.

double depression A moderately depressed mood that persists for at least 2 years and is punctuated by periods of major depression.

seasonal affective disorder (SAD) Recurrent depressive episodes in a seasonal pattern.

Seasonal affective disorder is not merely having the blues because of the weather. It appears to be due to reduced exposure to light in the winter months.

Who Is at Risk?

Approximately 18% of people in the United States meet the criteria for depression at some point in their lives (Kessler et al., 2012). On average, major depression lasts about 12 weeks (Eaton et al., 2008). However, without treatment, approximately 80% of individuals will experience at least one recurrence of the disorder (Judd, 1997; Mueller et al., 1999). Compared with people who have a single episode, individuals with recurrent depression have more severe symptoms, higher rates of depression in their families, more suicide attempts, and higher rates of divorce (Merikangas, Wicki, & Angst, 1994).

Similar to that of anxiety disorders, the rate of depression is much higher in women (22%) than in men (14%; Kessler et al., 2012). Socioeconomic standing has been invoked as an explanation for women's heightened risk: Their incomes are lower than those of men, and poverty could cause depression. Sex differences in hormones are another possibility: Estrogen, androgen, and progesterone influence depression; some women experience *postpartum depression* (depression following childbirth) due to changing hormone balances. It is also possible that the higher rate of depression in women reflects their greater willingness to face their depression and seek out help, leading to higher rates of diagnosis (Nolen-Hoeksema, 2008). Women have a tendency to accept, disclose, and ruminate on their negative emotions, whereas men are more likely to deny negative emotions and engage in self-distractions such as work and drinking alcohol.

Heritability estimates for major depression typically range from 33 to 45% (Plomin et al., 1997; Wallace, Schnieder, & McGuffin, 2002). However, as with most types of mental disorders, heritability rates vary as a function of severity. For example, a relatively large study of twins found that the concordance rates for severe major depression (defined as three or more episodes) were quite high, with a rate of 59% for identical twins and 30% for fraternal twins (Bertelsen, Harvald, & Hauge, 1977). In contrast, concordance rates for less severe major depression (defined as fewer than three episodes) fell to 33% for identical twins and 14% for fraternal twins. Heritability rates for persistent depressive disorder are low and inconsistent (Plomin et al., 1997). This makes depression about as heritable as complex medical conditions such as type 2 diabetes and asthma.

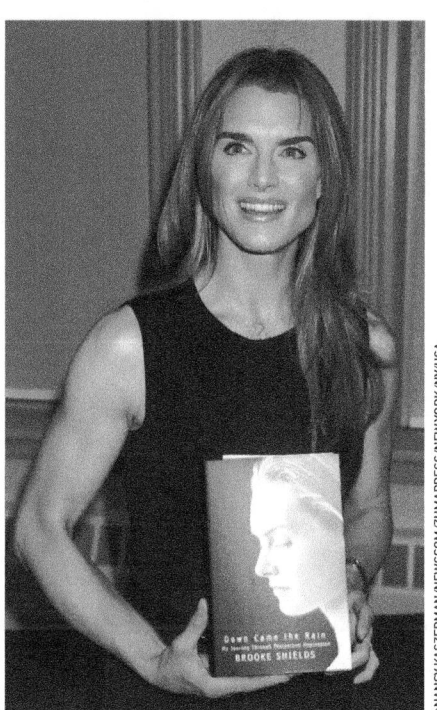

Postpartum depression can strike women out of nowhere, often causing new mothers to feel extreme sadness, guilt, and disconnection, and even to experience serious thoughts of suicide. The actress Brooke Shields wrote about her experience with postpartum depression in a popular book on this condition.

▶ Figure 15.4

GENE × ENVIRONMENT INTERACTIONS IN DEPRESSION Stressful life experiences are much more likely to lead to later depression among those with one, and especially two, short alleles of the serotonin transporter gene. Those with two long alleles, which are associated with more efficient serotonergic functioning, showed no increased risk of depression, even those who experienced severe maltreatment.

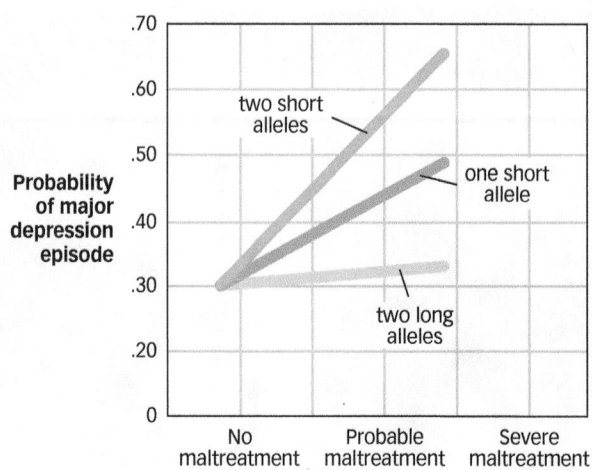

Neurotransmitters Play a Role, and So Does Stress

Beginning in the 1950s, researchers noticed that drugs that increased levels of the neurotransmitters norepinephrine and serotonin could sometimes reduce depression. This observation suggested that depression might be caused by an absolute or relative depletion of these neurotransmitters and sparked a revolution in the pharmacological treatment of depression (Schildkraut, 1965), leading to the development and widespread use of popular prescription drugs such as Prozac and Zoloft, which increase the availability of serotonin in the brain. Further research has shown, however, that reduced levels of these neurotransmitters cannot be the whole story regarding the causes of depression. For example, some studies have found *increases* in norepinephrine activity among depressed individuals (Thase & Howland, 1995). Moreover, even though these antidepressant medications change neurochemical transmission in less than a day, they typically take at least 2 weeks to relieve depressive symptoms. In many cases, they are not effective in decreasing depressive symptoms. A biochemical model of depression has yet to be developed that accounts for all the evidence.

Newer biological models of depression have tried to understand depression using a diathesis–stress framework. For instance, Avshalom Caspi and his colleagues (2003) found that stressful life events are much more likely to lead to depression among those with a certain genetic trait (vulnerability) related to the activity of the neurotransmitter serotonin, a finding showing that nature and nurture interact to influence brain structure, function, and chemistry in depression (see **FIGURE 15.4**).

Research also has begun to tell us what parts of the brain show abnormalities in depression. For instance, some important findings came out of a recent meta-analysis (which is a quantitative synthesis of the results of many individual studies) of 24 brain imaging studies. Results showed that when viewing negative stimuli (words or images), people suffering from depression showed both increased activity in regions of the brain associated with processing emotional information and decreased activity in areas associated with cognitive control (see **FIGURE 15.5**; Hamilton et al., 2012). Of course, this is not the whole picture; these findings don't explain all of the symptoms seen in depression, why and when depression comes and goes, or how treatment works. Given that depression does not arise due to a single gene or brain region, but likely from the interactions of different biological systems that each give rise to the different psychological traits seen in depression, it will likely be many years before we fully understand the biological causes of this disorder (Young et al., 2016).

	Structure	Activity in depression
A	Amygdala	Increased
B	Dorsal ACC	Increased
C	Insula and superior temporal gyrus	Increased
D	DLPFC	Decreased
E	Caudate body	Decreased

◄ **Figure 15.5**

THE BRAIN AND DEPRESSION When presented with negative information, people with depression show increased activation in regions of the brain associated with emotional processing, such as the amygdala, insula, and dorsal anterior cingulate cortex (ACC), and decreased activity in regions associated with cognitive control such as the dorsal striatum and dorsolateral prefrontal cortex (DLPFC; Hamilton et al., 2012).

Negative Thoughts Contribute to Depression

If optimists see the world through rose-colored glasses, people who suffer from depression tend to view the world through dark gray lenses. Their negative cognitive style is remarkably consistent and, some argue, begins in childhood with experiences that create a pattern of negative self thoughts (Blatt & Homann, 1992; Gibb, Alloy, & Tierney, 2001). One of the first theorists to emphasize the role of thought in depression, Aaron T. Beck (1967), noted that his depressed patients distorted perceptions of their experiences and embraced dysfunctional attitudes that promoted and maintained negative mood states. His observations led him to develop a *cognitive model of depression*, which states that biases in how information is attended to, processed, and remembered lead to and maintain depression.

Elaborating on this initial idea, researchers proposed a theory of depression that emphasizes the role of people's negative inferences about the causes of their experiences (Abramson, Seligman, & Teasdale, 1978). **Helplessness theory,** which is a part of the cognitive model of depression, maintains that *individuals who are prone to depression automatically attribute negative experiences to causes that are internal (i.e., their own fault), stable (i.e., unlikely to change), and global (i.e., widespread).* For example, a student at risk for depression might view a bad grade on a math test as a sign of low intelligence (internal) that will never change (stable) and that will lead to failure in all his or her future endeavors (global). In contrast, a student without this tendency might have the opposite response, attributing the grade to something external (poor teaching), unstable (a missed study session), and/or specific (boring subject).

The relationship between one's perceptions and depression has been further developed and supported over the past several decades. The update to Beck's cognitive model suggests that due to a combination of a genetic vulnerability and negative early life events, people with depression have developed a negative *schema* (described in the Development chapter). This negative schema is characterized by biases in:

▶ interpretations of information (a tendency to interpret neutral information negatively—seeing the world through gray glasses)

▶ attention (trouble disengaging from negative information)

▶ memory (better recall of negative information; Gotlib & Joormann, 2010)

For example, a student at risk for depression who gets a bad grade on a test might interpret a well-intentioned comment from the teacher ("Good job on the test") negatively ("She's being sarcastic!"); have trouble forgetting about both the test score

The cognitive model of depression is based on approaches to thinking developed by the Stoic philosophers of ancient Greece and Rome. Epictetus's famous quote, "Men are disturbed not by things, but by the principles and notions which they form concerning things," is commonly cited by cognitive theorists as a guiding principle of the cognitive model of depression.

helplessness theory The idea that individuals who are prone to depression automatically attribute negative experiences to causes that are internal (i.e., their own fault), stable (i.e., unlikely to change), and global (i.e., widespread).

bipolar disorder A condition characterized by cycles of abnormal, persistent high mood (mania) and low mood (depression).

and the perceived negative comment; and have better memory about this test in the future ("Sure, I did well on my English exam, but don't forget about that bad math test last month"). The presence of these biases may help to explain the internal, stable, and global attributions seen in depression. In addition, recent research suggests that some of the differences in brain structure and function seen in those with depression can help to explain some of these cognitive biases. For instance, people with depression show abnormalities in parts of the brain involved in attention and memory, especially when presented with negative information (Disner et al., 2011). Although we don't fully understand the causes of depression, pieces of the puzzle are being discovered and put together as you read this.

BIPOLAR DISORDER

If depression is distressing and painful, would the opposite extreme be better? Not for Julie, a 20-year-old college sophomore. When first seen by a clinician, Julie had gone 5 days without sleep and was extremely active and expressing bizarre thoughts and ideas. She proclaimed to friends that she did not menstruate because she was "of a third sex, a gender above the two human sexes." She claimed to be a "superwoman," capable of avoiding human sexuality and yet still able to give birth. Preoccupied with the politics of global disarmament, she felt that she had switched souls with the senior senator from her state, had tapped into his thoughts and memories, and could save the world from nuclear destruction. She began to campaign for an elected position in the U.S. government (even though no elections were scheduled at that time). Worried that she would forget some of her thoughts, she had been leaving hundreds of notes about her ideas and activities everywhere, including on the walls and furniture of her dormitory room (Vitkus, 1999).

In addition to her manic episodes, Julie had a history of depression. The diagnostic label for this constellation of symptoms is **bipolar disorder,** *a condition characterized by cycles of abnormal, persistent high mood (mania) and low mood (depression).* In about two thirds of people with bipolar disorder, manic episodes immediately precede or immediately follow depressive episodes (Whybrow, 1997). The depressive phase of bipolar disorder is often clinically indistinguishable from major depression (Johnson, Cuellar, & Miller, 2009). In the manic phase, which must last at least 1 week to meet *DSM* requirements, mood can be elevated, expansive, or irritable. Other prominent symptoms include grandiosity, decreased need for sleep, talkativeness, racing thoughts, distractibility, and reckless behavior (such as compulsive gambling, sexual indiscretions, and unrestrained spending sprees). Psychotic features such as hallucinations (erroneous perceptions) and delusions (erroneous beliefs) may be present, so the disorder can be misdiagnosed as schizophrenia (described in a later section of this chapter).

Here's how Kay Redfield Jamison (1995, p. 67) described her own experience with bipolar disorder in *An Unquiet Mind: A Memoir of Moods and Madness.*

> There is a particular kind of pain, elation, loneliness, and terror involved in this kind of madness. When you're high it's tremendous. The ideas and feelings are fast and frequent like shooting stars, and you follow them until you find better and brighter ones. . . . But, somewhere, this changes. The fast ideas are far too fast, and there are far too many; overwhelming confusion replaces clarity. Memory goes. Humor and absorption on friends' faces are replaced by fear and concern. Everything previously moving with the grain is now against—you are irritable, angry, frightened, uncontrollable, and enmeshed totally in the blackest caves of the mind. You never knew those caves were there. It will never end, for madness carves its own reality.

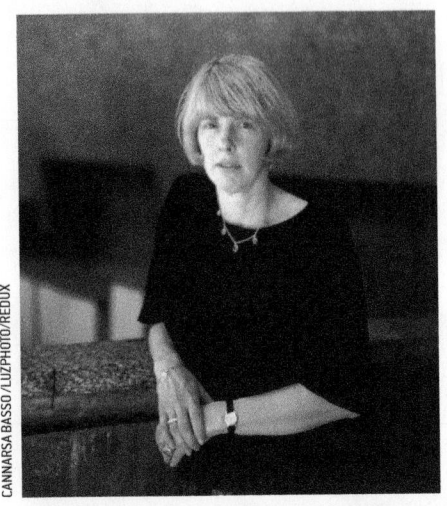

The psychologist Kay Redfield Jamison has written several best-selling books about her own struggles with bipolar disorder.

Who Is at Risk?

The lifetime risk for bipolar disorder is about 2.5% and does not differ between men and women (Kessler et al., 2012). Bipolar disorder is typically a recurrent condition, with approximately 90% of afflicted people suffering from several episodes over a lifetime (Coryell et al., 1995). About 10% of people with bipolar disorder have *rapid cycling bipolar disorder,* characterized by at least four mood episodes (either manic or depressive) every year. This form of the disorder is particularly difficult to treat (Post et al., 2008). Rapid cycling is more common in women than in men and is sometimes precipitated by taking certain kinds of antidepressant drugs (Liebenluft, 1996; Whybrow, 1997). Unfortunately, bipolar disorder tends to be persistent. In one study, 24% of the participants had relapsed within 6 months of recovery from an episode, and 77% had at least one new episode within 4 years of recovery (Coryell et al., 1995).

Some researchers have suggested that people with psychotic and mood (especially bipolar) disorders have higher creativity and intellectual ability (Andreasen, 2011). In bipolar disorder, this suggestion goes, before the mania becomes too pronounced, the energy, grandiosity, and ambition that it supplies may help people achieve great things. Notable individuals thought to have had the disorder include Isaac Newton, Vincent van Gogh, Abraham Lincoln, Ernest Hemingway, Winston Churchill, and Theodore Roosevelt.

Genetics and Life Situation Play a Role

Among the various mental disorders, bipolar disorder has one of the highest rates of heritability, with concordance from 40 to 70% for identical twins and 10% for fraternal twins (Craddock & Jones, 1999). Like most other disorders, bipolar disorder is likely *polygenic,* arising from the interaction of multiple genes that combine to create the symptoms observed in those with this disorder; however, these genes have been difficult to identify. Adding to the complexity, there also is evidence of *pleiotropic effects,* in which one gene influences a person's susceptibility to multiple disorders. For instance, one recent study revealed a shared genetic vulnerability for bipolar disorder and schizophrenia. The genes linked to both disorders are associated with compromised abilities both in filtering unnecessary information and recognition memory, as well as problems with dopamine and serotonin transmission—factors present in both types of disorders (Huang et al., 2010). A follow-up study examining more than 60,000 people revealed that common genetic risk factors are associated with bipolar disorder and schizophrenia, as well as major depression, autism spectrum disorder, and attention-deficit/hyperactivity disorder. These disorders share overlapping symptoms such as problems with mood regulation, cognitive impairments, and social withdrawal (Cross-Disorder Group of the Psychiatric Genomics Consortium, 2013). Findings like these are exciting because they help us begin to understand why we see similar symptoms in people with what we previously thought were unrelated disorders. Although some genetic links have been made, we currently lack an understanding of how different biological factors work together to cause the symptoms observed in bipolar and other disorders.

There is growing evidence that the epigenetic changes you learned about in the Neuroscience and Behavior chapter can help to explain how genetic risk factors influence the development of bipolar and related disorders. Remember how rat pups whose moms spent less time licking and grooming them experienced epigenetic changes (decreased DNA methylation) that led to a poorer stress response? As you might expect, these same kinds of epigenetic effects seem to help explain who develops symptoms of mental disorders and who doesn't. For instance, studies examining monozygotic twin pairs (identical twins, who share 100% of their DNA) in which one develops bipolar disorder or schizophrenia and one doesn't, reveal significant epigenetic differences between the two, with decreased methylation at genetic locations known to be important in brain development and the occurrence of bipolar disorders and schizophrenia (Dempster et al., 2011; Labrie, Pai, & Petronis, 2012).

expressed emotion A measure of how much hostility, criticism, and emotional overinvolvement that people communicate when speaking about a family member with a mental disorder.

Stressful life experiences often precede manic and depressive episodes (Johnson, Cuellar, et al., 2008). One study found that severely stressed individuals took an average of three times longer to recover from an episode than did individuals not affected by stress (Johnson & Miller, 1997). The stress–disorder relationship is not simple, however: High levels of stress have less impact on people with extraverted personalities than on those with more introverted personalities (Swednsen et al., 1995). Personality characteristics such as neuroticism and conscientiousness have also been found to predict increases in bipolar symptoms over time (Lozano & Johnson, 2001). Finally, people living with family members high in **expressed emotion,** which in this context is *a measure of how much hostility, criticism, and emotional overinvolvement people communicate when speaking about a family member with a mental disorder*, are more likely to relapse than people with supportive families (Miklowitz & Johnson, 2006). This is true not just of those with bipolar disorder: Expressed emotion is associated with higher rates of relapse across a wide range of mental disorders (Hooley, 2007).

Build to the Outcomes

1. What is a mood disorder?

2. What is the difference between depression and sadness?

3. What are the types of depressive disorders?

4. What factors may explain why women experience higher rates of depression than men?

5. How does the diathesis–stress framework help explain depression?

6. What is the helplessness theory?

7. What are the elements of the negative schema that characterizes the outlook of some people with depression?

8. What is bipolar disorder?

9. Why is bipolar disorder sometimes misdiagnosed as schizophrenia?

10. How does our understanding of epigenetics further our understanding of genetic risk factors?

11. How does stress relate to manic-depressive episodes?

12. Define *expressed emotion* in the context of mood disorders.

Schizophrenia and Other Psychotic Disorders: Losing the Grasp on Reality

Learning Outcomes

► Compare the negative, positive, and cognitive symptoms of schizophrenia.

► Describe the biological factors contributing to schizophrenia.

► Explain the evidence for the influence of environmental factors.

Margaret, a 39-year-old mother, believed that God was punishing her for marrying a man she did not love and bringing two children into the world. As her punishment, God had made her and her children immortal so that they would have to suffer in their unhappy home life forever—a realization that came to her one evening when she was washing dishes and saw a fork lying across a knife in the shape of a cross. Margaret found further support for her belief in two pieces of evidence: First, a local television station was rerunning old episodes of *The Honeymooners,* a 1950s situation comedy in which the main characters often argue and shout at each other. She saw this as a sign from God that her own marital conflict would go on forever. Second, she believed (falsely) that the pupils of her children's eyes were fixed in size and would neither dilate nor constrict—a sign of their immortality. At home, she would lock herself in her room for hours and sometimes days. The week before her diagnosis, she kept her 7-year-old son home from school so that he could join her and his 4-year-old sister in reading aloud from the Bible (Oltmanns et al., 1991). Margaret was suffering from the best-known, most widely studied psychotic disorder: schizophrenia. Schizophrenia is one of the most mystifying and devastating of all the mental disorders. Many people with this disorder experience a lifetime of suffering and impairment, but see Other Voices: Successful

Successful and Schizophrenic

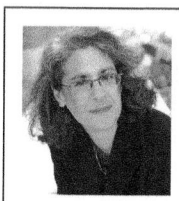

Elyn R. Saks is a law professor at the University of Southern California and the author of the memoir *The Center Cannot Hold: My Journey Through Madness.*

This chapter describes what we know about the characteristics and causes of mental disorders, and the next chapter describes how these disorders are commonly treated. For some of the more severe disorders, such as schizophrenia, the picture does not look good. People diagnosed with schizophrenia often are informed that it is a lifelong condition, and although current treatments show some effectiveness in decreasing the delusional thinking and hallucinations often present in those with schizophrenia, people with this disorder often are unable to hold down a full-time job, maintain healthy relationships, or achieve a high quality of life.

Elyn Saks is one such person. She received a diagnosis of schizophrenia and was informed of this prognosis. She described what happened next in a longer version of the following article, which appeared in the *New York Times.*

Thirty years ago, I was given a diagnosis of schizophrenia. My prognosis was "grave": I would never live independently, hold a job, find a loving partner, get married. My home would be a board-and-care facility, my days spent watching TV in a day room with other people debilitated by mental illness....

Then I made a decision. I would write the narrative of my life. Today I am a chaired professor at the University of Southern California Gould School of Law. I have an adjunct appointment in the department of psychiatry at the medical school of the University of California, San Diego. The MacArthur Foundation gave me a genius grant.

Although I fought my diagnosis for many years, I came to accept that I have schizophrenia and will be in treatment the rest of my life.... What I refused to accept was my prognosis.

Conventional psychiatric thinking and its diagnostic categories say that people like me don't exist. Either I don't have schizophrenia (please tell that to the delusions crowding my mind), or I couldn't have accomplished what I have (please tell that to U.S.C.'s committee on faculty affairs). But I do, and I have. And I have undertaken research with colleagues at U.S.C. and U.C.L.A. to show that I am not alone. There are others with schizophrenia and such active symptoms as delusions and hallucinations who have significant academic and professional achievements.

Over the last few years, my colleagues . . . and I have gathered 20 research subjects with high-functioning schizophrenia in Los Angeles. They suffered from symptoms like mild delusions or hallucinatory behavior. Their average age was 40. Half were male, half female, and more than half were minorities. All had high school diplomas, and a majority either had or were working toward college or graduate degrees. They were graduate students, managers, technicians and professionals, including a doctor, lawyer, psychologist and chief executive of a nonprofit group. At the same time, most were unmarried and childless, which is consistent with their diagnoses.... More than three-quarters had been hospitalized between two and five times because of their illness, while three had never been admitted.

How had these people with schizophrenia managed to succeed in their studies and at such high-level jobs? We learned that, in addition to medication and therapy, all the participants had developed techniques to keep their schizophrenia at bay. For some, these techniques were cognitive. An educator with a master's degree said he had learned to face his hallucinations and ask, "What's the evidence for that? Or is it just a perception problem?" Another participant said, "I hear derogatory voices all the time....You just gotta blow them off."...

Other techniques that our participants cited included controlling sensory inputs. For some, this meant keeping their living space simple (bare walls, no TV, only quiet music), while for others, it meant distracting music. "I'll listen to loud music if I don't want to hear things," said a participant who is a certified nurse's assistant. Still others mentioned exercise, a healthy diet, avoiding alcohol and getting enough sleep....

One of the most frequently mentioned techniques that helped our research participants manage their symptoms was work. "Work has been an important part of who I am," said an educator in our group. "When you become useful to an organization and feel respected in that organization, there's a certain value in belonging there." This person works on the weekends too because of "the distraction factor." In other words, by engaging in work, the crazy stuff often recedes to the sidelines....

That is why it is so distressing when doctors tell their patients not to expect or pursue fulfilling careers. Far too often, the conventional psychiatric approach to mental illness is to see clusters of symptoms that characterize people. Accordingly, many psychiatrists hold the view that treating symptoms with medication is treating mental illness. But this fails to take into account individuals' strengths and capabilities, leading mental health professionals to underestimate what their patients can hope to achieve in the world.... A recent New York Times Magazine article described a new company that hires high-functioning adults with autism, taking advantage of their unusual memory skills and attention to detail....

An approach that looks for individual strengths, in addition to considering symptoms, could help dispel the pessimism surrounding mental illness. Finding "the wellness within the illness," as one person with schizophrenia said, should be a therapeutic goal. Doctors should urge their patients to develop relationships and engage in meaningful work. They should encourage patients to find their own repertory of techniques to manage their symptoms and aim for a quality of life as they define it. And they should provide patients with the resources—therapy, medication and support—to make these things happen.

Elyn Saks's story is amazing and inspiring. It also is quite unusual. How should we incorporate stories like hers and the people in the research study she described? Are these people outliers—simply a carefully selected collection of people who had unusually favorable outcomes? (Given that Los Angeles is such a large city, it is reasonable to think one could amass a small sample of such cases.) Or has Professor Saks touched on an important limitation to the way in which the field currently conceptualizes, classifies, and treats mental disorders? Do we focus too much on what is wrong and on how professionalized health care can treat the pathology and not enough on what inherent strengths people have that can help them overcome their challenges, function at a high level, and achieve a high quality of life? These are all questions that are testable with the methods of psychological science, and the answers may help to improve the lives of many people.

Those suffering from schizophrenia often experience hallucinations and delusions, unable to determine what is real and what their own minds have created. The experience of John Nash, a Nobel Prize–winning economist with schizophrenia, was depicted in the book and movie *A Beautiful Mind*.

schizophrenia A disorder characterized by the profound disruption of basic psychological processes; a distorted perception of reality; altered or blunted emotion; and disturbances in thought, motivation, and behavior.

positive symptoms Thoughts and behaviors, such as delusions and hallucinations, present in schizophrenia but not seen in those without the disorder.

hallucination A false perceptual experience that has a compelling sense of being real despite the absence of external stimulation.

delusion A false belief, often bizarre and grandiose, that is maintained in spite of its irrationality.

disorganized speech A severe disruption of verbal communication in which ideas shift rapidly and incoherently among unrelated topics.

and Schizophrenic for a discussion of the fact that many with this disorder have very successful careers and fulfilling lives). A review of the symptoms of this disorder make clear why this condition can be so distressing and impairing.

SYMPTOMS AND TYPES OF SCHIZOPHRENIA

Schizophrenia is a psychotic disorder (*psychosis* is a break from reality) characterized by *the profound disruption of basic psychological processes; a distorted perception of reality; altered or blunted emotion; and disturbances in thought, motivation, and behavior*. Traditionally, schizophrenia was regarded primarily as a disturbance of thought and perception, in which the sense of reality becomes severely distorted and confused. However, this condition is now understood to take different forms affecting a wide range of functions. According to the *DSM–5*, schizophrenia is diagnosed when two or more symptoms emerge during a continuous period of at least 1 month, with signs of the disorder persisting for at least 6 months. The symptoms of schizophrenia often are separated into *positive, negative,* and *cognitive symptoms*.

Positive symptoms of schizophrenia include *thoughts and behaviors, such as delusions and hallucinations, not seen in those without the disorder*:

▶ **Hallucinations** are *false perceptual experiences that have a compelling sense of being real despite the absence of external stimulation*. The perceptual disturbances associated with schizophrenia can include hearing, seeing, smelling, or having a tactile sensation of things that are not there. Schizophrenic hallucinations are often auditory (e.g., hearing voices that no one else can hear). Among people with schizophrenia, some 65% report hearing voices repeatedly (Frith & Fletcher, 1995). The British psychiatrist Henry Maudsley (1886) long ago proposed that these voices are in fact produced in the mind of the person with schizophrenia, and recent research substantiates his idea. In one PET imaging study, auditory hallucinations were accompanied by activation in Broca's area (discussed in the Neuroscience and Behavior chapter), the part of the brain associated with the production of language (McGuire, Shah, & Murray, 1993). Unfortunately, the voices heard in schizophrenia seldom sound like the self or like a kindly uncle offering advice. They command, scold, suggest bizarre actions, or offer snide comments. One individual reported a voice saying, "He's getting up now. He's going to wash. It's about time" (Frith & Fletcher, 1995).

▶ **Delusions** are *false beliefs, often bizarre and grandiose, that are maintained in spite of their irrationality*. For example, an individual with schizophrenia may believe that he or she is Jesus Christ, Napoleon, Joan of Arc, or some other well-known person. Such delusions of identity have helped foster the misconception that schizophrenia involves multiple personalities. However, adopted identities in schizophrenia do not alternate, exhibit amnesia for each other, or otherwise "split." Delusions of persecution are also common. Some individuals believe that the CIA, demons, extraterrestrials, or other malevolent forces are conspiring to harm them or control their minds, which may represent an attempt to make sense of the tormenting delusions (Roberts, 1991). People with schizophrenia have little or no insight into their disordered perceptual and thought processes (Karow et al., 2007). Without understanding that they have lost control of their own minds, they may develop unusual beliefs and theories that attribute control to external agents.

▶ **Disorganized speech** is *a severe disruption of verbal communication in which ideas shift rapidly and incoherently among unrelated topics*. The abnormal speech patterns in schizophrenia reflect difficulties in organizing thoughts and focusing attention. Individuals often make irrelevant responses to questions, associate ideas loosely, and use words in peculiar ways. For example, asked by her doctor, "Can you tell me the name of this place?" one patient with schizophrenia responded, "I have not been a drinker for 16 years. I am taking a mental rest after a 'carter' assignment of 'quill.' You know, a 'penwrap.' I had contracts with Warner Brothers Studios and Eugene broke phonograph records but Mike protested. I have been with the police department for 35 years. I am made of flesh and blood—see, Doctor" [pulling up her dress] (Carson et al., 2000, p. 474).

▶ **Grossly disorganized behavior** is *behavior that is inappropriate for the situation or ineffective in attaining goals*, often with specific motor disturbances. An individual might exhibit constant childlike silliness, improper sexual behavior (such as masturbating in public), disheveled appearance, or loud shouting or swearing. Specific motor disturbances might include strange movements, rigid posturing, odd mannerisms, bizarre grimacing, or hyperactivity. **Catatonic behavior** is a marked decrease in all movement or an increase in muscular rigidity and overactivity. Individuals with catatonia may actively resist movement (when someone is trying to move them) or become completely unresponsive and unaware of their surroundings in a stupor. In addition, individuals receiving drug therapy may exhibit motor symptoms (such as rigidity or spasm) as a side effect of the medication. Indeed, the DSM–5 includes a diagnostic category labeled "medication-induced movement disorders" that identifies motor disturbances arising from medications of the sort commonly used to treat schizophrenia.

A person suffering from catatonic schizophrenia may assume an unusual posture and fail to move for hours.

Negative symptoms are *deficits in or disruptions of normal emotions and behaviors*. They include emotional and social withdrawal; apathy; poverty of speech; and other indications of the absence or insufficiency of normal behavior, motivation, and emotion. These symptoms refer to things missing in people with schizophrenia. Negative symptoms may rob people of emotion, for example, leaving them with flat, deadpan responses; their interest in people or events may be undermined, or their capacity to focus attention may be impaired.

Cognitive symptoms are *deficits in cognitive abilities, specifically in executive functioning, attention, and working memory*. These are the least noticeable symptoms because they are much less bizarre and public than the positive and negative symptoms. However, these cognitive deficits often play a large role in preventing people with schizophrenia from achieving a high level of functioning, such as maintaining friendships and holding down a job (Green et al., 2000).

Schizophrenia occurs in about 1% of the population (Jablensky, 1997) and is slightly more common in men than in women (McGrath et al., 2008). Early versions of the *DSM* suggested that schizophrenia might have a very early onset—in the form of infantile autism—but more recent studies suggest that these disorders are distinct and that schizophrenia rarely develops before early adolescence (Rapoport et al., 2009). The first episode typically occurs in late adolescence or early adulthood (Gottesman, 1991). Despite its relatively low frequency, schizophrenia is the primary diagnosis for nearly 40% of all admissions to state and county mental hospitals; it is the second most frequent diagnosis for inpatient psychiatric admission at other institutions (Rosenstein, Milazzo-Sayre, & Manderscheid, 1990). The disproportionate rate of hospitalization for schizophrenia is a testament to the devastation it causes in people's lives.

BIOLOGICAL FACTORS

In 1899, when the German psychiatrist Emil Kraepelin first described the syndrome we now know as schizophrenia, he remarked that the disorder was so severe that it

grossly disorganized behavior
Behavior that is inappropriate for the situation or ineffective in attaining goals, often with specific motor disturbances.

catatonic behavior A marked decrease in all movement or an increase in muscular rigidity and overactivity.

negative symptoms Deficits in or disruptions of normal emotions and behaviors (e.g., emotional and social withdrawal; apathy; poverty of speech; and other indications of the absence or insufficiency of normal behavior, motivation, and emotion) that are present in those with schizophrenia.

cognitive symptoms Deficits in cognitive abilities, specifically executive functioning, attention, and working memory, present in those with schizophrenia.

▶ **Figure 15.6**
AVERAGE RISK OF DEVELOPING SCHIZOPHRENIA The risk of schizophrenia among biological relatives is greater for those with greater degrees of relatedness. An identical (MZ) twin of a person with schizophrenia has a 48% risk of developing schizophrenia, for example. Offspring of two parents with schizophrenia have a 46% risk of developing this disorder (data from Gottesman, 1991).

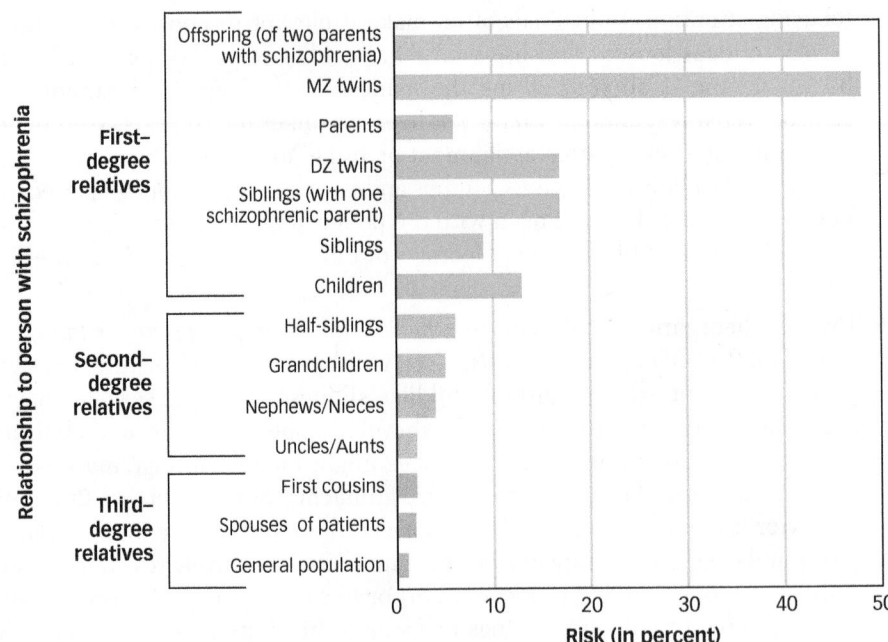

suggested "organic," or biological, origins. Over the years, accumulating evidence for the role of biology in schizophrenia has come from studies of genetic factors, biochemical factors, and neuroanatomy.

Genetic Factors and Environment Play a Role

Family studies indicate that the closer a person's genetic relatedness to a person with schizophrenia, the greater their likelihood of developing the disorder (Gottesman, 1991). As shown in **FIGURE 15.6**, concordance rates increase dramatically with biological relatedness. These rates are estimates and vary considerably from study to study, but almost every study finds the average concordance rates higher for identical twins (48%) than for fraternal twins (17%), which suggests a genetic component to the disorder (Torrey et al., 1994).

Although genetics clearly have a strong predisposing role in schizophrenia, considerable evidence suggests that environmental factors, such as prenatal and perinatal environments, also affect concordance rates (Jurewicz, Owen, & O'Donovan, 2001; Thaker, 2002; Torrey et al., 1994). For example, because approximately 70% of identical twins share the same prenatal blood supply, toxins in the mother's blood could contribute to the high concordance rate. More recent studies (discussed in the earlier section on bipolar disorder) are contributing to a better understanding of how environmental stressors can trigger epigenetic changes that increase susceptibility to this disorder.

The Precise Role of Neurotransmitters Has Yet to Be Fully Understood

During the 1950s, researchers discovered major tranquilizers that could reduce the symptoms of schizophrenia by lowering levels of the neurotransmitter dopamine. The effectiveness of many drugs in alleviating schizophrenic symptoms is related to the drugs' capacity to reduce dopamine's role in neurotransmission in certain brain tracts. This finding suggested the **dopamine hypothesis,** *the idea that schizophrenia involves an excess of dopamine activity.* The hypothesis has been invoked to explain why amphetamines, which increase dopamine levels, often exacerbate symptoms of schizophrenia (Harro, 2015).

dopamine hypothesis The idea that schizophrenia involves an excess of dopamine activity.

(a)   (b)

DR. KUNUGI

◄ Figure 15.7

ENLARGED VENTRICLES IN SCHIZOPHRENIA
These MRI scans of monozygotic twins reveal that (a) the twin affected by schizophrenia shows enlarged ventricles (all the central white space), compared with (b) the unaffected twin (Kunugi et al., 2003).

If only things were so simple. Considerable evidence suggests that this hypothesis is inadequate (Moncrieff, 2009). For example, many individuals with schizophrenia do not respond favorably to dopamine-blocking drugs (e.g., major tranquilizers), and those who do seldom show a complete remission of symptoms. Moreover, the drugs block dopamine receptors very rapidly, yet individuals with schizophrenia typically do not show a beneficial response for weeks. Finally, research has implicated other neurotransmitters in schizophrenia, suggesting that the disorder may involve a complex interaction among a host of different biochemicals (Risman et al., 2008; Sawa & Snyder, 2002). In sum, the precise role of neurotransmitters in schizophrenia has yet to be determined.

Research Has Identified Structural Changes in the Brain

When neuroimaging techniques became available, researchers immediately started looking for distinctive anatomical features of the brain in individuals with schizophrenia. The earliest observations revealed enlargement of the *ventricles,* hollow areas filled with cerebrospinal fluid, lying deep within the core of the brain (see **FIGURE 15.7**; Johnstone et al., 1976). In some individuals (primarily those with chronic, negative symptoms), the ventricles were abnormally enlarged, suggesting a loss of brain-tissue mass that could arise from an anomaly in prenatal development (Arnold et al., 1998; Heaton et al., 1994).

Understanding the significance of this brain abnormality for schizophrenia is complicated by several factors, however. First, such enlarged ventricles are found in only a minority of individuals with schizophrenia. Second, some individuals who do not have schizophrenia also show evidence of enlarged ventricles. Finally, this type of brain abnormality can be caused by the long-term use of some types of antipsychotic medications commonly prescribed for schizophrenia (Breggin, 1990; Gur et al., 1998).

Neuroimaging studies provide evidence of a variety of brain abnormalities associated with schizophrenia. Paul Thompson and his colleagues (2001) examined changes in the brains of adolescents whose MRI scans could be traced sequentially from the onset of schizophrenia. By superimposing the scans onto an image of a standardized brain, the researchers were able to detect progressive tissue loss beginning in the parietal lobe and eventually encompassing much of the brain (see **FIGURE 15.8**). All adolescents lose some gray matter over time in a kind of normal "pruning" of the brain, but in those developing schizophrenia, the loss was dramatic enough to seem pathological. A variety of specific brain changes found in other studies suggests a clear relationship between biological changes in the brain and the progression of schizophrenia (Cannon, 2015).

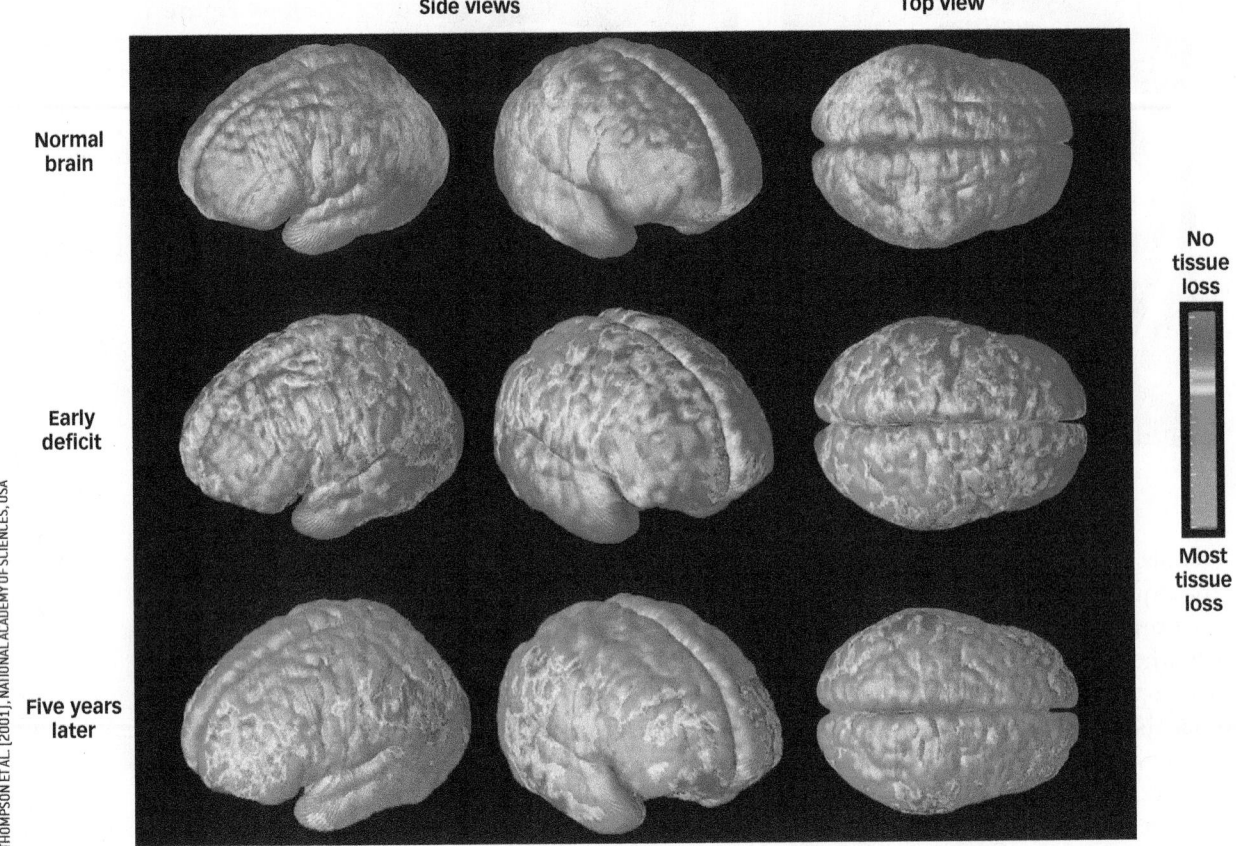

Side views | Top view

Normal brain

Early deficit

Five years later

No tissue loss

Most tissue loss

THOMPSON ET AL. (2001), NATIONAL ACADEMY OF SCIENCES, USA

▲ Figure 15.8

BRAIN TISSUE LOSS IN ADOLESCENT SCHIZOPHRENIA MRI scan composites reveal brain tissue loss in adolescents diagnosed with schizophrenia. Normal brains show minimal loss due to "pruning" (*top*). Early-deficit scans reveal loss in the parietal areas (*middle*); individuals at this stage may experience symptoms such as hallucinations or bizarre thoughts. Scans 5 years later reveal extensive tissue loss over much of the cortex (*bottom*); individuals at this stage are likely to suffer from delusions, disorganized speech and behavior, and negative symptoms such as social withdrawal (Thompson et al., 2001).

SOCIAL/PSYCHOLOGICAL FACTORS

With all these potential biological contributors to schizophrenia, you might think there would be few psychological or social causes of this disorder. However, several studies suggest that family environment plays a role in the development of and recovery from the condition. One large-scale study compared the risk of schizophrenia in children adopted into healthy families and those adopted into severely disturbed families (Tienari et al., 2004). (Disturbed families were defined as those with extreme conflict, lack of communication, or chaotic relationships.) Among children whose biological mothers had schizophrenia, the disturbed environment increased their likelihood of developing schizophrenia—an outcome that was not found among children who were also reared in disturbed families but whose biological mothers did *not* have schizophrenia. This finding provides support for the diathesis–stress model described earlier.

Build to the Outcomes

1. What is schizophrenia?

2. What are the positive, negative, and cognitive symptoms of schizophrenia?

3. What is the role of genetics in schizophrenia?

4. How do biochemical factors contribute to schizophrenia?

5. What changes appear in the brains of people with schizophrenia?

6. What environmental factors contribute to schizophrenia?

Disorders of Childhood and Adolescence

Most of the disorders described above can have their onset during childhood, adolescence, or adulthood. In fact, half of all disorders begin by age 14 and three quarters by age 24 (Kessler, Berglund, et al., 2005). Several of the disorders you have learned about tend not to begin until early adulthood, such as bipolar disorder and schizophrenia. However, other disorders *always*, by definition, begin in childhood or adolescence, and if they don't, you are never going to have them. These include autism spectrum disorder, attention-deficit/hyperactivity disorder, conduct disorder, intellectual disability (formerly called *mental retardation*), learning disorders, communication disorders, and motor skill disorders, in addition to many others. The first three are among the most common and best known, so we will review them briefly here.

AUTISM SPECTRUM DISORDER

Marco is a 4-year-old only child. His parents have become worried because, although his mother stays home with him all day and tries to talk with him and play with him, he still has not spoken a single word, and he shows little interest in trying. He spends much of his time playing with his toy trains, which seem to be the thing he enjoys most in life. He often sits for hours staring at spinning train wheels or pushing a single train back and forth, seeming completely in his own world, uninterested in playing with anyone else. Marco's parents have become concerned about his apparent inability to speak, lack of interest in others, and development of some peculiar mannerisms, such as flapping his arms repeatedly for no apparent reason.

Autism spectrum disorder (ASD) is *a condition beginning in early childhood in which a person shows persistent communication deficits as well as restricted and repetitive patterns of behaviors, interests, or activities*. In *DSM–5*, ASD now subsumes multiple disorders that were considered separate in *DSM–IV*: autistic disorder, Asperger's disorder, childhood disintegrative disorder, and pervasive developmental disorder not otherwise specified (i.e., these disorders are no longer recognized in the *DSM*).

The true rate of ASD is difficult to pinpoint, especially given the recent change in diagnostic definition. Estimates from the 1960s indicated that autism was a rare diagnosis, occurring in 4 per 10,000 children. Estimates have been creeping up over time and now stand at approximately 10 to 20 per 10,000 children. If one considers the full range of disorders that now fall under the ASD umbrella in the *DSM–5*, the rate is 60 per 10,000 children (Newschaffer et al., 2007). It is unclear whether this increased rate is due to increased awareness and recognition of ASD, better screening and diagnostic tools, or to some other factor. Boys have higher rates of ASD than girls by a ratio of about 4:1.

Early theories of autism described it as "childhood schizophrenia," but it is now understood to be separate from schizophrenia, which is rarely diagnosed in children, emerging mainly in adolescence or young adulthood (Kessler & Wang, 2008). ASD is currently viewed as a heterogeneous set of traits that cluster together in some families (heritability estimates for ASD are as high as 90%), leaving some children with just a few mild ASD traits and others with a more severe form of the disorder (Geschwind, 2009). Although the causes of ASD are not yet fully understood, one thing that is now clear is that despite a great deal of research examining the question, there is no evidence that ASD is caused by vaccinations (Mandy & Lai, 2016).

One current model suggested that ASD can be understood as an impaired capacity for *empathizing,* knowing the mental states of others, combined with a superior ability for *systematizing,* understanding the rules that organize the structure and function of objects (Baron-Cohen & Belmonte, 2005). Consistent with this model, brain imaging studies show that people with autism have comparatively decreased activity in regions

autism spectrum disorder (ASD) A condition beginning in early childhood in which a person shows persistent communication deficits as well as restricted and repetitive patterns of behaviors, interests, or activities.

Temple Grandin, a professor of animal sciences at Colorado State University, is living proof that people with autism spectrum disorder are able to have very successful professional careers.

Optimal Outcome in Autism Spectrum Disorder

What comes to mind when you think of the word *autism*? What kind of person do you imagine? If that person is an adult, what do you imagine that they do for a living? Can they hold a job? Can they care for themselves? Many people consider Autism Spectrum Disorder (ASD) a lifelong condition and believe that those affected will forever experience significant difficulties and disabilities in their interpersonal, education, and occupational functioning. However, recent studies are helping to change this outlook.

Deborah Fein and colleagues (2013) recently described a sample of people who were diagnosed with autism as children, but who no longer met the criteria for ASD. How could this be? For years, researchers have noticed that some portion of children diagnosed with autism later fail to meet diagnostic criteria. One recent review suggested that 3 to 25% of children ultimately lose their ASD diagnosis over time (Helt et al., 2008). There are several potential explanations for this change. The most obvious is that some portion of children diagnosed with ASD are misdiagnosed and don't really have this disorder. Perhaps they are overly shy, or quiet, or develop speech later than other children, and this is misinterpreted as ASD. Another possibility is that children who lose their ASD diagnosis had a milder form of the disorder and/or were identified and treated earlier. There is some support for this idea, as one recent study found that 17% of children diagnosed with ASD at age 2 no longer met the criteria for this disorder at age 4. The strongest predictors of this optimal outcome were

less severe symptoms, fewer repetitive behaviors, and stronger adaptive skills (Moulton et al., 2016).

The possibility of effectively treating ASD initially was raised in an important study by Ivar Lovaas in 1987. Lovaas assigned 19 children with autism to an intensive behavioral intervention in which they received over 40 hours per week of one-on-one behavior therapy for 2 years, and 40 children to control conditions in which they received fewer than 10 hours per week of treatment. Amazingly, the follow-up of the treated children revealed that 47% of those in the intensive behavior therapy condition obtained a normal level of intellectual and educational functioning—passing through a normal first grade class—compared with only 2% of those in the control conditions.

Extending this earlier work, Geraldine Dawson and colleagues are testing a program called the Early Start Denver Model (ESDM), an intensive behavioral intervention (20 hours per week for 2 years) similarly designed to improve outcomes among those with ASD. Using randomized, controlled trials, Dawson and her colleagues found that compared with those receiving standard community treatment, toddlers with ASD who received ESDM showed significant improvements in IQ (a 17-point rise!), language, adaptive and social functioning, and ASD diagnosis (Dawson et al., 2010). Many of these gains persisted when the children were 6 years old, two years after the treatment ended (Estes et al., 2015). Interestingly, children in the ESDM showed normalized brain activity after treatment (i.e., greater brain

activation when viewing faces), which was in turn associated with improved social behavior; those in the control condition showed the opposite pattern (Dawson et al., 2012).

Given that early detection and treatment can lead to such positive outcomes for those with ASD, should we be screening all young children for ASD so we can catch it early and intervene? This is an area of intense debate. The U.S. Preventive Services Task Force recently released a report concluding that there is insufficient evidence to conclude that the benefits of universal screening outweigh the potential risks (e.g., misdiagnosis of ASD) (Siu & U.S. Preventive Task force, 2016). However, Dawson (2016) and others argue that because we have methods of accurately detecting and effectively treating ASD in young children, we should screen all children for this disorder, so that we can maximize their chances of optimal outcomes. Researchers and policy makers will be working actively on this issue in the years ahead.

▲ Autism was once viewed as a condition with lifelong impairments. New research suggests that early intervention can help many of those in whom ASD is diagnosed to achieve normal levels of functioning.

associated with understanding the minds of others and greater activation in regions related to basic object perception (Sigman, Spence, & Wang, 2006).

Although many people with ASD experience impairments throughout their lives that prevent them from having relationships and holding down a job, many go on to very successful careers. This is often due to the unique strengths that some people with ASD have, such as the abilities to perceive or remember details or to master symbol systems such as mathematics or music (Happé & Vital, 2009). The renowned behavioral scientist and author Temple Grandin (2006) has written of her personal experience with autism. She was diagnosed with autism at age 3, started learning to talk late, and then suffered teasing for odd habits and "nerdy" behavior. Fortunately, she developed ways to cope and found a niche through her special talent—the ability to understand animal behavior (Sacks, 1996). She is now a Professor of Animal Sciences at Colorado State University; celebrated author of books such as *Animals in Translation;* designer of animal handling systems used widely in ranching, farming, and zoos; and the central character in an HBO movie based on her life. Temple Grandin's story lets us know that there are happy endings. Overall, those diagnosed with ASD as children have highly variable trajectories, with some achieving normal or better-than-normal functioning and others struggling with profound disorder. Autism is a childhood disorder that in adulthood can have many outcomes (see Hot Science: Optimal Outcome in Autism Spectrum Disorder).

ATTENTION-DEFICIT/HYPERACTIVITY DISORDER

Chances are you have had the experience of being distracted during a lecture or while reading one of your *other* textbooks. We all have trouble focusing from time to time. Far beyond normal distraction, **attention deficit/hyperactivity disorder (ADHD)** is *a persistent pattern of severe problems with inattention and/or hyperactivity or impulsiveness that cause significant impairments in functioning.* This is quite different from occasional mind wandering or bursts of activity. Meeting the criteria for ADHD requires having multiple symptoms of inattention (e.g., persistent problems with sustained attention, organization, memory, following instructions), hyperactivity–impulsiveness (e.g., persistent difficulties with remaining still, waiting for a turn, interrupting others), or both. Most children experience some of these behaviors at some point, but to meet the criteria for ADHD, a child has to have many of these behaviors for at least 6 months in at least two settings (e.g., home and school) to the point where they impair the child's ability to perform at school or get along at home.

Approximately 10% of boys and 4% of girls meet criteria for ADHD (Polanczyk et al., 2007). The *DSM–5* requires that symptoms of ADHD be present before the age of 12 in order to meet the criteria for this disorder. As you can imagine, children and adolescents with ADHD often struggle in the classroom. One recent study of 500 people with ADHD found that about half had a C average or lower, and about one third were in special classes (Biederman et al., 2006). For a long time ADHD was thought of as a disorder that affects only children and adolescents and that people "age out" of it. However, we now know that in many instances this disorder persists into adulthood. The same symptoms are used to diagnose both children and adults. (For example, children with ADHD may struggle with attention and concentration in the classroom, whereas adults may experience the same problems in meetings.) Approximately 4% of adults meet the criteria for ADHD; they are more likely to be male, divorced, and unemployed—and most did not receive any treatment for their ADHD (Kessler, Adler, et al., 2006). Unfortunately, most people still think of ADHD as a disorder of childhood and don't realize that adults can suffer from it as well. This could be why so few adults with ADHD receive treatment and why the disorder often wreaks havoc on job performance and relationships.

Because ADHD, like most disorders, is defined by the presence of a wide range of symptoms, it is unlikely that it emerges from one single cause or dysfunction. The exact cause of ADHD is not known, but there are some promising leads. Genetic studies suggest that there is a strong biological influence and estimate that the heritability of ADHD is 76% (Faraone et al., 2005). Brain imaging studies suggest that those with ADHD have smaller brain volumes (Castellanos et al., 2002) as well as structural and functional abnormalities in frontosubcortical networks associated with attention and behavioral inhibition (Makris et al., 2009). The good news is that current drug treatments for ADHD are effective and appear to decrease the risk of later psychological and academic problems (Biederman et al., 2009).

CONDUCT DISORDER

Michael is an 8-year-old boy whose mother brought him into a local clinic because his behavior had been getting progressively out of control, and his parents and

attention deficit/hyperactivity disorder (ADHD) A persistent pattern of severe problems with inattention and/or hyperactivity or impulsiveness that cause significant impairments in functioning.

Psychologists are attempting to identify the causes of conduct disorder in the hope of being able to decrease the harmful behaviors, such as bullying, that often accompany it.

teachers were no longer able to control him. Although Michael's two older brothers and little sisters got along perfectly fine at home and at school, Michael had always gotten into trouble. At home he routinely bullied his siblings, threw glasses and dishes at family members, and on numerous occasions punched and kicked his parents. Outside of the house, Michael had been getting into trouble for stealing from the local store, yelling at his teacher, and spitting at the principal of his school. The last straw came when Michael's parents found him trying to set fire to his bedspread one night. They tried punishing him by taking away his toys, restricting his privileges, and trying to encourage him with a sticker chart, but nothing seemed to change his behavior.

Conduct disorder is a condition in which a child or adolescent engages in a *persistent pattern of deviant behavior involving aggression to people or animals, destruction of property, deceitfulness or theft, or serious rule violations.* Approximately 9% of people in the United States report a lifetime history of conduct disorder (12% of boys and 7% of girls; Nock et al., 2006). This number may seem a bit high, but approximately 40% of those with conduct disorder have, on average, only 3 symptoms that cluster into one of three areas: rule breaking, theft/deceit, or aggression toward others. The other 60% have more symptoms, on average 6 to 8 of the 15 defined symptoms, with problems in many more areas and a much higher risk of having other mental disorders later in life (Nock et al., 2006).

Meeting the criteria for conduct disorder requires having any 3 of the 15 symptoms of conduct disorder. This means that approximately 32,000 different combinations of symptoms could lead to a diagnosis, which makes those with conduct disorder a pretty diverse group. This diversity makes it difficult to pin down the causes of conduct disorder. One thing that seems clear is that a wide range of genetic, biological, and environmental factors interact to produce this disorder. Indeed, risk factors for conduct disorder include maternal smoking during pregnancy, exposure to abuse and family violence during childhood, affiliation with deviant peer groups, and the presence of deficits in executive functioning (e.g., decision making, impulsiveness; Boden et al., 2010; Burke et al., 2002). Researchers currently are attempting to better understand the pathways through which inherited genetic factors interact with environmental stressors (e.g., childhood adversities) to create characteristics in brain structure and function (e.g., reduced activity in brain regions associated with planning and decision making) that interact with environmental factors (e.g., affiliation with deviant peers) to lead to the behaviors that are characteristic of conduct disorder. Not surprisingly, conduct disorder tends to be comorbid with other disorders characterized by problems with decision making and impulsiveness, such as ADHD, substance use disorders, and antisocial personality disorder, which is described in more detail in the next section.

conduct disorder A persistent pattern of deviant behavior involving aggression toward people or animals, destruction of property, deceitfulness or theft, or serious rule violations.

Build to the Outcomes

1. What is autism spectrum disorder (ASD)?

2. What is the relationship between ASD and empathy?

3. What is attention-deficit/hyperactivity disorder (ADHD)?

4. What are the criteria for an ADHD diagnosis?

5. What is conduct disorder?

6. How is it possible that there are 32,000 different combinations of symptoms that could lead to a diagnosis of conduct disorder? What does this say about the population of people who have been given this diagnosis?

Personality Disorders: Extreme Traits and Characteristics

As discussed in the chapter on Personalities, we all have one, and we all differ in the extent to which we have different ways of behaving, thinking, and feeling. Sometimes, personality traits can become so extreme that they can be considered mental disorders. **Personality disorders** are *enduring patterns of thinking, feeling, or relating to others or controlling impulses that deviate from cultural expectations and cause distress or impaired functioning.* Personality disorders begin in adolescence or early adulthood and are relatively stable over time. Let's look at the types of personality disorders and then take a closer look at one that sometimes lands people in jail: antisocial personality disorder.

TYPES OF PERSONALITY DISORDERS

The *DSM–5* lists 10 specific personality disorders (see **TABLE 15.3**). They fall into three clusters: (1) *odd/eccentric,* (2) *dramatic/erratic,* and (3) *anxious/inhibited.* Personality

Learning Outcomes

▶ Identify the three types of personality disorders.

▶ Explain the diagnostic signs of APD.

personality disorders Enduring patterns of thinking, feeling, or relating to others or controlling impulses that deviate from cultural expectations and cause distress or impaired functioning.

TABLE 15.3

Clusters of Personality Disorders

Cluster	Personality Disorder	Characteristics
A. Odd/Eccentric	Paranoid	Distrust in others, suspicion that people have sinister motives. Apt to challenge the loyalties of friends and read hostile intentions into others' actions. Prone to anger and aggressive outbursts but otherwise emotionally cold. Often jealous, guarded, secretive, overly serious.
	Schizoid	Extreme introversion and withdrawal from relationships. Prefers to be alone, little interest in others. Humorless, distant, often absorbed with own thoughts and feelings, a daydreamer. Fearful of closeness, with poor social skills, often seen as a "loner."
	Schizotypal	Peculiar or eccentric manners of speaking or dressing. Strange beliefs. "Magical thinking," such as belief in ESP or telepathy. Difficulty forming relationships. May react oddly in conversation, not respond, or talk to self. Speech elaborate or difficult to follow. (Possibly a mild form of schizophrenia.)
B. Dramatic/Erratic	Antisocial	Impoverished moral sense or "conscience." History of deception, crime, legal problems, impulsive and aggressive or violent behavior. Little emotional empathy or remorse for hurting others. Manipulative, careless, callous. At high risk for substance abuse and alcoholism.
	Borderline	Unstable moods and intense, stormy personal relationships. Frequent mood changes and anger, unpredictable impulses. Self-mutilation or suicidal threats or gestures to get attention or manipulate others. Self-image fluctuation and a tendency to see others as "all good" or "all bad."
	Histrionic	Constant attention seeking. Grandiose language, provocative dress, exaggerated illnesses, all to gain attention. Believes that everyone loves them. Emotional, lively, overly dramatic, enthusiastic, and excessively flirtatious. Shallow and labile emotions. "Onstage."
	Narcissistic	Inflated sense of self-importance, absorbed by fantasies of self and success. Exaggerates own achievement, assumes others will recognize they are superior. Good first impressions but poor longer-term relationships. Exploitative of others.
C. Anxious/Inhibited	Avoidant	Socially anxious and uncomfortable unless they are confident of being liked. In contrast with schizoid person, yearns for social contact. Fears criticism and worries about being embarrassed in front of others. Avoids social situations due to fear of rejection.
	Dependent	Submissive, dependent, requiring excessive approval, reassurance, and advice. Clings to people and fears losing them. Lacking self-confidence. Uncomfortable when alone. May be devastated by end of close relationship or suicidal if breakup is threatened.
	Obsessive-compulsive	Conscientious, orderly, perfectionist. Excessive need to do everything "right." Inflexibly high standards and caution can interfere with their productivity. Fear of errors can make them strict and controlling. Poor expression of emotions. (Not the same as obsessive-compulsive disorder.)

Information from *DSM–5* (American Psychiatric Association, 2013).

Ever browse a copy of *Architectural Digest* and wonder who would live in one of those perfect homes? A person with obsessive-compulsive personality disorder might fit right in. This personality disorder (characterized by excessive perfectionism) should not be mistaken, by the way, for obsessive-compulsive disorder—the anxiety disorder in which the person suffers from repeated unwanted thoughts or actions.

antisocial personality disorder (APD) A pervasive pattern of disregard for and violation of the rights of others that begins in childhood or early adolescence and continues into adulthood.

disorders have been a bit controversial for several reasons. First, critics question whether having a problematic personality is really a disorder. Given that approximately 15% of the U.S. population has a personality disorder according to the *DSM–5*, perhaps it might be better just to admit that a lot of people can be difficult to interact with and leave it at that. Another question is whether personality problems correspond to "disorders" in that there are distinct *types,* or whether such problems might be better understood as extreme values on trait *dimensions* such as the Big Five traits discussed in the Personality chapter (Trull & Durrett, 2005). In *DSM–IV*, personality disorders appeared as a separate type of disorder from all of the other disorders described above. (Specifically, those major disorders were all in a category called *Axis I*, and personality disorders were in *Axis II*.) However, in *DSM–5* personality disorders have earned equal footing as full-fledged disorders. One of the most thoroughly studied of all the personality disorders is antisocial personality disorder.

ANTISOCIAL PERSONALITY DISORDER

Henri Desiré Landru began using personal ads to attract a woman "interested in matrimony" in Paris in 1914, and he succeeded in seducing 10 of them. He bilked them of their savings, poisoned them, and cremated them in his stove, also disposing of a boy and two dogs along the way. He recorded his murders in a notebook and maintained a marriage and a mistress all the while. The gruesome actions of serial killers such as Landru leave us frightened and wondering; however, bullies, compulsive liars, and even drivers who regularly speed through a school zone share the same shocking blindness to human pain. The *DSM–5* includes the category of **antisocial personality disorder (APD)** and defines it as *a pervasive pattern of disregard for and violation of the rights of others that begins in childhood or early adolescence and continues into adulthood.*

Adults with an APD diagnosis typically have a history of *conduct disorder* before the age of 15. In adulthood, a diagnosis of APD is given to individuals who show three or more of a set of seven diagnostic signs: illegal behavior, deception, impulsivity, physical aggression, recklessness, irresponsibility, and a lack of remorse for wrongdoing. About 3.6% of the general population has APD, and the rate of occurrence in men is 3 times the rate in women (Grant et al., 2004).

The terms *sociopath* and *psychopath* describe people with APD who are especially coldhearted, manipulative, and ruthless—yet may be glib and charming (Cleckley, 1976; Hare, 1998). Although psychologists usually try to explain the development

Henri Desiré Landru (1869–1922) was a serial killer who met widows through ads he placed in newspapers' lonely-hearts columns. After obtaining enough information to embezzle money from them, he murdered 10 women and the son of one of the women. He was executed for serial murder in 1922.

of abnormal behavior as a product of childhood experiences or difficult life circumstances, those who work with APD seem less forgiving, often noting the sheer dangerousness of people with this disorder. Many people with APD do commit crimes, and many are caught because of the frequency and flagrancy of their infractions. Among 22,790 prisoners in one study, 47% of the men and 21% of the women were diagnosed with APD (Fazel & Danesh, 2002). Statistics such as these support the notion of a "criminal personality."

Both the early onset of conduct problems and the lack of success in treatment suggest that career criminality often has an internal cause (Lykken, 1995). Evidence of brain abnormalities in people with APD is also accumulating (Blair, Peschardt, & Mitchell, 2005). One line of investigation has looked at sensitivity to fear in psychopaths and individuals who show no such psychopathology. For example, criminal psychopaths who are shown negative emotional words such as *hate* or *corpse* exhibit less activity in the amygdala and hippocampus than do noncriminals (Kiehl et al., 2001). These two brain areas are involved in the process of fear conditioning (Patrick, Cuthbert, & Lang, 1994), so their relative inactivity in such studies suggests that psychopaths are less sensitive to fear than are other people. Violent psychopaths can target their aggression toward the self as well as others, often behaving in reckless ways that lead them to violent ends. It might seem peaceful to go through life "without fear," but perhaps fear is useful in keeping people from the extremes of antisocial behavior.

Build to the Outcomes

1. What are personality disorders?
2. What are the different types of personality disorders?
3. What are the characteristics of a person with antisocial personality disorder (APD)?
4. Why do prison statistics support the idea of a "criminal personality"?

Self-Harm Behaviors: Intentionally Injuring Oneself

We all have an innate drive to keep ourselves alive. We eat when we are hungry, get out of the way of fast-moving vehicles, and go to school so we can earn a living to keep ourselves, and our families, alive (see the discussion of evolutionary psychology in the Psychology: Evolution of a Science chapter). One of the most extreme manifestations of abnormal human behavior is revealed when a person acts in direct opposition to this drive for self-preservation and engages in intentionally self-destructive behavior. Accounts of people intentionally harming themselves date back to the beginning of recorded history. However, it is only over the past several decades that we have begun to gain an understanding of why people purposely do things to hurt themselves. *DSM–5* includes two self-destructive behaviors in its Section III (disorders in need of further study): suicidal behavior disorder and nonsuicidal self-injury disorder.

Learning Outcomes

▶ Explain the factors that increase the risk of suicide.

▶ Explain what is currently known to be the motivation behind nonsuicidal self-injury.

SUICIDAL BEHAVIOR

Tim, a 35-year-old accountant, had by all appearances been living a pretty happy, successful life. He was married to his high school sweetheart and had two young children. Over the past several years, though, his workload had increased, and he started to

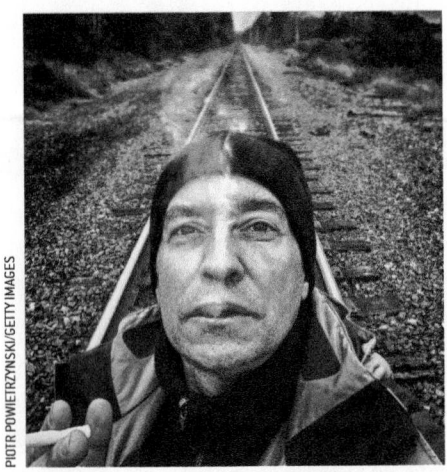

We all have an innate desire to keep ourselves alive. So why do some people purposely do things to harm themselves?

suicide Intentional self-inflicted death.

suicide attempt Engagement in potentially harmful behavior with some intention of dying.

experience severe job-related stress. At around the same time, he and his wife began to experience some financial problems, and his alcohol consumption increased, all of which put significant strain on the family and began to affect his work. Tim's coworkers noted that he had become pretty angry and agitated lately—even yelling at coworkers on a few occasions. One evening Tim and his wife got into a heated argument about the family's finances and Tim's excessive alcohol use; Tim went into the bathroom and swallowed a bottle full of prescription medicine in an effort to end his life. He was taken to the hospital and kept there to be treated for suicidal behavior.

Suicide, *intentional self-inflicted death*, is the tenth leading cause of death in the United States and the second leading cause of death among people 15 to 24 years old. It takes the lives of more than five times as many people as HIV/AIDS each year in the United States, and more than twice as many people as homicide (Hoyert & Xu, 2012). There are large demographic differences in the suicide rate. For instance, approximately 80% of suicides around the world occur among men. White people are much more likely to kill themselves than members of other racial and ethnic groups, accounting for 90% of all suicides (Centers for Disease Control and Prevention, 2013). Unfortunately, we currently do not have a good understanding of why these enormous sociodemographic differences exist.

Nonfatal **suicide attempts,** in which people engage in *potentially harmful behavior with some intention of dying*, occur much more frequently than suicide deaths. In the United States, approximately 15% of adults report that they have seriously considered suicide at some point in their lives, 5% have made a plan to kill themselves, and 5% have actually made a suicide attempt. The rates of these behaviors in the United States are slightly above the percentages seen across a wide range of countries, which are 9% (considered suicide), 3% (planned suicide), and 3% (made an attempt), respectively (Nock et al., 2008). As these numbers suggest, only one third of those who think about suicide actually go on to make a suicide attempt. Although many more men than women die by suicide, women experience suicidal thoughts and (nonfatal) suicide attempts at significantly higher rates than do men (Nock et al., 2008). Moreover, the rates of suicidal thoughts and attempts increase dramatically during adolescence and young adulthood. A recent study of a representative sample of approximately 10,000 U.S. adolescents revealed that suicidal thoughts and behaviors are virtually nonexistent before age 10 but increase dramatically from ages 12 to 18 (see **FIGURE 15.9**) before leveling off during early adulthood (Nock et al., 2013).

▶ Figure 15.9

AGE OF ONSET OF SUICIDAL BEHAVIOR DURING ADOLESCENCE A recent survey of a nationally representative sample of U.S. adolescents shows that although suicidal thoughts and behaviors are quite rare among children (the rate was 0.0 for ages 1–4), they increase dramatically starting at age 12 and continue to climb throughout adolescence (data from Nock et al., 2013).

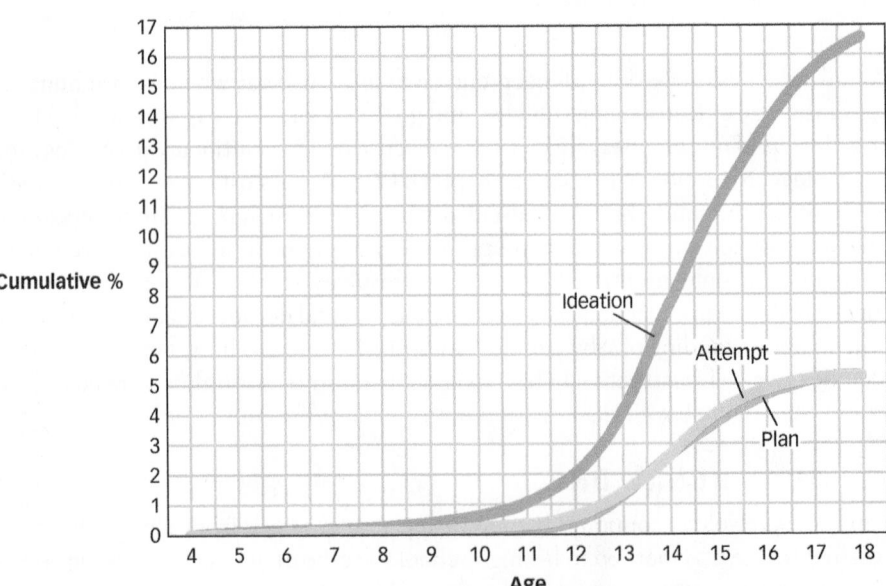

So the numbers are staggering, but *why* do people try to kill themselves? The short answer is: We do not yet know, and it's complicated. When interviewed in the hospital following their suicide attempt, most people who have tried to kill themselves report that they did so in order to escape from an intolerable state of mind or impossible situation (Boergers, Spirito, & Donaldson, 1998). Consistent with this explanation, research has documented that the risk of suicidal behavior is significantly increased if a person experiences factors that can create severely distressing states, such as the presence of multiple mental disorders (more than 90% of people who die by suicide have at least one mental disorder); the experience of significant negative life events during childhood and adulthood (e.g., physical or sexual assault); and the presence of severe medical problems (Nock, Borges, & Ono, 2012). The search is ongoing for a more comprehensive understanding of how and why some people respond to negative life events with suicidal thoughts and behaviors, as well as on methods of better predicting and preventing these devastating outcomes.

NONSUICIDAL SELF-INJURY

Louisa, an 18-year-old college student, secretly cuts her lower abdomen and upper thighs about once per week, typically when she is feeling intense anger and hatred, either toward herself or someone else. She has always had a bit of a "hot streak," as she calls it, but it wasn't until she turned 14 that she started to use self-injury as a way to calm herself down. Louisa says that she actually feels a little ashamed after each episode of cutting, but she doesn't know how else to calm down when she gets really upset, and so she has no plans to stop this behavior.

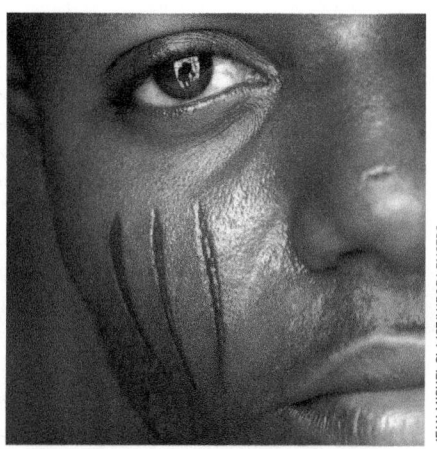

Although in Western cultures self-injury is considered to be pathological, in some parts of the world scarification of the skin is viewed as a rite of passage into adulthood and a symbol of one's tribe, as in the case of this young man from the Republic of Benin in West Africa.

Louisa is engaging in a behavior called **nonsuicidal self-injury (NSSI),** the *direct, deliberate destruction of body tissue in the absence of any intent to die*. NSSI has been reported since the beginning of recorded history; however, it is a behavior that appears to be on the rise over the past few decades. Recent studies suggest that as many as 15 to 20% of adolescents and 3 to 6% of adults report engaging in NSSI at some point in their lifetime (Muehlenkamp et al., 2012). The rates appear to be even between males and females, and for people of different races and ethnicities. Like suicidal behavior, NSSI is virtually absent during childhood, increases dramatically during adolescence, and then appears to decrease across adulthood.

In some parts of the world, cutting or scarification of the skin is socially accepted, and in some cases encouraged as a rite of passage (Favazza, 2011). In parts of the world where self-cutting is not socially encouraged, why would a person purposely hurt him- or herself if not to die? Recent studies suggest that people who engage in self-injury have very strong emotional and physiological responses to negative events, that they perceive this response as intolerable, and that NSSI serves to diminish the intensity of this response (Nock, 2009). There also is some evidence that in many instances, people engage in self-injury as a means to communicate distress or elicit help from others (Nock, 2010). Although we are beginning to get an understanding of why some people engage in NSSI, there are many aspects of this behavior that we do not yet understand, and the study of NSSI is an increasingly active area of research.

Unfortunately, like suicidal behavior, our understanding of the genetic and neurobiological influences on NSSI is limited, and there currently are no effective medications for these problems. There also is very limited evidence for behavioral interventions or prevention programs (Mann et al., 2005). So, whereas suicidal behavior and NSSI are some of the most disturbing and dangerous mental disorders, they also, unfortunately, are among the most perplexing. The field has made significant strides in our understanding of these behavior problems in recent years, but there is a long way to go before we are able to predict and prevent them accurately and effectively.

nonsuicidal self-injury (NSSI) Direct, deliberate destruction of body tissue in the absence of any intent to die.

Build to the Outcomes

1. What are the factors that research has uncovered that create the distressing states that can lead to suicide?

2. What reason has been given in hospital interviews for the suicide attempt?

3. What is nonsuicidal self-injury (NSSI)?

4. How does culture play a role in the view of self-injury as pathological?

5. Why might people engage in self-injury?

Chapter Review

Defining Mental Disorders: What Is Abnormal?

▶ The *DSM–5* is a classification system that defines a mental disorder as occurring when a person experiences disturbances of thought, emotion, or behavior that produce distress or impairment. The original volume provided a common language for talking about disorders, but diagnostic criteria were vague. The *DSM–5* includes detailed lists of criteria, including cultural considerations, designed to increase the validity of the process.

▶ The medical model conceptualizes abnormal thought and behaviors as illnesses with defined symptoms and possible cures.

▶ According to the biopsychosocial model, mental disorders arise from an interaction of biological, psychological, and social factors, often thought of as a combination of a diathesis (internal predisposition) and a stressor (environmental life event). The diathesis–stress model suggests that a person may be predisposed for a disorder that may or may not manifest depending on whether it is triggered by stress.

▶ The RDoC is a new classification system that focuses on biological, cognitive, and behavioral aspects of mental disorders.

▶ Psychiatric labels may create negative stereotypes and may be one reason that many people do not seek help.

Anxiety Disorders: Excessive Fear, Anxiety, and Avoidance

▶ People with anxiety disorders have irrational worries and fears that undermine their ability to function normally.

▶ Phobic disorders are characterized by excessive fear and avoidance of specific objects, activities, or situations. The preparedness theory posits that people are instinctively predisposed toward certain fears, and heritability studies support this idea. Temperament and the influence of environment are additional factors.

▶ People who suffer from panic disorder experience a sudden, terrifying attack of intense anxiety. Agoraphobia can lead people to be housebound for fear of public humiliation. Panic disorder has a hereditary component, and people who experience panic attacks may be hypersensitive to physiological signs of anxiety.

▶ Generalized anxiety disorder (GAD) involves a chronic state of anxiety, whereas phobic disorders involve anxiety tied to a specific object or situation. Biological explanations of GAD suggest a role for neurotransmitters, but the evidence is unclear. Life situation and experience play a role as well, supporting the diathesis–stress notion.

Obsessive-Compulsive Disorder: Persistent Thoughts and Repetitive Behaviors

▶ People with obsessive-compulsive disorder experience recurring, anxiety-provoking thoughts that compel them to engage in ritualistic, irrational behavior. Attempts to suppress this behavior have little or no benefit.

▶ OCD derives from concerns that could be real, supporting the preparedness theory. Studies indicate a moderate genetic link; one hypothesis implicates heightened neural activity in a portion of the basal ganglia.

Posttraumatic Stress Disorder: Distress and Avoidance After a Trauma

▶ Terrifying, life-threatening events, such as combat experience or rape, can lead to the development of posttraumatic stress disorder (PTSD), in which a person experiences chronic physiological arousal, unwanted thoughts or images of the event, and avoidance of things or situations that remind the person of the event.

▶ Research has identified neural correlates of PTSD.

Depressive and Bipolar Disorders: Extreme Highs and Lows

▶ Mood disorders are mental disorders in which a disturbance in mood is the predominant feature.

▶ Major depression (or unipolar depression) is characterized by a severely depressed mood and/or inability to experience pleasure lasting at least 2 weeks; symptoms include excessive self-criticism, guilt, difficulty concentrating, suicidal thoughts, sleep and appetite disturbances, and lethargy. Persistent depressive disorder, a related disorder, involves less severe symptoms that persist for at least 2 years. Some people experience depression in a seasonal pattern.

▶ Bipolar disorder is an unstable emotional condition involving extreme mood swings of depression and mania. The manic phase is characterized by periods of abnormally and persistently elevated, expansive, or irritable mood, lasting at least 1 week.

▶ Depression has at its roots socioecomonic, hormonal, genetic, and neural factors. Helplessness theory indicates that biases in how information is processed can lead to depression.

▶ Bipolar disorder has one of the highest rates of heritability. Epigenetics helps explain some of the genetic risk factors, a link to the influence of environment.

Schizophrenia and Other Psychotic Disorders: Losing the Grasp on Reality

▶ Schizophrenia is a severe psychological disorder involving hallucinations, disorganized thoughts and behavior, and emotional and social withdrawal.

▶ Positive symptoms are thoughts and behaviors *not* seen in those without the disorder; negative symptoms indicate an absence of normal behavior; cognitive symptoms are impairments in executive functioning, attention, and working memory.

▶ Schizophrenia affects only 1% of the population, but it accounts for a disproportionate share of psychiatric hospitalizations. The likelihood of getting the disorder increases with biological relatedness.

▶ The first drugs that reduced the availability of dopamine sometimes reduced the symptoms of schizophrenia, suggesting that the disorder involved an excess of dopamine activity, but recent research suggests that schizophrenia may involve a complex interaction among a variety of neurotransmitters.

▶ Brain changes are evident in people with schizophrenia, but evidence shows children whose biological mothers had schizophrenia are more likely to develop it if they are raised in an affected family.

Disorders of Childhood and Adolescence

▶ Some mental disorders always begin during childhood or adolescence, and in some cases (ASD, ADHD) persist into adulthood.

▶ Autism spectrum disorder (ASD) emerges in early childhood and is a condition in which a person has persistent communication deficits, including difficultly empathizing with others, as well as restricted and repetitive patterns of behavior, interests, or activities.

▶ Attention-deficit/hyperactivity disorder (ADHD) begins by age 12 and involves a persistent pattern of severe problems with inattention and/or hyperactivity or impulsiveness that cause significant impairments in functioning.

▶ Conduct disorder begins in childhood or adolescence and involves a persistent pattern of deviant behavior involving aggression toward people or animals, destruction of property, deceitfulness or theft, or serious rule violations. Because the diagnosis requires having any 3 of 15 symptoms, there are 32,000 different combinations. This suggests a wide diversity within the group of people who share this diagnosis.

Personality Disorders: Extreme Traits and Characteristics

▶ Personality disorders are enduring patterns of thinking, feeling, relating to others, or controlling impulses that cause distress or impaired functioning.

▶ They include three clusters: odd/eccentric, dramatic/erratic, and anxious/inhibited.

▶ Antisocial personality disorder (APD) is associated with a lack of moral emotions and behavior. People with antisocial personality disorder can be manipulative, dangerous, and reckless, often hurting others and sometimes hurting themselves.

Self-Harm Behaviors: Intentionally Injuring Oneself

▶ Suicide is among the leading causes of death in the United States and the world. Most people who die by suicide have a mental disorder. Suicide attempts most often are motivated by an attempt to escape intolerable mental states or situations.

▶ Nonsuicidal self-injury (NSSI), like suicidal behavior, increases dramatically during adolescence, but for many is a persistent problem throughout adulthood. Although NSSI is performed without suicidal intent, like suicidal behavior, it is most often motivated by an attempt to escape from painful mental states.

KEY CONCEPT QUIZ

1. The conception of psychological disorders as diseases that have symptoms and possible cures is referred to as
    a. the medical model.
    b. physiognomy.
    c. the root syndrome framework.
    d. a diagnostic system.

2. The *DSM–5* is best described as a
    a. medical model.
    b. classification system.
    c. set of theoretical assumptions.
    d. collection of physiological definitions.

3. *Comorbidity of disorders* refers to
    a. symptoms stemming from internal dysfunction.
    b. the relative risk of death arising from a disorder.
    c. the co-occurrence of two or more disorders in a single individual.
    d. the existence of disorders on a continuum from normal to abnormal.

4. Irrational worries and fears that undermine one's ability to function normally are an indication of
    a. a genetic abnormality.
    b. dysthymia.

    c. diathesis.
    d. an anxiety disorder.

5. A(n) _____ disorder involves anxiety tied to a specific object or situation.
    a. generalized anxiety
    b. environmental
    c. panic
    d. phobic

6. Kelly's fear of germs leads her to wash her hands repeatedly throughout the day, often for a half hour or more, under extremely hot water. From which disorder does Kelly suffer?
    a. panic attacks
    b. obsessive-compulsive disorder
    c. phobia
    d. generalized anxiety disorder

7. Extreme moods swings between _____ characterize bipolar disorder.
    a. depression and mania
    b. stress and lethargy
    c. anxiety and arousal
    d. obsessions and compulsions

8. Schizophrenia is characterized by which of the following?
   a. hallucinations
   b. disorganized thoughts and behavior
   c. emotional and social withdrawal
   d. all of the above

9. Autism spectrum disorder is characterized by which of the following?
   a. communication deficits and restricted, repetitive behavior
   b. hallucinations and delusions

   c. suicidal thoughts
   d. all of the above

10. In the United States, those at highest risk for suicide are
   a. men.
   b. White people.
   c. those with a mental disorder.
   d. all of the above

 LearningCurve   Don't stop now! Quizzing yourself is a powerful study tool. Go to LaunchPad to access the LearningCurve adaptive quizzing system and your own personalized learning plan. Visit launchpadworks.com.

KEY TERMS

mental disorder (p. 588)

medical model (p. 589)

Diagnostic and Statistical Manual of Mental Disorders (DSM) (p. 590)

comorbidity (p. 592)

biopsychosocial perspective (p. 593)

diathesis–stress model (p. 594)

Research Domain Criteria Project (RDoC) (p. 595)

anxiety disorder (p. 598)

phobic disorders (p. 598)

specific phobia (p. 598)

social phobia (p. 598)

preparedness theory (p. 599)

panic disorder (p. 600)

agoraphobia (p. 600)

generalized anxiety disorder (GAD) (p. 601)

obsessive-compulsive disorder (OCD) (p. 603)

posttraumatic stress disorder (PTSD) (p. 604)

mood disorders (p. 606)

major depressive disorder (or unipolar depression) (p. 606)

persistent depressive disorder (p. 606)

double depression (p. 606)

seasonal affective disorder (SAD) (p. 606)

helplessness theory (p. 609)

bipolar disorder (p. 610)

expressed emotion (p. 612)

schizophrenia (p. 614)

positive symptoms (p. 614)

hallucination (p. 614)

delusion (p. 614)

disorganized speech (p. 614)

grossly disorganized behavior (p. 615)

catatonic behavior (p. 615)

negative symptoms (p. 615)

cognitive symptoms (p. 615)

dopamine hypothesis (p. 616)

autism spectrum disorder (ASD) (p. 619)

attention-deficit/hyperactivity disorder (ADHD) (p. 621)

conduct disorder (p. 622)

personality disorders (p. 623)

antisocial personality disorder (APD) (p. 624)

suicide (p. 626)

suicide attempt (p. 626)

nonsuicidal self-injury (NSSI) (p. 627)

CHANGING MINDS

1. You catch a TV interview with a celebrity who describes his difficult childhood, living with a mother who suffered from major depression. "Sometimes my mother stayed in her bed for days, not even getting up to eat," he says. "At the time, the family hushed it up. My parents were immigrants, and they came from a culture where it was considered shameful to have mental problems. You are supposed to have enough strength of will to overcome your problems, without help from anyone else. So my mother never got treatment." How might the idea of a medical model of psychiatric disorders have helped this woman and her family in the decision whether to seek treatment?

2. You're studying for your upcoming psychology exam when your roommate breezes in, saying: "I was just at the gym and I ran into Sue. She's totally schizophrenic: nice one minute, mean the next." You can't resist the opportunity to set the record straight. What psychiatric disorder is your roommate (incorrectly) attributing to Sue? How is this different from schizophrenia?

3. A friend of yours has a family member who is experiencing severe mental problems, including delusions and loss of motivation. "We went to one psychiatrist," she says, "and got a diagnosis of schizophrenia. We went for a second opinion, and the other doctor said it was probably bipolar disorder. They're both good doctors, and they're both using the same *DSM*—how can they come up with different diagnoses?"

4. After reading the chapter, one of your classmates turns to you with a sigh of relief. "I finally figured it out. I have a deadbeat brother, who always gets himself into trouble and then blames other people for his problems. Even when he gets a ticket for speeding, he never thinks it's his fault—the police were picking on him, or his passengers were urging him to go too fast. I always thought he was just a loser, but now I realize he has a personality disorder!" Do you agree with your classmate's diagnosis of his brother? How would you caution your classmate about the dangers of self-diagnosis, or diagnosis of friends and family?

ANSWERS TO KEY CONCEPT QUIZ

1. a; 2. b; 3. c; 4. d; 5. c; 6. b; 7. a; 8. d; 9. a; 10. c.

 LaunchPad macmillan learning

LaunchPad features the full e-Book of *Psychology*, the LearningCurve adaptive quizzing system, videos, and a variety of activities to boost your learning. Visit LaunchPad at launchpadworks.com.

Treatment of Psychological Disorders

16

TODAY WE'RE GOING TO BE TOUCHING A DEAD MOUSE I saw in the alley outside my office building," Dr. Jenkins said. "Okay, let's do it, I'm ready," Christine responded. The pair walked down to the alley and spent the next 50 minutes touching, then stroking, the dead mouse. They then went back upstairs to plan out what other disgusting things Christine was going to touch over the next 7 days before coming back for her next therapy session. This is all part of the psychological treatment of Christine's obsessive-compulsive disorder (OCD). It is an approach called *exposure and response prevention* (ERP), in which people are gradually exposed to the content of their obsessions and prevented from engaging in their compulsions. Christine's obsessions include the fear that she is going to be contaminated by germs and die of cancer; her compulsive behavior involves several hours per day of washing her body and scrubbing everything around her with alcohol wipes in order to decrease the possibility of her developing cancer. After dozens and dozens of exposures, without performing the behaviors that they believe have been keeping them safe, people undergoing ERP eventually learn that their obsessive thoughts are not accurate and that they don't have to act out their compulsions. ERP can be a very scary treatment, but it has proven amazingly effective at decreasing obsessions and compulsions and helping people with OCD return to a high level of daily functioning. OCD was widely considered untreatable until the development of ERP, which is now considered to be the most effective way to treat OCD (Foa, 2010). ERP is just one of many approaches currently being used to help people to overcome the mental disorders you learned about in the last chapter.

Exposure-based treatments, in which a person learns to face the source of their fear and anxiety, have proven to be an effective way to treat anxiety disorders.

THERE ARE MANY DIFFERENT WAYS TO TREAT PSYCHOLOGICAL DISORDERS and to change the thoughts, behaviors, and emotions associated with them. In this chapter, we will explore the most common approaches to psychological treatment. We will examine why people need to seek psychological help in the first place, and then explore how psychotherapy for individuals is built on the major theories of the causes and cures of disorders, including psychoanalytic, humanistic, existential, behavioral, and cognitive theories. We also will consider biological approaches to treatment that focus on directly modifying brain structure and function. We'll discuss which treatments work and how we know what works best. We'll also look to the future by exploring some exciting new directions in the assessment and treatment of disorders using innovative technologies.

Treatment: Getting Help to Those Who Need It

Learning Outcomes

- Describe reasons people with mental disorders may fail to get treatment.
- Outline different approaches to treatment.

Estimates suggest that 46.4% of people in the United States suffer from a mental disorder at some point in their lifetime (Kessler, Berglund, et al., 2005), and 26.2% suffer from at least one disorder during a given year (Kessler, Chiu, et al., 2005). The personal costs of these disorders include anguish to the sufferers as well as interference in their ability to carry on the activities of daily life. Think about Christine from the example above. If she did not (or could not) seek treatment, she would continue to be crippled by her OCD, which was causing major problems in her life. She had to quit her job at the local coffee shop because she was no longer able to touch money or anything else that had been touched by other people without washing it first. Her relationship with her boyfriend was in trouble because he was growing tired of her constant reassurance seeking regarding cleanliness (hers and his). All of these problems were in turn increasing her anxiety and depression, making her obsessions even stronger. She desperately wanted and needed some way to break out of this vicious cycle. She needed an effective treatment.

The personal and social burdens associated with mental disorders are enormous. Mental disorders typically have earlier ages of onset than physical disorders and are associated with significant impairments in the ability to carry out daily activities, such as days out of school or work or problems in family and personal relationships. Impairments associated with mental disorders are as severe, and in many cases more severe, than those associated with physical disorders such as cancer, chronic pain, and heart disease (Ormel et al., 2008). For instance, a person with severe depression may be unable to hold down a job or even get organized enough to collect a disability check; people with many disorders stop getting along with family, caring for their children, or trying to help.

There are financial costs too. Depression is the second leading cause of all disability worldwide (Ferrari et al., 2013). People with severe depression often are unable to make it in to work due to their disorder, and even when they make it to work they often suffer from poor work performance. Recent estimates suggest that depression-related lost work productivity costs somewhere from $30 to $50 billion per year (Kessler, 2012). If we add in similar figures for anxiety disorders, psychotic disorders, substance disorders, and all other psychological problems, the overall costs are astronomical. In addition to the personal benefits of treatment, then, society also stands to benefit from the effective treatment of psychological disorders.

Do all people with a mental disorder receive treatment? Not by a long shot. Only about 18% of people in the United States with a mental disorder in a given 12-month period receive treatment during the same time frame. Treatment rates are even lower elsewhere around the world, especially in low-income or developing countries (Wang et al., 2007). Treatment rates are higher for those with more severe mental disorders. Approximately 40% of those in the United States with a serious mental disorder (one that substantially interferes with major life activities) have received treatment in the past year (Wang, Demler, & Kessler, 2002). However, it is clear from these numbers that most people with a mental disorder do not receive treatment, and among those who do, the average delay from onset until first receiving treatment is over a decade (Wang et al., 2004)!

WHY MANY PEOPLE FAIL TO SEEK TREATMENT

A physical symptom such as a toothache would send most people to the dentist—a trip that usually results in a successful treatment. The clear source of pain and the obvious solution make for a quick and effective response. In contrast, the path from a mental disorder to a successful treatment is often far less clear, and many people are less familiar with when they should seek treatment for a mental disorder or where they should go. In the case of mental disorders, people may fail to get treatment for a number of reasons. Here are three of the most often reported:

1. *People may not realize that they have a mental disorder that can be effectively treated.* Approximately 45% of those with a mental disorder who do not seek treatment report that they did not do so because they didn't think that they needed to be treated (Mojtabai et al., 2011). Mental disorders often are not taken nearly as seriously as physical illness, perhaps because the origin of mental illness is "hidden" and usually cannot be diagnosed by a blood test or X-ray. Moreover, although most people know what a toothache is and that it can be successfully treated, far fewer people know when they have a mental disorder and what treatments might be available.

2. *There may be barriers to treatment, such as beliefs and circumstances that keep people from getting help.* Individuals may believe that they should be able to handle things themselves. In fact, this is the primary reason that people with a mental disorder give for not seeking treatment (72.6%) and for dropping out of treatment prematurely (42.2%; Mojtabai et al., 2011). Other attitudinal barriers for not seeking treatment include believing that the problem was not that severe (16.9% of people not seeking treatment), the belief that treatment would be ineffective (16.4%), and perceived stigma from others (9.1%).

3. *Structural barriers prevent people from physically getting to treatment.* Like finding a good lawyer or plumber, finding the right psychologist can be more difficult than simply flipping through the yellow pages or searching online. This confusion is understandable given the plethora of different types of treatments available (see The Real World: Types of Psychotherapists). Once you find the therapist for you, you may encounter structural barriers related to not being able to afford treatment (15.3% of non-treatment seekers), lack of clinician availability (12.8%), inconvenience of attending treatment (9.8%), and trouble finding transportation to the clinic (5.7%; Mojtabai et al., 2011).

When your tooth hurts, you go to a dentist. But how do you know when to see a psychologist?

THE IMAGE BANK/GETTY IMAGES

Even when people seek and find help, they sometimes do not receive the most effective treatments, which further complicates things. For starters, most of the treatment of mental disorders is not provided by mental health specialists, but by general medical practitioners (Wang et al., 2007). And even when people make it to a mental health specialist, they do not always receive the most effective treatment possible. In fact, only a small percentage of those with a mental disorder (< 40%) receive what would be considered minimally adequate treatment, and only 15.3% of those with serious mental illness receive treatment that is considered minimally adequate. Inadequate treatment is especially a problem among those who are younger, African

Types of Psychotherapists

What do you do if you're ready to seek the help of a mental health professional? To whom do you turn? Therapists have widely varying backgrounds and training, and this affects the kinds of services they offer. Before you choose a therapist, it is useful to have an understanding of a therapist's background, training, and areas of expertise. There are several major "flavors."

- *Psychologist* A psychologist who practices psychotherapy holds a doctorate with specialization in clinical psychology (a PhD or PsyD). This degree takes about 5 years to complete and includes extensive training in therapy, the assessment of psychological disorders, and research. The psychologist will sometimes have a specialty, such as working with adolescents or helping people overcome sleep disorders, and will usually conduct therapy that involves talking. Psychologists must be licensed by the state, and most states require candidates to complete about 2 years of supervised practical training and a competency exam. If you look for a *psychologist* on the Internet or through a clinic, you will usually find someone with this background.

- *Psychiatrist* A psychiatrist is a medical doctor who has completed an M.D. with specialized training in assessing and treating mental disorders. Psychiatrists

can prescribe medications, and some also practice psychotherapy. General-practice physicians can also prescribe medications for mental disorders and often are the first to see people with such disorders because people consult them for a wide range of health problems. However, general-practice physicians do not typically receive much training in the diagnosis or treatment of mental disorders, and they do not practice psychotherapy

- *Clinical/psychiatric social worker* Social workers have a master's degree in social work and have training in working with people in dire life situations such as poverty, homelessness, or family conflict. Clinical or psychiatric social workers also receive special training to help people in these situations who have mental disorders. Social workers often work in government or private social service agencies and may also work in hospitals or have a private practice.

- *Counselor* Counselors have a wide range of training. To be a counseling psychologist, for example, requires a doctorate and practical training—the title uses that key term *psychologist* and is regulated by state laws. But states vary in how they define *counselor*. In some cases, a counselor must have a master's degree and extensive

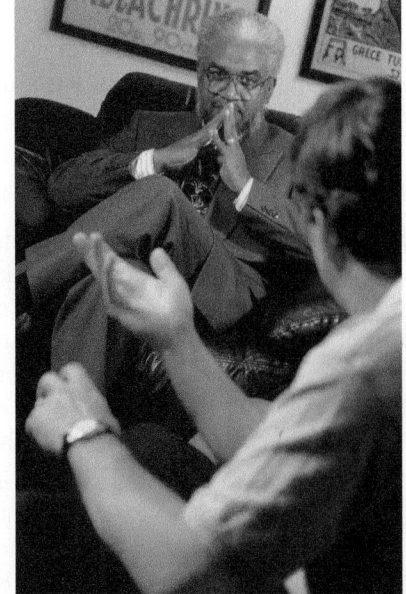

training in therapy, whereas in others, a counselor may have minimal training or relevant education. Counselors who work in schools usually have a master's degree and specific training in counseling in educational settings.

Some people offer therapy under made-up terms that sound professional—"mind/body healing therapist," for example, or "marital adjustment adviser." Often these terms are simply invented to mislead clients and avoid licensing boards, and the "therapist" may have no training or expertise at all. And, of course, there are a few people who claim to be licensed practitioners who are not: Louise Wightman, who had once worked as the stripper "Princess Cheyenne," was convicted of fraud in 2007 after conducting psychotherapy as a psychologist with dozens of clients. She claimed she didn't know the PhD degree she had purchased over the Internet was bogus (Associated Press, 2007). People who offer therapy may be well meaning and even helpful, but they might do harm, too. To be safe, it is important to shop wisely for a therapist whose training and credentials reflect expertise and inspire confidence.

How should you shop? One way is to start with people you know: your general-practice physician, a school counselor, or a trusted friend or family member who might know of a good therapist. Or you can visit your college clinic or hospital or contact the Web site of an organization such as the American Psychological Association that offers referrals to licensed mental health care providers. When you do contact someone, he or she will often be able to provide you with further advice about who would be just the right kind of therapist to consult.

Before you agree to see a therapist for treatment, you should ask questions such as those below to evaluate whether the therapist's style or background is a good match for your problem:

- What type of therapy do you practice?
- What types of problems do you usually treat?
- For how long do you usually see people in therapy?
- Will our work involve "talking" therapy, medications, or both?
- How effective is this type of therapy for the type of problem I'm having?
- What are your fees for therapy? Will health insurance cover them?

Not only will the therapist's answers to these questions tell you about his or her background and experience, but they will also tell you about his or her approach to treating clients. You can then make an informed decision about the type of service you need.

Although you should consider what type of therapist would best fit your needs, the therapist's personality and approach can sometimes be as important as his or her background or training. You should seek out someone who is willing and open to answer questions, who has a clear understanding about the type of problem leading you to seek therapy, and who shows general respect and empathy for you. A therapist is someone you are entrusting with your mental health, and you should enter into such a relationship only if you and the therapist have good rapport.

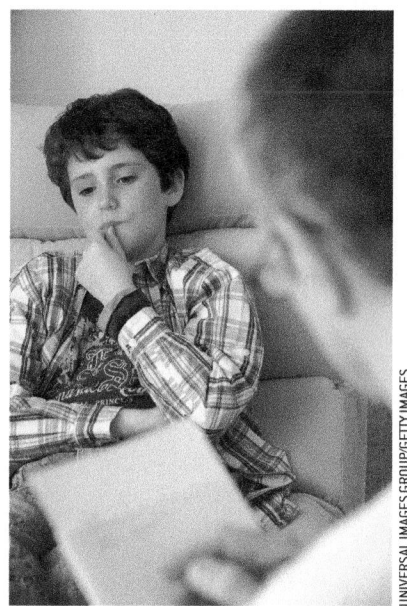

UNIVERSAL IMAGES GROUP/GETTY IMAGES

American, living in the southern United States, diagnosed with a psychotic disorder, and treated in a general medical setting (Wang et al., 2002). Clearly, before choosing or prescribing a therapy, we need to know what kinds of treatments are available and understand which treatments are best for particular disorders.

APPROACHES TO TREATMENT

Treatments can be divided broadly into two kinds: (1) psychological treatment, in which people interact with a clinician in order to use the environment to change their brain and behavior; and (2) biological treatment, in which the brain is treated directly with drugs, surgery, or some other direct intervention. In some cases, both psychological *and* biological treatments are applied. Christine's OCD, for example, might be treated not only with the ERP but also with medication that mitigates her obsessive thoughts and compulsive urges. For many years, psychological treatment was the main form of intervention for psychological disorders because few biological options were available. Folk remedies purporting to have a biological basis—such as hydrotherapy (pouring cold water on those with mental disorders), trephination (drilling holes in the skull to let the evil spirits escape), and bloodletting (the removal of blood from the body)—once were tried in efforts to cure psychological disorders (Note: Do not try these at home. Turns out they don't work.) As we learn more about the biology and chemistry of the brain, approaches to mental health that begin with the brain are becoming increasingly widespread. As you'll see later in the chapter, many effective treatments combine both psychological and biological interventions.

DATA VISUALIZATION
How Has the Rate of ADHD Diagnosis Changed Over Time?
Go to launchpadworks.com.

Build to the Outcomes

1. What are some of the personal, social, and financial costs of mental illness?

2. What are the obstacles to treatment for the mentally ill?

3. What are the two broad types of treatment?

Psychological Treatments: Healing the Mind Through Interaction

Learning Outcomes

▶ Outline the aspects of each approach to psychotherapy.

▶ Describe the pros and cons of group treatment.

Psychological therapy, or **psychotherapy**, *is an interaction between a socially sanctioned clinician and someone suffering from a psychological problem, with the goal of providing support or relief from the problem.* Over 500 different forms of psychotherapy exist. Although there are similarities among all the psychotherapies, each approach is unique in its goals, aims, and methods. A recent survey of psychotherapists asked them to describe their main theoretical orientation (Norcross & Rogan, 2013; see **FIGURE 16.1**). One out of four reported using **eclectic psychotherapy**, *a form of psychotherapy that involves drawing on techniques from different forms of therapy, depending on the client and the problem.* This approach allows therapists to apply an appropriate theoretical perspective suited to the problem at hand, rather than adhering to a single theoretical perspective for all clients and all types of problems. Nevertheless, as Figure 16.1 shows, the majority of psychotherapists use a single approach, such as psychodynamic therapy, humanistic and existential therapies, or behavioral and cognitive therapies. We'll examine each of those major approaches to psychotherapy in turn.

PSYCHODYNAMIC THERAPY

Psychodynamic psychotherapy has its roots in Freud's psychoanalytically oriented theory of personality. **Psychodynamic psychotherapies** *explore childhood events and encourage individuals to use this understanding to develop insight into their psychological problems.* Psychoanalysis was the first psychodynamic therapy to develop, but it has largely been replaced by modern psychodynamic therapies, such as interpersonal psychotherapy.

Psychoanalysis

As we saw in the Personality chapter, *psychoanalysis* assumes that people are born with aggressive and sexual urges that are repressed during childhood development through the use of defense mechanisms. Psychoanalysts encourage their clients to bring these repressed conflicts into consciousness so that the clients can understand them and reduce their unwanted influences. Psychoanalysts focus a great deal on early childhood events because they believe that urges and conflicts were likely to be repressed during this time.

psychotherapy An interaction between a socially sanctioned clinician and someone suffering from a psychological problem, with the goal of providing support or relief from the problem.

eclectic psychotherapy A form of psychotherapy that involves drawing on techniques from different forms of therapy, depending on the client and the problem.

psychodynamic psychotherapies Therapies that explore childhood events and encourage individuals to use this understanding to develop insight into their psychological problems.

▶ Figure 16.1
APPROACHES TO PSYCHOTHERAPY IN THE 21ST CENTURY This chart shows the percentage of psychologists who have various primary psychotherapy orientations (data from Norcross & Rogan, 2013).

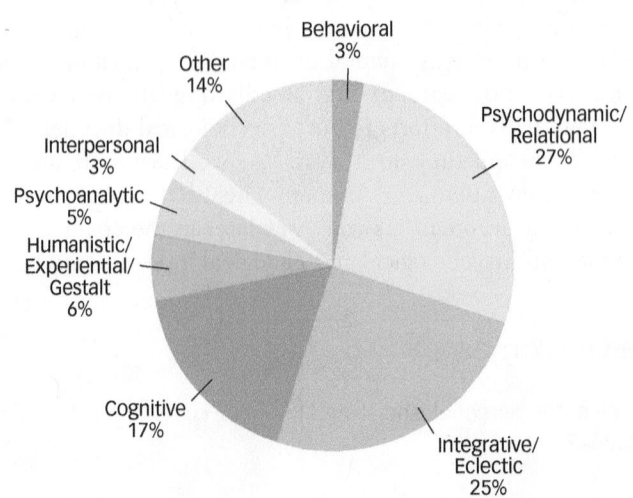

Traditional psychoanalysis involves four or five sessions per week over an average of 3 to 6 years (Ursano & Silberman, 2003). During a session, the client reclines on a couch, facing away from the analyst, who asks the client to express whatever thoughts and feelings come to mind. Occasionally, the therapist may comment on some of the information the client presents but does not express his or her values and judgments. The stereotypic image you might have of psychological therapy— a person lying on a couch talking to a person sitting in a chair—springs from this approach.

The goal of psychoanalysis is for the client to understand the unconscious in a process Freud called *developing insight*. A psychoanalyst can use several key techniques to help the client develop insight, including the following:

Free association. In free association, the client reports every thought that enters the mind, without censorship or filtering. This strategy allows the stream of consciousness to flow unimpeded. If the client stops, the therapist prompts further associations. ("And what does that make you think of?") The therapist may then look for themes that recur across therapy sessions.

Dream analysis. Psychoanalysis may treat dreams as metaphors that symbolize unconscious conflicts or wishes and that contain disguised clues that the therapist can help the client understand. A psychoanalytic therapy session might begin with an invitation for the client to recount a dream, after which the client might be asked to participate in the interpretation by freely associating to the dream.

Interpretation. This is the process by which the therapist deciphers the meaning (e.g., unconscious impulses or fantasies) underlying what the client says and does. Interpretation is used throughout therapy, during free association and dream analysis, as well as in other aspects of the treatment. During the process of interpretation, the therapist suggests possible meanings to the client, looking for signs that the correct meaning has been discovered.

Analysis of resistance. In the process of "trying on" different interpretations of the client's thoughts and actions, the therapist may suggest an interpretation that the client finds particularly unacceptable. **Resistance** is a *reluctance to cooperate with treatment for fear of confronting unpleasant unconscious material.* For example, the therapist might suggest that the client's problem with obsessive health worries could be traced to a childhood rivalry with her mother for her father's love and attention. The client could find the suggestion insulting and resist the interpretation. The therapist might interpret this resistance as a signal not that the interpretation is wrong but instead that the interpretation is on the right track. If a client always shifts the topic of discussion away from a particular idea, it might signal to the therapist that this is indeed an issue the client could be directed to confront in order to develop insight.

Through the course of meeting so frequently over such a long period of time, the client and psychoanalyst often develop a close relationship. Freud noticed this relationship developing in his analyses and was at first troubled by it: Clients would develop an unusually strong attachment to him, almost as though they were viewing him as a parent or a lover, and he worried that this could interfere with achieving the goal of insight. Over time, however, he came to believe that the development and resolution of this relationship was a key process of psychoanalysis. **Transference** occurs *when the analyst begins to assume a major significance in the client's life, and the client reacts to the analyst on the basis of unconscious childhood fantasies.* Successful psychoanalysis involves analyzing the transference so that the client understands this reaction and why it occurs.

In traditional psychoanalysis, the client lies on a couch, with the therapist sitting behind, out of the client's view.

"Before we begin, I'd like to say a few words about the concept of 'defence mechanisms'."

resistance A reluctance to cooperate with treatment for fear of confronting unpleasant unconscious material.

transference An event that occurs in psychoanalysis when the analyst begins to assume a major significance in the client's life, and the client reacts to the analyst on the basis of unconscious childhood fantasies.

In the movie *Good Will Hunting,* the lead character, played by Matt Damon, forms a strong bond with his therapist, played by Robin Williams. As in psychodynamic therapy, the therapist uses their relationship to help break down the patient's defense mechanisms and resolve an inner conflict. The amazing bond that was formed between therapist and patient and the life-changing treatment delivered are the stuff of therapists' dreams (and Hollywood scripts).

interpersonal psychotherapy (IPT) A form of psychotherapy that focuses on helping clients improve current relationships.

Psychodynamic Therapy

Freud's original version of psychoanalysis is practiced by only about 5% of clinicians today (see Figure 16.1). However, many of his insights and techniques remain very influential in a broader range of psychodynamic treatments used more frequently today (about 30% of therapists today use psychodynamic therapy), which differ from classic psychoanalysis in both their content and their procedures. One of the most common psychodynamic treatments is **interpersonal psychotherapy (IPT)**, *a form of psychotherapy that focuses on helping clients improve current relationships* (Weissman, Markowitz, & Klerman, 2000). In terms of content, rather than using free association, therapists using psychodynamic therapies such as IPT talk to clients about their interpersonal behaviors and feelings. They pay particular attention to the client's grief (an exaggerated reaction to the loss of a loved one), role disputes (conflicts with a significant other), role transitions (changes in life status, such as starting a new job, getting married, or retiring), or interpersonal deficits (lack of the necessary skills to start or maintain a relationship). The treatment focuses on interpersonal functioning with the assumption that, as interpersonal relations improve, symptoms will subside.

Modern psychodynamic psychotherapies such as IPT also differ from classical psychoanalysis in the procedures used. For starters, in modern psychodynamic therapy the therapist and client typically sit face to face. In addition, therapy is less intensive, with meetings often occurring only once a week and therapy lasting months rather than years. In contrast to classical psychoanalysis, modern psychodynamic therapists are more likely to see relief from symptoms as a reasonable goal for therapy (in addition to the goal of facilitating insight), and they are more likely to offer support or advice in addition to interpretation (Barber et al., 2013). Therapists are also now less likely to interpret a client's statements as a sign of unconscious sexual or aggressive impulses. However, other concepts, such as transference and fostering insight into unconscious processes, remain features of most psychodynamic therapies. Freud's couch casts a long shadow.

What Is the Evidence?

Although psychodynamic therapy has been around for a long time and continues to be widely practiced, there is limited evidence for its effectiveness. Some researchers suggest that there is evidence that psychodynamic therapies are effective (Shedler, 2010). However, in-depth studies that examine evidence from many prior studies find that IPT (one specific form of psychodynamic therapy) and cognitive behavior therapy (described below) are more effective than all other treatments, especially in the case of the treatment of depressive and anxiety disorders (Tolin, 2010; Watzke et al., 2012; Zhou et al., 2015). Moreover, there is some evidence that some of the aspects of psychodynamic therapy long believed to be effective may actually be harmful. For instance, research suggests that the more a therapist makes interpretations about perceived transference in the client, the worse the therapeutic alliance and the worse the clinical outcome (Henry et al., 1994).

HUMANISTIC AND EXISTENTIAL THERAPIES

Humanistic and existential therapies emerged in the middle of the 20th century, in part as a reaction to the negative views that psychoanalysis holds about human nature. Humanistic and existential therapies assume that human nature is generally positive, and they emphasize the natural tendency of each individual to strive for personal improvement. Humanistic and existential therapies share the assumption that psychological problems stem from feelings of alienation and loneliness, and that those feelings can be traced to failures to reach one's potential (in the humanistic approach) or from failures to find meaning in life (in the existential approach). Although interest in these approaches peaked in the 1960s and 1970s, some therapists continue to practice these approaches today. Two well-known types are person-centered therapy (a humanistic approach) and gestalt therapy (an existential approach).

Person-Centered Therapy

Person-centered therapy (or **client-centered therapy**) *assumes that all individuals have a tendency toward growth and that this growth can be facilitated by acceptance and genuine reactions from the therapist.* The psychologist Carl Rogers (1902–1987) developed person-centered therapy in the 1940s and 1950s (Rogers, 1951). Person-centered therapy assumes that each person is qualified to determine his or her own goals for therapy, such as feeling more confident or making a career decision, and even the frequency and length of therapy. In this type of nondirective treatment, the therapist tends not to provide advice or suggestions about what the client should be doing, but instead paraphrases the client's words, mirroring the client's thoughts and sentiments (e.g., "I think I hear you saying . . ."). Person-centered therapists believe that with adequate support, the client will recognize the right things to do.

Rogers encouraged person-centered therapists to demonstrate three basic qualities: congruence, empathy, and unconditional positive regard. Congruence means openness and honesty in the therapeutic relationship and ensuring that the therapist communicates the same message at all levels. For example, the therapist must communicate the same message in words, in facial expression, and in body language. Saying "I think your concerns are valid" while smirking simply will not do. Empathy is the continuous process of trying to understand the client by getting inside his or her way of thinking, feeling, and understanding the world. Interestingly, research has shown that the more empathic a client says the clinician is, the more similarity there is between the client's and therapist's levels of physiological arousal in that moment (Marci et al., 2007). This suggests that therapists who are being empathic may really be feeling some of what their clients are feeling. Seeing the world from the client's perspective enables the therapist to better appreciate the client's apprehensions, worries, or fears. Finally, the therapist must treat the client with unconditional positive regard by providing a nonjudgmental, warm, and accepting environment in which the client can feel safe expressing his or her thoughts and feelings.

The goal is not to uncover repressed conflicts, as in psychodynamic therapy, but instead to try to understand the client's experience and reflect that experience back to the client in a supportive way, encouraging the client's natural tendency toward growth. This style of therapy is reminiscent of psychoanalysis in its way of encouraging the client toward the free expression of thoughts and feelings.

Gestalt Therapy

Gestalt therapy was founded by Frederick "Fritz" Perls (1893–1970) and colleagues in the 1940s and 1950s (Perls, Hefferkine, & Goodman, 1951). **Gestalt therapy** *has the goal of helping the client become aware of his or her thoughts, behaviors, experiences, and feelings and to "own" or take responsibility for them.* Gestalt therapists are encouraged to be enthusiastic and warm toward their clients, an approach they share with person-centered therapists. To help facilitate the client's awareness, gestalt therapists also reflect back to the client their impressions of the client.

Gestalt therapy emphasizes the experiences and behaviors that are occurring at that particular moment in the therapy session. For example, if a client is talking about something stressful that occurred during the previous week, the therapist might shift the attention to the client's current experience by asking, "How do you feel as you describe what happened to you?" This technique is known as focusing. Clients are also encouraged to put their feelings into action. One way to do this is

person-centered therapy (or client-centered therapy) A form of psychotherapy that assumes that all individuals have a tendency toward growth and that this growth can be facilitated by acceptance and genuine reactions from the therapist.

gestalt therapy A form of psychotherapy whose goal is helping the client become aware of his or her thoughts, behaviors, experiences, and feelings and to "own" or take responsibility for them.

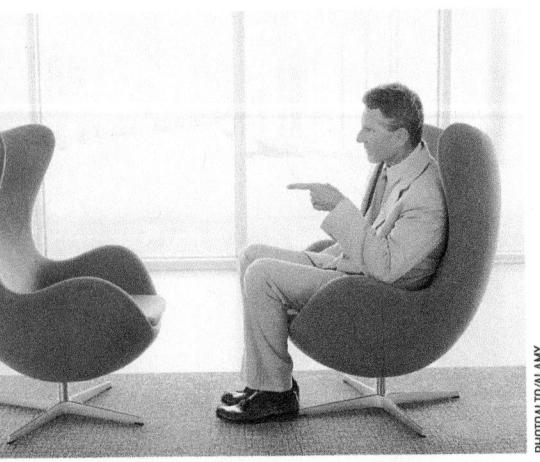

As part of gestalt therapy, clients may be encouraged to imagine that another person is sitting across from them in a chair. The client then moves from chair to chair, role-playing what he or she would say to the imagined person and how that person would answer.

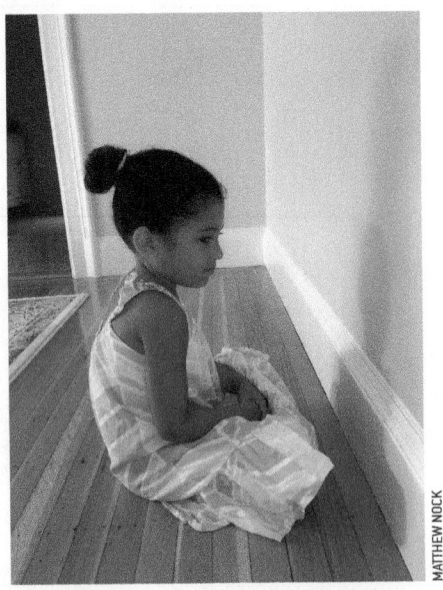

A behavioral psychologist might treat a temper tantrum using time-out for reinforcement, a method that is based on the behavioral principle of operant conditioning and that ensures that a child will not be rewarded for her undesired behavior.

behavior therapy A type of therapy that assumes that disordered behavior is learned and that symptom relief is achieved through changing overt maladaptive behaviors into constructive behaviors.

token economy A form of behavior therapy in which clients are given "tokens" for desired behaviors, which they can later trade for rewards.

the empty chair technique, in which the client imagines that another person (e.g., a spouse, a parent, a coworker) is in an empty chair, sitting directly across from the client. The client then moves from chair to chair, alternating from role-playing what he or she would say to the other person and how he or she imagines the other person would respond.

BEHAVIORAL AND COGNITIVE THERAPIES

Unlike the talk therapies described above, behavioral and cognitive treatments emphasize actively changing a person's current thoughts and behaviors as a way to mitigate or eliminate their psychopathology. In the evolution of psychological treatments, clients started out lying down in psychoanalysis, then sitting in psychodynamic and related approaches, but often stand and engage in behavior-change homework assignments in their everyday life in behavioral and cognitive therapies.

Behavior Therapy: Changing Maladaptive Behavior Patterns

Whereas Freud developed psychoanalysis as an offshoot of hypnosis and other techniques that other clinicians used before him, behavior therapy was developed on the basis of laboratory findings of earlier behavioral psychologists. As you read in the Psychology: Evolution of a Science chapter, behaviorists rejected theories that were based on "invisible" mental properties that were difficult to test and impossible to observe directly. Behaviorists found psychoanalytic ideas particularly hard to test: How do you know whether a person has an unconscious conflict or whether insight has occurred? Behavioral principles, in contrast, focused solely on behaviors that could be observed (e.g., avoidance of a feared object, such as refusing to get on an airplane). **Behavior therapy** assumes that *disordered behavior is learned and that symptom relief is achieved through changing overt, maladaptive behaviors into more constructive behaviors.* A variety of behavior therapy techniques have been developed for many disorders, based on the learning principles you encountered in the Learning chapter, including operant conditioning procedures (which focus on reinforcement and punishment) and classical conditioning procedures (which focus on extinction). Here are three examples of behavior therapy techniques in action:

Eliminating Unwanted Behaviors How would you change a 3-year-old boy's habit of throwing tantrums at the grocery store? A behavior therapist might investigate what happens immediately before and after the tantrum: Did the child get candy to "shut him up"? The study of operant conditioning shows that behavior can be influenced by its *consequences* (the reinforcing or punishing events that follow). Adjusting these might help change the behavior. Making the consequences less reinforcing (no candy!) and more punishing (a period of time-out facing the wall in the grocery store while the parent watches from nearby rather than providing a rush of attention) could eliminate the problem behavior.

Promoting Desired Behaviors Candy and time-outs can have a strong influence on child behavior, but they work less well with adults. How might you get an individual with schizophrenia to engage in activities of daily living? How would you get a cocaine addict to stop using drugs? A behavior therapy technique that has proven to be quite effective in such cases is the **token economy**, which involves *giving clients "tokens" for desired behaviors, which they can later trade for rewards.* For instance, in the case of cocaine dependence, the desired behavior is not using cocaine. Programs that reward non-use (verified by urine samples) with vouchers that can be exchanged for rewards such as money, bus passes, clothes, and so on, have shown an ability to significantly reduce cocaine use and associated psychological problems (Petry, Alessi, & Rash, 2013). Similar systems are used to promote desired behaviors in classrooms, the workplace, and commercial advertising (e.g., airline and credit card rewards programs).

Reducing Unwanted Emotional Responses One of the most powerful ways to reduce fear is by gradual exposure to the feared object or situation. **Exposure therapy** involves *confronting an emotion-arousing stimulus directly and repeatedly, ultimately leading to a decrease in the emotional response.* This technique depends on the processes of habituation and response extinction. For example, in Christine's case her clinician gradually exposed her to the content of her obsessions (dirt and germs), which became less and less distressing with repeated exposure (as she learned that no harm actually would come to her from coming into contact with the previously feared stimulus). Similarly, for clients who are afraid of social interaction and unable to function at school or work, a behavioral treatment might involve exposure first to imagined situations in which they talk briefly with one person, then talk a bit longer to a medium-sized group, and finally, give a speech to a large group. It's now known that *in vivo* (live) exposure is more effective than imaginary exposure (Choy, Fyer, & Lipsitz, 2007). In other words, if a person fears social situations, it is better for that person to practice social interaction than merely to imagine it. Behavioral therapists use an exposure hierarchy to accustom the client gradually to the feared object or situation. Easier situations are practiced first, and as fear decreases, the client progresses to more difficult or frightening situations (see **TABLE 16.1**). It is vitally important that the person continue to be exposed to the feared stimulus until their anxiety decreases. If they leave the situation before it does, this can reinforce their anxiety, because they fail to learn that the feared stimulus is not harmful and they learn that avoiding it decreases their anxiety. So if you have a fear of, say, public speaking, best to speak to increasingly large groups of people and to not leave each situation until your anxiety decreases!

Exposure therapy can also help people overcome unwanted emotional and behavioral responses through *exposure and response prevention.* Persons with OCD, for example, might have recurrent thoughts that their hands are dirty and need washing.

exposure therapy An approach to treatment that involves confronting an emotion-arousing stimulus directly and repeatedly, ultimately leading to a decrease in the emotional response.

TABLE 16.1

Exposure Hierarchy for Social Phobia

Item	Fear (0–100)
1. Have a party and invite everyone from work	99
2. Go to a holiday party for 1 hour without drinking	90
3. Invite Cindy to have dinner and see a movie	85
4. Go for a job interview	80
5. Ask boss for a day off work	65
6. Ask questions in a meeting at work	65
7. Eat lunch with coworkers	60
8. Talk to a stranger on the bus	50
9. Talk to cousin on the telephone for 10 minutes	40
10. Ask for directions at the gas station	35

Information from Ellis (1991).

An exposure therapy client with obsessive-compulsive disorder who fears contamination in public restrooms might be given the "homework" of visiting three such restrooms in a week, touching the toilets, and then *not* washing up.

Washing stops the uncomfortable feelings of contamination only briefly, though, and they wash again and again in search of relief. In exposure with response prevention, they might be asked in therapy to get their hands dirty on purpose (first by touching a coin picked up from the ground, then by touching a public toilet, and later by touching a dead mouse) and leave them dirty for hours. They may need to do this only a few times to break the cycle and be freed from the obsessive ritual (Foa et al., 2007).

Cognitive Therapy: Changing Distorted Thoughts

Whereas behavior therapy focuses primarily on changing a person's behavior, **cognitive therapy**, as the name suggests, focuses on *helping a client identify and correct any distorted thinking about self, others, or the world* (Beck, 2005). For example, behaviorists might explain a phobia as the outcome of a classical conditioning experience such as being bitten by a dog; the dog bite leads to the development of a dog phobia through the association of the dog with the experience of pain. Cognitive theorists might instead emphasize the *interpretation* of the event. It might not be the event itself that caused the fear, but rather the individual's beliefs and assumptions about the event and the feared stimulus. In the case of a dog bite, to explain the fear, cognitive theorists might focus on a person's new or strengthened belief that dogs are dangerous.

Cognitive therapies use a principal technique called **cognitive restructuring**, which involves *teaching clients to question the automatic beliefs, assumptions, and predictions that often lead to negative emotions and to replace negative thinking with more realistic and positive beliefs*. Specifically, clients are taught to examine the evidence for and against a particular belief or to be more accepting of outcomes that may be undesirable yet still manageable. For example, a depressed client may believe that she is stupid and will never pass her college courses—all on the basis of one poor grade. In this situation, the therapist would work with the client to examine the validity of this belief. The therapist would consider relevant evidence such as grades on previous exams, performance on other coursework, and examples of intelligence outside school. It may be that the client has never failed a course before and has achieved good grades in this particular course in the past. In this case, the therapist would encourage the client to consider all this information in determining whether she is truly "stupid." **TABLE 16.2** shows a variety

cognitive therapy Focuses on helping a client identify and correct any distorted thinking about self, others, or the world.

cognitive restructuring A therapeutic approach that teaches clients to question the automatic beliefs, assumptions, and predictions that often lead to negative emotions and to replace negative thinking with more realistic and positive beliefs.

TABLE 16.2

Common Irrational Beliefs and the Emotional Responses They Can Cause

Belief	Emotional Response
I have to get this done immediately.	Anxiety, stress
I must be perfect.	
Something terrible will happen.	
Everyone is watching me.	Embarrassment, social anxiety
I won't be able to make friends.	
People know something is wrong with me.	
I'm a loser and will always be a loser.	Sadness, depression
Nobody will ever love me.	
She did that to me on purpose.	Anger, irritability
He is evil and should be punished.	
Things ought to be different.	

Information from Ellis (1991).

of potentially irrational ideas that can unleash unwanted emotions such as anger, depression, or anxiety. Any of these irrational beliefs might bedevil a person with serious emotional problems if left unchallenged and are potential targets for cognitive restructuring. In therapy sessions, the cognitive therapist will help the client to identify evidence that supports, and fails to support, each negative thought in order to help the client generate more balanced thoughts that accurately reflect the true state of affairs. In other words, the clinician tries to remove the dark lens through which the client views the world, not with the goal of replacing it with rose-colored glasses, but instead with clear glass. Here is a brief sample transcript of what part of a cognitive therapy session might sound like.

The cognitive therapist Aaron Beck's approach to psychotherapy employs a direct and rational approach to help people change maladaptive thinking patterns.

Clinician	Last week I asked you to keep a thought record of situations that made you feel very depressed, at least one per day, and the automatic thoughts that popped into your mind. Were you able to do that?
Client	Yes.
Clinician	Great. Did you bring it in with you today?
Client	Yes, here it is.
Clinician	Wonderful, I'm glad you were able to complete this assignment. Let's take a look at this together. What's the first situation that you recorded?
Client	Well . . . I went out on Friday night with my friends, which I thought would be fun and help me to feel better. But I was feeling kind of down about things and I ended up not really talking to anyone, which led me to just sit in the corner and drink all night, which caused me to get so drunk that I passed out at the party. I woke up the next day feeling embarrassed and more depressed than ever.
Clinician	Okay, sounds like a tough situation. So the situation is you had too much to drink and passed out. The resulting emotion you had was depression. How intense was your feeling of depression on a scale of 0 to 100?
Client	Ninety.
Clinician	Okay, and what thoughts automatically popped into your head?
Client	I can't control myself. I'll never be able to control myself. My friends think I'm a loser and will never want to hang out with me again.
Clinician	Okay, and which of these thoughts led you to feel most depressed?
Client	That my friends think I'm a loser and won't want to hang out with me anymore.
Clinician	All right, so let's focus on that one for a minute. What evidence can you think of that supports this thought?
Client	Well . . . um . . . I got really drunk and so they *have* to think I'm a loser. I mean, who does that?
Clinician	Okay, write that down on your thought record in this column here. Anything else? Is there any other evidence you can think of that supports those thoughts?
Client	No.
Clinician	All right. Now let's take a moment to think about whether there is any evidence that doesn't support those thoughts. Did anything happen that suggests that your friends don't think you are a loser or that they do want to keep hanging out with you?
Client	Well . . . apparently some kids were making fun of me when I was passed out and my friends stopped them. And they also brought me home safely and then called the next day and joked about what happened and my one friend Tommy said something like "we've all been there" and that he wants to hang out again this weekend.

mindfulness meditation Teaches an individual to be fully present in each moment; to be aware of his or her thoughts, feelings, and sensations; and to detect symptoms before they become a problem.

cognitive behavioral therapy (CBT) A blend of cognitive and behavioral therapeutic strategies.

Clinician	Okay, great, write that down in this next column. This is very interesting. So on one hand, you feel depressed and have thoughts that you are a loser and your friends don't like you. But on the other hand, you have some pretty real-world evidence that even though you drank too much, they were still there for you and they do in fact want to hang out with you again, yes?
Client	Yeah, I guess you're right if you put it that way. I didn't think about it like that.
Clinician	So now if we were going to replace your first thoughts, which don't seem to have a lot of real-world evidence, with a more balanced thought based on the evidence, what would that new thought be?
Client	Probably something like, my friends probably weren't happy about the fact that I got so drunk because then they had to take care of me, but they are my friends and were there for me and want to keep hanging out with me.
Clinician	Excellent job. I think that sounds just right based on the evidence, write that down in the next column. And how much do you believe in this new thought on a scale of 0 to 100?
Client	I think it's actually pretty accurate, so I would say 95.
Clinician:	And thinking about this new more balanced thought rather than your first one, how would you rate your depression?
Client:	Much lower than before. Probably a 40. I'm still not happy that I got so drunk, but less depressed about my friends.

In addition to cognitive restructuring techniques, which try to change a person's thoughts to be more balanced or accurate, some forms of cognitive therapy also include techniques for coping with unwanted thoughts and feelings, techniques that resemble meditation (see the Consciousness chapter). Clients may be encouraged to attend to their troubling thoughts or emotions or be given meditative techniques that allow them to gain a new focus (Hofmann & Asmundson, 2008). One such technique, called **mindfulness meditation**, *teaches an individual to be fully present in each moment; to be aware of his or her thoughts, feelings, and sensations; and to detect symptoms before they become a problem.* Researchers found mindfulness meditation to be helpful for preventing relapse in depression. In one study, people recovering from depression were about half as likely to relapse during a 60-week assessment period if they received mindfulness meditation-based cognitive therapy than if they received treatment as usual (Teasdale, Segal, & Williams, 2000). Cognitive and cognitive behavioral therapies (covered below) do well in preventing relapse because once a person learns the skills taught in these therapies, they can continue to use them in future situations all on their own, without guidance from a clinician (DeRubeis, Siegle, & Hollon, 2008). This is in contrast to medications, which only work as long as they are present in the body.

Cognitive Behavioral Therapy: Blending Approaches

Historically, cognitive and behavioral therapies were considered distinct systems of therapy, and some people continue to follow this distinction, using solely behavioral *or* cognitive techniques. Today, the extent to which therapists use cognitive versus behavioral techniques depends on the individual therapist as well as the type of problem being treated. Most therapists working with anxiety and depression use *a blend of cognitive and behavioral therapeutic strategies,* often referred to as **cognitive behavioral therapy (CBT)**. In a way, this technique acknowledges that there may be behaviors that people cannot control through rational thought, but also that there are ways of helping people think more rationally when thought does play a role. In contrast to traditional behavior therapy and cognitive therapy, CBT is *problem focused*, meaning that it is undertaken for specific problems (e.g., reducing the frequency of panic attacks or returning to work after a bout of depression), and *action oriented*, meaning that the

How might the use of behavior-change homework improve the effectiveness of behavior therapy?

therapist tries to assist the client in selecting specific strategies to help address those problems. The client is expected to *do* things, such as engage in exposure exercises, practice behavior change skills or use a diary to monitor relevant symptoms (e.g., the severity of depressed mood, panic attack symptoms). This is in contrast to psychodynamic or other therapies where goals may not be explicitly discussed or agreed on and the client's only necessary action is to attend the therapy session.

CBT also contrasts with psychodynamic approaches in its assumptions about what the client can know. CBT is *transparent* in that nothing is withheld from the client. By the end of the course of therapy, most clients have a very good understanding of the treatment they have received as well as the specific techniques that are used to make the desired changes. For example, clients with OCD who fear contamination would feel confident in knowing how to confront feared situations such as public washrooms and why confronting these situations is helpful.

Cognitive behavioral therapies have been found to be effective for a number of disorders (Butler et al., 2006; see Hot Science: "Rebooting" Psychological Treatment). Substantial effects of CBT have been found for unipolar depression, generalized anxiety disorder, panic disorder, social phobia, posttraumatic stress disorder, and childhood depressive and anxiety disorders. CBT has moderate but less substantial effects for marital distress, anger, somatic disorders, and chronic pain.

GROUP TREATMENTS: HEALING MULTIPLE MINDS AT THE SAME TIME

It is natural to think of psychopathology as an illness that affects only the individual. A particular person "is depressed," for example, or "has anxiety." Yet each person lives in a world of other people, and interactions with others may intensify and even cause disorders. A depressed person may be lonely after moving away from friends and loved ones, or an anxious person could be worried about pressures from parents. These ideas suggest that people might be able to recover from disorders in the same way they got into them—not just as an individual effort, but through social processes.

Couples and Family Therapy

When a couple is "having problems," neither individual may be suffering from any psychopathology. Rather, it may be the relationship itself that is disordered. *In couples therapy*, a married, cohabitating, or dating couple is seen together in therapy to work on problems usually arising within the relationship. A traditional situation for couples therapy might involve a couple seeking help because they are unhappy with their relationship. In this scenario, both members of the couple are expected to attend therapy sessions and the problem is seen as arising from their interaction rather than from the problems of one half of the couple. Treatment strategies would target changes in *both* parties, focusing on ways to break their repetitive dysfunctional pattern.

In some cases, therapy with even larger groups is warranted. An individual may be having a problem—say, an adolescent is abusing alcohol—but the source of the problem is the individual's relationships with family members; perhaps the mother is herself an alcoholic who subtly encourages the adolescent to drink, and the father travels and neglects the family. In this case, it could be useful for the therapist to work with the whole group at once in *family therapy*—psychotherapy involving members of a family. Family therapy can be particularly effective when adolescent children are having problems (Masten, 2004).

In family therapy, the "client" is the entire family. Family therapists believe that problem behaviors exhibited by a particular family member are the result of a dysfunctional family. For example, an adolescent girl suffering from bulimia might be treated in therapy with her mother, father, and older brother. The therapist would

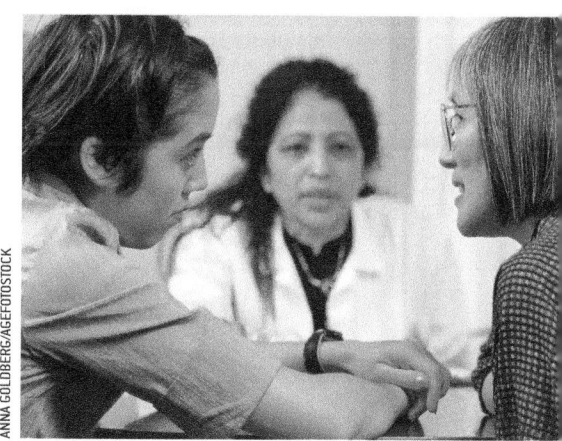

Families enter therapy for many reasons, sometimes to help particular members and other times because there are problems in one or more of the relationships in the family.

"Rebooting" Psychological Treatment

Modern psychotherapy has advanced far beyond the days of Freud and his free-associating patients. We now have more sophisticated treatments that have been developed on the basis of recent advances in psychological science and supported in experimental studies showing that they actually do decrease peoples' psychological suffering. However, psychological treatment is still pretty primitive in many ways. It usually involves a patient meeting once per week with a clinician who attempts to talk them out of their psychological disorder—just as it did in the earliest days of psychological treatment. In a recent paper, Alan Kazdin (and his student Stacey Blase) called for a "rebooting" of psychotherapy research and practice (Kazdin & Blase, 2011). What is needed, they argue, is a portfolio of treatment delivery approaches that take advantage of recent advances in technology.

Although most psychologists providing treatment to those with psychological disorders still employ traditional psychotherapy, researchers are developing and testing new methods of assessing and treating disorders that make creative use of new technologies. One of the most exciting recent advances in psychological treatment involves computerized training programs. For example, research suggests that biases in the ways that people process information cause psychological disorders. Cognitive bias modification (CBM) is a computerized intervention that focuses on eliminating these biases. Specifically, people with social anxiety show selective attention for threatening information. (For example, when shown a series of pairs of faces, they have an automatic tendency to look at the angrier one.) In one form of CBM for social anxiety, the patient completes a computerized training program in which he or she is repeatedly shown pairs of faces, one angry and one neutral, that flash on the screen very quickly (for 500 milliseconds), after which the letter "E" or "F" appears behind one of them. The patient's task is to indicate whether the

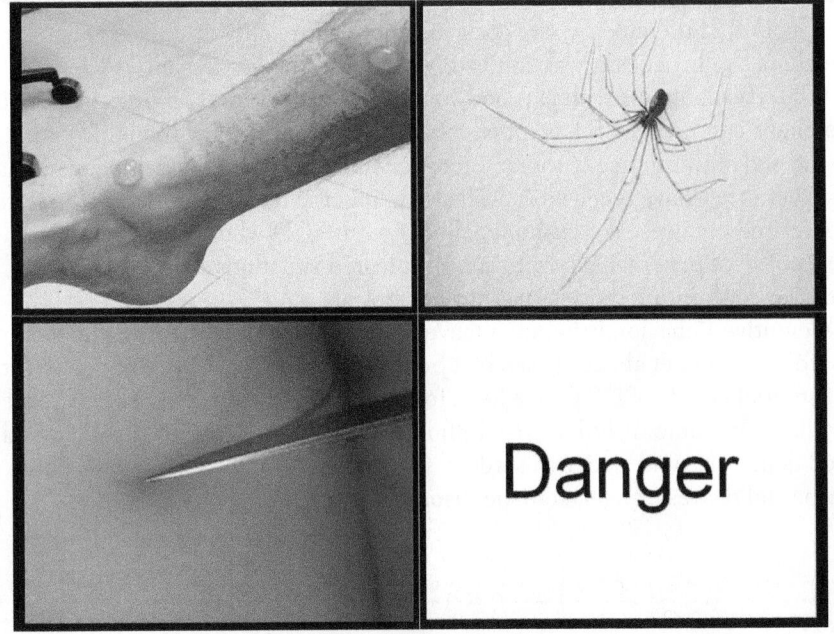

▲ In Therapeutic Evaluative Conditioning (TEC) patients are trained to repeatedly pair suicidal or self-injury-related images (*bottom left*) with aversive images (*top right*). Over time, people making such pairings develop an aversion to suicide/self-injury and show a decrease in these self-harm behaviors.

letter is an "E" or "F." In CBM, the "E" or "F" always, or nearly always, appears behind the neutral face, which over time teaches the person to ignore the angry face and attend to the neutral face, thus reducing the tendency to attend to threatening faces. A recent review of 15 experiments including over 1,000 people found that CBM was associated with a significant decrease in symptoms of social anxiety. However, the effects were relatively small and short lasting, leading the authors to conclude that this method is not yet ready for wide-scale use (Heeren et al., 2015).

Another smartphone-based app called Therapeutic Evaluative Conditioning (TEC) presents the user with several different images (see figure) and has them repeatedly pair suicidal or self-injury-related images with aversive images such as snakes or spiders. The idea is that, as with classical conditioning, by repeatedly pairing these images, over time people will come to associate the suicidal or self-injury-related images with the aversive feeling evoked by the pictures of snakes and spiders. Researchers found that in three different randomized controlled trials, people who played this matching game for a few minutes each day for one month showed significant reductions in self-injury and suicidal behavior (Franklin et al., 2016).

The development of computer- or smartphone-based interventions has been extremely exciting; however, one recent review found that very few interventions using mobile technologies have data supporting their effectiveness (Larsen, Nicholas, & Christensen, 2016). So although the development of computerized approaches has opened up lots of new opportunities for intervention, it is important that psychologists carefully evaluate which ones can help improve health outcomes and which are simply fancier ways of providing ineffective treatment.

work to understand how the family members relate to one another, how the family is organized, and how it changes over time. In discussions with the family, the therapist might discover that the parents' excessive enthusiasm about her brother's athletic career led the girl to try to gain their approval by controlling her weight to become "beautiful." Both couples and family therapy involve more than one person attending therapy together, and the problems and solutions are seen as arising from the *interactions* of these individuals rather than simply from any one individual.

Group Therapy

Taking these ideas one step further, if individuals (or families) can benefit from talking with a psychotherapist, perhaps they can also benefit from talking with other clients who are talking with the therapist. This is **group therapy**, *a type of therapy in which multiple participants (who often do not know one another at the outset) work on their individual problems in a group atmosphere.* The therapist in group therapy serves more as a group facilitator than as a personal therapist, conducting the sessions both by talking with individuals and by encouraging them to talk with each other. Group therapy is often useful for people who have a common problem, such as substance abuse, but it can also be beneficial for those with differing problems. It is important to note that group therapy is not an approach in itself but a mode of delivering treatment. That is, group therapy can be psychodynamic, cognitive, cognitive behavioral, and so on, in its approach.

Why do people choose group therapy? One advantage is that attending a group with others who have similar problems shows clients that they are not alone in their suffering. In addition, group members model appropriate behaviors for each other and share their insights about how to deal with their problems. Group therapy is often just as effective as individual therapy (e.g., Jonsson & Hougaard, 2008). So from a societal perspective, group therapy is much more efficient.

Group therapy also has disadvantages. It may be difficult to assemble a group of individuals who have similar needs. This is particularly an issue with CBT, which tends to focus on specific problems such as depression or panic disorder. Group therapy may become a problem if one or more members undermine the treatment of other group members. This can occur if some group members dominate the discussions, threaten other group members, or make others in the group uncomfortable (e.g., attempting to date other members). Finally, clients in group therapy get less attention than they might in individual psychotherapy.

Self-Help and Support Groups

Some important types of group therapy are *self-help groups* and *support groups,* which are discussion groups that focus on a particular disorder or difficult life experience and are often run by peers (rather than a clinician) who have themselves struggled with the same issues. The most famous self-help and support groups are Alcoholics Anonymous (AA), Gamblers Anonymous, and Al-Anon (a program for families and friends of those with alcohol problems). Other self-help groups offer support to cancer survivors or to parents of children with autism or to people with mood disorders, eating disorders, and substance abuse problems. In fact, self-help and support groups exist for just about every psychological disorder. In addition to being cost effective, self-help and support groups allow people to realize that they are not the only ones with a particular problem and give them the opportunity to offer guidance and support to each other arising from personal experiences of success.

In some cases, though, self-help and support groups can do more harm than good. Some members may be disruptive or aggressive or encourage each other to engage in behaviors that are countertherapeutic (e.g., avoiding feared situations or using alcohol to cope). People with moderate problems may be exposed to others with severe problems and may become oversensitized to symptoms they might not otherwise have found disturbing. Because self-help and support groups are usually not led by trained therapists, mechanisms to evaluate these groups or to ensure their quality are rarely in place.

AA has more than 2 million members in the United States, with 117,000 group meetings that occur around the world (Alcoholics Anonymous, 2016). Members are

group therapy A type of therapy in which multiple participants (who often do not know each other at the outset) work on their individual problems in a group atmosphere.

Self-help groups are a cost-effective, time-effective, and treatment-effective solution for dealing with some types of psychological problems. Many people like self-help groups, but are they effective? How could you test this?

encouraged to follow *12 steps* to reach the goal of lifelong abstinence from all drinking; the steps include believing in a higher power, practicing prayer and meditation, and making amends for harm to others. Most members attend group meetings several times per week, and between meetings they receive additional support from their "sponsor." A few studies examining the effectiveness of AA have been conducted, and it appears that individuals who participate tend to overcome problem drinking with greater success than those who do not participate in AA (Fiorentine, 1999; Morgenstern et al., 1997). However, several tenets of the AA philosophy are not supported by the research. We know that the general AA program is useful, but questions about which parts of this program are most helpful have yet to be studied.

Considered together, the many social approaches to psychotherapy reveal how important interpersonal relationships are for each of us. It may not always be clear how psychotherapy works, whether one approach is better than another, or what particular theory best explains how problems have developed. What is clear, however, is that social interactions among people—both in individual therapy and in all the different forms of therapy in groups—can be useful in treating psychological disorders.

Build to the Outcomes

1. What is the basis for psychoanalysis and its key techniques?

2. In what common ways do modern psychodynamic theories differ from Freudian analysis?

3. How does a humanistic view of human nature differ from a psychodynamic view?

4. What are the characteristics of person-centered and Gestalt therapies?

5. How do behavioral therapies compensate for what behaviorists saw as problems with psychoanalytic ideas?

6. What is the idea behind the concept of cognitive restructuring?

7. How is CBT both *problem focused* and *action oriented*?

8. When is group therapy the best option?

9. How do self-help and support groups differ from traditional psychotherapy?

Biological Treatments: Healing the Mind by Physically Altering the Brain

Learning Outcomes

▶ Explain how antipsychotic medications affect the brain.

▶ Identify the risks of antianxiety medications.

▶ Explain how modern antidepressants affect the brain.

▶ Identify which herbal supplements have been proven to be effective.

▶ Debate pros and cons of combining psychological therapy with drug therapy.

▶ Identify the more extreme treatment options when psychotherapy and medications are unsuccessful.

People have ingested foreign substances in an attempt to change or improve their mental state since the beginning of recorded history. Humans have been fermenting fruits and other natural substances to create alcohol since about 7000 BCE (McGovern et al., 2004). Over a period of more than 1,500 years, Greek physicians prescribed a substance called *theriac* to treat a wide range of ailments, including anxiety and depression. Theriac was composed of dozens of different ingredients (including red roses, carrots, and viper's flesh), although we now know that one ingredient in particular (opium) likely was responsible for its positive effects. More recently, physicians found that another substance also worked wonders as a cure for depression, headaches, indigestion, and a range of other problems. That substance was cocaine, and it turns out that it has many negative side effects, which led to it falling out of favor as a sanctioned medicine (Markel, 2011). Since then, drug treatments have been developed that don't lead users to feel euphoric (as is the case with opium and cocaine). Instead they target specific neurotransmitters in the brain that are believed to be involved in the causes of different mental disorders. These treatments have grown in variety, effectiveness, and popularity; they are now the most common medical approach in treating psychological disorders (see **FIGURE 16.2**).

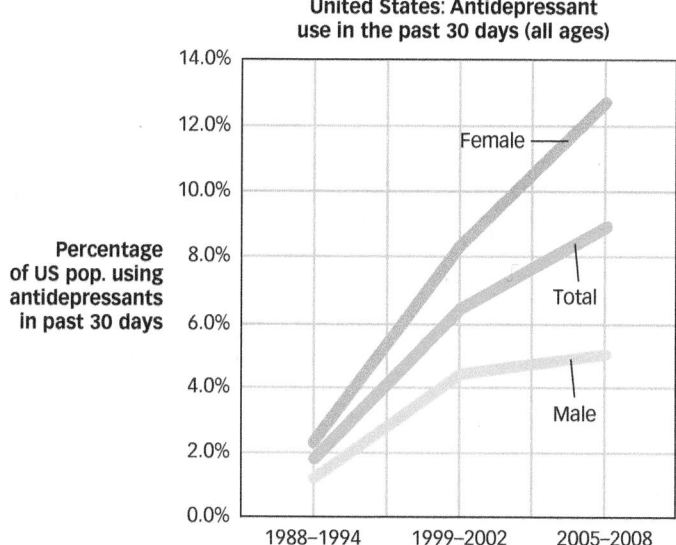

United States: Antidepressant use in the past 30 days (all ages)

Percentage of US pop. using antidepressants in past 30 days

Female

Total

Male

14.0%
12.0%
10.0%
8.0%
6.0%
4.0%
2.0%
0.0%

1988–1994   1999–2002   2005–2008

◄ Figure 16.2

ANTIDEPRESSANT USE The popularity of psychiatric medications has skyrocketed in recent years. A recent government report showed that the use of antidepressant medications rose 400% over the period from 1988 to 2008 (National Center for Health Statistics, 2012). This increase may be due to a number of factors, including the publication of data on the effectiveness of these medications, increasing efforts to disseminate them to prescribers, and enhanced efforts to market these drugs directly to consumers. The higher rates of use shown here for females may be due in part to the fact that women have higher rates of both depression and treatment use in general, compared with men.

ANTIPSYCHOTIC MEDICATIONS

The story of drug treatments for severe psychological disorders starts in the 1950s, with chlorpromazine (brand name Thorazine), which was originally developed as a sedative, but when administered to people with schizophrenia, often left them euphoric and docile, although they had formerly been agitated and incorrigible (Barondes, 2003). Chlorpromazine was the first in a series of **antipsychotic drugs**, which *treat schizophrenia and related psychotic disorders,* and completely changed the way schizophrenia was managed. Other related medications, such as thioridazine (Mellaril) and haloperidol (Haldol), followed. Before the introduction of antipsychotic drugs, people with schizophrenia often exhibited bizarre symptoms and were sometimes so disruptive and difficult to manage that the only way to protect them (and other people) was to keep them in hospitals for people with mental disorders, which were initially called *asylums* but now are referred to as *psychiatric hospitals* (see The Real World: Treating Severe Mental Disorders). In the period following the introduction of these drugs, the number of people in psychiatric hospitals decreased by more than two thirds. Antipsychotic drugs made possible the deinstitutionalization of hundreds of thousands of people and gave a major boost to the field of **psychopharmacology**, *the study of drug effects on psychological states and symptoms.*

Researchers believe that antipsychotic medications exert their effect by blocking dopamine receptors in parts of the brain such as the mesolimbic pathway: a pathway paved with dopamine neurons extending from the ventral tegmental area (VTA) to the Nucleus accumbens in the basal ganglia. (see the Neuroscience and Behavior chapter). The medications reduce dopamine activity in these areas. The effectiveness of schizophrenia medications led to the dopamine hypothesis (described in the Psychological Disorders chapter), suggesting that schizophrenia may be caused by excess dopamine in the synapse. Research has indeed found that dopamine overactivity in the mesolimbic pathway of the brain is related to the more bizarre positive symptoms of schizophrenia, such as hallucinations and delusions (Marangell et al., 2003).

Although antipsychotic drugs work well for positive symptoms, it turns out that negative symptoms of schizophrenia, such as emotional numbing and social withdrawal, may be related to dopamine *under*activity in the mesocortical pathways of the brain (connections between parts of the VTA and the cerebral cortex). This may help explain why antipsychotic medications do not relieve negative symptoms well. Instead of a medication that blocks dopamine receptors, negative symptoms require

antipsychotic drugs Medications that are used to treat schizophrenia and related psychotic disorders.

psychopharmacology The study of drug effects on psychological states and symptoms.

Treating Severe Mental Disorders

Society has never quite known what to do with people who have severe mental disorders. For much of recorded history, mentally ill people have been victims of maltreatment, languishing as paupers in the streets or, worse, suffering under inhumane conditions in prisons. It was something of a reform, then, when in the 18th century, the few private "madhouses" for the rich became models for the establishment of public asylums in England and France.

In North America, the asylum movement for humane treatment of the mentally ill was fostered initially by Dr. Benjamin Rush (a signer of the Constitution) and later by the mental health crusader Dorothea Dix. Dix visited jails and almshouses in Massachusetts and in 1843 reported to the legislature on widespread cruelty toward the insane. She developed a remarkably effective personal campaign across North America and Europe that eventually resulted in the building of hundreds of asylums for the mentally ill.

The creation of asylums encouraged humane treatment but did not guarantee it. London's St. Mary's of Bethlehem Hospital, known for inspiring the term *bedlam* (a contraction of the name "Bethlehem"), was typical—even charging visitors to view the inmates as a way of financing the institution. One visitor to this human zoo in 1753 remarked, "To my great surprise, I found at least a hundred people, who, having paid their two pence apiece, were suffered, unattended, to run rioting up and down the wards, making sport and diversion of the miserable inhabitants" (Hitchcock, 2005). To some degree, the abuse of insane in-

mates by jailers simply was transformed into the abuse of mental patients by asylum workers. For severe disorders, there often was no "treatment" at all, and the focus of the asylum instead was merely on custody (Jones, 1972).

These weaknesses of the asylum movement eventually led to another revolution in mental health treatment—the deinstitutionalization movement of the 1960s. Drugs were being discovered that helped people to manage their disorders and live outside hospitals. With the funding of a "community mental health" initiative by the Kennedy administration, dozens of mental hospitals across the United States were closed, and thousands of patients were trained to shop, cook, take public transportation, and otherwise deal with living outside a hospital setting. Former asylum patients were returned to their families or placed in foster homes or group apartments, but in too many cases they were simply released with nowhere to go and ultimately became homeless. Treatment of all but the most untreatable patients was managed through community mental health centers, which were support units to provide emergency inpatient care as needed but mainly supplying outpatient treatment and assistance in community living (Levine, 1981).

Has this experiment worked? On one hand, treatment for some severe disorders has improved since deinstitutionalization began. The basic drugs that helped people to manage their lives outside mental hospitals have been refined and improved. In addition, the conditions and treatments avail-

▲ What does a modern psychiatric hospital look like? In Hollywood movies, they typically are dirty, scary, and painted in drab gray or green, and it is always nighttime. In the real world, they look just like other hospital units in terms of cleanliness, scariness, paint scheme, and the experience of both day and night.

able in psychiatric hospitals have improved immensely. Contrary to what you may see in the movies, psychiatric units and hospitals look just like other medical floors in general hospitals.

However, outside the hospital walls, federal funding of the network of community mental health centers was abandoned by the Reagan administration in the 1980s, and state-funded programs and private managed care providers have not made up the difference (Cutler, Bevilacqua, & McFarland, 2003). So, although deinstitutionalization has allowed people with severe mental illnesses greater freedom from asylums, many of these people have ended up on the streets, where they remain homeless, poor, and vulnerable to danger. Treatment for those with serious mental illness has improved over the past 100 or more years, but we still clearly have a long way to go.

a medication that *increases* the amount of dopamine available at the synapse. This is a good example of how medical treatments can have broad psychological effects but do not target specific psychological symptoms.

Over the past few decades, a new class of antipsychotic drugs was introduced that includes clozapine (Clozaril), risperidone (Risperdal), and olanzepine (Zyprexa). These newer drugs are often referred to as *atypical* antipsychotics. (The older drugs are now often referred to as *conventional* or *typical* antipsychotics.) Unlike the older antipsychotic medications, these newer drugs appear to affect both the dopamine and serotonin systems, blocking both types of receptors. The ability to block serotonin receptors appears to be a useful addition, because enhanced serotonin activity in the brain has been implicated in some of the core difficulties in schizophrenia, such as cognitive and perceptual disruptions, as well as mood disturbances. This may explain why atypical antipsychotics work at least as well as older drugs for the positive symptoms of schizophrenia and also work fairly well for the negative symptoms (Bradford, Stroup, & Lieberman, 2002).

Like most medications, antipsychotic drugs have side effects, which can be sufficiently unpleasant that some people "go off their meds," preferring their symptoms to the drug. One side effect that often occurs with long-term use is *tardive dyskinesia,* a condition of involuntary movements of the face, mouth, and extremities. In fact, people often need to take another medication to treat the unwanted side effects of the conventional antipsychotic drugs. Side effects of the newer medications tend to be different from and sometimes milder than those of the older antipsychotics. For that reason, the atypical antipsychotics are now usually the front-line treatments for schizophrenia (Meltzer, 2013).

"The drug has, however, proved more effective than traditional psychoanalysis."

ANTIANXIETY MEDICATIONS

Antianxiety medications are *drugs that help reduce a person's experience of fear or anxiety.* The most commonly used antianxiety medications are the benzodiazepines, a type of tranquilizer that works by facilitating the action of the neurotransmitter gamma-aminobutyric acid (GABA). As you learned in the Neuroscience and Behavior chapter, GABA inhibits certain neurons in the brain. This inhibitory action can produce a calming effect for the person. Commonly prescribed benzodiazepines include diazepam (Valium), lorazepam (Ativan), and alprazolam (Xanax). The benzodiazepines typically take effect in a matter of minutes and are effective for reducing symptoms of anxiety disorders (Roy-Byrne & Cowley, 2002).

Nonetheless, doctors are relatively cautious when prescribing benzodiazepines. One concern is that these drugs have the potential for abuse. They are often associated with the development of *drug tolerance,* which is the need for higher dosages over time to achieve the same effects following long-term use (see the Consciousness chapter). Furthermore, after people become tolerant of the drug, they risk significant withdrawal symptoms when it's discontinued. Some withdrawal symptoms include increased heart rate, shakiness, insomnia, agitation, and anxiety—the very symptoms the drug was taken to eliminate! Therefore, people who take benzodiazepines for extended periods may have difficulty coming off these drugs and should discontinue their medications gradually to minimize withdrawal symptoms (Schatzberg, Cole, & DeBattista, 2003). Another consideration when prescribing benzodiazepines is their side effects. The most common side effect is drowsiness, although benzodiazepines

antianxiety medications Drugs that help reduce a person's experience of fear or anxiety.

If you watch television you have seen advertisements for specific drugs. Does this direct-to-consumer advertising really work? Sure does! One recent study sent people posing as patients to physicians' offices asking for specific drugs and found that patient requests had a huge impact on doctors' behavior: Those asking about specific drugs were much more likely to receive a prescription than those who did not make a request (Kravitz et al., 2005).

antidepressants A class of drugs that help lift people's moods.

can also have negative effects on coordination and memory. And benzodiazapines combined with alcohol can depress respiration, potentially causing accidental death.

When anxiety leads to insomnia, drugs known as hypnotics may be useful as sleep aids. One such drug, zolpidem (Ambien), is in wide use and is often effective, but with some reports of sleepwalking, sleep-eating, and even sleep-driving (Hughes, 2007). Another alternative for anxiety is buspirone (Buspar), which has been shown to reduce anxiety among individuals who suffer from generalized anxiety disorder (Roy-Byrne & Cowley, 2002).

ANTIDEPRESSANTS AND MOOD STABILIZERS

Antidepressants are *a class of drugs that help lift people's moods.* They were first introduced in the 1950s, when iproniazid, a drug that was used to treat tuberculosis, was found to elevate mood (Selikoff, Robitzek, & Ornstein, 1952). Iproniazid is a *mono-amine oxidase inhibitor (MAOI),* a medication that prevents the enzyme monoamine oxidase from breaking down neurotransmitters such as norepinephrine, serotonin, and dopamine. A second category of antidepressants introduced in the 1950s is the tricyclic antidepressants, including drugs such as imipramine (Tofranil) and amitriptyline (Elavil), which block the reuptake of norepinephrine and serotonin, thereby increasing the amount of neurotransmitter in the synaptic space between neurons. These two classes of antidepressants are used sparingly due to their side effects, which include potential dangerous increases in blood pressure, constipation, difficulty urinating, blurred vision, and racing heart (Marangell et al., 2003).

Among the most commonly used antidepressants today are the *selective serotonin reuptake inhibitors,* or SSRIs, which include drugs such as fluoxetine (Prozac), citalopram (Celexa), and paroxetine (Paxil). The SSRIs work by blocking the reuptake of serotonin in the brain, which makes more serotonin available in the synaptic space between neurons. The greater availability of serotonin in the synapse gives the neuron a better chance of "recognizing" and using this neurotransmitter in sending the desired signal. The SSRIs were developed on the basis of hypotheses that low levels of serotonin are a causal factor in depression. Supporting this hypothesis, SSRIs are effective for depression, as well as for a wide range of other problems. SSRIs are called *selective* because, unlike the tricyclic antidepressants, which work on the serotonin and norepinephrine systems, SSRIs work more specifically on the serotonin system (see **FIGURE 16.3**).

▶ Figure 16.3

ANTIDEPRESSANT DRUG ACTIONS
Antidepressant drugs, such as MAOIs, SSRIs, and tricyclic antidepressants, act on neurotransmitters such as serotonin, dopamine, and norepinephrine by inhibiting their breakdown and blocking reuptake. These actions make more of the neurotransmitter available for release and leave more of the neurotransmitter in the synaptic gap to activate the receptor sites on the postsynaptic neuron. These drugs relieve depression and often alleviate anxiety and other disorders.

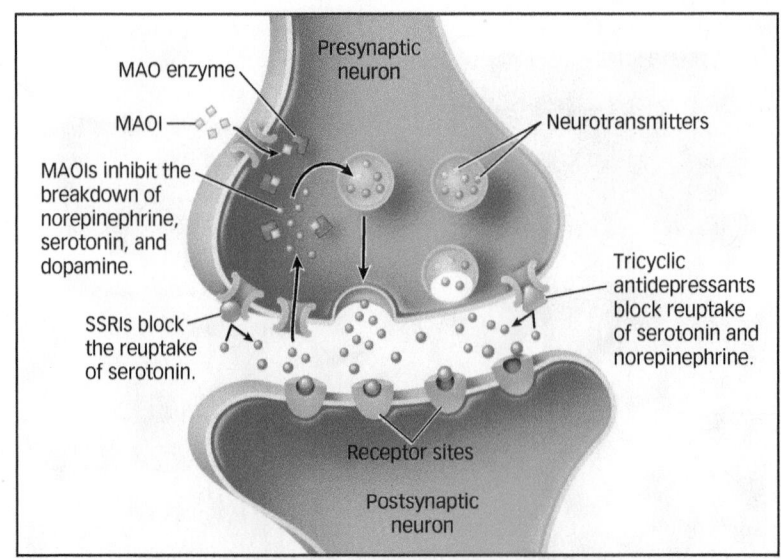

Finally, antidepressants such as venlafaxine (Effexor) and ibupropion (Wellbutrin) offer other alternatives. Effexor is an example of a serotonin and norepinephrine reuptake inhibitor (SNRI). Whereas SSRIs act only on serotonin, SNRIs act on both serotonin and norepinephrine. Wellbutrin, in contrast, is a norepinephrine and dopamine reuptake inhibitor. These and other newly developed antidepressants appear to have fewer (or at least different) side effects than the tricyclic antidepressants and MAOIs.

Antidepressants and Anxiety Disorders

Most antidepressants can take up to a month before they start to have an effect on mood. Besides relieving symptoms of depression, almost all of the antidepressants effectively treat anxiety disorders, and many of them can resolve other problems, such as eating disorders. In fact, several companies that manufacture SSRIs have marketed their drugs as treatments for anxiety disorders rather than for their antidepressant effects.

How well do antidepressants work in treating these conditions? Although many studies supported by drug companies show positive results, there is evidence that drug companies are more likely to publish results of studies that suggest their drugs are effective and less likely to publish results that suggest their drugs don't work. In one meta-analysis, researchers found that 97% of studies of antidepressants that found positive results (that is, results favoring the effectiveness of the drug) were published, compared with only 12% of studies that found negative results (Turner et al., 2008). Researchers getting access to unpublished data held by the U.S. Food and Drug Administration found that when combining *all* available data, antidepressants are only slightly more effective than a placebo (i.e., a sugar pill containing no active medicine) (Kirsch et al., 2008). These authors also found that antidepressants had stronger effects for some types of patients. (Check out A World of Difference: Differences in People's Responses to Treatment to learn more.)

Mood Stabilizers Are Used for Bipolar Disorder

Although antidepressants are commonly used to treat major depression, they are not recommended for treating bipolar disorder, which is characterized by manic or hypomanic episodes (see the Psychological Disorders chapter). Antidepressants are not prescribed because, in the process of lifting one's mood, they might actually trigger a manic episode in a person with bipolar disorder. Instead, bipolar disorder is treated with *mood stabilizers,* which are medications used to suppress swings between mania and depression. Commonly used mood stabilizers include lithium and valproate. Even in unipolar depression, lithium is sometimes effective when combined with traditional antidepressants in people who do not respond to antidepressants alone.

Lithium has been associated with possible long-term kidney and thyroid problems, so people taking lithium must monitor their blood levels of lithium on a regular basis. Furthermore, lithium has a precise range in which it is useful for each person, another reason it should be closely monitored with blood tests. Valproate, in contrast, does not require such careful blood monitoring. Although valproate may have side effects, it is currently the most commonly prescribed drug in the United States for bipolar disorder (Schatzberg et al., 2003). In sum, although antidepressants are effective for a wide variety of problems, mood stabilizers may be required when a person's symptoms include extreme swings between highs and lows, such as those experienced with bipolar disorder.

HERBAL AND NATURAL PRODUCTS

In a survey of more than 2,000 Americans, 7% of those suffering from anxiety disorders and 9% of those suffering from severe depression reported using alternative "medications" such as herbal medicines, megavitamins, homeopathic remedies, or

A WORLD OF DIFFERENCE

Differences in People's Responses to Treatment

We are all different. We like different foods, different music, different books, and so on. It turns out that we also differ in how we respond to treatments for psychological disorders. For instance, one recent study compared the decrease in symptoms of depression seen in 718 patients randomly assigned to receive either antidepressant medication or pill placebo (Fournier et al., 2010). Participants receiving medication showed a dramatic decrease in symptoms over the course of treatment. However, so did those taking placebo. Closer examination of the data revealed that for those with mild or moderate depression, placebo is just as effective as antidepressant medi-

cation at decreasing a person's symptoms, and it is only for people with severe depression that antidepressants seem to work better than placebo (see figure).

More recent research is further examining what predicts which kind of people will respond best to which kind of treatment. For instance, a recent study by Robert DeRubeis and colleagues (2014) found that data collected before people are randomized to a given treatment (e.g., cognitive behavioral therapy vs. medication) could be used to predict accurately which treatment would benefit them most. A follow-up study by DeRubeis and colleagues found a similar result in comparing two other kinds of treatment (i.e., cognitive

therapy and interpersonal psychotherapy; Huibers et al., 2015). In this study, patients who were randomly assigned to the treatment that was predicted to be more effective for them improved significantly more than those assigned to their nonoptimal treatment. Such findings suggest that in the future, psychologists will be able to collect information from new patients in order to determine which of the many available treatments will benefit them most. This personalized, or tailored, approach to treatment is likely to lead to much better outcomes for users of psychological services in the future, and in this way is expected to make a world of difference!

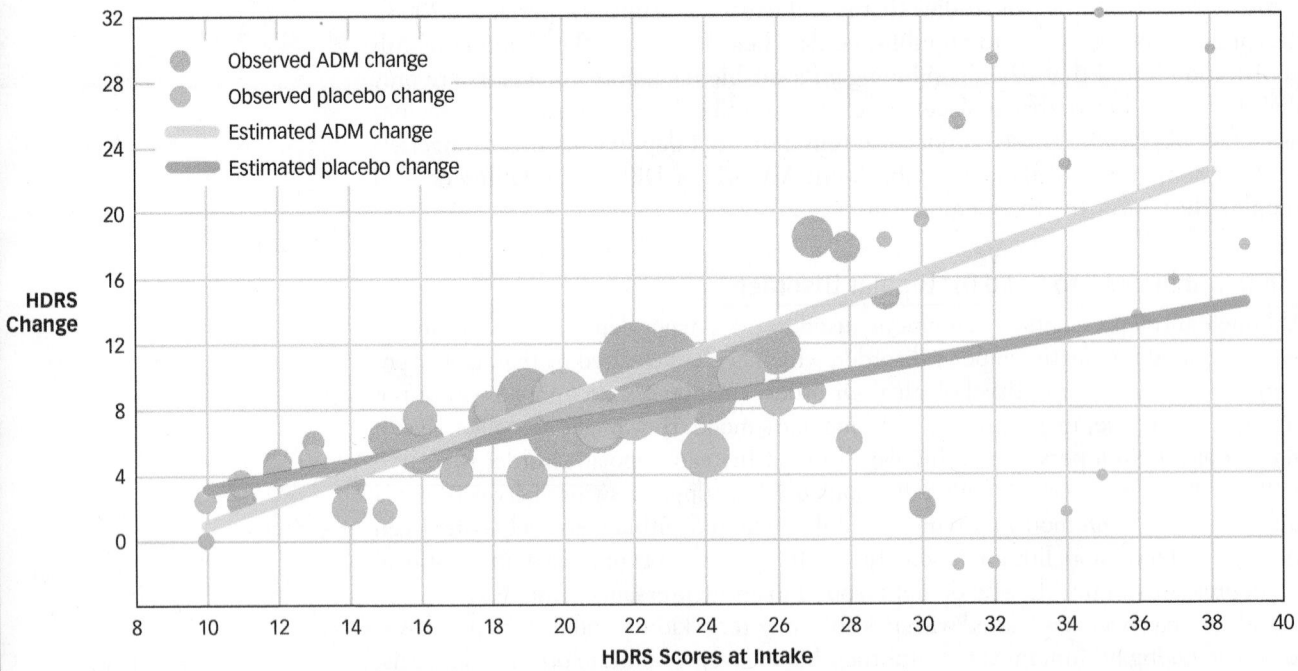

▲ A total of 713 depressed individuals from six different studies were given pills to treat their depression. Half were randomly assigned to receive an antidepressant medication (ADM) and half to receive a pill placebo. Importantly, the participants did not know if they were taking an antidepressant or simply a placebo. For those with mild or moderate depression, as measured by the Hamilton Depression Rating Scale (HDRS), antidepressants did not work any better than placebo. However, those with severe depression showed much greater improvement on antidepressants than on placebo. The circle size represents the number of people with data at each point (data from Fournier et al., 2010).

naturopathic remedies to treat these problems (Kessler et al., 2001). Major reasons people use these products are that they are easily available over the counter, are less expensive, and are perceived as "natural" alternatives to synthetic or manmade "drugs." Are herbal and natural products effective in treating mental health problems? Or are they just "snake oil"?

The answer to this question isn't simple. Herbal products are not considered medications by regulatory agencies such as the Food and Drug Administration, so they are exempt from rigorous research to establish their safety and effectiveness. Instead, herbal products are classified as nutritional supplements and regulated in the same way as food. There is little scientific information about herbal products, including possible interactions with other medications, possible tolerance and withdrawal symptoms, side effects, appropriate dosages, how they work, or even *whether* they work—and the purity of these products often varies from brand to brand (Jordan, Cunningham, & Marles, 2010).

There is research support for the effectiveness of some herbal and natural products, but the evidence is not overwhelming (Lake, 2009). Products such as inositol (a sugar alcohol), kava (an herb related to black pepper), omega-3 fatty acid (a fish oil), and SAM-e (an amino acid derivative) are sold as health foods and are described as having positive psychological effects of various kinds, but the evidence is mixed. For example, in the case of St. John's wort (a wort, it turns out, is an herb), some studies have shown it has an advantage over a placebo condition (e.g., Lecrubier et al., 2002) for the treatment of depression, whereas others show no advantage (e.g., Hypericum Depression Trial Study Group, 2002). Omega-3 fatty acids have been linked with lower rates of depression and suicide (see **FIGURE 16.4**), and several treatment studies have shown that omega-3s are superior to placebo at decreasing depression (Lewis et al., 2011; Parker et al., 2006). Overall, although herbal medications and treatments are worthy of continued research, these products should be closely monitored and used judiciously until more is known about their safety and effectiveness.

Phototherapy, *a therapy that involves repeated exposure to bright light,* is another natural treatment that may be helpful to people who have a seasonal pattern to their depression. This could include people suffering with seasonal affective disorder (SAD; see the Psychological Disorders chapter), or those who experience depression only in the winter months due to the lack of sunlight. Typically, people are exposed to bright light in the morning, using a lamp designed for this purpose. Phototherapy has not been as well researched as psychological treatment or medication, but the handful of studies available suggest it is about as effective as antidepressant medication in the treatment of SAD (Thaler et al., 2011).

COMBINING MEDICATION AND PSYCHOTHERAPY

Given that psychological treatments and medications both have shown an ability to treat mental disorders effectively, some natural next questions are: Which is more effective? Is the combination of psychological and medicinal treatments better than either by itself?

phototherapy A therapy that involves repeated exposure to bright light.

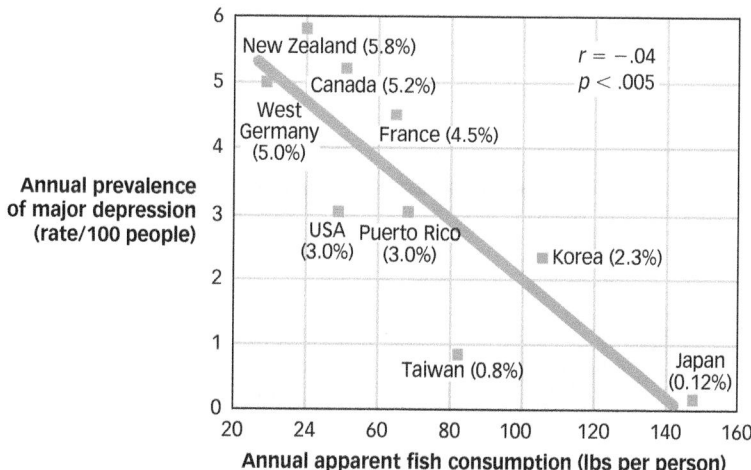

◄ Figure 16.4

OMEGA-3 FATTY ACIDS AND DEPRESSION Recent studies have shown that consumption of omega-3 fatty acids is associated with a wide range of positive mental health outcomes. For instance, Joe Hibbeln (1998) showed that countries that consume more fish (a main dietary source of omega-3s) have significantly lower rates of depression. But remember, correlation does not mean causation! It could be that some other factor explains this association. For instance, it could be that living closer to the ocean or a greater focus on health overall predicts both greater omega-3 consumption and lower rates of depression.

► **Figure 16.5**

THE EFFECTIVENESS OF MEDICATION PSYCHOTHERAPY AND MEDICINE FOR PANIC DISORDER One study of CBT and medication (imipramine) for panic disorder found that the effects of CBT, medication, and treatment that combined CBT and medication were not significantly different over the short term, though all three were superior to the placebo condition (Barlow et al., 2000).

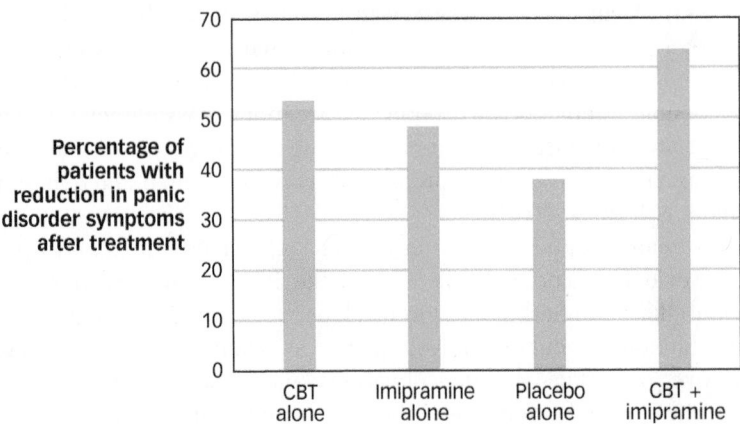

Many studies have compared psychological treatments, medications, and combinations of these approaches for addressing psychological disorders. The results of these studies often depend on the particular problem being considered. For example, in the cases of schizophrenia and bipolar disorder, researchers have found that medication is more effective than psychological treatment and so is considered a necessary part of treatment; recent studies have tended to examine whether adding psychotherapeutic treatments such as social skills training or cognitive behavioral treatment can be helpful. (They can.) In the case of mood and anxiety disorders, medication and psychological treatments are equally effective. One study compared cognitive behavior therapy, imipramine (the antidepressant also known as Tofranil), and the combination of these treatments (CBT plus imipramine) with a placebo (administration of an inert medication) for the treatment of panic disorder (Barlow et al., 2000). After 12 weeks of treatment, either CBT alone or imipramine alone was found to be superior to a placebo. For the CBT-plus-imipramine condition, the response rate also exceeded the rate for the placebo but was not significantly better than that for either CBT or imipramine alone. In other words, either treatment was better than nothing, but the combination of treatments was not significantly more effective than one or the other (see **FIGURE 16.5**). More is not always better (see Other Voices: Diagnosis: Human).

Given that both therapy and medications are effective, one question is whether they work through similar mechanisms. A study of people with social phobia examined patterns of cerebral blood flow following treatment using either citalopram (an SSRI) or CBT (Furmark et al., 2002). Participants in both groups were alerted to the possibility that they would soon have to speak in public. In both groups, those who responded to treatment showed decreased activation in the amygdala, hippocampus, and neighboring cortical areas during this challenge (see **FIGURE 16.6**). The amygdala, located next to the hippocampus (see Figure 6.20) plays a significant role in memory for emotional information. These findings suggest that both therapy and medication

► **Figure 16.6**

THE EFFECTS OF MEDICATION AND THERAPY IN THE BRAIN PET scans of individuals with social phobia showed similar reductions in activations of the amygdala–hippocampus region after they received treatment with CBT (*left*) and with citalopram (*right*), an SSRI (from Furmark et al., 2002).

COURTESY TOMAS FURMARK

Diagnosis: Human

SUSAN SYMONES/INFINITY PORTRAIT DESIGN

Ted Gup is an author and a fellow of the Edmond J. Safra Center for Ethics at Harvard University.

Should more people receive psychological treatment or medications? Or should fewer? On one hand, data indicate that most people with a mental disorder do not receive treatment and that untreated mental disorders are an enormous source of pain and suffering. On the other hand, some argue that we have become too quick to label normal human behavior as "disordered" and too willing to medicate any behavior, thought, or feeling that makes us uncomfortable. Ted Gup is one of these people. The following is a version of his op-ed piece that appeared in *The New York Times* on April 3, 2013 under the headline "Diagnosis: Human."

The news that 11 percent of school-age children now receive a diagnosis of attention deficit hyperactivity disorder—some 6.4 million—gave me a chill. My son David was one of those who received that diagnosis.

In his case, he was in the first grade. Indeed, there were psychiatrists who prescribed medication for him even before they met him. One psychiatrist said he would not even see him until he was medicated. For a year I refused to fill the prescription at the pharmacy. Finally, I relented. And so David went on Ritalin, then Adderall, and other drugs that were said to be helpful in combating the condition.

In another age, David might have been called "rambunctious." His battery was a little too large for his body. And so he would leap over the couch, spring to reach the ceiling and show an exuberance for life that came in brilliant microbursts.

As a 21-year-old college senior, he was found on the floor of his room, dead from a fatal mix of alcohol and drugs. The date was Oct. 18, 2011. No one made him take the heroin and alcohol, and yet I cannot help but hold myself and others to account. I had unknowingly colluded with a system that devalues talking therapy and rushes to medicate, inadvertently sending a message that self-medication, too, is perfectly acceptable.

My son was no angel (though he was to us) and he was known to trade in Adderall, to create a submarket in the drug among his classmates who were themselves all too eager to get their hands on it. What he did cannot be excused, but it should be understood. What he did was to create a market that perfectly mirrored the society in which he grew up, a culture where Big Pharma itself prospers from the off-label uses of drugs, often not tested in children and not approved for the many uses to which they are put.

And so a generation of students, raised in an environment that encourages medication, are emulating the professionals by using drugs in the classroom as performance enhancers.

And we wonder why it is that they use drugs with such abandon. As all parents learn—at times to their chagrin—our children go to school not only in the classroom but also at home, and the culture they construct for themselves as teenagers and young adults is but a tiny village imitating that to which they were introduced as children. . . .

Ours is an age in which the airwaves and media are one large drug emporium that claims to fix everything from sleep to sex. I fear that being human is itself fast becoming a condition. It's as if we are trying to contain grief, and the absolute pain of a loss like mine. We have become increasingly disassociated and estranged from the patterns of life and death, uncomfortable with the messiness of our own humanity, aging and, ultimately, mortality.

Challenge and hardship have become pathologized and monetized. Instead of enhancing our coping skills, we undermine them and seek shortcuts where there are none, eroding the resilience upon which each of us, at some point in our lives, must rely.

Have we gone too far in labeling and treatment of mental disorders? Or have we not gone far enough? On one hand, we shouldn't rush to diagnose and medicate normal behavior, but on the other hand, we must provide help to those who are suffering with a true mental disorder. One possible way forward is to ensure that people are diagnosed and treated only after a thorough evaluation by a well-trained professional. This way, we will know that a mental health professional has carefully considered whether the problems a person is having are truly disordered and in need of intervention, or just part of being human.

affect the brain in regions associated with a reaction to threat. Although we might expect that events that influence the brain should be physical—after all, the brain is a physical object—it is important to keep in mind that environmental learning experiences, such as psychological treatment, produce similar influences on the brain.

One complication in combining medication and psychotherapy is that these treatments are often provided by different people. Psychiatrists are trained in the administration of medication in medical school (and they may also provide psychological treatment), whereas psychologists provide psychological treatment but not medication. This means that the coordination of treatment often requires cooperation between psychologists and psychiatrists.

The question of whether psychologists should be licensed to prescribe medications has been a source of debate among psychologists and physicians (Fox et al., 2009). Only Louisiana and New Mexico currently allow licensed and specially trained

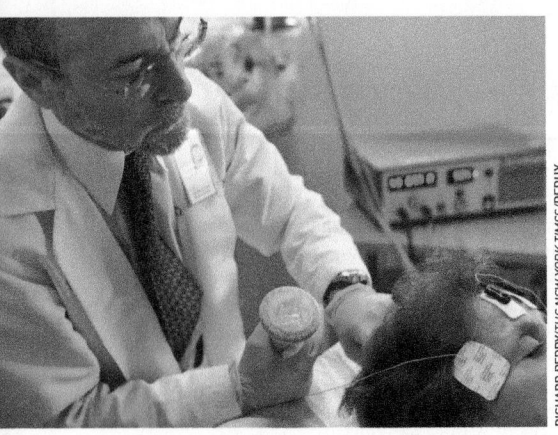

Electroconvulsive therapy (ECT) can be an effective treatment for severe depression. To reduce the side effects, it is administered under general anesthesia.

RICHARD PERRY/*THE NEW YORK TIMES*/REDUX

electroconvulsive therapy (ECT) A treatment that involves inducing a brief seizure by delivering an electrical shock to the brain.

transcranial magnetic stimulation (TMS) A treatment that involves placing a powerful pulsed magnet over a person's scalp to alter neuronal activity in the brain.

psychologists prescription privileges, but nine more states are currently considering it (Munsey, 2008). Opponents argue that psychologists do not have the medical training to understand how medications interact with other drugs. Proponents of prescription privileges argue that patient safety would not be compromised as long as rigorous training procedures were established. This issue remains a focus of debate, and at present, the coordination of medication and psychological treatment usually involves a team effort of psychiatry and psychology.

BIOLOGICAL TREATMENTS BEYOND MEDICATION

Medication can be an effective biological treatment, but for some people medications do not work, or side effects are intolerable. If this group of people doesn't respond to psychotherapy either, what other options do they have to achieve symptom relief? Some additional avenues of help are available, but some are risky or poorly understood.

One biological treatment sometimes used to treat severe mental disorders that do not respond to psychological treatment or medication is **electroconvulsive therapy (ECT)**, sometimes referred to as *shock therapy*, which is *a treatment that involves inducing a brief seizure by delivering an electrical shock to the brain*. The shock is applied to the person's scalp for less than a second. ECT is used primarily to treat severe depression that has not responded to antidepressant medications, although it may also be useful for treating bipolar disorder (Khalid et al., 2008; Poon et al., 2012). Patients are pretreated with muscle relaxants and are under general anesthetic, so they are not conscious of the procedure. The main side effect of ECT is impaired short-term memory, which usually improves over the first month or two after the end of treatment. In addition, patients undergoing this procedure sometimes report headaches and muscle aches afterward (Marangell et al., 2003). Despite these side effects, the treatment can be effective: ECT is more effective than simulated ECT, than placebo, and than antidepressant drugs such as tricyclics and MAOIs (Pagnin et al., 2008).

Another biological approach that does not involve medication is **transcranial magnetic stimulation (TMS)**, *a treatment that involves placing a powerful pulsed magnet over a person's scalp to alter neuronal activity in the brain*. As a treatment for depression, the magnet is placed just above the right or left eyebrow in an effort to stimulate the right or left prefrontal cortex (areas of the brain implicated in depression). TMS is an exciting development because it is noninvasive and has fewer side effects than ECT (see the Neuroscience and Behavior chapter). Side effects are minimal; they include mild headache and a small risk of seizure, but TMS has no impact on memory or concentration. Daily TMS applied to the left prefrontal cortex for 4 to 6 weeks has been found

Transcranial magnetic stimulation (TMS) is an exciting new technique that allows researchers and clinicians to change brain activity using a magnetic wand—no surgery is required.

BRUCE R. BENNETT/CORBIS

to be effective in the treatment of depression in patients who have not responded to medication (Perera et al., 2016). In fact, a study comparing TMS with ECT found that both procedures were effective, with no significant differences between them (Janicak et al., 2002). Other studies have found that TMS can also be used to treat auditory hallucinations in schizophrenia (Aleman, Sommer, & Kahn, 2007).

In very rare cases, **psychosurgery**, *the surgical destruction of specific brain areas,* may be used to treat psychological disorders. Psychosurgery has a controversial history, beginning in the 1930s with the invention of the lobotomy by the Portuguese physician Antonio Egas Moniz (1874–1955). After discovering that certain surgical procedures on animal brains calmed behavior, Moniz began to use similar techniques on violent or agitated human patients. Lobotomies involved inserting an instrument into the brain through the patient's eye socket or through holes drilled in the side of the head. The objective was to sever connections between the frontal lobes and inner brain structures such as the thalamus, known to be involved in emotion. Although some lobotomies produced highly successful results and Moniz received the 1949 Nobel Prize for his work, significant side effects such as extreme lethargy or childlike impulsiveness detracted from these benefits. Lobotomy was used widely for years, leaving many people devastated by these permanent side effects, and because of this, for many years there was a movement challenging the awarding of the Nobel Prize to Moniz. (It was never revoked.) The development of antipsychotic drugs during the 1950s provided a safer way to treat violent individuals and brought the practice of lobotomy to an end (Swayze, 1995).

Psychosurgery is rarely used these days and is reserved only for extremely severe cases for which no other interventions have been effective, and the symptoms of the disorder are intolerable to the patient. For instance, psychosurgery is sometimes used in severe cases of OCD in which the person is completely unable to function in daily life, and psychological treatment and medication are not effective. In contrast to the earlier days of lobotomy, when broad regions of brain tissue were destroyed, modern psychosurgery involves a very precise destruction of brain tissue in order to disrupt the brain circuits known to be involved in the generation of obsessions and compulsions. This increased precision has produced better results. For example, people suffering from OCD who fail to respond to treatment (including several trials of medications and cognitive behavioral treatment) may benefit from specific surgical procedures called *cingulotomy* and *anterior capsulotomy*. Cingulotomy involves destroying part of the corpus callosum (see Figure 3.18) and the cingulate gyrus (the ridge just above the corpus collosum). Anterior capsulotomy involves creating small lesions to disrupt the pathway between the caudate nucleus and the putamen. Because of the relatively small number of cases of psychosurgery, there are not as many studies of these techniques as there are for other treatments. However, available studies have shown that psychosurgery typically leads to substantial improvements in both the short and long term for people with severe OCD (Csigó et al., 2010; van Vliet et al., 2013).

A final approach, called *deep brain stimulation* (DBS), combines the use of psychosurgery with the use of electrical currents (as in ECT and TMS). In DBS, a treatment pioneered only recently, a small, battery-powered device is implanted in the body to deliver electrical stimulation to specific areas of the brain known to be involved in the disorder being targeted (**FIGURE 16.7**). This technique has been successful for OCD treatment (Abelson et al., 2009) and can provide benefits for people with a variety of neurologic conditions. The tremor that accompanies Parkinson's disease has proven to be treatable in this way (Perlmutter & Mink, 2006), as have some cases of severe depression that are otherwise untreatable (Mayberg et al., 2005). The early view of psychosurgery as a treatment of last resort is being replaced by a cautious hope that newer, focused treatments that target brain circuits known to be functioning abnormally in those with certain mental disorders can have beneficial effects (Ressler & Mayberg, 2007).

psychosurgery Surgical destruction of specific brain areas.

▶ **Figure 16.7**

DBS Deep brain stimulation involves the insertion of battery-powered electrodes that deliver electrical pulses to specific areas of the brain believed to be causing a person's mental disorder.

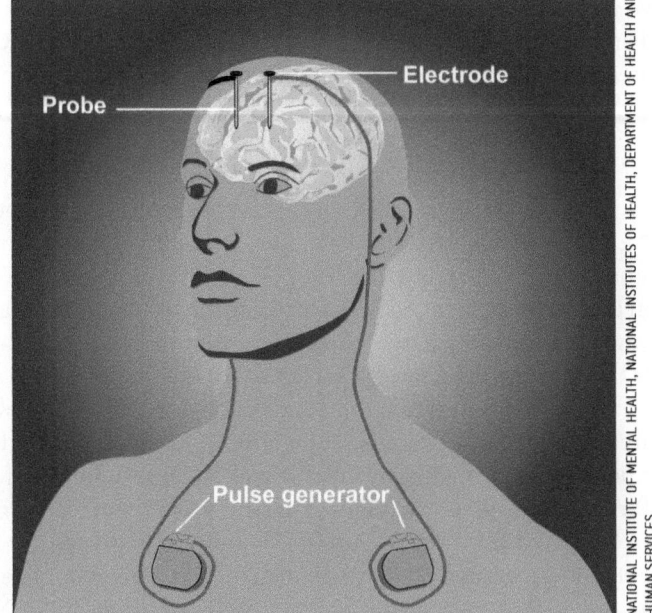

NATIONAL INSTITUTE OF MENTAL HEALTH, NATIONAL INSTITUTES OF HEALTH, DEPARTMENT OF HEALTH AND HUMAN SERVICES

Build to the Outcomes

1. What do antipsychotic drugs do?

2. What are the advantages of the newer, atypical antipsychotic medications?

3. What are some reasons for caution when prescribing antianxiety medications?

4. How do antidepressant drugs affect neurotransmitters?

5. Why are antidepressants not prescribed for bipolar disorder?

6. Why aren't herbal and natural products given the same scrutiny given to pharmacological drugs?

7. Which herbal remedies have been proven to be effective?

8. Do therapy and medications work similarly in treating mental illness?

9. What are the benefits of ECT? The risks?

10. What is the procedure for TMS?

11. When would the use of psychosurgery be appropriate?

Treatment Effectiveness: For Better or for Worse

Learning Outcomes

▶ Describe treatment illusions.

▶ Explain research methods used in treatment studies.

▶ Explain the criteria used to determine a treatment's effectiveness.

Think back to Christine and the dead mouse at the beginning of this chapter. What if, instead of exposure and response prevention, Christine had been assigned psychoanalysis or psychosurgery? Could these alternatives have been just as effective (and justified) for treating her OCD? Throughout this chapter, we have explored various psychological and biological treatments that might help people with psychological disorders. But do these treatments actually work? Which ones work better than the others?

As you learned in the Methods in Psychology chapter, pinning down a specific cause for an effect can be a difficult detective exercise. The detection is made even more difficult because people may approach treatment evaluation very unscientifically, often by simply noticing an improvement (or no improvement, or even a worsening of symptoms) and reaching a conclusion based on that sole observation. Determination of a treatment's effectiveness can be misdirected by illusions that can be overcome only by careful, scientific evaluation.

TREATMENT ILLUSIONS

Imagine you're sick, and the doctor says, "Take a pill." You follow the doctor's orders, and you get better. To what do you attribute your improvement? If you're like most people, you reach the conclusion that the pill cured you. That's one possible explanation, but there are at least three others: Maybe you would have gotten better anyway; maybe the pill wasn't the active ingredient in your cure; or maybe after you're better, you mistakenly remember having been more ill than you really were. These possibilities point to three potential illusions of treatment: illusions produced by natural improvement, by placebo effects, and by reconstructive memory.

Natural Improvement

Natural improvement is the tendency of symptoms to return to their mean or average level. The illusion in this case happens when you conclude mistakenly that a treatment has made you better when you would have gotten better anyway. People typically turn to therapy or medication when their symptoms are at their worst. When this is the case, the client's symptoms will often improve regardless of whether there was any treatment at all; when you're at rock bottom, there's nowhere to move but up. In most cases, for example, depression that becomes severe enough to make individuals candidates for treatment will tend to lift in several months *no matter what they do*. A person who enters therapy for depression may develop an illusion that the therapy works because the therapy coincides with the typical course of the illness and the person's natural return to health. How can we know if change was caused by the treatment or by natural improvement? As discussed in the Methods in Psychology chapter, we could do an experiment in which we assign half of the people who are depressed to receive treatment and the other half to receive no treatment, and then monitor them over time to see if the ones who got treatment actually show greater improvement. This is precisely how researchers test out different interventions, as described in more detail below.

Placebo Effects

Recovery could be produced by *nonspecific treatment effects* that are not related to the specific mechanisms by which treatment is supposed to be working. For example, the doctor prescribing the medication might simply be a pleasant and hopeful individual who gives the client a sense of hope or optimism that things will improve. Client and doctor alike might attribute the client's improvement to the effects of medication on the brain, whereas the true active ingredient was the warm relationship with the doctor or an improved outlook on life.

"If this doesn't help you don't worry, it's a placebo."

placebo An inert substance or procedure that has been applied with the expectation that it will produce a healing response.

Simply knowing that you are getting a treatment can be a nonspecific treatment effect. These instances include the positive influences that can be produced by a **placebo**, *an inert substance or procedure that has been applied with the expectation that it will produce a healing response.* For example, if you take a sugar pill that does not contain any painkiller for a headache thinking it is Tylenol or aspirin, this pill is a placebo. Placebos can have profound effects in the case of psychological treatments. Research shows that a large percentage of individuals with anxiety, depression, and other emotional and medical problems experience significant improvement after a placebo treatment (see The Real World: Treating Severe Mental Disorders and A World of Difference: Differences in People's Responses to Treatment).

Reconstructive Memory

A third treatment illusion can come about when the client's motivation to get well causes errors in *reconstructive memory* for the original symptoms. You might think that you've improved because of a treatment when in fact you're simply misremembering, mistakenly believing that your symptoms before treatment were worse than they actually were. This tendency was first observed in research examining the effectiveness of a study skills class (Conway & Ross, 1984). Some students who wanted to take the class were enrolled, but others were randomly assigned to a waiting list until the class could be offered again. When their study abilities were measured afterward, those students who took the class were no better at studying than their wait-listed counterparts. However, those who took the class *said* that they had improved. How could this be? Those participants recalled their study skills before the class as being worse than they actually had been. Conway and Ross (1984) dubbed this motivated reconstruction of the past "Getting What You Want by Revising What You Had." A client who forms a strong expectation of success in therapy might conclude later that even a useless treatment had worked wonders by recalling past symptoms and troubles as worse than they were and thereby making the treatment seem effective.

TREATMENT STUDIES: SEEKING EVIDENCE

How can we make sure that we are using treatments that actually work and not wasting time with procedures that may be useless or even harmful? Research psychologists use the approaches covered in the Methods in Psychology chapter to create experiments that test whether treatments are effective for the different mental disorders described in the Psychological Disorders chapter.

Treatment outcome studies are designed to evaluate whether a particular treatment works, often compared with some other treatment or a control condition. For example, to study the outcome of treatment for depression, researchers might compare the self-reported symptoms of two groups of people who were initially depressed: a group that received treatment for 6 weeks and a control group that had also been selected for the study but were assigned to a waiting list for later treatment and were simply tested 6 weeks after their selection. The outcome study could determine whether this treatment had any benefit.

Researchers use a range of methods to ensure that any observed effects are not due to the treatment illusions described earlier. For example, the treatment illusions caused by natural improvement and reconstructive memory happen when people compare their symptoms before treatment with their symptoms after treatment. To avoid this, a treatment (or experimental) group and a control group need to be randomly assigned to each condition and then compared at the end of treatment. That way, natural improvement or motivated reconstructive memory can't cause illusions of effective treatment.

But what should happen to the control group during the treatment? If they simply stay home waiting until they can get treatment later (a wait-list control group), they won't receive the placebo effects. So, ideally, a treatment should be assessed in a *double-blind experiment*, a study in which both the participant and the researcher/ therapist are uninformed about which treatment the participant is receiving. In drug studies, this isn't hard to arrange because active drugs and placebos can be made to look alike to both the participants and the researchers during the study. Keeping both participants and researchers "in the dark" is much harder in the study of psychological treatments; in fact, in most cases it is not possible. Both the participant and the therapist can easily notice the differences in treatments such as psychoanalysis and behavior therapy, for example, so there's no way to keep the beliefs and expectations of both participant and therapist completely out of the picture in evaluating psychotherapy effectiveness. Nevertheless, by comparing treatments either with no treatment or with other active interventions (such as other psychological treatments or medications), researchers can determine which treatments work and which are most effective for different disorders.

WHICH TREATMENTS WORK ACCORDING TO THE EVIDENCE?

The distinguished psychologist Hans Eysenck (1916–1997) reviewed the relatively few studies of psychotherapy effectiveness available in 1957 and raised a furor among therapists by concluding that psychotherapy—particularly psychoanalysis—not only was ineffective but seemed to *impede* recovery (Eysenck, 1957). Much larger numbers of studies have been examined statistically since then, and they support a more optimistic conclusion: The typical psychotherapy client is better off than three quarters of untreated individuals (Seligman, 1995; Smith, Glass, & Miller, 1980). Although critiques of psychotherapy continue to point out weaknesses in how clients are tested, diagnosed, and treated (Baker, McFall, & Shoham, 2009; Dawes, 1994), strong evidence generally supports the effectiveness of many treatments (Nathan & Gorman, 2007), including psychodynamic therapy (Shedler, 2010). The key question then becomes: Which treatments are effective for which problems (Hunsley & Di Giulio, 2002)?

One of the most enduring debates in clinical psychology concerns how the various psychotherapies compare with each other. Some psychologists have argued for years that evidence supports the conclusion that most psychotherapies work about equally well. In this view, common factors shared by all forms of psychotherapy, such as contact with and empathy from a professional, contribute to change (Luborsky et al., 2002; Luborsky & Singer, 1975). In contrast, others have argued that there are important differences among therapies and that certain treatments are more effective than others, especially for treating particular types of problems. For instance, studies of children, adolescents, and adults have revealed that for problems such as depression and anxiety, cognitive behavioral therapy (CBT) and interpersonal psychotherapy (IPT) lead to significant better outcomes than do other approaches (Tolin, 2010; Zhou et al., 2015). How can we make sense of these differing perspectives?

In 1995, the American Psychological Association (APA) published one of the first attempts to define criteria for determining whether a particular type of psychotherapy is effective for a particular problem (Task Force on Promotion and Dissemination of Psychological Procedures, 1995). The official criteria for empirically validated treatments defined two levels of empirical support: *well-established treatments,* those with a high level of support (e.g., evidence from several randomized controlled trials); and *probably efficacious treatments,* those with preliminary support. After these criteria were established, the APA published a list of empirically supported treatments (Chambless et al., 1998; Woody & Sanderson, 1998). Recent reviews of such treatments have highlighted several specific psychological treatments that have been shown to work as well as, or even better than, other available treatments, including medication (Barlow et al., 2013). **TABLE 16.3** lists several of these treatments.

TABLE 16.3

Selected List of Specific Psychological Treatments Compared With Medication or Other Treatments

Disorder	Treatment	Results
Depression	CBT	PT = meds; PT + meds > either alone
Panic disorder	CBT	PT > meds at follow-up; PT = meds at end of treatment; both > placebo
Posttraumatic stress disorder	CBT	PT > present-centered therapy
Insomnia	CBT	PT > medication or placebo
Depression and physical health in Alzheimer's patients	Exercise and behavioral management	PT > routine medical care
Gulf War veterans' illnesses	CBT and exercise	PT > Usual care or alternative treatments

Note: CBT = cognitive behavior therapy; PT = psychological treatment; Meds = medication.
Information from Barlow et al. (2013).

Some researchers and clinicians have questioned whether treatments shown to work in well-controlled studies conducted at university clinics will work in the real world. For instance, some psychologists have noted that most treatment studies reported in the literature do not have large numbers of participants who are of ethnic minority status, and so it is unclear if these treatments will work with ethnically and culturally diverse groups. One recent, comprehensive review of all available data suggests that despite gaps in the literature, where there are data available, results suggest that current evidence-based psychological treatments work as well with ethnic minority clients as with White clients (Miranda et al., 2005).

WAVEBREAK MEDIA LTD/ALAMY STOCK PHOTO

MARY KATE DENNY/PHOTOEDIT

Treatments that are shown to be effective in research studies (which often include only a small percentage of ethnic minority patients) have been found to work equally well with people of different ethnicities (Miranda et al., 2005).

Even trickier than the question of establishing whether a treatment works is whether a psychotherapy or medication might actually do harm. The dangers of drug treatment should be clear to anyone who has read a magazine ad for a drug and studied the fine print with its list of side effects, potential drug interactions, and complications. Many drugs used for psychological treatment may be addictive, creating long-term dependency with serious withdrawal symptoms. The strongest critics of drug treatment claim that drugs do no more than trade one unwanted symptom for another: depression for lack of sexual interest, anxiety for intoxication, or agitation for lethargy and dulled emotion (e.g., see Breggin, 2000).

The dangers of psychotherapy are more subtle, but one is clear enough in some cases that there is actually a name for it. **Iatrogenic illness** is *a disorder or symptom that occurs as a result of a medical or psychotherapeutic treatment itself* (e.g., Boisvert & Faust, 2002). Such an illness might arise, for example, when a psychotherapist becomes convinced that a client has a disorder that in fact the client does not have. As a result, the therapist works to help the client accept that diagnosis and participate in psychotherapy to treat that disorder. Being treated for a disorder can, under certain conditions, make a person show signs of that very disorder—and so an iatrogenic illness is born.

In some cases, clients who have been influenced through hypnosis and repeated suggestions in therapy come to believe that they have dissociative identity disorder (even coming to express multiple personalities) or to believe that they were subjected to traumatic events as a child and "recover" memories of such events when investigation reveals no evidence for these problems prior to therapy (Acocella, 1999; McNally, 2003; Ofshe & Watters, 1994). Some people enter therapy with a vague sense that something odd has happened to them, and emerge after hypnosis or other imagination-enhancing techniques with the conviction that their therapist's theory was right: They were abducted by space aliens (Clancy, 2005). Needless to say, a therapy that leads clients to develop such bizarre beliefs does more harm than good.

Just as psychologists have created lists of treatments that work, they also have begun to establish lists of treatments that *harm*. The purpose of doing so is to inform other researchers, clinicians, and the public which treatments they should avoid. Many people are under the impression that although every psychological treatment may not be effective, some treatment is better than no treatment. However, it turns out that a number of interventions intended to help alleviate people's symptoms actually make them worse! Did your high school have a D.A.R.E. (Drug Abuse and Resistance Education) program? Have you heard of critical-incident stress debriefing (CISD), Scared Straight, and boot-camp programs? They all sound as if they might work, but careful scientific experiments have determined that people who participate in these interventions are actually worse off after doing so (see **TABLE 16.4**; Lilienfeld, 2007)!

iatrogenic illness A disorder or symptom that occurs as a result of a medical or psychotherapeutic treatment itself.

TABLE 16.4

Some Psychological Treatments That Cause Harm

Type of Treatment	Potential Harm	Source of Evidence
CISD	Increased risk of PTSD	RCTs
Scared Straight	Worsening of conduct problems	RCTs
Boot-camp interventions for conduct problems	Worsening of conduct problems	Meta-analysis (review of studies)
DARE programs	Increased use of alcohol and drugs	RCTs

Note: CISD = critical-incident stress debriefing; PTSD = posttraumatic stress disorder; RCTs = randomized controlled trials
Information from Lilienfeld (2007).

To regulate the potentially powerful influence of therapies, psychologists hold themselves to a set of ethical standards for the treatment of people with mental disorders (American Psychological Association, 2002). Adherence to these standards is required for membership in the American Psychological Association, and state licensing boards also monitor adherence to ethical principles in therapy. These ethical standards include (1) striving to benefit clients and taking care to do no harm; (2) establishing relationships of trust with clients; (3) promoting accuracy, honesty, and truthfulness; (4) seeking fairness in treatment and taking precautions to avoid biases; and (5) respecting the dignity and worth of all people. When people suffering from mental disorders come to psychologists for help, adhering to these guidelines is the least that psychologists can do. Ideally, in the hope of relieving this suffering, they can do much more.

Build to the Outcomes

1. What are three kinds of treatment illusions?

2. What is the placebo effect?

3. What methods are used in treatment outcome studies?

4. Why is a double-blind experiment so important in assessing treatment effectiveness?

5. How do psychologists know which treatments work and which might be harmful?

6. How might psychotherapy cause harm?

Chapter Review

Treatment: Getting Help to Those Who Need It

▶ Mental illness is often misunderstood, and because of this, it too often goes untreated.

▶ Untreated mental illness can be extremely costly, affecting an individual's ability to function and also causing social and financial burdens.

▶ Many people who suffer from mental illness do not get the help they need: They may be unaware that they have a problem, they may be uninterested in getting help for their problem, or they may face structural barriers to getting treatment.

▶ Treatments include psychotherapy, which focuses on the mind; medical and biological methods, which focus on the brain and body; and the combination of the two approaches.

Psychological Treatments: Healing the Mind Through Interaction

▶ Psychodynamic therapies, including psychoanalysis, emphasize helping clients gain insight into their unconscious conflicts. Traditional psychoanalysis involves 4 to 5 sessions per week of treatment with a client lying on a couch and free-associating, whereas modern psychodynamic therapies involve one session per week with face-to-face interactions in which therapists help clients solve interpersonal problems.

▶ Humanistic approaches (e.g., person-centered therapy) and existential approaches (e.g., gestalt therapy) focus on helping people to develop a sense of personal worth.

▶ Behavior therapy applies learning principles to specific behavior problems.

▶ Cognitive therapy is focused on helping people to change the way they think about events in their lives, and teaching them to challenge irrational thoughts.

▶ Cognitive behavior therapy (CBT), which merges cognitive and behavioral approaches, has been shown to be effective for treating a wide range of psychological disorders.

▶ Group therapies target couples, families, or groups of clients brought together for the purpose of working together to solve their problems.

▶ Self-help and support groups, such as AA, are common in the United States and around the world but are not well studied.

Biological Treatments: Healing the Mind by Physically Altering the Brain

▶ Antipsychotic medications block dopamine receptors in parts of the brain, reducing dopamine activity. They are used to treat the positive symptoms of schizophrenia.

▶ Antianxiety medications are used to treat anxiety disorders but have the potential for abuse especially because of the development of drug tolerance.

▶ Antidepressants affect the level of serotonin in the brain and are used to treat depression and related disorders.

▶ Herbal and natural products are not considered medications by regulatory agencies and so are not subject to strict scrutiny. Although there is little scientific information on their effectiveness, some do indicate mild positive effects.

▶ Medications are often combined with psychotherapy. Evidence from a study on social phobia suggests that both affect the brain in regions associated with threat.

▶ Other biomedical treatments include electroconvulsive therapy (ECT), transcranial magnetic stimulation (TMS), and psychosurgery—this last used in extreme cases, when other methods of treatment have been exhausted.

Treatment Effectiveness: For Better or for Worse

▶ Observing improvement during treatment does not necessarily mean that the treatment was effective; it might instead reflect natural improvement,

nonspecific treatment effects (e.g., the placebo effect), and reconstructive memory processes.

▶ Treatment studies focus on both treatment outcomes and processes, applying scientific research methods such as double-blind techniques and placebo controls.

▶ Treatments for psychological disorders are generally more effective than no treatment at all, but some (e.g., cognitive behavior therapy and interpersonal psychotherapy) are more effective than others for certain disorders, and both medication and psychotherapy have dangers that ethical practitioners must consider carefully.

KEY CONCEPT QUIZ

1. Which of the following is NOT a reason that people fail to get treatment for mental illness?
   a. People may not realize that their disorder needs to be treated.
   b. Levels of impairment for people with mental illness are comparable to or higher than those of people with chronic medical illnesses.
   c. There may be barriers to treatment, such as beliefs and circumstances that keep people from getting help.
   d. Even people who acknowledge they have a problem may not know where to look for services.

2. Eclectic psychotherapy
   a. concentrates on the interpretation of dreams.
   b. introduces clients to strange situations.
   c. draws on techniques from different forms of therapy.
   d. focuses on the analysis of resistance.

3. The different psychodynamic therapies all share an emphasis on
   a. the influence of the collective unconscious.
   b. the importance of taking responsibility for psychological problems.
   c. combining behavioral and cognitive approaches.
   d. developing insight into the unconscious sources of psychological disorders.

4. Which type of therapy would likely work best for someone with an irrational fear of heights?
   a. psychodynamic
   b. gestalt
   c. behavioral
   d. humanistic

5. Mindfulness meditation is part of which kind of therapy?
   a. interpersonal
   b. humanistic
   c. psychodynamic
   d. cognitive

6. Which type of therapy emphasizes action on the part of the client, as well as complete transparency as to the specifics of the treatment?
   a. cognitive behavioral
   b. humanistic
   c. existential
   d. group

7. Examining the failure to reach one's potential reflects the _____ approach, whereas examining one's failure to find meaning in life reflects the _____ approach.
   a. cognitive; behavioral
   b. humanistic; existential
   c. psychodynamic; cognitive behavioral
   d. existential; humanistic

8. Antipsychotic drugs were developed to treat
   a. depression.
   b. schizophrenia.
   c. anxiety.
   d. mood disorders.

9. Atypical antipsychotic drugs
   a. act on different neurotransmitters depending on the individual.
   b. affect only the dopamine system.
   c. affect only the serotonin system.
   d. act on both the dopamine and serotonin systems.

10. Antidepressant medications have the strongest effects for people with _____ depression.
    a. no
    b. mild
    c. moderate
    d. severe

 LearningCurve Don't stop now! Quizzing yourself is a powerful study tool. Go to LaunchPad to access the LearningCurve adaptive quizzing system and your own personalized learning plan. Visit launchpadworks.com.

KEY TERMS

psychotherapy (p. 638)

eclectic psychotherapy (p. 638)

psychodynamic psychotherapies (p. 638)

resistance (p. 639)

transference (p. 639)

interpersonal psychotherapy (IPT) (p. 640)

person-centered therapy (or client-centered therapy) (p. 641)

gestalt therapy (p. 641)

behavior therapy (p. 642)

token economy (p. 642)

exposure therapy (p. 643)

cognitive therapy (p. 644)

cognitive restructuring (p. 644)

mindfulness meditation (p. 646)

cognitive behavioral therapy (CBT) (p. 646)

group therapy (p. 649)

antipsychotic drugs (p. 651)

psychopharmacology (p. 651)

antianxiety medications (p. 653)

antidepressants (p. 654)

phototherapy (p. 657)

electroconvulsive therapy (ECT) (p. 660)

transcranial magnetic stimulation (TMS) (p. 660)

psychosurgery (p. 661)

placebo (p. 664)

iatrogenic illness (p. 667)

CHANGING MINDS

1. One of your friends recently lost a close family member in a tragic car accident, and he's devastated. He hasn't been attending classes, and when you check up on him, you learn that he's not sleeping well or eating regularly. You want to help him but feel a little out of your depth, so you suggest he visit the campus counseling center and talk to a therapist. "Only crazy people go to therapy," he says. What could you tell your friend to dispel his assumption?

2. While you're talking to your bereaved friend, his roommate comes in. The roommate agrees with your suggestion about therapy but takes it further. "I'll give you the name of my therapist. He helped me quit smoking—he'll be able to cure your depression in no time." Why is it dangerous to assume that a good therapist can cure anyone and anything?

3. In the Methods in Psychology chapter you read about Louise Hay, whose bestselling book, *You Can Heal Your Life,* promotes a kind of psychotherapy: teaching readers how to change their thoughts and thereby improve not only their inner lives but also their physical health. The chapter quotes Hay as saying that scientific evidence is unnecessary to validate her claims. Is there a scientific basis for the major types of psychotherapy described in this chapter? How is scientific experimentation used to assess their effectiveness?

4. In June 2009, the pop icon Michael Jackson died after receiving a fatal dose of the anesthetic propofol, which is sometimes used off label as an antianxiety drug. An autopsy confirmed that his body contained a cocktail of prescription drugs, including the benzodiazepines lorazepam and diazepam. (Jackson's cardiologist, Dr. Conrad Murray, was later convicted of involuntary manslaughter for administering the fatal dose.) Other celebrities whose deaths have been attributed to medications commonly prescribed for anxiety and depression include Prince in 2016, Heath Ledger in 2008, and Anna Nicole Smith in 2007. "These drugs are dangerous," your roommate notes. "People who have psychological problems should seek out talk therapy for their problems and stay away from the medications, even if they're prescribed by a responsible doctor." You agree that medications can be dangerous if misused, but how would you justify the use of drug treatment for serious mental disorders?

ANSWERS TO KEY CONCEPT QUIZ

1. b; 2. c; 3. d; 4. c; 5. d; 6. a; 7. b; 8. b; 9. d; 10. d.

LaunchPad macmillan learning

LaunchPad features the full e-Book of *Psychology*, the LearningCurve adaptive quizzing system, videos, and a variety of activities to boost your learning. Visit LaunchPad at **launchpadworks.com.**

Glossary

absentmindedness A lapse in attention that results in memory failure. (p. 246)

absolute threshold The minimal intensity needed to just barely detect a stimulus in 50% of trials. (p. 127)

accommodation The process by which infants revise their schemas in light of new information. (p. 433)

accommodation The process whereby the eye maintains a clear image on the retina. (p. 133)

acetylcholine (ACh) A neurotransmitter involved in a number of functions, including voluntary motor control. (p. 84)

acquisition The phase of classical conditioning when the CS and the US are presented together. (p. 266)

action potential An electric signal that is conducted along a neuron's axon to a synapse. (p. 81)

activation–synthesis model The theory that dreams are produced when the brain attempts to make sense of random neural activity that occurs during sleep. (p. 194)

actor–observer effect The tendency to make situational attributions for our own behaviors while making dispositional attributions for the identical behavior of others. (p. 546)

adolescence The period of development that begins with the onset of sexual maturity (about 11 to 14 years of age) and lasts until the beginning of adulthood (about 18 to 21 years of age). (p. 448)

adulthood The stage of development that begins around 18 to 21 years and ends at death. (p. 460)

aggression Behavior whose purpose is to harm another. (p. 508)

agonists Drugs that increase the action of a neurotransmitter. (p. 85)

agoraphobia A specific phobia involving a fear of public places. (p. 600)

alcohol myopia A condition that results when alcohol hampers attention, leading people to respond in simple ways to complex situations. (p. 202)

algorithm A well-defined sequence of procedures or rules that guarantees a solution to a problem. (p. 374)

altered state of consciousness A form of experience that departs significantly from the normal subjective experience of the world and the mind. (p. 187)

altruism Behavior that benefits another without benefiting oneself. (p. 516)

amygdala A part of the limbic system that plays a central role in many emotional processes, particularly the formation of emotional memories. (p. 95)

anal stage The second psychosexual stage, in which experience is dominated by the pleasures and frustrations associated with the anus, retention and expulsion of feces and urine, and toilet training. (p. 487)

analogical problem solving The process of solving a problem by finding a similar problem with a known solution and applying that solution to the current problem. (p. 382)

anorexia nervosa An eating disorder characterized by an intense fear of being overweight and a severe restriction of food intake. (p. 329)

antagonists Drugs that block the function of a neurotransmitter. (p. 85)

anterograde amnesia The inability to transfer new information from the short-term store into the long-term store. (p. 226)

antianxiety medications Drugs that help reduce a person's experience of fear or anxiety. (p. 653)

antidepressants A class of drugs that help lift people's moods. (p. 654)

antipsychotic drugs Medications that are used to treat schizophrenia and related psychotic disorders. (p. 651)

antisocial personality disorder (APD) A pervasive pattern of disregard for and violation of the rights of others that begins in childhood or early adolescence and continues into adulthood. (p. 624)

anxiety disorder The class of mental disorders in which anxiety is the predominant feature. (p. 598)

aphasia Difficulty in producing or comprehending language. (p. 361)

apparent motion The perception of movement as a result of alternating signals appearing in rapid succession in different locations. (p. 148)

appraisal An evaluation of the emotion-relevant aspects of a stimulus. (p. 316)

approach motivation The motivation to experience a positive outcome. (p. 341)

area A1 A portion of the temporal lobe that contains the primary auditory cortex. (p. 154)

area V1 The part of the occipital lobe that contains the primary visual cortex. (p. 135)

assimilation The process by which infants apply their schemas in novel situations. (p. 433)

association areas Areas of the cerebral cortex that are composed of neurons that help provide sense and meaning to information registered in the cortex. (p. 99)

attachment The emotional bond that forms between newborns and their primary caregivers. (p. 443)

attention deficit/hyperactivity disorder (ADHD) A persistent pattern of severe problems with inattention and/or hyperactivity or impulsiveness that cause significant impairments in functioning. (p. 621)

attitude An enduring positive or negative evaluation of an object or event. (p. 533)

attribution An inference about the cause of a person's behavior. (p. 545)

autism spectrum disorder (ASD) A condition beginning in early childhood in which a person shows persistent communication deficits as well as restricted and repetitive patterns of behaviors, interests, or activities. (p. 619)

autonomic nervous system (ANS) A set of nerves that carries involuntary and automatic commands that control blood vessels, body organs, and glands. (p. 88)

availability bias The concept that items that are more readily available in memory are judged as having occurred more frequently. (p. 374)

avoidance motivation The motivation not to experience a negative outcome. (p. 341)

axon The part of a neuron that carries information to other neurons, muscles, or glands. (p. 77)

balanced placebo design A study design in which behavior is observed following the presence or absence of an actual stimulus and also following the presence or absence of a placebo stimulus. (p. 201)

basal ganglia A set of subcortical structures that directs intentional movements. (p. 95)

basilar membrane A structure in the inner ear that undulates when vibrations from the ossicles reach the cochlear fluid. (p. 153)

behavior Observable actions of human beings and nonhuman animals. (p. 3)

behavior therapy A type of therapy that assumes that disordered behavior is learned and that symptom relief is achieved through changing overt maladaptive behaviors into more constructive behaviors. (p. 642)

behavioral neuroscience An approach to psychology that links psychological processes to activities in the nervous system and other bodily processes. (p. 20)

behaviorism An approach that advocates that psychologists restrict themselves to the scientific study of objectively observable behavior. (p. 12)

belief An enduring piece of knowledge about an object or event. (p. 533)

belief bias The idea that people's judgments about whether to accept conclusions depend more on how believable the conclusions are than on whether the arguments are logically valid. (p. 391)

bias The distorting influences of present knowledge, beliefs, and feelings on recollection of previous experiences. (p. 253)

Big Five The traits of the five-factor model: openness to experience, conscientiousness, extraversion, agreeableness, and neuroticism. (p. 478)

binding problem How the brain links features together so that we see unified objects in our visual world rather than free-floating or miscombined features. (p. 140)

binge eating disorder An eating disorder characterized by recurrent and uncontrolled episodes of eating a large number of calories in a short time. (p. 328)

binocular disparity The difference in the retinal images of the two eyes that provides information about depth. (p. 147)

biofeedback The use of an external monitoring device to obtain information about a bodily function and possibly gain control over that function. (p. 567)

biological preparedness A propensity for learning particular kinds of associations over others. (p. 272)

biopsychosocial perspective Explains mental disorders as the result of interactions among biological, psychological, and social factors. (p. 593)

bipolar disorder A condition characterized by cycles of abnormal, persistent high mood (mania) and low mood (depression). (p. 610)

blind spot A location in the visual field that produces no sensation on the retina. (p. 135)

blocking A failure to retrieve information that is available in memory even though you are trying to produce it. (p. 247)

bulimia nervosa An eating disorder characterized by binge eating followed by compensatory behavior. (p. 329)

burnout A state of physical, emotional, and mental exhaustion resulting from long-term involvement in an emotionally demanding situation and accompanied by lowered performance and motivation. (p. 563)

bystander intervention The act of helping strangers in an emergency situation. (p. 515)

Cannon–Bard theory The theory that a stimulus simultaneously triggers activity in the body and emotional experience in the brain. (p. 313)

case method A procedure for gathering scientific information by studying a single individual. (p. 60)

catatonic behavior A marked decrease in all movement or an increase in muscular rigidity and overactivity. (p. 615)

category-specific deficit A neurological syndrome that is characterized by an inability to recognize objects that belong to a particular category, although the ability to recognize objects outside the category is undisturbed. (p. 371)

cell body (or soma) The part of a neuron that coordinates information-processing tasks and keeps the cell alive. (p. 77)

central nervous system (CNS) The part of the nervous system that is composed of the brain and spinal cord. (p. 87)

cephalocaudal rule The "top-to-bottom" rule that describes the tendency for motor skills to emerge in sequence from the head to the feet. (p. 432)

cerebellum A large structure of the hindbrain that controls fine motor skills. (p. 92)

cerebral cortex The outermost layer of the brain, visible to the naked eye and divided into two hemispheres. (p. 94)

change blindness Failure to detect changes to the visual details of a scene. (p. 149)

childhood The stage of development that begins at about 18 to 24 months and lasts until adolescence, which begins between 11 and 14 years. (p. 435)

chromosomes Strands of DNA wound around each other in a double-helix configuration. (p. 104)

chronic stressors Sources of stress that occur continuously or repeatedly. (p. 554)

chunking Combining small pieces of information into larger clusters or chunks that are more easily held in short-term memory. (p. 223)

circadian rhythm A naturally occurring 24-hour cycle. (p. 187)

classical conditioning A type of learning that occurs when a neutral stimulus produces a response after being paired with a stimulus that naturally produces a response. (p. 263)

cochlea A fluid-filled tube that is the organ of auditory transduction. (p. 153)

cocktail-party phenomenon A phenomenon in which people tune in one message even while they filter out others nearby. (p. 176)

cognitive behavioral therapy (CBT) A blend of cognitive and behavioral therapeutic strategies. (p. 646)

cognitive development The process by which infants and children gain the ability to think and understand. (p. 432)

cognitive dissonance An unpleasant state that arises when a person recognizes the inconsistency of his or her actions, attitudes, or beliefs. (p. 536)

cognitive enhancers Drugs that improve the psychological processes that underlie intelligent performance. (p. 422)

cognitive map A mental representation of the physical features of the environment. (p. 283)

cognitive neuroscience The field of study that attempts to understand the links between cognitive processes and brain activity. (p. 22)

cognitive psychology The scientific study of mental processes, including perception, thought, memory, and reasoning. (p. 19)

cognitive restructuring A therapeutic approach that teaches clients to question the automatic beliefs, assumptions, and predictions that often lead to negative emotions and to replace negative thinking with more realistic and positive beliefs. (p. 644)

cognitive symptoms Deficits in cognitive abilities, specifically executive functioning, attention, and working memory, present in those with schizophrenia. (p. 615)

cognitive therapy Focuses on helping a client identify and correct any distorted thinking about self, others, or the world. (p. 644)

cognitive unconscious All the mental processes that give rise to a person's thoughts, choices, emotions, and behavior even though they are not experienced by the person. (p. 184)

color-opponent system Theory stating that pairs of visual neurons work in opposition. (p. 138)

common knowledge effect The tendency for group discussions to focus on information that all members share. (p. 514)

comorbidity The co-occurrence of two or more disorders in a single individual. (p. 592)

companionate love An experience involving affection, trust, and concern for a partner's well-being. (p. 526)

comparison level The cost–benefit ratio that people believe they deserve or could attain in another relationship. (p. 526)

concept A mental representation that groups or categorizes shared features of related objects, events, or other stimuli. (p. 368)

concrete operational stage The stage of cognitive development that begins at about 6 years and ends at about 11 years, during which children learn how various actions, or *operations,* can affect or transform *concrete* objects. (p. 435)

conditioned response (CR) A reaction that resembles an unconditioned response but is produced by a conditioned stimulus. (p. 266)

conditioned stimulus (CS) A previously neutral stimulus that produces a reliable response in an organism after being paired with a US. (p. 266)

conduct disorder A persistent pattern of deviant behavior involving aggression toward people or animals, destruction of property, deceitfulness or theft, or serious rule violations. (p. 622)

cones Photoreceptors that detect color, operate under normal daylight conditions, and allow us to focus on fine detail. (p. 133)

conformity The tendency to do what others do simply because others are doing it. (p. 530)

conjunction fallacy When people think that two events are more likely to occur together than either individual event. (p. 375)

conscious motivations Motivations of which people are aware. (p. 341)

consciousness A person's subjective experience of the world and the mind. (pp. 5, 172)

conservation The notion that the quantitative properties of an object are invariant despite changes in the object's appearance. (p. 436)

consolidation The process by which memories become stable in the brain. (p. 227)

control group The group of participants who are not exposed to the particular manipulation, compared with the experimental group, in an experiment. (p. 54)

conventional stage A stage of moral development in which the morality of an action is primarily determined by the extent to which it conforms to social rules. (p. 446)

cooperation Behavior by two or more individuals that leads to mutual benefit. (p. 512)

corpus callosum A thick band of nerve fibers that connects large areas of the cerebral cortex on each side of the brain and supports communication of information across the hemispheres. (p. 98)

correlation Two variables are said to "be correlated" when variations in the value of one variable are synchronized with variations in the value of the other. (p. 48)

correlation coefficient A mathematical measure of both the direction and strength of a correlation, which is symbolized by the letter *r.* (p. 49)

correspondence bias The tendency to make a dispositional attribution even when we should instead make a situational attribution. (p. 545)

crystallized intelligence The ability to apply knowledge that was acquired through experience. (p. 405)

cultural psychology The study of how cultures reflect and shape the psychological processes of their members. (p. 25)

debriefing A verbal description of the true nature and purpose of a study. (p. 67)

deep structure The meaning of a sentence. (p. 352)

defense mechanisms Unconscious coping mechanisms that reduce anxiety generated by threats from unacceptable impulses. (p. 486)

deindividuation A phenomenon that occurs when immersion in a group causes people to become less aware of their individual values. (p. 515)

delusion A false belief, often bizarre and grandiose, that is maintained in spite of its irrationality. (p. 614)

demand characteristics Those aspects of an observational setting that cause people to behave as they think someone else wants or expects. (p. 41)

dendrite The part of a neuron that receives information from other neurons and relays it to the cell body. (p. 77)

dependent variable The variable that is measured in a study. (p. 54)

depressants Substances that reduce the activity of the central nervous system. (p. 200)

developmental psychology The study of continuity and change across the life span. (p. 428)

deviation IQ A statistic obtained by dividing a person's test score by the average test score of people in the same age group and then multiplying the quotient by 100 (see *ratio IQ*). (p. 398)

Diagnostic and Statistical Manual of Mental Disorders (DSM) A classification system that describes the features used to diagnose each recognized mental disorder and indicates how that disorder can be distinguished from other, similar problems. (p. 590)

diathesis–stress model Suggests that a person may be predisposed to a psychological disorder that remains unexpressed until triggered by stress. (p. 594)

dichotic listening A task in which people wearing headphones hear different messages presented to each ear. (p. 176)

diffusion chain A process in which individuals initially learn a behavior by observing another individual perform that behavior, and then become models from which other individuals learn the behavior. (p. 290)

diffusion of responsibility The tendency for individuals to feel diminished responsibility for their actions when they are surrounded by others who are acting the same way. (p. 515)

direct replication An experiment that uses the same procedures as a previous experiment but with a new sample. (p. 61)

discrimination The capacity to distinguish between similar but distinct stimuli. (p. 267)

disorganized speech A severe disruption of verbal communication in which ideas shift rapidly and incoherently among unrelated topics. (p. 614)

display rule A norm for the appropriate expression of emotion. (p. 321)

DNA methylation Adding a methyl group to DNA. (p. 106)

door-in-the-face technique An influence strategy that involves getting someone to deny an initial request. (p. 529)

dopamine A neurotransmitter that regulates motor behavior, motivation, pleasure, and emotional arousal. (p. 84)

dopamine hypothesis The idea that schizophrenia involves an excess of dopamine activity. (p. 616)

double depression A moderately depressed mood that persists for at least 2 years and is punctuated by periods of major depression. (p. 606)

double-blind observation A technique whose true purpose is hidden from both the observer and the person being observed. (p. 44)

drive An internal state caused by physiological needs. (p. 327)

drive-reduction theory A theory suggesting that organisms are motivated to reduce their drives. (p. 327)

drug tolerance The tendency for larger doses of a drug to be required over time to achieve the same effect. (p. 198)

dual process theories Theories that suggest that we have two different systems in our brains for processing information: one dedicated to fast, automatic, and unconscious processing, and the other dedicated to slow, effortful, and conscious processing. (p. 185)

dynamic unconscious An active system encompassing a lifetime of hidden memories, the person's deepest instincts and desires, and the person's inner struggle to control these forces. (p. 184)

echoic memory A fast-decaying store of auditory information. (p. 222)

eclectic psychotherapy A form of psychotherapy that involves drawing on techniques from different forms of therapy, depending on the client and the problem. (p. 638)

ego The component of personality, developed through contact with the external world, that enables us to deal with life's practical demands. (p. 485)

egocentrism The failure to understand that the world appears different to different people. (p. 436)

electroconvulsive therapy (ECT) A treatment that involves inducing a brief seizure by delivering an electrical shock to the brain. (p. 660)

electroencephalograph (EEG) A device used to record electrical activity in the brain. (p. 113)

electrooculograph (EOG) An instrument that measures eye movements. (p. 188)

embryonic stage The period of prenatal development that lasts from the 2nd week until about the 8th week. (p. 429)

emotion A positive or negative experience that is associated with a particular pattern of physiological activity. (p. 312)

emotion regulation The strategies people use to influence their own emotional experiences. (p. 317)

emotional expression An observable sign of an emotional state. (p. 318)

emotional intelligence The ability to reason about emotions and to use emotions to enhance reasoning. (p. 406)

empirical method A set of rules and techniques for observation. (p. 38)

empiricism The belief that accurate knowledge can be acquired through observation. (p. 36)

encoding specificity principle The idea that a retrieval cue can be an effective reminder when it helps re-create the specific way in which information was initially encoded. (p. 231)

encoding The process of transforming what we perceive, think, or feel into an enduring memory. (p. 216)

endocrine system A network of glands that produce and secrete into the bloodstream chemical messages known as hormones, which influence a wide variety of basic functions, including metabolism, growth, and sexual development. (p. 96)

endorphins Chemicals that act within the pain pathways and emotion centers of the brain. (p. 84)

epigenetic marks Chemical modifications to DNA that can turn genes on or off. (p. 106)

epigenetics The study of environmental influences that determine whether or not genes are expressed, or the degree to which they are expressed, without altering the basic DNA sequences that constitute the genes themselves. (p. 106)

episodic memory The collection of past personal experiences that occurred at a particular time and place. (p. 239)

equity A state of affairs in which the cost–benefit ratios of two partners are roughly equal. (p. 526)

evolutionary psychology A psychological approach that explains mind and behavior in terms of the adaptive value of abilities that are preserved over time by natural selection. (p. 22)

exemplar theory A theory of categorization that argues that we make category judgments by comparing a new instance with stored memories of other instances of the category. (p. 370)

existential approach A school of thought that regards personality as governed by an individual's ongoing choices and decisions in the context of the realities of life and death. (p. 489)

expectancy theory The idea that alcohol effects can be produced by people's expectations of how alcohol will influence them in particular situations. (p. 201)

experiment A technique for establishing the causal relationship between variables. (p. 53)

experimental group The group of participants who are exposed to a particular manipulation, compared with the control group, in an experiment. (p. 54)

explicit memory The act of consciously or intentionally retrieving past experiences. (p. 237)

exposure therapy An approach to treatment that involves confronting an emotion-arousing stimulus directly and repeatedly, ultimately leading to a decrease in the emotional response. (p. 643)

expressed emotion A measure of how much hostility, criticism, and emotional overinvolvement that people communicate when speaking about a family member with a mental disorder. (p. 612)

external validity An attribute of an experiment in which variables have been defined in a normal, typical, or realistic way. (p. 59)

extinction The gradual elimination of a learned response that occurs when the CS is repeatedly presented without the US. (p. 266)

extrinsic motivation A motivation to take actions that lead to reward. (p. 338)

facial feedback hypothesis The theory that emotional expressions can cause the emotional experiences they signify. (p. 320)

false recognition A feeling of familiarity about something that hasn't been encountered before. (p. 250)

family resemblance theory The concept that members of a category have features that appear to be characteristic of category members but may not be possessed by every member. (p. 369)

fast mapping The process whereby children can map a word onto an underlying concept after only a single exposure. (p. 355)

feature-integration theory The idea that focused attention is not required to detect the individual features that make up a stimulus but is required to bind those individual features together. (p. 141)

fetal alcohol syndrome (FAS) A developmental disorder that stems from heavy alcohol use by the mother during pregnancy. (p. 430)

fetal stage The period of prenatal development that lasts from the 9th week until birth. (p. 429)

fight-or-flight response An emotional and physiological reaction to an emergency that increases readiness for action. (p. 556)

fixation A phenomenon in which a person's pleasure-seeking drives become psychologically stuck, or arrested, at a particular psychosexual stage. (p. 486)

fixed-interval schedule (FI) An operant conditioning principle whereby reinforcers are presented at fixed time periods, provided that the appropriate response is made. (p. 278)

fixed-ratio schedule (FR) An operant conditioning principle whereby reinforcement is delivered after a specific number of responses have been made. (p. 278)

flashbulb memories Detailed recollections of when and where we heard about shocking events. (p. 254)

fluid intelligence The ability to solve and reason about novel problems. (p. 405)

foot-in-the-door technique A technique that involves making a small request and following it with a larger request. (p. 535)

formal operational stage The final stage of cognitive development that begins around the age of 11, during which children learn to reason about abstract concepts. (p. 436)

fovea An area of the retina where vision is the clearest and there are no rods at all. (p. 133)

framing effects A bias whereby people give different answers to the same problem depending on how the problem is phrased (or framed). (p. 376)

fraternal twins (or dizygotic twins) Twins who develop from two different eggs that were fertilized by two different sperm. (p. 409)

frequency distribution A graphical representation of measurements arranged by the number of times each measurement was made. (p. 44)

frontal lobe The region of the cerebral cortex that has specialized areas for movement, abstract thinking, planning, memory, and judgment. (p. 99)

frustration–aggression hypothesis A principle stating that animals aggress when their goals are frustrated. (p. 508)

full consciousness A level of consciousness in which you know and are able to report your mental state. (p. 179)

functional fixedness The tendency to perceive the functions of objects as unchanging. (p. 386)

functionalism The study of how mental processes enable people to adapt to their environments. (p. 7)

GABA (gamma-aminobutyric acid) The primary inhibitory neurotransmitter in the brain. (p. 84)

gate-control theory of pain A theory of pain perception based on the idea that signals arriving from pain receptors in the body can be stopped, or *gated*, by interneurons in the spinal cord via feedback from two directions. (p. 160)

gateway drug A drug whose use increases the risk of the subsequent use of more harmful drugs. (p. 205)

gene The major unit of hereditary transmission. (p. 104)

general adaptation syndrome (GAS) A three-stage physiological response that appears regardless of the stressor that is encountered. (p. 557)

generalization The CR is observed even though the CS is slightly different from the CS used during acquisition. (p. 267)

generalized anxiety disorder (GAD) A disorder characterized by chronic excessive worry accompanied by three or more of the following symptoms: restlessness, fatigue, concentration problems, irritability, muscle tension, and sleep disturbance. (p. 601)

genetic dysphasia A syndrome characterized by an inability to learn the grammatical structure of language despite having otherwise normal intelligence. (p. 359)

genital stage The fifth and final psychosexual stage, the time for the coming together of the mature adult personality with a capacity to love, work, and relate to others in a mutually satisfying and reciprocal manner. (p. 487)

germinal stage The 2-week period of prenatal development that begins at conception. (p. 429)

Gestalt psychology A psychological approach that emphasizes that we often perceive the whole rather than the sum of the parts. (p. 17)

gestalt therapy A form of psychotherapy whose goal is helping the client become aware of his or her thoughts, behaviors, experiences, and feelings and to "own" or take responsibility for them. (p. 641)

glial cells Support cells found in the nervous system. (p. 77)

glutamate The major excitatory neurotransmitter in the brain. (p. 84)

grammar A set of rules that specify how the units of language can be combined to produce meaningful messages. (p. 351)

grossly disorganized behavior Behavior that is inappropriate for the situation or ineffective in attaining goals, often with specific motor disturbances. (p. 615)

group A collection of people who have something in common that distinguishes them from others. (p. 513)

group polarization The tendency for groups to make decisions that are more extreme than any member would have made alone. (p. 514)

group therapy A type of therapy in which multiple participants (who often do not know each other at the outset) work on their individual problems in a group atmosphere. (p. 649)

groupthink The tendency for groups to reach consensus in order to facilitate interpersonal harmony. (p. 514)

habituation A general process in which repeated or prolonged exposure to a stimulus results in a gradual reduction in responding. (p. 262)

hair cells Specialized auditory receptor neurons embedded in the basilar membrane. (p. 153)

hallucination A false perceptual experience that has a compelling sense of being real despite the absence of external stimulation. (p. 614)

hallucinogens Drugs that alter sensation and perception and often cause visual and auditory hallucinations. (p. 204)

haptic perception The active exploration of the environment by touching and grasping objects with our hands. (p. 157)

harm reduction approach A response to high-risk behaviors that focuses on reducing the harm such behaviors have on people's lives. (p. 205)

health psychology The subfield of psychology concerned with ways psychological factors influence the causes and treatment of physical illness and the maintenance of health. (p. 552)

hedonic principle The claim that people are motivated to experience pleasure and avoid pain. (p. 326)

helplessness theory The idea that individuals who are prone to depression automatically attribute negative experiences to causes that are internal (i.e., their own fault), stable (i.e., unlikely to change), and global (i.e., widespread). (p. 609)

heritability A measure of the variability of behavioral traits among individuals that can be accounted for by genetic factors. (p. 107)

heritability coefficient A statistic (commonly denoted as h^2) that describes the proportion of the difference between people's IQ scores that can be explained by differences in their genes. (p. 410)

heuristic A fast and efficient strategy that may facilitate decision making but does not guarantee that a solution will be reached. (p. 374)

heuristic persuasion The process by which attitudes or beliefs are changed by appeals to habit or emotion. (p. 534)

hindbrain The area of the brain that coordinates information coming into and out of the spinal cord. (p. 92)

hippocampus A structure critical for creating new memories and integrating them into a network of knowledge so that they can be stored indefinitely in other parts of the cerebral cortex. (p. 95)

histone modification Adding chemical modifications to proteins called histones that are involved in packaging DNA. (p. 107)

homeostasis The tendency for a system to take action to keep itself in an optimal state. (p. 327)

human sexual response cycle The stages of physiological arousal during sexual activity. (p. 336)

humanistic psychology An approach to understanding human nature that emphasizes the positive potential of human beings. (p. 12)

hypnosis A social interaction in which one person (the hypnotist) makes suggestions that lead to a change in another person's (the subject's) subjective experience of the world. (p. 208)

hypnotic analgesia The reduction of pain through hypnosis in people who are susceptible to hypnosis. (p. 209)

hypothalamus A subcortical structure that regulates body temperature, hunger, thirst, and sexual behavior. (p. 94)

hypothesis A falsifiable prediction made by a theory. (p. 37)

hysteria A temporary loss of cognitive or motor functions, usually as a result of emotionally upsetting experiences. (p. 10)

iatrogenic illness A disorder or symptom that occurs as a result of a medical or psychotherapeutic treatment itself. (p. 667)

iconic memory A fast-decaying store of visual information. (p. 222)

id The part of the mind containing the drives present at birth; it is the source of our bodily needs, wants, desires, and impulses, particularly our sexual and aggressive drives. (p. 485)

identical twins (or monozygotic twins) Twins who develop from the splitting of a single egg that was fertilized by a single sperm. (p. 409)

illusions Errors of perception, memory, or judgment in which subjective experience differs from objective reality. (p. 17)

illusory conjunction A perceptual mistake whereby the brain incorrectly combines features from multiple objects. (p. 141)

immune system A complex response system that protects the body from bacteria, viruses, and other foreign substances. (p. 560)

implicit learning Learning that takes place largely independent of awareness of both the process and the products of information acquisition. (p. 295)

implicit memory The influence of past experiences on later behavior and performance, even without an effort to remember them or an awareness of the recollection. (p. 237)

inattentional blindness A failure to perceive objects that are not the focus of attention. (p. 149)

independent variable The variable that is manipulated in an experiment. (p. 54)

infancy The stage of development that begins at birth and lasts between 18 and 24 months. (p. 431)

informational influence A phenomenon that occurs when another person's behavior provides information about what is true. (p. 533)

informed consent A written agreement to participate in a study made by an adult who has been informed of all the risks that participation may entail. (p. 67)

insomnia Difficulty in falling asleep or staying asleep. (p. 191)

instrument Anything that can detect the condition to which an operational definition refers. (p. 40)

intelligence The ability to use one's mind to solve novel problems and learn from experience. (p. 396)

intermittent reinforcement An operant conditioning principle whereby only some of the responses made are followed by reinforcement. (p. 279)

intermittent reinforcement effect The fact that operant behaviors that are maintained under intermittent reinforcement schedules resist extinction better than those maintained under continuous reinforcement. (p. 280)

internal validity An attribute of an experiment that allows it to establish causal relationships. (p. 59)

internal working model of relationships A set of beliefs about the self, the primary caregiver, and the relationship between them. (p. 444)

interneurons Neurons that connect sensory neurons, motor neurons, or other interneurons. (p. 79)

interpersonal psychotherapy (IPT) A form of psychotherapy that focuses on helping clients improve current relationships. (p. 640)

intrinsic motivation A motivation to take actions that are themselves rewarding. (p. 338)

introspection The subjective observation of one's own experience. (p. 6)

ironic processes of mental control A mental process that can produce ironic errors because monitoring for errors can itself produce them. (p. 182)

James–Lange theory The theory that a stimulus triggers activity in the body, which in turn produces an emotional experience in the brain. (p. 312)

just noticeable difference (JND) The minimal change in a stimulus that can just barely be detected. (p. 129)

kin selection The process by which evolution selects for individuals who cooperate with their relatives. (p. 516)

language A system for communicating with others using signals that are combined according to rules of grammar and that convey meaning. (p. 351)

language acquisition device (LAD) A collection of processes that facilitate language learning. (p. 358)

latency stage The fourth psychosexual stage, in which the primary focus is on the further development of intellectual, creative, interpersonal, and athletic skills. (p. 487)

latent content A dream's true underlying meaning. (p. 194)

latent learning A process in which something is learned, but it is not manifested as a behavioral change until sometime in the future. (p. 282)

law of effect The principle that behaviors that are followed by a "satisfying state of affairs" tend to be repeated, and those that produce an "unpleasant state of affairs" are less likely to be repeated. (p. 274)

learning The acquisition, from experience, of new knowledge, skills, or responses that results in a relatively permanent change in the state of the learner. (p. 262)

limbic system A group of forebrain structures including the hypothalamus, the hippocampus, and the amygdala, which are involved in motivation, emotion, learning, and memory. (p. 95)

linguistic relativity hypothesis The proposal that language shapes the nature of thought. (p. 364)

locus of control A person's tendency to perceive the control of rewards as internal to the self or external in the environment. (p. 493)

long-term memory A type of storage that holds information for hours, days, weeks, or years. (p. 225)

long-term potentiation (LTP) A process whereby repeated communication across the synapse between neurons strengthens the connection, making further communication easier. (p. 230)

loss aversion The tendency to care more about avoiding losses than about achieving equal-size gains. (p. 342)

loudness A sound's intensity. (p. 151)

lymphocytes White blood cells that produce antibodies that fight infection, including T cells and B cells. (p. 560)

major depressive disorder (or unipolar depression) A disorder characterized by a severely depressed mood and/or inability to experience pleasure that lasts 2 or more weeks and is accompanied by feelings of worthlessness, lethargy, and sleep and appetite disturbance. (p. 606)

manifest content A dream's apparent topic or superficial meaning. (p. 194)

manipulation Changing a variable in order to determine its causal power. (p. 54)

marijuana (or cannabis) The leaves and buds of the hemp plant, which contain a psychoactive drug called tetrahydrocannabinol (THC). (p. 204)

matched pairs technique A technique whereby each participant is identical to one other participant in terms of a third variable. (p. 52)

matched samples technique A technique whereby the participants in two groups are identical in terms of a third variable. (p. 52)

mean The average value of all the measurements. (p. 44)

means–ends analysis A process of searching for the means or steps to reduce differences between the current situation and the desired goal. (p. 381)

median The value that is in the middle, that is, greater than or equal to half the measurements and less than or equal to half the measurements. (p. 44)

medical model An approach that conceptualizes abnormal psychological experiences as illnesses that, like physical illnesses, have biological and environmental causes, defined symptoms, and possible cures. (p. 589)

meditation The practice of intentional contemplation. (p. 566)

medulla An extension of the spinal cord into the skull that coordinates heart rate, circulation, and respiration. (p. 92)

memory The ability to store and retrieve information over time. (p. 216)

memory misattribution Assigning a recollection or an idea to the wrong source. (p. 248)

mental control The attempt to change conscious states of mind. (p. 181)

mental disorder A persistent disturbance or dysfunction in behavior, thoughts, or emotions that causes significant distress or impairment. (p. 588)

mere exposure effect The tendency for liking to increase with the frequency of exposure. (p. 520)

metabolism The rate at which energy is used by the body. (p. 334)

mind The private inner experience of perceptions, thoughts, memories, and feelings. (p. 3)

mind–body problem The issue of how the mind is related to the brain and body. (p. 174)

mindfulness meditation Teaches an individual to be fully present in each moment; to be aware of his or her thoughts, feelings, and sensations; and to detect symptoms before they become a problem. (p. 646)

minimal consciousness A low-level kind of sensory awareness and responsiveness that occurs when the mind inputs sensations and may output behavior. (p. 177)

Minnesota Multiphasic Personality Inventory (MMPI) A well-researched clinical questionnaire used to assess personality and psychological problems. (p. 473)

mirror neurons Neurons that are active when an animal performs a behavior, such as reaching for or manipulating an object, and are also activated when another animal observes that animal performing the same behavior. (p. 99)

mode The value of the most frequently observed measurement. (p. 44)

monocular depth cues Aspects of a scene that yield information about depth when viewed with only one eye. (p. 145)

mood disorders Mental disorders that have mood disturbance as their predominant feature. (p. 606)

morphemes The smallest meaningful units of language. (p. 351)

morphological rules A set of rules that indicate how morphemes can be combined to form words. (p. 351)

motivation The psychological cause of an action. (p. 325)

motor development The emergence of the ability to execute physical action. (p. 432)

motor neurons Neurons that carry signals from the spinal cord to the muscles to produce movement. (p. 78)

motor reflexes Specific motor responses that are triggered by specific patterns of sensory stimulation. (p. 432)

myelin sheath An insulating layer of fatty material. (p. 77)

myelination The formation of a fatty sheath around the axons of a neuron. (p. 430)

narcissism A trait that reflects a grandiose view of the self combined with a tendency to seek admiration from and exploit others. (p. 500)

narcolepsy A disorder in which sudden sleep attacks occur in the middle of waking activities. (p. 192)

narcotics (or opiates) Highly addictive drugs derived from opium that relieve pain. (p. 203)

nativism The philosophical view that certain kinds of knowledge are innate or inborn. (p. 3)

nativist theory The view that language development is best explained as an innate, biological capacity. (p. 358)

natural correlation A correlation observed in the world around us. (p. 50)

natural selection Charles Darwin's theory that the features of an organism that help it survive and reproduce are more likely than other features to be passed on to subsequent generations. (p. 7)

naturalistic observation A technique for gathering scientific information by unobtrusively observing people in their natural environments. (p. 41)

need for achievement The motivation to solve worthwhile problems. (p. 341)

negative symptoms Deficits in or disruptions of normal emotions and behaviors (e.g., emotional and social withdrawal; apathy; poverty of speech; and other indications of the absence or insufficiency of normal behavior, motivation, and emotion) that are present in those with schizophrenia. (p. 615)

nervous system An interacting network of neurons that conveys electrochemical information throughout the body. (p. 87)

neurons Cells in the nervous system that communicate with one another to perform information-processing tasks. (p. 77)

neurotransmitters Chemicals that transmit information across the synapse to a receiving neuron's dendrites. (p. 83)

night terrors (or sleep terrors) Abrupt awakenings with panic and intense emotional arousal. (p. 192)

nonshared environment Features of the environment that are not experienced by all relevant members of a household (see *shared environment*). (p. 411)

nonsuicidal self-injury (NSSI) Direct, deliberate destruction of body tissue in the absence of any intent to die. (p. 627)

norepinephrine A neurotransmitter that is particularly involved in states of vigilance or heightened awareness of dangers in the environment. (p. 84)

norm of reciprocity The unwritten rule that people should benefit those who have benefited them. (p. 529)

normal distribution A mathematically defined distribution in which the frequency of measurements is highest in the middle and decreases symmetrically in both directions. (p. 44)

normative influence A phenomenon that occurs when another person's behavior provides information about what is appropriate. (p. 529)

norms Customary standards for behavior that are widely shared by members of a culture. (p. 528)

obedience The tendency to do what powerful people tell us to do. (p. 532)

object permanence The fact that objects continue to exist even when they are not visible. (p. 434)

observational learning A condition in which an organism learns by watching the actions of others. (p. 290)

obsessive-compulsive disorder (OCD) A disorder in which repetitive, intrusive thoughts (obsessions) and ritualistic behaviors (compulsions) designed to fend off those thoughts interfere significantly with an individual's functioning. (p. 603)

occipital lobe A region of the cerebral cortex that processes visual information. (p. 98)

Oedipus conflict A developmental experience in which a child's conflicting feelings toward the opposite-sex parent are (usually) resolved by identifying with the same-sex parent. (p. 487)

olfactory bulb A brain structure located above the nasal cavity beneath the frontal lobes. (p. 163)

olfactory receptor neurons (ORNs) Receptor cells that initiate the sense of smell. (p. 162)

operant behavior Behavior that an organism performs that has some impact on the environment. (p. 274)

operant conditioning A type of learning in which the consequences of an organism's behavior determine whether it will repeat that behavior in the future. (p. 272)

operational definition A description of a property in concrete, measurable terms. (p. 40)

optimism bias A bias whereby people believe that, compared with other people, they are more likely to experience positive events and less likely to experience negative events in the future. (p. 377)

oral stage The first psychosexual stage, in which experience centers on the pleasures and frustrations associated with the mouth, sucking, and being fed. (p. 487)

organizational encoding The process of categorizing information according to the relationships among a series of items. (p. 219)

outcome expectancies A person's assumptions about the likely consequences of a future behavior. (p. 492)

panic disorder A disorder characterized by the sudden occurrence of multiple psychological and physiological symptoms that contribute to a feeling of stark terror. (p. 600)

parallel processing The brain's capacity to perform multiple activities at the same time. (p. 140)

parasympathetic nervous system A set of nerves that helps the body return to a normal resting state. (p. 89)

parietal lobe A region of the cerebral cortex whose functions include processing information about touch. (p. 98)

passionate love An experience involving feelings of euphoria, intimacy, and intense sexual attraction. (p. 526)

perception The organization, identification, and interpretation of a sensation in order to form a mental representation. (p. 126)

perceptual confirmation The tendency for people to see what they expect to see. (p. 540)

perceptual constancy A perceptual principle stating that even as aspects of sensory signals change, perception remains consistent. (p. 142)

peripheral nervous system (PNS) The part of the nervous system that connects the central nervous system to the body's organs and muscles. (p. 87)

persistence The intrusive recollection of events that we wish we could forget. (p. 254)

persistent depressive disorder The same cognitive and bodily problems as in depression are present, but they are less severe and last longer, persisting for at least 2 years. (p. 606)

person-centered therapy (or client-centered therapy) A form of psychotherapy that assumes that all individuals have a tendency toward growth and that this growth can be facilitated by acceptance and genuine reactions from the therapist. (p. 641)

person–situation controversy The question of whether behavior is caused more by personality or by situational factors. (p. 490)

personal constructs Dimensions people use in making sense of their experiences. (p. 491)

personality An individual's characteristic style of behaving, thinking, and feeling. (p. 472)

personality disorders Enduring patterns of thinking, feeling, or relating to others or controlling impulses that deviate from cultural expectations and cause distress or impaired functioning. (p. 623)

persuasion A phenomenon that occurs when a person's attitudes or beliefs are influenced by a communication from another person. (p. 534)

phallic stage The third psychosexual stage, in which experience is dominated by the pleasure, conflict, and frustration associated with the phallic-genital region as well as coping with powerful incestuous feelings of love, hate, jealousy, and conflict. (p. 487)

phenomenology The study of how things seem to the conscious person. (p. 172)

pheromones Biochemical odorants emitted by other members of its species that can affect an animal's behavior or physiology. (p. 163)

philosophical empiricism The view that all knowledge is acquired through experience. (p. 3)

phobic disorders Disorders characterized by marked, persistent, and excessive fear and avoidance of specific objects, activities, or situations. (p. 598)

phoneme The smallest unit of sound that is recognizable as speech rather than as random noise. (p. 351)

phonological rules A set of rules that indicate how phonemes can be combined to produce speech sounds. (p. 351)

phototherapy A therapy that involves repeated exposure to bright light. (p. 657)

phrenology A now discredited theory that specific mental abilities and characteristics, ranging from memory to the capacity for happiness, are localized in specific regions of the brain. (p. 5)

physiology The study of biological processes, especially in the human body. (p. 5)

pitch How high or low a sound is. (p. 151)

pituitary gland The "master gland" of the body's hormone-producing system, which releases hormones that direct the functions of many other glands in the body. (p. 96)

place code The process by which different frequencies stimulate neural signals at specific places along the basilar membrane, from which the brain determines pitch. (p. 155)

placebo An inert substance or procedure that has been applied with the expectation that it will produce a healing response. (p. 664)

pons A brain structure that relays information from the cerebellum to the rest of the brain. (p. 94)

population A complete collection of participants who might possibly be measured. (p. 60)

positive symptoms Thoughts and behaviors, such as delusions and hallucinations, present in schizophrenia but not seen in those without the disorder. (p. 614)

postconventional stage A stage of moral development in which the morality of an action is determined by a set of general principles that reflect core values. (p. 446)

posthypnotic amnesia The failure to retrieve memories following hypnotic suggestions to forget. (p. 208)

posttraumatic stress disorder (PTSD) A disorder characterized by chronic physiological arousal, recurrent unwanted thoughts or images of the trauma, and avoidance of things that call the traumatic event to mind. (p. 604)

power An instrument's ability to detect small magnitudes of the property. (p. 41)

practical reasoning The process of figuring out what to do, or reasoning directed toward action. (p. 389)

preconventional stage A stage of moral development in which the morality of an action is primarily determined by its consequences for the actor. (p. 446)

prejudice A positive or negative evaluation of another person based on their group membership. (p. 513)

preoperational stage The stage of cognitive development that begins at about 2 years and ends at about 6 years, during which children develop a preliminary understanding of the physical world. (p. 435)

preparedness theory The idea that people are instinctively predisposed toward certain fears. (p. 599)

primary sex characteristics Bodily structures that are directly involved in reproduction. (p. 448)

priming An enhanced ability to think of a stimulus, such as a word or object, as a result of a recent exposure to that stimulus. (p. 238)

proactive interference Situations in which information learned earlier impairs memory for information acquired later. (p. 245)

problem of other minds The fundamental difficulty we have in perceiving the consciousness of others. (p. 173)

procedural memory The gradual acquisition of skills as a result of practice, or "knowing how" to do things. (p. 237)

projective tests Tests designed to reveal inner aspects of individuals' personalities by analysis of their responses to a standard series of ambiguous stimuli. (p. 474)

prospect theory The theory that people choose to take on risk when evaluating potential losses and avoid risks when evaluating potential gains. (p. 377)

prospective memory Remembering to do things in the future. (p. 246)

prototype The "best" or "most typical" member of a category. (p. 369)

proximodistal rule The "inside-to-outside" rule that describes the tendency for motor skills to emerge in sequence from the center to the periphery. (p. 432)

psychoactive drugs Chemicals that influence consciousness or behavior by altering the brain's chemical message system. (p. 197)

psychoanalysis A therapeutic approach that focuses on bringing unconscious material into conscious awareness to better understand psychological disorders. (p. 10)

psychoanalytic theory An approach that emphasizes the importance of unconscious mental processes in shaping feelings, thoughts, and behavior. (p. 10)

psychodynamic approach An approach that regards personality as formed by needs, strivings, and desires largely operating outside of awareness—motives that also can produce emotional disorders. (p. 485)

psychodynamic psychotherapies Therapies that explore childhood events and encourage individuals to use this understanding to develop insight into their psychological problems. (p. 638)

psychology The scientific study of mind and behavior. (p. 2)

psychopharmacology The study of drug effects on psychological states and symptoms. (p. 651)

psychophysics Methods that measure the strength of a stimulus and the observer's sensitivity to that stimulus. (p. 127)

psychosexual stages Distinct early life stages through which personality is formed as children experience sexual pleasures from specific body areas and caregivers redirect or interfere with those pleasures. (p. 486)

psychosomatic illness An interaction between mind and body that can produce illness. (p. 574)

psychosurgery Surgical destruction of specific brain areas. (p. 661)

psychotherapy An interaction between a socially sanctioned clinician and someone suffering from a psychological problem, with the goal of providing support or relief from the problem. (p. 638)

puberty The onset of bodily changes associated with sexual maturity. (p. 448)

punisher Any stimulus or event that decreases the likelihood of the behavior that led to it. (p. 274)

random assignment A procedure that lets chance assign participants to the experimental or control group. (p. 56)

random sampling A technique for choosing participants that ensures that every member of a population has an equal chance of being included in the sample. (p. 60)

range The value of the largest measurement in a frequency distribution minus the value of the smallest measurement. (p. 46)

ratio IQ A statistic obtained by dividing a person's mental age by the person's physical age and then multiplying the quotient by 100 (see *deviation IQ*). (p. 398)

rational choice theory The classical view that we make decisions by determining how likely something is to happen, judging the value of the outcome, and then multiplying the two. (p. 373)

rational coping Facing a stressor and working to overcome it. (p. 565)

reaction time The amount of time taken to respond to a specific stimulus. (p. 5)

reappraisal Changing one's emotional experience by changing the way one thinks about the emotion-eliciting stimulus. (p. 317)

reasoning A mental activity that consists of organizing information or beliefs into a series of steps in order to reach conclusions. (p. 389)

rebound effect of thought suppression The tendency of a thought to return to consciousness with greater frequency following suppression. (p. 182)

receptors Parts of the cell membrane that receive the neurotransmitter and initiate or prevent a new electric signal. (p. 83)

reciprocal altruism Behavior that benefits another with the expectation that those benefits will be returned in the future. (p. 516)

reconsolidation The process whereby memories can become vulnerable to disruption when they are recalled, thus requiring them to be consolidated again. (p. 227)

referred pain Feeling of pain when sensory information from internal and external areas converges on the same nerve cells in the spinal cord. (p. 160)

reflex arc A neural pathway that controls reflex actions. (p. 90)

refractory period The time following an action potential during which a new action potential cannot be initiated. (p. 82)

reframing Finding a new or creative way to think about a stressor that reduces its threat. (p. 565)

rehearsal The process of keeping information in short-term memory by mentally repeating it. (p. 222)

reinforcement The consequences of a behavior determine whether it will be more or less likely to occur again. (p. 15)

reinforcer Any stimulus or event that increases the likelihood of the behavior that led to it. (p. 274)

relaxation response A condition of reduced muscle tension, cortical activity, heart rate, breathing rate, and blood pressure. (p. 567)

relaxation therapy A technique for reducing tension by consciously relaxing muscles of the body. (p. 567)

reliability The tendency for an instrument to produce the same measurement whenever it is used to measure the same thing. (p. 41)

REM sleep A stage of sleep characterized by rapid eye movements and a high level of brain activity. (p. 188)

representativeness heuristic A mental shortcut that involves making a probability judgment by comparing an object or event with a prototype of the object or event. (p. 376)

repression A mental process that removes unacceptable thoughts and memories from consciousness and keeps them in the unconscious. (p. 184)

repressive coping Avoiding feelings, thoughts, or situations that are reminders of a stressor and maintaining an artificially positive viewpoint. (p. 564)

Research Domain Criteria Project (RDoC) A new initiative that aims to guide the classification and understanding of mental disorders by revealing the basic processes that give rise to them. (p. 595)

resistance A reluctance to cooperate with treatment for fear of confronting unpleasant unconscious material. (p. 639)

response An action or physiological change elicited by a stimulus. (p. 13)

resting potential The difference in electric charge between the inside and outside of a neuron's cell membrane. (p. 80)

reticular formation A brain structure that regulates sleep, wakefulness, and levels of arousal. (p. 92)

retina A layer of light-sensitive tissue lining the back of the eyeball. (p. 133)

retrieval The process of bringing to mind information that has been previously encoded and stored. (p. 216)

retrieval cue External information that is associated with stored information and helps bring it to mind. (p. 231)

retrieval-induced forgetting A process by which retrieving an item from long-term memory impairs subsequent recall of related items. (p. 233)

retroactive interference Situations in which information learned later impairs memory for information acquired earlier. (p. 245)

retrograde amnesia The inability to retrieve information that was acquired before a particular date, usually the date of an injury or surgery. (p. 226)

rods Photoreceptors that become active under low-light conditions for night vision. (p. 133)

Rorschach Inkblot Test A projective technique in which respondents' inner thoughts and feelings are believed to be revealed by analysis of their responses to a set of unstructured inkblots. (p. 474)

sample A partial collection of people drawn from a population. (p. 60)

schemas Theories about the way the world works. (p. 433)

schizophrenia A disorder characterized by the profound disruption of basic psychological processes; a distorted perception of reality; altered or blunted emotion; and disturbances in thought, motivation, and behavior. (p. 614)

scientific method A procedure for finding truth by using empirical evidence. (p. 37)

seasonal affective disorder (SAD) Recurrent depressive episodes in a seasonal pattern. (p. 606)

second-order conditioning A type of learning where a CS is paired with a stimulus that became associated with the US in an earlier procedure. (p. 266)

secondary sex characteristics Bodily structures that change dramatically with sexual maturity but that are not directly involved in reproduction. (p. 448)

self-actualizing tendency The human motive toward realizing our inner potential. (p. 488)

self-concept A person's explicit knowledge of his or her own behaviors, traits, and other personal characteristics. (p. 495)

self-consciousness A distinct level of consciousness in which the person's attention is drawn to the self as an object. (p. 179)

self-esteem The extent to which an individual likes, values, and accepts the self. (p. 497)

self-fulfilling prophecy The tendency for people to behave as they are expected to behave. (p. 540)

self-regulation The exercise of voluntary control over the self to bring the self into line with preferred standards. (p. 580)

self-report A method in which a person provides subjective information about his or her own thoughts, feelings, or behaviors, typically via questionnaire or interview. (p. 473)

self-selection A problem that occurs when anything about a participant determines whether he or she will be included in the experimental or control group. (p. 55)

self-serving bias People's tendency to take credit for their successes but downplay responsibility for their failures. (p. 500)

self-verification The tendency to seek evidence to confirm the self-concept. (p. 497)

semantic encoding The process of relating new information in a meaningful way to knowledge that is already stored in memory. (p. 217)

semantic memory A network of associated facts and concepts that make up our general knowledge of the world. (p. 239)

sensation Simple stimulation of a sense organ. (p. 126)

sensitization A simple form of learning that occurs when presentation of a stimulus leads to an increased response to a later stimulus. (p. 262)

sensorimotor stage A stage of cognitive development that begins at birth and lasts through infancy, during which infants acquire information about the world by sensing it and moving around within it. (p. 433)

sensory adaptation The process whereby sensitivity to prolonged stimulation tends to decline over time as an organism adapts to current conditions. (p. 131)

sensory memory A type of storage that holds sensory information for a few seconds or less. (p. 221)

sensory neurons Neurons that receive information from the external world and convey this information to the brain via the spinal cord. (p. 78)

serial position effect The observation that the first few and last few items in a series are more likely to be recalled than the items in the middle. (p. 222)

serotonin A neurotransmitter that is involved in the regulation of sleep and wakefulness, eating, and aggressive behavior. (p. 84)

shaping Learning that results from the reinforcement of successive steps to a final desired behavior. (p. 280)

shared environment Features of the environment that are experienced by all relevant members of a household (see *nonshared environment*). (p. 411)

short-term memory A type of storage that holds nonsensory information for more than a few seconds but less than a minute. (p. 222)

sick role A socially recognized set of rights and obligations linked with illness. (p. 576)

signal detection theory Holds that the response to a stimulus depends on both a person's sensitivity to the stimulus in the presence of noise and the person's response criterion. (p. 129)

sleep apnea A disorder in which the person stops breathing for brief periods while asleep. (p. 191)

sleep paralysis The experience of waking up unable to move. (p. 192)

social cognition The processes by which people come to understand others. (p. 537)

social influence The ability to change or direct another person's behavior. (p. 527)

social loafing The tendency for people to expend less effort when in a group than when alone. (p. 515)

social phobia A disorder that involves an irrational fear of being publicly humiliated or embarrassed. (p. 598)

social psychology The study of the causes and consequences of sociality. (pp. 24, 508)

social support The aid gained through interacting with others. (p. 569)

social–cognitive approach An approach that views personality in terms of how the person thinks about the situations encountered in daily life and behaves in response to them. (p. 489)

somatic nervous system A set of nerves that conveys information between voluntary muscles and the central nervous system. (p. 87)

somatic symptom disorders The set of psychological disorders in which a person with at least one bodily symptom displays significant health-related anxiety, expresses disproportionate concerns about their symptoms, and devotes excessive time and energy to their symptoms or health concerns. (p. 574)

somnambulism (or sleepwalking) Occurs when a person arises and walks around while asleep. (p. 192)

source memory Recall of when, where, and how information was acquired. (p. 248)

specific phobia A disorder that involves an irrational fear of a particular object or situation that markedly interferes with an individual's ability to function. (p. 598)

spinal reflexes Simple pathways in the nervous system that rapidly generate muscle contractions. (p. 89)

spontaneous recovery The tendency of a learned behavior to recover from extinction after a rest period. (p. 267)

standard deviation A statistic that describes the average difference between the measurements in a frequency distribution and the mean of that distribution. (p. 47)

state-dependent retrieval The process whereby information tends to be better recalled when the person is in the same state during encoding and retrieval. (p. 231)

stereotype threat The fear of confirming the negative beliefs that others may hold. (pp. 420, 540)

stereotyping The process by which people draw inferences about others based on their knowledge of the categories to which others belong. (p. 538)

stimulants Substances that excite the central nervous system, heightening arousal and activity levels. (p. 202)

stimulus Sensory input from the environment. (p. 5)

storage The process of maintaining information in memory over time. (p. 216)

Strange Situation A behavioral test that is used to determine a child's attachment style. (p. 443)

stress The physical and psychological response to internal or external stressors. (p. 552)

stress-inoculation training (SIT) A reframing technique that helps people cope with stressful situations by developing positive ways to think about the situations. (p. 566)

stressors Specific events or chronic pressures that place demands on a person or threaten the person's well-being. (p. 552)

structuralism The analysis of the basic elements that constitute the mind. (p. 5)

subcortical structures Areas of the forebrain housed under the cerebral cortex near the very center of the brain. (p. 94)

subliminal perception Thought or behavior that is influenced by stimuli that a person cannot consciously report perceiving. (p. 185)

subtyping The tendency for people who receive disconfirming evidence to modify their stereotypes rather than abandon them. (p. 541)

suggestibility The tendency to incorporate misleading information from external sources into personal recollections. (p. 251)

suicide Intentional self-inflicted death. (p. 626)

suicide attempt Engagement in potentially harmful behavior with some intention of dying. (p. 626)

sunk-cost fallacy A framing effect in which people make decisions about a current situation on the basis of what they have previously invested in the situation. (p. 376)

superego The mental system that reflects the internalization of cultural rules, mainly learned as parents exercise their authority. (p. 485)

surface structure How a sentence is worded. (p. 352)

syllogistic reasoning Determining whether a conclusion follows from two statements that are assumed to be true. (p. 391)

sympathetic nervous system A set of nerves that prepares the body for action in challenging or threatening situations. (p. 88)

synapse The junction or region between the axon of one neuron and the dendrites or cell body of another. (p. 77)

syntactical rules A set of rules that indicate how words can be combined to form phrases and sentences. (p. 352)

systematic persuasion The process by which attitudes or beliefs are changed by appeals to reason. (p. 534)

taste buds The organ of taste transduction. (p. 164)

tectum A part of the midbrain that orients an organism in the environment. (p. 94)

tegmentum A part of the midbrain that is involved in movement and arousal. (p. 94)

telegraphic speech Speech that is devoid of function morphemes and consists mostly of content words. (p. 355)

telomerase An enzyme that rebuilds telomeres at the tips of chromosomes. (p. 558)

telomeres Caps at the ends of the chromosomes that prevent the chromosomes from sticking to each other. (p. 558)

temperaments Characteristic patterns of emotional reactivity. (p. 443)

template A mental representation that can be directly compared with a viewed shape in the retinal image. (p. 144)

temporal code The process whereby the cochlea registers low frequencies via the firing rate of action potentials entering the auditory nerve. (p. 155)

temporal lobe A region of the cerebral cortex responsible for hearing and language. (p. 99)

teratogens Any substances that pass from mother to unborn child and impair development. (p. 430)

terminal buttons Knoblike structures that branch out from an axon. (p. 83)

terror management theory The theory that people cope with their existential terror by developing a cultural worldview. (p. 343)

thalamus A subcortical structure that relays and filters information from the senses and transmits the information to the cerebral cortex. (p. 94)

Thematic Apperception Test (TAT) A projective technique in which respondents' underlying motives, concerns, and the way they see the social world are believed to be revealed through analysis of the stories they make up about ambiguous pictures of people. (p. 474)

theoretical reasoning (or discursive reasoning) Reasoning directed toward arriving at a belief. (p. 389)

theory A hypothetical explanation of a natural phenomenon. (p. 37)

theory of mind The understanding that the mind produces representations of the world and that these representations guide behavior. (p. 438)

third-variable correlation Two variables are correlated only because each is causally related to a third variable. (p. 51)

third-variable problem The fact that a causal relationship between two variables cannot be inferred from the naturally occurring correlation between them because of the ever-present possibility of third-variable correlation. (p. 53)

thought suppression The conscious avoidance of a thought. (p. 181)

timbre A listener's experience of sound quality or resonance. (p. 151)

token economy A form of behavior therapy in which clients are given "tokens" for desired behaviors, which they can later trade for rewards. (p. 642)

trait A relatively stable disposition to behave in a particular and consistent way. (p. 474)

transcranial magnetic stimulation (TMS) A treatment that involves placing a powerful pulsed magnet over a person's scalp to alter neuronal activity in the brain. (p. 660)

transduction The process that occurs when many sensors in the body convert physical signals from the environment into encoded neural signals sent to the central nervous system. (p. 127)

transfer-appropriate processing The process whereby memory is more likely to transfer from one situation to another when the encoding and retrieval contexts of the situations match. (p. 232)

transference An event that occurs in psychoanalysis when the analyst begins to assume a major significance in the client's life, and the client reacts to the analyst on the basis of unconscious childhood fantasies. (p. 639)

transience Forgetting what occurs with the passage of time. (p. 244)

two-factor theory of emotion The theory that emotions are based on inferences about the causes of physiological arousal. (p. 313)

two-factor theory of intelligence Spearman's theory suggesting that a person's performance on a test is due to a combination of general ability (g) and skills that are specific to the test (s). (p. 402)

Type A behavior pattern The tendency toward easily aroused hostility, impatience, a sense of time urgency, and competitive achievement strivings. (p. 561)

unconditioned response (UR) A reflexive reaction that is reliably produced by an unconditioned stimulus. (p. 265)

unconditioned stimulus (US) Something that reliably produces a naturally occurring reaction in an organism. (p. 265)

unconscious The part of the mind that operates outside of conscious awareness but influences conscious thoughts, feelings, and actions. (p. 10)

unconscious motivations Motivations of which people are not aware. (p. 341)

universality hypothesis The theory that emotional expressions have the same meaning for everyone. (p. 318)

validity The extent to which a concrete event defines a property. (p. 41)

variable A property whose value can vary across individuals or over time. (p. 48)

variable-interval schedule (VI) An operant conditioning principle whereby behavior is reinforced on the basis of an average time that has expired since the last reinforcement. (p. 278)

variable-ratio schedule (VR) An operant conditioning principle whereby the delivery of reinforcement is based on a particular average number of responses. (p. 279)

vestibular system The three fluid-filled semicircular canals and adjacent organs located next to the cochlea in the inner ear. (p. 161)

visual acuity The ability to see fine detail. (p. 131)

visual form agnosia The inability to recognize objects by sight. (p. 139)

visual imagery encoding The process of storing new information by converting it into mental pictures. (p. 218)

Weber's law States that the just noticeable difference of a stimulus is a constant proportion despite variations in intensity. (p. 129)

working memory A type of short-term storage that actively maintains information. (p. 223)

zygote A fertilized egg that contains chromosomes from both a sperm and an egg. (p. 429)

References

Aarts, H., Custers, R., & Marien, H. (2008). Preparing and motivating behavior outside of awareness. *Science, 319,* 1639.

Abel, T., Alberini, C., Ghirardi, M., Huang, Y.-Y., Nguyen, P., & Kandel, E. R. (1995). Steps toward a molecular definition of memory consolidation. In D. L. Schacter (Ed.), *Memory distortion: How minds, brains and societies reconstruct the past* (pp. 298–328). Cambridge, MA: Harvard University Press.

Abelson, J., Curtis, G., Sagher, O., Albucher, R., Harrigan, M., Taylor, S., . . . Giordani, B. (2009). Deep brain stimulation for refractory obsessive-compulsive disorder. *Biological Psychiatry, 57,* 510–516.

Abrams, M., & Reber, A. S. (1988). Implicit learning: Robustness in the face of psychiatric disorders. *Journal of Psycholinguistic Research, 17,* 425–439.

Abramson, L. Y., Seligman, M. E. P., & Teasdale, J. D. (1978). Learned helplessness in humans: Critique and reformulation. *Journal of Abnormal Psychology, 87,* 49–74.

Acar, O. A. & Ende, J. van den (2016). Knowledge distance, cognitive-search process, and creativity: The making of winning solutions in science contexts. *Psychological Science, 27,* 692–699.

Acevedo, B. P., & Aron, A. (2009). Does a long-term relationship kill romantic love? *Review of General Psychology, 13,* 59–65.

Acevedo-Garcia, D., McArdle, N., Osypuk, T. L., Lefkowitz, B., & Krimgold, B. K. (2007). *Children left behind: How metropolitan areas are failing America's children.* Boston: Harvard School of Public Health.

Achter, J. A., Lubinski, D., & Benbow, C. P. (1996). Multipotentiality among the intellectually gifted: "It was never there and already it's vanishing." *Journal of Counseling Psychology, 43,* 65–76.

Ackerman, P. L. (2014). Adolescent and adult intellectual development. *Current Directions in Psychological Science, 23*(4), 246–251. doi: 10.1177/0963721414534960

Acocella, J. (1999). *Creating hysteria: Women and multiple personality disorder.* San Francisco: Jossey-Bass.

Addis, D. R., Wong, A. T., & Schacter, D. L. (2007). Remembering the past and imagining the future: Common and distinct neural substrates during event construction and elaboration. *Neuropsychologia, 45,* 1363–1377.

Addis, D. R., Wong, A. T., & Schacter, D. L. (2008). Age-related changes in the episodic simulation of future events. *Psychological Science, 19,* 33–41.

Adelmann, P. K., & Zajonc, R. B. (1989). Facial efference and the experience of emotion. *Annual Review of Psychology, 40,* 249–280.

Adolph, K. E., Cole, W. G., Komati, M., Garciaguirre, J. S., Badaly, D., Lingeman, J. M., . . . Sotsky, R. B. (2012). How do you learn to walk? Thousands of steps and dozens of falls per day. *Psychological Science, 23*(11), 1387–1394. doi:10.1177/0956797612446346

Adolphs, R., Russell, J. A., & Tranel, D. (1999). A role for the human amygdala in recognizing emotional arousal from unpleasant stimuli. *Psychological Science, 10,* 167–171.

Adolphs, R., Tranel, D., Damasio, H., & Damasio, A. R. (1995). Fear and the human amygdala. *Journal of Neuroscience, 15,* 5879–5891.

Adorno, T. W., Frenkel-Brunswik, E., Levinson, D. J., & Sanford, R. N. (1950). *The authoritarian personality.* New York: Harper & Row.

Aggleton, J. (Ed.). (1992). *The amygdala: Neurobiological aspects of emotion, memory and mental dysfunction.* New York: Wiley-Liss.

Agin, D. (2007). *Junk science: An overdue indictment of government, industry, and faith groups that twist science for their own gain.* New York: Macmillan.

Agren, T., Engman, J., Frick, A., Björkstrand, J., Larsson, E. M., Furmark, T., & Fredrikson, M. (2012). Disruption of reconsolidation erases a fear memory trace in the human amygdala. *Science, 337,* 1550–1552.

Agthe, M., Spörrle, M., & Maner, J. K. (2010). Don't hate me because I'm beautiful: Anti-attractiveness bias in organizational evaluation and decision making. *Journal of Experimental Psychology, 46*(6), 1151–1154. doi:10.1016/j.jesp.2010.05.007

Aharon, I., Etcoff, N., Ariely, D., Chabris, C. F., O'Conner, E., & Breiter, H. C. (2001). Beautiful faces have variable reward value: fMRI and behavioral evidence. *Neuron, 32,* 537–551.

Ahlskog, J. E. (2011). Pathological behaviors provoked by dopamine agonist therapy of Parkinson's disease. *Physiology & Behavior, 104,* 168–172.

Ainslie, G. (2001). *Breakdown of will.* New York: Cambridge University Press.

Ainsworth, M. D. S., Blehar, M. C., Waters, E., & Wall, S. (1978). *Patterns of attachment: A psychological study of the strange situation.* Hillsdale, NJ: Erlbaum.

Ainsworth, S. E., & Maner, J. K. (2012). Sex begets violence: Mating motives, social dominance, and physical aggression in men. *Journal of Personality and Social Psychology, 103*(5), 819–829. doi: 10.1037/a0029428

Aksglaede, L., Sorensen, K., Petersen, J. H., Skakkebaek, N. E., & Juul, A. (2009). Recent decline in age at breast development: The Copenhagen puberty study. *Pediatrics, 123*(5), e932–e939.

Alasaari, J. S., Lagus, M., Ollila, H. M., Toivola, A., Kivimaki, M., Vahterra, J., . . . Paunio, T. (2012). Environmental stress affects DNA methylation of a CpG rich promoter region of serotonin transporter gene in a nurse cohort. *PLoS One, 7,* e45813. doi:10.1371/journal.pone.0045813

Albarracín, D., & Vargas, P. (2010). Attitudes and persuasion: From biology to social responses to persuasive intent. In S. T. Fiske, D. T. Gilbert, & G. Lindzey (Eds.), *The handbook of social psychology* (5th ed., Vol. 1, pp. 389–422). New York: Wiley.

Alcoholics Anonymous. (2016). Estimated worldwide A.A. individual and group membership. http://www.aa.org/assets/en_US/ smf-132_en.pdf. Accessed July 5, 2016.

Aleman, A., Sommer, I. E., & Kahn, R. S. (2007). Efficacy of slow repetitive transcranial magnetic stimulation in the treatment of resistant auditory hallucinations in schizophrenia: A meta-analysis. *Journal of Clinical Psychiatry, 68,* 416–421.

Alicke, M. D., Klotz, M. L., Breitenbecher, D. L., Yurak, T. J., & Vredenburg, D. S. (1995). Personal contact, individuation, and the better-than-average effect. *Journal of Personality and Social Psychology, 68,* 804–824.

Allen, J. G., Flanigan, S. S., LeBlanc, M., Vallarino, J., MacNaughton, P., Stewart, J. H., & Christiani, D. C. (2016). Flavoring chemicals in e-cigarettes: Diacetyl, 2,3-pentanedione, and acetoin in a sample of 51 products, including fruit-, candy-, and cocktail-flavored e-cigarettes. *Environmental Health Perspectives, 124*(6), 733–739.

Allen, P., Larøi, F., McGuire, P. K., & Aleman, A. (2008). The hallucinating brain: A review of structural and functional neuroimaging studies of hallucinations. *Neuroscience and Biobehavioral Reviews, 32,* 175–191.

Allison, D. B., Kaprio, J., Korkeila, M., Koskenvuo, M., Neale, M. C., & Hayakawa, K. (1996). The heritability of body mass index among an international sample of monozygotic twins reared apart. *International Journal of Obesity, 20*(6), 501–506.

Alloway, T. P., Gathercole, S. E., Kirkwood, H., & Elliott, J. (2009). The cognitive and behavioral characteristics of children with low working memory. *Child Development, 80,* 606–621.

Allport, G. W. (1937). *Personality: A psychological interpretation.* New York: Holt.

Allport, G. W. (1954). *The nature of prejudice.* Cambridge, MA: Addison-Wesley.

Allport, G. W., & Odbert, H. S. (1936). Trait-names: A psycholexical study. *Psychological Monographs, 47,* 592.

Alvarez, L. W. (1965). A pseudo experience in parapsychology. *Science, 148,* 1541.

Alvarez, L., & Eckholm, E. (2009, January 7). Purple heart is ruled out for traumatic stress. *New York Times.* http://www.nytimes.com/2009/01/08/us/08purple.html

American Psychological Association. (2002). *Ethical principles of psychologists and code of conduct.* Washington, DC: Author. Retrieved from apa.org/code/ethics/index.aspx [includes 2010 amendments].

American Psychological Association. (2005). *Resolution in favor of empirically supported sex education and HIV prevention programs for adolescents.* Washington, DC: Author.

American Psychological Association. (2009). *Report of the American Psychological Association task force on appropriate therapeutic responses to sexual orientation.* Washington, DC: Author.

Amos, N., & McCabe, M. P. (2015). Conceptualizing and measuring perceptions of sexual attractiveness: Are there differences across gender and sexual orientation? *Personality and Individual Differences, 76,* 111–122. doi: 10.1016/j.paid.2014.11.057

Anand, S., & Hotson, J. (2002). Transcranial magnetic stimulation: Neurophysiological applications and safety. *Brain and Cognition, 50,* 366–386.

Anderson, C. A. (1989). Temperature and aggression: Ubiquitous effects of heat on occurrence of human violence. *Psychological Bulletin, 106,* 74–96.

Anderson, C. A., Berkowitz, L., Donnerstein, E., Huesmann, L. R., Johnson, J. D., Linz, D., . . . Wartella, E. (2003). The influence of media violence on youth. *Psychological Science in the Public Interest, 4,* 81–110.

Anderson, C. A., Bushman, B. J., & Groom, R. W. (1997). Hot years and serious and deadly assault: Empirical tests of the heat hypothesis. *Journal of Personality and Social Psychology, 73,* 1213–1223.

Anderson, C. A., & Bushman, B. J. (2002). Human aggression. *Annual Review of Psychology, 53,* 27–51.

Anderson, C. A., Shibuya, A., Ihori, N., Swing, E. L., Bushman, B. J., Sakamoto, A., . . . Saleem, M. (2010). Violent video game effects on aggression, empathy, and prosocial behavior in Eastern and Western countries: A meta-analytic review. *Psychological Bulletin, 136*(2), 151–173. doi: 10.1037/a0018251

Anderson, J. R., & Schooler, L. J. (1991). Reflections of the environment in memory. *Psychological Science, 2,* 396–408.

Anderson, J. R., & Schooler, L. J. (2000). The adaptive nature of memory. In E. Tulving & F. I. M. Craik (Eds.), *Handbook of memory* (pp. 557–570). New York: Oxford University Press.

Anderson, M. C. (2003). Rethinking interference theory: Executive control and the mechanisms of forgetting. *Journal of Memory and Language, 49,* 415–445.

Anderson, M. C., Bjork, R. A., & Bjork, E. L. (1994). Remembering can cause forgetting: Retrieval dynamics in long-term memory. *Journal of Experimental Psychology: Learning, Memory, and Cognition, 20,* 1063–1087.

Anderson, M. C., Ochsner, K. N., Kuhl, B., Cooper, J., Robertson, E., Gabrieli, S. W., . . . Gabrieli, J. D. E. (2004). Neural systems underlying the suppression of unwanted memories. *Science, 303,* 232–235.

Anderson, M. L. (2008). Multiple inference and gender differences in the effects of early intervention: A reevaluation of the Abecedarian, Perry Preschool, and Early Training Projects. *Journal of the American Statistical Association, 103*(484), 1481–1495. doi: 10.1198/016214508000000841

Anderson, R. C., Pichert, J. W., Goetz, E. T., Schallert, D. L., Stevens, K. V., & Trollip, S. R. (1976). Instantiation of general terms. *Journal of Verbal Learning and Verbal Behavior, 15,* 667–679.

Andreasen, N. C. (2011). A journey into chaos: Creativity and the unconscious. *Mens Sana Monographs, 9,* 42–53.

Andrewes, D. (2001). *Neuropsychology: From theory to practice.* Hove, England: Psychology Press.

Andrews-Hanna, J. R. (2012). The brain's default network and its adaptive role in internal mentation. *Neuroscientist, 18,* 251–270.

Andrews, I. (1982). Bilinguals out of focus: A critical discussion. *International Review of Applied Linguistics in Language Teaching, 20,* 297–305.

Annis, L. F., & Annis, D. B. (1982). A normative study of students' reported preferred study techniques. *Literacy Research and Instruction, 21,* 201–207.

Ansfield, M., Wegner, D. M., & Bowser, R. (1996). Ironic effects of sleep urgency. *Behavior Research and Therapy, 34,* 523–531.

Ansuini, C. G., Fiddler-Woite, J., & Woite, R. S. (1996). The source, accuracy, and impact of initial sexuality information on lifetime wellness. *Adolescence, 31,* 283–289.

Antoni, M. H., Lehman, J. M., Klibourn, K. M., Boyers, A. E., Culver, J. L., Alferi, S. M., . . . Carver, C. S. (2001). Cognitive-behavioral stress management intervention decreases the prevalence of depression and enhances benefit finding among women under treatment for early-stage breast cancer. *Health Psychology, 20,* 20–32.

Apicella, C. L., Feinberg, D. R., & Marlowe, F. W. (2007). Voice pitch predicts reproductive success in male hunter-gatherers. *Biology Letters, 3*(6), 682–684. doi:10.1098/rsbl.2007.0410

Apperly, I. A., & Butterfill, S. A. (2009). Do humans have two systems to track beliefs and belief-like states? *Psychological Review, 116,* 953–970.

Arden, R., & Adams, M. J. (2016). A general intelligence factor in dogs. *Intelligence, 55,* 79–85. doi: 10.1016/j.intell.2016.01.008

Arellano, D., Varona, J., & Perales, F. (2008). Generation and visualization of emotional states in virtual characters. *Computer Animation and Virtual Worlds, 19*(3–4), 259–270.

Aristotle. (1998). *The Nichomachean ethics* (D. W. Ross, Trans.). Oxford, England: Oxford University Press. (Original work circa 350 BCE)

Armstrong, D. M. (1980). *The nature of mind.* Ithaca, NY: Cornell University Press.

Arnold, M. B. (Ed.). (1960). *Emotion and personality: Psychological aspects* (Vol. 1). New York: Columbia University Press.

Arnold, S. E., Trojanowski, J. Q., Gur, R. E., Blackwell, P., Han, L., & Choi, C. (1998). Absence of neurodegeneration and neural injury in the cerebral cortex in a sample of elderly patients with schizophrenia. *Archives of General Psychiatry, 55*, 225–232.

Aron, A., Fisher, H., Mashek, D., Strong, G., Li, H., & Brown, L. (2005). Reward, motivation, and emotion systems associated with early-stage intense romantic love. *Journal of Neurophysiology, 93*, 327–337.

Aronson, E. (1963). Effect of the severity of threat on the devaluation of forbidden behavior. *Journal of Abnormal and Social Psychology, 66*, 584–588.

Aronson, E. (1969). The theory of cognitive dissonance: A current perspective. In L. Berkowitz (Ed.), *Advances in experimental social psychology* (Vol. 4, pp. 1–34): Academic Press.

Aronson, E., & Mills, J. (1958). The effect of severity of initiation on liking for a group. *Journal of Abnormal and Social Psychology, 59*, 177–181.

Aronson, E., & Worchel, P. (1966). Similarity versus liking as determinants of interpersonal attractiveness. *Psychonomic Science, 5*, 157–158.

Aronson, E., Willerman, B., & Floyd, J. (1966). The effect of a pratfall on increasing interpersonal attractiveness. *Psychonomic Science, 4*, 227–228.

Aronson, J., & Steele, C. M. (2004). Stereotypes and the fragility of academic competence, motivation, and self-concept. In A. J. Elliot & C. S. Dweck (Eds.), *Handbook of competence and motivation* (pp. 436–456). New York: Guilford Press.

Asch, S. E. (1946). Forming impressions of personality. *Journal of Abnormal and Social Psychology, 41*, 258–290.

Asch, S. E. (1951). Effects of group pressure on the modification and distortion of judgments. In H. Guetzkow (Ed.), *Groups, leadership, and men* (pp. 177–190). Pittsburgh, PA: Carnegie Press.

Asch, S. E. (1955). Opinions and social pressure. *Scientific American, 193*, 31–35.

Asch, S. E. (1956). Studies of independence and conformity: 1. A minority of one against a unanimous majority. *Psychological Monographs: General and Applied, 70*, 1–70.

Aschoff, J. (1965). Circadian rhythms in man. *Science, 148*, 1427–1432.

Aserinsky, E., & Kleitman, N. (1953). Regularly occurring periods of eye motility, and concomitant phenomena, during sleep. *Science, 118*, 273–274.

Ashby, F. G., & Ell, S. W. (2001). The neurobiology of human category learning. *Trends in Cognitive Sciences, 5*, 204–210.

Ashby, F. G., & O'Brien, J. B. (2005). Category learning and multiple memory systems. *Trends in Cognitive Sciences, 9*, 83–89.

Ashcraft, M. H. (1998). *Fundamentals of cognition.* New York: Longman.

Associated Press. (2007). Former stripper guilty of posing as psychologist. *Boston Herald.* Retrieved from http://www.bostonherald.com.

Astington, J. W., & Baird, J. (2005). *Why language matters for theory of mind.* Oxford, England: Oxford University Press.

Atance, C. M., Bélanger, M., & Meltzoff, A. N. (2010). Preschoolers' understanding of others' desires: Fulfilling mine enhances my understanding of yours. *Developmental Psychology, 46*(6), 1505–1513. doi:10.1037/a0020374

Atkinson, R. C., & Shiffrin, R. M. (1968). Human memory: A proposed system and its control processes. In K. W. Spence & J. T. Spence (Eds.), *The psychology of learning and motivation* (Volume 2, pp. 89–195). New York: Academic Press.

Au, J., Sheehan, E., Tsai, N., Duncan, G. J., Buschkuehl, M., & Jaeggi, S. (2015). Improving fluid intelligence with training on working memory: A meta-analysis. *Psychonomic Bulletin & Review, 22*, 366–377.

Aviezer, H., Hassin, R. R., Ryan, J., Grady, C., Susskind, J., Anderson, A., . . . Bentin, S. (2008). Angry, disgusted, or afraid? Studies on the malleability of emotion perception. *Psychological Science, 19*, 724–732.

Avolio, B. J., & Waldman, D. A. (1994). Variations in cognitive, perceptual, and psychomotor abilities across the working life span: Examining the effects of race, sex, experience, education, and occupational type. *Psychology and Aging, 9*, 430–442.

Axelrod, R. (1984). *The evolution of cooperation.* New York: Basic Books.

Axelrod, R., & Hamilton, W. D. (1981). The evolution of cooperation. *Science, 211*, 1390–1396.

Ayduk, O., Shoda, Y., Cervone, D., & Downey, G. (2007). Delay of gratification in children: Contributions to social-personality psychology. In G. Downey, Y. Shoda, & C. Cervone (Eds.), *Persons in context: Building a science of the individual* (pp. 97–109). New York: Guilford Press.

Ayres, C. E. (1921). Instinct and capacity. 1. The instinct of belief-in-instincts. *Journal of Philosophy, 18*, 561–565.

Azuma, H., & Kashiwagi, K. (1987). Descriptors for an intelligent person: A Japanese study. *Japanese Psychological Research, 29*, 17–26.

Baars, B. J. (1986). *The cognitive revolution in psychology.* New York: Guilford Press.

Baca-Motes, K., Brown, A., Gneezy, A., Keenan, E. A., & Nelson, L. D. (2013). Commitment and behavior change: Evidence from the field. *Journal of Consumer Research, 39*(5), 1070–1084. doi:10.1086/667226

Back, M. D., Schmukle, S. C., & Egloff, B. (2008). Becoming friends by chance. *Psychological Science, 19*, 439–440.

Backman, C. W., & Secord, P. F. (1959). The effect of perceived liking on interpersonal attraction. *Human Relations, 12*, 379–384.

Bäckman, L., & Dixon, R. A. (1992). Psychological compensation: A theoretical framework. *Psychological Bulletin, 112*, 259–283.

Baddeley, A. D. (2001). Is working memory still working? *American Psychologist, 56*, 851–864.

Baddeley, A. D. (2012). Working memory: Theories, models, and controversies. *Annual Review of Psychology, 63*, 1–29.

Baddeley, A. D., Allen, R. J., & Hitch, G. J. (2011). Binding in visual working memory: The role of the episodic buffer. *Neuropsychologia, 49*, 1393–1400.

Baddeley, A. D., & Hitch, G. J. (1974). Working memory. In S. Dornic (Ed.), *Attention and performance* (Vol. 6, pp. 647–667). Hillsdale, NJ: Erlbaum.

Bagby, R. M., Levitan, R. D., Kennedy, S. H., Levitt, A. J., & Joffe, R. T. (1999). Selective alteration of personality in response to noradrenergic and serotonergic antidepressant medication in depressed sample: Evidence of non-specificity. *Psychiatry Research, 86*, 211–216.

Bahrick, H. P. (1984). Semantic memory content in permastore: 50 years of memory for Spanish learned in school. *Journal of Experimental Psychology: General, 113,* 1–29.

Bahrick, H. P. (2000). Long-term maintenance of knowledge. In E. Tulving & F. I. M. Craik (Eds.), *The Oxford handbook of memory* (pp. 347–362). New York: Oxford University Press.

Bahrick, H. P., Hall, L. K., & Berger, S. A. (1996). Accuracy and distortion in memory for high school grades. *Psychological Science, 7,* 265–271.

Bahrick, H. P., Hall, L. K., & DaCosta, L. A. (2008). Fifty years of college grades: Accuracy and distortions. *Emotion, 8,* 13–22.

Bailey, J. M., & Pillard, R. C. (1991). A genetic study of male sexual orientation. *Archives of General Psychiatry, 48,* 1089–1096.

Bailey, J. M., Pillard, R. C., Neale, M. C., & Agyes, Y. (1993). Heritable factors influence sexual orientation in women. *Archives of General Psychiatry, 50,* 217–223.

Bailey, J. M., Vasey, P. L., Diamond, L. M., Breedlove, S. M., Vilain, E., & Epprecht, M. (2016). Sexual orientation, controversy, and science. *Psychological Science in the Public Interest, 17*(2), 45–101. doi: 10.1177/1529100616637616

Bailey, J. M., & Zucker, K. J. (1995). Childhood sex-typed behavior and sexual orientation: A conceptual analysis and quantitative review. *Developmental Psychology, 31,* 43–55.

Baillargeon, R., Scott, R. M., & He, Z. (2010). False-belief understanding in infants. *Trends in Cognitive Sciences, 14*(3), 110–118.

Baillargeon, R., Spelke, E. S., & Wasserman, S. (1985). Object permanence in 5-month-old infants. *Cognition, 20,* 191–208.

Baker, D. P., Eslinger, P. J., Benavides, M., Peters, E., Dieckmann, N. F., & Leon, J. (2015). The cognitive impact of the education revolution: A possible cause of the Flynn Effect on population IQ. *Intelligence, 49,* 144–158. doi: 10.1016/j.intell.2015.01.003

Baker, E., Shelton, K. H., Baibazarova, E., Hay, D. F., & van Goozen, S. H. M. (2013). Low skin conductance activity in infancy predicts aggression in toddlers 2 years later. *Psychological Science, 24*(6), 1051–1056. doi:10.1177/0956797612465198

Baker, P. (2015, June 10). Michelle Obama talks about race and success, and makes it personal. *New York Times.* http://www.nytimes.com/2015/06/11/us/michelle-obama-king-college-prep-and-tuskegee-graduation-speeches.html

Baker, T. B., Brandon, T. H., & Chassin, L. (2004). Motivational influences on cigarette smoking. *Annual Review of Psychology, 55,* 463–491.

Baker, T. B., McFall, R. M., & Shoham, V. (2009). Current status and future prospects of clinical psychology: Toward a scientifically principled approach to mental and behavioral health care. *Psychological Science in the Public Interest, 9,* 67–103.

Baldwin, M. W., Carrell, S. E., & Lopez, D. F. (1989). Priming relationship schemas: My advisor and the pope are watching me from the back of my mind. *Journal of Experimental Social Psychology, 26,* 435–454.

Baler, R. D., & Volkow, N. D. (2006). Drug addiction: The neurobiology of disrupted self-control. *Trends in Molecular Medicine, 12,* 559–566.

Baltes, P. B., & Reinert, G. (1969). Cohort effects in cognitive development of children as revealed by cross-sectional sequences. *Developmental Psychology, 1,* 169–177.

Banaji, M. R., & Heiphetz, L. (2010). Attitudes. In S. T. Fiske, D. T. Gilbert, & G. Lindzey (Eds.), *The handbook of social psychology* (5th ed., Vol. 1, pp. 348–388). New York: Wiley.

Bandura, A. (1965). Influence of models' reinforcement contingencies on the acquisition of imitative responses. *Journal of Social and Personality Psychology, 1,* 589–595.

Bandura, A. (1977). *Social learning theory.* Englewood Cliffs, NJ: Prentice Hall.

Bandura, A. (1986). *Social foundations of thought and action: A social cognitive theory.* Englewood Cliffs, NJ: Prentice Hall.

Bandura, A. (1994). Social cognitive theory of mass communication. In J. Bryant & D. Zillmann (Eds.), *Media effects: Advances in theory and research* (pp. 61–90). Hillsdale, NJ: Erlbaum.

Bandura, A., Ross, D., & Ross, S. (1961). Transmission of aggression through imitation of adult models. *Journal of Abnormal and Social Psychology, 63,* 575–582.

Bandura, A., Ross, D., & Ross, S. (1963). Vicarious reinforcement and imitative learning. *Journal of Abnormal and Social Psychology, 67,* 601–607.

Banks, M. S., & Salapatek, P. (1983). Infant visual perception. In M. Haith & J. Campos (Eds.), *Handbook of child psychology: Biology and infancy* (pp. 435–572). New York: Wiley.

Banse, R., & Scherer, K. R. (1996). Acoustic profiles in vocal emotion expression. *Journal of Personality and Social Psychology, 70,* 614–636.

Barber, J. P., Muran, J. C., McCarthy, K. S., & Keefe, J. R. (2013). Research on dynamic therapies. In M. Lambert (Ed.), *Bergin and Garfield's handbook of psychotherapy and behavior change* (6th ed., pp. 443–494). Hoboken, NJ: Wiley.

Barber, S. J., Harris, C. B., & Rajaram, S. (2015). Why two heads apart are better than two heads together: Multiple mechanisms underlie the collaborative inhibition effect in memory. *Journal of Experimental Psychology: Learning, Memory, and Cognition, 41,* 559–566.

Barber, S. J., Rajaram, S., & Fox, E. B. (2012). Learning and remembering with others: The key role of retrieval in shaping group recall and collective memory. *Social Cognition, 30,* 121–132.

Bard, P. (1934). On emotional experience after decortication with some remarks on theoretical views. *Psychological Review, 41,* 309–329.

Bargh, J. A., & Chartrand, T. L. (1999). The unbearable automaticity of being. *American Psychologist, 54,* 462–479.

Bargh, J. A., Chen, M., & Burrows, L. (1996). The automaticity of social behavior: Direct effects of trait concept and stereotype activation on action. *Journal of Personality and Social Psychology, 71,* 230–244.

Bargh, J. A., Gollwitzer, P. M., Lee-Chai, A., Barndollar, K., & Trötschel, R. (2001). The automated will: Nonconscious activation and pursuit of behavioral goals. *Journal of Personality and Social Psychology, 81,* 1014–1027.

Bargh, J. A., Gollwitzer, P. M., & Oettingen, G. (2010). Motivation. In S. T. Fiske, D. T. Gilbert, & G. Lindzey (Eds.), *The handbook of social psychology* (5th ed., Vol. 1, pp. 263–311). New York: Wiley.

Bargh, J. A., & Morsella, E. (2008). The unconscious mind. *Perspectives on Psychological Science, 3,* 73–89.

Barker, A. T., Jalinous, R., & Freeston, I. L. (1985). Noninvasive magnetic stimulation of the human motor cortex. *Lancet, 2,* 1106–1107.

Barkow, J. (1980). Prestige and self-esteem: A biosocial interpretation. In D. R. Omark, F. F. Stayer, & D. G. Freedman (Eds.), *Dominance relations* (pp. 319–322). New York: Garland.

Barlow, D. H., Bullis, J. R., Comer, J. S., & Ametaj, A. A. (2013). Evidence-based psychological treatments: An update and a way forward. *Annual Review of Clinical Psychology, 9,* 1–27.

Barlow, D. H., Gorman, J. M., Shear, M. K., & Woods, S. W. (2000). Cognitive-behavioral therapy, imipramine, or their combination for panic disorder: A randomized controlled trial. *Journal of the American Medical Association, 283*(19), 2529–2536.

Barnier, A. J., Levin, K., & Maher, A. (2004). Suppressing thoughts of past events: Are repressive copers good suppressors? *Cognition and Emotion, 18,* 457–477.

Baron-Cohen, S. (1991). Do people with autism understand what causes emotion? *Child Development, 62,* 385–395.

Baron-Cohen, S., & Belmonte, M. K. (2005). Autism: A window onto the development of the social and analytic brain. *Annual Review of Neuroscience, 28,* 109–126.

Baron-Cohen, S., Leslie, A., & Frith, U. (1985). Does the autistic child have a "theory of mind"? *Cognition, 21,* 37–46.

Barondes, S. (2003). *Better than Prozac.* New York: Oxford University Press.

Barrett, L. F., Mesquita, B., & Gendron, M. (2011). Context in emotion perception. *Current Directions in Psychological Science, 20*(5), 286–290. doi: 10.1177/0963721411422522

Barrientos, R. M., Watkins, L. R., Rudy, J. W., & Maier, S. F. (2009). Characterization of the sickness response in young and aging rats following *E. coli* infection. *Brain, Behavior, and Immunity, 23,* 450–454.

Bartal, I. B.-A., Decety, J., & Mason, P. (2011). Empathy and pro-social behavior in rats. *Science, 334*(6061), 1427–1430.

Bartlett, F. C. (1932). *Remembering: A study in experimental and social psychology.* Cambridge, England: Cambridge University Press.

Bartol, C. R., & Costello, N. (1976). Extraversion as a function of temporal duration of electric shock: An exploratory study. *Perceptual and Motor Skills, 42,* 1174.

Bartoshuk, L. M. (2000). Comparing sensory experiences across individuals: Recent psychophysical advances illuminate genetic variation in taste perception. *Chemical Senses, 25,* 447–460.

Bartoshuk, L. M., & Beauchamp, G. K. (1994). Chemical senses. *Annual Review of Psychology, 45,* 419–445.

Basden, B. H., Basden, D. R., Bryner, S., & Thomas, R. L. (1997). A comparison of group and individual remembering: Does collaboration disrupt retrieval strategies? *Journal of Experimental Psychology: Learning, Memory, and Cognition, 23,* 1176–1191.

Basile, K. C., Chen, J., Black, M. C., & Saltzman, L. E. (2007). Prevalence and characteristics of sexual violence victimization among U.S. adults, 2001–2003. *Violence and Victims, 22*(4), 437–448.

Bass, C. & Halligan, P. (2014) Factitious disorders and malingering: Challenges for clinical assessment and management. *Lancet, 383,* 1422–1432.

Bates, E., & Goodman, J. C. (1997). On the inseparability of grammar and the lexicon: Evidence from acquisition, aphasia, and real-time processing. *Language and Cognitive Processes, 12,* 507–584.

Bates, T. C., Hansell, N. K., Martin, N. G., & Wright, M. J. (2016). When does socioeconomic status (SES) moderate the heritability of IQ? No evidence for g × SES interaction for IQ in a representative sample of 1176 Australian adolescent twin pairs. *Intelligence, 56,* 10–15. doi: 10.1016/j.intell.2016.02.003

Bateson, M., Nettle, D., & Roberts, G. (2006). Cues of being watched enhance cooperation in a real-world setting. *Biology Letters, 2*(3), 412–414.

Batson, C. D. (2002). Addressing the altruism question experimentally. In S. G. Post & L. G. Underwood (Eds.), *Altruism & altruistic love: Science, philosophy, & religion in dialogue* (pp. 89–105). London: Oxford University Press.

Batty, G. D., Deary, I. J., Schoon, I., & Gale, C. R. (2007). Mental ability across childhood in relation to risk factors for premature mortality in adult life: The 1970 British Cohort Study. *Journal of Epidemiology & Community Health, 61*(11), 997–1003. doi:10.1136/jech.2006.054494

Baumeister, R. F. (2000). Gender differences in erotic plasticity: The female sex drive as socially flexible and responsive. *Psychological Bulletin, 126,* 347–374.

Baumeister, R. F., Ainsworth, S. E., & Vohs, K. D. (2015). Are groups more or less than the sum of their members? The moderating role of individual identification. *Behavioral and Brain Sciences,* 1–38. doi: 10.1017/S0140525X15000618

Baumeister, R. F., Bratslavsky, E., Muraven, M., & Tice, D. M. (1998). Ego depletion: Is the active self a limited resource? *Journal of Personality and Social Psychology, 74,* 1252–1265.

Baumeister, R. F., Campbell, J. D., Krueger, J. I., & Vohs, K. D. (2003). Does high self-esteem cause better performance, interpersonal success, happiness, or healthier lifestyles? *Psychological Science in the Public Interest, 4,* 1–44.

Baumeister, R. F., Cantanese, K. R., & Vohs, K. D. (2001). Is there a gender difference in strength of sex drive? Theoretical views, conceptual distinctions, and a review of relevant evidence. *Personality and Social Psychology Review, 5,* 242–273.

Baumeister, R. F., & Leary, M. R. (1995). The need to belong: Desire for interpersonal attachments as a fundamental human motivation. *Psychological Bulletin, 117,* 497–529.

Baumeister, R. F., Smart, L., & Boden, J. M. (1996). Relation of threatened egotism to violence and aggression: The dark side of high self-esteem. *Psychological Review, 103,* 5–33.

Baumeister, R. F., Vohs, K. D., & Tice, D. M. (2007). The strength model of self-control. *Current Directions in Psychological Science, 16,* 351–355.

Baxter, L. R., Schwartz, J. M., Bergman, K. S., Szuba, M. P., Guze, B. H., Mazziotta, J. C., Alazraki, A., . . . Munford, P. (1992). Caudate glucose metabolic rate changes with both drug behavior therapy for obsessive-compulsive disorder. *Archives of General Psychiatry, 49,* 681–689.

Bayley, P. J., Frascino, J. C., & Squire, L. R. (2005). Robust habit learning in the absence of awareness and independent of the medial temporal lobe. *Nature, 436,* 550–553.

Bayley, P. J., Gold, J. J., Hopkins, R. O., & Squire, L. R. (2005). The neuroanatomy of remote memory. *Neuron, 46,* 799–810.

Beaty, R. E., Benedek, M., Silvia, P. J., & Schacter, D. L. (2016). Creative cognition and brain network dynamics. *Trends in Cognitive Sciences, 20,* 87–95.

Bechara, A., Damasio, A. R., Damasio, H., & Anderson, S. W. (1994). Insensitivity to future consequences following damage to human prefrontal cortex. *Cognition, 50,* 7–15.

Bechara, A., Damasio, H., Tranel, D., & Damasio, A. R. (1997). Deciding advantageously before knowing the advantageous strategy. *Science, 275,* 1293–1295.

Bechara, A., Dolan, S., Denburg, N., Hindes, A., & Anderson, S. W. (2001). Decision-making deficits, linked to a dysfunctional ventromedial prefrontal cortex, revealed in alcohol and stimulant abusers. *Neuropsychologia, 39,* 376–389.

Bechara, A., Tranel, D., & Damasio, H. (2000). Characterization of the decision-making deficit of patients with ventromedial prefrontal cortex lesions. *Brain, 123,* 2189–2202.

Beck, A. T. (1967). *Depression: Causes and treatment.* Philadelphia: University of Pennsylvania Press.

Beck, A. T. (2005). The current state of cognitive therapy: A 40-year retrospective. *Archives of General Psychiatry, 62,* 953–959.

Beckers, G., & Zeki, S. (1995). The consequences of inactivating areas V1 and V5 on visual motion perception. *Brain, 118,* 49–60.

Bedny, M., & Saxe, R. (2012). Insights into the origins of knowledge from the cognitive neuroscience of blindness. *Cognitive Neuropsychology, 29,* 56–84.

Beek, M. R., Levin, D. T., & Angelone, B. (2007). Change blindness: Beliefs about the roles of intention and scene complexity in change detection. *Consciousness and Cognition, 16,* 31–51.

Beesdo, K., Pine, D. S., Lieb, R., & Wittchen, H. U. (2010). Incidence and risk patterns of anxiety and depressive disorders and categorization of generalized anxiety disorder. *Archives of General Psychiatry, 67,* 47–57.

Békésy, G. von. (1960). *Experiments in hearing.* New York: McGraw-Hill.

Bell, A. P., Weinberg, M. S., & Hammersmith, S. K. (1981). *Sexual preference: Its development in men and women.* Bloomington: Indiana University Press.

Bell, R., Roer, J. P., & Buchner, A. (2015). Adaptive memory: Thinking about function. *Journal of Experimental Psychology: Learning, Memory, & Cognition, 41,* 1038–1048.

Belluck, P., & Carey, B. (2013, May 7). Psychiatry's guide is out of touch with science, experts say. *New York Times.* Retrieved from http://www.nytimes.com/2013/05/07/psychiatrys-new-guide-falls-short-experts-say.html

Belsky, J. (2012). The development of human reproductive strategies: Progress and prospects. *Current Directions in Psychological Science, 21*(5), 310–316. doi:10.1177/0963721412453588

Belsky, J., Ruttle, P. L., Boyce, W. T., Armstrong, J. M., & Essex, M. J. (2015). Early adversity, elevated stress physiology, accelerated sexual maturation, and poor health in females. *Developmental Psychology, 51*(6), 816–822. doi: 10.1037/dev0000017

Belsky, J., Spritz, B., & Crnic, K. (1996). Infant attachment security and affective-cognitive information processing at age 3. *Psychological Science, 7,* 111–114.

Bem, S. L. (1974). The measure of psychological androgyny. *Journal of Consulting and Clinical Psychology, 42,* 155–162.

Ben-Porath, Y. S., & Tellegen, A. (2008). *Minnesota Multiphasic Personality Inventory–2–Restructured Form: Manual for administration, scoring, and interpretation.* Minneapolis: University of Minnesota Press.

Benedek, M., Jauk, E., Fink, A., Koschutnig, K., Reishofer, G., Ebner, F., & Neubauer, A. C. (2014). To create or to recall? Neural mechanisms underlying the generation of creative new ideas. *NeuroImage, 88,* 125–133.

Benedetti, F., Maggi, G., & Lopiano, L. (2003). Open versus hidden medical treatment: The patient's knowledge about a therapy affects the therapy outcome. *Prevention & Treatment, 6,* Article 1. Retrieved from http://content.apa.org/psycarticles/ 2003-07872-001

Benedetti, F., Pollo, A., Lopiano, L., Lanotte, M., Vighetti, S., & Rainero, I. (2003). Conscious expectation and unconscious conditioning in analgesic, motor, and hormonal placebo/nocebo responses. *Journal of Neuroscience, 23,* 4315–4323.

Benenson, J. F., Markovits, H., Thompson, M. E., & Wrangham, R. W. (2011). Under threat of social exclusion, females exclude more than males. *Psychological Science, 22*(4), 538–544. doi: 10.1177/0956797611402511

Bennett, I. J., Romano, J. C., Howard, J. H., & Howard, D. V. (2008). Two forms of implicit learning in young adults with dyslexia. *Annals of the New York Academy of Sciences, 1145,* 184–198.

Benoit, R. G., & Anderson, M. C. (2012). Opposing mechanisms support the voluntary forgetting of unwanted memories. *Neuron, 76,* 450–460.

Benoit, S. C., Kemp, C. J., Elias, C. F., Abplanalp, W., Herman, J. P., Migrenne, S., . . . Clegg, D. J. (2009). Palmitic acid mediates hypothalamic insulin resistance by altering PKC-theta subcellular localization in rodents. *Journal of Clinical Investigation, 119*(9), 2577–2589.

Benson, H. (Ed.). (1990). *The relaxation response.* New York: Harper Torch.

Benson, H., Dusek, J. A., Sherwood, J. B., Lam, P., Bethea, C. F., Carpenter, W., . . . Hibberd, P. L. (2006). Study of the therapeutic effects of intercessory prayer (STEP) in cardiac bypass patients: A multicenter randomized trial of uncertainty and certainty of receiving intercessory prayer. *American Heart Journal, 151,* 934–942.

Bentz, D. & Schiller, D. (2015). Threat processing: Models and mechanisms. *WIREs Cognitive Science, 6,* 427–439.

Berger, H. (1929). Über das Elektrenkephalogramm des Menschen [Electroencephalogram of man]. *Archiv für Psychiatrie und Nervenkrankheiten, 87,* 527–570.

Berglund, H., Lindstrom, P., & Savic, I. (2006). Brain response to putative pheromones in lesbian women. *Proceedings of the National Academy of Sciences, USA, 103,* 8269–8274.

Bering, J. (2004). A critical review of the "enculturation hypothesis": The effects of human rearing on great ape social cognition. *Animal Cognition, 7,* 201–212.

Berkowitz, L. (1990). On the formation and regulation of anger and aggression: A cognitive-neoassociationistic analysis. *American Psychologist, 45,* 494–503.

Bernard, L. L. (1924). *Instinct: A study in social psychology.* New York: Holt.

Bernier, A., Beauchamp, M. H., Carlson, S. M., & Lalonde, G. (2015). A secure base from which to regulate: Attachment security in toddlerhood as a predictor of executive functioning at school entry. *Developmental Psychology, 51*(9), 1177–1189. doi: 10.1037/ dev0000032

Berridge, K. C. (2007). The debate over dopamine's role in reward: The case for incentive salience. *Psychopharmacology, 191,* 391–431.

Berry, D. S., & McArthur, L. Z. (1985). Some components and consequences of a babyface. *Journal of Personality and Social Psychology, 48,* 312–323.

Berry, J. W., Poortinga, Y. H., Segall, M. H., & Dasen, P. R. (1992). *Cross-cultural psychology: Research and applications.* New York: Cambridge University Press.

Berscheid, E., Dion, K., Walster, E., & Walster, G. W. (1971). Physical attractiveness and dating choice: A test of the matching hypothesis. *Journal of Experimental Social Psychology, 7*(2), 173–189.

Berscheid, E., & Reis, H. T. (1998). Interpersonal attraction and close relationships. In D. T. Gilbert, S. T. Fiske, & G. Lindzey (Eds.), *The handbook of social psychology* (4th ed., Vol. 2, pp. 193–281). New York: McGraw-Hill.

Bertelsen, B., Harvald, B., & Hauge, M. (1977). A Danish twin study of manic-depressive disorders. *British Journal of Psychiatry, 130,* 330–351.

Bertenthal, B. I., Rose, J. L., & Bai, D. L. (1997). Perception–action coupling in the development of visual control of posture. *Journal of Experimental Psychology: Human Perception & Performance, 23,* 1631–1643.

Berthoud, H.-R., & Morrison, C. (2008). The brain, appetite, and obesity. *Annual Review of Psychology, 59,* 55–92.

Best, J. B. (1992). *Cognitive psychology* (3rd ed.). New York: West Publishing.

Bettencourt, B. A., & Miller, N. (1996). Gender differences in aggression as a function of provocation: A meta-analysis. *Psychological Bulletin, 119,* 422–447.

Bhargava, S. (2011). Diagnosis and management of common sleep problems in children. *Pediatrics in Review, 32,* 91.

Bhattacharya, K., Ghosh, A., Monsivais, D., Dunbar, R. I. M., & Kaski, K. (2016). Sex differences in social focus across the life cycle in humans. *Royal Society Open Science, 3*(4).

Bialystok, E. (1999). Cognitive complexity and attentional control in the bilingual mind. *Child Development, 70,* 636–644.

Bialystok, E. (2009). Bilingualism: The good, the bad, and the indifference. *Bilingualism: Language and Cognitive Processes, 12,* 3–11.

Bialystok, E., Abutalebi, J., Bak, T. H., Burke, D. M., & Kroll, J. F. (2016). Aging in two languages: Implications for public health. *Ageing Research Reviews, 27,* 56–60.

Bialystok, E., Craik, F. I. M., & Luk, G. (2012). Bilingualism: Consequences for mind and brain. *Trends in Cognitive Sciences, 16,* 240–250.

Bickerton, D. (1990). *Language and species.* Chicago: University of Chicago Press.

Biederman, I. (1987). Recognition-by-components: A theory of human image understanding. *Psychological Review, 94,* 115–147.

Biederman, J., Faraone, S. V., Spencer, T. J., Mick, E., Monuteaux, M. C., & Aleardi, M. (2006). Functional impairments in adults with self-reports of diagnosed ADHD: A controlled study of 1001 adults in the community. *Journal of Clinical Psychiatry, 67,* 524–540.

Biederman, J., Monuteaux, M. C., Spencer, T., Wilens, T. E., & Faraone, S. V. (2009). Do stimulants protect against psychiatric disorders in youth with ADHD? A 10-year follow-up study. *Pediatrics, 124,* 71–78.

Bilalić, M., McLeod, P., & Gobet, F. (2008). Why good thoughts block better ones: The mechanisms of the pernicious Einstellung (set) effect. *Cognition, 108,* 652–661.

Billet, E., Richter, J., & Kennedy, J. (1998). Genetics of obsessive-compulsive disorder. In R. Swinson, M. Anthony, S. Rachman, & M. Richter (Eds.), *Obsessive-compulsive disorder: Theory, research, and treatment* (pp. 181–206). New York: Guilford Press.

Binet, A. (1905). New methods for the diagnosis of the intellectual level of subnormals. *L'Année psychologique, 12,* 191–244. Reprinted in A. Binet & T. Simon (1916). *The development of intelligence in children* (E. S. Kite, Trans.).Vineland, NJ: Publications of the Training School at Vineland.

Binet, A. (1909). *Les idées modernes sur les enfants* [Modern ideas about children]. Paris: Flammarion.

Binswanger, L. (1958). The existential analysis school of thought. In R. May (Ed.), *Existence: A new dimension in psychiatry and psychology* (pp. 191–213). New York: Basic Books.

Biro, S., Alink, L. R., van IJzendoorn, M. H., & Bakermans-Kranenburg, M. J. (2014). Infants' monitoring of social interactions: The effect of emotional cues. *Emotion, 14*(2), 263–271. doi: 10.1037/a0035589

Bjork, D. W. (1983). *The compromised scientist: William James in the development of American psychology.* New York: Columbia University Press.

Bjork, D. W. (1993). *B. F. Skinner: A life.* New York: Basic Books.

Bjork, E. L., & Bjork, R. A. (2011). Making things hard on yourself, but in a good way: Creating desirable difficulties to enhance learning. In M. A. Gernsbacher, R. W. Pewe, L. M. Hough, & J. R. Pomerantz (Eds.), *Psychology and the real world: Essays illustrating fundamental contributions to society* (pp. 56–64). New York: Worth Publishers.

Bjork, R. A. (1975). Retrieval as a memory modifier. In R. Solso (Ed.), Information processing and cognition: The Loyola Symposium (pp. 123–144). Hillsdale, NJ: Erlbaum.

Bjork, R. A. (2011). On the symbiosis of remembering, forgetting, and learning. In A. S. Benjamin (Ed.), *Successful remembering and successful forgetting: A festschrift in honor of Robert A. Bjork* (pp. 1–22). London: Psychology Press.

Bjork, R. A., & Bjork, E. L. (1988). On the adaptive aspects of retrieval failure in autobiographical memory. In M. M. Gruneberg, P. E. Morris, & R. N. Sykes (Eds.), *Practical aspects of memory: Current research and issues* (pp. 283–288). Chichester, UK: Wiley.

Bjork, R. A., Dunlosky, J., & Kornell, N. (2013). Self-regulated learning: Beliefs, techniques, and illusions. *Annual Review of Psychology, 64,* 417–444.

Blackburn, E. H., & Epel, E. S. (2012). Too toxic to ignore. *Nature, 490,* 169–171.

Blackburn, E. H., Epel, E. S., & Lin, J. (2015) Human telomere biology: A contributory and interactive factor in aging, disease risks, and protection. *Science, 350,* 1193–1198.

Blair, C. (2006). How similar are fluid cognition and general intelligence? A developmental neuroscience perspective on fluid cognition as an aspect of human cognitive ability. *Behavioral and Brain Sciences, 29*(2), 109–125 (article),125–160 (discussion). doi: 10.1017/S0140525X06009034

Blair, I. V. (2002). The malleability of automatic stereotypes and prejudice. *Personality and Social Psychology Review, 6,* 242–261.

Blair, J., Peschardt, K., & Mitchell, D. R. (2005). *Psychopath: Emotion and the brain.* Oxford: Blackwell.

Blascovich, J., & Tomaka, J. (1996). The biopsychosocial model of arousal regulation. In M. P. Zanna (Ed.), *Advances in experimental social psychology* (Vol. 28, pp. 1–51). San Diego, CA: Academic Press.

Blascovich, J., Mendes, W. B., Hunter, S. B., Lickel, B., & Kowai-Bell, N. (2001). Perceiver threat in social interactions with stigmatized others. *Journal of Personality and Social Psychology, 80,* 253–267.

Blasi, A. (1980). Bridging moral cognition and moral action: A critical review of the literature. *Psychological Bulletin, 88,* 1–45.

Blatt, S. J., & Homann, E. (1992). Parent–child interaction in the etiology of dependent and self-critical depression. *Clinical Psychology Review, 12,* 47–91.

Blesch, A., & Tuszynski, M. H. (2009). Spinal cord injury: Plasticity, regeneration and the challenge of translational drug development. *Trends in Neurosciences, 32,* 41–47.

Bliss, T. V. P. (1999). Young receptors make smart mice. *Nature, 401,* 25–27.

Bliss, T. V. P., & Lømo, W. T. (1973). Long-lasting potentiation of synaptic transmission in the dentate area of the anesthetized rabbit following stimulation of the perforant path. *Journal of Physiology, 232,* 331–356.

Bloch, C., Kaiser, A., Kuenzli, E., Zappatore, D., Haller, S., Franceschini, R., . . . Nitsch, C. (2009). The age of second language acquisition determines the variability in activation elicited by narration in three languages in Broca's and Wernicke's area. *Neuropsychologia, 47,* 625–633.

Bloch, L., Haase, C. M., & Levenson, R. W. (2014). Emotion regulation predicts marital satisfaction: More than a wives' tale. *Emotion, 14*(1), 130–144. doi: 10.1037/a0034272

Bloom, C. M., Venard, J., Harden, M., & Seetharaman, S. (2007). Non-contingent positive and negative reinforcement schedules of superstitious behaviors. *Behavioural Process, 75,* 8–13.

Blumen, H. M., & Rajaram, S. (2008). Influence of re-exposure and retrieval disruption during group collaboration on later individual recall. *Memory, 16,* 231–244.

Boden, J. M., Fergusson, D. M., & Horwood, L. J. (2010). Risk factors for conduct disorder and oppositional/defiant disorder: Evidence from a New Zealand birth cohort. *Journal of the American Academy of Child and Adolescent Psychiatry, 49,* 1125–1133.

Boecker, H., Sprenger, T., Spilker, M. E., Henriksen, G., Koppenhoefer, M., Wagner, K. J., . . . Tolle, T. R. (2008). The runner's high: Opioidergic mechanisms in the human brain. *Cerebral Cortex, 18,* 2523–2531.

Boehm, J. K., & Kubzansky, L. D. (2012). The heart's content: The association between positive psychological well-being and cardiovascular health. *Psychological Bulletin, 138,* 655–691.

Boehm, J. K., Williams, D. R., Rimm, E. B., Ryff, C., & Kubzansky, L. D. (2013). Relation between optimism and lipids in midlife. *American Journal of Cardiology, 111,* 1425–1431.

Boergers, J., Spirito, A., & Donaldson, D. (1998). Reasons for adolescent suicide attempts: Associations with psychological functioning. *Journal of the American Academy of Child and Adolescent Psychiatry, 37,* 1287–1293.

Boinski, S., Quatrone, R. P., & Swartz, H. (2000). Substrate and tool use by brown capuchins in Suriname: Ecological contexts and cognitive bases. *American Anthropologist, 102,* 741–761.

Boisvert, C. M., & Faust, D. (2002). Iatrogenic symptoms in psychotherapy: A theoretical exploration of the potential impact of labels, language, and belief systems. *American Journal of Psychotherapy, 56,* 244–259.

Bolger, N., Davis, A., & Rafaeli, E. (2003). Diary methods: Capturing life as it is lived. *Annual Review of Psychology, 54,* 579–616.

Bolton, G. E., & Ockenfels, A. (2000). ERC: A theory of equity, reciprocity, and competition. *American Economic Review, 90,* 166–193.

Boomsma, D., Busjahn, A., & Peltonen, L. (2002). Classical twin studies and beyond. *Nature Reviews Genetics, 3,* 872–882.

Bootzin, R. R., & Epstein, D. R. (2011). Understanding and treating insomnia. *Annual Review of Clinical Psychology, 7,* 435–458.

Bordone, V., Scherbov, S., & Steiber, N. (2015). Smarter every day: The deceleration of population ageing in terms of cognition. *Intelligence, 52,* 90–96. doi: 10.1016/j.intell.2015.07.005

Borghol, N., Suderman, M., McArdle, W., Racine, A., Hallett, M., Pembrey, M., . . . Szyf, M. (2012). Associations with early-life socioeconomic position in adult DNA methylation. *International Journal of Epidemiology, 41,* 62–74.

Borkenau, P., & Liebler, A. (1995). Observable attributes as manifestations and cues of personality and intelligence. *Journal of Personality, 63,* 1–25.

Borkevec, T. D. (1982). Insomnia. *Journal of Consulting and Clinical Psychology, 50,* 880–895.

Born, R. T., & Bradley, D. C. (2005). Structure and function of visual area MT. *Annual Review of Neuroscience, 28,* 157–189.

Börner, K., Klavans, R., Patek, M., Zoss, A. M., Biberstine, J. R., Light, R. P., . . . Boyack, K. W. (2012). Design and update of a classification system: The UCSD map of science. *PLoS ONE, 7,* e39464.

Bornstein, R. F. (1989). Exposure and affect: Overview and metaanalysis of research, 1968–1987. *Psychological Bulletin, 106,* 265–289.

Boroditsky, L. (2001). Does language shape thought? Mandarin and English speakers' conceptions of time. *Cognitive Psychology, 43,* 1–22.

Boroditsky, L., Fuhrman, O., & McCormick, K. (2011). Do English and Mandarin speakers think about time differently? *Cognition, 118,* 123–129.

Botwin, M. D., Buss, D. M., & Shackelford, T. K. (1997). Personality and mate preferences: Five factors in mate selection and marital satisfaction. *Journal of Personality, 65,* 107–136.

Bouchard, S. M., Brown, T. G., & Nadeau, L. (2012). Decision making capacities and affective reward anticipation in DWI recidivists compared to non-offenders: A preliminary study. *Accident Analysis and Prevention, 45,* 580–587.

Bouchard, T. J., & McGue, M. (2003). Genetic and environmental influences on human psychological differences. *Journal of Neurobiology, 54,* 4–45.

Bouton, M. E. (1988). Context and ambiguity in the extinction of emotional learning: Implications for exposure therapy. *Behaviour Research and Therapy, 26,* 137–149.

Bower, B. (1999, October 30). The mental butler did it—research suggests that subconscious affects behavior more than thought. *Science News, 156,* 208–282.

Bower, G. H. (1981). Mood and memory. *American Psychologist, 36,* 129–148.

Bower, G. H., Clark, M. C., Lesgold, A. M., & Winzenz, D. (1969). Hierarchical retrieval schemes in recall of categorical word lists. *Journal of Verbal Learning and Verbal Behavior, 8,* 323–343.

Bowers, K. S., Regehr, G., Balthazard, C., & Parker, D. (1990). Intuition in the context of discovery. *Cognitive Psychology, 22,* 72–110.

Bowlby, J. (1969). *Attachment and loss: Vol. 1. Attachment.* New York: Basic Books.

Bowlby, J. (1973). *Attachment and loss: Vol. 2. Separation.* New York: Basic Books.

Bowlby, J. (1980). *Attachment and loss: Vol. 3. Loss: Sadness and depression.* New York: Basic Books.

Boyack, K. W., Klavans, R., & Börner, K. (2005). Mapping the backbone of science. *Scientometrics, 64,* 351–374.

Boyd, R. (2008, February 7). Do people use only 10 percent of their brains? *Scientific American.* Retrieved from http://www.scientificamerican.com/article.cfm?id=people-only-use-10-percent-of-brain&page=2

Bozarth, M. A. (Ed.). (1987). *Methods of assessing the reinforcing properties of abused drugs.* New York: Springer-Verlag.

Bozarth, M. A., & Wise, R. A. (1985). Toxicity associated with longterm intravenous heroin and cocaine self-administration in the rat. *Journal of the American Medical Association, 254,* 81–83.

Brackett, M. A., & Mayer, J. D. (2003). Convergent, discriminant, and incremental validity of competing measures of emotional intelligence. *Personality and Social Psychology Bulletin, 29,* 1147.

Brackett, M. A., Rivers, S. E., Shiffman, S., Lerner, N., & Salovey, P. (2006). Relating emotional abilities to social functioning: A comparison of self-report and performance measures of emotional intelligence. *Journal of Personality and Social Psychology, 91,* 780.

Brackett, M. A., Warner, R. M., & Bosco, J. (2005). Emotional intelligence and relationship quality among couples. *Personal Relationships, 12*(2), 197–212.

Bradford, D., Stroup, S., & Lieberman, J. (2002). Pharmacological treatments for schizophrenia. In P. E. Nathan & J. M. Gorman (Eds.), *A guide to treatments that work* (2nd ed., pp. 169–199). New York: Oxford University Press.

Bradmetz, J., & Schneider, R. (2004). The role of the counterfactually satisfied desire in the lag between false-belief and false-emotion attributions in children aged 4–7. *British Journal of Developmental Psychology, 22,* 185–196.

Braet, W., & Humphreys, G. W. (2009). The role of reentrant processes in feature binding: Evidence from neuropsychology and TMS on late onset illusory conjunctions. *Visual Cognition, 17,* 25–47.

Brakefield, T. A., Mednick, S. C., Wilson, H. W., De Neve, J. E., Christakis, N. A., & Fowler, J. H. (2014). Same-sex sexual attraction does not spread in adolescent social networks. *Archives of Sexual Behavior, 43*(2), 335–344. doi: 10.1007/s10508-013-0142-9

Bramlett, M. D., & Mosher, W. D. (2002). *Cohabitation, marriage, divorce, and remarriage in the United States* (Vital and Health Statistics Series 23, No. 22). Hyattsville, MD: National Center for Health Statistics.

Brandt, K. R., Gardiner, J. M., Vargha-Khadem, F., Baddeley, A. D., & Mishkin, M. (2009). Impairment of recollection but not familiarity in a case of developmental amnesia. *Neurocase, 15,* 60–65.

Brant, A. M., Munakata, Y., Boomsma, D. I., Defries, J. C., Haworth, C. M. A., Keller, M. C., ... Hewitt, J. K. (2013). The nature and nurture of high IQ: An extended sensitive period for intellectual development. *Psychological Science, 24*(8), 1487–1495. doi: 10.1177/0956797612473119

Braun, A. R., Balkin, T. J., Wesensten, N. J., Gwadry, F., Carson, R. E., Varga, M., . . . Herskovitch, P. (1998). Dissociated pattern of activity in visual cortices and their projections during rapid eye movement sleep. *Science, 279,* 91–95.

Breazeal, C. (2009). Role of expressive behaviour for robots that learn from people. *Philosophical Transactions of the Royal Society, 364,* 3527–3538.

Breckler, S. J. (1994). Memory for the experiment of donating blood: Just how bad was it? *Basic and Applied Social Psychology, 15,* 467–488.

Brédart, S., & Valentine, T. (1998). Descriptiveness and proper name retrieval. *Memory, 6,* 199–206.

Bredy, T. W., Wu, H., Crego, C., Zellhoefer, J., Sun, Y. E., & Barad, M. (2007). Histone modifications around individual BDNF gene promoters in prefrontal cortex are associated with extinction of conditioned fear. *Learning and Memory, 14,* 268–276.

Breggin, P. R. (1990). Brain damage, dementia, and persistent cognitive dysfunction associated with neuroleptic drugs: Evidence, etiology, implications. *Journal of Mind and Behavior, 11,* 425–463.

Breggin, P. R. (2000). *Reclaiming our children.* Cambridge, MA: Perseus Books.

Brehm, S. S. (1992). *Intimate relationships* (2nd ed.). New York: McGraw-Hill.

Breland, K., & Breland, M. (1961). The misbehavior of organisms. *American Psychologist, 16,* 681–684.

Brennan, P. A., & Zufall, F. (2006). Pheromonal communication in vertebrates. *Nature, 444,* 308–315.

Brenninkmeijer, V., Vanyperen, N. W., & Buunk, B. P. (2001). I am not a better teacher, but others are doing worse: Burnout and perceptions of superiority among teachers. *Social Psychology of Education, 4*(3–4), 259–274.

Breslow, L., Pritchard, D. E., DeBoer, J., Stump, G. S., Ho, A. D., & Seaton, D. T. (2013). Studying learning in the worldwide classroom: Research into edX's first MOOC. *Research & Practice in Assessment, 8,* 13–25.

Brethel-Haurwitz, K. M., & Marsh, A. A. (2014). Geographical differences in subjective well-being predict extraordinary altruism. *Psychological Science, 25* (3), 762–771. doi: 10.1177/0956797613516148

Bretherton, I., & Munholland, K. A. (1999). Internal working models in attachment relationships: A construct revisited. In J. Cassidy & P. R. Shaver (Eds.), *Handbook of attachment: Theory, research and clinical applications* (pp. 89–114). New York: Guilford Press.

Brewer, J. A., Worhunsky, P. D., Gray, J. R., Tang, Y.-Y., Weber, J., & Kober, H. (2011). Meditation experience is associated with differences in default mode network activity and connectivity. *Proceedings of the National Academy of Sciences, 108,* 20254–20259.

Brewer, M. B. (1999). The psychology of prejudice: Ingroup love or outgroup hate? *Journal of Social Issues, 55*(3), 429–444. doi: 10.1111/0022-4537.00126

Brewer, W. F. (1996). What is recollective memory? In D. C. Rubin (Ed.), *Remembering our past: Studies in autobiographical memory* (pp. 19–66). New York: Cambridge University Press.

Briggs, J. (2000). Conflict management in a modern Inuit community. In P. P. Schweitzer, M. Biesele, & R. K. Hitchcock (Eds.), *Hunters and gatherers in the modern world: Conflict, resistance, and self-determination* (pp. 110–124). New York: Berghahn Books.

Broadbent, D. E. (1958). *Perception and communication.* London: Pergamon Press.

Broberg, D. J., & Bernstein, I. L. (1987). Candy as a scapegoat in the prevention of food aversions in children receiving chemotherapy. *Cancer, 60,* 2344–2347.

Broca, P. (1861). Remarques sur le siège de la faculté du langage articulé; suivies d'une observation d'aphémie (perte de la parole) [Remarks on the seat of the faculty of articulated language, following an observation of aphemia (loss of speech)]. *Bulletin de la Société Anatomique de Paris, 36,* 330–357.

Broca, P. (1863). Localisation des fonctions cérébrales: Siège du langage articulé [Localization of brain functions: Seat of the faculty of articulated language]. *Bulletin de la Société d'Anthropologie de Paris, 4,* 200–202.

Brock, A. (1993). Something old, something new: The "reappraisal" of Wilhelm Wundt in textbooks. *Theory & Psychology, 3*(2), 235–242.

Brody, N. (2003). Construct validation of the Sternberg Triarchic Abilities Test: Comment and reanalysis. *Intelligence, 31*(4), 319–329.

Brooks, D. (2012, May 3). The campus tsunami. *New York Times.* Retreived from http://www.nytimes.com/2012/05/04/opinion/brooks-the-campus-tsunami.html

Brooks, R., & Meltzoff, A. N. (2002). The importance of eyes: How infants interpret adult looking behavior. *Developmental Psychology, 38,* 958–966.

Brooks-Gunn, J., Graber, J. A., & Paikoff, R. L. (1994). Studying links between hormones and negative affect: Models and measures. *Journal of Research on Adolescence, 4,* 469–486.

Brosnan, S. F., & DeWaal, F. B. M. (2003). Monkeys reject unequal pay. *Nature, 425,* 297–299.

Brown, A. S. (2004). *The déjà vu experience.* New York: Psychology Press.

Brown, B. B., Mory, M., & Kinney, D. (1994). Casting crowds in a relational perspective: Caricature, channel, and context. In G. A. R. Montemayor & T. Gullotta (Eds.), *Advances in adolescent development: Personal relationships during adolescence* (Vol. 5, pp. 123–167). Newbury Park, CA: Sage.

Brown, J. D. (1993). Self-esteem and self-evaluation: Feeling is believing. In J. M. Suls (Ed.), *The self in social perspective: Psychological perspectives on the self* (Vol. 4, pp. 27–58). Hillsdale, NJ: Erlbaum.

Brown, J. D., & McGill, K. L. (1989). The cost of good fortune: When positive life events produce negative health consequences. *Journal of Personality and Social Psychology, 57,* 1103–1110.

Brown, L. E., Wilson, E. T., & Gribble, P. L. (2009). Repetitive transcranial magnetic stimulation to the primary cortex interferes with motor learning by observing. *Journal of Cognitive Neuroscience, 21,* 1013–1022.

Brown, P., Roediger, H. L. III, & McDaniel, M. A. (2014). *Make it stick: The science of successful learning.* Cambridge, MA: Harvard University Press.

Brown, R. (1958). *Words and things.* New York: Free Press.

Brown, R., & Hanlon, C. (1970). Derivational complexity and order of acquisition in child speech. In J. R. Hayes (Ed.), *Cognition and the development of language* (pp. 11–53). New York: Wiley.

Brown, R., & Kulik, J. (1977). Flashbulb memories. *Cognition, 5,* 73–99.

Brown, R., & McNeill, D. (1966). The "tip-of-the-tongue" phenomenon. *Journal of Verbal Learning and Verbal Behavior, 5,* 325–337.

Brown, R. P., Osterman, L. L., & Barnes, C. D. (2009). School violence and the culture of honor. *Psychological Science, 20*(11), 1400–1405.

Brown, S. C., & Craik, F. I. M. (2000). Encoding and retrieval of information. In E. Tulving & F. I. M. Craik (Eds.), *The Oxford handbook of memory* (pp. 93–107). New York: Oxford University Press.

Brown, T. A., & Barlow, D. H. (2002). Classification of anxiety and mood disorders. In D. H. Barlow (Ed.), *Anxiety and its disorders: The nature and treatment of anxiety and panic* (2nd ed.). New York: Guilford Press.

Brownell, K. D., Greenwood, M. R. C., Stellar, E., & Shrager, E. E. (1986). The effects of repeated cycles of weight loss and regain in rats. *Physiology and Behavior, 38,* 459–464.

Bruner, J. S. (1983). Education as social invention. *Journal of Social Issues, 39,* 129–141.

Brunet, A., Orr, S. P., Tremblay, J., Robertson, K., Nader, K., & Pitman, R. K. (2008). Effects of post-retrieval propranolol on psychophysiologic responding during subsequent script-driven traumatic imagery in posttraumatic stress disorder. *Journal of Psychiatric Research, 42,* 503–506.

Brunner, D. P., Dijk, D. J., Tobler, I., & Borbely, A. A. (1990). Effect of partial sleep deprivation on sleep stages and EEG power spectra. *Electroencephalography and Clinical Neurophysiology, 75,* 492–499.

Bryck, R. L., & Fisher, P. A. (2012). Training the brain: Practical applications of neural plasticity from the intersection of cognitive neuroscience, developmental psychology, and prevention science. *American Psychologist, 67,* 87–100.

Buchanan, C. M., Eccles, J. S., & Becker, J. B. (1992). Are adolescents the victims of raging hormones? Evidence for activational effects of hormones on moods and behavior at adolescence. *Psychological Bulletin, 111,* 62–107.

Buchanan, T. W. (2007). Retrieval of emotional memories. *Psychological Bulletin, 133,* 761–779.

Buck Louis, G. M., Gray, L. E., Marcus, M., Ojeda, S. R., Pescovitz, O. H., Witchel, S. F., . . . Euling, S. Y. (2008). Environmental factors and puberty timing: Expert panel research. *Pediatrics, 121*(Suppl. 3), S192–S207. doi: 10.1542/ peds1813E

Buckholtz, J. W., & Meyer-Lindenberg, A. (2012). Psychopathology and the human connectome: Toward a transdiagnostic model of risk for mental illness. *Neuron, 74,* 990–1003.

Buckley, C. (2007, January 3). Man is rescued by stranger on subway tracks. *New York Times.* http://www.nytimes.com/2007/01/03/ nyregion/03life.html

Buckner, R. L., Andrews-Hanna, J. R., & Schacter, D. L. (2008). The brain's default network: Anatomy, function, and relevance to disease. *Annals of the New York Academy of Sciences, 1124,* 1–38.

Buckner, R. L., Petersen, S. E., Ojemann, J. G., Miezin, F. M., Squire, L. R., & Raichle, M. E. (1995). Functional anatomical studies of explicit and implicit memory retrieval tasks. *The Journal of Neuroscience, 15,* 12–29.

Bunce, D. M., Flens, E. A., & Neiles, K. Y. (2011). How long can students pay attention in class? A study of student attention decline using clickers. *Journal of Chemical Education, 87,* 1438–1443.

Bureau of Justice Statistics. (2008). *Prisoners in 2007* (No. NCJ224280 by H. C. West & W. J. Sabol). Washington, DC: U.S. Department of Justice.

Burger, J. M. (1999). The foot-in-the-door compliance procedure: A multiple-process analysis and review. *Personality and Social Psychology Review, 3,* 303–325.

Burger, J. M. (2009). Replicating Milgram: Would people still obey today? *American Psychologist, 64,* 1–11.

Burger, J. M., & Burns, L. (1988). The illusion of unique invulnerability and the use of effective contraception. *Personality and Social Psychology Bulletin, 14,* 264–270.

Burger, J. M., Sanchez, J., Imberi, J. E., & Grande, L. R. (2009). The norm of reciprocity as an internalized social norm: Returning favors even when no one finds out. *Social Influence, 4*(1), 11–17.

Burgess E. W., & Wallin, P. (1953). *Engagement and marriage.* Philadelphia: J. B. Lippincott.

Burke, D., MacKay, D. G., Worthley, J. S., & Wade, E. (1991). On the tip of the tongue: What causes word failure in young and older adults? *Journal of Memory and Language, 30,* 237–246.

Burke, J. D., Loeber, R., & Birmaher, B. (2002). Oppositional defiant disorder and conduct disorder: Part II. A review of the past 10 years. *Journal of the American Academy of Child and Adolescent Psychiatry, 41,* 1275–1293.

Burkham, D. T., Ready, D. D., Lee, V. E., & LoGerfo, L. F. (2004). Social-class differences in summer learning between kindergarten and first grade: Model specification and estimation. *Sociology of Education, 77,* 1–31.

Burks, S. V., Carpenter, J. P., Goette, L., & Rustichini, A. (2009). Cognitive skills affect economic preferences, strategic behavior, and job attachment. *Proceedings of the National Academy of Sciences, 106*(19), 7745–7750. doi: 10.1073/pnas. 0812360106

Burns, D. J., Hwang, A. J., & Burns, S. A. (2011). Adaptive memory: Determining the proximate mechanisms responsible for the memorial advantages of survival processing. *Journal of Experimental Psychology: Learning, Memory, and Cognition, 37,* 206–218.

Burnstein, E., Crandall, C., & Kitayama, S. (1994). Some neo-Darwinian decision rules for altruism: Weighing cues for inclusive fitness as a function of the biological importance of the decision. *Journal of Personality and Social Psychology, 67,* 773–789.

Burris, C. T., & Branscombe, N. R. (2005). Distorted distance estimation induced by a self-relevant national boundary. *Journal of Experimental Social Psychology, 41,* 305–312.

Bushman, B. J., & Huesmann, L. R. (2010). Aggression. In S. T. Fiske, D. T. Gilbert, & G. Lindzey (Eds.), *The handbook of social psychology* (5th ed., Vol. 2, pp. 833–863). New York: Wiley.

Buss, D. M. (1985). Human mate selection. *American Scientist, 73,* 47–51.

Buss, D. M. (1989). Sex differences in human mate preferences: Evolutionary hypotheses tested in 37 cultures. *Behavioral and Brain Sciences, 12,* 1–49.

Buss, D. M. (1996). Social adaptation and five major factors of personality. In J. S. Wiggins (Ed.), *The five-factor model of personality: Theoretical perspectives* (pp. 180–208). New York: Guilford Press.

Buss, D. M. (1999). *Evolutionary psychology: The new science of the mind.* Boston: Allyn & Bacon.

Buss, D. M. (2000). *The dangerous passion: Why jealousy is as necessary as love and sex.* New York: Free Press.

Buss, D. M. (2007). The evolution of human mating. *Acta Psychologica Sinica, 39,* 502–512.

Buss, D. M., & Haselton, M. G. (2005). The evolution of jealousy. *Trends in Cognitive Sciences, 9,* 506–507.

Buss, D. M., & Schmitt, D. P. (1993). Sexual strategies theory: An evolutionary perspective on human mating. *Psychological Review, 100,* 204–232.

Butler, A. C., Chapman, J. E., Forman, E. M., & Beck, A. T. (2006). The empirical status of cognitive-behavioral therapy: A review of meta-analyses. *Clinical Psychology Review, 26,* 17–31.

Butler, M. A., Corboy, J. R., & Filley, C. M. (2009). How the conflict between American psychiatry and neurology delayed the appreciation of cognitive dysfunction in multiple sclerosis. *Neuropsychology Review, 19,* 399–410.

Butts, A. (2013, October 28). The "American smile." [Web log post.] Retrieved from http://www.speaking-denglish.com/2013/10/american-smile/

Byers-Heinlein, K., Burns, T. C., & Werker, J. F. (2010). The roots of bilingualism in newborns. *Psychological Science, 21*(3), 343–348. doi: 10.1177/0956797609360758

Byrne, D., Allgeier, A. R., Winslow, L., & Buckman, J. (1975). The situational facilitation of interpersonal attraction: A three-factor hypothesis. *Journal of Applied Social Psychology, 5,* 1–15.

Byrne, D., & Clore, G. L. (1970). A reinforcement model of evaluative responses. *Personality: An International Journal, 1,* 103–128.

Byrne, D., Ervin, C. R., & Lamberth, J. (1970). Continuity between the experimental study of attraction and real-life computer dating. *Journal of Personality and Social Psychology, 16,* 157–165.

Cabeza, R. (2002). Hemispheric asymmetry reduction in older adults: The HAROLD model. *Psychology and Aging, 17,* 85–100.

Cabeza, R., Rao, S., Wagner, A. D., Mayer, A., & Schacter, D. L. (2001). Can medial temporal lobe regions distinguish true from false? An event-related fMRI study of veridical and illusory recognition memory. *Proceedings of the National Academy of Sciences, USA, 98,* 4805–4810.

Cacioppo, J. T., & Patrick, B. (2008). *Loneliness: Human nature and the need for social connection.* New York: Norton.

Cahill, L., Haier, R. J., Fallon, J., Alkire, M. T., Tang, C., Keator, D., . . . McGaugh, J. L. (1996). Amygdala activity at encoding correlated with long-term, free recall of emotional information. *Proceedings of the National Academy of Sciences, USA, 93,* 8016–8021.

Cahill, L., & McGaugh, J. L. (1998). Mechanisms of emotional arousal and lasting declarative memory. *Trends in Neurosciences, 21,* 294–299.

Calder, A. J., Young, A. W., Rowland, D., Perrett, D. I., Hodges, J. R., & Etcoff, N. L. (1996). Facial emotion recognition after bilateral amygdala damage: Differentially severe impairment of fear. *Cognitive Neuropsychology, 13,* 699–745.

Calkins, M. W. (Ed.). (1930). *Mary Whiton Calkins* (Vol. 1). Worcester, MA: Clark University Press.

Callaghan, T., Rochat, P., Lillard, A., Claux, M. L., Odden, H., Itakura, S., . . . Singh, S. (2005). Synchrony in the onset of mental-state reasoning: Evidence from five cultures. *Psychological Science, 16,* 378–384.

Calvin, C. M., Deary, I. J., Fenton, C., Roberts, B. A., Der, G., Leckenby, N., & Batty, G. D. (2010). Intelligence in youth and all-cause-mortality: Systematic review with meta-analysis. *International Journal of Epidemiology, 40*(3), 626–644. doi:10.1093/ije/dyq190

Calvin, C. M., Deary, I. J., Fenton, C., Roberts, B. A., Der, G., Leckenby, N., & Batty, G. D. (2011). Intelligence in youth and all-cause-mortality: Systematic review with meta-analysis. *International Journal of Epidemiology, 40*(3), 626–644.

Cameron, C. D., & Payne, B. K. (2011). Escaping affect: How motivated emotion regulation creates insensitivity to mass suffering. *Journal of Personality and Social Psychology, 100*(1), 1–15.

Campbell, A. (1999). Staying alive: Evolution, culture, and women's intra-sexual aggression. *Behavioral & Brain Sciences, 22,* 203–252.

Campbell, C. M., & Edwards, R. R. (2012). Ethnic differences in pain and pain management. *Pain Management, 2,* 219–230.

Campbell, C. M., Edwards, R. R., & Fillingim, R. B. (2005). Ethnic differences in responses to multiple experimental pain stimuli. *Pain, 113,* 20–26.

Campbell, F. A., Ramey, C. T., Pungello, E., Sparling, J., & Miller-Johnson, S. (2002). Early childhood education: Young adult outcomes from the Abecedarian Project. *Applied Developmental Science, 6*(1), 42–57. doi: 10.1207/S1532480XADS0601_05

Cannon, T. D. (2015). How schizophrenia develops: Cognitive and brain mechanisms underlying onset of psychosis. *Trends in Cognitive Science, 19,* 744–756.

Cannon, W. B. (1929). *Bodily changes in pain, hunger, fear, and rage: An account of recent research into the function of emotional excitement* (2nd ed.). New York: Appleton-Century-Crofts.

Cantor, N. (1990). From thought to behavior: "Having" and "doing" in the study of personality and cognition. *American Psychologist, 45,* 735–750.

Caprioli, M. (2003). Gender equality and state aggression: The impact of domestic gender equality on state first use of force. *International Interactions, 29*(3), 195–214. doi: 10.1080/03050620304595

Carey, N. (2012). *The epigenetics revolution: How modern biology is rewriting our understanding of genetics, disease, and inheritance.* New York: Columbia University Press.

Carlson, C., & Hoyle, R. (1993). Efficacy of abbreviated progressive muscle relaxation training: A quantitative review of behavioral medicine research. *Journal of Consulting and Clinical Psychology, 61,* 1059–1067.

Carmena, J. M., Lebedev, M. A., Crist, R. E., O'Doherty, J. E., Santucci, D. M., Dimitrov, D. F., . . . Nicolelis, M. A. (2003). Learning to control a brain-machine interface for reaching and grasping by primates. *Public Library of Science Biology, 1,* 193–208.

Carmichael Olson, H., Streissguth, A. P., Sampson, P. D., Barr, H. M., Bookstein, F. L., & Thiede, K. (1997). Association of prenatal alcohol exposure with behavioral and learning problems in early adolescence. *Journal of the American Academy of Child & Adolescent Psychiatry, 36*(9), 1187–1194.

Carney, D. R., Cuddy, A. J. C., & Yap, A. J. (2010). Power posing: Brief nonverbal displays affect neuroendocrine levels and risk tolerance. *Psychological Science, 21*(10), 1363–1368. doi: 10.1177/0956797610383437

Carolson, E. A. (1998). A prospective longitudinal study of attachment disorganization/disorientation. *Child Development, 69,* 1107–1128.

Caron, M.-J., Mottron, L., Berthiaume, C., & Dawson, M. (2006). Cognitive mechanisms, specificity and neural underpinnings of visuospatial peaks in autism. *Brain, 129,* 1789–1802.

Carpenter, S. K. (2012). Testing enhances the transfer of learning. *Current Directions in Psychological Science, 21,* 279–283.

Carr, L., Iacoboni, M., Dubeau, M., Mazziotta, J. C., & Lenzi, G. L. (2003). Neural mechanisms of empathy in humans: A relay from neural systems for imitation to limbic areas. *Proceedings of the National Academy of Sciences, USA, 100,* 5497–5502.

Carroll, J. B. (1993). *Human cognitive abilities.* Cambridge: Cambridge University Press.

Carson, R. C., Butcher, J. N., & Mineka, S. (2000). *Abnormal psychology and modern life* (11th ed.). Boston: Allyn & Bacon.

Carstensen, L. L. (1992). Social and emotional patterns in adulthood: Support for socioemotional selectivity theory. *Psychology and Aging, 7,* 331–338.

Carstensen, L. L., & Fredrickson, B. L. (1998). Influence of HIV status and age on cognitive representations of others. *Health Psychology, 17*, 1–10.

Carstensen, L. L., Pasupathi, M., Mayr, U., & Nesselroade, J. R. (2000). Emotional experience in everyday life across the adult life span. *Journal of Personality and Social Psychology, 79*, 644–655.

Carstensen, L. L., & Turk-Charles, S. (1994). The salience of emotion across the adult life span. *Psychology and Aging, 9*, 259–264.

Carver, C. S. (2006). Approach, avoidance, and the self-regulation of affect and action. *Motivation and Emotion, 30*, 105–110.

Carver, C. S., Lehman, J. M., & Antoni, M. H. (2003). Dispositional pessimism predicts illness-related disruption of social and recreational activities among breast cancer patients. *Journal of Personality and Social Psychology, 84*, 813–821.

Carver, C. S., & White, T. L. (1994). Behavioral inhibition, behavioral activation, and affective responses to impending reward and punishment: The bis/bas scales. *Journal of Personality and Social Psychology, 67*(2), 319–333.

Casasanto, D., & Boroditsky, L. (2008). Time in the mind: Using space to think about time. *Cognition, 106*, 579–593.

Casazza, K., Fontaine, K. R., Astrup, A., Birch, L. L., Brown, A. W., Bohan Brown, M. M., . . . Allison, D. B. (2013). Myths, presumptions, and facts about obesity. *New England Journal of Medicine, 368*(5), 446–454.

Case, A., & Deaton, A. (2015) Rising morbidity and mortality in midlife among white non-Hispanic Americans in the 21st century. *Proceedings of the National Academy of Sciences, 112*, 15078–15083.

Caspi, A., & Herbener, E. S. (1990). Continuity and change: Assortative marriage and the consistency of personality in adulthood. *Journal of Personality and Social Psychology, 58*, 250–258.

Caspi, A., Lynam, D., Moffitt, T. E., & Silva, P. A. (1993). Unraveling girls' delinquency: Biological, dispositional, and contextual contributions to adolescent misbehavior. *Developmental Psychology, 29*, 19–30.

Caspi, A., Roberts, B. W., & Shiner, R. L. (2005). Personality development: Stability and change. *Annual Review of Psychology, 56*, 453–484.

Caspi, A., Sugden, K., Moffitt, T. E., Taylor, A., Craig, I. W., Harrington, H., . . . Poulton, R. (2003). Influence of life stress on depression: Moderation by a polymorphism in the 5-HTT gene. *Science, 301*, 386–389.

Castel, A. D., McCabe, D. P., & Roediger, H. L. III. (2007). Illusions of competence and overestimation of associate memory for identical items: Evidence from judgments of learning. *Psychonomic Bulletin & Review, 14*, 197–111.

Castellani, R. J., Perry, G., & Iverson, G. L. (2015). Chronic effects of mild neurotrauma: Putting the cart before the horse? *Journal of Neuropathology & Experimental Neurology, 74*, 493–499.

Castellanos, F. X., Patti, P. L., Sharp, W., Jeffries, N. O., Greenstein, D. K., Clasen, L. S., . . . Rapoport, J. L. (2002). Developmental trajectories of brain volume abnormalities in children and adolescents with attention-deficit/hyperactivity disorder. *Journal of the American Medical Association, 288*, 1740–1748. doi: 10.1001/jama.288.14.1740

Catrambone, R. (2002). The effects of surface and structural feature matches on the access of story analogs. *Journal of Experimental Psychology: Learning, Memory, & Cognition, 28*, 318–334.

Cattell, R. B. (1950). *Personality: A systematic, theoretical, and factual study.* New York: McGraw-Hill.

Ceci, S. J. (1991). How much does schooling influence general intelligence and its cognitive components? A reassessment of the evidence. *Developmental Psychology, 27*, 703–722.

Ceci, S. J., DeSimone, M., & Johnson, S. (1992). Memory in context: A case study of "Bubbles P.," a gifted but uneven memorizer. In D. J. Herrmann, H. Weingartner, A. Searleman, & C. McEvoy (Eds.), *Memory improvement: Implications for memory theory* (pp. 169–186). New York: Springer-Verlag.

Ceci, S. J., Ginther, D. K., Kahn, S., & Williams, W. M. (2014). Women in academic science: A changing landscape. *Psychological Science in the Public Interest, 15*(3), 75–141. doi: 10.1177/1529100614541236

Ceci, S. J., & Williams, W. M. (1997). Schooling, intelligence, and income. *American Psychologist, 52*, 1051–1058.

Ceci, S. J., Williams, W. M., & Barnett, S. M. (2009). Women's underrepresentation in science: Sociocultural and biological considerations. *Psychological Bulletin, 135*(2), 218–261. doi:10.1037/a0014412

Centers for Disease Control and Prevention. (2002, June 28). Youth risk behavior surveillance. *Surveillance Summary, 51*(SS-4), 1–64. Washington, DC: Author.

Centers for Disease Control and Prevention. (2012). Monitoring selected national HIV prevention and care objectives by using HIV surveillance data—United States and 6 U.S. dependent areas—2010. *HIV Surveillance Supplemental Report, 17*(No. 3, part A).

Centers for Disease Control and Prevention. (2013). *Injury prevention and control: Data and statistics (WISQARS).* Retrieved from http://www.cdc.gov/injury/wisqars/index.html

Centers for Disease Control and Prevention. (2015). Current cigarette smoking among adults—United States, 2005–2014. *Morbidity and Mortality Weekly Report, 64*, 1233–1240.

Centola, D., & Baronchelli, A. (2015). The spontaneous emergence of conventions: An experimental study of cultural evolution. *Proceedings of the National Academy of Sciences, 112*(7), 1989–1994. doi: 10.1073/pnas.1418838112

Cepeda, N. J., Pashler, H., Vul, E., Wixted, J. T., & Rohrer, D. (2006). Distributed practice in verbal recall tests: A review and quantitative synthesis. *Psychological Bulletin, 132*, 354–380.

Chabris, C. F., Hebert, B. M., Benjamin, D. J., Beauchamp, J., Cesarini, D., van der Loos, M., & Laibson, D. (2012). Most reported genetic associations with general intelligence are probably false positives. *Psychological Science, 23*(11), 1314–1323. doi: 10.1177/0956797611435528

Chabris, C., & Simons, D. (2010). *The invisible gorilla: And other ways our intuitions deceive us.* New York: Crown.

Chabris, C., & Simons, D. (2012, November 16). Using just 10% of your brains? Think again. *Wall Street Journal Online.* Retrieved from http://online.wsj.com/article/SB10001424127887324556304578119351874212 18.html

Chaiken, S. (1980). Heuristic versus systematic information processing and the use of source versus message cues in persuasion. *Journal of Personality and Social Psychology, 39*, 752–766.

Chalmers, D. (1996). *The conscious mind: In search of a fundamental theory.* New York: Oxford University Press.

Chambless, D. L., Baker, M. J., Baucom, D. H., Beutler, L. E., Calhoun, K. S., Crits-Christoph, P., . . . Woody, S. R. (1998). Update on empirically validated therapies, II. *Clinical Psychologist, 51*(1), 3–14.

Chandler, J., & Schwarz, N. (2009). How extending your middle finger affects your perception of others: Learned movements influence concept accessibility. *Journal of Experimental Social Psychology, 45*, 123–128.

Chandrashekar, J., Hoon, M. A., Ryba, N. J., & Zuker, C. S. (2006). The receptors and cells for human tastes. *Nature, 444*, 288–294.

Chang, P. P., Ford, D. E., Meoni, L. A., Wang, N., & Klag, M. J. (2002). Anger in young men and subsequent premature cardiovascular disease. *Archives of Internal Medicine, 162,* 901–906.

Chaplin, T. M., & Aldao, A. (2013). Gender differences in emotion expression in children: A meta-analytic review. *Psychological Bulletin, 139,* 735–765.

Charles, S. T., Reynolds, C. A., & Gatz, M. (2001). Age-related differences and change in positive and negative affect over 23 years. *Journal of Personality and Social Psychology, 80,* 136–151.

Charness, N. (1981). Aging and skilled problem solving. *Journal of Experimental Psychology: General, 110,* 21–38.

Charpak, G., & Broch, H. (2004). *Debunked! ESP, telekinesis, and other pseudoscience* (B. K. Holland, Trans.). Baltimore: Johns Hopkins University Press.

Chartrand, T. L., & Bargh, J. A. (1999). The chameleon effect: The perception-behavior link and social interaction. *Journal of Personality and Social Psychology, 76,* 893–910.

Chartrand, T. L., & Kay, A. (2006). *Mystery moods and perplexing performance: Consequences of succeeding and failing at a nonconscious goal.* Unpublished manuscript.

Chen, E., Cohen, S., & Miller, G. E. (2010). How low socio-economic status affects 2-year hormonal trajectories in children. *Psychological Science, 21*(1), 31–37.

Chen, Q. & Yan, Z. (2015). Does multitasking with mobile phones affect learning? A review. *Computers in Human Behavior, 54,* 34–42.

Cheney, D. L., & Seyfarth, R. M. (1990). *How monkeys see the world.* Chicago: University of Chicago Press.

Cheng, D. T., Disterhoft, J. F., Power, J. M., Ellis, D. A., & Desmond, J. E. (2008). Neural substrates underlying human delay and trace eyeblink conditioning. *Proceedings of the National Academy of Sciences, USA, 105,* 8108–8113.

Cherlin, A. J. (Ed.). (1992). *Marriage, divorce, remarriage* (2nd ed.). Cambridge, MA: Harvard University Press.

Cherry, C. (1953). Some experiments on the recognition of speech with one and two ears. *Journal of the Acoustical Society of America, 25,* 275–279.

Chetty, R., Stepner, M., Abraham, S., Lin, S., Scuderi, B., Turner, N., . . . Cutler, D. (2016). The association between income and life expectancy in the United States, 2001–2014. *Journal of the American Medical Association, 315*(16), 1750–1766.

Chivers, M. L., Rieger, G., Latty, E., & Bailey, J. M. (2004). A sex difference in the specificity of sexual arousal. *Psychological Science, 15,* 736–744.

Chivers, M. L., Seto, M. C., & Blanchard, R. (2007). Gender and sexual orientation differences in sexual response to sexual activities versus gender of actors in sexual films. *Journal of Personality and Social Psychology, 93,* 1108–1121.

Choi, I., Nisbett, R. E., & Norenzayan, A. (1999). Causal attribution across cultures: Variation and universality. *Psychological Bulletin, 125,* 47–63.

Chomsky, N. (1957). *Syntactic structures.* The Hague: Mouton.

Chomsky, N. (1959). A review of *Verbal Behavior* by B. F. Skinner. *Language, 35,* 26–58.

Chomsky, N. (1986). *Knowledge of language: Its nature, origin, and use.* New York: Praeger.

Chorover, S. L. (1980). *From Genesis to genocide: The meaning of human nature and the power of behavior control.* Cambridge, MA: MIT Press.

Choy, Y., Fyer, A. J., & Lipsitz, J. D. (2007). Treatment of specific phobia in adults. *Clinical Psychology Review, 27,* 266–286.

Christakis, N. A., & Fowler, J. H. (2007). The spread of obesity in a large social network over 32 years. *New England Journal of Medicine, 357*(4), 370–379.

Christianson, S.-Å., & Loftus, E. F. (1987). Memory for traumatic events. *Applied Cognitive Psychology, 1,* 225–239.

Chui, H., Hoppmann, C. A., Gerstorf, D., Walker, R., & Luszcz, M. A. (2014). Social partners and momentary affect in the oldest-old: The presence of others benefits affect depending on who we are and who we are with. *Developmental Psychology, 50*(3), 728–740. doi: 10.1037/a0033896

Chung, G. H., Flook, L., & Fuligni, A. J. (2009). Daily family conflict and emotional distress among adolescents from Latin American, Asian, and European backgrounds. *Developmental Psychology, 45,* 1406–1415.

Cialdini, R. B. (2005). Don't throw in the towel: Use social influence research. *American Psychological Society, 18,* 33–34.

Cialdini, R. B. (2013). The focus theory of normative conduct. In P. A. M. van Lange, A. W. Kruglanski, & E. T. Higgins (Eds.), *Handbook of theories of social psychology* (Vol. 3, pp. 295–312). New York: Sage.

Cialdini, R. B., & Goldstein, N. J. (2004). Social influence: Compliance and conformity. *Annual Review of Psychology, 55*(1), 591–621. doi: 10.1146/annurev.psych.55.090902.142015

Cialdini, R. B., Trost, M. R., & Newsom, J. T. (1995). Preference for consistency: The development of a valid measure and the discovery of surprising behavioral implications. *Journal of Personality and Social Psychology, 69,* 318–328.

Cialdini, R. B., Vincent, J. E., Lewis, S. K., Catalan, J., Wheeler, D., & Darby, B. L. (1975). Reciprocal concessions procedure for inducing compliance: The door-in-the-face technique. *Journal of Personality and Social Psychology, 31,* 206–215.

Ciarrochi, J. V., Chan, A. Y., & Caputi, P. (2000). A critical evaluation of the emotional intelligence concept. *Personality & Individual Differences, 28,* 539.

Ciarrochi, J., Heaven, P. C. L., & Skinner, T. (2012). Cognitive ability and health-related behaviors during adolescence: A prospective study across five years. *Intelligence, 40*(4), 317–324. doi: 10.1016/j.intell.2012.03.003

Cicchetti, D., & Toth, S. L. (1998). Perspectives on research and practice in developmental psychopathology. In I. E. Sigel & K. A. Renninger (Eds.), *Handbook of child psychology: Vol. 4. Child psychology in practice* (5th ed., pp. 479–583). New York: Wiley.

Clancy, S. A. (2005). *Abducted: How people come to believe they were kidnapped by aliens.* Cambridge, MA: Harvard University Press.

Clark-Polner, E., Johnson, T., & Barrett, L. F. (2016). Multivoxel pattern analysis does not provide evidence to support the existence of basic emotions. *Cerebral Cortex.* First published online February 29, 2016. doi: 10.1093/cercor/bhw028

Clark, C. A., & Dagher, A. (2014). The role of dopamine in risk taking: A specific look at Parkinson's disease and gambling. *Frontiers in Behavioral Neuroscience, 8,* 196. doi: 10.3389/fnbeh.2014.00196

Clark, I. A., & Maguire, E. A. (2016). Remembering preservation in hippocampal amnesia. *Annual Review of Psychology, 67,* 51–82.

Clark, M. S., & Lemay, E. P. (2010). Close relationships. In S. T. Fiske, D. T. Gilbert, & G. Lindzey (Eds.), *The handbook of social psychology* (5th ed., Vol. 2). New York: Wiley.

Clark, R. D., & Hatfield, E. (1989). Gender differences in receptivity to sexual offers. *Journal of Psychology and Human Sexuality, 2,* 39–55.

Cleckley, H. M. (1976). *The mask of sanity* (5th ed.). St. Louis: Mosby.

Coates, T. (2015). *Between the world and me.* New York: Spiegel & Grau.

Coe, C. L., & Lubach, G. R. (2008). Fetal programming prenatal origins of health and illness. *Current Directions in Psychological Science, 17,* 36–41.

Cogan, R., Cogan, D., Waltz, W., & McCue, M. (1987). Effects of laughter and relaxation on discomfort thresholds. *Journal of Behavioral Medicine, 10,* 139–144.

Coghill, R. C., McHaffie, J. G., & Yen, Y. (2003). Neural correlates of individual differences in the subjective experience of pain. *Proceedings of the National Academy of Sciences, USA, 100,* 8538–8542.

Cohen, A. O., Breiner, K., Steinberg, L., Bonnie, R. J., Scott, E. S., Taylor-Thompson, K. A., . . . Casey, B. J. (2016). When is an adolescent an adult? Assessing cognitive control in emotional and nonemotional contexts. *Psychological Science, 27*(4), 549–562.

Cohen, D., Nisbett, R. E., Bowdle, B. F., & Schwarz, N. (1996). Insult, aggression, and the southern culture of honor: An "experimental ethnography." *Journal of Personality and Social Psychology, 70,* 945–960.

Cohen, G. (1990). Why is it difficult to put names to faces? *British Journal of Psychology, 81,* 287–297.

Cohen, S. (1988). Psychosocial models of the role of social support in the etiology of physical disease. *Health Psychology, 7,* 269–297.

Cohen, S. (1999). Social status and susceptibility to respiratory infections. *New York Academy of Sciences, 896,* 246–253.

Cohen, S., Frank, E., Doyle, W. J., Skoner, D. P., Rabin, B. S., & Gwaltney, J. M., Jr. (1998). Types of stressors that increase susceptibility to the common cold in healthy adults. *Health Psychology, 17,* 214–223.

Cohen-Kettenis, P. T., & Pfäfflin, F. (2003). *Transgenderism and intersexuality in childhood and adolescence: Making choices.* Thousand Oaks, CA: SAGE.

Coifman, K. G., Bonanno, G. A., Ray, R. D., & Gross, J. J. (2007). Does repressive coping promote resilience? Affective-autonomic response discrepancy during bereavement. *Journal of Personality and Social Psychology, 92,* 745–758.

Coker, T. R., Austin, S. B., & Schuster, M. A. (2010). The health and health care of lesbian, gay, and bisexual adolescents. *Annual Review of Public Health, 31,* 457–477. doi: 10.1146/ annurev. publhealth.012809.103636

Colcombe, S. J., Erickson, K. I., Scalf, P. E., Kim, J. S., Prakesh, R., McAuley, E., . . . Kramer, A. F. (2006). Aerobic exercise training increases brain volume in aging humans. *Journals of Gerontology Series A: Biological Sciences and Medical Sciences, 61,* 1166–1170.

Colcombe, S. J., Kramer, A. F., Erickson, K. I., Scalf, P., McAuley, E., Cohen, N. J., . . . Elavsky, S. (2004). Cardiovascular fitness, cortical plasticity, and aging. *Proceedings of the National Academy of Sciences, USA, 101,* 3316–3321.

Cole, M. (1996). *Cultural psychology: A once and future discipline.* Cambridge, MA: Belknap Press of Harvard University Press.

Coman, A., Manier, D., & Hirst, W. (2009). Forgetting the unforgettable through conversation: Social shared retrieval-induced forgetting of September 11 memories. *Psychological Science, 20,* 627–633.

Condon, J. W., & Crano, W. D. (1988). Inferred evaluation and the relation between attitude similarity and interpersonal attraction. *Journal of Personality and Social Psychology, 54,* 789–797.

Conklin, Q., King, B., Zanesco, A., Pokorny, J., Hamidi, A., Lin, J., . . . Saron, C. (2015). Telomere lengthening after three weeks of an intensive insight meditation retreat. *Psychoneuroendocrinology, 61,* 26–27.

Conley, T. D. (2011). Perceived proposer personality characteristics and gender differences in acceptance of casual sex offers. *Journal of Personality and Social Psychology, 100*(2), 309–329. doi: 10.1037/ a0022152

Conley, T. D., Moors, A. C., Matsick, J. L., Ziegler, A., & Valentine, B. A. (2011). Women, men, and the bedroom: Methodological and conceptual insights that narrow, reframe, and eliminate gender differences in sexuality. *Current Directions in Psychological Science, 20*(5), 296–300. doi: 10.1177/0963721411418467

Connolly, B. & Fox, S. H. (2014). Treatment of cognitive, psychiatric, and affective disorders associated with Parkinson's disease. *Neurotherapeutics, 11,* 78–91.

Conway, M., & Ross, M. (1984). Getting what you want by revising what you had. *Journal of Personality and Social Psychology, 47,* 738–748.

Cook, M., & Mineka, S. (1989). Observational conditioning of fear to fear-relevant versus fear-irrelevant stimuli in rhesus monkeys. *Journal of Abnormal Psychology, 98*(4), 448–459.

Cook, M., & Mineka, S. (1990). Selective associations in the observational conditioning of fear in rhesus monkeys. *Journal of Experimental Psychology: Animal Behavior Process, 16,* 372–389.

Coontz, P. (2008). The responsible conduct of social research. In K. Yang & G. J. Miller (Eds.), *Handbook of research methods in public administration* (pp. 129–139). Boca Raton, FL: Taylor & Francis.

Cooper, H., Nye, B., Charlton, K., Lindsay, J., & Greathouse, S. (1996). The effects of summer vacation on achievement test scores: A narrative and meta-analytic review. *Review of Educational Research, 66*(3), 227–268.

Cooper, J., & Fazio, R. H. (1984). A new look at dissonance theory. In L. Berkowitz (Ed.), *Advances in experimental social psychology* (Vol. 17, pp. 229–266). New York: Academic Press.

Cooper, J. C., Hollon, N. G., Wimmer, G. E., & Knutson, B. (2009). Available alternative incentives modulate anticipatory nucleus accumbens activation. *Social Cognitive and Affective Neuroscience, 4,* 409–416.

Cooper, J. M., & Strayer, D. L. (2008). Effects of simulator practice and real-world experience on cell-phone-related driver distraction. *Human Factors, 50,* 893–902.

Cooper, J. R., Bloom, F. E., & Roth, R. H. (2003). *Biochemical basis of neuropharmacology.* New York: Oxford University Press.

Cooper, M. L. (2006). Does drinking promote risky sexual behavior? A complex answer to a simple question. *Current Directions in Psychological Science, 15,* 19–23.

Cooper, W. H., & Withey, W. J. (2009). The strong situation hypothesis. *Personality and Social Psychology Review, 13,* 62–72.

Corbetta, M., Shulman, G. L., Miezin, F. M., & Petersen, S. E. (1995). Superior parietal cortex activation during spatial attention shifts and visual feature conjunction. *Science, 270,* 802–805.

Cordaro, D. T., Keltner, D., Tshering, S., Wangchuk, D., & Flynn, L. M. (2016). The voice conveys emotion in ten globalized cultures and one remote village in Bhutan. *Emotion, 16*(1), 117–128. doi: 10.1037/emo0000100

Coren, S. (1997). *Sleep thieves.* New York: Free Press.

Corkin, S. (2002). What's new with the amnesic patient HM? *Nature Reviews Neuroscience, 3,* 153–160.

Corkin, S. (2013). *Permanent present tense: The unforgettable life of the amnesic patient, H.M.* New York: Basic Books.

Correll, J., Park, B., Judd, C. M., & Wittenbrink, B. (2002). The police officer's dilemma: Using ethnicity to disambiguate potentially threatening individuals. *Journal of Personality and Social Psychology, 83,* 1314–1329.

Correll, J., Park, B., Judd, C. M., Wittenbrink, B., Sadler, M. S., & Keesee, T. (2007). Across the thin blue line: Police officers and racial bias in the decision to shoot. *Journal of Personality and Social Psychology, 92,* 1006–1023.

Correll, J., Wittenbrink, B., Crawford, M. T., & Sadler, M. S. (2015). Stereotypic vision: How stereotypes disambiguate visual stimuli. *Journal of Personality and Social Psychology, 108*(2), 219–233. doi: 10.1037/pspa0000015

Corsi, P. (1991). *The enchanted loom: Chapters in the history of neuroscience.* New York: Oxford University Press.

Corti, E. (1931). *A history of smoking* (P. England, Trans.). London: Harrap.

Coryell, W., Endicott, J., Maser, J. D., Mueller, T., Lavori, P., & Keller, M. (1995). The likelihood of recurrence in bipolar affective disorder: The importance of episode recency. *Journal of Affective Disorders, 33,* 201–206.

Costa, P. T., Terracciano, A., & McCrae, R. R. (2001). Gender differences in personality traits across cultures: Robust and surprising findings. *Journal of Personality and Social Psychology, 81,* 322–331.

Costanza, A., Weber, K., Gandy, S., Bouras, C., Hof, P. R., Giannakopoulos, G., & Canuto, A. (2011). Contact sport–related chronic traumatic encephalopathy in the elderly: Clinical expression and structural substrates. *Neuropathology and Applied Neurobiology, 37,* 570–584.

Cottrell, C. A., Neuberg, S. L., & Li, N. P. (2007). What do people desire in others? A sociofunctional perspective on the importance of different valued characteristics. *Journal of Personality and Social Psychology, 92,* 208–231.

Cox, D., & Cowling, P. (1989). *Are you normal?* London: Tower Press.

Coyne, J. A. (2000, April 3). Of vice and men: Review of R. Tornhill and C. Palmer, *A natural history of rape. New Republic,* pp. 27–34.

Craddock, N., & Jones, I. (1999). Genetics of bipolar disorder. *Journal of Medical Genetics, 36,* 585–594.

Craik, F. I. M., Barense, M. D., Rathbone, C. J., Grusec, J. E., Stuss, D. T., Gao, F., . . . Black, S. E. (2014). VL: A further case of erroneous recollection. *Neuropsychologia, 56,* 367–380.

Craik, F. I. M., Govoni, R., Naveh-Benjamin, M., & Anderson, N. D. (1996). The effects of divided attention on encoding and retrieval processes in human memory. *Journal of Experimental Psychology: General, 125,* 159–180.

Craik, F. I. M., & Tulving, E. (1975). Depth of processing and the retention of words in episodic memory. *Journal of Experimental Psychology: General, 104,* 268–294.

Cramer, R. E., Schaefer, J. T., & Reid, S. (1996). Identifying the ideal mate: More evidence for male–female convergence. *Current Psychology, 15,* 157–166.

Crane, C. A., Godleski, S. A., Przybyla, S. M., Schlauch, R. C., & Testa, M. (2015). The proximal effects of acute alcohol consumption on male-to-female aggression: A meta-analytic review of the experimental literature. *Trauma, Violence, & Abuse.* doi: 10.1177/1524838015584374

Craske, M. G. (1999). *Anxiety disorders: Psychological approaches to theory and treatment.* Boulder, CO: Westview Press.

Creery, J. D., Oudiette, D., Antony, J. W., & Paller, K. A. (2015). Targeted memory reactivation during sleep depends on prior learning. *Sleep, 38,* 755–763.

Crick, N. R., & Grotpeter, J. K. (1995). Relational aggression, gender, and social-psychological adjustment. *Child Development, 66,* 710–722.

Crocker, J., & Wolfe, C. T. (2001). Contingencies of self-worth. *Psychological Review, 108*(3), 593–623.

Crombag, H. F. M., Wagenaar, W. A., & Van Koppen, P. J. (1996). Crashing memories and the problem of "source monitoring." *Applied Cognitive Psychology, 10,* 95–104.

Cross, E. S., Kraemer, D. J. M., Hamilton, A. F. de C., Kelley, W. M., & Grafton, S. T. (2009). Sensitivity of the action observation network to physical and observational learning. *Cerebral Cortex, 19,* 315–326.

Cross, P. (1977). Not can but will college teachers be improved? *New Directions for Higher Education, 17,* 1–15.

Cross-Disorder Group of the Psychiatric Genomics Consortium. (2013). Identification of risk loci with shared effects on five major psychiatric disorders: A genome-wide analysis. *Lancet, 381,* 1371–1379.

Csigó, K., Harsányi, A., Demeter, G., Rajkai, C., Németh, A., & Racsmány, M. (2010). Long-term follow-up of patients with obsessive-compulsive disorder treated by anterior capsulotomy: A neuropsychological study. *Journal of Affective Disorders, 126,* 198–205.

Csikszentmihalyi, M. (1990). *Flow: The psychology of optimal experience.* New York: Harper & Row.

Cuc, A., Koppel, J., & Hirst, W. (2007). Silence is not golden: A case of socially shared retrieval-induced forgetting. *Psychological Science, 18,* 727–733.

Cuddy, A. J. C., Fiske, S. T., & Glick, P. (2007). The BIAS map: Behaviors from intergroup affect and stereotypes. *Journal of Personality and Social Psychology, 92*(4), 631–648. doi: 10.1037/0022-3514.92.4.631

Cummins, D. D. (2012). *Good thinking: Seven powerful ideas that influence the way we think.* New York: Cambridge University Press.

Cunningham, M. R., Barbee, A. P., & Pike, C. L. (1990). What do women want? Facial metric assessment of multiple motives in the perception of male facial physical attractiveness. *Journal of Personality and Social Psychology, 59,* 61–72.

Cunningham, M. R., Roberts, A. R., Barbee, A. P., Druen, P. B., & Wu, C.-H. (1995). "Their ideas of beauty are, on the whole, the same as ours": Consistency and variability in the cross-cultural perception of female physical attractiveness. *Journal of Personality and Social Psychology, 68,* 261–279.

Cunningham, W. A., & Brosch, T. (2012). Motivational salience: Amygdala tuning from traits, needs, values, and goals. *Current Directions in Psychological Science, 21*(1), 54–59.

Curran, J. P., & Lippold, S. (1975). The effects of physical attraction and attitude similarity on attraction in dating dyads. *Journal of Personality, 43,* 528–539.

Curtiss, S. (1977). *Genie: A psycholinguistic study of a modern-day "wildchild."* New York: Academic Press.

Cutler, D. L., Bevilacqua, J., & McFarland, B. H. (2003). Four decades of community mental health: A symphony in four movements. *Community Mental Health Journal, 39,* 381–398.

D'Agostino, P. R., & Fincher-Kiefer, R. (1992). Need for cognition and correspondence bias. *Social Cognition, 10,* 151–163.

Dabbs, J. M., Bernieri, F. J., Strong, R. K., Campo, R., & Milun, R. (2001). Going on stage: Testosterone in greetings and meetings. *Journal of Research in Personality, 35,* 27–40.

Dabbs, J. M., Carr, T. S., Frady, R. L., & Riad, J. K. (1995). Testosterone, crime, and misbehavior among 692 male prison inmates. *Personality and Individual Differences, 18,* 627–633.

Dael, N., Mortillaro, M., & Scherer, K. R. (2012). Emotion expression in body action and posture. *Emotion, 12,* 1085–1101.

Dagher, A., & Robbins, T. W. (2009). Personality, addiction, dopamine: Insights from Parkinson's disease. *Neuron, 61,* 502–510.

Dalton, P. (2003). Olfaction. In H. Pashler & S. Yantis (Eds.), *Stevens' handbook of experimental psychology: Vol. 1. Sensation and perception* (3rd ed., pp. 691–746). New York: Wiley.

Daly, M., & Wilson, M. (1988). Evolutionary social psychology and family homicide. *Science, 242,* 519–524.

Damasio, A. R. (1989). Time-locked multiregional retroactivation: A systems-level proposal for the neural substrates of recall and recognition. *Cognition, 33,* 25–62.

Damasio, A. R. (1994). *Descartes' error: Emotion, reason, and the human brain.* New York: Putnam.

Damasio, A. R. (2005). *Descartes' error: Emotion, reason, and the human brain.* New York: Penguin.

Damasio, A. R., Grabowski, T. J., Bechara, A., Damasio, H., Ponto, L. L. B., Parvisi, J., & Hichwa, R. D. (2000). Subcortical and cortical brain activity during the feeling of self-generated emotions. *Nature Neuroscience, 3,* 1049–1056.

Damasio, H., Grabowski, T. J., Tranel, D., Hichwa, R. D., & Damasio, A. R. (1996). A neural basis for lexical retrieval. *Nature, 380,* 499–505.

Damsma, G., Pfaus, J. G., Wenkstern, D., Phillips, A. G., & Fibiger, H. C. (1992). Sexual behavior increases dopamine transmission in the nucleus accumbens and striatum of male rats: Comparison with novelty and locomotion. *Behavioral Neurosciences, 106,* 181–191.

Daneshvar, D. H., Nowinski, C. J., McKee, A. C., & Cantu, R. C. (2011). The epidemiology of sport-related concussion. *Clinical Sports Medicine, 30,* 1–17.

Daniel, H. J., O'Brien, K. F., McCabe, R. B., & Quinter, V. E. (1985). Values in mate selection: A 1984 campus survey. *College Student Journal, 19,* 44–50.

Danner, U. N., Ouwehand, C., van Haastert, N. L., Homsveld, H., & de Ridder, D. T. (2012). Decision-making impairments in women with binge eating disorder in comparison with obese and normal weight women. *European Eating Disorders Review, 20,* e56–e62.

Dar-Nimrod, I., & Heine, S. J. (2006). Exposure to scientific theories affects women's math performance. *Science, 314,* 435.

Darley, J. M., & Berscheid, E. (1967). Increased liking caused by the anticipation of interpersonal contact. *Human Relations, 10,* 29–40.

Darley, J. M., & Gross, P. H. (1983). A hypothesis-confirming bias in labeling effects. *Journal of Personality and Social Psychology, 44,* 20–33.

Darley, J. M., & Latané, B. (1968). Bystander intervention in emergencies: Diffusion of responsibility. *Journal of Personality and Social Psychology, 8,* 377–383.

Darwin, C. (1998). *The expression of the emotions in man and animals* (P. Ekman, Ed.). New York: Oxford University Press. (Original work published 1872)

Darwin, C. (2007). *The expression of the emotions in man and animals.* New York: Bibliobazaar. (Original work published 1899)

Darwin, C. J., Turvey, M. T., & Crowder, R. G. (1972). An auditory analogue of the Sperling partial report procedure: Evidence for brief auditory storage. *Cognitive Psychology, 3,* 255–267.

Dasgupta, N. (2013). Implicit attitudes and beliefs adapt to situations: A decade of research on the malleability of implicit prejudice, stereotypes, and the self-concept. *Advances in Experimental Social Psychology, 47,* 233–279. doi: 10.1016/B978-0-12-407236-7.00005-X

Dauer, W., & Przedborski, S. (2003). Parkinson's disease: Mechanisms and models. *Neuron, 39,* 889–909.

Daum, I., Schugens, M. M., Ackermann, H., Lutzenberger, W., Dichgans, J., & Birbaumer, N. (1993). Classical conditioning after cerebellar lesions in humans. *Behavioral Neuroscience, 107,* 748–756.

Davidson, R. J., Ekman, P., Saron, C., Senulis, J., & Friesen, W. V. (1990). Emotional expression and brain physiology I: Approach/withdrawal and cerebral asymmetry. *Journal of Personality and Social Psychology, 58,* 330–341.

Davidson, R. J., Putnam, K. M., & Larson, C. L. (2000). Dysfunction in the neural circuitry of emotion regulation—a possible prelude to violence. *Science, 289,* 591–594.

Davies, G, Tenesa, A., Payton, A., Yang, J., Harris, S. E., Liewald, D., . . . Deary, I. J. (2011). Genome-wide association studies establish that human intelligence is highly heritable and polygenic. *Molecular Psychiatry, 16*(10), 996–1005. doi: 10.1038/mp2011.85

Davies, G. (1988). Faces and places: Laboratory research on context and face recognition. In G. M. Davies & D. M. Thomson (Eds.), *Memory in context: Context in memory* (pp. 35–53). New York: Wiley.

Davila Ross, M., Menzler, S., & Zimmermann, E. (2008). Rapid facial mimicry in orangutan play. *Biology Letters, 4*(1), 27–30.

Davis, C. (2008, March 30). Simon Cowell admits to using Botox. *People Magazine.* Retrieved from http://www.people.com/people/article/0,,20181478,00.html

Davis, C. J., Bowers, J. S., & Memon, A. (2011). Social influence in televised election debates: A potential distortion of democracy. *PLosONE, 6*(3), e18154.

Davis, J. L., Senghas, A., Brandt, F., & Ochsner, K. N. (2010). The effects of BOTOX injections on emotional experience. *Emotion, 10*(3), 433–440. doi: 10.1037/a0018690

Davis, S., & Wahlin-Jacobsen, S. (2015). Testosterone in women–the clinical significance. *Lancet Diabetes & Endocrinology, 3,* 980–992.

Dawes, R. M. (1994). *House of cards: Psychology and psychotherapy built on myth.* New York: Free Press.

Dawood, K., Kirk, K. M., Bailey, J. M., Andrews, P. W., & Martin, N. G. (2005). Genetic and environmental influences on the frequency of orgasm in women. *Twin Research, 8,* 27–33.

Dawson, G. (2016). Why it's important to continue universal autism screening while research fully examines its impact. *JAMA Pediatrics, 170,* 527–528.

Dawson, G., Jones, E. J. H., Merkle, K., Venema, K., Lowry, R., Faja, S., . . . Webb, S. J. (2012). Early behavioral intervention is associated with normalized brain activity in young children with autism. *Journal of the American Academy of Child and Adolescent Psychiatry, 51,* 1150–1159.

Dawson, G., Rogers, S., Munson, J., Smith, M., Winter, J., Greenson, J., . . . Varley, J. (2010). Randomized, controlled trial of an intervention for toddlers with autism: The Early Start Denver Model. *Pediatrics, 125,* e17–e23.

Dawson, M., Soulieres, I., Gernsbacher, M. A., & Mottron, L. (2007). The level and nature of autistic intelligence. *Psychological Science, 18,* 657–662.

Day, J. J., & Sweatt, J. D. (2011). Epigenetic mechanisms in cognition. *Neuron, 70,* 813–829.

Dayan, P., & Huys, Q. J. M. (2009). Serotonin in affective control. *Annual Review of Neuroscience, 32,* 95–126.

de Araujo, I. E., Rolls, E. T., Velazco, M. I., Margot, C., & Cayeux, I. (2005). Cognitive modulation of olfactory processing. *Neuron, 46,* 671–679.

De Bolle, M., De Fryut, F., McCrae, R. R., Löckenhoff, C. E., Costa, P. T. Jr., Aguilar-Valfae, M. E., . . . Terrecciano, A. (2015). The emergence of sex differences in personality traits in early adolescence: A cross-sectional, cross-cultural study. *Journal of Personality and Social Psychology, 108,* 171–185.

de Craen, A. J. M., Moerman, D. E., Heisterkamp, S. H., Tytgat, G. N. J., Tijssen, J. G. P., & Kleijnen, J. (1999). Placebo effect in the treatment of duodenal ulcer. *British Journal of Clinical Pharmacology, 48,* 853–860.

de Rosnay, M., Pons, F., Harris, P. L., & Morrell, J. M. B. (2004). A lag between understanding false belief and emotion attribution in young children: Relationships with linguistic ability and mothers' mental-state language. *British Journal of Developmental Psychology,* 24(1), 197–218.

De Vries, M. H., Barth, A. C. R., Maiworm, S., Knecht, S., Zwitserlood, P., & Flöel, A. (2010). Electrical stimulation of Broca's area enhances implicit learning of an artificial grammar. *Journal of Cognitive Neuroscience, 22,* 2427–2436.

de Waal, F. B. M. (2012). The antiquity of empathy. *Science, 336*(6083), 874–876. doi: 10.1126/science.1220999

De Witte, P. (1996). The role of neurotransmitters in alcohol dependency. *Alcohol & Alcoholism, 31*(Suppl. 1), 13–16.

De Wolff, M., & van IJzendoorn, M. H. (1997). Sensitivity and attachment: A meta-analysis on parental antecedents of infant attachment. *Child Development, 68,* 571–591.

Deák, G. O. (2006). Do children really confuse appearance and reality? *Trends in Cognitive Sciences, 10*(12), 546–550.

Deary, I. J. (2000). *Looking down on human intelligence: From psychometrics to the brain.* New York: Oxford University Press.

Deary, I. J. (2012). Intelligence. *Annual Review of Psychology, 63*(1), 453–482. doi:10.1146/annurev-psych-120710-100353

Deary, I. J., Batty, G. D., & Gale, C. R. (2008). Bright children become enlightened adults. *Psychological Science, 19*(1), 1–6.

Deary, I. J., Batty, G. D., Pattie, A., & Gale, C. R. (2008). More intelligent, more dependable children live longer: A 55-year longitudinal study of a representative sample of the Scottish nation. *Psychological Science, 19,* 874.

Deary, I. J., Taylor, M. D., Hart, C. L., Wilson, V., Smith, G. D., Blane, D., & Starr, J. M. (2005). Intergenerational social mobility and mid-life status attainment: Influences of childhood intelligence, childhood social factors, and education. *Intelligence, 33*(5), 455–472. doi: 10.1016/j.intell.2005.06.003

Deary, I. J., Weiss, A., & Batty, G. D. (2011). Intelligence and personality as predictors of illness and death: How researchers in differential psychology and chronic disease epidemiology are collaborating to understand and address health inequalities. *Psychological Science in the Public Interest, 11*(2), 53–79. doi: 10.1177/1529100610387081

Deci, E. L. (1971). Effects of externally mediated rewards on intrinsic motivation. *Journal of Personality and Social Psychology, 18,* 105–115.

Deci, E. L., Koestner, R., & Ryan, R. M. (1999). A meta-analytic review of experiments examining the effects of extrinsic rewards on intrinsic motivation. *Psychological Bulletin, 125,* 627–668.

Deese, J. (1959). On the prediction of occurrence of particular verbal intrusions in immediate recall. *Journal of Experimental Psychology, 58,* 17–22.

DeFelipe, J., & Jones, E. G. (1988). *Cajal on the cerebral cortex: An annotated translation of the complete writings.* New York: Oxford University Press.

Degenhardt, L., Chiu, W. T., Sampson, N., Kessler, R. C., Anthony, J. C., Angermeyer, M., . . . Wells, J. E. (2008). Toward a global view of alcohol, tobacco, cannabis, and cocaine use: Findings from the WHO World Mental Health surveys. *PLoS Medicine, 5,* e141.

Dekker, M. C., & Koot, H. M. (2003). DSM–IV disorders in children with borderline to moderate intellectual disability: I. Prevalence and impact. *Journal of the American Academy of Child and Adolescent Psychiatry, 42*(8), 915–922. doi: 10.1097/01.CHI.0000046892.27264.1A

Dekker, S., Lee, N. C., Howard-Jones, P., & Jolles, J. (2012). Neuromyths in education: Prevalence and predictors of misconceptions among teachers. *Frontiers in Psychology, 3,* 429. doi: 10.3389/fpsyg.2012.00429

Delgado, M. R., Frank, R. H., & Phelps, E. A. (2005). Perceptions of moral character modulate the neural systems of reward during the trust game. *Nature Neuroscience, 8,* 1611–1618.

Del Vicario, M., Bessi, A., Zollo, F., Petroni, F., Scalåa, A., Caldarelli, G., ... Quattrociocchi, W. (2016). The spreading of misinformation online. *Proceedings of the National Academy of Sciences, 113*(3), 554–559. doi: 10.1073/pnas.1517441113

Demb, J. B., Desmond, J. E., Wagner, A. D., Vaidya, C. J., Glover, G. H., & Gabrieli, J. D. E. (1995). Semantic encoding and retrieval in the left inferior prefrontal cortex: A functional MRI study of task difficulty and process specificity. *Journal of Neuroscience, 15,* 5870–5878.

Dement, W. C. (1959, November 30). Dreams. *Newsweek.*

Dement, W. C. (1978). *Some must watch while some must sleep.* New York: Norton.

Dement, W. C. (1999). *The promise of sleep.* New York: Delacorte Press.

Dement, W. C., & Kleitman, N. (1957). The relation of eye movements during sleep to dream activity: An objective method for the study of dreaming. *Journal of Experimental Psychology, 53,* 339–346.

Dement, W. C., & Wolpert, E. (1958). Relation of eye movements, body motility, and external stimuli to dream content. *Journal of Experimental Psychology, 55,* 543–553.

Dempster, E. L., Pidsley, R., Schalkwyk, L. C., Owens, S., Georgiades, A., Kane, F., . . . Mill, J. (2011). Disease-associated epigenetic changes in monozygotic twins discordant for schizophrenia and bipolar disorder. *Human Molecular Genetics, 20,* 4786–4796.

Dennett, D. (1991). *Consciousness explained.* New York: Basic Books.

Denny, B. T., & Ochsner, K. N. (2014). Behavioral effects of longitudinal training in cognitive reappraisal. *Emotion, 14*(2), 425–433. doi: 10.1037/a0035276

DePaulo, B. M., Charlton, K., Cooper, H., Lindsay, J. J., & Muhlenbruck, L. (1997). The accuracy–confidence correlation in the detection of deception. *Personality and Social Psychology Review, 1,* 346–357.

DePaulo, B. M., Lindsay, J. J., Malone, B. E., Muhlenbruck, L., Charlton, K., & Cooper, H. (2003). Cues to deception. *Psychological Bulletin, 129,* 74–118.

DePaulo, B. M., & Morris, W. L. (2006). The unrecognized stereotyping and discrimination against singles. *Current Directions in Psychological Science, 15,* 251–254.

DePaulo, B. M., Stone, J. I., & Lassiter, G. D. (1985). Deceiving and detecting deceit. In B. R. Schlenker (Ed.), *The self and social life* (pp. 323–370). New York: McGraw-Hill.

Der, G., Batty, G. D., & Deary, I. J. (2009). The association between IQ in adolescence and a range of health outcomes at 40 in the 1979 U.S. national longitudinal study of youth. *Intelligence, 37*(6), 573–580.

DeRubeis, R. J., Cohen, Z. D., Forand, N. R., Fournier, J. C., Gelfand, L. A., & Lorenzo-Luaces, L. (2014). The personalized advantage index: Translating research on prediction into individualized treatment recommendations: A demonstration. *PLoS ONE, 9,* e83875.

DeRubeis, R. J., Siegle, G. J., & Hollon, S. D. (2008). Cognitive therapy versus medication for depression: Treatment outcomes and neural mechanisms. *Nature Reviews Neuroscience, 9,* 788–796.

DesJardin, J. L., Eisenberg, L. S., & Hodapp, R. M. (2006). Sound beginnings: Supporting families of young deaf children with cochlear implants. *Infants and Young Children, 19,* 179–189.

Des Jarlais, D. C., McKnight, C., Goldblatt, C., & Purchase, D. (2009). Doing harm reduction better: Syringe exchange in the United States. *Addiction, 104*(9), 1331–1446.

D'Esposito, M. & Postle, B. R. (2015). The cognitive neuroscience of working memory. *Annual Review of Psychology, 66*, 115–142.

DeVilliers, P. (2005). The role of language in theory-of-mind development: What deaf children tell us. In J. W. Astington & J. A. Baird (Eds.), *Why language matters for theory of mind* (pp. 266–297). Oxford: Oxford University Press.

DeYoung, C. G., & Gray, J. R. (2009). Personality neuroscience: Explaining individual differences in affect, behavior, and cognition. In P. J. Corr & G. Matthews (Eds.), *The Cambridge handbook of personality psychology* (pp. 323–346). New York: Cambridge University Press.

DeYoung, C. G., Hirsh, J. B., Shane, M. S., Papademetris, X., Rajeevan, N., & Gray, J. R. (2010). Testing predictions from personality neuroscience: Brain structure and the Big Five. *Psychological Science, 21*, 820–828.

Diaconis, P., & Mosteller, F. (1989). Methods for studying coincidences. *Journal of the American Statistical Association, 84*, 853–861.

Diano, S., Farr, S. A., Benoit, S. C., McNay, E. C., da Silva, I., Horvath, B., . . . Horvath, T. L. (2006). Ghrelin controls hippocampal spine synapse density and memory performance. *Nature Neuroscience, 9*(3), 381–388.

Dickens, W. T., & Flynn, J. R. (2001). Heritability estimates versus large environmental effects: The IQ paradox resolved. *Psychological Review, 108*, 346–369.

Dickinson, A., Watt, A., & Griffiths, J. H. (1992). Free-operant acquisition with delayed reinforcement. *Quarterly Journal of Experimental Psychology Section B: Comparative and Physiological Psychology, 45*, 241–258.

Didden, R., Sigafoos, J., Lang, R., O'Reilly, M., Drieschner, K., & Lancioni, G. E. (2012). Intellectual disabilities. In P. Sturmey & M. Hersen (Eds.), *Handbook of evidence-based practice in clinical psychology.* Hoboken, NJ: Wiley. doi: 10.1002/9781118156391.ebcp001006

DiDonato, T. E., Ullrich, J., & Krueger, J. I. (2011). Social perception as induction and inference: An integrative model of intergroup differentiation, ingroup favoritism, and differential accuracy. *Journal of Personality and Social Psychology, 100*(1), 66–83. doi: 10.1037/a0021051

Diederich, N. J., & Goetz, C. G. (2008). The placebo treatments in neurosciences: New insights from clinical and neuroimaging studies. *Neurology, 71*, 677–684.

Diekelmann, S., & Born, J. (2010). The memory function of sleep. *Nature Reviews Neuroscience, 11*, 114–126.

Dietary Guidelines Advisory Committee. (2005). *Dietary guidelines for Americans 2005.* Retrieved October 15, 2007, from http://www.health.gov/dietaryguidelines

Dijksterhuis, A. (2004). Think different: The merits of unconscious thought in preference development and decision making. *Journal of Personality and Social Psychology, 87*, 586–598.

Dimberg, U. (1982). Facial reactions to facial expressions. *Psychophysiology, 19*, 643–647.

Dion, K., Berscheid, E., & Walster, E. (1972). What is beautiful is good. *Journal of Personality and Social Psychology, 24*, 285–290.

Dion, K. L. (2005). Marital status as stimulus variable and subject variable. *Psychological Inquiry, 16*, 104–110.

Disner, S. G., Beevers, C. G., Haigh, E. A., & Beck, A. T. (2011). Neural mechanisms of the cognitive model of depression. *Nature Reviews Neuroscience, 12*, 467–477.

Dittrich, W. H., Troscianko, T., Lea, S., & Morgan, D. (1996). Perception of emotion from dynamic point-light displays represented in dance. *Perception, 25*, 727–738. doi: 10.3389/fpsyg.2011.00337

Dolcos, F. (2014). Current emotion research in cognitive neuroscience: Linking enhancing and impairing effects of emotion on cognition. *Emotion Review, 6*, 362–375.

Dollard, J., Doob, L. W., Miller, N. E., Mowrer, O. H., & Sears, R. R. (1939). *Frustration and aggression.* Oxford: Yale University Press.

Domhoff, G. W. (2007). Realistic simulation and bizarreness in dream content: Past findings and suggestions for future research. In D. B. P. McNamara (Ed.), *The new science of dreaming: Content, recall, and personality correlates* (Vol. 22, pp. 1–27). Westport, CT: Praeger.

Domingue, B. W., Fletcher, J., Conley, D., & Boardman, J. D. (2014). Genetic and educational assortative mating among US adults. *Proceedings of the National Academy of Sciences, 111*(22), 7996–8000. doi: 10.1073/pnas.1321426111

Domjan, M. (2005). Pavlovian conditioning: A functional perspective. *Annual Review of Psychology, 56*, 179–206.

Donner, T. H., Kettermann, A., Diesch, E., Ostendorf, F., Villiringer, A., & Brandt, S. A. (2002). Visual feature and conjunction searches of equal difficulty engage only partially overlapping frontoparietal networks. *NeuroImage, 15*, 16–25.

Dornbusch, S. M., Hastorf, A. H., Richardson, S. A., Muzzy, R. E., & Vreeland, R. S. (1965). The perceiver and perceived: Their relative influence on categories of interpersonal perception. *Journal of Personality and Social Psychology, 1*, 434–440.

Dorus, S., Vallender, E. J., Evans, P. D., Anderson, J. R., Gilbert, S. L., Mahowald, M., . . . Lahn, B. T. (2004). Accelerated evolution of nervous system genes in the origin of *Homo sapiens. Cell, 119*, 1027–1040.

Dostoevsky, F. (1988). *Winter notes on summer impressions* (D. Patterson, Trans.). Evanston, IL: Northwestern University Press. (Original work published 1863)

Dovidio, J. F., & Gaertner, S. L. (2010). Intergroup bias. In S. T. Fiske, D. T. Gilbert, & G. Lindzey (Eds.), *The handbook of social psychology* (5th ed., Vol. 2, pp. 1085–1121). New York: Wiley.

Downer, J. D. C. (1961). Changes in visual gnostic function and emotional behavior following unilateral temporal damage in the "splitbrain" monkey. *Nature, 191*, 50–51.

Downing, P. E., Chan, A. W. Y., Peelen, M. V., Dodds, C. M., & Kanwisher, N. (2006). Domain specificity in visual cortex. *Cerebral Cortex, 16*, 1453–1461.

Draguns, J. G., & Tanaka-Matsumi, J. (2003). Assessment of psychopathology across and within cultures: Issues and findings. *Behaviour Research and Therapy, 41*, 755–776.

Druckman, D., & Bjork, R. A. (1994). *Learning, remembering, believing: Enhancing human performance.* Washington, DC: National Academy Press.

Duchaine, B. & Yovel, G. (2015). A revised neural framework for face processing. *Annual Review of Vision Science, 1*, 393–416.

Duckworth, A. L., & Seligman, M. E. P. (2005). Self-discipline outdoes IQ in predicting academic performance of adolescents. *Psychological Science, 16*, 939–944.

Dudai, Y. (2012). The restless engram: Consolidations never end. *Annual Review of Neuroscience, 35*, 227–247.

Dudycha, G. J., & Dudycha, M. M. (1933). Some factors and characteristics of childhood memories. *Child Development, 4*, 265–278.

Duenwald, M. (2002, September 12). Students find another staple of campus life: Stress. *New York Times.* Retrieved from http://www.nytimes.com/2002/09/17/health/students-find-another-staple-of-campus-life-stress.html?pagewanted=all&src=pm

Duff, M. C., Kurczek, J., Rubin, R., Cohen, N. J., & Tranel, D. (2013). Hippocampal amnesia disrupts creative thinking. *Hippocampus, 23*, 1143–1149.

Duffy, K. A., & Chartrand, T. L. (2015) The extravert advantage: How and when extraverts build rapport with other people. *Psychological Science, 26,* 1795–1802.

Duncan, G. J., Yeung, W. J., Brooks-Gunn, J., & Smith, J. R. (1998). How much does childhood poverty affect the life chances of children? *American Sociological Review, 63,* 406–423.

Duncker, K. (1945). On problem-solving. (L. S. Lees, Trans.). *Psychological Monographs, 58*(5), i–113.

Dunham, Y., Chen, E. E., & Banaji, M. R. (2013). Two signatures of implicit intergroup attitudes: Developmental invariance and early enculturation. *Psychological Science, 6,* 860–868. doi: 10.1177/0956797612463081

Dunlap, K. (1919). Are there any instincts? *Journal of Abnormal Psychology, 14,* 307–311.

Dunlop, S. A. (2008). Activity-dependent plasticity: Implications for recovery after spinal cord injury. *Trends in Neurosciences, 31,* 410–418.

Dunlosky, J., & Rawson, K. A. (2012). Overconfidence produces underachievement: Inaccurate self-evaluations undermine students' learning and retention. *Learning and Instruction, 22,* 271–280.

Dunlosky, J., & Thiede, K. W. (2013). Four cornerstones of calibration research: Why understanding students' judgments can improve their achievement. *Learning and Instruction, 24,* 58–61.

Dunlosky, J., Rawson, K. A., Marsh, E. J., Nathan, M. J., & Willingham, D. T. (2013). Improving students' learning with effective learning techniques: Promising directions from cognitive and educational psychology. *Psychological Science in the Public Interest, 14*(1), 4–58.

Dunphy, D. C. (1963). The social structure of urban adolescent peer groups. *Sociometry, 26,* 230–246.

Dutton, D. G., & Aron, A. P. (1974). Some evidence for heightened sexual attraction under conditions of high anxiety. *Journal of Personality and Social Psychology, 30,* 510–517.

Duval, S., & Wicklund, R. A. (1972). *A theory of objective self awareness.* New York: Academic Press.

Dyer, D., Dalzell, F., & Olegario, F. (2004). *Rising Tide: Lessons from 165 years of brand building at Procter & Gamble.* Cambridge, MA: Harvard Business School Press.

Eagly, A. H., Ashmore, R. D., Makhijani, M. G., & Longo, L. C. (1991). What is beautiful is good, but . . . : A meta-analytic review of research on the physical attractiveness stereotype. *Psychological Bulletin, 110,* 109–128.

Eagly, A. H., & Steffen, V. J. (1986). Gender and aggressive behavior: A meta-analytic review of the social psychological literature. *Psychological Bulletin, 100,* 309–330.

Eagly, A. H., & Wood, W. (1999). The origins of sex differences in human behavior: Evolved dispositions versus social roles. *American Psychologist, 54,* 408–423.

Eastwick, P. W., Eagly, A. H., Finkel, E. J., & Johnson, S. E. (2011). Implicit and explicit preferences for physical attractiveness in a romantic partner: A double dissociation in predictive validity. *Journal of Personality and Social Psychology, 101*(5), 993–1011. doi: 10.1037/a0024061

Eastwick, P. W., Finkel, E. J., Mochon, D., & Ariely, D. (2007). Selective versus unselective romantic desire: Not all reciprocity is created equal. *Psychological Science, 18,* 317–319.

Eaton, W. W., Shao, H., Nestadt, G., Lee, B. H., Bienvenu, O. J., & Zandi, P. (2008). Population-based study of first onset and chronicity of major depressive disorder. *Archives of General Psychiatry, 65,* 513–520.

Ebbinghaus, H. (1964). *Memory: A contribution to experimental psychology.* New York: Dover. (Original work published 1885)

Eddy, D. M. (1982). Probabilistic reasoning in clinical medicine: Problems and opportunities. In D. Kahneman, P. Slovic, & A. Tversky (Eds.), *Judgments under uncertainty: Heuristics and biases* (pp. 249–267). New York: Cambridge University Press.

Edgerton, V. R., Tillakaratne, J. K. T., Bigbee, A. J., deLeon, R. D., & Roy, R. R. (2004). Plasticity of the spinal neural circuitry after injury. *Annual Review of Neuroscience, 27,* 145–167.

Edwards, W. (1955). The theory of decision making. *Psychological Bulletin, 51,* 201–214.

Efferson, C., Lalive, R., & Fehr, E. (2008). The coevolution of cultural groups and ingroup favoritism. *Science, 321,* 1844–1849.

Eich, J. E. (1980). The cue-dependent nature of state-dependent retention. *Memory & Cognition, 8,* 157–173.

Eich, J. E. (1995). Searching for mood dependent memory. *Psychological Science, 6,* 67–75.

Eichenbaum, H. (2008). *Learning & memory.* New York: Norton.

Eichenbaum, H., & Cohen, N. J. (2001). *From conditioning to conscious recollection: Memory systems of the brain.* New York: Oxford University Press.

Eimas, P. D., Siqueland, E. R., Jusczyk, P., & Vigorito, J. (1971). Speech perception in infants. *Science, 171,* 303–306.

Einstein, G. O., & McDaniel, M. A. (1990). Normal aging and prospective memory. *Journal of Experimental Psychology: Learning, Memory, and Cognition, 16,* 717–726.

Einstein, G. O., & McDaniel, M. A. (2005). Prospective memory: Multiple retrieval processes. *Current Direction in Psychological Science, 14,* 286–290.

Eisenberg, N., Fabes, R. A., Guthrie, I. K., & Reiser, M. (2000). Dispositional emotionality and regulation: Their role in predicting quality of social functioning. *Journal of Personality and Social Psychology, 78,* 136.

Eisenberg, N., Hofer, C., Sulik, M. J., & Liew, J. (2014). The development of prosocial moral reasoning and a prosocial orientation in young adulthood: Concurrent and longitudinal correlates. *Developmental Psychology, 50*(1), 58–70. doi: 10.1037/ a0032990

Eisenberger, N. I., Lieberman, M. D., & Williams, K. D. (2003). Does rejection hurt? An fMRI study of social exclusion. *Science, 302,* 290–292. doi: 10.1126/science.1089134

Eisenegger, C., Haushofer, J., & Fehr, E. (2011). The role of testosterone in social interaction. *Trends in Cognitive Sciences, 15*(6), 263–271. doi: 10.1016/j.tics.2011.04.008

Eisenegger, C., Naef, M., Snozzi, R., Heinrichs, M., & Fehr, E. (2010). Prejudice and truth about the effect of testosterone on human bargaining behaviour. *Nature, 463,* 356–359.

Ekman, P. (1965). Differential communication of affect by head and body cues. *Journal of Personality and Social Psychology, 2,* 726–735.

Ekman, P. (1972). Universals and cultural differences in facial expressions of emotion. In J. K. Cole (Ed.), *Nebraska Symposium on Motivation, 1971* (pp. 207–283). Lincoln: University of Nebraska Press.

Ekman, P. (1992). *Telling lies.* New York: Norton.

Ekman, P. (2003). Darwin, deception, and facial expression. *Annals of the New York Academy of Sciences, 1000,* 205–221.

Ekman, P. (2016). What scientists who study emotion agree about. *Perspectives on Psychological Science, 11*(1), 31–34.

Ekman, P., & Friesen, W. V. (1968). Nonverbal behavior in psychotherapy research. In J. M. Shlien (Ed.), *Research in psychotherapy* (Vol. 3, pp. 179–216). Washington, DC: American Psychological Association.

Ekman, P., & Friesen, W. V. (1971). Constants across cultures in the face and emotion. *Journal of Personality and Social Psychology, 17,* 124–129.

Ekman, P., & Friesen, W. V. (1982). Felt, false, and miserable smiles. *Journal of Nonverbal Behavior, 6,* 238–252.

Ekman, P., Levenson, R. W., & Friesen, W. V. (1983). Autonomic nervous system activity distinguishes among emotions. *Science, 221,* 1208–1210.

Elbogen, E. B., & Johnson, S. C. (2009). The intricate link between violence and mental disorder. *Archives of General Psychiatry, 66*(2), 152–161.

Eldridge, L. L., Knowlton, B. J., Furmanski, C. S., Bookheimer, S. Y., & Engel, S. A. (2000). Remembering episodes: A selective role for the hippocampus during retrieval. *Nature Neuroscience, 3,* 1149–1152.

Eldridge, M. A., Barnard, P. J., & Bekerian, D. A. (1994). Autobiographical memory and daily schemas at work. *Memory, 2,* 51–74.

Elfenbein, H. A. (2013). Nonverbal dialects and accents in facial expressions of emotion. *Emotion Review, 5*(1), 90–96. doi: 10.1177/1754073912451332

Elfenbein, H. A., & Ambady, N. (2002). On the universality and cultural specificity of emotion recognition: A meta-analysis. *Psychological Bulletin, 128,* 203–235.

Elfenbein, H. A., Der Foo, M. D., White, J., & Tan, H. H. (2007). Reading your counterpart: The benefit of emotion recognition accuracy for effectiveness in negotiation. *Journal of Nonverbal Behavior, 31,* 205–223.

Ellemers, N. (2012). The group self. *Science, 336*(6083), 848–852. doi: 10.10.1126/science.1220987

Ellenbogen, J. M., Payne, J. D., & Stickgold, R. (2006). The role of sleep in declarative memory consolidation: Passive, permissive, or none? *Current Opinion in Neurobiology, 16,* 716–722.

Elliott, R., Sahakian, B. J., Matthews, K., Bannerjea, A., Rimmer, J., & Robbins, T. W. (1997). Effects of methylphenidate on spatial working memory and planning in healthy young adults. *Psychopharmacology, 131,* 196–206.

Ellis, A. (1991). *Reason and emotion in psychotherapy.* New York: Carol.

Ellis, B. J., & Garber, J. (2000). Psychosocial antecedents of variation in girls' pubertal timing: Maternal depression, stepfather presence, and marital and family stress. *Child Development, 71,* 485–501.

Ellis, E. M. (1983). A review of empirical rape research: Victim reactions and response to treatment. *Clinical Psychology Review, 3,* 473–490.

Ellis, L., & Ames, M. A. (1987). Neurohormonal functioning in sexual orientation: A theory of homosexuality–heterosexuality. *Psychological Bulletin, 101,* 233–258.

Ellman, S. J., Spielman, A. J., Luck, D., Steiner, S. S., & Halperin, R. (1991). REM deprivation: A review. In S. J. Ellman & J. S. Antrobus (Eds.), *The mind in sleep: Psychology and psychophysiology* (2nd ed., pp. 329–376). New York: Wiley.

Ellsworth, P. C., & Scherer, K. R. (2003). Appraisal processes in emotion. In R. J. Davidson, K. R. Scherer, & H. H. Goldsmith (Eds.), *The handbook of affective science* (pp. 572–595). New York: Oxford University Press.

Emerson, R. C., Bergen, J. R., & Adelson, E. H. (1992). Directionally selective complex cells and the computation of motion energy in cat visual cortex. *Vision Research, 32,* 203–218.

Epel, E. S., Blackburn, E. H., Lin, J., Dhabhar, F. S., Adler, N.E., Morrow, J. D., & Cawthorn, R. M. (2004). Accelerated telomere shortening in response to life stress. *Proceedings of the National Academy of Sciences, 101,* 17312–17315.

Epel, E. S., Daubenmier, J., Moskowitz, J. T., Foldman, S., & Blackburn, E. H. (2009). Can meditation slow rate of cellular aging? Cognitive stress, mindfulness, and telomerase. *Annals of the New York Academy of Sciences, 1172,* 34–53.

Epley, N., & Waytz, A. (2010). Mind perception. In S. T. Fiske, D. T. Gilbert, & G. Lindzey (Eds.), *The handbook of social psychology* (5th ed., Vol. 1, pp. 498–541). New York: Wiley.

Epstein, R. (2007a). *The case against adolescence: Rediscovering the adult in every teen.* New York: Quill Driver.

Epstein, R. (2007b). The myth of the teen brain. *Scientific American Mind, 18,* 27–31.

Erffmeyer, E. S. (1984). Rule-violating behavior on the golf course. *Perceptual and Motor Skills, 59,* 591–596.

Ericsson, K. A., & Charness, N. (1999). Expert performance: Its structure and acquisition. In S. J. Ceci & W. M. Williams (Eds.), *The nature–nurture debate: The essential readings* (pp. 200–256). Oxford, England: Blackwell.

Erikson, E. H. (1959). *Identity and the life cycle.* New York: International Universities Press.

Espy, K. A., Fang, H., Johnson, C., Stopp, C., Wiebe, S. A., & Respass, J. (2011). Prenatal tobacco exposure: Developmental outcomes in the neonatal period. *Developmental Psychology, 47*(1), 153–169. doi: 10.1037/a0020724

Estes, A., Munson, J., Rogers, S. J., Greenson, J., Winter, J., & Dawson, G. (2015). Long-term outcomes of early intervention in 6-year-old children with Autism Spectrum Disorder. *Journal of the American Academy of Child and Adolescent Psychiatry, 54,* 580–587.

Etcoff, N. (1999). *Survival of the prettiest: The science of beauty.* New York: Doubleday.

Evans, G. W. (2004). The environment of childhood poverty. *American Psychologist, 59*(2), 77–92.

Evans, G. W. (2006). Child development and the physical environment. *Annual Review of Psychology, 57,* 423–451.

Evans, G. W., & Stecker, R. (2004). Motivational consequences of environmental stress. *Journal of Environmental Psychology, 24,* 143–165.

Evans, J. St. B., Barston, J. L., & Pollard, P. (1983), On the conflict between logic and belief in syllogistic reasoning. *Memory & Cognition, 11,* 295–306.

Evans, P. D., Gilbert, S. L., Mekel-Bobrov, N., Vallender, E. J., Anderson, J. R., Vaez-Azizi, L. M., . . . Lahn, B. T. (2005). Microcephalin, a gene regulating brain size, continues to evolve adaptively to humans. *Science, 309,* 1717–1720.

Evans, S. W., & Kim, P. (2012). Childhood poverty and young adults' allostatic load: The mediating role of childhood cumulative risk exposure. *Psychological Science, 23*(9), 979–983. doi: 10.1177/0956797612441218

Everson, S. A., Lynch, J. W., Chesney, M. A., Kaplan, G. A., Goldberg, D.E., Shade, S. B., . . . Salonen, J. T. (1997). Interaction of workplace demands and cardiovascular reactivity in progression of carotid atherosclerosis: Population based study. *British Medical Journal, 314,* 553–558.

Exner, J. E. (1993). *The Rorschach: A comprehensive system: Vol. 1. Basic Foundations.* New York: Wiley.

Eysenck, H. J. (1957). The effects of psychotherapy: An evaluation. *Journal of Consulting Psychology, 16,* 319–324.

Eysenck, H. J. (1967). *The biological basis of personality.* Springfield, IL: Charles C Thomas.

Eysenck, H. J. (1990). Biological dimensions of personality. In L. A. Pervin (Ed.), *Handbook of personality: Theory and research* (pp. 244–276). New York: Guilford Press.

Falk, R., & McGregor, D. (1983). The surprisingness of coincidences. In P. Humphreys, O. Svenson, & A. Vari (Eds.), *Analysing* *and aiding decision processes* (pp. 489–502). New York: North Holland.

Fancher, R. E. (1979). *Pioneers in psychology.* New York: Norton.

Fantz, R. L. (1964). Visual experience in infants: Decreased attention to familiar patterns relative to novel ones. *Science, 164,* 668–670.

Farah, M. J., & Rabinowitz, C. (2003). Genetic and environmental influences on the organization of semantic memory in the brain: Is "living things" an innate category? *Cognitive Neuropsychology, 20,* 401–408.

Farah, M. J., Illes, J., Cook-Deegan, R., Gardner, H., Kandel, E., King, P., . . . Wolpe, P. R. (2004) Neurocognitive enhancement: What can we do and what should we do? *Nature Reviews Neuroscience, 5,* 421–426.

Faraone, S. V., Perlis, R. H., Doyle, A. E., Smoller, J. W., Goralnick, J. J., Holmgren, M. A., & Sklar, P. (2005). Molecular genetics of attention-deficit/hyperactivity disorder. *Biological Psychiatry, 57,* 1313–1323.

Farivar, R. (2009). Dorsal–ventral integration in object recognition. *Brain Research Reviews, 61,* 144–153.

Farooqi, I. S., Bullmore, E., Keogh, J., Gillard, J., O'Rahilly, S., & Fletcher, P. C. (2007). Leptin regulates striatal regions and human eating behavior. *Science, 317,* 1355.

Farooqi, I. S., Matarese, G., Lord, G. M., Keogh, J. M., Lawrence, E., Agwu, C., & O'Rahilly, S. (2002). Beneficial effects of leptin on obesity, T cell hyporesponsiveness, and neuroendocrine/metabolic dysfunction of human congenital leptin deficiency. *Journal of Clinical Investigation, 110*(8), 1093–1103.

Farrar, M. J. (1990). Discourse and the acquisition of grammatical morphemes. *Journal of Child Language, 17,* 607–624.

Farrelly, D., Lazarus, J., & Roberts, G. (2007). Altruists attract. *Evolutionary Psychology, 5,* 313–329.

Favazza, A. (2011). *Bodies under siege: Self-mutilation, nonsuicidal self-injury, and body modification in culture and psychiatry.* Baltimore: Johns Hopkins University Press.

Fazel, S., & Danesh, J. (2002). Serious mental disorder in 23,000 prisoners: A review of 62 surveys. *Lancet, 359,* 545–550.

Fechner, G. T. (1966). *Elements of psychophysics* (H. E. Alder, Trans.). New York: Holt, Rinehart and Winston. (Original work published 1860)

Feczer, D., & Bjorklund, P. (2009). Forever changed: Posttraumatic stress disorder in female military veterans, a case report. *Perspectives in Psychiatric Care, 45,* 278–291.

Fehr, E., & Gaechter, S. (2002). Altruistic punishment in humans. *Nature, 415,* 137–140.

Fein, D., Barton, M., Eigsti, I.-M., Kelley, E., Naigles, L., Schultz, R. T., . . . Tyson, K. (2013). Optimal outcome in individuals with a history of autism. *Journal of Child Psychology and Psychiatry, 54,* 195–205.

Fein, S., Goethals, G. R., & Kugler, M. B. (2007). Social influence on political judgments: The case of presidential debates. *Political Psychology, 28,* 165–192.

Feinberg, M., Willer, R., & Schultz, M. (2014). Gossip and ostracism promote cooperation in groups. *Psychological Science. 25*(3), 656–664. doi: 10.1177/0956797613510184

Feinberg, T. E. (2001). *Altered egos: How the brain creates the self.* New York: Oxford University Press.

Feingold, A. (1992a). Gender differences in mate selection preferences: A test of the parental investment model. *Psychological Bulletin, 112,* 125–139.

Feingold, A. (1992b). Good-looking people are not what we think. *Psychological Bulletin, 111,* 304–341.

Feinstein, J. S., Buzza, C., Hurlemann, R., Follmer, R. L., Dahdaleh, N. S., Coryell, W. H., . . . Wemmie, J. A. (2013).

Fear and panic in humans with bilateral amygdala damage. *Nature Neuroscience, 16*(3), 270–272.

Feldman, D. E. (2009). Synaptic mechanisms for plasticity in neocortex. *Annual Review of Neuroscience, 32,* 33–55.

Ferguson, C. J. (2010). Blazing angels or resident evil? Can violent video games be a force for good? *Review of General Psychology, 14*(2), 68–81. doi: 10.1037/a0018941

Fernald, A., Marchman, V. A., & Weisleder, A. (2013). SES differences in language processing skill and vocabulary are evident at 18 months. *Developmental Science, 16,* 234–248.

Fernandez Nievas, I. F. & Thaver, D. (2015) Work-life balance: A different scale for doctors. *Frontiers in Pediatrics, 3,* 115.

Fernbach, P. M., Rogers, T., Fox, C. R., & Sloman, S. A. (2013). Political extremism is supported by an illusion of understanding. *Psychological Science, 24*(6), 939–946.

Fernyhough, C. (2012). *Pieces of light: The new science of memory.* London: Profile Books.

Ferrari, A . J., Charlson, F. J., Norman, R. E., Patten, S. B., Freedman, G., Murray, C. J. L., . . . Whiteford, H. A. (2013). Burden of depressive disorders by country, sex, age, and year: Findings from the Global Burden of Disease Study 2010. *PLoS Medicine, 10,* e1001547.

Ferster, C. B., & Skinner, B. F. (1957). *Schedules of reinforcement.* New York: Appleton-Century-Crofts.

Festinger, L. (1957). *A theory of cognitive dissonance.* Stanford, CA: Stanford University Press.

Festinger, L., & Carlsmith, J. M. (1959). Cognitive consequences of forced compliance. *Journal of Abnormal and Social Psychology, 58,* 203–210.

Festinger, L., Schachter, S., & Back, K. (1950). *Social pressures in informal groups: A study of human factors in housing.* Oxford: Harper & Row.

Field, G. C. (1921). Faculty psychology and instinct psychology. *Mind, 30,* 257–270.

Fields, G. (2009, May 14). White House czar calls for end to "War on Drugs." *Wall Street Journal.* Retrieved from http://online.wsj.com/article/SB124225891527617397.html

Fields, H. L., & Levine, J. D. (1984). Placebo analgesia: A role for endorphins? *Trends in Neurosciences, 7,* 271–273.

Finkel, E. J., Cheung, E. O., Emery, L. F., Carswell, K. L., & Larson, G. M. (2015). The suffocation model: Why marriage in America is becoming an all-or-nothing institution. *Current Directions in Psychological Science, 24*(3), 238–244. doi: 10.1177/0963721415569274

Finkel, E. J., & Eastwick, P. W. (2009). Arbitrary social norms influence sex differences in romantic selectivity. *Psychological Science, 20,* 1290–1295.

Finkelstein, E. A., Trogdon, J. G., Cohen, J. W., & Dietz, W. (2009). Annual medical spending attributable to obesity: Payer- and service-specific estimates. *Health Affairs, 28*(5), w822–w831.

Finkelstein, K. E. (1999, October 17). In concert, searchers retrieve Yo-Yo Ma's lost Stradivarius. *New York Times.* http://www.nytimes.com/1999/10/17/nyregion/in-concert-searchers-retrieve-yo-yo-ma-s-lost-stradivarius.html

Finn, R. (1991). Different minds. *Discover, 12,* 54–59.

Fiore, A. T., Taylor, L. S., Zhong, X., Mendelsohn, G. A., & Cheshire, C. (2010). Who's right and who writes: People, profiles, contacts, and replies in online dating. *Proceedings of Hawaii International Conferences on Systems Science, 43,* Persistent Conversation minitrack.

Fiorentine, R. (1999). After drug treatment: Are 12-step programs effective in maintaining abstinence? *American Journal of Drug and Alcohol Abuse, 25,* 93–116.

Fiorillo, C. D., Newsome, W. T., & Schultz, W. (2008). The temporal precision of reward prediction in dopamine neurons. *Nature Neuroscience, 11*, 966–973.

Fischer, P., Krueger, J. I., Greitemeyer, T., Vogrincic, C., Kastenmüller, A., Frey, D., … Kainbacher, M. (2011). The bystander-effect: A meta-analytic review on bystander intervention in dangerous and non-dangerous emergencies. *Psychological Bulletin, 137*(4), 517–537. doi: 10.1037/a0023304

Fisher, R. J., & Ma, Y. (2014). The price of being beautiful: Negative effects of attractiveness on empathy for children in need. *Journal of Consumer Research, 41*(2), 436–450. doi: 10.1086/676967

Fisher, R. P., & Craik, F. I. M. (1977). The interaction between encoding and retrieval operations in cued recall. *Journal of Experimental Psychology: Human Learning and Perception, 3*, 153–171.

Fiske, S. T. (1998). Stereotyping, prejudice, and discrimination. In D. T. Gilbert, S. T. Fiske, & G. Lindzey (Eds.), *The handbook of social psychology* (4th ed., Vol. 2, pp. 357–411). New York: McGraw-Hill.

Fiske, S. T. (2010). *Social beings: A core motives approach to social psychology*. Hoboken, NJ: Wiley.

Fleeson, W. (2004). Moving personality beyond the person-situation debate: The challenge and opportunity of within-person variability. *Current Directions in Psychological Science, 13*, 83–87.

Flegal, K. M., & Troiano, R. P. (2000). Changes in the distribution of body mass index of adults and children in the U.S. population. *International Journal of Obesity, 24*, 807–818.

Fletcher, G. J. O., Simpson, J. A., Thomas, G., & Giles, L. (1999). Ideals in intimate relationships. *Journal of Personality and Social Psychology, 76*, 72–89. doi: 10.1037/0022-3514.76.1.72

Fletcher, P. C., Shallice, T., & Dolan, R. J. (1998). The functional roles of prefrontal cortex in episodic memory. I. Encoding. *Brain, 121*, 1239–1248.

Flor, H., Nikolajsen, L., & Jensen, T. S. (2006). Phantom limb pain: A case of maladaptive CNS plasticity? *Nature Reviews Neuroscience, 7*, 873–881.

Flynn, E. (2008). Investigating children as cultural magnets: Do young children transmit redundant information along diffusion chains? *Philosophical Transactions of the Royal Society of London Series B, 363*, 3541–3551.

Flynn, E., & Whiten, A. (2008). Cultural transmission of tool-use in young children: A diffusion chain study. *Social Development, 17*, 699–718.

Flynn, J. R. (2012). *Are we getting smarter? Rising IQ in the twenty-first century*. New York: Cambridge University Press.

Foa, E. B. (2010). Cognitive behavioral therapy of obsessive-compulsive disorder. *Dialogues in Clinical Neuroscience, 12*, 199–207.

Foa, E. B., Liebowitz, M. R., Kozak, M. J., Davies, S., Campeas, R., Franklin, M. E., . . . Tu, X. (2007). Randomized, placebo-controlled trial of exposure and ritual prevention, clomipramine, and their combination in the treatment of obsessive-compulsive disorder. *Focus, 5*, 368–380.

Foa, E. B., & Meadows, E. A. (1997). Psychosocial treatments for posttraumatic stress disorder: A critical review. *Annual Review of Psychology, 48*, 449–480.

Foa, E. B. & McLean, C. P. (2016) The efficacy of exposure therapy for anxiety-related disorders and its underlying mechanisms: The case of OCD and PTSD. *Annual Review of Clinical Psychology, 12*, 1–28.

Fogassi, L., Ferrari, P. F., Gesierich, B., Rozzi, S., Chersi, F., & Rizzolatti, G. (2005). Parietal lobe: From action organization to intention understanding. *Science, 308*, 662–667.

Forkstam, C., Hagoort, P., Fernández, G., Ingvar, M., & Petersson, K. M. (2006). Neural correlates of artificial syntactic structure classification. *NeuroImage, 32*, 956–967.

Fornito, A., Zalesky, A., & Breakspear, M. (2015). The connectomics of brain disorders. *Nature Reviews Neuroscience, 16*, 159–172.

Foroni, F., & Semin, G. R. (2009). Language that puts you in touch with your bodily feelings: The multimodal responsiveness of affective expressions. *Psychological Science, 20*(8), 974–980.

Fournier, J. C., DeRubeis, R., Hollon, S. D., Dimidjian, S., Amsterdam, J. D., Shelton, R. C., & Fawcett, J. (2010). Antidepressant drug effects and depression severity. *Journal of the American Medical Association, 303*, 47–53.

Fouts, R. S., & Bodamer, M. (1987). Preliminary report to the National Geographic Society on "Chimpanzee intrapersonal signing." *Friends of Washoe, 7*, 4–12.

Fox, M. J. (2009). *Always looking up*. New York: Hyperion.

Fox, P. T., Mintun, M. A., Raichle, M. E., Miezin, F. M., Allman, J. M., & Van Essen, D. C. (1986). Mapping human visual cortex with positron emission tomography. *Nature, 323*, 806–809.

Fox, R. E., DeLeon, P. H., Newman, R., Sammons, M. T., Dunivin, D. L., & Baker, D. C. (2009). Prescriptive authority and psychology: A status report. *American Psychologist, 64*, 257–268.

Fragaszy, D. M., Izar, P., Visalberghi, E., Ottoni, E. B., & de Oliveria, M. G. (2004). Wild capuchin monkeys (*Cebus libidinosus*) use anvils and stone pounding tools. *American Journal of Primatology, 64*, 359–366.

Franchow, E. I., & Suchy, Y. (2015). Naturally-occurring expressive suppression in daily life depletes executive functioning. *Emotion, 15*(1), 78–89. doi: 10.1037/emo0000013

Francis, D., Diorio, J., Liu, D., & Meaney, M. J. (1999). Nongenomic transmission across generations of maternal behavior and stress responses in the rat. *Science, 286*, 1155–1158.

Frank, M. G., Ekman, P., & Friesen, W. V. (1993). Behavioral markers and recognizability of the smile of enjoyment. *Journal of Personality and Social Psychology, 64*, 83–93.

Frank, M. G., & Stennet, J. (2001). The forced-choice paradigm and the perception of facial expressions of emotion. *Journal of Personality and Social Psychology, 80*, 75–85.

Frankl, V. (2000). *Man's search for meaning*. New York: Beacon Press.

Franklin, J. C., Fox, K. R., Franklin, C. R., Kleiman, E. M., Ribeiro, J. D., Jaroszewski, A. C., . . . Nock, M. K. (2016). A brief mobile app reduces nonsuicidal and suicidal self-injury: Evidence from three randomized controlled trials. *Journal of Consulting and Clinical Psychology, 84*, 544–557.

Fratkin, J. L., Sinn, D. L., Patall, E. A., & Gosling, S. D. (2013). Personality consistency in dogs: A meta-analysis. *PLoS ONE, 8*, e54907.

Fredman, T., & Whiten, A. (2008). Observational learning from tool using models by human-reared and mother-reared capuchin monkeys (*Cebus apella*). *Animal Cognition, 11*, 295–309.

Fredrickson, B. L. (2000). Cultivating positive emotions to optimize health and well-being. *Prevention and Treatment, 3*, Article 0001a. doi: 10.1037/1522-3736.3.1.31a.

Freedman, J. (1978). *Happy people: What happiness is, who has it, and why*. New York: Harcourt Brace Jovanovich.

Freedman, J. L., & Fraser, S. C. (1966). Compliance without pressure: The foot-in-the-door technique. *Journal of Personality and Social Psychology, 4*, 195–202.

Freeman, S., Walker, M. R., Borden, R., & Latané, B. (1975). Diffusion of responsibility and restaurant tipping: Cheaper by the bunch. *Personality and Social Psychology Bulletin, 1*, 584–587.

French, H. W. (1997, February 26). In the land of the small it isn't easy being tall. *New York Times*. Retrieved from http://www.nytimes.com/1997/02/26/world/in-the-land-of-the-small-it-isn-t-easy-being-tall.html

Freud, S. (1938). The psychopathology of everyday life. In A. A. Brill (Ed.), *The basic writings of Sigmund Freud* (pp. 38–178). New York: Basic Books. (Original work published 1901)

Freud, S. (1965). *The interpretation of dreams* (J. Strachey, Trans.). New York: Avon. (Original work published 1900)

Freund, A. M., & Blanchard-Fields, F. (2014). Age-related differences in altruism across adulthood: Making personal financial gain versus contributing to the public good. *Developmental Psychology, 50*(4), 1125–1136. doi: 10.1037/a0034491

Frick, R. W. (1985). Communicating emotion: The role of prosodic features. *Psychological Bulletin, 97*, 412–429.

Fried, P. A., & Watkinson, B. (2000). Visuoperceptual functioning differs in 9- to 12-year-olds prenatally exposed to cigarettes and marijuana. *Neurotoxicology and Teratology, 22*, 11–20.

Friedlander, L., & Desrocher, M. (2006). Neuroimaging studies of obsessive-compulsive disorder in adults and children. *Clinical Psychology Review, 26*, 32–49.

Friedman, J. M. (2003). A war on obesity, not the obese. *Science, 299*(5608), 856–858.

Friedman, J. M., & Halaas, J. L. (1998). Leptin and the regulation of body weight in mammals. *Nature, 395*(6704), 763–770.

Friedman, M., & Rosenman, R. H. (1974). *Type A behavior and your heart*. New York: Knopf.

Friedman, S. L., & Boyle, D. E. (2008). Attachment in U.S. children experiencing nonmaternal care in the early 1990s. *Attachment & Human Development, 10*(3), 225–261.

Friedman-Hill, S. R., Robertson, L. C., & Treisman, A. (1995). Parietal contributions to visual feature binding: Evidence from a patient with bilateral lesions. *Science, 269*, 853–855.

Friesen, W. V. (1972). *Cultural differences in facial expressions in a social situation: An experimental test of the concept of display rules* (Doctoral dissertation, University of California, San Francisco).

Frith, C. D., & Fletcher, P. (1995). Voices from nowhere. *Critical Quarterly, 37*, 71–83.

Frith, U. (2003). *Autism: Explaining the enigma*. Oxford: Blackwell.

Fry, D. P. (2012). Life without war. *Science, 336*(6083), 879–884. doi: 10.1126/science.1217987

Fryer, A. J., Mannuzza, S., Gallops, M. S., Martin, L. Y., Aaronson, C., Gorman, J. M., . . . Klein, D. F. (1990). Familial transmission of simple phobias and fears: A preliminary report. *Archives of General Psychiatry, 47*, 252–256.

Fu, F., Tarnita, C. E., Christakis, N. A., Wang, L., Rand, D. G., & Novak, M. A. (2012). Evolution of in-group favoritism. *Scientific Reports, 2*, Article 460. doi: 10.1038/srep00460

Fukui, H., Murai, T., Fukuyama, H., Hayashi, T., & Hanakawa, T. (2005). Functional activity related to risk anticipation during performance of the Iowa gambling task. *NeuroImage, 24*, 253–259.

Funder, D. C. (2001). Personality. *Annual Review of Psychology, 52*, 197–221.

Furmark, T., Tillfors, M., Marteinsdottir, I., Fischer, H., Pissiota, A., Långström, B., & Fredrikson, M. (2002). Common changes in cerebral blood flow in patients with social phobia treated with citalopram or cognitive behavioral therapy. *Archives of General Psychiatry, 59*(5), 425–433.

Furnham, A. (2001). Self-estimates of intelligence: Culture and gender difference in self and other estimates of both general (g) and multiple intelligences. *Personality and Individual Differences, 31*(8), 1381–1405. doi: 10.1016/S0191-8869(00)00232-4

Fuss, J., Steinle, J., Bindila, L., Auer, M.K., Kirchherr, H., Lutz, B., & Gass, P. (2015). A runner's high depends on cannabinoid receptors in mice. *PNAS, 112*, 13105-13108.

Fuster, J. M. (2003). *Cortex and mind*. New York: Oxford University Press.

Gadermann, A. M., Alonso, J., Vilagut, G., Zaslavsky, A. M., & Kessler, R. C. (2012). Comorbidity and disease burden in the National Comorbidity Survey Replication (NCS-R). *Depression and Anxiety, 29*, 797–806.

Gais, S., & Born, J. (2004). Low acetylcholine during slow-wave sleep is critical for declarative memory consolidation. *Proceedings of the National Academy of Sciences, USA, 101*, 2140–2144.

Galati, D., Scherer, K. R., & Ricci-Bitt, P. E. (1997). Voluntary facial expression of emotion: Comparing congenitally blind with normally sighted encoders. *Journal of Personality and Social Psychology, 73*, 1363–1379.

Gale, C. R., Batty, G. D., McIntosh, A. M., Porteous, D. J., Deary, I. J., & Rasmussen, F. (2012). Is bipolar disorder more common in highly intelligent people? A cohort study of a million men. *Molecular Psychiatry, 18*(2), 190–194. doi: 10.1038/mp.2012.26

Gale, C. R., Batty, G. D., Tynelius, P., Deary, I. J., & Rasmussen, F. (2010). Intelligence in early adulthood and subsequent hospitalization for mental disorders. *Epidemiology, 21*(1), 70–77. doi: 10.1097/EDE.0b013e3181c17da8

Galef, B. (1998). Edward Thorndike: Revolutionary psychologist, ambiguous biologist. *American Psychologist, 53*, 1128–1134.

Galanter, E. (1962). Contemporary psychophysics. In R. Brown, E. Galanter, E. H. Hess, & G. Mandler (Eds.), *New directions in psychology*. New York: Holt, Rinehart, & Winston.

Gallistel, C. R. (2000). The replacement of general-purpose learning models with adaptively specialized learning modules. In M. S. Gazzaniga (Ed.), *The new cognitive neurosciences* (pp. 1179–1191). Cambridge, MA: MIT Press.

Gallo, D. A. (2006). *Associative illusions of memory*. New York: Psychology Press.

Gallo, D. A. (2010). False memories and fantastic beliefs: 15 years of the DRM illusion. *Memory & Cognition, 38*, 833–848.

Gallup (2014, July 9). Obesity linked to lower social well-being. Retrieved from http://www.gallup.com/poll/172253/obesity-linked-lower-social.aspx

Gallup (2014, July 10). Older Americans feel best about their physical appearance. Retrieved from http://www.gallup.com/poll/172361/older-americans-feel-best-physical-appearance.aspx

Gallup (2015, October 21). In US, 58% back legal marijuana use. Retrieved from http://www.gallup.com/poll/186260/back-legal-marijuana.aspx

Gallup, G. G. (1977). Self-recognition in primates: A comparative approach to the bidirectional properties of consciousness. *American Psychologist, 32*, 329–338.

Gallup, G. G. (1997). On the rise and fall of self-conception in primates. *Annals of the New York Academy of Sciences, 818*, 73–84.

Gallup, G. G., & Frederick, D. A. (2010). The science of sex appeal: An evolutionary perspective. *Review of General Psychology, 14*(3), 240–250. doi: 10.1037/a0020451

Galton, F. (1869). *Hereditary genius: An inquiry into its laws and consequences*. London: Macmillan/Fontana.

Gangestad, S. W., & Haselton, M. G. (2015). Human estrus: Implications for relationship science. *Current Opinion in Psychology, 1*, 45–51.

Ganzel, B. L., Kim, P., Glover, G. H., & Temple, E. (2008). Resilience after 9/11: Multimodal neuroimaging evidence for stress-related change in the healthy adult brain. *NeuroImage, 40*, 788–795.

Garb, H. N. (1998). *Studying the clinician: Judgment research and psychological assessment*. Washington, DC: American Psychological Association.

Garcia, J. (1981). Tilting at the windmills of academe. *American Psychologist 36*, 149–158.

Garcia, J., & Koelling, R. A. (1966). Relation of cue to consequence in avoidance learning. *Psychonomic Science, 4*, 123–124.

Garcia-Moreno, C., Jansen, H. A. F. M., Ellsberg, M., Heise, L., & Watts, C. H. (2006). Prevalence of intimate partner violence: Findings from the WHO multi-country study on women's health and domestic violence. *Lancet, 368*(9543), 1260–1269. doi: 10.1016/S0140-6736(06)69523-8

Gardner, M., & Steinberg, L. (2005). Peer influence on risk taking, risk preference, and risky decision making in adolescence and adulthood: An experimental study. *Developmental Psychology, 41*,(4), 625–635. doi:10.1037/0012-1649.41.4.625

Gardner, R. A., & Gardner, B. T. (1969). Teaching sign language to a chimpanzee. *Science, 165*, 664–672.

Garland, A. F., & Zigler, E. (1999). Emotional and behavioral problems among highly intellectually gifted youth. *Roeper Review, 22*(1), 41.

Garrett, B. L. (2011). *Convicting the innocent: Where criminal prosecutions go wrong*. Cambridge, MA: Harvard University Press.

Gaser, C., & Schlaug, G. (2003). Brain structures differ between musicians and nonmusicians. *Journal of Neuroscience, 23*, 9240–9245.

Gates, F. J. (2011). *How many people are lesbian, gay, bisexual, and transgender?* Los Angeles: UCLA School of Law, Williams Institute. Retrieved from http://williamsinstitute.law.ucla.edu/wp-content/uploads/Gates-How-Many-People-LGBT-Apr-2011.pdf

Gathercole, S. E. (2008). Nonword repetition and word learning: The nature of the relationship. *Applied Psycholinguistics, 27*, 513–543.

Gazzaniga, M. S. (2006). Forty-five years of split brain research and still going strong. *Nature Reviews Neuroscience, 6*, 653–659.

Gazzaniga, M. S. (Ed.). (2000). *The new cognitive neurosciences*. Cambridge, MA: MIT Press.

Ge, D., Fellay, J., Thompson, A. J., Simon, J. S., Shianna, K. V., Urban, T. J., . . . Goldstein, D. B. (2009). Genetic variation in il28b predicts hepatitis C treatment-induced viral clearance. *Nature, 461*, 399–401.

Ge, X. J., Conger, R. D., & Elder, G. H. (1996). Coming of age too early: Pubertal influences on girls' vulnerability to psychological distress. *Child Development, 67*, 3386–3400.

Ge, X. J., Conger, R. D., & Elder, G. H., Jr. (2001). Pubertal transition, stressful life events, and the emergence of gender differences in adolescent depressive symptoms. *Developmental Psychology, 37*(3), 404–417. doi: 10.1037/0012-1649.37.3.404

Ge, X. J., & Natsuaki, M. N. (2009). In search of explanations for early pubertal timing effects on developmental psychopathology. *Current Directions in Psychological Science, 18*, 327–331.

Geen, R. G. (1984). Preferred stimulation levels in introverts and extraverts: Effects on arousal and performance. *Journal of Personality and Social Psychology, 46*, 1303–1312.

Gegenfurtner, K. R., Bloj, M., & Toscani, M. (2015). The many colours of 'the dress'. *Current Biology, 25*, R543–R544.

Gegenfurtner, K. R., & Kiper, D. C. (2003). Color vision. *Annual Review of Neuroscience, 26*, 181–206.

Geier, A., Wansink, B., & Rozin, P. (2012). Red potato chips: Segmentation cues substantially decrease food intake. *Health Psychology, 31*, 398–401.

Gendron, M., Roberson, D., van der Vyver, J. M., & Barrett, L. F. (2014). Perceptions of emotion from facial expressions are not culturally universal: Evidence from a remote culture. *Emotion, 14*, 251–262. do: 10.1037/a0036052

Gerbasi, M. E., & Prentice, D. A. (2013). The self- and other-interest inventory. *Journal of Personality and Social Psychology, 105*(3), 495–514. doi: 10.1037/a0033483

Gershoff, E. T. (2002). Corporal punishment by parents and associated child behaviors and experiences: A meta-analytic and theoretical review. *Psychological Bulletin, 128*, 539–579.

Geschwind, D. H. (2009). Advances in autism. *Annual Review of Medicine, 60*, 67–80.

Gibb, B. E., Alloy, L. B., & Tierney, S. (2001). History of childhood maltreatment, negative cognitive styles, and episodes of depression in adulthood. *Cognitive Therapy and Research, 25*, 425–446.

Gibbons, F. X. (1990). Self-attention and behavior: A review and theoretical update. In M. P. Zanna (Ed.), *Advances in experimental social psychology* (Vol. 23, pp. 249–303). San Diego: Academic Press.

Gick, M. L., & Holyoak, K. J. (1980). Analogical problem solving. *Cognitive Psychology, 12*, 306–355.

Giedd, J. N., Blumenthal, J., Jeffries, N. O., Castellanos, F. X., Liu, H., Zijdenbos, A., . . . Rapoport, J. L. (1999). Brain development during childhood and adolescence: A longitudinal MRI study. *Nature Neuroscience, 2*, 861–863.

Gierlach, E., Blesher, B. E., & Beutler, L. E. (2010). Cross-cultural differences in risk perceptions of disasters. *Risk Analysis, 30*, 1539–1549.

Gigone, D., & Hastie, R. (1993). The common knowledge effect: Information sharing and group judgment. *Journal of Personality and Social Psychology, 54*, 959–974.

Gilbert, D. T. (1991). How mental systems believe. *American Psychologist, 46*, 107–119.

Gilbert, D. T. (1998). Ordinary personology. In D. T. Gilbert, S. T. Fiske, & G. Lindzey (Eds.), *The handbook of social psychology* (4th ed., Vol. 2, pp. 89–150). New York: McGraw-Hill.

Gilbert, D. T. (2006). *Stumbling on happiness*. New York: Knopf.

Gilbert, D. T., Brown, R. P., Pinel, E. C., & Wilson, T. D. (2000). The illusion of external agency. *Journal of Personality and Social Psychology, 79*, 690–700.

Gilbert, D. T., Gill, M. J., & Wilson, T. D. (2002). The future is now: Temporal correction in affective forecasting. *Organizational Behavior and Human Decision Processes, 88*, 430–444.

Gilbert, D. T., & Malone, P. S. (1995). The correspondence bias. *Psychological Bulletin, 117*, 21–38.

Gilbert, D. T., Pelham, B. W., & Krull, D. S. (1988). On cognitive busyness: When persons perceivers meet persons perceived. *Journal of Personality and Social Psychology, 54*, 733–740.

Gilbertson, M. W., Shenton, M. E., Ciszewski, A., Kasai, K., Lasko, N. B., Orr, S. P., & Pitman, R. K. (2002). Smaller hippocampal volume predicts pathological vulnerability to psychological trauma. *Nature Neuroscience, 5*, 1242–1247.

Gillespie, C. F., & Nemeroff, C. B. (2007). Corticotropin-releasing factor and the psychobiology of early-life stress. *Current Directions in Psychological Science, 16*, 85–89.

Gillette, J., Gleitman, H., Gleitman, L., & Lederer, A. (1999). Human simulation of vocabulary learning. *Cognition, 73*, 135–176.

Gilligan, C. (1982). *In a different voice: Psychological theory and women's development*. Cambridge, MA: Harvard University Press.

Gilovich, T. (1991). *How we know what isn't so: The fallibility of human reason in everyday life.* New York: Free Press.

Gino, F., & Pierce, L. (2009). The abundance effect: Unethical behavior in the presence of wealth. *Organizational Behavior and Human Decision Processes, 109*(2), 142–155. doi: 10.1016/j.obhdp.2009.03.003

Ginzburg, K., Solomon, Z., & Bleich, A. (2002). Repressive coping style, acute stress disorder, and posttraumatic stress disorder after myocardial infarction. *Psychosomatic Medicine, 64,* 748–757.

Giovanello, K. S., Schnyer, D. M., & Verfaellie, M. (2004). A critical role for the anterior hippocampus in relational memory: Evidence from an fMRI study comparing associative and item recognition. *Hippocampus, 14,* 5–8.

Gladue, B. A. (1994). The biopsychology of sexual orientation. *Current Directions in Psychological Science, 3,* 150–154.

Glanzer, M. & Cunitz, A. R. (1966). Two storage mechanisms in free recall. *Journal of Verbal Learning and Verbal Behavior, 5,* 351–360.

Glass, D. C., & Singer, J. E. (1972). *Urban stress.* New York: Academic Press.

Glenwick, D. S., Jason, L. A., & Elman, D. (1978). Physical attractiveness and social contact in the singles bar. *Journal of Social Psychology, 105,* 311–312.

Glick, D. M., & Orsillo, S. M. (2015). An investigation of the efficacy of acceptance-based behavioral therapy for academic procrastination. *Journal of Experimental Psychology: General, 144,* 400–409.

Glynn, L. M., & Sandman, C. A. (2011). Prenatal origins of neurological development: A critical period for fetus and mother. *Current Directions in Psychological Science, 20*(6), 384–389. doi: 10.1177/0963721411422056

Gneezy, U., & Rustichini, A. (2000). A fine is a price. *Journal of Legal Studies, 29,* 1–17.

Gobert, A., Rivet, J. M., Cistarelli, L., Melon, C., & Millan, M. J. (1999). Buspirone modulates basal and fluoxetine-stimulated dialysate levels of dopamine, noradrenaline, and serotonin in the frontal cortex of freely moving rats: Activation of serotonin 1A receptors and blockade of alpha2-adrenergic receptors underlie its actions. *Neuroscience, 93,* 1251–1262.

Goddard, H. H. (1913). *The Kallikak family: A study in the heredity of feeble-mindedness.* New York: Macmillan.

Godden, D. R., & Baddeley, A. D. (1975). Context-dependent memory in two natural environments: On land and underwater. *British Journal of Psychology, 66,* 325–331.

Goehler, L. E., Gaykema, R. P. A., Hansen, M. K., Anderson, K., Maier, S. F., & Watkins, L. R. (2000). Vagal immune-to-brain communication: A visceral chemosensory pathway. *Autonomic Neuroscience: Basic and Clinical, 85,* 49–59.

Goetzman, E. S., Hughes, T., & Klinger, E. (1994). *Current concerns of college students in a midwestern sample.* (Unpublished report, University of Minnesota, Morris).

Goff, L. M., & Roediger, H. L., III. (1998). Imagination inflation for action events—repeated imaginings lead to illusory recollections. *Memory & Cognition, 26,* 20–33.

Goldman, M. S., Brown, S. A., & Christiansen, B. A. (1987). Expectancy theory: Thinking about drinking. In H. T. Blane & K. E. Leonard (Eds.), *Psychological theories of drinking and alcoholism* (pp. 181–266). New York: Guilford Press.

Goldstein, M. H., Schwade, J. A., Briesch, J., & Syal, S. (2010). Learning while babbling: Prelinguistic object-directed vocalizations signal a readiness to learn. *Infancy, 15,* 362–391.

Gomez, C., Argandota, E. D., Solier, R. G., Angulo, J. C., & Vazquez, M. (1995). Timing and competition in networks representing ambiguous figures. *Brain and Cognition, 29,* 103–114.

Gontier, N. (2008). Genes, brains, and language: An epistemological examination of how genes can underlie human cognitive behavior. *Review of General Psychology, 12,* 170–180.

Gonzaga, G. C., Keltner, D., Londahl, E. A., & Smith, M. D. (2001). Love and the commitment problem in romantic relations and friendship. *Journal of Personality and Social Psychology, 81,* 247–262.

Goodale, M. A., & Milner, A. D. (1992). Separate visual pathways for perception and action. *Trends in Neurosciences, 15,* 20–25.

Goodale, M. A., & Milner, A. D. (2004). *Sight unseen.* Oxford: Oxford University Press.

Goodale, M. A., Milner, A. D., Jakobson, L. S., & Carey, D. P. (1991). A neurological dissociation between perceiving objects and grasping them. *Nature, 349,* 154–156.

Gootman, E. (2003, March 3). Separated at birth in Mexico, united at campuses on Long Island. *New York Times.* Retrieved from http://www.nytimes.com/2003/03/03/nyregion/separated-at-birth-in-mexico-reunited-at-campuses-on-li.html?_r=0

Gopnik, A. (2012). Scientific thinking in young children: Theoretical advances, empirical research, and policy implications. *Science, 337*(6102), 1623–1627. doi: 10.1126/science.1223416

Gopnik, A., & Astington, J. W. (1988). Children's understanding of representational change and its relation to the understanding of false belief and the appearance reality distinction. *Child Development, 59,* 26–37.

Gopnik, M. (1990a). Feature-blind grammar and dysphasia. *Nature, 344,* 715.

Gopnik, M. (1990b). Feature blindness: A case study. *Language Acquisition: A Journal of Developmental Linguistics, 1,* 139–164.

Gorczynski, P., & Faulkner, G. (2011). Exercise therapy for schizophrenia. *Cochrane Database of Systematic Reviews, 5,* CD004412.

Gordon, P. (2004). Numerical cognition without words: Evidence from Amazonia. *Science, 306,* 496–499.

Gorno-Tempini, M. L., Price, C. J., Josephs, O., Vandenberghe, R., Cappa, S. F., Kapur, N., & Frackowiak, R. S. (1998). The neural systems sustaining face and proper-name processing. *Brain, 121,* 2103–2118.

Gosling, S. D. (1998). Personality dimensions in spotted hyenas (*Crocuta crocuta*). *Journal of Comparative Psychology, 112,* 107–118.

Gosling, S. D. (2008). Personality in non-human animals. *Social and Personality Psychology Compass, 2,* 985–1001.

Gosling, S. D., & John, O. P. (1999). Personality dimensions in nonhuman animals: A cross-species review. *Current Directions in Psychological Science, 8,* 69–75.

Gosling, S. D., Rentfrow, P. J., & Swann, W. B., Jr. (2003). A very brief measure of the Big-Five personality domains. *Journal of Research in Personality, 37,* 504–528.

Gotlib, I. H., & Joormann, J. (2010). Cognition and depression: Current status and future directions. *Annual Review of Clinical Psychology, 6,* 285–312.

Gottesman, I. I. (1991). *Schizophrenia genesis: The origins of madness.* New York: Freeman.

Gottesman, I. I., & Hanson, D. R. (2005). Human development: Biological and genetic processes. *Annual Review of Psychology, 56,* 263–286.

Gottfredson, L. S. (1997). Mainstream science on intelligence: An editorial with 52 signatories, history, and bibliography. *Intelligence, 24,* 13–23.

Gottfredson, L. S. (2003). Dissecting practical intelligence theory: Its claims and evidence. *Intelligence, 31*(4), 343–397.

Gottfredson, L. S., & Deary, I. J. (2004). Intelligence predicts health and longevity, but why? *Current Directions in Psychological Science, 13,* 1–4.

Gottfried, J. A. (2008). Perceptual and neural plasticity of odor quality coding in the human brain. *Chemosensory Perception, 1,* 127–135.

Gouldner, A. W. (1960). The norm of reciprocity. *American Sociological Review, 25,* 161–178.

Grady, C. L., Haxby, J. V., Horwitz, B., Schapiro, M. B., Rapoport, S. I., Ungerleider, L. G., . . . Herscovitch, P. (1992). Dissociation of object and spatial vision in human extrastriate cortex: Age-related changes in activation of regional cerebral blood flow measured with [15O] water and positron emission tomography. *Journal of Cognitive Neuroscience, 4*(1), 23–34. doi: 10.1162/jocn.1992.4.1.23

Graf, P., & Schacter, D. L. (1985). Implicit and explicit memory for new associations in normal subjects and amnesic patients. *Journal of Experimental Psychology: Learning, Memory, and Cognition, 11,* 501–518.

Grant, A. M. (2008). Personal life coaching for coaches-in-training enhances goal attainment, insight, and learning. *Coaching, 1*(1), 54–70.

Grant, B. F., Hasin, D. S., Stinson, F. S., Dawson, D. A., Chou, S. P., & Ruan, W. J. (2004). Prevalence, correlates, and disability of personality disorders in the U.S.: Results from the National Epidemiologic Survey on Alcohol and Related Conditions. *Journal of Clinical Psychiatry, 65,* 948–958.

Grassian, S. (2006). Psychiatric effects of solitary confinement. *Washington University Journal of Law and Policy, 22,* 1–24.

Gray, H. M., Gray, K., & Wegner, D. M. (2007). Dimensions of mind perception. *Science, 315,* 619.

Gray, J. A. (1970). The psychophysiological basis of introversion–extraversion. *Behavior Research and Therapy, 8,* 249–266.

Gray, J. A. (1990). Brain systems that mediate both emotion and cognition. *Cognition and Emotion, 4,* 269–288.

Greely, H., Sahakian, B., Harris, J., Kessler, R. C., Gazzaniga, M., Campbell, P., & Farah, M. J. (2008). Towards responsible use of cognitive enhancing drugs by the healthy. *Nature, 456*(7223), 702–705.

Green, C. S., & Bavelier, D. (2007). Action video-game experience alters the spatial resolution of vision. *Psychological Science, 18,* 88–94.

Green, D. A., & Swets, J. A. (1966). *Signal detection theory and psychophysics.* New York: Wiley.

Green, M. F., Kern, R. S., Braff, D. L., & Mintz, J. (2000). Neurocognitive deficits and functional outcome in schizophrenia: Are we measuring the "right stuff"? *Schizophrenia Bulletin, 26,* 119–136.

Green, S. K., Buchanan, D. R., & Heuer, S. K. (1984). Winners, losers, and choosers: A field investigation of dating initiation. *Personality and Social Psychology Bulletin, 10,* 502–511.

Greenberg, J., Pyszczynski, T., Solomon, S., Rosenblatt, A., Veeder, M., Kirkland, S., & Lyon, D. (1990). Evidence for terror management theory II: The effects of mortality salience on reactions to those who threaten or bolster the cultural worldview. *Journal of Personality and Social Psychology, 58,* 308–318.

Greenberg, J., Solomon, S., & Arndt, J. (2008). A basic but uniquely human motivation: Terror management. In J. Y. Shah & W. L. Gardner (Eds.), *Handbook of motivation science* (pp. 114–134). New York: Guilford Press.

Greene, J. (2013). *Moral tribes: Emotion, reason, and the gap between us and them.* New York: Penguin.

Greene, J. D., Sommerville, R. B., Nystrom, L. E., Darley, J. M., & Cohen, J. D. (2001). An fMRI investigation of emotional engagement in moral judgment. *Science, 293,* 2105–2108.

Greenspan, L., & Deardorff, J. (2014). *The new puberty: How to navigate early development in today's girls.* Emmaus, PA: Rodale Books.

Greenwald, A. G. (1992). New look 3: Unconscious cognition reclaimed. *American Psychologist, 47,* 766–779.

Greenwald, A. G., & Nosek, B. A. (2001). Health of the Implicit Association Test at age 3. *Zeitschrift für Experimentelle Psychologie, 48,* 85–93.

Greenwald, A. G., McGhee, D. E., & Schwartz, J. L. K. (1998). Measuring individual differences in implicit cognition: The implicit association test. *Journal of Personality and Social Psychology, 74,* 1464–1480.

Gropp, E., Shanabrough, M., Borok, E., Xu, A. W., Janoschek, R., Buch, T., . . . Brüning, J. C. (2005). Agouti-related peptide-expressing neurons are mandatory for feeding. *Nature Neuroscience, 8,* 1289–1291.

Gross, J. J. (1998). Antecedent- and response-focused emotion regulation: Divergent consequences for experience, expression, and physiology. *Journal of Personality and Social Psychology, 74,* 224–237.

Gross, J. J. (2002). Emotion regulation: Affective, cognitive, and social consequences. *Psychophysiology, 39,* 281–291.

Gross, J. J., & Muñoz, R. F. (1995). Emotion regulation and mental health. *Clinical Psychology: Science and Practice, 2,* 151–164.

Groves, B. (2004, August 2). Unwelcome awareness. *San Diego Union-Tribune,* p. 24.

Grün, F., & Blumberg, B. (2006). Environmental obesogens: Organotins and endocrine disruption via nuclear receptor signaling. *Endocrinology, 147,* s50–s55.

Guerin, S. A., Robbins, C. A., Gilmore, A. W., & Schacter, D. L. (2012a). Interactions between visual attention and episodic retrieval: Dissociable contributions of parietal regions during gist-based false recognition. *Neuron, 75,* 1122–1134.

Guerin, S. A., Robbins, C. A., Gilmore, A. W., & Schacter, D. L. (2012b). Retrieval failure contributes to gist-based false recognition. *Journal of Memory and Language, 66,* 68–78.

Guilford, J. P. (1967). *The nature of human intelligence.* New York: McGraw-Hill.

Guillery, R. W., & Sherman, S. M. (2002). Thalamic relay functions and their role in corticocortical communication: Generalizations from the visual system. *Neuron, 33,* 163–175.

Gup, T. (2013, April 3). Diagnosis: Human. *New York Times.* Retrieved from http://www.nytimes.com/2013/04/03/opinion/diagnosis-human.html

Gur, R. E., Cowell, P., Turetsky, B. I., Gallacher, F., Cannon, T., Bilker, W., & Gur, R. C. (1998). A follow-up magnetic resonance imaging study of schizophrenia: Relationship of neuroanatomical changes to clinical and neurobehavioral measures. *Archives of General Psychiatry, 55,* 145–152.

Gurwitz, J. H., McLaughlin, T. J., Willison, D. J., Guadagnoli, E., Hauptman, P. J., Gao, X., & Soumerai, S. B. (1997). Delayed hospital presentation in patients who have had acute myocardial infarction. *Annals of Internal Medicine, 126,* 593–599.

Gusnard, D. A., & Raichle, M. E. (2001). Searching for a baseline: Functional imaging and the resting human brain. *Nature Reviews Neuroscience, 2,* 685–694.

Gustafsson, J.-E. (1984). A unifying model for the structure of intellectual abilities. *Intelligence, 8,* 179–203.

Gutchess, A. H., & Schacter, D. L. (2012). The neural correlates of gist-based true and false recognition. *NeuroImage, 59,* 3418–3426.

Guthrie, R. V. (2000). Kenneth Bancroft Clark (1914–). In A. E. Kazdin (Ed.), *Encyclopedia of Psychology* (Vol. 2, p. 91). Washington, DC: American Psychological Association.

Haase, C. M., Heckhausen, J., & Wrosch, C. (2013). Developmental regulation across the life span: Toward a new synthesis. *Developmental Psychology, 49*(5), 964–972. doi: 10.1037/a0029231

Hackman, D. A., & Farah, M. J. (2008). Socioeconomic status and the developing brain. *Trends in Cognitive Sciences, 13,* 65–73.

Hackman, J. R., & Katz, N. (2010). Group behavior and performance. In S. T. Fiske, D. T. Gilbert, & G. Lindzey (Eds.), *The handbook of social psychology* (5th ed., Vol. 2, pp. 1208–1251). New York: Wiley.

Haddadin, S., Liu, J., Cash, S. S., van der Smagt, P., & Donoghue, J. P. (2012). Reach and grasp by people with tetraplegia using a neurally controlled robotic arm. *Nature, 485,* 372–377.

Haedt-Matt, A. A., & Keel, P. K. (2011). Revisiting the affect regulation model of binge eating: A meta-analysis of studies using ecological momentary assessment. *Psychological Bulletin, 137*(4), 660–681.

Haggard, P., & Tsakiris, M. (2009). The experience of agency: Feelings, judgments, and responsibility. *Current Directions in Psychological Science, 18,* 242–246.

Haidt, J. (2001). The emotional dog and its rational tail: A social intuitionist approach to moral judgment. *Psychological Review, 108,* 814–834.

Haidt, J. (2006). *The happiness hypothesis: Finding modern truth in ancient wisdom.* New York: Basic Books.

Haidt, J., & Keltner, D. (1999). Culture and facial expression: Open-ended methods find more expressions and a gradient of recognition. *Cognition and Emotion, 13*(3), 225–266.

Haines, M. M., Stansfeld, S. A., Job, R. F., Berglund, B., & Head, J. (2001). Chronic aircraft noise exposure, stress responses, mental health and cognitive performance in school children. *Psychological Medicine, 31,* 265–277.

Halim, M. L., Ruble, D. N., Tamis-LeMonda, C. S., Zosuls, K. M., Lurye, L. E., & Greulich, F. K. (2014). Pink frilly dresses and the avoidance of all things "girly": Children's appearance rigidity and cognitive theories of gender development. *Developmental Psychology, 50*(4), 1091–1101. doi: 10.1037/a0034906

Hallett, M. (2000). Transcranial magnetic stimulation and the human brain. *Nature, 406,* 147–150.

Halliday, R., Naylor, H., Brandeis, D., Callaway, E., Yano, L., & Herzig, K. (1994). The effect of D-amphetamine, clonidine, and yohimbine on human information processing. *Psychophysiology, 31,* 331–337.

Halpern, B. (2002). Taste. In H. Pashler & S. Yantis (Eds.), *Stevens' handbook of experimental psychology: Vol. 1. Sensation and perception* (3rd ed., pp. 653–690). New York: Wiley.

Halpern, D. F., Benbow, C. P., Geary, D. C., Gur, R. C., Hyde, J. S., & Gernsbacher, M. A. (2007). The science of sex differences in science and mathematics. *Psychological Science in the Public Interest, 8*(1), 1–51.

Hambrick, D. Z., Oswald, F. L., Altmann, E. M., Meinz, E. J., Gobet, F., & Campitelli, G. (2013). Deliberate practice: Is that all it takes to become an expert? *Intelligence, 45,* 34–45. doi: 10.1016/j.intell.2013.04.001

Hamermesh, D. S., & Biddle, J. E. (1994). Beauty and the labor market. *American Economic Review, 84,* 1174–1195.

Hamilton, A. F., & Grafton, S. T. (2006). Goal representation in human anterior intraparietal sulcus. *Journal of Neuroscience, 26,* 1133–1137.

Hamilton, A. F., & Grafton, S. T. (2008). Action outcomes are represented in human inferior frontoparietal cortex. *Cerebral Cortex, 18,* 1160–1168.

Hamilton, D. L., & Gifford, R. K. (1976). Illusory correlation in interpersonal perception: A cognitive basis of stereotypic judgements. *Journal of Experimental Social Psychology, 12,* 392–407.

Hamilton, J. P., Etkin, A., Furman, D. J., Lemus, M. G., Johnson, R. F., & Gotlib, I. H. (2012). Functional neuroimaging of major depressive disorder: A meta-analysis and new integration of baseline activation and neural response data. *American Journal of Psychiatry, 169,* 693–703.

Hamilton, J. P., Glover, G. H., Hsu, J. J., Johnson, R. F., & Gotlib, I. H. (2010). Modulation of subgenual anterior cingulated cortex activity with real-time neurofeedback. *Human Brain Mapping, 32,* 22–31.

Hamilton, W. D. (1964). The genetical evolution of social behaviour. *Journal of Theoretical Biology, 7,* 1–16.

Hamlin, J. K., Mahajan, N., Liberman, Z., & Wynn, K. (2013). Not like me = bad: Infants prefer those who harm dissimilar others. *Psychological Science, 24*(4), 589–594. doi: 10.1177/0956797612457785

Hamlin, J. K., & Steckler, C. M. (2015). The moral infant: On the roots of moral reasoning and behavior in the first two years, in R. Scott & S. Kosslyn (Eds.), *Emerging trends in the social and behavioral sciences.* Hoboken, NJ: Wiley.

Hamlin, J. K., Wynn, K., & Bloom, P. (2007). Social evaluation by preverbal infants. *Nature, 450*(7169), 557–559.

Hammersla, J. F., & Frease-McMahan, L. (1990). University students' priorities: Life goals vs. relationships. *Sex Roles, 23,* 1–14.

Hannon, E. E., & Trainor, L. J. (2007). Music acquisition: Effects of enculturation and formal training on development. *Trends in Cognitive Sciences, 11,* 466–472.

Hansen, E. S., Hasselbalch, S., Law, I., & Bolwig, T. G. (2002). The caudate nucleus in obsessive-compulsive disorder. Reduced metabolism following treatment with paroxetine: A PET study. *International Journal of Neuropsychopharmacology, 5,* 1–10.

Happé, F. & Frith, U. (2006). The weak coherence account: Detail-focused cognitive style in autism spectrum disorders. *Journal of Autism and Developmental Disorders, 36,* 5–25.

Happé, F. G. E. (1995). The role of age and verbal ability in the theory of mind performance of subjects with autism. *Child Development, 66,* 843–855.

Happé, F. G. E., & Vital, P. (2009). What aspects of autism predispose to talent? *Philosophical Transactions of the Royal Society B: Biological Science, 364,* 1369–1375.

Harand, C., Bertran, F., La Joie, R., Landeau, B., Mézenge, F., Desgranges, B., . . . Rauchs, G. (2012). The hippocampus remains activated over the long term for the retrieval of truly episodic memories. *PLoS ONE, 7,* e43495. doi: 10.1371/journal.pone.0043495

Harding, C. M., Brooks, G. W., Ashikaga, T., Strauss, J. S., & Brier, A. (1987). The Vermont longitudinal study of persons with severe mental illness, II: Long-term outcome of subjects who retrospectively met DSM-III criteria for schizophrenia. *American Journal of Psychiatry, 144,* 727–735.

Hare, R. D. (1998). *Without conscience: The disturbing world of the psychopaths among us.* New York: Guilford Press.

Harkness, S., Edwards, C. P., & Super, C. M. (1981). Social roles and moral reasoning: A case study in a rural African community. *Developmental Psychology, 17,* 595–603.

Harlow, H. F. (1958). The nature of love. *American Psychologist, 13,* 573–685.

Harlow, H. F., & Harlow, M. L. (1965). The affectional systems. In A. M. Schrier, H. F. Harlow, & F. Stollnitz (Eds.), *Behavior of nonhuman primates* (Vol. 2, pp. 287–334). New York: Academic Press.

Harlow, J. M. (1848). Passage of an iron rod through the head. *Boston Medical and Surgical Journal, 39,* 389–393.

Harman, O. & Dietrich, M. R. (Eds.) (2013). *Outsider science: Routes to innovation in biology*. Chicago: University of Chicago Press.

Harmon-Jones, E., Harmon-Jones, C., & Levy, N. (2015). An action-based model of cognitive-dissonance processes. *Current Directions in Psychological Science, 24*(3), 184–189. doi: 10.1177/0963721414566449

Harris, B. (1979). Whatever happened to Little Albert? *American Psychologist, 34,* 151–160.

Harris, P. L., de Rosnay, M., & Pons, F. (2005). Language and children's understanding of mental states. *Current Directions in Psychological Science, 14,* 69–73.

Harris, P. L., Johnson, C. N., Hutton, D., Andrews, G., & Cooke, T. (1989). Young children's theory of mind and emotion. *Cognition and Emotion, 3,* 379–400.

Harro, J. (2015). Neuropsychiatric adverse effects of amphetamine and methamphetamine. *International Review of Neurobiology, 120,* 179–204.

Hart, B., & Risley, T. R. (1995). *Meaningful differences in the everyday experience of young American children*. Baltimore: Brookes.

Hart, B. L. (1988). Biological basis of the behavior of sick animals. *Neuroscience and Biobehavioral Reviews, 12,* 123–137.

Hart, C.L. (2013). *High price: A neuroscientist's journey of self-discovery that challenges everything you know about drugs and society*. New York: Harper Collins.

Hart, W., Albarracin, D., Eagly, A. H., Lindberg, M. J., Merrill, L., & Brechan, I. (2009). Feeling validated versus being correct: A meta-analysis of selective exposure to information. *Psychological Bulletin, 135,* 555–588.

Hartshorne, H., & May, M. (1928). *Studies in deceit*. New York: Macmillan.

Hartshorne, J. K., & Germine, L. T. (2015). When does cognitive functioning peak? The asynchronous rise and fall of different cognitive abilities across the life span. *Psychological Science, 26* (4), 433–443. doi: 10.1177/0956797614567339

Haslam, C., Wills, A. J., Haslam, S. A., Kay, J., Baron, R., & McNab, F. (2007). Does maintenance of colour categories rely on language? Evidence to the contrary from a case of semantic dementia. *Brain and Language, 103,* 251–263.

Hassabis, D., Kumaran, D., Vann, S. D., & Maguire, E. A. (2007). Patients with hippocampal amnesia cannot imagine new experiences. *Proceedings of the National Academy of Sciences, USA, 104,* 1726–1731.

Hasselmo, M. E. (2006). The role of acetylcholine in learning and memory. *Current Opinion in Neurobiology, 16,* 710–715.

Hassin, R. R., Bargh, J. A., & Zimerman, S. (2009). Automatic and flexible: The case of non-conscious goal pursuit. *Social Cognition, 27,* 20–36.

Hassmen, P., Koivula, N., & Uutela, A. (2000). Physical exercise and psychological well-being: A population study in Finland. *Preventive Medicine, 30,* 17–25.

Hasson, U., Hendler, T., Bashat, D. B., & Malach, R. (2001). Vase or face? A neural correlate of shape-selective grouping processes in the human brain. *Journal of Cognitive Neuroscience, 13,* 744–753.

Hatemi, P. K., Gillespie, N. A., Eaves, L. J., Maher, B. S., Webb, B. T., Heath, A. C., . . . Martin, N. G. (2011). A genome-wide analysis of liberal and conservative political attitudes. *Journal of Politics, 73,* 271–285.

Hatfield, E. (1988). Passionate and companionate love. In R. J. Sternberg & M. L. Barnes (Eds.), *The psychology of love* (pp. 191–217). New Haven, CT: Yale University Press.

Hatfield, E., & Rapson, R. L. (1992). Similarity and attraction in close relationships. *Communication Monographs, 59,* 209–212.

Hausser, M. (2000). The Hodgkin-Huxley theory of the action potential. *Nature Neuroscience, 3,* 1165.

Havas, D. A., Glenberg, A. M., Gutowski, K. A., Lucarelli, M. J., & Davidson, R. J. (2010). Cosmetic use of botulinum toxin-A affects processing of emotional language. *Psychological Science, 21*(7), 895–900. doi:10.1177/0956797610374742

Hawley, P. H. (2002). Social dominance and prosocial and coercive strategies of resource control in preschoolers. *International Journal of Behavioral Development, 26,* 167–176.

Haworth, C. M. A., Wright, M. J., Luciano, M., Martin, N. G., de Geus, E. J. C., van Beijsterveldt, C. E. M., . . . Plomin, R. (2010). The heritability of general cognitive ability increases linearly from childhood to young adulthood. *Molecular Psychiatry, 15*(11), 1112–1120. doi: 10.1038/mp.2009.55

Haxby, J. V., Gobbini, M. I., Furey, M. L., Ishai, A., Schouten, J. L., & Pietrini, P. (2001). Distributed and overlapping representations of faces and objects in ventral temporal cortex. *Science, 293,* 2425–2430.

Hayes, J. E., Bartoshuk, L. M., Kidd, J. R., & Duffy, V. B. (2008). Supertasting and PROP bitterness depends on more than the TAS2R38 gene. *Chemical Senses, 23,* 255–265.

Hayes, K., & Hayes, C. (1951). The intellectual development of a home-raised chimpanzee. *Proceedings of the American Philosophical Society, 95,* 105–109.

Hayes, S. C., Strosahl, K., & Wilson, K. G. (1999). *Acceptance and commitment therapy: An experiential approach to behavior change*. New York: Guilford Press.

Hay-McCutcheon, M. J., Kirk, K. I., Henning, S. C., Gao, S. J., & Qi, R. (2008). Using early outcomes to predict later language ability in children with cochlear implants. *Audiology and Neuro-Otology, 13,* 370–378.

Heath, S. B. (1983). *Way with words: Language, life and work in communities and classrooms*. Cambridge: Cambridge University Press.

Heatherton, T. F., & Weinberger, J. L. (Eds.). (1994). *Can personality change?* Washington, DC: American Psychological Association.

Heaton, R., Paulsen, J. S., McAdams, L. A., Kuck, J., Zisook, S., Braff, D., . . . Jeste, D. V. (1994). Neuropsychological deficits in schizophrenia: Relationship to age, chronicity, and dementia. *Archives of General Psychiatry, 51,* 469–476.

Heavey, C. L., Hurlburt, R. T., & Lefforge, N. L. (2012). Toward a phenomenology of feelings. *Emotion, 12*(4), 763–777.

Hebb, D. O. (1949). *The organization of behavior*. New York: Wiley.

Hebl, M. R., & Heatherton, T. F. (1997). The stigma of obesity in women: The difference is Black and White. *Personality and Social Psychology Bulletin, 24,* 417–426.

Hebl, M. R., & Mannix, L. M. (2003). The weight of obesity in evaluating others: A mere proximity effect. *Personality and Social Psychology Bulletin, 29,* 28–38.

Hedges, L. V., & Nowell, A. (1995). Sex differences in mental test scores, variability, and numbers of high-scoring individuals. *Science, 269*(5220), 41–45.

Heeren, A., Moqoase, C., Philippot, P., & McNally, R. J. (2015). Attention bias modification for social anxiety: A systematic review and meta-analysis. *Clinical Psychology Review, 40,* 76–90.

Heerey, E. A., Keltner, D., & Capps, L. M. (2003). Making sense of self-conscious emotion: Linking theory of mind and emotion in children with autism. *Emotion, 3,* 394–400.

Heine, S. J., & Lehman, D. R. (1995). Cultural variation in unrealistic optimism: Does the West feel more invulnerable than the East? *Journal of Peronality and Social Psychology, 68,* 595–607.

Heiy, J. E., & Cheavens, J. S. (2014). Back to basics: A naturalistic assessment of the experience and regulation of emotion. *Emotion,* 14(5), 878–891. doi: 10.1037/a0037231

Helliwell, J., & Grover, S. (2014, December). How's life at home? New evidence on marriage and the set point for happiness. NBER Working Paper No. 20794.

Helt, M., Kelley, E., Kinsbourne, M., Pandey, J., Boorstein, H., Herbert, M., & Fein, D. (2008). Can children with autism recover? If so, how? *Neuropsychology Review,* 18, 339–366.

Henderlong, J., & Lepper, M. R. (2002). The effects of praise on children's intrinsic motivation: A review and synthesis. *Psychological Bulletin,* 128, 774–795.

Henrich, J., Heine, S. J., & Norenzayan, A. (2010). Most people are not WEIRD. *Nature,* 466, 29.

Henry, W. P., Strupp, H. H., Schacht, T. E., & Gaston, L. (1994). Psychodynamic approaches. In A. E. Bergin & S. L. Garfield (Eds.), *Handbook of psychotherapy and behavior change* (pp. 467–508). New York: Wiley.

Herman, C. P., Roth, D. A., & Polivy, J. (2003). Effects of the presence of others on food intake: A normative interpretation. *Psychological Bulletin,* 129, 873–886.

Herman-Giddens, M. E., Steffes, J., Harris, D., Slora, E., Hussey, M., Dowshen, S. A., & Reiter, E. O. (2012). Secondary sexual characteristics in boys: Data from the pediatric research in office settings network. *Pediatrics,* 130(5), e1058–e1068. doi: 10.1542/peds.2011-3291

Herring, M. P., Puetz, T. W., O'Connor, P. J., & Dishman, R. K. (2010). Effect of exercise training on depressive symptoms among patients with chronic illness: A systematic review and meta-analysis of randomized controlled trials. *Archives of Internal Medicine,* 172, 101–111.

Herrnstein, R. J. (1977). The evolution of behaviorism. *American Psychologist,* 32, 593–603.

Hertenstein, M. J., Holmes, R., McCullough, M., & Keltner, D. (2009). The communication of emotion via touch. *Emotion,* 9, 566–573.

Hertig, M. M., & Nagel, B. J. (2012). Aerobic fitness relates to learning on a virtual Morris water maze task and hippocampal volume in adolescents. *Behavioral Brain Research,* 233, 517–525.

Herz, R. S., & von Clef, J. (2001). The influence of verbal labeling on the perception of odors. *Perception,* 30, 381–391.

Hettema, J. M., Neale, M. C., & Kendler, K. S. (2001). A review and meta-analysis of the genetic epidemiology of anxiety disorders. *American Journal of Psychiatry,* 158, 1568–1578.

Heyes, C. (2016). Born pupils? Natural pedagogy and cultural pedagogy. *Perspectives on Psychological Science,* 11(2), 280–295. doi: 10.1177/1745691615621276

Heyes, C. M., & Foster, C. L. (2002). Motor learning by observation: Evidence from a serial reaction time task. *Quarterly Journal of Experimental Psychology (A),* 55, 593–607.

Heyman, G. M. (2009). *Addiction: A disorder of choice.* Cambridge, MA: Harvard University Press.

Heymsfield, S. B., Greenberg, A. S., Fujioka, K., Dixon, R. M., Kushner, R., Hunt, T., . . . McCarnish, M. (1999). Recombinant leptin for weight loss in obese and lean adults: A randomized, controlled, dose-escalation trial. *Journal of the American Medical Association,* 282(16), 1568–1575.

Hibbeln, J. R. (1998). Fish consumption and major depression. *Lancet,* 351, 1213.

Hickok, G. (2009). Eight problems for the mirror neuron theory of action understanding in monkeys and humans. *Journal of Cognitive Neuroscience,* 21, 1229–1243.

Higgins, E. T. (1987). Self-discrepancy theory: A theory relating self and affect. *Psychological Review,* 94, 319–340.

Higgins, E. T. (1997). Beyond pleasure and pain. *American Psychologist,* 52, 1280–1300.

Hilgard, E. R. (1965). *Hypnotic susceptibility.* New York: Harcourt, Brace and World.

Hilgard, E. R. (1986). *Divided consciousness: Multiple controls in human thought and action.* New York: Wiley-Interscience.

Hillman, C. H., Erickson, K. I., & Kramer, A. F. (2008). Be smart, exercise your heart: Exercise effects on brain and cognition. *Nature Reviews Neuroscience,* 9, 58–65.

Hilts, P. (1995). *Memory's ghost: The strange tale of Mr. M and the nature of memory.* New York: Simon & Schuster.

Hine, T. (1995). *The total package: The evolution and secret meanings of boxes, bottles, cans, and tubes.* Boston: Little, Brown.

Hintzman, D. L., Asher, S. J., & Stern, L. D. (1978). Incidental retrieval and memory for coincidences. In M. M. Gruneberg, P. E. Morris, & R. N. Sykes (Eds.), *Practical aspects of memory* (pp. 61–68). New York: Academic Press.

Hirschberger, G., Florian, V., & Mikulincer, M. (2002). The anxiety buffering function of close relationships: Mortality salience effects on the readiness to compromise mate selection standards. *European Journal of Social Psychology,* 32, 609–625.

Hirsh-Pasek, K., Adamson, L. B., Bakeman, R., Owen, M. T., Golinkoff., R. M., Pace, A., . . . & Suma, K. (2015). The contribution of early communication quality to low-income children's language success. *Psychological Science,* 26, 1071–1083.

Hirst, W., & Echterhoff, G. (2012). Remembering in conversations: The social sharing and reshaping of memory. *Annual Review of Psychology,* 63, 55–79.

Hirst, W., Phelps, E. A., Buckner, R. L., Budson, A. E., Cuc, A., Gabrieli, J. D. E., . . . Vaidya, C. J. (2009). Long-term memory for the terrorist attack of September 11: Flashbulb memories, event memories, and the factors that influence their retention. *Journal of Experimental Psychology: General,* 138, 161–176.

Hirst, W., Phelps, E. A., Meksin, R., Vaidya, C. J., Johnson, M. K., Mitchell, K. J., . . . Olsson, A. (2015). A ten-year follow-up of a study of memory for the attack of September 11, 2001: Flashbulb memories and memories for flashbulb events. *Journal of Experimental Psychology: General,* 144, 604–623.

Hirstein, W., & Ramachandran, V. S. (1997). Capgras syndrome: A novel probe for understanding the neural representation of the identity and familiarity of persons. *Proceedings: Biological Sciences,* 264, 437–444.

Hitchcock, S. T. (2005). *Mad Mary Lamb: Lunacy and murder in literary London.* New York: Norton.

Hobson, J. A. (1988). *The dreaming brain.* New York: Basic Books.

Hobson, J. A., & McCarley, R. W. (1977). The brain as a dream-state generator: An activation–synthesis hypothesis of the dream process. *American Journal of Psychiatry,* 134, 1335–1368.

Hochberg, L. R., Bacher, D., Jarosiewicz, B., Masse, N. Y., Simeral, J. D., Vogel, J. . . . Donoghue, J. P. (2012). Reach and grasp by people with tetraplegia using a neurally controlled robotic arm. *Nature,* 485, 372–377.

Hockley, W. E. (2008). The effects of environmental context on recognition memory and claims of remembering. *Journal of Experimental Psychology: Learning, Memory, and Cognition,* 34, 1412–1429.

Hodgkin, A. L., & Huxley, A. F. (1939). Action potential recorded from inside a nerve fibre. *Nature,* 144, 710–712.

Hodson, G., & Sorrentino, R. M. (2001). Just who favors the ingroup? Personality differences in reactions to uncertainty in the minimal group paradigm. *Group Dynamics, 5,* 92–101.

Hoek, H. W. (2006). Incidence, prevalence and mortality of anorexia nervosa and other eating disorders. *Current Opinion in Psychiatry, 19*(4), 389–394. doi: 10.1097/01.yco.0000228759.95237.78

Hoek, H. W., & van Hoeken, D. (2003). Review of the prevalence and incidence of eating disorders. *International Journal of Eating Disorders, 34,* 383–396.

Hoffrage, U., & Gigerenzer, G. (1996). The impact of information representation on Bayesian reasoning. In G. Cottrell (Ed.), *Proceedings of the Eighteenth Annual Conference of the Cognitive Science Society* (pp. 126–130). Mahwah, NJ: Erlbaum.

Hoffrage, U., & Gigerenzer, G. (1998). Using natural frequencies to improve diagnostic inferences. *Academic Medicine, 73,* 538–540.

Hofmann, S. G., & Asmundson, G. J. G. (2008). Acceptance and mindfulness-based therapy: New wave or old hat? *Clinical Psychology Review, 28,* 1–16.

Hofmann, W., Vohs, K. D., & Baumeister, R. F. (2012). What people desire, feel conflicted about, and try to resist in everyday life. *Psychological Science, 23,* 582–588.

Hogan, M. J., & Strasburger, V. C. (2008). Body image, eating disorders, and the media. *Adolescent Medicine: State of the Art Reviews, 19*(3), 521–46, x–xi. Retrieved from http://www.ncbi.nlm.nih.gov/pubmed/19227390

Hollins, M. (2010). Somesthetic senses. *Annual Review of Psychology, 61,* 243–271.

Holloway, G. (2001). *The complete dream book: What your dreams tell about you and your life.* Naperville, IL: Sourcebooks.

Holman, E. A., Silver, R. C., Poulin, M., Andersen, J., Gil-Rivas, V., & McIntosh, D. N. (2008). Terrorism, acute stress, and cardiovascular health. *Archives of General Psychiatry, 65,* 73–80.

Holman, M. A., Carlson, M. L., Driscoll, C. L. W., Grim, K. J., Petersson, R., Sladen, D. P., & Flick, R. P. (2013). Cochlear implantation in children 12 months of age or younger. *Otology & Neurology, 34,* 251–258.

Holmbeck, G. N., & O'Donnell, K. (1991). Discrepancies between perceptions of decision making and behavioral autonomy. In R. L. Paikoff (Ed.), *New directions for child development: Shared views in the family during adolescence* (no. 51, pp. 51–69). San Francisco: Jossey-Bass.

Holmes, J., Gathercole, S. E., & Dunning, D. L. (2009). Adaptive training leads to sustained enhancement of poor working memory in children. *Developmental Science, 12,* F9-F15.

Holmes, T. H., & Rahe, R. H. (1967). The social readjustment rating scale. *Journal of Psychosomatic Research, 11,* 213–318.

Holt-Lunstad, J., Smith, T. B., Baker, M., Harris, T., & Stephenson, D. (2015). Loneliness and social isolation as risk factors for mortality: A meta-analytic review. *Perspectives on Psychological Science, 10*(2), 227–237. doi: 10.1177/1745691614568352

Hölzel, B. K., Carmody, J., Vangel, M., Congleton, C., Yerramsetti, S. M., Gard, T., & Lazar, S. W. (2011). Mindfulness practice leads to increases in regained gray matter density. *Psychiatry Research: Neuroimaging, 191*(1), 36–43.

Homans, G. C. (1961). *Social behavior.* New York: Harcourt, Brace and World.

Homonoff, T. (2013, March 27). Can small incentives have large effects? The impact of taxes versus bonuses on disposable bag use. Working Papers (Princeton University. Industrial Relations Section). Retrieved from http://arks.princeton.edu/ark:/88435/dsp014q77fr47j

Hooley, J. M. (2007). Expressed emotion and relapse of psychopathology. *Annual Review of Clinical Psychology, 3,* 329–352.

Hopper, L. M., Flynn, E. G., Wood, L. A. N., & Whiten, A. (2010). Observational learning of tool use in children: Investigating cultural spread through diffusion chains and learning mechanisms through ghost displays. *Journal of Experimental Child Psychology, 106,* 82–97.

Horn, J. L., & Cattell, R. B. (1966). Refinement and test of the theory of fluid and crystallized general intelligences. *Journal of Educational Psychology, 5,* 253–270.

Horner, A. J., Bisby, J. A., Bush, D., Lin, W.-J., & Burgess, N. (2015). Evidence for holistic episodic recollection via hippocampal pattern completion. *Nature Communications, 6,* 7462. doi: 10.1038/ncomms8462

Horner, V., Whiten, A., Flynn, E., & de Waal, F. B. M. (2006). Faithful replication of foraging techniques along cultural transmission chains by chimpanzees and children. *Proceedings of the National Academy of Sciences, USA, 103,* 13878–13883.

Horrey, W. J., & Wickens, C. D. (2006). Examining the impact of cell phone conversation on driving using meta-analytic techniques. *Human Factors, 48,* 196–205.

Horta, B. L., Victoria, C. G., Menezes, A. M., Halpern, R., & Barros, F. C. (1997). Low birthweight, preterm births and intrauterine growth retardation in relation to maternal smoking. *Pediatrics and Perinatal Epidemiology, 11,* 140–151.

Hosking, S. G., Young, K. L., & Regan, M. A. (2009). The effects of text messaging on young drivers. *Human Factors, 51,* 582–592.

Howard, I. P. (2002). Depth perception. In S. Yantis & H. Pashler (Eds.), *Stevens' handbook of experimental psychology: Vol. 1. Sensation and perception* (3rd ed., pp. 77–120). New York: Wiley.

Howard, J. H., Jr., & Howard, D. V. (1997). Age differences in implicit learning of higher order dependencies in serial patterns. *Psychology and Aging, 12,* 634–656.

Howard, M. O., Brown, S. E., Garland, E. L., Perron, B. E., & Vaughn, M. G. (2011). Inhalant use and inhalant use disorders in the United States. *Addiction Science & Clinical Practice, 6,* 18–31.

Howes, M., Siegel, M., & Brown, F. (1993). Early childhood memories—accuracy and affect. *Cognition, 47,* 95–119.

Hoyert, D. L., & Xu, J. (2012). Deaths: Preliminary data for 2011. *National Vital Statistics Reports, 61,* 1–51.

Huang, J., Perlis, R. H., Lee, P. H., Rush, A. J., Fava, M., Sachs, G. S., . . . Smoller, J. W. (2010). Cross-disorder genomewide analysis of schizophrenia, bipolar disorder, and depression. *American Journal of Psychiatry, 167,* 1254–1263.

Hubel, D. H. (1988). *Eye, brain, and vision.* New York: Freeman.

Hubel, D. H., & Wiesel, T. N. (1962). Receptive fields, binocular interaction and functional architecture in the cat's visual cortex. *Journal of Physiology, 160,* 106–154.

Hubel, D. H., & Wiesel, T. N. (1998). Early exploration of the visual cortex. *Neuron, 20,* 401–412.

Huesmann, L. R., Moise-Titus, J., Podolski, C.-L., & Eron, L. D. (2003). Longitudinal relations between children's exposure to TV violence and their aggressive and violent behavior in young adulthood: 1977–1992. *Developmental Psychology, 39,* 201–221.

Hughes, J. R. (2007). A review of sleepwalking (somnambulism): The enigma of neurophysiology and polysomnography with differential diagnosis of complex partial seizures. *Epilepsy & Behavior, 11,* 483–491.

Hughes, S., Power, T., & Francis, D. (1992). Defining patterns of drinking in adolescence: A cluster analytic approach. *Journal of Studies on Alcohol, 53,* 40–47.

Huibers, M. J., Cohen, Z. D., Lemmens, L. H., Arntz, A., Peeters, F. P., Cuijpers, P., & DeRubeis, R. J. (2015). Predicting optimal outcomes in cognitive therapy or interpersonal psychotherapy for depressed individuals using the personalized advantage index approach. *PLoS ONE, 10,* e0140771.

Hull, C. L. (1943). *Principles of behavior.* New York: Appleton-Century-Crofts.

Hunsley, J., & Di Giulio, G. (2002). Dodo bird, phoenix, or urban legend? The question of psychotherapy equivalence. *Scientific Review of Mental Health Practice, 1,* 13–24.

Hunt, E. B. (2011). *Human intelligence.* New York: Cambridge University Press.

Hunt, L. L., Eastwick, P. W., & Finkel, E. J. (2015). Leveling the playing field: Longer acquaintance predicts reduced assortative mating on attractiveness. *Psychological Science, 26*(7), 1046–1053. doi: 10.1177/0956797615579273

Hurvich, L. M., & Jameson, D. (1957). An opponent process theory of color vision. *Psychological Review, 64,* 384–404.

Hussey, E., & Safford, A. (2009). Perception of facial expression in somatosensory cortex supports simulationist models. *Journal of Neuroscience, 29*(2), 301–302.

Huttenlocher, P. R. (1979). Synaptic density in human frontal cortex—developmental changes and effects of aging. *Brain Research, 163,* 195–205.

Huxley, A. (1932). *Brave new world.* London: Chatto and Windus.

Huxley, A. (1954). *The doors of perception.* New York: Harper & Row.

Hyde, J. S. (2005) The gender similarities hypothesis. *American Psychologist, 60,* 581–592.

Hyde, K. L., Lerch, J., Norton, A., Forgeard, M., Winner, E., Evans, A. C., & Schlaug, G. (2009). Musical training shapes structural brain development. *Journal of Neuroscience, 29,* 3019–3025.

Hyman, I. E., Jr., & Pentland, J. (1996). The role of mental imagery in the creation of false childhood memories. *Journal of Memory and Language, 35,* 101–117.

Hyman, I. E., Jr., Boss, S. M., Wise, B. M., McKenzie, K. E., & Caggiano, J. M. (2010). Did you see the unicycling clown? Inattentional blindness while walking and talking on a cell phone. *Applied Cognitive Psychology, 24*(5), 597–607.

Hyman, I. E., Sarb, B. A., & Wise-Swanson, B. M. (2014). Failure to see money on a tree: Inattentional blindness for objects that guided behavior. *Frontiers in Psychology, 5,* 336. doi: 10.3389/fpsyg.2014.00356

Hypericum Depression Trial Study Group. (2002). Effect of *Hypericum perforatum* (St. John's wort) in major depressive disorder: A randomized controlled trial. *Journal of the American Medical Association, 287,* 1807–1814.

Iacoboni, M. (2009). Imitation, empathy, and mirror neurons. *Annual Review of Psychology, 60,* 653–670.

Iacoboni, M., Molnar-Szakacs, I., Gallese, V., Buccino, G., Mazziotta, J. C., & Rizzolatti, G. (2005). Grasping the intentions of others with one's own mirror neuron system. *PLoS Biology, 3,* 529–535.

Ichheiser, G. (1949). Misunderstandings in human relations: A study in false social perceptions. *American Journal of Sociology, 55* (Pt. 2):1–70.

Identifying the culprit: Assessing eyewitness identification (2014). Washington, DC: National Academies Press.

Imbo, I., & LeFevre, J.-A. (2009). Cultural differences in complex addition: Efficient Chinese versus adaptive Belgians and Canadians. *Journal of Experimental Psychology: Learning, Memory, and Cognition, 35,* 1465–1476.

Inciardi, J. A. (2001). *The war on drugs III.* New York: Allyn & Bacon.

Ingvar, M., Ambros-Ingerson, J., Davis, M., Granger, R., Kessler, M., Rogers, G. A., . . . Lynch, G. (1997). Enhancement by an ampakine of memory encoding in humans. *Experimental Neurology, 146,* 553–559.

Inniss, D., Steiger, H., & Bruce, K. (2011). Threshold and subthreshold post-traumatic stress disorder in bulimic patients: Prevalences and clinical correlates. *Eating and Weight Disorders, 16*(1), e30–6. doi: 10.1007/BF03327518

Inui, A. (2001). Ghrelin: An orexigenic and somatotrophic signal from the stomach. *Nature Reviews Neuroscience, 2,* 551–560.

Irvine, J. T. (1978). Wolof magical thinking: Culture and conservation revisited. *Journal of Cross-Cultural Psychology, 9,* 300–310.

Isaacowitz, D. M. (2012). Mood regulation in real time: Age differences in the role of looking. *Current Directions in Psychological Science, 21*(4), 237–242. doi: 10.1177/0963721412448651

Isaacowitz, D. M., & Blanchard-Fields, F. (2012). Linking process and outcome in the study of emotion and aging. *Perspectives on Psychological Science, 7*(1), 3–17. doi: 10.1177/1745691611424750

Isabelle, R. A. (1993). Origins of attachment: Maternal interactive behavior across the first year. *Child Development, 64,* 605–621.

Isenberg, D. J. (1986). Group polarization: A critical review and meta-analysis. *Journal of Personality and Social Psychology, 50*(6), 1141–1151. doi: 10.1037/0022-3514.50.6.1141

Ittelson, W. H. (1952). *The Ames demonstrations in perception.* Princeton, NJ: Princeton University Press.

Iturrate, I., Chavarriaga, R., Montesano, L., Minguez, J., & del R. Millán, J. (2015). Teaching brain-machine interfaces as an alternative paradigm to neuroprosthetics control. *Scientific Reports, 5,* Article number: 13893. doi: 10.1038/srep13893

Iverson, G. L. (2015). Suicide and chronic traumatic encephalopathy. *Journal of Neuropsychiatry & Clinical Neurosciences, 28*(1), 9–16. doi: 10.1176/appi.neuropsych.15070172

Izard, C. E. (1971). *The face of emotion.* New York: Appleton-Century-Crofts.

Jablensky, A. (1997). The 100-year epidemiology of schizophrenia. *Schizophrenia Research, 28,* 111–125.

Jaccard, J., Dittus, P. J., & Gordon, V. V. (1998). Parent–adolescent congruency in reports of adolescent sexual behavior and in communications about sexual behavior. *Child Development, 69,* 247–261.

Jacobs, B. L. (1994). Serotonin, motor activity, and depression-related disorders. *American Scientist, 82,* 456–463.

Jacobson, E. (1932). The electrophysiology of mental activities. *American Journal of Psychology, 44,* 677–694.

Jacobson, T., & Hoffman, V. (1997). Children's attachment representations: Longitudinal relations to school behavior and academic competency in middle childhood and adolescence. *Developmental Psychology, 33,* 703–710.

Jaeger, A., Eisenkraemer, R. E., & Stein, L. M. (2015). Test-enhanced learning in third-grade children. *Educational Psychology, 35,* 513–521.

Jaeggi, S. M., Buschkuehl, M., Jonides, J., & Perrig, W. J. (2008). Improving fluid intelligence with training on working memory. *Proceedings of the National Academy of Sciences, USA, 105,* 6829–6833. doi: 10.1073/pnas.0801268105

Jaffee, S., & Hyde, J. S. (2000). Gender differences in moral orientation: A meta-analysis. *Psychological Bulletin, 126,* 703–726.

Jahoda, G. (1993). *Crossroads between culture and mind.* Cambridge, MA: Harvard University Press.

James, T. W., Culham, J., Humphrey, G. K., Milner, A. D., & Goodale, M. A. (2003). Ventral occipital lesions impair object recognition but not object-directed grasping: An fMRI study. *Brain, 126,* 2463–2475.

James, W. (1884). What is an emotion? *Mind, 9,* 188–205.

James, W. (1890). *The principles of psychology.* Cambridge, MA: Harvard University Press.

James, W. (1911). *Memories and studies.* New York: Longman.

Jamieson, J. P., Koslov, K., Nock, M. K., & Mendes, W. B. (2013). Experiencing discrimination increases risk-taking. *Psychological Science, 24,* 131–139.

Jamieson, J. P., Mendes, W. B., Blackstock, E., & Schmader, T. (2010). Turning the knots in your stomach into bows: Reappraising arousal improves performance on the GRE. *Journal of Experimental Social Psychology, 46,* 208–212.

Jamieson, J. P., Nock, M. K., & Mendes, W. B. (2013). Changing the conceptualization of stress in social anxiety disorder: Affective and physiological consequences. *Clinical Psychological Science, 1*(4), 363–374. doi: 10.1177/2167702613482119

Jamison, K. R. (1993). *Touched with fire: Manic-depressive illness and the artistic temperament.* New York: Free Press.

Janicak, P. G., Dowd, S. M., Martis, B., Alam, D., Beedle, D., Krasuski, J., . . . Viana, M. (2002). Repetitive transcranial magnetic stimulation versus electroconvulsive therapy for major depression: Preliminary results of a randomized trial. *Biological Psychiatry, 51,* 659–667.

Janis, I. L. (1982). *Groupthink: Scientific studies of policy decisions and fiascoes.* Boston: Houghton-Mifflin.

Jarvella, R. J. (1970). Effects of syntax on running memory span for connected discourse. *Psychonomic Science, 19,* 235–236.

Jarvella, R. J. (1971). Syntactic processing of connected speech. *Journal of Verbal Learning and Verbal Behavior, 10,* 409–416.

Jausovec, N., & Jausovec, K. (2005). Differences in induced gamma and upper alpha oscillations in the human brain related to verbal performance and emotional intelligence. *International Journal of Psychophysiology, 56,* 223.

Jausovec, N., Jausovec, K., & Gerlic, I. (2001). Differences in even-trelated and induced electroencephalography patterns in the theta and alpha frequency bands related to human emotional intelligence. *Neuroscience Letters, 311,* 93.

Jaynes, J. (1976). *The origin of consciousness in the breakdown of the bicameral mind.* London: Allen Lane.

Jenkins, H. M., Barrera, F. J., Ireland, C., & Woodside, B. (1978). Signal-centered action patterns of dogs in appetitive classical conditioning. *Learning and Motivation, 9,* 272–296.

Jenkins, J. G., & Dallenbach, K. M. (1924). Obliviscence during sleep and waking. *American Journal of Psychology, 35,* 605–612.

John, O. P., Naumann, L. P., & Soto, C. J. (2008). Paradigm shift to the integrative Big-Five trait taxonomy: History, measurement, and conceptual issues. In O. P. John, R. W. Robins, & L. A. Pervin (Eds.), *Handbook of personality: Theory and research* (pp. 114–158). New York: Guilford Press.

John, O. P., & Srivastava, S. (1999). The Big Five trait taxonomy: History, measurement, and theoretical perspectives. In L. A. Pervin & O. P. John (Eds.), *Handbook of personality: Theory and research* (2nd ed., pp. 102–138). New York: Guilford Press.

Johnson, C. A., Xiao, L., Palmer, P., Sun, P., Wang, Q., Wei, Y. L., . . . Bechara, A. (2008). Affective decision-making deficits, linked to

dysfunctional ventromedial prefrontal cortex, revealed in 10th-grade Chinese adolescent binge drinkers. *Neuropsychologia, 46,* 714–726.

Johnson, D. H. (1980). The relationship between spike rate and synchrony in responses of auditory-nerve fibers to single tones. *Journal of the Acoustical Society of America, 68,* 1115–1122.

Johnson, D. R., & Wu, J. (2002). An empirical test of crisis, social selection, and role explanations of the relationship between marital disruption and psychological distress: A pooled time-series analysis of four-wave panel data. *Journal of Marriage and the Family, 64,* 211–224.

Johnson, J. D., Noel, N. E., & Sutter-Hernandez, J. (2000). Alcohol and male sexual aggression: A cognitive disruption analysis. *Journal of Applied Social Psychology, 30,* 1186–1200.

Johnson, J. S., & Newport, E. L. (1989). Critical period effects in second language learning: The influence of maturational state on the acquisition of English as a second language. *Cognitive Psychology, 21,* 60–99.

Johnson, K. (2002). Neural basis of haptic perception. In H. Pashler & S. Yantis (Eds.), *Stevens' handbook of experimental psychology: Vol. 1. Sensation and perception* (3rd ed., pp. 537–583). New York: Wiley.

Johnson, M. H., Dziurawiec, S., Ellis, H. D., & Morton, J. (1991). Newborns' preferential tracking of face-like stimuli and its subsequent decline. *Cognition, 40,* 1–19.

Johnson, M. K., Hashtroudi, S., & Lindsay, D. S. (1993). Source monitoring. *Psychological Bulletin, 114,* 3–28.

Johnson, N. J., Backlund, E., Sorlie, P. D., & Loveless, C. A. (2000). Marital status and mortality: The National Longitudinal Mortality Study. *Annual Review of Epidemiology, 10,* 224–238.

Johnson, S. C., Dweck, C. S., & Chen, F. S. (2007). Evidence for infants' internal working models of attachment. *Psychological Science, 18,* 501–2. doi: 10.1111/j.1467-9280.2007.01929.x

Johnson, S. L., Cuellar, A. K., & Miller, C. (2009). Unipolar and bipolar depression: A comparison of clinical phenomenology, biological vulnerability, and psychosocial predictors. In I. H. Gottlib & C. L. Hammen (Eds.), *Handbook of depression* (2nd ed., pp. 142–162). New York: Guilford Press.

Johnson, S. L., Cuellar, A. K., Ruggiero, C., Winnett-Perman, C., Goodnick, P., White, R., & Miller, I. (2008). Life events as predictors of mania and depression in bipolar 1 disorder. *Journal of Abnormal Psychology, 117,* 268–277.

Johnson, S. L., & Miller, I. (1997). Negative life events and time to recover from episodes of bipolar disorder. *Journal of Abnormal Psychology, 106,* 449–457.

Johnston, L., Bachman, J., & O'Malley, P. (1997). *Monitoring the future.* Ann Arbor, MI: Institute for Social Research.

Johnstone, E. C., Crow, T. J., Frith, C., Husband, J., & Kreel, L. (1976). Cerebral ventricular size and cognitive impairment in chronic schizophrenia. *Lancet, 2,* 924–926.

Jokela, M., Elovainio, M., Singh-Manoux, A., & Kivimaki, M. (2009). IQ, socioeconomic status, and early death: The US National Longitudinal Survey of Youth. *Psychosomatic Medicine, 71*(3), 322–328. doi: 10.1097/PSY.0b013e31819b69f6

Jonas, E., Graupmann, V., Kayser, D. N., Zanna, M., Traut-Mattausch, E., & Frey, D. (2009). Culture, self, and the emergence of reactance: Is there a "universal" freedom? *Journal of Experimental Social Psychology, 45,* 1068–1080.

Jones, B. C., Little, A. C., Penton-Voak, I. S., Tiddeman, B. P., Burt, D. M., & Perrett, D. I. (2001). Facial symmetry and judgements of apparent health: Support for a "good genes" explanation of the attractiveness–symmetry relationship. *Evolution and Human Behavior, 22,* 417–429.

Jones, E. E., & Harris, V. A. (1967). The attribution of attitudes. *Journal of Experimental Social Psychology, 3,* 1–24.

Jones, E. E., & Nisbett, R. E. (1972). The actor and the observer: Divergent perceptions of the causes of behavior. In E. E. Jones, D. E. Kanouse, H. H. Kelley, R. E. Nisbett, S. Valins, & B. Weiner (Eds.), *Attribution: Perceiving the causes of behavior* (pp. 79–94). Morristown, NJ: General Learning Press.

Jones, K. (1972). *A history of mental health services.* London: Routledge and Kegan Paul.

Jones, L. M., & Foshay, N. N. (1984). Diffusion of responsibility in a nonemergency situation: Response to a greeting from a stranger. *Journal of Social Psychology, 123,* 155–158.

Jones, S. S. (2007). Imitation in infancy. *Psychological Science, 18*(7), 593–599.

Jonsson, H., & Hougaard, E. (2008). Group cognitive behavioural therapy for obsessive-compulsive disorder: A systematic review and meta-analysis. *Acta Psychiatrica Scandinavica, 117,* 1–9.

Jordan, S. A., Cunningham, D. G., & Marles, R. J. (2010). Assessment of herbal medicinal products: Challenges and opportunities to increase the knowledge base for safety assessment. *Toxicology and Applied Pharmacology, 243,* 198–216.

Judd, L. L. (1997). The clinical course of unipolar major depressive disorders. *Archives of General Psychiatry, 54,* 989–991.

Judd, T. (2014). Making sense of multitasking: The role of Facebook. *Computers & Education, 70,* 194–202.

Jung-Beeman, M. (2005). Bilateral brain processes for comprehending natural language. *Trends in Cognitive Sciences, 9,* 512–518.

Jung-Beeman, M., Bowden, E. M., Haberman, J., Frymiare, J. L., Arambel-Liu, S., Greenblatt, R., . . . Kounios, J. (2004). Neural activity when people solve verbal problems with insight. *PLoS Biology, 2,* 500–510.

Jurewicz, I., Owen, R. J., & O'Donovan, M. C. (2001). Searching for susceptibility genes in schizophrenia. *European Neuropsychopharmacology, 11,* 395–398.

Kaas, J. H. (1991). Plasticity of sensory and motor maps in adult mammals. *Annual Review of Neuroscience, 14,* 137–167.

Kagan, J. (1997). Temperament and the reactions to unfamiliarity. *Child Development, 68,* 139–143.

Kahneman, D. (2011). *Thinking fast and slow.* New York: Farrar, Straus and Giroux.

Kahneman, D., & Deaton, A. (2010). High income improves evaluation of life but not emotional well-being. *Proceedings of the National Academy of Sciences, 107,* 16489–16493.

Kahneman, D., Krueger, A. B., Schkade, D. A., Schwarz, N., & Stone, A. A. (2004). A survey method for characterizing daily life experience: The day reconstruction method. *Science, 306,* 1776–1780.

Kahneman, D., & Tversky, A. (1973). On the psychology of prediction. *Psychological Review, 80,* 237–251.

Kahneman, D., & Tversky, A. (1979). Prospect theory: An analysis of decision under risk. *Econometrica, 47,* 263–291.

Kahneman, D., & Tversky, A. (1984). Choices, values, and frames. *American Psychologist, 39,* 341–350.

Kalb. J. (2015, January 12). Give me a smile. *New Yorker.*

Kalokerinos, E. K., Greenaway, K. H., & Denson, T. F. (2015). Reappraisal but not suppression downregulates the experience of positive and negative emotion. *Emotion, 15*(3), 271–275. doi: 10.1037/emo0000025

Kamin, L. J. (1959). The delay-of-punishment gradient. *Journal of Comparative and Physiological Psychology, 52,* 434–437.

Kamiya, J. (1969). Operant control of the EEG alpha rhythm and some of its reported effects on consciousness. In C. S. Tart (Ed.), *Altered states of consciousness* (pp. 519–529). Garden City, NY: Anchor Books.

Kan, P. F., & Kohnert, K. (2008). Fast mapping by bilingual pre-school children. *Journal of Child Language, 35,* 495–514.

Kandel, E. R. (2000). Nerve cells and behavior. In E. R. Kandel, G. H. Schwartz, & T. M. Jessell (Eds.), *Principles of neural science* (pp. 19–35). New York. McGraw-Hill.

Kandel, E. R. (2006). *In search of memory: The emergence of a new science of mind.* New York: Norton.

Kang, S. H. K., McDermott, K. B., & Roediger, H. L. III. (2007). Test format and corrective feedback modify the effect of testing on long-term retention. *European Journal of Cognitive Psychology, 19,* 528–558.

Kann, L., Kinchen, S., Shanklin, S. L., Flint, K. H., Hawkins, J., Harris, W. A., . . . Zaza, S. (2014). *Youth risk behavior surveillance—United States, 2013.* MMWR 2014;63(SS6304). U.S. Centers for Disease Control and Prevention. Retrieved from http://www.cdc.gov/mmwr/pdf/ss/ss6304.pdf

Kanwisher, N. (2000). Domain specificity in face perception. *Nature Neuroscience, 3,* 759–763.

Kanwisher, N., McDermott, J., & Chun, M. M. (1997). The fusiform face area: A module in human extrastriate cortex specialized for face perception. *Journal of Neuroscience, 17,* 4302–4311.

Kanwisher, N., & Yovel, G. (2006). The fusiform face area: A cortical region specialized for the perception of faces. *Philosophical Transactions of the Royal Society (B), 361,* 2109–2128.

Kapur, S., Craik, F. I. M., Tulving, E., Wilson, A. A., Houle, S., & Brown, G. M. (1994). Neuroanatomical correlates of encoding in episodic memory: Levels of processing effects. *Proceedings of the National Academy of Sciences, USA, 91,* 2008–2011.

Karau, S. J., & Williams, K. D. (1993). Social loafing: A meta-analytic review and theoretical integration. *Journal of Personality and Social Psychology, 65,* 681–706.

Karow, A., Pajonk, F. G., Reimer, J., Hirdes, F., Osterwald, C., Naber, D., & Moritz, S. (2007). The dilemma of insight into illness in schizophrenia: Self- and expert-rated insight and quality of life. *European Archives of Psychiatry and Clinical Neuroscience, 258,* 152–159.

Karpicke, J. D. (2012). Retrieval-based learning: Active retrieval promotes meaningful learning. *Current Directions in Psychological Science, 21,* 157–163.

Karpicke, J. D., & Blunt, J. R. (2011). Retrieval practice produces more learning than elaborative studying with concept mapping. *Science, 331,* 772–775.

Karpicke, J. D., & Roediger, H. L., III. (2008). The critical importance of retrieval for learning. *Science, 319,* 966–968.

Karpicke, J. D. & Aue, W. R. (2015). The testing effect is alive and well with complex materials. *Educational Psychology Review, 27,* 317–326.

Kassam, K. S., Gilbert, D. T., Swencionis, J. K., & Wilson, T. D. (2009). Misconceptions of memory: The Scooter Libby effect. *Psychological Science, 20,* 551–552.

Kasser, T., & Sharma, Y. S. (1999). Reproductive freedom, educational equality, and females' preference for resource-acquisition characteristics in mates. *Psychological Science, 10,* 374–377.

Kassin, S. M. (2007). Internalized false confessions. In M. Toglia, J. Read, D. Ross, & R. Lindsay (Eds.), *Handbook of eyewitness psychology: Volume 1, Memory for events* (pp. 175–192). Mahwah, NJ: Erlbaum.

Kassin, S. M. (2015). The social psychology of false confessions. *Social Issues and Policy Review, 9,* 25–51.

Katon, W. (1994). Primary care—psychiatry panic disorder management. In B. E. Wolfe & J. D. Maser (Eds.), *Treatment of panic disorder: A consensus development conference* (pp. 41–56). Washington, DC: American Psychiatric Press.

Kaufman, A. S. (2001). WAIS-III IQs, Horn's theory, and generational changes from young adulthood to old age. *Intelligence, 29,* 131–167.

Kaufman, L. (2009, January 30). Utilities turn their customers green, with envy. *New York Times.* Retrieved from http://www.nytimes.com/2009/01/31/science/earth/31compete.html

Kawakami, K., Dovidio, J. F., Moll, J., Hermsen, S., & Russin, A. (2000). Just say no (to stereotyping): Effects of training in the negation of stereotypic associations on stereotype activation. *Journal of Personality and Social Psychology, 78,* 871–888.

Kayyal, M., Widen, S., & Russell, J. A. (2015). Context is more powerful than we think: Contextual cues override facial cues even for valence. *Emotion, 15*(3), 287–291. doi: 10.1037/ emo0000032

Kazdin, A. E., & Blaise, S. L. (2011). Rebooting psychotherapy research and practice to reduce the burden of mental illness. *Perspectives on Psychological Science, 6,* 21–37.

Keane, T. M., Marshall, A. D., & Taft, C. T. (2006). Posttraumatic stress disorder: Etiology, epidemiology, and treatment outcome. *Annual Review of Clinical Psychology, 2,* 161–197.

Keefe, F. J., Abernathy, A. P., & Campbell, L. C. (2005). Psychological approaches to understanding and treating disease-related pain. *Annual Review of Psychology, 56,* 601–630.

Keefe, F. J., Lumley, M., Anderson, T., Lynch, T., & Carson, K. L. (2001). Pain and emotion: New research directions. *Journal of Clinical Psychology, 57,* 587–607.

Kelley, H. H. (1967). Attribution theory in social psychology. In D. Levine (Ed.), *Nebraska Symposium on Motivation* (Vol. 15, pp. 192–238). Lincoln: University of Nebraska Press.

Kelley, M. R., Neath, I., & Surprenant, A. M. (2013). Three more semantic serial position functions and a SIMPLE explanation. *Memory & Cognition, 41,* 600–610.

Kelley, W. M., Macrae, C. N., Wyland, C. L., Caglar, S., Inati, S., & Heatherton, T. F. (2002). Finding the self? An event-related fMRI study. *Journal of Cognitive Neuroscience, 14,* 785–794.

Kelly, G. (1955). *The psychology of personal constructs.* New York: Norton.

Kelm, Z., Womer, J., Walter, J. K., & Feudtner, C. (2014) Interventions to cultivate physician empathy: A systematic review. *BMC Medical Education, 14,* 219.

Keltner, D. (1995). Signs of appeasement: Evidence for the distinct displays of embarrassment, amusement, and shame. *Journal of Personality and Social Psychology, 68,* 441–454.

Keltner, D., & Buswell, B. N. (1996). Evidence for the distinctness of embarrassment, shame, and guilt: A study of recalled antecedents and facial expressions of emotion. *Cognition and Emotion, 10,* 155–171.

Keltner, D., & Haidt, J. (1999). Social functions of emotions at four levels of analysis. *Cognition and Emotion, 13,* 505–521.

Keltner, D., & Harker, L. A. (1998). The forms and functions of the nonverbal signal of shame. In P. Gilbert & B. Andrews (Eds.), *Shame: Interpersonal behavior, psychopathology, and culture* (pp. 78–98). New York: Oxford University Press.

Keltner, D., & Shiota, M. N. (2003). New displays and new emotions: A commentary on Rozin and Cohen (2003). *Emotion, 3,* 86–91.

Kendler, K. S., Hettema, J. M., Butera, F., Gardner, C. O., & Prescott, C. A. (2003). Life event dimensions of loss, humiliation, entrapment, and danger in the prediction of onsets of major depression and generalized anxiety. *Archives of General Psychiatry, 60,* 789–796.

Kendler, K. S., Myers, J., & Prescott, C. A. (2002). The etiology of phobias: An evaluation of the stress–diathesis model. *Archives of General Psychiatry, 59,* 242–248.

Kenrick, D. T., Sadalla, E. K., Groth, G., & Trost, M. R. (1990). Evolution, traits, and the stages of human courtship: Qualifying the parental investment model. *Journal of Personality, 58,* 97–116.

Kensinger, E. A., & Schacter, D. L. (2005). Emotional content and reality monitoring ability: fMRI evidence for the influence of encoding processes. *Neuropsychologia, 43,* 1429–1443.

Kensinger, E. A., & Schacter, D. L. (2006). Amygdala activity is associated with the successful encoding of item, but not source, information for positive and negative stimuli. *The Journal of Neuroscience, 26,* 2564–2570.

Kensinger, E. A., Clarke, R. J., & Corkin, S. (2003). What neural correlates underlie successful encoding and retrieval? A functional magnetic resonance imaging study using a divided attention paradigm. *Journal of Neuroscience, 23,* 2407–2415.

Keo-Meier, C. L., Herman, L. I., Reisner, S. L., Pardo, S. T., Sharp, C., & Babcock, J. C. (2015). Testosterone treatment and MMPI–2 improvement in transgender men: A prospective controlled study. *Journal of Consulting and Clinical Psychology, 83,* 143–156.

Kephart, W. M. (1967). Some correlates of romantic love. *Journal of Marriage and the Family, 29,* 470–474.

Kerr, N. L., & Tindale, R. S. (2004). Group performance and decision making. *Annual Review of Psychology, 55,* 623–655. doi: 10.1146/annurev.psych.55.090902.142009

Kershaw, T. C., & Ohlsson, S. (2004). Multiple causes of difficulty in insight: The case of the nine-dot problem. *Journal of Experimental Psychology: Learning, Memory, and Cognition, 30,* 3–13.

Kertai, M. D., Pal, N., Palanca, B. J., Lin, N., Searleman, S. A., Zhang, L., . . . B-Unaware Study Group. (2010). Association of perioperative risk factors and cumulative duration of low bispectral index with intermediate-term mortality after cardiac surgery in the B-Unaware trial. *Anesthesiology, 112*(5), 1116–1127.

Kessler, R. C. (2012). The costs of depression. *Psychiatric Clinics of North America, 35,* 1–14.

Kessler, R. C., & Üstün, T. B. (Eds.). (2008). *The WHO Mental Health surveys: Global perspectives on the epidemiology of mental health.* Cambridge: Cambridge University Press.

Kessler, R. C., Adler, L., Barkley, R., Biederman, J., Connors, C. K., Demler, O., . . . Zaslavsky, A. M. (2006). The prevalence and correlates of adult ADHD in the United States: Results from the National Comorbidity Study Replication. *American Journal of Psychiatry, 163,* 716–723.

Kessler, R. C., Angermeyer, M., Anthony, J. C., deGraaf, R., Demyittenaere, K., Gasquet, I., . . . Üstün, T. B. (2007). Lifetime prevalence and age-of-onset distributions of mental disorders in the World Health Organization World Mental Health Survey Initiative. *World Psychiatry, 6,* 168–176.

Kessler, R. C., Berglund, P., Demler, M. A., Jin, R., Merikangas, K. R., & Walters, E. E. (2005). Lifetime prevalence and age-of-onset distributions of *DSM–IV* disorders in the National Comorbidity Survey replication. *Archives of General Psychiatry, 62,* 593–602.

Kessler, R. C., Chiu, W. T., Dernier, O., & Walters, E. E. (2005). Prevalence, severity, and comorbidity of 12-month *DSM–IV* disorders in the National Comorbidity Survey replication. *Archives of General Psychiatry, 62,* 617–627.

Kessler, R. C., Demler, O., Frank, R. G., Olfson, M., Pincus, H. A., Walters, E. E., . . . Zaslavsky, A. M. (2005). Prevalence and treatment of mental disorders, 1990 to 2003. *New England Journal of Medicine, 352*(24), 2515–2523.

Kessler, R. C., Petukhova, M., Sampson, N. A., Zaslavsky, A. M., & Wittchen, H. U. (2012). Twelve-month and lifetime prevalence and lifetime morbid risk of anxiety and mood disorders in the United States. *International Journal of Methods in Psychiatric Research, 21*(3), 169–184.

Kessler, R. C., Soukup, J., Davis, R. B., Foster, D. F., Wilkey, S. A., Van Rompay, M. I., & Eisenberg, D. M. (2001). The use of complementary and alternative therapies to treat anxiety and depression in the United States. *American Journal of Psychiatry, 158*, 289–294.

Kessler, R. C., & Wang, P. S. (2008). The descriptive epidemiology of commonly occurring mental disorders in the United States. *Annual Reviews of Public Health, 29*, 115–129.

Keuler, D. J., & Safer, M. A. (1998). Memory bias in the assessment and recall of pre-exam anxiety: How anxious was I? *Applied Cognitive Psychology, 12*, S127–S137.

Khalid, N., Atkins, M., Tredget, J., Giles, M., Champney-Smith, K., & Kirov, G. (2008). The effectiveness of electroconvulsive therapy in treatment-resistant depression: A naturalistic study. *Journal of ECT, 24*, 141–145.

Khalid, R. (1991). Personality and academic achievement: A thematic apperception perspective. *British Journal of Projective Psychology, 36*, 25–34.

Khan, R. M., Luk, C.-H., Flinker, A., Aggarwal, A., Lapid, H., Haddad, R., & Sobel, N. (2007). Predicting odor pleasantness from odorant structure: Pleasantness as a reflection of the physical world. *Journal of Neuroscience, 27*, 10015–10023.

Kiecolt-Glaser, J. K., Garner, W., Speicher, C., Penn, G., & Glaser, R. (1984). Psychosocial modifiers of immunocompetence in medical students. *Psychosomatic Medicine, 46*, 7–14.

Kiefer, H. M. (2004, May 25). *Americans unruffled by animal testing.* Retrieved from http://www.gallup.com/poll/11767/Americans-Unruffled-Animal-Testing.aspx

Kiefer, M., Schuch, S., Schenk, W., & Fiedler, K. (2007). Mood states modulate activity in semantic brain areas during emotional word encoding. *Cerebral Cortex, 17*, 1516–1530.

Kiehl, K. A., Smith, A. M., Hare, R. D., Mendrek, A., Forster, B. B., Brink, J., & Liddle, P. F. (2001). Limbic abnormalities in affective processing by criminal psychopaths as revealed by functional magnetic resonance imaging. *Biological Psychiatry, 50*, 677–684.

Kihlstrom, J. F. (1985). Hypnosis. *Annual Review of Psychology, 36*, 385–418.

Kihlstrom, J. F., Beer, J. S., & Klein, S. B. (2002). Self and identity as memory. In M. R. Leary & J. P. Tangney (Eds.), *Handbook of self and identity* (pp. 68–90). New York: Guilford Press.

Killingsworth, M. A., & Gilbert, D. T. (2010). A wandering mind is an unhappy mind. *Science, 330*, 932.

Kim, G., Walden, T. A., & Knieps, L. J. (2010). Impact and characteristics of positive and fearful emotional messages during infant social referencing. *Infant Behavior and Development, 33*, 189–195.

Kim, J. W., & King, B. G. (2014). Seeing stars: Matthew effects and status bias in Major League Baseball umpiring. *Management Science, 60*(11), 2619–2644. doi: 10.1287/mnsc.2014.1967

Kim, U. K., Jorgenson, E., Coon, H., Leppert, M., Risch, N., & Drayna, D. (2003). Positional cloning of the human quantitative trait locus underlying taste sensitivity to phenylthiocarbamide. *Science, 299*, 1221–1225.

Kinney, D. A. (1993). From nerds to normals—the recovery of identity among adolescents from middle school to high school. *Sociology of Education, 66*, 21–40.

Kirchner, W. H., & Towne, W. F. (1994). The sensory basis of the honeybee's dance language. *Scientific American, 270*(6), 74–80.

Kirsch, I., Cardena, E., Derbyshire, S., Dienes, Z., Heap, M., Kallio, S., . . . Whalley, M. (2011). Definitions of hypnosis and hypnotizability and their relation to suggestion and suggestibility: A consensus statement. *Contemporary Hypnosis and Integrative Therapy, 28*, 107–115.

Kirsch, I., Deacon, B. J., Huedo-Medine, T. B., Scoboria, A., Moore, T. J., & Johnson, B. T. (2008). Initial severity and antidepressant benefits: A meta-analysis of data submitted to the Food and Drug Administration. *PLoS Medicine, 5*, e45.

Kirwan, C. B., Bayley, P. J., Galvan, V. V., & Squire, L. R. (2008). Detailed recollection of remote autobiographical memory after damage to the medial temporal lobe. *Proceedings of the National Academy of Sciences, USA, 105*, 2676–2680.

Kish, S. J., Lerch, J., Furukawa, Y. , Tong, J., McCluskey, T., Wilkins, D., . . . Bioleau, I. (2010). Decreased cerebral cortical serotonin transporter binding in ecstacy users: A positron emission tomography [^{11}c] DASB and structural brain imaging study. *Brain, 133*, 1779–1797.

Klarer, M., Arnold, M., Günther, L., Winter, C., Langhans, W., & Meyer, U. (2014) Gut vagal afferents differentially modulate innate anxiety and learned fear. *Journal of Neuroscience, 34*, 7067–7076.

Klein, C. T. F., & Helweg-Larsen, M. (2002). Perceived control and the optimistic bias: A meta-analytic review. *Psychology and Health, 17*, 437–446.

Klein, S. B. (2004). The cognitive neuroscience of knowing one's self. In M. Gazzaniga (Ed.), *The cognitive neurosciences* (3rd ed., pp. 1007–1089). Cambridge, MA: MIT Press.

Klein, S. B., Robertson, T. E., & Delton, A. W. (2011). The future-orientation of memory: Planning as a key component mediating the high levels of recall found with survival processing. *Memory, 19*, 121–139.

Klein, S. B., & Thorne, B. M. (2007). *Biological psychology.* New York: Worth Publishers.

Klingberg, T. (2010). Training and plasticity of working memory. *Trends in Cognitive Sciences, 14*, 317–324.

Klinger, E. (1975). Consequences of commitment to and disengagement from incentives. *Psychological Review, 82*, 1–25.

Klinger, E. (1977). *Meaning and void.* Minneapolis: University of Minnesota Press.

Klump, K. L., Strober, M., Bulik, C. M., Thornton, L., Johnson, C., Devlin, B., . . . Kaye, W. H. (2004). Personality characteristics of women before and after recovery from an eating disorder. *Psychological Medicine, 34*(8), 1407–1418. doi: 10.1017/S0033291704002442

Klüver, H., & Bucy, P. C. (1937). "Psychic blindness" and other symptoms following bilateral temporary lobectomy in rhesus monkeys. *American Journal of Physiology, 119*, 352–353.

Knowlton, B. J., Ramus, S. J., & Squire, L. R. (1992). Intact artificial grammar learning in amnesia: Dissociation of classification learning and explicit memory for specific instances. *Psychological Science, 3*, 173–179.

Knutson, B., Adams, C. M., Fong, G. W., & Hommer, D. (2001). Anticipation of increasing monetary reward selectively recruits nucleus accumbens. *Journal of Neuroscience, 21*, 159.

Knutson, B., Wolkowitz, O. M., Cole, S. W., Chan, T., Moore, E. A., Johnson, R. C., Reus, V. I. (1998). Selective alteration of personality and social behavior by serotonergic intervention. *American Journal of Psychiatry, 155*, 373–379.

Kobasa, S. (1979). Stressful life events, personality, and health: An inquiry into hardiness. *Journal of Personality and Social Psychology, 37,* 1–11.

Koehler, J. J. (1993). The influence of prior beliefs on scientific judgments of evidence quality. *Organizational Behavior and Human Decision Processes, 56,* 28–55.

Koenigs, M., Young, L., Adolphs, R., Tranel, D., Cushman, F., Hauser, M., & Damasio, A. (2007). Damage to the prefrontal cortex increases utilitarian moral judgements. *Nature, 446,* 908–911.

Koffka, K. (1935). *Principles of Gestalt psychology.* New York: Harcourt, Brace and World.

Kohlberg, L. (1958). *The development of modes of thinking and choices in years 10 to 16* (Unpublished doctoral dissertation, University of Chicago).

Kohlberg, L. (1963). Development of children's orientation towards a moral order: I. Sequencing in the development of moral thought. *Vita Humana, 6,* 11–36.

Kohlberg, L. (1986). A current statement on some theoretical issues. In S. Modgil & C. Modgil (Eds.), *Lawrence Kohlberg: Concensus and controversy* (pp. 485–546). Philadelphia: Falmer.

Kolbert, E. (2009, July 20). XXXL. *The New Yorker,* pp. 73–77.

Kohler, P. K., Manhart, L. E., & Lafferty, E. (2008). Abstinence-only and comprehensive sex education and the initiation of sexual activity and teen pregnancy. *Journal of Adolescent Health, 42,* 344–351.

Kolb, B., & Whishaw, I. Q. (2003). *Fundamentals of human neuropsychology* (5th ed.). New York: Worth Publishers.

Koller, D. (2011, December 5). Death knell for the lecture: Technology as a passport to personalized education. Retrieved from http://www.nytimes.com/2011/12/06/science/daphne-koller-technology-as-a-passport-to-personalized-education.html?pageswanted=all

Kolotkin, R. L., Meter, K., & Williams, G. R. (2001). Quality of life and obesity. *Obesity Reviews, 2,* 219–229.

Komter, A. (2010). The evolutionary origins of human generosity. *International Sociology, 25*(3), 443–464.

Konen, C. S., & Kastner, S. (2008). Two hierarchically organized neural systems for object information in human visual cortex. *Nature Neuroscience, 11,* 224–231.

Koole, S. L., Dijksterhuis, A., & van Knippenberg, A. (2001). What's in a name: Implicit self-esteem and the automatic self. *Journal of Personality and Social Psychology, 80,* 669–685.

Koss, M. P. (1990). The women's mental health research agenda: Violence against women. *American Psychologist, 45,* 374–380.

Kosslyn, S. M., Alpert, N. M., Thompson, W. L., Chabris, C. F., Rauch, S. L., & Anderson, A. K. (1993). Visual mental imagery activates topographically organized visual cortex: PET investigations. *Journal of Cognitive Neuroscience, 5,* 263–287.

Kosslyn, S. M., Pascual-Leone, A., Felician, O., Camposano, S., Keenan, J. P., Thompson, W. L., . . . Alpert, N. M. (1999). The role of area 17 in visual imagery: Convergent evidence from PET and rTMS. *Science, 284,* 167–170.

Kosslyn, S. M., Thompson, W. L., Constantini-Ferrando, M. F., Alpert, N. M., & Spiegel, D. (2000). Hypnotic visual illusion alters color processing in the brain. *American Journal of Psychiatry, 157,* 1279–1284.

Kounios, J., & Beeman, M. (2009). The Aha! moment. *Current Directions in Psychological Science, 18,* 210–216.

Kounios, J., & Beeman, M. (2015). *The eureka factor: Aha moments, creative insight, and the brain.* New York: Random House.

Kounios, J., Frymiare, J. L., Bowden, E. M., Fleck, J. I., Subramaniam, K., Parrish, T. B., & Jung-Beeman, M. (2006). The prepared mind: Neural activity prior to problem presentation predicts subsequent solution by sudden insight. *Psychological Science, 17,* 882–890.

Kraemer, H. C., Shrout, P. E., & Rubio-Stipec, M. (2007). Developing the *Diagnostic and Statistical Manual–V:* What will "statistical" mean in *DSM–V? Social Psychiatry and Psychiatric Epidemiology, 42,* 259–267.

Kraus, M. W., Piff, P. K., & Keltner, D. (2011). Social class as culture: The convergence of resources and rank in the social realm. *Current Directions in Psychological Science, 20*(4), 246–250. doi: 10.1177/0963721411414654

Kraus, N., & Chandrasekaran, B. (2010). Music training for the development of auditory skills. *Nature Reviews Neuroscience, 11,* 599–605.

Kravitz, D. J., Saleem, K. S., Baker, C. I., & Mishkin, M. (2011). A new neural framework for visuospatial processing. *Nature Reviews Neuroscience, 12,* 217–230.

Kravitz, D. J., Saleem, K. S., Baker, C. I., Ungerleider, L. G., & Mishkin, M. (2013). The ventral visual pathway: An expanded neural framework for the processing of object quality. *Trends in Cognitive Sciences, 17,* 26–49.

Kravitz, R. L., Epstein, R. M., Feldman, M. D., Franz, C. E., Azari, R., Wilkes, M. S., . . . Franks, P. (2005). Influence of patients' requests for direct-to-consumer advertised antidepressants: A randomized controlled trial. *Journal of the American Medical Association, 293,* 1995–2002.

Kredlow, M. A., & Otto, M. W. (2015). Interference with the reconsolidation of trauma-related memories in adults. *Depression and Anxiety, 32,* 32–37.

Kringelbach, M. L., O'Doherty, J., Rolls, E. T., & Andrews, C. (2003). Activation of the human orbitofrontal cortex to a liquid food stimulus is correlated with its subjective pleasantness. *Cerebral Cortex, 13,* 1064–1071.

Kristensen, P., & Bjerkedal, T. (2007). Explaining the relation between birth order and intelligence. *Science, 316,* 1717.

Kroeze, W. K., & Roth, B. L. (1998). The molecular biology of serotonin receptors: Therapeutic implications for the interface of mood and psychosis. *Biological Psychiatry, 44,* 1128–1142.

Kruk, M. R., Halasz, J., Meelis, W., & Haller, J. (2004). Fast positive feedback between the adrenocortical stress response and a brain mechanism involved in aggressive behavior. *Behavioral Neuroscience, 118,* 1062–1070.

Kubovy, M. (1981). Concurrent-pitch segregation and the theory of indispensable attributes. In M. Kubovy & J. R. Pomerantz (Eds.), *Perceptual organization* (pp. 55–96). Hillsdale, NJ: Erlbaum.

Kucyi, A., & Davis, K. D. (2015). The dynamic pain connectome. *Trends in Neurosciences, 38,* 86–95.

Kuhl, B. A., Dudukovic, N. M., Kahn, I., & Wagner, A. D. (2007). Decreased demands on cognitive control reveal the neural processing benefits of forgetting. *Nature Neuroscience, 10,* 908–917.

Kuhl, P., & Rivera-Gaxiola, M. (2008). Neural substrates of language acquisition. *Annual Review of Neuroscience, 31,* 511–534.

Kuhl, P. K. (2010). Brain mechanisms in early language acquisition. *Neuron, 67,* 713–727.

Kuhl, P. K., & Meltzoff, A. N. (1996). Infant vocalizations in response to speech: Vocal imitation and developmental change. *Journal of the Acoustical Society of America, 100*(4), 2425. doi: 10.1121/1.417951

Kuhn, S., & Gallinat, J. (2012). The neural correlates of subjective pleasantness. *NeuroImage, 61,* 289–294.

Kunda, Z. (1990). The case for motivated reasoning. *Psychological Bulletin, 108,* 480–498.

Kunda, Z., & Oleson, K. C. (1997). When exceptions prove the rule: How extremity of deviance determines the impact of deviant examples on stereotypes. *Journal of Personality and Social Psychology, 72,* 965–979.

Kundakovic, M., Gudsnuk, K, Herbstman, J. B., Tang, D. L., Perera, F. P., & Champagne, F. A. (2015). DNA methylation of BDNF as a biomarker of early-life adversity. *Proceedings of the National Academy of Sciences USA, 112,* 6807–6813.

Kunugi, H., Urushibara, T., Murray, R. M., Nanko, S., & Hirose, T. (2003). Prenatal underdevelopment and schizophrenia: A case report of monozygotic twins. *Psychiatry and Clinical Neurosciences, 57,* 271–274.

Kunz, P. R., & Woolcott, M. (1976). Season's greetings: From my status to yours. *Social Science Research, 5,* 269–278.

Kvavilashvili, L., Mirani, J., Schlagman, S., Foley, K., & Kornbrot, D. E. (2009). Consistency of flashbulb memories of September 11 over long delays: Implications for consolidation and wrong time slice hypotheses. *Journal of Memory and Language, 61,* 556–572.

Kwon, M.-K., Setoodehnia, M., Baek, J., Luck, S. J., & Oakes, L. M. (2016). The development of visual search in infancy: Attention to faces versus salience. *Developmental Psychology, 52*(4), 537–555. doi: 10.1037/dev0000080

LaBar, K. S., & Phelps, E. A. (1998). Arousal-mediated memory consolidation: Role of the medial temporal lobe in humans. *Psychological Science, 9,* 490–493.

Labrie, V., Pai, S., & Petronis, A. (2012). Epigenetics of major psychosis: Progress, problems, and perspectives. *Trends in Genetics, 28,* 427–435.

Lacey, H. P., Smith, D. M., & Ubel, P. A. (2006). Hope I die before I get old: Mispredicting happiness across the adult lifespan. *Journal of Happiness Studies, 7*(2), 167–182. doi: 10.1007/s10902-005-2748-7

Lachman, R., Lachman, J. L., & Butterfield, E. C. (1979). *Cognitive psychology and information processing: An introduction.* Hillsdale, NJ: Erlbaum.

Lackner, J. R., & DiZio, P. (2005). Vestibular, proprioceptive, and haptic contributions to spatial orientation. *Annual Review of Psychology, 56,* 115–147.

Lafer-Sousa, R., Hermann, K. L., & Conway, B. R. Striking individual differences in color perception uncovered by "the dress" photograph. *Current Biology, 25,* R1–R2.

LaFraniere, S. (2007, July 4). In Mauritania, seeking to end an overfed ideal. *New York Times.* Retrieved from http://www.nytimes.com/2007/07/04/world/africa/04mauritania.html?pagewanted=all

Lai, C. K., Lehr, S. A., Cerruti, C., Joy-Gaba, J. A., Teachman, B. A., Koleva, S. P., . . . Hawkins, C. B. (2014). Reducing implicit racial preferences: I. A comparative investigation of 17 interventions. *Journal of Experimental Psychology. General, 143*(4), 1765–1785. doi: 10.1037/a0036260

Lai, Y., & Siegal, J. (1999). Muscle atonia in REM sleep. In B. Mallick & S. Inoue (Eds.), *Rapid eye movement sleep* (pp. 69–90). New Delhi: Narosa Publishing House.

Lake, J. (2009). Natural products used to treat depressed mood as monotherapies and adjuvants to antidepressants: A review of the evidence. *Psychiatric Times, 26,* 1–6.

Lakhan, S. E., & Kirchgessner, A. (2012, March 12). Chronic traumatic encephalopathy: The dangers of getting "dinged." *Springer Plus,* 1:2. doi:10.1186/2193-1801-1-2

Lakin, J. M. (2013). Sex differences in reasoning abilities: Surprising evidence that male–female ratios in the tails of the quantitative reasoning distribution have increased. *Intelligence, 41*(4), 263–274. doi: 10.1016/j.intell.2013.04.004

Lakshminarayanan, V. R., Chen, M. K., & Santos, L. R. (2011). The evolution of decision-making under risk: Framing effects in monkey risk preferences. *Journal of Experimental Social Psychology, 47*(3), 689–693. doi: 10.1016/j.jesp.2010.12.011

Lam, L. L., Emberly, E., Fraser, H. B., Neumann, S. M., Chen, E., Miller, G. E., . . . Kobor, M. S. (2012). Factors underlying variable DNA methylation in a human community cohort. *Proceedings of the National Academy of Sciences, USA, 109*(Suppl. 2), 17253–17260.

Lamb, M. E., Sternberg, K. J., & Prodromidis, M. (1992). Nonmaternal care and the security of infant/mother attachment: A reanalysis of the data. *Infant Behavior & Development, 15,* 71–83.

Landauer, T. K., & Bjork, R. A. (1978). Optimum rehearsal patterns and name learning. In M. M. Gruneberg, P. E. Morris, & R. N. Sykes (Eds.), *Practical aspects of memory* (pp. 625–632). New York: Academic Press.

Lane, J. D., Harris, P. L., Gelman, S. A., & Wellman, H. M. (2014). More than meets the eye: Young children's trust in claims that defy their perceptions. *Developmental Psychology, 50*(3), 865–871. doi: 10.1037/a0034291

Lang, F. R., & Carstensen, L. L. (1994). Close emotional relationships in late life: Further support for proactive aging in the social domain. *Psychology and Aging, 9,* 315–324.

Langleben, D. D., Loughead, J. W., Bilker, W. B., Ruparel, K., Childress, A. R., Busch, S. I., & Gur, R. C. (2005). Telling truth from lie in individual subjects with fast event-related fMRI. *Human Brain Mapping, 26,* 262–272.

Langlois, J. H., Kalakanis, L., Rubenstein, A. J., Larson, A., Hallam, M., & Smoot, M. (2000). Maxims or myths of beauty? A meta-analytic and theoretical review. *Psychological Bulletin, 126,* 390–423.

Langlois, J. H., Ritter, J. M., Casey, R. J., & Sawin, D. B. (1995). Infant attractiveness predicts maternal behaviors and attitudes. *Developmental Psychology, 31,* 464–472.

LaPierre, S., Boyer, R., Desjardins, S., Dubé, M., Lorrain, D., Préville, M., & Brassard, J. (2012). Daily hassles, physical illness, and sleep problems in older adults with wishes to die. *International Psychogeriatrics, 24,* 243–252.

Lareau, A. (2003). *Unequal childhoods: Class, race, and family life.* Berkeley: University of California Press.

Lariviére, V., Haustein, S., & Börner, K. (2015). Long-distance interdisciplinarity leads to higher scientific impact. *PLoS ONE, 10,* e0122565.

Larrick, R. P., Timmerman, T. A., Carton, A. M., & Abrevaya, J. (2011). Temper, temperature, and temptation: Heat-related retaliation in baseball. *Psychological Science, 22*(4), 423–428. doi:10.1177/0956797611399292

Larsen, M. E., Nicholas, J., & Christensen, H. (2016). A systematic assessment of smartphone tools for suicide prevention. *PLoS ONE, 11,* e0152285.

Larsen, S. F. (1992). Potential flashbulbs: Memories of ordinary news as baseline. In E. Winograd & U. Neisser (Eds.), *Affect and accuracy in recall: Studies of "flashbulb memories"* (pp. 32–64). New York: Cambridge University Press.

Larson, R., & Richards, M. H. (1991). Daily companionship in late childhood and early adolescence—changing developmental contexts. *Child Development, 62,* 284–300.

Lashley, K. S. (1960). In search of the engram. In F. A. Beach, D. O. Hebb, C. T. Morgan, & H. W. Nissen (Eds.), *The neuropsychology of Lashley* (pp. 478–505). New York: McGraw-Hill.

Latané, B., Williams, K., & Harkins, S. (1979). Many hands make light the work: The causes and consequences of social loafing. *Journal of Personality and Social Psychology, 37,* 822–832.

Lattal, K. A. (2010). Delayed reinforcement of operant behavior. *Journal of the Experimental Analysis of Behavior, 93,* 129–139.

Laupa, M., & Turiel, E. (1986). Children's conceptions of adult and peer authority. *Child Development, 57,* 405–412.

Lavie, P. (2001). Sleep–wake as a biological rhythm. *Annual Review of Psychology, 52,* 277–303.

Lawrence, N. S., Jollant, F., O'Daly, O., Zelaya, F., & Phillips, M. L. (2009). Distinct roles of prefrontal cortical subregions in the Iowa Gambling Task. *Cerebral Cortex, 19,* 1134–1143.

Lawton, M. P., Kleban, M. H., Rajagopal, D., & Dean, J. (1992). The dimensions of affective experience in three age groups. *Psychology and Aging, 7,* 171–184.

Lazarus, R. S. (1984). On the primacy of cognition. *American Psychologist, 39,* 124–129.

Lazarus, R. S., & Alfert, E. (1964). Short-circuiting of threat by experimentally altering cognitive appraisal. *Journal of Abnormal and Social Psychology, 69,* 195–205.

Lazarus, R. S., & Folkman, S. (1984). *Stress, appraisal, and coping.* New York: Springer.

Le, B., & Agnew, C. R. (2003). Commitment and its theorized determinants: A meta–analysis of the Investment Model. *Personal Relationships, 10*(1), 37–57. doi: 10.1111/1475-6811.00035

Leader, T., Mullen, B., & Abrams, D. (2007). Without mercy: The immediate impact of group size on lynch mob atrocity. *Personality and Social Psychology Bulletin, 33*(10), 1340–1352.

Leary, M. R. (1990). Responses to social exclusion: Social anxiety, jealousy, loneliness, depression, and low self-esteem. *Journal of Social and Clinical Psychology, 9,* 221–229.

Leary, M. R. (2010). Affiliation, acceptance, and belonging: The pursuit of interpersonal connection. In S. T. Fiske, D. T. Gilbert, & G. Lindzey (Eds.), *The handbook of social psychology* (5th ed., Vol. 2, pp. 864–897). New York: Wiley.

Leary, M. R., & Baumeister, R. F. (2000). The nature and function of self-esteem: Sociometer theory. In M. P. Zanna (Ed.), *Advances in experimental social psychology* (Vol. 32, pp. 1–62). San Diego: Academic Press.

Leary, M. R., Britt, T. W., Cutlip, W. D., & Templeton, J. L. (1992). Social blushing. *Psychological Bulletin, 112,* 446–460.

Lecky, P. (1945). *Self-consistency: A theory of personality.* New York: Island Press.

Lecrubier, Y., Clerc, G., Didi, R., & Kieser, M. (2002). Efficacy of St. John's wort extract WS 5570 in major depression: A double-blind, placebo-controlled trial. *American Journal of Psychiatry, 159,* 1361–1366.

Lederman, S. J., & Klatzky, R. L. (2009). Haptic perception: A tutorial. *Attention, Perception, & Psychophysics, 71,* 1439–1459.

LeDoux, J. E. (1992). Brain mechanisms of emotion and emotional learning. *Current Opinion in Neurobiology, 2,* 191–197.

LeDoux, J. E., Iwata, J., Cicchetti, P., & Reis, D. J. (1988). Different projections of the central amygdaloid nucleus mediate autonomic and behavioral correlates of conditioned fear. *Journal of Neuroscience, 8,* 2517–2529.

Lee, D. N., & Aronson, E. (1974). Visual proprioceptive control of standing in human infants. *Perception & Psychophysics, 15,* 529–532.

Lee, L., Loewenstein, G., Ariely, D., Hong, J., & Young, J. (2008). If I'm not hot, are you hot or not? Physical-attractiveness evaluations and dating preferences as a function of one's own attractiveness. *Psychological Science, 19,* 669–677.

Lee, M. H., Smyser, C. D., & Shimoy, J. S. (2013). Resting-state fMRI: A review of methods and clinical applications. *American Journal of Neuroradiology, 34,* 1866–1872. doi: 10.3174/ ajnr.A3263

Lefcourt, H. M. (1982). *Locus of control: Current trends in theory and research* (2nd ed.). Hillsdale, NJ: Erlbaum.

Leff, S. S., Waasdorp, T. E., & Crick, N. R. (2010). A review of existing relational aggression programs: Strengths, limitations, and future direction. *School Psychology Review, 39,* 508–535.

Legare, C. H., & Nielseon, M. (2015). Imitation and innovation: The dual engines of cultural learning. *Trends in Cognitive Sciences, 19,* 688–699.

Legenbauer, T., Vocks, S., Schäfer, C., Schütt-Strömel, S., Hiller, W., Wagner, C., & Vögele, C. (2009). Preference for attractiveness and thinness in a partner: Influence of internalization of the thin ideal and shape/weight dissatisfaction in heterosexual women, heterosexual men, lesbians, and gay men. *Body Image, 6*(3), 228–234. doi: 10.1016/j.bodyim.2009.04.002

Lemay, E. P. (2016). The forecast model of relationship commitment. *Journal of Personality and Social Psychology, 111*(1), 34–52. doi: 10.1037/pspi0000052

Lempert, D. (2007). *Women's increasing wage penalties from being overweight and obese.* Washington, DC: U.S. Bureau of Labor Statistics.

Lenoir, M., Serre, F., Chantin, L., & Ahmed, S. H. (2007). Intense sweetness surpasses cocaine reward. *PLoS ONE, 2,* e698.

Lenton, A. P., & Francesconi, M. (2010). How humans cognitively manage an abundance of mate options. *Psychological Science, 21*(4), 528–533. doi: 10.1177/0956797610364958

Lentz, M. J., Landis, C. A., Rothermel, J., & Shaver, J. L. (1999). Effects of selective slow wave sleep disruption on musculoskeletal pain and fatigue in middle-aged women. *Journal of Rheumatology, 26,* 1586–1592.

Leon, D. A., Lawlor, D. A., Clark, H., Batty, G. D., & Macintyre, S. (2009). The association of childhood intelligence with mortality risk from adolescence to middle age: Findings from the Aberdeen children of the 1950s cohort study. *Intelligence, 37*(6), 520–528.

Lepage, M., Ghaffar, O., Nyberg, L., & Tulving, E. (2000). Prefrontal cortex and episodic memory retrieval mode. *Proceedings of the National Academy of Sciences, USA, 97,* 506–511.

LePort, A. K. R., Mattfield, A. T., Dickinson-Anson, H., Fallon, J. H., Stark, C. E. L., Kruggel, F., . . . McGaugh, J. L. (2012). Behavioral and neuroanatomical investigation of highly superior autobiographical memory (HSAM). *Neurobiology of Learning and Memory, 98,* 78–92.

Lepper, M. R., Greene, D., & Nisbett, R. E. (1973). Undermining children's intrinsic interest with extrinsic rewards: A test of the "overjustification" hypothesis. *Journal of Personality and Social Psychology, 28,* 129–137.

Lerman, D. (2006). Consumer politeness and complaining behavior. *Journal of Services Marketing, 20,* 92–100.

Lerman, D. C., & Vorndran, C. M. (2002). On the status of knowledge for using punishment: Implications for treating behavior disorders. *Journal of Applied Behavior Analysis, 35,* 4312–4464.

Lerner, J. S., Li, Y., Valdesolo, P., & Kassam, K. S. (2015). Emotion and decision making. *Annual Review of Psychology, 66,* 799–823. doi: 10.1146/annurev-psych-010213-115043

Leung, A. K.-Y., & Cohen, D. (2011). Within- and between-culture variation: Individual differences and the cultural logics of honor, face, and dignity cultures. *Journal of Personality and Social Psychology, 100*(3), 507–526. doi: 10.1037/a0022151

Levelt Committee, Noort Committee, Drenth Committee. (2012, November 28). *Flawed science: The fraudulent research practices of social psychologist Diederik Stapel.* Retrieved from http://www.tilburguniversity.edu/nl/nieuws-en-agenda/finalreportLevelt.pdf

Levenson, J. M., & Sweatt, J. D. (2005). Epigenetic mechanisms in memory formation. *Nature Reviews Neuroscience, 6,* 108–118.

Levenson, R. W., Cartensen, L. L., Friesen, W. V., & Ekman, P. (1991). Emotion, physiology, and expression in old age. *Psychology and Aging, 6,* 28–35.

Levenson, R. W., Ekman, P., & Friesen, W. V. (1990). Voluntary facial action generates emotion-specific autonomic nervous system activity. *Psychophysiology, 27,* 363–384.

Levenson, R. W., Ekman, P., Heider, K., & Friesen, W. V. (1992). Emotion and automatic nervous system activity in the Minangkabau of West Sumatra. *Journal of Personality and Social Psychology, 62,* 972–988.

Levin, R., & Nielsen, T. (2009). Nightmares, bad dreams, and emotion dysregulation: A review and new neurocognitive model of dreaming. *Current Directions in Psychological Science, 18,* 84–88.

Levine, M. (1981). *History and politics of community mental health.* New York: Oxford University Press.

Levine, R. V., & Norenzayan, A. (1999). The pace of life in 31 countries. *Journal of Cross-Cultural Psychology, 30*(2), 178–205.

Levy, J., Trevarthen, C., & Sperry, R. W. (1972). Perception of bilateral chimeric figures following hemispheric disconnection. *Brain, 95,* 61–78.

Lewin, K. (1936). *Principles of topological psychology.* New York: McGraw-Hill.

Lewin, K. (1951). Behavior and development as a function of the total situation. In K. Lewin (Ed.), *Field theory in social science: Selected theoretical papers* (pp. 791–843). New York: Harper & Row.

Lewis, M., & Brooks-Gunn, J. (1979). *Social cognition and the acquisition of self.* New York: Plenum Press.

Lewis, M. B. (2012). Exploring the positive and negative implications of facial feedback. *Emotion, 12*(4), 852–859.

Lewis, M. D., Hibbeln, J. R., Johnson, J. E., Lin, Y. H., Hyun, D. Y., & Loewke, J. D. (2011). Suicide deaths of active-duty U. S. military and omega-3 fatty acid status: A case control comparison. *Journal of Clinical Psychiatry, 72,* 1585–1590.

Lewontin, R., Rose, S., & Kamin, L. J. (1984). *Not in our genes.* New York: Pantheon.

Li, N. P., Yong, J. C., Tov, W., Sng, O., Fletcher, G. J. O., Valentine, K. A., ... Balliet, D. (2013). Mate preferences do predict attraction and choices in the early stages of mate selection. *Journal of Personality and Social Psychology, 105*(5), 757–776. doi: 10.1037/a0033777

Li, R., Polat, U., Makous, W., & Bavelier, D. (2009). Enhancing the contrast sensitivity function through action video game training. *Nature Neuroscience, 12,* 549–551.

Li, Y. J., Johnson, K. A., Cohen, A. B., Williams, M. J., Knowles, E. D., & Chen, Z. (2012). Fudamental(ist) attribution error: Protestants are dispositionally focused. *Journal of Personality and Social Psychology, 102*(2), 281–290. doi: 10.1037/ a0026294

Libet, B. (1985). Unconscious cerebral initiative and the role of conscious will in voluntary action. *Behavioral and Brain Sciences, 8,* 529–566.

Liebenluft, E. (1996). Women with bipolar illness: Clinical and research issues. *American Journal of Psychiatry, 153,* 163–173.

Lieberman, M. D., Inagaki, T. K., Tabibnia, G., & Crockett, M. J. (2011). Subjective responses to emotional stimuli during labeling, reappraisal, and distraction. *Emotion, 11,* 468–480.

Lieberman, M. D., & Rosenthal, R. (2001). Why introverts can't always tell who likes them: Multitasking and nonverbal decoding. *Journal of Personality and Social Psychology, 80,* 294–310.

Liebowitz, M. R., Gorman, J. M., Fyer, A. J., Levitt, M., Dillon, D., Levy, G., . . . Davies, S. O. (1985). Lactate provocation of panic attacks: II. Biochemical and physiological findings. *Archives of General Psychiatry, 42,* 709–719.

Lifshitz, M., Aubert Bonn, N., Fischer, A., Kashem, I. R., & Raz, A. (2013). Using suggestion to modulate automatic processes: From Stroop to McGurk and beyond. *Cortex, 49*(2), 463–473. doi: 10.1016/j.cortex.2012.08.007

Lilienfeld, S. O. (2007). Psychological treatments that cause harm. *Perspectives on Psychological Science, 2,* 53–70.

Lilienfeld, S. O., Lynn, S. J., & Lohr, J. M. (Eds.). (2003). *Science and pseudoscience in clinical psychology.* New York: Guilford Press.

Lilienfeld, S. O., Wood, J. M., & Garb, H. N. (2000). The scientific status of projective techniques. *Psychological Science in the Public Interest, 1,* 27–66.

Lindenberger, U., & Baltes, P. B. (1994). Sensory functioning and intelligence in old age: A strong connection. *Psychology and Aging, 9*(3), 339–355. doi: 10.1037/0882-7974.9.3.339

Lindenberger, U., & Baltes, P. B. (1997). Intellectual functioning in old and very old age: Cross-sectional results from the Berlin aging study. *Psychology and Aging, 12,* 410–432.

Lindquist, K., & Barrett, L. F. (2008). Constructing emotion: The experience of fear as a conceptual act. *Psychological Science, 19,* 898–903.

Lindquist, S. I., & McLean, J. P. (2011). Daydreaming and its correlates in an educational environment. *Learning and Individual Differences, 21,* 158–167.

Lindstrom, M. (2005). *Brand sense: How to build powerful brands through touch, taste, smell, sight and sound.* London: Kogan Page.

Liou, A. P., Paziuk, M., Luevano, J.-M., Machineni, S., Turnbaugh, P. J., & Kaplan, L. M. (2013). Conserved shifts in the gut microbiota due to gastric bypass reduce host weight and adiposity. *Science Translational Medicine, 5*(178), 178ra41–178ra41.

Little, B. R. (1983). Personal projects: A rationale and method for investigation. *Environment and Behavior, 15,* 273–309.

Liu, D., Diorio, J., Tannenbaum, B., Caldji, C., Francis, D., Freedman, A., . . . Meaney, M. J. (1997). Maternal care, hippocampal glucocorticoid receptors, and hypothalamic–pituitary–adrenal responses to stress. *Science, 277,* 1659–1662.

Liu, D., Wellman, H. M., Tardif, T., & Sabbagh, M. A. (2008). Theory of mind development in Chinese children: A meta-analysis of false belief understanding across cultures and languages. *Developmental Psychology, 44,* 523–531.

Livingstone, M., & Hubel, D. (1988). Segregation of form, color, movement, and depth: Anatomy, physiology, and perception. *Science, 240,* 740–749.

Locksley, A., Ortiz, V., & Hepburn, C. (1980). Social categorization and discriminatory behavior: Extinguishing the minimal intergroup discrimination effect. *Journal of Personality and Social Psychology, 39,* 773–783.

Loehlin, J. C. (1973). Blood group genes and Negro–White ability differences. *Behavior Genetics, 3*(3), 263–270.

Loehlin, J. C. (1992). *Genes and environment in personality development.* Newbury Park, CA: Sage.

Loftus, E. F. (1993). The reality of repressed memories. *American Psychologist, 48,* 518–537.

Loftus, E. F. (2003). Make-believe memories. *American Psychologist, 58,* 867–873.

Loftus, E. F., & Ketchum, K. (1994). *The myth of repressed memory.* New York: St. Martin's Press.

Loftus, E. F., & Klinger, M. R. (1992). Is the unconscious smart or dumb? *American Psychologist, 47,* 761–765.

Loftus, E. F., & Pickrell, J. E. (1995). The formation of false memories. *Psychiatric Annals, 25,* 720–725.

Lonegran, M. H., Olivera-Figueroa, L. A., Pitman, R. K., & Brunet, A. (2013). Propranolol's effects on the consolidation and reconsolidation of long-term emotional memory in healthy participants: A meta-analyis. *Journal of Psychiatry & Neuroscience, 38,* 222–231.

Lopes, P. N., Grewal, D., Kadis, J., Gall, M., & Salovey, P. (2006). Emotional intelligence and positive work outcomes. *Psichothema, 18,* 132.

Lord, C. G., Ross, L., & Lepper, M. R. (1979). Biased assimilation and attitude polarization: The effects of prior theories on subsequently considered evidence. *Journal of Personality and Social Psychology, 37,* 2098–2109.

Lorenz, K. (1952). *King Solomon's ring.* New York: Crowell.

Lovaas, O. I. (1987). Behavioral treatment and normal educational and intellectual functioning in young autistic children. *Journal of Consulting and Clinical Psychology, 55,* 3–9.

Low, J., & Watts, J. (2013). Attributing false beliefs about object identity reveals a signature blind spot in humans' efficient mind-reading system. *Psychological Science, 24*(3), 305–311. doi: 10.1177/0956797612451469

Lozano, B. E., & Johnson, S. L. (2001). Can personality traits predict increases in manic and depressive symptoms? *Journal of Affective Disorders, 63,* 103–111.

Luborsky, L., & Singer, B. (1975). Comparative studies of psychotherapies: Is it true that "everyone has won and all must have prizes"? *Archives of General Psychiatry, 32*(8), 995–1008.

Luborsky, L., Rosenthal, R., Diguer, L., Andrusyna, T. P., Berman, J. S., Levitt, J. T., . . . Krause, E. D. (2002). The dodo bird verdict is alive and well—mostly. *Clinical Psychology: Science and Practice, 9,* 2–12.

Lucas, R. E., Clark, A. E., Georgellis, Y., & Diener, E. (2003). Reexamining adaptation and the set point model of happiness: Reactions to changes in marital status. *Journal of Personality and Social Psychology, 84,* 527–539.

Lucas, R. E., & Dyrenforth, P. S. (2005). The myth of marital bliss? *Psychological Inquiry, 16*(2/3), 111–115.

Ludwig, A. M. (1966). Altered states of consciousness. *Archives of General Psychiatry, 15,* 225–234.

Lurquin, J. H., Michaelson, L. E., Barker, J. E, Gustavson, D. E., von Bastian, C. C., Carruth, N. P., & Miyake, A. (2016). No evidence of the ego-depletion effect across task characteristics and individual differences: A pre-registered study. *PLoS ONE, 11*(2), e0147770.

Luthar, S. S., & Ciciolla, L. (2016). What it feels like to be a mother: Variations by children's developmental stages. *Developmental Psychology, 52*(1), 143–154. doi: 10.1037/dev0000062

Lykken, D. T. (1995). *The antisocial personalities.* Hillsdale, NJ: Erlbaum.

Lynn, M., & Shurgot, B. A. (1984). Responses to lonely hearts advertisements: Effects of reported physical attractiveness, physique, and coloration. *Personality and Social Psychology Bulletin, 10,* 349–357.

Lynn, R. (2009). What has caused the Flynn effect? Secular increases in the development quotients of infants. *Intelligence, 37*(1), 16–24.

Lynn, R. (2013). Who discovered the Flynn effect? A review of early studies of the secular increase of intelligence. *Intelligence, 41*(6), 765–769. doi: 10.1016/j.intell.2013.03.008

Lyons, D. E., Young, A. G., & Keil, F. C. (2007). The hidden structure of overimitation. *Proceedings of the National Academy of Sciences, 104*(50), 19751–19756. doi: 10.1073/pnas.0704452104.

Lythcott-Haims, J. (2015). *How to raise an adult.* New York: Henry Holt.

Lyubomirsky, S. (2008). *The how of happiness: A scientific approach to getting the life you want.* New York: Penguin.

Lyubomirsky, S., & Lepper, H. S. (1999). A measure of subjective happiness: Preliminary reliability and construct validation. *Social Indicators Research, 46,* 137–155.

MacCann, C., Joseph, D. L., Newman, D. A., & Roberts, R. D. (2014). Emotional intelligence is a second-stratum factor of intelligence: Evidence from hierarchical and bifactor models. *Emotion, 14*(2), 358–374. doi: 10.1037/a0034755

MacDonald, S., Uesiliana, K., & Hayne, H. (2000). Cross-cultural and gender differences in childhood amnesia. *Memory, 8,* 365–376.

MacGregor, J. N., Ormerod, T. C., & Chronicle, E. P. (2001). Information processing and insight: A process model of performance on the nine-dot and related problems. *Journal of Experimental Psychology: Learning, Memory, and Cognition, 27,* 176–201.

Mackey, A. P., Hill, S. S., Stone, S. I., & Bunge, S. A. (2011). Differential effects of reasoning and speed training in children. *Developmental Science, 14,* 582–590. doi: 10.1111/j.1467-7687.2010.01005x

Maclean, P. D. (1970). The triune brain, emotion, and scientific bias. In F. O. Schmitt (Ed.), *The neurosciences: A second study program* (pp. 336–349). New York: Rockefeller University Press.

MacLeod, M. D. (2002). Retrieval-induced forgetting in eyewitness memory: Forgetting as a consequence of remembering. *Applied Cognitive Psychology, 16,* 135–149.

MacLeod, M. D., & Saunders, J. (2008). Retrieval inhibition and memory distortion: Negative consequences of an adaptive process. *Current Directions in Psychological Science, 17,* 26–30.

Macmillan, M. (2000). *An odd kind of fame: Stories of Phineas Gage.* Cambridge, MA: MIT Press.

Macmillan, N. A., & Creelman, C. D. (2005). *Detection theory.* Mahwah, NJ: Erlbaum.

Macrae, C. N., Bodenhausen, G. V., Milne, A. B., & Jetten, J. (1994). Out of mind but back in sight: Stereotypes on the rebound. *Journal of Personality and Social Psychology, 67,* 808–817.

Macrae, C. N., Moran, J. M., Heatherton, T. F., Banfield, J. F., & Kelley, W. M. (2004). Medial prefrontal activity predicts memory for self. *Cerebral Cortex, 14,* 647–654.

Maddi, S. R., Harvey, R. H., Khoshaba, D. M., Fazel, M., & Resurreccion, N. (2009). Hardiness training facilitates performance in college. *Journal of Positive Psychology, 4,* 566–577.

Maddi, S. R., Kahn, S., & Maddi, K. L. (1998). The effectiveness of hardiness training. *Consulting Psychology Journal: Practice and Research, 50,* 78–86.

Maddox, G. B., & Balota, D. A. (2015). Retrieval practice and spacing effects in young and older adults: An examination of the benefits of desirable difficulty. *Memory & Cognition, 43,* 760–774.

Maddux, W. W., Mullen, E., & Galinsky, A. D. (2008). Chameleons bake bigger pies and take bigger pieces: Strategic behavioral mimicry facilitates negotiation outcomes. *Journal of Experimental Social Psychology, 44,* 461–468.

Madigan, S., Atkinson, L., Laurin, K., & Benoit, D. (2013). Attachment and internalizing behavior in early childhood: A meta-analysis. *Developmental Psychology, 49*(4), 672–689. doi: 10.1037/a0028793

Madore, K. P., Addis, D. , & Schacter, D. L. (2015). Creativity and memory: Effects of an episodic specificity induction on divergent thinking. *Psychological Science, 26*, 1461–1468.

Maes, M. (1995). Evidence for an immune response in major depression: A review and hypothesis. *Progress in Neuro-Psychopharmacology and Biological Psychiatry, 19*, 11–38.

Maguire, E. A., Woollett, K., & Spiers, H. J. (2006). London taxi drivers and bus drivers: A structural MRI and neuropsychological analysis. *Hippocampus, 16*, 1091–1101.

Mahajan, N., Martinez, M. A., Gutierrez, N. L., Diesendruck, G., Banaji, M. R., & Santos, L. R. (2011). The evolution of intergroup bias: Perceptions and attitudes in rhesus macaques. *Journal of Personality and Social Psychology, 100*(3), 387–405. doi: 10.1037/a0022459

Mahon, B. Z., & Caramazza, A. (2009). Concepts and categories: A cognitive neuropsychological perspective. *Cognitive Neuropsychology, 60*, 27–51.

Mahon, B. Z., Anzellotti, S., Schwarzbach, J., Zampini, M., & Caramazza, A. (2009). Category-specific organization in the human brain does not require visual experience. *Neuron, 63*, 397–405.

Mahowald, M., & Schenck, C. (2000). REM sleep parasomnias. In M. Kryger, T. Roth, & W. Dement (Eds.), *Principles and practices of sleep medicine* (3rd ed., pp. 724–741). Philadelphia: Saunders.

Maier, S. F., & Watkins, L. R. (1998). Cytokines for psychologists: Implications of bidirectional immune-to-brain communication for understanding behavior, mood, and cognition. *Psychological Review, 105*, 83–107.

Maier, S. F., & Watkins, L. R. (2000). The immune system as a sensory system: Implications for psychology. *Current Directions in Psychological Science, 9*, 98–102.

Major, B., Mendes, W. B., & Dovidio, J. F. (2013). Intergroup relations and health disparities: A social psychological perspective. *Health Psychology, 32*, 514–524.

Makin, J. E., Fried, P. A., & Watkinson, B. (1991). A comparison of active and passive smoking during pregnancy: Long-term effects. *Neurotoxicology and Teratology, 16*, 5–12.

Makris, N. , Biederman, J., Monuteaux, M. C., & Seidman, L. J. (2009). Towards conceptualizing a neural systems-based anatomy of attention-deficit/hyperactivity disorder. *Developmental Neuroscience, 31*, 36–49.

Malina, R. M., Bouchard, C., & Beunen, G. (1988). Human growth: Selected aspects of current research on well-nourished children. *Annual Review of Anthropology, 17*, 187–219.

Malooly, A. M., Genet, J. J., & Siemer, M. (2013). Individual differences in reappraisal effectiveness: The role of affective flexibility. *Emotion, 13*(2), 302–313. doi: 10.1037/a0029980

Mampe, B., Friederici, A. D., Christophe, A., & Wermke, K. (2009). Newborns' cry melody is shaped by their native language. *Current Biology, 19*, 1–4.

Mandle, C. L., Jacobs, S. C., Arcari, P. M., & Domar, A. D. (1996). The efficacy of relaxation response interventions with adult patients: A review of the literature. *Journal of Cardiovascular Nursing, 10*, 4–26.

Mandler, G. (1967). Organization and memory. In K. W. Spence & J. T. Spence (Eds.), *The psychology of learning and motivation* (Vol. 1, pp. 327–372). New York: Academic Press.

Mandy, W., & Lai, M. C. (2016). The role of the environment in the developmental psychopathology of autism spectrum condition. *Journal of Child Psychology and Psychiatry, 57*, 271–292.

Mankiw, N. G., & Weinzierl, M. (2010). The optimal taxation of height: A case study of utilitarian income redistribution. *American Economic Journal: Economic Policy, 2*, 155–176.

Mann, J. J. (2005). The medical management of depression. *New England Journal of Medicine, 353*, 1819–1834.

Mann, J. J., Apter, A., Bertolote, J., Beautrais, A., Currier, D., Haas, A., . . . Hendin, H. (2005). Suicide prevention strategies: A systematic review. *Journal of the American Medical Association, 294*(16), 2064–2074. doi: 10.1001/jama.294.16.2064

Marangell, L. B., Silver, J. M., Goff, D. M., & Yudofsky, S. C. (2003). Psychopharmacology and electroconvulsive therapy. In R. E. Hales & S. C. Yudofsky (Eds.), *The American Psychiatric Publishing textbook of clinical psychiatry* (4th ed., pp. 1047–1149). Washington, DC: American Psychiatric Publishing.

March of Dimes. (2010). *Smoking during pregnancy.* http://www.marchofdimes.com/professionals/14332_1171.asp

Marci, C. D., Ham, J., Moran, E., & Orr, S. P. (2007). Physiologic correlates of perceived therapist empathy and social-emotional process during psychotherapy. *Journal of Nervous and Mental Disease, 195*, 103–111.

Marcus, G. (2012, December 3). Neuroscience fiction. *New Yorker.* http://www.newyorker.com/online/blogs/newsdesk/2012/12/what-neuroscience-really-teaches-us-and-what-it-doesnt.html

Marcus, G. B. (1986). Stability and change in political attitudes: Observe, recall, and "explain." *Political Behavior, 8*, 21–44.

Markel, H. (2011). *An anatomy of addiction: Sigmund Freud, William Halsted, and the miracle drug cocaine.* New York: Pantheon.

Markus, H. (1977). Self-schemata and processing information about the self. *Journal of Personality and Social Psychology, 35*, 63–78.

Marlatt, G. A., & Rohsenow, D. (1980). Cognitive processes in alcohol use: Expectancy and the balanced placebo design. In N. K. Mello (Ed.), *Advances in substance abuse: Behavioral and biological research* (pp. 159–199). Greenwich, CT: JAI Press.

Marlatt, G. A., & Witkiewitz, K. (2010). Update on harm reduction policy and intervention research. *Annual Review of Clinical Psychology, 6*, 591–606.

Marmot, M. G., Stansfeld, S., Patel, C., North, F., Head, J., White, L., . . . Feeney, A. (1991). Health inequalities among British civil servants: The Whitehall II study. *Lancet, 337*, 1387–1393.

Marr, D., & Nishihara, H. K. (1978). Representation and recognition of the spatial organization of three-dimensional shapes. *Proceedings of the Royal Society B: Biological Sciences, 200*, 269–294.

Marsolek, C. J. (1995). Abstract visual-form representations in the left cerebral hemispheres. *Journal of Experimental Psychology: Human Perception and Performance, 21*, 375–386.

Martin, A. (2007). The representation of object concepts in the brain. *Annual Review of Psychology, 58*, 25–45.

Martin, A., & Caramazza, A. (2003). Neuropsychological and neuroimaging perspectives on conceptual knowledge: An introduction. *Cognitive Neuropsychology, 20*, 195–212.

Martin, A., & Chao, L. L. (2001). Semantic memory and the brain: Structure and processes. *Current Opinion in Neurobiology, 11*, 194–201.

Martin, K. D., & Hill, R. P. (2012). Life satisfaction, self-determination, and consumption adequacy at the bottom of the pyramid. *Journal of Consumer Research, 38*, 1155–1168.

Martin, M. J., Blozis, S. A., Boeninger, D. K., Masarik, A. S., & Conger, R. D. (2014). The timing of entry into adult roles and changes in trajectories of problem behaviors during the transition to adulthood. *Developmental Psychology, 50*(11), 2473–2484. doi: 10.1037/a0037950

Martin, N. G., Eaves, L. J., Geath, A. R., Jarding, R., Feingold, L. M., & Eysenck, H. J. (1986). Transmission of social attitudes. *Proceedings of the National Academy of Sciences, USA, 83*, 4364–4368.

Martins, S. S., Sampson, L., Cerda, M., & Galea, S. (2015). Worldwide prevalence and trends in unintentional drug overdose: A systematic review of the literature. *American Journal of Public Health, 105*, E29–E49.

Marucha, P. T., Kiecolt-Glaser, J. K., & Favagehi, M. (1998). Mucosal wound healing is impaired by examination stress. *Psychosomatic Medicine, 60,* 362–365.

Marzuk, P. M., Tardiff, K., Leon, A. C., Hirsch, C., Portera, L., Iqbal, M. I., . . . Hartwell, N. (1998). Ambient temperature and mortality from unintentional cocaine overdose. *Journal of the American Medical Association, 279,* 1795–1800.

Maslach, C. (2003). Job burnout: New directions in research and intervention. *Current Directions in Psychological Science, 12,* 189–192.

Maslow, A. (1943). A theory of human motivation. *Psychological Review, 50,* 370–396.

Maslow, A. H. (1937). Dominance-feeling, behavior, and status. In R. J. Lowry (Ed.), *Dominance, self-esteem, self-actualization: Germinal papers by A. H. Maslow* (pp. 49–70). Monterey, CA: Brooks-Cole.

Maslow, A. H. (1954). *Motivation and personality.* New York: Harper & Row.

Mason, M. F., Norton, M. I., Van Horn, J. D., Wegner, D. M., Grafton, S. T., & Macrae, C. N. (2007). Wandering minds: The default network and stimulus-independent thought. *Science, 3154,* 393–395.

Masten, A. S. (2004). Family therapy as a treatment for children: A critical review of outcome research. *Family Process, 18,* 323–335.

Masters, W. H., & Johnson, V. E. (1966). *Human sexual response.* Boston: Little, Brown.

Mather, M., & Carstensen, L. L. (2003). Aging and attentional biases for emotional faces. *Psychological Science, 14,* 409–415.

Mather, M., & Carstensen, L. L. (2005). Aging and motivated cognition: The positivity effect in attention and memory. *Trends in Cognitive Sciences, 9*(10), 496–502.

Mather, M., Canli, T., English, T., Whitfield, S., Wais, P., Ochsner, K., . . . Cartensen, L. L. (2004). Amygdala responses to emotionally valenced stimuli in older and younger adults. *Psychological Science, 15,* 259–263.

Matsumoto, D., & Willingham, B. (2009). Spontaneous facial expressions of emotion of congenitally and noncongenitally blind individuals. *Journal of Personality and Social Psychology, 96,* 1–10.

Mattar, A. A. G., & Gribble, P. L. (2005). Motor learning by observing. *Neuron, 46,* 153–160.

Matthews, G., & Gilliland, K. (1999). The personality theories of H. J. Eysenck and J. A. Gray: A comparative review. *Personality and Individual Differences, 26,* 583–626.

Matzel, L. D., Han, Y. R., Grossman, H., Karnik, M. S., Patel, D., Scott, N., . . . Gandhi, C. C. (2003). Individual differences in the expression of a general learning ability in mice. *Journal of Neuroscience, 23*(16), 6423–6433.

Maudsley, H. (1886). *Natural causes and supernatural seemings.* London: Kegan Paul, Trench.

Maus, G. W., Ward, J., Nijhawan, R., & Whitney, D. (2013). The perceived position of moving objects: Transcranial magnetic stimulation of area MT+ reduces the flash-lag effect. *Cerebral Cortex, 23,* 241–247.

Max, A. (2006, September 16). Dutch reach new heights. *USA Today.* Retrieved from http://usatoday30.usatoday.com/news/ offbeat/2006-09 -16-dutch-tall_x.htm

May, R. (1983). *The discovery of being: Writings in existential psychology.* New York: Norton.

Mayberg, H., Lozano, A., Voon, V., McNeely, H., Seminowicz, D., Hamani, C., . . . Kennedy, S. H. (2005). Deep brain stimulation for treatment-resistant depresssion. *Neuron, 45,* 651–660.

Mayer, J. D., Caruso, D. R., & Salovey, P. (1999). Emotional intelligence meets traditional standards for an intelligence. *Intelligence, 27,* 267.

Mayer, J. D., Caruso, D. R., Zigler, E., & Dreyden, J. I. (1989). Intelligence and intelligence-related personality traits. *Intelligence, 13*(2), 119–133. doi: 10.1016/0160-2896(89)90011-1

Mayer, J. D., Roberts, R. D., & Barsade, S. G. (2008). Human abilities: Emotional intelligence. *Annual Review of Psychology, 59,* 507–536.

Maynard-Smith, J. (1965). The evolution of alarm calls. *American Naturalist, 100,* 637–650.

McAdams, D. (1993). *The stories we live by: Personal myths and the making of the self.* New York: Morrow.

McCabe, S. E., Knight, J. R., Teter, C. J., & Wechsler, H. (2005). Nonmedical use of prescription stimulants among U.S. college students: Prevalence and correlates from a national survey. *Addiction, 100,* 96–106.

McClelland, D. C., Atkinson, J. W., Clark, R. A., & Lowell, E. L. (1953). *The achievement motive.* New York: Appleton-Century-Crofts.

McCrae, R. R., & Costa, P. T. (1999). A five-factor theory of personality. In L. A. Pervin & O. P. John (Eds.), *Handbook of personality: Theory and research* (pp. 139–153). New York: Guilford Press.

McCrea, S. M., Buxbaum, L. J., & Coslett, H. B. (2006). Illusory conjunctions in simultanagnosia: Coarse coding of visual feature location? *Neuropsychologia, 44,* 1724–1736.

McDaniel, M. A., Thomas, R. C., Agarwal, P. K., McDermott, K. B., & Roediger, H. L. (2013). Quizzing in middle-school science: Successful transfer performance on classroom exams. *Applied Cognitive Psychology, 27,* 360–372.

McDermott, K. B., Agarwal, P. K., D'Antonio, L., Roediger, H. L., & McDaniel, M. A. (2014). Both multiple-choice and short-answer quizzes enhance later exam performance in middle and high school classes. *Journal of Experimental Psychology: Applied, 20,* 3–21.

McDougall, W. (1930). The hormic psychology. In C. Murchison (Ed.), *Psychologies of 1930* (pp. 3–36). Worcester, MA: Clark University Press.

McElwain, N. L., Booth-LaForce, C., & Wu, X. (2011). Infant–mother attachment and children's friendship quality: Maternal mental state talk as an intervening mechanism. *Developmental Psychology, 47*(5), 1295–1311. doi: 10.1037/a0024094

McEvoy, S. P., Stevenson, M. R., McCartt, A. T., Woodward, M., Haworth, C., Palamara, P., & Circarelli, R. (2005). Role of mobile phones in motor vehicle crashes resulting in hospital attendance: A case-crossover study. *British Medical Journal, 331,* 428–430.

McFall, R. M., & Treat, T. A. (1999). Quantifying the information value of clinical assessments with signal detection theory. *Annual Review of Psychology, 50,* 215–241.

McFarlane, A. H., Norman, G. R., Streiner, D. L., Roy, R., & Scott, D. J. (1980). A longitudinal study of the influence of the psychosocial environment on health status: A preliminary report. *Journal of Health and Social Behavior, 21,* 124–133.

McGarty, C., & Turner, J. C. (1992). The effects of categorization on social judgement. *British Journal of Social Psychology, 31,* 253–268.

McGaugh, J. L. (2000). Memory: A century of consolidation. *Science, 287,* 248–251.

McGaugh, J. L. (2006). Make mild moments memorable: Add a little arousal. *Trends in Cognitive Sciences, 10,* 345–347.

McGaugh, J. L. (2015). Consolidating memories. *Annual Review of Psychology, 66,* 1–24.

McGovern, P. E., Zhang, J., Tang, J., Zhang, Z., Hall, G. R., Moreau, R. A., . . . Wang, C. (2004). Fermented beverages of pre- and proto-historic China. *Proceedings of the National Academy of Sciences of the United States of America, 101,* 17593–17598.

McGowan, P. O., Sasaki, A., D'Alessio, A. D., Dymov, S., Labonté, B., Szyf, M., . . . Meaney, M. J. (2009). Epigenetic regulation of the glucocorticoid receptor in human brain associates with childhood abuse. *Nature Neuroscience, 12,* 342–348.

McGowan, P. O., Suderman, M., Sasaki, A., Huang, T. C. T., Hallett, M., Meaney, J. J., & Szyf, M. (2011). Broad epigenetic signature of maternal care in the brain of adult rats. *PLoS One, 6*(2), e14739. doi: 10.1371/journal.pone.0014739

McGrath, J., Saha, S., Chant, D., & Welham, J. (2008). Schizophrenia: A concise overview of incidence, prevalence, and mortality. *Epidemiologic Reviews, 30,* 67–76.

McGue, M., & Bouchard, T. J. (1998). Genetic and environmental influences on human behavioral differences. *Annual Review of Neuroscience, 21,* 1–24.

McGuire, P. K., Shah, G. M., & Murray, R. M. (1993). Increased blood flow in Broca's area during auditory hallucinations in schizophrenia. *Lancet, 342,* 703–706.

McIntyre, S. H., & Munson, J. M. (2008). Exploring cramming: Student behaviors, beliefs, and learning retention in the Principles of Marketing course. *Journal of Marketing Education, 30,* 226–243.

McKee, A. C., Cantu, R. C., Nowinski, C. J., Hedley-Whyte, E. T., Gavett, B. E., Budson, A. E., . . . Stern, R. A. (2009). Chronic traumatic encephalopathy in athletes: Progressive tauopathy after repetitive head injury. *Journal of Neuropathology and Experimental Neurology, 68,* 709–735.

McKetin, R., Ward, P. B., Catts, S. V., Mattick, R. P., & Bell, J. R. (1999). Changes in auditory selective attention and event-related potentials following oral administration of D-amphetamine in humans. *Neuropsychopharmacology, 21,* 380–390.

McKinney, C. H., Antoni, M. H., Kumar, M., Tims, F. C., & McCabe, P. M. (1997). Effects of guided imagery and music (GIM) therapy on mood and cortisol in healthy adults. *Health Psychology, 16,* 390–400.

McLaughlin, K. A., Nandi, A., Keyes, K. M., Uddin, M., Aiello, A. E., Galea, S., & Koenen, K. C. (2012). Home foreclosure and risk of psychiatric morbidity during the recent financial crisis. *Psychological Medicine, 42,* 1441–1448.

McLean, K. C. (2008). The emergence of narrative identity. *Social and Personality Psychology Compass, 2*(4), 1685–1702.

McNally, R. J. (2003). *Remembering trauma.* Cambridge, MA: Belknap Press of Harvard University Press.

McNally, R. J., & Clancy, S. A. (2005). Sleep paralysis, sexual abuse, and space alien abduction. *Transcultural Psychiatry, 42,* 113–122.

McNally, R. J., & Geraerts, E. (2009). A new solution to the recovered memory debate. *Perspective on Psychological Science, 4,* 126–134.

McNally, R. J., & Steketee, G. S. (1985). Etiology and maintenance of severe animal phobias. *Behavioral Research and Therapy, 23,* 431–435.

McNeilly, A. S., Robinson, I. C., Houston, M. J., & Howie, P. W. (1983). Release of oxytocin and prolactin in response to suckling. *British Medical Journal, 286,* 257–259.

McRae, C., Cherin, E., Yamazaki, G., Diem, G., Vo, A. H., Russell, D., . . . Freed, C. R. (2004). Effects of perceived treatment on quality of life and medical outcomes in a double-blind placebo surgery trial. *Archives of General Psychiatry, 61,* 412–420.

Mead, G. H. (1934). *Mind, self, and society.* Chicago: University of Chicago Press.

Mead, M. (1968). *Sex and temperament in three primitive societies.* New York: Dell. (Original work published 1935)

Meaidi, A., Jennum, P., Ptito, M., & Kupers, R. (2014). The sensory construction of dreams and nightmare frequency in congenitally blind and late blind individuals. *Sleep Medicine, 15,* 586–595.

Meaney, M. J., & Ferguson-Smith, A. C. (2010). Epigenetic regulation of the neural transcriptome: The meaning of the marks. *Nature Neuroscience, 13,* 1313–1318.

Means, B., Toyama, Y., Murphy, R., Bakia, M., & Jones, K. (2010). *Evaluation of evidence based practices in online learning: Meta-analysis and review of online learning studies.* Washington, DC: U.S. Department of Education. Retrieved from https://www2.ed.gov/rschstat/eval/tech/evidence-based-practices/finalreport.pdf

Mechelli, A., Crinion, J. T., Noppeney, U., O'Doherty, J., Ashburner, J., Frackowiak, R. S., & Price, C. J. (2004). Neurolinguistics: Structural plasticity in the bilingual brain. *Nature, 431,* 757.

Medin, D. L., & Schaffer, M. M. (1978). Context theory of classification learning. *Psychological Review, 85,* 207–238.

Medvec, V. H., Madey, S. F., & Gilovich, T. (1995). When less is more: Counterfactual thinking and satisfaction among Olympic medalists. *Journal of Personality and Social Psychology, 69,* 603–610.

Meeren, H. K. M., van Heijnsbergen, C. C. R. J., & de Gelder, B. (2005). Rapid perceptual integration of facial expression and emotional body language. *Proceedings of the National Academy of Sciences, USA, 102*(45), 16518–16523.

Mehl, M. R., Vazire, S., Ramirez-Esparza, N., Slatcher, R. B., & Pennebaker, J. W. (2009). Are women really more talkative than men? *Science, 317,* 82.

Mehu, M., & Scherer, K. R. (2015). Emotion categories and dimensions in the facial communication of affect: An integrated approach. *Emotion, 15*(6), 798–811. doi: 10.1037/a0039416

Meindl, J. N., & Casey, L. B. (2012). Increasing the suppressive effect of delayed punishers: A review of basic and applied literature. *Behavioral Interventions, 27,* 129–150.

Meins, E. (2003). Emotional development and attachment relationships. In A. Slater & G. Bremner (Eds.), *An introduction to developmental psychology* (pp. 141–164). Malden, MA: Blackwell.

Meins, E., Fernyhough, C., Fradley, E., & Tuckey, M. (2001). Rethinking maternal sensitivity: Mothers' comments on infants' mental processes predict security of attachment at 12 months. *Journal of Child Psychology & Psychiatry & Allied Disciplines, 42,* 637–648.

Meisel, S. R., Dayan, K. I., Pauzner, H., Chetboun, I., Arbel, Y., & David, D. (1991). Effect of Iraqi missile war on incidence of acute myocardial infarction and sudden death in Israeli citizens. *Lancet, 338,* 660–661.

Mekel-Bobrov, N., Gilbert, S. L., Evans, P. D., Vallender, E. J., Anderson, J. R., Hudson, R. R., . . . Lahn, B. T. (2005). Ongoing adaptive evolution of ASPM, a brain size determinant in *Homo sapiens. Science, 309,* 1720–1722.

Melander, E. (2005). Gender equality and intrastate armed conflict. *International Studies Quarterly, 49*(4), 695–714. doi: 10.1111/j.1468-2478.2005.00384.x

Mellon, R. C. (2009). Superstitious perception: Response-independent reinforcement and punishment as determinants of recurring eccentric interpretations. *Behaviour Research and Therapy, 47,* 868–875.

Meltzer, A. L., McNulty, J. K., Jackson, G. L., & Karney, B. R. (2014). Sex differences in the implications of partner physical attractiveness for the trajectory of marital satisfaction. *Journal of Personality and Social Psychology, 106*(3), 418–428. doi: 10.1037/a0034424

Meltzer, H. Y. (2013). Update on typical and atypical antipsychotic drugs. *Annual Review of Medicine, 64*, 393–406.

Meltzoff, A. N. (1995). Understanding the intentions of others: Reenactment of intended acts by 18-month-old children. *Developmental Psychology, 31*, 838–850.

Meltzoff, A. N. (2007). "Like me": A foundation for social cognition. *Developmental Science, 10*(1), 126–134. doi: 10.1111/j.1467-7687 .2007.00574x

Meltzoff, A. N., Kuhl, P. K., Movellan, J., & Sejnowski, T. J. (2009). Foundations for a new science of learning. *Science, 325*, 284–288.

Meltzoff, A. N., & Moore, M. K. (1977). Imitation of facial and manual gestures by human neonates. *Science, 198*, 75–78.

Melzack, R., & Wall, P. D. (1965). Pain mechanisms: A new theory. *Science, 150*, 971–979.

Mendes, W. B., Blascovich, J., Hunter, S. B., Lickel, B., & Jost, J. T. (2007). Threatened by the unexpected: Physiological responses during social interactions with expectancy-violating partners. *Journal of Personality and Social Psychology, 92*, 698–716.

Mendes, W. B., Blascovich, J., Lickel, B., & Hunter, S. (2002). Challenge and threat during social interaction with White and Black men. *Personality & Social Psychology Bulletin, 28*, 939–952.

Mendle, J. (2014). Beyond pubertal timing: New directions for studying individual differences in development. *Current Directions in Psychological Science, 23*(3), 215–219. doi: 10.1177/0963721414530144

Mendle, J., Harden, K. P., Brooks-Gunn, J., & Graber, J. A. (2010). Development's tortoise and hare: Pubertal timing, pubertal tempo, and depressive symptoms in boys and girls. *Developmental Psychology, 46*(5), 1341–1353. doi: 10.1037/a0020205

Mendle, J., Turkheimer, E., & Emery, R. E. (2007). Detrimental psychological outcomes associated with early pubertal timing in adolescent girls. *Developmental Review, 27*, 151–171.

Mennella, J. A., Johnson, A., & Beauchamp, G. K. (1995). Garlic ingestion by pregnant women alters the odor of amniotic fluid. *Chemical Senses, 20*, 207–209.

Merikangas, K. R., Wicki, W., & Angst, J. (1994). Heterogeneity of depression: Classification of depressive subtype by longitudinal course. *British Journal of Psychiatry, 164*, 342–348.

Mervis, C. B., & Bertrand, J. (1994). Acquisition of the Novel Name–Nameless Category (N3C) principle. *Child Development, 65*, 1646–1662. doi: 10.2307/1131285

Merzenich, M. M., Recanzone, G. H., Jenkins, W. M., & Grajski, K. A. (1990). Adaptive mechanisms in cortical networks underlying cortical contributions to learning and nondeclarative memory. *Cold Spring Harbor Symposia on Quantitative Biology, 55*, 873–887.

Mesoudi, A., Chang, L., Dall, S. R. X., & Thornton, A. (2015). The evolution of individual and cultural variation in social learning. *Trends in Ecology & Evolution, 31*, 215–225.

Messick, D. M., & Cook, K. S. (1983). *Equity theory: Psychological and sociological perspectives.* New York: Praeger.

Meston, C. M., & Buss, D. M. (2007). Why humans have sex. *Archives of Sexual Behavior, 36*, 477–507.

Mestre, J. M., Guil, R., Lopes, P. N., Salovey, P., & Gil-Olarte, P. (2006). Emotional intelligence and social and academic adaptation to school. *Psicothema, 18*, 112.

Mestry, N., Donnelly, N., Meneer, T., & McCarthy, R. A. (2012). Discriminating Thatcherised from typical faces in a case of prosopagnosia. *Neuropsychologia, 50*, 3410–3418.

Metcalfe, J. (2009). Metacognitive judgments and control of study. *Current Directions in Psychological Science, 18*, 159–163.

Metcalfe, J., Casal-Roscum, L., Radin, A., & Friedman, D. (2015). On teaching old dogs new tricks. *Psychological Science, 26*, 1833–1842. doi: 10.1177/0956797615597912

Metcalfe, J., & Finn, B. (2008). Evidence that judgments of learning are causally related to study choice. *Psychonomic Bulletin & Review, 15*, 174–179.

Metcalfe, J., & Wiebe, D. (1987). Intuition in insight and noninsight problem solving. *Memory & Cognition, 15*, 238–246.

Methven, L., Allen, V. J., Withers, G. A., & Gosney, M. A. (2012). Ageing and taste. *Proceedings of the Nutrition Society, 71*, 556–565.

Meyer-Bahlberg, H. F. L., Ehrhardt, A. A., Rosen, L. R., & Gruen, R. S. (1995). Prenatal estrogens and the development of homosexual orientation. *Developmental Psychology, 31*, 12–21.

Michaela, R., Florian, S., Gert, G. W., & Ulman, L. (2009). Seeking pleasure and seeking pain: Differences in prohedonic and contrahedonic motivation from adolescence to old age. *Psychological Science, 20*(12), 1529–1535.

Michelson, D., Pollack, M., Lydiard, R. D., Tamura, R., Tepner, R., & Tollefson, G. (1999). Continuing treatment of panic disorder after acute responses: Randomized, placebo-controlled trial with fluoxetine. The Fluoxetine Panic Disorder Study Group. *British Journal of Psychiatry, 174*, 213–218.

Mikels, J. A., Maglio, S. J., Reed, A. E., & Kaplowitz, L. J. (2011). Should I go with my gut? Investigating the benefits of emotion-focused decision making. *Emotion, 11*(4), 743–753.

Mikels, J. A., & Shuster, M. M. (2016). The interpretative lenses of older adults are not rose-colored—just less dark: Aging and the interpretation of ambiguous scenarios. *Emotion, 16*(1), 94–100.

Miklowitz, D. J., & Johnson, S. L. (2006). The psychopathology and treatment of bipolar disorder. *Annual Review of Clinical Psychology, 2*, 199–235.

Mikolajczak, M., Avalosse, H., Vancorenland, S., Verniest, R., Callens, M., van Broeck, N., ... Mierop, A. (2015). A nationally representative study of emotional competence and health. *Emotion, 15*(5), 653–667. doi: 10.1037/emo0000034

Milgram, S. (1963). Behavioral study of obedience. *Journal of Abnormal and Social Psychology, 67*, 371–378.

Milgram, S. (1974). *Obedience to authority.* New York: Harper & Row.

Milgram, S., Bickman, L., & Berkowitz, O. (1969). Note on the drawing power of crowds of different size. *Journal of Personality and Social Psychology, 13*, 79–82.

Miller, A. J. (1986). *The obedience experiments: A case study of controversy in social science.* New York: Praeger.

Miller, C., Seckel, E., & Ramachandran, V. S. (2012). Using mirror box therapy to treat phantom pain in Haitian earthquake victims. *Journal of Vision, 12*, article 1323. doi: 10.1167/12.9.1323

Miller, D. T., & Prentice, D. A. (1996). The construction of social norms and standards. In E. T. Higgins & A. W. Kruglanski (Ed.), *Social psychology: Handbook of basic principles* (pp. 799–829). New York: Guilford Press.

Miller, D. T., & Ratner, R. K. (1998). The disparity between the actual and assumed power of self-interest. *Journal of Personality and Social Psychology, 74*, 53–62.

Miller, D. T., & Ross, M. (1975). Self-serving biases in the attribution of causality: Fact or fiction? *Psychological Bulletin, 82*, 213–225.

Miller, G. A. (1956). The magical number seven, plus or minus two: Some limits on our capacity for processing information. *Psychological Review, 63*, 81–96.

Miller, N. E. (1960). Motivational effects of brain stimulation and drugs. *Federation Proceedings, 19,* 846–854.

Miller, T. W. (Ed.). (1996). *Theory and assessment of stressful life events.* Madison, CT: International Universities Press.

Miller, W. R., & Rollnick, S. (2012). *Motivational interviewing: Helping people change* (3rd ed.). New York: Guilford Press.

Mills, P. J., & Dimsdale, J. E. (1991). Cardiovascular reactivity to psychosocial stressors. A review of the effects of beta-blockade. *Psychosomatics, 32,* 209–220.

Milne, E., & Grafman, J. (2001). Ventromedial prefrontal cortex lesions in humans eliminate implicit gender stereotyping. *Journal of Neuroscience, 21,* 1–6.

Milner, A. D., & Goodale, M. A. (1995). *The visual brain in action.* Oxford: Oxford University Press.

Milner, B. (1962). Laterality effects in audition. In V. B. Mountcastle (Ed.), *Interhemispheric relations and cerebral dominance* (pp. 177–195). Baltimore: Johns Hopkins University Press.

Mineka, S., & Cook, M. (1988). Social learning and the acquisition of snake fear in monkeys. In T. Zentall & B. G. Galef, Jr. (Eds.), *Social learning* (pp. 51–73). Hillsdale, NJ: Erlbaum.

Mineka, S., & Ohman, A. (2002). Born to fear: Non-associative vs. associative factors in the etiology of phobia. *Behaviour Research and Therapy, 40,* 173–184.

Mingroni, M. A. (2007). Resolving the IQ paradox: Heterosis as a cause of the Flynn effect and other trends. *Psychological Review, 114,* 806–829.

Minsky, M. (1986). *The society of mind.* New York: Simon & Schuster.

Minson, J. A., & Mueller, J. S. (2012). The cost of collaboration: Why joint decision making exacerbates rejection of outside information. *Psychological Science, 23*(3), 219–224. doi: 10.1177/0956797611429132

Miranda, J., Bernal, G., Lau, A., Kihn, L., Hwang, W. C., & LaFramboise, T. (2005). State of the science on psychological interventions for ethnic minorities. *Annual Review of Clinical Psychology, 1,* 113–142.

Mischel, W. (1968). *Personality and assessment.* New York: Wiley.

Mischel, W. (2004). Toward an integrative science of the person. *Annual Review of Psychology, 55,* 1–22.

Mischel, W., Ayduk, O., Baumeister, R. F., & Vohs, K. D. (2004). Willpower in a cognitive-affective processing system: The dynamics of delay of gratification. In *Handbook of self-regulation: Research, theory, and applications* (pp. 99–129). New York: Guilford Press.

Mischel, W., & Shoda, Y. (1999). Integrating dispositions and processing dynamics within a unified theory of personality: The cognitive-affective personality system. In L. A. Pervin & O. P. John (Eds.), *Handbook of personality: Theory and research.* New York: Guilford Press.

Mischel, W., Shoda, Y., & Rodriguez, M. L. (1989). Delay of gratification in children. *Science, 244,* 933–938.

Mishra, A., & Mishra, H. (2010). Border bias: The belief that state borders can protect against disasters. *Psychological Science, 21*(11), 1582–1586. doi: 10.1177/0956797610385950

Mita, T. H., Dermer, M., & Knight, J. (1977). Reversed facial images and the mere-exposure hypothesis. *Journal of Personality and Social Psychology, 35,* 597–601.

Mitchell, J. P. (2006). Mentalizing and Marr: An information processing approach to the study of social cognition. *Brain Research, 1079,* 66–75.

Mitchell, J. P., Heatherton, T. F., & Macrae, C. N. (2002). Distinct neural systems subserve person and object knowledge. *Proceedings of the National Academy of Sciences, USA, 99,* 15238–15243.

Mitchell, K. J., & Johnson, M. K. (2009). Source monitoring 15 years later: What have we learned from fMRI about the neural mechanisms of source memory? *Psychological Bulletin, 135,* 638–677.

Miura, I. T., Okamoto, Y., Kim, C. C., & Chang, C. M. (1994). Comparisons of children's cognitive representation of number: China, France, Japan, Korea, Sweden and the United States. *International Journal of Behavioral Development, 17,* 401–411.

Miyamoto, Y., Ma, X., & Petermann, A. G. (2014). Cultural differences in hedonic emotion regulation after a negative event. *Emotion, 14*(4), 804–815. doi: 10.1037/a0036257

Moffitt, T. E. (1993). Adolescence-limited and life-course-persistent antisocial behavior: A developmental taxonomy. *Psychological Review, 100,* 674–701.

Moffitt, T. E. (2005). Genetic and environmental influences on antisocial behaviors: Evidence from behavioral-genetic research. *Advances in Genetics, 55,* 41–104.

Moghaddam, B., & Bunney, B. S. (1989). Differential effect of cocaine on extracellular dopamine levels in rat medial prefrontal cortex and nucleus accumbens: Comparison to amphetamine. *Synapse, 4,* 156–161.

Mojtabai, R., Olfson, M., Sampson, N. A., Jin, R., Druss, B., Wang, P. S., . . . Kessler, R. C. (2011). Barriers to mental health treatment: Results from the National Comorbidity Survey replication. *Psychological Medicine, 41*(8), 1751–1761.

Mokdad, A. H., Ford, E. S., Bowman, B. A., Dietz, W. H., Vinicor, F., Bales, V. S., & Marks, J. S. (2003). Prevalence of obesity, diabetes, and obesity-related health risk factors, 2001. *Journal of the American Medical Association, 289*(1), 76–79. doi: 10.1001/jama.289.1.76

Molden, D., Lee, A. Y., & Higgins, E. T. (2009). Motivations for promotion and prevention. In J. Shah & W. Gardner (Eds.), *Handbook of motivation science* (pp. 169–187). New York: Guilford Press.

Molloy, L. E., Gest, S. D., Feinberg, M. E., & Osgood, D. W. (2014). Emergence of mixed-sex friendship groups during adolescence: Developmental associations with substance use and delinquency. *Developmental Psychology, 50*(11), 2449–2461. doi: 10.1037/a0037856

Monahan, J. (1992). Mental disorder and violent behavior: Perceptions and evidence. *American Psychologist, 47,* 511–521.

Monahan, J. L., Murphy, S. T., & Zajonc, R. B. (2000). Subliminal mere exposure: Specific, general, and diffuse effects. *Psychological Science, 11,* 462–466.

Moncrieff, J. (2009). A critique of the dopamine hypothesis of schizophrenia and psychosis. *Harvard Review of Psychiatry, 17,* 214–225.

Montag, C., Błaszkiewicz, K., Sariyska, R., Lachman, B., Andone, I., Trendafilov, B., . . . Markowetz, A. (2015). Smartphone usage in the 21st century: Who is active on WhatsApp? *BMC Research Notes, 81*(1), 331.

Montague, C. T., Farooqi, I. S., Whitehead, J. P., Soos, M. A., Rau, H., Wareham, N. J., . . . O'Rahilly, S. (1997). Congenital leptin deficiency is associated with severe early-onset obesity in humans. *Nature, 387*(6636), 903–908.

Montenigro, P. H., Corp, D. T., Stein, T. D., Cantu, R. C., & Stern, R. A. (2015). Chronic traumatic encephalopathy: Historical origins and current perspective. *Annual Review of Clinical Psychology, 11,* 309–330.

Mook, D. G. (1983). In defense of external invalidity. *American Psychologist, 38,* 379–387.

Moon, S. M., & Illingworth, A. J. (2005). Exploring the dynamic nature of procrastination: A latent growth curve analysis of academic procrastination. *Personality and Individual Differences, 38*, 297–309.

Moore, D. W. (2003). *Public lukewarm on animal rights.* Retrieved from http://www.gallup.com/poll/8461/publiclukewarm-animal-rights.aspx

Moore, E. G. J. (1986). Family socialization and the IQ test performance of traditionally and transracially adopted Black children. *Developmental Psychology, 22*, 317–326.

Moore, K. L. (1977). *The developing human* (2nd ed.). Philadelphia: Saunders.

Moore, L. (2012, August 31). American's future has to be multilingual. *The Washington Diplomat.* Retrieved from http://www.wash-diplomat.com/index.php?option=com_content&view=article&id=8549:op-ed-americans-future-has-to-be-multilingual&catid=1492:september -2012&Itemid=504

Moran, P., Klinteberg, B. A., Batty, G. D., & Vågerö, D. (2009). Brief report: Childhood intelligence predicts hospitalization with personality disorder in adulthood: Evidence from a population-based study in Sweden. *Journal of Personality Disorders, 23*(5), 535–540. doi: 10.1521/pedi.2009.23.5.535

Moray, N. (1959). Attention in dichotic listening: Affective cues and the influence of instructions. *Quarterly Journal of Experimental Psychology, 11*, 56–60.

Moreno, S., Marques, C., Santos, A., Santos, M., Castro, S. L., & Besson, M. (2009). Musical training influences linguistic abilities in 8-year-old children: More evidence for brain plasticity. *Cerebral Cortex, 19*, 712–723.

Morgenstern, J., Labouvie, E., McCrady, B. S., Kahler, C. W., & Frey, R. M. (1997). Affiliation with Alcoholics Anonymous after treatment: A study of its therapeutic effects and mechanisms of action. *Journal of Consulting and Clinical Psychology, 65*, 768–777.

Morin, A. (2002). Right hemisphere self-awareness: A critical assessment. *Consciousness & Cognition, 11*, 396–401.

Morin, A. (2006). Levels of consciousness and self-awareness: A comparison of various neurocognitive views. *Consciousness & Cognition, 15*, 358–371.

Morin, C. M., Bélanger, L., LeBlanc, M., Ivers, H., Savard, J., Espie, C. A., . . . Grégoire, J. P. (2009). The natural history of insomnia: A population-based 3-year longitudinal study. *Archives of Internal Medicine, 169*, 447–453.

Morris, C. D., Bransford, J. D., & Franks, J. J. (1977). Levels of processing versus transfer-appropriate processing. *Journal of Verbal Learning and Verbal Behavior, 16*, 519–533.

Morris, R. G., Anderson, E., Lynch, G. S., & Baudry, M. (1986). Selective impairment of learning and blockade of long-term potentiation by an N-methyl-D-aspartate receptor antagonist, AP5. *Nature, 319*, 774–776.

Morris, T. L. (2001). Social phobia. In M. W. Vasey & M. R. Dadds (Eds.), *The developmental psychopathology of anxiety* (pp. 435–458). New York: Oxford University Press.

Morrow, D., Leirer, V., Altiteri, P., & Fitzsimmons, C. (1994). When expertise reduces age differences in performance. *Psychology and Aging, 9*, 134–148.

Moruzzi, G., & Magoun, H. W. (1949). Brain stem reticular formation and activation of the EEG. *Electroencephalography and Clinical Neurophysiology, 1*, 455–473.

Moscovitch, M. (1994). Memory and working-with-memory: Evaluation of a component process model and comparisons with other models. In D. L. Schacter & E. Tulving (Eds.), *Memory systems 1994* (pp. 269–310). Cambridge, MA: MIT Press.

Moscovitch, M., Cabeza, R., Winocur, G., & Nadel, L. (2016). Episodic memory and beyond: The hippocampus and cortex in transformation. *Annual Review of Psychology, 67*, 105–134.

Moscovitch, M., Nadel, L., Winocur, G., Gilboa, A., & Rosenbaum, R. S. (2006). The cognitive neuroscience of remote episodic, semantic and spatial memory. *Current Opinion in Neurobiology, 16*, 179–190.

Motley, M. T., & Baars, B. J. (1979). Effects of cognitive set upon laboratory induced verbal (Freudian) slips. *Journal of Speech & Hearing Research, 22*, 421–432.

Moulin, C. J. A., Conway, M. A., Thompson, R. G., James, N., & Jones, R. W. (2005). Disordered memory awareness: Recollective confabulation in two cases of persistent déjà vecu. *Neuropsychologia, 43*, 1362–1378.

Moulin, C. J. A. (2013). Disordered recognition memory: Recollective confabulation. *Cortex, 49*, 1541–1552.

Moulton, E., Barton, M., Robins, D. L., Abrams, D. N., & Fein, D. (2016) Early characteristics of children with ASD who demonstrate optimal progress between age two and four. *Journal of Autism and Developmental Disorders, 46*, 2160–2173.

Moura, A. C. A. de, & Lee, P. C. (2004). Capuchin stone tool use in Caatinga dry forest. *Science, 306*, 1909.

Mroczek, D. K., & Spiro, A. (2005). Change in life satisfaction during adulthood: Findings from the Veterans Affairs Normative Aging Study. *Journal of Personality and Social Psychology, 88*, 189.

Muehlenkamp, J. J., Claes, L., Havertape, L., & Plener, P. L. (2012). International prevalence of adolescent non-suicidal self-injury and deliberate self-harm. *Child and Adolescent Psychiatry and Mental Health, 6*(10). doi: 10.1156/1753-2000-6-10

Mueller, T. E., Gavin, L. E., & Kulkarni, A. (2008). The association between sex education and youth's engagement in sexual intercourse, age at first intercourse, and birth control use at first sex. *Journal of Adolescent Health, 42*(1), 89–96.

Mueller, T. I., Leon, A. C., Keller, M. B., Solomon, D. A., Endicott, J., Coryell, W., . . . Maser, J. D. (1999). Recurrence after recovery from major depressive disorder during 15 years of observational follow-up. *American Journal of Psychiatry, 156*, 1000–1006.

Muenter, M. D., & Tyce, G. M. (1971). L-dopa therapy of Parkinson's disease: Plasma L-dopa concentration, therapeutic response, and side effects. *Mayo Clinic Proceedings, 46*, 231–239.

Mullen, M. K. (1994). Earliest recollections of childhood: A demographic analysis. *Cognition, 52*, 55–79.

Muller, M. N., & Wrangham, R. W. (2004). Dominance, aggression and testosterone in wild chimpanzees: A test of the "challenge hypothesis." *Animal Behaviour, 67*, 113–123.

Munsey, C. (2008, February). Prescriptive authority in the states. *Monitor on Psychology, 39*, 60.

Murayama, K., Miyatsu, T., Buchli, D., & Storm, B. C. (2014). Forgetting as a consequence of retrieval: A meta-analytic review of retrieval-induced forgetting. *Psychological Bulletin, 140*, 1383–1409.

Murphy, N. A., Hall, J. A., & Colvin, C. R. (2003). Accurate intelligence assessments in social interactions: Mediators and gender effects. *Journal of Personality, 71*, 465–493.

Murray, C. (2002). *IQ and income inequality in a sample of sibling pairs from advantaged family backgrounds.* Paper presented at the 114th Annual Meeting of the American Economic Association.

Murray, H. A. (1943). *Thematic Apperception Test manual.* Cambridge, MA: Harvard University Press.

Murray, H. A., & Kluckhohn, C. (1953). Outline of a conception of personality. In C. Kluckhohn, H. A. Murray, & D. M. Schneider

(Eds.), *Personality in nature, society, and culture* (2nd ed., pp. 3–52). New York: Knopf.

Myers, D. G., & Diener, E. (1995). Who is happy? *Psychological Science, 6,* 10–19.

Myers, D. G., & Lamm, H. (1975). The polarizing effect of group discussion. *American Scientist, 63*(3), 297–303.

Myles, P. S., Leslie, K., McNell, J., Forbes, A., & Chan, M. T. V. (2004). Bispectral index monitoring to prevent awareness during anaesthesia: The B-Aware randomized controlled trial. *Lancet, 363,* 1757–1763.

Nadasdy, A. (1995). Phonetics, phonology, and applied linguistics. *Annual Review of Applied Linguistics, 15,* 68–77.

Nader, K., & Hardt, O. (2009). A single standard for memory: The case of reconsolidation. *Nature Reviews Neuroscience, 10,* 224–234.

Nader, K., Shafe, G., & LeDoux, J. E. (2000). Fear memories require protein synthesis in the amygdala for reconsolidation after retrieval. *Nature, 406,* 722–726.

Nagasako, E. M., Oaklander, A. L., & Dworkin, R. H. (2003). Congenital insensitivity to pain: An update. *Pain, 101,* 213–219.

Nagell, K., Olguin, R. S., & Tomasello, M. (1993). Processes of social learning in the tool use of chimpanzees (*Pan troglodytes*) and human children (*Homo sapiens*). *Journal of Comparative Psychology, 107,* 174–186.

Nairne, J. S., Pandeirada, J. N. S., & Thompson, S. R. (2008). Adaptive memory: The comparative value of survival processing. *Psychological Science, 19,* 176–180.

Nairne, J. S., Thompson, S. R., & Pandeirada, J. N. S. (2007). Adaptive memory: Survival processing enhances retention. *Journal of Experimental Psychology: Learning, Memory, and Cognition, 33,* 263–273.

Nakazato, M., Murakami, N., Date, Y., Kojima, M., Matsuo, H., Kangawa, K., & Matsukura, S. (2001). A role for ghrelin in the central regulation of feeding. *Nature, 409,* 194–198.

Naqvi, N., Shiv, B., & Bechara, A. (2006). The role of emotion in decision making: A cognitive neuroscience perspective. *Current Directions in Psychological Science, 15,* 260–264.

Nash, G. (2001). The subversive male: Homosexual and bestial images on European Mesolithic rock art. In L. Bevan (Ed.), *Indecent exposure: Sexuality, society and the archaeological record* (pp. 43–55). Glasgow: Cruithne Press.

Nassi, J. J., & Callaway, E. M. (2009). Parallel processing strategies of the primate visual system. *Nature Reviews Neuroscience, 10,* 360–372.

Nathan, P. E., & Gorman, J. M. (2007). *A guide to treatments that work* (3rd ed.). New York: Oxford University Press.

National Center for Health Statistics. (2012). *Health, United States, 2011* (with special feature on socioeconomic status and health). Hyattsville, MD: Author.

National Center for Health Statistics. (2016a). Health of Black or African American non-Hispanic population. Atlanta: Centers for Disease Control and Prevention. Retrieved from http://www.cdc.gov/nchs/fastats/black-health.htm

National Center for Health Statistics. (2016b). Child health. Atlanta: Centers for Disease Control and Prevention. Retrieved from http://www.cdc.gov/nchs/fastats/child-health.htm

National Research Council. (2003). *The polygraph and lie detection.* Washington, DC: National Academies Press.

Neihart, M. (1999). The impact of giftedness on psychological well-being: What does the empirical literature say? *Roeper Review, 22*(1), 10.

Neimark, J. (2004, July/August). The power of coincidence. *Psychology Today,* pp. 47–52.

Neimeyer, R. A., & Mitchell, K. A. (1988). Similarity and attraction: A longitudinal study. *Journal of Social and Personal Relationships, 5,* 131–148.

Neisser, U. (1967). *Cognitive psychology.* New York: Appleton-Century-Crofts.

Neisser, U. (Ed.). (1998). *The rising curve: Long-term gains in IQ and related measures.* Washington, DC: American Psychological Association.

Neisser, U., & Harsch, N. (1992). Phantom flashbulbs: False recollections of hearing the news about *Challenger.* In E. Winograd & U. Neisser (Eds.), *Affect and accuracy in recall: Studies of "flashbulb memories"* (pp. 9–31). Cambridge: Cambridge University Press.

Neisser, U., Boodoo, G., Bouchard, T. J., Jr., Boykin, A. W., Brody, N., Ceci, S. J., . . . Loehlin, J. C. (1996). Intelligence: Knowns and unknowns. *American Psychologist, 51,* 77–101.

Nelson, A. B., & Kreitzer, A. C. (2015). Reassessing models of basal ganglia function and dysfunction. *Annual Review of Neuroscience, 37,* 117–135.

Nelson, C. A., Zeanah, C. H., Fox, N. A., Marshall, P. J., Smyke, A. T., & Guthrie, D. (2007). Cognitive recovery in socially deprived young children: The Bucharest early intervention project. *Science, 318,* 1937–1940.

Nemeth, C., & Chiles, C. (1988). Modelling courage: The role of dissent in fostering independence. *European Journal of Social Psychology, 18,* 275–280.

Nes, L. S. & Sergerstrom, S. C. (2006). Dispositional optimism and coping: A meta-analytic review. *Personality and Social Psychology Review, 10,* 235–251.

Neuberg, S. L., Kenrick, D. T., & Schaller, M. (2010). Evolutionary social psychology. In S. T. Fiske, D. T. Gilbert, & G. Lindzey (Eds.), *The handbook of social psychology* (5th ed., Vol. 2, pp. 761–796). New York: Wiley.

Neugebauer, R., Hoek, H. W., & Susser, E. (1999). Prenatal exposure to wartime famine and development of antisocial personality in early adulthood. *Journal of the American Medical Association, 282,* 455–462.

Newbold, R. R., Padilla-Banks, E., Snyder, R. J., & Jefferson, W. N. (2005). Developmental exposure to estrogenic compounds and obesity. *Birth Defects Research Part A: Clinical and Molecular Teratology, 73,* 478–480.

Newell, A., Shaw, J. C., & Simon, H. A. (1958). Elements of a theory of human problem solving. *Psychological Review, 65,* 151–166.

Newman, A. J., Bavelier, D., Corina, D., Jezzard, P., & Neville, H. J. (2002). A critical period for right hemisphere recruitment in American Sign Language processing. *Nature Neuroscience, 5,* 76–80.

Newman, J. P., Wolff, W. T., & Hearst, E. (1980). The feature-positive effect in adult human subjects. *Journal of Experimental Psychology: Human Learning and Memory, 6,* 630–650.

Newman, M. G., & Stone, A. A. (1996). Does humor moderate the effects of experimentally induced stress? *Annals of Behavioral Medicine, 18,* 101–109.

Newschaffer, C. J., Croen, L. A., Daniels, J., Giarelli, E., Grether, J. K., Levy, S. E., . . . Windham, G. C. (2007). The epidemiology of autism spectrum disorders. *Annual Review of Public Health, 28,* 235–258.

Newsome, W. T., & Paré, E. B. (1988). A selective impairment of motion perception following lesions of the middle temporal visual area (MT). *Journal of Neuroscience, 8,* 2201–2211.

Neylan, T. C., Metzler, T. J., Best, S. R., Weiss, D. S., Fagan, J. A., Libermans, A., . . . Marmar, C. R. (2002). Critical incident exposure and sleep quality in police officers. *Psychosomatic Medicine, 64,* 345–352.

Ng, M., Fleming, T., Robinson, M., Thomson, B., Graetz, N., Margono, C., ... Gakidou, E. (2016). Global, regional, and national prevalence of overweight and obesity in children and adults during 1980–2013: A systematic analysis for the Global Burden of Disease Study 2013. *Lancet, 384,* 766–781. doi: 10.1016/S0140-6736(14)60460-8

Niaura, R., Todaro, J. F., Stroud, L., Spiro, A. III, Ward, K. D., & Weiss, S. (2002). Hostility, the metabolic syndrome, and incident coronary heart disease. *Health Psychology, 21,* 588–593.

Nicoladis, E., & Genesee, F. (1997). Language development in preschool bilingual children. *Journal of Speech-Language Pathology & Audiology, 21,* 258–270.

Nicolas, S., Andrieu, B., Croizet, J.-C., Sanitioso, R. B., & Burman, J. T. (2013). Sick? Or slow? On the origins of intelligence as a psychological object. *Intelligence, 41*(5), 699–711. doi: 10.1016/j.intell.2013.08.006

Niedenthal, P. M., Barsalou, L. W., Winkielman, P., Krauth-Gruber, S., & Ric, F. (2005). Embodiment in attitudes, social perception, and emotion. *Personality and Social Psychology Review, 9*(3), 184–211.

Nikles, C. D., II, Brecht, D. L., Klinger, E., & Bursell, A. L. (1998). The effects of current concern- and nonconcern-related waking suggestions on nocturnal dream content. *Journal of Personality and Social Psychology, 75,* 242–255.

Nikolaev, B., & Salahodjaev, R. (2016). The role of intelligence in the distribution of national happiness. *Intelligence, 56,* 38–45. doi: 10.1016/j.intell.2016.02.006

Nir, Y., & Tononi, G. (2010). Dreaming and the brain: From phenomenology to neurophysiology. *Trends in Cognitive Sciences, 14*(2), 88–100.

Nisbett, R. E. (2009). *Intelligence and how to get it.* New York: Norton.

Nisbett, R. E., Aronson, J., Blair, C., Dickens, W., Flynn, J., Halpern, D. F., & Turkheimer, E. (2012). Intelligence: New findings and theoretical developments. *American Psychologist, 67*(2), 130–159. doi: 10.1037/a0026699

Nisbett, R. E., Caputo, C., Legant, P., & Maracek, J. (1973). Behavior as seen by the actor and as seen by the observer. *Journal of Personality and Social Psychology, 27,* 154–164.

Nisbett, R. E., & Cohen, D. (1996). *Culture of honor: The psychology of violence in the South.* Boulder, CO: Westview Press.

Nissen, M. J., & Bullemer, P. (1987). Attentional requirements of learning: Evidence from performance measures. *Cognitive Psychology, 19,* 1–32.

Nock, M. K. (2009). Why do people hurt themselves? New insights into the nature and functions of self-injury. *Current Directions in Psychological Science, 18,* 78–83. doi: 10.1111/j.1467-8721.2009.01613.x

Nock, M. K. (2010). Self-injury. *Annual Review of Clinical Psychology, 6,* 339–363. doi: 10.1146/annurev.clinpsy.121208.131258

Nock, M. K., Borges, G., Bromet, E. J., Alonso, J., Angermeyer, M., Beautrais, A., . . . Williams, D. (2008). Cross-national prevalence and risk factors for suicidal ideation, plans, and attempts. *British Journal of Psychiatry, 192,* 98–105.

Nock, M. K., Borges, G., & Ono, Y. (Eds.). (2012). *Suicide: Global perspectives from the WHO World Mental Health Surveys.* New York: Cambridge University Press.

Nock, M. K., Green, J. G., Hwang, I., McLaughlin, K. A., Sampson, N. A., Zaslavsky, A. M., & Kessler, R. C. (2013). Prevalence, correlates and treatment of lifetime suicidal behavior among adolescents: Results from the National Comorbidity Survey Replication–Adolescent Supplement (NCSA–A). *Journal of the American Medical Association Psychiatry, 70*(3), 300–310. doi: 10.1001/2013.jamapsychiatry.55

Nock, M. K., Holmberg, E. G., Photos, V. I., & Michel, B. D. (2007). Structured and semi-structured interviews. In M. Hersen & J. C. Thomas (Eds.), *Handbook of clinical interviewing with children* (pp. 30–49). Thousand Oaks, CA: Sage.

Nock, M. K., Kazdin, A. E., Hiripi, E., & Kessler, R. C. (2006). Prevalence, subtypes, and correlates of *DSM–IV* conduct disorder in the National Comorbidity Survey Replication. *Psychological Medicine, 36,* 699–710.

Nolen-Hoeksema, S. (2008). Gender differences in coping with depression across the lifespan. *Depression, 3,* 81–90.

Norby, S. (2015). Why forget? On the adaptive value of memory loss. *Perspectives on Psychological Science, 10,* 551–578.

Norcross, J. C., Hedges, M., & Castle, P. H. (2002). Psychologists conducting psychotherapy in 2001: A study of the Division 29 membership. *Psychotherapy: Theory/Research/Practice/Training, 39,* 97–102.

Norcross, J. C., & Rogan, J. D. (2013). Psychologists conducting psychotherapy in 2012: Current practices and historical trends among Division 29 members. *Psychotherapy, 50,* 490–495.

Norrholm, S. D., & Ressler, K. J. (2009). Genetics of anxiety and trauma-related disorders. *Neuroscience, 164,* 272–287.

Norton, M. I., Frost, J. H., & Ariely, D. (2007). Less is more: The lure of ambiguity, or why familiarity breeds contempt. *Journal of Personality and Social Psychology, 92*(1), 97–105. doi: 10.1037/0022-3514.92.1.97

Nosanchuk, T. A., & Lightstone, J. (1974). Canned laughter and public and private conformity. *Journal of Personality and Social Psychology, 29,* 153–156.

Nowak, M. A. (2006). Five rules for the evolution of cooperation. *Science, 314,* 1560–1563.

Nuttin, J. M. (1985). Narcissism beyond Gestalt and awareness: The name letter effect. *European Journal of Social Psychology, 15,* 353–361.

Nyborg, H., & Jensen, A. R. (2001). Occupation and income related to psychometric g. *Intelligence, 29,* 45–55.

Oately, K., Keltner, D., & Jenkins, J. M. (2006). *Understanding emotions* (2nd ed.). Malden, MA: Blackwell.

O'Brien, J. L., O'Keefe, K. M., LaViolette, P. S., DeLuca, A. N., Blacker, D., Dickerson, B. C., & Sperling, R. A. (2010). Longitudinal fMRI in elderly reveals loss of hippocampal activation with clinical decline. *Neurology, 74,* 1969–1976.

Ochsner, K. N. (2000). Are affective events richly recollected or simply familiar? The experience and process of recognizing feelings past. *Journal of Experimental Psychology: General, 129,* 242–261.

Ochsner, K. N., Bunge, S. A., Gross, J. J., & Gabrieli, J. D. E. (2002). Rethinking feelings: An fMRI study of the cognitive regulation of emotion. *Journal of Cognitive Neuroscience, 14,* 1215–1229.

Ochsner, K. N., Ray, R. R., Hughes, B., McRae, K., Cooper, J. C., Weber, J., . . . Gross, J. J. (2009). Bottom-up and top-down processes in emotion generation: Common and distinct neural mechanisms. *Psychological Science, 20,* 1322–1331.

O'Connor, T. G., & Rutter, M. (2000). Attachment disorder following early severe deprivation: Extension and longitudinal follow-up. *Journal of the American Academy of Child and Adolescent Psychiatry, 39,* 703–712.

O'Doherty, J. P., Dayan, P., Friston, K., Critchley, H., & Dolan, R. J. (2003). Temporal difference models and reward-related learning in the human brain. *Neuron, 38,* 329–337.

Ofshe, R. J. (1992). Inadvertent hypnosis during interrogation: False confession due to dissociative state, misidentified multiple personality, and the satanic cult hypothesis. *International Journal of Clinical and Experimental Hypnosis, 40,* 125–126.

Ofshe, R., & Watters, E. (1994). *Making monsters: False memories, psychotherapy, and sexual hysteria.* New York: Scribner/Macmillan.

Ohayon, M. M. (2002). Epidemiology of insomnia: What we know and what we still need to learn. *Sleep Medicine, 6,* 97–111.

Ohayon, M. M., Guilleminault, C., & Priest, R. G. (1999). Night terrors, sleepwalking, and confusional arousals in the general population: Their frequency and relationship to other sleep and mental disorders. *Journal of Clinical Psychiatry, 60,* 268–276.

Öhman, A. (1996). Preferential preattentive processing of threat in anxiety: Preparedness and attentional biases. In R. M. Rapee (Ed.), *Current controversies in the anxiety disorders.* New York: Guilford Press.

Öhman, A., Dimberg, U., & Öst, L. G. (1985). Animal and social phobias: Biological constraints on learned fear responses. In S. Reiss & R. Bootzin (Eds.), *Theoretical issues in behavior therapy* (pp. 123–175). New York: Academic Press.

Okuda, J., Fujii, T., Ohtake, H., Tsukiura, T., Tanji, K., Suzuki, K., . . . Yamadori, A. (2003). Thinking of the future and the past: The roles of the frontal pole and the medial temporal lobes. *NeuroImage, 19,* 1369–1380.

Okulicz-Kozaryn, A. (2011). Europeans work to live and Americans live to work (Who is happy to work more: Americans or Europeans?) *Journal of Happiness Studies, 12*(2), 225–243.

Olatunji, B. O., & Wolitzky-Taylor, K. B. (2009). Anxiety sensitivity and the anxiety disorders: A meta-analytic review and synthesis. *Psychological Bulletin, 135,* 974–999.

O'Laughlin, M. J., & Malle, B. F. (2002). How people explain actions performed by groups and individuals. *Journal of Personality and Social Psychology, 82,* 33–48.

Olausson, P. O., Haglund, B., Weitoft, G. R., & Cnattingius, S. (2001). Teenage child-bearing and long-term socioeconomic consequences: A case study in Sweden. *Family Planning Perspectives, 33,* 70–74.

Olds, J. (1956, October). Pleasure center in the brain. *Scientific American, 195,* 105–116.

Olds, J., & Fobes, J. I. (1981). The central basis of motivation: Intracranial self-stimulation studies. *Annual Review of Psychology, 32,* 523–574.

Olds, J., & Milner, P. (1954). Positive reinforcement produced by electrical stimulation of septal areas and other regions of rat brains. *Journal of Comparative and Physiological Psychology, 47,* 419–427.

Ollers, D. K., & Eilers, R. E. (1988). The role of audition in infant babbling. *Child Development, 59,* 441–449.

Olofsson, J. K., Bowman, N. E., Khatibi, K., & Gottfried, J. A. (2012). A time-based account of the perception of odor objects and valences. *Psychological Science, 23,* 1224–1232.

Olsson, A., Kopsida, E., Sorjonen, K., & Savic, I. (2016). Testosterone and estrogen impact social evaluations and vicarious emotions: A double-blind placebo-controlled study. *Emotion, 16,* 515–523.

Olsson, A., & Phelps, E. A. (2007). Social learning of fear. *Nature Neuroscience, 10,* 1095–1102.

Oltmanns, T. F., Neale, J. M., & Davison, G. C. (1991). *Case studies in abnormal psychology* (3rd ed.). New York: Wiley.

Olton, D. S., & Samuelson, R. J. (1976). Remembrance of places passed: Spatial memory in rats. *Journal of Experimental Psychology: Animal Behavior Processes, 2,* 97–116.

Ongley, S. F., & Malti, T. (2014). The role of moral emotions in the development of children's sharing behavior. *Developmental Psychology, 50*(4), 1148–1159. doi: 10.1037/a0035191

Onishi, K. H., & Baillargeon, R. (2005). Do 15-month-old infants understand false beliefs? *Science, 308,* 255–258.

Ono, K. (1987). Superstitious behavior in humans. *Journal of the Experimental Analysis of Behavior, 47,* 261–271.

Ophir, E., Nass, C., & Wagner, A. D. (2009). Cognitive control in media multitaskers. *Proceedings of the National Academy of Sciences, USA, 106,* 15583–15587.

Orban, P., Lungu, O., & Doyon, J. (2008). Motor sequence learning and developmental dyslexia. *Annals of the New York Academy of Sciences, 1145,* 151–172.

Ormel, J., Petukhova, M., Chatterji, S., Aguilar-Gaxiola, S., Alonso, J., Angermeyer, M. C., . . . Kessler, R. C. (2008). Disability and treatment of specific mental and physical disorders across the world: Results from the WHO World Mental Health Surveys. *British Journal of Psychiatry, 192,* 368–375.

Oswald, L., Taylor, A. M., & Triesman, M. (1960). Discriminative responses to stimulation during human sleep. *Brain, 83,* 440–453.

Otto, M. W., Henin, A., Hirshfeld-Becker, D. R., Pollack, M. H., Biederman, J., & Rosenbaum, J. F. (2007). Posttraumatic stress disorder symptoms following media exposure to tragic events: Impact of 9/11 on children at risk for anxiety disorders. *Journal of Anxiety Disorders, 21,* 888–902.

Oudiette, D. & Paller, K. A. (2013). Upgrading the sleeping brain with targeted memory reactivation. *Trends in Cognitive Sciences, 17,* 142–149.

Owens, W. A. (1966). Age and mental abilities: A second adult followup. *Journal of Educational Psychology, 57,* 311–325.

Oztekin, I., Curtis, C. E., & McElree, B. (2009). The medial temporal lobe and left inferior prefrontal cortex jointly support interference resolution in verbal working memory. *Journal of Cognitive Neuroscience, 21,* 1967–1979.

Pagnin, D., de Queiroz, V., Pini, S., & Cassano, G. B. (2008). Efficacy of ECT in depression: A meta-analytic review. *Focus, 6,* 155–162.

Paivio, A. (1971). *Imagery and verbal processes.* New York: Holt, Rinehart and Winston.

Paivio, A. (1986). *Mental representations: A dual coding approach.* New York: Oxford University Press.

Palermo, T. M., Eccleston, C., Lewandowski, A. S., Williams, A. C., & Morley, S. (2011). Randomized controlled trials of psychological therapies for management of chronic pain in children and adolescents: An updated meta-analytic review. *Pain, 148,* 387–397.

Paluck, B. L., & Green, D. P. (2009). Prejudice reduction: What works? A review and assessment of research and practice. *Annual Review of Psychology, 60,* 339–367.

Pandit, J. J., Andrade, J., Bogod, D. G., Hitchman, J. M., Jonker, W. R....Cook, T. M. (2014). The 5th National Audit Project (NAP5) on accidental awareness during general anaesthesia: Summary of main findings and risk factors. *Anaesthesia, 69,* 1089–1101.

Pantev, C., Oostenveld, R., Engelien, A., Ross, B., Roberts, L. E., & Hoke, M. (1998). Increased auditory cortical representation in musicians. *Nature, 392,* 811–814.

Papez, J. W. (1937). A proposed mechanism of emotion. *Archives of Neurology and Pathology, 38,* 725–743.

Parbery-Clark, A., Skoe, E., & Kraus, N. (2009). Musical experience limits the degradative effects of background noise on the neural processing of sound. *Journal of Neuroscience, 11,* 14100–14107.

Parbery-Clark, A., Strait, D. L., Anderson, S., Hittner, E., & Kraus, N. (2011). Musical experience and the aging auditory system: Implications for cognitive abilities and hearing speech in noise. *PLoS One, 6,* e18082.

Parbery-Clark, A., Tierney, A., Strait, D. L., & Kraus, N. (2012). Musicians have fine-tuned neural distinction of speech syllables. *Neuroscience, 219,* 111–119.

Park, B., & Hastie, R. (1987). Perception of variability in category development: Instance- versus abstraction-based stereotypes. *Journal of Personality and Social Psychology, 53*(4), 621–635. doi: 10.1037/0022-3514.53.4.621

Park, D. C., & McDonough, I. M. (2013). The dynamic aging mind: Revelations from functional neuroimaging research. *Perspectives on Psychological Science, 8*(1), 62–67. doi: 10.1177/1745691612469034

Park, D. C., Polk, T. A., Park, R., Minear, M., Savage, A., & Smith, M. R. (2004). Aging reduces neural specialization in ventral visual cortex. *Proceedings of the National Academy of Sciences, USA, 101*(35), 13091–13095. doi: 10.1073/pnas.0405148101

Parker, E. S., Cahill, L. S., & McGaugh, J. L. (2006). A case of unusual autobiographical remembering. *Neurocase, 12,* 35–49.

Parker, G., Gibson, N. A., Brotchie, H., Heruc, G., Rees, A. M., & Hadzi-Pavlovic, D. (2006). Omega-3 fatty acids and mood disorders. *American Journal of Psychiatry, 163,* 969–978.

Parker, H. A., & McNally, R. J. (2008). Repressive coping, emotional adjustment, and cognition in people who have lost loved ones to suicide. *Suicide and Life-Threatening Behavior, 38,* 676–687.

Parkin, B. L., Ekhtiari, H., & Walsh, V. F. (2015). Non-invasive brain stimulation in cognitive neuroscience: A primer. *Neuron, 87,* 932–945.

Parkinson, B., & Totterdell, P. (1999). Classifying affect-regulation strategies. *Cognition and Emotion, 13,* 277–303.

Parrott, A. C. (2001). Human psychopharmacology of Ecstasy (MDMA): A review of 15 years of empirical research. *Human Psychopharmacology, 16,* 557–577.

Parrott, A. C., Morinan, A., Moss, M., & Scholey, A. (2005). *Understanding drugs and behavior.* Chichester, UK: Wiley.

Parsons, T. (1975). The sick role and the role of the physician reconsidered. *Milbank Memorial Fund Quarterly, Health and Society, 53*(3), 257–278.

Pascual-Ferrá, P., Liu, Y., & Beatty, M. J. (2012). A meta-analytic comparison of the effects of text messaging to substance-induced impairment on driving performance. *Communication Research Reports, 29,* 229–238.

Pascual-Leone, A., Amedi, A., Fregni, F., & Merabet, L. B. (2005). The plastic human brain cortex. *Annual Review of Neuroscience, 28,* 377–401.

Pascual-Leone, A., Houser, C. M., Reese, K., Shotland, L. I., Grafman, J., Sato, S., . . . Cohen, L. G. (1993). Safety of rapid-rate transcranial magnetic stimulation in normal volunteers. *Electroencephalography and Clinical Neurophysiology, 89,* 120–130.

Passini, F. T., & Norman, W. T. (1966). A universal conception of personality structure? *Journal of Personality and Social Psychology, 4,* 44–49.

Pasupathi, M., McLean, K. C., & Weeks, T. (2009). To tell or not to tell: Disclosure and the narrative self. *Journal of Personality, 77,* 1–35.

Patall, E. A., Cooper, H., & Robinson, J. C. (2008). The effects of choice on intrinsic motivation and related outcomes: A meta-analysis of research findings. *Psychological Bulletin, 134*(2), 270–300.

Patihis, L., Frenda, S. J., LePort, A. K. R., Petersen, N., Nichols, R. M., Stark, C. E. L., . . . Loftus, E. F. (2013). False memories in highly superior autobiographical memory individuals. *Proceedings of the National Academy of Sciences USA, 110,* 20947–20952.

Patrick, C. J., Cuthbert, B. N., & Lang, P. J. (1994). Emotion in the criminal psychopath: Fear image processing. *Journal of Abnormal Psychology, 103,* 523–534.

Patterson, C. J. (2013). Sexual orientation and family lives. In G. W. Peterson & K. R. Bush (Eds.), *The handbook of marriage and the family.* New York: Springer.

Pavlidis, I., Eberhardt, N. L., & Levine, J. A. (2002). Human behaviour: Seeing through the face of deception. *Nature, 415,* 35.

Pavlidou, E. V., Williams, J. M., & Kelly, L. M. (2009). Artificial grammar learning in primary school children with and without developmental dyslexia. *Annals of Dyslexia, 59,* 55–77.

Pavlov, I. P. (1923a). New researches on conditioned reflexes. *Science, 58,* 359–361.

Pavlov, I. P. (1923b, July 23). Pavloff. *Time, 1*(21), 20–21.

Pavlov, I. P. (1927). *Conditioned reflexes.* Oxford: Oxford University Press.

Payne, J. D., Kensinger, E. A., Wamsley, E., Spreng, R. N., Alger, S., Gibler, K., . . . & Stickgold, R. (2015). Napping and the selective consolidation of negative aspects of scenes. *Emotion, 15,* 176–186.

Payne, J. D., Schacter, D. L., Propper, R., Huang, L., Wamsley, E., Tucker, M. A., . . . Stickgold, R. (2009). The role of sleep in false memory formation. *Neurobiology of Learning and Memory, 92,* 327–334.

Payne, J. D., Stickgold, R., Swanberg, K., & Kensinger, E. A. (2008). Sleep preferentially enhances memory for emotional components of scenes. *Psychological Science, 19,* 781–788.

Pearce, J. M. (1987). A model of stimulus generalization for Pavlovian conditioning. *Psychological Review, 84,* 61–73.

Pearson, J., & Kosslyn, S. M. (2015). The heterogeneity of mental representation: Ending the imagery debate. *Proceedings of the National Academy of Sciences USA, 112,* 10089–10092.

Peck, J., & Shu, S. B. (2009). The effect of mere touch on perceived ownership. *Journal of Consumer Research, 36,* 434–447.

Peelen, M. V., & Kastner, S. (2009). A nonvisual look at the functional organization of visual cortex. *Neuron, 63,* 284–286.

Peissig, J. J., & Tarr, M. J. (2007). Visual object recognition: Do we know more now than we did 20 years ago? *Annual Review of Psychology, 58,* 75–96.

Pelham, B. W. (1985). Self-investment and self-esteem: Evidence for a Jamesian model of self-worth. *Journal of Personality and Social Psychology, 69,* 1141–1150.

Pelham, B. W., Carvallo, M., & Jones, J. T. (2005). Implicit egotism. *Current Directions in Psychological Science, 14,* 106–110.

Pelham, B. W., Mirenberg, M. C., & Jones, J. T. (2002). Why Susie sells seashells by the seashore: Implicit egotism and major life decisions. *Journal of Personality and Social Psychology, 82,* 469–487.

Penfield, W., & Rasmussen, T. (1950). *The cerebral cortex of man: A clinical study of localization of function.* New York: Macmillan.

Pennebaker, J. W. (1980). Perceptual and environmental determinants of coughing. *Basic and Applied Social Psychology, 1,* 83–91.

Pennebaker, J. W. (1989). Confession, inhibition, and disease. *Advances in Experimental Social Psychology, 22,* 211–244.

Pennebaker, J. W., & Chung, C. K. (2007). Expressive writing, emotional upheavals, and health. In H. Friedman & R. Silver (Eds.), *Handbook of health psychology* (pp. 263–284). New York: Oxford University Press.

Pennebaker, J. W., Kiecolt-Glaser, J. K., & Glaser, R. (1988). Disclosure of traumas and immune function: Health implications for psychotherapy. *Journal of Consulting and Clinical Psychology, 56,* 239–245.

Pennebaker, J. W., & Sanders, D. Y. (1976). American graffiti: Effects of authority and reactance arousal. *Personality and Social Psychology Bulletin, 2,* 264–267.

Penner, L. A., Albrecht, T. L., Orom, H., Coleman, D. K., & Underwood, W. (2010). Health and health care disparities. In J. F. Dovidio, M. Hewstone, P. Glick, & V. M. Esses (Eds.), *The Sage handbook of prejudice, stereotyping and discrimination* (pp. 472–489). Thousand Oaks, CA: Sage.

Perenin, M.-T., & Vighetto, A. (1988). Optic ataxia: A specific disruption in visuomotor mechanisms. I. Different aspects of the deficit in reaching for objects. *Brain, 111,* 643–674.

Perera, T., George, M. S., Grammer, G., Janicak, P. G., Pascual-Leone, A., & Wirecki, T. S. (2016). The Clinical TMS Society consensus review and treatment recommendations for TMS therapy for major depressive disorder. *Brain Stimulation, 9,* 336–346.

Perilloux, H. K., Webster, G. D., & Gaulin, S. J. C. (2010). Signals of genetic quality and maternal investment capacity: The dynamic effects of fluctuating asymmetry and waist-to-hip ratio on men's ratings of women's attractiveness. *Social Psychological and Personality Science, 1*(1), 34–42. doi: 10.1177/1948550609349514

Perlmutter, J. S., & Mink, J. W. (2006). Deep brain stimulation. *Annual Review of Neuroscience, 29,* 229–257.

Perloff, L. S., & Fetzer, B. K. (1986). Self-other judgments and perceived vulnerability to victimization. *Journal of Personality and Social Psychology, 50,* 502–510.

Perls, F. S., Hefferkine, R., & Goodman, P. (1951). *Gestalt therapy: Excitement and growth in the human personality.* New York: Julian Press.

Perrett, D. I., Burt, D. M., Penton-Voak, I. S., Lee, K. J., Rowland, D. A., & Edwards, R. (1999). Symmetry and human facial attractiveness. *Evolution and Human Behavior, 20,* 295–307.

Perrett, D. I., Rolls, E. T., & Caan, W. (1982). Visual neurones responsive to faces in the monkey temporal cortex. *Experimental Brain Research, 47,* 329–342.

Perry, R., & Sibley, C. G. (2012). Big Five personality prospectively predicts social dominance orientation and right wing authoritarianism. *Personality and Individual Differences, 52,* 3–8.

Pessiglione, M., Seymour, B., Flandin, G., Dolan, R. J., & Frith, C. D. (2006). Dopamine-dependent prediction errors underpin reward-seeking behavior in humans. *Nature, 442,* 1042–1045.

Petersen, A. C., & Grockett, L. (1985). Pubertal timing and grade effects on adjustment. *Journal of Youth and Adolescence, 14,* 191–206.

Petersen, J. L., & Hyde, J. S. (2010). A meta-analytic review of research on gender differences in sexuality, 1993–2007. *Psychological Bulletin, 136*(1), 21–38. doi:10.1037/a0017504

Peterson, C., & Siegal, M. (1999). Representing inner worlds: Theory of mind in autistic, deaf and normal hearing children. *Psychological Science, 10,* 126–129.

Peterson, C., Slaughter, V., Moore, C., & Wellman, H. M. (2016). Peer social skills and theory of mind in children with autism, deafness, or typical development. *Developmental Psychology, 52*(1), 46–57. doi: 10.1037/a0039833

Peterson, C., Wang, Q., & Hou, Y. (2009). "When I was little": Childhood recollections in Chinese and European Canadian grade school children. *Child Development, 80,* 506–518.

Peterson, G. B. (2004). A day of great illumination: B. F. Skinner's discovery of shaping. *Journal of the Experimental Analysis of Behavior, 82,* 317–328.

Peterson, L. R., & Peterson, M. J. (1959). Short-term retention of individual verbal items. *Journal of Experimental Psychology, 58,* 193–198.

Peterson, S. E., Fox, P. T., Posner, M. I., Mintun, M. A., & Raichle, M. E. (1989). Positron emission tomographic studies of the processing of single words. *Journal of Cognitive Neuroscience, 1,* 154–170.

Petersson, K. M., Forkstam, C., & Ingvar, M. (2004). Artificial syntactic violations activate Broca's region. *Cognitive Science, 28,* 383–407.

Petitto, L. A., & Marentette, P. F. (1991). Babbling in the manual mode: Evidence for the ontogeny of language. *Science, 251,* 1493–1496.

Petrie, K. P., Booth, R. J., & Pennebaker, J. W. (1998). The immunological effects of thought suppression. *Journal of Personality and Social Psychology, 75,* 1264–1272.

Petry, N. M., Alessi, S. M., & Rash, C. J. (2013). Contingency management treatments decrease psychiatric symptoms. *Journal of Consulting and Clinical Psychology, 81*(5), 926–931. doi: 10.1037/a0032499

Petty, R. E., & Cacioppo, J. T. (1986). The elaboration likelihood model of persuasion. In L. Berkowitz (Ed.), *Advances in experimental social psychology* (Vol. 19, pp. 123–205). New York: Academic Press.

Petty, R. E., Cacioppo, J. T., & Goldman, R. (1981). Personal involvement as a determinant of argument-based persuasion. *Journal of Personality and Social Psychology, 41,* 847–855.

Petty, R. E., & Wegener, D. T. (1998). Attitude change: Multiple roles for persuasion variables. In D. T. Gilbert, S. T. Fiske, & G. Lindzey (Eds.), *The handbook of social psychology* (4th ed., Vol. 1, pp. 323–390). Boston: McGraw-Hill.

Pew Research Center for People & the Press. (1997). *Motherhood today: A tougher job, less ably done.* Washington, DC: Author.

Pew Research Center for People & the Press. (2009). *Growing old in America: Expectations vs. reality.* Retrieved from http://pewsocialtrends.org/pubs/736/getting-old-in-america

Pham, M. T., Lee, L., & Stephen, A. T. (2012). Feeling the future: The emotional oracle effect. *Journal of Consumer Research, 39*(3), 461–477.

Phelan, J., Link, B., Stueve, A., & Pescosolido, B. (1997, August). *Public conceptions of mental illness in 1950 in 1996: Has sophistication increased? Has stigma declined?* Paper presented at the American Sociological Association, Toronto, Ontario.

Phelps, E. A. (2006). Emotion and cognition: Insights from studies of the human amygdala. *Annual Review of Psychology, 24,* 27–53.

Phelps, E. A., & LeDoux, J. L. (2005). Contributions of the amygdala to emotion processing: From animal models to human behavior. *Neuron, 48,* 175–187.

Phillips, F. (2002, January 24). Jump in cigarette sales tied to Sept. 11 attacks. *Boston Globe,* p. B1.

Phills, C. E., Kawakami, K., Tabi, E., Nadolny, D., & Inzlicht, M. (2011). Mind the gap: Increasing associations between the self and Blacks with approach behaviors. *Journal of Personality and Social Psychology, 100*(2), 197–210. doi: 10.1037/a0022159

Piaget, J. (1954). *The child's conception of number.* New York: Norton.

Piaget, J. (1965). *The moral judgment of the child.* New York: Free Press. (Original work published 1932)

Piaget, J. (1977). The first year of life of the child. In H. E. Gruber & J. J. Voneche (Eds.), *The essential Piaget: An interpretive reference and guide* (pp. 198–214). New York: Basic Books. (Original work published 1927)

Piaget, J., & Inhelder, B. (1969). *The psychology of the child* (H. Weaver, Trans.). New York: Basic Books.

Piantadosi, S. T., & Kidd, C. (2016). Extraordinary intelligence and the care of infants. *Proceedings of the National Academy of Sciences, 113* (2016), 1–6. doi: 10.1073/pnas.1506752113

Piazza, J. R., Charles, S. T., Sliwinski, M. J., Mogle, J., & Almeida, D. M. (2013). Affective reactivity to daily stressors and long-term risk of reporting a chronic physical health condition. *Annals of Behavioral Medicine, 45,* 110–120.

Pietschnig, J., & Voracek, M. (2015). One century of global IQ gains: A formal meta-analysis of the Flynn effect (1909–2013). *Perspectives on Psychological Science, 10*(3), 282–306. doi: 10.1177/1745691615577701

Piff, P. K., Kraus, M. W., Côté, S., Cheng, B. H., & Keltner, D. (2010). Having less, giving more: The influence of social class on prosocial behavior. *Journal of Personality and Social Psychology, 99*(5), 771–784. doi: 10.1037/a0020092

Piff, P. K., Stancato, D. M., Côté, S., Mendoza-Denton, R., & Keltner, D. (2012). Higher social class predicts increased unethical behavior. *Proceedings of the National Academy of Sciences of the United States of America, 109*(11), 4086–4091. doi: 10.1073/pnas.1118373109

Pinel, J. P. J., Assanand, S., & Lehman, D. R. (2000). Hunger, eating, and ill health. *American Psychologist, 55,* 1105–1116.

Pines, A. M. (1993). Burnout: An existential perspective. In W. B. Schaufeli, C. Maslach, & T. Marek (Eds.), *Professional burnout: Recent developments in theory and research* (pp. 33–51). Washington, DC: Taylor & Francis.

Pinker, S. (1994). *The language instinct.* New York: Morrow.

Pinker, S. (1997a). Evolutionary psychology: An exchange. *New York Review of Books, 44,* 55–58.

Pinker, S. (1997b). *How the mind works.* New York: Norton.

Pinker, S. (2003). *The blank slate: The modern denial of human nature.* New York: Viking.

Pinker, S. (2007, March 19). A history of violence: We're getting nicer every day. *The New Republic Online.* Retrieved from https://newrepublic.com/article/64340/history-violence-were-getting-nicer-every-day

Pinker, S., & Bloom, P. (1990). Natural language and natural selection. *Behavioral and Brain Sciences, 13,* 707–784.

Pitcher, D., Garrido, L., Walsh, V., & Duchaine, B. C. (2008). Transcranial magnetic stimulation disrupts the perception and embodiment of facial expressions. *Journal of Neuroscience, 28*(36), 8929–8933.

Plassman, H., O'Doherty, J., Shiv, B., & Rangel, A. (2008). Marketing actions can modulate neural representations of experienced pleasantness. *Proceedings of the National Academy of Sciences, USA, 105,* 1050–1054.

Platek, S. M., Critton, S. R., Myers, T. E., & Gallup, G. G. Jr. (2003). Contagious yawning: The role of self-awareness and mental state attribution. *Cognitive Brain Research, 17,* 223–227.

Plato. (1956). *Protagoras* (O. Jowett, Trans.). New York: Prentice Hall. (Original work circa 380 BCE)

Plomin, R., & Caspi, A. (1999). Behavioral genetics and personality. In L. A. Pervin & O. P. John (Eds.), *Handbook of personality: Theory and research* (Vol. 2, pp. 251–276). New York: Guilford Press.

Plomin, R., & Spinath, F. M. (2004). Intelligence: Genetics, genes, and genomics. *Journal of Personality and Social Psychology, 86,* 112–129.

Plomin, R., DeFries, J. C., McClearn, G. E., & McGuffin, P. (2001). *Behavioral genetics* (4th ed.). New York: W. H. Freeman.

Plomin, R., DeFries, J. C., McClearn, G. E., & Rutter, M. (1997). *Behavioral genetics* (3rd ed.). New York: W. H. Freeman.

Plomin, R., Haworth, C. M. A., Meaburn, E. L., Price, T. S., Wellcome Trust Case Control Consortium 2, & Davis, O. S. P. (2013). Common DNA markers can account for more than half of the genetic influence on cognitive abilities. *Psychological Science, 24*(4), 562–568. doi: 10.1177/0956797612457952

Plomin, R., Scheier, M. F., Bergeman, C. S., Pedersen, N. L., Nesselroade, J. R., & McClearn, G. E. (1992). Optimism, pessimism, and mental health: A twin/adoption analysis. *Personality and Individual Differences, 13,* 921–930.

Plotnik, J. M., de Waal, F. B. M., & Reiss, D. (2006). Self-recognition in an Asian elephant. *Proceedings of the National Academy of Sciences, USA, 103,* 17053–17057.

Polanczyk, G., de Lima, M. S., Horta, B. L., Biederman, J., & Rohde, L. A. (2007). The worldwide prevalence of ADHD: A systemic review and metaregression analysis. *American Journal of Psychiatry, 164,* 942–948.

Polderman, T. J. C., Benyamin, B., de Leeuw, C. A., Sullivan, P. F., van Bochoven, A., Visscher, P. M., & Posthuma, D. (2015). Meta-analysis of the heritability of human traits based on fifty years of twin studies. *Nature Genetics, 47*(7), 702–709. doi: 10.1038/ng.3285

Poliak, S., & Peles, E. (2003). The local differentiation of myelinated axons at nodes of Ranvier. *Nature Reviews Neuroscience, 4,* 968–980.

Polivy, J., & Herman, C. P. (1992). Undieting: A program to help people stop dieting. *International Journal of Eating Disorders, 11,* 261–268.

Polivy, J., & Herman, C. P. (2002). If at first you don't succeed: False hopes of self-change. *American Psychologist, 57,* 677–689.

Polzanczyk, G., de Lima, M. S., Horta, B. L., Biederman, J., & Rohde, L. A. (2007). The worldwide prevalence of ADHD: A systematic review and metaregression analysis. *American Journal of Psychiatry, 164,* 942–948.

Pond, R. S., DeWall, C. N., Lambert, N. M., Deckman, T., Bonser, I. M., & Fincham, F. D. (2012). Repulsed by violence: Disgust sensitivity buffers trait, behavioral, and daily aggression. *Journal of Personality and Social Psychology, 102*(1), 175–188. doi: 10.1037/a0024296

Poole, D. A., Lindsay, S. D., Memon, A., & Bull, R. (1995). Psychotherapy and the recovery of memories of childhood sexual abuse: U.S. and British practitioners' opinions, practices, and experiences. *Journal of Consulting and Clinical Psychology, 63,* 426–487.

Poon, S. H., Sim, K., Sum, M. Y., Kuswanto, C. N., & Baldessarini, R. J. (2012). Evidence-based options for treatment-resistant adult bipolar disorder patients. *Bipolar Disorders, 14,* 573–584.

Pope, A. W., & Bierman, K. L. (1999). Predicting adolescent peer problems and antisocial activities: The relative roles of aggression and dysregulation. *Developmental Psychology, 35,* 335–346.

Porter, S., & ten Brinke, L. (2008). Reading between the lies: Identifying concealed and falsified emotions in universal facial expressions. *Psychological Science, 19,* 508–514.

Portocarrero, J. S., Burright, R. G., & Donovick, P. J. (2007). Vocabulary and verbal fluency of bilingual and monolingual college students. *Archives of Clinical Neuropsychology, 22,* 415–422.

Posner, M. I., & Raichle, M. E. (1994). *Images of mind.* New York: W. H. Freeman and Company.

Post, R. M., Frye, M. A., Denicoff, G. S., Leverich, G. S., Dunn, R. T., Osuch, E. A., . . . Jajodia, K. (2008). Emerging trends in the treatment of rapid cycling bipolar disorder: A selected review. *Bipolar Disorders, 2,* 305–315.

Posthuma, D., & de Geus, E. J. C. (2006). Progress in the molecular-genetic study of intelligence. *Current Directions in Psychological Science, 15,* 151–155.

Postman, L., & Underwood, B. J. (1973). Critical issues in interference theory. *Memory & Cognition, 1,* 19–40.

Postmes, T., & Spears, R. (1998). Deindividuation and anti-normative behavior: A meta-analysis. *Psychological Bulletin, 123,* 238–259.

Powell, R. A., Symbaluk, D. G., MacDonald, S. E., & Honey, P. L. (2009). *Introduction to learning and behavior* (3rd ed.). Belmont, CA: Wadsworth Cengage Learning.

Power, M. L., & Schulkin, J. (2009). *The evolution of obesity.* Baltimore: Johns Hopkins University Press.

Prakash, R. S., Voss, M. W., Erickson, K. I., & Kramer, A. F. (2015). Moving towards a healthier brain and mind. *Annual Review of Psychology, 66,* 769–797.

Prasada, S., & Pinker, S. (1993). Generalizations of regular and irregular morphology. *Language and Cognitive Processes, 8,* 1–56.

Pressman, S. D., Cohen, S., Miller, G. E., Barkin, A., Rabin, B. S., & Treanor, J. J. (2005). Loneliness, social network size, and immune response to influenza vaccination in college freshmen. *Health Psychology, 24,* 297–306.

Price, J. L., & Davis, B. (2008). *The woman who can't forget: The extraordinary story of living with the most remarkable memory known to science.* New York: Free Press.

Prior, H., Schwartz, A., & Güntürkün, O. (2008). Mirror-induced behavior in the magpie (*Pica pica*): Evidence of self-recognition. *PLoS Biology, 6,* e202.

Prochaska, J. J., & Sallis, J. F. (2004). A randomized controlled trial of single versus multiple health behavior change: Promoting physical activity and nutrition among adolescents. *Health Psychology, 23,* 314–318.

Procopio, M., & Marriott, P. (2007). Intrauterine hormonal environment and risk of developing anorexia nervosa. *Archives of General Psychiatry, 64*(12), 1402–1407.

Protzko, J. (2015). The environment in raising early intelligence: A meta-analysis of the fadeout effect. *Intelligence, 53,* 202–210. doi: 10.1016/j.intell.2015.10.006

Protzko, J. (2016). Does the raising IQ-raising g distinction explain the fadeout effect? *Intelligence, 56,* 65–71. doi: 10.1016/j.intell.2016.02.008

Protzko, J., Aronson, J., & Blair, C. (2013). How to make a young child smarter: Evidence from the database of raising intelligence. *Perspectives on Psychological Science, 8*(1), 25–40. doi: 10.1177/1745691612462585

Provencal, N., & Binder, E. B. (2015). The neurobiological effects of stress as contributors to psychiatric disorders: Focus on epigenetics. *Current Opinion in Neurobiology, 30,* 31–37.

Provine, R. R. (2000). *Laughter: A scientific investigation.* New York: Viking.

Pruitt, D. G. (1998). Social conflict. In D. T. Gilbert, S. T. Fiske, & G. Lindzey (Eds.), *The handbook of social psychology* (4th ed., Vol. 2, pp. 470–503). New York: McGraw-Hill.

Punjabi, N. M. (2008). The epidemiology of adult obstructive sleep apnea. *Proceedings of the American Thoracic Society, 5,* 136–143.

Puterman, E., Lin, J., Blackburn, E. H., O'Donovan, A., Adler, N., & Epel, E. (2010). The power of exercise: Buffering the effect of chronic stress on telomere length. *PLoS ONE, 5,* e10837.

Pyc, M. A., & Rawson, K. A. (2009). Testing the retrieval effort hypothesis: Does greater difficulty correctly recalling information lead to higher levels of memory? *Journal of Memory and Language, 60,* 437–447.

Pyers, J. E., & Senghas, A. (2009). Language promotes false-belief understanding: Evidence from learners of a new sign language. *Psychological Science, 20*(7), 805–812.

Pyers, J. E., Shusterman, A., Senghas, A., Spelke, E. S., & Emmorey, K. (2010). Evidence from an emerging sign language reveals that language supports spatial cognition. *Proceedings of the National Academy of Sciences, USA,107,* 12116–12120.

Pyszczynski, T., Holt, J., & Greenberg, J. (1987). Depression, self-focused attention, and expectancies for positive and negative future life events for self and others. *Journal of Personality and Social Psychology, 52,* 994–1001.

Quattrone, G. A. (1982). Behavioral consequences of attributional bias. *Social Cognition, 1,* 358–378.

Querleu, D., Lefebvre, C., Titran, M., Renard, X., Morillon, M., & Crepin, G. (1984). Réactivité de nouveau-né de moins de deux heures de vie à la voix maternelle [Reactivity of a newborn at less than two hours of life to the mother's voice]. *Journal de Gynécologie Obstétrique et de Biologie de la Reproduction, 13,* 125–134.

Quiroga, R. (2016). Neuronal codes for visual perception and memory. *Neuropsychologia, 83,* 227–241.

Quiroga, R. Q., Reddy, L., Kreiman, G., Koch, C., & Fried, I. (2005). Invariant visual representation by single neurons in the human brain. *Nature, 435,* 1102–1107.

Qureshi, A., & Lee-Chiong, T. (2004). Medications and their effects on sleep. *Medical Clinics of North America, 88,* 751–766.

Rabbitt, P., Diggle, P., Holland, F., & McInnes, L. (2004). Practice and drop-out effects during a 17-year longitudinal study of cognitive aging. *Journal of Gerontology: Psychological Sciences and Social Sciences, 59*(2), 84–97.

Rabin, L. A., Fogel, J., & Nutter-Upham, K. E. (2011). Academic procrastination in college students: The role of self-reported executive function. *Journal of Clinical and Experimental Neuropsychology, 33,* 344–357.

Race, E., Keane, M. M., & Verfaellie, M. (2011). Medial temporal lobe damage causes deficits in episodic memory and episodic future thinking not attributable to deficits in narrative construction. *Journal of Neuroscience, 31,* 10262–10269.

Radford, E., & Radford, M. A. (1949). *Encyclopedia of superstitions.* New York: Philosophical Library.

Rahe, R. H., Meyer, M., Smith, M., Klaer, G., & Holmes, T. H. (1964). Social stress and illness onset. *Journal of Psychosomatic Research, 8,* 35–44.

Raichle, M. E. (2015). The brain's default mode network. *Annual Review of Neuroscience, 38,* 433–447.

Raichle, M. E., & Mintun, M. A. (2006). Brain work and brain imaging. *Annual Review of Neuroscience, 29,* 449–476.

Rajaram, S. (2011). Collaboration both hurts and helps memory: A cognitive perspective. *Current Directions in Psychological Science, 20,* 76–81.

Rajaram, S., & Pereira-Pasarin, L. P. (2010). Collaborative memory: Cognitive research and theory. *Perspectives on Psychological Science, 6,* 649–663.

Ramachandran, V. S., & Altschuler, E. L. (2009). The use of visual feedback, in particular mirror visual feedback, in restoring brain function. *Brain, 132,* 1693–1710.

Ramachandran, V. S., & Blakeslee, S. (1998). *Phantoms in the brain: Probing the mysteries of the human mind.* New York: Morrow.

Ramachandran, V. S., & Brang, D. (2015). Phantom touch. In T. J. Prescott, E. Ahissar, & E. Izhikevich (Eds.), *Scholarpedia of Touch* (pp. 377–386). Amsterdam: Atlantis Press.

Ramachandran, V. S., Brang, D., & McGeoch, P. D. (2010). Dynamic reorganization of referred sensations by movements of phantom limbs. *NeuroReport, 21,* 727–730.

Ramachandran, V. S., Rodgers-Ramachandran, D., & Stewart, M. (1992). Perceptual correlates of massive cortical reorganization. *Science, 258,* 1159–1160.

Ramirez-Esparza, N., Gosling, S. D., Benet-Martinez, V., & Potter, J. P. (2004). Do bilinguals have two personalities? A special case of cultural frame-switching. *Journal of Research in Personality, 40,* 99–120.

Rand, D. G., & Nowak, M. A. (2016). Human cooperation. *Trends in Cognitive Sciences, 17*(8), 413–425. doi: 10.1016/j.tics.2013.06.003

Randles, D., Inzlicht, M., Proulx, T., Tullett, A. M., & Heine, S. J. (2015). Is dissonance reduction a special case of fluid compensation? Evidence that dissonant cognitions cause compensatory affirmation and abstraction. *Journal of Personality and Social Psychology, 108*(5), 697–710. doi: 10.1037/a0038933

Rapaport, D. (1946). *Diagnostic psychological testing: The theory, statistical evaluation, and diagnostic application of a battery of tests.* Chicago: Year Book Publishers.

Rapoport, J., Chavez, A., Greenstein, D., Addington, A., & Gogtay, N. (2009). Autism-spectrum disorders and childhood onset schizophrenia: Clinical and biological contributions to a relationship revisited. *Journal of the American Academy of Child and Adolescent Psychiatry, 48,* 10–18.

Rappoport, J. L. (1990). Obsessive-compulsive disorder and basal ganglia dysfunction. *Psychological Medicine, 20,* 465–469.

Ratliff, K. A., & Oishi, S. (2013). Gender differences in implicit self-esteem following a romantic partner's success or failure. *Journal of Personality and Social Psychology, 105*(4), 688–702. doi: 10.1037/a0033769

Rauschecker, J. P., & Scott, S. K. (2009). Maps and streams in the auditory cortex: Nonhuman primates illuminate human speech processing. *Nature Neuroscience, 12,* 718–724.

Raven, J., Raven, J. C., & Court, J. H. (2004). *Manual for Raven's Progressive Matrices and Vocabulary Scales.* San Antonio: Harcourt Assessment.

Raz, A., Fan, J., & Posner, M. I. (2005). Hypnotic suggestion reduces conflict in the brain. *Proceedings of the National Academy of Sciences, 102,* 9978–9983.

Raz, A., Shapiro, T., Fan, J., & Posner, M. I. (2002). Hypnotic suggestion and the modulation of Stroop interference. *Archives of General Psychiatry, 59,* 1155–1161.

Raz, N. (2000). Aging of the brain and its impact on cognitive performance: Integration of structural and functional findings. In F. I. M. Craik & T. A. Salthouse (Eds.), *The handbook of aging and cognition* (pp. 1–90). Mahwah, NJ: Erlbaum.

Read, K. E. (1965). *The high valley.* London: Allen and Unwin.

Reber, A. S. (1967). Implicit learning of artificial grammars. *Journal of Verbal Learning and Verbal Behavior, 6,* 855–863.

Reber, A. S. (1996). *Implicit learning and tacit knowledge: An essay on the cognitive unconscious.* New York: Oxford University Press.

Reber, A. S., & Allen, R. (2000). Individual differences in implicit learning. In R. G. Kunzendorf & B. Wallace (Eds.), *Individual differences in conscious experience* (pp. 227–247). Philadelphia: John Benjamins.

Reber, A. S., Walkenfeld, F. F., & Hernstadt, R. (1991). Implicit learning: Individual differences and IQ. *Journal of Experimental Psychology: Learning, Memory, and Cognition, 17,* 888–896.

Reber, P. J. (2013). The neual basis of implicit learning and memory: A review of neuropsychological and neuroimaging research. *Neuropsychologia, 51,* 2026–2042.

Reber, P. J., Gitelman, D. R., Parrish, T. B., & Mesulam, M. M. (2003). Dissociating explicit and implicit category knowledge with fMRI. *Journal of Cognitive Neuroscience, 15,* 574–583.

Recanzone, G. H., & Sutter, M. L. (2008). The biological basis of audition. *Annual Review of Psychology, 59,* 119–142.

Rechsthaffen, A., Gilliland, M. A., Bergmann, B. M., & Winter, J. B. (1983). Physiological correlates of prolonged sleep deprivation in rats. *Science, 221,* 182–184.

Redick, T. S. (2015). Working memory training and interpreting interactions in intelligence interventions. *Intelligence, 50,* 14–20.

Redick, T. S., Shipstead, Z., Harrison, T. L., Hicks, K. L., Fried, D. E., Hambrick, D. Z., . . . Engle, R. W. (2013). No evidence of intelligence improvement after working memory training: A randomized, placebo-controlled study. *Journal of Experimental Psychology: General, 142,* 359–379. doi: 10.1037/a002908

Reed, C. L., Klatzky, R. L., & Halgren, E. (2005). What vs. where in touch: An fMRI study. *NeuroImage, 25,* 718–726.

Reed, D. R. (2008). Birth of a new breed of supertaster. *Chemical Senses, 33,* 489–491.

Reed, G. (1988). *The psychology of anomalous experience* (rev. ed.). Buffalo, NY: Prometheus Books.

Reeve, C. L., Heggestad, E. D., & Lievens, F. (2009). Modeling the impact of test anxiety and test familiarity on the criterion-related validity of cognitive ability tests. *Intelligence, 37*(1), 34–41. doi: 10.1016/j.intell.2008.05.003

Regan, P. C. (1998). What if you can't get what you want? Willingness to compromise ideal mate selection standards as a function of sex, mate value, and relationship context. *Personality and Social Psychology Bulletin, 24,* 1294–1303.

Regier, T., & Kay, P. (2009). Language, thought, and color: Whorf was half right. *Trends in Cognitive Sciences, 13,* 439–446.

Reichbach, G. L. (2012, May 16). A judge's plea for pot [op-ed article]. *New York Times.* Retrieved from http://www.nytimes.com/2012/05/17/opinion/a-judges-plea-for-medical-marijuana.html

Reis, H. T., Maniaci, M. R., Caprariello, P. S., Eastwick, P. W., & Finkel, E. J. (2011). Familiarity does indeed promote attraction in live interaction. *Journal of Personality and Social Psychology, 101*(3), 557–570. doi: 10.1037/a0022885

Reiss, D., & Marino, L. (2001). Mirror self-recognition in the bottlenose dolphin: A case of cognitive convergence. *Proceedings of the National Academy of Sciences, USA, 98,* 5937–5942.

Reissland, N. (1988). Neonatal imitation in the first hour of life: Observations in rural Nepal. *Developmental Psychology, 24,* 464–469.

Renner, K. E. (1964). Delay of reinforcement: A historical review. *Psychological Review, 61,* 341–361.

Renner, M. J., & Mackin, R. (1998). A life stress instrument for classroom use. *Teaching of Psychology, 25,* 46–48.

Rensink, R. A. (2002). Change detection. *Annual Review of Psychology, 53,* 245–277.

Rensink, R. A., O'Regan, J. K., & Clark, J. J. (1997). To see or not to see: The need for attention to perceive changes in scenes. *Psychological Science, 8,* 368–373.

Repacholi, B. M., & Gopnik, A. (1997). Early reasoning about desires: Evidence from 14- and 18-month-olds. *Developmental Psychology, 33,* 12–21.

Rescorla, R. A. (2006). Stimulus generalization of excitation and inhibition. *Quarterly Journal of Experimental Psychology, 59,* 53–67.

Ressler, K. J., & Mayberg, H. S. (2007). Targeting abnormal neural circuits in mood and anxiety disorders: From the laboratory to the clinic. *Nature Neuroscience, 10,* 1116–1124.

Ressler, K. J., & Nemeroff, C. B. (1999). Role of norepinephrine in the pathophysiology and treatment of mood disorders. *Biological Psychiatry, 46,* 1219–1233.

Rice, K. G., Richardson, C. M. E., & Clark, D. (2012). Perfectionism, procrastination, and psychological distress. *Journal of Counseling Psychology, 39,* 288–302.

Richards, M., Black, S., Mishra, G., Gale, C. R., Deary, I. J., & Batty, D. G. (2009). IQ in childhood and the metabolic syndrome in middle age: Extended follow-up of the 1946 British birth cohort study. *Intelligence, 37*(6), 567–572.

Richards, M. H., Crowe, P. A., Larson, R., & Swarr, A. (1998). Developmental patterns and gender differences in the experience of peer companionship during adolescence. *Child Development, 69,* 154–163.

Richardson, D. S. (2014). Everyday aggression takes many forms. *Current Directions in Psychological Science, 23*(3), 220–224. doi: 10.1177/0963721414530143

Richert, E. S. (1997). Excellence with equity in identification and programming. In N. Colangelo & G. A. Davis (Eds.), *Handbook of gifted education* (2nd ed., pp. 75–88). Boston: Allyn & Bacon.

Richters, J., de Visser, R., Rissel, C., & Smith, A. (2006). Sexual practices at last heterosexual encounter and occurrence of orgasm in a national survey. *Journal of Sex Research, 43,* 217–226.

Ridenour, T. A., & Howard, M. O. (2012). Inhalants abuse: Status of etiology and intervention. In J. C. Verster, K. Brady, M. Galanter, & P. Conrod (Eds.), *Drug abuse and addiction in medical illness: Causes, consequences, and treatment* (pp. 189–199). New York: Springer.

Rieber, R. W. (Ed.). (1980). *Wilhelm Wundt and the making of scientific psychology.* New York: Plenum Press.

Rieger, G., Linsenmeier, J. A., Gygax, L., Garcia, S., & Bailey, J. M. (2010). Dissecting "gaydar": Accuracy and the role of masculinity–femininity. *Archives of Sexual Behavior, 39,* 124–140.

Rimer, J., Dwan, K., Lawlor, D. A., Greig, C. A., McMurdo, M., Morley, W., & Mead, G. E. (2012). Exercise for depression. *Cochrane Database of Systematic Reviews, 7,* CD004366.

Ringach, D. L., & Jentsch, J. D. (2009). We must face the threats. *Journal of Neuroscience, 29,* 11417–11418.

Risko, E. F., Anderson, N., Sarwal, A., Engelhardt, M., & Kingstone, A. (2012). Every attention: Variation in mind wandering and memory in a lecture. *Applied Cognitive Psychology, 26,* 234–242.

Risman, J. E., Coyle, J. T., Green, R. W., Javitt, D. C., Benes, F. M., Heckers, S., & Grace, A. A. (2008). Circuit-based framework for understanding neurotransmitter and risk gene interactions in schizophrenia. *Trends in Neurosciences, 31,* 234–242.

Rivera, L. A. (2012) Hiring as cultural matching: The case of elite professional service firms. *American Sociological Review, 77,* 999–1022.

Rizzolatti, G. (2004). The mirror-neuron system and imitation. In S. Hurley & N. Chater (Eds.), *Perspectives on imitation: From mirror neurons to memes* (pp. 55–76). Cambridge, MA: MIT Press.

Rizzolatti, G., & Craighero, L. (2004). The mirror-neuron system. *Annual Review of Neuroscience, 27,* 169–192.

Rizzolatti, G., & Sinigaglia, C. (2010). The functional role of the parieto-frontal mirror circuit. *Nature Reviews Neuroscience, 11,* 264–274.

Roberson, D., Davidoff, J., Davies, I. R. L., & Shapiro, L. R. (2004). The development of color categories in two languages: A longitudinal study. *Journal of Experimental Psychology: General, 133,* 554–571.

Roberts, G. A. (1991). Delusional belief and meaning in life: A preferred reality? *British Journal of Psychiatry, 159,* 20–29.

Roberts, G. A., & McGrady, A. (1996). Racial and gender effects on the relaxation response: Implications for the development of hypertension. *Biofeedback and Self-Regulation, 21,* 51–62.

Robertson, L. C. (1999). What can spatial deficits teach us about feature binding and spatial maps? *Visual Cognition, 6,* 409–430.

Robertson, L. C. (2003). Binding, spatial attention and perceptual awareness. *Nature Reviews Neuroscience, 4,* 93–102.

Robins, L. N., Helzer, J. E., Hesselbrock, M., & Wish, E. (1980). Vietnam veterans three years after Vietnam. In L. Brill & C. Winick (Eds.), *The yearbook of substance use and abuse* (Vol. 11). New York: Human Sciences Press.

Robins, R. W., Fraley, R. C., & Krueger, R. F. (Eds.). (2007). *Handbook of research methods in personality psychology.* New York: Guilford Press.

Robinson, A., & Clinkenbeard, P. R. (1998). Giftedness: An exceptionality examined. *Annual Review of Psychology, 49,* 117–139.

Robinson, D. N. (1995). *An intellectual history of psychology.* Madison: University of Wisconsin Press.

Rodieck, R. W. (1998). *The first steps in seeing.* Sunderland, MA: Sinauer.

Roediger, H. L. III. (2000). Why retrieval is the key process to understanding human memory. In E. Tulving (Ed.), *Memory, consciousness, and the brain: The Tallinn conference* (pp. 52–75). Philadelphia: Psychology Press.

Roediger, H. L. III, & Craik, F. I. M. (Eds.). *Varieties of memory and consciousness: Essays in honor of Endel Tulving* (pp. 3–41). Hillsdale, NJ: Erlbaum.

Roediger, H. L. III, & Karpicke, J. D. (2006). Test-enhanced learning: Taking memory tests improves long-term retention. *Psychological Science, 17,* 249–255.

Roediger, H. L. III, & McDermott, K. B. (1995). Creating false memories: Remembering words not presented in lists. *Journal of Experimental Psychology: Learning, Memory, and Cognition, 21,* 803–814.

Roediger, H. L. III, & McDermott, K. B. (2000). Tricks of memory. *Current Directions in Psychological Science, 9,* 123–127.

Roediger, H. L. III, Weldon, M. S., & Challis, B. H. (1989). Explaining dissociations between implicit and explicit measures of retention: A processing account. In H. L. Roediger & F. I. M. Craik (Eds.), *Varieties of memory and consciousness: Essays in honour of Endel Tulving* (pp. 3–39). Hillsdale, NJ: Erlbaum.

Rogers, C. R. (1951). *Client-centered therapy: Its current practice, implications, and theory.* Boston: Houghton Mifflin.

Rogers, T. B., Kuiper, N. A., & Kirker, W. S. (1977). Self-reference and the encoding of personal information. *Journal of Personality and Social Psychology, 35,* 677–688.

Rohrer, D. (2015). Student instruction should be distributed over long time periods. *Educational Psychology Review, 27,* 635–643.

Rohrer, D., Dedrick, R. F., & Sterschic, S. (2015). Interleaved practice improves mathematics learning. *Journal of Educational Psychology, 107,* 900–908.

Roig, M., Skriver, K., Lundbye-Jensen, J., Kiens, B., & Nielsen, J. B. (2012). A single bout of exercise improves motor memory. *PLoS One, 7,* e44594. doi: 10.1371/journal.pone.0044594

Roisman, G. I., Masten, A. S., Coatsworth, J. D., & Tellegen, A. (2004). Salient and emerging developmental tasks in the transition to adulthood. *Child Development, 75,* 123–133. doi: 10.1111/j.1467-8624.2004.00658.x

Rolls, E. T. (2015). Taste, olfactory, and food reward value processing in the human brain. *Progress in Neurobiology, 127–128,* 64–90.

Romero-Corral, A., Montori, V. M., Somers, V. K., Korinek, J., Thomas, R. J., Allison, T. G., . . . Lopez-Jiminez, F. (2006). Association of body weight with total mortality and with cardiovascular events in coronary artery disease: A systematic review of cohort studies. *Lancet, 368*(9536), 666–678.

Ronay, R., & Galinsky, A. D. (2011). Lex talionis: Testosterone and the law of retaliation. *Journal of Experimental Social Psychology, 47*(3), 702–705. doi: 10.1016/j.jesp.2010.11.009

Rondan, C., & Deruelle, C. (2004). Face processing in high functioning autistic adults: A look into spatial frequencies and the inversion effect. *Journal of Cognitive and Behavioral Psychotherapies, 4,* 149–164.

Roney, J. R., & Simmons, Z. L. (2013). Hormonal predictors of women's sexual desire in normal menstrual cycles. *Hormones and Behavior, 63,* 636–645.

Rosch, E. H. (1973). Natural categories. *Cognitive Psychology, 4,* 328–350.

Rosch, E. H. (1975). Cognitive representations of semantic categories. *Journal of Experimental Psychology: General, 104,* 192–233.

Rosch, E. H., & Mervis, C. B. (1975). Family resemblances: Studies in the internal structure of categories. *Cognitive Psychology, 7,* 573–605.

Rose, S. P. R. (2002). Smart drugs: Do they work? Are they ethical? Will they be legal? *Nature Reviews Neuroscience, 3,* 975–979.

Roseman, I. J. (1984). Cognitive determinants of emotion: A structural theory. *Review of Personality and Social Psychology, 5,* 11–36.

Roseman, I. J., & Smith, C. A. (2001). Appraisal theory: Overview, assumptions, varieties and controversies. In K. R. Scherer, A. Schorr, & T. Johnstone (Eds.), *Appraisal processes in emotion: Theory, methods, research* (pp. 3–19). New York: Oxford University Press.

Rosenbaum, J. E. (2009). Patient teenagers? A comparison of the sexual behavior of virginity pledgers and matched nonpledgers. *Pediatrics, 123*(1), e110–e120.

Rosenberg, M. (1965). *Society and the adolescent self-image.* Princeton, NJ: Princeton University Press.

Rosenberg, T. (2013, March 27). The destructive influence of imaginary peers. *New York Times.* Retrieved from http://opinionator.blogs .nytimes.com/2013/03/27the-destructive-influence-of-imaginary-peers/

Rosenhan, D. (1973). On being sane in insane places. *Science, 179,* 250–258.

Rosenkranz, K., Williamon, A., & Rothwell, J. C. (2007). Motorcortical excitability and synaptic plasticity is enhanced in professional musicians. *Journal of Neuroscience, 27,* 5200–5206.

Rosenstein, M. J., Milazzo-Sayre, L. J., & Manderscheid, R. W. (1990). Characteristics of persons using specifically inpatient, outpatient, and partial care programs in 1986. In M. A. Sonnenschein (Ed.), *Mental health in the United States* (pp. 139–172). Washington, DC: U.S. Government Printing Office.

Rosenthal, R., & Fode, K. L. (1963). The effect of experimenter bias on the performance of the albino rat. *Behavioral Science, 8,* 183–189.

Roser, M. E., Aslin, R. N., McKenzie, R., Zahra, D., & Fiser, J. (2015). Enhanced visual statistical learning in adults with autism. *Neuropsychology, 29,* 163–172.

Ross, L. (1977). The intuitive psychologist and his shortcomings: Distortions in the attribution process. *Advances in Experimental Social Psychology, 10,* 173–220.

Ross, L., Amabile, T. M., & Steinmetz, J. L. (1977). Social roles, social control, and biases in social-perception processes. *Journal of Personality and Social Psychology, 35,* 485–494.

Ross, L., & Nisbett, R. E. (1991). *The person and the situation.* New York: McGraw-Hill.

Ross, M., Blatz, C. W., & Schryer, E. (2008). Social memory processes. In H. L. Roediger III (Ed.), *Learning and memory: A comprehensive reference* (Vol. 2, pp. 911–926). Oxford: Elsevier.

Rossano, F., Carpenter, M., & Tomasello, M. (2012). One-year-old infants follow others' voice direction. *Psychological Science, 23*(11), 1298–1302. doi: 10.1177/0956797612450032

Rosvall, M., & Bergstrom, C. T. (2008). Maps of random walks on complex networks reveal community structure. *Proceedings of the National Academy of Sciences, USA, 105,* 1118–1123.

Roth, B., Becker, N., Romeyke, S., Schäfer, S., Domnick, F., & Spinath, F. M. (2015). Intelligence and school grades: A meta-analysis. *Intelligence, 53,* 118–137. doi: 10.1016/j.intell.2015.09.002

Roth, H. P., & Caron, H. S. (1978). Accuracy of doctors' estimates and patients' statements on adherence to a drug regimen. *Clinical Pharmacology and Therapeutics, 23,* 361–370.

Rothbart, M. K., & Bates, J. E. (1998). Temperament. In W. Damon (Series Ed.) & N. Eisenberg (Vol. Ed.), *Handbook of child psychology: Vol. 3. Social, emotional and personality development* (5th ed., pp. 105–176). New York: Wiley.

Rothbaum, B. O., & Schwartz, A. C. (2002). Exposure therapy for posttraumatic stress disorder. *American Journal of Psychotherapy, 56,* 59–75.

Rotter, J. B. (1966). Generalized expectancies for internal versus external locus of control of reinforcement. *Psychological Monographs: General and Applied, 80,* 1–28.

Rotton, L. (1992). Trait humor and longevity: Do comics have the last laugh? *Health Psychology, 11,* 262–266.

Roy-Byrne, P. P., & Cowley, D. (1998). *Pharmacological treatment of panic, generalized anxiety, and phobic disorders.* New York: Oxford University Press.

Roy-Byrne, P. P., & Cowley, D. S. (2002). Pharmacological treatments for panic disorder, generalized anxiety disorder, specific phobia, and social anxiety disorder. In P. E. Nathan & J. M. Gorman (Eds.), *A guide to treatments that work* (2nd ed., pp. 337–365). New York: Oxford University Press.

Rozenblit, L., & Keil, F. C. (2002). The misunderstood limits of folk science: An illusion of explanatory depth. *Cognitive Science, 26,* 521–562.

Rozin, P. (1968). Are carbohydrate and protein intakes separately regulated? *Journal of Comparative and Physiological Psychology, 65,* 23–29.

Rozin, P., Bauer, R., & Catanese, D. (2003). Food and life, pleasure and worry, among American college students: Gender differences and regional similarities. *Journal of Personality and Social Psychology, 85,* 132–141.

Rozin, P., Dow, S., Moscovitch, M., & Rajaram, S. (1998). What causes humans to begin and end a meal? A role for memory for what has been eaten, as evidenced by a study of multiple meal eating in amnesic patients. *Psychological Science, 9,* 392–396.

Rozin, P., Kabnick, K., Pete, E., Fischler, C., & Shields, C. (2003). The ecology of eating: Smaller portion size in France than in the United States helps to explain the French paradox. *Psychological Science, 14,* 450–454.

Rozin, P., & Kalat, J. W. (1971). Specific hungers and poison avoidance as adaptive specializations of learning. *Psychological Review, 78,* 459–486.

Rozin, P., Scott, S., Dingley, M., Urbanek, J. K., Jiang, H., & Kaltenbach, M. (2011). Nudge to nobesity: I. Minor changes in accessibility decrease food intake. *Judgment and Decision Making, 6,* 323–332.

Rozin, P., Trachtenberg, S., & Cohen, A. B. (2001). Stability of body image and body image dissatisfaction in American college students over about the last 15 years. *Appetite, 37,* 245–248.

Rubin, M., & Badea, C. (2012). They're all the same! . . . but for several different reasons: A review of the multicausal nature of perceived group variability. *Current Directions in Psychological Science, 21*(6), 367–372. doi: 10.1177/0963721412457363

Rubin, Z. (1973). *Liking and loving.* New York: Holt, Rinehart & Winston.

Rubin-Fernandez, P., & Geurts, B. (2012). How to pass the false-belief task before your fourth birthday. *Psychological Science, 24*(1), 27–33. doi: 10.1177/0956797612447819

Rudman, L. A., Ashmore, R. D., & Gary, M. L. (2001). "Unlearning" automatic biases: The malleability of implicit prejudice and stereotypes. *Journal of Personality and Social Psychology, 81,* 856–868.

Rummer, R., Schweppe, J., Schlegelmilch, R., & Grice, M. (2014). Mood is linked to vowel type: The role of articulatory movements. *Emotion, 14*(2), 246–250. doi: 10.1037/a0035752

Running, C. A., Craig, B. A., & Mattes, R. D. (2015). Oleogustus: The unique taste of fat. *Chemical Senses, 40,* 507–516.

Rusbult, C. E., & Van Lange, P. A. M. (2003). Interdependence, interaction and relationships. *Annual Review of Psychology, 54,* 351–375.

Ruscio, A. M., Stein, D. J., Chiu, W. T., & Kessler, R. C. (2010). The epidemiology of obsessive-compulsive disorder in the National Comorbidity Survey Replication. *Molecular Psychiatry, 15,* 53–63.

Rushton, J. P., & Templer, D. I. (2009). National differences in intelligence, crime, income, and skin color. *Intelligence, 37*(4), 341–346.

Russell, B. (1945). *A history of Western philosophy.* New York: Simon & Schuster.

Russell, J. A. (1980). A circumplex model of affect. *Journal of Personality and Social Psychology, 39,* 1161–1178.

Russell, J., Gee, B., & Bullard, C. (2012). Why do young children hide by closing their eyes? Self-visibility and the developing concept of self. *Journal of Cognition and Development, 13*(4), 550–576. doi: 10.1080/15248372.2011.594826

Rutledge, R. B., Lazzaro, S. C., Lau, B., Myers, C. E., Gluck, M. A., & Glimcher, P. W. (2009). Dopaminergic drugs modulate learning rates and perseveration in Parkinson's patients in a dynamic foraging task. *Journal of Neuroscience, 29,* 15104–15114.

Rutter, M., O'Connor, T. G., & the English and Romanian Adoptees Study Team. (2004). Are there biological programming effects for psychological development? Findings from a study of Romanian adoptees. *Developmental Psychology, 40,* 81–94.

Rutter, M., & Silberg, J. (2002). Gene–environment interplay in relation to emotional and behavioral disturbance. *Annual Review of Psychology, 53,* 463–490.

Ryan, R. M., & Deci, E. L. (2000). Self-determination theory and the facilitation of intrinsic motivation, social development, and well-being. *American Psychologist, 55,* 68–78.

Sachs, J. S. (1967). Recognition of semantic, syntactic, and lexical changes in sentences. *Psychonomic Bulletin & Review, 1,* 17–18.

Sacks, O. (1995). *An anthropologist on Mars.* New York: Knopf.

Sacks, O. (1996). *An anthropologist on Mars* (ppbk). Visalia, CA: Vintage.

Saffran, J. R., Aslin, R. N., & Newport, E. I. (1996). Statistical learning by 8-month-old infants. *Science, 274,* 1926–1928.

Sahakian, B., & Morein-Zamir, S. (2007). Professor's little helper. *Nature, 450*(7173), 1157–1159.

Saks, E. R. (2013, January 25). Successful and schizophrenic. *New York Times.* Retrieved from http://www.nytimes.com/2013/01/27/opinion/sunday/schizophrenic-not-stupid.html

Sakuraba, S., Sakai, S., Yamanaka, M., Yokosawa, Y., & Hirayama, K. (2012). Does the human dorsal stream really process a category for tools? *Journal of Neuroscience, 32,* 3949–3953.

Sallet, J., Mars, R. B., Noonan, M. P., Andersson, J. L., O'Reilly, J. X., Jbabdi, S., . . . Rushworth, M. F. S. (2011). Social network size affects neural circuits in macaques. *Science, 334*(6056), 697–700. doi: 10.1126/science.1210027

Salmon, D. P., & Bondi, M. W. (2009). Neuropsychological assessment of dementia. *Annual Review of Psychology, 60,* 257–282.

Salovey, P., & Grewal, D. (2005). The science of emotional intelligence. *Current Directions in Psychological Science, 14*(6), 281–285.

Salthouse, T. A. (1984). Effects of age and skill in typing. *Journal of Experimental Psychology: General, 113,* 345–371.

Salthouse, T. A. (1987). Age, experience, and compensation. In C. Schooler & K. W. Schaie (Eds.), *Cognitive functioning and social structure over the life course* (pp. 142–150). Norwood, NJ: Ablex.

Salthouse, T. A. (1996a). General and specific mediation of adult age differences in memory. *Journal of Gerontology: Series B: Psychological Sciences and Social Sciences, 51B,* P30–P42.

Salthouse, T. A. (1996b). The processing-speed theory of adult age differences in cognition. *Psychological Review, 103,* 403–428.

Salthouse, T. A. (2000). Pressing issues in cognitive aging. In D. Park & N. Schwartz (Eds.), *Cognitive aging: A primer* (pp. 43–54). Philadelphia: Psychology Press.

Salthouse, T. A. (2001). Structural models of the relations between age and measures of cognitive functioning. *Intelligence, 29,* 93–115.

Salthouse, T. A. (2006). Mental exercise and mental aging. *Perspectives on Psychological Science, 1*(1), 68–87.

Salthouse, T. A. (2015). Do cognitive interventions alter the rate of age-related cognitive change? *Intelligence, 53,* 86–91. doi: 10.1016/j.intell.2015.09.004

Salvatore, J. E., Kuo, S. I.-C., Steele, R. D., Simpson, J. A., & Collins, W. A. (2011). Recovering from conflict in romantic relationships: A developmental perspective. *Psychological Science, 22*(3), 376–383. doi: 10.1177/0956797610397055

Sampson, R. J., & Laub, J. H. (1995). Understanding variability in lives through time: Contributions of life-course criminology. *Studies of Crime Prevention, 4,* 143–158.

Sara, S. J. (2000). Retrieval and reconsolidation: Toward a neurobiology of remembering. *Learning & Memory, 7,* 73–84.

Sarris, V. (1989). Max Wertheimer on seen motion: Theory and evidence. *Psychological Research, 51,* 58–68.

Sarter, M. (2006). Preclinical research into cognition enhancers. *Trends in Pharmacological Sciences, 27,* 602–608.

Sasanuma, S. (1975). Kana and kanji processing in Japanese aphasics. *Brain and Language, 2,* 369–383.

Satcher, D. (2001). *The Surgeon General's call to action to promote sexual health and responsible sexual behavior.* Washington, DC: U.S. Government Printing Office.

Satterwhite, C. L., Torrone, E., Meites, E., Dunne, E. F., Mahajan, R., Ocfernia, M. C., . . . Weinstock, H. (2013). Sexually transmitted infections among U.S. women and men: Prevalence and incidence estimates, 2008. *Sexually Transmitted Diseases, 40*(3), 187–193.

Savage, C. R., Deckersbach, T., Heckers, S., Wagner, A. D., Schacter, D. L., Alpert, N. M., . . . Rauch, S. L. (2001). Prefrontal regions supporting spontaneous and directed application of verbal learning strategies: Evidence from PET. *Brain, 124,* 219–231.

Savage-Rumbaugh, S., & Lewin, R. (1996). *Kanzi: The ape on the brink of the human mind*. New York: Wiley.

Savage-Rumbaugh, S., Shanker, G., & Taylor, T. J. (1998). *Apes, language, and the human mind*. Oxford: Oxford University Press.

Savic, I., Berglund, H., & Lindstrom, P. (2005). Brain response to putative pheromones in homosexual men. *Proceedings of the National Academy of Sciences, USA, 102*, 7356–7361.

Savic, I., & Lindstrom, P. (2008). PET and MRI show differences in cerebral asymmetry and functional connectivity between homo- and heterosexual subjects. *Proceedings of the National Academy of Sciences, USA, 105*(27), 9403–9408.

Savin-Williams, R. C., & Vrangalova, Z. (2013). Mostly heterosexual as a distinct sexual orientation group: A systematic review of the empirical evidence. *Developmental Review, 33*, 58–88.

Sawa, A., & Snyder, S. H. (2002). Schizophrenia: Diverse approaches to a complex disease. *Science, 295*, 692–695.

Sawyer, T. F. (2000). Francis Cecil Sumner: His views and influence on African American higher education. *History of Psychology, 3*(2), 122–141.

Scarborough, E., & Furumoto, L. (1987). *Untold lives: The first generation of American women psychologists*. New York: Columbia University Press.

Scarr, S., Pakstis, A. J., Katz, S. H., & Barker, W. B. (1977). Absence of a relationship between degree of White ancestry and intellectual skills within a Black population. *Human Genetics, 39*(1), 69–86.

Schachter, S. (1982). Recidivism and self-cure of smoking and obesity. *American Psychologist, 37*, 436–444.

Schachter, S., & Singer, J. E. (1962). Cognitive, social, and psychological determinants of emotional state. *Physiological Review, 69*, 379–399.

Schacter, D. L. (1987). Implicit memory: History and current status. *Journal of Experimental Psychology: Learning, Memory, and Cognition, 13*, 501–518.

Schacter, D. L. (1996). *Searching for memory: The brain, the mind, and the past*. New York: Basic Books.

Schacter, D. L. (1999). The seven sins of memory: Insights from psychology and cognitive neuroscience. *American Psychologist, 54*(3), 182–203.

Schacter, D. L. (2001a). *Forgotten ideas, neglected pioneers: Richard Semon and the story of memory*. Philadelphia: Psychology Press.

Schacter, D. L. (2001b). *The seven sins of memory: How the mind forgets and remembers*. Boston: Houghton Mifflin.

Schacter, D. L. (2012). Adaptive constructive processes and the future of memory. *American Psychologist, 67*, 603–613.

Schacter, D. L., & Addis, D. R. (2007). The cognitive neuroscience of constructive memory: Remembering the past and imagining the future. *Philosophical Transactions of the Royal Society of London, B, 362*, 773–786.

Schacter, D. L., Addis, D. R., & Buckner, R. L. (2008). Episodic simulation of future events: Concepts, data, and applications. *Annals of the New York Academy of Sciences, 1124*, 39–60.

Schacter, D. L., Addis, D. R., Hassabis, D., Martin, V. C., Spreng, R. N., & Szpunar, K. K. (2012). The future of memory: Remembering, imagining, and the brain. *Neuron, 16*, 582–583.

Schacter, D. L., Alpert, N. M., Savage, C. R., Rauch, S. L., & Albert, M. S. (1996). Conscious recollection and the human hippocampal formation: Evidence from positron emission tomography. *Proceedings of the National Academy of Sciences, USA, 93*, 321–325.

Schacter, D. L., & Curran, T. (2000). Memory without remembering and remembering without memory: Implicit and false memories.

In M. S. Gazzaniga (Ed.), *The new cognitive neurosciences* (2nd ed., pp. 829–840). Cambridge, MA: MIT Press.

Schacter, D. L., Dobbins, I. G., & Schnyer, D. M. (2004). Specificity of priming: A cognitive neuroscience perspective. *Nature Reviews Neuroscience, 5*, 853–862.

Schacter, D. L., Gaesser, B., & Addis, D. R. (2013). Remembering the past and imagining the future in the elderly. *Gerontologist, 59*(2), 143–151. doi: 10.1159/000342198

Schacter, D. L., Guerin, S. A., & St. Jacques, P. L. (2011). Memory distortion: An adaptive perspective. *Trends in Cognitive Sciences, 15*, 467–474.

Schacter, D. L., Harbluk, J. L., & McLachlan, D. R. (1984). Retrieval without recollection: An experimental analysis of source amnesia. *Journal of Verbal Learning and Verbal Behavior, 23*, 593–611.

Schacter, D. L., Israel, L., & Racine, C. A. (1999). Suppressing false recognition in younger and older adults: The distinctiveness heuristic. *Journal of Memory and Language, 40*, 1–24.

Schacter, D. L., & Loftus, E. F. (2013). Memory and law: What can cognitive neuroscience contribute? *Nature Neuroscience, 16*, 119–123.

Schacter, D. L., Reiman, E., Curran, T., Yun, L. S., Bandy, D., McDermott, K. B., & Roediger, H. L., III. (1996). Neuroanatomical correlates of veridical and illusory recognition memory: Evidence from positron emission tomography. *Neuron, 17*, 267–274.

Schacter, D. L. & Szpunar, K. K. (2015). Enhancing attention and memory during video-recorded lectures. *Scholarship of Teaching and Learning in Psychology, 1*, 60–71.

Schacter, D. L., & Tulving, E. (1994). *Memory systems 1994*. Cambridge, MA: MIT Press.

Schacter, D. L., Wagner, A. D., & Buckner, R. L. (2000). Memory systems of 1999. In E. Tulving & F. I. M. Craik (Eds.), *The Oxford handbook of memory* (pp. 627–643). New York: Oxford University Press.

Schacter, D. L., Wig, G. S., & Stevens, W. D. (2007). Reductions in cortical activity during priming. *Current Opinion in Neurobiology, 17*, 171–176.

Schafer, R. B., & Keith, P. M. (1980). Equity and depression among married couples. *Social Psychology Quarterly, 43*, 430–435.

Schaie, K. W. (1996). *Intellectual development in adulthood: The Seattle Longitudinal Study*. New York: Cambridge University Press.

Schaie, K. W. (2005). *Developmental influences on adult intelligence: The Seattle Longitudinal Study*. New York: Oxford University Press.

Schapira, A. H. V., Emre, M., Jenner, P., & Poewe, W. (2009). Levodopa in the treatment of Parkinson's disease. *European Journal of Neurology, 16*, 982–989.

Schatzberg, A. F., Cole, J. O., & DeBattista, C. (2003). *Manual of clinical psychopharmacology* (4th ed.). Washington, DC: American Psychiatric Publishing.

Scheibe, S., Sheppes, G., & Staudinger, U. M. (2015). Distract or reappraise? Age-related differences in emotion-regulation choice. *Emotion, 15*, 677–681. doi: 10.1037/a0039246

Schenk, T., Ellison, A., Rice, N., & Milner, A. D. (2005). The role of V5/MT+ in the control of catching movements: An rTMS study. *Neuropsychologia, 43*, 189–198.

Scherer, K. R. (1999). Appraisal theory. In T. Dalgleish & M. Power (Eds.), *Handbook of cognition and emotion* (pp. 637–663). New York: Wiley.

Scherer, K. R. (2001). The nature and study of appraisal: A review of the issues. In K. R. Scherer, A. Schorr, & T. Johnstone (Eds.), *Appraisal processes in emotion: Theory, methods, research* (pp. 369–391). New York: Oxford University Press.

Schiff, M., Duyme, M., Stewart, J., Tomkiewicz, S., & Feingold, J. (1978). Intellectual status of working-class children adopted early in upper-middle-class families. *Science, 200,* 1503–1504.

Schildkraut, J. J. (1965). The catecholamine hypothesis of affective disorders: A review of supporting evidence. *American Journal of Psychiatry, 122,* 509–522.

Schiller, D., Monfils, M. H., Raio, C. M., Johnson, D. C., LeDoux, J. E., & Phelps, E. A. (2010). Preventing the return of fear in humans using reconsolidation update mechanisms. *Nature, 463,* 49–54.

Schilling, O. K., Wahl, H.-W., & Wiegering, S. (2013). Affective development in advanced old age: Analyses of terminal change in positive and negative affect. *Developmental Psychology, 49*(5), 1011–1020. doi: 10.1037/a0028775

Schlesinger, J. (2012). *The insanity hoax: Exposing the myth of the mad genius.* Ardsley-on-Hudson, NY: Shrinktunes Media.

Schmader, T., Johns, M., & Forbes, C. (2008). An integrated process model of stereotype threat effects on performance. *Psychological Review, 115,* 336–356.

Schmidt, F. L., & Hunter, J. E. (1998). The validity and utility of selection methods in personnel psychology: Practical and theoretical implications of 85 years of research findings. *Psychological Bulletin, 124,* 262–274.

Schmitt, D. P., Jonason, P. K., Byerley, G. J., Flores, S. D., Illbeck, B. E., O'Leary, K. N., & Qudrat, A. (2012). A reexamination of sex differences in sexuality: New studies reveal old truths. *Current Directions in Psychological Science, 21*(2), 135–139. doi: 10.1177/0963721412436808

Schmitt, D. P., Realo, A., Voracek, M., & Allik, J. (2008). Why can't a man be more like a woman? Sex differences in personality traits across 55 cultures. *Journal of Personality and Social Psychology, 94,* 168–182.

Schneider, B. H., Atkinson, L., & Tardif, C. (2001). Child–parent attachment and children's peer relations: A quantitative review. *Developmental Psychology, 37,* 86–100.

Schnorr, J. A., & Atkinson, R. C. (1969). Repetition versus imagery instructions in the short- and long-term retention of paired associates. *Psychonomic Science, 15,* 183–184.

Schoenemann, P. T., Sheenan, M. J., & Glotzer, L. D. (2005). Prefrontal white matter volume is disproportionately larger in humans than in other primates. *Nature Neuroscience, 8,* 242–252.

Schonberg, T., O'Doherty, J. P., Joel, D., Inzelberg, R., Segev, Y., & Daw, N. D. (2009). Selective impairment of prediction error signaling in human dorsolateral but not ventral striatum in Parkinson's disease patients: Evidence from a model-based fMRI study. *NeuroImage, 49,* 772–781.

Schott, B. J., Henson, R. N., Richardson-Klavehn, A., Becker, C., Thoma, V., Heinze, H. J., & Duzel, E. (2005). Redefining implicit and explicit memory: The functional neuroanatomy of priming, remembering, and control of retrieval. *Proceedings of the National Academy of Sciences, USA, 102,* 1257–1262.

Schouwenburg, H. C. (1995). Academic procrastination: Theoretical notions, measurement, and research. In J. R. Ferrari, J. L. Johnson, & W. G. McCown (Eds.), *Procrastination and task avoidance: Theory, research, and treatment* (pp. 71–96). New York: Plenum Press.

Schreiner, C. E., Read, H. L., & Sutter, M. L. (2000). Modular organization of frequency integration in primary auditory cortex. *Annual Review of Neuroscience, 23,* 501–529.

Schreiner, C. E., & Winer, J. A. (2007). Auditory cortex mapmaking: Principles, projections, and plasticity. *Neuron, 56,* 356–365.

Schubert, T. W., & Koole, S. L. (2009). The embodied self: Making a fist enhances men's power-related self-conceptions. *Journal of Experimental Social Psychology, 45,* 828–834.

Schulreich, S., Gerhardt, H., & Heekeren, H. R. (2016). Incidental fear cues increase monetary loss aversion. *Emotion, 16*(3), 402–412 doi: 10.1037/emo0000124

Schultz, D., Izard, C. E., & Bear, G. (2004). Children's emotion processing: Relations to emotionality and aggression. *Development and Psychopathology, 16*(2), 371–387.

Schultz, D. P., & Schultz, S. E. (1987). *A history of modern psychology* (4th ed.). San Diego: Harcourt Brace Jovanovich.

Schultz, W. (2006). Behavioral theories and the neurophysiology of reward. *Annual Review of Psychology, 57,* 87–115.

Schultz, W. (2007). Behavioral dopamine signals. *Trends in Neurosciences, 30,* 203–210.

Schultz, W., Dayan, P., & Montague, P. R. (1997). A neural substrate of prediction and reward. *Science, 275,* 1593–1599.

Schwartz, B. L. (2002). *Tip-of-the-tongue states: Phenomenology, mechanisms, and lexical retrieval.* Mahwah, NJ: Erlbaum.

Schwartz, C. E., Wright, C. I., Shin, L. M., Kagan, J., & Rauch, S. L. (2003). Inhibited and uninhibited infants "grown up": Adult amygdalar response to novelty. *Science, 300,* 1952–1953.

Schwartz, H. A., Eichstaedt, J. C., Kern, M. L., Dziurzynski, L., Ramones, S. M., Agrawal, M., . . . Ungar, L. H. (2013). Personality, gender, and age in the language of social media: The open-vocabulary approach. *PLoS ONE, 8,* e73791.

Schwartz, J. H., & Westbrook, G. L. (2000). The cytology of neurons. In E. R. Kandel, G. H. Schwartz, & T. M. Jessell (Eds.), *Principles of neural science* (pp. 67–104). New York: McGraw-Hill.

Schwartz, S., & Maquet, P. (2002). Sleep imaging and the neuropsychological assessment of dreams. *Trends in Cognitive Sciences, 6,* 23–30.

Schwartzman, A. E., Gold, D., & Andres, D. (1987). Stability of intelligence: A 40-year follow-up. *Canadian Journal of Psychology, 41,* 244–256.

Schwarz, N. (2012). Feelings-as-information theory. In P. A. M. Van Lange, A. W. Kruglanski, & E. T. Higgins (Eds.), *Handbook of theories of social psychology* (Vol. 1, pp. 289–308). Thousand Oaks, CA: SAGE.

Schwarz, N., & Clore, G. L. (1983). Mood, misattribution, and judgments of well-being: Informative and directive functions of affective states. *Journal of Personality and Social Psychology, 45,* 513–523.

Schwarz, N., Mannheim, Z., & Clore, G. L. (1988). How do I feel about it? The informative function of affective states. In K. Fiedler & J. Forgas (Eds.), *Affect cognition and social behavior: New evidence and integrative attempts* (pp. 44–62). Toronto: C. J. Hogrefe.

Schweizer, T. A., Ware, J., Fischer, C. E., Craik, F. I. M., & Bialystok, E. (2012). Bilingualism as a contributor to cognitive reserve: Evidence from brain atrophy in Alzheimer's disease. *Cortex, 48,* 991–996.

Scoville, W. B., & Milner, B. (1957). Loss of recent memory after bilateral hippocampal lesions. *Journal of Neurology, Neurosurgery, and Psychiatry, 20,* 11–21.

Scribner, S. (1975). Recall of classical syllogisms: A cross-cultural investigation of errors on logical problems. In R. J. Falmagne (Ed.), *Reasoning: Representation and process in children and adults* (pp. 153–173). Hillsdale, NJ: Erlbaum.

Scribner, S. (1984). Studying working intelligence. In B. Rogoff & J. Lave (Eds.), *Everyday cognition: Its development in social context* (pp. 9–40). Cambridge, MA: Harvard University Press.

Sedlmeier, P., Eberth, J., Schwarz, M., Zimmermann, D., Haarig, F., Jaeger, S., & Kunze, S. (2012). The psychological effects of meditation: A meta-analysis. *Psychological Bulletin, 138,* 1139–1171.

Seeman, T. E., Dubin, L. F., & Seeman, M. (2003). Religiosity/spirituality and health: A critical review of the evidence for biological pathways. *American Psychologist, 58,* 53–63.

Segall, M. H., Lonner, W. J., & Berry, J. W. (1998). Cross-cultural psychology as a scholarly discipline: On the flowering of culture in behavioral research. *American Psychologist, 53*(10), 1101–1110.

Sehulster, J. R. (1989). Content and temporal structure of autobiographical knowledge: Remembering twenty-five seasons at the Metropolitan Opera. *Memory & Cognition, 17,* 590–596.

Seidman, G. (2013). Self-presentation and belonging on Facebook: How personality influences social media use and motivations. *Personality and Individual Differences, 54,* 402–407.

Seligman, M. E. P. (1971). Phobias and preparedness. *Behavior Therapy, 2,* 307–320.

Seligman, M. E. P. (1995). The effectiveness of psychotherapy: The consumer reports study. *American Psychologist, 48,* 966–971.

Selikoff, I. J., Robitzek, E. H., & Ornstein, G. G. (1952). Toxicity of hydrazine derivatives of isonicotinic acid in the chemotherapy of human tuberculosis. *Quarterly Bulletin of SeaView Hospital, 13,* 17–26.

Selye, H., & Fortier, C. (1950). Adaptive reaction to stress. *Psychosomatic Medicine, 12,* 149–157.

Semenza, C. (2009). The neuropsychology of proper names. *Mind & Language, 24,* 347–369.

Semenza, C., & Zettin, M. (1989). Evidence from aphasia for the role of proper names as pure referring expressions. *Nature, 342,* 678–679.

Senghas, A., Kita, S., & Ozyurek, A. (2004). Children create core properties of language: Evidence from an emerging sign language in Nicaragua. *Science, 305,* 1782.

Senior, J. (2014). *All joy and no fun: The paradox of modern parenthood.* New York: Harper-Collins.

Senju, A., Maeda, M., Kikuchi, Y., Hasegawa, T., Tojo, Y., & Osanai, H. (2007). Absence of contagious yawning in children with autism spectrum disorder. *Biology Letters, 3*(6), 706–708.

Senju, A., Southgate, V., Snape, C., Leonard, M., & Csibra, G. (2011). Do 18-month-olds really attribute mental states to others? A critical test. *Psychological Science, 22*(7), 878–880. doi: 10.1177/0956797611411584

Senju, A., Southgate, V., White, S., & Frith, U. (2009). Mindblind eyes: An absence of spontaneous theory of mind in Asperger syndrome. *Science, 325,* 883–885.

Serpell, R. (1974). Aspects of intelligence in a developing country. *African Social Research, 17,* 578–596.

Seybold, K. S., & Hill, P. C. (2001). The role of religion and spirituality in mental and physical health. *Current Directions in Psychological Science, 10,* 21–23.

Seymour, K., Clifford, C. W. G., Logothetis, N. K., & Bartels, A. (2010). Coding and binding of color and form in visual cortex. *Cerebral Cortex, 20*(8), 1946–1954. doi: 10.1093/cercor/bhp265

Shafritz, K. M., Gore, J. C., & Marois, R. (2002). The role of the parietal cortex in visual feature binding. *Proceedings of the National Academy of Sciences, USA, 99,* 10917–10922.

Shah, J. Y., Higgins, E. T., & Friedman, R. S. (1998). Performance incentives and means: How regulatory focus influences goal attainment. *Journal of Personality and Social Psychology, 74,* 285–293.

Shahaeian, A., Peterson, C. C., Slaughter, V., & Wellman, H. M. (2011). Culture and the sequence of steps in theory of mind development. *Developmental Psychology, 47*(5), 1239–1247. doi: 10.1037/a0023899

Shallcross, A. J., Ford, B. Q, Floerke, V. A., & Mauss, I. B. (2013). Getting better with age: The relationship between age, acceptance, and negative affect. *Journal of Personality and Social Psychology, 104*(4), 734–749. doi: 10.1037/a0031180

Shallice, T., Fletcher, P., Frith, C. D., Grasby, P., Frackowiak, R. S. J., & Dolan, R. J. (1994). Brain regions associated with acquisition and retrieval of verbal episodic memory. *Nature, 368,* 633–635.

Shariff, A. F., & Tracy, J. L. (2011). What are emotion expressions for? *Current Directions in Psychological Science, 20*(6), 395–399.

Sharot, T. (2011). *The optimism bias: A tour of the irrationally positive brain.* New York: Pantheon Books.

Shaw, J. & Porter, S. (2015). Constructing rich false memories of committing crime. *Psychological Science, 26,* 291–301.

Shaw, J. S., Bjork, R. A., & Handal, A. (1995). Retrieval-induced forgetting in an eyewitness paradigm. *Psychonomic Bulletin & Review, 13,* 1023–1027.

Shedler, J. (2010). The efficacy of psychodynamic psychotherapy. *American Psychologist, 65,* 98–109.

Sheehan, P. (1979). Hypnosis and the process of imagination. In E. Fromm & R. S. Shor (Eds.), *Hypnosis: Developments in research and new perspectives* (pp. 293–319). Chicago: Aldine.

Sheese, B. E., & Graziano, W. G. (2005). Deciding to defect: The effects of video-game violence on cooperative behavior. *Psychological Science, 16,* 354–357.

Shen, H., Wan, F., & Wyer, R. S. (2011). Cross-cultural differences in the refusal to accept a small gift: The differential influence of reciprocity norms on Asians and North Americans. *Journal of Personality and Social Psychology, 100*(2), 271–281. doi: 10.1037/a0021201

Shepherd, G. M. (1988). *Neurobiology.* New York: Oxford University Press.

Shepperd, J., Malone, W., & Sweeny, K. (2008). Exploring the causes of the self-serving bias. *Social and Personality Psychology Compass, 2*(2), 895–908.

Sherry, S. B., & Hall, P. A. (2009). The perfectionism model of binge eating: Tests of an integrative model. *Journal of Personality and Social Psychology, 96*(3), 690–709.

Shiffman, S., Gnys, M., Richards, T. J., Paty, J. A., & Hickcox, M. (1996). Temptations to smoke after quitting: A comparison of lapsers and maintainers. *Health Psychology, 15,* 455–461.

Shih, M., Pittinsky, T. L., & Ambady, N. (1999). Stereotype susceptibility: Identity salience and shifts in quantitative performance. *Psychological Science, 10,* 80–83.

Shimamura, A. P., & Squire, L. R. (1987). A neuropsychological study of fact memory and source amnesia. *Journal of Experimental Psychology: Learning, Memory, and Cognition, 13,* 464–473.

Shin, H., & Ryan, A. M. (2014). Early adolescent friendships and academic adjustment: Examining selection and influence processes with longitudinal social network analysis. *Developmental Psychology, 50*(11), 2462–2472. doi: 10.1037/a0037922

Shin, L. M., Rauch, S. L., & Pitman, R. K. (2006). Amygdala, medial prefrontal cortex, and hippocampal function in PTSD. *Annals of the New York Academy of Science, 1071,* 67–79.

Shinskey, J. L., & Munakata, Y. (2005). Familiarity breeds searching. *Psychological Science, 16*(8), 596–600.

Shipstead, Z., Redick, T. S., & Engle, R. W. (2012). Is working memory training effective? *Psychological Bulletin, 138,* 628–654.

Shiv, B., Loewenstein, G., Bechara, A., Damasio, H., & Damasio, A. R. (2005). Investment behavior and the negative side of emotion. *Psychological Science, 16,* 435–439.

Shomstein, S., & Yantis, S. (2004). Control of attention shifts between vision and audition in human cortex. *Journal of Neuroscience, 24,* 10702–10706.

Shore, C. (1986). Combinatorial play: Conceptual development and early multiword speech. *Developmental Psychology, 22,* 184–190.

Shultz, S., & Dunbar, R. (2012). Encephalization is not a universal macroevolutionary phenomenon in mammals but is associated with sociality. *Proceedings of the National Academy of Sciences,107,* 21582–21586.

Shweder, R. A. (1991). *Thinking through cultures: Expeditions in cultural psychology.* Cambridge, MA: Harvard University Press.

Shweder, R. A., & Sullivan, M. A. (1993). Cultural psychology: Who needs it? *Annual Review of Psychology, 44,* 497–523.

Siegel, A., Roeling, T. A. P., Gregg, T. R., & Kruk, M. R. (1999). Neuropharmacology of brain-stimulation-evoked aggression. *Neuroscience and Biobehavioral Reviews, 23,* 359–389.

Siegel, E. H., Sands, M. K., Condon, P., Chang, Y., Dy, J., Quigley, K. S., & Barrett, L. F. (2015). Emotion fingerprints or emotion populations? A meta-analytic investigation of autonomic features of emotion categories. Unpublished manuscript.

Siegel, S. (1976). Morphine analgesia tolerance: Its situational specificity supports a Pavlovian conditioning model. *Science, 193,* 323–325.

Siegel, S. (1984). Pavlovian conditioning and heroin overdose: Reports by overdose victims. *Bulletin of the Psychonomic Society, 22,* 428–430.

Siegel, S. (2005). Drug tolerance, drug addiction, and drug anticipation. *Current Directions in Psychological Science, 14,* 296–300.

Siegel, S., Baptista, M. A. S., Kim, J. A., McDonald, R. V., & Weise-Kelly, L. (2000). Pavlovian psychopharmacology: The associative basis of tolerance. *Experimental and Clinical Psychopharmacology, 8,* 276–293.

Sigman, M., Spence, S. J., & Wang, T. (2006). Autism from developmental and neuropsychological perspectives. *Annual Review of Clinical Psychology, 2,* 327–355.

Sigurdsson, T., Doyere, V., Cain, C. K., & LeDoux, J. E. (2007). Long-term potentiation in the amygdala: A cellular mechanism of fear learning and memory. *Neuropharmacology, 52,* 215–227.

Silvani, A., Calandra-Buonaura, G., Dampney, R. A., & Cortelli, P. (2016). Brain-heart interactions: Physiology and clinical implications. *Philosophical Transactions of the Royal Society, A,* 347 doi: 10.1098/rsta.2015.0181

Silverman, A. M., Gwinn, J. D., & Van Boven, L. (2014). Stumbling in their shoes: Disability simulations reduce judged capabilities of disabled people. *Social Psychological and Personality Science, 6*(4), 464–471. doi: 10.1177/1948550614559650

Simon, L. (1998). *Genuine reality: A life of William James.* New York: Harcourt Brace.

Simon, R. W. (2008). The joys of parenthood reconsidered. *Contexts, 7,* 40–45.

Simons, D. J., & Chabris, C. F. (1999). Gorillas in our midst: Sustained inattentional blindness for dynamic events. *Perception, 28,* 1059–1074.

Simons, D. J., & Levin, D. T. (1998). Failure to detect changes to people during a real-world interaction. *Psychonomic Bulletin & Review, 5,* 644–649.

Simons, D. J., & Rensink, R. A. (2005). Change blindness: Past, present, and future. *Trends in Cognitive Sciences, 9,* 16–20.

Simonton, D. K. (2006). Presidential IQ, openness, intellectual brilliance, and leadership: Estimates and correlations for 42 U.S. chief executives. *Political Psychology, 27*(4), 511–526. doi: 10.1111/j.1467-9221.2006.00524.x

Simonton, D. K. (2014). The mad-genius paradox: Can creative people be more mentally healthy but highly creative people more mentally ill? *Perspectives on Psychological Science, 9*(5), 470–480. doi: 10.1177/1745691614543973

Simpson, A., & Riggs, K. J. (2011). Three- and 4-year-olds encode modeled actions in two ways leading to immediate imitation and delayed emulation. *Developmental Psychology, 47*(3), 834–840. doi: 10.1037/a0023270

Simpson, E. L. (1974). Moral development research: A case study of scientific cultural bias. *Human Development, 17,* 81–106.

Simpson, J. A., Campbell, B., & Berscheid, E. (1986). The association between romantic love and marriage: Kephart (1967) twice revisited. *Personality and Social Psychology Bulletin, 12,* 363–372.

Simpson, J. A., Collins, W. A., & Salvatore, J. E. (2011). The impact of early interpersonal experience on adult romantic relationship functioning: Recent findings from the Minnesota Longitudinal Study of Risk and Adaptation. *Current Directions in Psychological Science, 20*(6), 355–359. doi: 10.1177/0963721411418468

Simpson, J. A., Collins, W. A., Tran, S., & Haydon, K. C. (2007). Attachment and the experience and expression of emotions in romantic relationships: A developmental perspective. *Journal of Personality and Social Psychology, 92*(2), 355–367. doi: 10.1037/0022-3514.92.2.355

Simpson, S. J., & Raubenheimer, D. (2014). Perspective: Tricks of the trade. *Nature, 508,* S66. doi: 10.1038/508S66a

Singer, P. (1975). *Animal liberation: A new ethics for our treatment of animals.* New York: Random House.

Singer, T., Seymour, B., O'Doherty, J., Kaube, H., Dolan, R. J., & Frith, C. D. (2004). Empathy for pain involves the affective but not sensory components of pain. *Science, 303,* 1157–1162.

Singh, D. (1993). Adaptive significance of female physical attractiveness: Role of waist-to-hip ratio. *Journal of Personality and Social Psychology, 65,* 293–307.

Sirois, F. M. (2015). Is procrastination a vulnerability factor for hypertension and cardiovascular disease? Testing an extension of the procrastination–health model. *Journal of Behavioral Medicine, 38,* 578–589.

Siu, A. L., & U.S. Preventive Services Task Force. (2016). Screening for Autism Spectrum Disorder in young children: U.S. Preventive Services Task Force recommendation statement. *JAMA, 315,* 691–696.

Skinner, B. F. (1938). *The behavior of organisms: An experimental analysis.* New York: Appleton-Century-Crofts.

Skinner, B. F. (1948). "Superstition" in the pigeon. *Journal of Experimental Psychology, 38,* 168–172.

Skinner, B. F. (1950). Are theories of learning necessary? *Psychological Review, 57,* 193–216.

Skinner, B. F. (1953). *Science and human behavior.* New York: Macmillan.

Skinner, B. F. (1957). *Verbal behavior.* New York: Appleton-Century-Crofts.

Skinner, B. F. (1958). Teaching machines. *Science, 129,* 969–977.

Skinner, B. F. (1971). *Beyond freedom and dignity.* New York: Bantam Books.

Skinner, B. F. (1972). The operational analysis of psychological terms. In B. F. Skinner, *Cumulative record* (3rd ed., pp. 370–384). New York: Appleton-Century-Crofts. (Original work published 1945)

Skinner, B. F. (1979). *The shaping of a behaviorist: Part two of an autobiography.* New York: Knopf.

Skinner, B. F. (1986). *Walden II.* Englewood Cliffs, NJ: Prentice Hall. (Original work published 1948)

Skoe, E. & Kraus, N. (2013). Musical training heightens auditory brainstem function during sensitive periods in development. *Frontiers in Psychology, 4,* 622. doi: 10.3389/fpsyg.2013.00622

Skoe, E., Krizman, J., Anderson, S., & Kraus, N. (2015). Stability and plasticity of auditory brainstem function across the lifespan. *Cerebral Cortex, 25,* 1415–1426.

Skotko, B. G., Levine, S. P., & Goldstein, R. (2011). Self-perceptions from people with Down syndrome. *American Journal of Medical Genetics Part A, 155*(10), 2360–2369. doi: 10.1002/ajmg.a.34235

Slagter, H. A. (2012). Conventional working memory training may not improve intelligence. *Trends in Cognitive Sciences, 16,* 582–583.

Slater, A., Morison, V., & Somers, M. (1988). Orientation discrimination and cortical function in the human newborn. *Perception, 17,* 597–602.

Slotnick, S. D., & Schacter, D. L. (2004). A sensory signature that distinguished true from false memories. *Nature Neuroscience, 7,* 664–672.

Smart, E., Smart, L., & Morton, L. (2003). *Bringing Elizabeth home: A journey of faith and hope.* New York: Doubleday.

Smetacek, V. (2002). Balance: Mind-grasping gravity. *Nature, 415,* 481.

Smetana, J. G. (1981). Preschool children's conceptions of moral and social rules. *Child Development, 52,* 1333–1336.

Smetana, J. G., & Braeges, J. L. (1990). The development of toddlers' moral and conventional judgments. *Merrill-Palmer Quarterly, 36,* 329–346.

Smith, A. R., Chein, J., & Steinberg, L. (2014). Peers increase adolescent risk taking even when the probabilities of negative outcomes are known. *Developmental Psychology, 50*(5), 1564–1568. doi: 10.1037/a0035696

Smith, A. R., Seid, M. A., Jimanez, L. C., & Wcislo, W. T. (2010). Socially induced brain development in a facultatively eusocial sweat bee *Megalopta genalis* (Halictidae). *Proceedings of the Royal Society B: Biological Sciences.* doi: 10.1098/rspb .2010.0269

Smith, C. N., Frascino, J. C., Hopkins, R. O., & Squire, L. R. (2013). The nature of anterograde and retrograde impairment after damage to the medial temporal lobe. *Neuropsychologia, 51,* 2709–2714.

Smith, E. E., & Jonides, J. (1997). Working memory: A view from neuroimaging. *Cognitive Psychology, 33,* 5–42.

Smith, M. L., Glass, G. V., & Miller, T. I. (1980). *The benefits of psychotherapy.* Baltimore: Johns Hopkins University Press.

Smith, N., & Tsimpli, I.-M. (1995). *The mind of a savant.* Oxford: Oxford University Press.

Snedeker, J., Geren, J., & Shafto, C. (2007). Starting over: International adoption as a natural experiment in language development. *Psychological Science, 18,* 79–87.

Snedeker, J., Geren, J., & Shafto, C. (2012). Disentangling the effects of cognitive development and linguistic expertise: A longitudinal study of the acquisition of English in internationally adopted children. *Cognitive Psychology, 65,* 39–76.

Sneed, J. R. (2005). Models of the aging self. *Journal of Social Issues, 61*(2), 375–388.

Soderstrom, N. C., & Bjork, R. A. (2014). Testing facilitates the regulation of subsequent study time. *Journal of Memory and Language, 73,* 99–115.

Sodian, B., & Kristen-Antonow, S. (2015). Declarative joint attention as a foundation of theory of mind. *Developmental Psychology, 51*(9), 1190–1200. doi: 10.1037/dev0000039

Sokol-Hessner, P., Lackovic, S. F., Tobe, R. H., Camerer, C. F., Leventhal, B. L., & Phelps, E. A. (2015). Determinants of propanolol's selective effect on loss aversion. *Psychological Science, 26,* 1123–1130.

Solomon, J., & George, C. (1999). The measurement of attachment security in infancy and childhood. In J. Cassidy & P. R. Shaver (Eds.), *Handbook of attachment: Theory, research and clinical applications* (pp. 287–316). New York: Guilford Press.

Solomon, S., Greenberg, J., & Pyszczynski, T. (1991). A terror management theory of social behavior: The psychological functions of self-esteem and cultural worldviews. In M. P. Zanna (Ed.), *Advances in experimental social psychology* (Vol. 24, pp. 93–159). New York: Academic Press.

Solomon, S., Greenberg, J., & Pyszczynski, T. (2004). The cultural animal: Twenty years of terror management theory and research. In J. Greenberg, S. L. Koole, & T. Pyszczynski (Eds.), *Handbook of experimental existential psychology* (pp. 13–34). New York: Guilford Press.

Somerville, L. H., Jones, R. M., Ruberry, E. J., Dyke, J. P., Glover, G., & Casey, B. J. (2013). The medial prefrontal cortex and the emergence of self-conscious emotion in adolescence. *Psychological Science, 24*(8), 1554–1562. doi: 10.1177/0956797613475633

Son, L. K., & Metcalfe, J. (2000). Metacognitive and control strategies in study-time allocation. *Journal of Experimental Psychology: Learning, Memory, and Cognition, 26,* 204–221.

Sonnby-Borgstrom, M., Jonsson, P., & Svensson, O. (2003). Emotional empathy as related to mimicry reactions at different levels of information processing. *Journal of Nonverbal Behavior, 27,* 3–23.

Southgate, V., Senju, A., & Csibra, G. (2007). Action anticipation through attribution of false belief by two-year-olds. *Psychological Science, 18,* 587–592.

Sparrow, B., Liu, J., & Wegner, D. M. (2011). Google effects on memory: Cognitive consequence of having information at our fingertips. *Science, 333,* 776–778.

Spearman, C. (1904). "General intelligence," objectively determined and measured. *American Journal of Psychology, 15,* 201–293.

Speisman, J. C., Lazarus, R. S., Moddkoff, A., & Davison, L. (1964). Experimental reduction of stress based on ego-defense theory. *Journal of Abnormal and Social Psychology, 68,* 367–380.

Spelke, E. S. (2005). Sex differences in intrinsic aptitude for mathematics and science: A critical review. *The American Psychologist, 60*(9), 950–958. doi: 10.1037/0003-066X.60.9.950

Spencer, L. G. (1929). *Illustrated phrenology: The science and art teaching how to read character; A manual of mental science.* London: L. N. Fowler & Company.

Sperling, G. (1960). The information available in brief visual presentations. *Psychological Monographs, 74*(11), 1–29.

Sperry, R. W. (1964). The great cerebral commissure. *Scientific American, 210,* 42–52.

Spielmann, S. S., MacDonald, G., Maxwell, J. A., Joel, S., Peragine, D., Muise, A., & Impett, E. A. (2013). Settling for less out of fear of being single. *Journal of Personality and Social Psychology, 105*(6), 1049–1073. doi: 10.1037/a0034628

Spinoza, B. (1982). *The ethics and selected letters* (S. Feldman, Ed., & S. Shirley, Trans.). Indianapolis: Hackett. (Original work published 1677)

Spitz, R. A. (1949). Motherless infants. *Child Development, 20,* 145–155.

Sprecher, S. (1999). "I love you more today than yesterday": Romantic partners' perceptions of changes in love and related affect over time. *Journal of Personality and Social Psychology, 76,* 46–53.

Spunt, R. P., Meyer, M. L., & Lieberman, M. D. (2015). The default mode of human brain function primes the intentional stance. *Journal of Cognitive Neuroscience, 27*(6), 1116–1124. doi: 10.1162/jocn_a_00785

Squire, L. R. (1992). Memory and the hippocampus: A synthesis from findings with rats, monkeys, and humans. *Psychological Review, 99*, 195–231.

Squire, L. R. (2009). The legacy of patient HM for neuroscience. *Neuron, 61*, 6–9.

Squire, L. R., & Kandel, E. R. (1999). *Memory: From mind to molecules.* New York: Scientific American Library.

Squire, L. R., Knowlton, B., & Musen, G. (1993). The structure and organization of memory. *Annual Review of Psychology, 44*, 453–495.

Squire, L. R., & Wixted, J. T. (2011). The cognitive neuroscience of memory since HM. *Annual Review of Neuroscience, 34*, 259–288.

Srivistava, S., John, O. P., Gosling, S. D., & Potter, J. (2003). Development of personality in early and middle adulthood: Set like plaster or persistent change? *Journal of Personality and Social Psychology, 84*, 1041–1053.

Sroufe, L. A., Egeland, B., & Kruetzer, T. (1990). The fate of early experience following developmental change: Longitudinal approaches to individual adaptation in childhood. *Child Development, 61*, 1363–1373.

Staddon, J. E. R., & Simmelhag, V. L. (1971). The "superstition" experiment: A reexamination of its implications for the principles of adaptive behavior. *Psychological Review, 78*, 3–43.

Stahl, A. E., & Feigenson, L. (2015). Observing the unexpected enhances infants' learning and exploration. *Science, 348*(6230), 91–94. doi: 10.1126/science.aaa3799

St. Jacques, P. L., & Schacter, D. L. (2013). Modifying memory: Selectively enhancing and updating personal memories for a museum tour by reactivating them. *Psychological Science, 24*, 537–543.

Stanca, L. (2016). The geography of well-being: Do children make us happy, where, and why? *World Happiness Report.* Retrieved from http://worldhappiness.report/

Stanovich, K. E. (2009). *What intelligence tests miss: The psychology of rational thought.* New Haven, CT: Yale University Press.

Stanovich, K. E., & West, R. F. (2000). Individual differences in reasoning: Implications for the rationality debate? *Behavioral and Brain Sciences, 23*, 645–726.

Statton, M. A., Encarnacion, M., Celnik, P., & Bastian, A. J. (2015). A single bout of moderate aerobic exercise improves motor skill acquisition. *PLoS One.* doi: 10.1371/journal.pone.0141393

Staw, B. M., & Hoang, H. (1995). Sunk costs in the NBA: Why draft order affects playing time and survival in professional basketball. *Administrative Science Quarterly, 40*, 474–494.

Steele, C. M., & Aronson, J. (1995). Stereotype threat and the intellectual test performance of African Americans. *Journal of Personality and Social Psychology, 69*, 797–811.

Steele, C. M., & Josephs, R. A. (1990). Alcohol myopia: Its prized and dangerous effects. *American Psychologist, 45*, 921–933.

Steele, H., Steele, M., Croft, C., & Fonagy, P. (1999). Infant-mother attachment at one year predicts children's understanding of mixed emotions at six years. *Social Development, 8*, 161–178.

Stein, D. J., Phillips, K. A., Bolton, D., Fulford, K. W. M., Sadler, J. Z., & Kendler, K. S. (2010). What is a mental/ psychiatric disorder? From *DSM–IV* to *DSM–V. Psychological Medicine, 40*(11), 1759–1765. doi:10.1017/S0033291709992261.

Stein, M., Federspiel, A., Koenig, T., Wirth, M., Lehmann, C., Wiest, R., . . . Dierks, T. (2009). Reduced frontal activation with increasing second language proficiency. *Neuropsychologia, 47*, 2712–2720.

Stein, M. B. (1998). Neurobiological perspectives on social phobia: From affiliation to zoology. *Biological Psychiatry, 44*, 1277–1285.

Stein, M. B., Chavira, D. A., & Jang, K. L. (2001). Bringing up bashful baby: Developmental pathways to social phobia. *Psychiatric Clinics of North America, 24*, 661–675.

Steinbaum, E. A., & Miller, N. E. (1965). Obesity from eating elicited by daily stimulation of hypothalamus. *American Journal of Physiology, 208*, 1–5.

Steinberg, L. (1999). *Adolescence* (5th ed.). Boston: McGraw-Hill.

Steinberg, L. (2007). Risk taking in adolescence: New perspectives from brain and behavioral science. *Current Directions in Psychological Science, 16*(2), 55–59. doi: 10.1111/j.1467-8721.2007.00475x

Steinberg, L., & Monahan, K. C. (2007). Age differences in resistance to peer influence. *Developmental Psychology, 43*, 1531–1543.

Steinberg, L., & Morris, A. S. (2001). Adolescent development. *Annual Review of Psychology, 52*, 83–110.

Steiner, F. (1986). Differentiating smiles. In E. Branniger-Huber & F. Steiner (Eds.), *FACS in psychotherapy research* (pp.139–148). Zurich: Universität Zürich, Department of Clinical Psychology.

Steiner, J. E. (1973). The gustofacial response: Observation on normal and anencephalic newborn infants. In J. F. Bosma (Ed.), *Fourth symposium on oral sensation and perception: Development in the fetus and infant* (DHEW 73–546; pp. 254–278). Bethesda, MD: U.S. Department of Heath, Education, and Welfare.

Steiner, J. E. (1979). Human facial expressions in response to taste and smell stimulation. *Advances in Child Development and Behavior, 13*, 257–295.

Stellar, J. R., Kelley, A. E., & Corbett, D. (1983). Effects of peripheral and central dopamine blockade on lateral hypothalamic self-stimulation: Evidence for both reward and motor deficits. *Pharmacology, Biochemistry, and Behavior, 18*, 433–442.

Stellar, J. R., & Stellar, E. (1985). *The neurobiology of motivation and reward.* New York: Springer-Verlag.

Stelmack, R. M. (1990). Biological bases of extraversion: Psychophysiological evidence. *Journal of Personality, 58*, 293–311.

Stephens, R. S. (1999). Cannabis and hallucinogens. In B. S. McCrady & E. E. Epstein (Eds.), *Addictions: A comprehensive guidebook* (pp. 121–140). New York: Oxford University Press.

Sterelny, K., & Griffiths, P. E. (1999). *Sex and death: An introduction to philosophy of biology.* Chicago: University of Chicago Press.

Stern, J. A., Brown, M., Ulett, A., & Sletten, I. (1977). A comparison of hypnosis, acupuncture, morphine, Valium, aspirin, and placebo in the management of experimentally induced pain. In W. E. Edmonston (Ed.), *Conceptual and investigative approaches to hypnosis and hypnotic phenomena* (Vol. 296, pp. 175–193). New York: New York Academy of Sciences.

Stern, W. (1914). *The psychological methods of testing intelligence* (G. M. Whipple, Trans.). Baltimore: Warwick & York.

Sternberg, R. J. (1986). A triangular theory of love. *Psychological Review, 93*, 119–135.

Sternberg, R. J. (1999). The theory of successful intelligence. *Review of General Psychology, 3*(4), 292–316. doi: 10.1037/1089-2680.3.4.292

Sternberg, R. J. (2006). The Rainbow Project: Enhancing the SAT through assessments of analytical, practical, and creative skills. *Intelligence, 34*(4), 321–350. doi: 10.1016/j.intell.2006.01.002

Sternberg, R. J., & Grigorenko, E. L. (2004). Intelligence and culture: How culture shapes what intelligence means, and the implications for a science of well-being. *Philosophical Transaction of the Royal Society B*, 1427–1434. doi: 10.1093/acprof: oso/9780198567523.003.0014

Stevens, G., & Gardner, S. (1982). *The women of psychology* (Vol. 1). Rochester: Schenkman Books.

Stevens, J. (1988). An activity approach to practical memory. In M. M. Gruneberg, P. E. Morris, & R. N. Sykes (Eds.), *Practical aspects of memory: Current research and issues* (Vol. 1, pp. 335–341). New York: Wiley.

Stevens, L. A. (1971). *Explorers of the brain.* New York: Knopf.

Stevenson, R. J., & Boakes, R. A. (2003). A mnemonic theory of odor perception. *Psychological Review, 110,* 340–364.

Stevenson, R. J., & Wilson, D. A. (2007). Odour perception: An object-recognition approach. *Perception, 36,* 1821–1833.

Stewart-Williams, S. (2004). The placebo puzzle: Putting together the pieces. *Health Psychology, 23,* 198–206.

Stickgold, R., Hobson, J. A., Fosse, R., & Fosse, M. (2001). Sleep, learning, and dreams: Off-line memory reprocessing. *Science, 294,* 1052–1057.

Stickgold, R., Malia, A., Maguire, D., Roddenberry, D., & O'Connor, M. (2000). Replaying the game: Hypnagogic images in normals and anmesics. *Science, 290,* 350–353.

Stigler, J. W., Shweder, R., & Herdt, G. (Eds.). (1990). *Cultural psychology: Essays on comparative human development.* Cambridge: Cambridge University Press.

Stone, A. A., Schwartz, J. E., Broderick, J. E., & Deaton, A. (2010). A snapshot of the age distribution of psychological well-being in the United States. *Proceedings of the National Academy of Sciences, USA, 107*(22), 9985–9990. doi: 10.1073/pnas.1003744107

Stone, J., Perry, Z. W., & Darley, J. M. (1997). "White men can't jump": Evidence for the perceptual confirmation of racial stereotypes following a basketball game. *Basic and Applied Social Psychology, 19,* 291–306.

Stoodley, C. J., Ray, N., J., Jack, A., & Stein, J. F. (2008). Implicit learning in control, dyslexic, and garden-variety poor readers. *Annals of the New York Academy of Sciences, 1145,* 173–183.

Storm, B. C., Bjork, E. L., Bjork, R. A., & Nestojko, J. F. (2006). Is retrieval success a necessary condition for retrieval-induced forgetting? *Psychonomic Bulletin & Review, 2,* 249–253.

Storm, B. C., & Stone, S. M. (2015). Saving-enhanced memory: The benefits of saving on the learning and remembering of new information. *Psychological Science, 26,* 182–188.

Storms, M. D. (1973). Videotape and the attribution process: Reversing actors' and observers' points of view. *Journal of Personality and Social Psychology, 27,* 165–175.

Strack, F., Martin, L. L., & Stepper, S. (1988). Inhibiting and facilitating conditions of the human smile: A nonobtrusive test of the facial feedback hypothesis. *Journal of Personality and Social Psychology, 54,* 768–777.

Strayer, D. L., Drews, F. A., & Johnston, W. A. (2003). Cell phone–induced failures of visual attention during simulated driving. *Journal of Experimental Psychology: Applied, 9,* 23–32.

Streissguth, A. (2007). Offspring effects of prenatal alcohol exposure from birth to 25 years: The Seattle Prospective Longitudinal Study. *Journal of Clinical Psychology in Medical Settings, 14*(2), 81–101. doi: 10.1007/s10880-007-9067-6

Streissguth, A. P., Barr, H. M., Bookstein, F. L., Sampson, P. D., & Carmichael Olson, H. (1999). The long-term neurocognitive consequences of prenatal alcohol exposure: A 14-year study. *Psychological Science, 10,* 186–190.

Striano, T., & Reid, V. M. (2006). Social cognition in the first year. *Trends in Cognitive Sciences, 10*(10), 471–476.

Strickland, L. H. (1991). Russian and Soviet social psychology. *Canadian Psychology, 32,* 580–595.

Striegel-Moore, R. H., & Bulik, C. M. (2007). Risk factors for eating disorders. *American Psychologist, 62,* 181–198.

Strohmetz, D. B., Rind, B., Fisher, R., & Lynn, M. (2002). Sweetening the till: The use of candy to increase restaurant tipping. *Journal of Applied Social Psychology, 32,* 300–309.

Stroop, J. P. (1935). Studies of interference in serial verbal reactions. *Journal of Experimental Psychology, 18,* 643–661.

Strueber, D., Lueck, M., & Roth, G. (2006). The violent brain. *Scientific American Mind, 17,* 20–27.

Stuss, D. T., & Benson, D. F. (1986). *The frontal lobes.* New York: Raven Press.

Substance Abuse and Mental Health Services Administration. (2005). *Results from the 2004 National Survey on Drug Use and Health: National findings* (DHHS Publication No. SMA 05-4062, NSDUH Series H-28). Rockville, MD: U.S. Department of Health and Human Services.

Suchman, A. L., Markakis, K., Beckman, H. B., & Frankel, R. (1997). A model of empathic communication in the medical interview. *Journal of the American Medical Association, 277,* 678–682.

Suddendorf, T., & Corballis, M. C. (2007). The evolution of foresight: What is mental time travel and is it unique to humans? *Behavioral and Brain Sciences, 30,* 299–313.

Suderman, M., McGowan, P. O., Sasaki, A., Huang, T. C. T., Hallett, M. T., Meaney, M. J., . . . Szyf, M. (2012). Conserved epigenetic sensitivity to early life experiences in the rat and human hippocampus. *Proceedings of the National Academy of Sciences, USA, 109*(Suppl. 2), 17266–17272.

Sulloway, F. J. (1992). *Freud, biologist of the mind.* Cambridge, MA: Harvard University Press.

Sundet, J. M., Eriksen, W., & Tambs, K. (2008). Intelligence correlations between brothers decrease with increasing age difference: Evidence for shared environmental effects in young adults. *Psychological Science, 19,* 843–847.

Sunstein, S. (2015, September 19). Making government logical. *New York Times.* Retrieved from http://www.nytimes.com/2015/09/20/opinion/sunday/cass-sunstein-making-government-logicalhtml.html

Suri, G., Whittaker, K., & Gross, J. J. (2015). Launching reappraisal: It's less common than you might think. *Emotion, 15*(1), 73–77. doi: 10.1037/emo0000011

Susman, S., Dent, C., McAdams, L., Stacy, A., Burton, D., & Flay, B. (1994). Group self-identification and adolescent cigarette smoking: A 1-year prospective study. *Journal of Abnormal Psychology, 103,* 576–580.

Susser, E. B., Brown, A., & Matte, T. D. (1999). Prenatal factors and adult mental and physical health. *Canadian Journal of Psychiatry, 44*(4), 326–334.

Suthana, N., & Fried, I. (2012). Percepts to recollections: Insights from single neuron recordings in the human brain. *Trends in Cognitive Sciences, 16,* 427–436.

Sutin, A. R., Stephan, Y., & Terracciano, A. (2015). Weight discrimination and risk of mortality. *Psychological Science, 26*(11), 1803–1811. http://doi.org/10.1177/0956797615601103

Suzuki, L. A., & Valencia, R. R. (1997). Race–ethnicity and measured intelligence: Educational implications. *American Psychologist, 52,* 1103–1114.

Swami, V., Pietschnig, J., Bertil, B., Nader, I. W., Stieger, S., & Voracek, M. (2012) Personality differences between tattooed and non-tattooed individuals. *Psychological Reports: Mental & Physical Health, 111,* 97–106.

Swami, V., & Tovée, M. J. (2008). The muscular male: A comparison of the physical attractiveness preferences of gay and heterosexual men. *International Journal of Men's Health, 7*(1), 59–71. doi: 10.3149/jmh.0701.59

Swann, W. B. Jr. (1983). Self-verification: Bringing social reality into harmony with the self. In J. M. Suls & A. G. Greenwald (Eds.), *Psychological perspectives on the self* (Vol. 2, pp. 33–66). Hillsdale, NJ: Erlbaum.

Swann, W. B. Jr. (2012). Self-verification theory. In P. Van Lang, A. Kruglanski, & E. T. Higgins (Eds.), *Handbook of theories of social psychology* (pp. 23–42). London: Sage.

Swann, W. B., Jr., & Rentfrow, P. J. (2001). Blirtatiousness: Cognitive, behavioral, and physiological consequences of rapid responding. *Journal of Personality and Social Psychology, 181*(6), 1160–1175.

Swayze, V. W., II. (1995). Frontal leukotomy and related psychosurgical procedures before antipsychotics (1935–1954): A historical overview. *American Journal of Psychiatry, 152,* 505–515.

Swednsen, J., Hammen, C., Heller, T., & Gitlin, M. (1995). Correlates of stress reactivity in patients with bipolar disorder. *American Journal of Psychiatry, 152,* 795–797.

Sweeny, K., Carroll, P. J., & Shepperd, J. A. (2006). Is optimism always best? Future outlooks and preparedness. *Current Directions in Psychological Science, 15,* 302–306.

Swencionis, J. K., & Fiske, S. T. (2016) Promote up, ingratiate down: Status comparisons drive warmth-competence tradeoffs in impression management. *Journal of Experimental Social Psychology, 64,* 27–34.

Swets, J. A., Dawes, R. M., & Monahan, J. (2000). Psychological science can improve diagnostic decisions. *Psychological Science in the Public Interest, 1,* 1–26.

Swinkels, A. (2003). An effective exercise for teaching cognitive heuristics. *Teaching of Psychology, 30,* 120–122.

Szechtman, H., & Woody, E. Z. (2006). Obsessive-compulsive disorder as a disturbance of security motivation: Constraints on comorbidity. *Neurotoxicity Research, 10,* 103–112.

Szpunar, K. K. (2010). Episodic future thought: An emerging concept. *Perspectives on Psychological Science, 5,* 142–162.

Szpunar, K. K., Khan, N. Y., & Schacter, D. L. (2013). Interpolated memory tests reduce mind wandering and improve learning of online lectures. *Proceedings of the National Academy of Sciences, USA, 110,* 6313–6317.

Szpunar, K. K., Watson, J. M., & McDermott, K. B. (2007). Neural substrates of envisioning the future. *Proceedings of the National Academy of Sciences, USA, 104,* 642–647.

Tajfel, H., Billig, M. G., Bundy, R. P., & Flament, C. (1971). Social categorization and intergroup behaviour. *European Journal of Social Psychology, 1,* 149–178.

Tajfel, H., & Turner, J. C. (1986). The social identity theory of intergroup behavior. In S. Worchel & W. G. Austin (Eds.), *Psychology of intergroup relations* (pp. 7–24). Chicago: Nelson.

Tajfel, H., & Wilkes, A. L. (1963). Classification and quantitative judgement. *British Journal of Psychology, 54,* 101–114.

Takahashi, K. (1986). Examining the Strange Situation procedure with Japanese mothers and 12-month-old infants. *Developmental Psychology, 22,* 265–270.

Tamir, M., Bigman, Y. E., Rhodes, E., Salerno, J., & Schreier, J. (2015). An expectancy-value model of emotion regulation: Implications for motivation, emotional experience, and decision making. *Emotion, 15*(1), 90–103. http://doi.org/10.1037/emo0000021

Tamir, M., & Ford, B. Q. (2012). Should people pursue feelings that feel good or feelings that do good? Emotional preferences and well-being. *Emotion, 12,* 1061–1070.

Tamminga, C. A., Nemeroff, C. B., Blakely, R. D., Brady, L., Carter, C. S., Davis, K. L., . . . Suppes, T. (2002). Developing novel treatments for mood disorders: Accelerating discovery. *Biological Psychiatry, 52,* 589–609.

Tanaka, F., Cicourel, A., & Movellan, J. R. (2007). Socialization between toddlers and robots at an early childhood education center. *Proceedings of the National Academy of Sciences, USA, 104*(46), 17954–17958.

Tang, D. W., Fellows, L. K., & Dagher, A. (2014). Behavioral and neural valuation of foods is driven by implicit knowledge of caloric content. *Psychological Science, 25*(12), 2168–2176. doi: 10.1177/0956797614552081

Tang, G., Gudsnuk, K., Kuo, S.-H., Cotrina, M. L., Rosoklija, G., Sosunov, A., . . . Sulzer, D. (2014). Loss of mTOR-dependent macroautophagy causes autistic-like synaptic pruning deficits. *Neuron, 83*(5), 1131–43. doi: 10.1016/j.neuron.2014.07.040

Tang, Y.-P., Shimizu, E., Dube, G. R., Rampon, C., Kerchner, G. A., Zhuo, M., . . . Tsien, J. Z. (1999). Genetic enhancement of learning and memory in mice. *Nature, 401,* 63–69.

Tang, Y. Y., Lu, Q., Fan, M., Yang, Y., & Posner, M. I. (2012). Mechanisms of white matter changes induced by meditation. *Proceedings of the National Academy of Sciences,109,* 10570–10574.

Tarantino, N., Tully, E. C., Garcia, S. E., South, S., Iacono, W. G., & McGue, M. (2014). Genetic and environmental influences on affiliation with deviant peers during adolescence and early adulthood. *Developmental Psychology, 50*(3), 663–673. doi: 10.1037/a0034345

Tarr, M. J., & Vuong, Q. C. (2002). Visual object recognition. In S. Yantis & H. Pashler (Eds.), *Stevens' handbook of experimental psychology: Vol. 1. Sensation and perception* (3rd ed., pp. 287–314). New York: Wiley.

Tart, C. T. (Ed.). (1969). *Altered states of consciousness.* New York: Wiley.

Task Force on Promotion and Dissemination of Psychological Procedures. (1995). Training in and dissemination of empirically validated psychological treatments: Report and recommendations. *Clinical Psychologist, 48,* 3–23.

Taylor, D., & Lambert, W. (1990). *Language and culture in the lives of immigrants and refugees.* Austin, TX: Hogg Foundation for Mental Health.

Taylor, E. (2001). *William James on consciousness beyond the margin.* Princeton, NJ: Princeton University Press.

Taylor, S. E. (1989). *Positive illusions.* New York: Basic Books.

Taylor, S. E. (2002). *The tending instinct: How nurturing is essential to who we are and how we live.* New York: Times Books.

Taylor, S. E., & Brown, J. D. (1988). Illusion and well-being: A social psychological perspective on mental health. *Psychological Bulletin, 103,* 193–210.

Taylor, S. E., & Fiske, S. T. (1975). Point-of-view and perceptions of causality. *Journal of Personality and Social Psychology, 32,* 439–445.

Teasdale, J. D., Segal, Z. V., & Williams, J. M. G. (2000). Prevention of relapse/recurrence in major depression by mindfulness-based cognitive therapy. *Journal of Consulting and Clinical Psychology, 68,* 615–623.

Telch, M. J., Lucas, J. A., & Nelson, P. (1989). Non-clinical panic in college students: An investigation of prevalence and symptomology. *Journal of Abnormal Psychology, 98,* 300–306.

Tellegen, A., & Atkinson, G. (1974). Openness to absorbing and self-altering experiences ("absorption"), a trait related to hypnotic susceptibility. *Journal of Abnormal Psychology, 83,* 268–277.

Tellegen, A., Lykken, D. T., Bouchard, T. J., Wilcox, K., Segal, N., & Rich, A. (1988). Personality similarity in twins reared together and apart. *Journal of Personality and Social Psychology, 54,* 1031–1039.

Terman, L. M. (1916). *The measurement of intelligence.* Boston: Houghton Mifflin.

Terman, L. M., & Oden, M. H. (1959). *Genetic studies of genius: Vol. 5. The gifted group at mid-life.* Stanford, CA: Stanford University Press.

Tesser, A. (1991). Emotion in social comparison and reflection processes. In J. Suls & T. A. Wills (Ed.), *Social comparison: Contemporary theory and research* (pp. 117–148). Hillsdale, NJ: Erlbaum.

Teuscher, U., & Teuscher, C. (2007). Reconsidering the double standard of aging: Effects of gender and sexual orientation on facial attractiveness ratings. *Personality and Individual Differences, 42*(4), 631–639. doi: 10.1016/j.paid.2006.08.020

Tews, M. J., Stafford, K., & Tracey, J. B. (2011) What matters most? The perceived importance of ability and personality for hiring decisions. *Cornell Hospitality Quarterly, 52,* 94–101.

Teyler, T. J., & DiScenna, P. (1986). The hippocampal memory indexing theory. *Behavioral Neuroscience, 100,* 147–154.

Thaker, G. K. (2002). Current progress in schizophrenia research. Search for genes of schizophrenia: Back to defining valid phenes. *Journal of Nervous and Mental Disease, 190,* 411–412.

Thaler, K., Delivuk, M., Chapman, A., Gaynes, B. N., Kaminski, A., & Gartlehner, G. (2011). Second-generation antidepressants for seasonal affective disorder. *Cochrane Database of Systematic Reviews, CD008591.*

Thaler, R. H. (1988). The ultimatum game. *Journal of Economic Perspectives, 2,* 195–206.

Thase, M. E., & Howland, R. H. (1995). Biological processes in depression: An updated review and integration. In E. E. Beckham & W. R. Leber (Eds.), *Handbook of depression* (2nd ed., pp. 213–279). New York: Guilford Press.

Thibaut, J. W., & Kelley, H. H. (1959). *The social psychology of groups.* New York: Wiley.

Thoma, S. J., Narvaez, D., Rest, J., & Derryberry, P. (1999). Does moral judgment development reduce to political attitudes or verbal ability? Evidence using the defining issues test. *Educational Psychology Review, 11,* 325–341.

Thomaes, S., Bushman, B. J., Stegge, H., & Olthof, T. (2008). Trumping shame by blasts of noise: Narcissism, self-esteem, shame, and aggression in young adolescents. *Child Development, 79*(6), 1792–1801.

Thomas, A., & Chess, S. (1977). *Temperament and development.* New York: Brunner/Mazel.

Thomason, M., & Thompson, P. M. (2011). Diffusion imaging, white matter, and psychopathology. *Annual Review of Clinical Psychology, 7,* 63–85.

Thompson, B., Coronado, G., Chen, L., Thompson, L. A., Halperin, A., Jaffe, R., . . . Zbikowski, S. M. (2007). Prevalence and characteristics of smokers at 30 Pacific Northwest colleges and universities. *Nicotine & Tobacco Research, 9,* 429–438.

Thompson, C. P., Skowronski, J., Larsen, S. F., & Betz, A. (1996). *Autobiographical memory: Remembering what and remembering when.* Mahwah, NJ: Erlbaum.

Thompson, P. M., Giedd, J. N., Woods, R. P., MacDonald, D., Evans, A. C., & Toga, A. W. (2000). Growth patterns in the developing brain detected by using continuum mechanical tensor maps. *Nature, 404,* 190–193.

Thompson, P. M., Vidal, C., Giedd, J. N., Gochman, P., Blumenthal, J., Nicolson, R., . . . Rapoport, J. L. (2001). Accelerated gray matter loss in very early-onset schizophrenia. *Proceedings of the National Academy of Sciences, USA, 98,* 11650–11655.

Thompson, R. F. (2005). In search of memory traces. *Annual Review of Psychology, 56,* 1–23.

Thomson, D. M. (1988). Context and false recognition. In G. M. Davies & D. M. Thomson (Eds.), *Memory in context: Context in memory* (pp. 285–304). Chichester, UK: Wiley.

Thorndike, E. L. (1898). Animal intelligence: An experimental study of associative processes in animals. *Psychological Review Monograph Supplements, 2,* i–109.

Thornhill, R., & Gangestad, S. W. (1993). Human facial beauty: Averageness, symmetry, and parasite resistance. *Human Nature, 4,* 237–269.

Thornhill, R., & Gangestad, S. W. (1999). The scent of symmetry: A human sex pheromone that signals fitness? *Evolution and Human Behavior, 20,* 175–201.

Thurber, J. (1956). *Further fables of our time.* New York: Simon & Schuster.

Thurstone, L. L. (1938). *Primary mental abilities.* Chicago: University of Chicago Press.

Tice, D. M., & Baumeister, R. F. (1997). Longitudinal study of procrastination, performance, stress, and health: The costs and benefits of dawdling. *Psychological Science, 8*(6), 454–458.

Tienari, P., Wynne, L. C., Sorri, A., Lahti, I., Läksy, K., Moring, J., . . . Wahlberg, K. E. (2004). Genotype–environment interaction in schizophrenia-spectrum disorder: Long-term follow-up study of Finnish adoptees. *British Journal of Psychiatry, 184,* 216–222.

Tierney, A. T., Krizman, J., & Kraus, N. (2015). Music training alters the course of adolescent auditory development. *Proceedings of the National Academy of Science, 112,* 10062–10067.

Timmerman, T. A. (2007). "It was a thought pitch": Personal, situational, and target influences on hit-by-pitch events across time. *Journal of Applied Psychology, 92,* 876–884.

Titchener, E. B. (1896). *An outline of psychology.* New York: Macmillan.

Todd, A. R., Bodenhausen, G. V., Richeson, J. A., & Galinsky, A. D. (2011). Perspective taking combats automatic expressions of racial bias. *Journal of Personality and Social Psychology, 100*(6), 1027–1042. doi: 10.1037/a0022308

Todd, J. T., & Morris, E. K. (1992). Case histories in the great power of steady misrepresentation. *American Psychologist, 47*(11), 1441–1453.

Toga, A. W., Clark, K. A., Thompson, P. M., Shattuck, D. W., & Van Horn, J. D. (2012). Mapping the human connectome. *Neurosurgery, 71,* 1–5.

Tolin, D. F. (2010). Is cognitive-behavioral therapy more effective than other therapies? A meta-analytic review. *Clinical Psychology Review, 30,* 710–720.

Tolman, E. C., & Honzik, C. H. (1930a). "Insight" in rats. *University of California Publications in Psychology, 4,* 215–232.

Tolman, E. C., & Honzik, C. H. (1930b). Introduction and removal of reward and maze performance in rats. *University of California Publications in Psychology, 4,* 257–275.

Tolman, E. C., Ritchie, B. F., & Kalish, D. (1946). Studies in spatial learning: I: Orientation and short cut. *Journal of Experimental Psychology, 36,* 13–24.

Tomasello, M., & Call, J. (2004). The role of humans in the cognitive development of apes revisited. *Animal Cognition, 7,* 213–215.

Tomasello, M., Davis-Dasilva, M., Camak, L., & Bard, K. (1987). Observational learning of tool use by young chimpanzees. *Human Evolution, 2,* 175–183.

Tomasello, M., Savage-Rumbaugh, S., & Kruger, A. C. (1993). Imitative learning of actions on objects by children, chimpanzees, and enculturated chimpanzees. *Child Development, 64,* 1688–1705.

Tomkins, S. S. (1981). The role of facial response in the experience of emotion. *Journal of Personality and Social Psychology, 40,* 351–357.

Tooby, J., & Cosmides, L. (2000). Mapping the evolved functional organization of mind and brain. In M. S. Gazzaniga (Ed.), *The cognitive neurosciences* (pp. 1185–1198). Cambridge, MA: MIT Press.

Tootell, R. B. H., Reppas, J. B., Dale, A. M., Look, R. B., Sereno, M. I., Malach, R., . . . Rosen, B. R. (1995). Visual-motion aftereffect in human cortical area MT revealed by functional magnetic resonance imaging. *Nature, 375,* 139–141.

Torgensen, S. (1986). Childhood and family characteristics in panic and generalized anxiety disorder. *American Journal of Psychiatry, 143,* 630–639.

Torrey, E. F., Bower, A. E., Taylor, E. H., & Gottesman, I. I. (1994). *Schizophrenia and manic-depressive disorder: The biological roots of mental illness as revealed by the landmark study of identical twins.* New York: Basic Books.

Tracy, J. L., & Beall, A. T. (2011). Happy guys finish last: The impact of emotion expressions on sexual attraction. *Emotion, 11*(6), 1379–1387. doi: 10.1037/a0022902

Tracy, J. L., Randles, D., & Steckler, C. M. (2015). The nonverbal communication of emotions. *Current Opinion in Behavioral Sciences, 3,* 25–30.

Tracy, J. L., Shariff, A. F., Zhao, W., & Henrich, J. (2013). Cross-cultural evidence that the noverbal expression of pride is an automatic status signal. *Journal of Experimental Psychology: General, 142*(1), 163–180.

Tranter, L. J., & Koutstaal, W. (2007). Age and flexible thinking: An experimental demonstration of the beneficial effects of increased cognitively stimulating activity on fluid intelligence in healthy older adults. *Neuropsychology, Development, and Cognition. Section B, Aging, Neuropsychology and Cognition, 15,* 184–207.

Treede, R. D., Kenshalo, D. R., Gracely, R. H., & Jones, A. K. (1999). The cortical representation of pain. *Pain, 79,* 105–111.

Treisman, A. (1998). Feature binding, attention and object perception. *Philosophical Transactions of the Royal Society B, 353,* 1295–1306.

Treisman, A. (2006). How the deployment of attention determines what we see. *Visual Cognition, 14,* 411–443.

Treisman, A., & Gelade, G. (1980). A feature integration theory of attention. *Cognitive Psychology, 12,* 97–136.

Treisman, A., & Schmidt, H. (1982). Illusory conjunctions in the perception of objects. *Cognitive Psychology, 14,* 107–141.

Trivers, R. L. (1972). Parental investment and sexual selection. In B. Campbell (Ed.), *Sexual selection and the descent of man, 1871–1971* (pp. 139–179). Chicago: Aldine.

Trull, T. J., & Durrett, C. A. (2005). Categorical and dimensional models of personality disorder. *Annual Review of Clinical Psychology, 1,* 355–380.

Tucker, E. (2003, June 25). Move over, Fido! Chickens are becoming hip suburban pets. *USA Today.* Retrieved from http://usatoday30.usatoday.com/money/2003-06-25-pet-chickens_x.htm

Tucker-Drob, E. M., & Bates, T. C. (2016). Large cross-national differences in Gene × Socioeconomic Status interaction on intelligence. *Psychological Science, 27*(2), 138–149. doi: 10.1177/0956797615612727

Tucker-Drob, E. M., Briley, D. A., & Harden, K. P. (2013). Genetic and environmental influences on cognition across development and context. *Current Directions in Psychological Science, 22*(5), 349–355. doi: 10.1177/0963721413485087

Tucker-Drob, E. M., Rhemtulla, M., Harden, K. P., Turkheimer, E., & Fask, D. (2010). Emergence of a Gene × Socioeconomic Status interaction on infant mental ability between 10 months and 2 years. *Psychological Science, 22*(1), 125–133. doi: 10.1177/0956797610392926

Tuerlinckx, F., De Boeck, P., & Lens, W. (2002). Measuring needs with the Thematic Apperception Test: A psychometric study. *Journal of Personality and Social Psychology, 82,* 448–461.

Tulving, E. (1972). Episodic and semantic memory. In E. Tulving & W. Donaldson (Eds.), *Organization of memory* (pp. 381–403). New York: Academic Press.

Tulving, E. (1983). *Elements of episodic memory.* Oxford: Clarendon Press.

Tulving, E. (1985). Memory and consciousness. *Canadian Psychologist, 25,* 1–12.

Tulving, E. (1998). Neurocognitive processes of human memory. In C. von Euler, I. Lundberg, & R. Llins (Eds.), *Basic mechanisms in cognition and language* (pp. 261–281). Amsterdam: Elsevier.

Tulving, E., Kapur, S., Craik, F. I. M., Moscovitch, M., & Houle, S. (1994). Hemispheric encoding/retrieval asymmetry in episodic memory: Positron emission tomography findings. *Proceedings of the National Academy of Sciences, USA, 91,* 2016–2020.

Tulving, E., & Pearlstone, Z. (1966). Availability versus accessibility of information in memory for words. *Journal of Verbal Learning and Verbal Behavior, 5,* 381–391.

Tulving, E., & Schacter, D. L. (1990). Priming and human memory systems. *Science, 247,* 301–306.

Tulving, E., Schacter, D. L., & Stark, H. (1982). Priming effects in word-fragment completion are independent of recognition memory. *Journal of Experimental Psychology: Learning, Memory, and Cognition, 8,* 336–342.

Tulving, E., & Thompson, D. M. (1973). Encoding specificity and retrieval processes in episodic memory. *Psychological Review, 80,* 352–373.

Turiel, E. (1998). The development of morality. In N. Eisenberg (Ed.), *Handbook of child psychology: Vol. 3. Social, emotional and personality development* (pp. 863–932). New York: Wiley.

Turkheimer, E., Haley, A., Waldron, M., D'Onofrio, B., & Gottesman, I. I. (2003). Socioeconomic status modifies heritability of IQ in young children. *Psychological Science, 14,* 623–628.

Turner, D. C., Robbins, T. W., Clark, L., Aron, A. R., Dowson, J., & Sahakian, B. J. (2003). Cognitive enhancing effects of modafinil in healthy volunteers. *Psychopharmacology, 165,* 260–269.

Turner, D. C., & Sahakian, B. J. (2006). Neuroethics of cognitive enhancement. *BioSocieties, 1,* 113–123.

Turner, E. H., Matthews, A. M., Linardatos, E., Tell, R. A., & Rosenthal, R. (2008). Selective publication of antidepressant trials and its influence on apparent efficacy. *New England Journal of Medicine, 358,* 252–260.

Turner, M. E., & Pratkanis, A. R. (1998). Twenty-five years of groupthink theory and research: Lessons from the evaluation of a theory. *Organizational Behavior and Human Decision Processes, 73*(2–3), 105–115. doi: 10.1006/obhd.1998.2756

Tversky, A., & Kahneman, D. (1973). Availability: A heuristic for judging frequency and probability. *Cognitive Psychology, 5,* 207–232.

Tversky, A., & Kahneman, D. (1974). Judgment under uncertainty: Heuristics and biases. *Science, 185,* 1124–1131.

Tversky, A., & Kahneman, D. (1981). The framing of decisions and the psychology of choice. *Science, 211,* 453–458.

Tversky, A., & Kahneman, D. (1983). Extensional versus intuitive reasoning: The conjunction fallacy in probability judgment. *Psychological Review, 90,* 293–315.

Tversky, A., & Kahneman, D. (1992). Advances in prospect theory: Cumulative representation of uncertainty. *Journal of Risk and Uncertainty, 5,* 297–323.

Twenge, J. M., Campbell, W. K., & Foster, C. A. (2003). Parenthood and marital satisfaction: A meta-analytic review. *Journal of Marriage and Family, 65,* 574–583.

Tyler, T. R. (1990). *Why people obey the law.* New Haven, CT: Yale University Press.

U.S. Census Bureau. (2012). *The 2012 statistical abstract: National data book.* Washington, DC: Author.

Umberson, D., Williams, K., Powers, D. A., Liu, H., & Needham, B. (2006). You make me sick: Marital quality and health over the life course. *Journal of Health and Social Behavior, 47,* 1–16.

Uncapher, M. R., & Rugg, M. D. (2008). Fractionation of the component processes underlying successful episodic encoding: A combined fMRI and divided-attention study. *Journal of Cognitive Neuroscience, 20,* 240–254.

Ungerleider, L. G., & Mishkin, M. (1982). Two cortical visual systems. In D. J. Ingle, M. A. Goodale, & R. J. W. Mansfield (Eds.), *Analysis of visual behavior* (pp. 549–586). Cambridge, MA: MIT Press.

Urban, N. B. L., Girgis, R. R., Talbot, P. S., Kegeles, L. S., Xu, X., Frankie, W. G., . . . Laruelle, M. (2012). Sustained recreational use of ecstasy is associated with altered pre- and postsynaptic markers of serotonin transmission in neocortical areas: A PET study with [11c] DASB and [11c] MDL 100907. *Neuropsychopharmacology, 37,* 1465–1473.

Ursano, R. J., & Silberman, E. K. (2003). Psychoanalysis, psychoanalytic psychotherapy, and supportive psychotherapy. In R. E. Hales & S. C. Yudofsky (Eds.), *The American Psychiatric Publishing textbook of clinical psychiatry* (4th ed., pp. 1177–1203). Washington, DC: American Psychiatric Publishing.

Uskul, A. K., & Over, H. (2014). Responses to social exclusion in cultural context: Evidence from farming and herding communities. *Journal of Personality and Social Psychology, 106*(5), 752–771. doi: 10.1037/a0035810

Vacha, E., & McBride, M. (1993). Cramming: A barrier to student success, a way to beat the system, or an effective strategy? *College Student Journal, 27,* 2–11.

Vafaei, A., Ahmed, T., Falcão Freire A., Zunzunegui, M. V., & Guerra, R. O. (2016) Depression, sex and gender roles in older adult populations: The international mobility in aging studies (IMIAS). *PLoS ONE, 11,* e0146867.

Valentine, T., Brennen, T., & Brédart, S. (1996). *The cognitive psychology of proper names: On the importance of being Ernest.* London: Routledge.

Valentová, J., Roberts, S. C., & Havlíček, J. (2013). Preferences for facial and vocal masculinity in homosexual men: The role of relationship status, sexual restrictiveness, and self-perceived masculinity. *Perception, 42* (2), 187–197. doi: 10.1068/p6909

Vallacher, R. R., & Wegner, D. M. (1985). *A theory of action identification.* Hillsdale, NJ: Erlbaum.

Vallacher, R. R., & Wegner, D. M. (1987). What do people think they're doing? Action identification and human behavior. *Psychological Review, 94,* 3–15.

Vallender, E. J., Mekel-Bobrov, N., & Lahn, B. T. (2008). Genetic basis of human brain evolution. *Trends in Neurosciences, 31,* 637–644.

van Anders, S. M. (2012). Testosterone and sexual desire in healthy women and men. *Archives of Sexual Behavior, 41,* 1471–1484.

van den Boom, D. C. (1994). The influence of temperament and mothering on attachment and exploration: An experimental manipulation of sensitive responsiveness among lower-class mothers with irritable infants. *Child Development, 65,* 1457–1477.

van den Boom, D. C. (1995). Do first year intervention effects endure? Follow-up during toddlerhood of a sample of Dutch irritable infants. *Child Development, 66,* 1798–1816.

van Dis, I., Kromhout, D., Geleijnse, J. M., Boer, J. M. A., & Verschuren, W. M. M. (2009). Body mass index and waist circumference predict both 10-year nonfatal and fatal cardiovascular disease risk: Study conducted in 20,000 Dutch men and women aged 20–65 years. *European Journal of Cardiovascular Prevention & Rehabilitation, 16*(6), 729–734.

Van Dongen, E. V., Thielen, J.-W., Takashima, A., Barth, M., & Fernandez, G. (2012). Sleep supports selective retention of associative memories based on relevance for future utilization. *PLoS One, 7,* e43426. doi: 10.1371/journal.pone.0043426

Van Gog, T., Kester, L., Dirkx, K., Hoogerheide, V., Boerboom, J., & Verkoeijen, P. P. J. L. (2015). Testing after worked example study does not enhance delayed problem-solving performance compared to restudy. *Educational Psychology Review, 27,* 265–289.

van Honk, J., & Schutter, D. J. L. G. (2007). Testosterone reduces conscious detection of signals serving social correction: Implications for antisocial behavior. *Psychological Science, 18,* 663–667.

van IJzendoorn, M. H., Juffer, F., & Klein Poelhuis, C. W. (2005). Adoption and cognitive development: A meta-analytic comparison of adopted and nonadopted children's IQ and school performance. *Psychological Bulletin, 131,* 301–316.

van IJzendoorn, M. H., & Kroonenberg, P. M. (1988). Cross-cultural patterns of attachment: A meta-analysis of the strange situation. *Child Development, 59,* 147–156.

van IJzendoorn, M. H., & Sagi, A. (1999). Cross-cultural patterns of attachment: Universal and contextual dimensions. In J. Cassidy & P. R. Shaver (Eds.), *Handbook of attachment: Theory, research and clinical applications* (pp. 713–734). New York: Guilford Press.

van Ittersum, K., & Wansink, B. (2012). Plate size and color suggestibility: The Delboeuf illusion's bias on serving and eating behavior. *Journal of Consumer Research, 39,* 121–130.

Van Lange, P. A. M., Rinderu, M., & Bushman, B. J. (2016). Aggression and violence around the world: A model of CLimate, Aggression, and Self-control in Humans (CLASH). *Behavioral and Brain Sciences, 23,* 1–63.

Van Laningham, J., Johnson, D. R., & Amato, P. (2001). Marital happiness, marital duration, and the U-shaped curve: Evidence from a five-wave panel study. *Social Forces, 79,* pp. 1313–1341.

van Praag, H. (2009). Exercise and the brain: Something to chew on. *Trends in Neuroscience, 32,* 283–290.

van Stegeren, A. H., Everaerd, W., Cahill, L., McGaugh, J. L., & Gooren, L. J. G. (1998). Memory for emotional events: Differential effects of centrally versus peripherally acting blocking agents. *Psychopharmacology, 138,* 305–310.

Van Vliet, I. M., van Well, E. P., Bruggeman, R., Campo, J. A., Hijman, R., Van Megen, H. J., . . . Van Rijen, P. C. (2013). An evaluation of irreversible psychosurgical treatment of patients with obsessive-compulsive disorder in the Netherlands, 2001–2008. *Journal of Nervous and Mental Disease, 201,* 226–228.

Vargha-Khadem, F., Gadian, D. G., Copp, A., & Mishkin, M. (2005). FOXP2 and the neuroanatomy of speech and language. *Nature Reviews Neuroscience, 6,* 131–138.

Vargha-Khadem, F., Gadian, D. G., Watkins, K. E., Connelly, A., Van Paesschen, W., & Mishkin, M. (1997). Differential effects of early hippocampal pathology on episodic and semantic memory. *Science, 277,* 376–380.

Vazire, S., & Mehl, M. R. (2008). Knowing me, knowing you: The relative accuracy and unique predictive validity of self-ratings and other ratings of daily behavior. *Journal of Personality and Social Psychology, 95,* 1202–1216.

Veldhuizen, M. G., Douglas, D., Aschenbrenner, K., Gitelman, D. R., & Small, D. M. (2011). The anterior insular cortex represents breaches of taste identity expectation. *Journal of Neuroscience, 31,* 14735–14744.

Vinter, A., & Perruchet, P. (2002). Implicit motor learning through observational training in adults and children. *Memory & Cognition, 30,* 256–261.

Vitkus, J. (1999). *Casebook in abnormal psychology* (4th ed.). New York: McGraw-Hill.

Vondra, J. I., Shaw, D. S., Swearingen, L., Cohen, M., & Owens, E. B. (2001). Attachment stability and emotional and behavioral regulation from infancy to preschool age. *Development and Psychopathology, 13,* 13–33.

Von Frisch, K. (1974). Decoding the language of the bee. *Science, 185,* 663–668.

von Stumm, S., & Plomin, R. (2015). Socioeconomic status and the growth of intelligence from infancy through adolescence. *Intelligence, 48,* 30–36. doi: 10.1016/j.intell.2014.10.002

Voon, V., Pessiglione, M., Brezing, C., Gallea, C., Fernandez, H. H., Dolan, R. J., & Hallett, M. (2010). Mechanisms underlying dopamine-mediated reward bias in compulsive behaviors. *Neuron, 65,* 135–142.

Vorster, A. P. & Born, J. (2015). Sleep and memory in mammals, birds and invertebrates. *Neuroscience and Biobehavioral Reviews, 50,* 103–119.

Vortac, O. U., Edwards, M. B., & Manning, C. A. (1995). Functions of external cues in prospective memory. *Memory, 3,* 201–219.

Vrij, A., Granhag, P. A., Mann, S., & Leal, S. (2011). Outsmarting the liars: Toward a cognitive lie detection approach. *Current Directions in Psychological Science, 20*(1), 28–32.

Vukasović, T., & Bratko, D. (2015) Heritability of personality: A meta-analysis of behavior genetic studies. *Psychological Bulletin, 141,* 769–785.

Vygotsky, L. S. (1978). *Mind in society: The development of higher psychological processes.* Cambridge, MA: Harvard University Press.

Wade, N. J. (2005). *Perception and illusion: Historical perspectives.* New York: Springer.

Wade, S. E., Trathen, W., & Schraw, G. (1990). An analysis of spontaneous study strategies. *Reading Research Quarterly, 25,* 147–166.

Wadhwa, P. D., Sandman, C. A., & Garite, T. J. (2001). The neurobiology of stress in human pregnancy: Implications for prematurity and development of the fetal central nervous system. *Progress in Brain Research, 133,* 131–142.

Wager, T., & Atlas, L. Y. (2013). How is pain influenced by cognition? Neuroimaging weighs in. *Perspectives on Psychological Science, 8,* 91–97.

Wager, T. D., Rilling, J., K., Smith, E. E., Sokolik, A., Casey, K. L., Davidson, R. J., . . . Cohen, J. D. (2004). Placebo-induced changes in fMRI in the anticipation and experience of pain. *Science, 303,* 1162–1167.

Wagner, A. D., Schacter, D. L., Rotte, M., Koutstaal, W., Maril, A., Dale, A. M., . . . Buckner, R. L. (1998). Remembering and forgetting of verbal experiences as predicted by brain activity. *Science, 281,* 1188–1190.

Wagner, G., & Morris, E. (1987). Superstitious behavior in children. *Psychological Record, 37,* 471–488.

Wai, J., Putallaz, M., & Makel, M. C. (2012). Studying intellectual outliers: Are there sex differences, and are the smart getting smarter? *Current Directions in Psychological Science, 21*(6), 382–390. doi: 10.1177/0963721412455052

Wakefield, J. C. (2007). The concept of mental disorder: Diagnostic implications of the harmful dysfunction analysis. *World Psychiatry, 6,* 149–56.

Walden, T. A., & Ogan, T. A. (1988). The development of social referencing. *Child Development, 59,* 1230–1240.

Waldfogel, S. (1948). The frequency and affective character of childhood memories. *Psychological Monographs, 62*(4), i–39. doi: 10.1037/h0093581

Walker, C. (1977). Some variations in marital satisfaction. In R. C. J. Peel (Ed.), *Equalities and inequalities in family life* (pp. 127–139). London: Academic Press.

Walker, L. J. (1988). The development of moral reasoning. *Annals of Child Development, 55,* 677–691.

Walker, N. P., McConville, P. M., Hunter, D., Deary, I. J., & Whalley, L. J. (2002). Childhood mental ability and lifetime psychiatric contact. *Intelligence, 30*(3), 233–245. doi: 10.1016/S0160-2896(01)00098-8

Wallace, J., Schnieder, T., & McGuffin, P. (2002). Genetics of depression. In I. H. Gottlieb & C. L. Hammen (Eds.), *Handbook of depression* (pp. 169–191). New York: Guilford Press.

Wallbott, H. G. (1998). Bodily expression of emotion. *European Journal of Social Psychology, 28,* 879–896.

Walster, E., Aronson, V., Abrahams, D., & Rottmann, L. (1966). Importance of physical attractiveness in dating behavior. *Journal of Personality and Social Psychology, 4,* 508–516.

Walster, E., Walster, G. W., & Berscheid, E. (1978). *Equity: Theory and research.* Boston: Allyn & Bacon.

Walton, D. N. (1990). What is reasoning? What is an argument? *Journal of Philosophy, 87,* 399–419.

Walton, G. M., & Spencer, S. J. (2009). Latent ability: Grades and test scores systematically underestimate the intellectual ability of negatively stereotyped students. *Psychological Science, 20,* 1132–1139.

Waltzman, S. B. (2006). Cochlear implants: Current status. *Expert Review of Medical Devices, 3,* 647–655.

Wamsley, E. J., & Stickgold, R. (2011). Memory, sleep, and dreaming: Experiencing consolidation. *Sleep Medicine Clinics, 6,* 97–108.

Wang, J. L., Jackson, L. A., Zhang, D. J., & Su, Z. Q. (2012). The relationships among the Big Five personality factors, self-esteem, narcissism, and sensation seeking to Chinese university students' uses of social networking sites (SNSs). *Computers in Human Behavior, 28,* 2313–2319.

Wang, P. S., Aguilar-Gaxiola, S., Alonso, J., Angermeyer, M. C., Borges, G., Bromet, E. J., . . . Wells, J. E. (2007). Use of mental health services for anxiety, mood, and substance disorders in 17 countries in the WHO World Mental Health Surveys. *Lancet, 370,* 841–850.

Wang, P. S., Berglund, P. A., Olfson, M., & Kessler, R. C. (2004). Delays in initial treatment contact after first onset of a mental disorder. *Health Services Research, 39*, 393–415.

Wang, P. S., Berglund, P., Olfson, M., Pincus, H. A., Wells, K. B., & Kessler, R. C. (2005). Failure and delay in initial treatment contact after first onset of mental disorders in the National Comorbidity Survey Replication. *Archives of General Psychiatry, 62*(6), 629–640.

Wang, P. S., Demler, O., & Kessler, R. C. (2002). Adequacy of treatment for serious mental illness in the United States. *American Journal of Public Health, 92*, 92–98.

Wang, S.-H., & Baillargeon, R. (2008). Detecting impossible changes in infancy: A three-system account. *Trends in Cognitive Sciences, 12*(1), 17–23.

Wang, S. M., Allen, R. J., Lee, J. R., & Hsieh, C. E. (2015). Evaluating the developmental trajectory of the episodic buffer component of working memory and its relation to word recognition in children. *Journal of Experimental Child Psychology, 133*, 16–28.

Wang, W., & Parker, K. (2014). Record share of Americans have never married as values, economics and gender patterns change. Washington, DC: Pew Research Center's Social & Demographic Trends project. Retrieved from http://www.pewsocialtrends.org/2014/09/24/record-share-of-americans-have-never-married/

Wansink, B., & Linder, L. R. (2003). Interactions between forms of fat consumption and restaurant bread consumption. *International Journal of Obesity, 27*, 866–868.

Wansink, B., Painter, J. E., & North, J. (2005). Bottomless bowls: Why visual cues of portion size may influence intake. *Obesity Research, 13*, 93–100.

Wansink, B., & Wansink, C. S. (2010). The largest last supper: Depictions of food portions and plate size increased over the millennium. *International Journal of Obesity, 34*, 943–944.

Ward, B. W., Dahlhamer, J. M., Galinsky, A. M., & Joestl, S. S. (2014). Sexual orientation and health among US adults: National Health Interview Survey, 2013. *National Health Statistics Reports, 15*, 1–10.

Ward, J., Parkin, A. J., Powell, G., Squires, E. J., Townshend, J., & Bradley, V. (1999). False recognition of unfamiliar people: "Seeing film stars everywhere." *Cognitive Neuropsychology, 16*, 293–315.

Warneken, F., & Tomasello, M. (2009). Varieties of altruism in children and chimpanzees. *Trends in Cognitive Sciences, 13*, 397–402.

Warren, K. R., & Hewitt, B. G. (2009). Fetal alcohol spectrum disorders: When science, medicine, public policy, and laws collide. *Developmental Disabilities Research Reviews, 15*, 170–175.

Warren, M. T., Wray-Lake, L., Rote, W. M., & Shubert, J. (2016). Thriving while engaging in risk? Examining trajectories of adaptive functioning, delinquency, and substance use in a nationally representative sample of adolescents. *Developmental Psychology, 52*(2), 296–310. doi: 10.1037/a0039922

Warrington, E. K., & McCarthy, R. A. (1983). Category specific access dysphasia. *Brain, 106*, 859–878.

Warrington, E. K., & Shallice, T. (1984). Category specific semantic impairments. *Brain, 107*, 829–854.

Watanabe, S., Sakamoto, J., & Wakita, M. (1995). Pigeons' discrimination of painting by Monet and Picasso. *Journal of the Experimental Analysis of Behavior, 63*, 165–174.

Waters, T. E. A., Fraley, R. C., Groh, A. M., Steele, R. D., Vaughn, B. E., Bost, K. K., . . . Roisman, G. I. (2015). The latent structure of secure base script knowledge. *Developmental Psychology, 51*(6), 823–830. doi: 10.1037/dev0000012

Watkins, L. R., & Maier, S. F. (2005). Immune regulation of central nervous system functions: From sickness responses to pathological pain. *Journal of Internal Medicine, 257*, 139–155.

Watson, D., & Pennebaker, J. W. (1989). Health complaints, stress, and distress: Exploring the central role of negative affectivity. *Psychological Review, 96*, 234–254.

Watson, D., & Tellegen, A. (1985). Toward a consensual structure of mood. *Psychological Bulletin, 98*, 219–235.

Watson, J. B. (1913). Psychology as the behaviorist views it. *Psychological Review, 20*, 158–177.

Watson, J. B., & Rayner, R. (1920). Conditioned emotional reactions. *Journal of Experimental Psychology, 3*, 1–14.

Watson, R. I. (1978). *The great psychologists.* New York: Lippincott.

Watt, H. J. (1905). Experimentelle Beitraege zu einer Theorie des Denkens [Experimental contributions to a theory of thinking]. *Archiv fuer die gesamte Psychologie, 4*, 289–436.

Watzke, B., Rüddel, H., Jürgensen, R., Koch, U., Kristen, L., Grothgar, B., & Schulz, H. (2012). Longer term outcome of cognitive-behavioural and psychodynamic psychotherapy in routine mental health care: Randomised controlled trial. *Behaviour Research and Therapy, 50*, 580–387.

Weaver, I. C. G., Cervoni, N., Champagne, F. A., D'Alessio, A. C., Sharma, S., Seckl, J. R., . . . Meaney, M. J. (2004). Epigenetic programming by maternal behavior. *Nature Neuroscience, 7*, 847–854.

Webb, T. L., Miles, E., & Sheeran, P. (2012). Dealing with feeling: A meta-analysis of the effectiveness of strategies derived from the process model of emotion regulation. *Psychological Bulletin, 138*(4), 775–808.

Weber, R., & Crocker, J. (1983). Cognitive processes in the revision of stereotypic beliefs. *Journal of Personality and Social Psychology, 45*, 961–977.

Webster Marketon, J. I., & Glaser, R. (2008). Stress hormones and immune function. *Cellular Immunology, 252*, 16–26.

Wechsler, H., & Nelson, T. F. (2001). Binge drinking and the American college student: What's five drinks? *Psychology of Addictive Behaviors, 15*(4), 287–291. doi: 10.1037/0893-164X.15.4.287

Wegner, D. M. (1989). *White bears and other unwanted thoughts.* New York: Viking.

Wegner, D. M. (1994a). Ironic processes of mental control. *Psychological Review, 101*, 34–52.

Wegner, D. M. (1994b). *White bears and other unwanted thoughts: Suppression, obsession, and the psychology of mental control.* New York: Guilford Press.

Wegner, D. M. (1997). Why the mind wanders. In J. D. Cohen & J. W. Schooler (Eds.), *Scientific approaches to consciousness* (pp. 295–315). Mahwah, NJ: Erlbaum.

Wegner, D. M. (2002). *The illusion of conscious will.* Cambridge, MA: MIT Press.

Wegner, D. M. (2009). How to think, say, or do precisely the worst thing for any occasion. *Science, 325*, 48–51.

Wegner, D. M., Ansfield, M., & Pilloff, D. (1998). The putt and the pendulum: Ironic effects of the mental control of action. *Psychological Science, 9*, 196–199.

Wegner, D. M., Broome, A., & Blumberg, S. J. (1997). Ironic effects of trying to relax under stress. *Behavior Research and Therapy, 35*, 11–21.

Wegner, D. M., Erber, R., & Raymond, P. (1991). Transactive memory in close relationships. *Journal of Personality and Social Psychology, 61*, 923–929.

Wegner, D. M., Erber, R. E., & Zanakos, S. (1993). Ironic processes in the mental control of mood and mood-related thought. *Journal of Personality and Social Psychology, 65,* 1093–1104.

Wegner, D. M., & Gilbert, D. T. (2000). Social psychology: The science of human experience. In H. Bless & J. Forgas (Eds.), *The message within: Subjective experience in social cognition and behavior* (pp. 1–9). Philadelphia: Psychology Press.

Wegner, D. M., Schneider, D. J., Carter, S. R., & White, T. L. (1987). Paradoxical effects of thought suppression. *Journal of Personality and Social Psychology, 53,* 5–13.

Wegner, D. M., Vallacher, R. R., Macomber, G., Wood, R., & Arps, K. (1984). The emergence of action. *Journal of Personality and Social Psychology, 46,* 269–279.

Wegner, D. M., & Wenzlaff, R. M. (1996). Mental control. In E. T. Higgins & A. Kruglanski (Eds.), *Social psychology: Handbook of basic mechanisms and processes* (pp. 466–492). New York: Guilford Press.

Wegner, D. M., Wenzlaff, R. M., & Kozak, M. (2004). Dream rebound: The return of suppressed thoughts in dreams. *Psychological Science, 15,* 232–236.

Wegner, D. M., & Zanakos, S. (1994). Chronic thought suppression. *Journal of Personality, 62,* 615–640.

Weiner, W. J., Shulman, L. M., & Lang, A. E. (2013). *Parkinson's disease* (3rd ed.). Baltimore: Johns Hopkins University Press.

Weinstein, N. D. (1980). Unrealistic optimism about future life events. *Journal of Personality and Social Psychology, 39,* 806–820.

Weintraub, D., Papay, K., & Siderowf, A. (2013). Screening for impulse control symptoms in patients with de novo Parkinson disease: A case-control study. *Neurology, 80,* 176–180.

Weir, C., Toland, C., King, R. A., & Martin, L. M. (2005). Infant contingency/extinction performance after observing partial reinforcement. *Infancy, 8,* 63–80.

Weisberg, R. (1999). Creativity and knowledge: A challenge to theories. In R. J. Sternberg (Ed.), *Handbook of creativity* (pp. 226–250). Cambridge: Cambridge University Press.

Weiser, M., Zarka, S., Werbeloff, N., Kravitz, E., & Lubin, G. (2010). Cognitive test scores in male adolescent cigarette smokers compared to non-smokers: A population-based study. *Addiction, 105*(2), 358–363. doi: 10.1111/j.1360-0443.2009.02740.x

Weisfeld, G. (1999). *Evolutionary principles of human adolescence.* New York: Basic Books.

Weiss, K. J., & Curcio Alexander, J. (2013). Sex, lies, and statistics: Inferences from the child sexual abuse accommodation syndrome. *Journal of the American Academy of Psychiatry and the Law, 41,* 412–420.

Weissenborn, R. (2000). State-dependent effects of alcohol on explicit memory: The role of semantic associations. *Psychopharmacology, 149,* 98–106.

Weissman, M. M., Markowitz, J. C., & Klerman, G. L. (2000). *Comprehensive guide to interpersonal psychotherapy.* New York: Basic Books.

Weldon, M. S. (2001). Remembering as a social process. In D. L. Medin (Ed.), *The psychology of learning and motivation: Advances in research and theory* (Vol. 40, pp. 67–120). San Diego, CA: Academic Press.

Wellman, H. M., Fang, F., Liu, D., Zhu, L., & Liu, L. (2006). Scaling theory-of-mind understandings in Chinese children. *Psychological Science, 17,* 1075–1081. doi: 10.1111/j.1467-9280.2006.01830.x

Wenzlaff, R. M., & Wegner, D. M. (2000). Thought suppression. In S. T. Fiske (Ed.), *Annual review of psychology* (Vol. 51, pp. 51–91). Palo Alto, CA: Annual Reviews.

Wernicke, K. (1874). *Der Aphasische Symptomenkomplex* [The aphasic symptom complex]. Breslau: Cohn and Weigart.

Wertheimer, M. (1982). *Productive thinking.* Chicago: University of Chicago Press. (Originally published 1945)

Wesch, N. N., Law, B., & Hall, C. R. (2007). The use of observational learning by athletes. *Journal of Sport Behavior, 30,* 219–231.

Westrin, A., & Lam, R. W. (2007). Seasonal affective disorder: A clinical update. *Journal of Clinical Psychiatry, 19,* 239–246.

Wexler, K. (1999). Maturation and growth of grammar. In W. C. Ritchie & T. K. Bhatia (Eds.), *Handbook of child language acquisition* (pp. 55–110). San Diego: Academic Press.

Whalen, P. J., Rauch, S. L., Etcoff, N. L., McInerney, S. C., Lee, M. B., & Jenike, M. A. (1998). Masked presentations of emotional facial expressions modulate amygdala activity without explicit knowledge. *Journal of Neuroscience, 18,* 411–418.

Whalley, L. J., & Deary, I. J. (2001). Longitudinal cohort study of childhood IQ and survival up to age 76. *British Medical Journal, 322,* 1–5.

Wheatley, T., & Haidt, J. (2005). Hypnotic disgust makes moral judgments more severe. *Psychological Science, 16,* 780–784.

Wheeler, M. A., Petersen, S. E., & Buckner, R. L. (2000). Memory's echo: Vivid recollection activates modality-specific cortex. *Proceedings of the National Academy of Sciences, USA, 97,* 11125–11129.

White, F. J. (1996). Synaptic regulation of mesocorticolimbic dopamine neurons. *Annual Review of Neuroscience, 19,* 405–436.

White, G. M., & Kirkpatrick, J. (Eds.). (1985). *Person, self, and experience: Exploring pacific ethnopsychologies.* Berkeley: University of California Press.

White, N. M., & Milner, P. M. (1992). The psychobiology of reinforcers. *Annual Review of Psychology, 41,* 443–471.

Whitney, D., Ellison, A., Rice, N. J., Arnold, D., Goodale, M., Walsh, V., & Milner, D. (2007). Visually guided reaching depends on motion area MT+. *Cerebral Cortex, 17,* 2644–2649.

Whorf, B. (1956). *Language, thought, and reality.* Cambridge, MA: MIT Press.

Whybrow, P. C. (1997). *A mood apart.* New York: Basic Books.

Wibowo, E., & Wassersurg, R. (2014). Estrogen in men. *American Scientist, 102,* 452–459.

Wicker, B., Keysers, C., Plailly, J., Royet, J.-P., Gallese, V., & Rizzolatti, G. (2003). Both of us disgusted in My insula: The common neural basis of seeing and feeling disgust. *Neuron, 40,* 655–664.

Wicklund, R. (1975). Objective self-awareness. In L. Berkowitz (Ed.), *Advances in experimental social psychology* (Vol. 8, pp. 233–275). New York: Academic Press.

Wiebe, S. A., Fang, H., Johnson, C., James, K. E., & Espy, K. A. (2014). Determining the impact of prenatal tobacco exposure on self-regulation at 6 months. *Developmental Psychology, 50*(6), 1746–1756. doi: 10.1037/a0035904

Wiederman, M. W. (1997). Pretending orgasm during sexual intercourse: Correlates in a sample of young adult women. *Journal of Sex & Marital Therapy, 23,* 131–139.

Wiegner, L., Hange, D., Björkelund, C., & Ahlbrig, G. Jr. (2015). Prevalence of perceived stress and associations to symptoms of exhaustion, depression, and anxiety in a working age population seeking primary care: An observational study. *BMC Family Practice, 16,* 38.

Wiener, D. N. (1996). *B. F. Skinner: Benign anarchist.* Boston: Allyn & Bacon.

Wiesenthal, D. L., Austrom, D., & Silverman, I. (1983). Diffusion of responsibility in charitable donations. *Basic and Applied Social Psychology, 4,* 17–27.

Wig, G. S., Buckner, R. L., & Schacter, D. L. (2009). Repetition priming influences distinct brain systems: Evidence from task-evoked data and resting-state correlations. *Journal of Neurophysiology, 101,* 2632–2648.

Wiggs, C. L., & Martin, A. (1998). Properties and mechanisms of perceptual priming. *Current Opinion in Neurobiology, 8,* 227–233.

Wilcoxon, H. C., Dragoin, W. B., & Kral, P. A. (1971). Illness-induced aversions in rats and quail: Relative salience of visual and gustatory cues. *Science, 171,* 826–828.

Wiley, J. L. (1999). Cannabis: Discrimination of "internal bliss"? *Pharmacology, Biochemistry, & Behavior, 64,* 257–260.

Wilhelm, I., Dieckelmann, S., Molzow, I., Ayoub, A., Molle, M., & Born, J. (2011). Sleep selectively enhances memories expected to be of future relevance. *Journal of Neuroscience, 31,* 1563–1569.

Wilkinson, L., Teo, J. T., Obeso, I., Rothwell, J. C., & Jahanshahi, M. (2010). The contribution of primary motor cortex is essential for probabilistic implicit sequence learning: Evidence from theta burst magnetic stimulation. *Journal of Cognitive Neuroscience, 22,* 427–436.

Williams, A. C. (2002). Facial expression of pain: An evolutionary account. *Behavioral and Brain Sciences, 25,* 439–488.

Williams, C. M., & Kirkham, T. C. (1999). Anandamide induces overeating: Mediation by central cannabinoid (CB1) receptors. *Psychopharmacology, 143,* 315–317.

Williams, K. D. (2007). Ostracism. *Annual Review of Psychology, 58,* 425–452. doi: 10.1146/annurev.psych.58.110405.085641

Williams, K. D., Nida, S. A., Baca, L. D., & Latané, B. (1989). Social loafing and swimming: Effects of identifiability on individual and relay performance of intercollegiate swimmers. *Basic and Applied Social Psychology, 10,* 73–81.

Williams, W. M. & Ceci, S. J. (2015). National hiring experiments reveal 2:1 faculty preference for women on STEM tenure track. *Proceedings of the National Academy of Sciences, 112,* 5360–5365.

Willingham, D. T. (2007). Critical thinking: Why is it so hard to teach? *American Educator, 31*(2), 8–19.

Wilson, K., & Korn, J. H. (2007). Attention during lectures: Beyond ten minutes. *Teaching of Psychology, 34,* 85–89.

Wilson, T. D. (2002). *Strangers to ourselves: Discovering the adaptive unconscious.* Cambridge, MA: Harvard University Press.

Wilson, T. D. (2009). Know thyself. *Perspectives on Psychological Science, 4,* 384–389.

Wilson, T. D. (2011). *Redirect: The surprising new science of psychological change.* New York: Little, Brown.

Wilson, T. D. (2012, July 12). Stop bullying the "soft" sciences. *Los Angeles Times.* Retrieved from http://articles.latimes.com/2012/jul/12/opinion/la-oe-wilson-social-sciences-20120712

Wilson, T. D., & Lassiter, G. D. (1982). Increasing intrinsic interest with superfluous extrinsic constraints. *Journal of Personality and Social Psychology, 42,* 811–819.

Wilson, T. D., Meyers, J., & Gilbert, D. T. (2003). "How happy was I, anyway?" A retrospective impact bias. *Social Cognition, 21,* 421–446.

Wilson, T. D., Reinhard, D. A., Westgate, E. C., Gilbert, D. T., Ellerbeck, N., Hahn, C., . . . Shaked, A. (2014). Just think: The challenges of the disengaged mind. *Science, 345,* 75–77.

Wimber, M., Alink, A., Charest, I., Kriegeskorte, N., & Anderson, M.C. (2015). Retrieval induces adaptive forgetting of competing memories via cortical pattern suppression. *Nature Neuroscience, 18,* 582–589.

Wimber, M., Rutschmann, R. N., Greenlee, M. W., & Bauml, K.-H. (2009). Retrieval from episodic memory: Neural mechanisms of interference resolution. *Journal of Cognitive Neuroscience, 21,* 538–549.

Wimmer, H., & Perner, J. (1983). Beliefs about beliefs: Representations and constraining function of wrong beliefs in young children's understanding of deception. *Cognition, 13,* 103–128.

Winawer, J., Witthoft, N., Frank, M. C., Wu, L., Wade, A. R., & Boroditsky, L. (2007). Russian blues reveal effects of language on color discrimination. *Proceedings of the National Academy of Sciences, USA, 104,* 7780–7785.

Windeler, J., & Kobberling, J. (1986). Empirische Untersuchung zur Einschatzung diagnostischer Verfahren am Beispiel des Haemoccult-Tests [An empirical study of the value of diagnostic procedures using the example of the hemoccult test]. *Klinische Wochenscrhrift, 64,* 1106–1112.

Windham, G. C., Eaton, A., & Hopkins, B. (1999). Evidence for an association between environmental tobacco smoke exposure and birthweight: A meta-analysis and new data. *Pediatrics and Perinatal Epidemiology, 13,* 35–57.

Winkler, A. D., Spillmann, L., Werner, J. S., & Webster, M. A. (2015). Asymmetries in blue-yellow color perception and in the color of 'the dress.' *Current Biology, 25,* R547–R548.

Winner, E. (2000). The origins and ends of giftedness. *American Psychologist, 55,* 159–169.

Winocur, G., Moscovitch, M., & Bontempi, B. (2010). Memory formation and long-term retention in humans and animals: Convergence towards a transformation account of hippocampal–neocortical interactions. *Neuropsychologia, 48,* 2339–2356.

Winter, L., & Uleman, J. S. (1984). When are social judgments made? Evidence for the spontaneousness of trait inferences. *Journal of Personality and Social Psychology, 47,* 237–252.

Winterer, G., & Weinberger, D. R. (2004). Genes, dopamine and cortical signal-to-noise ratio in schizophrenia. *Trends in Neuroscience, 27,* 683–690.

Wise, R. A. (1989). Brain dopamine and reward. *Annual Review of Psychology, 40,* 191–225.

Wise, R. A. (2005). Forebrain substrates of reward and motivation. *Journal of Comparative Neurology, 493,* 115–121.

Wittchen, H., Knauper, B., & Kessler, R. C. (1994). Lifetime risk of depression. *British Journal of Psychiatry, 165,* 16–22.

Wittgenstein, L. (1999). *Philosophical investigations.* Upper Saddle River, NJ: Prentice Hall. (Originally published 1953)

Wixted, J. T., & Ebbensen, E. (1991). On the form of forgetting. *Psychological Science, 2,* 409–415.

Wolf, J. R., Arkes, H. R., & Muhanna, W. A. (2008). The power of touch: An examination of the effect of duration of physical contact on the valuation of objects. *Judgment and Decision Making, 3,* 476–482.

Wolff, P., & Holmes, K. J. (2011). Linguistic relativity. *WIRES Cognitive Science, 2,* 253–265.

Wong, D. T., Bymaster, F. P., & Engleman, E. A. (1995). Prozac (fluoxetine, Lilly 110140), the first selective serotonin uptake inhibitor and an antidepressant drug: Twenty years since its first publication. *Life Sciences, 57,* 411–441.

Wood, A., Rychlowska, M., & Niedenthal, P. M. (2016). Heterogeneity of long-history migration predicts emotion recognition accuracy. *Emotion, 16*(4), 413–420. doi: 1037/emo0000137

Wood, J. M., & Bootzin, R. R. (1990). Prevalence of nightmares and their independence from anxiety. *Journal of Abnormal Psychology, 99,* 64–68.

Wood, J. M., Bootzin, R. R., Rosenhan, D., Nolen-Hoeksema, S., & Jourden, F. (1992). Effects of the 1989 San Francisco earthquake on frequency and content of nightmares. *Journal of Abnormal Psychology, 101,* 219–224.

Woods, S. C., Seeley, R. J., Porte, D., Jr., & Schwartz, M. W. (1998). Signals that regulate food intake and energy homeostasis. *Science, 280,* 1378–1383.

Woody, S. R., & Nosen, E. (2008). Psychological models of phobic disorders and panic. In M. M. Anthony & M. B. Stein (Eds.), *Oxford handbook of anxiety and related disorders* (pp. 209–224). New York: Oxford University Press.

Woody, S. R., & Sanderson, W. C. (1998). Manuals for empirically supported treatments: 1998 update. *Clinical Psychologist, 51,* 17–21.

Woolf, S. H., & Purnell, J. Q. (2016). The good life: Working together to promote opportunity and improve population health and well-being. *Journal of the American Medical Association, 315*(16), 1706–1708. doi: 10.1001/jama.2016.4263.

Woumans, E., Santens, P., Sieben, A., Versijpt, J., Stevens, M., & Duyck, W. (2015). Bilingualism delays clinical manifestation of Alzheimer's disease. *Bilingualism: Language and Cognition, 18,* 568–574.

Wrangham, R., & Peterson, D. (1997). *Demonic males: Apes and the origin of human violence.* New York: Mariner.

Wraw, C., Deary, I. J., Gale, C. R., & Der, G. (2015). Intelligence in youth and health at age 50. *Intelligence, 53* (2015), 23–32.

Wren, A. M., Seal, L. J., Cohen, M. A., Brynes, A. E., Frost, G. S., Murphy, K. G., . . . Bloom, S. R. (2001). Ghrelin enhances appetite and increases food intake in humans. *Journal of Clinical Endocrinology and Metabolism, 86,* 5992–5995.

Wrenn, C. C., Turchi, J. N., Schlosser, S., Dreiling, J. L., Stephenson, D. A., & Crawley, J. N. (2006). Performance of galanin transgenic mice in the 5-choice serial reaction time attentional task. *Pharmacology Biochemistry and Behavior, 83,* 428–440.

Wulf, S. (1994, March 14). Err Jordan. *Sports Illustrated.* Retrieved from http://www.si.com/vault/1994/03/14/130652/err-jordan-try-as-he-might-michael-jordan-has-found-baseball-beyong-his-grasp

Wundt, W. (1900–1920). *Völkerpsychologie. Eine untersuchung der entwicklungsgesetze von sprache, mythos und sitte* [Völkerpsychologie: An examination of the developmental laws of language, myth, and custom]. Leipzig: Engelmann & Kroner.

Yamaguchi, S. (1998). Basic properties of umami and its effects in humans. *Physiology and Behavior, 49,* 833–841.

Yang, S., & Sternberg, R. J. (1997). Conceptions of intelligence in ancient Chinese philosophy. *Journal of Theoretical and Philosophical Psychology, 17,* 101–119.

Yeo, B. T. T., Krienen, F. M., Sepulcre, J., Sabuncu, M. R., Lashkari, D., Hollinshead, M., . . . Buckner, R. L. (2011). The organization of the human cerebral cortex estimated by intrinsic functional connectivity. *Journal of Neurophysiology, 106,* 1125–1165.

Yeshurun, Y., & Sobel, N. (2010). An odor is not worth a thousand words: From multidimensional odors to unidimensional odor objects. *Annual Review of Psychology, 61,* 219–241.

Yik, M., Russell, J. A., & Steiger, J. H. (2011). A 12-point circumplex structure of core affect. *Emotion, 11*(4), 705–731.

Young, J. J., Silber, T., Bruno, D., Galatzer-Levy, I. R., Pomara, N., & Marmar, C. R. (2016). Is there progress? An overview of selecting biomarker candidates for major depressive disorder. *Frontiers in Psychiatry, 7,* 72.

Young, R. M. (1990). *Mind, brain, and adaptation in the nineteenth century: Cerebral localization and its biological context from Gall to Ferrier.* New York: Oxford University Press.

Yu, Y., & Kushnir, T. (2014). Social context effects in 2- and 4-year-olds' selective versus faithful imitation. *Developmental Psychology, 50*(3), 922–933. doi: 10.1037/a0034242

Yucha, C., & Gilbert, C. D. (2004). *Evidence-based practice in biofeedback and neurofeedback.* Colorado Springs: Association for Applied Psychophysiology and Biofeedback.

Yuill, N., & Perner, J. (1988). Intentionality and knowledge in children's judgments of actor's responsibility and recipient's emotional reaction. *Developmental Psychology, 24,* 358–365.

Yzerbyt, V., & Demoulin, S. (2010). Intergroup relations. In S. T. Fiske, D. T. Gilbert, & G. Lindzey (Eds.), *The handbook of social psychology* (5th ed., Vol. 2, pp. 1024–1083). New York: Wiley.

Zahn-Waxler, C., Radke-Yarrow, M., Wagner, E., & Chapman, M. (1992). Development of concern for others. *Developmental Psychology, 28,* 126–136.

Zajonc, R. B. (1968). Attitudinal effects of mere exposure. *Journal of Personality and Social Psychology, 9,* 1–27.

Zajonc, R. B. (1989). Feeling the facial efference: Implications of the vascular theory of emotion. *Psychological Review, 96,* 395–416.

Zebrowitz, L. A., Hall, J. A., Murphy, N. A., & Rhodes, G. (2002). Looking smart and looking good: Facial cues to intelligence and their origins. *Personality and Social Psychology Bulletin, 28,* 238–249.

Zebrowitz, L. A., & Montepare, J. M. (1992). Impressions of baby-faced individuals across the life span. *Developmental Psychology, 28,* 1143–1152.

Zeki, S. (1993). *A vision of the brain.* London: Blackwell Scientific.

Zeki, S. (2001). Localization and globalization in conscious vision. *Annual Review of Neuroscience, 24,* 57–86.

Zentall, T. R., Sutton, J. E., & Sherburne, L. M. (1996). True imitative learning in pigeons. *Psychological Science, 7,* 343–346.

Zentner, M., & Mitura, K. (2012). Stepping out of the caveman's shadow: Nations' gender gap predicts degree of sex differentiation in mate preferences. *Psychological Science, 23*(10), 1176–1185. doi: 10.1177/0956797612441004

Zerwas, S., & Bulik, C. M. (2011). Genetics and epigenetics of eating disorders. *Psychiatric Annals, 41*(11), 532–538. doi: 10.3928/00485713-20111017-06

Zhang, T. Y., & Meaney, M. J. (2010). Epigenetics and the environmental regulation of the genome and its function. *Annual Review of Psychology, 61,* 439–466.

Zhong, C.-B., Bohns, V. K., & Gino, F. (2010). Good lamps are the best police: Darkness increases dishonesty and self-interested behavior. *Psychological Science, 21*(3), 311–314. doi: 10.1177/0956797609360754

Zhou, X., Hetrick, S. E., Cuijpers, P., Qin, B., Barth, J., Whittington, C. J., . . . Xie, P. (2015). Comparative efficacy and acceptability of psychotherapies for depression in children and adolescents: A systematic review and network analysis. *World Psychiatry, 14,* 207–222.

Zihl, J., von Cramon, D., & Mai, N. (1983). Selective disturbance of movement vision after bilateral brain damage. *Brain, 106,* 313–340.

Zillmann, D., Katcher, A. H., & Milavsky, B. (1972). Excitation transfer from physical exercise to subsequent aggressive behavior. *Journal of Experimental Psychology, 8,* 247–259.

Zimbardo, P. (2007). *The Lucifer effect: Understanding how good people turn evil.* New York: Random House.

Zimprich, D., & Martin, M. (2002). Can longitudinal changes in processing speed explain longitudinal age changes in fluid intelligence? *Psychology and Aging, 17,* 690–695.

Zuckerman, M., & Driver, R. E. (1985). Telling lies: Verbal and nonverbal correlates of deception. In W. Seigman & S. Feldstein (Eds.), *Multichannel integrations of nonverbal behavior* (pp. 129–147). Hillsdale, NJ: Erlbaum.

Zuckerman, M., DePaulo, B. M., & Rosenthal, R. (1981). Verbal and nonverbal communication of deception. In L. Berkowitz (Ed.), *Advances in experimental social psychology* (Vol. 14, pp. 1–59). New York: Academic Press.

Name Index

Subject Index

Note: Page numbers followed by f indicate figures; those followed by t indicate tables.